February 27–March 2, 2019
Minneapolis, MN, USA

Association for
Computing Machinery

Advancing Computing as a Science & Profession

SIGCSE'19

Proceedings of the 50th ACM Technical Symposium on Computer Science Education

Sponsored by:

ACM SIGCSE

Symposium Co-Chairs:

Elizabeth K. Hawthorne & Manuel A. Pérez-Quiñones

Program Co-Chairs:

Sarah Heckman & Jian Zhang

Association for
Computing Machinery

Advancing Computing as a Science & Profession

The Association for Computing Machinery
2 Penn Plaza, Suite 701
New York, New York 10121-0701

ISBN: 978-1-4503-5890-3 (Digital)

ISBN: 978-1-4503-6742-4 (Print)

Additional copies may be ordered prepaid from:

ACM Order Department
PO Box 30777
New York, NY 10087-0777, USA

Phone: 1-800-342-6626 (USA and Canada)
+1-212-626-0500 (Global)
Fax: +1-212-944-1318
E-mail: acmhelp@acm.org
Hours of Operation: 8:30 am – 4:30 pm ET

Welcome from the SIGCSE Chair

Welcome to the 50th SIGCSE Technical Symposium on Computer Science Education (the 2019 Symposium), the premiere technical conference for computer science educators. The 2019 Symposium is sponsored by the Association for Computing Machinery (ACM) Special Interest Group on Computer Science Education (SIGCSE).

SIGCSE has the third largest membership of any of ACM's Special Interest Groups (SIG), and is among the oldest SIGs. Only ten SIGs were founded prior to 1968 when SIGCSE was formed, and two other SIGs shared their 50th anniversary in 2018 with SIGCSE. The SIGCSE Board and many other SIGCSE volunteers celebrated the 50th anniversary last year, but I would like to give a special thanks to two people. Briana Morrison, who is on the SIGCSE Board, created a series of weekly postings about SIGCSE's anniversary. These postings were shared on the listserv and published on SIGCSE's web site, and I know that many of you, myself included, enjoyed them. I would also like to thank Jane Prey, who is a long-time SIGCSE volunteer and previous SIGCSE award winner, for her work as the guest editor of a special issue of ACM Inroads celebrating SIGCSE's anniversary.

However, the celebration for the SIG is far from over. This year marks the 50th Technical Symposium, an achievement that even fewer SIGs share, as only six ACM SIGs have conferences that have been held 50 or more times. Further, the SIGCSE Symposium is thriving. The past several years have seen large increases in attendance at the conference, and this year will be even better thanks in part to the 50th anniversary committee. Adrienne Decker, who is a SIGCSE Board member and chairing the committee, Carl Alphonce, and Kurt Eiselt have worked for more than a year to put together a series of special events at the 50th Symposium. There will be a track focused on anniversary content that includes peer-reviewed papers and panels and invited discussants. Previous conference co-chairs have been invited to attend the conference and will be recognized for their work. The Travel Grant program has been expanded to 50 people for the anniversary, which should bring a new group of educators to our community. There will be special ribbons, stickers, and mementos for all attendees, and there will be a 50th anniversary booth and signage throughout the conference providing information about the conference history. Finally, the committee has worked with a historian, the Charles Babbage Institute, and Computing Educator's Oral History Project to bring content to attendees and have attendees contribute to the organizations' initiatives. On behalf of the SIGCSE Board I would like to thank the 50th anniversary committee for all of their hard work.

Of course, none of the activities at the 2019 Symposium would have been possible without the dedicated effort of conference co-chairs Manuel Pérez-Quiñones and Beth Hawthorne. They have spent countless hours ensuring that the 50th Technical Symposium will an event to remember. They and their committee of nearly 100 people have put together an engaging and innovative program, created opportunities for networking, and handled all the issues big and small that come with a conference of this size. On behalf of the SIGCSE organization and Board, I thank Manuel and Beth for their hard work, innovative ideas, excellent communication, and sense of humor.

Along with everything else you can expect to see this year, the conference provides us with a chance to honor two people for their contributions to computer science education and the SIGCSE community. The annual SIGCSE award for Outstanding Contribution to Computer Science Education will be given to Mark Guzdial at the University of Michigan. Mark has worked to transform wide-scale teaching practice through contextualized computing education, most notably with the Media Computation curriculum, advocated and supported policy changes supporting computing for all in many states in the U.S., published core research in computing education over decades, and helped to foster the next generation of computing educators through his mentorship. It is difficult to find someone in the SIGCSE community who has not read something written by Mark, including the thousands of regular readers of his long-standing blog on computing education. He has also contributed significantly as an organizer of two SIGCSE conferences and served on the SIGCSE Board. Mark has touched the computing education community and SIGCSE in many ways throughout the years, and our community is better for it. The annual SIGCSE award for Lifetime Service will be given to Gloria Childress Townsend at DePauw University. Gloria has worked tirelessly on behalf of diversity and inclusion in computing. She was a co-founder and co-facilitator of the SIGCSE Committee on Expanding the Women-in-Computing Community, a committee that has led birds-of-a-feather sessions at the Technical Symposium annually since 2005. Gloria worked for decades with ACM-W serving on the Executive Board and as ACM-W chair. She conceived of the idea of small regional celebrations of women in computing and worked as a guide and leader for these celebrations as they spread from the United States across the globe. Her extensive service to the computing education community has helped it to reach people who might not have joined without her hard work. Please join me and the rest of the SIGCSE Board in congratulating both of them on their well-deserved awards.

The 50th SIGCSE Technical Symposium will be an amazing event. I hope that you enjoy the celebrations, learn something new about computing education, meet new colleagues and friends, and stay warm in chilly Minneapolis. Enjoy the conference!

Amber Settle
SIGCSE Chair, 2016-2019

SIGCSE 2019 Chairs Welcome

Welcome to the 50th ACM Technical Symposium on Computer Science Education! Our theme this year is Celebrating the 50 Technical Symposia that has taken us from a small gathering of Computing Education enthusiasts in Texas in 1970 to the largest computing education conference in the world. The first SIGCSE Technical Symposium had over 40 papers submitted, 18 of them were accepted. For the 50th symposium, we received 526 paper submissions and accepted 169. In addition, the program has grown to include the ACM Student Research Competition, posters, demos, birds-of-a-feather, panels, special sessions, pre-symposium events, and workshops. Including all tracks, we received 994 submissions, from over 50 countries, with a total of 2668 unique authors representing over 800 organizations. And the participating organizations cover the gamut of K-12, community colleges, public and private universities and colleges, non-profits, corporate entities, government offices, and national laboratories. The growth of this conference parallels the growth of interest in the understanding and study of computing. We have plenty of reasons to celebrate the 50th gathering of our community.

With the growth of the computing education community, so has grown attendance at SIGCSE. In 1972 attendance was around 300 participants. Last year attendance surpassed 1500, and it was the third year in a row with record attendance. What is often missed is that conferences like SIGCSE are run by volunteers. All reviewers, associate program chairs, committee members, symposium and program chairs, and students are volunteers. All are giving their time to help participate in the dissemination of the greatest ideas and research results having to do with computing education.

The 2019 program continues to grow. This year we have a number of presentations exploring our history - in a special 50th celebration track, alongside of the now traditional coverage of topics in computing education, including active learning, AP exams, CS1, computational thinking, issues of diversity, tools, assessment, curriculum issues, etc. As is customary, we have other events that share our passion for computing education and are co-located with us. RESPECT 2019, the fourth international conference on Research on Equity and Sustained Participation in Engineering, Computing, and Technology will take place on Wednesday. We also have the SIGCSE sponsored New Chairs Roundtable as well as a number of pre-symposia, workshops, sponsored and affiliated events to complement our already robust offerings.

We are honored to have Dr. Freeman Habrowski, III, President of the University of Maryland, Baltimore County as our opening keynote. Among his many accomplishments, he chaired the committee that produced the National Academies' report, *Expanding Underrepresented Minority Participation: America's Science and Technology Talent at the Crossroads.* He will share a 50-year perspective on American society with a particular focus on technology, student success, and inclusion in computing.

We are also honored to have Dr. Blair Taylor of Towson University who consults with the NSA's College of Cyber, as a subject matter expert on long-term strategies to build the nation's cyber workforce. In the closing keynote, Dr. Taylor will share her experiences and perspectives on the future of integrating cybersecurity into computer science education.

The SIGCSE Symposium promotes high-quality scholarship and community engagement around computer science education. We continued the practice of reviewer discussions, an expanded associate program committee, and three paper submissions tracks, recognizing the differences in scope and review criteria between (1) CS education research, (2) experience reports and tools, and (3) curricula initiatives. In 2019, we changed the paper length up to a full 6 pages of content with a 7th page available for acknowledgments and references. These innovations have made our reviewing process more tailored and transparent. 797 volunteers provided each Paper with at least 5 reviews; and all other submissions with at least 3 reviews. Reviewers, along with 69 Associate Program Chairs and 14 Track Chairs, discussed submissions to come to a consensus. Program Chairs made final selections based on recommendations, importance, novelty, and timeliness. Table 1 table shows the number of submissions reviewed and accepted in each category.

Table 1: SIGCSE 2019 Submission and Acceptance Statistics

Track	# Submitted	# Accepted	Acceptance Rate
Papers (CS Education Research, Experience Reports and Tools, Curricula Initiatives)	526	169	32%
Panels	40	18	45%
Special Sessions	28	15	54%
Workshops	57	30	53%
ACM Student Research Competition	35	19	54%
Birds of a Feather	58	30	52%
Demos	24	11	46%
Lightning Talks	29	22	76%
Nifty Assignments	53	6	11%
Posters	144	90	63%

We are privileged to have exhibitors and supporters who champion CS education. This year's supporters include: Platinum: GitHub Education, Google, and Microsoft; Gold: Codio, Intel, Oracle Academy, Turing's Craft, and zyBooks; Silver: ABET, IBM, Gradescope by Turnitin, Mimir, and Vocareum; and Bronze: AnitaB.org.

This year the Program Chairs selected three best papers from each of the paper tracks for their accomplishment of high quality, novelty and broad appeal to reviewers. All best papers received at least one nomination from reviewers, high ratings, and excellent comments from reviewers. The top three papers in each track are shown below and highlighted throughout the printed program.

Best Papers for CS Education Research		
1	First Things First: Providing Metacognitive Scaffolding for Interpreting Problem Prompts James Prather *Abilene Christian University*, Raymond Pettit *Abilene Christian* University, Brett A. Becker *University College Dublin*, Paul Denny *The University of Auckland*, Dastyni Loksa *University of Washington*, Alani Peters *Abilene Christian University*, Zachary Albrecht *Abilene Christian University*, Krista Masci *Abilene Christian University*	Fri 11:10am Hyatt: Greenway J (2nd floor)
2	Assessing Incremental Testing Practices and Their Impact on Project Outcomes Ayaan M. Kazerouni *Virginia Tech*, Clifford A. Shaffer *Virginia Tech*, Stephen H. Edwards *Virginia Tech*, Francisco Servant *Virginia Tech*	Thu 3:45pm Hyatt: Greenway D/E (2nd floor)
3	Exploring the Value of Different Data Sources for Predicting Student Performance in Multiple CS Courses Soohyun Nam Liao *University of California, San Diego*, Daniel Zingaro *University of Toronto Mississauga*, Christine Alvarado *University of California, San Diego*, William G. Griswold *University of California, San Diego*, Leo Porter *University of California at San Diego*	Thu 11:10am Millennium: Grand South (1st floor)
Best Papers for Experience Reports and Tools		
1	Computer Science Principles for Teachers of Blind and Visually Impaired Students Andreas Stefik *University of Nevada, Las Vegas*, Richard E. Ladner *University of Washington*, William Allee *University of Nevada, Las Vegas*, Sean Mealin *North Carolina State University*	Fri 2:10pm Millennium: Grand South (1st floor)
2	Developing Soft and Technical Skills Through Multi-Semester, Remotely Mentored, Community-Service Projects Janet Davis *Whitman College*, Samuel A. Rebelsky *Grinnell College*	Thu 11:10am Hyatt: Greenway J (2nd floor)
3	Visualizing Classic Synchronization Problems: Dining Philosophers, Producers-Consumers, and Readers-Writers Joel C. Adams *Calvin College*, Elizabeth R. Koning *Calvin College*, Christiaan D. Hazlett *University of Illinois at Urbana-Champaign*	Fri 4:35pm Millennium: Grand South (1st floor)
Best Papers for Curricula Initiatives		
1	');DROP TABLE textbooks;--: An Argument for SQL Injection Coverage in Database Textbooks Cynthia Taylor *Oberlin College*, Saheel Sakharkar *University of Illinois at Chicago*	Thu 2:10pm Hyatt: Greenway A (2nd floor)
2	A Flexible Curriculum for Promoting Inclusion through Peer Mentorship Heather Pon-Barry *Mount Holyoke College*, Audrey St. John *Mount Holyoke College*, Becky Wai-Ling Packard *Mount Holyoke College*, Barbara Rotundo *Mount Holyoke College*	Sat 12:05pm Hyatt: Greenway J (2nd floor)
3	PythonSneks: An Open-Source, Instructionally-Designed Introductory Curriculum with Action-Design Research Austin Cory Bart *University of Delaware*, Allie Sarver *Virginia Tech*, Michael Friend *Virginia Tech*, Larry Cox *Virginia Tech*	Thu 1:45pm Millennium: Grand Central (1st floor)

This event owes many thanks to the SIGCSE Board for their guidance over the years. In addition, many organizations and their representatives had a hand in the success of this event. In no particular order: the planners at dLPLAN Meetings | Events: Dorothea Heck, Peggy Robins, Angelina Palmieri, and Betsy Fenwick; the Symposium Site Coordinators: Bob Beck and Paul Tymann; the ACM staff: April Mosqus and Donna Cappo; representatives from Sheridan: Lisa Tolles; Bill Guckert from WRG Design, Cindy Lathrop from the Hyatt Regency Minneapolis, and Melissa Jetson from Meet Minneapolis. We thank our home institutions for their generous support by allowing us to devote time to serve the SIGCSE community.

Finally, we are tremendously grateful for the engagement and support of the SIGCSE community and countless volunteers over the first 50 Symposia, and we look forward to the continued growth of this vibrant academic community. Let the celebration begin!

Elizabeth K. Hawthorne
Symposium Co-Chair
Union County College

Manuel A. Pérez-Quiñones
Symposium Co-Chair
University of North Carolina at Charlotte

Sarah Heckman
Program Co-Chair
North Carolina State University

Jian Zhang
Program Co-Chair
Texas Woman's University

Table of Contents

Paper Session: Tools 1

Session Chair: Charles Dierbach *(Towson University)*

Paper Session: Practice & Problems

Session Chair: Paul Denny *(The University of Auckland)*

Paper Session: Process & Performance

Session Chair: Razvan Alexandru Mezei *(Saint Martin's University)*

Paper Session: Autograders

Session Chair: Karen Jin *(University of New Hampshire)*

Paper Session: Capstones & Projects

Session Chair: Michelle Friend *(University of Nebraska Omaha)*

Special Session: SIGCSE Reads 2019: Discussion and Q & A

Session: SIGCSE@50 - CS1

Session Chair: James Caristi *(Valparaiso University)*

Paper Session: Camps

Session Chair: William H. Bares *(College of Charleston)*

Paper Session: Story & Video

Session Chair: Caroline Budwell *(Virginia Commonwealth University)*

Paper Session: Games & Gamification

Session Chair: Kalpathi Subramanian *(University of North Carolina at Charlotte)*

Paper Session: Testing 1

Session Chair: Mohsen Dorodchi *(University of North Carolina at Charlotte)*

Panel: The Reality of Inclusion:

Special Session: ACM Task Force on Data Science Education

Panel: CS Principles Higher Education Pathways

Session: SIGCSE@50 - Computing Education Research

Session: Morning Keynote & 2019 SIGCSE Award for Outstanding Contribution to Computer Science Education

Session Chairs: Elizabeth K. Hawthorne *(Union County College)*;
Manuel A. Pérez-Quiñones *(University of North Carolina at Charlotte)*

Paper Session: Online

Session Chair: Bernd Bruegge *(Technical University Munich)*

Paper Session: Mistakes and Errors

Session Chair: Ben Stephenson *(University of Calgary)*

Paper Session: Instruments 1

Session Chair: Steven Bogaerts *(DePauw University)*

Paper Session: Testing 2

Session Chair: Clifford A. Shaffer *(Virginia Tech)*

Paper Session: Teaching Practice 2

Session Chair: Matthew Hertz *(University at Buffalo)*

Paper Session: Assessment 2

Session Chair: Eileen T. Kraemer *(Clemson University)*

Paper Session: CS1 1

Session Chair: Eric Fouh *(University of Pennsylvania)*

Panel: This is What Diversity Looks Like

Panel: Civic Engagement Across the Computing Curriculum

Special Session: Exploring our Privilege: Activities and Discussions

Special Session: Computing Curricula 2020: Introduction and Community Engagement

Special Session: A Discussion of Research Practice Partnerships in CS Education

Session: SIGCSE@50 - Equity

Paper Session: Professional Tools & Practice

Session Chair: Roberto Hoyle *(Oberlin College)*

Paper Session: Student Success

Session Chair: Craig Zilles *(University of Illinois at Urbana-Champaign)*

Paper Session: Instruments 2

Session Chair: Emily Lovell *(Berea College)*

Paper Session: Security 1

Session Chair: Sotirios Kentros *(Salem State University)*

Special Session: Leading Conversations about Microaggressions, Bias, and Other Difficult Topics

Panel: Wrestling with Retention in the CS Major: Report from the ACM Retention Committee

Panel: Why and How to Spend a Sabbatical in Industry

Session: SIGCSE@50 - CS0

Session Chair: Leigh Ann Delyser *(CSforALL)*

Paper Session: Physical Computing

Session Chair: Barbara Anthony *(Southwestern University)*

Paper Session: Professional Skills

Session Chair: Victoria Hong *(St. Joseph's College)*

Paper Session: Attitudinal

Session Chair: Bob Edmison *(Virginia Tech)*

Special Session: Microteaching

Panel: Community College Transfer Pathways

Special Session: Curious about Student Participation in Humanitarian Open Source Software?

Session: SIGCSE@50 - Broadening Participation

Session Chair: Alison Derbenwick Miller *(Oracle)*

Session: Keynote

Session Chair: Elizabeth K. Hawthorne *(Union County College)*

Paper Session: Professional Development 1

Session Chair: Diana Cukierman *(Simon Fraser University)*

Paper Session: REU

Session Chair: Aarathi Prasad *(Skidmore College)*

Paper Session: Expectations

Session Chair: Brian Harrington *(University of Toronto Scarborough)*

Paper Session: Outreach

Session Chair: Alison Clear *(Eastern Institute of Technology)*

Paper Session: Theory & Mat

Session Chair: Shanon Reckinger *(University of Illinois Chicago)*

Paper Session: Pair Programming

Session Chair: Albert Chan *(Fayetteville State University)*

Paper Session: CSP

Session Chair: Joshua Elder *(CSforALL)*

Session: SIGCSE@50 - Historical Perspectives

Paper Session: Professional Development 2

Session Chair: Valerie Summet *(Rollins College)*

Paper Session: Mentorship

Session Chair: Janet Davis *(Whitman College)*

Paper Session: Engagement

Session Chair: Gloria Washington *(Howard University)*

Paper Session: Access

Session Chair: Jennifer Parham-Mocello *(Oregon State University)*

Paper Session: Culture & Language

Session Chair: Andrew J. Ko *(University of Washington)*

Paper Session: Inclusion

Session Chair: Brandon Myers *(University of Iowa)*

Paper Session: Blocks

Session Chair: Denise Case *(Northwest Missouri State University)*

Special Session: Women and Girls of Color in Computing

Special Session: Demystifying Language about Students' Varied Identities

Session: Nifty Assignments

Session Chairs: Nick Parlante *(Stanford University)*, Julie Zelenski *(Stanford University)*

Panel: Making K-12 CS Education Accessibility a Norm, not an Exception

Wednesday Workshops

Friday Workshops

Saturday Workshops

Birds of a Feather Flock #1

Session Chair: Mary Anne Egan *(Siena College)*, Mark Sherriff *(University of Virginia)*

Birds of a Feather Flock #2

Session Chairs: Mary Anne Egan *(Siena College)*, Mark Sherriff *(University of Virginia)*

Poster Session #1

Session Chairs: Laurence D. Merkle *(Air Force Institute of Technology)*,
S. Monisha Pulimood *(The College of New Jersey)*

Poster Session #2

Session Chairs: Laurence D. Merkle *(Air Force Institute of Technology)*,
S. Monisha Pulimood *(The College of New Jersey)*

Poster Session #3

Session Chairs: Laurence D. Merkle *(Air Force Institute of Technology)*, S. Monisha Pulimood *(The College of New Jersey)*

Lightning Talks #1

Session Chairs: Lina Battestilli *(NC State University)*, Peter-Michael Osera *(Grinnell College)*

Lightning Talks #2

Session Chairs: Lina Battestilli *(NC State University)*, Peter-Michael Osera *(Grinnell College))*

Demonstrations

Session Chairs: Lina Battestilli *(NC State University)*, Peter-Michael Osera *(Grinnell College)*

ACM SRC: ACM Student Research Competition

Session Chairs: Jessica Schmidt *(NC State University)*, Stephen Hughes *(Coe College)*

Recipients of the SIGCSE Award for Outstanding Contribution to Computer Science Education

1981 **William F. Atchison**, *University of Maryland*
1982 **Alan Perlis**, *Yale University*
1983 **Karl V . Karlstrom**, *Prentice-Hall*
1985 **Elliot I. Organick**, *University of Utah*
1986 **Donald Knuth**, *Stanford University*
1987 **Niklaus Wirth**, *ETH, Zurich*
1988 **Grace Murray Hopper**, *Rear Admiral, USN, Digital Equipment Corp.*
1989 **Edsger W. Dijkstra**, *The University of Texas at Austin*
1990 **Curriculum '68 Committee**:
William F. Atchison, Samuel D. Conte, John Hamblen, Thomas E. Hull, Thomas A. Keenan, William B. Kehl, Edward J. McClusey, Silvio O. Navarro, Werner Rheinboldt, Earl J. Schweppe, William Viavant, David M. Young, Jr.
1991 **David Gries**, *Cornell University*
1992 **Daniel D. McCracken**, *City College, City University of New York*
1993 **Alan C. Kay**, *Apple Computer*
1994 **Norman E. Gibbs**, *Software Engineering Institute*
1995 **Robert M. Aiken**, *Temple University*
1996 **Nell B. Dale**, *The University of Texas at Austin*
1997 **Andrew Tannenbaum**, *Vrije University*
1998 **William A. Wulf**, *University of Virginia and National Academy of Engineering*
1999 **Peter J. Denning**, *George Mason University*
2000 **Andries Van Dam**, *Brown University*
2001 **Allen B. Tucker**, *Bowdoin College*
2002 **Elliot Soloway**, *University of Michigan*
2003 **Eric Roberts**, *Stanford University*
2004 **Mordechai Ben-Ari**, *Weizmann Institute of Science*
2005 **Kim Bruce**, *Williams College*
2006 **Richard Pattis**, *Carnegie Mellon University*
2007 **Judith Gal-Ezer,** *Open University of Israel* and **John Hughes**, *University of Technology, Sydney*
2008 **Randy Pausch,** *Carnegie Mellon University*
2009 **Elliot B. Koffman**, *Temple University*
2010 **Sally Fincher,** *University of Kent, Canterbury*
2011 **Matthias Felleisen,** *Northeastern University*
2012 **Harold (Hal) Abelson,** *Massachusetts Institute of Technology*
2013 **Michael Kölling**, *University of Kent, Canterbury*
2014 **Robert M. Panoff,** *The Shodor Education Foundation, Inc.*
2015 **Mark Allen Weiss,** *Florida International University*
2016 **Jan Cuny,** *National Science Foundation*
2017 **Gail Chapman,** *Exploring Computer Science*
2018 **Tim Bell**, *University of Canterbury, New Zealand*
2019 **Mark Guzdial**, *University of Michigan*

Recipients of the SIGCSE Lifetime Service Award

1997 **Richard Austing**, *University of Maryland*
1998 **Della Bonnette**, *University of Southwestern Louisiana*
1999 **Robert Aiken**, *Temple University*
2000 **James E. Miller**, *University of Southern Mississippi*
2001 **Lillian N. (Boots) Cassel**, *Villanova University*
2002 **Joe Turner**, *Clemson University and Zayed University*
2003 **Harriet Taylor**, *National Science Foundation and Louisiana State University*
2004 **Bruce Klein**, *Grand V alley State University*
2005 **Andrew McGettrick**, *University of Strathclyde*
2006 **Joyce Currie Little**, *Towson State University*
2007 **John Impagliazzo**, *Hofstra University*
2008 **Dennis Frailey**, *Raytheon Corporation*
2009 **Michael J. Clancy**, *University of California, Berkeley*
2010 **Peter Denning**, *Naval Postgraduate School*
2011 **Gordon Davies**, *Open University*
2012 **Jane Prey**, *Microsoft Research*
2013 **Henry Walker**, *Grinnell College*
2014 **Andrea Lawrence**, *Spelman College*
2015 **Frank H. Young**, *Rose-Hulman Institute of Technology*
2016 **Barbara Boucher Owens**, *Southwestern University*
2017 **Mats Daniels**, *Uppsala University*
2018 **Eric Roberts**, *Stanford University*
2019 **Gloria Childress Townsend**, *DePauw University*

SIGCSE 2019 Technical Symposium Organization

Symposium Co-Chairs: Elizabeth K. Hawthorne *(Union County College, USA)*
Manuel A. Pérez-Quiñones *(University of North Carolina at Charlotte, USA)*

Program Co-Chairs: Sarah Heckman *(North Carolina State University, USA)*
Jian Zhang *(Texas Woman's University, USA)*

Program Committee

Special Sessions and Panels Co-Chairs: Christina Gardner-McCune (*University of Florida, USA)*
Alvaro Monge *(California State University, Long Beach, USA)*

Workshop Co-Chairs: Brett Becker *(University College Dublin, Ireland)*
Pam Cutter *(Kalamazoo College, USA)*

Poster Co-Chairs: Laurence D. Merkle *(Air Force Institute of Technology, USA)*
S. Monisha Pulimood *(The College of New Jersey, USA)*

Birds of a Feather Co-Chairs: Mary Anne Egan *(Siena College, USA)*
Mark Sherriff *(University of Virginia, USA)*

Demos and Lightning Talks Co-Chairs: Lina Battestilli *(North Carolina State University, USA)*
Peter-Michael Osera *(Grinnell College, USA)*

Student Research Competition Co-Chairs: Jessica Schmidt *(North Carolina State University, USA)*
Stephen Hughes *(Coe College, USA)*

Nifty Assignments Co-Chairs: Nick Parlante *(Stanford University, USA)*
Julie Zelenski *(Stanford University, USA)*

Organizing Committee

Accessibility Chair Stacy Branham *(University of California, Irvine, USA)*

Pre-Symposium & Affiliated Events: John Dougherty *(Haverford College, USA)*
Diana Cukierman *(Simon Fraser University, Canada)*

Registration: Lynn Degler *(Rose-Hulman Institute of Technology, USA)*
Cary Laxer *(Rose-Hulman Institute of Technology, USA)*
Laurence D. Merkle *(Air Force Institute of Technology, USA)*

Publications: Ruth Anderson (*University of Washington, USA*)

Database Administrator: Leen-Kiat Soh (*University of Nebraska, Lincoln, USA*)
Mark Sherriff (*University of Virginia, USA*)

Webmaster: Josh Hug (*University of California, Berkeley, USA*)
Matt Jadud *(Bates College, USA)*

Treasurer: Paul Tymann *(Rochester Institute of Technology, USA)*

Evaluations: Phil East (*University of Northern Iowa, USA)*

Supporter/Exhibitor Liaison: Dave Musicant *(Carleton College, USA)*
Jodi Tims *(Baldwin Wallace University, USA)*

Student Volunteers & Activities: Sara Melnick *(Independent)*
Darakhshan Mir *(Bucknell University, USA)*
Samuel A. Rebelsky *(Grinnell College, USA)*

K-12 Liaison: Leigh Ann Sudol-DeLyser *(CSforALL, USA)*
Ria Galanos *(Thomas Jefferson High School for Science and Technology, USA)*

Community College Liaison: Cara Tang *(Portland Community College, USA)*

International Liaison: Jennifer Campbell *(University of Toronto, Canada)*

Kids' Camp: Dale-Marie Wilson *(University of North Carolina at Charlotte, USA)*
Meghan Allen *(University of British Columbia, Canada)*

Puzzles, Social, & Board Games: Steven Wolfman *(University of British Columbia, Canada)*
Zach Butler *(Rochester Institute of Technology, USA)*

Publicity and Social Media: Adam Blank *(University of Washington, USA)*
John Lewis *(Virginia Tech, USA)*

Local Arrangements: Jigang Liu *(Metropolitan State University, USA)*

50th Celebration Planning Committee: Adrienne Decker *(University at Buffalo, USA)*
Kurt Eiselt *(University of California, Davis, USA)*
Carl Alphonce *(University at Buffalo, USA)*

International Committee Members: Meghan Allen *(The University of British Columbia, Canada)*
Miles Berry *(University of Roehampton, United Kingdom)*
Karen Bradshaw *(Rhodes University, South Africa)*
Ernesto Cuadros-Vargas *(UTEC, Peru)*
Paul Denny *(University of Auckland, New Zealand)*
Rita Garcia *(Adelaide, Australia)*
Orit Hazzan *(Technion, Israel)*
Arto Hellas *(University of Helsinki, Finland)*
Carsten Kleiner *(Hochschule Hannover, Germany)*
Wendy Powley *(Queen's University, Canada)*
Marco Silva *(Federal University of Technology, Brazil)*
Abhijat Vichare *(Persistent, India)*
Hironori Washizaki *(Waseda University, Japan)*
Gary Wong *(University of Hong Kong, Hong Kong)*
Ming Zhang *(Peking University, China)*

Associate Program Chairs: Eric Aaron *(Colby College, USA)*
Joel C. Adams *(Calvin College, USA)*
Rajeev Agrawal *(US Army Engineer Research and Development Center, USA)*
Meghan Allen *(The University of British Columbia, Canada)*
Carl Alphonce *(University at Buffalo, USA)*
Christine Alvarado *(University of California San Diego, USA)*
Ruth Anderson *(University of Washington, USA)*
Barbara Anthony *(Southwestern University, USA)*
Julio César Bahamón *(University of North Carolina at Charlotte, USA)*
Mark Bailey *(Hamilton College, USA)*
Tiffany Barnes *(North Carolina State University, USA)*
Brett A. Becker *(University College Dublin, Ireland)*
Marie Bienkowski *(SRI International, USA)*
Kevin Buffardi *(California State University - Chico, USA)*
Alistair Campbell *(Hamilton College, USA)*
Paul Cao *(University of California San Diego, USA)*
Albert Chan *(Fayetteville State University, USA)*
Peter J. Clarke *(Florida International University, USA)*
Steve Cooper *(University of Nebraska-Lincoln, USA)*
Ernesto Cuadros-Vargas *(San Pablo Catholic University, Peru)*
Adrienne Decker *(University at Buffalo, USA)*
Leigh Ann DeLyser *(CSforALL, USA)*
Mohsen Dorodchi *(University of North Carolina at Charlotte, USA)*
John P. Dougherty *(Haverford College, USA)*
Maureen Doyle *(Northern Kentucky University, USA)*
Joshua Eckroth *(Stetson University, USA)*
Stephen Edwards *(Virginia Tech, USA)*
Matthew Forshaw *(Newcastle University, United Kingdom)*
Allan Fowler *(Kennesaw State University, USA)*
Michelle Friend *(University of Nebraska Omaha, USA)*
Chris Gregg *(Stanford University, USA)*
Cecily Heiner *(Southern Utah University, USA)*
Sharon Hsiao *(Arizona State University, USA)*
Helen Hu *(Westminster College, USA)*
Mark J. Johnson *(Central College, USA)*
Maria Jump *(Northeastern University -- Charlotte, USA)*
Carsten Kleiner *(University of Applied Science and Arts Hannover, Germany)*
Andrew J. Ko *(University of Washington, USA)*
Stephan Krusche *(Technical University of Munich, Germany)*
David Levine *(Saint Bonaventure University, USA)*
Andrew Luxton-Reilly *(The University of Auckland, New Zealand)*

Associate Program Chairs (continued):

Bruce R. Maxim *(University of Michigan, USA)*
Lester I. McCann *(University of Arizona, USA)*
Susan Mengel *(Texas Tech University, USA)*
Laurence D. Merkle *(Air Force Institute of Technology, USA)*
Craig Miller *(DePaul University, USA)*
Robert Noonan *(William and Mary, USA)*
Jody Paul *(Metropolitan State University of Denver, USA)*
Leo Porter *(University of California San Diego, USA)*
Wendy Powley *(Queen's University, Canada)*
Samuel A. Rebelsky *(Grinnell College, USA)*
Suzanne Rivoire *(Sonoma State University, USA)*
Susan Rodger *(Duke University, USA)*
Ingrid Russell *(University of Hartford, USA)*
Mark Sherriff *(University of Virginia, USA)*
Swapneel Sheth *(University of Pennsylvania, USA)*
Simon *(University of Newcastle, Australia)*
Melissa Stange *(Lord Fairfax Community College, USA)*
Ben Stephenson *(University of Calgary, Canada)*
Jim Teresco *(Siena College, USA)*
Luther Tychonievich *(University of Virginia, USA)*
Paul Tymann *(Rochester Institute of Technology, USA)*
Frank Vahid *(University of California, Riverside, USA)*
Jan Vahrenhold *(Westfälische Wilhelms-Universität Münster, Germany)*
Abhijat Vichare *(Abhijat Research and Software, India)*
Ellen Walker *(Hiram College, USA)*
Henry Walker *(Grinnell College, USA)*
Charles Wallace *(Michigan Technological University, USA)*
Ursula Wolz *(Bennington College, USA)*

ACM Student Research Competition (SRC) Reviewers

Mohammad Q. Azhar (BMCC, The City University Of New York)
Doug Baldwin (SUNY Geneseo)
Judith Bayard Cushing (The Evergreen State College)
David Bunde (Knox College)
Michael Cotterell (University of Georgia)
Barb Cutler (Rensselaer Polytechnic Institute)
Mohsen Dorodchi (University of North Carolina at Charlotte)
Maureen Doyle (Northern Kentucky University)
Hillary Fleenor (Columbus State University)
Eric Fouh (Lehigh University)
S. Jane Fritz (St. Joseph's College)
J Paul Gibson (Mines Telecom)
Carlos Guerrero (Universitat de les Illes Balears)
Geoffrey Herman (University of Illinois at Urbana-Champaign)
Roberto Hoyle (Oberlin College)
Dugald Hutchings (Elon University)
Wei Jin (Georgia Gwinnett College)
Lisa Lacher (University of Houston - Clear Lake)
David Levine (Saint Bonaventure University)
Zilu Liang (Tokyo Institute of Technology)
Sa Liu (Harrisburg University of Science and Technology)
James McGuffee (Christian Brothers University)
Chao Mei (University of Texas at San Antonio)
Xenia Mountrouidou (College of Charleston)
Dave Musicant (Carleton College)
Arnold Pears (KTH Royal Institute of Technology)
Yang Song (University of North Carolina Wilmington)
Izak Van Zyl (Cape Peninsula University of Technology)
Ellen Walker (Hiram College)
Nikhil Yadav (St. John's University)
Jeong Yang (Texas A&M University-San Antonio)
Lan Yang (California State Polytechnic University, Pomona)

BOF Reviewers

Shakil Akhtar (Clayton State University)
Mark Allison (University of Michigan-Flint)
Nada Basit (University of Virginia)
Michael Bauer (Leeward Community College)
Leland Beck (San Diego State University)
Marjahan Begum (Copenhagen Business School)
Christopher Bohn (University of Nebraska-Lincoln)
Dennis Bouvier (Southern Illinois University Edwardsville)
Kevin Buell (Arizona State University)
Deanne Cranford-Wesley (Forsyth Technical Community College)
Rosiane de Freitas (IComp/UFAM)
Toby Donaldson (Simon Fraser University)
Huseyin Ergin (Ball State University)
Razieh Fathi (University at Buffalo)
Yujian Fu (Alabama A&M University)
Anna Förster (University of Bremen)
Charles Garrod (Carnegie Mellon University)
Chris Gregg (Stanford University)
Caroline Hardin (University of Wisconsin-Madison)
Cinda Heeren (UBC)
Michael Hilton (Carnegie Mellon University)
Thomas Horton (Univ. of Virginia, Dept. of Computer Science)
Justin Hsia (University of Washington)
Jim Huggins (Kettering University)
Colin Johnson (University of Kent)
Deborah Kariuki (CSForAll)
Richard Kick (Newbury Park High School)
Joan Krone (Denison University)
David Largent (Ball State University)
Melinda Mcdaniel (Georgia Institute of Technology)
Charlie Mcdowell (UC Santa Cruz)
Alvaro Monge (California State University Long Beach)
Krish Narayanan (Eastern Michigan University)
Keith O'Hara (Bard College)
Swati Padhee (Wright State University)
James Paterson (Glasgow Caledonian University)
Fabio Petrillo (Universite du Quebec a Chicoutimi)
Donna Reese (Mississippi State University)
Matt Roberts (Macquarie University)
Jason Schultz (Bemidji State University)
Amber Solomon (Georgia Institute of Technology)
Lei Tang (Rice University)
Fatma Tarlaci (Stanford University)
George Thomas (University of Wisconsin Oshkosh)
Kim Tracy (Rose-Hulman Institute of Technology)
Anthony Varghese (University of Wisconsin-River Falls)

Demonstration Reviewers

Michal Aibin (British Columbia Institute of Technology)
David Arnow (Brooklyn College (CUNY))

Ajay Bandi (Northwest Missouri State University)
James Chegwidden (Tarrant County College)
Josh Dehlinger (Towson University)
Kathleen Ericson (University of Tennessee at Martin)
Paul Fodor (Stony Brook University)
Adam Gaweda (North Carolina State University)
Olga Glebova (Georgia State University)
Javier Gonzalez-Sanchez (Arizona State University)
Marco Aurélio Graciotto Silva (Federal University of Technology - Paraná)
James Heliotis (Rochester Institute of Technology)
Kimberly Hermans (University of California, Irvine)
David Hovemeyer (York College of Pennsylvania)
Hasan Jamil (University of Idaho)
Amir Kamil (University of California, Berkeley)
Young Lee (none)
Idongesit Mkpong-Ruffin (Faulkner University)
Jared O'Leary (BootUp)
Lawrence Osborne (Lamar University Faculty)
Christian Roberson (Florida Southern College)
Raja Sooriamurthi (Carnegie Mellon University)
William Thacker (Winthrop University)

Lightning Talk Reviewers

Reem Ali (University of Minnesota)
Meghan Allen (The University of British Columbia)
Beverly Bachmayer (Intel)
Matthew Barr (University of Glasgow)
Lillian Cassel (Villanova University)
Albert Chan (Fayetteville State University)
Edward Chapin (University of Maryand Eastern Shore)
Jonathan Corley (University of West Georgia)
Diana Cukierman (Simon Fraser University)
Venu Dasigi (Bowling Green State University)
Alex Edgcomb (Sr. Software Engineer at zyBooks. Research Specialist at UC Riverside.)
Heidi Ellis (Western New England University)
Theodore Hays (Clemson University Undergraduate Research Team)
Cruz Izu (The University of Adelaide)
James Kolasa (Bluegrass Community and Technical College)
Violetta Lonati (University of Milan)
Manuel Martins Barata (ISEL - Instituto Superior de Engenharia de Lisboa)
Razvan Alexandru Mezei (Saint Martin's University)
Diba Mirza (University of California Santa Barbara)
Christopher Moretti (Princeton University)
Briana Morrison (University of Nebraska at Omaha)
Anurag Nagar (The University of Texas at Dallas)
Peter Ohmann (College of St. Benedict / St. John's University)
Andrew Rasmussen (Chicago Public Schools)
Tim Sisson (Cleveland State University)
Nadine von Frankenberg Und Ludwigsdorff (Technical University of Munich)
Kendra Walther (University of Southern California)
Arthur Yanushka (Christian Brothers University)

Nifty Assignment Reviewers

Joseph Ahor Abandoh-Sam (Valley View University)
Owen Astrachan (Duke University)
Arvind Bhusnurmath (University of Pennsylvania)
James H. Davenport (University of Bath)
Giuseppe De Ruvo (The University of Auckland)
Zhijiang Dong (Middle Tennessee State University)
Colin S. Gordon (Drexel University)
Jean Goulet (Universite de Sherbrooke)
Michael Guerzhoy (Princeton University)
Fahmida Hamid (University of North Texas)
Nadeem Hamid (Berry College)
Matthew Hertz (University at Buffalo)
Sarah J Huibregtse (Rochester Institute of Technology)
Janet Jenkins (University of North Alabama)
Osvaldo Jimenez (University of the Pacific)
Pankaj Kamthan (Concordia University)
Amanpreet Kapoor (University of Florida)
Bo Kim (Southern New Hampshire University)
Ana Paula Ludtke Ferreira (Universidade Federal do Pampa)
Suzanne Matthews (United States Military Academy)
Afsaneh Minaie (Utah Valley University)
Benjamin Mitchell (Villanova University)
Linda Null (The Pennsylvania State University)
Joe Politz (University of California San Diego)
Aarathi Prasad (Skidmore College)

John Rager (Amherst College)
Saquib Razak (Carnegie Mellon University)
David Reed (Creighton University)
Mike Scott (University of Texas at Austin - Computer Science Departmnet)
Nigamanth Sridhar (Cleveland State University)
Ben Stephenson (University of Calgary)
Amber Stubbs (Simmons College)
Deborah Trytten (University of Oklahoma)
Giovanni Vincenti (University of Baltimore)
Alan Whitehurst (Southern Virginia University)
Victor Winter (University of Nebraska at Omaha)

Panel Session Reviewers

Andrew Allen (Georgia Southern University)
Alice Armstrong (Shippensburg University)
Cathy Bareiss (Olivet Nazarene University)
Arvind Bhusnurmath (University of Pennsylvania)
Carlos Cabrera (Florida International University)
Cengiz Gunay (Georgia Gwinnett College)
Hoda Hosny (AUC Egypt)
Justin Hsia (University of Washington)
Joseph Isaac (University of Florida)
Yerika Jimenez (University of Florida)
Colin Johnson (University of Kent)
Amanpreet Kapoor (University of Florida)
Joe Kmoch (JK Consulting)
Joaquim Madeira (University of Aveiro)
Robyn Moncrief (National Louis University)
Dave Musicant (Carleton College)
Keith O'Hara (Bard College)
Peter-Michael Osera (Grinnell College)
Imani Palmer (University of Illinois at Urbana-Champaign)
Rosario Robinson (FocusGears)
Jerry Roth (Vanderbilt University)
Anya Tafliovich (University of Toronto)
Terry Tang (Rice University)
S. Rebecca Thomas (Bard College)
Hakan Tuzun (Hacettepe University)
Linda Werner (University of CA, Santa Cruz)
Howard Whitston (University of South Alabama)
Adrienne Decker (University at Buffalo)

Paper Reviewers

Joseph A. Abandoh-Sam (Valley View University)
Ahmed Abukmail (University of Houston-Clear Lake)
Donald Acton (The University of British Columbia)
Joshua Adams (Saint Leo University)
Paul Addison (Ivy Tech Community College)
Ashish Aggarwal (University of Florida)
Irfan Ahmed (Virginia Commonwealth University)
Michal Aibin (British Columbia Institute of Technology)
Efthimia Aivaloglou (Open Universiteit)
Mete Akcaoglu (Michigan State University)
Bita Akram (North Carolina State University)
Saeed Al-Haj (Ohio Northern University)
Hisham Al-Mubaid (University of Houston-clear lake)
Jennifer Albert (The Citadel)
Ibrahim Albluwi (Princeton University)
Farha Ali (Lander University)
Mark Allison (University of Michigan-Flint)
Cecilia Ovesdotter Alm (Rochester Institute of Technology)
Roberto Almeida Bittencourt (UEFS - State University of Feira de Santana)
Asm Iftekhar Anam (University of Wisconsin - Green Bay)
Maurício Aniche (Delft University of Technology)
Craig Anslow (Victoria University of Wellington)
Gabriella Anton (Northwestern University)
Vaibhav Anu (Montclair State University)
John Anvik (Department of Mathematics and Computer Science, University of Lethbridge)
Ajayi Anwansedo (Southern University and A & M)
Saira Anwar (Purdue University)
Eduardo Aranha (UFRN)
Luis Gustavo J. Araujo (State University of Feira de Santana)
António Araújo (University of Porto)
Alex Aravind (University of Northern British Columbia)
David Arnow (Brooklyn College (CUNY))
Muhammad Rizwan Asghar (The University of Auckland)
Thomas Babbitt (USMA)
Monica Babes-Vroman (Rutgers University)
Donald Bagert (Benedictine College)
Connor Bain (Northwestern Universtiy)
Doug Baldwin (SUNY Geneseo)
Robert Ball (Weber State University)
Michael Ball (University of California, Berkeley)
Ajay Bandi (Northwest Missouri State University)
Shankar M. Banik (The Citadel)
William Bares (College of Charleston)
Lecia Barker (University of Colorado Boulder)

Ian Barland (Radford University)
David Barnes (University of Kent)
Matthew Barr (University of Glasgow)
Phillip Barry (University of Minnesota)
Lina Battestilli (North Carolina State University)
Daniel Bauer (Columbia University)
Michael Bauer (Leeward Community College)
Judith Bayard Cushing (The Evergreen State College)
Marjahan Begum (Copenhagen Business School)
Fabiane Benitti (UFSC)
Angela Berardinelli (Mercyhurst University)
Mario Luca Bernardi (Giustino Fortunato University)
Andrew Berns (University of Northern Iowa)
Gianmario Besana (DePaul University)
Bradley Beth (The University of Texas at Austin)
Arnab Bhattacharya (Indian Institute of Technology, Kanpur)
Debasis Bhattacharya (University of Hawaii Maui College)
Saúl Blanco (Indiana University Bloomington)
Michael Bloodgood (The College of New Jersey)
Richard Blumenthal (Regis University)
Ryan Bockmon (Univeristy of Nebraska - Lincoln)
Elizabeth Boese (University of Colorado - Boulder)
Steven Bogaerts (DePauw University)
Christopher Bohn (University of Nebraska-Lincoln)
Bill Booth (Baylor University)
Otto Borchert (Missouri Southern State University)
João Marcelo Borovina Josko (Federal Universty of ABC - Sao Paulo - Brazil)
Durell Bouchard (Roanoke College)
Eric Bouwers (Squla)
Jeremy Bradbury (University of Ontario Institute of Technology)
Andrej Brodnik (University of Ljubljana)
Neil Brown (King's College London)
Glenn Bruns (California State University Monterey Bay)
Dennis Brylow (Marquette University)
Karan K. Budhraja (University of Maryland, Baltimore County)
Philip Buffum (North Carolina State University)
David Burlinson (University of North Carolina at Charlotte)
Jeffrey Bush (University of Colorado Boulder)
Zack Butler (Rochester Institute of Technology)
Candido Cabo (City University of New York)
Ricardo Caceffo (University of Campinas (Unicamp), Brazil)
Yu Cai (Michigan Technological University)
Andre P. Calitz (none)
Jennifer Campbell (University of Toronto)
Soraya Cardenas (Cascadia College)
Lori Carter (Point Loma Nazarene University)
Leandro Carvalho (Institute of Computing - Universidade Federal do Amazonas)
Lillian Cassel (Villanova University)
Francisco Enrique Vicente Castro (Worcester Polytechnic Institute)
Veronica Catete (North Carolina State University)
Veronica Catete (North Carolina State University)
Sharath Chandrashekhara (University at Buffalo)
Bruce Char (Drexel University Department of Computer Science)
Ankur Chattopadhyay (University of Wisconsin - Green Bay)
James Chegwidden (Tarrant County College)
Robert Chen (Framingham State University (retired))
Juan Chen (College of Computer, National University of Defense Technology, China)
Wai Chong Chia (Sunway University)
Sridhar Chimalakonda (Indian Institute of Technology - Tirupati)
Donald Chinn (University of Washington)
Vanea Chiprianov (University of Pau)
Radhouane Chouchane (Columbus State University)
Cheng Yu Chung (Arizona State University)
Christos Chytas (Carl von Ossietzky Universität Oldenburg)
John Cigas (Park University)
Dawn Cizmar (St. Edwards University)
Jaclyn Cohen (Open.Michigan Initiative)
Rachel Cole (Research Alliance for New York City Schools)
Randy Connolly (Mount Royal University)
Phillip Conrad (UC Santa Barbara)
Jonathan Corley (University of West Georgia)
Mary Courtney (Pace University)
Andrew Csizmadia (Newman University)
Kathryn Cunningham (Georgia Institute of Technology)
Edwin Curran (University of Ulster)
Mónica Isabel T. Da Costa (EST - IPCB)
Omar Darwish (Texas Woman's Univery)
Venu Dasigi (Bowling Green State University)

James H. Davenport (University of Bath)
Karen C. Davis (Miami University)
Don Davis (University of Texas at San Antonio)
Rosiane de Freitas (IComp/UFAM)
Giuseppe De Ruvo (The University of Auckland)
Debzani Deb (Winston-salem state university)
Nasrin Dehbozorgi (University of North Carolina at Charlotte)
Josh Dehlinger (Towson University)
Fabian Deitelhoff (FH Dortmund)
Rafael Del Vado Vírseda (Universidad Complutense de Madrid. Departamento de Sistemas Informáticos y Computación)
Marie-Anne Demuynck (Texas Woman's University)
Yuli Deng (Arizona State University)
Kamyar Dezhgosha (University of Illinois at Springfield)
Christo Dichev (WSSU)
Darina Dicheva (Winston-Salem State University)
Suzanne W. Dietrich (Arizona State University)
Betsy DiSalvo (Georgia Institute of Technology)
Zachary Dodds (Harvey Mudd College)
Anca Doloc-Mihu (Georgia Gwinnett College)
Robert Domanski (City University of New York)
Toby Donaldson (Simon Fraser University)
Yihuan Dong (North Carolina State University)
Zhijiang Dong (Middle Tennessee State University)
John Dooley (Knox College)
Felicia Doswell (Norfolk State University)
John A. Doucette (New College of Florida)
Toby Dragon (Ithaca College)
J. Philip East (University of Northern Iowa)
Alex Edgcomb (Sr. Software Engineer at zyBooks. Research Specialist at UC Riverside.)
Bob Edmison (Virginia Tech)
John Edwards (Utah State University)
Roger Eggen (University of North Florida)
Jesse Eickholt (Central Michigan University)
Farjana Eishita (University of New Orleans)
Yasmine El-Glaly (Rochester Institute of Technology)
Daniel Ellsworth (Colorado College)
Richard Enbody (Michigan State University)
Kirankumar Eranki (Indian Institute of Technology Bombay)
Huseyin Ergin (Ball State University)
Barbara Ericson (University of Michigan)
Yadran Eterovic (Pontificia Universidad Catlica de Chile)
Cheri Fancsali (Research Alliance for NYC Schools)
Mohammed Farghally (Virginia Tech)
Mojtaba Sedigh Fazli (University of Georgia)
Yvon Feaster (Clemson University)
Alan Fekete (The University of Sydney)
Russell Feldhausen (Kansas State University)
Maria Lydia Fioravanti (University of São Paulo)
Hillary Fleenor (Columbus State University)
Paul Fodor (Stony Brook University)
Daniel Fokum (The University of the West Indies)
Samantha S. Foley (University of Wisconsin-La Crosse)
Anna Förster (University of Bremen)
Eric Fouh (Lehigh University)
Susan Eileen Fox (Macalester College)
Ellen Francine Barbosa (ICMC/USP)
Anna Frankfurt (University of Prince Edward Island)
Diana Franklin (UChicago STEM Education)
Gordon Fraser (University of Passau)
Frank Friedman (Temple University)
Ilenia Fronza (Free University of Bolzano / Bozen)
Yujian Fu (Alabama A&M University)
Muztaba Fuad (Winston-Salem State University)
Ramona Fuentes-Valdéz (Tecnológico de Monterrey)
Paulo Gabriel Gadelha Queiroz (ufersa)
Dilrukshi Gamage (University of Moratuwa)
Saturnino Garcia (University of San Diego)
Christina Gardner-McCune (University of Florida)
Charles Garrod (Carnegie Mellon University)
Megean Garvin (UMBC)
Alessio Gaspar (University of South Florida Polytechnic)
Isabela Gasparini (UDESC)
Adam Gaweda (North Carolina State University)
Edward F. Gehringer (North Carolina State University)
Alexandra Gendreau Chakarov (University of Colorado Boulder)
Paul Gestwicki (Ball State University)
Uttam Ghosh (Vanderbilt University)
Nasser Giacaman (The University of Auckland)
J Paul Gibson (Mines Telecom)
Niki Gitinabard (North Carolina State University)

Richard Glassey (Robert Gordon University)
Ira Goldstein (Siena College)
Mercedes Gómez-Albarrán (Universidad Complutense de Madrid)
Javier Gonzalez-Huerta (Blekinge Institue of Technology)
Javier Gonzalez-Sanchez (Arizona State University)
Ana I. González-Tablas (University Carlos III de Madrid)
Colin S. Gordon (Drexel University)
Jean Goulet (Universite de Sherbrooke)
Marco Aurélio Graciotto Silva (Federal University of Technology - Paraná)
Joanthan Gratch (Texas Woman's University)
Jean M. Griffin (Google)
Tor-Morten Grønli (Westerdals Oslo ACT)
Joshua Gross (Blackburn)
Carlos Guerrero (Universitat de les Illes Balears)
Francisco J. Gutierrez (Computer Science Department, University of Chile)
Mandlenkosi Gwetu (UKZN)
Steve Hadfield (US Air Force Academy)
Ayman Hajja (College Of Charleston)
Hossein Hakimzadeh (Indiana University Bloomington)
Margeret Hall (School of Interdisciplinary Informatics, University of Nebraska Omaha)
Ranette Halverson (Midwestern State University)
Tom Halverson (Dakota State University)
Alan Hamlett (WakaTime)
Sally Hamouda (Rhode IslandCollege)
Meng Han (Kennesaw State University)
Qiang Hao (Computer Science & SMATE, Western Washington University)
David Harvie (United States Military Academy)
J. Scott Hawker (Rochester Institute of Technology)
Elizabeth Hawthorne (Union County College)
Alan Hayes (University of Bath)
Orit Hazzan (Technion - Israel Institute of Technology)
Bastiaan Heeren (Open University, The Netherlands)
Fredrik Heintz (Linköping University)
David Heise (Lincoln University)
Arto Hellas (University of Helsinki)
Shelly Heller (George Washington University)
Austin Henley (University of Tennessee)
Julie Henry (PreCISE - UNamur)
Suvineetha Herath (Carl Sandburg College)
Geoffrey Herman (University of Illinois at Urbana-Champaign)
Kimberly Hermans (University of California, Irvine)
Arnon Hershkovitz (Tel Aviv University)
Matthew Hertz (University at Buffalo)
Michael Hewner (Rose Hulman Institute of Techonology)
Timothy Highley (La Salle University)
Curt Hill (Valley City State University)
Michael Hilton (Carnegie Mellon University)
Mark Holliday (Western Carolina University)
Charles G Hoot (NW Missouri State University)
Cay Horstmann (San Jose State University)
Thomas B. Horton (Univ. of Virginia, Dept. of Computer Science)
David Hovemeyer (York College of Pennsylvania)
Christopher Hovey (University of Colorado Boulder)
Brian Howard (DePauw University)
Iris Howley (Williams College)
Aleata Hubbard (WestEd)
Jim Huggins (Kettering University)
Janet Hughes (The Open University)
Sarah J Huibregtse (Rochester Institute of Technology)
Dugald Hutchings (Elon University)
Nicole Hutchins (Vanderbilt University)
Jorge Eduardo Ibarra-Esquer (Universidad Autónoma de Baja California)
Ahmed Ibrahim (University of Virginia)
Michelle Ichinco (University of Massachusetts Lowell)
Md Athar Imtiaz (The University of Auckland)
Cruz Izu (The University of Adelaide)
Jana Jackova (Matej Bel University)
Filip Jagodzinski (Western Washington University)
Eissa Jamil (Edge Technovations LLC)
Hasan Jamil (University of Idaho)
Gayithri Jayathirtha (University of Pennsylvania)
Johan Jeuring (Open Universiteit Nederland and Universiteit Utrecht)
Osvaldo Jimenez (University of the Pacific)
Yerika Jimenez (University of Florida)
Haojian Jin (Carnegie Mellon University)
Karen Jin (University of New Hampshire)
Wei Jin (Georgia Gwinnett College)
Mike Jipping (Hope College)
William Joel (Graphics Research Group / WCSU)
Jeremiah Johnson (University of New Hampshire)
Julie Johnson (Vanderbilt University)
Chris Johnson (University of Wisconsin, Eau Claire)

Naomi Johnson (University of Virginia)
Maria José Marcelino (University of Coimbra)
Swaroop Joshi (The Ohio State University)
Dennis Kafura (Virginia Tech)
Antti-Juhani Kaijanaho (University of Jyvaskyla, Faculty of Information Technology)
Tetsuro Kakeshita (Saga University)
Maria Kallia (King's College London)
Amanpreet Kapoor (University of Florida)
Amey Karkare (Indian Institute of Technology, Kanpur)
Ayaan Kazerouni (Virginia Tech)
William Kerney (Clovis Community College)
Fazel Keshtkar (ST John's University)
Daehee Kim (California State University - Stanislaus)
Meen Chul Kim (Drexel University)
Bo Kim (Southern New Hampshire University)
Jason King (North Carolina State University)
Jason King (North Carolina State University)
Styliani Kleanthous (University of Cyprus)
Devorah Kletenik (City University of New York)
John Kloosterman (University of Michigan)
Jane Kochanov (Penn State Harrisburg)
Kyu Han Koh (California State University, Stanislaus)
Tobias Kohn (University of Cambridge)
James Kolasa (Bluegrass Community and Technical College)
Meir Komar (JCT)
G. Ayorkor Korsah (Ashesi University)
Brittany Ann Kos (University of Colorado Boulder)
Joan Krone (Denison University)
Jw Kruger (Unisa SBL)
Shreya Kumar (University of Notre Dame)
Zachary Kurmas (Grand Valley State University)
Clif Kussmaul (Muhlenberg College)
Lisa Lacher (University of Houston - Clear Lake)
Richard Ladner (University of Washington)
Christopher I. G. Lanclos (Mississippi State University)
Dieter Landes (University of Applied Sciences and Arts)
Matthew Lang (Google)
Joan Langdon (Bowie State University)
Yedidyah Langsam (City University of New York)
D. Brian Larkins (Rhodes College)
John Lasseter (Hobart & William Smith Colleges)
Celine Latulipe (University of North Carolina at Charlotte)
Alina Lazar (Youngstown State University)
Akos Ledeczi (Vanderbilt University)
Annie En-Shiun Lee (University of Waterloo)
Gilliean Lee (Lander University)
Irene Lee (Massachusetts Institute of Technology)
Michael Lee (New Jersey Institute of Technology)
Tsee Lee (Brooklyn Technical High School)
Young Lee (none)
Zachary Lehman (University of California, Los Angeles)
Chi-Un Lei (The University of Hong Kong)
Juho Leinonen (University of Helsinki)
Pedro Leite (Donnelly College)
Matt Lepinski (New College of Florida)
Terry Letsche (Wartburg College)
Kees Leune (Adelphi University)
Grace Lew (Biola University)
Gary Lewandowski (Xavier University)
Peilong Li (University of Massachusetts Lowell)
Toby Jia-Jun Li (Human-Computer Interaction Institute, Carnegie Mellon University)
Zilu Liang (Tokyo Institute of Technology)
Chun Wai Liew (Lafayette College)
Mark Liffiton (Illinois Wesleyan University)
Seongtaek Lim (Cornell Tech)
Yu-Tzu Lin (National Taiwan Normal University)
Panos Linos (Butler University)
Joshua Littenberg-Tobias (MIT)
Hong Liu (Indiana University Kokomo)
Jiangjiang Liu (Lamar)
Qiang Liu (College of Computer, National University of Defense Technology)
Jigang Liu (Metropolitan State University)
Li Liu (California State University, Northridge)
Matija Lokar (University of Ljubljana)
Violetta Lonati (University of Milan)
Dobrila Lopez (Curtin University)
Leonardo Lucena (Instituto Federal do Rio Grande do Norte)
Marcia Lucena (UFRN)
Stephanie Ludi (University of North Texas)
Ana Paula Ludtke Ferreira (Universidade Federal do Pampa)
Roman Lysecky (University of Arizona)
Nicholas Lytle (North Carolina State University)
Reza M. Parizi (Kennesaw State University)
David Malan (Harvard University)
Samuel Mann (Otago Polytechnic)
Farshid Marbouti (San Jose State University)

Daniela Marghitu (Auburn University)
Thomas Marlowe (Seton Hall University)
Maíra Marques Samary (Universidad de Chile)
Manuel Martins Barata (ISEL - Instituto Superior de Engenharia de Lisboa)
Julian Mason (Toyota Research Institute)
Raina Mason (Southern Cross University)
William Mason (Georgia Institute of Technology)
Ecivaldo Matos (UFBA - Universidade Federal da Bahia)
Suzanne Matthews (United States Military Academy)
Bruce Maxwell (Colby College)
Keith Maycock (National College of Ireland)
Chris Mayfield (James Madison University)
Jean Mayo (Michigan Technological University)
Robert McCloskey (University of Scranton)
O. William Mcclung (Nebraska Wesleyan University)
Frank Mccown (Harding University)
Chris McDonald (The Univ. of Western Australia)
Charlie Mcdowell (UC Santa Cruz)
James McGuffee (Christian Brothers University)
John McManus (Randolph-Macon College)
Pedro Medeiros (Universidade Nova de Lisboa- Dep. Informática)
Chao Mei (KENNESAW STATE UNIVERSITY Search)
Alexandra Mendes (Teesside University)
Suzanne Menzel (Indiana University Bloomington)
Jose Carlos Metrolho (IPCB)
Razvan Alexandru Mezei (Saint Martin's University)
Afsaneh Minaie (Utah Valley University)
Mia Minnes (University of California San Diego)
Jose Miro-Julia (UIB)
Diba Mirza (University of California Santa Barbara)
Allison Mishkin (University of Oxford)
Amitabh Mishra (University of West Florida)
Sumita Mishra (Rochester Institute of Technology)
Benjamin R. Mitchell (Villanova University)
Idongesit Mkpong-Ruffin (Faulkner University)
Karina Mochetti (UFF)
Selvarajah Mohanarajah (UNC-Pembroke)
Gabriela Moise (Petroleum-Gas University of Ploiesti)
Mattia Monga (Università degli Studi di Milano - Dip. di Informatica)
Alvaro Monge (California State University Long Beach)
Christopher Moretti (Princeton University)
Michael Morgan (Monash University)
Mirella M. Moro (Univ. Federal de Minas Gerais - UFMG)
Niema Moshiri (University of California San Diego)
Frank Moss (Claremont Graduate University)
Sukanya Kannan Moudgalya (Michigan State University)
Xenia Mountrouidou (College of Charleston)
Michael G Murphy (retired)
Paolo Musmarra (Università degli Studi di Salerno)
Brandon Myers (University of Iowa)
Muhammad Nadeem (Mississippi State University)
Anurag Nagar (The University of Texas at Dallas)
Pedro Najera (Tecnologico de Monterrey, Campus Cuernavaca)
Fabiola Nakamura (Universidade Federal do Amazonas)
Mourya Reddy Narasareddygari (North Dakota State University)
Mamoun Nawahdah (Birzeit University)
Fariha Naz (Simon Fraser University)
Patrick Ndayizigamiye (University of KwaZulu-Natal)
Marion Neumann (Washington Universoty in St. Louis)
Ha Nguyen (University of California-Irvine)
Jaye Nias (Spelman College)
Delmer Nicholson (University of Cincinnati Clermont College)
Emma Norling (The University of Sheffield)
Cindy Norris (Appalachian State University)
Sarah M North (Kennesaw State University)
Theodore S. Norvell (Memorial University of Newfoundland)
Linda Null (The Pennsylvania State University)
Brian O'Neill (Western New England University)
Suhaib Obeidat (Bloomfield College)
Peter Ohmann (College of St. Benedict / St. John's University)
Edward Okie (Radford University)
Oluwakemi Ola (UBC)
John Oliver (Cal Poly)
Lawrence Osborne (Lamar University Faculty)
Radek Oslejsek (Masaryk University)
Joseph Osunde (The Open University, United Kingdom)

Vanessa Stangherlin Machado Paixão-Cortes (PUCRS / URI)
Yin Pan (none)
Greta Pangborn (Saint Michael's College)
Katarina Pantic (Utah State University)
Jennifer Parham-Mocello (Oregon State University)
Joonsuk Park (University of Richmond)
Younghee Park (San Jose State University)
Youngki Park (Chuncheon National University of Education)
Young Park (Bradley University)
Hyesung Park (Georgia Gwinnett College)
Rob Parke (University of Southern California)
Miranda Parker (Georgia Institute of Technology)
Rick Parker (University of Colorado Boulder)
Pablo Parra (University of Alcala)
Leo Natan Paschoal (University of São Paulo)
James Paterson (Glasgow Caledonian University)
Joslenne Pena (The Pennsylvania State University)
Bin Peng (Park University)
Markeya Peteranetz (University of Nebraska-Lincoln)
Teresa Peterman (GVSU)
Andrew Petersen (University of Toronto)
Peter Peterson (University of Minnesota)
Zachary Peterson (Cal Poly, San Luis Obispo)
Iasonas Petras (Princeton University)
Fabio Petrillo (Universite du Quebec a Chicoutimi)
Raymond Pettit (University of Virginia)
Matthew Peveler (Rensselaer Polytechnic Institute)
Phu H. Phung (University of Dayton)
Gustavo Pinto (UFPA)
Blagovesta Pirelli (Ecole Polytechnique Fédérale de Lausanne)
Lambros Piskopos (Wilbur Wright College)
Enrico Pontelli (New Mexico State University)
Jari Porras (LUT)
Lori Postner (Nassau Community College)
James Prather (Abilene Christian University)
Thomas W. Price (North Carolina State University)
Abena Primo (Huston-Tillotson University)
Christopher Proctor (Stanford University)
Lauren Provost (Simmons College)
Keith Quille (Institute of Technology Tallaght)
Beth Quinn (NCWIT)
John Rager (Amherst College)
Saty Raghavachary (University of Southern California)
Brian Railing (Carnegie Mellon University)
Sagar Raina (Mount Saint Mary College)
Rajendra Raj (Rochester Institute of Techinology)
Damith Chatura Rajapakse (National University of Singapore)
Raghuram Ramanujan (Davidson College)
Devina Ramduny-Ellis (Greenhead College)
Shikha Raturi (University of the South Pacific)
Saquib Razak (Carnegie Mellon University)
Elissa M. Redmiles (University of Maryland)
Michael Redmond (La Salle University, Philadelphia, PA, USA)
Donna Reese (Mississippi State University)
Christine Reilly (Skidmore College)
Yolanda Reimer (University of Montana)
Detlef Rick (University of Hamburg)
Charles Riedesel (University of Nebraska - Lincoln)
Kathryn E Ringland (Northwestern University)
Kelly Rivers (Carnegie Mellon University)
Christian Roberson (Florida Southern College)
Nicholas Rosasco (Valparaiso University)
Joel Ross (U Washington iSchool)
Guido Rößling ()
Anthony Ruocco (Roger Williams University)
Ryan Rybarczyk (Butler University)
Mehran Sahami (Stanford University)
Mariam Salloum (UC Riverside)
Ian Sanders (unisa)
Kari Sandouka (Dordt College)
Sreecharan Sankaranarayanan (Carnegie Mellon University)
Cassandra Scharber (University of Minnesota)
Jessica Young Schmidt (North Carolina State University)
Karl Schmitt (Valparaiso University)
Kaye Schroeder (National American University, The College of St. Scholastica)
Jason Schultz (Bemidji State University)
Stephanie Schwartz (Millersville University)
Michael James Scott (Falmouth University)
Bruno Sena (University of São Paulo)
Mazyar Seraj (University of Bremen)
Adolfo Gustavo Serra Seca Neto (UTFPR)

Christian Servin (El Paso Community College)
Michael Shah (Tufts University)
Bonita Sharif (University of Nebraska - Lincoln)
Mohamed Shehab (University of North Carolina at Charlotte)
Amit Shesh (Northeastern University)
Yasuto Shirai (Shizuoka University)
Angela Siegel (Dalhousie University)
Bill Siever (Washington University)
Scott Sigman (Drury University)
Jorge Silveyra (Muhlenberg College)
Maninder Singh (North Dakota State University)
Tim Sisson (Cleveland State University)
Harvey Siy (University of Nebraska at Omaha)
Thérèse Smith (Worcester Polytechnic Institute)
Takako Soma (Illinois College)
Raja Sooriamurthi (Carnegie Mellon University)
Shvetha Soundararajan (George Mason University)
Greg Speegle (Baylor University)
Ellen Spertus (Mills College)
Nathan Sprague (James Madison University)
Nigamanth Sridhar (Cleveland State University)
Bernhard Standl (Vienna University of Technology)
Andreas Steffens (RWTH Aachen University)
Kristin Stephens-Martinez (University of California, Berkeley)
Tom Stokke (University of North Dakota)
Jeffrey Stone (The Pennsylvania State University)
Kristina Striegnitz (Union College)
Kalpathi Subramanian (The University of N Carolina at Charlotte)
Valerie Summet (Rollins College)
Durga Suresh-Menon (Wentworth Institute of Technology)
Valdemar Švábenský (Masaryk University)
Alaaeddin Swidan (Delft University of Technology)
Claudia Szabo (The University of Adelaide)
Toni Taipalus (University of Jyväskylä)
Robert Tairas (Vanderbilt University)
Paul Talaga (University of Indianapolis)
Burcin Tamer (Computing Research Association)
Sheng Tan (Florida State University)
Fatma Tarlaci (Stanford University)
Micah Taylor (The University of North Carolina at Chapel Hill)
Cynthia Taylor (Oberlin College)
Rita Tesseroli (UFPR)
William Thacker (Winthrop University)
Anastasios Theodoropoulos (University of Peloponnese)
Charles Thevathayan (RMIT University)
George Thomas (University of Wisconsin Oshkosh)
Megan Thomas (California State University, Stanislaus)
Brian Thoms (California State University Channel Islands)
Armando Maciel Toda (University of São Paulo)
Kim Tracy (Rose-Hulman Institute of Technology)
Christian Trefftz (Grand Valley State University)
Deborah Trytten (University of Oklahoma)
Jennifer Tsan (North Carolina State University)
Liviana Tudor (Petroleum-Gas University of Ploiesti, Romania)
Claude Turner (Norfolk State University)
Martin Ukrop (Faculty of Informatics, Masaryk University, Czech Republic)
Ian Utting (University of Kent)
David Valentine (Grove City College)
Eliana Valenzuela-Andrade (University of Puerto Rico at Arecibo)
Robert Van Camp (Marietta College)
Sarah Van Wart (University of California, Berkeley)
Izak Van Zyl (Cape Peninsula University of Technology)
James Vanderhyde (Saint Xavier University)
Anthony Varghese (University of Wisconsin-River Falls)
Jorge Vasconcelos (National Autonomous University of Mexico (UNAM))
Nanette Veilleux (Simmons College)
J. Ángel Velázquez-Iturbide (Universidad Rey Juan Carlos)
Gabriela Vilanova (UNPA)
Giovanni Vincenti (University of Baltimore)
Rebecca Vivian (The University of Adelaide)
David Voorhees (Le Moyne College)
Jan Vykopal (Masaryk University)
Rosita Wachenchauzer (Universidad Nacional de Tres de Febrero)
Amber Wagner (Kennesaw State University)
Sally K Wahba (NetApp)
Mike Wallinga (Northwestern College)
Kendra Walther (University of Southern California)
Patrick Wang (Institut Supérieur d'Électronique de Paris)
Sujing Wang (Lamar University)
Yi Wang (Rochester Institute of Technology)
Stan Warford (Pepperdine University)
Jayce R. Warner (The University of Texas at Austin)
Kevin Waterman (EDC)
Andrew Watkins (Baldwin Wallace University)

Neftali Watkinson (University of California, Irvine)
Josh Weese (Kansas State University)
Bingyang Wei (Texas Christian University)
Dee Weikle (James Madison University)
Troy Weingart (United Stated Air Force Academy Dept of Computer Science)
David Weintrop (University of Maryland)
Richard Weiss (The Evergreen State College)
Kevin Wendt (University of Minnesota)
Xiaojing Weng (The Education University of Hong Kong)
Elizabeth White (George Mason University)
Alan Whitehurst (Southern Virginia University)
Michael Whitney (Winthrop University)
Eliane Wiese (University of Utah)
Jim Williams (University of Wisconsin-Madison)
Craig Wills (Worcester Polytechnic Institute)
Victor Winter (University of Nebraska at Omaha)
Zoe Wood (Cal Poly)
Heather Wright (Computing Research Association)
Jinyue Xia (University Of North Carolina Charlotte)
Benjamin Xie (University of Washington)
Mamta Yadav (Texas A&M University - Corpus Christi)
Nikhil Yadav (St. John's University)
Jeong Yang (Texas A&M University-San Antonio)
Lan Yang (California State Polytechnic University, Pomona)
Arthur Yanushka (Christian Brothers University)
Sejong Yoon (The College of New Jersey)
Timothy Yuen (University of Texas at San Antonio)
Zhen Zeng (Arizona State Univeristy)
Jinghua Zhang (Winston-Salem State University)
Yuanlin Zhang (Texas Tech University)
Ming Zhao (Arizona State University)
Rui Zhi (North Carolina State University)
Craig Zilles (University of Illinois at Urbana-Champaign)

Poster Reviewers

Seth Adjei (Northern Kentucky University)
Ashish Aggarwal (University of Florida)
Jennifer Albert (The Citadel)
Gabriella Anton (Northwestern University)
Saira Anwar (Purdue University)
Luis Gustavo J. Araujo (State University of Feira de Santana)
Monica Babes-Vroman (Rutgers University)
Donald Bagert (Benedictine College)
Michael Ball (University of California, Berkeley)
Mario Luca Bernardi (Giustino Fortunato University)
Bradley Beth (The University of Texas at Austin)
Manish Bhatt (University of New Orleans)
Esdras Bispo Jr. (Federal University of Goiás)
Jeremy Bradbury (University of Ontario Institute of Technology)
Andrej Brodnik (University of Ljubljana)
Ricardo Caceffo (University of Campinas (Unicamp), Brazil)
Ankur Chattopadhyay (University of Wisconsin - Green Bay)
Radhouane Chouchane (Columbus State University)
Vincent Cicirello (Stockton University)
Alison Clear (EIT)
Phillip Conrad (UC Santa Barbara)
Andrew Csizmadia (Newman University)
Fabian Deitelhoff (FH Dortmund)
Gabriella Dodero (ASLERD)
Mohsen Dorodchi (University of North Carolina at Charlotte)
Felicia Doswell (Norfolk State University)
Bob Edmison (Virginia Tech)
Kurt Eiselt (University of California, Davis)
Daniel Ellsworth (Colorado College)
Yadran Eterovic (Pontificia Universidad Catlica de Chile)
Mohammed Farghally (Virginia Tech)
Russell Feldhausen (Kansas State University)
Ronald Finkbine (Indiana University Southeast)
Susan Eileen Fox (Macalester College)
Kathleen Freeman (University of Oregon)
Ilenia Fronza (Free University of Bolzano / Bozen)
Alessio Gaspar (University of South Florida Polytechnic)
Richard Glassey (Robert Gordon University)
Mark Gondree (Sonoma State University)
Ana I. González-Tablas (University Carlos III de Madrid)
Isabela Hidalgo (University of South Florida)
Timothy Highley (La Salle University)
José Ramón Hilera (Universidad de Alcalá)
Brian Howard (DePauw University)
Jana Jackova (Matej Bel University)
Yerika Jimenez (University of Florida)
Kartik Palani Kartik Palani (University of Illinois at Urbana-Champaign)

Fazel Keshtkar (ST John's University)
Edward Kim (Villanova University)
Meen Chul Kim (Drexel University)
Carsten Kleiner (University of Applied Science and Arts Hannover)
Joe Kmoch (JK Consulting)
Kyu Han Koh (California State University, Stanislaus)
Joan Langdon (Bowie State University)
Bobby Law (Glasgow Caledonian University)
Alina Lazar (Youngstown State University)
Christopher League (LIU Brooklyn)
Chi-Un Lei (The University of Hong Kong)
Peilong Li (University of Massachusetts Lowell)
Yu-Tzu Lin (National Taiwan Normal University)
Qiang Liu (College of Computer, National University of Defense Technology)
Nicholas Lytle (North Carolina State University)
Mirella M. Moro (Univ. Federal de Minas Gerais - UFMG)
Joaquim Madeira (University of Aveiro)
Olaf Manuel Maennel (Tallinn University of Technology)
Maria Jose Marcelino (University of Coimbra)
Bruce Maxwell (Colby College)
Lester McCann (University of Arizona)
Ralph Eric McGregor (Bridgewater College)
Pedro Medeiros (Universidade Nova de Lisboa- Dep. Informática)
Alexandra Mendes (Teesside University)
Jose Carlos Metrolho (IPCB)
Gabriela Moise (Petroleum-Gas University of Ploiesti)
Niema Moshiri (University of California San Diego)
Shamsi Moussavi (MassBay Community College)
Srikanth Mudigonda (Saint Louis University)
Paolo Musmarra (Università degli Studi di Salerno)
Nilufer Onder (Michigan Technological University)
Daniel Paiva (Universidade Tecnológica Federal do Paraná)
Youngki Park (Chuncheon National University of Education)
Matthew Peveler (Rensselaer Polytechnic Institute)
Enrico Pontelli (New Mexico State University)
Sagar Raina (Mount Saint Mary College)
Ali Raza (University of Colorado Boulder)
Detlef Rick (University of Hamburg)
Charles Riedesel (University of Nebraska - Lincoln)
Marc Rigas (The Pennsylvania State University)
Suzanne Rivoire (Sonoma State University)
Kaye Schroeder (National American University, The College of St. Scholastica)
Ching-Kuang Shene (Michigan Technological University)
Yasuto Shirai (Shizuoka University)
Bill Siever (Washington University)
Maninder Singh (North Dakota State University)
Varsha Srikanth Koushik (University of Colorado Boulder)
Melissa Stange (Lord Fairfax Community College)
Andreas Steffens (RWTH Aachen University)
Paul Talaga (University of Indianapolis)
Rita Tesseroli (UFPR)
Brian Thoms (California State University Channel Islands)
Armando Toda (University of São Paulo)
Tammy Vandegrift (University of Portland)
Jorge Vasconcelos (National Autonomous University of Mexico (UNAM))
Rebecca Vivian (The University of Adelaide)
Amber Wagner (Kennesaw State University)
Patrick Wang (Institut Supérieur d'Électronique de Paris)
Howard Whitston (University of South Alabama)
Craig Wills (Worcester Polytechnic Institute)
Steven Wolfman (The University of British Columbia)
Fan Yang (Stanford University)
H. Kai Yang (Seattle College)
Yueming Yang (Baldwin Wallace University)
Jones Yu (Wentworth Institute of Technology)
Yuanlin Zhang (Texas Tech University)

Special Session Reviewers

Andrew Allen (Georgia Southern University)
Isabel Azevedo (ISEP)
Beverly Bachmayer (Intel)
Leland Beck (San Diego State University)
S. Jane Fritz (St. Joseph's College)
Olga Glebova (Georgia State University)
Mark Gondree (Sonoma State University)
Colin Johnson (University of Kent)
Michael Kirkpatrick (James Madison University)
Swathi Kurunji (Teradata)
Steven Mcgee (The Learning Partnership)

Louis Mchugh (Illinois Institute of Technology)

Sara More (Johns Hopkins Department of Computer Science)

Imani Palmer (University of Illinois at Urbana-Champaign)

Andy Rasmussen (Chicago Public Schools)

Matt Roberts (Macquarie University)

Tobias Rocha (UFRN)

Rehmat Ullah (Hongik University)

Tammy Vandegrift (University of Portland)

Ming Zhang (Peking University)

Sanja Zivanovic (Barry University)

Workshop Reviewers

Raman Adaikkalavan (Indiana University South Bend)

Mohammad Q. Azhar (BMCC, The City University Of New York)

Luciana Benotti (Universidad Nacional de Cordoba)

Marc Berges (Technische Universität München, TUM School of Education)

Erik Brunvand (University of Utah)

David Bunde (Knox College)

Richard Burns (West Chester University)

Michael Cotterell (University of Georgia)

Lawrence D'Antonio (Ramapo College)

Luigi De Russis (Politecnico di Torino)

Nate Derbinsky (Northeastern University)

Priscilla Dodds (Georgia State University)

Ali Ebnenasir (Michigan Technological University)

Kathleen Ericson (University of Tennessee at Martin)

Mark Floryan (University of Virginia)

Joshua T. Guerin (University of Tennessee at Martin)

Yasemin Gulbahar (Ankara University)

Brian Harrington (University of Toronto)

Cinda Heeren (UBC)

Wen-Jung Hsin (Park University)

Kartik Palani Kartik Palani (University of Illinois at Urbana-Champaign)

Anastasia Kurdia (Tulane University)

David Largent (Ball State University)

Cam Macdonell (MacEwan University)

Melinda Mcdaniel (Georgia Institute of Technology)

Srikanth Mudigonda (Saint Louis University)

Daniel Costa De Paiva (Universidade Tecnológica Federal do Paraná)

Shari Plantz-Masters (Regus University)

Joe Politz (University of California San Diego)

Traci Sarmiento (United States Air Force Academy)

Ching-Kuang Shene (Michigan Technological University)

Varsha Srikanth Koushik (University of Colorado Boulder)

Nadine von Frankenberg Und Ludwigsdorff (Technical University of Munich)

Steven Wolfman (The University of British Columbia)

Jidong Xiao (Boise State University)

Fan Yang (Stanford University)

Rina Zviel-Girshin (Ruppin Academic Center)

SIGCSE 2019 Sponsors & Supporters

Platinum Supporters:

Gold Supporters:

Silver Supporters:

Bronze Supporters:

Beauty and Joy of Computing:

2016–17 Findings from an AP CS Principles course

June Mark
Education Development Center
Waltham, MA 02453
jmark@edc.org

Kelsey Klein
Education Development Center
Waltham, MA 02453
kklein@edc.org

ABSTRACT

In 2016–17, the College Board launched the Advanced Placement (AP) Computer Science Principles (CSP) course and exam. The AP CSP course was designed with the goal of broadening participation in computer science, and aims to introduce students to the creative aspects of computing by engaging students in developing computational artifacts related to their interests. The big ideas of the course include programming, abstraction, algorithms, data and information, the Internet, and also the global and societal impacts of computing.

With support from the National Science Foundation (NSF), the Beauty and Joy of Computing in New York City partnership created the Beauty and Joy of Computing (BJC) course that is aligned to the AP CSP framework and endorsed by the College Board. The partnership recruited over 100 NYC teachers to implement the course, provided professional development (PD) and implementation support, and conducted research on the course implementation and the effects on teachers and students.

This paper reports on findings from the implementation of BJC as an AP CSP course in NYC from the 2016–17 school year. It addresses student performance on a content knowledge assessment, a survey of students' attitudes toward computer science, and the 2017 AP CSP exam. Given the intentional design of the BJC course and AP CSP framework to address diversity and equity, student outcomes are also disaggregated by gender and race/ethnicity.

KEYWORDS

computer science education, K-12 curriculum, Computer Science Principles

ACM Reference format:

June Mark and Kelsey Klein. 2019. Beauty and Joy of Computing: 2016-17 Findings from an AP CS Principles course. In *Proceedings of the 50th ACM Technical Symposium on Computer Science Education*, Minneapolis, Minnesota USA, February 27-March 2, 2019 (SIGCSE'19), ACM, NY, NY, USA, 7 pages. DOI: 10.1145/3287324.3287375

1 Introduction

The National Science Foundation (NSF) and the College Board developed the Advanced Placement (AP) Computer Science Principles (CSP) course and framework to broaden participation in computer science (CS), especially among females and students from racial and ethnic groups historically underrepresented in CS, and to provide an engaging and lively introduction to CS for high school students [1, 2, 3, 4]. The course was part of an NSF-led initiative (CS10K) to train 10,000 high school teachers to teach CS [5, 6]. Following pilots at the college and high school levels, CSP became an official AP course during the 2016–17 school year with the first administration of the CSP exam taking place in May 2017.

To support adoption of AP CSP, the NSF and other organizations funded a number of projects to develop curriculum materials aligned to the AP CSP framework and to provide professional development (PD) for high school teachers to become aware of curricular options, learn about pedagogical practices that support equitable CS instruction, and to plan for implementation and use in their own schools and classrooms [3, 7]. The Beauty and Joy of Computing (BJC) curriculum, described here, grows out of one of those curriculum development and implementation efforts.

2 About BJC and the BJC4NYC partnership

BJC was initially developed at the University of California, Berkeley (UCB) as a course for non-CS majors using the Snap*!* visual programming language [8]. In 2014, with support from the NSF, UCB partnered with Education Development Center (EDC) to create, test, and refine BJC, a yearlong high school AP CSP course adapted from the college-level course of the same name. In the BJC for NYC (BJC4NYC) partnership, the NYC Department of Education (NYCDOE) and the Foundation for Computer Science in NYC (CSNYC) partnered with EDC and UCB to recruit and train over 100 BJC teachers from a demographically representative set of NYC high schools. North Carolina State University (NCSU) joined the partnership to support BJC PD beyond NYC, and to develop online resources for teacher PD. The BJC4NYC partnership goals were to attract more female, black, and Latinx students in NYC to the joy of programming, the beauty of the intellectual ideas behind CS, and the social impacts of technology. The results of the partnership include the creation of the BJC curriculum for high school use, alignment to the AP CSP framework and endorsement of the course by the College Board, recruitment of more than 100 NYC teachers to implement the course, and the provision of more than six weeks of PD and ongoing implementation support for three cohorts of NYC teachers. The PD and supports were designed to increase teachers' CS content knowledge and prepare them to teach BJC. Beyond NYC, NCSU has led PD for hundreds of BJC teachers across the country [9, 10].

BJC was designed to be a version of AP CSP that would deepen students' understanding by placing more emphasis on programming than the framework requires. This choice came from the authors' desire to provide students with engaging computer science experiences that are fun, and that help students feel competent and confident that they can "do" computer science. BJC is designed so that students can see the power of their own logic and the beauty and elegance of the code they create to express their creativity, especially on projects that are personally relevant and interesting. A key goal of the course is that students experience programming itself as something they enjoy and know they can do.

Moreover, programming is central to developing important ideas and ways of thinking (e.g., abstraction and algorithmic thinking) that are characteristic of computer science. The programming content features recursion and higher-order functions because of the powerful and beautiful way that they exemplify abstraction, one of the core ideas in computer science and the AP CSP framework. Traditionally, higher-order functions have been considered too difficult for high school students. The authors hypothesized that the explicit visual representations that the blocks-based programming language Snap*!* provides will make higher-order functions accessible to a diverse population of high school students. The non-programming parts of the course focus on the social implications of computing, and give students opportunities to analyze computing innovations balancing optimism about the affordances of computer technologies with a critical stance toward specific uses.

3 Related Research

Attention to broadening participation in CS has grown as projections for future jobs in the computer science and science, technology, engineering and mathematics (STEM) fields have rapidly increased [11], along with the recognition that there is a need to diversify the STEM workforce. In 2011, blacks and Hispanics made up just 13% of the STEM workforce even though they were 26% of the workforce at large, and there were twice as many men employed in a STEM occupation as women [12]. Of CS degrees awarded in 2016, 76% were to white or Asian students, and 79% were to male students [13]. This has led to the recognition that access to computer science is an equity issue, and there is a need for more opportunities for students to engage with computer science ideas and practices in K–12 education, and greater encouragement to pursue computer science in college and careers.

The need for more opportunities for students to learn CS in high school is particularly pronounced for female students and students from racial and ethnic groups historically underrepresented in computing and technology (URG). Buzzetto-More and colleagues found that inadequate programming skills from coursework prior to college is a barrier to minorities participating in computing disciplines in college [14]. The College Board has reported that students who take AP computer science are eight times more likely to major in CS [15]. Chute found that lack of exposure to STEM was a contributing factor to low rates in minority and female participation [16]. Research points to the need for contextualizing the study of CS in order to engage these students. The National Center for Women & Information Technology (NCWIT) encourages schools to make CS curricula relevant to students, to recruit female and URG students, and to use inclusive pedagogies [17]. Estrada et al. point to the importance of personal relevance and beneficial uses of technology, which they argue may be more important in attracting URG students [18]. One target of state- and district-level CS4All initiatives has been to broaden students' participation in CS courses, especially among female and URG students, and especially in high school courses such as AP CSP.

Given that the AP CSP course and exam are so new, there is little research data or findings on the effects of the AP CSP course and associated curriculum programs to date. The extant literature focuses on describing the goals and ideas behind the CS Principles framework and course including course goals, big ideas, and computational thinking practices [3, 4, 19, 20]; and describes curriculum and PD efforts aimed at preparing teachers to teach AP CSP courses and introducing teachers to equitable pedagogies for teaching CS [9, 21, 22, 23, 24]. Many CS education initiatives have focused heavily on teacher PD as essential to realizing the goals of broader access and participation in CS. Findings about what contributes to effective PD for teaching AP CSP is now emerging from these teacher PD efforts. Guidance on teacher PD in CS includes recommendations to customize PD to support teachers with varied CS backgrounds, attend to novice teachers' content knowledge, contextualize PD experiences in classroom curricula and pedagogy, focus on increasing access and equity, and encourage collaboration and community among teachers [9, 22, 25, 26]. Support and funding for PD opportunities in CS by the NSF, Infosys, and other funders has catalyzed the spread of CS courses and instruction in K–12 schools [27]. Some research details teachers' experiences teaching AP CSP, along with discussion of the challenges encountered teaching CSP [28, 29]. In terms of outcomes, Hamlen and colleagues reported on teacher and student effects resulting from an AP CSP PD project [30]. There is a need for more literature examining the effects of AP CSP programs on teacher and student outcomes, including CS participation, CS knowledge, and attitudes toward CS.

4 Broadening CS Participation in High School

The introduction of the AP CSP course and exam sought to broaden participation in CS by making the field more attractive to women and black, Hispanic, and Native American students, groups historically underrepresented in CS. The goals included increasing the proportion of female and URG students enrolling in AP computer science courses and passing the AP CS exams. Participation in AP CS A (a Java-based programming course), the only AP computer science course being offered prior to the introduction of AP CSP, is dominated by white and Asian males. The early College Board data on the impact of the CSP course on student participation are encouraging. With the launch of AP CSP in 2016–17—the biggest launch of a new AP course in College Board history—there was a 79% jump in participation, with over 100,000 students taking an AP CS exam, either AP CS A or AP CSP. Moreover, in the first year of AP CSP, the number of girls who took an AP CS course more than doubled, as did the numbers of Hispanic/Latinx and black/African American students. In 2018, there was a 50% rise in the number of students taking the AP CSP exam, from 50,000 students in 2017 to 76,000 students in 2018. From 2017 to 2018, there were also substantive gains in the number of black, Hispanic/Latinx, and female students taking and passing the AP CSP exam. Access to and participation in AP CSP is a critical lever for diversifying CS enrollment in high school, and for increasing students' opportunities to consider CS-related opportunities in colleges and careers [31, 32, 33]. As a result of AP CSP, participation in CS is growing, and the greatest gains in participation are among females, black, and Hispanic/Latinx students. The studies reported here focus on the outcomes related to the implementation of one specific curriculum, Beauty and Joy of Computing, designed to be aligned to the AP CSP framework.

5 Research Goals and Context

In addition to developing the high school version of the BJC curriculum and providing PD for teachers in NYC who use BJC, our NSF-funded project conducted a set of research and evaluation activities, partnering with Haynie Research and Evaluation. The goals of the data collection and analyses were three-fold:

1) to inform design as well as revisions to curriculum materials,

2) to report on project quality and effectiveness, and

3) to report research-based knowledge to the CS education field.

To this end, the partnership supported implementation and collected teacher and student data for three years looking at teacher outcomes, and student gains in content knowledge and attitudes toward computer science prior to and after taking a BJC AP CSP course. The data presented here, from two sub-studies, largely addresses student outcomes, and is from school year 2016–17, the second year of project data collection and the first year the AP CSP exam was offered. Sub-study 1 was specifically interested in a subset of the BJC research study results on the student survey and content assessment. Supplementing other BJC student data collection in NYC, the first year of AP CSP administration allowed us to see how BJC students fared on the AP CSP exam compared to students who were taught AP CSP content not using BJC. Sub-study 2 aimed to analyze the results of all students in NYC who took the AP CSP exam in 2017, specifically comparing BJC and non-BJC students.

6 Research Questions

The research questions reported here in this paper include:

1. Has participation in BJC AP CSP broadened student participation in CS?
2. Do students enrolled in a BJC AP CSP course gain in content knowledge from the beginning to end of the year? Are student gains similar when disaggregated by gender and URG status?
3. Do students enrolled in a BJC AP CSP course gain in interest, confidence, belongingness, and identification with computing? Are student gains similar when disaggregated by gender and URG status?
4. How do summative AP test scores of BJC students in NYC compare to other students in NYC not taught with the BJC curriculum?

7 Methodology

Below we describe our research samples, data collection procedures, instrumentation, and data analysis methods for BJC4NYC student participation data and both sub-studies.

7.1 Data Collection Procedures

Student participation in BJC data collection procedures. NYCDOE tracked student enrollment in BJC courses in NYC. Information on student enrollment overall and by subgroups of interest (e.g., gender and race) was collected, summarized, and provided by NYCDOE.

Sub-study 1 participants and data collection procedures. All students enrolled in a BJC AP CSP course in NYC were asked to complete a content assessment and an attitude survey at the beginning (October–December 2016) and end (May–June 2017) of the 2016–17 school year. Students were included as BJC research participants if they completed all four data collection instruments: the pre- and post-course content assessments and the pre- and post-course surveys. In 2016–17, the sample included 311 students across 24 NYC high schools. A majority of the sample was female (54%), non-URG (63%), and juniors in high school (57%); just 10% of students had taken a CS course previously. Student content assessments and attitude surveys were administered online via SurveyMonkey using links provided to them by their teacher.

Sub-study 2 participants and data collection procedures. In May 2017, 2,854 students took the 2017 AP CSP exam in NYC. Demographically, students were 57% male, 43% female; 13% black, 20% Hispanic with 33% of students from underrepresented racial and ethnic groups and 65% were designated as in poverty based on eligibility for free or reduced price lunch or identification by the NYCDOE Human Resources Administration as receiving certain types of public assistance. Thirty percent of students who took the 2017 AP CSP exam in NYC were taught using the BJC curriculum. NYCDOE's Research and Policy Support Group (RPSG) provided the 2017 AP CSP exam scores for NYC students through a data request.

Note that the sub-study 1 and sub-study 2 samples overlap but neither is completely inclusive of the other. Specifically, some of the AP CSP exam takers in NYC participated in the BJC research study (sample 1), and not all BJC research study participants took the AP CSP exam (sample 2).

7.2 Instrumentation

The measures used in this study include:

Student Enrollment Memorandum. NYCDOE wrote a memorandum summarizing student enrollment in BJC courses across NYC. Summary information was included overall and by student demographics.

Content Assessment. The pre- and post-course student content assessment was developed by using released AP CSP items, UCB BJC assessments, and parallel items developed by BJC curriculum developers, AP CSP curriculum developers and CS content knowledge experts. The assessment is made up of 30 items intended to measure AP CSP Big Ideas 2–7 (Abstraction, Data and Information, Algorithms, Programming, The Internet, and Global Impact) as well as the BJC-specific topics of recursion and higher order functions. Big Idea 1 (Creativity) is not covered on the assessment as it is an overarching concept that is not explicitly assessed on the AP CSP Exam [1]. Two items were removed prior to analysis because of mistakes in the item wording or in the response options. The assessment provides two overall sum-scores: one for the AP CSP Big Ideas (21 items, Cronbach's alpha = 0.80) and one for the BJC-specific topics (7 items, Cronbach's alpha = 0.53). Given Cronbach's alpha for the BJC-specific topics sub-score does not meet the standard of 0.70, only students' Big Ideas sub-score was analyzed.

Attitude Survey. The pre- and post-course student attitude surveys were adapted from [34, 35, 36] and included scales to measure CS-related confidence (Cronbach's alpha = 0.79), interest (Cronbach's alpha = 0.91), belongingness (Cronbach's alpha = 0.77), and identity (Cronbach's alpha = 0.84). Belongingness refers to the feeling that you fit in and there are others like you in CS, while identity refers to whether or not you and others you know view yourself as a CS person. Confidence, interest, and belongingness were rated on a 4-point Likert scale from strongly disagree to strongly agree; identity was rated on a 3-point scale (1=No, not at all; 2=Maybe, at least a little; 3=Yes, very much).

2017 AP CSP Exam. The 2017 AP CSP exam was administered on Friday, May 5, 2017 to students across the United States. Scores range from 1 to 5; a score of 3 or above is a passing score.

7.3 Data Analysis

To answer the first research question, student enrollment information was captured from NYCDOE's memorandum on BJC enrollment in NYC. To answer the second and third research questions, pre-course and post-course student content assessment and attitude survey data collected from BJC research participants in NYC high schools were analyzed using the following analytic procedures. Scale scores were calculated for content knowledge (AP CSP Big Ideas) by summing the corresponding items and for attitudes toward CS (interest, confidence, belongingness, and identity) by averaging the corresponding items. The mean of each scale was calculated for pre- and post-course data. Then, dependent samples t-tests were run to determine if the mean values changed significantly from pre- to post-course. In addition, gain scores were calculated from pre- to post-course by subtracting pre-course scores from post-course scores, and regression analyses were run on the gain scores by gender and URG status to determine if students underrepresented in CS make similar gains as those not underrepresented. Results are also presented for the regression analyses with a school sample size variable, or the number of research participants in the school, included as a covariate to take into account the variation in the number of students from each school in the sample, which ranged from 1 to 74 students. To answer the fourth research question, frequency distributions and passing rates were calculated for the overall NYC sample; for the sample after taking into account large, demographically unique schools; and broken out by curriculum (taught AP CSP with the BJC curriculum versus not with the BJC curriculum). The chi-square test of association was used to determine if there were significant differences in AP CSP exam scores by curriculum. IBM's SPSS Statistics version 24 was used to analyze all research study data.

8 Findings

Given the broadening participation goals of BJC and the AP CSP course, we first report BJC student participation findings, followed by the student outcome findings for our two sub-studies.

8.1 Student participation

Student enrollment for BJC classes in NYC during 2016–17 was 1,383 students. Of those students, 43% were female, and 57% were male. Reported race/ethnicity showed black 27%, Hispanic 28%, Asian 23%, white 19%, multi-racial 1%, and Native American 1%. Students were mostly juniors (33%) and seniors (44%); 18% were ninth and tenth graders. Sixty percent of BJC4NYC students received free or reduced price lunch, 2% were ELs, and 7% were students with disabilities. Students were enrolled in schools that covered all five boroughs of NYC. Many of the participating schools did not previously have CS programs or the ability to offer them until this opportunity. Student data for 2017–18 are still being collected; however, the preliminary student enrollment for BJC classes in NYC is 2,383 students, showing gains in percentages of female (49%), black (33%), and Hispanic (29%) students.

8.2 Sub-study 1

Students showed significant pre- to post-course gains in AP CSP Big Ideas content knowledge; specifically, average scores increased from 9.09 pre-course to 10.75 post-course for a significant gain of 1.66 ($p < 0.001$, Cohen's $d = 0.43$). URG status and gender are significant factors for content knowledge; non-URG and male students performed significantly better on the content assessment than URG and female students, respectively, both at pre-course and at post-course ($p < 0.05$ for all, Cohen's d ranged from 0.30 to 0.63). See figure 1, below, for pre- and post-course means overall and by subgroup. But for gains, there was no gender difference on the content assessment with male scores increasing from pre- to post-course by an average of 2.00 and female scores increasing by an average of 1.52 (p = 0.299). By contrast, non-URG students both started and ended the course with higher scores and showed significantly greater gains on the content assessment than URG students (gains of 2.10 and 0.92, respectively, p = 0.011, d = 0.31). School sample size was also included in a set of regression analyses as a covariate. After taking into account school sample size, gender remained insignificant; however, URG status changed from significant to insignificant (p = 0.698). Thus, after taking into account the number of research participants in each school, non-URG and URG students had similar gains on the content assessment pre- to post-course. In short, female and URG students achieved similar gains on the content assessment as male and non-URG students, respectively, taking into account school sample size.

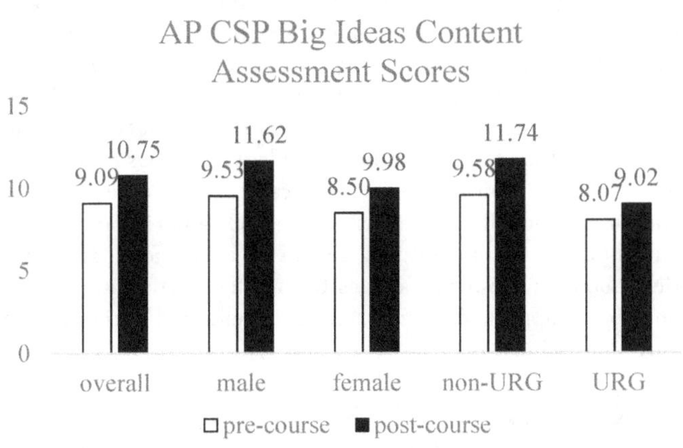

Figure 1: Pre- and post-course content assessment scores

Figure 2 below contains student pre- and post-course means for variables measuring student attitudes toward CS. Significant, positive differences were found from pre- to post-course for confidence (p = 0.015, d = 0.14) and identity (p = 0.001, d = 0.20); no significant gains were found for interest or belongingness. Overall, male students and non-URG students reported more positive attitudes toward CS than females and URG students. However, females and URG students showed similar gains in confidence, interest, belongingness, and identity from pre- to post-course as males and non-URG students, respectively. As with the content assessment results, school sample size was then included in the model. After taking into account school sample size, gender and URG status still were not significant predictors of the CS attitude gain scores.

	Pre-Course	Post-Course
Attitude Scale	Mean (SD)	Mean (SD)
Confidence	2.80 (0.55)	2.87 (0.55)
Interest	2.91 (0.64)	2.93 (0.70)
Belongingness	3.02 (0.49)	3.07 (0.50)
Identity	2.01 (0.53)	2.10 (0.52)

Figure 2: Average scores (and standard deviations) for the four student pre- and post-course attitudes toward CS scales

8.3 Sub-study 2

The overall passing rate for the 2017 AP CSP exam in NYC was 72.7%. Of the 30% of students who took the 2017 AP CSP exam in NYC and were taught with the BJC curriculum, 67.2% passed the 2017 AP CSP exam. However, the student demographics of those two groups differed. Because over 50% of NYC students who took the AP CSP exam were from two high-performing high schools that had student demographics that differed from the norms for the city's schools overall, additional analyses were conducted without those two schools.

Two participating high schools—we call them North and South—had significantly different demographics from other NYC schools, and one of the schools was a selective high school requiring an entrance exam in NYC. They had 1,519 and 135 students take the 2017 AP CSP Exam, respectively. Together, students from these two schools made up 58% of NYC students who took the 2017 AP CSP exam. Demographically, these schools have significantly fewer URG students, students with individualized education plans (IEP), and students designated as in poverty. Both schools were also significantly more likely to have sophomores and significantly less likely to have seniors sitting for the exam. Because of the size and demographic make-up of the schools, these two schools were removed prior to additional analysis. Both schools had a pass rate over 90% on the 2017 AP CSP exam. At North HS, 131 of 1519 students were taught using BJC; their pass rate was 100% compared to 91.6% for students not taught with BJC. At South HS, all 135 students were taught using BJC, and their pass rate was 91.8%.

Excluding these two schools, 1,192 students (42% of NYC AP CSP exam takers) from 75 schools took the exam in NYC. The remaining students, demographically, were mostly juniors and seniors; 54% male; 61% URG; and 77.5% designated as in poverty. Of these students, only 45.9% passed the 2017 AP CSP Exam, with 19% receiving a score of 1 and 35.2% receiving a score of 2. Excluding North and South High Schools, almost half of students who took the 2017 AP CSP Exam in NYC were taught using BJC, and students taught with the BJC curriculum passed at a significantly higher rate (54.2%) than students not taught with BJC (37.7%).

9 Limitations

The results reported here are limited in several ways. For sub-study 1, the biggest limitation is teacher and student response rates. Over half of teachers trained to teach BJC in 2015–16 or 2016–17 did not collect student data in 2016–17. Of the teachers who did collect student data, classroom response rates varied considerably from 25% to 100%. Data collection may have been limited because research incentives are not permitted for teachers in NYC. For sub-study 2, the biggest limitation was that classification of BJC curriculum use to either users or non-users was based on our knowledge of curriculum use gathered from College Board data, teacher surveys, and NYCDOE records. However, this data is incomplete, and our records about use of the BJC curriculum could not be verified for some teachers. In addition, it is possible that there are teachers who used BJC but did not indicate use to the College Board, or did not attend the NYCDOE-sponsored PD, and therefore, we were unaware of their use.

Furthermore, there are limitations that span the entire study. First, due to small sample sizes for most schools, our analyses could not take into account the nesting of students within schools, teachers, and classrooms. In the final year of project data collection, we hope to have a large enough sample to conduct analyses that do take this nesting into account. Relatedly, we do not take into account teacher or school-level factors that likely impact students' scores on the attitude survey, content assessment, and 2017 AP CSP exam, nor do we take into account student factors beyond gender and URG status. Finally, there is limited research on the validity of the measures used, including for the 2017 AP CSP exam. While all scales and assessments were developed thoughtfully and then tested, little exists in the field of computer science by which to validate them. In addition, it is important to note that these results are preliminary, and further analysis of the 2016–2017 results are underway. Also underway is analysis of subsequent administrations of the attitude survey, content assessment, and AP CSP exam accounting for these limitations.

10 Discussion and Implications

A number of state- and district-wide efforts are currently aimed at broadening participation in computer science in K–12 schools across the U.S. Particular attention at the high school level has been focused on the introduction and implementation of a new AP course, CSP, designed both to attract a broader audience of students to computer science and to engage them in the important content ideas and characteristic ways of thinking employed in the field of computer science. In the last decade, a number of curriculum programs have emerged to support schools in offering the AP CSP course. The College Board provides teachers and schools with links to a set of curriculum programs that have been reviewed and endorsed for the AP CSP course [7].

In the results reported here, we are encouraged about the gains in participation in CS in NYC, particularly among female, black, and Hispanic students. To continue to attract greater numbers of these students, active recruitment is needed, and there is still much to do to ensure that these students have multiple experiences that continue to spark their CS interests, and encourage them to pursue CS and CS-related courses and careers. It is also essential to dig deeper into the results to examine whether the demographics of the BJC AP CSP classrooms in NYC schools mirror the overall demographics of their school populations, and that gains in access and achievement are similar across different student groups. As for achievement gains, while we saw similar gains on the content assessment for females and males, as well as for URG and non-URG students when taking into account the variation in school research sample size, males and non-URG students started out scoring higher on the content assessment at pre-test. What earlier CS experiences need to be provided to close these starting achievement gaps?

In addition, implementation efforts found that there were substantive differences in the school contexts where the BJC AP CSP course was introduced. For some schools, the BJC course was the very first AP course offered at the school, and many students in these schools often did not see themselves as ready to take an AP course or exam, and some students were not accustomed to the level of demand expected in the course. We feel that it is critical to better understand the broader contexts of the schools where AP CSP is being implemented, and to develop and test the needed supports so that rigorous CS courses can be implemented and sustained in diverse school settings.

Since these implementation efforts are all relatively new, there is great interest in understanding the successes and challenges of introducing CS through the AP CSP course. There is also a demand for evidence that demonstrates the AP CSP course and the curriculum programs developed to support teaching and learning CSP are increasing participation as desired, and also showing desirable outcomes for teacher and student learning. Moreover, it is critical to examine student outcomes particularly for students from groups historically underrepresented in computing, including female students, black, and Hispanic/Latinx students. The results of this work can advance knowledge in the field about promising strategies to broaden participation in CS and about supports for successful implementation of rigorous CS curricula and instruction.

ACKNOWLEDGMENTS

This material is based upon work supported by the National Science Foundation under Grant No. 1441075. Any opinions, findings, and conclusions or recommendations expressed in this material are those of the author(s) and do not necessarily reflect the views of the National Science Foundation. We would like to acknowledge the efforts of Kathleen Haynie and Hetal Thukral of Haynie Research and Evaluation who served as external evaluators for the BJC4NYC partnership, and contributed to the analyses of the teacher and student outcomes for the project. We also want to thank our partners at the NYCDOE, particularly Michelle Kennedy, for assistance in recruitment, implementation support, and data collection and analysis. We also thank the BJC curriculum development team for their passion and dedication to developing curriculum that inspire students to love CS.

REFERENCES

[1] College Board. 2017. AP Computer Science Principles: Including the Curriculum Framework (Fall 2017). Retrieved August 30, 2018 from https://apcentral.collegeboard.org/pdf/ap-computer-science-principles-course-and-exam-description.pdf

[2] College Board. 2018. Computer Science Principles: Course details. Retrieved August 30, 2018 from https://advancesinap.collegeboard.org/stem/computer-science-principles/course-details

[3] Marie desJardins. 2015. Creating AP CS Principles: Let many flowers bloom. ACM Inroads 6, 4 (Dec. 2015), 60-66. DOI: 10.1145/2835852

[4] Richard Kick and Frances P. Trees. 2015. AP CS Principles: Engaging, challenging, and rewarding. ACM Inroads 6, 1 (March 2015), 42–45. DOI: 10.1145/2710672

[5] Jan Cuny. 2012. Transforming high school computing. ACM Inroads. 3, 2 (June 2012), 32.

[6] Owen Astrachan, Jan Cuny, Chris Stephenson, and Cameron Wilson. 2011. The CS10K Project: Mobilizing the community to transform high school computing. In Proceedings of the 42nd ACM Technical Symposium on Computer Science Education (SIGCSE '11). ACM Press, New York, NY, 85-86.

[7] College Board. 2018. Adopt Ready-to-Use Curricula: Providers of AP CSP Curricula and Pedagogical Support. Retrieved August 28, 2018 from https://apcentral.collegeboard.org/courses/ap-computer-science-principles/classroom-resources/curricula-pedagogical-support

[8] Brian Harvey. 2012. The Beauty and Joy of Computing: Computer science for everyone. In Constructionism: Theory, Practice, and Impact Conference Proceedings. Athens, Greece, 33-39.

[9] Thomas W. Price, Veronica Catete, Jennifer Albert, Tiffany Barnes, and Daniel D. Garcia. 2016. Lessons learned from "BJC" CS Principles professional development. In Proceedings of the 47th ACM Technical Symposium on Computer Science Education (SIGCSE '16). ACM Press, New York, NY, 467-472.

[10] Meghana Subramaniam and Veronica Catete. 2017. A pathway to strengthening support for Beauty and Joy of Computing teachers. In Proceedings of the 48th ACM Technical Symposium on Computer Science Education (SIGCSE '17). ACM Press, New York, NY, 779-780.

[11] Bureau of Labor Statistics, U.S. Department of Labor, 2018. Occupational Outlook Handbook: Computer and Information Technology Occupations. Retrieved April 18, 2018, from https://www.bls.gov/ooh/computer-and-information-technology/home.htm

[12] Liana Christin Landivar. 2013. Disparities in STEM employment by sex, race, and Hispanic origin. Disparities in STEM employment by sex, race, and Hispanic origin. Disparities in STEM employment by sex, race, and Hispanic origin. Education Review. 29, 6, 911–922.

[13] Data USA. (n.d.). Computer science: Diversity. Retrieved from https://datausa.io/profile/cip/110701/#demographics

[14] Nicole A. Buzzetto-More and Ojiabo Ukoha, and Narenda Rustagi. 2010. Unlocking the barriers to women and minorities in computer science and information systems studies: Results from a multi-methodological study conducted at two minority serving institutions. Journal of Information Technology Education: Research, 9, 115–131.

[15] Krista D. Mattern, Emily J. Shaw, and Maureen Ewing. 2011. Advanced Placement Exam Participation Is AP Exam Participation and Performance Related to Choice of College Major? The College Board. Report 2011-6.

[16] Eleanor Chute. 2009, February 10. Lack of diversity part of equation in STEM fields. Retrieved from http://www.post-gazette.com/news/education/2009/02/10/Lack-of-diversity-part-of-equation-in-STEM-fields/stories/200902100187.

[17] National Center for Women & Information Technology. 2009, November 19. Moving beyond computer literacy: Why schools should teach computer science. Retrieved from https://www.ncwit.org/resources/moving-beyond-computer-literacy-why-schools-should-teach-computer-science/moving-beyond

[18] Mica Estrada, Myra Burnett, Andrew G. Campbell, Patricia B. Campbell, Wilfred F. Denetclaw, Carlos G. Gutiérrez, Sylvia Hurtado,... and Maria Elena Zavala. 2016. Improving underrepresented minority student persistence in STEM. CBE Life Sciences Education, 15(3). https://doi.org/10.1187/cbe.16-01-0038

[19] Owen Astrachan, Tiffany Barnes, Daniel D. Garcia, Jody Paul, Beth Simon, and Larry Snyder. 2011. CS Principles: Piloting a new course at national scale. In Proceedings of the 42nd ACM Technical Symposium on Computer Science Education (SIGCSE '11). ACM Press, New York, NY, 397-398.

[20] Owen Astrachan and Amy Briggs. 2012. The CS Principles Project. ACM Inroads. 3, 2 (June 2012), 38-42.

[21] Jane Margolis, Joanna Goode, and Gail Chapman. 2015. An equity lens for scaling: A critical juncture for exploring computer science. ACM Inroads 6, 3 (Sept. 2015), 58–66. DOI: 10.1145/2794294

[22] Jeff Gray, Kathy Haynie, Sheryl Packman, Mary Boehm, Carol Crawford, and Deepa Muralidhar. 2015. A mid-project report on a statewide professional development model for CS Principles. In Proceedings of the 46th ACM Technical Symposium on Computer Science Education (SIGCSE '15). ACM Press, New York, NY, 380–385.

[23] Ralph Morelli, Chinma Uche, Pauline Lake, and Lawrence Baldwin. 2015. Analyzing year one of a CS Principles PD project. In Proceedings of the 46th ACM Technical Symposium on Computer Science Education (SIGCSE '15). ACM Press, New York, NY, 368-373.

[24] Jan Cuny, Diane A. Baxter, Daniel D. Garcia, Jeff Gray, and Ralph Morelli. 2014. CS Principles professional development: Only 9,500 to go! Lessons learned from our CS10K summer 2013 PD. In Proceedings of the 45th ACM Technical Symposium on Computer Science Education (SIGCSE '14). ACM Press, New York, NY, 543–544.

[25] K–12 Computer Science Framework Steering Committee. 2016. K–12 Computer Science Framework. Retrieved from www.k12cs.org

[26] Jeanne Century, Michael Lach, Heather King, Sarah Rand, Courtney Heppner, Baker Franke, and Jean Westrick. 2013. Building an Operating System for Computer Science. Chicago, IL: CEMSE, University of Chicago with UEI, University of Chicago. Retrieved August 30, 2018 from http://outlier.uchicago.edu/computerscience/OS4CS/

[27] Infosys Limited. 2016. Infosys Foundation USA partners with the National Science Foundation and DonorsChoose.org to pioneer a new model of public-private-community collaboration for computer science education. (April 2016). Retrieved August 30, 2018 from https://www.infosys.com/newsroom/press-releases/Pages/new-private-public-community-collaboration.aspx

[28] Richard Kick. 2012. Computer Science Principles at Newbury Park High School. ACM Inroads 3, 2 (June 2012), 75-77. DOI: 10.1145/2189835.2189859

[29] Jean Griffin, Tammy Pirmann, and Brent Gray. 2016. Two teachers, two perspectives on CS Principles. In Proceedings of the 47th ACM Technical Symposium on Computer Science Education (SIGCSE '16). ACM Press, New York, NY, 461-466.

[30] Karla Hamlen, Nigamanth Sridhar, Lisa Bievenue, Debbie K. Jackson, and Anil Lalwani. 2018. Effects of teacher training in a Computer Science Principles curriculum on teacher and student skills, confidence, and beliefs. In Proceedings of the 49th ACM Technical Symposium on Computer Science Education (SIGCSE '18). ACM Press, New York, NY, 741-746.

[31] College Board. 2018. AP computer science expansion. Retrieved August 30, 2018 from https://reports.collegeboard.org/ap-program-results/ap-computer-science-expansion

[32] College Board. 2018. More students than ever are participating and succeeding in Advanced Placement (February 2018). Retrieved August 30, 2018 from https://www.collegeboard.org/releases/2018/more-students-than-ever-are-participating-and-succeeding-in-advanced-placement

[33] College Board. 2018. Number of female and underrepresented students taking AP computer science courses spikes again. (Aug. 2018). Retrieved August 27, 2018 from https://www.collegeboard.org/membership/all-access/counseling-admissions-financial-aid-academic/number-girls-and-underrepresented

[34] Andrew Hoegh and Barbara Moskal. 2009. Examining science and engineering students' attitudes toward computer science. Presentation at the 39th ASEE/IEE Frontiers in Education Conference. October 2009.

[35] Clayton Lewis, Michele H. Jackson, and William M. Waite. 2010. Student and faculty attitudes and beliefs about computer science. Communications of the ACM. 53, 78-85.

[36] Eric N. Wiebe, Laurie Williams, Kai Yang, and Carol Miller. 2003. Report No.: NCSU CSC TR-2003-1. Dept. of Computer Science, NC State University, Raleigh, NC.

Implementing EarSketch: Connecting Classroom Implementation to Student Outcomes

Tom McKlin
The Findings Group
125 E. Trinity Place, Ste 249
Decatur, Georgia USA
tom@thefindingsgroup.org

Dana Wanzer
The Findings Group
125 E. Trinity Place, Ste 249
Decatur, Georgia USA
dana@thefindingsgroup.org

Taneisha Lee
The Findings Group
125 E. Trinity Place, Ste 249
Decatur, Georgia USA
taneisha@thefindingsgroup.org

Brian Magerko
Digital Media Program
Georgia Institute of Technology
85 Fifth Street NW
Atlanta, Georgia USA
magerko@gatech.edu

Doug Edwards
Center for Education Integrating Science Mathematics and Computing
Georgia Institute of Technology
Atlanta, Georgia USA
doug.edwards@ceismc.gatech.edu

Sabrina Grossman
Center for Education Integrating Science Mathematics and Computing
Georgia Institute of Technology
Atlanta, Georgia USA
sabrina.grossman@ceismc.gatech.edu

Jason Freeman
Center for Music Technology
Georgia Institute of Technology
840 McMillan Street
Atlanta, Georgia USA
jason.freeman@gatech.edu

ABSTRACT

The expansion of computer science into more classrooms invites researchers and evaluators to shift their focus from predominantly measuring student-level factors to measuring both student- and classroom-level variables. Research presented in this article uses multi-level modeling to study student-level factors within the larger context of classroom-level factors. Specifically, we analyze EarSketch, a collaborative and authentic learning tool, that introduces students to programming through music remixing, has previously been shown to increase student engagement, and increases learners' intentions to persist in computing.

This article presents classroom implementation frameworks commonly used in math and science education but rarely, if ever, applied to computer science. The results from a multi-level modeling analysis show that classroom implementation correlates with students' intentions to persist in computing but may not be related to student attitudes toward computing or content knowledge acquisition. Further analysis reveals that one of the five classroom implementation factors, elaboration, emerges as the most salient. This article triangulates these results with qualitative findings from school administrators and teachers, and the article concludes by theorizing how classroom implementation frameworks may be adapted to meet the unique needs of computer science teachers, learners, researchers, evaluators, and curriculum developers.

SIGCSE '19, February 27-March 2, 2019, Minneapolis, MN, USA

ACM ISBN 978-1-4503-5890-3/19/02...$15.00
https://doi.org/10.1145/3287324.3287379

KEYWORDS: Computer science education, creativity, STEAM, music, broadening participation

ACM Reference format:

Tom McKlin, Dana Wanzer, Taneisha Lee, Brian Magerko, Doug Edwards, Sabrina Grossman, and Jason Freeman. 2019. Implementing EarSketch: Connecting Classroom Implementation to Student Outcomes. In *Proceedings of 50th ACM Technical Symposium on Computer Science Education (SIGCSE '19), February 27-Mar. 2, 2019, Minneapolis, MN, USA.* ACM, NY, NY, USA, 7 pages. https://doi.org/*10.1145/3287324.3287379*

1 INTRODUCTION

The expansion of computer science curricula into more classrooms requires that evaluators and researchers study how teachers implement curricula. This paper proposes that we incorporate classroom implementation, the study of enacted curriculum, into research and evaluation designs as outcome variables for professional learning and predictors of student success. This paper describes EarSketch, the EarSketch curriculum, how it was enacted by 18 computer science teachers, the variation across teachers, and how that variation may affect student success.

1.1 EarSketch

EarSketch seeks to engage diverse student populations in introductory computer science by emphasizing the personally expressive role of computing in the domain of music. EarSketch students learn elements of computing and sample-based music composition (i.e. composition using musical beats, samples, and effects). They write Python or JavaScript code to algorithmically create music in popular genres and use fundamental computing concepts such as loops, lists, and user-defined functions to manipulate musical samples, beats, and effects.

EarSketch is a web-based learning platform that includes a Python and JavaScript code editor with both text and blocks-based modes;

a multi-track digital audio workstation view that shows the musical results of code execution; an audio loop library with 4000+ musical clips in a variety of popular music genres that serve as building blocks for new musical compositions; and an inline curriculum, with student and teacher-facing components, that is closely aligned with Computer Science Principles [8].

The design of EarSketch leverages music's potential as a hook to engage students in computing, as well as the natural conceptual parallels between the two disciplines. It affords an "immediate opportunity to act" [5] in that students with no prior musical or computational background can quickly become musically expressive, writing a few lines of code to assemble audio clips from the loop library. EarSketch is also perceived to be authentic [19][25] by students; it utilizes industry-relevant programming languages, borrows heavily from music production paradigms in its user interface and API, and incorporates popular musical styles and content created by well-known engineers and producers.

1.2 EarSketch Curriculum

The EarSketch curriculum is aligned with the programming standards of the College Board's Advanced Placement (AP) Computer Science Principles (CSP) course, as well as a related (non-AP) Computer Science Principles course that is a standard high-school course in the state of Georgia. The course introduces students to the creative aspects of programming, abstractions, algorithms, large data sets, the Internet, cybersecurity, and the impacts of computing across multiple domains [2]. AP CSP does not mandate a specific programming language or problem domain: students submit performance tasks created with a programming language or environment of their choice, and they take a language-agnostic end-of-course exam.

The EarSketch curriculum for CSP consists of a 10-to-12-week module that covers the CSP learning objectives for programming and many of the objectives for creativity, abstraction, and algorithms. We have also provided scaffolding and support for teachers in three areas: a) teaching materials that include day-by-day lesson plans, slides, worksheets, mini-tasks, videos, project descriptions and rubrics, assessments, and integration guides; b) face-to-face and online professional development that introduces teachers to EarSketch, the curriculum, and new pedagogical practices such as studio-based learning; and c) a community where teachers can ask questions, share materials, and review additional training resources in both an online website and a series of in-person events.

The EarSketch CSP module is organized into three units that have teacher lesson plans based on the 5E instructional model. Bybee et al. [4] describe the 5E model as a series of instructional phases designed to help learners better understand scientific and technical knowledge, attitude, and skills. The phases of the model are:

1. Engagement: Accessing prior knowledge and helping students become curious about a new topic.
2. Exploration: Experiencing a common set of activities to facilitate the growth of concepts, processes, and skills. This may include lab activities that use prior knowledge to generate new ideas, explore questions, and conduct an investigation.
3. Explanation: Opportunities for students to demonstrate conceptual understanding, process skills, or behaviors. Learners explain their understanding of the concept which guides students toward deeper understanding.
4. Elaboration: Additional activities and new experiences that challenge and extend students' conceptual understanding.
5. Evaluation: Students assess their understanding and abilities and demonstrate progress toward achieving educational objectives.

Further, each unit has an authentic challenge that requires the student to code musical concepts to satisfy the musical and technical criteria of the challenge. For example, the first challenge requires the student to select a client that could be a business in their community or a school organization. The student must develop a short musical introduction for a client advertisement that applies research on how tempo and pitch affect mood. Students share their music and code with their classmates, teacher, and client to see if the intended mood is elicited and also discuss their code. Based on the feedback, they then iterate on their creation to reach a final product. In open-ended projects such as the above challenge, there is no single, correct solution. Students must collaborate and communicate with their classmates, their teacher, and external partners to iteratively refine the project goals, assess work in progress, and devise new musical and computational strategies to address feedback. The EarSketch CSP module follows this studio-based learning (SBL) approach across all three units: a) designing an artifact; b) presenting work to peers and teachers, along with a detailed justification of the decisions made; c) discussing the work of peers and offering feedback; and d) revising work based on feedback [14].

1.3 Theory of Change

The EarSketch team modified its original theory of change [10][19], which only included student-level variables, to account for classroom-level variables (*self-efficacy, classroom implementation,* and *teacher CS content knowledge* prior to entering the program). A theory of change is a tool that illustrates how and why a desired change occurs [1]. The updated EarSketch theory of change (see Figure 1) posits that classroom variables combined with a learning environment conducive to music and computing contribute to changes in student attitudes, which then lead to changes in two important student outcomes: increased computer science content knowledge and an intention to persist in future computing education and computing-centric careers.

2 CLASSROOM IMPLEMENTATION

Observations and interviews with EarSketch teachers reveal that they may approach implementation in different ways. Indeed, Kilpatrick [17] cautions that two classrooms using the same curriculum may look very different. The learning activities may vary widely, may afford different learning opportunities for students, and ultimately may produce different learning outcomes. Variation in classrooms using the same curriculum reveals the importance of measuring classroom implementation. Chval et al. [7] recommend a systematic examination of curriculum enactment to determine whether, how, and under what conditions differences in implementation affect classroom activities and student success.

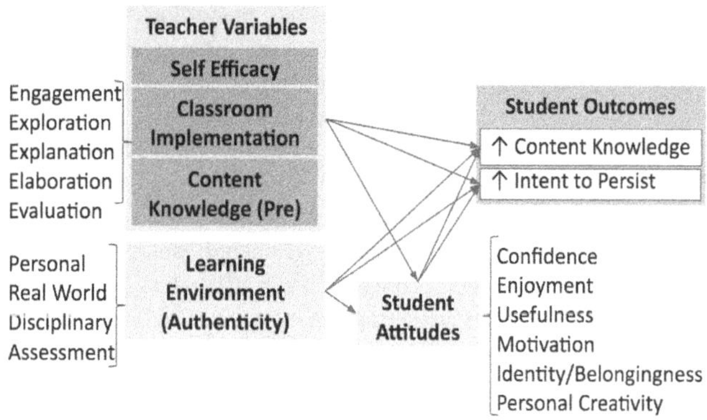

Figure 1. EarSketch Theory of Change

2.1 Consider the Teacher

We must consider the teacher's role in relation to the curriculum and our own perspectives on teaching in order to adequately measure classroom implementation. Implementing a curriculum may have many meanings ranging from the teacher as simply the curriculum deliverer to the teacher as the curriculum co-creator. Snyder et al. [26] offer three conceptualizations of teaching: 'teacher as consumer', 'teacher as shaper', and 'teacher as creator.' Under the **'teacher as consumer'** model, one measures "fidelity," the degree to which the curriculum is delivered as intended to discern factors that facilitate or inhibit intended implementation. The intent of the curriculum designers is central, and some argue that the first step is to interview curriculum authors to understand curriculum design while others discern authors' intent through the curriculum and supporting materials. Mathematics researchers have used two broad approaches to measuring fidelity: some measure fidelity as a binary operation in which the curriculum either is or is not implemented with fidelity while others measure the degree to which the curriculum is implemented as intended. The **'teacher as shaper'** model measures mutual adaptations which are modifications that teachers make to enact the curriculum to meet student, classroom, and school contextual needs. Teachers are 'active implementers' who modify the curriculum to meet their students' needs. An important consideration within the 'mutual adaptation' camp is to discern which adaptations acceptably comply with the authors' original intent and which are unacceptable deviations. In the **'teacher as creator'** model, one measures enactment which is the jointly-created experience of the curriculum among teacher and students. Chval et al. [7] cite Ben-Peretz [3] who describes curriculum development as a two-stage process: the first stage is the authors' conceptualization of the curriculum and support materials; the second stage is the teachers' adaptations, alterations, and translations of these materials to specific students in specific classrooms.

2.2 The Need for Measuring Classroom Implementation in CS Education

The expansion of K-12 Computer Science education in recent years means that researchers may treat the classroom as a unit of analysis. More classrooms [9], the Computer Science Principles framework [2], and numerous curricula make it imperative that researchers consider classroom implementation as a critical variable in program theories of change.

Further, a 2017 empowerment evaluation [12] conducted among CS education evaluators prior to and during the NSF CISE/EHR 2017 meeting revealed six pressing evaluation needs. Two needs are important to this work: CS education evaluators expressed a need to better assess the quality of instructional strategies and to better assess the quality of curriculum materials. Additionally, the NSF-funded Evaluation Working Group collected data across all CS10K projects and found that only 23% report classroom implementation measures [11].

This study presents one initial approach to measuring classroom implementation, and we offer it as an early example upon which to improve the capacity of researchers and evaluators at using classroom implementation as a set of variables to both help explain student success and describe the effects of professional learning and curriculum support materials.

2.3 Approaches to Measuring Implementation

Space constraints prohibit a thorough review of all approaches to measuring implementation; however, the following two approaches offer unique and applicable perspectives. First, Century's [6] framework consists of four broad areas and proposes multiple data sources (observations, focus groups/interviews, teacher and student surveys, enactment checklists, and data from the school's student information system). The first component, *what the curriculum guides teachers to do,* addresses time spent on instruction, the order of lessons, materials used in each lesson, lesson preparation, readings, assessments, and instructional delivery formats required by the intervention. The second, *what teachers know,* includes teacher background knowledge and specific knowledge needed to enact the intervention. The third component, *how teachers interact,* includes pedagogical actions such as facilitating student engagement with the content, with each other, and with the teacher; and facilitating student autonomy, risk taking, and interest. This component focuses on the roles teachers play to facilitate student engagement while the fourth component focuses directly on student engagement. The final component, *how and in what ways students engage,* measures students engaging with each other, with the content, and with instructional materials and activities.

Second, Huntley [16] describes classroom observation as the gold standard and uses the concerns-based adoption model to develop innovation configuration maps. This model [3] posits that instructional behaviors either align with the intent of the curriculum developers or fall outside of the curriculum developer's intent. Innovation configuration (IC) maps are rubrics that describe the degree to which classroom practice is faithful to the curriculum designer's intent. Maps are developed by interviewing curriculum designers to understand what classroom practices are consistent with their intent and which ones are not, which practices are acceptable and which are not. The concerns-based adoption model assumes that an innovation (such as curriculum materials) may take many different forms when implemented, and innovation configuration maps are diagnostic tools that carefully describe the ideal way of implementing an innovation and variations of the ideal. An IC map is a grid in which the rows represent major components of the innovation and the columns represent variations of implementation. The first column represents the ideal implementation; the second column is an acceptable variation of an ideal implementation that still falls within the curriculum envelope. The third and fourth columns describe implementations that fall outside of the acceptable curriculum envelope. For computer science curricula, we might develop an innovation configuration map for major components like Introducing a Concept, Facilitating Pair Programming, or Modeling Programming.

3 METHODS

3.1 Procedures

Participating teachers attended a summer professional learning workshop and received ongoing support during the academic year. The workshop consisted of three day-long, face-to-face sessions combined with a month-long asynchronous online session. These two learning events are designed to prepare teachers to teach the Computer Science Principles programming unit (Big Idea 5). The 18 teachers taught 882 students during the 2017-18 school year. Of those, 473 (53.6%) students consented to participate in the study.

3.2 Assessment Instruments

This study examines the theory of change to discern whether the overall theory holds and to determine how classroom-level variables relate to student attitudes and student success. While the theory of change suggests causality, the statistical approaches below show correlation and cannot prove causality.

3.2.1 Self Efficacy

We administered a 16-item self-efficacy survey to teachers [27] that measures five subconstructs: *Computing Pedagogical Knowledge Self Efficacy, Instructional Self Efficacy, Engagement Self Efficacy, Disciplinary Self Efficacy,* and *Outcome Expectancy.* The instrument was administered upon entry (pre) into the program and then after teachers finished teaching all EarSketch units (post). For this analysis, we used responses from the post administration.

3.2.2 Classroom Implementation

We administered an enactment checklist to teachers for three lessons over the course of the EarSketch module. The self-report enactment checklist was adapted from two prior projects [13][21] that focused on curriculum development and implementation. The enactment surveys were constructed as an efficient method to measure curriculum implementation with multiple teachers in diverse geographic settings. The self-reported enactment checklist was used during curriculum implementation and supported by teacher interviews and observations. Data from the checklist aligned with teacher responses from interviews, encouraging continued use of this tool when evaluating enactment on a large scale curricular intervention.

The first step in development of the checklists was to identify the critical components, or essential program elements of the curriculum [20][6]. In EarSketch, these critical components were defined by the learning goals of each lesson. These learning goals were organized on the enactment checklist using the 5E instructional model to match the lesson plan format provided to the teachers. The enactment checklist asks teachers whether and to what degree they used curriculum resources and the percentage of students engaged in each stage of the lesson.

3.2.3 Content Knowledge

We measured computing content knowledge for both students and teachers using a 20-item, language agnostic instrument developed by the EarSketch team with support from an Advanced Placement Computer Science teacher. The assessment is aligned with the College Board's AP CSP Framework [8] and measures objectives 5.1.1-5.4.1 (Big Idea 5: Programming). We administered the assessment as a traditional pre-post test to both students and teachers. Students took the test before and after the EarSketch units; teachers took the test during professional learning and again after teaching the EarSketch units. The assessment addresses the essential knowledge areas appropriate for multiple-choice format. The team also conducted think-aloud interviews with high school computer science students to verify that students accurately interpret the items. Findings were also triangulated through six focus groups with a representative sample of students.

3.2.4 Learning Environment and Student Attitudes

The EarSketch student survey measures students' perceptions of the learning environment (whether they perceive it to be authentic to making music and to computing) along with attitudes (*confidence, enjoyment, importance, motivation, identity, intent to persist,* and *personal creativity*). See Engelman et al. [10] and McKlin et al. [19] for more on the student survey, particularly *authenticity* and *personal creativity.* The student survey contains subscales from the Computer Science Attitude Survey (CSAS) [28] and the Computer Attitude Questionnaire (CAQ) [18]. The student survey was administered at the end of the unit as a retrospective pre-post, except for the authenticity scale which was administered as a post-only scale. (Students cannot rate the *authenticity* of a learning environment prior to experiencing the learning environment.)

3.2.5 Qualitative Analyses

Teachers and administrators participated in 30 – 60 minute semi-structured interviews after teaching the EarSketch module. Interviews were audio recorded and transcribed verbatim. The first cycle of coding involved creating attribute (school district, number of years teaching CSP, etc.) and structural codes [24]. Structural codes identify content-based phrases related to implementation, decision making in selecting CS curriculum and courses, experiences with EarSketch, differing interest and engagement by subgroups, factors that enhance teaching, and types of support needed to teach CSP with EarSketch. During the second cycle of coding, pattern coding was used to develop major themes.

3.3 Multi-Level Modeling

We used multilevel modeling (MLM) to answer the question: How do classroom-level variables (*teaching efficacy, classroom implementation, and content knowledge*) and student perceptions of the learning environment relate to student attitudes and student outcomes? Multilevel modeling (MLM) is a statistical approach that accounts for grouped data [15]. This is important to use because individuals in a group tend to be more similar than individuals across groups. This study has two levels of data: students (level 1 data) are grouped within classrooms (level 2 data). *Teaching efficacy, classroom implementation,* and *teacher content knowledge (pre)* are classroom-level data (level 2 data) while student ratings of the *learning environment (authenticity)*, the six student attitudinal constructs, and student outcomes (*content knowledge* and *intent to persist*) are student-level data (level 1 data). We performed three MLMs: one for each of the three outcomes (*student attitudes, student content knowledge,* and *intent to persist*). The first step is to determine what percentage of the outcome at the student-level is predicted by classroom-level variables. The second step includes all student-level predictors. The third step adds the classroom-level predictors to see how well they predict the outcome above and beyond the student-level predictors.

4 RESULTS

4.1 Percentage of Each Outcome Predicted by Classroom Variables

The first step is determining what percentage of the outcome at the student-level is explained by the grouping structure of the data by calculating the Intraclass Correlation Coefficient (ICC). These analyses essentially run a simple regression with only the grouping variable as a predictor of each of the three outcomes. The ICC values indicate 21% of the variation in student attitudes, 32% of the variation in student content knowledge, and 13% of the variation in students' intention to persist is explained by classroom membership. These findings indicate that a significant portion of the variation in student outcomes is explained by the students' classroom. The following analyses examine which student- and classroom-level variables contribute to the variation in student outcomes.

4.2 Student- and Classroom-Level Predictors of Project Outcomes

Table 1 shows the results of three MLM analyses. Each analysis uses a different outcome variable (*student attitudes, student content knowledge, and students' intention to persist*). Each analysis contains two models: model 1 uses student-level variables to predict the outcome variable, and model 2 adds classroom-level variables to the student-level variables. For example, the first MLMs in Table 1 use student attitudes as the outcome variable: Model 1 shows that *authenticity* (student perceptions that the learning environment is authentic) and attitudes toward computing upon entering the program both significantly predict post student attitudes. Model 2 adds classroom-level variables and shows that they do not significantly predict student attitudes over and above the student-level variables. The same is true for student content knowledge; adding classroom-level variables does not significantly improve the model's ability to explain content knowledge growth. However, two classroom-level variables (teacher scores on the content knowledge assessment at pre and the composite classroom implementation score) significantly predict students' intention to persist in computing.

Table 1: MLM Results Across Student Outcomes

Student Attitudes (post)	**Model 1**	**Model 2**
Student-level variables		
Authenticity	**.275 (.04)***	**.220 (.04)***
Attitudes (Pre)	**.591 (.04)***	**.635 (.04)***
Classroom-level variables		
Self-efficacy		-.047 (.06)
CKA (Pre)		.109 (.06)+
Implementation		.089 (.06)+
Content Knowledge (Post)	**Model 1**	**Model 2**
Student-level variables		
Authenticity	.065 (.05)+	.031 (.05)
Attitudes (Pre)	.048 (.05)+	.014 (.05)
CKA (Pre)	**.585 (.05)***	**.594 (.07)***
Classroom-level variables		
Self-efficacy		.034 (.11)
CKA (Pre)		-.004 (.13)
Implementation		-.028 (.11)
Intent to Persist (Post)	**Model 1**	**Model 2**
Student-level variables		
Authenticity	**.156 (.04)***	**.119 (.04)***
Attitudes (Pre)	-.028 (.07)	.013 (.07)
Intent to Persist (Pre)	**.717 (.07)***	**.738 (.07)***
Classroom-level variables		
Self-efficacy		-.049 (.04)
CKA (Pre)		**.094 (.04)***
Implementation		**.100 (.04)***

Note: Values shown are the Standardized Beta (standardized error) coefficients. * indicates $p < .05$; + indicates $p < .10$

4.3 Classroom Implementation Factors

Given the significant relationship between classroom implementation and students' intention to persist in computing, we further asked which aspects of classroom implementation (i.e., engagement, exploration, explanation, elaboration, evaluation), if any, correlate with students' intentions to persist. Table 2 shows the results of an MLM analysis extending beyond Model 2 of Table 1 for Intent to Persist. It included all student-level and classroom-level variables, but instead of including Implementation as a single variable, it includes the 5Es of implementation individually. Results indicate that elaboration (i.e., additional activities and new experiences that challenge and extend students' conceptual understanding and skills) is the most salient factor related to students' intent to persist.

Table 2: Elaboration is the Most Salient Classroom Implementation Factor

Classroom Implementation Factor	Intent to Persist Model 3
Engagement	-.013 (.04)
Exploration	-.043 (.06)
Explanation	.028 (.07)
Elaboration	**.061 (.03)***
Evaluation	-.067 (.05)+

Note: This model also includes student-level variables and the other classroom-level variables (teacher self-efficacy, teacher CKA at pre) but they are not shown here as values are similar to those from Table 1 Model 2 for Intent to Persist. * indicates $p < .05$ + indicates $p < .10$

4.4 Results from teacher and administrator interviews

Having found a significant relationship between classroom implementation and students' intentions to persist and further finding that elaboration is a critical component of classroom implementation, we sought to understand this relationship through interviews with school administrators and teachers. The following administrator observed a class as students completed their mini-tasks, EarSketch elaboration projects that extend students' conceptual understanding in CS and music.

[A]s a district administrator, how we kind of view the effectiveness of a curriculum is if you can walk in and ask the students 'What are you learning? Why are you learning it? How does it apply to this class?' During the EarSketch modules, they've been very good at explaining what they're doing, and why they're doing it, and how it applies to computer science.

A first year EarSketch and experienced CSP teacher shared an experience with students creating and sharing their mini-tasks.

"they're able to create something. It's theirs. They can show it to their friends. A lot of them like that aspect of it, that they're able to show them...They will say, "Hey, this is what I made in EarSketch. This is similar to what you just made in GarageBand." They can sit there and actually have a conversation about that, and that's not something they were not doing before [EarSketch]. So, to have them really engage in that way...They can see the benefit of what they're learning, that real-world connection right away. I think that's what's so beneficial with using EarSketch, because they can see it.

Qualitative findings also support the relationship between implementation and students' intent to persist in future computing education. The following first year EarSketch and experienced CSP teacher shared how using EarSketch resulted in a larger number of students enrolling in the next-level computing course, AP Computer Science.

As a result of us using EarSketch, they're a lot more confident, and many of them have signed up for AP Computer Science when they would not have before...Because now they feel like, Yeah, I can do this. I'm not afraid of programming. I'm not afraid of doing an actual language. So, I actually have, besides the seniors which I do have which is only like 4, the rest of the class is underclassmen, and the majority of them have signed up for AP Computer Science.

When asked about student interest in computer science careers, teachers shared that the EarSketch course may motivate students to gather information about related post-secondary education and careers in computer science.

I have some students who, because we did EarSketch, they've researched Georgia Tech and their Music Technology Department. So, I did have some kids do research there. I've had some kids who say, "Hey, [teacher's name], how can I get other skills? How can I do other things outside of EarSketch, but still learn programming?" So, I've had some kids who have looked online and done some research on how to take additional computer science classes and coding classes.

I have a lot of kids in my CSP courses. I even have some in my intro course in Web Design who say, "Hey, this is what I want to do. What schools should I be looking at? What jobs are available if I want to go this route?" Most of them want to know how much money they can make.

5 DISCUSSION

This paper presents an initial approach for measuring classroom implementation. This work indicates that classroom level variables explain a large enough portion of the variation in student outcomes to necessitate further study, finds that classroom level variables affect students' intention to persist in computing, and shows that one element of classroom implementation stands out: elaboration (additional activities and new experiences that challenge and extend students' conceptual skills). Qualitative findings from administrators and teachers describe students who appear more capable of associating their work with real-world disciplinary endeavors in computing and music and appear motivated to pursue further high-school and post-secondary education in computing and music technology.

We also base our classroom implementation on the 5E model of instruction. While initially reasonable, we perceive that a better approach would be to incorporate a framework that is more sensitive to classroom-based phenomena. We perceive that Century's four-stage model or Huntley's CBAM approach might be more sensitive to the shifts in classroom implementation because these models are tied to the observable enactment of the curriculum rather than lesson plans. Two new instruments [22] [23] have emerged from Century's work that offer promise for the measurement of classroom implementation in future studies.

6 ACKNOWLEDGEMENTS

The EarSketch project receives funding from the National Science Foundation (1417835 and 1649671). EarSketch is available online at earsketch.gatech.edu.

7 REFERENCES

[1] Annie E. Casey Foundation and Organizational Research Services. 2004. Theory of Change: A practical tool for action, results and learning. Retrieved March 3, 2016 from: http://www.aecf.org/m/resourcedoc/aecf- theoryofchange-2004.pdf

[2] Astrachan, O. et al. (2011). CS principles: piloting a new course at national scale. Proceedings of the 42nd ACM technical symposium on Computer science education (New York, NY, USA, 2011), 397–398.

[3] Ben-Peretz, M. (1990). The Teacher-Curriculum Encounter: Freeing Teachers from the Tyranny of Texts. Albany, NY: SUNY Press.

[4] Bybee, R., Taylor, J., Gardner, A., Van Scotter, P., Powell, J., Westbrook, A., & Landes, N. (2006). *The BSCS 5E Instructional Model: Origins and Effectiveness.* Colorado Springs, CO: BSCS. Retrieved from https://bscs.org/sites/default/files/_legacy/BSCS_5E_Instructional_Model-Full_Report.pdf

[5] Carroll, J. 1998. Minimalism Beyond the Nurnberg Funnel. MIT Press.

[6] Century, J., Rudnick, M., & Freeman, C. (2010). A Framework for Measuring Fidelity of Implementation: A Foundation for Shared Language and Accumulation of Knowledge. American Journal of Evaluation, 31(2), 199–218. https://doi.org/10.1177/1098214010366173

[7] Chval, K., Wilson, L. D., Ziebarth, S., Heck, D. J., & Weiss, I. R. (2012). Introduction. In Approaches to Studying the Enacted Mathematics Curriculum (pp. 1–18). Charlotte, N.C: Information Age Publishing.

[8] College Board. 2016. AP Computer Science Principles Curriculum Framework Accessed March 3, 2016 from https://secure-media.collegeboard.org/digitalServices/pdf/ap/ap-computer-science- principles-course-and-exam-description.pdf

[9] College Board Communications. (2018, June 12). AP Computer Science Principles participation grows by over 50% in Year Two. Retrieved from https://www.collegeboard.org/membership/all-access/counseling-admissions-academic/ap-computer-science-principles-participation

[10] Engelman, S., Magerko, B., McKlin, T., Miller, M., Edwards, D., & Freeman, J. (2017). Creativity in Authentic STEAM Education with EarSketch (pp. 183–188). ACM Press. https://doi.org/10.1145/3017680.3017763

[11] Evaluation Working Group. (2017). CS10K Common Data Elements: Year 3 Common Data Collection Report (2016-2017). Amherst, MA: SageFox Consulting Group. Retrieved from http://sagefoxgroup.com/dev/wp-content/uploads/2018/02/Combined-CS10K-Year-3-Report-2018.pdf

[12] Fetterman, D., Haynie, K., McKlin, T., Ravitz, J., Bates, T., DuBow, W., ... Tiffany-Morales, J. (2017, November). *Building a Computer Science and STEM Evaluation Learning Community: Using Empowerment Evaluation and Technology Tools.* Presented at the American Evaluation Association, Washington, DC.

[13] Gale, J., Grossman, S., Ryan, M., Newton, S., Usselman, M. (2018). Exploring curriculum implementation using self-report enactment checklists. Paper presented at National Association of Research in Science Teaching conference. (Atlanta, GA).

[14] Hendrix, D. et al. 2010. Implementing studio-based learning in CS2. Proceedings of the 41st ACM technical symposium on Computer science education (New York, NY, USA, 2010), 505–509.

[15] Hox, J. J. (2002). Multilevel analysis: Techniques and applications. Mahwah, NJ: Erlbaum.

[16] Huntley, M. A. (2012). Using concerns-based adoption model theory to develop tools to examine variations in mathematics textbook implementation. In D. J. Heck, K. B. Chval, I. R. Weiss, & S. W. Ziebarth (Eds.), Approaches to studying the enacted mathematics curriculum. Charlotte, N.C: Information Age Publishing.

[17] Kilpatrick, J. (2003). What works? In S. L. Senk & D. R. Thompson (Eds.), Standards-based school mathematics curricula: What are they? What do students learn? (pp. 471–488). Mahwah: Erlbaum.

[18] Knezek, G. and Christensen, R. 1996. Validating the Computer Attitude Questionnaire (CAQ). Presented at Annual Meeting of the Southwest Education Research Association (New Orleans, Louisiana, January 26, 1996). AMSERA'96.

[19] McKlin, T., Magerko, B., Lee, T., Wanzer, D., Edwards, D., & Freeman, J. (2018). Authenticity and Personal Creativity: How EarSketch Affects Student Persistence (pp. 987–992). ACM Press. https://doi.org/10.1145/3159450.3159523

[20] Mowbray, C. T., Holter, M. C., Teague, G. B., & Bybee, D. (2003). Fidelity Criteria: Development, Measurement, and Validation. American Journal of Evaluation, 24(3), 315–340. https://doi.org/10.1177/109821400302400303

[21] Newton, Sunni H.; Gale, Jessica; Alemdar, Meltem; and Wind, Stefanie. (2018) "Assessment of Practice-Focused Middle School Science Modules". Interdisciplinary STEM Teaching & Learning Conference. (Savannah, GA) https://digitalcommons.georgiasouthern.edu/stem/2018/2018/37

[22] Outlier Research & Evaluation (September, 2017). BASICS Study ECS Student Implementation and Contextual Factor Questionnaire Measures [Measurement scales]. Chicago, IL; Outlier Research & Evaluation at UChicago STEM Education | University of Chicago. Retrieved from http://outlier.uchicago.edu/basics/resources/Measures- StudentImplementation/

[23] Outlier Research & Evaluation (September, 2017). BASICS Study ECS Teacher Implementation and Contextual Factor Questionnaire Measures [Measurement scales]. Chicago, IL; Outlier Research & Evaluation at UChicago STEM Education | University of Chicago. Retrieved from http://outlier.uchicago.edu/basics/resources/Measures- TeacherImplementation/

[24] Saldaña, J. (2013). The coding manual for qualitative researchers. Thousand Oaks, CA: Sage

[25] Shaffer, D.W., and Resnick, M. 1999. Thick Authenticity: New media and authentic learning. Journal of Interact. Learn. Res. 10, 2, 195-215.

[26] Snyder, J., Bolin, F., & Zumwalt, K. (1992). Curriculum implementation. In *Handbook of research on curriculum: A project of the American Educational Research Association* (pp. 402–435). New York, NY: Macmillan.

[27] Yoon Yoon, S., Evans, M. G., & Strobel, J. (2014). Validation of the Teaching Engineering Self-Efficacy Scale for K-12 Teachers: A Structural Equation Modeling Approach: Validation of the Teaching Engineering Self-Efficacy Scale. *Journal of Engineering Education, 103*(3), 463–485. https://doi.org/10.1002/jee.20049

[28] Wiebe, E., Williams, L., Yang, K., and Miller, C. 2003. Computer science attitude survey. Comput. Scie. 14.

[29] American Psychological Association. (2010). *Publication manual of the American Psychological Association* (6th ed). Washington, DC: American Psychological Association.

Food for Thought: Supporting African American Women's Computational Algorithmic Thinking in an Intro CS Course

Yolanda A. Rankin
School of Information
Florida State University
Tallahassee, FL USA
yrankin@fsu.edu

Jakita O. Thomas
Comp Sci & SW Engineering
Auburn University
Auburn, AL USA
jnt0020@auburn.edu

India Irish
School of Interactive Computing
Georgia Tech
Atlanta, GA USA
indiai@gatech.edu

ABSTRACT

African American women who have little if any experience in computer programming prior to matriculation into college often struggle in introductory CS courses that emphasize programming from the outset. These same students feel underprepared and disadvantaged, oftentimes choosing to withdraw from such courses which contributes to the underrepresentation of African American women in CS. The challenge lies in creating equitable learning environments that bridge students' everyday experiences to fundamental CS concepts. In this experience report, we introduce *the Dessert Wars Challenge*, an alternative pedagogical strategy that leverages students' everyday experiences with food to forge meaningful connections to CS. We examine how African American women's participation in the *Dessert Wars Challenge* supports the development of their Computational Algorithmic Thinking (CAT) capabilities, the ability to design, implement, assess and adapt algorithms, and contributes to their retention in a college-level introductory CS course.

CCS CONCEPTS

• Social and professional topics ~ Computer Science Education

KEYWORDS: African American women; computational algorithmic thinking; food

ACM Reference format:
Yolanda A. Rankin, Jakita O. Thomas, India Irish. 2019. Food for Thought: Supporting African American Women's Computational Algorithmic Thinking in an Intro CS Course. In *Proceedings of 50th ACM Technical Symposium on Computer Science Education (SIGCSE '19), February 27-Mar. 2, 2019, Minneapolis, MN, USA.* ACM, New York, NY, USA, 7 pages. https://doi.org/10.1145/3287324.3287484

1 INTRODUCTION

Prior research demonstrates that one of the obstacles in increasing the representation of women in Computer Science (CS) is their lack of experience in computer programming prior to matriculation into college [1, 8]. The lack of prior programming experience is acutely relevant to underrepresented populations due to the lack of exposure and access to computing resources in K-12 education [11]. Such lack of experience creates inequitable learning environments in which underrepresented populations (i.e., African American women) struggle to achieve academically, resulting in decreased retention of such populations in CS higher education.

While many African American women enter college with little if any CS-related experiences, cooking and food touch the lives of every individual in every culture and from every walk of life [16]. All students have funds of knowledge or everyday experiences with eating or preparing food, ranging from the simple act of fixing a bowl of cereal for breakfast to cooking a main entrée for dinner [13]. Leveraging students' funds of knowledge about food, we seek to create equity, equal access to resources and learning opportunities for all students regardless of their prior knowledge or experiences, in the CS classroom setting. Hence, we introduce the *It's All in the Mix* module, a series of food-focused activities that bridge students' every day experiences with food to Computational Algorithmic Thinking (CAT)---the ability to design, implement, and assess the design and implementation of algorithms to solve a broad range of problems [16-17, 23, 25]. CAT makes explicit a critical aspect of computational thinking through its focus on understanding how learners identify and understand a problem, articulate an algorithm or set of algorithms in the form of a solution to the problem, and evaluate the solution based on some set of criteria [23, 25-27].

In this experience report, we focus on one specific food-related activity within the module---the *Dessert Wars Challenge*, and how it supports student development of CAT capabilities in an introductory CS course offered on an all-women Historically Black college campus. Our research explores the following questions: 1. What are African American women's perceptions of the *Dessert Wars Challenge* learning activity? 2. How does participation in the *Dessert Wars Challenge* support students' developing CAT capabilities? This experience report makes three contributions. First, building upon existing CS education research, we leverage students' funds of knowledge [13] about food as the context for African American women to develop their CAT capabilities in an introductory CS course. Second, we demonstrate that the integration of CS unplugged activities into introductory CS courses creates a level playing field for all students to succeed, thereby increasing the retention of African American women.

ACM ISBN 978-1-4503-5890-3/19/02..$15.00
https://doi.org/10.1145/3287324.3287484

Third, we outline the implications for creating equitable learning experiences for underrepresented populations.

2 MOTIVATION

Our research is motivated by two factors: 1. the need to increase the representation of African American women in computing; and 2. leveraging students' everyday experiences with food as the context for Computational Algorithmic Thinking (CAT).

2.1 AFRICAN AMERICAN WOMEN IN CS

Statistics show that the percentage of African American women receiving Bachelor's degrees in CS has significantly dropped over a ten-year period (2004 – 2014) even though the enrollment in CS courses at the college level has increased in recent years [14, 29]. Multiple strategies have been employed to increase the participation of African American women in the field of CS. For example, Dahlberg et al. [7] broaden participation in CS via the STARS Alliance, a network of CS programs sponsored on multiple university/college campuses in the U.S. that target African American undergraduate students. Scott & White [22] embed culturally responsive pedagogy into CS curriculum to empower African American middle school girls to utilize technology to fight social injustices. Thomas [23] examines the longitudinal development of CAT capabilities in African American middle school girls as they learn how to create multiple video games for different platforms. However, less research has specifically emphasized the inclusion of equity as a key component in the design of learning experiences that retain African American women in CS.

2.2 FOOD AS THE CONTEXT FOR CAT

Computational Algorithmic Thinking (CAT) focuses specifically on the process of designing, articulating, implementing, adapting, and discarding algorithms as needed to determine the "right" solution to a problem [23, 25]. The introductory CS course featured in our study emphasizes CAT to support students' understanding of what CS is and how computer scientists approach and solve problems in a step-by-step, logical, and creative manner. Most importantly, the course intentionally introduces algorithms as a precursor to programming, creating a level playing field for students who may not have any prior programming experience [8].

One area in which students have prior, though tacit, knowledge of algorithms is in the context of using a recipe to prepare a dish. Prior research demonstrates that cooking and baking activities can provide an effective context for helping students to develop scientific reasoning skills [3, 10, 19]. Because cooking, eating, and engaging with food are common experiences that cut across culture, race, age, and socio-economic status, students have funds of knowledge---ways of knowing of, talking about, and interacting with food in their everyday experiences---that we intentionally draw upon in the classroom setting [13]. These funds of knowledge allow us to leverage students' everyday experiences with food as the context for students to develop their CAT capabilities [2, 16, 17].

Leveraging Schneider & Gersting's [20] definition of an algorithm---a set of well-ordered and unambiguous instructions that are feasibly computable and halt in a finite amount of time, we utilize food as a bridge to CS for several reasons. First, recipes represent a specific set of ordered instructions inclusive of specific ingredients, their corresponding amounts and the specific order in which ingredients are mixed together and manipulated (e.g., baked in an oven) to create the final dish. Second, writing a recipe represents the process of designing an algorithm. Third, following a recipe to prepare a dish models the act of implementing an algorithm. Fourth, the result, an edible dish, represents the output of the algorithm while tasting the dish is indicative of algorithm assessment. Finally, cooking requires the element of creativity, something that students often mistakenly think is undervalued in CS. The goal is to bridge students' funds of knowledge about food to CAT development in an entry level CS college course.

3 DESSERT WARS CHALLENGE

Inspired by popular reality TV cooking shows, we have developed the *It's All in the Mix* module as part of a college-level introductory CS course. This course satisfies the CS requirement for STEM majors and is the first CS course in the curriculum for CS majors. *It's All in the Mix* currently consists of a set of integrated food-focused activities---*Peanut Butter and Jelly Sandwich*, *Dessert Wars Challenge*, and Make My Dish---that expose students to CAT through the design, implementation, assessment, and adaptation of recipes [8,14,16-17]. For the purposes of this paper, we specifically focus on the *Dessert Wars Challenge* because this challenge emphasizes the role of creativity in algorithm design. Students work together to create unique desserts using a variety of available ingredients. The learning objectives are: 1. to collaboratively write a well-defined recipe for a unique dessert based upon a set of ingredients; and 2. to collaboratively create a unique dessert using the set of available ingredients.

3.1 SETTING & PARTICIPANTS

The introductory CS course was offered at a Historically Black liberal arts women's college in the southeastern United States. Thirty-five African American women enrolled in the CS course - 24 during Spring 2015 and 11 during Spring 2016. All 35 women signed IRB to participate in the *Dessert Wars Challenge*. The same instructor taught both course sections. During the first week of classes in both sections, students completed a survey to measure their prior knowledge of CS concepts and prior computer programming experience. More than 80% of the students did not understand how to design, implement or evaluate algorithms as a problem-solving technique nor did they have any prior experience writing code.

3.2 SPRING 2015 INTRO TO CS COURSE

For the first enactment of the *Dessert Wars Challenge* in Spring 2015, students were divided into teams of 4-5 students. A variety of ingredients, including yogurt, blackberries, strawberries, blueberries, sliced almonds, chopped walnuts, pecan chips, chocolate syrup, caramel topping, whipped cream, and vanilla wafers along with bowls, napkins, and plastic utensils were placed on a table. Each team was given 5 minutes to view the ingredients and brainstorm about ideas for creating a unique dessert and 10 minutes to select the ingredients to make their desserts and write the corresponding recipe for their concoctions. Teams were free to use any or as much of the ingredients on the table with no further instructions about making their desserts. After 10 minutes, each team presented their dessert and corresponding recipe to be judged by the teaching assistants. Each team received feedback about their dessert based on presentation, originality, documented recipe, and taste. The instructor facilitated a class discussion about the similarities (e.g., use of same ingredients) and the differences (e.g., layering of ingredients, etc.) of each of the recipes and how these differences exemplified the role of creativity in algorithm design. Leveraging reflective practice [20] as a tool for learning, students completed an online journal entry after the activity.

3.3 SPRING 2016 INTRO TO CS COURSE

For the second enactment in Spring 2016, the instructor modified the *Dessert Wars Challenge* based upon student feedback received in Spring 2015. The food-related activity took place in an on-campus kitchen lab space consisting of a stove, refrigerator, oven, and plenty of counter top/work spaces. Eleven students self-selected their team members, resulting in 5 teams of 2-3 students each. The instructor provided explicit instructions about the required components for creating the unique dessert. Each team was required to choose ingredients that represented each component of the dessert: 1. dessert base---short cake or vanilla wafers; 2. filling---vanilla yogurt, strawberry yogurt or whip cream; 3. fruit---raspberries, strawberries, or blueberries, or pineapple chunks; 4. Nuts---sliced almonds, pecan chips, or walnut pieces; and 5. toppings---chocolate syrup, caramel or whip cream. All ingredients were separated per team and placed in different work spaces designated for each team. Paper bowls and plates, plastic cutlery, and napkins as well as extra ingredients were placed on the kitchen counter. Each team was allowed 5 minutes to view the selection of ingredients and 15 minutes to write and execute a recipe of the team's unique dessert. Each team then placed the final creation of their desserts on a serving table. Next, teams turned in their recipes of their desserts before randomly being assigned to create another's team dessert. The result was then placed next to the original dessert and using the criteria of presentation, originality, documented recipe, and taste, evaluated by the instructor and teaching assistants. The instructor led a group discussion that compared the similarities and differences in the two implementations of each team's dessert, asking students to assess any differences of the two desserts and what attributed to those differences while highlighting characteristics of well-defined algorithms. Finally, students completed their online reflective journals to capture their impressions of the food-focused activity.

3.4 DATA COLLECTION AND ANALYSIS

We intentionally chose to utilize self-reflection journals to capture students' perceptions of their learning experiences in their own words to empower their voices to be heard. This was terribly important to the authors since African American women in CS are often characterized by numerical data under the heading "women of color" (which only tells half of the story), or they are rendered invisible under the assumingly homogenous category of gender [12,15,29]. To assist students with their journal entries, we prompted them to answer the following questions: 1. What was easy about the *Dessert Wars Challenge*? 2. What was difficult about the *Dessert Wars Challenge*? 3. What suggestions do you have for improving this learning activity? 4. What did you learn about algorithms as a result of participating in the *Dessert Wars Challenge*? 5. Would you recommend the *Dessert Wars Challenge* as a required activity for this course? Using SurveyMonkey, we collected online reflective journal entries for the *Dessert Wars Challenge* in both sections and imported entries into NVivo. Content analysis was performed over the full set of students' responses to identify categories of emergent themes for each question. For example, similar student responses to the question "What was difficult about the *Dessert Wars Challenge*?" were grouped together (i.e., "The most difficult part was making a dish that was creative," "It was difficult to create an intricate dessert," "Being creative so our dessert wasn't like everyone else's," etc.) based upon similar phrases and meaning to identify the categorical theme of creating a unique dessert. Using this same process for questions 1 – 4, we identified 15 emergent themes for the category of ***easy***, 11 emergent themes for the category of ***difficult***, and 13 emergent themes for the category of ***suggestions***.

Because the initial focus was on the design of the food-focused learning activity in Spring 2015, we gauged the impact of student participation in the *Dessert Wars Challenge* on their algorithm design capabilities in the Spring 2016 semester. All 11 students in the Spring 2016 course section were given the following test question for evaluation: Write an algorithm that gets the price for item A plus the quantity purchased of each item. The algorithm prints the total costs of all items purchased, including a 6% sales tax. Using Schneider & Gersting's [19] definition of an algorithm, we derived the following rubric to evaluate students' test answers: 1. The algorithm must include ordered steps; 2. The algorithm must get the price and quantity of item as inputs; 3. The algorithm must include primitive operations, conditional statements or repetitive statements; 4. The algorithm must correctly calculate the total price inclusive of the 6% tax; 5. The algorithm must explicitly halt in a finite amount of time (e.g., final step of stop). Using the predefined rubric, two raters separately coded students' test answers and then discussed and resolved differences to achieve 90% inter-rater reliability.

4 RESULTS

We analyzed students' online reflective journals for both course sections and assessed students' responses to the test question below.

4.1 SPRING 2015 STUDENT REFLECTIONS

Students identified several easy concepts as a result of participating in the *Dessert Wars Challenge*. We identified 8 emergent themes for the category of ***easy*** (e.g., choosing the ingredients, creating the dessert, writing the recipe/algorithm, etc.). Fifty percent (12 students) thought it was easy to be creative, the dominant emergent category. See Table 1. This suggested that the variety in the selection of ingredients and working collaboratively promoted thinking outside the box. For example, one student asked permission to leave the classroom to go get popsicle sticks to help her teammates to create a unique presentation of their dessert, giving them a competitive edge. Twenty-five percent (6 students) identified the second dominant emergent category of ***easy*** to be writing the recipe/algorithm. This suggested that working together as a team made it easier to write and execute the recipe in a short timeframe.

We identified 5 emergent themes for the category of ***difficult*** (e.g., the act of being creative, incorporating different operations into a recipe, logistical problems encountered during the food-related activity, etc.). Seventy-one percent of students identified the dominant category of ***difficult*** to be logistics for enacting the food-related activity. See Table 1. Students indicated that the time constraints, limited amount of ingredients, insufficient workspace and number of students in one group made it difficult for them to complete the activity. Time became the contributing factor as students had to manage their time wisely while they worked together to brainstorm ideas for their desserts and then simultaneously write the recipe while making the dessert with whatever ingredients were still available at the time of implementation. Teams that quickly figured out and agreed upon which to dessert to make had the advantage of access to the entire selection of ingredients while some groups had access to only a limited set of ingredients due to spending more time on planning.

We identified 9 emergent themes for ***suggestions*** (e.g., more structure for the food-related activity, more variety and amount of ingredients, student selected team members, creating more desserts, etc.). When asked how we could improve the *Dessert Wars Challenge*, students made several recommendations: 1. Give teams more time to really think about what dessert they want to create and sufficient time to do so; 2. Create a separate, designated workspace for each team so that students are not on top of each other as they work together to create their desserts; 3. Separate the ingredients and supplies per team so that each team has the same selection and amount of ingredients and supplies; and 4. Provide more structure/instructions for the food-related activity; 5. Allow teams to select their own members. Based upon student feedback, the instructor re-designed the food-related activity.

4.2 SPRING 2016 STUDENT REFLECTIONS

We had slightly different results for the category of ***easy*** in the Spring 2016 enactment of the *Dessert Wars Challenge*, identifying 7 emergent themes. Sixty-four percent (7 students) identified logistics for enacting the food-related activity as the dominant ***easy*** category. Students indicated that the re-design of this activity better facilitated students' ability to carry out the different tasks of brainstorming, writing the recipe, making the dessert and then using another team's recipe to make the second dessert. Because of the small sample size (N=11), no more than 2 students reported any other tasks as being easy.

While we identified 6 emergent themes for the category of ***difficult***, five of those themes were reported by no more than 18% (2 students). The dominant emergent theme of ***difficulty*** was time constraint. However, this theme was reported by only 27% (3 students), suggesting that majority of students had sufficient time to construct their dessert.

Between Spring 2015 and Spring 2016, the instructor re-designed the *Dessert Wars Challenge* informed by 2015 student feedback. For example, the instructor made sure that the learning activity took place in the on-campus kitchen lab which had plenty of workspace for each team to maneuver as they worked together to create a unique dessert. Each team also had a selection of the same amount and variety of ingredients so that no team had the advantage over another team. Consequently, we identified only 4 emergent themes for ***suggestions*** (i.e., more variety of ingredients, more time, more rules and no suggestions) with students reporting fewer logistical problems and more satisfaction with the food-related activity. Sixty-four percent (7 students) in the Spring 2016 course made no suggestions for improving the food-related activity and thought it was well structured. Only 2 students suggested using typical ingredients for desserts indicating that some students were not familiar with desserts that included some of the ingredients (e.g., sliced almonds). (Note: the total percentage for Spring 2016 equals more than 100% because students made multiple suggestions.)

Table 1: Comparison of Course Enactments

	Spring 2015 (N=24)	Spring 2016 (N=11)
Easy Tasks	-Being creative (50%) -Writing the recipe (25%)	Logistics for enacting food activity (64%)
Difficult Tasks	Logistics for enacting food activity (71%)	Time constraint (27%)
Suggestions	-More time -Larger workspace -More ingredients -Same amount of ingredients per team -Self-selected teams -More structure	-Fine as is -Use typical dessert ingredients

4.3 SELF-REPORTED LEARNING OUTCOMES

Because we had such a small sample size in each course section, we combined students' online journal entries for both enactments to identify emergent themes for the category of ***self-reported learning***. We identified 11 unique emergent themes for both course sections. Fifty-four (54%) (19 students) self-reported the dominant emergent theme of learning how to apply the characteristics of well-written algorithms. Students revealed that they had a better understanding of the characteristics of well-constructed algorithms, citing the use of clear, organized and precise instructions as a requirement for writing algorithms. Fourteen percent (5 students) identified the second dominant emergent theme of self-reported learning to be creativity (e.g., "I learned that the construction of an algorithm can greatly affect the outputs of a problem...that the inputs given can be the same, but with different algorithms the results will vary."). This supports the potential of the *Dessert Wars Challenge* to promote creativity while utilizing students' implicit knowledge of recipes to develop new funds of knowledge of algorithms as creative problem-solving tools [13].

4.4 ALGORITHMIC DESIGN

The question remained as to whether the *Dessert Wars Challenge* provided adequate support to assist African American undergraduate women with algorithm design in an academic setting. We gauged the impact of student participation in the *Dessert Wars Challenge* on their ability to design algorithms in the Spring 2016 semester. The majority demonstrated the ability to write well-defined algorithms. Using the rubric defined in the previous section (i.e., ordered steps, halts in finite amount of time, etc.), we coded all 11 students' answers to the cash register problem. Fifty-five percent (6 students) received full credit for their algorithm while the remaining 45% received partial credit. All 11 students wrote algorithms that consisted of primitive operations (e.g., Set variable Price to X.XX). Nine percent (1 student) included a conditional statement in her algorithm because she created her algorithm as a flow chart, suggesting that she preferred flow charts to pseudocode when designing algorithms. Ninety-one percent (10 students) accepted price and quantity of an item as inputs and correctly calculated the total price including the 6% sales tax. Only 27% (3 students) did not order their steps nor did they include a halt statement in their algorithms.

5 PUTTING THE PIECES TOGETHER

The *Dessert Wars Challenge* has revealed several insights for designing equitable learning experiences in CS when teaching underrepresented populations such as African American women.

5.1 STUDENTS' DEVELOPING CAT CAPABILITIES

Based upon students' feedback, the *Dessert Wars Challenge* did provide sufficient motivation and a situated context for African American women to develop their CAT capabilities, specifically their ability to design and implement algorithms. Using a Likert scale from 1 (strongly disagree) to 5 (strongly agree), 89% (31 students) recommended that we keep this food activity as a required part of the introductory CS course. Though students perceived the time constraint to inhibit creativity, the teams rose to the challenge and created unique desserts using the predetermined selection of ingredients. Students successfully articulated algorithms in two different contexts---first, as recipes of desserts which are exemplars of algorithms and second, as a solution to the cashier problem mentioned above. A few students even created real life scenarios (i.e., "Bill wants to buy 6 basketballs for $10 each.") to situate their algorithmic solutions. Students' ability to perform both activities confirmed previous research which explored the potential of food-related activities to serve as a bridge between students' tacit knowledge of algorithms in the context of recipes and their explicit knowledge of the design and implementation of algorithms as a problem-solving tool in an academic setting [20]. Furthermore, qualitative analysis of students' online reflective journals suggested that students thought critically about the characteristics of a well-defined algorithm and developed skills to write precise and organized algorithms with little if any ambiguity. One student wrote, "I learned that an algorithm must be written out in a manner so the algorithm can be executed exactly. This is where being unambiguous comes into play." Such evidence emphasizes the potential of the *Dessert Wars Challenge* to support students' developing CAT capabilities.

5.2 RETAINING AFRICAN AMERICAN WOMEN

Comparing the percentage of students who completed the Spring 2015 course to the percentage of students who completed the Spring 2016 course, we had retention rate of 96% (lost 1 student due to health issues) and a retention rate of 100%, respectively, even when students did not have passing grades at midterm. When comparing the retention rate for both course sections to the same introductory CS course taught in Spring 2017 by the same instructor but without the inclusion of the food-related activities, we saw a decreased retention rate of 79% with poor academically performing students dropping the class at midterms. We posited that 21% (7 students out of the initial enrollment of 33 students) dropped the class because more instructional time was spent on learning how to write Python code in the first few weeks of the course with less time allocated for extending students' funds of knowledge to their understanding of the concept of algorithms, how to design them and the correlation between algorithmic design and programming. Anecdotally, students in the 2017 course complained about the fast pace of the course as they struggled with the programming concepts, especially since most of the students had no programming experience prior to taking the introductory CS course.

In comparison to predominantly White institutions (PWIs), 100% of students enrolled in all three sections of the introductory CS course were African American women. Furthermore, the all-women's southern liberal arts institution and the classroom environment embodied inclusion and challenged the status quo of African American women not representing a critical mass of the STEM student population. In addition, the instructor shared the same ethnicity, gender and life experiences as her students, positioning the instructor to be a role model to other African American women in STEM and CS. Thus, the initial starting point in the course represented a level playing field, since the young women were not a minority nor were they subject to a hostile learning environment that conveyed the message that African American women do not belong in CS. This course also elevated and honored the intersectional experiences of these students, being both African American and female in a Computing space, which is also rare in STEM [5,6,24]. Additionally, the instructor also willingly relinquished some of her power as the instructor to welcome an opportunity for students to criticize her pedagogical strategy, an act of inclusion and an invitation for joint ownership which engaged the African American women as co-designers in creating a more equitable learning experience. These situational factors constituted a more equitable learning environment than most CS departments at PWIs. However, without the inclusion of *It's All in the Mix* even in this nurturing learning environment, retention of African American women in introductory CS courses still presented quite a challenge.

5.3 LIMITATIONS OF THE STUDY

Due to the small sample size (N=35), we cannot generalize our preliminary findings. One future research goal is to compare the CAT capabilities of larger student populations who engage in the *Dessert Wars Challenge* with those who do not, exploring ways to scaffold students' CAT capability development. Because food serves as the context for CAT capability development, it is not clear if we would see similar retention rates if we were to conduct the same study with African American undergraduate students of both sexes. We plan to explore gender differences in retention rates and learning outcomes in future research.

6 CONCLUSION

In summary, effective pedagogical strategies which target African American women are crucial to the retention of this population in CS. This paper describes an alternative pedagogical approach that leverages African American women's everyday experiences with food to develop their CAT capabilities in a college level introductory CS course. Integration of food-related activities creates an equitable learning experience, increasing student retention in the college-level introductory CS course.

REFERENCES

[1] Barker, L.J., McDowell, C., and Kalahar, K. (2009). Exploring Factors that Influence Computer Science Introductory Course Students to Persist in the Major. In Proceedings of the 40th SIGCSE Technical Symposium on Computer Science Education (Chattanooga, Tennessee, March 2009).

[2] Choi, Jaz Hee-jeong, Comber, Robert, & Linehan, Conor (2013) Food for thought : designing for critical reflection on food practices. *Interactions, 20*(1), pp. 46-47.

[3] Clegg, T., Bonsignore, E., Yip, J., Gelderblom, H., Kuhn, A., Valenstein, T., Lewittes, B., and Druin, A. (2012). Technology for promoting scientific practice and personal meaning in life-relevant learning. In Proc. Interaction Design and Children 2012.

[4] Cohoon, J.M. and Aspray, W. 2008. Retaining women in undergraduate computing. In Women and information technology: Research on underrepresentation. MIT Press, Cambridge, MA, 2006, 137-180.

[5] Collins, Patricia Hill and Bilge, Sirma. 2016. *Intersectionality.* Polity Press.

[6] Crenshaw, K., (1993). "Demarginalizing the Intersection of Race and Sex: A Black Feminist Critique of Antidiscrimination Doctrine, Feminist Theory and Antiracist Politics." In Feminist Legal Theory: Foundations, edited by D. K. Weisberg, Temple University Press, Philadelphia, PA pp. 383-95.

[7] Dahlberg, T., Barnes, T., Buch, K., & Rorrer, A. (2011). "The STARS Alliance: viable Strategies for Attracting, Retaining, Supporting, and Developing Underrepresented Students in Computing," *ACM Transactions on Computing Education 2011.*

[8] Davis, J. & Rebelsky, S. A. (2007). Food-first computer science: starting the first course right with PB&J. In *Proceedings of ACM Special Interest Group on Computer Science Education Conference (SIGCSE '07),* pp. 372-376. Covington, KY USA, ACM Press.

[9] Denning, P.J. and McGettrick, A. 2005. Recentering Computer Science. Communications of the ACM, 51:8, pp. 15-19.

[10] Ericson, Barbara, Parker, Miranda, and Engelman, Shelly (2016). Sisters Rise Up 4 CS: Helping female students pass the advanced placement computer science A exam. In *Proceedings of ACM Special Interest Group on Computer Science Education Conference (SIGCSE '16),* pp. 309-314. Memphis, TN USA, ACM Press.

[11] Gardner, C. M., Clegg, T. L., Williams, O. L. & Kolodner, J. L., (2006). Messy learning environments: busy hands and less engaged minds. In Proc. International Conference of the Learning Sciences (ICLS 2006), ISLS.

[12] Google Inc. & Gallup Inc. (2016, February). Computer Science Learning: Closing the Gap: Black Students. Findings from: Diversity Gaps in Computer Science: Exploring the Underrepresentation of Girls, Blacks and Hispanics (Issue Brief No. 2). Retrieved from https://goo.gl/FIhXKp.

[13] Hodari, A. K., Ong, M., Ko, L. T., & Kachchaf, R. R. (2014). New Enactments of Mentoring and Activism U.S. Women of Color in Computing Education and Careers. In Proceedings of the tenth annual conference on International Computing Education Research Pp. 83-90.

[14] Lewandowski, G. and Morehead, A. (1998). Computer science through the eyes of dead monkeys: Learning styles and interaction in CS I. In Proceedings of the Twenty-Ninth SIGCSE Technical Symposium on Computer Science Education (Atlanta, Georgia, United States, February 26 - March 01, 1998). D. Joyce and J. Impagliazzo, Eds. SIGCSE '98. ACM Press, New York, NY, 312-316. DOI= http://doi.acm.org/10.1145/273133.274319

[15] Moje, E. B., Ciechanowski, K. M., Kramer, K., Ellis, L., Carillo, R., & Collazo, T. (2004). Working toward third space in content area literacy: an examination of everyday funds of knowledge and discourse. Reading Research Quarterly Vol. 39, No. 1 January/February/March 2004. Pp. 38-70.

[14] National Science Foundation, National Center for Science and Engineering Statistics. 2015. *Women, Minorities, and Persons with Disabilities in Science and Engineering: 2015.* Special Report NSF 15-311. Arlington, VA. Available at http://www.nsf.gov/statistics/wmpd/.

[15] Ong, M. 2011. The Status of Women of Color in Computer Science. Communications of the ACM, 54, 7, (Jul. 2011), 1-3.

[16] Rankin, Y. A. & Thomas, J. O. (2017). Leveraging Food as the Context for Developing Computational Algorithmic Thinking in an Entry Level College Course. In Y. A. Rankin & J. O. Thomas (Eds.) *Moving Students of Color from Consumers to Producers of Technology.* IGI Global Publishers Hershey, PA.

[17] Rankin, Y. A. & Thomas, J. O. (2016). Leveraging Food to Achieve 100% Retention in an Intro CS Course. *Journal of Computing Sciences in Colleges*

[18] Rheingans, Penny, Dias-Espinoza, Crystal, D'Eramo, Erica, and Ireland, Danyelle (2018). A Model for Increasing Gender Diversity in Technology. In *Proceedings of ACM Special Interest Group on Computer Science Education Conference (SIGCSE '18),* pp. 459-464, Baltimore, MD USA, ACM Press.

[19] Rowat, A. C., Naveen, N. S., Pia, M. S., Campàs, O., Castells, P., Rosenberg, D., Brenner, M. P., & Weitz, D. A. (2014). The kitchen as a physics classroom. Physics Education, Volume 49, Number 5

[20] Schneider, G. M. & Gersting, J. L. (2013). *Invitation to Computer Science, 6th Edition.* Boston, MA: Course Technology, Cengage Learning, 4-16.

[21] Schön, D. (1983). The Reflective Practitioner: How professionals think in action. London: Temple Smith

[22] Scott, K. A., & White, M. A. (2013). CompuGirls' Standpoint Culturally Responsive Computing and Its Effect on Girls of Color. *Urban Education* September 2013 Vol. 48, No. 5 pp. 657-681.

[23] Thomas, Jakita O., (2018). The Computational Algorithmic Thinking (CAT) Capability Flow: an approach to articulating CAT Capabilities over Time in African-American Middle-School Girls. In *Proceedings of ACM Special Interest Group on Computer Science Education Conference (SIGCSE '18),* pp. 149-154. Baltimore, MD USA, ACM Press.

[24] Thomas, J. O., Joseph, N., Williams, A.*, Crum, C.*, Burge, J. (2018). Speaking Truth To Power: Exploring the Intersectional Experiences of Black women in Computing. In J. Payton and G. Thiruvathukal (Eds.). (2018). *Proceedings of the 3rd Annual Conference for Research On Equity & Sustained Participation in Computing, Engineering, & Technology* (RESPECT ' 18). Baltimore, MD, USA: IEEE Xplore.

[25] Thomas, J. O. (2014). Supporting Computational Algorithmic Thinking (SCAT): Development of a complex cognitive capability in African-American middle-school girls. In *Proceedings of ACM Special Interest Group on Computer Science Education Conference (SIGCSE '14),* (Atlanta, Georgia USA), ACM Press.

[26] Wing, J. (2011). Research notebook: Computational thinking—What and why? The Link Magazine, Spring. Carnegie Mellon University, Pittsburgh. Retrieved from http://link.cs.cmu.edu/article.php?a=600

[27] Wing, J.M. (2006). Computational Thinking. In *Communications of the ACM Viewpoint,* March 2006, pp. 33-35.

[28] Zarrett, N. R., & Malanchuk, O. (2005). Who's Computing? Gender and race differences in young adults' decisions to pursue an information technology career. *New Directions for Child and Adolescent Development,* 65-84.

[29] Zweben, S. & Bizot, B. (2017). Taulbee 2015 Survey Continued Booming Undergraduate CS Enrollment; Doctoral Degree Production Dips Slightly. Computing Research News May 2017 Vol 28/No. 5, pp. 2 -60.

This is What Diversity Looks Like*

Making CS Curriculum Culturally Relevant for Spanish-speaking Communities

Joseph Carroll-Miranda†
University of Puerto Rico
Río Piedras Campus
San Juan, PR
joseph.carroll@upr.edu

Patricia Ordonez
University of Puerto Rico
Río Piedras Campus
San Juan, PR
patricia.ordonez@upr.edu

Edusmildo Orozco
University of Puerto Rico
Río Piedras Campus
San Juan, PR
edusmildo.orozco1@upr.edu

Milagros Bravo
University of Puerto Rico
Río Piedras Campus
San Juan, PR
milabravo@gmail.com

Michelle Borrero
University of Puerto Rico
Río Piedras Campus
San Juan, PR
michelle.borrero@upr.edu

Luis Lopez
University of Puerto Rico
Río Piedras Campus
San Juan, PR
luis.lopez58@upr.edu

Gerriann Houser
University of Puerto Rico
Río Piedras Campus
San Juan, PR
gerriann.houser@upr.edu

Eliud Gerena
University of Puerto Rico
Río Piedras Campus
San Juan, PR
eliud.gerena@upr.edu

Dale Reed
(moderator)
University of Chicago at Illinois
Chicago, IL
dalereed@gmail.com

Brenda Santiago
University of Puerto Rico
Río Piedras Campus
San Juan, PR
brenda.santiago@upr.edu

Agustin Corchado
University of Puerto Rico
Río Piedras Campus
San Juan, PR
agustin.corchado1@upr.edu

Andreshka Santana
University of Puerto Rico
Rio Piedras Campus
San Juan, PR
andreshka.santana@upr.edu

ABSTRACT

Exploring Computer Science (ECS) [1] spawned from the need to provide access to Computer Science to everyone in the US. The success and commitment to equity and diversity of the ECS curriculum in Latina/o communities inspired an interdisciplinary group of educators from the University of Puerto Rico to tackle the lack of K-12 CSE on the island. This group recognized the need to implode the self-perception of Latinas (os) as being foreign to computing by educating them about Computer Science. Teachers were identified as the catalyst change agents to transform Puerto Ricans students into contributors and creators of technology through computing. The intended audience for this panel consists of practitioners and creators of curriculum looking for creative strategies to engage students from diverse cultural backgrounds in computing using their native language.

CCS CONCEPTS

• Social and professional topics → Professional topics → Computing education → K-12 education • Social and professional topics → Professional topics → Computing education → Model curricula

SIGCSE '19, February 27-March 2, 2019, Minneapolis, MN, USA

ACM ISBN 978-1-4503-5890-3/19/02
https://doi.org/10.1145/3287324.3287339.

KEYWORDS

ECS; Translation; Culturally Relevant Curriculum; Cultural and Linguistic Equivalence; Professional Development

ACM Reference format:

Joseph Carroll-Miranda, Patricia Ordo n ez, Edusmildo Orozco, Mila Bravo, Michelle Borrero, Luis Lo pez, Gerriann Houser, Eliud Gerena, Dale Reed, Brenda Santiago, Agustín Corchado, and Andreska Santana. 2019. This is What Diversity Looks Like: Making ECS Culturally Relevant for Spanish-speaking Puerto Ricans. In *Proceedings of ACM SIGCSE Symposium (SIGCSE 2019). ACM, Minneapolis, MN, USA, 2 pages.*

1 Summary Topic

The daunting task of integrating CSE into the high school curriculum requires a system wide coherent vision that harmonizes, across all levels, an effective process of systemic change in education [2]. The first step in accomplishing this task was to find a curriculum that successfully engaged Latino students. After five UPR professors attended ECS-PDs across the US, the need for both a Spanish ECS curriculum and PD was evident. This panel of experts will share the experiences of translating ECS curriculum into Spanish, offering ECS PD in Spanish, implementing the ECS curriculum in the classroom, developing a Research Practitioner Partnership [3], and using a cultural linguistic equivalence model for the validation of the translated ECS curriculum.

2 Panel Structure

Each panelist will be given 10 minutes to present his or her respective positions. Following the presentation, the moderator will facilitate the audience discussion. We anticipate questions about culturally relevant adaptations of the ECS curriculum implementation and how Puerto Rico's cultural and linguistic equivalence model can be applied to other Spanish speaking communities in the U.S.

3 General Reflections

As the lead facilitator of both ECS PDs offered in Puerto Rico in Spanish, the moderator will share his experiences. The unique ways in which facilitating this PD stands out include stories of resilience, creativity, musicality and passion. Furthermore, discussion of these cultural differences will help participants develop meaningful culturally relevant experiences with students of diverse backgrounds.

4 Why Translate ECS Curriculum?

The cultural differences experienced by a first cohort of educators during ECS PD in the US, made evident the need to have both ECS curriculum and PD available in Spanish. The language barrier became a serious stumbling block not only during the PD, but in the first attempt of implementing the ECS curriculum in PR. The presenter will share how cultural differences impede the effective implementation of ECS curriculum amongst a Spanish-speaking population and emphasize the benefits of having the curriculum in Spanish.

5 Facilitating a CS PD in Spanish

ECS PD was offered in Spanish in the summers of 2017 and 2018. As one of the first Spanish-speaking ECS facilitators, the experience of offering this PD allowed for cultural and linguistic adaptations to flourish organically. Several language issues that arose from the ECS translation. The presenter will share some of the most memorable vignettes, share the results of pre- and post-tests on both CS content and CS self-efficacy during the second ECS PD in PR.

6 Lessons from the field

After the first ECS PD in Spanish in the summer of 2017, a cohort of 10 educators set out to implement ECS in their classrooms. The destructive effects of both Hurricane Irma and Maria combined with administrative obstacles prevented a full implementation of ECS. Nevertheless, this cohort of teachers integrated ECS into their classes. The presenter will share the results of classroom visits using the ECS observation protocols, and share a diverse set of strategies used to teach ECS in Puerto Rico.

7 The Research Practitioner Partnership Journey

The community of educators orbiting ECS [4] facilitated the process of creating the first Research Practitioner Partnership (RPP) in Puerto Rico. This RPP (AIPE in Spanish) has been instrumental in the process of validating both the ECS curriculum and PD with respect to cultural linguistic equivalence. The presenter will share how the collaborative and equitable nature of the RPP has created a simultaneous bottom up and top bottom synergy that is catapulting the implementation of a CS curriculum in Puerto Rico.

8 A Model of cultural linguistic equivalence

The presenter's vast experience working with the translation of research instruments into Spanish [5] has served as a cornerstone of a cultural linguistic equivalence model for the validation of ECS curriculum's translation. This five phase model for translation and the research driven experiences with this model will be presented to encourage its use in other cultural and linguistic contexts.

REFERENCES

[1] J. Margolis, J. Goode and J. Flapan, ""A Critical Crossroads for Computer Science for All: 'Identifying Talent' or 'Building Talent,' and What Difference does it Make?. "," in *Moving Students of Color from Consumers of Technology to Producers of Technology*. Moving Students of Color from Consumers of Technology to Producers of Technology., 2016, pp. 1-23.

[2] J. Kania and M. Kramer, "Collective Impact," *Stanford Social Innovation Review*, pp. 36-41, Winter 2011.

[3] W. Penuel and D. R. Galagher, Creating Research-Practice in Education, Cambridge, MA: Creating research-practice in education, 2017.

[4] J. Ryoo, J. Goode and J. Margolis, "It takes a village: supporting inquiry- and equity-oriented computer science pedagogy through a professional learning community," 2016.

[5] M. Bravo, "Instrument Development: Cultural Adaptations for Ethnic Minority Research," in *Handbook of Racial and Ethnic Minority Psychology*, Sage Publications, pp. 220234.

Civic Engagement Across the Computing Curriculum

Mark Goadrich (Moderator)
Hendrix College
Conway, AR, USA
goadrich@hendrix.edu

Michael Goldweber
Xavier University
Cincinatti, OH, USA
goldweber@xavier.edu

Matthew Jadud
Bates College
Lewiston, ME, USA
matthew.c@jadud.com

S. Monisha Pulimood
The College of New Jersey
Ewing, NJ, USA
pulimood@tcnj.edu

Samuel A. Rebelsky
Grinnell College
Grinnell, IA, USA
rebelsky@grinnell.edu

ABSTRACT

As outlined in the ACM Computer Science Curricula 2013 Guidelines section on Social Issues and Professional Practice, "Students must also be exposed to the larger societal context of computing to develop an understanding of the relevant social [and] ethical ... issues." [1] In this panel, we demonstrate diverse approaches used to achieve this goal with respect to civic engagement. Drawing from experiences with non-major, introductory computing, mobile applications, software engineering, and interdisciplinary courses, we discuss how to move beyond surface-level discussions of ethical case studies toward an integration of civic engagement activities and personal reflection into standard computing curriculum.

CCS CONCEPTS

• **Applied computing → Computing in government**; **Education**;

KEYWORDS

Civic Engagement, Computing for Social Good, Social Issues

1 SUMMARY

Many standard computing courses can be enhanced with opportunities for civic engagement. Our experiences show that with careful planning and support, incorporating civic engagement can increase student motivation and success, and open new pathways for underrepresented groups in computing. Our intended panel audience is computing educators seeking advice and direction on how to begin implementing civic engagement in their courses. We are also targeting educators looking to share their own civic engagement experiences and build community.

2 PANEL STRUCTURE

After a very brief introduction from each panelist (5 minutes total), the moderator will ask the panel to comment on the following questions, with the goal of drawing out common themes and connections among the panelists on their experiences with civic engagement and computing curriculum.

- How do you involve civic engagement in your courses?
- How do you assess student success?
- What external resources helped or barriers hindered you?
- What lessons have you learned?

We recognize that our positions cannot cover the full spectrum of civic engagement experiences. Thus, each of these questions will also be posed to the audience to enlarge the conversation. Discussion on each question will be limited to 10 minutes, leaving 30 minutes for audience questions and participation.

3 POSITION STATEMENTS

3.1 Mark Goadrich

In fall of 2017, I enhanced our CS1 course at Hendrix with civic engagement modules. The first project in our introductory computer science course consisted of students coding a simple question/answer situation. I required their program help the user understand a civic process, such as applying to be a U.S. citizen, or determining which permits were required for renovating a home in a historic district, and provided sample output for one such situation. With a civic direction and purpose for the project, we found that students spent much more time on this project than in previous semesters. The students became very invested and engaged in getting all of the details correct, often going above and beyond the requirements to earn full credit. Second, I created a lab exercise on civic hacking to visualize freely-available data from our local government website. Given the GPS locations for local educational institutions and for tornado sirens inside city limits, students were tasked to determine if there was sufficient overlap between the effective siren range and the schools. In a follow-up survey, I was encouraged that my students were able to extrapolate their experience to other civic hacking activities, such as investigating pedestrian safety, or relationships between crime and police station locations.

3.2 Michael Goldweber

In the Computing for Social Good in Education (CSG-Ed) literature there is a four-level taxonomy of how "green" an assignment or exercise can be. These levels range from level 1: redefining an existing project with a CSG-Ed narrative, up to level 4: a real world problem brought by or solved for real stakeholders. In the fall of

SIGCSE '19, February 27-March 2, 2019, Minneapolis, MN, USA

ACM ISBN 978-1-4503-5890-3/19/02.
https://doi.org/10.1145/3287324.3287335

2017 I offered an experimental course: "Open-Ended Problem Solving" with the goal of undertaking a level 4 project. After consulting with various community partners, I decided to focus on the current opioid epidemic. After spending a crash course on the opioid epidemic through guest lectures by community partners, students, in hackathon fashion engaged in an ideation phase. Once there were n reasonably developed ideas, there was a voting phase to select the 3 most popular projects. Finally, students, through preference voting, were assigned to project teams. Each team, composed of 6-8 students, self-organized to tackle their selected problems. Focusing on two week sprints, all teams adopted the agile approach. All in all there were 5 sprints: an insufficient number to bring any of the apps to completion. While I was pleased with the educational experience -students were very successful in their interactions with community partners and in identifying new technologies, algorithms, and concepts they then went on to master- the unrealized potential of bringing these apps to market left all feeling unsatisfied. This is, however, a common pitfall with level 4 projects. Unexpectedly, I received a $25k grant to hire students to complete 2 of the apps. Six students were hired, none of whom were enrolled in the original class; testing both the quality of documentation and students' ability to perform a project handoff. By the conclusion of the summer, both apps had received approval from our primary community partners and are awaiting Google and Apple approval.

3.3 Matthew Jadud

At Bates College, during our 5-week intensive "short term," where students enroll in one course, we (Jadud and co-educator Hamish Cameron) offered *Community Engaged Computing*, an introductory course with 14 first- through final-year students. The course met four mornings per week (2hrs) and two afternoons (3hrs), plus community engagement time on Fridays (2hrs). The course involved learning the fundamentals of programming in App Inventor, a community-engaged design process, and two series of readings: one on the history of immigration in Lewiston, Maine (*Making Refuge: Somali Bantu Refugees and Lewiston, Maine* by Catherine Besteman) and a series of readings on creativity and creative process. The community partner in this project was an affinity group of middle-school aged Somali and Somali Bantu girls who met weekly after school for community and mutual support. The team of Bates college students who chose to work with this group (three women and one man) first developed a short lesson for the students to introduce them to programming in App Inventor, and then used the images and resources from this project to develop a replicable protocol for turning these images and stories into a mural. This work was carried out in close collaboration with Erica Mott (artist, choreographer) and Justice Roe (muralist) in Chicago, Ill. The product of the collaboration was then hung in the Hyde Park Art Center, and will later be presented in venues local to Lewiston.

3.4 S. Monisha Pulimood

I teach Software Engineering, a Computer Science major requirement, and have found that traditional projects that appeal to some students do not resonate with others. Inspired by research that shows that students, particularly those from underrepresented groups, are more engaged by projects that address a social need, I explored collaborations with other disciplines and community partners. Supported by NSF Award No. 1141170, a colleague from Journalism and I developed and tested a curricular model that enables students with diverse perspectives and disciplinary backgrounds to learn how to collaborate and integrate concepts from their respective fields to develop computational solutions for complex real-world problems. This includes coordinated, but separately taught, courses and collaboration with a community partner. The pilot consisted of a multi-semester collaboration between students in computer science, journalism and interactive multimedia classes who worked in partnership with Habitat for Humanity, to create a web-based application to identify pollutants in properties being considered for redevelopment. Interdisciplinary collaborative classes emphasize problem-solving in a gender-neutral, culturally and ethnically diverse community, and provide an engaging learning environment in which students solve problems together with their peers from other disciplines. Moreover, students are motivated to explore social justice issues more deeply, and understand how they can use their disciplinary backgrounds to address a community-identified need. My classes continue to collaborate with other local non-profits, such as the local food bank. The software engineering course is now designated as meeting the Advanced Community Engaged Learning requirement for students.

3.5 Samuel A. Rebelsky

For the past four years, the emphasis of our software design course has been multi-semester projects in which small teams (4-6 student) build non-mission-critical software for community nonprofits. Students have developed a wide variety of projects, including a text notification system for a local preschool, a grant management system for the umbrella for local nonprofits, and a directory tailored toward a local retirement home. Our partner nonprofits report that they can rarely afford the commercial equivalents to the software the students develop, which gives the partners patience when projects take more time than predicted. Students report that knowing the software they write will actually make a difference in the local community helps motivate and incentivize them. Although most projects take a year or more to develop, students typically work on a project for only a semester, giving them a more realistic software development experience, one in which they regularly join projects in progress. As they work with non-technical partners and grow in their understanding of the broader context of the projects they are developing, students also build their "soft" skills.

ACKNOWLEDGMENTS

Mark Goadrich's work was supported by Project Pericles. S. M. Pulimood's work was partially supported by the National Science Foundation (NSF) under Grant No. DUE-1141170. Any opinions, findings and conclusions or recommendations expressed in this material are those of the author(s) and do not necessarily reflect the views of the NSF.

REFERENCES

[1] Association for Computing Machinery (ACM) Joint Task Force on Computing Curricula and IEEE Computer Society. 2013. *Computer Science Curricula 2013: Curriculum Guidelines for Undergraduate Degree Programs in Computer Science*. ACM, New York, NY, USA. 999133.

Exploring our Privilege: Activities and Discussions

Miranda Parker
College of Computing
Georgia Tech
Atlanta, GA, USA
miranda.parker@gatech.edu

Jason T. Black
School of Business and Industry
Florida A&M Univ.
Tallahassee, FL, USA
Jason.Black@famu.edu

Helen H. Hu
Computer Science Dept.
Westminster College
Salt Lake City, UT USA
hhu@westminstercollege.edu

Colleen M. Lewis
Computer Science Dept.
Harvey Mudd College
Claremont, CA, USA
lewis@cs.hmc.edu

ABSTRACT

A meritocracy is an environment in which rewards are based solely on ability. The concept of privilege runs counter to this idea. Privilege is an unearned, unasked for advantage gained because of the way society views an aspect of your identity such as race, ethnicity, gender, perceived socioeconomic status, and language. Privilege can affect our students experiences in the classroom and beyond. However, privilege does not have to be viewed as an entitlement, but rather an opportunity to level the playing field for all people. In this session, we seek to visually display the world of privilege through adapting interactive activities known as a privilege walk and an asset walk. Come to learn and meet with other attendees who want to create a more inclusive society.

CCS CONCEPTS

• **Social and professional topics~Computer science education**

KEYWORDS

Privilege; accessibility; inclusive teaching; equity; justice.

1 OBJECTIVE

Privilege is an unearned, unasked for advantage gained because of the way society views an aspect of your identity such as race, ethnicity, gender, perceived socioeconomic status, and language [2]. In this session, we seek to visually display the world of privilege through adapting interactive activities known as a privilege walk and an asset walk. We want to help attendees of SIGCSE discover the combinations of privilege and lack of advantage in their identity [4]. We also want to help attendees acknowledge where privilege gives them power, and learn strategies to redistribute that power. This workshop was very positively received at the Grace Hopper Celebration of Women in Computing in 2014 where we had approximately 300 attendees.

We hope to create a safe space for attendees to reflect on the ways that society's power structures have impacted their lives and given them unearned advantages. We also want to facilitate productive discussions about privilege and how it manifests itself in our lives and society.

In addition to educating attendees about privilege, we would like to give them tools to become effective allies and redistribute their privilege. Discussions about privilege can happen anytime and anywhere, and we would like to leave the attendees with the tools to fully participate in these conversations, and to create safe spaces of their own.

2 SESSION OUTLINE

We have outlined below the approximate duration and description of each section of the session based upon running this workshop at GHC in 2014.

2.1 Goals and Key Terms (5 minutes)

The facilitators will introduce the concepts of meritocracy and privilege and explain the purpose of the exercise. The facilitators will emphasize that it is natural to feel guilty as we become more aware of our privileges, but that this process is important for being an effective ally.

2.2 Privilege Walk (10 minutes)

The facilitators will read a series of statements based on an article by McIntosh [1] such as "I am never asked to speak for all the people of my racial group." After each statement is read, the participant will raise their hand if they identify with the statement. Attendees will be asked to pause and look around the room. This will be a silent and reflective exercise and attendees will be asked to tally the total number of times they raised their hand.

2.3 Initial Reactions (5 minutes)

After the statements are finished, the facilitators will invite attendees to share their initial reactions to the exercise with the entire audience. This will introduce themes for later discussion by small groups.

2.4 Small Group Discussion (20 minutes)

Attendees will be organized into small discussion groups, which provides an additional opportunity for SIGCSE members to get to know each other. In these groups, attendees will discuss their reactions to the exercise and share statements that surprised or affected them.

SIGCSE '19, February 27-March 2, 2019, Minneapolis, MN, USA

ACM ISBN 978-1-4503-5890-3/19/02.
https://doi.org/10.1145/3287324.3287512

2.5 Asset Walk (10 minutes)

The facilitators will present some strengths and weakness of the privilege walk activity. The facilitator will then read a different set of statements that highlight the ways in which particular types of adversity build strengths that are often overlooked. This set of statements known as an asset walk were developed by Oropeza Fujimoto & Fujimoto [3].

2.6 Brainstorming in Groups (10 minutes)

Attendees will brainstorm in their groups additional privileges they have that were not mentioned or assets they have from having faced adversity that were not mentioned. By being proactive in addressing our privilege we can take ownership and this can be an important way to address the guilt that can be triggered by these discussions.

2.7 Allyship and Q&A (15 minutes)

The facilitators will bring the entire audience back together to close the activity with a discussion of allyship and Q&A with the Special Session facilitators.

3 EXPECTATIONS

This session will be aimed at anyone who is interested in discovering more about the interaction between their identity and society. Attendees will have the opportunity to examine the effects of unequal power distribution on their opportunities and lives. Attendees will also get to discuss strategies to use their privilege to help others, change societal patterns of oppression, and create a more inclusive classroom or research group. Handouts and a link to the handouts will be made available for attendees wanting a copy of the privilege and asset walk questions, a tip sheet on allyship, and the references we cite here and in the presentation.

4 SUITABILITY FOR A SPECIAL SESSION

The flexibility of a Special Session provides the opportunity for SIGCSE attendees to participate in two powerful activities (a privilege and asset walk) and in-depth discussion with other attendees.

5 PRESENTERS

5.1 Miranda Parker, Georgia Tech

Miranda Parker is a Human-Centered Computing PhD candidate at Georgia Institute of Technology. As a CS education researcher, Miranda explores issues of privilege in the CS classroom. She looks at how a student's race, gender, socioeconomic status, and other aspects of their identity shape their CS learning experience.

5.2 Jason T. Black, Florida A&M University

Dr. Black, Associate Professor in Business Information Systems, holds a MS degree in CS from Georgia Tech, and a PhD in CS from Florida State University. Dr. Black has a research background in mobile computing, collaborative learning and educational technology. Dr. Black founded and directed the NSF-funded African-American Women in CS Scholarship program, and a founding partner in the NSF-funded STARS Alliance for Diversity in Computing. Dr. Black also is working in Big Data, Social Computing, Social Media, and Entrepreneurship.

5.3 Helen H. Hu, Westminster College

Helen Hu is a Professor and Chair of CS at Westminster College. She the PI on a NSF project, focused on Process Oriented Guided Inquiry Learning (POGIL) in Introductory CS. The POGIL approach has been shown in other STEM disciplines to increase student learning and retention, particularly for students from underrepresented populations. Helen Hu leads a large number of outreach programs in Utah, including a project that introduced Exploring CS course to over 200 Utah high schools.

5.4 Colleen Lewis, Harvey Mudd College

Colleen Lewis is an Associate Professor of CS at Harvey Mudd College. Colleen researches how people learn CS and how people feel about learning CS. Her research seeks to identify effective teaching practices for creating equitable learning spaces for all students. Lewis is the PI for CSTeachingTips.org, a NSF-sponsored project for disseminating effective CS teaching practices.

5 REFERENCES

[1] McIntosh, Peggy. "White Privilege: Unpacking the Invisble Knapsack." Peace and Freedom. July 1989. http://www.library.wisc.edu/EDVRC/docs/public/pdfs/LIReadings/InvisibleKnapsack.pdf

[2] Oluo, Ijeoma. (2018). So you want to talk about race. Hachette UK.

[3] Oropeza Fujimoto, M. & Fujimoto, E. (2016). CSU Fullerton, U.S.A.; I-Chen Huang – Wenzao Uruline College of Languages, Taiwan. (Responding to Unpacking the Invisible Knapsack by McIntosh, P. 1988 and extending the work of Yosso, T. 2005.) (REVISED JULY 2016). https://profteacher.files.wordpress.com/2016/11/community-cultural-wealth-walk-revised-july-2016-by-oropeza-fujimoto-huangin-progress.pdf

[4] Watt, Sherry. (2007). "Difficult Dialogues, Privilege and Social Justice: Uses of the Privileged Identity Exploration Model in Student Affairs Practice." The College Student Affairs Journal. Spring 2007. Vol 26, No 2. Pages 114-126. http://files.eric.ed.gov/fulltext/EJ899385.pdf.

Computing Curricula 2020: Introduction and Community Engagement

Alison Clear
Eastern Institute of Technology
School of Computing
Auckland, New Zealand 1010
+64 9 9799406
aclear@eit.ac.nz

Allen Parrish
Mississippi State University
Computer Science and Engineering
Mississippi State, MS 39762 USA
+1 662-325-6586
allen.parrish@msstate.edu

John Impagliazzo
Hofstra University
Department of Computer Science
Hempstead, New York USA
+1 631-513-2833
john.impagliazzo@hofstra.edu

Ming Zhang
Peking University
School of EECS
100871, Beijing, China
+86 10.62765825
mzhang_cs@pku.edu.cn

ABSTRACT

This session presents an overview of the *Computing Curricula 2020 (CC2020)* project and provides a status report for the project. CC2020 seeks to generate a modern revision of the well-known CC2005 document by reflecting a more current view of computing, including the addition of new and emerging sub-disciplines like cybersecurity and data science. Further, CC2020 proposes a competency-based characterization of computing, as well as a bottom-up organization of computing into its sub-disciplines based on an analysis of competencies. This session imparts the results of the project to date and provides an opportunity for participants to infuse new ideas on the current computing disciplinary landscape, as well as input for the competency model it proposes.

CCS CONCEPTS

• Social and professional topics • Model Curricula

KEYWORDS

Computing model curricula, disciplinary taxonomy, competencies, CC2020, CC2005.

ACM Reference format:

Alison Clear, Allen Parrish, John Impagliazzo, Ming Zhang, 2019. Computing Curricula 2020: Introduction and Community Engagement. In *Proceedings of ACM Special Interest Group on Computer Science Education. ACM, New York, NY, USA, 2 pages.* https://doi.org/10.1145/3287324.3287517.

ACM ISBN 978-1-4503-5890-3/19/02.
https://doi.org/10.1145/3287324.3287517

1 OBJECTIVE

This session will present an overview of the global project *Computing Curricula 2020 (CC2020)* and it provide a status report on its activities. CC2020 is a joint project launched by professional computing societies worldwide to examine the current state of curricular guidelines for academic programs granting degrees in computing and to provide a vision for the future of computing. The goal of the initiative is to produce a comprehensive report that compares these guidelines to situate and contextualize them in the landscape of computing education. Ultimately, the project strives to help programs prepare graduates both academically and professionally to meet the challenges in the mid-2020s and beyond. The international scope of the project should perk the interest of many members of the SIGCSE community because the global presence as the 2019 symposium and the special interest participants have in matters of curricular developments and research. Additionally, CC2020 is a priority of the ACM Education Council and the ACM Education Board.

The CC2020 project is sponsored principally by the Association for Computing Machinery (ACM) and the IEEE Computer Society. Additional sponsors include the Association for Information Systems (AIS), and Association for Information Technology Professionals (AITP/EDSIG). Project collaborators include Special Interest Group for Computer Human Interaction (SIGCHI), Information Processing Society of Japan (IPSJ), Information-Technology Promotion Agency (IPA) of Japan, Chinese Computing Federation (CCF), Conferencia Latinoamericana de Informática (CLEI) "Latin-American Conference on Informatics," and Computer Society of India (CSI). The project team consists of a task force of 36 members representing 16 countries and six continents. A steering committee of 13 members functions as an executive board to manage the project.

This special session has two principal objectives. First, the session provides an opportunity to communicate the results and status of the project to potential stakeholders within the computing education community and to SIGCSE participants. Second, the session will allow the project team to engage with stakeholders to obtain feedback that may become part of the project. The session not only conveys information, but it provides a forum for lively interaction on a project that will likely change the landscape of computing education communities.

2 OUTLINE

Each of the authors are responsible for a critical role in the CC2020 project. Alison Clear and Allen Parrish are co-chairs of the CC2020 project representing ACM and IEEE, respectively. John Impagliazzo chairs the competency group that is responsible for developing computing competencies for the future. Ming Zhang is a member of the CC2020 steering committee with the responsibility of ensuring that the project has universal participation on a global scale, particularly in China.

The following outline for the special session has two interwoven parts that includes informing the audience of the project and allowing many opportunities for audience interaction and discussion.

- Introduction (5 mins) – Clear introduces CC2020 and provides a general background on the project.
- Review of CC2005 (5 min) – Clear provides a review of CC2005 and its significance.
- Progress and Competencies (10 min) – Impagliazzo discusses the current progress of the project (from [1, 2, 3]), along with an overview of the competencies and their meaning.
- Report structure (10 mins) – Parrish discusses the structure of the final report and demonstrates the current prototype of the visualization tool under construction.
- Global Outreach (10 mins) – Zhang discusses the importance of the CC2020 to a global community of computing educators and worldwide industries.
- Group Brainstorming (20 minutes) – Clear facilitates group brainstorming exercises that involve (a) developing a list of new and emerging computing disciplines that should be part of the CC2020 report, and (b) assessing some developed competencies for a computing discipline to determine where limitations might exist.
- Report Out (10 minutes) – Parrish directs a group summarization of the activities presented.
- Closure (5 mins) – Clear summarizes the session and suggests "next steps" activities.

3 EXPECTATIONS

The goal of the CC2020 project is to publish a written report and a dynamic set of tools for exploring the competency space used to define computing and its disciplines. The audience of this special session would consist of computing faculty members, ideally from a variety of computing disciplines, including those that are emerging. The audience will learn many of the details of a project that is global in scope and that should exhibit significant influence on the way institutions might form computing curricula over the next decade. Feedback from the audience should inform the presenters on new insights of special interest to the project through group discussions, general discourse, and from the reporting process.

REFERENCES

[1] M. Jafar, L. Waguespack and J. Babb, "A Visual Analytics Approach to Gain Insight into the Structure of Computing Curricula, *2017 Proceedings of the EDSIG Conference,* Austin, TX, ISSN: 2473-3857 V3 n4377.

[2] H. Topi, "Role of Information Systems in the CC2020 Initiative," *ACM Inroads,* December 2017, vol 8, no 4.

[3] J. Impagliazzo and A. Pears, "The CC2020 Project – Computing Curricula Standards for 2020 and Beyond," *Proceedings of Educon,* 2018.

Special Session: A Discussion of Research Practice Partnerships in CS Education

Leigh Ann DeLyser
CSforALL
New York, NY
leighann@csforall.org

Joshua Elder
CSforALL
New York, NY
Joshua@csforall.org

Alan Peterfreund
SageFox Consulting Group
Amherst, MA
apeterfreund@sagefoxgroup.com

Stacey Sexton
SageFox Consulting Group
Amherst, MA
ssexton@sagefoxgroup.com

ABSTRACT

In the summer of 2017, the National Science Foundation funded a cohort of Research Practice Partnership (RPP) projects focused on expanding access to Computer Science Education in the United States. Funded as one of the RPP projects was the RPPforCS project, a collaboration between Sagefox Consulting and CSforAll. The project operates as a community of practice for the individual RPP projects, holding regular webinars, producing a newsletter, and curating a discussion forum on Slack. In this special session we propose a structured poster session specifically for the RPP projects funded by the NSF.

ACM Reference format:
Leigh Ann DeLyser, Joshua Elder, Alan Peterfreund, and Stacey Sexton. 2019. Special Session: A Discussion of Research Practice Partnerships in CS Education. In *Proceedings of ACM Special Interest Group on Computer Science Education, Minneapolis, MN, USA, February 2019 (SIGCSE'19),* 2 pages. https://doi.org/10.1145/3287324.3287523

1 OBJECTIVE

The SIGCSE conference covers a wide variety of topics related to Computer Science (CS) education. The National Science Foundation is a primary funder of much of the research conducted by the SIGCSE community and therefore an important influencer in the types of projects proposed and focal topics to be covered.

Research-Practice Partnerships are a relatively new research methodology, both in general education research and in CS education research and the SIGCSE community.[3] A Research-Practice Partnership (RPP) is a design-based implementation research [2] approach to address research questions or problems that arise in authentic practice settings. These settings could be formal or informal education settings (i.e., classrooms or out-of-school spaces).

As a new research methodology and as a priority for NSF, it is important for the SIGCSE community to learn about RPPs, see examples of RPPs in practice, and understand the data and analysis that RPPs produce. To meet this goal, we propose a special session in the form of a structured poster session to enable the 23 funded projects participating in the RPPforCS project to display posters about their design, execution, and early results after year 1.

A structured poster session would represent a new type of session for SIGCSE, although they are common at the American Education Research Association (AERA) annual meeting. Structured poster sessions are organized around a specific topic or theme and, in addition to typical poster presentations, include a discussion with a moderator and discussant who reflect at the end of the session and encourage attendee discussion. The structured poster session format will enable the SIGCSE community to identify posters specifically focused on the topic of RPPs, engage in a broader discussion around RPPs, and grow the community knowledge base for a NSF multi-year funded program. [1]

2 ABOUT RPPFORCS

The RPPforCS project is a National Science Foundation funded collaboration between SageFox Consulting and CSforALL to build the capacity of NSF funded CSforALL:Research-Practice Partnership[1] evaluators and researchers to study, understand, and report on the project efforts and to establish a participant-driven multi-site research agenda for the NSF CSforALL:RPP program. The project uses a connected community of practice in order to promote dissemination and provide formative feedback to projects and the broader community of CS education research practice partnerships.

The project was started in 2017, coincident with the funding of the first cohort of NSF awardees, and has made efforts to connect the community of project teams through online communication channels, webinars, and in person meetings. Additionally, the project convenes a researcher and evaluator working group to discuss the potential for shared measures used across projects.

3 SESSION OUTLINE

A structured poster session includes three components. First, the session moderator introduces the session and gives each presenter 15-30 seconds to introduce their poster's title and general theme. Second, attendees visit the posters that are of interest to them. Third, the moderator reconvenes the group to the central presentation and introduces the discussant who facilitates a conversation relevant to the theme of the session and informed by the posters.

SIGCSE'19, February 2019, Minneapolis, MN, USA

ACM ISBN 978-1-4503-5890-3/19/02.
https://doi.org/10.1145/3287324.3287523

Figure 1: Map of RPPforCS Participating Projects

The posters will be representative of the projects funded by the NSF CSforALL:RPP[1] program. Due to the large number of projects (24) there is not space in this proposal to include a description of the data and results from all projects. The projects span small, medium, and large awards as defined by the NSF, and represent a national geographic spread of projects. Figure 1 shows the geographic distribution of the projects in the RPPforCS community.

For this special session, we propose the following session outline:

- Introduction (10 minutes, Joshua Elder): Joshua Elder from CSforALL and the RPPforCS project will introduce the RPPforCS project and facilitate the individual poster introductions from presentation leads.
- Poster Presentations (45 minutes, Individual Project Leads): Individual projects will present posters in an open format. Attendees are free to walk from poster to poster and speak with the presenters.
- Discussion (20 minutes, Leigh Ann DeLyser): Leigh Ann DeLyser from CSforALL and RPPforCS will offer a brief synthesizing summary of the posters and facilitate a discussion of the posters, theme of the session, and implications for the SIGCSE community.

4 EXPECTATIONS

SIGCSE attendees in the session will be expected to (1) visit individual posters and attend to the materials presented, and (2) participate in a discussion of RPPs and implications for the SIGCSE community. Because the session will reflect the landscape of funded RPP projects from the National Science Foundation [1], it will be geared toward CS education implementation in K-12 schools in the United States.

Poster presenters will be expected to prepare a poster related to their NSF funded CSforALL:RPP project. Posters will need to contain both a description of the Research Practice Partnership as well as data from the first year of implementation of the project. Poster presenters will be prepared to discuss both the methods and research design of the project as well as the data presented.

5 BENEFIT TO THE SIGCSE COMMUNITY

The session has a twofold benefit for the SIGCSE community. First, the ability to attend a session with a large number (potentially 24) of examples of a new research methodology is of general benefit to all researchers interested in current and relevant education research. Second, because Research-Practice Partnerships are currently a key NSF priority, the CS education community can benefit from a discussion of the design and implementation experiences of these funded projects.

REFERENCES

[1] Computer science for all (csforall:rpp) researcher practitioner partnerships.

[2] T. Anderson and J. Shattuck. Design-based research: A decade of progress in education research? *Educational researcher*, 41(1):16–25, 2012.

[3] C. E. Coburn, W. R. Penuel, and K. E. Geil. Practice partnerships: A strategy for leveraging research for educational improvement in school districts. *William T. Grant Foundation*, 2013.

Going Beyond the Platitudes of Equity: Developing a Shared Vision for Equity in Computer Science Education

Jean Ryoo[1]*, Gail Chapman[2], Julie Flapan[1], Joanna Goode[3], Jane Margolis[1], Christine Ong[1], Cynthia Estrada[1], Max Skorodinsky[3], Tiera Tanksley[1], Jamika D. Burge[4], Ryoko Yamaguchi[4], Frieda McAlear[5], Allison Scott[5], Alexis Martin[5], Sonia Koshy[5], Kamau Bobb[6], Lien Diaz[6]

[1] UCLA "REAL-CS", Los Angeles, CA {jeanryoo@ucla.edu; flapan@gseis.ucla.edu; margolis@gseis.ucla.edu; ong@cresst.org; cynthiaestradag@ucla.edu; tctanksl@ucla.edu}

[2] Exploring Computer Science "REAL-CS", Eugene, OR {chapgail@gmail.com}

[3]University of Oregon "REAL-CS", Eugene, OR {goodej@uoregon.edu; makseem@uoregon.edu}

[3] "Bright-CS", Arlington, VA {jamika.burge@gmail.com; ryamaguchi@plusalpharesearch.com}

[4] Kapor Center, Oakland, CA {friedam@kaporcenter.org; allison@kaporcenter.org; alexis@kaporcenter.org; sonia@kaporcenter.org}

[5] Georgia Tech, Atlanta, GA {kamau.bobb@cc.gatech.edu; ldiaz@cc.gatech.edu}

*Moderator

ABSTRACT

Efforts to broaden participation in computing address how systemic school structures, educator preparation, and curriculum can provide inclusive learning spaces for all students. The emerging multiplicity of scholarship in computer science (CS) education forwards diverse voices, perspectives, and positionalities, and together, provide a rich set of evidence-based narratives that can transform K-12 policies and practices. The four projects featured in this panel bring together CS education efforts with varying methodologies focused on equity-oriented pedagogies and learning for all youth across the US. This panel will focus not only on sharing the multi-pronged efforts of the featured projects, but also on developing a shared vision among participants and panelists for what "equity" can and should be in the future of both SIGCSE and CS education as we celebrate SIGCSE's 50th anniversary. By highlighting the work of *projects* rather than *individuals* in this panel, audience members will have the opportunity to learn about how collaborative efforts create and examine contexts for equity in CS education across diverse stakeholders, while also providing a richer base for constructing visions of equity that go beyond mere platitudes, toward action items for broadening participation in computing.

1. SUMMARY

The Computer Science for All Movement is gaining momentum nationwide as administrators, educators, parents, students, and researchers recognize the pressing need to democratize access to quality computing education for *all* students [e.g., 1, 2, etc.]. This effort to broaden participation in computing is a united response to research revealing that youth of color and females have been systematically denied access to CS courses and inclusive pedagogy, especially in low-income schools, resulting in segregated CS education and career pathways [3]. The variety of efforts to broaden participation in computing—with the creation of new curricula, teacher education programs, policy, and assessments—has led to a growing body of research focused on equity in CS education. Yet questions remain about the impacts of CS for All efforts on historically underrepresented students' experiences and engagement with CS, teachers' perceptions of their roles in broadening participation in computing, pedagogical practices for inclusive CS learning, and structures/policies impacting teaching and learning.

Responding to SIGCSE's 50th anniversary call to create a vision for the next 50 years—especially around topics of broadening participation, diversity, and K-12 education—this panel brings together four different CS education efforts focused on equity-related issues in CS education. Representing a range of methodologies and contexts across the US (from research-practice partnerships to non-profits to university organizations) that seek to have direct impact on supporting equity-oriented pedagogies and learning experiences for *all* youth, presenters will share how: (1) equity is being defined in their research/program, and (2) their CS for All efforts impact equity issues in CS education. This will be followed by an effort to design a shared vision not only for what we believe "equity" should mean for SIGCSE and the CS for All movement, but also, going beyond the platitudes of equity, what it should look like to take action based on this shared vision.

2. PANEL STRUCTURE

Unlike a traditional SIGCSE panel that typically highlights only 4 *individual* panelists, this panel brings together a larger number of people to represent 4 different *collaborative projects* geared toward addressing equity issues in CS education. While only one individual from each project will represent the teams on stage during brief panel presentations, all team members will be present to participate in the interactive aspects of this panel. We believe that having many people at the table representing collaborative work offers a more accurate representation of what the CS for All movement involves: not individuals working independently, but many people coming together to address equity issues pressing in their communities or in the nation at large. The goal of the panel is to share a range of perspectives across collaborators who have expertise in research, pedagogy, professional development, policy, and institutional change, toward developing a shared vision of what "equity" can and should look like, as well as specific action items to work toward for the SIGCSE and CS for All community. As such, the panel will begin with a 5-minute introduction to the session by the

SIGCSE '19, February 27-March 2, 2019, Minneapolis, MN, USA

ACM ISBN 978-1-4503-5890-3/19/02.
https://doi.org/10.1145/3287324.3287331

moderator introducing the panelists and panel goals. This will be followed by 10-minute presentations by each project in which panelists will explain how their projects: 1) define equity in their work, and 2) seek to address inequity in CS education across either formal or informal K-12 learning contexts while addressing where they see room for improvement. Then, audience members can ask panelists (and their team members in the room) specific questions during a 10-minute Q & A, allowing time for attendees to digest ideas shared thus far. This will be followed by a 20-minute activity in which panelists and audience members will work together to create a shared definition of "equity" for CS education, as well as action items we want both the SIGCSE and CS Education community at large to achieve within the next 50 years. Following this discussion, the moderator will incorporate all ideas from the panel toward developing a white paper (authorship including all willing panelists and audience members) to share with the SIGCSE community at large. This white paper will describe the range of ideas shared during the panel, offering a starting point for how our community of scholars, educators, students, parents, and community organizers can continue to take action, so that computing can truly be for *all* in the next 50 years of SIGCSE and beyond.

3. "REAL-CS" Team (UCLA + Univ of OR)

"REAL-CS" (Researching Equity, Access, & Learning in CS Education, funded by the NSF) brings together educators and researchers across the University of Oregon and UCLA to address equity issues in high school CS education across three strands: 1) teacher education and professional development; 2) policy and public engagement; 3) student learning research. Building on over a decade of research focused on democratizing access to K-12 CS education for youth historically underrepresented in CS [3, 4], the creation of the Exploring Computer Science curriculum and professional development [5], and policy/outreach efforts [6, 7], the REAL-CS team offers insights into how our current project supports equity-oriented teacher learning and practice, efforts to ensure CS for All reaches youth throughout the state of California, and why student identity is important to support within the context of introductory CS high school classrooms.

4. "BRIGHT-CS" Team

BRIGHT-CS (*Building Student Retention through Individuated Guided coHort Training in CS*) is an NSF-funded research project that harnesses the power of mentoring, peer learning, grit and resilience to put cohorts of middle school black girls at the core of the STEM-CS pipeline model. BRIGHT-CS supports two objectives: 1) to create a computing learning ecosystem for K-12 students, particularly focused on black girls [8, 9, 10]; and 2) to research the impact of the learning ecosystem in a longitudinal manner. To create a computing learning ecosystem, we use a cohort model of positive peer and near-peer mentors among black girls in computing with an emphasis on (1) empowerment and leadership development for black girls, (2) comprehensive computer science and computational thinking experiences, and (3) partnerships with schools, colleges/universities, and non-profit and community organizations. In investigating the effectiveness of this learning ecosystem, an important outcome of this research is to determine and inform best practices for broadening participation to other student groups traditionally viewed as marginalized.

5. Kapor Center

The Kapor Center investigates how to broaden participation in computing for underrepresented students (with a particular focus on girls of color) through: 1) analyses of differing levels of access to CS courses in California school districts, 2) examinations of strategies and interventions to bring about more equitable outcomes for all students, and 3) providing direct programs for low-income first-generation high school students to learn rigorous CS. The Kapor Center also documents obstacles and barriers to participation that exist despite access to CS courses, to directly inform the design and implementation of the next generation of computing education initiatives. Kapor Center findings contribute to ongoing district and state-level implementation plans, such that continuous improvement can be made to increase the number of girls and underrepresented students with access to CS courses, enrolled in CS courses, and demonstrating successful completion and persistence in computing sequences. This research on models for broadening participation in computing education can be utilized across local districts, states, and at the national level.

6. Constellations Ctr for Equity in Computing

The Constellations Center views equity as a structural matter. Students of color are facing all of the challenges associated with the intersection of race, class, and education in computing education that manifests itself in their having unfair access to capable teachers of CS or schools that engender the composite set of skills upon which a solid computing education can be built. As a pledge to provide access to high level computing education to underrepresented students, the Center's solution to this crisis is to build and deploy a hybrid model with solid instruction of online computing content and a professional development strategy that builds teacher efficacy over time. This hybrid instruction model alleviates novice computing teachers from being the sole subject matter experts and allows them the opportunity to increase their efficacy in the knowledge and skills comprised in the computing course they are facilitating over a sustained period of time.

7. REFERENCES

[1] Smith, M. 2016. *Computer Science for All.* The White House President Barack Obama. https://obamawhitehouse.archives.gov/blog/2016/01/30/computer-science-all.

[2] CS for All. https://www.csforall.org.

[3] Margolis, J., Holme, J., Estrella, R., Goode, J., & Nao, K. 2017. *Stuck in the shallow end: Education, race, and computing*, revised ed. MIT Press.

[4] Exploring Computer Science. http://exploringcs.org.

[5] Goode, J. & Chapman, G. 2016. *Exploring Computer Science Curriculum.* University of Oregon.

[6] Alliance for California Computing Education for Students and Schools (ACCESS). http://access-ca.org.

[7] Computer Science for California (CS for CA). http://access-ca.org/csforca/.

[8] Traphagen, K., & Traill, S. (2014). How Cross Sector Collaborations are Advancing STEM Learning. Los Altos, CA: Noyce Foundation.

[9] Casey, B. (2012). STEM Education: Preparing for the Jobs of the Future. Washington DC: US Congress Joint Economic Committee.

[10] National Science Foundation, & National Center for Science and Engineering Statistics. (2013). Women, Minorities, and Persons with Disabilities in Science and Engineering 2013 (Special Report NSF 13-304). Arlington, VA: National Science Foundation

Interactive Peer-Led Code Reviews in CS2 Curricula

Ryan Rybarczyk
Butler University
4600 Sunset Avenue
Indianapolis IN 46208
rrybarcz@butler.edu

Lingma Acheson
Indiana University-Purdue University Indianapolis
723 W. Michigan St.
Indianapolis IN 46202
linglu@cs.iupui.edu

ABSTRACT

Previous work demonstrated an effective strategy on how to teach two programming languages (Java and C++) side-by-side in a Computer Science II (CS2) course. The goal of this approach was twofold: first, to stress the importance of programming language selection as part of a career preparation module; secondly, to improve the overall success and satisfaction of the students. The results of this work led to additional questions, including how students (peers) could be leveraged to act as instructors in laboratory settings to aid in a peer-led learning exercise. One of the unique challenges associated with CS2 curricula is the varying degree of student experiences and expertise when entering the course. Course surveys have demonstrated that a subset of the student population enter the course with significant programming experience, while others report no prior experience with programming or programming languages. It is therefore the role of the instructor, to find the proper balance within the course in order to satisfy all students' learning needs. In the original work it was indicated, via student post-completion surveys, that peer-led discussion of coding "best practices" could improve overall student outcomes. This survey provided the motivation for this paper. In this paper, we propose using interactive peer-led code reviews to help introduce the students to widely accepted practices found throughout industry while allowing them to better master the material through a shared learning experience. We provide an outline for how this can be achieved in an existing course structure and discuss the outcomes from this study.

CCS CONCEPTS

• **Computing education → Computer Science Education**; *computer science education, curriculum*;

KEYWORDS

CS2, Curriculum, Peer-led Instruction, Career Preparation

SIGCSE '19, February 27-March 2, 2019, Minneapolis, MN, USA

ACM ISBN 978-1-4503-5890-3/19/02...$15.00
https://doi.org/10.1145/3287324.3287442

ACM Reference format:
Ryan Rybarczyk, Lingma Acheson. 2019. Interactive Peer-Led Code Reviews in CS2 Curricula. In *Proceedings of the 50th ACM Technical Symposium on Computer Science Education (SIGCSE '19). February 27-March 2, 2019, Minneapolis, MN, USA*, ACM, NY, NY, USA, 7 pages. DOI: https://doi.org/10.1145/3287324.3287442

1 INTRODUCTION

One of the unique challenges associated with teaching the Computer Science (CS) curriculum at the university/college level is the varying background of student knowledge (in computing and programming) within introductory courses, Computer Science I and II (CS1/CS2) [2]. These courses are designed such that they cover a vast expanse of material and in some instances may necessitate that the instructor make assumptions as to the level, or proficiency, of the students' in the course when designing lectures, exercises and assignments. One of the suggested solutions to mitigate this problem is the use of peer-led instruction [3]. In this particular method of instruction, the instructor of the course leverages the experience of student peers to assist in the learning process. In [1], it was proposed how two object-oriented (OO) programming languages could successfully be taught side-by-side in an effort to improve overall student learning outcomes. This work provided many answers to the original questions, but also brought up new and interesting questions that needed to be further investigated. One of these questions presented was how to best utilize student peers within a classroom or laboratory setting. To broaden this point we wanted to focus both on current students as well as former students serving as peer leaders within the classroom.

In this paper, we are proposing the use of interactive peer-led code reviews as a means to improve overall student retention, increase student satisfaction, and to better prepare the students for their future careers in field of CS. We have created a sample implementation and a set of important questions that should be discussed as part of this peer-led exercise. Additionally, we describe how this approach can easily be implemented as part of any CS2 curriculum. We conclude this paper by demonstrating that through the use of peer-led instruction, specifically in the form of interactive peer-led code reviews, this proposed method can succeed in improved retention of students, higher student satisfaction, and overall student learning and career preparation within a CS undergraduate degree program.

2 PEER-LED INSTRUCTION & LEARNING

Peer-led instruction and learning is a well-studied topic in the area of STEM education. Discussions on peer-led instruction and its implementation can be found in [4]. In this paper, we have chosen to focus on the methodology of the Peer-led Team Learning (PLTL) approach as we believe this pedagogy provides the most benefit within our given problem area. We will now briefly describe this concept to provide background for our work.

2.1 Peer-led Team Learning

The concept of PLTL has been a popular research topic in the field of STEM education for the last two decades. The PLTL approach is a socio-collaborative pedagogical methodology in which students are organized into small groups, with the support and guidance of a more senior student(s) that serves as a peer leader, to engage as a cohort in problem-solving exercises that involve problems that are complex enough to invite the sharing of conceptual knowledge, differing problem-solving procedures, justification of ideas, and consensus building [4]. The goal of this approach is to provide a community-based learning environment in which the students work together through the free exchange of ideas and knowledge. The PLTL methodology can be implemented in all types of STEM courses, class sizes, and institution types [4] and thus, is a perfect fit for our specific problem. We will now briefly describe how we have adapted this model to fit the needs and the resources available to our specific department.

2.1.1 Adapted PLTL

In our adapted model of the PLTL methodology, peers are leveraged in assisting other students to help master course content through laboratory or recitation-style sessions. This role of assisting can manifest itself in many different forms and can be adapted to the needs of the specific course and/or instructor. In the case of laboratory instruction, students who have successfully completed the course are invited back to be hired as Peer Leaders (PL). In this role, the PL are expected to help run a given laboratory session and answer any questions the students have with respect to course content or their assignments. Each PL goes through departmental training to properly educate them on their role within the course as well as to provide them with a clear outline as to their expected performance.

In addition to using PL in the course, we can also leverage the students themselves to aid in this learning process. One such application of using student peers for instruction is that of pair programming [5, 6]. This area focuses on the physiological impact that working with a student peer has on the ability to learn course content and its relationship with the ability to improve overall student performance. In this paper, we attempt to leverage both the work done in the PLTL community (through the use of PL) as well as the work done in pair programming community (through the use of interactive peer-led code reviews).

3 CAREER PREPARATION

One of the key goals of any instructor, at any educational level, is the ability to adequately prepare students' for successful entry into the next phase of their career. This process is often augmented by existing dedicated services offered as part of a college or university. These services provide students with resources (e.g., resume building and preparation) that can help them in their transition from academia into the workforce. This guidance often is not fully utilized by most students until they reach their final year of study. An alternative option that can be provided to students, at all academic levels, is that of integrating career guidance and preparation into existing course curriculum. In this paper we have chosen to focus on program or major specific guidance and not the general guidance provided by these academic units of the college or university.

Part of implementing this approach to career guidance and preparation into the curriculum is the requirement of adhering to existing standards and course expectations. For instance, the required course content must not suffer as a result of such integration and instead should only be augmented. In the module, as described in [1], the goal was to provide students with an overview of what a degree in CS will yield them upon graduation, specifically what would be expected of them in the workforce. This was not simply meant to be a tool to promote the generalized content associated with career options, guidance, and preparation but rather, is meant as a tool that can help provide hands-on practical experience and exposure to activities and challenges that students will face in their careers.

In this paper, we are proposing to augment this existing approach by leveraging the use of PL as guides to younger more novice students. In this approach, the PL are not only leading, or helping facilitate the classroom discussion, but rather they are serving as peer-guidance counselors. One common question that instructors frequently get asked when discussing course material, specifically in introductory style courses, is that of: "*When are we ever going to use this?*" This question can quickly be answered by the instructor and practical examples given, but can take on an entirely different meaning of importance with the student who has asked the question when that same information comes from a peer. Building a sense of belonging and peer acceptance is a primary goal of this updated career preparation module.

4 INTERACTIVE PEER-LED CODE REVIEWS

In this section, we will introduce our proposed inclusion of interactive peer-led code reviews into an example CS2 course in which two languages (C++ and Java) are introduced and taught in a side-by-side approach. Our motivation for exploring the use of peer-led code reviews came from a literature review of techniques [7-11] to improve student retention. Before providing the details on how this implementation was achieved, we will provide a short background on the previous work done and the necessary changes to the course structure that arose as part of this proposed teaching strategy.

4.1 Existing Course Structure

Python is the first programming language introduced to students in our department as part of the CS1 course. The use of this language as an introductory teaching language is widespread [12] and our department has observed the same success that others have found when implementing this as first language to CS majors. Students tend to leave this course with a better understanding on how to program and feel comfortable with the constructs of what a programming language is and how it can be used. These same students when transitioning to our CS2 course, in which OO concepts are taught, often hit a road block due to an increase in difficulty of not only the OO content but the need to learn new programming languages. In exploring this sudden struggle we have concluded that it is no different than when a student learns a secondary language after "mastering" a primary natural language.

In the case of a students' transition from Python to C++/Java, syntax suddenly plays a much larger role in the success or failure of a programs completion. This problem is further exacerbated by the fact that many students now enter colleges or universities with significant programming experience, while others may have zero experience in the field, thus leaving them to feel isolated and alone in the learning process.

The existing CS2 course structure therefore necessitated a refresh on those CS1 concepts – with specific focus on the programming that was done in that course. This refresher topic allows for the students to provide their feedback on the language (Python) and what they felt was its strengths and weaknesses.

We have taken an approach that will help to ease the students into the learn process of the CS2 content by allowing them to find an initial comfort zone with the course content and their peers in the course. While most students only provide critiques regarding the languages' (Python) strengths, most notably due to their familiarity with one and only one programming language, those students with a more diverse programming background will provide feedback regarding its limitations, or their perceived weaknesses, of the language. This type of feedback session can then be leveraged to serve as the "jumping off point" for our further discussion into two brand new languages and introduction to OO concepts.

Through this integration of early feedback sessions – specifically those in which all students feel welcome to participate, we can build a community of comfort in which the students feel confidence in their abilities and willingness to explore and learn together as a cohort. Engaging the students in group conversation, in which they are the leaders and can actively and intelligently discuss the pros/cons of a given language, helps to build their confidence at a time in the semester where it can yield substantial benefit. This sense of self-efficacy [13] provides the basis for students to be much more willing to tackle difficult challenges and be more willing to explore interesting topics together as a learning group.

4.2 Modified Course Structure

At this point, we are ready to transition into teaching our first new language of the semester: the C programming language. For most students this language is completely foreign and its heavy emphasis on the importance of syntax can overwhelm those students who previously felt comfortable with Python, and its relaxed syntactical rules. This is an excellent opportunity to discuss with the students the relationship between programming languages and natural languages and how each are learned. Most students will have taken a secondary language either in their K-12 education or as part of their college or university requirements. A discussion on the similarities between learning a new natural language and learning a new programming language can help to break down some of the barriers that some students have during this transition. Much work has been done in this area of study regarding natural language learning and its relationship with learning new programming languages [14, 15]. In our discussion, we use this more as a motivating factor than a pedagogical approach and instead try and establish a comfort or familiarity level with the students.

In order to introduce our first interactive peer-led code review, we created a laboratory assignment that had the students split into two units, with one unit writing a "Hello World" program in Python and the other unit writing a "Hello World" program in C. Here each unit consisted of 5 students. At this point in the course we have introduced the C programming language sufficient enough that this task can be completed.

Once each unit had completed their respective task they were once again reunited into a single group with each unit presenting their work to the other unit. It was the responsibility of each unit to explain what they did to solve their task. While both units had an idea of the syntax of each language, this exercise was intended to really allow each unit of students to ask questions in a much more informal manner. The focus of this exercise was to put the students in a comfortable and safe environment in which to learn directly from each other rather than from a PL or instructor. After this initial ice-breaker exercise, the students were asked to provide feedback. Each unit surveyed responded that they felt much more inclined to ask questions and felt more confident in their individual abilities.

The first programming assignment given as part of the course is designed to test the students' knowledge of the concept recursion. They are required to use recursion to solve the task of reversing a word – in this case their first name. This assignment serves as the basis for the upcoming interactive peer-led code reviews. In this instance, an instructor solution is shown to the students after their submissions as a way to guide them through this learning a new language and it syntactical rules.

Our original goal of teaching two languages side-by-side was to provide an environment in which the students focus more on deeper questions regarding the semantics of their programs rather than questions on the syntax of the language itself. This experience has shown that the students, over the course of trial and error, will come to an understanding of the basic syntactic features of a programming language. Here, we are referring to these key syntactic features to be those that prevent compilation from occurring.

One common syntactic feature of the two programming languages (C++ and Java) is that of the presence of an end of statement semicolon. This transition to using end of statement semicolons, in these two languages, comes as a shock to most students whose only programming experience comes from CS1 and their use of Python. This behavior and strict adherence to this type of syntax is not found in Python. Through trial and error and through repetitive exercises, as well as interactive peer-led reviews, this ability to move past the more trivial questions regarding syntax can take place. The goal is to put the students in situations where

Table 1: **Code Review Sessions**

Session	Description
1	Python vs. C
2	C Syntax
3	C++ vs. C
4	C++ vs. Java
5	Assignment Code Reviews*
	Assignment #3
	Assignment #4
	Assignment #5
	Assignment #6

***Note:** These sessions occurred after every assignment.

this behavior is learned from doing rather than just from pure instruction.

One way to achieve this desired behavior is to stress how the syntax of a programming language, like C++ or Java, is no different than punctuation of a natural language. One common example given is that all sentences in the English language end in some form of punctuation – with most ending with a period. If we take this same approach with our programs – where most statements end with a semicolon the students can quickly memorize this fact. This does not prevent all student syntactic errors, as students will have a tendency to place a semicolon at the end of **every** line, but it will help to reduce the overall error rate within their programs.

We can then leverage this instruction when introducing interactive peer-led code reviews. Instead of only lecturing this fact, we argue to let the students' themselves explore this idea in practice and learn through one another. Thus, when a student incorrectly uses a semicolon on a line in which one should not be used (e.g., with an if-statement) then other students (their peers) can recognize this and alert the student of their mistake. This positive and peer-led reinforcement learning allows the student to make the mistake but be alerted by peers rather than by a PL or an instructor. We believe this type of approach helps to build their confidence. At the same time, this same student who was alerted to their error will be given a chance to critique others' work in the future and through their own mistakes have gained the insight of its consequences and be able to recognize its presence in others work.

In this paper, we argue that this process benefits the students two-fold, in terms of career preparation: first, the students are less negative towards other students with the knowledge that their work will also be critiqued; second, the student gains a different perspective on not only their work but code styles in general. When we say "overly negative," we do not mean that students will be hesitant to provide a critique in an effort to speed up the process, but rather being negative just out of spite. This is a point that needs to be clearly distinguished with the students, that it is "ok" to provide critical feedback when necessary.

After each subsequent assignment submission, as shown in Table 1, the students were given one laboratory session in which samples of student submissions were anonymized and presented for the class to critique. These student samples were selected at random and the students were unaware of whose work was being shown. The purpose of this exercise was to allow the students, themselves, to critique the submission much like an instructor, or grader, would do. The sessions were structured such that a PL would begin by asking for opinions on the code. These could be on any aspect – either syntactically or semantically. A sample of these can be seen in Fig. 1.

If the discussion between students became heated or was stalled for any reason it would be the responsibility of the PL to move the discussion along. In certain instances, when the students' had little to say about a particular piece of code, the PL could interject and begin to ask questions, as shown in Fig. 1, or highlight areas that they may have noticed as part of the submission. The goal of this exercise was to continue to emphasize that the focus should be more on the semantics of a program than its syntax. Allowing PL to draw the students' attention to particular or unique behaviors found in the code.

Two primary questions arose out of this exercise: first, will students be receptive to peer-led code reviews or will they view them negatively and unnecessary? Second, will the constructive feedback, provided by peers, lead to improved proficiency in programming and thus improved retention?

5 EXPERIMENTATION

One of the primary questions that was raised, in [1], was what content must be sacrificed in order to achieve the integration of this new component. In this section we outline how we evaluated this new teaching module as part of the CS2 curricula without sacrificing the core content of the course. We will now provide an outline for how this was achieved in practice.

5.1 Experimental Setup

The CS2 course in which this proposed approach was implemented, consisted of a sixteen week (fifteen instructional weeks) semester. The class met twice a week with both a lecture and a laboratory component. Students were only required to attend one laboratory session per week but have the option to attend both sessions if they so desired. The lectures were traditional in nature with the instructor presenting content and demonstrating examples through live coding exercises. The laboratory sessions had both an instructor as well as two PL present during each session. Due to a large class size (> 120 students), the instructor rotated between the two laboratory classrooms during each session. The laboratory classrooms could accommodate 35 students (≈17 students per PL) and were configured in a setup with one student per machine.

Few alterations were necessary in terms of the existing course content due to the nature of the existing lecture format. Small

1. What do you like about this block of code?
2. What do you not like about this block of code?
3. Do you notice any syntax errors in the code?
4. What is your opinion on the programmers commenting sty
5. What is your opinion on the programmers' use of variables
6. Do we think the code will compile and run?
7. Is there potential for code reuse here?
8. Is this "dead code" – if so, should we remove it?

Figure 1: **Sample Code Review Questions**

Announcements

- Assignment #6 – Due 12/11/2017

Task 1 (5 minutes)

- Introduce the exercise for Lab #13 & attendance sign-in.

Task 2 (35 minutes)

- Break into groups of two (2) again – ideally you should find a new partner for this week than the one you had in the last lab. The purpose behind this constant switching is to get your acclimated to working with different individuals to solve a problem.
- This week, in our final organized lab, we are going to explore the concept of algorithms in more detail as well as the opportunity to further explore Polymorphism.
- Using the same exercise as last week (e.g. Checking & Savings) – make use of Polymorphism when constructing the application.
    - How could you force the respective Derived classes (Gold Checking and Silver Checking) to inherit and override methods defined in the Base class (Checking)?
    - What would be the mechanism you would use in C++ to accomplish this?
        - If you wrote your exercise in Java – how could you achieve this same behavior in Java?
            - We did not discuss this (yet) in lecture – so this may take some additional research on your part to determine how to make this behavior "happen" in Java.
    - Write the code necessary to emulate this behavior for the exercise application.
        - What is the amount of effort required to make this happen?
            - What impact did your original design have in this ease of modification? If any?

Figure 2: Sample Laboratory Session Handout

modifications were made, most notably introducing samples of code that were written outside of the live demonstrations and then solicited responses from the class on their opinions of the code. In some instances, these examples would contain errors that would be discovered by the class and then a discussion would ensue on how to properly correct them. This structure allowed the students to continue to focus more on the semantics of solving problems rather than getting bogged down in the syntactical details of each respective language.

We felt that by shifting some of this work (of teaching syntactical details) to the laboratory sessions, where the students could obtain hands-on practice, would create a much more interactive lecture environment where deeper questions could be asked. One of the key pieces of feedback collected after the initial attempts at the course redesign was the importance of the laboratory sessions to "work out the kinks" with the syntactical details of each language and to receive feedback or ask questions about the active assignment.

The laboratory component of the course, as a result, needed a dramatic overhaul. Traditionally, the laboratory component was utilized as either an extensive of lecture, in which the students would have an opportunity to be engaged in hands-on exercises, or one in which the PL would serve as peer mentors in our adapted PLTL model. With the inclusion of interactive peer-led code reviews the PL role would once again change.

To keep students informed on the changes and what to expect the instructor published laboratory handouts which described each sessions goals. A sample list of one of these sessions' goals can be seen in Fig. 2. In addition to this laboratory handout, the PL and the instructor would have weekly meetings in which laboratory session expectations were discussed. This weekly feedback session also provided a mechanism to collect additional information regarding student performance.

As this was the first implementation of this approach in the course, it was decided to make periodic checkpoints in which both the instructor as well as the PL would survey each laboratory session and ask for student feedback on the approach. This would allow for any adjustments in the moment rather than after the fact. This was an assumption that was made during the course redesign in order to best accommodate the needs of all the students and ensure that the learning objectives were still being met.

6 RESULTS

Anonymous surveys were conducted and progress tracked of students' progression. All of the surveys conducted were voluntary in nature and were not required as part of the course. An argument against this approach is that there would be no incentive for the students to participate. What we found, through our initial introductory survey, was that students indicated that they were more in favor of participating in surveys in which their feedback was actually "heard" and applied in practice. Since this overall implementation was carried out over two full semesters (Fall and Spring) it was possible to evaluate over 260 students. The PL were also surveyed as part of this exercise. Since their role was modified in how the laboratory sessions were conducted we wanted to collect their feedback about their experiences with respect to this proposed change.

The goal of all of the surveys conducted was to gauge how impactful the interactive peer-led code reviews were in terms of overall student performance and meeting the learning objectives. When we examined the preliminary surveys, those related to the small sample units, we found that overall student satisfaction was positive. In this survey, 100% of the students responded that they were in favor of the interactive peer-led code reviews moving forward in the course. Additional comments spoke in favor of the hands-on interaction as well as allowing students to aid in their respective learning rather than being lectured to or given instructions from a PL. This motivated a much more broad experiment in applying the interactive peer-led code reviews to the entire laboratory session and to student work.

In the first few laboratory sessions in which interactive peer-led code reviews were performed the student responses were somewhat

Please circle the option that best fits your feelings on this course and the use of peer-led code reviews.

1. Do you feel that the peer-led code reviews improve your confidence in learning the programming languages for this course?
    A. Yes
    B. No
    C. Not Sure

2. Do you feel more confident in your programming abilities after participating in a peer-led cc review?
    A. Yes
    B. No
    C. Not Sure

3. Do you feel that this course provided you with the necessary skills to be successful in your f course work in Computer Science?
    A. Satisfied
    B. Neutral
    C. Not Satisfied

Figure 3: Sample Student Survey

mixed. An example of a student survey can be seen in Fig. 3. In this case, approximately 67% of students responded that they were in favor of the code reviews. While this favorable rate was lower than expected it was not entirely unexpected. We believe that this is the result of the fact that the initial samples of code that were shown to the students were not their own, and thus were not related to their assignment. With the introduction of student-based code reviews, as mentioned in Section 5, the time for assignment question/answer was also dramatically reduced. This no doubt influenced the students' response rates on this survey. One other factor to mention was that despite the students feeling more engaged and more comfortable with their peers, the concept of a code review was still a foreign to most and three of the students reported that they felt uncomfortable giving critical feedback to their peers.

After the initial trial period was completed, the interactive peer-led code reviews began to look at code samples from the students' own assignments, as indicated in Table 1. In order to further adapt the trial run, and to account for some of those uneasy feelings that students reported, we allowed for the students to resubmit their code based upon the feedback that they received. One obvious question that arises as a result of this decision is the impact of seeing another student's submission would have on academic integrity. This is a valid concern and one that was heavily weighed when making this decision. It was determined that while this would definitely be a concern, in an effort to truly highlight the importance of peer-led code reviews we needed to demonstrate, in the moment, the justification to well thought out critiques and their impact on the overall product or deliverable.

The results of this exercise were much more favorable with 88% of students reporting satisfaction with this approach. This figure was strictly related to the live interactive peer-led session. An option was given to students, who still did not feel comfortable with an interactive peer-led critique, to opt out and instead work independently. We want to stress that as with the surveys, participation in the code review process was voluntary. We chose to stress the importance of anonymous code and thus students were not aware of what code samples came from what student. Each student was also given the option of a one-on-one meeting with a PL, or the instructor, to have a full code review in which they could engage in active discussion about their individual submission. In this process, the correctness of the code was not analyzed but rather if areas could be improved or cleaned up with respect syntax and/or commenting in their code.

The final analysis that was performed as part of this work was carried out for two motivating reasons: first, we wanted to explore what impact this type of peer-led process had on overall student success in the course; second, we wanted to continue to explore the benefit of the proposed side-by-side approach, as described in [1]. We compared two corresponding semesters, as this was a critique of the original work and one that we wanted to properly address in this work. When performing this empirical analysis to our study we found that the Fail rate of the students dropped each semester by over 4%, as shown in Fig. 4, compared to the previous related semesters (85 and 124 students respectively). While additional semesters testing needs to be conducted, these results have demonstrated that this approach has proven to be promising and

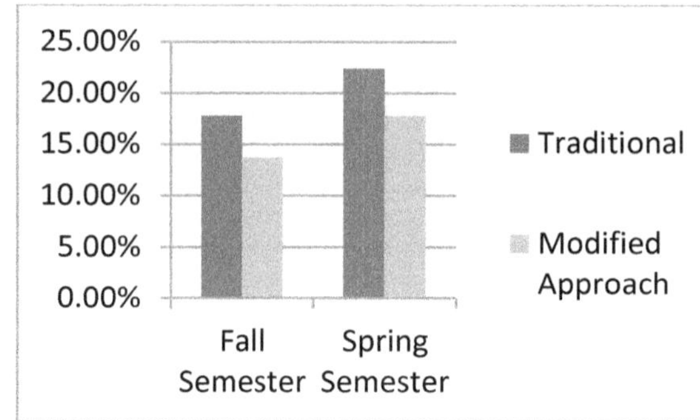

Figure 4: CS2 Failure Rate

provides a good indication that this yields a net benefit to the overall student learning process in our CS2 course.

7 CONCLUSIONS

In summary, we have described how to utilize interactive peer-led code reviews to improve overall student satisfaction and performance as part of a CS2 course. We have leveraged the existing career preparation and guidance modules to teach of the importance of peer-led code reviews as part of the expectations the students will face when entering the workforce. We have demonstrated that this approach will also increase student satisfaction within the structure and content of the course. Increased student confidence and a stronger sense of belonging within the degree program were also positive outcomes of this work. Empirically, we have shown that the Fail rate, between corresponding semesters, has decreased while at the same time the enrollment in the course has increased (+85 students). We believe that this preliminary result demonstrates that through peer-led learning activities, students will perform at a higher level and earn the success that they so desire in the CS2 course.

Future work includes examining the impact of this approach on the trial group of students as they matriculate through the program and on to graduation and subsequently enter the workforce. We believe that initially introducing the students to individuals already in the workforce, potentially recent graduates of our program, allowing them to be exposed to this concept which will carry more weight with the students' opinions on the use of such a practice. This can be achieved by leveraging industrial partners. Finally, continuing work in the area of study around the PLTL approach and our specific flavor of this methodology is being carried out to better understand how the model, when applied to CS, can bring about improved student success, retention, and a sense of belonging.

REFERENCES

[1] R. Rybarczyk and L. Acheson, "Integrating A Career Preparedness Module into CS2 Curricula Through The Teaching C++ and Java Side-by-Side," in *Proceedings of the 49th ACM Technical Symposium on Computer Science Education*, 2018, pp. 592-597.

[2] H. M. Walker, "ACM RETENTION COMMITTEE Retention of students in introductory computing courses: curricular issues and approaches," *ACM Inroads*, vol. 8, pp. 14-16, 2017.

[3] S. Horwitz, S. H. Rodger, M. Biggers, D. Binkley, C. K. Frantz, D. Gundermann, *et al.*, "Using peer-led team learning to increase participation and success of under-represented groups in introductory computer science," in *ACM SIGCSE Bulletin*, 2009, pp. 163-167.

[4] L. Gafney and P. Varma-Nelson, *Peer-led team learning: Evaluation, dissemination, and institutionalization of a college level initiative* vol. 16: Springer Science & Business Media, 2008.

[5] M. O. Smith, A. Giugliano, and A. DeOrio, "Long Term Effects of Pair Programming," *IEEE Transactions on Education*, 2017.

[6] T. H. DeClue, "Pair programming and pair trading: effects on learning and motivation in a CS2 course," *Journal of Computing Sciences in colleges*, vol. 18, pp. 49-56, 2003.

[7] G. Gonzalez, "A systematic approach to active and cooperative learning in CS1 and its effects on CS2," *ACM SIGCSE Bulletin*, vol. 38, pp. 133-137, 2006.

[8] P. Lasserre and C. Szostak, "Effects of team-based learning on a CS1 course," in *Proceedings of the 16th annual joint conference on Innovation and technology in computer science education*, 2011, pp. 133-137.

[9] H. Pon-Barry, A. S. John, B. W.-L. Packard, and C. Stephenson, "Addressing the CS capacity challenge by improving undergraduate peer mentoring," *ACM Inroads*, vol. 8, pp. 43-47, 2017.

[10] Z. Wood and A. Keen, "Building Worlds: Bridging Imperative-First and Object-Oriented Programming in CS1-CS2," in *Proceedings of the 46th ACM Technical Symposium on Computer Science Education*, 2015, pp. 144-149.

[11] C. D. Hundhausen, A. Agrawal, and P. Agarwal, "Talking about code: Integrating pedagogical code reviews into early computing courses," *ACM Transactions on Computing Education (TOCE)*, vol. 13, p. 14, 2013.

[12] R. J. Enbody, W. F. Punch, and M. McCullen, "Python CS1 as preparation for C++ CS2," *ACM SIGCSE Bulletin*, vol. 41, pp. 116-120, 2009.

[13] S. R. Portnoff, "The introductory computer programming course is first and foremost a language course," *ACM Inroads*, vol. 9, pp. 34-52, 2018.

[14] S. R. Portnoff, "(1) The case for using foreign language pedagogies in introductory computer programming instruction (2) A contextualized pre-AP computer programming curriculum: Models and simulations for exploring real-world cross-curricular topics," California State University, Los Angeles, 2016.

[15] S. A. Robertson and M. P. Lee, "The application of second natural language acquisition pedagogy to the teaching of programming languages—a research agenda," *ACM SIGCSE Bulletin*, vol. 27, pp. 9-12, 1995.

Static Analyses in Python Programming Courses

David Liu
University of Toronto
david@cs.toronto.edu

Andrew Petersen
University of Toronto Mississauga
petersen@cs.toronto.edu

ABSTRACT

Students learning to program often rely on feedback from the compiler and from instructor-provided test cases to help them identify errors in their code. This feedback focuses on functional correctness, and the output, which is often phrased in technical language, may be difficult to for novices to understand or effectively use. Static analyses may be effective as a complementary aid, as they can highlight common errors that may be potential sources of problems. In this paper, we introduce PyTA, a wrapper for pylint that provides custom checks for common novice errors as well as improved messages to help students fix the errors that are found. We report on our experience integrating PyTA into an existing online system used to deliver programming exercises to CS1 students and evaluate it by comparing exercise submissions collected from the integrated system to previously collected data. This analysis demonstrates that, for students who chose to read the PyTA output, we observed a decrease in time to solve errors, occurrences of repeated errors, and submissions to complete a programming problem. This suggests that PyTA, and static analyses in general, may help students identify functional issues in their code not highlighted by compiler feedback and that static analysis output may help students more quickly identify debug their code.

CCS CONCEPTS

• **Social and professional topics** → *Computer science education.*

ACM Reference Format:
David Liu and Andrew Petersen. 2019. Static Analyses in Python Programming Courses. In *Proceedings of the 50th ACM Technical Symposium on Computer Science Education (SIGCSE '19), February 27-March 2, 2019, Minneapolis, MN, USA.* ACM, New York, NY, USA, 6 pages. https://doi.org/10.1145/3287324.3287503

1 INTRODUCTION

The debugging capabilities of novice programmers is of great importance to their overall success. In a study performed on novice computer science students, Ahmadzadeh et. al. noted that while less than half of the students who were good programmers were good debuggers, the majority of good debuggers were good programmers [1]. Debugging, however, is a difficult task for novices. The lack of experience novices possess regarding debugging strategies results in attempts at abstract debugging techniques which have seemingly little to do with the actual errors present in their code. This can culminate to novices eventually giving up altogether and instead simply trying fixes at random [11]. The difficulty students experience with this have been found to be at least partially attributed to the error messages they are presented with. Students often find these messages confusing due to reasons such as their technicality, brevity, and lack of visual aid [12, 18].

The confusion students face from standard error messages is not their only barrier. Novices could also use assistance with detecting errors involving semantics and logic [1]. For example, in our experience, students frequently write loops that always return in the first iteration. While this error may be obvious to a more experienced programmer or easy to find for a user with training in using a debugger, a novice still struggling with the concept of loops may have difficulty detecting this error. In particular, in data we collected for this report, one student made 15 consecutive submissions containing a loop that would always return on the first iteration. The student never seemed to realize that the cause of the error was an if/else statement within the loop. Instead, the student first made numerous modifications to the condition of the statement, and later proceeded to include an additional if/else statement within the block of the original if/else statement, eventually solving the programming exercise on the 38th submission. Conventional compiler (or language runtime) error messages provided no aid in this situation or with other common novice issues such as maintaining consistent indentation in Python.

While errors in logic and various coding malpractices cannot be detected with standard error messages, they can be detected using static analysis. In this paper, we introduce a static analysis tool for Python called PyTA[1] that has been designed to identify common CS1 student errors and to provide intuitive error messages to aid them in debugging. To demonstrate how easy it is to add static analysis support to a course, we integrated PyTA into our online exercise system. When students submit their code, they are presented with both the standard errors detected by Python and errors reported by PyTA. We then evaluate the impact of the additional feedback on student performance, hoping to see students repeating errors less often and correcting logic errors more efficiently.

2 RELATED WORK

Providing enhanced error messages to assist novices in debugging has been attempted numerous times before. A number of these efforts have focused on improving compiler error messages, and results have been mixed. Rigby and Thompson [14] compare the usability of Eclipse to Gild, a perspective intended to be more appropriate for novices. One of the improvements that Gild made is the incorporation of more novice friendly descriptions of common

SIGCSE '19, February 27-March 2, 2019, Minneapolis, MN, USA

ACM ISBN 978-1-4503-5890-3/19/02...$15.00
https://doi.org/10.1145/3287324.3287503

[1] PyTA is freely available. Please visit http://www.cs.toronto.edu/~david/pyta/quick_start.html for a quick start guide and https://github.com/pyta-uoft/pyta to access the project source code.

compiler errors. In a study of 6 students who had 25 minutes to complete tasks for each IDE it was found that students using Gild had fewer errors and asked fewer questions, but neither of these differences were statistically significant. Becker [3] used Decaf, a Java editor, which provided enhancements for 30 different compiler error messages such as displaying the error in less technical terms, and providing suggestions to resolve it. In addition to the enhanced messages, steps were taken to improve readability such as only displaying the first enhanced error message. The enhanced editor was used for a four-week period by more than 200 students, and they found a reduced number of overall errors, errors per student, and repeated errors. For 8 of these errors there was a statistically significant reduction. Qualitative data also indicated the tool was less frustrating for students and made learning programming easier.

In contrast, both Denny et al. [6] and Pettit et al. [13] found little evidence that compiler error messages improved student outcomes. Denny et al. implemented an enhanced feedback system to users of CodeWrite, a web based tool for students to solve problems in Java [6]. They found that compiler error messages were sometimes ambiguous, so static analysis of code was performed to identify additional errors. The feedback provided by CodeWrite includes the line an identified error occurs on, as well as a more detailed explanation of the cause of the error. However, after analyzing data from 83 students in a CS1 course, it was concluded that enhanced feedback provided no significant benefit. Pettit et al. performed similar work at their institution and concur, stating that despite positive feedback from both students and instructors, they saw no measurable benefit in terms of a reduction in student submissions to programming problems [13].

To resolve these contradictory findings, Becker et al. [4] ran a controlled experiment where students identified and resolved syntax errors in code. They found that the enhanced errors did help, with students able to fix more errors with the enhanced support, but they also found that the enhanced errors did not reduce the number of non-compiling submissions or increase overall student performance. This suggests that compiler error messages can be improved but that more comprehensive supports are required.

A number of other efforts have utilized static analyses to identify and explain common errors, often with positive results. Flowers et al. [8] developed Gauntlet, a pre-compiler used to assist novice programmers by preprocessing Java code and providing more understandable explanations for common errors. From the use of Gauntlet for 18 months in a core CS1 course, it was determined that Gauntlet reduced the frustration caused during the debugging process, improved the quality if students' work, and lessened the amount of assistance sought after by students.

Truong et al. [19] created a static analysis tool to be used in aiding the students in writing better quality Java programs. The tool performed two analyses that examine the quality of the submitted code and how close the structure of the student's code is to a sample solution. At the time of the writing of their paper, the tool had been used in tutorial exercises with positive feedback overall.

Hristova et al. [9] created a static analysis tool, Expresso, intended to be used to assist novice programmers in identifying errors in their code in Java. The tool was created after research was performed on the most common Java errors as well as determining that the functionality of other existing tools did not coincide with the researchers' needs. Twenty of these errors were deemed essential and Espresso provides enhanced messages for these errors as well as suggested solutions. The authors of Espresso believe it will be useful for introductory Java classes, although at the time of the writing of the paper it had not yet been tested in a classroom environment.

Ayewah et al. [2] created FindBugs, an industrial strength tool for finding bugs in Java codebases. While not specifically built for novice programmers, it has been successfully applied to student code and found to be effective at finding such errors [17].

Schorsch [15] notes that even when there are no syntax errors in a program, logic errors can still result in an unexpected output. The Code Analyzer for Pascal (CAP) is a static analysis tool that was created to provide feedback on not only syntax errors, but logic and stylistic errors as well. This tool was used in a CS1 course of 520 students and a qualitative analysis of students' opinions were positive overall and instructors teaching the course all noticed in an increased quality of student programs. Delev and Gjorgjevikj [5] report their findings on common errors of C source code written by novice programmers detected by two different static analysis tools. Clang Static Analyzer and CppCheck were both run 13,960 source code files and the desired data was parsed from their reports. The results of the reports indicate a large presence of stylistic errors as well as errors that novices tend to not notice such as "uninitialized variable". The authors also note some of the students had more difficulty locating errors than fixing them, indicating the localization of errors through static analysis can be advantageous to the learning environment.

Most recently, Edwards et al. [7] collected errors from over 500,000 student program submissions using the Java static analysis tools Checkstyle and PMD. The authors highlighted some of the most common non-syntax related errors occurring in Java submissions and discussed how the frequency of errors detected by static analysis relate to factors such as experience with programming and time spent working on a problem. The authors also identify a number of problems with using static analysis for student programming problems, one of the largest of which is that students can perceive the errors detected by static analysis as purely cosmetic and begin to ignore them.

Overall, these efforts suggest that compiler error messages are difficult to use and that static analyses can provide additional information that students can use to more effectively debug programs. However, the messages presented must be carefully curated so that students value them, rather than dismissing them as addressing style. Furthermore, while a number of tools have been developed for a range of languages, relatively little work (excepting [7, 8] has been performed that demonstrates that these tools are effective within a classroom setting.

3 BACKGROUND

The two main tools described in this paper are PCRS [20] and PyTA [10]. PCRS is an open-source application for bundling interactive programming exercises with video-based instruction and has been presented previously. PyTA, the focus of this report, is a publicly available Python module[2] which uses existing static

[2] See https://github.com/pyta-uoft/pyta.

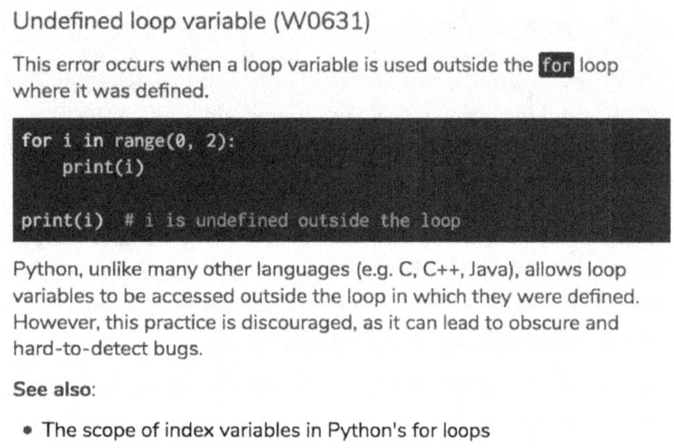

Undefined loop variable (W0631)

This error occurs when a loop variable is used outside the `for` loop where it was defined.

```
for i in range(0, 2):
    print(i)

print(i)  # i is undefined outside the loop
```

Python, unlike many other languages (e.g. C, C++, Java), allows loop variables to be accessed outside the loop in which they were defined. However, this practice is discouraged, as it can lead to obscure and hard-to-detect bugs.

See also:

- The scope of index variables in Python's for loops

Figure 1: Example error message provided by PyTA

code analysis, provided by pylint [16], to help students find and fix common coding errors in introductory Python courses.

PyTA takes the form of a pylint wrapper [16] with numerous custom checkers and was developed with novice programmers in mind. It provides a number of custom analyses targeting common introductory errors, and it provides custom messages for warnings and errors that help identify possible causes for the message. Figure 1 provides an example of the information provided to help students diagnose errors. As shown in the figure, each message provides both a text description as well as an example and then information about why the error or warning is problematic.

To demonstrate how PyTA can be utilized by a variety of tools, we integrated it into PCRS so that students completing Python coding problems online would receive additional feedback. Integration into the system required about 20 hours of work by an undergraduate student unfamiliar with both projects.

When a student submitted a solution to a coding problem, they were presented with three pieces of feedback. The first was a message explaining if their submission passed or failed overall, along with the performance (pass or fail) of their submission on individual test cases. Second, they were provided with the errors, if any, emitted by the standard Python interpreter. Finally, for evaluation purposes, students were provided with a drop down box that, when clicked, provided the results of PyTA on their submission. The dropdown box allowed us to determine when students at least viewed the extra PyTA information.

3.1 Evaluation

We evaluated PyTA in a CS1 course taught at a large, research-intensive North American university. Over 11 weeks, students taking the course were provided with 40 Python coding exercises hosted on PCRS. The coding exercises consisted of a section of starter code for a function or class along with a docstring explaining what the final functionality of the function or class should be. The exercises were short with solutions averaging 6.30 lines, and students were given unlimited attempts to complete each one. These exercises accounted for 10% percent of a student's final grade.

Students were also provided with an introduction to PyTA in the form of additional exercises posted in PCRS. These exercises consist of a function or class with complete, but slightly erroneous, code. Students were expected to submit the code once, to see the PyTA output, and then to update the code to remove the PyTA error. The errors covered in these questions consisted of the most common errors that occurred in the previous offering of the course.

For each submission, a unique but not identifying student ID, the problem ID, the submitted code, the standard Python errors caused by the code, a time stamp of the submission, and the submission result (pass or fail) was recorded. Student interaction with the PyTA output was also stored: the output of PyTA and the number of times the PyTA dropdown box was clicked. Overall, 114865 submissions were collected from 750 students.

Control data was obtained from student submissions in a previous year. The content of the course was similar over both years, was taught by the same head instructor, and has comparable tutorial and PCRS exercises. However, PyTA output was not available for these students, so the control dataset includes PCRS submissions of coding exercises that were completed with no PyTA intervention. 106467 submissions were collected from 504 students.

3.2 Methods

To evaluate the impact of PyTA support, we take a quantitative approach. We count the number of submissions where a student responded to the intervention by clicking on the PyTA dropdown box to get additional information. We also investigate measures indicative of a student's performance on a programming exercise such as the number of submissions and the number of occurrences of particular errors. We compare these measures across the intervention and control groups.

Before analyzing the data, steps were taken to clean it. Since students are given unlimited attempts, they occasionally submitted an empty submission to examine the test cases or error messages as a form of hint. Similarly, students would occasionally submit identical code multiple times in a row, perhaps in frustration or in response to network latency. This inflates the number of errors and does not indicate anything of the students' capabilities, so all empty or repeated submissions were removed.

We also removed all submissions to optional programming exercises, since students choosing to complete these problems may not be indicative of the general course population. Finally, the problems intended to be an introduction to PyTA were removed, as the code provided in these problems was intentionally erroneous and since these problems were not provided to the control group.

4 DATA

In this section, we discuss the the PyTA usage habits of the students in the intervention group and how the performance of these students differs from that of the control group. We also perform inter-group comparisons of the intervention group based on their usage of PyTA. In the comparisons, we focus on five exemplar programming exercises, numbered in order of increasing difficulty as determined by the average number of submissions required to successfully solve the problem.

Table 1: Number of PyTA Clicks in a Sequence of Submissions

Number of Clicks	Count of Sequences	% Sequences
0	21172	67.68
1	5476	17.51
2	2032	6.50
3	1031	3.30
4	537	1.72
5+	1032	3.30

4.1 Do students use PyTA?

In order to determine if students were making use of PyTA, an event was recorded whenever a student clicked on the drop down box that contained the PyTA output. Of the submissions recorded for the required problems 28.6% were followed by a click on the PyTA dropdown box. Usage per sequence of submissions is similar to usage per submission. A sequence of submissions is defined as the collection of submissions made by a student for a particular problem. There were 31280 sequences of submissions with 32.3% of these viewing the PyTA output at some point in the sequence.

We used usage statistics to identify three categories of students from the intervention group. The categories consist of students who use PyTA frequently, infrequently, and an average amount as determined by mean absolute deviation. The usage of PyTA was measured by the average number of submissions that occur between students examining the results of the static analysis. We classified frequent users as those that used PyTA more than once every 2.04 submissions, infrequent users as those that used PyTA less than once every 4.54 submissions, and average users as those who used PyTA between the amounts of the frequent and infrequent groups. There are 133 frequent users, 138 infrequent users, and 478 average users.

Table 2 shows the average grades that each of the groups received for their assignments and exams, displayed in the order in which these assessments were due or taken. We see that that frequent user groups consistently perform approximately 3-5% better than the average usage group, and the average usage group consistently performs approximately 8-10% better than the infrequent users group. For this table, we used two sample t-tests to compare the marks. The difference in mark is always significant when comparing the frequent and average users group to the infrequent users group, but is only significant for the midterm when comparing frequent and average users. In all tables, superscript X denotes a p-value of <0.05 when compared with the group in the same row in column X, and superscript X^* denotes a p-value of <0.01.

4.2 Do students repeat errors less often?

We define a repeated error as an error of a specific type (as identified by PyTA) that occurs on consecutive submissions. We do not consider whether the error appears in a different location in the code; if the same error is reported in two consecutive submissions, it is a repeated error.

A Wilcoxon two sided rank sum test was performed on the control and intervention groups for each of the problems; a rank

Table 2: Average grade received on assignments and examinations

Category	*Frequent*	*Average*	*Infrequent*
Assignment 1	83.09^{3^*}	80.34^{3^*}	$70.36^{1^*,2^*}$
Assignment 2	72.02^{3^*}	68.45^{3^*}	$60.63^{1^*,2^*}$
Assignment 3	44.99^{3^*}	40.38^{3^*}	$31.93^{1^*,2^*}$
Midterm	$58.55^{2,3^*}$	$53.37^{1,3^*}$	$43.94^{1^*,2^*}$
Term Test	70.52^{3^*}	67.68^{3^*}	$58.44^{1^*,2^*}$
Exam	59.20^{3^*}	54.80^{3^*}	$43.49^{1^*,2^*}$
Course	66.01^{3^*}	62.61^{3^*}	$52.45^{1^*,2^*}$

sum was used since the distributions of submissions typically have a long tail (are not normal). Table 3 shows the average number of repeated errors that occur in a submission for the 3 categories of the intervention group as well as the control group for each problem. In the first four problems examined, the control group maintains the highest percentage of repeated errors, seeing increases of more than 9% compared to the overall intervention group. All such differences were found to be significant. The frequent users group mostly sees the fewest percentage of repeated errors (except problem 4), but differences between the frequent and average groups are only significant for problem 2. The infrequent initially repeat errors less than the average user. In the most difficult two problems, the difference is significant.

4.3 Do students require fewer submissions to correct errors?

We define the submissions required to fix an error as the number of submissions after an occurrence of an error before that error is completely resolved. Completely resolved means that no later submission contains an occurrence of that error. We focus on only the top ten most common errors.

As seen in Table 4 the control group requires more submissions to resolve these errors in every case when compared to the overall intervention group. In the majority of these cases the differences are significant. In addition, the frequent users group solves errors in the fewest number of submissions as compared to the average and infrequent users. The differences in submissions required to solve any error between these groups never surpasses 1, although the largest differences are seen when comparing the frequent and infrequent groups for errors E9996 (always returning in a loop) and W0311 (bad indentation).

4.4 Do students pass exercises in fewer submissions?

Table 5 shows that the overall intervention group always requires less submissions than the control group, and in particular requires 2.54 fewer submissions for problem 2. Only the first three problems see significant differences between the two groups. Comparing the students in the intervention group: the frequent user group consistently requires the fewest submissions to solve each of the problems when comparing to the average and infrequent users groups, with the average users often requiring at least 25% more submissions than the frequent users and the infrequent users requiring more

Table 3: Average percent of errors repeated per submission

Problem	*Frequent*	*Average*	*Infrequent*	*Overall*	*Control*
1	11.11	18.00	11.43	15.86^{5*}	27.22^{4*}
2	17.13^{2}	22.85^{1}	19.47	21.34^{5*}	43.00^{4*}
3	12.95	14.924	15.44	14.82^{5*}	26.55^{4*}
4	16.37^{3}	12.28^{3*}	$23.11^{1,2*}$	15.77^{5*}	24.66^{4*}
5	18.35^{3*}	18.96^{3*}	$29.45^{1*,2*}$	21.28^{5}	23.96^{4}

Table 4: Average number of submissions to correct an error

Error Code	Description	*Frequent*	*Average*	*Infrequent*	*Overall*	*Control*
E0001-1	Invalid syntax	1.64	1.77	1.79	1.76	1.78
E0001-2	Unexpected indent	1.49	1.56	1.77	1.61^{5*}	1.73^{4*}
E0602	Undefined variable	$1.35^{2*,3*}$	$1.48^{1*,3}$	$1.58^{1*,2}$	1.49	1.54
E1101	No member	1.44^{3}	1.79	1.87^{1}	1.71	1.82
E9996	Always returning in a loop	$1.58^{2*,3*}$	2.06^{1*}	2.22^{1*}	2.06^{5*}	2.46^{4*}
W0104	Pointless statement	1.49	1.71	1.89	1.73^{5*}	1.97^{4*}
W0311	Bad indentation	1.72	1.90	2.23	1.98^{5}	2.50^{4}
W0612	Unused variable	$1.45^{2*,3*}$	1.78^{1*}	1.89^{1*}	1.78^{5*}	2.17^{4*}
W0613	Unused argument	1.53^{3*}	1.61^{3*}	$1.83^{1*,2*}$	1.65^{5*}	1.86^{4*}
W0621	Redefined outer name	2.20	2.27	2.26	2.26^{5*}	2.83^{4*}

than double the amount of submissions for problems 4 and 5. Nearly all of such differences are found to be significant, with the exception of the differences seen in the first problem. The average users group also see significantly fewer required submissions when compared to the infrequent users.

5 DISCUSSION

In each point of comparison, the intervention group performs better than the control group, and the users who frequently use PyTA perform better than the average and infrequent users. While this is positive and aligns with our hopes that providing additional, improved feedback from PyTA would lead to improved performance, the evidence only describes correlations; we cannot, with our study design, claim a causal relationship. It is, indeed, likely that frequent users would have higher course performance simply because they are likely to be students who use any and all resources available to master the course material.

In addition to limitations in the design of the evaluation of this tool, there are a number of other threats to validity that must be considered. The higher performance of the intervention group, overall, is more suggestive, but we still cannot guarantee that the difference is caused by PyTA. The instructors believed that students would perform better with the assistance of PyTA, so they did not feel that they could, ethically, restrict access to the tool. All students were allowed equal access. This made it necessary to perform a comparison with a previous year rather than separating students into those who receive assistance from PyTA and those who do not. The difference in populations is, by itself, a possible threat to validity. Performance did not improve gradually; the intervention groups solve problems faster and with less errors than the control group from the first week.

This effect could be caused by differences in instruction between the two years. While most of the material remained the same, one major difference between the two years was the inclusion of additional practice problems in the form of an introduction to PyTA. While the problems did not require students to write new code, they did require that students identify and fix errors, which may have resulted in the immediate improvement in performance in the problems students were required to submit.

A similar pattern holds within the three intervention groups themselves. The users who frequently use PyTA tend to outperform both the average and infrequent users. While we hope this is a result of their PyTA usage habits, their performance is higher than the other groups at the start. This suggests that the performance of students in these groups is a result of their attitudes or habits – not just PyTA usage. For example, the students who utilized PyTA the most probably also make maximal use of other resources (including the introduction to PyTA), leading them to perform better than students who do not, as a habit, use all of the information available.

Another possibility is that student performance may have increased as they received problems similar to those given in the previous year, so answers to these problems may have become more available. The online problems could be completed anywhere, and as a result, we cannot guarantee that students did not obtain assistance from outside sources. Since the solutions only involve a few lines of code, it is very difficult to tell if it is not the students' own work. Requiring that exercises be completed during tutorial sessions under the supervision of someone such as a teaching assistant may have helped prevent these cases. However, the purpose of tutorials is to proceed through more complicated exercises and review coding concepts, so this option was unavailable.

Table 5: Average number of submissions to pass an exercise

Problem	*Frequent*	*Average*	*Infrequent*	*Overall*	*Control*
1	1.31	1.50	1.55	1.47^{5^*}	1.68^{4^*}
2	$3.17^{2^*,3^*}$	$4.22^{1^*,3}$	$5.50^{1^*,2}$	4.24^{5^*}	6.78^{4^*}
3	$2.71^{2^*,3^*}$	$3.64^{1^*,3}$	$5.08^{1^*,2}$	3.70^{5^*}	5.04^{4^*}
4	$3.46^{2^*,3^*}$	5.23^{1^*}	8.07^{1^*}	5.35	5.91
5	$4.20^{2^*,3^*}$	$6.23^{1^*,3}$	$8.46^{1^*,2}$	6.19	6.91

Our final concern was our inability to determine if students were actually paying attention to the information provided to them in the PyTA dropdown box. Analyzing the click events can only tell us which students are accessing PyTA messages. It does not tell us if students are reading the messages or are just giving it a passing glance. In the future, eye tracking technology could be used to determine if the students are paying attention to the messages and whether they spend significant time perusing the messages.

6 CONCLUSION

The default Python syntax and runtime errors is a limited resource that is not easily accessible to novice programmers. Python makes use of a small number of error messages, making it difficult for students to use the messages to identify the source of the error. In addition, the errors do not detect many logical mistakes novices make. This insufficient feedback results in novices struggling with debugging and repeatedly making the same errors in logic, style, and syntax.

In this report, we present PyTA, a static analysis tool designed to check for common student errors and to present warnings and errors with effective, easy-to-understand messages. To evaluate the effectiveness of PyTA in a CS1 context, we integrated it into PCRS and used it to provide additional feedback when students completed online programming exercises. We compared student submissions in a year where PyTA was available to one where it was not and found that, overall, there is a significant reduction in the number of repeated errors per submission, submissions to pass a programming exercise, and submissions required to solve the most common errors. These effects were also seen when we compared students who used PyTA frequently to those who used it infrequently.

These results suggest that PyTA, and static analysis in general, may be an effective complement to language errors for students and may assist them with identifying and resolving common errors. We were able to integrate PyTA into our existing toolset with a minimal amount of effort and hope that other institutions will consider adopting it for their Python courses.

ACKNOWLEDGMENTS

We gratefully acknowledge the contributions of the many undergraduates at our institution who have contributed to the development of PyTA and PCRS. Special thanks goes to Kaveh Parsaie for his work integrating PyTA into PCRS and for his efforts to collect and analyze data on its impact.

REFERENCES

[1] Marzieh Ahmadzadeh, Dave Elliman, and Colin Higgins. 2005. An analysis of patterns of debugging among novice computer science students. *Acm sigcse bulletin* 37, 3 (2005), 84–88.

[2] Nathaniel Ayewah, David Hovemeyer, J David Morgenthaler, John Penix, and William Pugh. 2008. Using static analysis to find bugs. *IEEE software* 25, 5 (2008).

[3] Brett A Becker. 2016. An effective approach to enhancing compiler error messages. In *Proceedings of the 47th ACM Technical Symposium on Computing Science Education*. 126–131.

[4] Brett A. Becker, Kyle Goslin, and Graham Glanville. 2018. The Effects of Enhanced Compiler Error Messages on a Syntax Error Debugging Test. In *Proceedings of the 49th ACM Technical Symposium on Computer Science Education (SIGCSE '18)*. ACM, New York, NY, USA, 640–645. https://doi.org/10.1145/3159450.3159461

[5] Tomche Delev and Dejan Gjorgjevikj. 2017. Static analysis of source code written by novice programmers. In *Global Engineering Education Conference (EDUCON), 2017 IEEE*. 825–830.

[6] Paul Denny, Andrew Luxton-Reilly, and Dave Carpenter. 2014. Enhancing syntax error messages appears ineffectual. In *Proceedings of the 2014 conference on Innovation & technology in computer science education*. 273–278.

[7] Stephen H. Edwards, Nischel Kandru, and Mukund B.M. Rajagopal. 2017. Investigating Static Analysis Errors in Student Java Programs. In *Proceedings of the 2017 ACM Conference on International Computing Education Research (ICER '17)*. 65–73. https://doi.org/10.1145/3105726.3106182

[8] Thomas Flowers, Curtis A Carver, and James Jackson. 2004. Empowering students and building confidence in novice programmers through Gauntlet. In *Frontiers in Education, 2004. FIE 2004. 34th Annual*. T3H–10.

[9] Maria Hristova, Ananya Misra, Megan Rutter, and Rebecca Mercuri. 2003. Identifying and correcting Java programming errors for introductory computer science students. In *ACM SIGCSE Bulletin*, Vol. 35. 153–156.

[10] David Liu. [n. d.]. PyTA. https://github.com/pyta-uoft/pyta. Accessed: 2018-08-31.

[11] Laurie Murphy, Gary Lewandowski, Renée McCauley, Beth Simon, Lynda Thomas, and Carol Zander. 2008. Debugging: the good, the bad, and the quirky–a qualitative analysis of novices' strategies. In *ACM SIGCSE Bulletin*, Vol. 40. 163–167.

[12] Marie-Hélène Nienaltowski, Michela Pedroni, and Bertrand Meyer. 2008. Compiler error messages: What can help novices?. In *ACM SIGCSE Bulletin*, Vol. 40. 168–172.

[13] Raymond S. Pettit, John Homer, and Roger Gee. 2017. Do Enhanced Compiler Error Messages Help Students?: Results Inconclusive.. In *Proceedings of the 2017 ACM SIGCSE Technical Symposium on Computer Science Education (SIGCSE '17)*. ACM, New York, NY, USA, 465–470. https://doi.org/10.1145/3017680.3017768

[14] Peter C Rigby and Suzanne Thompson. 2005. Study of novice programmers using Eclipse and Gild. In *Proceedings of the 2005 OOPSLA workshop on Eclipse technology eXchange*. 105–109.

[15] Tom Schorsch. 1995. CAP: an automated self-assessment tool to check Pascal programs for syntax, logic and style errors. In *ACM SIGCSE Bulletin*, Vol. 27. 168–172.

[16] Sylvain Thénault. [n. d.]. Pylint. https://www.pylint.org/. Accessed: 2018-08-31.

[17] Marco Torchiano, Maurizio Morisio, et al. 2010. Assessing the precision of findbugs by mining java projects developed at a university. In *Mining Software Repositories (MSR), 2010 7th IEEE Working Conference on*. IEEE, 110–113.

[18] V Javier Traver. 2010. On compiler error messages: what they say and what they mean. *Advances in Human-Computer Interaction* 2010 (2010).

[19] Nghi Truong, Paul Roe, and Peter Bancroft. 2004. Static analysis of students' Java programs. In *Proceedings of the Sixth Australasian Conference on Computing Education-Volume 30*. 317–325.

[20] Daniel Zingaro, Yuliya Cherenkova, Olessia Karpova, and Andrew Petersen. 2013. Facilitating Code-writing in PI Classes. In *Proceeding of the 44th ACM Technical Symposium on Computer Science Education (SIGCSE '13)*. 585–590.

Using GitHub in the Classroom Predicts Student Learning Outcomes and Classroom Experiences: Findings from a Survey of Students and Teachers

Courtney Hsing
GitHub Education
courtkh@github.com

Vanessa Gennarelli
GitHub Education
mozzadrella@github.com

ABSTRACT

GitHub is a widely-used software development platform that supports version control, collaborative development, and project hosting. Currently, an estimated 18,000 educators use GitHub in programming classrooms. Depending on how GitHub is implemented in the classroom, students may rely on GitHub for activities such as, submitting assignments, collaborating on group projects, and receiving feedback. Despite GitHub's growing presence in programming classrooms, to date, few studies have explored how GitHub and the design of its implementation shape students' learning outcomes and classroom experiences. Building on previous research, we investigated how students in classrooms that used GitHub (GitHub classrooms), as opposed to classrooms that did not use GitHub (non-GitHub classrooms), differed across key variables. We surveyed 7530 students and 300 educators from GitHub and non-GitHub classrooms. Overall, we found that using GitHub in the classroom predicted better learning outcomes and classroom experiences. For example, students felt more prepared for the future, and they felt a greater sense of belonging in the classroom and in the field. Importantly, the design of implementation affected learning outcomes. For example, of the students who used GitHub in the classroom and received instructor feedback, those who received (versus did not receive) feedback via GitHub benefited more from the feedback. We discuss best practices for maximizing benefits to student learning when implementing GitHub in the classroom, study limitations, and future research directions. Our research is a step towards understanding how GitHub, a tool with a growing presence in programming classrooms, impacts students' learning experiences.

KEYWORDS

GitHub; education; learning outcomes

SIGCSE '19, February 27-March 2, 2019, Minneapolis, MN, USA

ACM ISBN 978-1-4503-5890-3/19/02...$15.00
https://doi.org/10.1145/3287324.3287460

ACM Reference format

Courtney Hsing and Vanessa Gennarelli. 2019. Using GitHub in the Classroom Predicts Student Learning Outcomes and Classroom Experiences: Findings from a Survey of Students and Teachers. In *Proceedings of 50th ACM Technical Symposium on Computer Science Education (SIGCSE '19), February 27-March 2, 2019, Minneapolis, MN, USA.* ACM, NY, NY, USA, 7 pages.
https://doi.org/10.1145/3287324.3287460

1. INTRODUCTION

GitHub is a widely-used software development platform that supports version control, collaborative development, and project hosting. With more than 1.8 million businesses and organizations using GitHub [5], it is recognized as an industry standard. In fact, many developers feel that knowing how to use GitHub is an essential part of securing a job [15]. Currently, an estimated 18,000 educators use GitHub in programming classrooms [14]. Depending on how GitHub is implemented in the classroom, students may rely on GitHub for activities such as, submitting assignments, collaborating on group projects, and receiving feedback. Unsurprisingly, the general idea of using GitHub in the classroom has generated interest not only among educators, but also among researchers interested in the implications GitHub has for student learning outcomes. To understand how GitHub can impact the student experience, we will review the general trends uncovered by previous research.

First, using GitHub in the classroom gives students the chance to learn how to use a popular industry tool. Research supports that one of the main motivations instructors have for implementing GitHub in the classroom is to help students develop familiarity with an important industry tool, thus making students more competitive on the job market [3]. Further, students mentioned the importance of publicly presenting their work on GitHub and that it is common for employers to refer to GitHub during the hiring process [3]. Research also supports that industry collaborations may encourage students to take assignments more seriously, invest greater effort, find assignments more meaningful, and be more motivated to perform well on assignments [9].

Next, by encouraging students to use GitHub for collaborative activities, such as peer reviews and group projects, instructors may facilitate students' development of communication, teamwork, and critical analysis skills [2]. Soft skills are important when working in industry, and computer science and software engineering education have begun to adopt a pedagogy that focuses on soft skills in addition to technical skills [3]. In a study where instructors were interviewed, they noted that using

GitHub in their courses effectively introduced students to collaborative practices essential to software development (e.g., cross-team collaboration, peer review) [3]. Further, a survey study found that students preferred the collaborative platform over more traditional individual assignments [8]. One of the key advantages students observed was that GitHub facilitated teamwork and collaboration, allowing students to connect with peers for help outside of the classroom and learn from each other's ideas [8].

In addition, research supports that using GitHub in the classroom boosts student engagement, the overall energy that a student invests in the academic experience [6]. By facilitating student contributions and cross-team collaboration, the use of GitHub enables a participatory culture where students feel their contributions are impactful [3]. Further, in one study, researchers interviewed instructors and found that some instructors use students' contributions on GitHub as materials for discussion in class, thus participation is incentivized because student contributions can direct class discussions [15]. Indeed, past research found that one main motivation instructors have for implementing GitHub in the classroom is to offer students the opportunity to directly influence the course and contribute to course materials (e.g., via pull requests) [3], creating novel ways for students to be involved in the classroom.

Lastly, although past research has not directly addressed this specific idea, using GitHub in the classroom may strengthen the sense of belonging students feel within the classroom because it allows students to collaborate and contribute to each other's learning process. Research finds that, more collaborative projects, where students work closely with peers, can foster a stronger sense of belonging [7]. Importantly, students' sense of belonging can positively predict variables tied to academic success, such as intrinsic motivation and academic self-efficacy [4]. Self-efficacy, the degree to which individuals feel capable of accomplishing a task, is essential to student success because it can protect students' confidence and help them persist when they encounter setbacks [11]. In addition, GitHub supports interactions with individuals in industry [3] and may promote a sense of belonging to the field. For instance, in a past study, an instructor reported that unregistered students and other GitHub users visited and "starred" their class's public repositories, establishing a connection between students and others in the field [15]. Research suggests that improving students' sense of belonging can have a protective effect on retention and increase achievement motivation [13, 10].

Building on previous research, we investigated how students in classrooms that used GitHub, as opposed to classrooms that did not use GitHub, differed across key variables. Our research deviated from previous studies in several ways. Notably, to date, studies on the use of GitHub in the classroom have relied on data from qualitative studies that mostly focus on instructors' perceptions of student learning. Although these approaches have highlighted important issues, trends, and ideas, we aim to build a deeper understanding of students' experiences and also draw comparisons between the students' and instructors' perceptions. Lastly, we hope to extend our understanding of how GitHub shapes student learning outcomes and experiences by measuring additional relevant outcome variables.

2. RESEARCH

This section describes the research methodology: the research questions, the survey used to collect data, and the participants.

2.1 Research Questions

R1: Does using (versus not using) GitHub in the classroom predict students' learning outcomes? Past research suggests that using GitHub in the classroom may boost student engagement [6], and encourage class participation [15]. In the survey, we asked students to rate how much they learned about teamwork and collaboration, popular tools, and project management from 1(very little) to 5 (very much). We also asked instructors to rate their students using the same survey items and scale. We hypothesized that, based on student and teacher responses, using (versus not using) GitHub in the classroom predicts learning more about collaboration, popular tools, and project management.

R2: Does using (versus not using) GitHub in the classroom predict students' feelings of preparation for the future? Research suggests that collaborative activities, such as peer reviews and group projects facilitated by GitHub, may strengthen students' development of skills important when working in industry in the future [2]. In the survey, students rated how much 1(very little) to 5 (very much) their course has prepared them for a future internship or career, being a part of the developer community, developing a portfolio of their work, and taking more advanced courses. We hypothesized that, based on student and teacher responses, using (versus not using) GitHub in the classroom predicts feeling more prepared for all measured domains.

R3: How is the implementation of GitHub in the classroom associated with students' classroom experiences? Using GitHub in the classroom may strengthen the sense of belonging students feel within the classroom. Research finds that, more collaborative projects, where students work closely with peers, can foster a stronger sense of belonging [7]. In addition, GitHub supports interactions with individuals in the broader developer community and may promote a students' sense of belonging to the field. We predicted that, using (versus not using) GitHub in the classroom predicts a greater sense of belonging both in the classroom and in the field.

To assess students' sense of belonging in the classroom and in the field, students were asked to rate the following items using a scale of 1(strongly disagree) to 7(strongly agree), and we created a composite score by averaging ratings across each set of three items. Items were adapted from a previous study [12].

Belonging in the classroom

1. My contributions in my course are valued.
2. I feel comfortable in my course.
3. People in my course accept me.

Belonging in the field

1. I see myself as part of the developer community.
2. I feel that I am a member of the developer community.
3. I feel a sense of belonging to the developer community.

R4: How does the design of implementation predict outcomes related to classroom learning? Lastly, because GitHub is a tool with diverse features and can be implemented flexibly in the classroom, we wanted to examine whether the design of implementation can predict outcomes related to classroom learning. First, we assessed how the number of features students used in the classroom is associated with positive learning outcomes and feelings of preparation for the future. We expected that using more GitHub features in the classroom is associated with greater positive learning outcomes and feelings of preparation for the future. In addition, we investigated how using GitHub as a tool to deliver feedback may predict the perceived effectiveness of feedback.

GitHub allows students to receive line-specific feedback from their instructors or peers via pull requests. Because detailed informational feedback tends to increase student self-efficacy and learning strategies [1], relying on GitHub may make students better learners who use feedback effectively. We measured students' perceptions of instructor and peer feedback by asking them to rate the following items from 1(strongly disagree) to 7(strongly agree)

Instructor feedback:

1. I understand the instructor's feedback.
2. I pay attention to the instructor's feedback.
3. I use the instructor's feedback effectively.
4. I find the instructor's feedback helpful.
5. The instructor understands my needs as a student.

Peer feedback:

1. I understand feedback from peers.
2. I pay attention to feedback from peers.
3. I use feedback from peers effectively.
4. I find feedback from peers helpful.

We hypothesized that, based on student and teacher responses, using (versus not using) GitHub to deliver feedback generally predicts greater effectiveness of peer and instructor feedback. However, we did not have specific predictions for how using (versus not using) GitHub to deliver feedback predicts the extent to which students pay attention to instructor and peer feedback, because it is unclear how the manner in which feedback is delivered would shape students' motivation to attend to feedback.

2.2 Methodology

Two surveys were designed to collect student and instructor responses. The student survey assessed students' perceptions and experiences in the classroom, and the instructor survey asked instructors to report on their impressions of students' learning experiences.

We invited 459,558 students (9.9% high school; 69.4% college; 3.3% non-traditional; 17.4% other) and 17,806 instructors (15.3% high school; 62.6% college; 2.0% non-traditional; 20.1% other) to participate in our study. Recipients had verified student or instructor status through GitHub and received a link to the online survey via email. In addition, to be eligible for the survey, the recipient must have either taken or taught a class with a programming component in the past semester. 7530 students and 300 instructors who either used or did not use GitHub in the classroom during the most recent semester completed our survey. The response rate of student recipients was 1.6% and the completion rate was 82.1%, and the response rate of instructor recipients was 1.7% and the completion rate was 85.0%. Tables 1 and 2 provide more information on the student and instructor participants' demographic information.

Table 1: Student and instructor respondents' use of GitHub in the classroom

	Students	Instructors
Used GitHub in the classroom	37.2%	67.0%
Did not use GitHub in the classroom	62.8%	33.0%

Table 2: Student and instructor respondents' gender

	Students	Instructors
Female	8.5%	6.9%
Male	90.0%	91.5%
Non-binary	1.0%	0.8%
Prefer to self-describe	0.5%	0.8%

3. RESULTS

Next, we present the results of our survey research.

3.1 Learning outcomes

To examine how implementing GitHub in the classroom predicts students' learning outcomes, we compared self-reported responses from students who used and students who did not use GitHub in the classroom during the previous semester. We also compared responses about students' experiences from teachers who implemented and from teachers who did not implement GitHub in the classroom. First, we examined how much students felt they learned about, and how much instructors felt their students learned about teamwork and collaboration, popular industry tool(s), and project management through their programming course. Separate analyses were conducted to examine teacher perceptions of students' learning outcomes. We used the Welch's t-test, accounting for unequal variance and unequal sample sizes.

In line with our hypothesis, we found that students who used GitHub in the classroom (M = 3.65, SD = 1.30) felt they learned more about teamwork and collaboration than students who did not use GitHub in the classroom (M = 2.78, SD = 1.47; $t(5743)$ = 25.60, p < 0.01). Instructors who used GitHub in the classroom (M = 3.12, SD = 1.44) also felt their students learned more about teamwork and collaboration than students who did not use GitHub in the classroom (M = 2.51, SD = 1.31; $t(277)$ = 3.44, p < 0.01). Results suggest that students who used GitHub in the classroom may have developed more skills necessary for collaborative work.

In addition, in line with our predictions, students who used GitHub in the classroom (M = 3.72, SD = 1.14) felt they learned more about popular industry tool(s) than students who did not use GitHub in the classroom (M = 2.86, SD = 1.38; $t(6032)$ = 28.01,

$p < 0.01$). Similarly, instructors who used GitHub in the classroom (M = 3.78, SD = 1.04) felt their students learned more about popular industry tool(s) than students who did not use GitHub in the classroom (M = 3.24, SD = 1.20; $t(161) = 3.66$, $p < 0.01$). Thus, using GitHub in the classroom may lead students to feel better prepared for working in industry.

Lastly, students who used GitHub in the classroom (M = 3.53, SD = 1.23) felt they learned more about project management than students who did not use GitHub in the classroom (M = 2.68, SD = 1.38; $t(5697) = 26.54$, $p < 0.01$). In line these results, instructors who used GitHub in the classroom (M = 2.95, SD = 1.15) felt their students learned more about project management than students who did not use GitHub in the classroom (M = 2.41, SD = 1.24; $t(276) = 3.62$, $p < 0.01$). These findings suggest using GitHub in the classroom may help students build skills important for tackling project objectives.

3.2 Preparation for the future

To examine how implementing GitHub in the classroom predicts students' feelings of preparation for the future, we compared self-reported responses about their own experiences from students who used and students who did not use GitHub in the classroom during the most recent semester. Again, we also compared responses about students' experiences from teachers who implemented and from teachers who did not implement GitHub in the classroom. We examined how much students felt their course prepared them, and how much instructors felt their course prepared their students for a future internship or career, being a part of the developer community, developing a portfolio of their work, and taking more advanced courses. Again, separate analyses were conducted to examine teacher perceptions of students' learning outcomes.

Consistent with our hypothesis, we found that students who used GitHub in the classroom (M = 3.84, SD = 1.12) felt more prepared for a future internship or career than students who did not use GitHub in the classroom (M = 3.25, SD = 1.30; $t(5826) = 19.77$, $p < 0.01$). However, when we compared instructors who used (M = 3.83, SD = 1.01) versus did not use GitHub in the classroom (M = 3.67, SD = 1.02), we found no difference in their ratings of students' preparation for a future internship or career, $t(276) = 1.23$, p =.22. This suggests, although instructors saw a connection between their course and students' future career regardless of using GitHub, students who used GitHub in the classroom found their courses more valuable to their future.

In addition, as predicted, we found that students who used GitHub in the classroom (M = 3.68, SD = 1.22) felt more prepared for being a part of the developer community than students who did not use GitHub in the classroom (M = 2.82, SD = 1.38; $t(5717) = 27.09$, $p < 0.01$). Similarly, instructors who used GitHub in the classroom (M = 3.37, SD = 1.22) felt their students were more prepared for being a part of the developer community than those who did not use GitHub in the classroom (M = 2.75, SD = 1.20; $t(276) = 3.99$, $p < 0.01$). Results suggest that students may feel more fit to contribute to the developer community after a semester of using GitHub in the classroom.

Supporting our predictions, we also found that students who used GitHub in the classroom (M = 3.58, SD = 1.30) felt more prepared for developing a portfolio of their work than students who did not use GitHub in the classroom (M = 2.85, SD = 1.40; $t(5516) = 21.66$, $p < 0.01$). In line with these results, instructors who used GitHub in the classroom (M = 3.37, SD = 1.23) also felt their students were more prepared for developing a portfolio of their work than students who did not use GitHub in the classroom (M = 2.77, SD = 1.11; $t(276) = 3.96$, $p < 0.01$).

Lastly, we found that students who used GitHub in the classroom (M = 3.88, SD = 1.14) felt more prepared for taking more advanced courses than students who did not use GitHub in the classroom (M = 3.70, SD = 1.24; $t(5529) = 5.97$, $p < 0.01$). However, instructors who did (M = 3.84, SD = 1.07) versus did not (M = 4.05, SD = 0.91) implement GitHub in the classroom showed no significant difference in ratings of students' preparedness for taking more advanced courses, $t(275) = 1.67$, p = 0.10. This suggests, although instructors may see a connection between their course and more advanced courses regardless of using GitHub in the classroom, perhaps using GitHub in the classroom helps highlight that connection for students.

3.3 Classroom experiences

Next, to investigate how implementing GitHub in the classroom predicts students' classroom experiences, we compared responses from students who used and students who did not use GitHub in the classroom. Specifically, we focused on students' sense of belonging in the class and in the field. We also examined students' likelihood to recommend their course to others, and to take a similar course in the future. Because these questions centered on students' personal feelings and perceptions to which instructors may have less insight, we did not assess instructors' perceptions of how students felt.

Consistent with our hypothesis, we found that students who used GitHub in the classroom (M = 5.78, SD = 0.99) felt a greater sense of belonging in the classroom than students who did not use GitHub in the classroom (M = 5.49, SD = 1.12; $t(5620.04) = 11.23$, $p < 0.01$). In addition, students who used GitHub in the classroom (M = 5.49, SD = 1.26) also felt a greater sense of belonging in the field than students who did not use GitHub in the classroom (M = 5.05, SD = 1.52; $t(5883) = 12.90$, $p < 0.01$). Findings suggest that using GitHub in the classroom may help students feel like they are a part of a larger community of people, and that their contributions are valued.

In addition, as predicted, students who used GitHub in the classroom (M = 5.90, SD = 1.30) were more likely to recommend their course to others than students who did not use GitHub in the classroom (M = 5.50, SD = 1.58; $F(1,34) = 3.55$, $p < 0.01$). Students who used GitHub in the classroom (M = 5.78, SD = 1.43) also felt they were more likely to take a similar course in the future than students who did not use GitHub in the classroom (M = 5.43, SD = 1.70; $t(5939) = 9.09$, $p < 0.01$). These results suggest students may enjoy and value their courses when they use GitHub in the classroom.

3.4 Design of implementation

Lastly, to explore how the design of implementation affects classroom learning, we conducted analyses focused on the way

GitHub was used in the classroom. Running separate regression analyses, we found that the number of GitHub features used in the classroom predicted various student learning outcomes and feelings of preparation for the future. Specifically, using more GitHub features in the classroom predicted students learning more about teamwork and collaboration ($b = .17$, $t(2505) = 15.74$, $p < 0.01$), popular industry tools ($b = .11$, $t(2504) = 10.95$, $p = < 0.01$), and project management ($b = .16$, $t(2505) = 15.34$, $p < 0.01$). In addition, using more GitHub features in the classroom also predicted students feeling more prepared for a future internship and career ($b = .11$, $t(2501) = 11.40$, $p < 0.01$), being a part of the developer community ($b = .15$, $t(2500) = 14.78$, $p < 0.01$), developing a portfolio of their work ($b = .15$, $t(2499) = 13.65$, $p < 0.01$), and taking more advanced courses ($b = .09$, $t(2488) = 9.26$, $p < 0.01$). Consistent with our predictions, results suggest that it may not simply be the implementation of GitHub in the classroom that matters, but how GitHub is used in the classroom may be a key predictor of positive learning outcomes and experiences.

To further assess how the design of implementation affects classroom learning, we explored how feedback is perceived by students when it is delivered via GitHub. One way in which instructors use GitHub in the classroom is as a tool for feedback communication, and we examined students' perceptions of feedback effectiveness when feedback is delivered via GitHub versus not via GitHub. Of the students who used GitHub in the classroom and received instructor feedback, students who received feedback via GitHub ($M = 6.01$, $SD = 1.07$) (versus not via GitHub ($M = 5.72$, $SD = 1.34$)) perceived feedback as more helpful, $t(790) = 4.43$, $p < 0.01$. Compared to students who did not receive feedback via GitHub ($M = 5.58$, $SD = 1.40$), students who did receive feedback via GitHub ($M = 5.90$, $SD = 1.18$) also felt their needs were better understood by their instructor, $t(733) = 4.48$, $p < 0.01$. Lastly, students who received feedback via GitHub ($M = 5.99$, $SD = 1.13$) felt they used the instructor's feedback more effectively than students who did not receive feedback via GitHub ($M = 5.81$, $SD = 1.18$, $t(666) = 2.67$, $p = .008$). However, there was no difference in students' understanding of instructor feedback ($t(1659) = 0.38$, $p = 0.70$) and the extent to which they pay attention to instructor feedback ($t(1668) = 1.04$, $p = 0.30$) when it was delivered via GitHub versus not via GitHub. In contrast, instructors reported no difference in feedback effectiveness across items when feedback is delivered via GitHub versus not via GitHub. Results suggest that student and teacher perceptions may not be in line with each other. Interestingly, delivering instructor feedback via GitHub seemed to impact students' perceptions that involved use or application of feedback, but not necessarily how much students paid attention to or understood feedback. One potential explanation is that the manner in which feedback is delivered may not shape students' willingness to attend to feedback or their ability to comprehend the feedback. However, how feedback is communicated may influence its perceived value and thus impact the extent to which students feel understood by their instructors.

We also assessed students' perceptions of peer feedback effectiveness when feedback is delivered via GitHub versus not via GitHub. Of the students who used GitHub in the classroom and received peer feedback, students who received feedback via GitHub ($M = 5.96$, $SD = 1.10$) (versus not via GitHub ($M = 5.76$, $SD = 1.25$)) perceived feedback as more helpful, $t(682) = 2.50$, $p < 0.01$. Compared to students who did not receive peer feedback via GitHub ($M = 5.68$, $SD = 1.17$), students who received peer feedback via GitHub ($M = 5.99$, $SD = 1.03$) also felt they used the feedback more effectively, $t(687) = 4.14$, $p < 0.01$. However, there was no difference in students' understanding of peer feedback ($t(980) = 1.74$, $p = 0.08$), or in the extent to which students paid attention to peer feedback ($t(988) = 1.24$, $p = 0.22$). when it was delivered via GitHub versus not via GitHub. In contrast, instructors reported no difference in peer feedback effectiveness across items when feedback is delivered via GitHub versus not via GitHub.

4. DISCUSSION

Overall, we found that students who used GitHub in the classroom tended to have better student learning outcomes, feel more prepared for the future, and report more positive classroom experiences. In addition, we learned that although using GitHub in the classroom is an important predictor of learning outcomes, the design of implementation mattered. Thus, it is important to consider how students will interact with GitHub when implementing it in the classroom.

We found that students who used (versus did not use) GitHub in the classroom felt they learned more about teamwork and collaboration, popular industry tool(s), and project management via their programming course. These findings suggest students can build skills necessary for working with others in industry by using GitHub in the classroom. Collaborative experiences between students may make them more effective developers in industry, and it is likely that other platforms that facilitate similar experiences can also generate such benefits.

Next, we found that students who used GitHub in the classroom felt more prepared for their future career, being part of the developer community, developing a portfolio of their work, and taking more advanced courses. Research supports that one of the main motivations instructors have for implementing GitHub in the classroom is to help make students more competitive on the job market [3]. Based on our findings, students do perceive benefits in line with instructors' motivations to implement GitHub in the classroom. However, instructor and student findings were not completely in line with each other. Specifically, instructors reported no difference in student preparation for taking more advanced courses and for a future internship or career. One possible explanation is that students and teachers consider different sets of skills when evaluating student preparedness across domains, but further research is necessary to understand the discrepancies in responses.

In addition, our data supported that students who used GitHub in the classroom felt a greater sense of belonging in the classroom. One potential explanation is that using GitHub in the classroom allows students to collaborate and contribute to each other's learning process. Research finds that, more collaborative projects, where students work closely with peers, can foster a stronger sense of belonging [7]. Importantly, students' sense of belonging can positively predict variables tied to academic success, such as intrinsic motivation and academic self-efficacy [4]. We also found that using GitHub in the classroom may promote a greater sense of belonging in the field more generally. One potential explanation is that GitHub supports interactions with individuals in industry. For instance, in a previous study, the researchers reported that unregistered students and other GitHub users visited and "starred" their public repositories, establishing a connection between students and others in the field [15].

Lastly, we learned that the design of implementation may impact student's learning outcomes and preparation for the future. For instance, using more features within GitHub may predict greater student learning outcomes. Because GitHub can be flexibly used in the classroom for tasks ranging from distributing classroom content to providing line-by-line feedback via pull requests, it is unsurprising that engaging more deeply with GitHub may boost benefits associated with using it. Further, we uncovered that receiving instructor and peer feedback via GitHub may have boosted students' perceptions of the feedback's value. In particular, using GitHub in the classroom predicted students' effective use of feedback and perception of feedback as helpful, but not students' attention towards or understanding of feedback. Importantly, students who received instructor feedback via GitHub felt better understood by their instructor. These findings highlight future avenues for research. For example, from this survey, we did not learn how students are actually applying instructor feedback when it is delivered via GitHub or via other means. It may be the case that receiving feedback via GitHub improved students' perceptions of the feedback but did not impact how students actually applied the feedback. However, it may also be the case that students are better able to apply feedback when it is delivered via GitHub versus via other means. Developing a deeper understanding of how students perceive and apply feedback delivered via different means will help instructors leverage tools that enhance their teaching. Lastly, it is unclear why instructors' responses were not in line with that of students'. One possibility is that instructors lack insight to students' more private experiences that meaningfully shift relative to the use of GitHub in the classroom to deliver feedback.

4.1 Limitations

Our research is a step towards understanding the impact associated with using GitHub in the classroom. However, there are a few notable limitations of the research that should be considered. First, our student and instructor participants may have been more experienced with using GitHub than the average user of GitHub because we only recruited participants who had verified student or instructor status through GitHub. It is possible that the average student would benefit even more from using GitHub in the classroom than our participants because they were learning a valuable industry tool with which they were less familiar. On the other hand, it is possible that the average student would benefit less from using GitHub in the classroom than our participants because they may be less committed to learning GitHub. To improve the generalizability of our findings, future research should attempt to replicate our pattern of results using a sample more representative of the average student using GitHub in the classroom.

In addition, the replication of findings is especially important because our effects are small. Although it may be the case that the benefits associated with using GitHub are small, another reason could be that we recruited a diverse sample of participants who used GitHub in various types of classrooms. Thus, it is possible that examining the effect of using GitHub in a more controlled classroom study would produce larger effects. Although we cannot be fully confident in these results without replication and further research, the pattern of results was mostly consistent across variables. Overall, our findings support that using GitHub in the classroom is associated with positive student learning outcomes and experiences.

Lastly, our study design did not allow us to draw conclusions regarding causality. Although we could determine how students who used (versus did not use) GitHub in the classroom differed, our correlational data did not reveal how using GitHub in the classroom caused change in students' learning outcomes and experiences. So, although we could examine the relationship between key variables and make inferences about causality, we did not collect data that directly examined causality. Future research may use the experimental method to explore whether implementing GitHub in the classroom causes change in students' learning outcomes and experiences. For example, researchers may randomly assign classes to either implement or not implement GitHub in the classroom, and observe how the two conditions differ on key variables.

5. CONCLUSION

Our research provides preliminary evidence illustrating how using GitHub in the classroom may benefit student learning and classroom experiences. Results highlight the potential impact of using GitHub in the classroom on student learning outcomes, and suggests using GitHub in the classroom positively predicts learning outcome variables. Importantly, the design of GitHub implementation matters and our results support that how students use GitHub in the classroom may impact learning outcomes. Combined with further research, our findings may be used to inform best practices for implementing GitHub in the classroom.

REFERENCES

[1] Butler, D.L., & Winne, P.H. (1995). Feedback and self-regulated learning: A theoretical synthesis. *Review of Educational Research, 65*, 245-281.

[2] Falkner, K., & Falkner, N.J.G. (2012). Supporting and structuring "contributing student pedagogy" in computer science curricula. *Computer Science Education, 22*, 413-443.

[3] Feliciano, J., Storey, M., & Zagalsky, A., (2016). Student experiences using GitHub in software engineering courses: A case study. *ICSE '16 Companion*, 1-10.

[4] Freeman, T.M., Anderman, L.H., & Jensen, J.M. (2007). Sense of belonging in college freshmen at the classroom and campus levels. *Journal of Experimental Education. 75*, 203-220.

[5] GitHub. (n.d.). Retrieved August 1, 2018, from http://github.com

[6] Gunnarsson, S., Larsson, P., Mansson, S., Martensson, E., & Sonnerup, J. (2017). Enhancing student engagement using GitHub as an educational tool. *Introduction to Teaching and Learning in Higher Education.* 1-14.

[7] Kember, D., Lee, K., & Li, N. (2001). Cultivating a sense of belonging in part-time students. *International Journal of Lifelong Education. 20,* 326-341.

[8] Kertész, C. (2015). Using GitHub in the classroom - a collaborative learning experience. *International Symposium for Design and Technology in Electronic Packaging,* Braşov, Romania, 381-386.

[9] Marcketti, S.B., & Karpova, E.E. (2014). Getting ready for the real world: Student perspectives on bringing industry collaboration into the classroom. *Journal of Family and Consumer Sciences, 106,* 27-31.

[10] O'Keefe, P. (2013). A sense of belonging: Improving student retention. *College Student Journal. 47,* 605-613.

[11] Pajares, F. (1996). Self-efficacy beliefs in academic settings. *Review of Educational Research, 66,* 543-578.

[12] Trujillo, G., & Tanner, K.D. (2014). Considering the role of affect in learning: Monitoring students' self-efficacy, sense of belonging, and science identity. *CBE – Life Sciences Education, 13,* 6-15.

[13] Walton, G.M., Cohen, G.L., Cwir, D., & Spencer, S.J. (2012). Mere belonging: The power of social connections. *Journal of Personality and Social Psychology, 102,* 513-532.

[14] Wan, T. (2018, June, 19). *GitHub's new education bundle equips students with industry-standard coding* tools. Retrieved from https://www.edsurge.com

[15] Zagalsky, A., Feliciano, J., Storey, M.A., Zhao, Y., & Wang, W. (2015). The emergence of github as a collaborative platform for education. *In Proc. of the 18th ACM Conference on Computer Supported Cooperative Work & Social Computing,* 1906-1917.

Early Programming Education and Career Orientation: The Effects of Gender, Self-Efficacy, Motivation and Stereotypes

Efthimia Aivaloglou
Open University of the Netherlands
fenia.aivaloglou@ou.nl

Felienne Hermans
Leiden Institute of Advanced Computer Science
f.f.j.hermans@liacs.leidenuniv.nl

ABSTRACT

Programming education currently begins at the elementary school age. In this paper we are exploring what affects the learning performance of young students in programming classes. We present the results collected during an eight-week experimental Scratch programming course run in elementary schools. We emphasize factors that have been found to affect learning performance in adult students, including self-efficacy and motivation, and measure how they affect students of this age group. We further explore the students' view of programming as a career path, and measure the effects of the course, their performance, and the stereotypes that they assume for computer scientists. We find that students' intrinsic and extrinsic motivation and previous programming experience are important factors, being strongly correlated with their self-efficacy and their inclination towards a CS career. For female students only, we also find CS career orientation to be strongly correlated with their self-efficacy.

CCS CONCEPTS

• **Social and professional topics** → *Computing education*; *Gender*;

KEYWORDS

self-efficacy, CS career orientation, programming education, Scratch, K12

ACM Reference Format:

Efthimia Aivaloglou and Felienne Hermans. 2019. Early Programming Education and Career Orientation:, The Effects of Gender, Self-Efficacy, Motivation and Stereotypes. In *Proceedings of the 50th ACM Technical Symposium on Computer Science Education (SIGCSE '19), February 27-March 2, 2019, Minneapolis, MN, USA*, Jennifer B. Sartor, Theo D'Hondt, and Wolfgang De Meuter (Eds.). ACM, New York, NY, USA, 7 pages. https://doi.org/10.1145/3287324.3287358

1 INTRODUCTION

An increasing number of countries are currently enriching their elementary school education with computing and programming courses [3], using Scratch and other languages specifically designed for early programming education. Moving the introduction of programming from universities to high schools and to elementary schools means that programming education needs to adjust —not only in terms of programming environments, but also in terms of pedagogical approaches.

The literature has suggested several factors that influence learning performance in programming. These include age [8, 16, 18], previous programming experience [2, 15, 20] and self-efficacy [12, 15, 17]. Self-efficacy represents the belief that one can successfully execute behaviours required to produce a desired outcome [4]. In education research, self-efficacy has become one of the most important variables that helps explain the relationship between past performance and future results [12], even in middle-school students [5]. Self-efficacy beliefs have been found to affect career orientation, through impacting the choice of students' college major [10, 17].

In this paper, we are interested in the factors that affect the performance of elementary school students in this new subject. We want to determine if the factors that have been found to apply to university-level students also apply to early programming education. At the same time, we want to examine if the early introduction of programming can affect career orientation, and if elementary school students hold specific stereotypes on computer scientists that have been found to be common [11] and to affect their orientation towards CS studies.

Specifically, we are examining the following research questions:

RQ1 How is the learning performance of elementary school students affected by their self-efficacy and their intrinsic and extrinsic motivation within the context of a programming course?

RQ2 What is the effect of those factors, of the course, as well as of established stereotypes on CS scientists, on the selection of programming/CS as a future career path?

RQ3 Does age, gender and previous programming experience affect those factors and relationships?

To answer our research questions, we designed and ran an experimental programming course, teaching Scratch during a series of eight lessons to elementary school students and measuring their performance, self-efficacy and career orientation throughout the course.

The results show that (1) students' intrinsic and extrinsic motivation are strongly correlated with their self-efficacy and, for the case of intrinsic motivation, their inclination towards a CS career, (2) students' previous programming experience is related to their extrinsic motivation, self-efficacy and CS career orientation, (3) the self-efficacy of female students is strongly correlated with their CS career orientation, and (4) course performance and stereotypical beliefs have no significant effect on CS career orientation.

SIGCSE '19, February 27-March 2, 2019, Minneapolis, MN, USA

ACM ISBN 978-1-4503-5890-3/19/02...$15.00
https://doi.org/10.1145/3287324.3287358

2 BACKGROUND AND RELATED WORK

The relationship between performance and self-efficacy of university level students has been widely studied. In [15] it was found that, in the context of a CS1 course, self-efficacy affected course performance, was influenced by previous programming experience and increased as students progressed through the course. The Motivated Strategies for Learning Questionnaire (MSLQ) was used in a study with 39 university students in their introductory programming course where it was found that, of all motivational and learning strategies scales in the MSLQ, self-efficacy had the strongest correlation with the students' course performance [19]. Examining the relationships between MSLQ scores and academic performance, Credé and Phillips found that the self-efficacy scores had within the highest observed validities for grades in individual classes [6]. Lishinski et al. examined the interaction of self-efficacy and intrinsic and extrinsic goal orientation and their impact on students performance in a CS1 course, and found that the self-efficacy of female students had a different connection to performance than that of their male peers [12]. Examining the benefits of prior programming experience on the performance of students of CS1 courses, Wilcox and Lionelle also found gender differences, with inexperienced students performing similarly, but female students with prior programming experience outperforming their male peers [20].

A number of studies have been carried out on teaching programming concepts to novice programmers with block-based languages in general, and with Scratch in particular. Scratch was taught in middle-school classes containing a total of 46 students in the study presented in [13]. Evaluating the internalization of programming concepts, it was found that students had problems with concepts related to initialization, variables and concurrency. In [21], Wilson et al. presented an eight-week Scratch course given to four primary school classes with a total of 60 students aged eight to eleven, and evaluated it by analysing the projects that the students created. Seiter and Foreman [18] proposed a model for assessing computational thinking in primary school students and applied it on 150 Scratch projects, finding that design patterns requiring understanding of parallelization, conditionals and, especially, variables were under-represented until a certain age. Programming abstractions related to variables and procedures were also found to be underutilized in a dataset of 250 thousand Scratch programs [1]. During an online Scratch course with over two thousand active participants, students over twelve years of age were measured to perform significantly better in questions related to operators and procedures [8].

On the topic of CS career orientation, strong social support and high self-efficacy have been found to be associated with strong orientation of undergraduates toward CS careers [17]. Lewis et al. found that university-level students measure their fit in CS according to their beliefs on stereotypical traits of computer scientists [11]. Discrepancies between self-beliefs and perceptions of professionals in science-related disciplines are known to be associated with lower interest in those disciplines [9]. This indicates that stereotypical beliefs about computer scientists might affect the attractiveness of CS as a career path. Using a draw-a-computer-scientist test, eight and nine year old students were found to most often draw male computer scientists working alone and performing actions connected to technology in general but not specific to computer science [7].

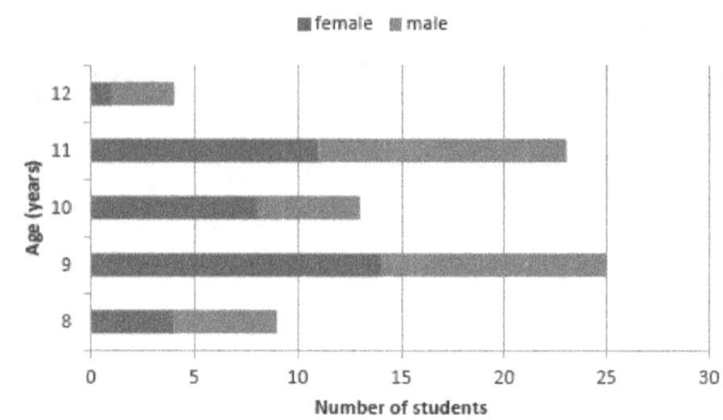

Figure 1: Age and gender of the participants

3 METHODOLOGY

3.1 Participants

The subjects in our study are 74 students attending the three last grades (grades six, seven and eight, aged up to twelve years) of two public elementary schools in the Netherlands. 35 of the students were attending a traditional school, while 39 were attending a bilingual Montessori school. To cater for limitations in the classroom size, in each school the children were randomly separated into two groups, resulting in a total of four groups. The lessons were given during regular school hours and were taught by the authors.

Figure 1 shows the gender and age distribution of the children participating in the experiment. Almost half of the students (38, or 51.35%) are female. The ages vary from eight to twelve years, with an average of 9.84 years.

3.2 Materials and measures

The materials used in the experiment include the lessons materials, a student profile & background questionnaire, where the students reported their age, gender, previous programming experience and whether they know any computer scientists in their social cycle, tests measuring their performance, and questionnaires measuring their self-efficacy, motivation, CS career orientation, beliefs and fit on stereotypes.[1]

3.2.1 Lessons material. The course was composed of eight hour-long lessons, spread in the same number of weeks. It started with one introductory lesson for each group, in which we set up the computers and created Scratch accounts for the students. In addition to that, we showed them a demo of how Scratch works and the basic idea of Scratch, that you can control a sprite on the screen with blocks.

We utilized the Scratch teaching material developed for the online introductory Scratch programming course presented in reference [8], which has been used by over 12,000 children to date.

[1]The tests and questionnaires are available at https://goo.gl/ZpZGFe

3.2.2 Learning performance. To gain an understanding on the progress of the students towards learning about programming concepts, we used an interim and a final test at the fifth and the eighth week respectively. The tests included a total of 17 questions, eleven of which were multiple choice and six were free text, which were graded manually. Four of the questions (three multiple choice and one free text) were not taken into account, following common practice to discard questions with less than 25% success rate as too hard to be representative. For the remaining questions, all answers received the same weight towards the final scores. As a result, the test scores in the interim and the final tests are calculated as the total correct answers divided by the number of questions.

3.2.3 Self-efficacy and motivation assessment. To measure the students' self-efficacy beliefs and extrinsic and intrinsic motivation we used the self-efficacy, extrinsic goal orientation and intrinsic goal orientation subscales of the MSLQ [14]. MSLQ consists of fifteen subscales designed from classic social-cognitive learning theories and is widely used as a self-report instrument for measuring student motivation and learning strategies and for subsequently predicting academic performance [6]. The self-efficacy subscale comprises of eight statements which assess both expectancy for success in the course and self-efficacy. They include judgements about the student's abilities to accomplish tasks, as well as about her confidence in her skills to perform those tasks.

Using questionnaires at the beginning, the middle and the end of the course, the students rated themselves on a seven point likert-scale from 'does not apply at all to me' to 'very true of me'. As specified in the MSLQ, students' self-efficacy scores were computed by taking the average of the points given to the eight statements of each questionnaire. The extrinsic and intrinsic motivation scores were similarly calculated, using the corresponding MSLQ subscales.

3.2.4 Stereotypes, student fit and career orientation. We measured the students' belief and fit to four stereotypical traits of computer scientists [11]: *Singularly focused*, indicating that CS requires an obsession with CS, *asocial*, indicating that computer scientists have limited social skills, *competitive*, and *male*. The student profile & background questionnaire included self-assessment statements for each of the singularly focused, asocial and competitive traits, where the students rated their fit on a seven point likert-scale from 'does not apply at all to me' to 'very true of me'. Using the same scale, the students replied to the statement 'I want to become a programmer when I grow up' at the beginning, middle and end of the course.

The students' beliefs regarding the stereotypes were measured using statements like 'Programmers love programming and prefer it over other hobbies' for the singularly focused, asocial, competitive and male traits, where they indicated their beliefs on a seven point likert-scale.

3.3 Data collection and analysis

Table 1 summarizes the timeline of the data collection activities throughout the course. In the first week, the students were given the profile & background questionnaire, which included the self-assessments for stereotypes fit and career orientation. The questionnaires containing the MSLQ subscales for self-efficacy, intrinsic and extrinsic goal orientation were given in the second week, along with the questions on their beliefs on stereotypes. The students' progress was measured using tests at the middle and at the end of the course, following a repeated self-efficacy and career orientation assessment.

Table 1: Lessons and data collection timeline

Week 1	Student profile & background questionnaire Stereotypes fit self-assessment CS career orientation assessment Setup & introductory Scratch lesson
Week 2	Self-efficacy assessment Intrinsic & extrinsic goal orientation Stereotypes beliefs Lesson 1 (from [8])
Week 3	Lesson 2
Week 4	Lesson 3
Week 5	Self-efficacy assessment CS career orientation assessment Interim test Lesson 4
Week 6	Lesson 5
Week 7	Lesson 6
Week 8	Self-efficacy assessment CS career orientation assessment Final test

To answer **RQ1**, we analysed the students' test results and looked at individual correlations with their motivation and self-efficacy measurements. For **RQ2**, we calculated the students' fit to each of the stereotypical traits by comparing the scores they gave to their beliefs about computer scientists to their self-assessment scores. We then examined correlations between the fit, the aforementioned factors and the students' self-declared CS career orientation. To answer **RQ3**, we looked at individual correlations and correlation differences between girls and boys, students with and without prior programming experience, and groups of different ages, which were tested for significance. We used the Pearson correlation coefficient for calculating all p-values presented in the results (unless otherwise indicated).

4 RESULTS

Table 2 presents descriptive statistics of the various types of data collected during the experiment. In the following sections, we present the results obtained for each of the research questions.

4.1 RQ1: Learning performance

Learning performance was measured using interim and final tests, the results of which are summarized in Figure 2. Figures 3 and 4 show the results of the self-efficacy and the intrinsic and extrinsic motivation measurements.

Analysing the motivation and self-efficacy measurements in relation to the test results, we found no significant correlation. In other words, the motivation and self-efficacy appear to have no significant effect on the performance of the students on the tests.

Table 2: Descriptive statistics of collected data. Test scores have a maximum value of one, all other items are on a seven point likert-scale.

	N	Avg	Mean	StdDev
Self-efficacy Initial	74	5.11	5.25	1.09
Self-efficacy Interim	73	5.18	5.25	1.10
Self-efficacy Final	66	5.33	5.56	1.04
Intrinsic Goal Orientation	74	5.01	5.00	1.21
Extrinsic Goal Orientation	74	4.37	4.25	1.37
Test Score Interim	71	0.41	0.33	0.23
Test Score Final	66	0.50	0.43	0.21
CS Career Orientation Initial	73	2.71	2.00	1.59
CS Career Orientation Interim	73	2.70	3.00	1.66
CS Career Orientation Final	66	2.89	3.00	1.91

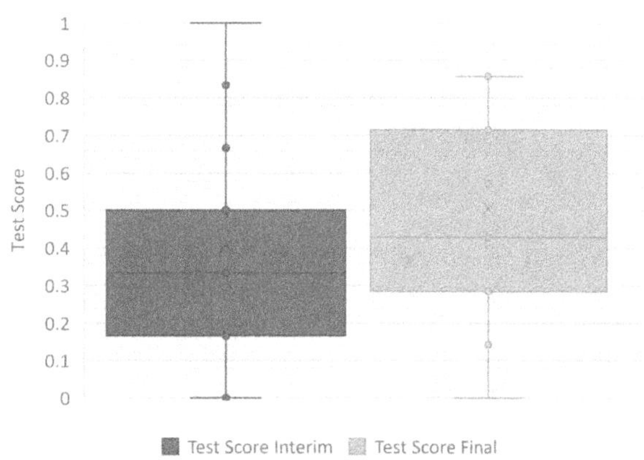

Figure 2: Test results

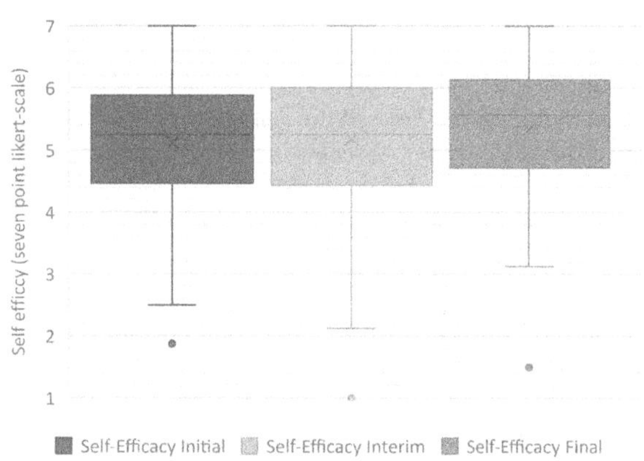

Figure 3: Self-efficacy measurements

Examining the interactions between self-efficacy and motivation, we found strong correlations: extrinsic motivation was significantly correlated with the self-efficacy measurements throughout

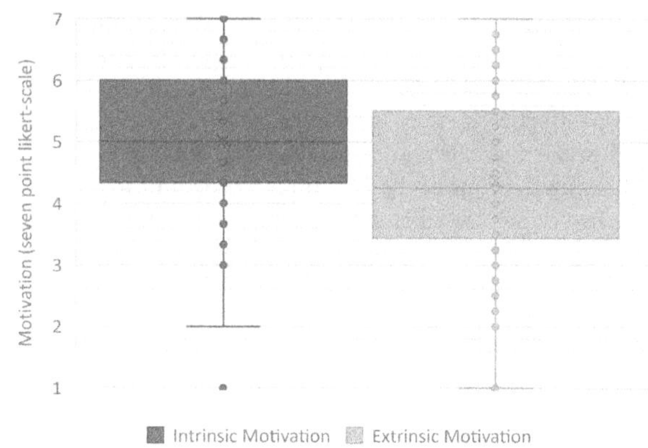

Figure 4: Motivation measurements

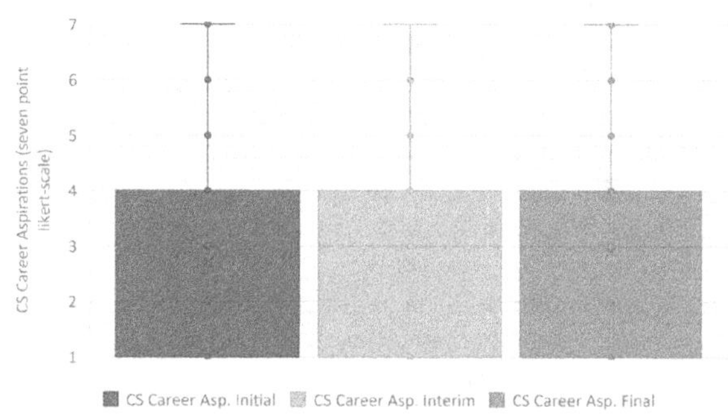

Figure 5: Responses to CS career orientation questions

the course ($p < 0.001$ in all three cases). The same applies for intrinsic motivation ($p < 0.001$ for the initial and interim self-efficacy measurements, $p = 0.002$ for the final one).

> The test performance of the students was not significantly affected by their self-efficacy or motivation. Self-efficacy was measured to be strongly correlated with both intrinsic and extrinsic motivation.

4.2 RQ2: Programming career orientation

The attractiveness of programming as a future career path was measured using self-assessment questions, the results of which are summarized in Figure 5.

The course did not affect the CS career orientation of the students: there was no significant difference between the repeated CS career orientation measurements during the course. Test performance also appears to have no effect on the measurements. This, however, does not apply for self-efficacy, especially in the middle of the course, when a strong correlation with CS career orientation exists ($p = 0.011$ for the interim measurements of the two variables). This correlation is attributed only to female students, which we examine separately in Section 4.3.

The strongest factor impacting the selection of programming as a future career path is found to be the students' intrinsic motivation, which is significantly correlated with the initially measured CS

Table 3: Students' perceptions on the stereotypical traits of programmers (converted to 0 to 1 scale)

Stereotypical trait	N	Avg	Mean	StdDev
Male	66	0.55	0.50	0.20
Social	74	0.56	0.50	0.24
Competitive	74	0.49	0.50	0.29
Singulary focused	74	0.63	0.67	0.29

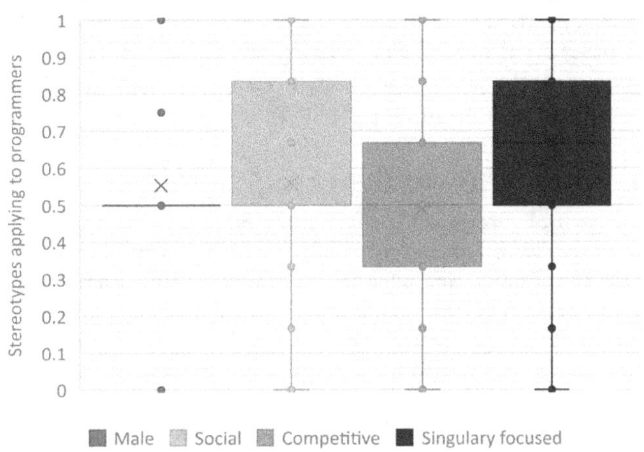

Figure 6: Student perceptions on stereotypical traits of programmers

career orientation (p = 0.029). The same effect was not significant for extrinsic motivation.

Next we examined the students' perceptions on stereotypical traits of computer scientists. Figure 6 and Table 3 summarize the students' responses to the statements described in Section 3.2.4. The results suggest that the students are not inclined towards any particular beliefs about computer scientists. Moreover, the students' fit to the stereotypical traits based on their self-assessment scores was found to have no significant effect on their CS career orientation.

> The students' inclination towards a CS career was strongly correlated with their intrinsic motivation for the course and their self-efficacy in the middle of the course. Their course performance and stereotypical beliefs have no significant effect on CS career orientation.

4.3 RQ3: Age, experience and gender effects

The *age* of the students was found to have no effect on their performance, career orientation, or any other of the examined variables.

In contrast, *previous programming experience* was a factor with strong effects. It was significantly correlated with the extrinsic motivation for the course (p = 0.005), as well as with the CS career orientation (p = 0.025 for the initial measurement and p = 0.031 for the interim one). It was also found to be significantly correlated with the initial and interim self-efficacy (p = 0.001 for both measurements).

Table 4: Gender differences in self-efficacy – test performance correlation (p-values)

Correlation	Females	Males
Self Eff. Initial - Test Score Interim	0.334	0.320
Self Eff. Interim - Test Score Interim	0.162	0.224
Self Eff. Final - Test Score Final	0.909	0.925

We further examined the effect of *gender* in the relationship between test performance and self-efficacy. Table 4 summarizes the results. For female students, the correlation is stronger than for male students, but it does not become significant throughout the course.

Regarding CS career orientation, no significant difference was found between male and female students. However, the factors that affect the attractiveness of programming as a career path were found to be different: For female students, a significant correlation was found between their CS career orientation measurement at the middle of the course and their self-efficacy measurements (p = 0.018 for the interim self-efficacy measurement and p =0.022 for the final one). This correlation was not significant for male students.

Examining students' perceptions on stereotypical traits of computer scientists, female students disagreed about the Male trait. A significant difference (Chi-square test, p = 0.014) was found between the answers of male and female students on the Male trait. In other words, female students replied that programming is a profession more for women, while male students that it is more for men.

> The students' previous programming experience is strongly correlated with their extrinsic motivation, self-efficacy and CS career orientation. For female students only, their CS career orientation is significantly related to their self-efficacy.

5 DISCUSSION

Having previous programming experience was a strong factor in our study: it was found to be significantly correlated with extrinsic motivation, CS career orientation and self-efficacy. This strong effect of prior experience has also be found to apply to CS1 courses [2, 15, 20]. In our experiment, there might be an additional reason for this observation: that programming experience, before our experimental courses, could have been obtained only through home-based or extra-curricular activities (we have confirmed that no previous programming lessons were given to the participants within the school environment). Therefore, having prior programming experience indicates that the students had sought to learn programming themselves, or were encouraged by their environment towards programming, and this proved to give them a significant head start in the course.

The age of the students was found to have no significant effect on their performance. This might be attributed to the fact that the age range was not large, with the majority of the students being from nine to eleven years old. A study on an online Scratch course has found performance differences to be significant after the age of twelve years [8]. Moreover, between elementary school children, differences can become apparent in the context of specific programming concepts like conditionals or repetitions [16, 18], which were not studied seperately in this experiment.

Beliefs on stereotypical traits of computer scientists have been found to affect how university-level students measure their fit in CS [11]. Fit is important, because discrepancies between self-beliefs and perceptions of professionals in science-related disciplines are associated with lower interest in those disciplines [9]. The effect of students' fit to stereotypical traits was not measured in our experiment, because the students were not measured to hold any of the four stereotypes about computer scientists. This might be attributed to their age; we could assume that perceptions about stereotypical traits of computer scientists have not been developed yet for this age group. Even the Male trait was not assumed, with students favouring neutral or their own gender as typical for the profession. It is therefore to be expected that their CS career orientation was not related to any of the already documented stereotypical traits of computer scientists.

Related to our findings on gender differences on self-efficacy is the work of Lishinski et al. [12]. In their work, they found self-efficacy to be correlated with motivation, but also to have a gender-dependent feedback loop with course performance. Female students of the CS1 course were found to adjust their self-efficacy beliefs based on their performance more efficiently than male students, which could cause them to disengage from CS because they were more prone to internalize early failures in the course.

In our study, we did not observe significant correlations between test performance and self-efficacy. We speculate that this might be due to the tests being too hard for the students to be representative of their course performance, or to the students of this age group not being experienced enough with written tests to produce results indicative of their learning progress. As a result, we believe that the tests grades, depicted in Figure 2, are too low to represent the students' performance distribution or to be correlated with self-efficacy measurements. We did, however, observe a gender difference related to self-efficacy: its correlation with CS career orientation, which was stronger for female students. We believe that, in view of the gender participation gap in CS, the implications of those differences are significant: possible performance failures in early programming courses could lead young girls to prematurely reject a CS career believing, for example, that programming is 'not their thing'. A qualitative study would be useful in further examining this implication.

5.1 Threats to validity

A threat to the validity of our evaluation concerns the participants in our experiment, who might not be representative of all students or even of all students in our country. To mitigate this effect we ran the experiment in four groups from two different public schools. The schools were selected based on factors that are not relevant to the experiment (mainly, their proximity to the university).

Another threat to the validity of our results is the possible influence of the course tutors on the students, on their performance and on their beliefs about the stereotypical traits of computer scientists. While this effect cannot be measured, we compared the results obtained from the students that were taught by each author and found no significant differences in any of the metrics.

With respect to instruments used during the experiments, students might have been too young to understand the statements used for their self-assessment of stereotypical traits. During the courses, students asked for explanations regarding some traits (for example, for the social one), while we had to adjust the explanation of others to make them more understandable. For example, we had to explain the 'singularly focused' with the statement 'Programmers love programming and prefer it over other hobbies'. The same applies for the students' self-assessment of self-efficacy and motivation which was based on MSLQ, where they needed explanations for some of its statements. When explanations were needed, we ensured that we provided them to all four groups of the experiment. However, it was outside the scope of our study to create a verified self-efficacy assessment instrument for elementary school students.

6 CONCLUDING REMARKS

The goal of this paper is to examine what affects the learning performance of school-aged children during an introductory programming course, and whether the course or other factors could affect their CS career orientation. To this end, we taught a series of eight Scratch lessons to elementary school students, measuring their performance, self-efficacy and career orientation throughout the course.

We found the students' intrinsic and extrinsic motivation and previous programming experience to be important factors, being significantly correlated with their self-efficacy and their inclination towards a CS career. The students were not measured to believe to any of the documented stereotypes about computer scientists, which could be attributed to their young age. Our study highlighted gender differences, with the CS career orientation of female students being more related to their self-efficacy. We believe that, in view of the gender participation gap in CS, the implications of those differences are significant and worth exploring further through qualitative studies.

Our research gives rise to other directions for future work. Firstly, we intend to replicate these findings on a larger scale. An intermediate, but necessary, step towards this direction is devising self-assessment instruments for self-efficacy and motivation that are targeted to younger audiences.

ACKNOWLEDGMENTS

We would like to thank the teachers and students of the schools involved in this research. We are grateful for your support in organizing and giving the lessons.

REFERENCES

[1] Efthimia Aivaloglou, Felienne Hermans, Jesús Moreno-León, and Gregorio Robles. 2017. A Dataset of Scratch Programs: Scraped, Shaped and Scored. In *Proceedings of the 14th International Conference on Mining Software Repositories (MSR '17)*. IEEE Press, Piscataway, NJ, USA, 511–514. https://doi.org/10.1109/MSR.2017.45

[2] Christine Alvarado, Gustavo Umbelino, and Mia Minnes. 2018. The Persistent Effect of Pre-College Computing Experience on College CS Course Grades. In *Proceedings of the 49th ACM Technical Symposium on Computer Science Education (SIGCSE '18)*. ACM, New York, NY, USA, 876–881.

[3] Computing at School Working Group. 2012. *Computer Science: A Curriculum for Schools.*

[4] A. Bandura. 1977. Self-efficacy: toward a unifying theory of behavioral change. *Psychological review* 2, 84 (1977), 191–215.

[5] Shari L. Britner and Frank Pajares. 2006. Sources of science self-efficacy beliefs of middle school students. *Journal of Research in Science Teaching* 43, 5 (2006), 485–499.

[6] Marcus Credé and L. Alison Phillips. 2011. A meta-analytic review of the Motivated Strategies for Learning Questionnaire. *Learning and Individual Differences* 21, 4 (2011), 337 – 346.

[7] Alexandria K. Hansen, Hilary A. Dwyer, Ashley Iveland, Mia Talesfore, Lacy Wright, Danielle B. Harlow, and Diana Franklin. 2017. Assessing Children's Understanding of the Work of Computer Scientists: The Draw-a-Computer-Scientist Test. In *Proceedings of the 2017 ACM SIGCSE Technical Symposium on Computer Science Education (SIGCSE '17)*. ACM, New York, NY, USA, 279–284. https://doi.org/10.1145/3017680.3017769

[8] Felienne Hermans and Efthimia Aivaloglou. 2017. Teaching Software Engineering Principles to K-12 Students: A MOOC on Scratch. In *Proceedings of the 39th International Conference on Software Engineering: Software Engineering and Education Track*. IEEE Press, Piscataway, NJ, USA, 13–22.

[9] James Daniel Lee. 1998. Which Kids Can "Become" Scientists? Effects of Gender, Self-Concepts, and Perceptions of Scientists. *Social Psychology Quarterly* 61, 3 (1998), 199–219.

[10] Robert W Lent and Gail Hackett. 1987. Career self-efficacy: Empirical status and future directions. *Journal of Vocational Behavior* 30, 3 (1987), 347 – 382.

[11] Colleen M. Lewis, Ruth E. Anderson, and Ken Yasuhara. 2016. "I Don'T Code All Day": Fitting in Computer Science When the Stereotypes Don'T Fit. In *Proceedings of the 2016 ACM Conference on International Computing Education Research*. ACM, 23–32.

[12] Alex Lishinski, Aman Yadav, Jon Good, and Richard Enbody. 2016. Learning to Program: Gender Differences and Interactive Effects of Students' Motivation, Goals, and Self-Efficacy on Performance. In *Proceedings of the 2016 ACM Conference on International Computing Education Research*. ACM, 211–220.

[13] Orni Meerbaum-Salant, Michal Armoni, and Mordechai (Moti) Ben-Ari. 2010. Learning Computer Science Concepts with Scratch. In *Proceedings of the Sixth International Workshop on Computing Education Research*. ACM, 69–76.

[14] R. Paul, S. Smith, M. L. Genthon, G. G. Martens, C. L. Hauen, G. G. Martens, M. Genthon, and P. Wren. 1991. *Technical Report No. 91-B-004: A Manual for the Use of the Motivated Strategies for Learning Questionnaire (MSLQ)*. Technical Report. The Regents of The University of Michigan.

[15] Vennila Ramalingam, Deborah LaBelle, and Susan Wiedenbeck. 2004. Self-efficacy and Mental Models in Learning to Program. In *Proceedings of the 9th Annual SIGCSE Conference on Innovation and Technology in Computer Science Education*. ACM, 171–175.

[16] Kathryn M. Rich, Carla Strickland, T. Andrew Binkowski, Cheryl Moran, and Diana Franklin. 2017. K-8 Learning Trajectories Derived from Research Literature: Sequence, Repetition, Conditionals. In *Proceedings of the 2017 ACM Conference on International Computing Education Research (ICER '17)*. ACM, New York, NY, USA, 182–190.

[17] Mary Beth Rosson, John M. Carroll, and Hansa Sinha. 2011. Orientation of Undergraduates Toward Careers in the Computer and Information Sciences: Gender, Self-Efficacy and Social Support. *Trans. Comput. Educ.* 11, 3, Article 14 (Oct. 2011), 23 pages.

[18] Linda Seiter and Brendan Foreman. 2013. Modeling the Learning Progressions of Computational Thinking of Primary Grade Students. In *Proceedings of the Ninth Annual International ACM Conference on International Computing Education Research*. ACM, 59–66.

[19] Christopher Watson, Frederick W.B. Li, and Jamie L. Godwin. 2014. No Tests Required: Comparing Traditional and Dynamic Predictors of Programming Success. In *Proceedings of the 45th ACM Technical Symposium on Computer Science Education*. ACM, 469–474.

[20] Chris Wilcox and Albert Lionelle. 2018. Quantifying the Benefits of Prior Programming Experience in an Introductory Computer Science Course. In *Proceedings of the 49th ACM Technical Symposium on Computer Science Education (SIGCSE '18)*. ACM, New York, NY, USA, 80–85.

[21] Amanda Wilson, Thomas Hainey, and Thomas Connolly. 2012. Evaluation of computer games developed by primary school children to gauge understanding of programming concepts. In *European Conference on Games Based Learning*. Academic Conferences International Limited, 549.

The Academic Enhancement Program: Assessing Programs Designed to Support Student Success

Diana Cukierman
School of Computing Science
Simon Fraser University
Burnaby B.C. Canada
diana@sfu.ca

Donna McGee Thompson
Student Learning Commons
Simon Fraser University
Burnaby B.C. Canada
dmcthomp@sfu.ca

Wayne Sun
Institutional Research and Planning
Simon Fraser University
Burnaby B.C. Canada
wayne_sun@sfu.ca

ABSTRACT

The Academic Enhancement Program (AEP) aims to help students succeed in their post-secondary studies by incorporating learning strategies and academic reflection activities into core first-year Computing Science (CS). Initially offered in a single CS course at our institution, the AEP has since been run as a required component in several CS courses. It has also been adapted collaboratively in other universities, and is customizable to other disciplines with plans to expand into other departments. We have regularly evaluated AEP based on students', academic advisors' and instructors' perceptions to support the continual improvement of the program. The current study relied on both students' self-perception and course performance data in two sections of the same course, with the same instructor, contents, and exams, where only students in one section participated in the program. Employing linear regression, this study sought to determine what non-trivial factors account for student success, measured by final exam scores. We determined that 22% of the variance in student success measured by final exam scores can be accounted for by basis of admission, admission GPA, number of credits registered in, and a newly defined construct embodying student CS programming background experience. While our model did not include AEP as a predictive factor, we are encouraged that 77% of AEP participants said that they would continue to use study skills learned in AEP in future courses. Implications for further investigation of learning support programs are discussed.

KEYWORDS: Introductory computing science, Predictors of course success, Learning support programs, Measuring programs success, Measuring student satisfaction, Student Experience.

ACM Reference format:
Diana Cukierman, Donna McGee Thompson and Wayne Sun. 2019. The Academic Enhancement Program: Assessing Programs Designed to Support Student Success. In *Proceedings of 50th ACM Technical Symposium on Computer Science Education (SIGCSE '19), February 27-March 2, 2019, Minneapolis, MN, USA.* ACM, New York, NY, USA, 7 pages. https://doi.org/10.1145/3287324.3287422

ACM ISBN 978-1-4503-5890-3/19/02...$15.00
https://doi.org/10.1145/3287324.3287422

1 Introduction and Background

In our respective roles as a computing science instructor, learning specialist, and research analyst within a university, we believe that students entering post-secondary studies benefit from being exposed to learning concepts that allow them to gain awareness about academic undergraduate culture, learning techniques, and basic learning theory, including ways to cope with study demands within specific disciplines, such as CS. We also believe it is important for students to experience rich student-to-student interactions and start forming a support community early in their studies. Post-secondary institutions have recognized the importance of providing learning strategies instruction and offering opportunities for enhanced student experience. Many institutions, including our own university, offer learning strategies workshops and tutoring to support student success. More recently, campuses have also become increasingly concerned with "student experience", which our institution has defined as becoming more "student-focused and holistically supportive [and providing an] accessible, healthy learning environment where students feel a sense of belonging" [16]. Academic programs that are aligned with the principles of student experience consider the whole student when developing and delivering curriculum. These campus programs, usually delivered by student services or learning assistance centres, offer valuable opportunities for student support.

Discipline-oriented learning-strategy instruction models have also been developed in some academic institutions. Paired learning support complements particular university courses in which the learned strategies can be directly applied[1]. Examples of paired learning support include adjunct courses and supplemental instruction [1,10]. In supplemental instruction (SI), optional weekly review sessions are offered to students in courses with a high risk for failure. These sessions are facilitated by trained successful previous students, who integrate course-relevant study skills [18]. Paired learning support may be less common in computing science and engineering than in other disciplines. According to data on supplemental instruction courses, compiled from Spring 2002 to Fall 2013, only 2% of the 5686 supplemental instruction courses, delivered in the USA, were in computing science [9]. However, these studies reveal benefits similar to those reported in other disciplines, such as higher average grades for participants over non-participants; a contribution to lower attrition rates; and learning gains, especially for disadvantaged, at-risk, or high-risk students [11,12,17].

The Academic Enhancement Program (AEP) aims to create a disciplinary relevant experience for CS students by making learning strategies and academic reflection activities an integral part of courses. In its development and delivery, we have also intentionally made efforts to support the overall wellness of students. The AEP therefore has two primary interacting objectives: 1) enhanced academic performance, and 2) improved student experience (the AEP was recognized as one of two "2014 SFU Champions for a Healthy Campus Community). This paper focuses on a study we conducted in one component of the program - AEP 101 - to assess these two objectives of the program.

1.1 The Academic Enhancement Program

The Academic Enhancement Program supports the academic success of students in CS by incorporating at least one academic and learning strategies workshop or assignment into select lower division CS courses. The AEP focuses on "learning about learning", potentially scaffolding the development of transferable self-regulation, study, and organizational skills relevant to CS courses. The AEP (www.cs.sfu.ca/CC/AEP/) is a collaborative program between the School of Computing Science and the Student Learning Commons (SLC) at Simon Fraser University. The program is co-developed and co-coordinated by a teaching faculty member in the School of CS and a learning specialist from the SLC.

Our institution is a Canadian comprehensive university with a population of more than 35,000 students across three campuses. The School of Computing Science offers undergraduate, master's, and doctoral degrees and has more than 1,300 registered undergraduate majors. The SLC is an academic success centre that assists and supports students in their academic pursuits, providing writing and learning support. The AEP program has been running successfully in the School of Computing Science every semester since 2006, and more recently in Engineering Science (ES). In 2008, the CS undergraduate program committee approved the AEP as a required component of selected courses. To date, more than 5,000 students have participated in AEP activities. We developed the AEP in response to our concern, shared by Computing Science (CS) educators and academic advisors, that increasingly students are struggling in first-year post-secondary CS courses and are unfamiliar with learning and study strategies that will best support their academic success. However, the program is not meant as a remedial activity for selected students, rather it is incorporated into courses for all students, and course points are provided in agreement with the instructors. A key component of our model is that we bring the activities directly into the class. Often the students needing the most support do not have the time or impetus to attend workshops offered on campus (through the SLC, Career Services, and Health and Counselling Services, for example) on their own, or may not even be aware of such resources. While the program involves just one activity (either workshop session or report) per course per semester, students may participate in AEP activities in different courses across two or more semesters, hence providing the effect of an extended program, and offering opportunities to reinforce core concepts.

The AEP provides students with reflection and discussion opportunities in the form of either learning workshops or reflective writing activities, tailored to the needs of the class. Students are invited to reflect and to discuss among peers, with facilitation from trained learning and discipline specialists, on their current academic experience. These types of activities are rare in disciplines such as Computing Science or Engineering. It is also uncommon in these disciplines to have dialogue and reflection opportunities among peers in small groups or with faculty especially in first-year courses as they typically have high enrollments, and these types of courses are not oriented around reflective discussion. It may therefore be especially important to deliver such programs within these disciplines. To date we have developed three workshops (AEP 101, AEP 102 and AEP 103) tailored to different courses and focusing on different aspects of learning and academic wellness topics. The AEP also provides the option of an "Assignment" component that encourages students to learn and reflect about a topic of their choice related to student success, wellness and connected to their discipline of study. The assignment allows that all students in the course may participate in an AEP activity, even those that may not have been able to attend a workshop session. There is only one intervention per course, be it a course-associated workshop or the elective assignment. Students receive course marks for these activities, up to 3% of the course grade, in agreement with the course instructor. We also suggest optional related activities to do in class to reinforce concepts seen in the AEP activity.

1.2 AEP 101 Workshop

AEP 101 is a two-hour academic and learning strategies workshop tailored to the course contents. The workshop is offered multiple times to allow students to attend a time that fits within their schedule. In the case of scheduling conflicts with the AEP 101 workshop sessions, students are encouraged to complete the AEP Assignment referred to above. The workshop is run by two co-facilitators, one a specialist in learning, and the other a CS faculty member or CS graduate student (who may or not be the course instructor) in a small group setting of up to 30 students. Facilitators briefly present materials and guide highly participatory activities related to time- and self-management, and using appropriate study strategies for CS programming courses. We begin AEP 101 by presenting students the "Ladder to Success", a framework to guide learners through five steps for successively addressing academic barriers: (1)The first step is 'Identification' of barriers and attribution of problems to controllable factors. (2) Next is 'Planning', in particular, adoption of time management strategies. (3) Then comes the 'Study Strategies' component, in which we introduce students to a series of processes for learning CS concepts, including reiterative problem solving. We stress that in programming courses, even at an introductory level, students need to apply more sophisticated learning strategies than memorization, which may be adequate in other disciplines. We also stress the variety and range of complexity in questions and skills that are part of the course learning outcomes and in general in the discipline, and correspondingly we encourage students to adopt a range of study strategies. (4) The proactive 'Help seeking' step invites students to dialogue and share ideas to solve concrete situations within the university context and identify other resources for help. (5) The 'Reflection' step concludes the workshop, and invites students to visualize the whole Ladder to Success framework as adaptable to addressing challenges in general through successive iterations of the process. For more details about the AEP we refer the reader to [6,7,8] and the AEP website www.cs.sfu.ca/CC/AEP/.

1.3 Rationale to do this study

While we have regularly evaluated AEP based on student surveys and interviews with academic advisors and instructors, no experimental study has been performed to determine causal effects of AEP or other factors. However, we have received very positive feedback including anecdotal evidence that students keep applying strategies learned at AEP years after [7,8]. This inspired an initial linear regression analysis [6] to obtain quantitative evidence for potential predictors. Recent studies have found that predictors of success in first-year CS courses include having good comfort level, mathematical background, programming background, self-efficacy in the discipline, and self-attribution of success to luck (the latter being negatively correlated) [15,14,4,3]. Background has been measured testing students with early i-clicker quizzes and with early course surveys [13,19]. Students' achievement goals have also been investigated as predictors of success within multi-institutional studies [19]. The present study hopes to further develop our earlier model [6] and discover non-trivial predictors of introductory CS course success, with predictors based on students' self-perception. We also specifically seek to provide additional evidence for success of the AEP. Having two sections of the same course offered simultaneously by the same instructor allowed for the evaluation of AEP, which is in direct response to the call for further CS education research studies. (e.g. [5])

2. Method

This study was conducted following a quasi-experimental design using natural groups with pre-test and post-test analysis. Predictor variables were discovered via linear regression modelling, while results of student perceptions from course surveys are presented. A CS1 course offered in the Fall of 2017 comprised of two class sections (D100 and D200) provided us the opportunity to design a "quasi experimental" study. Both sections were taught by the same instructor, first author of this paper, therefore the study and analysis should not be affected by an instructor effect. The learning objectives, class materials, exercises, assignments, quiz, midterm, and final exam were essentially identical; the final exam was taken by all the students at the same time. The quiz, midterm and final exam were of similar difficulty. The quiz had a weighting of 5%, the midterm 10% and the final exam 49%, for both groups. Students enrolled in the D100 course section were offered the opportunity to participate in AEP (a weighting of 2% for the course), but could for whatever reason choose not to complete AEP activities. To compensate for the difference in percentages in the course, D100 had assignments weigh 26% of the course, while D200 had their assignments weigh 28%. The choice of which section to assign AEP activities was random, without knowledge of section composition. The AEP activities were placed after the quiz and before the midterm. The students in our control group were in the D200 class section. They were not provided an AEP option nor assigned any alternative activity or assignment. Both courses were marked separately, but were marked by the same team of teaching assistants and instructor, with identical rubrics.

Table 1: Timeline of Class Section

D100	Beg Sem Survey	Quiz (pre-test, week 6)	AEP (week 7)	Survey End Sem	Final Exam (post-test)
D200	Beg Sem Survey	Quiz (pre-test, week 6)		Survey End Sem	Final Exam (post-test)

Students were categorized into two distinct groups: 1) those who completed AEP activities (YesAEP), and 2) those who did not complete any AEP activities (NoAEP). There did not appear to be any biased difference in the thirteen students who did not participate in AEP but who were offered to do the activity. As such, these students were included in the NoAEP group.

Table 2: Completion of AEP Activities by Course Section

Section	YesAEP	NoAEP
D100	170	13
D200	-	175
Grand Total	170	188

In order to evaluate AEP and determine whether or not it was a factor in predicting final exam score, this categorization was used within a linear regression model. Final course grade was not used as the outcome as this grade included group work, which would be difficult to separate on an individual student basis. We aimed to use final exam score as our outcome measure, although we also investigated other self-perception measures obtained from surveying students. There are many possible factors that may account for the variance in the final exam score [3,14,15]. Our study takes CS background experience into consideration as a predictor when assessing AEP. The definition of background experience is complex and can be subjective. As such, it was decided that the results from a combination of three questions from a survey conducted at the beginning of the course would be used to determine a student's background experience in the subject matter. The questions used to form the CS background construct are:

Question 1: Do I have programming experience?
- None,
- Less than 5 hours,
- More than 5, less than 30 hours,
- More than 30, less than 100 hours,
- More than 100 hours

Question 2: When was it the last time that I did any programming?
- I never did any programming,
- Within the last two months,
- Within the last two semesters,
- Within the last 2 years,
- More than 2 years ago

Question 3: What do I feel about my background in Computing Science and Programming?
- I have a very strong background,
- I have medium or basic background,
- I had quite a good background but I have forgotten a lot,
- I feel comfortable using my computer (laptop / smartphone / iPad, etc.) but I have very weak (or almost none) background in programming,
- I am not too comfortable using a computer (laptop / smartphone, etc.) and I have very weak (or almost none) background in programming

Based on the answers to these questions, students were categorized into the following background experience groups:
1. No background experience
2. Weak background experience
3. Medium background experience
4. Strong background experience
5. Exclude from project[1]

Completion of this survey was voluntary and therefore not all students were assigned a background experience. Only those students with an assigned background are included in the analysis. Due to the number of students with Medium or Strong background experience, this information was included in the linear regression model as a categorical variable. Students were classified into two groups: 1) No or Weak background experience and 2) Medium or Strong background experience. Other student demographic information was obtained from the university's Student Information Management System to be used in determining which non-trivial variables may account for the variance in final exam scores. These variables included: Basis of admission (Secondary vs. Post-secondary), Admission GPA, Gender, Citizenship (Domestic vs. International), Age as at September 1, 2017, Student Year Level, Number of Credits Registered in Fall 2017, Computing Science Major. Note also that the survey was conducted as a confidential survey, allowing only our Institutional Research and Planning (IRP) department to link student demographic data with background experience. The instructor was only provided the list of students who completed the surveys, allowing her to give students 0.5% course bonus points for participating in the questionnaire. Additional analysis was completed on the beginning of term survey as well as a survey administered at an end of the term. These surveys provide additional details about how students learn and what activities assist in their learning. SAS Enterprise Guide was used to perform a backward elimination linear regression analysis on the variables described above using a 95% confidence level threshold. It should be noted that there are unknown or unmeasured factors that may have an effect on the final exam score. Because these factors could not be included in the analysis, the model has limited utility for prediction. If these unknown factors had been included in the model, they might have changed the results.

[1] Since students are able to answer these questions however they choose, this category was created to capture answers to the three survey questions that are not logical. For example, it would not seem logical for a student to answer 'None' to the question of 'Do I have programming experience?', 'I never did any programming' to the question 'When was it the last time that I did any programming?', and 'I have a very strong background' to the question 'What do I feel about my background in Computing Science and Programming?'

3. Results

Aside from participation in AEP activities, there are differences in the student composition between the two groups within this study, especially within the variables under consideration for modelling.

Table 3: Demographic Data by Group

	YesAEP	NoAEP
Average Admission GPA[2]	3.99	3.66
Secondary School Basis of Admission	93%	70%
Computing Science Major	64%	30%
International Citizenship	11%	21%
Medium or Strong Background Experience	24%	13%
Students in 2nd or 3rd year	16%	42%
New student[3]	69%	39%

This study was not able to control for the differences between the two groups since there was no absolute method to ensure that AEP was presented to randomly selected individuals. While this is not ideal, the study was conducted in the best possible manner given the constraints of the registration system. This study does however follow principles dealing with nonequivalent control groups. By examining the quiz scores we observe that there is no statistically significant difference between the two groups (i.e. they are similar

[2] Based on a 4.33 GPA scale.

[3] New student refers to an individual who was not previously a student in our university, was admitted with a Secondary School basis of admission, and did not have any transfer credits.

with respect to quiz scores: YesAEP: 62.6%, NoAEP: 60.3%). Additionally, final exam scores show that there is a statistically significant difference (YesAEP: 70.5%, NoAEP: 63.3%). With these pre-test and post-test results, we have confidence in possibly attributing variance of final exam to the AEP. Furthermore, using a two sample T-test we observe that the difference between pre-test and post-test scores (with averages YesAEP: 7.9% and NoAEP: 3.0%) is significant. In particular, and as expected, the construct that we defined based on survey responses to measure students' CS background proved to be a strong predictor of final exam scores. As shown in Table 4, students who were categorized as having strong background in CS (given their responses) performed better than those that did not, regardless of which group of students (YesAEP or NoAEP) they were in. Using Two-Sample t-Tests *within each student group* we are able to confirm our intuition.

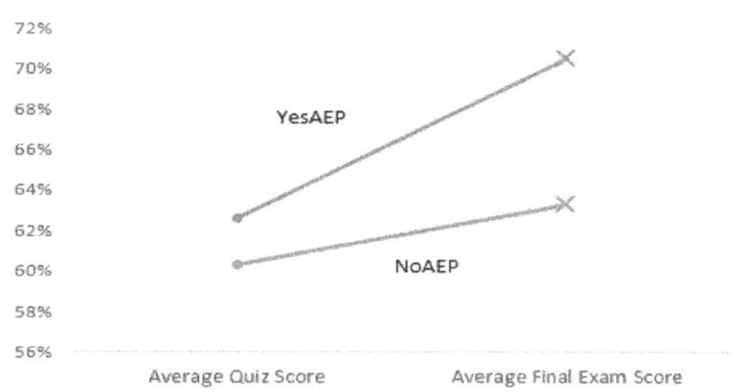

Figure 1: Pre-test and Post-test Analysis

Table 4: Average Final Exam Score by Background Experience and Student Group

Background Experience	YesAEP	NoAEP
No or Weak Background	66.6%	61.6%
Medium or Strong Background	83.2%	75.2%

However, using Two-Sample t-Tests between student groups *within each background category,* we did not find any evidence that suggests that the difference in final exam scores between the groups of students is statistically significant. Based on the analysis above, there is clearly some factor(s) that are affecting final exam score besides background experience. Using linear regression we were able to combine both categorical and continuous variables to determine which factor(s) account for the variance within final exam score. There is evidence that some factor(s) between these two groups are significant predictors on final exam scores. The linear regression model resulted in an R^2 of 0.2177, indicating that this overall model accounts for 22% of the variance in final exam score. Final exam scores (graded out of 62) were converted to a percentage for a scale out of 100%. The model indicates that with 95% confidence:

• Secondary school basis of admission has a negative impact on the final exam score. This is intuitive as secondary school students have no university level experience, which may affect their performance.

• For every point increase in admission GPA (4.33 scale), there is a 27% increase in final exam score on average.

• Having medium or strong background experience will increase final exam score by 13% on average.

• For every one credit increase in registration, there is a 1% increase in final exam score on average. While initially this may seem counterintuitive, students who take more credits are more likely to be full-time students who can place more attention and focus on their studies.

3.1 Selected results about Survey questions

Based on these results, AEP is not a predictor of final exam score. However, student perceptions of the program may reveal that AEP has some impact on student study habits or add value to their academic experiences. Here we consider responses to the surveys conducted at the beginning and at the end of the term. While both groups of respondents felt less confident or supported at the end of the course compared to the beginning, YesAEP respondents felt slightly more academically supported at the institution (YesAEP: 59% Strongly agreed/Agreed at the beginning vs. 51% Strongly agreed/Agreed at the end), compared to NoAEP: (61% Strongly agreed/Agreed at the beginning vs. 44% Strongly agreed/Agreed at the end). Additionally, YesAEP respondents remained confident in their ability to develop positive study strategies (67% Strongly agreed/Agreed at the beginning vs. 66% Strongly agreed/Agreed at the end), while NoAEP respondents felt less confident (63% Strongly agreed/Agreed at the beginning vs. 55% Strongly agreed/Agreed at the end). Differences between beginning of term and end of term responses are significantly different. Additionally, over 44% of YesAEP respondents Strongly agreed/Agreed that being aware of and reflecting about topics discussed in the AEP workshop or report helped them improve as a student in the course as well as in general. Another positive result we discovered, is that 77% of YesAEP respondents said that they will continue to use study skills learned in AEP in future courses. The drop in student perceptions of the course and their university experience satisfaction by student group is much higher in NoAEP compared to YesAEP (as shown in Figure 3). In the end of term survey, 73% of NoAEP respondents Strongly agreed/Agreed that they need to improve their study strategies and 52% would like to participate in study strategies/academic wellness workshops in the future.

4. Discussion

Systematically examining educational programs such as the AEP and the possible effects of such programs is important to furthering continual development of CS education. Designing true experiments in the classroom is challenging since random assignment to different educational programs may not be possible or desirable. This study was implemented within the parameters of the registration system; we implemented a quasi experiment to take advantage of the naturally formed two sections of an introductory CS and programming course. With this design we intended to support that the AEP may have a possible causal effect on students' final exam scores. We also conducted a linear regression to confirm which variables may explain variances in student success. Students in the two sections differed on several factors and these non-trivial differences may or may not have impacted their course success. Nonetheless, using pre-test and post-test analysis we determined that students were not significantly different at least on quiz results, which we used as a pre-test measure. As a post-test measure we used the final exam scores, where the exam took place after the intervention (AEP). The final exam scores differed significantly between the two groups. Thus the study followed principles dealing with nonequivalent control groups, and given the pre-test and post-test scores observed we can confidently say that the group exposed to the AEP program improved in their test results significantly more than the group that was not exposed (Figure 1 above). Given these observations, we have confidence in possibly attributing variance of final exam scores to the AEP.

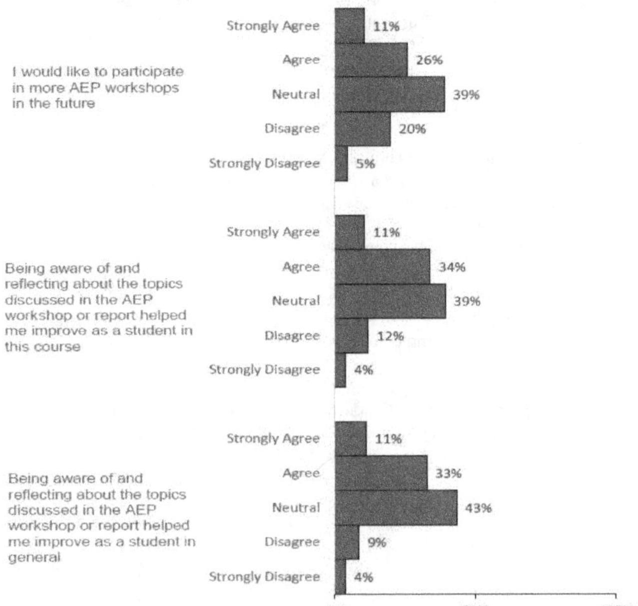

Figure 2: AEP Experience for Respondents from Course Section D100 who Completed AEP Activities

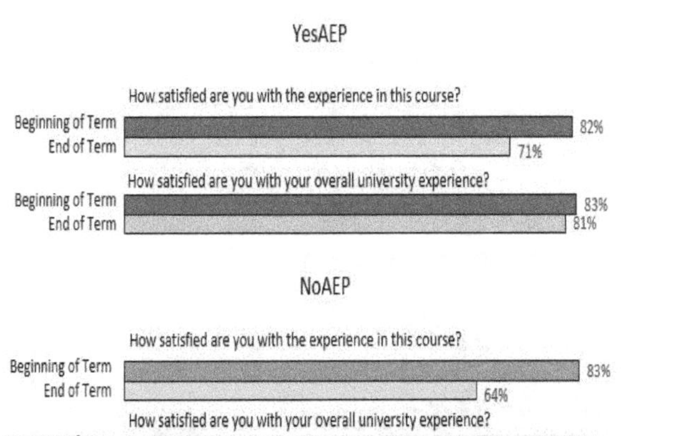

Figure 3: Student Perceptions at the Beginning and End of Term by Student Group (Percentage of Very Satisfied/Satisfied Respondents)

Performing a linear regression allowed us to confirm that 22% of variance in final exam scores can be explained by admission GPA, background experience, number of credits registered in, and being admitted from a secondary school. "Background experience" is a construct that we newly defined and included in the linear regression. We defined this construct embodying background in computing sciences and programming with a scale that was derived from responses to self-perception student surveys.

If a student has a medium or strong background as we defined it, then on average final exam scores would increase by 13% with respect to no or low background. AEP, while not a predictor, still holds value to students through positive perceptions and anecdotal evidence. Given that the goal of AEP is to have long-term effects, we are encouraged that 77% of respondents said that they will continue to use study skills learned in AEP in future courses. Selected excerpts from students include:

"... I have encountered some solutions to a very common issue that affects my study habits: the lack of concentration. I have learned the possible causes of this problem and also some solutions that I [will] certainly put into practice..."

"Overall, I really think that this exercise has been very useful. ...The workshop was very good. ...I shall go to more workshops in the future, not necessarily just for an AEP assignment, but for my own learning."

"...showed me that I had neglected something which I hadn't really thought of as a need...I now realize that I can't simply neglect my entire personal life for academic. Personal balance is a complement to academic success."

We also observed that student satisfaction with the course and university (a very subjective perception) dropped from the beginning of the semester to the end of the semester. Very interestingly, however, we observe that the levels of NoAEP respondents dropped by a larger percentage compared to YesAEP respondents (Figure 3). This result encourages us to further investigate the significance of these lower satisfaction scores, perhaps attenuated by the AEP, and possibly revise our constructs to more easily measure statistical significance. We acknowledge that this study has its limitations, as we were not able to randomly assign which students were exposed to AEP activities and were therefore not able to conduct a true experiment. In addition, it should be noted that there are many other unknown or unmeasurable factors that may have an effect on the final exam score. Because these factors could not be included in the analysis, the model has limited utility for prediction. If these unknown factors had been included in the model, they might have changed the results. Naturally, we endorse further investigation of the AEP to discover other non-trivial predictor variables to provide more evidence that these types of learning interventions accomplish their objectives. The fact that students report that they will persist with the skills acquired in AEP, presents opportunities for longitudinal studies to measure long-term effects and whether future success can be attributed to AEP. We are also interested in determining if discipline is significant with respect to the success of students or whether subject matter is irrelevant for AEP activities. While this study did present results from student perceptions via survey analysis, it may be valuable to expand survey questions to obtain more quantifiable data for significance testing. Focus groups of students may be beneficial for these purposes.

REFERENCES

[1] D. Arendale. 2002. History of supplemental instruction (SI): Mainstreaming of developmental education. In D. B. Lundell and J. L. Higbee (Eds.), Histories of Developmental Education. Minneapolis, MN: Center for Research on Developmental Education and Urban Literacy, General College, University of Minnesota, USA15-27

[2] L.J. Barker, C. McDowell, K. Kalahar. 2009. Exploring Factors that Influence Computer Science Introductory Course Students to Persist in The Major. In Proceedings of SIGCSE '09, Proceedings of the 40th ACM technical symposium on Computer science education, Chatanooga, Tenessee, ACM, USA, 153-157.

[3] P. Byrne, G. Lyons. 2001. The effect of Student Attributes on Success in Programming. Proceedings of the 6th annual conference on Innovation and technology in computer science education, ACM. Canterbury, UK, 49-52

[4] W. B. Cantwell, S. Shrock. 2001. Contributing to Success in an Introductory Computer Science Course: A study of Twelve Factors. Proceedings of SIGCSE 2001: Proceedings of the thirty-second SIGCSE technical symposium on Computer Science Education, Charlotte, NC, USA: ACM, 184-188

[5] M. Craig. 2018. Scholarly Evaluation of Teaching Interventions in Computer Science. (Keynote Presentation) WCCCE 2018, Western Canadian Conference on Computing Science Education. Victoria, B.C., Canada

[6] D. Cukierman. 2015. Predicting Success in University First Year Computing Science Courses: The Role of Student Participation in Reflective Learning Activities and in I-clicker Activities. ITiCSE 2015: Proceedings of the 2015 ACM Conference on Innovation and Technology in Computer Science Education. ACM. Vilnius, Lithuania, 248-253

[7] D. Cukierman, and D. McGee Thompson. 2009. "The Academic Enhancement Program: Encouraging Students to Learn about Learning as Part of their Computing Science Courses", ACM SIGCSE Bulletin, 41(3), 171-175, September 2009. Also Proceedings of ITICSE 2009, 14th Annual Conference on Innovation and Technology in Computer Science Education, Paris, France, July 2009: ACM

[8] R. Egan, D. Cukierman, and D. McGee Thompson. 2011. The Academic Enhancement Program in Introductory CS: A Workshop Framework Description and Evaluation. Proceedings of Iticse 2011, 16th Annual Conference on Innovation and Technology in Computer Science Education, Darmstadt, Germany: ACM, 278-282

[9] S. Guloy , F. Salimi, D. Cukierman, D. McGee Thompson. 2017. Insights on supporting learning during computing science and engineering students' transition to university: A design-oriented, mixed methods exploration of instructor and student perspectives. Higher Education Journal. Special Issue: Transition to Higher Education, DOI: 10.1007/s10734-016-0097-6: Springer, 479-497

[10] J.L. Higbee, D.R. Arendale, D.B. Lundell. 2005. Using theory and research to improve access and retention in developmental education. New Directions for Community Colleges, 2005(129), 5-15.

[11] J. Malm, L. Bryngfors, L. L. Mörner. 2012. Supplemental instruction for improving first year results in engineering studies. Studies in Higher Education, 37(6), 655-666.

[12] A. McCarthy, B. Smuts, M. Cosser. 1997. Assessing the effectiveness of supplemental instruction: A critique and a case study. Studies in Higher Education, 22(2), 221-231.

[13] L. Porter, D. Zingaro, R. Lister.2014. Predicting student success using fine grain clicker data. ICER 2014 - Proceedings of the 10th Annual International Conference on International Computing Education Research. 10.1145/2632320.2632354.51-58

[14] N. Rountree, J. Rountree, A. Robins, and R. Hanna . 2004. Interacting Factors that Predict Success and Failure in a CS1 Course. INROADS, The SIGCSE Bulletin. 36(4): ACM, 101-104

[15] Simon, S. Fincher , A. Robins , B. Baker, I. Box, Q. Cutts, M. de Raadt, P. Haden , J. Hamer, M. Hamilton & R. Lister , M. Petre , K. Sutton, & D. Tolhurst, and J. Tutty. 2006. Predictors of Success in a First Programming Course. Proceedings of ACE 2006, Australasian Computing Education Conference, Conferences in Research and Practice in Information Technology, 52: Australian Computer Society, Inc.189-196

[16] Student Experience Initiative, Simon Fraser University. https://www.sfu.ca/vpacademic/SEI.html. Accessed 1 December 2018

[17] T. J. Webster, K. C. Dee. 1998. Supplemental instruction integrated into an introductory engineering course. Journal of Engineering Education, 87(4), 377-383.

[18] G.E. Widmar. 1994. Supplemental Instruction: From small beginnings to a national program. In D. C. Martin & Arendale, D. R. (Eds.), Supplemental Instruction: Increasing achievement and retention. Jossey-Bass, 3-10.

[19] D. Zingaro, M. Craig, L. Porter, B. A. Becker, Y. Cao, P. Conrad, D. Cukierman, A Hellas, D. Loksa, N. Thota. 2018. Achievement Goals in CS1: Replication and Extension, in Proceedings of SIGCSE 2018 the 49th ACM Technical Symposium on Computer Science Education, February 2018, Baltimore, Maryland, USA, 687-692.

Speed and Studying: Gendered Pathways to Success

Iman YeckehZaare
University of Michigan School of Information
Ann Arbor, MI
oneweb@umich.edu

Paul Resnick
University of Michigan School of Information
Ann Arbor, MI
presnick@umich.edu

ABSTRACT

In an introductory Python programming course intended for non-majors with little prior CS experience, with 85 male and 108 female students, we were able to capture electronic traces of students' studying and problem-solving. There was no significant difference in final exam scores by gender but we found that female students spent 12.1 more hours studying over the semester while male students on average earned 2.7 more points per hour of solving problem set questions over the first half of the semester. We were able to capture their learning behavior because students studied using the Runestone interactive textbook and completed weekly problem sets in the same platform for the first half of the semester. We analyzed these logs to determine three quantities for each student. One is study time, as measured by total use of Runestone outside of weekly assignments. The second is speed, as measured by the number of points students earned per hour working on problem sets. The third is earliness, as measured by how far before the deadlines they worked on weekly assignments. We conclude that male students were faster at completing problem sets early in the semester but that female students found an alternative pathway to success.

CCS CONCEPTS

• **Social and professional topics → Model curricula**; **Gender**;

KEYWORDS

Diversity, Gender, Programming, Procrastination, Technology Skills, Education, Interactive Textbook

ACM Reference Format:
Iman YeckehZaare and Paul Resnick. 2019. Speed and Studying: Gendered Pathways to Success. In *Proceedings of the 50th ACM Technical Symposium on Computer Science Education (SIGCSE '19), February 27-March 2, 2019, Minneapolis, MN, USA.* ACM, New York, NY, USA, 6 pages. https://doi.org/10.1145/3287324.3287417

1 INTRODUCTION

Recently, numerous studies in SIGCSE and other venues have expressed their concerns about women's declining enrollment and increasing dropouts in computer science related courses and their involvement in the technology industry. They have also proposed methods to make teaching and curriculum design more gender-inclusive and initiated programs to foster women's success in technology-related fields [1, 3, 6, 10, 14, 21].

Computer Research Association (CRA) reported that in 2017, women accounted for only 19.0% of students who were awarded a computer science Bachelor's degree, 12.6% in computer engineering, and 25.0% in information sciences [22]. Similarly, a recent *New York Times* article [8] highlighted gender discrimination in the tech companies and reported among employees under 25, women's average salary is 29% less than men. More broadly, women hold only 11% of administrative positions and ownership of only 5% of technology-oriented start-ups in Silicon Valley. More importantly, women leave their career in the technology industry at a rate of 41%, which is twice as men's quitting rate. Many who leave jobs cite workplace culture issues [18].

In a study on 1,319 first-year undergraduate students with twice as many women as men, Beyer [2] discovered a positive effect of students' judgment of their first programming course instructor and pedagogical practices on taking more computer science courses. More importantly, they found significant correlations between a higher possibility of taking programming courses with higher technology self-efficacy and engagement in computer science; and lower conscientiousness, openness to experiences, and social relationships. They encourage instructors, curriculum designers, and business owners to consider these factors in improving gender-inclusiveness in computer science courses and technology-related careers. From another point of view, Harrington et al. [7] asked students to predict their grade as a bonus question at the end of the final exam and found that on average students overestimate their grades. However, although female and male students achieved similar exam grades, women underpredicted their grades more than men, which may be a reason for their higher dropouts.

Throughout six years of longitudinal study on 672 participants, Brainard and Carlin [4] identified the difficulty to find women role models in computing careers, separation from learning communities, and inappropriate instructions as main factors contributing to women's high attrition rate in engineering programs. Besides, other studies have found the reason in a common belief of inferior family-life among computer engineering practitioners. Rheingans et al. [14] report on the success of the CWIT Scholar program to empower female students through developing supportive communities of women who collaborate to improve technology education among female students.

From another perspective, Murphy et al. [11], in a study of those graduated with a computing major, found that because female in comparison with male students had less pre-college programming experience, introduction to computer science related courses were more challenging for them, though they caught up over time. Other

SIGCSE '19, February 27-March 2, 2019, Minneapolis, MN, USA

ACM ISBN 978-1-4503-5890-3/19/02...$15.00
https://doi.org/10.1145/3287324.3287417

studies [9, 10, 17, 19] have also reported women's lower pre-college computer science background in comparison with men.

It is less clear from the prior literature whether differences in performance between male and female students persist in those courses that have taken active steps to reduce stereotype threat and make the course environment more interesting to and supportive of female students. It is also less clear from the prior literature whether, in courses that have erased gender gaps in enrollment, there are systematic differences by gender in the behaviors of students. For example, are female students more conscientious in starting assignments earlier or completing problem sets? Do they spend more time studying? And if there are such differences, do they help female students to compensate for less prior knowledge, confidence, or interest in computing?

We have a unique opportunity to answer these questions, based on data from a course at the University of Michigan, School of Information that has consistently attracted roughly equal numbers of male and female students. An interactive textbook automatically captured indicators of behaviors such as starting early on problem sets, completing problems quickly, and total time studying. We conduct a mediation analysis to test whether these factors vary by gender and whether they explain differences in exam performance. We conclude that although male and female students had approximately equal success in the course, they followed somewhat different paths to success.

2 LEARNING ENVIRONMENT AND TECHNOLOGY USED

We report on an introductory Python programming course in Winter 2018. The course is geared toward students who do not intend to major in computer science, and most but not all students have no prior programming experience. It serves a pre-requisite for an upper-division major that involves additional programming courses but much less than typical computer science majors. The course also serves many other non-CS majors from around the campus.

2.1 Course Design

In addition to the fundamentals of Python programming, this course introduces students to the fields of information science and human-computer interaction. Furthermore, it covers the foundations of retrieving data from the Internet, manipulating and storing data, open-source software development, and redundancy and compression. For final projects, students were expected to write a program that downloads data from at least two sources (e.g., from Twitter, the *New York Times*, or a weather site) and combine and present it in some creative way.

The course has been designed and administered with a view toward making it attractive to both male and female students. Students are encouraged to work with others on problem sets. Multiple group office hours every week and random assignment to groups in weekly discussion sections facilitate study group formation. Music, art, and language are as likely to show up in programming tasks as are math or sports. We have encouraged diverse students to apply for instructional assistant positions, in order to serve as role models. Grades are assigned on an absolute scale rather than a curve so that there is no need for students to compete with each other. Few students drop out or fail. The course has grown to about 200 students per semester, with female students making up 49.8% of all enrollments from 2013-2017. Female students continued on to second-level programming courses at equal or higher rates than male students.

The pedagogy is based on active learning. Students are expected to study specific sections of a textbook prior to attending lectures. Both lectures and discussions involve frequent opportunities for students to answer questions and interact with each other. Furthermore, the textbook itself provides many interaction opportunities, as described in Section 2.3.

2.2 Student Demographics

- **Gender**: 85 (44.04%) male and 108 (55.96%) female.
- **English speakers**: 150 (77.77%) natives and 43 (22.28%) non-native speakers.
- **Ethnicity**: 120 (62.18%) white, 48 (24.87%) Asian, and 25 (12.95%) other ethnicities.
- **First term of enrollment at the university**: 38 (19.69%) enrolled in 2014 or earlier, 28 (14.51%) in 2015, 52 (26.94%) in 2016, and 75 (38.86%) in 2017 or 2018.
- **Parents' highest degree**: 42 (21.76%) Doctorate, 73 (37.82%) Masters, 47 (24.35%) Bachelors, 31 (16.06%) others.

2.3 The Runestone Interactive Textbook

The Runestone Interactive textbook[1] is an open-source platform that enables authors to create interactive textbooks and instructors to assemble assignments from those interactive elements. More than 20,000 students a day use it worldwide in over 600 high schools and colleges [2]. As with any webpage, a textbook page can include text, images, videos, and external links. Pages can also include interactive elements, such as [5]:

- Multiple choice questions;
- Fill-in-the-blank questions;
- Mixed up code problems (Parsons problems) where students have to rearrange code blocks in the correct order and with the correct indentation;
- Step-by-step code execution simulations, where students can be asked to predict the impact of various steps;
- Active code boxes where students can edit and run code.

These interactive elements provide students with immediate feedback. For example, the active code boxes can include "unit tests" that tell the student whether the code they executed does what the code was supposed to do. Assignments consist of collections of these interactive elements where the students' actions are graded. The system logs student actions, including a timestamp for each page load and a timestamp when the student submits each problem set question.

3 MEASURES AND MODEL

Our primary interest is in assessing whether there are systematic differences in activity patterns in the course between male and female students, whether those explain any differences in exam

[1] http://runestoneinteractive.org/

[2] http://runestoneinteractive.org/about.html

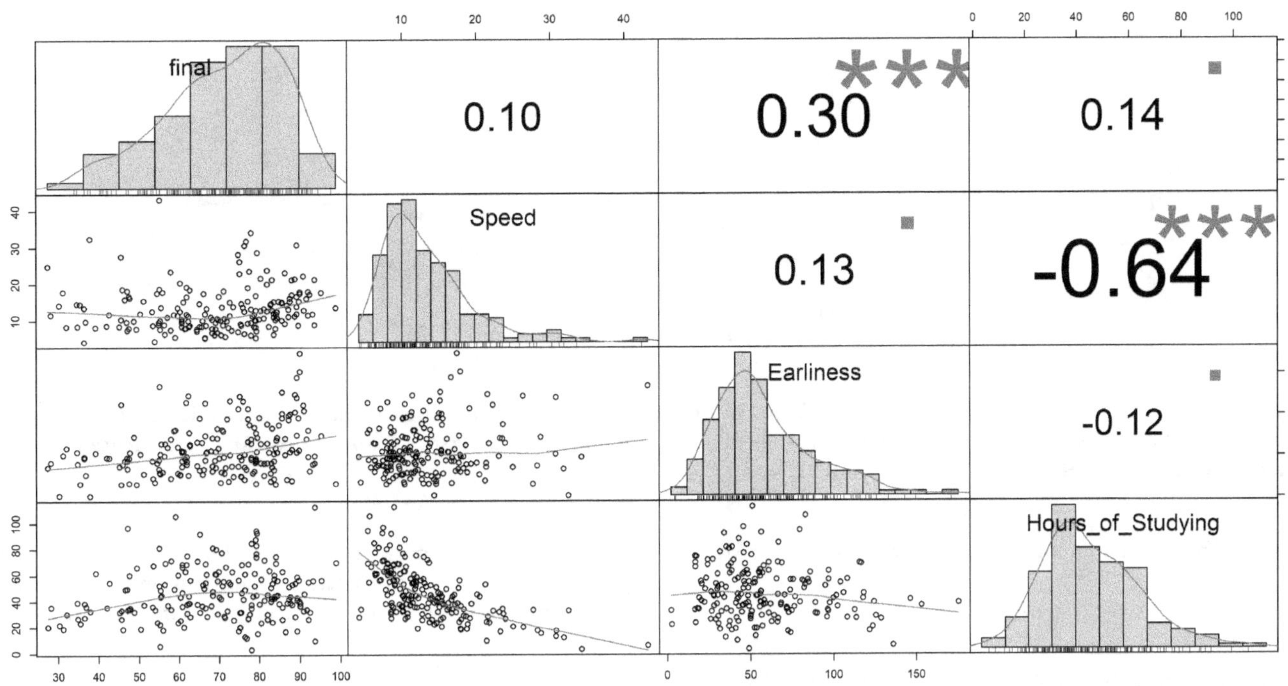

Figure 1: Correlation matrix between numerical variables, with their distributions [12]. Distributions and names of variables are located on the diagonal of the diagram. Each number indicates the correlation between the variables on the corresponding row and column. Stars indicate the significance level of each correlation (. : $P \leq 0.1$, * : $P \leq 0.05$, ** : $P \leq 0.01$, * * * : $P \leq 0.001$).

performance, and whether there is any residual difference in exam performance between male and female students. We begin by describing our measures, and then describe the statistical models that we will estimate.

3.1 Measures

Figure 1 shows correlations among the following four measures[3]:

Hours of Studying. We started the timer for a "session" with each page load. We marked the end of a session when another page was loaded or after five minutes without a logged interaction on the page; thus, our measure of session length probably slightly overestimates some of the sessions that actually ended after less than five minutes. There was also a review practice tool that re-presented past problems to students; we similarly calculated sessions lengths for the use of the practice tool. We then added up the time in all the sessions for each student, excluding the pages for problem sets.

The distribution of the total number of hours each student spent on studying the textbook over the semester was: Mean 45.966; Range [2.998, 112.398]; Quartiles 32.106, 43.709, 57.219.

Speed. We define a student's speed as the number of points earned per hour of working on problem sets, i.e., how fast each student found the correct answers to the problem sets. Since some session lengths may be slightly overestimated, the points per hour may be slightly underestimated. Each problem set was worth 100 points; most students earned all or almost all the points. A faster speed may indicate greater facility with the material (completing the questions faster) but may also be an indicator of less thoroughness in working through concepts rather than just rushing to get answers.

The first five weekly problems sets were administered in the Runestone environment; after that, the instructor moved the problem sets out of RuneStone to a complete Python environment. Thus, speed is only measured for the first five problem sets.

The distribution of problem set points per hour was: Mean 13.287; Range [0.000, 43.188]; Quartiles 8.812, 11.765, 16.008.

Earliness. We encouraged students to work toward a soft deadline of Friday afternoons but offered a two-day grace period. We computed a measure of how far in advance of the Sunday hard deadline students worked. For each code run that the student submitted for any problem in a problem set, we computed the number of hours between that action and the deadline for that problem set. We then averaged over all code runs. We interpret earliness as a good study habit, the reverse of procrastination. Again, this was computed only for the first five problem sets, where actions were recorded in Runestone.

The distribution of earliness was: Mean 58.028, Range [2.268, 175.420]; Quartiles 36.994, 50.777, 73.310.

Final exam grade. The final exam was administered as a pencil and paper exam, with multiple choice, short answer, and coding

[3]We have conducted all the analysis in R language [13] using RStudio software [16].

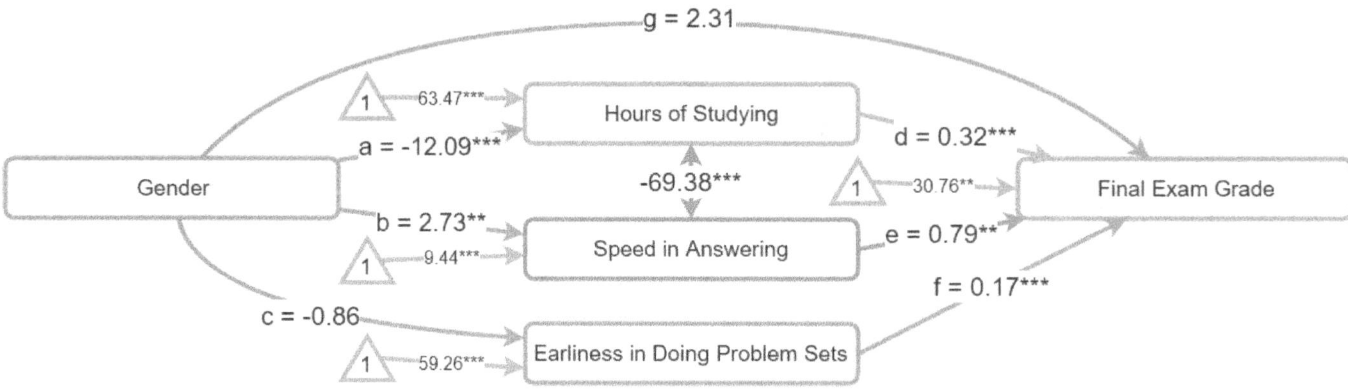

Figure 2: Path model predicting final exam score from the other four variables. One-directional arrows indicate the effects. The two-directional arrow shows the covariance of Hours of Studying and Speed. Arrows from the rectangles indicate constants in each regression model ($*: P \leq 0.05$, $**: P \leq 0.01$, $***: P \leq 0.001$)

questions. The distribution of exam grades was as follows: Mean 69.0%; Range [18.4%, 98.8%]; quartiles 58.8%, 71.2%, 82.4%.

3.2 Model

We conducted a mediation analysis to understand the correlation of gender with exam performance as mediated by Hours of Studying, Speed, and Earliness. We conducted the analysis using the *sem* command in lavaan R package [15]. It is equivalent to estimating a regression model predicting final exam score from the other four variables and separate regression models simultaneously predicting each of the behavior measures from gender. That determined the path coefficients displayed in Figure 2. The *sem* command also determines confidence intervals for the composite mediation effects of gender as mediated by each of the three behavior measures.

4 RESULTS

The mean final exam scores were 68.885% and 69.096%, respectively, for male and female students. The difference was not statistically significant t(182.06) = 0.088, p = 0.930 (Figure 3 - A). Controlling for the activity measures, there still was no statistically significant difference by gender. In both cases, we see no significant difference between grades achieved by each gender. There were, however, different pathways to success.

The results of the mediation analysis are summarized in Table 1 and visualized in the path diagram in Figure 2. Female students spent 12.086 more hours studying the textbook, on average. The mean hours of studying were 39.077 and 51.387, respectively, for male and female students and the difference was t(181.15) = 4.522, p = 0.000 (Figure 3 - C). Studying more was associated with higher final exam grades. Line 19 in Table 1 shows that in final exams female students got on average 3.923% higher grades than male students through dedicating more hours for studying the textbook.

Male students, on the other hand, were faster at completing problem sets, earning 2.727 more points per hour on average. The mean speed in answering problem sets were 14.715 and 12.164, respectively, for male and female students and the difference was t(128.25) = -2.704, p = 0.008 (Figure 3 - B). Speed was also associated with higher final exam grades. Line 20 in Table 1 shows that because of their higher speed in answering questions, male students got on average 2.144% higher final exam grades in comparison with female students.

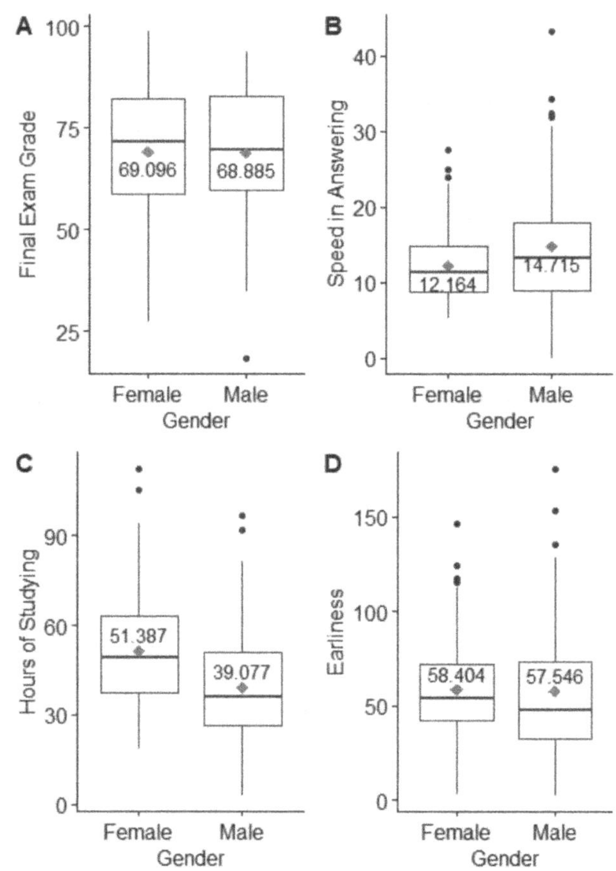

Figure 3: Box-plots of the study measurements across gender. Means are reported on each plot [20].

Table 1: Results of the Structural Equation Modeling. The first three lines show gender as a predictor of Hours of Studying, Speed, and Earliness (baseline gender is female.) The next four lines show the regression predicting final exam score. Line 8 indicates the covariance of Hours of Studying and Speed. Lines 9 - 12 show intercepts of the regressions. Lines 13 - 16 indicate the variances. The last four lines provide p-values and confidence intervals for the composite effects of pathways.

Line Num	Left-hand Side	Op.	Right-hand Side	Label	Estimates	Std.Err	Z-value	P-value	CI.lower	CI.upper
1	Hours_of_Studying	~	gender	a	-12.086	2.776	-4.354	0.000	-17.528	-6.606
2	Speed	~	gender	b	2.727	0.930	2.932	0.003	1.001	4.660
3	Earliness	~	gender	c	-0.857	4.557	-0.188	0.851	-9.349	8.571
4	final	~	Hours_of_Studying	d	0.325	0.084	3.884	0.000	0.153	0.480
5	final	~	Speed	e	0.786	0.302	2.604	0.009	0.201	1.374
6	final	~	Earliness	f	0.168	0.036	4.691	0.000	0.098	0.237
7	final	~	gender	g	2.312	2.354	0.982	0.326	-2.400	6.815
8	Hours_of_Studying	~~	Speed		-69.381	9.232	-7.515	0.000	-90.385	-53.526
9	Hours_of_Studying	~1			63.473	4.196	15.127	0.000	55.434	71.819
10	Speed	~1			9.437	1.200	7.864	0.000	7.002	11.727
11	Earliness	~1			59.261	6.438	9.204	0.000	46.445	71.790
12	final	~1			30.757	8.961	3.433	0.001	14.319	49.257
13	Hours_of_Studying	~~	Hours_of_Studying		349.473	39.403	8.869	0.000	281.742	437.384
14	Speed	~~	Speed		36.317	5.508	6.594	0.000	27.259	49.350
15	Earliness	~~	Earliness		934.376	115.700	8.076	0.000	731.932	1195.748
16	final	~~	final		214.969	19.702	10.911	0.000	183.160	263.142
17	gender	~~	gender		0.246	0.000	NA	NA	0.246	0.246
18	gender	~1			1.438	0.000	NA	NA	1.438	1.438
19	ad	:=	a*d	ad	-3.923	1.390	-2.822	0.005	-7.062	-1.638
20	be	:=	b*e	be	2.144	0.978	2.192	0.028	0.648	4.588
21	cf	:=	c*f	cf	-0.144	0.789	-0.182	0.856	-1.743	1.408
22	total	:=	g+ad+be+cf	total	0.389	2.350	0.166	0.868	-4.295	4.903

Finally, earliness in working on problem sets was associated with higher final exam grades, but there was no significant difference in earliness between male and female students. The mean earliness were 57.546 and 58.404, respectively, for male and female students and the difference was $t(155.79) = 0.187$, $p = 0.85$ (Figure 3 - D).

5 DISCUSSION

Contrary to previous literature describing differences in performance by gender in introductory programming courses, we do not find a statistically significant difference in final exam scores. Some gender differences remained, however.

Male students were faster at completing tasks on problem sets. One possible interpretation is that they were more skilled. This could have arisen from greater background knowledge, less confidence, stereotype threat, or other factors described in prior literature. Another possible interpretation, however, is that female students were more thorough in their approach to problem sets. Early in the course, it is sometimes possible to solve problem set assignments with syntactic matching or trial and error. Perhaps male students were more prone to try things until something worked and then move on without reflecting or taking the time to fully understand and internalize the material.

Female students spent considerably more hours studying. One possible interpretation, consistent with the skill interpretation of the speed difference, is that they recognized an initial skill deficit and compensated by studying more in order to erase that skill deficit. However, in a more detailed analysis of data, not reported here due to space limitations, there is no indication that the speed difference declines over time, as one would expect if study hours were erasing an initial skill deficit. Instead, we speculate that extra studying may lead to a different form of understanding that does not lead to improved speed on problem sets. That is, we speculate that both speed and the latent understanding that comes from more studying are separate dimensions of skill that both help with exam performance. It would be an interesting avenue for future research to theorize about what is involved in that latent understanding, and devise a way to measure it directly.

As expected, earliness was also positively correlated with exam performance. Instructors, ourselves included, often counsel students to start early on assignments, and it seems that that is good advice. Whether starting early directly leads to more learning or whether it is merely symptomatic of students who are better organized and more committed to a course is not clear. It was surprising, however, that there was no significant difference in earliness between male and female students, given the popular lore that female students have less attention and executive function problems.

The finding that there are multiple pathways to success has some design implications for instructors. Some students may develop skills that are apparent in the speed with which they solve programming exercises; everyone should be given ample opportunities to develop these skills through repeated practice. Other students, however, may also succeed through a process that develops understanding but less speed. It is not clear how to facilitate that learning, but we speculate that conceptual questions which trigger introspection of mental models may be especially valuable. At a minimum, it may be helpful for instructors to validate for students that understanding concepts well and developing speed at solving problems are complementary approaches, where either one may partially compensate for the other in a programmer's work.

6 CONCLUSION

In a course that has been honed over several years to be appealing and supportive to all genders, we found that male and female students performed equally well on the final exam but there were gender differences in the pathways they followed. Male students on average earned 2.7 more points per hour of solving the problem set questions over the first half of the semester, while female students spent 12.1 more hours studying over the semester. Both of these were positively correlated with exam performance.

REFERENCES

[1] Christine Alvarado, Cynthia Bailey Lee, and Gary Gillespie. 2014. New CS1 pedagogies and curriculum, the same success factors?. In *Proceedings of the 45th ACM technical symposium on Computer science education.* ACM, 379–384.

[2] Sylvia Beyer. 2014. Why are women underrepresented in Computer Science? Gender differences in stereotypes, self-efficacy, values, and interests and predictors of future CS course-taking and grades. *Computer Science Education* 24, 2-3 (2014), 153–192.

[3] Sylvia Beyer, Kristina Rynes, Julie Perrault, Kelly Hay, and Susan Haller. 2003. Gender differences in computer science students. *ACM SIGCSE Bulletin* 35, 1 (2003), 49–53.

[4] Suzanne G Brainard and Linda Carlin. 1998. A six-year longitudinal study of undergraduate women in engineering and science. *Journal of Engineering Education* 87, 4 (1998), 369–375.

[5] Barbara J Ericson, Lauren E Margulieux, and Jochen Rick. 2017. Solving Parsons problems versus fixing and writing code. In *Proceedings of the 17th Koli Calling Conference on Computing Education Research.* ACM, 20–29.

[6] Denise Gürer and Tracy Camp. 2002. An ACM-W literature review on women in computing. *ACM SIGCSE Bulletin* 34, 2 (2002), 121–127.

[7] Brian Harrington, Shichong Peng, Xiaomeng Jin, and Minhaz Khan. 2018. Gender, confidence, and mark prediction in CS examinations. In *Proceedings of the 23rd Annual ACM Conference on Innovation and Technology in Computer Science Education.* ACM, 230–235.

[8] Anita Hill. 2017. Anita Hill: Class Actions Could Fight Discrimination in Tech. https://www.nytimes.com/2017/08/08/opinion/anita-hill-women-in-tech-should-take-sexism-to-court.html?mcubz=3&_r=0

[9] Hilary M Lips and Linda Temple. 1990. Majoring in computer science: Causal models for women and men. *Research in Higher Education* 31, 1 (1990), 99–113.

[10] Jane Margolis and Allan Fisher. 2003. *Unlocking the clubhouse: Women in computing.* MIT press.

[11] Laurie Murphy, Brad Richards, Renée McCauley, Briana B Morrison, Suzanne Westbrook, and Timothy Fossum. 2006. Women catch up: gender differences in learning programming concepts. In *ACM SIGCSE Bulletin*, Vol. 38. ACM, 17–21.

[12] Brian G. Peterson and Peter Carl. 2018. *PerformanceAnalytics: Econometric Tools for Performance and Risk Analysis.* https://CRAN.R-project.org/package=PerformanceAnalytics R package version 1.5.2.

[13] R Core Team. 2018. *R: A Language and Environment for Statistical Computing.* R Foundation for Statistical Computing, Vienna, Austria. https://www.R-project.org/

[14] Penny Rheingans, Erica D'Eramo, Crystal Diaz-Espinoza, and Danyelle Ireland. 2018. A Model for Increasing Gender Diversity in Technology. In *Proceedings of the 49th ACM Technical Symposium on Computer Science Education.* ACM, 459–464.

[15] Yves Rosseel. 2012. lavaan: An R Package for Structural Equation Modeling. *Journal of Statistical Software* 48, 2 (2012), 1–36. http://www.jstatsoft.org/v48/i02/

[16] RStudio Team. 2015. *RStudio: Integrated Development Environment for R.* RStudio, Inc., Boston, MA. http://www.rstudio.com/

[17] Marian Gunsher Sackrowitz and Ann Parker Parelius. 1996. *An unlevel playing field: Women in the introductory computer science courses.* Vol. 28. ACM.

[18] Allison Scott, Freada Kapor Klein, and Uriridiakoghene Onovakpuri. 2017. Tech Leavers Study. https://www.kaporcenter.org/tech-leavers/ [Online; posted 1-December-2018].

[19] Greg Scragg and Jesse Smith. 1998. A study of barriers to women in undergraduate computer science. *ACM SIGCSE Bulletin* 30, 1 (1998), 82–86.

[20] Hadley Wickham. 2016. *ggplot2: Elegant Graphics for Data Analysis.* Springer-Verlag New York. http://ggplot2.org

[21] Ursula Wolz, Lina Battestilli, Bruce Maxwell, Susan Rodger, and Michelle Trim. 2018. Best Practices in Academia to Remedy Gender Bias in Tech. In *Proceedings of the 49th ACM Technical Symposium on Computer Science Education.* ACM, 672–673.

[22] Stuart Zweben and Betsy Bizot. 2018. 2017 Taulbee survey. *Computing* 30, 5 (2018).

An Item Response Theory Evaluation of a Language-Independent CS1 Knowledge Assessment

Benjamin Xie
University of Washington
The Information School, DUB Group
Seattle, Washington, USA
bxie@uw.edu

Matthew J. Davidson
University of Washington
College of Education
Seattle, Washington, USA
mattjd@uw.edu

Min Li
University of Washington
College of Education
Seattle, Washington, USA
minli@uw.edu

Andrew J. Ko
University of Washington
The Information School, DUB Group
Seattle, Washington, USA
ajko@uw.edu

ABSTRACT

Tests serve an important role in computing education, measuring achievement and differentiating between learners with varying knowledge. But tests may have flaws that confuse learners or may be too difficult or easy, making test scores less valid and reliable. We analyzed the Second Computer Science 1 (SCS1) concept inventory, a widely used assessment of introductory computer science (CS1) knowledge, for such flaws. The prior validation study of the SCS1 used Classical Test Theory and was unable to determine whether differences in scores were a result of question properties or learner knowledge. We extended this validation by modeling question difficulty and learner knowledge separately with Item Response Theory (IRT) and performing expert review on problematic questions. We found that three questions measured knowledge that was unrelated to the rest of the SCS1, and four questions were too difficult for our sample of 489 undergrads from two universities.

CCS CONCEPTS

• **Social and professional topics** → **Student assessment**;

KEYWORDS

validity; assessment; item response theory; CS1; concept inventory

ACM Reference Format:

Benjamin Xie, Matthew J. Davidson, Min Li, and Andrew J. Ko. 2019. An Item Response Theory Evaluation of a Language-Independent CS1 Knowledge Assessment. In *Proceedings of the 50th ACM Technical Symposium on Computer Science Education (SIGCSE '19), February 27-March 2, 2019, Minneapolis, MN, USA.* ACM, New York, NY, USA, 7 pages. https://doi.org/10.1145/3287324.3287370

SIGCSE '19, February 27-March 2, 2019, Minneapolis, MN, USA

ACM ISBN 978-1-4503-5890-3/19/02...$15.00
https://doi.org/10.1145/3287324.3287370

1 INTRODUCTION: IMPROVING MEASUREMENT OF CS KNOWLEDGE

Assessment is key to measuring knowledge, skills, and abilities related to computing [34]. For an instructor, assessments can differentiate between students' level of knowledge, helping personalize instruction. For learners, assessments can help them identify what they do and do not understand. For researchers and instructional designers, assessments can help measure the effect of interventions.

One recent and widely-used assessment is the Second Computer Science 1 (*SCS1*) concept inventory. The SCS1 was developed by Parker, Guzdial, & Engleman [26] as a replication to another concept inventory [33, 35]. The SCS1 is a multiple-choice exam which covers introductory computer science (*CS1*) knowledge, but does so with a language-independent pseudo-code. In the three years since the SCS1 was published, researchers have used it to measure students' CS1 knowledge before and after a course [12, 26, 36, 37] as part of pre-test/post-test studies [4], CS teachers' knowledge [26], and pre-CS1 students' knowledge [23].

The SCS1 is one of few CS concept inventories that has undergone validation to evaluate the validity and reliability of its test scores [26]. *Validation* is a process that involves evaluating the plausibility and appropriateness of proposed interpretations and uses of assessment scores [11, 13]. The validation process involves *iteratively* developing an assessment and an argument that specifies how to interpret assessment scores, and then challenging the argument to identify further improvements to the argument. Validation studies can identify if a test is too easy or too difficult for the target population [1], as well as whether surface features of questions [6] (e.g. wording of problem, style of code) confound the score [5, 16].

Through validation, we can produce evidence (empirical, theoretical, and argumentative) to support the interpretations of test scores for a proposed use. This evidence can better inform us as to which test questions are most effective at differentiating high- and low-performing students, helping us to further refine both specific questions and the set of questions included in the test as a whole. Ultimately, this evidence builds a case for the validity of interpretations of SCS1 scores as a measure of CS1 knowledge.

Validation is an iterative process, so we extended the prior validation study of the SCS1 to better understand how it measures test-takers. Parker, Guzdial, & Engleman [26] evaluated the SCS1 following Classical Test Theory (CTT)[1] [1], but CTT has limitations which make results challenging to interpret and generalize.

In this paper, we extended the validation of the SCS1 using Item Response Theory (IRT) [8], a widely used technique in the field of psychometrics. By using IRT, we can produce evidence on the quality of the SCS1 which can better generalize to the population of CS1 learners and distinguish between question difficulty and learner knowledge. We sought to answer the following questions: **RQ1**: *Do all the SCS1 questions measure the same underlying construct (CS1 knowledge)?* **RQ2**: *For what levels of CS1 knowledge does the SCS1 measure well?* **RQ3**: *How closely do the difficulty levels of the SCS1 questions align with the knowledge levels of our sample group?* **RQ4**: *What do the response patterns of problematic questions reveal?*

2 IRT VS. CLASSICAL TEST THEORY

Classical test theory (CTT) assumes a model where a learner's observed score is a combination of their unobserved *true score* and a certain amount of measurement error [24]. CTT attempts to measure this error by deriving test parameters on the basis of *total* scores for the learners in the sample [1]. CTT is useful as an initial analysis of data [11] but has three major limitations: 1) statistics such as test reliability, item difficulty, and item discrimination are *sample-dependent* [1, 38], 2) a learner's test score is an unspecified (at least in CTT) combination of a learner's knowledge and question properties (e.g. difficulty) [38]; 3) the model of observed score being a composite of true score and error is *unfalsifiable* [20].

In contrast, Item Response Theory [8, 20] provides more sample-agnostic statistics which estimate learner knowledge and question properties separately using falsifiable models. IRT analyzes each question and each learners' performance on a question separately, estimating question-level and test-level parameters, as well as learners' knowledge levels. This provides unique estimates of the difficulty and discrimination of each question for learners of different knowledge levels. Furthermore, these estimates generalize beyond the specific sample of learners. It does this by estimating the correspondence between unobserved latent variables (e.g. people's CS1 knowledge, difficulty of questions) and observable evidence of knowledge (e.g., people's responses to questions). By fitting response data to a model (e.g. logistic or multinomial), we can estimate question parameters (e.g. difficulty) with fewer assumptions about the characteristics of the sample. We can also make predictive statements about learner performance based on knowledge level.

IRT helps reason about the relationship between question difficulty and learner knowledge by placing people and questions on the *same* (typically unidimensional) continuum. It is centered at 0, which represents the ability level (herein *knowledge level*[2]) for the average test-taker of the population. If a test-taker's predicted knowledge level is greater than the difficulty of the question, they are more likely to get the question correct. Figure 1 shows an example of such a continuum. This continuum helps model the relationship between a learner's latent knowledge level and their observed item performance as a monotonically increasing function.

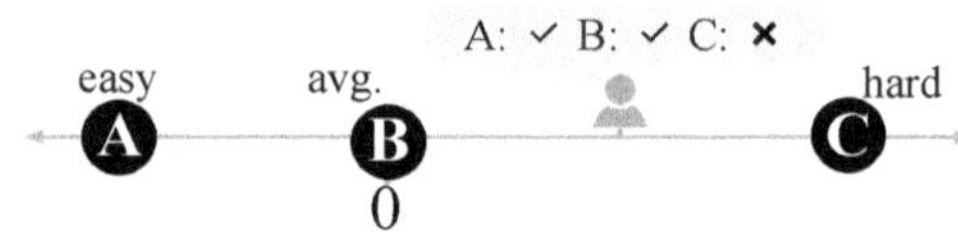

Figure 1: Representation of latent variable continuum with 3 questions (*A*, *B*, *C*). Because this learner's knowledge level is greater than the difficulties of *A* and *B*, we would predict they get those questions correct. Their level is lower than *C*'s difficulty, so we predict they get that question wrong. Zero reflects the knowledge level for the average test-taker.

Within IRT, a useful test question differentiates well between people located at different points on the continuum (having different knowledge levels) [8]. A question differentiates best between learners who have knowledge levels nearer to its difficulty. For most IRT models, the estimated difficulty of a question is the knowledge level at which a learner has an even chance (i.e. 50% probability) of answering correctly. Referring back to Figure 1, question *B* would better differentiate between learners with average knowledge levels (around 0), meaning some people would get B correct and others would not. In contrast, question *A* would be too easy to provide useful information about learners with an average knowledge level (almost everyone would get *A* correct). In addition to difficulty, some IRT models (including three models fitted below) estimate discrimination for each test question. *Discrimination* is how well a question distinguishes between knowledge levels–a high discrimination value means the probability of a learner answering correctly changes significantly based on their knowledge level. With discrimination, we can see if questions at the same difficulty level provide more or less information about learners' knowledge.

3 DATA: HUNDREDS OF SCS1 RESPONSES

The data we analyzed with IRT were responses to the SCS1, a 27 question multiple choice assessment of CS1 knowledge [26, 35]. The SCS1 covered nine concepts: *basics, conditionals, definite/for loops, indefinite/while loops, logical operators, arrays, recursion, function parameters,* and *function return values.* We began with SCS1 responses from 507 undergrad students about to begin 1 of 3 different courses at the University of Washington, Seattle (UW) and Georgia Institute of Technology (GT), large public universities in the United States. The data were collected for studies which used the SCS1 as a pre- and post-test to measure learning outcomes for different CS courses. We choose to analyze only pre-test data so the differences in interventions would not affect responses. Two of these courses (at different universities) administered the SCS1 within the first week of a CS1-level course, so we referred to these learners as *pre-CS1.* The third course administered the SCS1 within the first week of a CS2-level course (client-side web development), so we referred to these students as *pre-CS2.*

We only considered responses from test-takers who spent 10-70 minutes taking the SCS1. We chose the lower bound in the time limit to attempt to filter out random guessing; we choose the upper bound because the SCS1 is only supposed to take one hour.

[1] Sec. 3.2 of [26] mentioned "IRT analysis" of the SCS1, but we interpreted this as item-level analysis that follows CTT.

[2] We avoided using common IRT terms for comprehensibility. We will refer to items as *questions*, the instrument by name or as a *test*, the latent construct as *CS1 knowledge*, the item parameter as *difficulty* and the person parameter as *knowledge level*, or *knowledge/difficulty* when showing the latent variable continuum.

We also only considered test-takers who attempted at least 10 questions. The online format of the SCS1 made it such that learners could only see one question at a time and could not continue until they selected an answer, potentially forcing them to guess. So as soon as a test-taker stopped responding to a question, all further questions were left unanswered. Thus, the number of non-responses was monotonically increasing. So, we used the elbow method [29] to identify a cutoff of 10; after filtering by time and attempted questions, the number of responses decreased from 507 to 489.

Our sample had 118 responses from UW (54 pre-CS1, 64 pre-CS2) and 371 responses from GT (all pre-CSE1). While most of the sample were about to begin a CS1 course, surveys indicated that many had prior programming experience. At least half of the pre-CS1 learners from UW had prior programming experience (27/54 respondents), typically in the form of a high school course or independent learning. We only had demographic information for learners from UW, which was self-reported and had some non-response. Half (60/118) of the UW students identified as male, 38% as female, and 1 student as non-binary; the ratio of male to female was approximately equal between the pre-CS1 and pre-CS2 courses. Over 70% (87/118) were between 18-22 years old, with the remainder being older; most of the older respondents were pre-CS2. Survey respondents were predominantly Asian/Pacific Islander 46% (55/118) or 31% White/Caucasian, with only 6% reporting as minority or multi-ethnic. Java was most commonly known programming language, with 55% (66/118) of respondents reporting at least minimal proficiency in it; a majority of them were pre-CS2. We had no demographic data from GT.

4 IRT ANALYSIS: MODELING W/ 2PL

To understand how well the SCS1 measured achievement, we verified IRT assumptions then fit the response data to a logistic model.

4.1 Verifying IRT assumptions

4.1.1 Verifying conditional item independence. This assumption is that responses to a question are independent of responses to any other item, conditional on the learner's achievement level. This assumption enables us to calculate the probability of a response pattern by taking the product of the product of the probabilities of each individual response.

We justify conditional item independence through argumentation. While carryover effects [1] between questions are to some extent inevitable, we argue that conditional item independence is still valid because the online medium of the SCS1 exam only allowed respondents to see one question at a time. Furthermore, navigating back to previously attempted questions was difficult, as respondents would have had to go linearly back across previous questions and the questions pertaining to the same concept tended to be separate from each other. So, we assumed conditional item independence to be true.

4.1.2 RQ1: Verifying unidimensionality with CFA. The second assumption is *unidimensionality*, which states that only one unobserved "trait" is being measured by all of the questions [8, 31]. While the SCS1 measures nine concepts, unidimensionality would suggest that they are all related through the underlying trait of CS1 knowledge. This assumption allows us to use more standard IRT models that assume that achievement level is a singular construct that translates monotonically to more correct responses (i.e. a learner higher in the trait will generally answer more questions correctly). If the unidimensionality assumption were not valid, then more complex multidimensional IRT (mIRT) would be required [9].

To test whether a unidimensional IRT model was an acceptable for the SCS1, we conducted a *confirmatory factor analysis* (CFA). CFA, tests whether the relationship observed between variables in the collected data fits a predefined relationship. Because the goal is to see whether a unidimensional model is acceptable, each of the 27 SCS1 questions was specified to load onto a *single* latent variable, CS1 knowledge. The hypothesis was that a single underlying factor will explain sufficient observed variation in all questions.

The CFA was fit in R using the `cfa` function [28]; because test responses are dichotomous, we chose diagonally weighted least squares (WLSMV) as the estimation method. This method assumed that the underlying factor is normally distributed, but does not assume that the observed variables are [19]. To make the model identified, the variance of the latent factor was constrained to 1, so that factor loadings could be estimated for all questions.

Model fit appeared good. The model χ^2 tested the hypothesis that the model fits the data perfectly. $\chi^2(324) = 356.01$ (p=0.11), so we failed to reject that hypothesis. The comparative fit index (CFI), which compares the fit of our model to a null model, was 0.98 ($> .90$ is acceptable). The root mean square error of approximation (RMSEA) measures model fit with a penalty for more complex models. We found RMSEA = .014, which is acceptable (≤ 0.1). Finally, the standardized root mean square residual (SRMR) is based on the overall difference between the observed and estimated correlation matrices. We found SRMR = .079, which is also acceptable (≤ 0.8). These values all indicate acceptable model fit [14, 30], meaning one factor likely explains variation in these test items.

Table 1 shows the standardized factor loadings for each item, which can be interpreted as regression coefficients. For example, squaring the loading of Q3 (0.58) shows that CS1 knowledge explains $\approx$ 34% of the variation in scores for Q3. We found that a majority of the items had weak to moderate direct effects from the factor. Q20, 24, and 27 all showed poor loading on the factor. In addition to being low magnitude, each of those loadings were not found to be significantly different from zero. These particular items did not appear to be related to the factor of CS1 knowledge.

Table 1 also shows the change in Cronbach's α for each item. Cronbach's α is a measure of internal-consistency reliability. We found that $\alpha = 0.700$, an acceptable level given the SCS1 is primarily used for research and is not a high-stakes test [18, 25]. The table shows the change to α if a question is removed, which we would expect to be negative. If α actually *increased*, that would suggest that question is potentially problematic as the internal consistency of the SCS1 improved. We found that α increased when the same 3 questions which had poor factor loadings (20, 24, 27) were removed.

The residual covariance matrix also suggested that questions 20, 24, and 27 fit poorly. So, we removed these questions.

After dropping these 3 questions and re-running CFA, the α improved to 0.723. Omitting these questions also resulted in a better fitting model, $\chi^2(252) = 271.9$, p=0.19, CFI = 0.99, RMSEA = .013, and SRMR = .076. These fit indices suggest that a single factor of CS1 knowledge sufficiently explained variation in the SCS1 questions.

Table 1: Standardized factor loadings and change in α levels for SCS1 questions. High loading is ideal, suggesting a strong association between a question and the underlying factor (CS1 knowledge). α should be non-increasing.

Num	Factor loading (w/ std. error)	Change in α	Num	Factor loading (w/ std. error)	Change in α
1	0.49 (0.06)	-0.02	15	0.31 (0.08)	0.00
2	0.36 (0.06)	-0.01	16	0.68 (0.06)	-0.02
3	0.58 (0.05)	-0.02	17	0.46 (0.07)	-0.01
4	0.43 (0.08)	-0.01	18	0.16 (0.08)	0.00
5	0.29 (0.09)	0.00	19	0.68 (0.05)	-0.02
6	0.35 (0.06)	-0.01	20**	0.07 (0.08)	+0.01
7	0.46 (0.08)	-0.01	21	0.29 (0.07)	0.00
8	0.39 (0.07)	-0.01	22	0.35 (0.07)	-0.01
9	0.55 (0.06)	-0.02	23	0.43 (0.06)	-0.01
10	0.41 (0.06)	-0.01	24**	0.04 (0.08)	+0.01
11	0.38 (0.07)	-0.01	25	0.28 (0.06)	0.00
12	0.54 (0.06)	-0.02	26	0.43 (0.07)	-0.01
13	0.24 (0.08)	0.00	27**	-0.05 (0.07)	+0.01
14	0.47 (0.06)	-0.01			

** denotes a problematic question dropped from our analysis

4.2 IRT Model Fitting

After verifying the IRT assumptions of unidimensionality and local independence, we fit the response data to models. To evaluate question difficulty and discrimination, we fit the data to dichotomous IRT models with increasing number of parameters. More complex models tend to fit data better, but tend to be less generalizable. Therefore, we choose to fit four common models beginning with the simplest. We fit the Rasch, 1 Parameter Logistic (1PL), 2 Parameter Logistic (2PL), and 3 Parameter Logistic (3PL) models [8] to the data with `question.fit` function from the ltm package in R [27]. We assessed model performance using Akaike information criterion (AIC) and Bayesian information criterion (BIC) [15]. Information criteria transform the log-likelihood of a model by penalizing more complex models (models with more estimated parameters). These criteria can be used to compare similar models to ensure the best fit with the simplest model. We used a χ^2 test to check question fit.

Table 2 compares model performance. We selected the 2PL model because all 24 questions fit. We found it unusual that the 2PL model reported a greater BIC than the less complex Rasch and 1PL models, but we decided having all the questions fitting was more important.

Table 2: Dichotomous model performance. 2PL fit best.

Model	AIC	BIC	Questions that do not fit model
rasch	13104.7	13205.3	3, 19
1PL	13063.7	13168.5	3, 9, 16, 19, 23
2PL	**13018.3**	**13219.6**	**(all questions fit)**
3PL	12974.2	13276.1	3, 6, 22

For 2PL, the probability of learner x getting question j correct given a learner's knowledge level θ, question difficulty α_j, and question discrimination δ_j is $p(x_j = 1|\theta, \alpha_j, \delta_j) = \frac{e^{\alpha_j(\theta-\delta_j)}}{1+e^{\alpha_j(\theta-\delta_j)}}$.

While we present results for pre-CS1 and pre-CS2 students together, we also used CTT to ensure that any issues we identified were consistent between the two groups. We used CTT measures because did not have appropriate sample sizes to model pre-CS1 and pre-CS2 students separately with IRT.

Table 3: Question parameters for 2PL model. Questions should have $|\delta_j| \leq 3$ and $\alpha_j > 0$, with ** denoting issues.

j	δ_j (SE)	α_j (SE)	j	δ_j (SE)	α_j (SE)
1	1.16 (0.2)	0.91 (0.15)	13**	**3.99 (1.34)**	**0.40 (0.14)**
2	0.89 (0.23)	0.63 (0.13)	14	1.13 (0.21)	0.82 (0.14)
3	0.27 (0.1)	1.26 (0.19)	15**	**3.11 (0.81)**	0.51 (0.14)
4	2.26 (0.42)	0.73 (0.15)	16	1.28 (0.16)	1.35 (0.2)
5**	**3.91 (1.13)**	0.49 (0.15)	17	1.68 (0.29)	0.81 (0.15)
6	0.99 (0.25)	0.59 (0.13)	18**	**5.07 (2.55)**	**0.25 (0.13)**
7	2.33 (0.41)	0.79 (0.16)	19	0.74 (0.11)	1.53 (0.22)
8	1.60 (0.33)	0.66 (0.13)	21	1.58 (0.44)	0.47 (0.12)
9	1.16 (0.18)	1.00 (0.16)	22	1.36 (0.33)	0.57 (0.13)
10	1.27 (0.27)	0.68 (0.13)	23	0.08 (0.13)	0.79 (0.14)
11	1.90 (0.39)	0.63 (0.14)	25	0.78 (0.28)	0.47 (0.12)
12	0.63 (0.13)	1.06 (0.17)	26	1.77 (0.31)	0.78 (0.15)

4.3 Difficulty & Discrimination (RQ2)

Table 3 shows the 2PL model parameters and their standard error (SE). The difficulty means that a learner with exactly that knowledge level should have a 50% chance of answering correctly. Because most questions have a positive difficulty (δ_j) and 0 represents the average knowledge, the SCS1 is a difficult test. Question difficulty (and learner knowledge) represents the number of standard deviations from the mean (z-score). So, difficulty should range from -3 to 3, theoretically accounting for > 99.9% of learners' knowledge levels.

We found that Q5, 13, 15, and 18 are potentially too difficult. For these four questions, only 12-21% of pre-CS1 students got them correct, confirming these questions as being difficult for pre-CS1 students. For the pre-CS2 students, the more difficult questions were Q15 (19% got correct) and Q13 (25%), whereas Q5 (30%) and Q18 (31%) were still difficult but perhaps acceptably so.

The discrimination parameter (α_j) tells us how effectively a question differentiates among learners located near that question's difficulty. More specifically, we can interpret the discrimination to say that a greater α_j means that question j provides more information about learners with a knowledge level near the question's difficulty (δ_j), but this information more rapidly decreases for learners further away from the question's difficulty. Visually, a larger discrimination parameter translates to a steeper logit regression line, such as Q19 in Figure 2. Q19 does an excellent job distinguishing between learners around 0.75, but provides almost no information for learners above 2 or below 0 (average).

While a great discrimination parameter is desirable, there is disagreement on which values are "acceptable." For example, de Ayala 2009 defined 0.8-2.5 as an acceptable discrimination parameter range [8], whereas Baker 2001 defined 0.01 – 0.34 as "very low" and 0.35 – 0.64 as "low" discrimination [2]. We flagged Q13 ($\alpha_{13} = 0.40$) and Q18 ($\alpha_{18} = 0.25$) as having potentially problematic discrimination because their discrimination parameters were the lowest among all questions. We used point-biserial correlations (a CTT measure of discrimination [1]) to check discrimination for pre-CS1 and pre-CS2 students separately. Both Q13 and Q18 had a low point-biserial correlation (< 0.30) for both pre-CS1 ($r_{pre-CS1,Q13} = 0.10, r_{pre-CS1,Q18} = 0.18$) and pre-CS2 ($r_{pre-CS2,Q13} = 0.20, r_{pre-CS2,Q18} = 0.28$) students. Because these questions have high difficulty and pre-CS2 learners had more knowledge, it followed that the discrimination for pre-CS2 students were slightly higher (but still too low).

4.4 Estimates of learner knowledge (RQ3)

To better contextualize the difficulty of the SCS1, we used our 2PL model to estimate learner knowledge, something that IRT can measure but CTT cannot. Learner knowledge estimates are summary measures of the posterior distribution of CS1 knowledge conditioned on estimates of question difficulty and observed learner performance [8]. We used `ltm::factor.scores()` [27] with the mean of the posterior distribution as our estimator [3].

Figure 3 shows the relationship between learner knowledge and question difficulty. The estimated learner knowledge from our sample is on the left side, with estimated question difficulties on the right, allowing a clear comparison of learner knowledge to question difficulty levels. Learners in our sample had knowledge ranging from -1.73 to 2.93 and the distribution had a positive/right skew, largely because of the 13% of the sample who were pre-CS2.

With the learner knowledge estimates, we have stronger evidence to suggest that Q5, 13, 14, and 18 (noted as problematic in Table 3) are too difficult. This can clearly be seen in Figure 3 because these questions are above even the highest knowledge learner. These questions have an estimated difficulty greater than all 489 learners in the sample. Furthermore, the difficulty parameters of these questions are ≥ 3, and both knowledge and difficulty are z-scores on a normal distribution, so we would expect only 0.13% of the population to have a knowledge level of 3 or greater. So, these questions should undergo review for revision or removal.

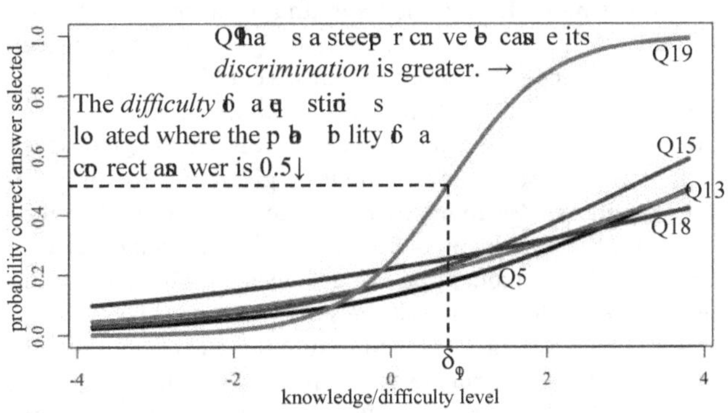

Figure 2: Item characteristic curves for an acceptable question (Q19) and four problematic ones in the SCS1. The flatness of the logistic curves for Q5, 13, 15, and 18 reflect the low/poor discrimination (as reported in Table 3).

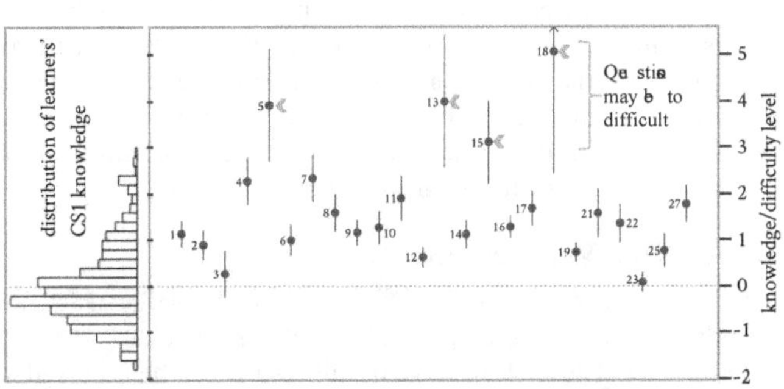

Figure 3: Wright map [10] showing the relationship between learner knowledge (left, ranging from -1.73 to 2.93, mean: 0.00, med.: -0.17) and question difficulty w/ std. error (right).

4.5 Responses for removed questions (RQ4)

Three additional questions that may require revision or removal from the SCS1 are the questions that we dropped prior to running our analysis due to poor factor loadings (Q20, 24, 27; see Table 1). While we dropped these questions because their response patterns deviated from our expectation, factor analysis did not inform us as to *how* these response patterns differed.

Analyzing responses to each incorrect option can provide insight into potential issues relating to test design and learner misconceptions. Each SCS1 question was multiple choice and had 1 correct option and 4 incorrect options, known as *distractors*. Ideally, distractors reflect common misconceptions. But in practice, some options may not represent a common misconception, resulting in the option rarely being selected for learners regardless of knowledge level. We would expect learners of lesser knowledge levels to more frequently select a distractor instead of the correct answer. If learners with greater knowledge levels systematically continue to select a distractor over the correct option, this could suggest confusion relating to the design of the question or a gap in instruction as learners consistently exhibit a misconception. So, we expect the frequency of distractor selection to decrease as knowledge increases.

To better understand how response patterns from dropped questions deviated, we used the IRT-based Nominal Response Model (NRM) [7, 8]. Whereas the 2PL model only considered whether a learner got a question correct or not, the NRM computes the probability of a learner choosing each of the answer options, taking into account the question's difficulty and the learner's knowledge.

In Figure 4, we plotted the probability of learners with varying knowledge levels selecting responses for the three dropped SCS1 questions compared to Q19 (a more ideal question). Each line within a graph represents the probability of a learner selecting a response option as a function of the their knowledge level, with the highest line being the answer choice with the highest probability. For example, for Q19, option C (the correct answer) was the choice with the highest probability for learners with knowledge levels around 0.4 or higher; for learners with knowledge levels around −1.4 or lower, option A was the most probable choice. Q19 displays the expected relationship for a well-functioning question, where learners with more knowledge are more likely to choose the correct answer. In contrast, Q20, 24, and 27 are problematic as they show that learners with more CS1 knowledge (further to the right) are *less* likely to choose the correct answer.

4.6 Expert review of problematic questions

With factor analysis and IRT modeling, we identified specific SCS1 questions that were problematic and may require revision. We said these questions were problematic because they may assess knowledge that is different from the rest of the SCS1 (based on their low factor loadings, Table 1) or too difficult (δ_j too great, Table 3) for the target population of CS1 learners. The next step would be to review these flagged questions to understand exactly what about these questions makes them problematic. One way to do this is with expert review [1, 8]. To conduct expert review, somebody with Educational Psychology and domain-specific expertise (about CS1, in this case) reviews questions that a validation study identified as potentially problematic. For this paper, the authors conducted the

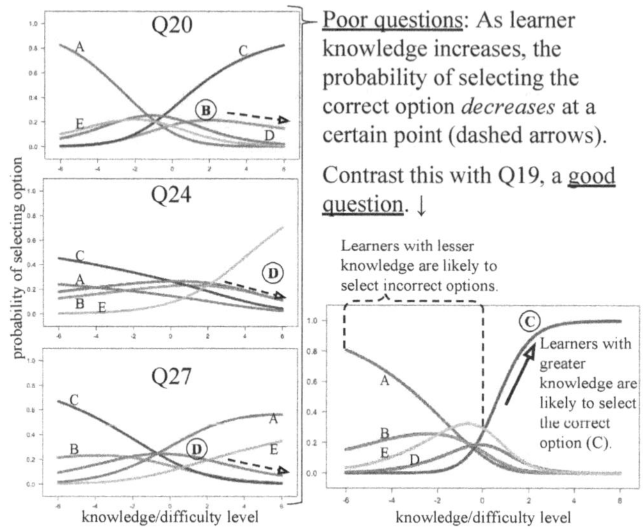

Figure 4: Item characteristic plots for NRM model for dropped questions (Q20, 24, 27) and a good question (Q19) for contrast. Plots show the relationship between learner knowledge and responses. Correct responses are circled.

expert review. In this section, we provide a more detailed explanation of our findings relating to 2 questions which we dropped from the analysis. To maintain the integrity of the SCS1, we were unable to show any of its questions (see Section 6 to access SCS1).

When reviewing the dropped questions (Q20, Q24, Q27), we first identified patterns across all 3 questions. The questions assessed knowledge of function scope (Q20, 27) and recursion (Q24). Prior work has found that both concepts are challenging for CS1 students [17, 32]. Furthermore, scope and recursion have more prominent roles in some programming paradigms than others. For example, almost all pre-CS2 students in our sample took a CS1 course that taught programming in R for working with data; within that curriculum, recursion was not taught and scope was only briefly covered.

We focused our expert review on the questions relating to scope. We looked at the SCS1 to contextualize the patterns in distractor selection for learners of varying knowledge levels (Figure 4). We found that for both questions, learners with below average knowledge (< 0) would select a distractor suggesting a misconception on code tracing; learners with above average knowledge (> 0) would select the distractor which reflected tracing the code correctly but lacking knowledge relating to scope. These similarities in response pattern suggest that these questions may assess similar knowledge and we may be able to drop one of them or revise one to assess different misconceptions relating to scope. Furthermore, the poor factor loading between these questions and the rest of the SCS1 suggest that this knowledge may be somewhat different from other CS1 concepts, or may not be covered sufficiently in CS1 courses.

Further expert review would involve examining the rest of the questions flagged as problematic in Table 3. Because of expert blind spot [22], expert review often includes cognitive interviews with the target population. Then, we can keep, revise, or remove questions.

5 DISCUSSION

In this paper, we conducted a validation study of the SCS1 using IRT to identify differences in question difficulty, discrimination, and response patterns relative to learner knowledge. From this, we found that 3 SCS1 questions may assess knowledge that is different from the rest of the test, and 4 other questions were too difficult for all 489 students in our sample, and potentially too difficult for the target population of CS1 learners. For the 3 questions that may assess different knowledge, we looked at which options were chosen, which further confirmed that the knowledge those questions measured may have been different. Finally, we conducted an expert review to better understand differences in learners' errors.

One way to interpret these results is that they are useful in identifying potentially problematic questions so we can improve the SCS1. In the previous section, we provided an example of how we could do that with expert review of flagged questions. This revealed that, at least in the populations we studied, scope and recursion may not have been covered in their prior coursework. It also revealed opportunity to drop or revise 1 question because it is redundant. However, it is important to conduct cognitive interviews with the target population to verify results from expert review.

Another way to interpret these results is that similar results could have been found through less complex means. Indeed, a limitation to IRT is the complexity of the analysis and requirements for a large sample size. But while CTT might have revealed *that* the test was hard, IRT revealed *how* and *for whom* each question was difficult. In particular, IRT estimated question difficulty and learner knowledge separately so that we could better distinguish whether a question was truly difficult or we happened to have learners with low knowledge levels. With this, we can better justify whether a question is appropriate for a given purpose or certain target population. We found that some items of the SCS1 were too difficult for the population of CS1 learners. Furthermore, there are additional IRT techniques that can help identify whether questions work differently for learners at the same knowledge level but with different characteristics (e.g. males and females) [21], as well as methods which can model tests that measure multiple knowledge constructs [9]. Many aspects of IRT can be useful in future work.

Beyond demonstrating the potential value of IRT, our results have practical implications for research and teaching. First, as with any instrument, the SCS1 needs more refinement to improve the validity of its measurements. Our results suggest that prior work using it as a pre-test may have risked encountering floor effects because of the test's difficulty. At its current level of difficulty, the SCS1 may be more appropriate only as a post-test. This suggests the need for additional instruments that help us measure prior knowledge more reliably, especially as more diverse learners, with more varied prior knowledge, begin to engage in computing education.

6 ACKNOWLEDGEMENTS

This material is based upon work supported by the National Science Foundation under Grant No. 1703304, 1735123, 1314399, 1639576, 1829590, and 12566082. Archive of full results can be accessed at github.com/codeandcognition/archive-2019sigcse-xie. We thank Miranda Parker and Mark Guzdial for collecting, sharing, and helping interpret the data. To access the SCS1, contact authors of [26].

REFERENCES

[1] Mary J. Allen and Wendy M. Yen. 2001. *Introduction to Measurement Theory.* Waveland Press.

[2] Frank B. Baker. 2001. *The Basics of Item Response Theory. Second Edition.* ERIC Clearinghouse on Assessment and Evaluation.

[3] R Darrell Bock and Robert J Mislevy. 1982. Adaptive EAP estimation of ability in a microcomputer environment. *Applied psychological measurement* 6, 4 (1982), 431–444.

[4] Peter L. Bonate. 2000. *Analysis of Pretest-Posttest Designs.* CRC Press.

[5] Dennis Bouvier, Ellie Lovellette, John Matta, Bedour Alshaigy, Brett A. Becker, Michelle Craig, Jana Jackova, Robert McCartney, Kate Sanders, and Mark Zarb. 2016. Novice Programmers and the Problem Description Effect. In *Proceedings of the 2016 ITiCSE Working Group Reports (ITiCSE '16).* ACM, New York, NY, USA, 103–118. https://doi.org/10.1145/3024906.3024912

[6] Michelle Craig, Jacqueline Smith, and Andrew Petersen. 2017. Familiar Contexts and the Difficulty of Programming Problems. In *Proceedings of the 17th Koli Calling International Conference on Computing Education Research (Koli Calling '17).* ACM, New York, NY, USA, 123–127. https://doi.org/10.1145/3141880.3141898

[7] R. Darrell Bock. 1972. Estimating item parameters and latent ability when responses are scored in two or more nominal categories. *Psychometrika* 37, 1 (01 Mar 1972), 29–51. https://doi.org/10.1007/BF02291411

[8] R. J. De Ayala. 2009. *The theory and practice of item response theory.* Guilford Press.

[9] Johannes Hartig and Jana Höhler. 2009. Multidimensional IRT Models for the Assessment of Competencies. *Studies in Educational Evaluation* 35, 2-3 (June 2009), 57–63. https://doi.org/10.1016/j.stueduc.2009.10.002

[10] David Torres Irribarra and Rebecca Freund. 2016. IRT Item-Person Map with 'ConQuest' Integration.

[11] Natalie Jorion, Brian D. Gane, Katie James, Lianne Schroeder, Louis V. DiBello, and James W. Pellegrino. 2015. An Analytic Framework for Evaluating the Validity of Concept Inventory Claims. *Journal of Engineering Education* 104, 4 (Oct. 2015), 454–496. https://doi.org/10.1002/jee.20104

[12] David Joyner. 2018. Toward CS1 at Scale: Building and Testing a MOOC-for-Credit Candidate. In *Proceedings of the Fifth Annual ACM Conference on Learning at Scale - L@S '18.* ACM Press, London, United Kingdom, 1–10. https://doi.org/10.1145/3231644.3231665

[13] Michael Kane. 2009. Articulating a Validity Argument. In *The Routledge Handbook of Language Testing.* Routledge. https://doi.org/10.4324/9780203181287.ch2

[14] R.B. Kline. 2011. *Principles and Practice of Structural Equation Modeling, Third Edition.* Guilford Publications.

[15] Sadanori Konishi and G. Kitagawa. 2008. *Information Criteria and Statistical Modeling.* Springer, New York.

[16] K Kotovsky, J.R Hayes, and H.A Simon. 1985. Why Are Some Problems Hard? Evidence from Tower of Hanoi. *Cognitive Psychology* 17, 2 (April 1985), 248–294. https://doi.org/10.1016/0010-0285(85)90009-X

[17] Amruth N. Kumar. 2001. Learning the Interaction Between Pointers and Scope in C++. *SIGCSE Bull.* 33, 3 (June 2001), 45–48. https://doi.org/10.1145/507758.377466

[18] Charles E. Lance, Marcus M. Butts, and Lawrence C. Michels. 2006. The Sources of Four Commonly Reported Cutoff Criteria: What Did They Really Say? *Organizational Research Methods* 9, 2 (April 2006), 202–220. https://doi.org/10.1177/1094428105284919

[19] Cheng-Hsien Li. 2016. Confirmatory factor analysis with ordinal data: Comparing robust maximum likelihood and diagonally weighted least squares. *Behavior Research Methods* 48, 3 (01 Sept. 2016), 936–949. https://doi.org/10.3758/s13428-015-0619-7

[20] Frederic M. Lord. 1980. *Applications of Item Response Theory to Practical Testing Problems.* Lawrence Erlbaum Associates, Inc.

[21] Patrícia Martinková, Adéla Drabinová, Yuan-Ling Liaw, Elizabeth A. Sanders, Jenny L. McFarland, and Rebecca M. Price. 2017. Checking Equity: Why Differential Item Functioning Analysis Should Be a Routine Part of Developing Conceptual Assessments. *Cell Biology Education* 16, 2 (2017), rm2. https://doi.org/10.1187/cbe.16-10-0307

[22] Mitchell J Nathan, Kenneth R Koedinger, and Martha W Alibali. 2001. Expert Blind Spot: When Content Knowledge Eclipses Pedagogical Content Knowledge. *Proceeding of the Third International Conference on Cognitive Science* (2001), 6.

[23] Greg L. Nelson, Benjamin Xie, and Andrew J. Ko. 2017. Comprehension First: Evaluating a Novel Pedagogy and Tutoring System for Program Tracing in CS1. In *2017 ACM Int'l Computing Education Research Conf. (ICER '17).* ACM, 2–11.

[24] Melvin R Novick. 1966. The axioms and principal results of classical test theory. *Journal of mathematical psychology* 3, 1 (1966), 1–18.

[25] Jum C. Nunnally. 1978. *Psychometric Theory* (2d ed. ed.). McGraw-Hill, New York.

[26] Miranda C. Parker, Mark Guzdial, and Shelly Engleman. 2016. Replication, Validation, and Use of a Language Independent CS1 Knowledge Assessment. In *2016 ACM Int'l Computing Education Research Conf. (ICER '16).* ACM, 93–101.

[27] Dimitris Rizopoulos. 2018. Latent Trait Models under IRT.

[28] Yves Rosseel. 2018. *The Lavaan Tutorial.* Technical Report. Ghent University.

[29] Marko Sarstedt and Erik Mooi. 2014. *Cluster Analysis.* Springer Berlin Heidelberg, Berlin, Heidelberg, 273–324. https://doi.org/10.1007/978-3-642-53965-7_9

[30] James B. Schreiber, Amaury Nora, Frances K. Stage, Elizabeth A. Barlow, and Jamie King. 2006. Reporting Structural Equation Modeling and Confirmatory Factor Analysis Results: A Review. *The Journal of Educational Research* 99, 6 (2006), 323–338. https://doi.org/10.3200/JOER.99.6.323-338

[31] A.H. Segars. 1997. Assessing the Unidimensionality of Measurement: A Paradigm and Illustration within the Context of Information Systems Research. *Omega* 25, 1 (Feb. 1997), 107–121. https://doi.org/10.1016/S0305-0483(96)00051-5

[32] Raja Sooriamurthi. 2001. Problems in Comprehending Recursion and Suggested Solutions. In *Proceedings of the 6th Annual Conference on Innovation and Technology in Computer Science Education (ITiCSE '01).* ACM, New York, NY, USA, 25–28. https://doi.org/10.1145/377435.377458

[33] Allison Elliott Tew. 2010. *Assessing Fundamental Introductory Computing Concept Knowledge in a Language Independent Manner.* Ph.D. Dissertation. Georgia Institute of Technology.

[34] A. E. Tew and B. Dorn. 2013. The Case for Validated Tools in Computer Science Education Research. *Computer* 46, 9 (Sept. 2013), 60–66. https://doi.org/10.1109/MC.2013.259

[35] Allison Elliott Tew and Mark Guzdial. 2011. The FCS1: A Language Independent Assessment of CS1 Knowledge. In *Proceedings of the 42Nd ACM Technical Symposium on Computer Science Education (SIGCSE '11).* ACM, New York, NY, USA, 111–116. https://doi.org/10.1145/1953163.1953200

[36] Dion Timmermann and Christian Kautz. 2016. Design of Open Educational Resources for a Programming Course with a Focus on Conceptual Understanding. In *Proceedings of the 44th SEFI Annual Conference.* Tampere, Finland.

[37] D. Timmermann, C. Kautz, and V. Skwarek. 2016. Evidence-Based Re-Design of an Introductory Course "Programming in C". In *2016 IEEE Frontiers in Education Conference (FIE).* 1–5. https://doi.org/10.1109/FIE.2016.7757492

[38] Colin S. Wallace and Janelle M. Bailey. 2010. Do Concept Inventories Actually Measure Anything? *Astronomy Education Review* 9, 1 (Dec. 2010). https://doi.org/10.3847/AER2010024

A Gap Analysis of Noncognitive Constructs in Evaluation Instruments Designed for Computing Education

Monica M. McGill
Knox College
Galesburg, IL, USA
mmmcgill@knox.edu

Adrienne Decker
University at Buffalo
Buffalo, NY, USA
adrienne@buffalo.edu

Tom McKlin
The Findings Group
Decatur, GA, USA
tom@thefindingsgroup.org

Kathy Haynie
Haynie Research and Evaluation
Skillman, NJ, USA
kchaynie@alumni.stanford.edu

ABSTRACT

A growing body of evidence indicates that there is a deep effect of noncognitive factors on academic achievement and learning. In this study, we analyzed a set of 31 evaluation instruments designed to measure noncognitive constructs (e.g., self-efficacy, confidence, motivation) within computing education. Using the Lee and Shute framework, we assigned each of the 115 unique constructs found in the instruments into one of the four components (Student Engagement, Learning Strategies, School Climate, Social-familial Influences) and their subcomponents to determine which constructs are most frequently measured. We found that the majority of constructs were designed to measure Student Engagement (Affect and Cognition) and School Climate (Teacher Variables). Constructs measuring Learning Strategies and Social-Familial Influences (e.g., homework strategies, peer influences) occur the least. This study may enable further discussions of what noncognitive factors are/are not currently being measured within the computing education community.

CCS CONCEPTS

• **Social and professional topics → Computing education; Computing education programs; Computer science education.**

KEYWORDS

Evaluation, assessment, constructs, noncognitive, education

ACM Reference Format:
Monica M. McGill, Adrienne Decker, Tom McKlin, and Kathy Haynie. 2019. A Gap Analysis of Noncognitive Constructs in Evaluation Instruments Designed for Computing Education. In *Proceedings of the 50th ACM Technical Symposium on Computer Science Education (SIGCSE '19), February 27-March 2, 2019, Minneapolis, MN, USA.* ACM, New York, NY, USA, Article 4, 7 pages. https://doi.org/10.1145/3287324.3287362

ACM ISBN 978-1-4503-5890-3/19/02.
https://doi.org/10.1145/3287324.3287362

1 INTRODUCTION

A growing body of empirical evidence indicates that noncognitive factors significantly affect academic achievement and learning [3, 11, 18, 28]. Most importantly, noncognitive factors are strongly related to the limited participation of women and minority students in computer science [11]. Studies have shown that non-majority students often feel that they do not belong in CS, and perceive that CS is the domain of white males, and does not serve socially progressive agendas (e.g. programming for good) nor allow for creative expression [11, 21, 30].

Farkus defines noncognitive constructs as "...any skills, behaviors, habits, tendencies, traits, and disposition that are typically not measured by tests" (see Figure 1) [10]. Examples of noncognitive constructs include self-efficacy, study skills of students, support of family and friends, and sense of belonging [10, 11, 22]. Although the terms *cognitive* and *noncognitive* are currently understood as interdependent in the fields of psychology, education, and economics, we concur with Farrington, et al., that maintaining a distinction between the two can shed further light on research-based factors within the field of educational psychology [11].

Figure 1: ©The Consortium on Chicago School Research and Jeff Hall Design [11]. Used with permission.

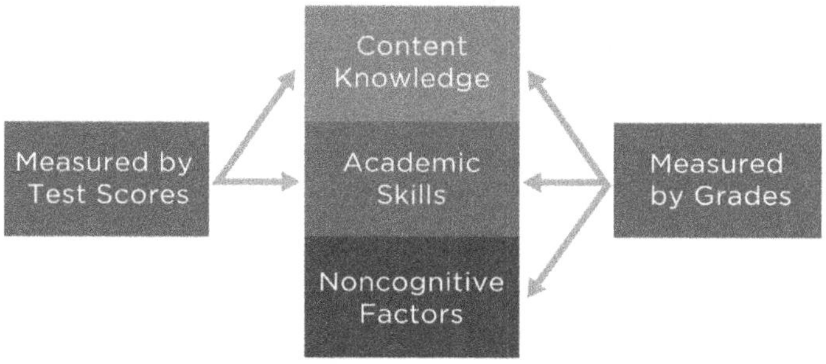

This study provides a taxonomy of existing research-based evaluation instruments that measure noncognitive constructs in computing education. Our overarching research question is: *Which noncognitive constructs are and are not currently being measured in instruments specifically designed for evaluating the impact of computing education?*

This meta-analytic research is relevant for CS education researchers who want to strengthen and improve the quality of their research and CS education evaluators intending to utilize rigorous evaluation instruments for measuring noncognitive factors. It is also foundational for practitioners and policy-makers who want to expand the repertoire of existing instruments by creating scales for measuring constructs that are not yet measured [11, 28].

2 BACKGROUND

Several frameworks model the affect noncognitive constructs have on student achievement. Farrington et al. identify five categories of noncognitive factors as well as their interdependencies [11]:

- Academic behaviors (attending class, doing homework, etc.)
- Academic perseverance (e.g. grit, self-control, self-discipline)
- Academic mindsets (e.g. positive or negative mindsets related to belonging, abilities, competencies)
- Learning strategies (e.g. study skills, metacognitive strategies, self-regulated learning), and
- Social skills (e.g. interpersonal skills, empathy, cooperation)

Farrington et al. make a strong case that not only do these factors influence academic achievement, they also influence later life outcomes, including success in the labor market. They further note that recent research indicates that emphasizing noncognitive learner factors "would yield high payoffs in improved educational outcomes as well as reduced racial/ethnic and gender disparities in school performance and educational attainment" [11, Chapter 1].

This model focuses on noncognitive factors centered on the learner. In contrast, Marzano's model was developed based on effect size through meta-studies. Three groupings (student-level, teacher-level, and school-level) were created based on the most significant effect sizes [22]. This model includes teacher-level factors (e.g. individual teacher effects, instructional strategies, curriculum design) and school-level factors (e.g. guaranteed/viable curriculum, challenging goals, effective feedback, parental/ community involvement, safe/orderly environment, and collegiality/ professionalism). This model acknowledges the breadth of variables outside students' control that have been shown to impact achievement.

Lee & Shute propose a *Personal and Social Contextual Factors* framework. Similar to Marzano, their well-defined framework was formed through an extensive analysis of effect sizes reported by several longitudinal meta-studies of the impact of noncognitive factors on learning and student achievement [18]. Like other frameworks, Lee & Shute recognize the reciprocity between the components and subcomponents–they interact and influence each other.

The four major components of this model (Student Engagement, Learning Strategies, School Climate, Social-familial Influences) each have several subcomponents (see Figure 2). *Student Engagement* has three: *behavior* defined as "students' external behaviors indicative of their interest and investment in learning activities"; *cognitive-motivational engagement* defined as "students' decisions, beliefs, and willingness to expand their efforts to learn and overcome challenging situations"; and *emotional engagement* defined as "student's affective reactions and feelings toward learning in general, as well as toward school, teachers, and classmates" [18](pp. 4-5).

Learning Strategies also has three subcomponents: cognitive, metacognitive, and behavioral learning strategies. *Cognitive strategies* refers to "skills that support learners as they develop internal procedures that enable them to perform complex tasks". *Metacognitive strategies* refers to "the abilities of learners to acknowledge, monitor, and evaluate their own cognitive processes as well as their strengths and weaknesses as learners." *Behavioral learning strategies* refers to "habitual activities that students employ during learning to manage and control their own behavior...behavior of others...and resources" [18](p 7). Learning strategies is further divided into individual constructs due to their well-studied impact on student achievement: time management, test-taking strategies, help-seeking, homework management, and test-taking skills.

School Climate is defined as "organizational characteristics that are persistent in and unique to a particular school" with four subcomponents: *academic emphasis* (students', parents', teachers', and administrators' "perception[s] of the importance of academic achievement"), *teacher variables* ("what teachers do in the classroom and how they interact with students and other teachers"), *principal leadership* ("principal's ability to influence the actions of school community members including teachers, parents, students, and district or state personnel"), and *other school climate variables* (e.g. sufficient resources, appropriate space, extracurricular activities).

Social-familial Influences are influences outside of school that impact student achievement. Lee & Shute note two subcomponents: *parental involvement* (general attitudinal and behavioral components of parental involvement on student achievement) and *peer influences* (peer support, attitudes, and achievement levels).

For the remainder of this article, we adapt Lee & Shute's terms, referring to Student-Personal and Social-Contextual as *factors*, Student Engagement, Learning Strategies, School Climate, and Social-Familial Influences as *components*, and any category underneath

Figure 2: Lee & Shute model [18]. * indicates that the subcomponent has additional constructs discussed in section 4.

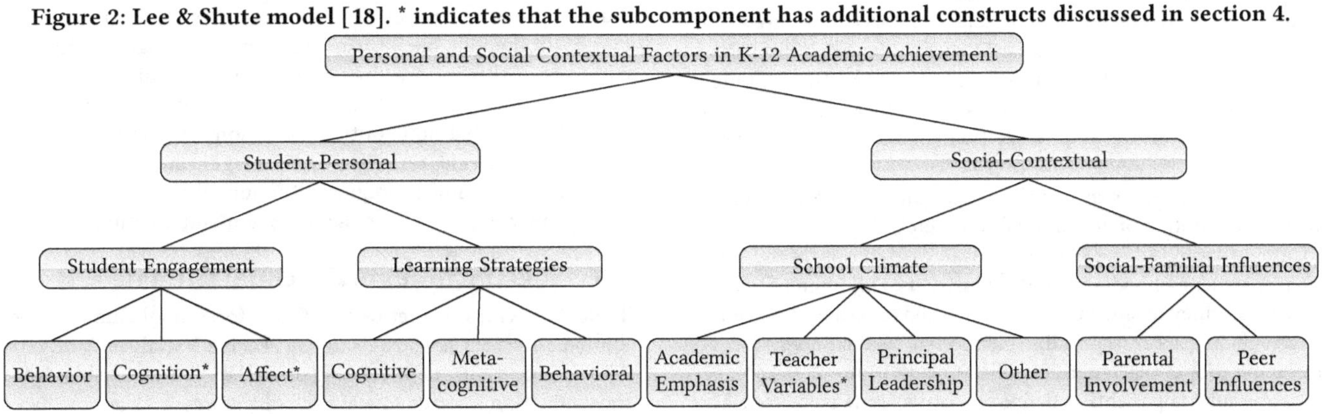

these as *subcomponents*. Subcomponents are further broken into *constructs* in the results section.

3 METHODOLOGY

To identify the noncognitive constructs being measured by evaluation instruments designed for computing education, we first needed to identify a set of instruments to study. To do so, we:

- Examined 297 articles published from 2012 to 2016 in the https://csedresearch.org database (2012-2016), noting instruments used in studies [23],
- Searched several online databases for instruments, including American Evaluation Association [2], STELAR [9] The Pear Institute [27], Institute for the Integration of Technology into Teaching and Learning [13], MSPNet [12], Engineering is Elementary [25], and
- Used search engines to perform searches based on relevant keywords (e.g., computer science, inventory, survey, instrument, evaluation, interest, self-efficacy, etc.).

After creating the initial set, we solicited the CS education community for additional instruments using the SIGCSE-Members listserv and computing education social media sites. With a total of 47 evaluation instruments, we reviewed each instrument to determine if it measured cognitive or noncognitive factors or assessed programs, or a combination of these. Due to limited space, we include the final list of instruments analyzed in this study in the Appendix of the companion paper published in these same proceedings [7].

Since noncognitive constructs may explain changes in student success in computing education, we carefully reviewed each of the 31 instruments to identify the noncognitive constructs that they set out to measure. Construct identification was completed by two independent coders. To help ensure inter-rater reliability, each coder was given an initial set of five instruments from which to identify constructs. This was done by examining the instruments and locating articles by the authors that defined the constructs measured. They then compared the constructs that they identified, resolving any discrepancies through discussion. The remaining instruments were divided among each coder, who then independently verified the constructs measured within each.

Many of the constructs found are documented in general education research literature and some in computer science education literature (e.g., sense of belonging, identity, anxiety, grit, interest, cognitive load, self efficacy) [1, 4, 5, 11, 14, 18, 19, 22, 24, 29]. As our use of these constructs in computer science interventions grows, so does our need to organize them for further analysis and discussion. After reviewing several models, we chose to adopt Lee & Shute's model for categorizing the constructs due to its holistic structure in terms of the learning ecosystem. By using this model, we could identify where our current use of psychosocial constructs within these instruments flourish as well as those that fall short, all within the broader context of educational research.

Categorization of the constructs was carried out by the same two researchers who identified the constructs. Full intercoder reliability was achieved since the coders worked together to place the constructs in the corresponding components/subcomponents. To determine proper placement, the formal definitions of the components and subcomponents as defined by Lee & Shute were used. The coders worked together to discuss where each construct (from each of the evaluation instruments) belonged within the framework. For example, Fixed Mindset was measured in one of the instruments. We then took the construct as it was defined in the instrument and evaluated the components and subcomponents. Based on these definitions, we determined that Fixed Mindset was a Student Engagement factor related to Cognitive-Motivational Engagement. From there, we then decided it fit best within the Attribution for Success/Failure category. This process continued until each construct from each of the instruments was assigned to an appropriate subcomponent.

4 RESULTS

This section provides the resulting grouping of constructs within the components and subcomponents of the Lee & Shute model. This section is divided into four subsections aligned with the components of the Lee & Shute model: *Student Engagement, Learning Strategies, School Climate,* and *Social-Familial Influences.* We conclude with a summary of how well each component is covered.

In each of the tables provided, we list each subcomponent and, when available, individual constructs identified by Lee & Shute within each subcomponent. We then show the constructs from the evaluation instruments within each where it made the most sense. For a few of these constructs, placement was less than a perfect match. We note these particular constructs with two asterisks (**).

4.1 Student-Personal: Student Engagement

We found many constructs for Student Engagement across the 31 instruments (Table 1). Lee & Shute identify seven constructs in the Cognition subcomponent (e.g., Attribution for Success/Failure, Confidence, Goal Orientation) and four constructs within Affect (e.g., Feelings toward school/learning, Interest/Curiosity) as having a profound impact on student achievement. We placed constructs from the instruments in the components where they best fit.

The Cognition and Affect subcomponents are captured more robustly in this set of instruments than Behavior, which only had six constructs. Some are measured more frequently than others. Self-concept, self-discipline, and feeling proud of academic accomplishments were measured less frequently than sense of belonging, self-efficacy, and intent/curiosity.

4.2 Student-Personal: Learning Strategies

Table 2 provides the set of subcomponents for Learning Strategies. We found that one instrument covered the cognitive strategies category of this model (instances and sources of repairs). Metacognition and behavioral strategies are weakly covered. We particularly note that none of the evaluation instruments evaluated behavioral strategies related to time management, test-taking strategies, or note-taking strategies, although all have been shown to significantly impact student achievement and learning.

4.3 Social-Contextual: School Climate

Table 3 provides the set of constructs for School Climate. Lee & Shute define four constructs under Teacher Variables: Motivation, Affect, Cognition, and Meta-Cognition. We placed constructs from the evaluation instruments in each of these four as appropriate.

Table 1: Student-Personal Factors: Student Engagement

Behavioral Engagement	Cognitive-Motivational Engagement	Emotional Engagement (Affect)
Contributions to small group work Engagement in cognitively demanding work Engagement in discussion Degree to which computer game was incorporated in leisure time and perceptions of it as leisure activity** Participation in activities Work autonomously	***Attribution for Success/Failure*** Cognitive Load** Fixed mindset Risk-taking ***Confidence*** Confidence in Using Computers Confidence: working w/computing professionals ***Goal Orientation*** Intent to major in CS Intent to attend graduate school Perceived relevance to future Perceived relevance to future career Usefulness of learning computing skills** (2) ***Outcome Expectancy*** Expectancy value Outcome expectancy beliefs toward computers ***Self-Concept*** Ability to perform leadership skills within group Beliefs about CS ability Confidence to independently control game Creative Tendencies Effective motivation in CS/programming ***Self-Discipline*** Grit Motivation and Persistence Persistence using computers in future ***Self-Efficacy*** Computer Self-Efficacy (2) Confidence: learning CS/programming Confidence: ability for complex programming tasks Confidence: ability for independence/persistence Confidence: ability for self-regulation Confidence: ability for simple programming tasks Confidence: ability to learn CS (2) Confidence: ability to use computers Perceptions of computing ability Self-efficacy conducting research	***Feelings toward school/learning*** Attitudes towards CS Attitudes towards computing Beliefs about using email for learning** Computer anxiety (4) Computer enjoyment/liking (2) Computer "Self-efficacy" (appears to measure affect)** (2) Empathy Enjoyment of outreach activities** Enjoyment using computer game for learning Enjoyment using computers to solve problems Excitement working with CS professionals Real-world connections** ***Feeling proud of academic accomplishments*** Attitude toward success in CS ***Sense of belonging/identification*** Beliefs about CS in relation to ethnic identity** CS identity Engagement by gender/race** Perceptions of CS field and profession Perceptions of CS professionals (2) Perceptions of CS as field for males (3) Perceptions of HFOSS community Professional/Scientist identity formation Sense of belonging in CS Sense of belonging in activity ***Interest/Curiosity*** Curiosity Experiences that influenced students including events/activities that may have piqued their interest How activity participation impacted choice of major Interest in CS (5) Interest in CS Careers (2) Interest in further explorations of CS (2)

Table 2: Student-Personal Factors: Learning Strategies

Cognition	Meta-Cognition	Behavior	
Instances and sources of repairs (Statement or question correction by teacher or student)	Is focus of learning on the "how" or the "why" Knowledge Transfer Perception of impact of a computer game on learning Problem solving strategies Self-assessed level of technological adoption	***Help-seeking***	Help-seeking and coping behaviors
		Homework Management	Study Habits
		Time Management, Test-taking and Note-taking Strategies	*none*

Table 3: Social-Contextual Factors: School Climate

Academic Emphasis	Teacher Variables		Other School Variables
Like/dislike of school	***Motivation*** Accommodating of computers Attitudes about computing Beliefs about CS teaching ability Beliefs about impact of technology on society Beliefs about requiring CS Beliefs about productivity of technology Beliefs about teaching ability (general) Concern over impact of technology Feelings about technology in classroom Perceptions of computers Perception of value of learning CS skills Significance of learning about technology Resourcefulness and coping Utility of technology ***Affect*** Attitude toward teaching CS curriculum Anxiety toward technology Avoidance/Acceptance of technology Comfort with technology Enthusiasm/Enjoyment of technology Interest in Technology	***Cognition*** Absorption of technology into their lives Competency with technology use in IT education Email for classroom learning Interaction with technology (e.g., email) Perception of cognitive demand in CS ***Meta-Cognition*** Confidence in ability to write a program Innovativeness Self-efficacy in teaching programming and CT	Community support for CS Community values/perceptions of CS How students receive help Instructional Style Interactions between students and teacher Nature of discourse in the classroom Resources available to students *Note: We found no constructs in any of the instruments that measured **Principal Leadership** subcomponent with respect to computing.*

Table 4: Social-Contextual Factors: Social-Familial Influences

Parental Involvement	Peer Influences
Importance of learning computing	Friends/family in CS
Perceptions of careers in computing	Friends/family interest in CS
Perspective on computing	
Support for pursuit of computing careers	

While there is moderate coverage of the teacher variables across the 31 instruments, many of these are related to technology in the classroom and not particularly focused on computer science education. We also found that one subcomponent, Principal Leadership, receives no coverage and only found one construct across the instruments that covers Academic Emphasis.

4.4 Social-Contextual: Social-Familial Influences

Social-Familial components are not well covered by the current set of constructs within the instruments we analyzed (see Table 4). Parental involvement is covered by only four constructs. We placed two constructs within peer influences, although we note that they may not be a perfect fit within the Lee & Shute model.

4.5 Summary

We found a total of 132 constructs being measured across the 31 instruments, with 115 of those being unique scales (or subscales) or uniquely contextualized into a program, course, or learning (see Table 5). At the component level, over half (56.5%) of the unique constructs measured Student Engagement and almost a third (31.3%) measured School Climate. The least measured were Learning Strategies (7.0%) and Social-Familial Influences (5.2%).

The vast majority (75.6%) of unique constructs measured were in just three subcomponents: Student Engagement: Affect (25.2% of the unique constructs), Student Engagement: Cognition (26.1%), and School Climate: Teacher Variables (24.3%). Digging deeper, the 29 unique constructs measured in the Affect subcomponent were found across a subset of the 31 evaluation instruments, indicating that instrument authors have developed different instruments that measure a similar construct. For example, six instruments measure the construct *Interest in CS*: Computing Attitudes Survey [8], BASICS Study Student Implementation Questionnaire [26], Computer Science Attitude Survey [17], Robotics Activities Attitudes Scale [6], and Computer Science Attitude and Identity Survey [31].

The fewest constructs measured were School Climate: Principal Leadership (0 constructs found), Learning Strategies: Cognition (1), School Climate: Academic Emphasis (1) , Learning Strategies: Behavior (2), and Social-Familial Influences: Peer Influences (2).

5 DISCUSSION

This works applies a well-established taxonomy of noncognitive factors in K-12 learning (Lee & Shute) to the current body of instruments in the computing education literature, using a categorization that has not been previously accomplished in our field. There are several limitations. The study is based on a framework that was designed based on studies from K-12 education. Therefore, though

Table 5: Number of constructs measured framed in the major components and subcomponents (Lee & Shute)

Component	Subcomponent	Total Constructs	Unique Constructs
Student Engagement	Behavior	6	6
	Cognition	33	30
	Affect	43	29
	Subtotal	***82***	***65***
Learning Strategies	Cognition	1	1
	Meta-Cognition	5	5
	Behavior	2	2
	Subtotal	***8***	***8***
School Climate	Academic Emphasis	1	1
	Teacher Variables	28	28
	Principal Leadership	0	0
	Other	7	7
	Subtotal	***36***	***36***
Social-Familial Influences	Parental Involvement	4	4
	Peer Influences	2	2
	Subtotal	***6***	***6***
TOTAL		***132***	***115***

it may identify gaps in the instruments, it may miss others in higher education. Likewise, we worked with a limited set of evaluation instruments (31). Adding additional instruments to the set could improve the robustness of the list of noncognitive constructs that are measured.

We hope that this study initiates further discussion within the computing education research community, addressing questions such as:

(1) What is the nature of computer science learning, including knowledge, engagement, instructional and learning strategies, and social and contextual factors?
(2) What are our models of learning in computer science education, and how do these incorporate noncognitive factors?
(3) What assessments are needed to measure critical cognitive and noncognitive factors in computer science learning?
(4) How well does the current body of valid measures meet the community's needs to measure diverse and informative theories of change?
(5) What additional measures are needed to determine computer science implementations, outcomes and mitigating factors?

This current study has made a critical contribution to answer questions 1, 2, and 3, and provides an analysis of question 4 based on the Lee & Shute framework and the current published computer science research literature. For question 5, about additional measures needed (and if we take the Lee & Shute framework as a given representation of the noncognitive domain in computer science education), Table 5 indicates: (1) there is currently a large number of constructs within most dimensions of student engagement, (2) measures of very few constructs within the learning strategies factor currently exist, (3) a very large number of teacher variable constructs have existing measures, although principal leadership and school climate academic emphasis measures are lacking and (4) a small number of measures exist for social-family influences. These results suggest that a focus on the development and validation of learning strategy measures (for a variety of constructs and in a variety of contexts) is arguably a top priority.

The work to organize psychosocial constructs is promising in a number of ways. First, this work may help identify the participants who are measured more frequently. It may reveal that our instruments provide little data on women and underrepresented minorities and therefore little information on the constructs that predict success among these populations. Further, this organizational structure may also reveal that we primarily measure student participants, and that we have not adequately expanded our analyses to include classroom, school, and district-level variables that contribute to student success.

Second, an organizational structure may help to determine which constructs and components account for the greatest variance in student success. We recognize that one next step is to gather effect size information that connects constructs and components of the framework to measures of student success. This may open the door for synthesis research and meta-analyses that look across studies to find effects that may otherwise not appear [16].

Finally, many programs currently measure identity and belonging among computer science students. These related constructs are occasionally used synonymously or as a single set of items for measuring both. This framework may move us toward greater sensitivity among all our instruments to differentiate closely related constructs. Improved sensitivity may also help reveal the difference between learning computer science and other STEM disciplines [15]. For example, Lishinski et al. (2017) reveal that students have strong emotional reactions to programming exercises, a psychosocial construct that may be unique to CS and that may explain some of the variance in student success [20].

6 CONCLUSION

The analogy we often use to guide this work is that we are looking for the psychosocial equivalent of the periodic table to help researchers see the landscape of constructs that inform student success, to understand the unique weight of each construct for whom and under what conditions, and to reveal gaps in our toolbox of psychosocial measures. Researchers and evaluators face an ever growing number of possible tools to help measure interventions, and as these tools grow, we must collectively become adept at matching the most sensitive and accurate instruments to more discerning and unique theories of change. To do that, we need a framework that serves as a concept map and also a guide telling us whether the instrument will validly and reliably measure our theory. Our use of the Lee & Shute framework is only a starting point in the classification of evaluation instruments designed for computing education research. We encourage researchers and evaluators to offer critiques that expand upon and improve the framework and the instruments as well.

ACKNOWLEDGMENTS

This material is based upon work supported by the U.S. National Science Foundation uder Grant Nos. 1625335, 1649671, 1745199, and 1757402.

REFERENCES

[1] Jeff Allen, Steven B Robbins, and Richard Sawyer. 2009. Can measuring psychosocial factors promote college success? *Applied Measurement in Education* 23, 1 (2009), 1–22.

[2] American Evaluation Association. 2018. American Evaluation Association. http://www.eval.org/

[3] John D Bransford, Ann L Brown, and Rodney R Cocking. 2000. *How People Learn: Brain, Mind, Experience, and School.* National Academy Press. http://books.nap.edu/catalog/9853.html

[4] Tor Busch. 1996. Gender, group composition, cooperation, and self-efficacy in computer studies. *Journal of educational computing research* 15, 2 (1996), 125–135.

[5] Jeanne Century, Mollie Rudnick, and Cassie Freeman. 2010. A framework for measuring fidelity of implementation: A foundation for shared language and accumulation of knowledge. *American Journal of Evaluation* 31, 2 (2010), 199–218.

[6] Jennifer Cross, Emily Hamner, Lauren Zito, Illah Nourbakhshh, and Debra Bernstein. 2016. Development of an assessment for measuring middle school student attitudes towards robotics activities. In *Frontiers in Education Conference (FIE), 2016 IEEE.* IEEE, 1–8.

[7] Adrienne Decker and Monica M. McGill. 2019. A Topical Review of Evaluation Instruments for Computing Education. In *Proceedings of the 50th ACM Technical Symposium on Computer Science Education.* ACM.

[8] Brian Dorn and Allison Elliott Tew. 2015. Empirical validation and application of the computing attitudes survey. *Computer Science Education* 25, 1 (2015), 1–36.

[9] Inc. Education Development Center. [n. d.]. STELAR. http://stelar.edc.org/resources

[10] George Farkas. 2003. Cognitive skills and noncognitive traits and behaviors in stratification processes. *Annual review of sociology* 29, 1 (2003), 541–562.

[11] Camille A Farrington, Melissa Roderick, Elaine Allensworth, Jenny Nagaoka, Tasha Seneca Keyes, David W Johnson, and Nicole O Beechum. 2012. *Teaching Adolescents to Become Learners: The Role of Noncognitive Factors in Shaping School Performance–A Critical Literature Review.* ERIC.

[12] Center for School Reform at TERC. [n. d.]. MSPMaterials. http://hub.mspnet.org/index.cfm/msp_tools

[13] Institute for the Integration of Technology into Teaching and Learning. [n. d.]. UNT Institute for the Integration of Technology. https://iittl.unt.edu/content/instruments

[14] Catherine Good, Aneeta Rattan, and Carol S Dweck. 2012. Why do women opt out? Sense of belonging and women's representation in mathematics. *Journal of personality and social psychology* 102, 4 (2012), 700.

[15] Mark Guzdial. 2018. Learning Computer Science Is Different Than Learning Other STEM Disciplines. https://cacm.acm.org/blogs/blog-cacm/224105-learning-computer-science-is-different-than-learning-other-stem-disciplines/fulltext. Accessed: 2010-07-21.

[16] John Hattie. 2008. *Visible learning: A synthesis of over 800 meta-analyses relating to achievement.* routledge.

[17] Andrew Hoegh and Barbara M Moskal. 2009. Examining science and engineering students' attitudes toward computer science. In *Frontiers in Education Conference, 2009. FIE'09. 39th IEEE.* IEEE, 1–6.

[18] Jihyun Lee and Valerie J Shute. 2010. Personal and social-contextual factors in K–12 academic performance: An integrative perspective on student learning. *Educational Psychologist* 45, 3 (2010), 185–202.

[19] Jihyun Lee and Lazar Stankov. 2018. Non-cognitive predictors of academic achievement: Evidence from TIMSS and PISA. *Learning and Individual Differences* 65 (2018), 50–64.

[20] Alex Lishinski, Aman Yadav, and Richard Enbody. 2017. Students' Emotional Reactions to Programming Projects in Introduction to Programming: Measurement Approach and Influence on Learning Outcomes. In *Proceedings of the 2017 ACM Conference on International Computing Education Research.* ACM, 30–38.

[21] J. Margolis and A. Fisher. 2003. *Unlocking the Clubhouse: Women in Computing.* MIT Press. https://books.google.com/books?id=StwGQw45YoEC

[22] Robert J Marzano. 2003. *What works in schools: Translating research into action.* ASCD.

[23] Monica M McGill, Adrienne Decker, and Zachary Abbott. 2018. Improving Research and Experience Reports of Pre-College Computing Activities: A Gap Analysis. In *Proceedings of the 49th ACM Technical Symposium on Computer Science Education.* ACM, 964–969.

[24] Briana B Morrison, Brian Dorn, and Mark Guzdial. 2014. Measuring cognitive load in introductory CS: adaptation of an instrument. In *Proceedings of the tenth annual conference on International computing education research.* ACM, 131–138.

[25] Boston Museum of Science. 2018. Research Instruments. https://www.eie.org/engineering-elementary/research/research-instruments

[26] University of Chicago Outlier Resesarch & Evaluation, UChicago STEM Education. 2017. BASICS Study Student Implementation Questionnaire. http://outlier.uchicago.edu/basics/resources/Measures-StudentImplementation/

[27] Afterschool PEAR (Program in Education and Resiliency). [n. d.]. PearInstitute. http://www.pearweb.org/atis/tools/jump

[28] Jeffrey A Rosen, Elizabeth J Glennie, Ben W Dalton, Jean M Lennon, and Robert N Bozick. 2010. *Noncognitive Skills in the Classroom: New Perspectives on Educational Research.* ERIC.

[29] Lazar Stankov, Suzanne Morony, and Yim Ping Lee. 2014. Confidence: the best non-cognitive predictor of academic achievement? *Educational Psychology* 34, 1 (2014), 9–28.

[30] Jennifer Wang, Sepehr Hejazi Moghadam, and Juliet Tiffany-Morales. 2017. Social Perceptions in Computer Science and Implications for Diverse Students. In *Proceedings of the 2017 ACM Conference on International Computing Education Research (ICER '17).* ACM, New York, NY, USA, 47–55. https://doi.org/10.1145/3105726.3106175

[31] Alicia N Washington, Shaefny Grays, and Sudhipta Dasmohapatra. 2016. The Computer Science Attitude and Identity Survey (CSAIS): A Novel Tool for Measuring the Impact of Ethnic Identity in Underrepresented Computer Science Students. In *Proceedings of the ASEE's 123rd Annual Conference & Exposition 2016.*

Electronic Textiles in Computer Science Education:

A Synthesis of Efforts to Broaden Participation, Increase Interest, and Deepen Learning

Gayithri Jayathirtha†
Graduate School of Education
University of Pennsylvania
Philadelphia PA USA
gayithri@gse.upenn.edu

Yasmin B. Kafai
Graduate School of Education
University of Pennsylvania
Philadelphia PA USA
kafai@upenn.edu

ABSTRACT

Just over a decade ago, various electronic textile construction kits have emerged with Arduino-based microcontrollers, sensors, and actuators that can be sewn together with conductive thread to create wearables augmented with new functionalities. These kits were designed to broaden participation in and perspectives about computing along with introducing learners to powerful ideas about circuitry and coding. In this paper, we synthesize 46 studies that have introduced crafts, circuitry, and coding concepts with e-textiles in K-16 education. We found that e-textiles have been successful in broadening participation and increasing interest in computing for many youth and adults, especially from underrepresented groups, inside and outside of school. While the e-textiles construction kits have been successful in deepening learning of circuitry concepts, learning of computer science, especially advanced concepts, has been far less attended to with the exception of projects designed by undergraduate students with already significant disciplinary expertise. In the discussion, we suggest directions for future research such as bringing more computing into e-textile designs, creating assessments to capture coding and circuitry learning, and developing models for more advanced projects to leverage the potential of e-textiles for computer science education.

CCS CONCEPTS

• Applied computing → Education → Interactive Learning Environments

KEYWORDS

Electronic textiles, computational construction kits, computer science education, gender and diversity

†Corresponding Author

SIGCSE '19, February 27-March 2, 2019, Minneapolis, MN, USA.

ACM ISBN 978-1-4503-5890-3/19/02...$15.00.
DOI: https://doi.org/10.1145/3287324.32873430

ACM Reference format:

Gayithri Jayathirtha and Yasmin Kafai. 2019. Electronic Textiles in Computer Science Education: A Synthesis of Efforts to Broaden Participation, Increase Interest, and Deepen Learning. In *Proceedings of the 50th ACM Technical Symposium on Computer Science Education (SIGCSE '19). Feb. 27-Mar. 2, 2019, Minneapolis, MN, USA.* ACM, New York, NY, USA. 7 pages. https://doi.org/10.1145/3287324.3287343

1 Introduction

To address the underrepresentation of women and minorities in the tech industry [1], many efforts are underway to broaden participation in K-12 computer science (CS) education, motivate interest in computing and not only introduce but also deepen their understanding of computational ideas. Many outreach efforts such as Code Start, Girls Who Code, and Black Girls Code (for example, [2]) and community spaces such as Computer Clubhouses [3] have provided opportunities for underrepresented groups to learn computer programming. Programming tools such as Scratch [4], Alice [5] and others have been designed to provide a low threshold for exploring computational ideas and connect to a variety of interests. Further, high school curricula such as *Exploring Computer Science* [6] have been developed to introduce computing to students in under-resourced communities.

One aspect that has not received as much attention is the introduction of new tools, materials and practices for learning computer science which challenge traditional conceptions of computing. One such example are electronic textiles (hereafter: e-textiles) that connect computing and crafting—two activities not commonly associated with each other—combining traditionally masculine activities of computing and engineering with the more traditionally feminine activities of sewing and crafting [7]. E-textile construction kits provide electronic components such as LED lights, sensors, and microcontrollers with sewable interface that can be stitched on clothing, accessories, and toys using conductive thread, and usually programmed through the conventional Arduino IDE. Over the last decade, numerous e-textile construction kits have been developed [8]. Four of these—the LilyPad Arduino (Sparkfun), micro:bit (BBC), and Flora and the Circuit Playground (Adafruit) have moved into commercial production and distribution, making these kits broadly accessible and more affordable for K-16 education. At the same time, dozens of studies have been conducted in which hundreds of learners of all ages and backgrounds have engaged with e-textiles inside and outside of school.

In this paper, we take stock of the overall contribution of e-textiles to computer science education. The introduction of e-textiles as an alternative to construction kits focused on robotics and gaming has been accompanied by hopes to broaden participation, increase interest in computing and further the learning of computing concepts. With many individual studies involving e-textiles completed, this comprehensive review will provide a more systematic and cumulative account on the trends in the field at large. Given the still exploratory nature of the research studies and the current state of computer science education [9], we conducted a meta-synthesis [10] rather than a meta-analysis which would be more suitable for fields with more statistical studies. Meta-syntheses have been common in public health and medical fields but are now finding more reception in educational contexts [11]. By searching through databases and consulting with experts in the field, we developed a repository of empirical studies on e-textiles to address the following research questions: (1) To what degree have e-textiles succeeded in broadening participation of underrepresented groups in computing? (2) To what degree have e-textiles raised students' interest in computing? and (3) What can students learn when making e-textile projects? In the discussion we address critical issues and outline steps for further research.

2 Background

The first e-textiles construction kit consisted of bulky, repurposed computer components connected together and attached to clothing to make a musical jacket, one that allowed the wearer to play music using the embroidered sections on its front [12]. Almost a decade later, the arrival of the Arduino board, a low-cost, open-source microcontroller led to the development of the LilyPad Arduino [7]. The LilyPad Arduino, prototyped by Buechley on a fabric substrate in a university research lab was later developed and distributed by Sparkfun (see Figure 1, left) as a printed circuit board with metal-coated holes, but with the same Arduino microcontroller and programmable input/output pins. Development of peripheral electronic components such as LED lights, temperature and light sensors, and switches soon followed these initial efforts. More recently, Adafruit Industries also developed similar boards such as Circuit Playground, this time with more on-board sensors such as accelerometer, temperature, and light sensors (see Figure 1, right), making it easier to realize interactive artifacts. Other commercially-available, simplified e-textile construction kits such as LilyTiny, Gemma and Flora provide pre-programmed functionalities or fewer input and output pins. In addition, researchers have developed other versions such as Teeboards [13] and Quilt Snaps [7, 14], but these have not gone into commercial distribution.

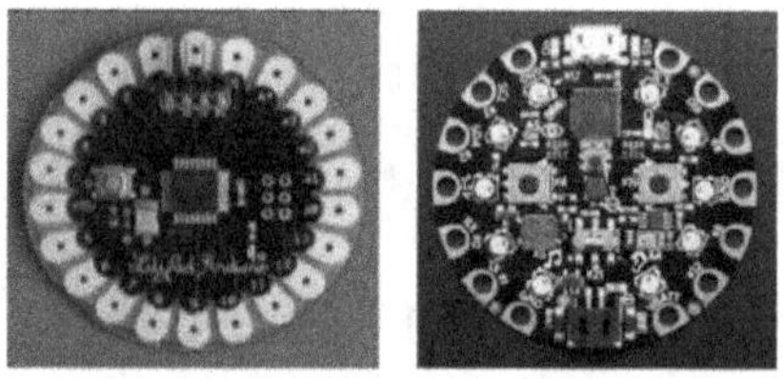

Figure 1: LilyPad Arduino board showing the sewable and electronic holes (left); Adafruit Circuit Playground board with many more on-board sensors (right)

One of the attractions for developing e-textiles for Buechley and colleagues was that "textile crafts might prove to be an effective means of promoting girls' enthusiasm toward programming and engineering" (p. 56) [14]. This aspect of broadening participation in computing was confirmed when Buechley and Hill [15] conducted a study of projects made with the Lilypad in "the wild" comparing them to typical Arduino-based projects. They studied the sales records of LilyPad and Arduino boards from the SparkFun site and analyzed the publicly-available project details to understand gender composition of the customers. Although a much smaller proportion of the overall customer base purchased LilyPad (12%) compared to Arduino (91%), they noted that only 2% of the Arduino customers were female while 35% of the LilyPad customers were female. Further, 65% of the LilyPad projects were developed by female makers, which is much higher than the small proportion (2%) of the Arduino projects where the makers were female. Buechley and Hill's [15] findings revealed that indeed new tools such as LilyPad Arduino can create new computing communities. With e-textiles moving into K-16 education, one of our central questions was whether this trend of increasing gender diversity among participants in computation would continue. Furthermore, we sought to see if the innovative sewable interface of e-textiles kits broadened participation across dimensions other than gender to include learners from groups underrepresented in computing.

A second intention of e-textiles was not only to broaden participation in computing but also to raise interest in computing by providing materials such as textiles and activities such as sewing which have been associated more with feminine traditions [16]. Individual programs such as Digital Youth Divas [17] and Gwen Girls [18] have taken advantage of this intersection of gendered disciplines. In addition, these programs involving e-textiles have also been designed to draw girls specifically from underrepresented groups. The early research in computer science education provides ample evidence that girls have not been interested in computing. Work by Yardi and Bruckman found that teenagers perceived computing as "boring, solitary and irrelevant to the real-world" (p. 42) [19]. Thus, we not only need to introduce more girls and learners from underrepresented communities in computation but we also need to address how e-textiles improve their interest in and perceptions about computing.

Finally, Buechley and colleagues saw potential to study the learning of computational concepts and practices as they engage with e-textiles [14]. Kafai, Fields and Searle's [20] study highlighted the rich possibility of computational learning within the context of a high school e-textiles class. Students developed computational concepts such as data, conditionals, loops, etc., and practices such as testing and debugging, thinking iteratively, etc., as they made e-textiles artifacts. Learning with e-textiles not only involved computational concepts but also circuit design, a topic traditionally housed in science education. In addition, the extensive crafting involved in making e-textiles artifacts demands creative thinking as learners wrestle with embedding circuitry and coding while attending to artistic and aesthetic dimensions. Through this synthesis, we attempt to assess in which ways the promises of e-textiles to broaden participation, increase interest, and deepen learning have been realized in K-16 education.

3 Synthesis Approach

We conducted a meta-synthesis [10] of all the literature on e-textiles published between 2007 and 2018 by focusing on searches of databases and information from colleagues working in the field. We started with systematic searches across digital libraries and conference proceedings as published in ACM Digital Library, ProQuest, EBSCO, JSTOR, and Google Scholar with keywords such as "electronic textiles," "wearables," "LilyPad Arduino" and "Circuit Playground". Furthermore, we reached out to the key contributors in the field seeking their input on our search and providing copies of publications not captured in the search.

At the conclusion of this process, our repository had 110 papers including reviews, commentaries, tool design, and evaluation studies. For the inclusion in our synthesis, we selected studies that satisfied the following criteria: (a) used e-textiles construction kits with a group of learners, either K-12 students or adults; (b) were situated in school classrooms and out-of-school settings such as after-school clubs, library workshops, or summer programs; and (c) involved examination of outcomes of learning, focusing on academic content of circuit design, computation, and/or outcomes of learner interest in and attitude towards computation. For example, a paper by Kim, Paulos, and Gross [51] that designed and prototyped an e-textile wearable without direct educational implications was not included in our synthesis. These selection criteria resulted in a final list of 46 studies. We then extracted from each paper demographic details about the learners (age, gender and ethnicity, if available); the duration, context and intention of the study; e-textile construction kits used; and the types of artifacts made by learners. We further categorized academic outcomes into the following topics: (1) interests and attitudes towards CS; (2) learning about circuits, and (3) learning about computation, ranging from basic ideas such as sequencing and variables to more advanced ideas of programming analog sensors and actuators. Some studies addressed more than one topic. We note that 43 out of the 46 studies included in our synthesis employed qualitative methods using participant observations, interviews, or student journal entries for data collection. Only three of the studies employed mixed methods and a quasi-experimental design (see [21, 22, 23]).

4 Findings

We present the key findings from our synthesis in the sections below, starting with a general overview of who participated, where and what participants did with e-textiles followed by a closer examination of outcomes focused on broadening participation, increasing interest, and deepening learning with e-textiles.

4.1 Engaging with E-Textiles

Across all studies included in our synthesis, a total of more than 1,300 youth and adults participated in different kinds of e-textiles activities, with an average group size of 27 learners [23, 24, 25]. The majority of studies involved middle (44%) and high school (40%) youth between the ages of 12-18 years followed by elementary school students (13%) of ages 8-11 years. Only 10 studies involved adults such as undergraduate and graduate college students [26, 27, 28, 29] as well as science and computer science teachers [30, 31, 32] among others [7, 14, 33].

On average, most workshops or classes were 15 hours in duration. Looking at the contexts in which these studies were conducted, more than half (56%) took place in out-of-school spaces such as after-school classes, computer clubs, summer camps and museums [22, 34, 35] while 40% of them took place within formal learning spaces such as grade-school classrooms and university-level courses (e.g., [26, 36, 37]). Hackathon competitions [29], teacher professional development [31], and online platforms [38] were other rare sites of research and mostly frequented by adult participants.

What kind of e-textile artifacts did participants make with these construction kits? We identified two distinct artifacts and approaches: (1) repurposing old clothing and textile accessories and (2) sewing new textile toys and accessories. In the first category, we found that participants augmented—often their own—tote bags, jackets, hats, and shoes with new features and functionalities (see [7, 25, 35]). In the second category, participants sewed from scratch textile artifacts such as bracelets, bookmarks, and interactive monsters (eg., [39, 40]) using the templates developed by Qiu and colleagues [41]. The LilyPad construction kit along with text-based Arduino programming or block-based Modkit programming language were used most frequently in these designs, with only a few studies using the other commercially available Circuit Playgrounds [30] or other sewable microcontrollers such as Adafruit Flora [21].

Across both approaches, basic projects involved students stitching simple lighting circuits to backpacks or making artifacts such as wristbands and represented the most frequent e-textile designs. Slightly advanced projects often included interactive artifacts using digital inputs such as buttons and switches. More advanced projects involved analog sensors and used the sensor output to trigger certain behaviors such as playing music or making lights blink in different patterns but were far less prominent [26, 29]. We will discuss below the ramifications of these project designs on learning outcomes across the field at large.

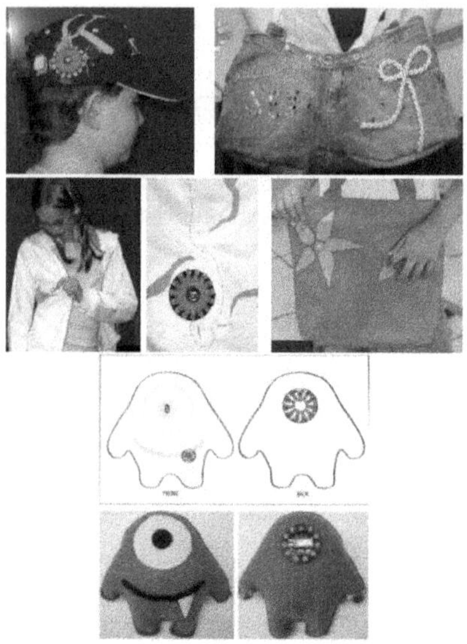

Figure 2a: Repurposing existing textiles (from left to right): hat, pants, jacket (with detail), and tote bag (drawn from [34, 25]); Figure 2b: Sewing new projects from Buechley and Qiu's [42] *Sew Electric*: template (upper row), plush toy monsters (lower row)

4.2 Broadening Participation in Computing

Of the 46 studies included in our synthesis, more than half (56%) focused on broadening perspectives about computing. One expectation of introducing e-textile construction kits was to make computing activities more accessible to a wider range of participants, particularly girls and women. Among the studies (only 73% of all the studies) that provided this demographic detail, 61% (567/928) of the participants were female while 39% (361/928) were male. This proportion, surprisingly, is very similar to what Buechley and Hill [15] observed in their survey of the LilyPad Arduino projects in the wild as discussed in the background section. This large proportion of women and girls participating in computation while making with e-textiles alone is a promising finding in support of broadening participation, especially when compared to what is known about the participation of women and girls in other computing activities. For instance, only 30% of total participants in the first LEGO robotics competition were girls [43], and girls comprised of only 22% of students who took AP Computer Science classes across the nation in 2015 (CSForAll).

Another dimension of broadening participation that emerged from our review concerned the ethnicity of participants. While less than half of the studies (49%) provided this demographic information, it is nonetheless an important factor. Close to half (48%) of the learners came from underrepresented groups such as Hispanics/Latinos, African-Americans and American Indians, followed by 37% who identified as Caucasian and 11% who identified as Asian, Pacific Islander or mixed; 4% declined to racially identify themselves. Many e-textiles programs were targeted outreach efforts to bring underrepresented student groups into computing (eg., [17, 18]) thus explaining the large number of underrepresented participants in e-textile activities. However, we have to note that acknowledging the demographic details of the participants becomes extremely important, especially in this day and age when we want to work towards making computing education more equitable. Overall, based on the information available, we can conclude that the use of e-textile construction kits was not only successful in broadening participation by including a larger percentage of women and girls but surprisingly included also large number of participants from ethnically underrepresented groups.

4.3 Increasing Interest in Computing

The use of e-textile construction kits did not only attract diverse groups into computation but also increased interest in and develop positive attitudes towards computing among K-16 learners. We already noted that a majority (56%) of the studies in our synthesis intended to broaden participants' perspectives about computing, either by providing more opportunities to be creative and express themselves or develop computing identities. Participants across all age groups—from elementary students to science teachers—reported more positive attitudes towards circuitry and computing after working with e-textiles (see [13, 17, 20, 21, 39]). A few studies noted that one of the reasons why e-textiles led to such positive attitudes towards computing was related to participants' ability to customize their e-textile artifacts according to their personal and cultural interests. For instance, Fields and Kafai [35] observed middle and high school students interweave their personal interests in anime characters into e-textiles projects in school while Pinkard and colleagues [17] saw girls adopting flowers from a favorite meme to make fabric e-flowers. This finding also applied to older learners: Fields and King [27] observed adult learners integrating their knowledge from homes with e-textiles while Lovell and Buechley [39] saw older participants create personally meaningful artifacts such as bike speedometers.

Likewise, cultural interests also found room in e-textiles (e.g., [27, 32, 37]). For instance, Kutznetsov and colleagues [18] observed e-textiles artifacts to serve as "healing materials" for at-risk African American girls (ages 10-12 years) with opportunities to express themselves in creative ways while Kafai and her colleagues [20] saw Native American students design artifacts that echoed elements of their culture such as native flowers and plants in a project quilt. While the above studies pointed at possible cultural connections that increased interest among young learners, Davis and colleagues' study [21] comparing e-textiles Arduino kit with the functionally similar traditional Arduino kit in an all-girls high school observed that the traditional Arduino construction kit produced the same positive effect on girls' self-identification with computing as the e-textiles kit. Lack of clear reasons for this observation forced the researchers to hypothesize that the context in which the study was conducted, an all-girls middle school, did not allow for gender-based stereotypes to appear and influence computing learning in this context. Furthermore, they highlighted the need for further examination of the relationship between the gendered nature of e-textiles activity and girls' perception about computing. Our synthesis also highlighted the need for studies to further examine the nuances of interactions to tease out the elements of tool design and learning environments that provide these unique opportunities for creative expression with computing.

4.4 Deepening Learning of Circuitry and Computing

Studies that examined learning of academic content fell along a wide spectrum—from basic circuitry and computing ideas such as instruction sequencing to more advanced ideas of integrating multiple analog inputs and outputs. Almost a third of the 46 studies focused on learning academic content, either circuitry or computing, by making e-textiles. Out of these 16 studies, eight of them investigated learning of simple circuit concepts such as polarity and eight on basic computing concepts such as digital input/outputs and control flow. Only four studies examined more advanced programming concepts in making e-textiles such as analog inputs and outputs, data structures, and nested conditionals. Although some of the advanced projects demanded design and implementation of complex circuits and sophisticated crafting, very few studies systematically examined the influence of these domains on developing computational ideas [28]. In contrast to the previous sections that provided ample evidence of broadening participation and increasing interest in computing, learning academic content, in particular more advanced computing concepts was limited when making e-textiles.

The most compelling evidence of learning with e-textiles comes from students' understanding of circuit design. Peppler and Glosson [22] explored early on this possibility of using e-textiles to introduce circuitry concepts such as current flow, connections and polarity as students sewed on simple circuits onto their t-shirts. In this study, significant changes between pre- and post-tests clearly indicate that a class of 17 middle school students improved understanding of simple circuitry concepts after making e-textile wearables. A later quasi-experimental study by Tofel-Grehl and colleagues [23] provided additional evidence that 75 students in science classes learned significantly better about circuit design when working with e-textiles than those who learned about circuits with traditional circuitry construction kits such as breadboards and alligator clips. Using a multiple-choice assessment instrument crafted from standardized test items, researchers attributed the differences in student understanding to the nature of e-textile components that allowed for mistakes that would then lead to better learning by debugging and fixing errors. Components such as un-insulated conductive thread increased transparency since they afforded unique opportunities for students to explore concepts such as current flow and short circuits when compared to conventional circuit construction kits.

Along with studying students' learning of basic circuit design nine studies examined students' learning of simple computing concepts such as variables, instruction sequencing, and simple digital input/output. Most of these studies involved students sewing actuators such as LEDs, sometimes including input devices such as buttons and switches, and programming using simple variables, binary operators, and conditional statements to produce different light patterns (see [39, 41, 44]). For example, students employed multiple lights and buttons to make interactive wall murals that would display different lighting patterns when the user pressed definite combinations of these buttons. As noted in section 4.1, most of these student projects were limited to making artifacts such as bracelets, murals or accessories augmented with simple interaction. This need to diversifying project ideas was noted in Peppler and colleagues [50] study where they conducted an expert analysis of 166 e-textiles projects online to identify creativity in these projects only to find that even experts found that a good majority of them were mostly basic, "first LED" projects.

Only four studies reported students making artifacts that involved more advanced computational constructs such as analog inputs and outputs, arrays, and complex control-flows, integration of multiple sensors and actuators (see [26, 27, 29, 45]). For instance, in Eisenberg and colleagues' [26] semester-long seminar, undergraduate engineering students developed e-textile projects such as heating-and-cooling jacket and lighting-cum-music t-shirt that utilized a wide range of electronic components while in Richard and colleagues' [29] overnight hackathon, teams of undergraduate engineering and design students crafted wearable music players and game controllers, sensory reactive clothing for babies, and responsive purses. These e-textile projects involved computational concepts beyond conditional and event-based programming to include data processing from multiple sensors and program actuators from a wider electronics community.

5 Discussion

Our synthesis of introducing e-textiles during the last decade revealed not only promising outcomes but also raised several issues if we want to further computer science education with e-textiles. We were heartened to see that engagement with e-textiles resulted in broadening participation and increasing interest in computing for significant numbers of youth and adults, especially from underrepresented groups. Furthermore, we identified limited efforts to explore and examine possibilities for deeper learning of more advanced computational concepts. Some studies provided examples of e-textile projects with more advanced computational concepts such as handing analog data or designing sophisticated control flows using loops and conditionals, but these were designed by undergraduate students with already significant disciplinary expertise in engineering, computation or arts. The findings of this synthesis thus provide directives for moving forward in the following directions: developing a better understanding of learning with e-textiles, creating assessments for understanding learning with e-textiles, and promoting the design of more advanced e-textile projects in K-12 CS education.

5.1 Understanding Learning with E-Textiles

Our synthesis demonstrated that e-textiles broadened participation in computing to include not only women but also learners from underrepresented groups. However, the exact reasons how these construction kits are drawing newer groups of participants into computing are unknown. While some of the studies alluded to the degree of personalization that these kits afford, there could be other reasons too. For example, Tofel-Grehl and colleagues' [23] study pointed out the different kinds of familial connections students drew on as they made e-textiles artifacts. Similarly, Searle and colleagues [37] noted how students were drawing on their familial and cultural funds of knowledge as they learned computing in classrooms. These are important connections but not yet well-understood in CS education research. A more in-depth exploration of these connections will advance our understanding of their role in developing computing identities and agency. Overall, there is a need for studies that further examine learning in these contexts to understand the features of these construction kits that enable broadening of participation and engage in learning.

5.2 Assessing Learning with E-Textiles

In our synthesis, we reviewed separately the multiple domains of coding or circuitry involved in learning with e-textiles, but there is a definite need to better understand the integrated or intersectional nature of problem-solving that happens as learners make and debug e-textiles projects. Many projects in computer science now promote learning integrated with other STEM subjects—just like e-textiles do—but there is little knowledge of how such integrations can be most productively facilitated for learners. For understanding learning about computational concepts and practices, we have just started developing measures that capture the intersectional nature of learning about circuitry and computing with e-textiles [44]. However, we know that crafting and aesthetics are also intertwined in the context of learning with e-textiles [20, 28]. We should capture learning outcomes that provide a more holistic assessment, not privileging one academic domain over the other. One possible approach is through portfolios that ask students to document and reflect upon their learning with e-textiles [46, 47]. Here learners can describe their artifacts with photos, annotated blueprints of circuit diagrams and Arduino code as a part of documenting their process and practices, moving the focus away from a final product. Furthermore, they can also describe challenges they had to overcome [46] which have proven to be insightful in understanding student gains in computational concepts, practices and perspectives [48]. Nevertheless, we see a need to push development of different assessments formats that allow us to capture the complexities of learning about computation with e-textiles.

5.3 Developing Advanced E-Textiles Projects

Our synthesis also identified the critical need to develop more complex e-textile activities that raise the ceiling of what students can learn about computing. We have a few examples from undergraduate classes and hackathons [26, 28, 29] where learning with e-textile projects expanded by bringing together an eclectic set of hardware such as fans, solar panels, fabric insulators, electroluminescent films, MP3 players with other microcontroller boards. These examples suggest that the introductory toolkit needs to include a wider variety of input and output devices so that novices can explore a more diverse set of computational ideas. To introduce such projects to K-12 students will also require careful consideration and design of scaffolds.

When e-textile construction kits were introduced over a decade ago they offered to broaden participation and increase interest in computing. While some of these promises have been realized there is a need to design tools, activities and pathways that provide opportunities for learners to explore a wider range of computational concepts, thereby enabling deeper learning. The promise of e-textiles to expand the landscape of computer science education to broaden participation and increase interest among learners from underrepresented groups will only gain strength with more research to foster deeper computational learning and assessment.

ACKNOWLEDGMENTS

This work was supported by the National Science Foundation grant to Yasmin Kafai, Jane Margolis, and Joanna Goode (#1509245/1512760/1510725). Any opinions, findings, conclusions or recommendations expressed in this paper are those of the authors and do not necessarily reflect the views of either NSF or the University of Pennsylvania. Special thanks to Deborah Fields, Debora Lui, Justice T. Walker, and Mia Shaw for their valuable feedback.

REFERENCES

[1] Jane Margolis and Rachel Estrella. 2017. *Stuck in the shallow end: education, race, and computing*, The MIT Press, Cambridge, MA, USA.

[2] Jeff Stern, Emily Reid, and Kari Bancroft. 2015. Teaching introductory computer science for a diverse student body: Girls who code style. In *Proceedings of the 46th ACM Technical Symposium on Computer Science Education*, ACM, 2015, 705-705.

[3] Yasmin B. Kafai, Kylie A. Peppler, and Robbin N. Chapman. 2009. *The Computer Clubhouse: Constructionism and Creativity in Youth Communities. Technology, Education–Connections.* Teachers College Press. 1234 Amsterdam Avenue, New York, NY, USA.

[4] Mitchel Resnick, John Maloney, Andrés Monroy-Hernández, Natalie Rusk, Evelyn Eastmond, Karen Brennan, Amon Millner, ... and Yasmin B. Kafai. 2009. Scratch: programming for all. *Communications of the ACM* 52, 11 (2009), 60-67.

[5] Caitlin Kelleher and Randy Pausch. 2005. Lowering the barriers to programming: A taxonomy of programming environments and languages for novice programmers. *ACM Computing Surveys (CSUR)* 37, no. 2 (2005): 83-137.

[6] Jane Margolis and Joanna Goode. 2016. Ten lessons for computer science for all. *ACM Inroads* 7, 4 (2016), 52-56.

[7] Leah Buechley. 2006. A construction kit for electronic textiles. In *Wearable Computers, 10th IEEE International Symposium 2006*, 83-90.

[8] Leah Buechley, Kylie Peppler, Michael Eisenberg, and Kafai Yasmin. 2013. *Textile Messages: Dispatches from the World of E-Textiles and Education. New Literacies and Digital Epistemologies. Volume 62.* Peter Lang Publishing Group. 29 Broadway 18th Floor, New York, NY 10006, 2013.

[9] Mark Guzdial. 2015. Learner-centered design of computing education: Research on computing for everyone. *Synthesis Lectures on Human-Centered Informatics* 8, 6 (2015), 1-165.

[10] Harsh Suri and David Clarke. 2009. Advancements in research synthesis methods: From a methodologically inclusive perspective. *Review of Educational Research* 79, 1 (2009), 395-430.

[11] Harsh Suri. 2013. Epistemological pluralism in research synthesis methods. *International journal of qualitative studies in education* 26, 7 (2013), 889-911.

[12] Maggie Orth, Rehmi Post, and Emily Cooper. 1998. Fabric computing interfaces. In *CHI 98 conference summary on Human factors in computing systems*, ACM, 1998, 331-332.

[13] Grace Ngai, Stephen CF Chan, Joey CY Cheung, and Winnie WY Lau. 2009. The TeeBoard: an education-friendly construction platform for e-textiles and wearable computing. In *Proceedings of the SIGCHI Conference on Human Factors in Computing Systems*, ACM, 2009, 249-258.

[14] Leah Buechley, Nwanua Elumeze, and Michael Eisenberg. 2006. Electronic/computational textiles and children's crafts. In *Proceedings of the 2006 conference on Interaction design and children*, ACM, 2006, 49-56.

[15] Leah Buechley and Benjamin M. Hill. 2010. LilyPad in the wild: how hardware's long tail is supporting new engineering and design communities. In *Proceedings of the 8th ACM conference on designing interactive systems*, ACM, 2010, 199-207.

[16] Leah Buechley and Michael Eisenberg. 2008. The LilyPad Arduino: Toward wearable engineering for everyone. *IEEE Pervasive Computing* 7, 2 (2008), 12-15.

[17] Nichole Pinkard, Sheena Erete, Caitlin K. Martin, and Maxine McKinney de Royston. 2017. Digital Youth Divas: Exploring narrative-driven curriculum to spark middle school girls' interest in computational activities. *Journal of the Learning Sciences* 26, 3 (2017), 477-516.

[18] S. Kutznetsov, L. Trutoiu, C. Kute, I. Howley, D. Siewiorek, and E. Paulos. 2011. Breaking Boundaries: Mentoring with Wearable Computing. In *Proceedings of CHI 2011*, 2957-2966.

[19] Sarita Yardi and Amy Bruckman. 2007. What is computing?: bridging the gap between teenagers' perceptions and graduate students' experiences. In *Proceedings of the third International workshop on Computing Education Research*, ACM, 2007, 39-50.

[20] Yasmin B. Kafai, Deborah Fields, and Kristin Searle. 2014. Electronic textiles as disruptive designs: Supporting and challenging maker activities in schools. *Harvard Educational Review* 84, no. 4 (2014): 532-556.

[21] Richard L. Davis, Christopher Proctor, Michelle Friend, and Paulo Blikstein. 2018. Solder and Wire or Needle and Thread: Examining the Effects of Electronic Textile Construction Kits on Girls' Attitudes Towards Computing and Arts. In *Proceedings of the International Conference of Learning Sciences*, 2018, 800-808.

[22] Kylie Peppler and Diane Glosson. 2013. Stitching circuits: Learning about circuitry through e-textile materials. *Journal of Science Education and Technology* 22, 5 (2013), 751-763.

[23] Colby Tofel-Grehl, Deborah Fields, Kristin Searle, Cathy Maahs-Fladung, David Feldon, Grace Gu, and Chongning Sun. 2017. Electrifying engagement in middle school science class: improving student interest through e-textiles. *Journal of Science Education and Technology* 26, 4 (2017), 406-417.

[24] Yasmin B. Kafai and Kylie A. Peppler. 2014. Transparency Reconsidered: Creative, Critical, and Connected Making with E-textiles. *DIY citizenship: Critical making and social media* (2014), 179-188.

[25] Eva-Sophie Katterfeldt, Nadine Dittert, and Heidi Schelhowe. 2009. EduWear: smart textiles as ways of relating computing technology to everyday life. In *Proceedings of the 8th International Conference on Interaction Design and Children*, ACM, 2009, 9-17.

[26] Michael Eisenberg, Ann Eisenberg, and Yingdan Huang. 2013. Bringing e-textiles into engineering education. *Textile Messages: Dispatches from the world of e-textiles and education* (2013), 121-129.

[27] Deborah A. Fields and Whitney L. King. 2014. So, I think I'm a programmer now. Developing connected learning for adults in a university craft technologies course. In *Learning and Becoming in Practice: The International Conference of the Learning Sciences (ICLS)*, 1, 927-936.

[28] Victor R. Lee and Deborah A. Fields. 2017. A rubric for describing competences in the areas of circuitry, computation, and crafting after a course using e-textiles. *The International Journal of Information and Learning Technology* 34, 5 (2017), 372-384.

[29] Gabriela T. Richard, Yasmin B. Kafai, Barrie Adleberg, and Orkan Telhan. 2015. StitchFest: Diversifying a College Hackathon to broaden participation and perceptions in computing. In *Proceedings of the 46th ACM Technical Symposium on Computer Science Education*, ACM, 2015, 114-119.

[30] Deborah A. Fields, Debora Lui, and Yasmin B. Kafai. 2017. Teaching computational thinking with electronic textiles: High school teachers' contextualizing strategies in exploring computer science. *Siu-cheung KONG The Education University of Hong Kong, Hong Kong* (2017), 67-72.

[31] Kristin A. Searle, Colby Tofel-Grehl, and Vicki Allan. 2016. The E-Textiles Bracelet Hack: Bringing Making to Middle School Classrooms. In *Proceedings of the 6th Annual Conference on Creativity and Fabrication in Education*, ACM, 2016, 107-110.

[32] Colby Tofel-Grehl and Kristin Searle. 2017. Critical Reflections on Teacher Conceptions of Race as Related to the Effectiveness of Science Learning. *Journal of Multicultural Affairs* 2, 1 (2017), 4.

[33] Leah Buechley, Mike Eisenberg, and Nwanua Elumeze. 2007. Towards a curriculum for electronic textiles in the high school classroom. In *ACM SIGCSE Bulletin*, 39 (3), 28-32.

[34] Leah Buechley, Mike Eisenberg, Jaime Catchen, and Ali Crockett. 2008. The LilyPad Arduino: using computational textiles to investigate engagement, aesthetics, and diversity in computer science education. In *Proceedings of the SIGCHI conference on Human Factors in Computing Systems*, ACM, 2008, 423-432.

[35] Deborah A. Fields and Y. B. Kafai. 2011. Crafting Identities: E-Textile Artifacts as Mediators in High Tech Communities. In H. Spada, G. Stahl (Eds), N. Miyake, & N. Law (Eds), Connecting Computer Supported Collaborative Learning to policy and practices: CSCL '11 community events proceedings, 2, Short Papers & Posters, International Society of the Learning Sciences, 910- 911.

[36] Deborah A. Fields, Yasmin B. Kafai, Tomoko Nakajima, and Joanna Goode. "Teaching Practices for Making E-Textiles in High School Computing Classrooms." In *Proceedings of the 7th Annual Conference on Creativity and Fabrication in Education*, p. 5. ACM, 2017.

[37] Kristin A. Searle and Yasmin B. Kafai. 2015. Boys' Needlework: Understanding Gendered and Indigenous Perspectives on Computing and Crafting with Electronic Textiles. In *International Computing Education Research*, 2015, 31-39.

[38] Emily Lovell and Leah Buechley. 2011. LilyPond: an online community for sharing e-textile projects. In *Proceedings of the 8th ACM Conference on Creativity and Cognition*, ACM, 2011, 365-366.

[39] Debora Lui, Breanne K. Litts, Sari Widman, Justice T. Walker, and Yasmin B. Kafai. 2016. Collaborative Maker Activities in the Classroom: Case Studies of High School Student Pairs' Interactions in Designing Electronic Textiles. In *Proceedings of the 6th Annual Conference on Creativity and Fabrication in Education*, ACM, 2016, 74-77.

[40] Anne Weibert, Andrea Marshall, Konstantin Aal, Kai Schubert, and Jennifer Rode. 2014. Sewing interest in E-textiles: analyzing making from a gendered perspective. In *Proceedings of the 2014 conference on Designing Interactive Systems*, ACM, 2014, 15-24.

[41] Kanjun Qiu, Leah Buechley, Edward Baafi, and Wendy Dubow. 2013. A curriculum for teaching computer science through computational textiles. In *Proceedings of the 12th International Conference on Interaction Design and Children*, ACM, 2013, 20-27.

[42] Leah Buechley and Kanjun Qiu. 2014. *Sew electric.*

[43] Alan Melchior, Tracy Cutter, and Faye Cohen. 2004. Evaluation of FIRST LEGO league. *Waltham, MA: Center for Youth and Communities, Heller Graduate School, Brandeis University.*

[44] Breanne K. Litts, Yasmin B. Kafai, Kristin A. Searle, and Emily Dieckmeyer. 2016. Perceptions of Productive Failure in Design Projects: High School Students' Challenges in Making Electronic Textiles. In *Proceedings of International Conference of Learning Sciences*, 2016.

[45] Orkan Telhan, Yasmin B. Kafai, and Breanne K. Litts. 2016. Designing for Connected Making: Supports for Collaboration and Community building in Crafting Activities. *Makeology Volume 1: Makerspaces as Learning Environments* (2016), 223-236

[46] Debora Lui, Gayithri Jayathirtha, Deborah A. Fields, Mia Shaw, and Yasmin Kafai. 2018. Design Considerations for Capturing Computational Thinking Practices in High School Students' Electronic Textile Portfolios. In *Proceedings of International Conference of Learning Sciences*, 2018, 721-728.

[47] Owen Astrachan and Amy Briggs. 2012. The CS principles project. *ACM Inroads* 3, no. 2, 38-42.

[48] Yasmin B. Kafai, Kristin Searle, Crîstobal Martinez, and Bryan Brayboy. 2014. Ethnocomputing with electronic textiles: culturally responsive open design to broaden participation in computing in American Indian youth and communities. In *Proceedings of the 45th ACM Technical Symposium on Computer Science Education*, ACM, 2014, 241-246.

[49] Gayithri Jayathirtha, Deborah A. Fields, and Yasmin B. Kafai. 2018. Computational concepts, practices, and collaboration in high school students' debugging electronic textile projects." In *Conference Proceedings of International Conference on Computational Thinking Education 2018*. 27-32.

[50] Kylie Peppler, Diane Glosson, Yasmin Kafai, Deborah Fields, and Kristin Searle. 2011. Articulating creativity in a new domain: expert insights from the field of e-textiles. In *Proceedings of the 8th ACM conference on Creativity and Cognition*, ACM, 2011, 385-386.

[51] Sunyoung Kim, Eric Paulos, and Mark D. Gross. 2010. WearAir: expressive t-shirts for air quality sensing." In *Proceedings of the fourth International Conference on Tangible, Embedded, and Embodied Interaction*, ACM, 2010, 295-296.

Evaluation of Peer Instruction for Cybersecurity Education

Pranita Deshpande
Department of Computer Science
University of New Orleans
pdeshpa1@my.uno.edu

Cynthia B. Lee
Computer Science Department
Stanford University
cbl@stanford.edu

Irfan Ahmed*
Department of Computer Science
Virginia Commonwealth University
iahmed3@vcu.edu

ABSTRACT

Peer instruction pedagogy is a student-centric approach that encourages students to read lecture material before coming to class and engages them in class via group discussion and preplanned conceptual questions. Peer instruction has shown promising results in core computer science courses such as Theory of Computation and Computer Architecture, as well as reducing failure rates and improving student retention in computer science major. This paper presents the results of the first-ever attempt to replicate these results in a cybersecurity course, using an action research methodology to implement and evaluate peer instruction in a semester-long cybersecurity course, Introduction to Computer Security. The evaluation consists of quizzes, subjective exams, peer instruction questions, and attitudinal surveys gathered over two control semesters and one peer instruction condition semester. We find evidence of learning gains during group discussion and improvements in dropout and failure rates compared to traditional lecture classes. In attitudinal surveys, most students report that they would recommend that other instructors use peer instruction.

ACM Reference format:
Pranita Deshpande, Cynthia B. Lee, and Irfan Ahmed. 2019. Evaluation of Peer Instruction for Cybersecurity Education. In *Proceedings of the 50th ACM Technical Symposium on Computer Science Education, Minneapolis, MN, USA, February 27-March 2, 2019 (SIGCSE '19),* ACM, New York, NY. 6 pages. DOI: http://dx.doi.org/10.1145/3287324.3287403

1 INTRODUCTION

Peer instruction is a well-defined teaching protocol designed for active engagement of students in class [3, 26]. It involves conceptual multiple-choice questions and group discussion activities aimed to provoke deep conceptual thinking in students. We aimed to test whether peer instruction could be effective in dealing with the challenges of cybersecurity education, including encouraging out-of-box thinking, developing a mindset of both attacker and defender, and attaining a deep working knowledge of cybersecurity tools and techniques [1, 2, 4–8, 11, 13, 14, 22–25].

Peer instruction requires students to read introductory expository material before coming to class, then engages students in reflection and clarification of the challenging parts of the reading via preplanned conceptual questions on important target concepts. In a peer instruction classroom, lecture is organized into a set of multiple choice questions. To discuss a concept, the instructor poses a question, first giving students a moment to consider and respond individually, then directing students to discuss in small groups to resolve any discrepancies in their responses or reasoning.

A robust body of research, summarized in Section 2, shows that use of peer instruction promotes greater student learning than traditional lecture. Inspired by the success of peer instruction in computer science courses, we implement and evaluate peer instruction in a semester-long cybersecurity course, Introduction to Computer Security. This paper presents the evaluation results of the implementation and compares them with a traditional lecture approach, based on three semesters' worth of data (two traditional lecture, and one peer instruction).

Roadmap. Section 2 presents the peer instruction methodology and related work. Section 3 discusses the implementation details in the computer security classes followed by the data collection and analysis results in sections 4 and 5. Section 6 concludes the paper.

2 BACKGROUND/RELATED WORK

2.1 Peer Instruction Methodology

Peer instruction is a teaching protocol comprised of before-class and in-class activities.

Before class. Before-class activities are aimed to have students familiarize themselves with the basics of topics for the next class meeting. They may include reading material, online videos, or other resources. A low-stakes quiz is given with the activities to incentivize the students to complete the work.

In class. The instructor divides a lecture into a series of peer instruction questions. Each question targets a certain concept. The instructor typically provides 60-90 seconds to the students to respond to the question individually, and then allows the students to discuss their answers with fellow students in small groups. The discussion typically lasts for two to three minutes. After the discussion, students respond to the question again, possibly changing their answer in light of new information from their peers. Clickers are used to collect the students' responses of on instructor's computer to allow the instructor to gauge classwide performance in real time. As needed, the instructor may choose to further discuss the concept, or move ahead with the next part of the lecture.

2.2 Related Work

Peer instruction is widely adopted and studied in many science disciplines. This section limits the scope to the pertinent efforts on the evaluation of peer instruction.

Peer instruction, as described in this paper, originated with Eric Mazur, a physics professor. The superiority of peer instruction over traditional lecture in physics classes was demonstrated in a 10-year, 6000-student study by Crouch *et. al* [10].

*Ahmed completed this work while he was at the University of New Orleans

SIGCSE '19, February 27-March 2, 2019, Minneapolis, MN, USA

ACM ISBN 978-1-4503-5890-3/19/02...$15.00.
DOI: http://dx.doi.org/10.1145/3287324.3287403

Peer instruction is now widely used—and studied—in computer science. In one study, students in a peer instruction course achieved 6% higher grades on the final exam compared to traditional lecture-centric approach [27]. In another, a trio of introductory programming course best practices, including peer instruction, improved retention in the computer science major by 31% [21].

Looking at a broader range of four courses (CS1, CS1.5, Theory of Computation, and Computer Architecture), the use of peer instruction reduced the failure rate by 61% on average [18].

A particular challenge of teaching cybersecurity is the centrality of the need for learners (and practitioners) to apply their knowledge to new and different contexts. Ronald *et al.* Cortright et al. [9] attempted to test the hypothesis that peer instruction enhanced meaningful learning and the student's ability to solve novel problems and the ability to apply the knowledge to different new and existing contexts. They performed the study in an undergraduate physiology class of 38 students. They equally divided the student population into two groups. The lecture consists of short presentations. Each presentation followed a multiple-choice quiz. One group answered the questions individually while the other during peer instruction discussion. Their results validated the hypothesis.

Peer instruction has been deployed and tested in a short cybersecurity course/workshop. Johnson *et. al* [15, 16] developed 108 peer instruction questions for a digital forensics course, and report results from piloting a subset of these questions in a four-hour long workshop to evaluate the peer instruction methodology. Their evaluation results showed the learning gain via quiz and clicker questions by 34% and 13% respectively.

Esper *et. al* [12] adopted peer instruction in a software engineering course that had 189 students. They made slight modification in the standard peer instruction methodology. A clicker question is initially shown without answers and then, the instructor asks the students to call out suggestions for the answers. Both the students and instructor proposed a potential answer choices with discussions of those answers. Their survey results showed that 28% students would not recommend peer instruction for teaching because correct answers are not given and clicker questions are not clear.

3 PEER INSTRUCTION IMPLEMENTATION

We gather data over three semesters (Fall 2015, Fall 2016 and Fall 2017) consisting of quizzes, subjective exams, peer instruction questions and surveys. The first two semesters are based on traditional lectures while in the latter semester, the course is revised to incorporate peer instruction methodology.

Peer instruction is evaluated in terms of dropout and failure rates, student learning gain during the group discussion, and survey on students' experience and usage of clickers.

The evaluation results show that peer instruction improves the dropout rate by 4% and the failure rate by 13% and 3% in quizzes and subjective exams on average respectively, when compared with traditional lecture classes. The survey results show that 77% students find the group discussion with fellow students useful to understand the computer security concepts. 70% students would recommend peer instruction be adopted by other instructors.

Course. We choose the *introduction to computer security* course to evaluate the effectiveness of peer instruction methodology for cybersecurity education. The course is taught at both undergraduate and graduate levels and provides a broad overview of cybersecurity and covers at least four cybersecurity areas i.e., user authentication, malicious software, buffer overflow, and cryptographic tools. The course is offered regularly once or twice in a year as needed.

Table 1: Number of students enrolled in the introduction to computer security course.

Teaching Method	Student Population
Traditional Lecture	42
Peer Instruction	33

Table 2: Data collection instruments

Quiz Questions	Subjective Exams	Clicker Questions	Survey Questions
29	17	18	19

Table 3: Survey on students background and interest in computer security

Survey Question	Fall 2015	Fall 2016	Fall 2017
Previously taken any coursework related to computer security	22%	16%	28%
Intend to specialize in computer security field	48%	63%	49%
Intend to take additional computer security course after this class	70%	74%	64%

Instructor. The course instructor is an experienced teacher who taught several cybersecurity graduate and undergraduate courses. The instructor taught the *introduction to computer security* course five times before implementing the peer instruction in the course. The course evaluations by students are typically around 4.5 out of 5.0, which validate the high quality of instruction.

Peer Instruction Activities. Recall that peer instruction teaching involves before-class and in-class activities. For the implementation, the students are given reading assignments to cover before-class activities. Each assignment expects the students to read a book chapter of the topic discussed next week in class. The students are given at least one-week time to finish an assignment.

During class, the instructor asks peer instruction questions on a target topic and let students discuss their answers in small groups (consisting of typically four to five students). Clickers are used to collect the responses. The instructor also used his lecture slides to discuss the topics as needed.

4 DATA COLLECTION

To assess the effectiveness of peer instruction in terms of student failure rate and learning gain, we develop and utilize four different instruments for data collection i.e., Quiz, Subjective Exam, Clicker Questions and Survey (refer to Table 2 for a summary). Figure 1 shows the timeline of data collection activities in a semester. The semester starts with a before-class reading assignment. The students are given a week to complete it while the instructor uses this week to discuss the syllabus, introduce the course activities, go through

Table 4: Survey on the reasons for enrolling in computer security

Survey Question	Fall 2015	Fall 2016	Fall 2017
Interested in subject matter	96%	90%	88%
Times of class is favorable for schedule	28%	16%	27%
Other classes wanted were full	9%	26%	30%
Prerequisite for other classes	13%	37%	30%

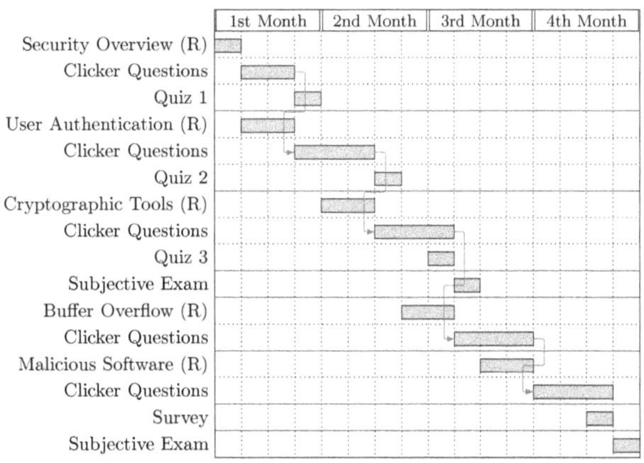

Figure 1: Timeline of the data collection using quizzes, survey, subject exams, and clicker questions. Each box represents a week. 'R' identifies before-class reading activities on five topics.

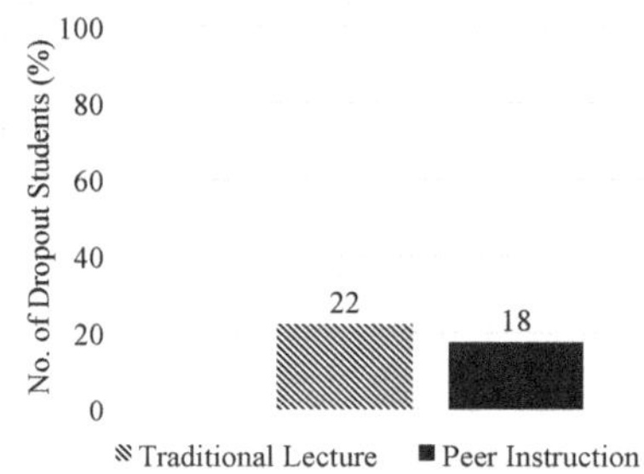

Figure 2: Student dropout rate for traditional lecture and peer instruction

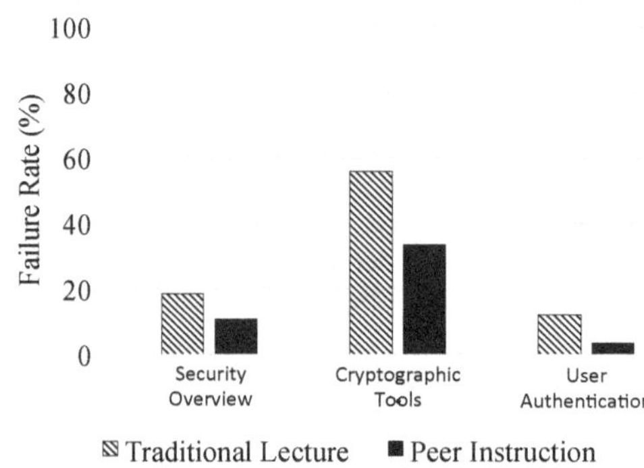

Figure 3: Failure rate in *quizzes* for peer instruction and traditional lecture in three cybersecurity topics i.e., security overview, user authentication, and cryptographic tools.

hands-on assignments, and initiate discussion on computer security to raise the students' interest on the subject matter. The rest of the semester comprises of periodic reading assignments and data collection activities.

We have collected the data for three semesters i.e., Fall 2015, Fall 2016, and Fall 2017. The first two uses *traditional lecture* approach while the latter implements *peer instruction.* Table 1 shows the enrollment number for these two approaches. This section further describes the data collection instruments.

Quiz. Three quizzes are developed to assess the student knowledge on three topics i.e., computer security overview, user authentication, and cryptographic tools. The students are given (at least a week) time to prepare for the quizzes after the lectures on the respective topics are completed in class. The quiz questions are designed to be straight forward with correct set of choices. To quantify the student responses, each correct question is given one mark.

Subjective Exam. The exams are midterm and final tests consisting of subjective questions to evaluate the understanding of the students on five cybersecurity topics, i.e., computer security overview, buffer overflow, user authentication, malicious software, and cryptographic tools. The duration of an exam is one hour and fifteen minutes. The students are advised to provide direct and concise answers to the questions. A standard rubric of correct answers is used to quantify the level of understanding of students on the topics.

Clicker Questions. The clicker questions are the peer instruction questions used for the lecture in class. Clickers are used to record the polls of a question before and after the student discussion in small groups. The polling results of the questions are an effective means to measure the learning gains of students at micro-scale as a result of peer discussion. Eighteen questions are used for five topics. Unfortunately, we could not collect the peer instruction data on one topic i.e., security overview. The other data is collected, analyzed and presented in this paper.

Surveys . We utilize an attitudinal survey to record the students' experience and opinions on clickers and peer instructions. The survey instrument is provided by Beth Simon and Leo Porter of UC San Diego, and Cynthia Lee of Stanford University. Results from this survey instrument have been published for numerous peer instruction courses, providing useful comparisons for our evaluation of peer instruction for cybersecurity (*e.g.*, [17][19][20]).

The survey gathers information on prior usage of clickers, course preparation, peer discussion, clicker usage, and lecture pacing. It contains 19 questions that are designed with a Likert scale. The survey is given to students at the end of semester in class and provided ample time to complete.

5 DATA ANALYSIS

We analyze the data to measure the effectiveness of peer instruction in terms of dropout and failure rates, student learning gain during

Table 5: Student Survey on Peer instruction lecture preparation, peer instruction, and clicker usage

Survey Questions	Average Opinion
Thinking about clicker questions on my own, before discussing with people around me, helped me learn course material.	70%
I read The required material before the lectures.	60%
Most of the time my group actually discussed the clicker question.	87%
Discussing course topics with my seatmate in the class helped me better understand the course material	77%
The immediate feedback from the clickers helped me focus on weakness in my understanding of the course	77%
Knowing the right answer is the only important part of the clicker question.	30%
Generally, by the time we finished with a question and discussion, I felt pretty clear about it.	80%
Clickers are an easy-to-use class collaboration tool.	77%
Clickers helped me pay attention in the class compared to traditional lectures	73%
Using clickers with discussion is valuable for my learning.	67%
I recommend that other instructors use this approach (reading quizzes, clickers, in-class discussion) in their courses.	70%

Table 6: Student survey on peer instruction implementation

<table>
<tr><td colspan="5">From the point of helping me learn, the content of clicker questions was</td></tr>
<tr><td>Much too hard
0%</td><td>Too hard
6.66%</td><td>OK
80%</td><td>Too easy
13.33%</td><td>Much too easy
0%</td></tr>
<tr><td colspan="5">In general, the instructor gave us enough time to read and understand the questions before the first vote.</td></tr>
<tr><td>No, far too little time
0%</td><td>No, too little time
0%</td><td>OK amount of time
80%</td><td>Yes, too much time
13.33%</td><td>Yes, far too much time
6.66%</td></tr>
<tr><td colspan="5">Which of the following best describes your discussion practices in this group?</td></tr>
<tr><td>I always discuss with the group around me, it helps me learn
66.66%</td><td>I always discuss with the group around me, I don't really learn, but I stay awake
10%</td><td>I sometimes discuss, it depends
22.33%</td><td>I rarely discuss, I don't think I get a lot out of it
0%</td><td>I rarely discuss, I'm too shy
0%</td></tr>
<tr><td colspan="5">The amount of time generally allowed for peer discussion was</td></tr>
<tr><td>Much too short
3.33%</td><td>Too short
11%</td><td>About right
89%</td><td>Too long
0%</td><td>Much too long
0%</td></tr>
<tr><td colspan="5">In general, the time allowed for class-wide discussion (after the group vote) was</td></tr>
<tr><td>Much too short
0%</td><td>Too short
6.66%</td><td>About right
70%</td><td>Too long
23.33%</td><td>Much too long
0%</td></tr>
<tr><td colspan="5">In general, it was helpful for the instructor to begin class-wide discussion by having students give an explanation.</td></tr>
<tr><td colspan="2">N/A - The instructor rarely did this
16.66%</td><td colspan="2">It's not helpful to hear other students' explanations
10%</td><td>It was helpful to hear other students' explanations
73.33%</td></tr>
<tr><td colspan="5">The professor explained the value of using clickers in this class.</td></tr>
<tr><td>Not at all
0%</td><td colspan="2">Somewhat, but I was still unclear why we were doing it
10%</td><td>Yes, they explained it well
83.33%</td><td>Yes, they explained it too much
6.66%</td></tr>
</table>

group discussions, and students' experience on clicker usage and peer instruction teaching methodology. Tables 4 and 3 summarize the students' background and interest in computer security. Only 30% students have some prior understanding of cybersecurity. However, 96% students are interested to learn cybersecurity. Around 75% students intend to take more cybersecurity courses and 50% would specialize in this area.

5.1 Dropout Rate

At the university, the students may drop the course within two weeks after the semester starts without any official record. After two weeks, the students have six weeks to drop the course with a "W" (or Withdraw) grade recorded.

Figure 2 shows the dropout rate for both traditional lecture classes, and peer instruction classes. We notice that the dropout rate is reduced by 4% in peer instruction classes from the classes taught with the traditional lecture approach.

5.2 Failure Rate

To measure the students' performance in the course for both traditional and peer instruction classes, we obtain failure rate in quizzes and subjective exams. The university policy defines that the passing grades are A, B, and C and the failing grades are D, and F. If a student scores less than 70% marks, he/she will be considered failed.

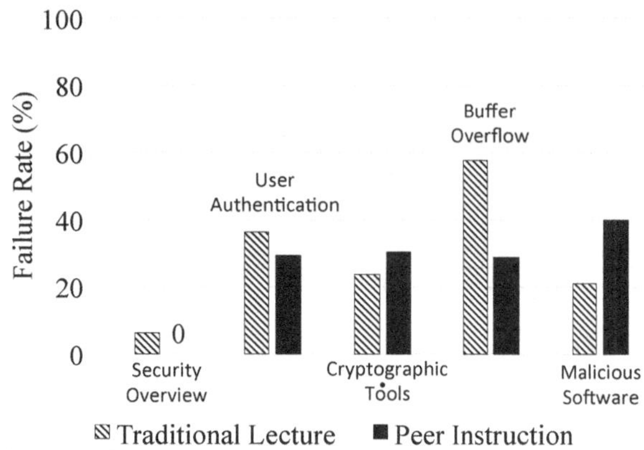

Figure 4: Failure rate in the *subjective exam* for five topics i.e., introductory computer security, user authentication, and cryptographic tools) in the peer instruction class and traditional lecture class

Class Quiz. Figure 3 presents the failure rate in quiz exams for both traditional-lecture and peer instruction classes. The results show consistent improvements in the failure rates for peer instruction. In particular, failure rate in security overview, cryptographic tools, and user authentication topics are reduced by 8%, 22%, and 8% respectively.

Subjective Exam. Figure 4 shows the failure rate of the subjective exams for the five topics (i.e., computer security overview, buffer overflow, user authentication, malicious software, and cryptographic tools) taught at both traditional-lecture and peer instruction classes. We notice substantial improvements in the failure rate. In particular, the failure rate for the topic, security overview is reduced to zero in peer instruction. We also notice some exceptions such as cryptographic tools where the failure rate is increased for peer instruction. We reevaluated the student answers of the questions on this topic. In particular, we found that a significant number of students misunderstood the following question.

Question on Cryptographic Tools: `How can message authentication be achieved using one-way hash function with 1) Symmetric encryption and 2) Public-key encryption.`

Apparently, they ignore the one-way hash function and assume that the question asks about the symmetric and Public-key encryption schemes. Some students derive message authentication through encryption without computing and utilizing cryptographic hash values. If the question is rephrased and restructured, it will likely reduce the failure rate on this topic.

Overall, we notice that the peer instruction reduces the failure rate by 3% on average when compared with the traditional lecture classes.

5.3 Learning Gain during Group Discussions

Figure 5 presents the results of the clicker responses of the students before and after the group discussions. We notice clear evidence of improvement in the correct answers by the students after the discussions.

To our surprise, some students chose an option from clickers that were not given in the questions. In particular, we observed

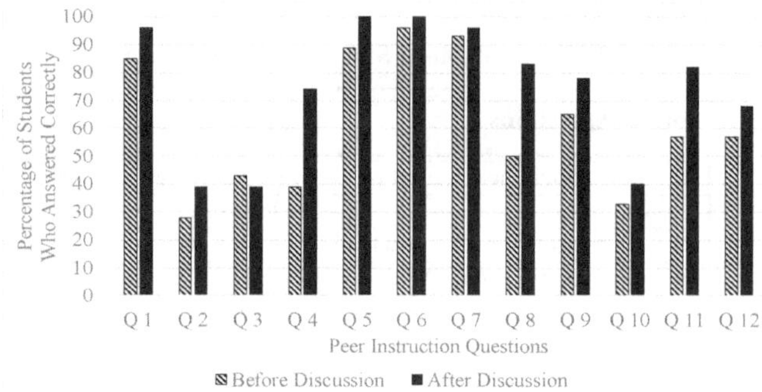

Figure 5: Percentage of the students who respond to the peer instruction questions correctly

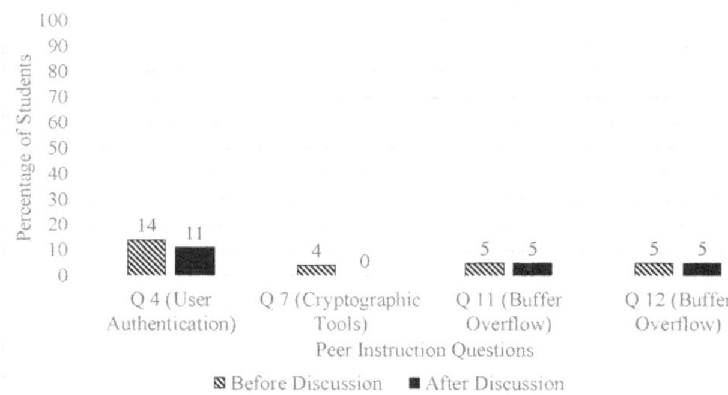

Figure 6: Percentage of the students who respond to the peer instruction questions with the clicker choices that are not given in the questions

these choices in the questions 4, 7, 11, and 12 on three topics: user authentication, cryptographic tools, and buffer overflow. Figure 6 shows the percentage of the students who have selected unexpected clicker options. Following is an example of such question.

Question on Buffer Overflow: `Which of the following describes a buffer overflow attack?`

A Exploiting the traffic flow mechanism in a buffer and blocking packets from reaching their destination.
B Flooding a buffer with server requests and overflowing the network bandwidth.
C Attempting to store more input in a data holding area than capacity allocates.
D An attacker fills the target buffer with malicious code

The above question has four choices: `A`, `B`, `C`, and `D`. However, some students respond with `E` from clickers. It shows that these students do not pay attention to the questions. We also notice in Figure 6 that some of these students change their responses after the group discussions, depicting that they start paying attention during the discussions.

5.4 Survey

Table 5 presents the results of the student attitudinal survey portion of the peer instruction evaluation. It shows that the most of the students find it useful to think about a clicker question before discussing it with other students and the discussion helps them understand the concept better. 70% of students would recommend peer instruction be adopted by other instructors.

Table 6 summarizes the students opinion about the peer instruction classes. It shows that the students have a generally positive experience of the classes. They have adequate time to understand the questions and vote for the correct answer. 80% students agree that the allowable duration for group discussions is sufficient.

6 CONCLUSION

We implemented and evaluated peer instruction in a semester-long course, introduction to computer security. The evaluation results were compared with traditional lecture classes in terms of dropout rate, failure rate, and student learning gain. Peer instruction showed promising results. The overall dropout rate was reduced by 4% and failure rate by 13% and 3% for quiz and subjective exams respectively when compared with traditional lecture classes. The survey results showed that 77% students found the discussions in small groups useful to understand the computer security concepts. The overall student experience of peer instruction was positive and majority students would recommend peer instruction be adopted by other instructors.

7 ACKNOWLEDGEMENT

This work was in part supported by the NSF grants # 1500101 and 1623276.

REFERENCES

[1] I. Ahmed, S. Obermeier, S. Sudhakaran, and V. Roussev. 2017. Programmable Logic Controller Forensics. *IEEE Security Privacy* 15, 6 (November 2017), 18–24. DOI: http://dx.doi.org/10.1109/MSP.2017.4251102

[2] Irfan Ahmed, Golden G. Richard, Aleksandar Zoranic, and Vassil Roussev. 2015. Integrity Checking of Function Pointers in Kernel Pools via Virtual Machine Introspection. In *Information Security*, Yvo Desmedt (Ed.). Springer International Publishing, Cham, 3–19.

[3] Irfan Ahmed and Vassil Roussev. 2018. Peer Instruction Teaching Methodology for Cybersecurity Education. *IEEE Security Privacy* 16, 4 (July 2018).

[4] Irfan Ahmed, Vassil Roussev, and Aisha Ali Gombe. 2015. Robust Fingerprinting for Relocatable Code. In *Proceedings of the 5th ACM Conference on Data and Application Security and Privacy (CODASPY '15)*. ACM, New York, NY, USA, 219–229. DOI: http://dx.doi.org/10.1145/2699026.2699104

[5] Irfan Ahmed, Vassil Roussev, William Johnson, Saranyan Senthivel, and Sneha Sudhakaran. 2016. A SCADA System Testbed for Cybersecurity and Forensic Research and Pedagogy. In *Proceedings of the 2Nd Annual Industrial Control System Security Workshop (ICSS '16)*. ACM, New York, NY, USA, 1–9. DOI: http://dx.doi.org/10.1145/3018981.3018984

[6] Sajal Bhatia, Sunny Behal, and Irfan Ahmed. 2018. *Distributed Denial of Service Attacks and Defense Mechanisms: Current Landscape and Future Directions.* Springer International Publishing, Cham, 55–97. DOI: http://dx.doi.org/10.1007/978-3-319-97643-3_3

[7] Manish Bhatt and Irfan Ahmed. 2018. Leveraging relocations in ELF-binaries for Linux kernel version identification. *Digital Investigation* 26 (2018), S12 – S20. DOI: http://dx.doi.org/https://doi.org/10.1016/j.diin.2018.04.022

[8] Manish Bhatt, Irfan Ahmed, and Zhiqiang Lin. 2018. Using Virtual Machine Introspection for Operating Systems Security Education. In *Proceedings of the 49th ACM Technical Symposium on Computer Science Education*. ACM, 396–401.

[9] Ronald N Cortright, Heidi L Collins, and Stephen E DiCarlo. 2005. Peer instruction enhanced meaningful learning: ability to solve novel problems. *Advances in physiology education* 29, 2 (2005), 107–111.

[10] Catherine H Crouch and Eric Mazur. 2001. Peer instruction: Ten years of experience and results. *American journal of physics* 69, 9 (2001), 970–977.

[11] Pranita Deshpande and Irfan Ahmed. 2019. Topological Scoring of Concept Maps for Cybersecurity Education. In *Proceeding of the 50th ACM Technical Symposium on Computer Science Education (SIGCSE '19)*.

[12] Sarah Esper. 2014. A Discussion on Adopting Peer Instruction in a Course Focused on Risk Management. *J. Comput. Sci. Coll.* 29, 4 (April 2014), 175–182. http://dl.acm.org/citation.cfm?id=2591468.2591496

[13] Jonathan Grimm, Irfan Ahmed, Vassil Roussev, Manish Bhatt, and ManPyo Hong. 2018. Automatic Mitigation of Kernel Rootkits in Cloud Environments. In *Information Security Applications*, Brent ByungHoon Kang and Taesoo Kim (Eds.). Springer International Publishing, Cham, 137–149.

[14] Salman Javaid, Aleksandar Zoranic, Irfan Ahmed, and Golden G Richard III. 2012. Atomizer: Fast, Scalable and Lightweight Heap Analyzer for Virtual Machines in a Cloud Environment. In *Proceedings of the 6th Layered Assurance Workshop (ACSAC'12)*.

[15] William Johnson, Irfan Ahmed, Vassil Roussev, and Cynthia B. Lee. 2017. Peer Instruction for Digital Forensics. In *2017 USENIX Workshop on Advances in Security Education (ASE 17)*. USENIX Association, Vancouver, BC.

[16] William E. Johnson, Allison Luzader, Irfan Ahmed, Vassil Roussev, Golden G. Richard III, and Cynthia B. Lee. 2016. Development of Peer Instruction Questions for Cybersecurity Education. In *2016 USENIX Workshop on Advances in Security Education (ASE 16)*. USENIX Association, Austin, TX. https://www.usenix.org/conference/ase16/workshop-program/presentation/johnson

[17] Cynthia Bailey Lee, Saturnino Garcia, and Leo Porter. 2013. Can Peer Instruction Be Effective in Upper-division Computer Science Courses? *Trans. Comput. Educ.* 13, 3, Article 12 (Aug. 2013), 22 pages.

[18] Leo Porter, Cynthia Bailey Lee, and Beth Simon. 2013. Halving fail rates using peer instruction: a study of four computer science courses. In *Proceeding of the 44th ACM technical symposium on Computer science education*. ACM, 177–182.

[19] Leo Porter, Dennis Bouvier, Quintin Cutts, Scott Grissom, Cynthia Lee, Robert McCartney, Daniel Zingaro, and Beth Simon. 2016. A Multi-institutional Study of Peer Instruction in Introductory Computing. In *Proceedings of the 47th ACM Technical Symposium on Computing Science Education (SIGCSE '16)*. ACM, New York, NY, USA, 358–363. DOI: http://dx.doi.org/10.1145/2839509.2844642

[20] Leo Porter, Saturnino Garcia, John Glick, Andrew Matusiewicz, and Cynthia Taylor. 2013. Peer Instruction in Computer Science at Small Liberal Arts Colleges. In *Proceedings of the 18th ACM Conference on Innovation and Technology in Computer Science Education (ITiCSE '13)*. ACM, New York, NY, USA, 129–134. DOI: http://dx.doi.org/10.1145/2462476.2465587

[21] Leo Porter and Beth Simon. 2013. Retaining Nearly One-third More Majors with a Trio of Instructional Best Practices in CS1. In *Proceeding of the 44th ACM Technical Symposium on Computer Science Education (SIGCSE '13)*. ACM, New York, NY, USA, 165–170. DOI: http://dx.doi.org/10.1145/2445196.2445248

[22] Vassil Roussev, Irfan Ahmed, and Thomas Sires. 2014. Image-based Kernel Fingerprinting. *Digit. Investig.* 11, S2 (Aug. 2014), S13–S21. DOI: http://dx.doi.org/10.1016/j.diin.2014.05.013

[23] Vassil Roussev, Andres Barreto, and Irfan Ahmed. 2016. API-Based Forensic Acquisition of Cloud Drives. In *Advances in Digital Forensics XII*, Gilbert Peterson and Sujeet Shenoi (Eds.). Springer International Publishing, Cham, 213–235.

[24] Saranyan Senthivel, Irfan Ahmed, and Vassil Roussev. 2017. SCADA network forensics of the PCCC protocol. *Digital Investigation* 22 (2017), S57 – S65. DOI: http://dx.doi.org/https://doi.org/10.1016/j.diin.2017.06.012

[25] Saranyan Senthivel, Shrey Dhungana, Hyunguk Yoo, Irfan Ahmed, and Vassil Roussev. 2018. Denial of Engineering Operations Attacks in Industrial Control Systems. In *Proceedings of the Eighth ACM Conference on Data and Application Security and Privacy (CODASPY '18)*. ACM, New York, NY, USA, 319–329. DOI: http://dx.doi.org/10.1145/3176258.3176319

[26] Beth Simon and Quintin Cutts. 2012. Peer Instruction: A Teaching Method to Foster Deep Understanding. *Commun. ACM* 55, 2 (Feb. 2012), 27–29. DOI: http://dx.doi.org/10.1145/2076450.2076459

[27] Beth Simon, Julian Parris, and Jaime Spacco. 2013. How We Teach Impacts Student Learning: Peer Instruction vs. Lecture in CS0. In *Proceeding of the 44th ACM Technical Symposium on Computer Science Education (SIGCSE '13)*. ACM, New York, NY, USA, 41–46. DOI: http://dx.doi.org/10.1145/2445196.2445215

From Midshipmen to Cyber Pros: Training Minority Naval Reserve Officer Training Corp Students for Cybersecurity

Naja A. Mack
University of Florida
Gainesville, FL
najamac@ufl.edu

Kevin Womack
Morehouse College
Atlanta, GA
kevin.womack@morehouse.edu

Earl W. Huff, Jr.
Clemson University
Clemson, SC
earlh@clemson.edu

Robert Cummings
Morehouse College
Atlanta, GA
robert.cummings@morehouse.edu

Negus Dowling
Morehouse College
Atlanta, GA
negus.dowling@morehouse.edu

Kinnis Gosha
Morehouse College
Atlanta, GA
kinnis.gosha@morehouse.edu

ABSTRACT

Computing is not only a fundamental part of our daily lives — our national security depends on it. It is essential that members of the Reserve Officer Training Corps (ROTC) be well-versed in computing techniques designed to combat cyber-attacks that continually improve in sophistication and frequency levels. Through computer science education, prospective military leaders are being taught the critical and analytical thinking skills necessary to address these threats. This paper outlines and discusses how underrepresented minority Naval Reserve Officer Training Corps (NROTC) midshipmen, with the majority having little-to-no programming skills or background, were taught the foundational aspects of computer science and exposed to specific cybersecurity concepts in a 15-week program. The program produced many insightful outcomes, one being the development of a tool that collected and analyzed publicly available social media data through the application of data mining algorithms and techniques. Additionally, interviews, which were conducted upon the completion of the program, documented notable findings on the program's effectiveness and on key concepts for teaching computer science to minority beginners.

CCS CONCEPTS

• Social and professional topics → Computer science education; • Applied computing → Military;

KEYWORDS

cybersecurity, programming, data mining, military, rotc

ACM Reference Format:

Naja A. Mack, Kevin Womack, Earl W. Huff, Jr., Robert Cummings, Negus Dowling, and Kinnis Gosha. 2019. From Midshipmen to Cyber Pros: Training Minority Naval Reserve Officer Training Corp Students for Cybersecurity. In *Proceedings of the 50th ACM Technical Symposium on Computer Science Education (SIGCSE '19), February 27-March 2, 2019, Minneapolis, MN, USA.* ACM, New York, NY, USA, 5 pages. https://doi.org/10.1145/3287324.3287500

SIGCSE '19, February 27-March 2, 2019, Minneapolis, MN, USA

ACM ISBN 978-1-4503-5890-3/19/02...$15.00
https://doi.org/10.1145/3287324.3287500

1 INTRODUCTION

As people's lives become increasingly immersed in the digital realm, it is necessary for developers and consumers to acquire knowledge in security to protect against intrusion and exploitation [2]. A recent report on cyber-related threats [3] showed an increase in remote entry attempts and dangerous user behavior, thus creating opportunities for attackers to exploit vulnerable systems. Primarily, the government, financial, professional and information sectors receive the highest volume and variety of malicious activity [3]. Cybersecurity represents the body of technologies, processes, and practices used to protect networks, devices, elections, programs, and data from a variety of attacks and unauthorized access [9]. With technology becoming a more significant part of our lives, cybersecurity will continue to be an integral aspect of personal and professional careers. More important than ever before, the basic foundations of cybersecurity should be instilled in job trainings, educational programs, and even in academic majors.

This paper presents findings from a 15-week program in which members of the Naval Reserve Officer Training Corps (NROTC) from three Historically Black Colleges and Universities (HBCUs), Morehouse College, Spelman College, and Clark Atlanta University, were taught core concepts in computer science and cybersecurity and tasked to develop a tool for threat and vulnerability analysis. Results from post-program interviews helped highlight program efficacy and offered suggestions

2 LITERATURE REVIEW

2.1 Computer Science Education for Non-Majors

The retention, and ultimate success, of students across the nation, has been an ongoing issue within the computer science community. The Theory of Constructivism, while seemingly encompassing most students, explains fallacies and learning deficits [1, 11]. It posits that students do not receive information as it is taught; instead, they fabricate their version of the information provided, based on prior knowledge or experience, an attempt to conceptualize processes and manifest them in the form of something familiar [1, 6]. Because computer science can be articulated in an unfamiliar manner, many students misunderstand the teachings and therefore struggle in, even basic introductory courses, which are typical requirements for 4-year degrees in post-secondary education [7].

At the heart of the problem is students' lack of interest in the subject itself, which is attributed to factors such as voluntary disengagement of the student, redundant communicative media programs, and perceived lack of relevant examples of computing in everyday life [8, 11]. A disengaged student will often revert to memorization, rather than investing the time and energy in understanding the material. As a result, critical thinking skills are not fostered, potentially leading to failure in these introductory courses. Secondly, the ability to relate what is learned to something familiar is crucial to retention. One study found that students learn better if they can relate the material at hand to something they enjoy or like; however, this can be difficult to do when learning computer science [8]. The question then becomes: How do we bridge the gap between programming and relevant real-world applications, when most introductory courses exclude examples or projects that illustrate how computer science can be applied to solve issues in today's society?

2.2 Computer Science, Cybersecurity and ROTC

The foundation of an understanding of cybersecurity is developed during the learning of fundamental programming concepts, like iteration and data structures. Many institutions of higher education have implemented labs or programming competitions to pique the interest of students in hopes to garner the interest of sharp, young, and impressionable minds [4]. Schools across the nation are using Computer Science to assess how vulnerable people are being hacked on email and social media platforms [5].

Colleges, universities, and service academies possess the tools necessary to produce cyber-literate leaders. Moreover, while there is a high demand for these leaders, few institutions provide the framework that properly combines computer science with other departments and programs to demonstrate how the field can be applied. Computer Science should be integrated into all programs in order to produce the most cyber-competent leaders. Because of the vital role that they play in the creation of future military leaders, the U.S. service academies have already begun to spearhead computer science synthesized programs. The Military Academy CYBER Education Working Group was established in 2012 with the goal of augmenting undergraduate cyber education at the military academies. The Working Group believes that cyber education should include knowledge that all officers, cyber leaders and all highly technical officers should know [10].

3 PROGRAM OVERVIEW

The program enabled NROTC midshipmen from three Historically Black Colleges and Universities (HBCUs) in Atlanta, GA, Morehouse College, Spelman College, and Clark Atlanta University, to contribute technically to cyber, and electronic warfare (EW) technology domains through a rigorous, product-oriented research-and-development (R&D) program. The ultimate deliverable of the program with the Navy ROTC midshipmen was to produce a functional beta version of a data mining tool that would stream tweets from a user account and perform informative analysis on the retrieved tweets. The cohort sessions were scheduled to take place over 15 weeks, with the first three weeks at the close of the Fall semester and 12 working weeks in the following Spring semester. Two undergraduate research assistants, both African-American males and a postdoctoral researcher, an African-American female, were appointed to the project to assist in supporting the midshipmen's learning. They were also responsible for maintaining the gradual progression of the software engineering behind the prototype. In order to facilitate learning while also aiming to complete the team project by the end of the program period, one-hour class sessions were held at the beginning of every week. Sessions were, often led by the undergraduate assistants and overseen by the postdoctoral researcher, with supplemental office hours available by appointment later in the week. With the limited experience of the program participants, classes covered Python basics such as:

1. Basic Syntax - Students learned fundamental commands that store variables, print messages, and perform mathematical operations
2. Loops - Students learned the structure of various loops and wrote their own to solve their own problems.
3. Functions - Students learned how to create functions to reduce repeated code and increase usability.
4. Lists - Students learned how to create and iterate through lists.

After learning python basics, the midshipmen learned how to carefully integrate Tweepy, an importable application programming interface (API) library that would be used for collecting and analyzing publicly available user information and tweets.

3.1 Participants

There were 18 total Navy ROTC midshipmen program participants (7 female and 11 male), 3 of whom were Computer Science majors (2 female and 1 male). About 40% of the total cohort were STEM majors at the time of enrollment in the program. In comparison to other cohorts within the same grant, the backgrounds and majors of this particular group of midshipmen were rather unconventional. At other institutions, cohorts were chosen to be purely STEM majors, or even solely computer science majors. The purpose in opting for diversity was the hope that students of different areas of study could bring varying viewpoints to the team project, which would ultimately make for a better, more user-friendly tool. Furthermore, selecting students of various majors would give project leaders the chance to introduce students of different majors to programming and computer science.

3.2 In-Class Activities

With tight deadlines on the team project, making sure that no midshipman was left behind in the content of the lectures was a top priority. To address this, the undergraduate assistants and their post-doctoral advisor developed strategic assignments that were to be completed during class meetings to check the understanding and comprehension of the midshipmen. The assignments ranged in difficulty from practicing simple arithmetic and assignment logic in the Python IDLE shell to complex function definitions and implementations, looping over complex data structures, and capturing user input to create simple applications to be run in the terminal.

At the initial cohort meetings, lessons were taught in a lecture style with simple coding exercises that would be done as a class, typically at the end of the slide deck of that day's session. For example, with the Python IDLE shell projected on the screen, one of the undergraduate assistants would ask the class what one should type to perform some assignment and arithmetic logic; together the class would tell the assistant what to type at the prompt. Later in the program, in-class assignments/activities and completeness checks were introduced, while pair-programming was phased out. Program participants were given assignments that were to be developed individually and submitted as a Python file. These Python files required the midshipmen to create more complex programs that included function definition, looping, and basic data structures, specifically lists and dictionaries.

3.3 Team Project

The team project given to the midshipmen was to create a data mining tweet analysis tool that would hypothetically provide a military team with enough relevant information to identify a user that could pose a potential threat to national security. The software application would be built entirely in Python, utilizing the Tweepy API library for extracting tweets and user data from Twitter and Tkinter to design an acceptable user interface. The software tool was collectively designed to perform four main functions:

(1) Create a basic user profile when given a user's Twitter handle;
(2) Create a customized/filtered user profile given a user's Twitter handle;
(3) Perform overall text analysis that would provide a word-cloud of the most frequently used words in the tweets of a particular profile given a user's Twitter handle and identify the five most frequently used words; and
(4) Perform overall sentiment analysis that would provide the percentage of positive, negative, and neutral tweets for a profile given a user's Twitter handle.

The midshipmen utilized the knowledge of Python basics and data structures from in-class activities and assignments in four distinct teams. Each team worked to deliver one of the four aforementioned basic requirements of the software to the best of their ability. The undergraduate assistants and the post-doctoral researcher were available for support for any issues that would arise; but ultimately, the midshipmen were actual owners of the project in its totality. Weekly sprints were utilized with team syncs at the beginning of each week to allow the program leaders to check in on the progress of the students in their respective tasks. Upon its completion in a month's time, the software tool was presented to program directors and leaders to secure further funding for continued learning and research.

3.4 Program Evaluation

Instructors were interviewed on the following areas to offer insight on the effectiveness of the program: the midshipmen's performance during the development of the tool, the tool's effectiveness to produce intended results, the tool's usability, and the tool's prospective user experience. Instructors, as well as 14 of the 18 midshipmen, were also interviewed with oepen and close ended questions on the learning experience, the program's strengths and weaknesses, and individual learning and teaching preferences. Results were analyzed through inductive qualitative content analysis.

4 RESULTS

4.1 Team Project

The instructors of the program were interviewed to assess the outcome of the developed tool. While developing the tool, the instructors agreed that the biggest challenge was getting the midshipmen to retain the Python programming concepts. Additionally, teamwork difficulties, including poor communication, lack of responsibility and accountability for individual tasks, and poor collaboration skills, interfered with the development of the tool. Nevertheless, the tool was completed to specification, and its usability was assessed. One instructor praised the success of the tool's demo. Another instructor believed the tool was usable at the minimum requirements and could use further aesthetic and GUI improvements and usability testing. The instructors agreed that the effectiveness of the tool matched its intention. However, there was still room for fine-tuning if the tool were to be regularly used. According to the instructors, potential users in cybersecurity would have high value in using the tool that the midshipmen built.

4.2 Midshipmen Interviews

The midshipmen were asked a series of yes/no questions. Three (22%) of the midshipmen experienced coding in a course prior to the program. Twelve (86%) midshipmen agreed to being more interested in computer science than in the beginning of the program, while 2 (14%) of them disagreed. Only one (7%) of the midshipmen believed it was not necessary to take a computer science or Python course prior to the program. All of midshipmen surveyed believed actual semester courses, apart from lab sessions, would improve their training. The majority of the midshipmen (86%) agreed that the lab was a good learning environment and that having a different environment to learn in was effective. Furthermore, the majority (86%) also preferred to figure out the homework on their own; further elaboration on this topic varied in rationale, including reasonings like being comfortable with problem-solving independently and time-consumption of walking through homework versus figuring it out independently. On the subject of out-of-class assignments, 92% of the midshipmen surveyed believed that the homework assignments were relevant, as their skills practiced through homework were applicable in later use in developing the data mining tool.

Midshipmen were also asked a series of additional open-ended questions on the topic of the varying instruction styles exercised in the program. The students ultimately preferred the teaching techniques of Powerpoints, learning supplemented with examples, working hands-on with assignments, and learning concepts prior to practicing them (as opposed to an examples-first approach). Although suggestions to improve teaching methods varied, many agreed with increasing the number of hands-on assignments. Furthermore, the results suggest that the midshipmen strongly liked computer science after completing the program and found it very necessary for the future. The midshipmen believed participation in the program enhanced their resumes and skillsets, aligning them more closely to serve in a cybersecurity field post-graduation. They generally had no problems with the time allotted to execute activities or assignments and their challenges in the program varied person-to-person; namely completing the homework, participating successfully in group assignments, and independent pacing proved to be some of the pain points, to name a few. Group learning preference varied as there was no significant skew in the survey results toward working alone or in a group. It is to be noted that the midshipmen would have liked to see the assignments be more concept-specific, an increased amount of homework for more opportunities for practice, and a better distribution of skill amongst group members in the team assignment.

4.3 Instructor Interviews

The instructors were asked a series of open-ended questions. The first questions were on teaching methods. Instructors varied between preferring instruction in the format of Powerpoints and interactive exercises. The instructors agreed instruction could have been improved by paying better attention to detail and by making the increase in difficulty gradual. Instructors also agreed the time spent in sessions were productive. Having two undergraduate assistant instructors was favored, particularly with the ability to be hands-on with the midshipmen. Having a lead instructor of the program was also favored to keep order and organization. Having consistent source material helped with lesson-planning as well as being equipped with the necessary tools; although a dedicated computer lab would've helped.

Instructors were also questioned on factors that differentiated and affected students directly. Having a course dedicated for such a program as an elective was determined to be beneficial. Prerequisite coding experience requirements were recommended depending on the task and rigor that the tool needs to be. Challenges occurred with teaching the midshipmen jargon at the same time as coding instruction, as well as ensuring the tool in the team project was working. Instructors believed the midshipmen had the most challenge with retaining the concepts and, more so, being able to explain them. There was no significant variance in coding performance between STEM and non-STEM midshipmen students, though students did vary in personality and persistence. One factor of persistence that was noticed was a midshipmen's visitation with the instructors during the instructor's office hours.

5 DISCUSSION

5.1 Team Project

The challenges the midshipmen faced in developing the tool more than likely originated from a lack of understanding that ultimately affected how individuals on a team communicated with each other and took ownership of individual tasks. This notion is supported by other accounts of teamwork improving when the tool development progressed, as students had better retained basic computer programming concepts. While the software application built by novice students is in beta version, the midshipmen's work and success has been measured with a focus on base-level usability and effectiveness. This will allow prospective users to see value in the product and support its continued development as the midshipmen continue to learn about computer science and enhance their skill.

5.2 Midshipmen Interviews

After interviewing the midshipmen, a few things became rather clear about the program. Primarily, the work and material covered sparked an interest in the students, most of whom have never been exposed to computer programming. Additionally, the program succeeded in maintaining the interest of the more experienced students. Taking a Python class before coding a tool in Python would facilitate a Python-based coding program, but it is not necessary, so long as the program includes enough time to educate its participants. Providing a space exclusively for work was shown to have led to an increase in focus and productivity during these sessions.

Personality variances between students may also account for the willingness to work independently or with teams. On the one hand, figuring out homework on a student's own account forced them to review and develop their own understanding of the Powerpoint material presented in the sessions. Therefore, having a consistent course structure with homework for students to work independently may be integral to teaching minority military students computer programming. All but one midshipman believed homework helped build skills in which they would later apply to the data mining tool. The one midshipman who believed homework was not relevant to their success specified that the inactive periods between and difficulty of each assignment varied so significantly that they felt that they had a good grasp of the lab material one week and would then feel completely confused by the next.

Instructing minority students with little knowledge of computer science can be executed in a range of techniques. Namely, showing examples presented in a structured way and allowing students to perform hands-on activities. Examples and hands-on activities that are grounded in relatable and applicable topics garnered the interest of just about every student without fail, which would support the claim that computer science interest and enjoyment increases when students are aware of the myriad of possibilities for creativity and discovery within the field. Interestingly, as pacing and group work were revealed as challenges, students did not believe the time allotted to assignments were problematic. Teaching how to pace working on computer science assignments for both group assignments and independent work may be useful in the instruction of beginner minority students.

5.3 Instructor Interviews

From the viewpoint of the instructor, the interviews provided insight on teaching methods, necessary prerequisites for beginner programmers, and student factors. As teaching format preference varied between instructors, it is noted that instructors should respond to what attracts their students the best as well as how they are most comfortable instructing. Regardless, thorough instruction is necessary to train students successfully. As students who are new to programming are bound to find challenges, the difficulty of assignments may best be instructed by arranging topics from least difficult to most difficult; this suggestion may not be as feasible while developing a tool due to tool development ordinal constraints.

As one-hour sessions were productive in the instructor and student perspective, it seems to be other teaching strategies that will more significantly determine what time is needed. Scheduling course materials can factor in the number and effectiveness of instructor assistants who can better interact with students individually and minimize whole-class review time, as a lead instructor orchestrates the program. Having credible and consistent source material can be a way to maintain organization. Having a dedicated lab and/or elective course can also help maintain the organization of the course and reduce the workload and expectancies of the students.

Beginner students of any major do not need a coding prerequisite for enrolling a computer programming course with tool development unless the tool is required to be highly intricate; the more intricate, the more coding knowledge a student would need. There should be emphasis on educating students on jargon, as jargon between student and instructor was a recurrent theme in challenges for both instructors and students. In many cases, students could code but had troubles explaining what they were doing or asking for assistance, contributing to confusion and lack of productivity. Personality and persistence were also confounding variables in a students' performance interfering with a student's ability to work independently and with groups, their motivation to get the intended results even through challenging moments, and their willingness to ask for help and visit instructors during office hours. Personality and persistence must be taken into account for students as students will vary how they understand instruction and how they will go about completing tasks.

5.4 Other Program Insights

There were periods of transition, not only in instruction style, but also in the degree of productivity throughout the course. Initially, PowerPoint lectures in-class lecturing was the only methods for learning that were utilized and proved itself to be non-conducive for knowledge retention. Often by the next lecture, students would have a difficult time recalling what was reviewed in the previous week. When homework, examples, and hands-on activities were incorporated regularly, there was a noticeable improvement in knowledge retention and positive attitude amongst the vast majority of the students. Though pushback came from the program participants at first, it became clear after a short time that interactive assignments were the only way to honestly check for understanding and guarantee participant engagement in the program. Genuinely interested and curious midshipmen improved their coding abilities tremendously from the level at which they began.

5.5 Limitations

As a specific program with only 18 midshipmen participants, some of the insight may not be completely generalizable. Qualitative analysis was conducted solely, complimenting the sample size and nature of the study. Therefore, the generalizability of findings may vary due to confounding variables that were either overlooked or not deemed necessary to cover through interviews. For example, the confounding variables of personality and self-efficacy, which were noticed during data analysis, were not directly assessed, yet were mentioned significantly. In addition, though there is no evidence to suggest, like any interview, there may have been instances of interviewee bias, leniency in rating the performance of the course, and accounts misrepresented through socially popular word choice. Findings support a contextualized understanding of a computer science course experience with novice computer programming students who were minority and military affiliated.

6 CONCLUSION

The course on cybersecurity fundamentals and the development of a data mining tool were successful, despite the lack of computer programming skills the majority of midshipmen had prior to the start of the program. The course experience evaluation, conducted by interviews, provided insight on teaching strategies and the most prominent challenges of new computer programmers. It is intended for this program to continue with plans to develop more in-depth tools. Future studies of the program will incorporate new confounding variables discovered through this study for more precise data analyses as well as incorporating growth measures and quantitative measures for increased generalizability and more rigorous insight.

ACKNOWLEDGMENTS

This material is also based in part upon work supported by the Defense Technical Information Center under Contract Number FA8075-14-D-0018-0026. Any opinions, findings, and conclusions or recommendations expressed in this material are those of the author(s) and do not necessarily reflect the views of the Defense Technical Information Center.

This material is also based in part upon work supported by the National Science Foundation under Grant Number 1547793. Any opinions, findings, and conclusions or recommendations expressed in this material are those of the author(s) and do not necessarily reflect the views of the National Science Foundation.

REFERENCES

[1] Mordechai Ben-Ari. 2001. Constructivism in computer science education. *Journal of Computers in Mathematics and Science Teaching* 20, 1 (2001), 45–73.
[2] Laurence Bradford. 2018. What You Need To Know About Cybersecurity In 2018. https://www.forbes.com/sites/laurencebradford/2018/03/30/why-people-should-learn-about-cybersecurity-in-2018/#5341dcba5d00
[3] Kwan Brown, Rebekah Lin and Bob Rudis. 2018. Quarterly Threat Report. https://www.rapid7.com/globalassets/_pdfs/research/rapid7-threat-report-2018-q2.pdf
[4] Art Conklin. 2005. The use of a collegiate cyber defense competition in information security education. In *Proceedings of the 2nd annual conference on Information security curriculum development*. ACM, 16–18.
[5] Arthur Conklin, Raymond E Cline, and Tiffany Roosa. 2014. Re-engineering cybersecurity education in the US: an analysis of the critical factors. In *System Sciences (HICSS), 2014 47th Hawaii International Conference on*. IEEE, 2006–2014.
[6] Steve Cooper and Steve Cunningham. 2010. Teaching computer science in context. *Acm Inroads* 1, 1 (2010), 5–8.
[7] Andrea Forte and Mark Guzdial. 2005. Motivation and nonmajors in computer science: identifying discrete audiences for introductory courses. *IEEE Transactions on Education* 48, 2 (2005), 248–253.
[8] Mark Guzdial and Elliot Soloway. 2002. Teaching the Nintendo generation to program. *Commun. ACM* 45, 4 (2002), 17–21.
[9] Nate Lord. 2018. What is Cyber Security? https://digitalguardian.com/blog/what-cyber-security
[10] Edward Sobiesk, Jean Blair, Gregory Conti, Michael Lanham, and Howard Taylor. 2015. Cyber education: a multi-level, multi-discipline approach. In *Proceedings of the 16th Annual Conference on Information Technology Education*. ACM, 43–47.
[11] Zoë J Wood, John Clements, Zachary Peterson, David Janzen, Hugh Smith, Michael Haungs, Julie Workman, John Bellardo, and Bruce DeBruhl. 2018. Mixed Approaches to CS0. (2018).

Topological Scoring of Concept Maps for Cybersecurity Education

Pranita Deshpande
Department of Computer Science
University of New Orleans
pdeshpa1@my.uno.edu

Irfan Ahmed*
Department of Computer Science
Virginia Commonwealth University
iahmed3@vcu.edu

ABSTRACT

Concept maps are a well-known pedagogical tool for organizing and representing knowledge and developing a deep understanding of concepts. Unfortunately, the grading of concept maps tends to be manual and tedious thereby, posing serious limitation for an instructor to use them in class efficiently. To automate the assessment and grading, the topology and structural features of concept maps are utilized. However, they have never been explored for cybersecurity education. This paper evaluates the effectiveness of topological scoring of the concept maps for two cybersecurity courses: digital forensics, and SCADA system security. We create a dataset of 41 high-quality concept maps developed with expert knowledge. We utilize waterloo rubric to manually validate the quality of the concept maps based-on their contents and further compare the rubric outcome (obtained via manual analysis) with the automated topological scoring of the maps. The evaluation results show that the topological scoring is promising. However, it is not equally effective and warrants for advanced techniques to better utilize the topology of the maps. The dataset is made publicly available for further research on this topic.

ACM Reference format:
Pranita Deshpande and Irfan Ahmed. 2019. Topological Scoring of Concept Maps for Cybersecurity Education. In *Proceedings of the 50th ACM Technical Symposium on Computer Science Education, Minneapolis, MN, USA, February 27-March 2, 2019 (SIGCSE '19),* ACM, New York, NY, 7 pages.
DOI: http://dx.doi.org/10.1145//3287324.3287495

1 INTRODUCTION

Concept maps are a visual tool for organizing and representing knowledge. They include concepts, represented as text boxes, and relationships between pairs of concepts indicated by a connecting link. The most abstract concepts are placed at the top the diagram, while progressively more specific ones are placed underneath them. This simple design allows seamless and effective linking and exploration of concept at different levels of detail.

Research has shown that concept mapping is beneficial for student learning, if it is used as an integral, on-going feature of the learning process, and not as an isolated activity at the beginning and/or end of a semester [13]. Concept maps are effective for students to clarify their knowledge structures [8]. The students who learn through concept maps have better learning outcomes over traditional approaches [22].

Unfortunately, the grading of concept maps tends to be manual and tedious thereby, posing serious limitation for an instructor to use them in class efficiently. The topology and structural features of concept maps are considered promising for automating the assessment and grading of concept maps. However, they have never been explored for cybersecurity education. The concept maps for cybersecurity can be quite different from other areas of computer science including the frequency of keywords and phrases, interdisciplinary topics, and dynamic subject area [2, 3, 5–7, 9–11, 17, 19, 24–27].

In this paper, we present a dataset of 41 concept maps for two cybersecurity courses (developed with expert knowledge) to support research in this direction. The courses are digital forensics, and supervisory control and data acquisition (SCADA) system security. We utilize the Waterloo rubric [1] to establish the ground truth about the quality of the maps. The rubric evaluates five elements of a concept map i.e., breadth of net, interconnectedness, use of descriptive links, efficient links, layout and development over the time, and identifies the quality of a map as either Excellent, Good, Poor, or Fail.

We further utilize the ground-truth to evaluate the effectiveness of a recent state-of-the-art topological scoring method [12]. The method uses the structural features of a concept map (i.e., branch point count, average words per concept, concept count, linking phrase, orphan count, proposition count, Root child count, sub-map count) and provides a topological score. The evaluation results show that the topological scoring is promising. However, they are not equally effective as compared to the Rubric and require more research in this domain. The dataset is made publicly available at gitlab for other researchers to use [14]

Contributions. We summarize the contribution of the paper as follows:

- *Concept Map Dataset* We develop the first dataset of concept maps for cybersecurity courses and make it publicly available for research and education.
- *Establish the Ground Truth* We assess and record the quality of the maps (ground-truth) in the datasets using the Waterloo Rubric.
- *Identify an Open Research Problem* We point out (via experimental analysis) that topological scoring requires attention from education research community to develop effective

*Ahmed completed this work while he was at the University of New Orleans

SIGCSE '19, February 27-March 2, 2019, Minneapolis, MN, USA.

ACM ISBN 978-1-4503-5890-3/19/02...$15.00
DOI: http://dx.doi.org/10.1145//3287324.3287495

solutions for automated assessment and grading of concept maps. Our dataset is useful for the research in this direction.

Roadmap. The rest of the paper is organized as follows: Section 2 presents the related work. Section 3 discusses the datasets including steps to create concept maps and guidelines from our experience, followed by concept map examples in section 4. Sections 5 and 6 presents the evaluation methods and results. Section 7 concludes the paper.

2 RELATED WORK

Concept mapping has received relatively little attention in cybersecurity education as compared to other pedagogical techniques such as peer instruction [4, 15, 20, 21].

Dexter [16] uses concept maps to detail required concepts for cybersecurity management, delving into sub- topics such as malicious behavior (deployment of code and usage of vulnerability scanners) on an organization's network targeting their information assets and perimeter defenses such as firewalls, routers, and IDS systems. The author also uses the concept maps to highlight policies and technologies that are key to an organizations cybersecurity management.

Tanner and Dampier [28] highlight the potential use of concept maps in digital forensic investigations, detailing in concept maps the six phases of the digital investigative process (identification, collection, preservation, examination, analysis, and presentation) as well as important procedures and concepts within each phase such as chain of custody or software used in particular phases. The authors note that the maps could be tailored on a per-investigation process to display contexts of specific evidence such as a suspect property and case timeline, and how each piece of evidence was examined. Tanner and Dampier further detail how case-specific concept maps may be shared by the law enforcement community as well as how a concept map could be shown in court in order to detail a complex investigative process.

Hay *et al.* [18] describe the pedagogical use of concept mapping in a general higher educational context, and summarize prior use of concept maps in both the teaching and learning processes. The authors focus on the usage of concept mapping to measure students prior knowledge, as well as allowing for the instructor to teach new material in the context of students prior understanding. They suggest that concept mapping be performed both by students and instructors, and identify several core practice of responsible university teaching that could be accomplished through concept mapping such as measuring the prior knowledge of students, presenting in a deliberate manner in the context of a known student knowledge base, and measuring change among the student population so that learning (where it occurs) is identified and the causes of non-learning are addressed.

3 DEVELOPING A CONCEPT MAP DATASET

Overview. Concept map is a graphical tool to represent concepts and the relationships among them on a particular topic. The mapping organizes the concepts in a hierarchy, with the most general ones at the top of the map and the most specific concepts at the bottom. The concepts are connected through arrows (or links) and propositions—a word or phrase describing the link. Concept mapping is a cognitively intensive task that examines the level of a student's understanding of concepts. It is particularly useful for in-class activities and homework assignments, and offers opportunities to improve the effectiveness of the instruction.

Concept mapping can be used to measure the level of a student's understanding of cybersecurity concepts throughout the course, via Concept map-based exercises. In particular, a poorly constructed (by a student) map that has missing links and gaps in logic, or incorrect information can allow the instructor to quickly correct misconceptions developed by a student.

Conversely, instructors can use a correct map in class as the basis for in-class discussion. The map requires students to actively build their understanding of foundational concepts, and allow them to reason about the bigger picture and the connections among concepts.

Steps to Create a Concept Map. We use the following systematic approach to develop a concept map.

(1) Select a target concept.
(2) Identify keywords that represent some aspect of the concept.
(3) Recognize any relationships among the keywords in appropriate words and phrases and then,
(4) Draw the concept map; circle the keywords and connect them with the relationship words/phrases.

Guidelines of Do's and Don'ts. From our experience of developing and improving concept maps including several revisions, and reviews and comments from other participants, we develop a guideline list of *Do's and Don'ts* while developing a concept map.

- A connection between two nodes should be unidirectional.
- A connecting phrase should describe the relationship between two nodes clearly. Otherwise, avoid such connections and elaborate them with additional keyword(s) between them.
- A connecting loop across one or multiple nodes tend to create confusion and should be avoided.

Dataset Details. We develop the concept maps for two cybersecurity courses: digital forensics, and SCADA system security.

Digital forensics is defined as the application of scientific tools and methods to identify, collect, and analyze digital artifacts in support of legal proceedings [23]. We have developed 19 concept maps for digital forensics investigation course. The course provides an introduction to digital forensics, and then covers the first response and evidence handling, file systems, memory forensics, and tools for investigation. The maps are divided into six different course modules. The distribution of the concept maps with respect to their topics are presented in Table 1 and described as follows.

- *Introduction to digital forensics* covers the concept maps on digital evidence including the location, type and documentation of evidence, types of digital forensics investigation, and legal aspects.
- *First response and evidence handling* covers the concept maps on how a digital forensics investigator should respond to a case before starting the investigation, what are

Topics	# of Concept Maps
Introduction to digital forensics	4
First response and evidence handling	2
Investigation steps	3
File systems	5
Memory Forensics	2
Tools for investigation	3
TOTAL	19

Table 1: Concept maps for digital forensics

the necessary steps and procedures which should be taken care of and how the evidence should be handled.

- *Investigation steps* focus on the steps/tasks that should be performed during a forensic investigation including the acquisition and analysis of the evidence, and the reporting that describes the entire investigation procedure and give a conclusion to a case.
- *File systems* covers the concept maps on file system investigation including an overview of different file systems, file allocation table, new technology file system, and investigating tips and techniques on file system.
- *Memory Forensics* covers the concept maps on memory analysis and live forensics including an explanation of volatility data and how important the data is for investigation.
- *Tools for investigation* covers the concept maps on the usage of different tools and techniques for file system investigation including sleuth kit, and windows registry and web browser investigation.

SCADA systems control major portions of the U.S. critical infrastructure — power grid, pipe-lines, water management, etc. — and protecting their integrity and availability is of primary importance to national security. We have developed 22 concept maps for the SCADA security course work. The course is designed for computer science students who have no understanding of control system and cover topics from introductory to advance level. The maps are divided for five different course modules, starting from an introduction to SCADA systems and then, covers PLC programming, communication protocols, and cyberattacks and security solution. The distribution of concept maps with respect to their topics are presented in Table 2 and described as follows.

- *Introduction to SCADA Systems* covers the basic concepts of a SCADA system, and its components, provides a brief understanding of some physical processes.
- *Programming of the Programmable Logic Controllers (PLC)* mainly covers Ladder Logic programming including rules to write a program and addressing formats of PLC
- *SCADA communication protocols* covers two protocols, Modbus and DNP3 along with the header and message formats.
- *SCADA Vulnerabilities and Attack* covers real-world attacks and vulnerabilities including the attack taxonomies on MODBUS and DNP3 protocols.
- *SCADA security solutions* covers security solution for SCADA systems such as PLC code detection.

Topics	# of Concept Maps
Introduction to SCADA Systems	4
PLC Programming	3
SCADA communication protocols	6
SCADA Vulnerabilities and Attack	5
SCADA security solutions	4
TOTAL	22

Table 2: Concept maps for SCADA system security

4 EXAMPLES OF CONCEPT MAPS

This section presents two examples of the concept maps from digital forensics and SCADA system.

4.1 SCADA System: *Working of a Conveyor Belt*

The main components of a typical conveyor belt are drives, actuators, controllers, monitors and sensors. Programmable logic controller (PLC) receives an input signal from proximity sensor that shows that an object is placed on the belt. The PLC runs its control logic and sends an output signal to Servo drive to move the conveyor belt to make some space for the next object. The whole conveyor belt physical process can be remotely monitored by using human-machine-interface (HMI) and the data received by the HMI is also stored in historian. There are two types of sensors proximity sensor and photo eye sensor, which detects the presence of the object using beam of light and electromagnetic field respectively.

Figure 1 shows the concept map on the working and components of a conveyor belt. The map consists of four levels of hierarchy, and mostly uses succinct phrases to link two nodes. Nodes are also using short descriptive phrases or long words. To develop this map, we use our systematic approach as follows:

- The target concept addresses a typical working model of conveyor belt including its components.
- We select the keywords including components, sensors and actuators used and how it was used.
- To connect the nodes that can make sufficient understanding of their relationships, we mostly use phrases, instead of words.

4.2 Digital Forensics: *Handling Digital Evidence*

When a forensic investigator collects an evidence from a crime scene, it is required that the evidence is handled properly, which typically involves five stages i.e., storage of evidence, disposition, transporting, documentation, and packing of evidence. *Storing of evidence* imposes rules and regulation such as access to storage must be limited and monitored, chain of custody should be maintained,login and log out details of who, what, when, where and why. *Transporting the evidence* includes protecting portable devices and media from external corruption, determining if a suspect computer should remain powered up, what applications and other processes were active. *Documenting the evidence* records where the evidence was found, what state it was in, model number, serial numbers, and time and date of evidence collection. After the investigation is done evidence must be *destroyed* or *returned.*

Figure 2 shows the concept map explaining the stages of evidence handling. The map consists of three levels of hierarchy. The nodes

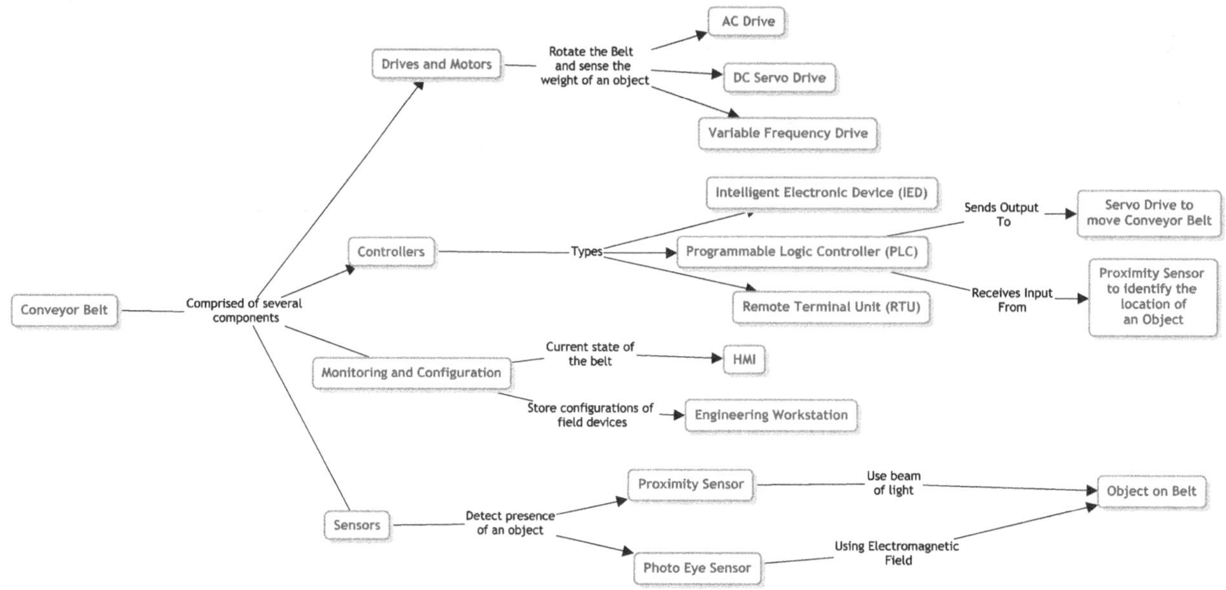

Figure 1: Working of ICS with Conveyor as an example

and connecting links are self explanatory phrases. To develop this map, we use our systematic approach as follows:

- The targeted concept is the concept of handling of digital evidence.
- Key nodes indicated the actions and duties to be performed in each individual stage.
- connecting nodes indicate the different stages in digital evidence handling

5 CONCEPT MAP ASSESSMENT METHODS

We utilize two different assessment methods for concept maps: the Waterloo Rubric [1], and Topological Scoring [12]. The rubric via manual analysis established the ground truth for the concept maps in the datasets. The scoring is an automated method to assess the quality of the maps.

5.1 Waterloo Rubric (*manual analysis)*

The Waterloo Rubrics is developed by the University of Waterloo for the assessment of the concept maps [1]. The rubric identifies the quality of the maps at four levels i.e. *Excellent, Good, Poor,* and *Fail* based-on the following six elements i.e., *breadth of net, interconnectedness, use of descriptive links, efficient links, layout,* and *development time.*

Breadth of net evaluates the significance of target concepts and their description in multiple levels. For *excellent,* a map includes important concepts and describe them in multiple levels. However, for *fail,* a map misses many important concepts.

Interconnectedness evaluates the number of concepts interlinked with other concepts. For *excellent,* all concepts are interlinked, and for *fail,* few concepts are interlinked.

Use of descriptive links evaluates the quality of description as accurately defined to vague and incorrectly defined. The first is ranked as *excellent* while the later is *fail.*

Efficient links evaluates the uniqueness of the information of the links and the quality of description of the relationships among the nodes. For *excellent,* each link type is distinct and clearly describes the relationship, while for *fail,* most links are vaguely described, and not distinct from each other.

Layout evaluates the physical layout of a concept map including its size to be fit in one page, and hierarchical structure. For *excellent,* maps fit in one page and have clear multiple hierarchy, while for *fail,* map consists of multiple pages and has no hierarchical organization.

Development over time evaluates whether a concept map is built incrementally as therm progress and new concepts are learned. for *excellent,* final map shows considerable cognitive progression from base map and a significantly greater depth of understanding of the domain. while for *fail* final map shows no significant cognitive profession from the base map and no increase in the understanding of the domain.

5.2 Topological Scoring (*automated analysis)*

Topological scoring [12] utilizes structural features of a concept map to compute a score between zero and six, where higher score indicates higher quality of the map. A brief description of the features are as follows:

Average Words per Concept is the total count of words, as separated by whitespace, in all concepts divided by the number of concept in a map. Concise concepts are important to the taxonomy score.

Branch Point Count is the total number of concepts and linking phrases that have at least one incoming connection and more than one outgoing connection.

Concept Count is the number of concept in a map.

Linking Phrase Count is the number of linking phrases in a map.

Orphan Count is the number of concepts in the map that have no connections.

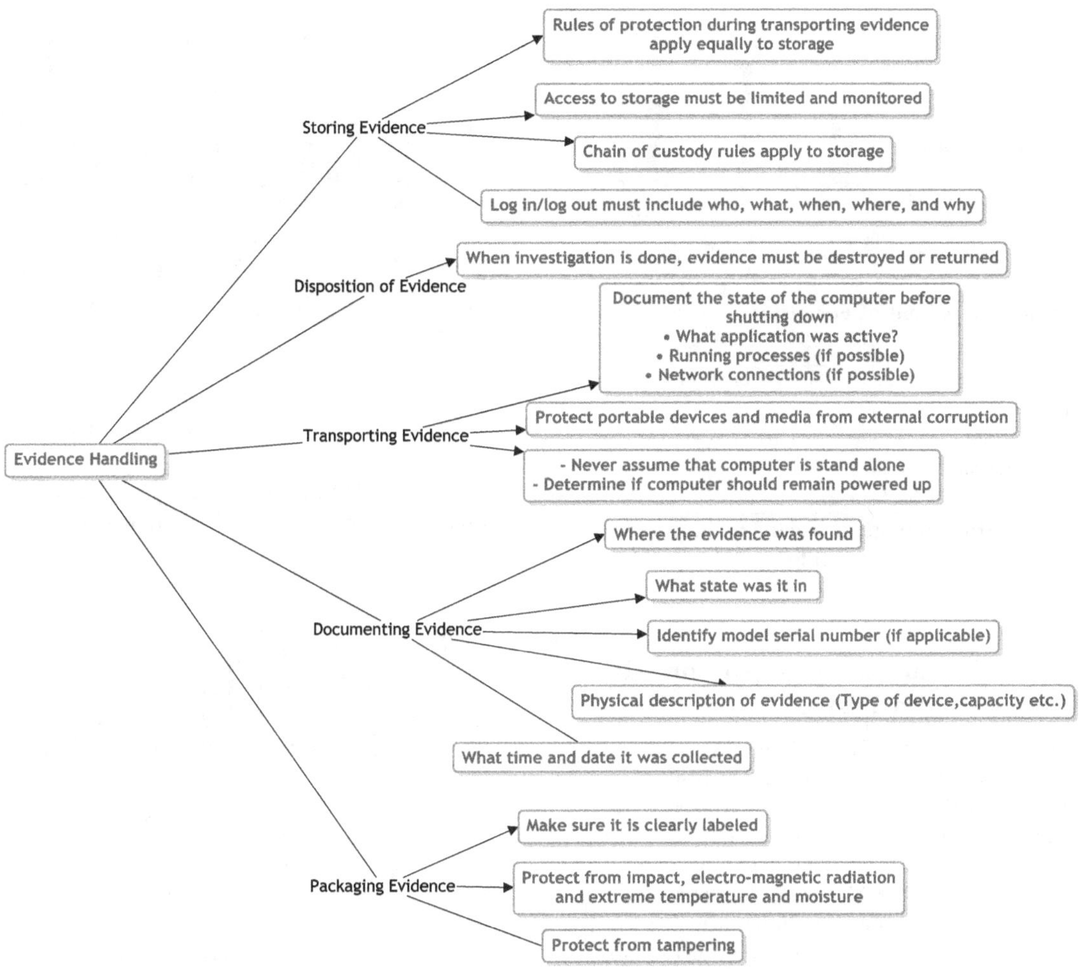

Figure 2: Different stages of handling of digital evidence

Proposition Count is the number of propositions (i.e. concept-linking phrase-concept) in a map.
Root Child Count is the number of concepts in a map that has an incoming connection from a root concept. A root concept is defined as one that has outgoing connections but no incoming connections.
Sub Map Count is the number of root concepts found in a map.
Taxonomy Score is the topological taxonomy score computed for a map.

6 ASSESSMENT RESULTS

We obtain the results of the Waterloo rubric and topological scoring on the concept maps of both courses and then, compare them to measure the effectiveness of the automated scoring method.

6.1 Waterloo Rubric

Figure 3 shows the assessment results on the concept maps of SCADA system security for each element of rubric. The results show that most of the maps are graded either excellent or good. For instance, using *breadth of net*, 14 maps are graded to excellent where as 7 maps are good. Similarly, using *interconnectedness*, 8 maps are excellent, where as 12 maps are good.

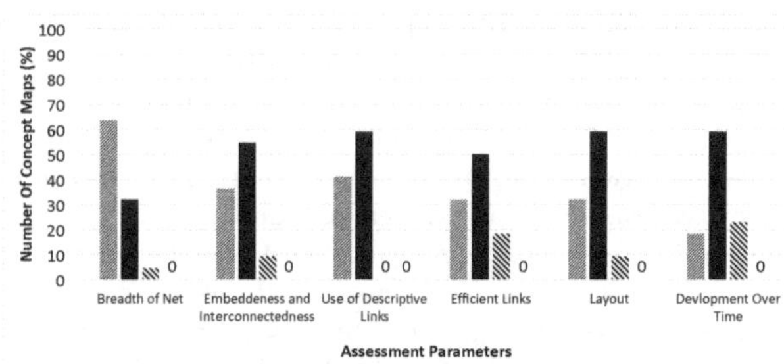

Figure 3: Rubric Assessment of SCADA system concept maps

Figure 4 shows the assessment results on the concept maps of digital forensics. The results validate the high quality of concept maps using each element separately. For instance, *breadth of net* identifies 13 and 5 maps as excellent and good; *Interconnectedness* identifies 11 and 7 maps as excellent and good respectively.

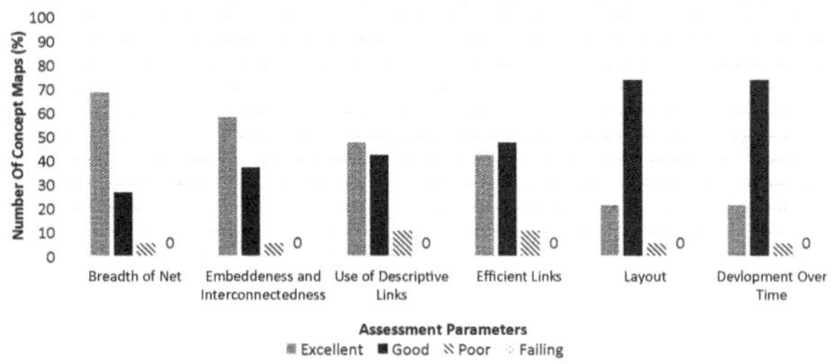

Figure 4: Rubric Assessment of Forensics concept maps

Accuracy Level	SCADA (%)	Forensics (%)
Accurate	13.64	0
Close to accurate	22.73	10.53
Close to inaccurate	27.27	31.58
Inaccurate	36.36	57.89

Table 3: Accuracy of the topological scoring when compared with the ground truth of Waterloo Rubric

6.2 Topological Scoring and Comparison with the Rubric (Ground Truth)

Analysis of Topological Scores. Figure 5 and 6 show the topological scores and the comparison with the Rubric results on the concept map of both SCADA system and digital forensics respectively. Recall that higher score refers to higher quality of a concept map. The results show that most of the maps have moderate scores. In particular, out of 22 maps of SCADA system, 8 maps score a rank of 2 or below where as 14 maps score 3 and above including 6 maps have the rank of five or higher. Furthermore, out of 19 maps of forensics, 9 maps score the rank of 2 and higher whereas 10 maps have the score of 1. Highest rank of a concept map is 4 for the topic of "report writing of investigation".

Comparison between Topological Scores and Waterloo Rubric. The Rubric grading is the ground truth. It assesses the quality of a concept map based-on content manually. To compare the ground truth with the automated topological scores, we normalized the rubric scale between zero and six where the distance between two consecutive levels (such as Excellent and Good) is 1.5.

Figures 5 and 6 shows the comparison between the ground truth rubric and topological score. We quantify the effectiveness of the scoring as accurate, close to accurate, close to inaccurate, and inaccurate. If the result of ground truth and scoring is same, it is accurate. If the score deviates one level from the ground truth, it is close to accurate. Two and three level deviations corresponds to close to inaccurate, and inaccurate respectively.

Table 3 summarize the results for the concept maps of both courses. It shows that the scoring achieves some level of accuracy. However, it is not significant and requires further research on this topic.

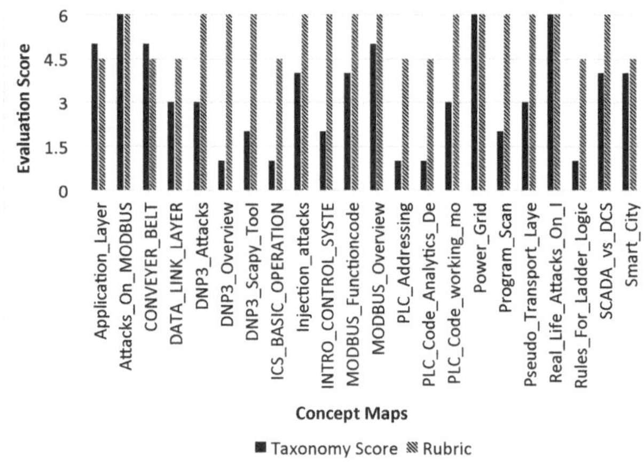

Figure 5: SCADA System Security - Comparison between the Waterloo Rubric and Topological Scoring

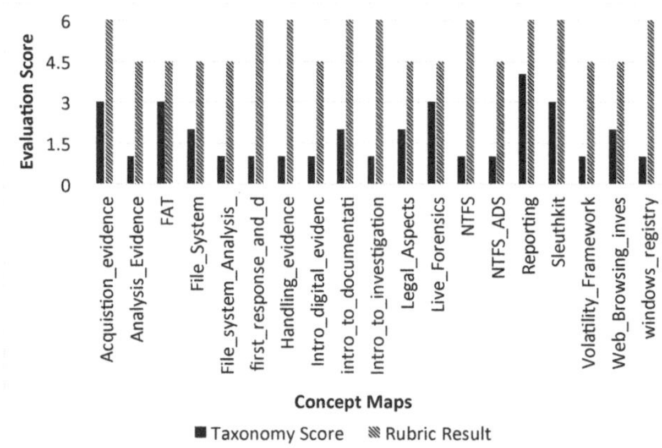

Figure 6: Digital Forensics - Comparison between the Waterloo Rubric and Topological Scoring

7 CONCLUSION

The paper presented a dataset of 41 concept maps for two cybersecurity courses useful for improving students' learning experience in class. We evaluated the quality of the maps using two well-known techniques. One was the Waterloo Rubric (manual assessment) based-on the six elements of quality (such as breadth of net, interconnectedness, and use of descriptive links) to classify a map into excellent, good, poor, and fail. The other was topological scoring (automated assessment) based-on the structural features of a map to compute the rank between zero and six.

The evaluation results showed that the rubric identified most of the maps as Excellent or Good and provided the ground-truth about the quality of the maps. However, when we compared the topological scoring with the ground-truth, the scoring did not achieve significant accuracy thereby, pointing out an open research problem for automated assessment and grading of concept maps.

8 ACKNOWLEDGEMENT

This work was in part supported by the NSF grants # 1500101 and 1623276.

REFERENCES

[1] 2016. Rubric for Assessing Concept Maps (Centre for Teaching Excellence, University of Waterloo). https://uwaterloo.ca/centre-for-teaching-excellence/sites/ca.centre-for-teaching-excellence/files/uploads/files/rubric_for_assessing_concept_maps.pdf. (2016).

[2] I. Ahmed, S. Obermeier, S. Sudhakaran, and V. Roussev. 2017. Programmable Logic Controller Forensics. *IEEE Security Privacy* 15, 6 (November 2017), 18–24. https://doi.org/10.1109/MSP.2017.4251102

[3] Irfan Ahmed, Golden G. Richard, Aleksandar Zoranic, and Vassil Roussev. 2015. Integrity Checking of Function Pointers in Kernel Pools via Virtual Machine Introspection. In *Information Security*, Yvo Desmedt (Ed.). Springer International Publishing, Cham, 3–19.

[4] Irfan Ahmed and Vassil Roussev. 2018. Peer Instruction Teaching Methodology for Cybersecurity Education. *IEEE Security Privacy* 16, 4 (July 2018).

[5] Irfan Ahmed, Vassil Roussev, and Aisha Ali Gombe. 2015. Robust Fingerprinting for Relocatable Code. In *Proceedings of the 5th ACM Conference on Data and Application Security and Privacy (CODASPY '15)*. ACM, New York, NY, USA, 219–229. https://doi.org/10.1145/2699026.2699104

[6] Irfan Ahmed, Vassil Roussev, William Johnson, Saranyan Senthivel, and Sneha Sudhakaran. 2016. A SCADA System Testbed for Cybersecurity and Forensic Research and Pedagogy. In *Proceedings of the 2Nd Annual Industrial Control System Security Workshop (ICSS '16)*. ACM, New York, NY, USA, 1–9. https://doi.org/10.1145/3018981.3018984

[7] Irfan Ahmed, Aleksandar Zoranic, Salman Javaid, Golden Richard, and Vassil Roussev. 2013. Rule-Based Integrity Checking of Interrupt Descriptor Tables in Cloud Environments. In *Advances in Digital Forensics IX*, Gilbert Peterson and Sujeet Shenoi (Eds.). Springer Berlin Heidelberg, Berlin, Heidelberg, 305–328.

[8] Williams M. Akinsanya, C. 2004. *Concept mapping for meaningful learning*. Report. 41–46 pages.

[9] Sajal Bhatia, Sunny Behal, and Irfan Ahmed. 2018. *Distributed Denial of Service Attacks and Defense Mechanisms: Current Landscape and Future Directions*. Springer International Publishing, Cham, 55–97. https://doi.org/10.1007/978-3-319-97643-3_3

[10] Manish Bhatt and Irfan Ahmed. 2018. Leveraging relocations in ELF-binaries for Linux kernel version identification. *Digital Investigation* 26 (2018), S12 – S20. https://doi.org/10.1016/j.diin.2018.04.022

[11] Manish Bhatt, Irfan Ahmed, and Zhiqiang Lin. 2018. Using Virtual Machine Introspection for Operating Systems Security Education. In *Proceedings of the 49th ACM Technical Symposium on Computer Science Education*. ACM, 396–401.

[12] Alberto J Cañas, Larry Bunch, Joseph D Novak, and Priit Reiska. 2013. Cmapanalysis: An extensible concept map analysis tool. *Journal for Educators, Teachers and Trainers* (2013).

[13] A. Cañas. 2003. *A Summary of Literature Pertaining to the Use of Concept Mapping Techniques and Technologies for Education and Performance Support*. Report.

[14] Pranita Deshpande and Irfan Ahmed. 2018 (accessed July 23, 2018). *Concept Map Datasets for Cybersecurity Courses*. https://gitlab.com/iahmed4/concept-map-datasets-for-cybersecurity-courses

[15] Pranita Deshpande and Irfan Ahmed. 2019. Evaluation of Peer Instruction for Cybersecurity Education. In *Proceeding of the 50th ACM Technical Symposium on Computer Science Education (SIGCSE '19)*.

[16] J. Dexter. 2002. *The Cyber Security Management System: A Conceptual Mapping*. Report. SANS Institute.

[17] Jonathan Grimm, Irfan Ahmed, Vassil Roussev, Manish Bhatt, and ManPyo Hong. 2018. Automatic Mitigation of Kernel Rootkits in Cloud Environments. In *Information Security Applications*, Brent ByungHoon Kang and Taesoo Kim (Eds.). Springer International Publishing, Cham, 137–149.

[18] David Hay, Ian Kinchin, and Simon Lygo-Baker. 2008. Making learning visible: the role of concept mapping in higher education. *Studies in Higher Education* 33, 3 (2008), 295–311. https://doi.org/10.1080/03075070802049251

[19] Salman Javaid, Aleksandar Zoranic, Irfan Ahmed, and Golden G Richard III. 2012. Atomizer: Fast, Scalable and Lightweight Heap Analyzer for Virtual Machines in a Cloud Environment. In *Proceedings of the 6th Layered Assurance Workshop (ACSAC'12)*.

[20] William Johnson, Irfan Ahmed, Vassil Roussev, and Cynthia B. Lee. 2017. Peer Instruction for Digital Forensics. In *2017 USENIX Workshop on Advances in Security Education (ASE 17)*. USENIX Association, Vancouver, BC.

[21] William E. Johnson, Allison Luzader, Irfan Ahmed, Vassil Roussev, Golden G. Richard III, and Cynthia B. Lee. 2016. Development of Peer Instruction Questions for Cybersecurity Education. In *2016 USENIX Workshop on Advances in Security Education (ASE 16)*. USENIX Association, Austin, TX. https://www.usenix.org/conference/ase16/workshop-program/presentation/johnson

[22] Paul Kim and Claudia Olaciregui. 2008. The effects of a concept map-based information display in an electronic portfolio system on information processing and retention in a fifth-grade science class covering the Earth's atmosphere. 39, 4 (2008), 700–714.

[23] Vassil Roussev. 2016. Digital forensic science: issues, methods, and challenges. *Synthesis Lectures on Information Security, Privacy, & Trust* 8, 5 (2016), 1–155.

[24] Vassil Roussev, Irfan Ahmed, and Thomas Sires. 2014. Image-based Kernel Fingerprinting. *Digit. Investig.* 11, S2 (Aug. 2014), S13–S21. https://doi.org/10.1016/j.diin.2014.05.013

[25] Vassil Roussev, Andres Barreto, and Irfan Ahmed. 2016. API-Based Forensic Acquisition of Cloud Drives. In *Advances in Digital Forensics XII*, Gilbert Peterson and Sujeet Shenoi (Eds.). Springer International Publishing, Cham, 213–235.

[26] Saranyan Senthivel, Irfan Ahmed, and Vassil Roussev. 2017. SCADA network forensics of the PCCC protocol. *Digital Investigation* 22 (2017), S57 – S65. https://doi.org/10.1016/j.diin.2017.06.012

[27] Saranyan Senthivel, Shrey Dhungana, Hyunguk Yoo, Irfan Ahmed, and Vassil Roussev. 2018. Denial of Engineering Operations Attacks in Industrial Control Systems. In *Proceedings of the Eighth ACM Conference on Data and Application Security and Privacy (CODASPY '18)*. ACM, New York, NY, USA, 319–329. https://doi.org/10.1145/3176258.3176319

[28] April Tanner and David Dampier. 2009. Concept Mapping for Digital Forensic Investigations. In *Advances in Digital Forensics V*, Gilbert Peterson and Sujeet Shenoi (Eds.). Springer Berlin Heidelberg, Berlin, Heidelberg, 291–300.

Automated Critique of Early Programming Antipatterns*

Leo C. Ureel II
Michigan Technological University
Houghton, Michigan
ureel@mtu.edu

Charles Wallace
Michigan Technological University
Houghton, Michigan
wallace@mtu.edu

ABSTRACT

The introductory programming lab, with small cycles of teaching, coding, testing, and critique from instructors, is an extraordinarily productive learning experience for novice programmers. We wish to extend the availability of such critique through automation, capturing the essence of interaction between student and instructor as closely as possible. Integrated Development Environments and Automated Grading Systems provide constant feedback through static analysis and unit testing. But we also wish to tailor automated feedback to acknowledge commonly recurring issues with novice programmers, in keeping with the practice of a human instructor. We argue that the kinds of mistakes that novice programmers make, and the way they are reported to the novices, deserve special care.

In this paper we provide examples of early programming antipatterns that have arisen from our teaching experience, and describe different ways of identifying and dealing with them automatically through our tool WebTA. Novice students may produce code that is close to a correct solution but contains syntactic errors; WebTA attempts to salvage the promising portions of the student's submission and suggest repairs that are more meaningful than typical compiler error messages. Alternatively, a student misunderstanding may result in well-formed code that passes unit tests yet contains clear design flaws; through additional analysis, WebTA can identify and flag them. Finally, certain types of antipattern can be anticipated and flagged by the instructor, based on the context of the course and the programming exercise; WebTA allows for customizable critique triggers and messages.

CCS CONCEPTS

• **Social and professional topics → Computer science education**; **CS1**; • **Applied computing → Computer-assisted instruction**; • **Software and its engineering → Patterns**; *Object oriented languages*;

KEYWORDS

CS1, design patterns, autograder, critiquing systems

*This work is supported by the National Science Foundation under grant DUE-1504860.

SIGCSE '19, February 27-March 2, 2019, Minneapolis, MN, USA

ACM ISBN 978-1-4503-5890-3/19/02...$15.00
https://doi.org/10.1145/3287324.3287463

ACM Reference Format:
Leo C. Ureel II and Charles Wallace. 2019. Automated Critique of Early Programming Antipatterns. In *Proceedings of the 50th ACM Technical Symposium on Computer Science Education (SIGCSE '19), February 27-March 2, 2019, Minneapolis, MN, USA.* ACM, New York, NY, USA, 7 pages. https://doi.org/10.1145/3287324.3287463

1 INTRODUCTION

Many automatic approaches have been developed for evaluating student programs [6, 7, 13]. Often these tools function as autograders, supporting the instructor in testing and grading programs submitted by large numbers of students. However, automated assessment can also be used to provide students with feedback before submitting code for grading. Program characteristics assessed dynamically include functionality, efficiency, and testing coverage. In addition, static analysis tools can be used to assess program characteristics such as coding style, programming errors, software metrics, and adherence to good design principles.

Our automated code critique tool *WebTA* falls into this latter category. WebTA acts as an assistant to the student, commenting on intermediate code iterations during development, and then as a traditional autograder for final submissions. Our inspiration is the computer lab experience, where students engage in tight loops of coding, testing, and critique, with human lab instructors providing continuous feedback. We wish to simulate as closely as possible the experience of interacting with a human mentor.

With this aim, we wish to detect and comment on programming and design flaws early in the process. Through our experience as instructors, we can anticipate *antipatterns*, commonly occurring practices that reflect misunderstandings or poor design choices [5], and plan interventions accordingly. Many studies of novice programmers point out how student misconceptions, particularly concerning the object-oriented paradigm, are manifested as antipatterns [4, 11, 17, 21].

Some early programming antipatterns cut across traditional boundaries of syntactic wellformedness or behavioral correctness, and therefore require special effort to detect. WebTA constructs an Abstract Syntax Tree for student code and performs analysis on this structure to detect certain kinds of anomalous code—some syntactically well-formed, others not.

Furthermore, we want to tailor our feedback to be most effective for learning. Messages that may be appropriate for a general purpose Integrated Development Environment like Eclipse may be confusing, misleading, or even intimidating for novices, and this can have detrimental effects on their persistence in studying computing [2]. Another risk of cryptic error messages is that they may inoculate students against carefully reading such feedback.

From our experience teaching introductory programming, the following categories of antipattern have emerged:

- Some antipatterns result in syntactically ill-formed code, but we do not wish to report them with a standard compile-time error message; the standard message may be quite opaque and confusing, whereas we can say something more relevant and meaningful to a novice student.
- Other antipatterns do not result in compile time errors and have no effect on behavior, thus are not detectable through testing. A human instructor looking at student code would note such "code smells" [10, 15] and call them out. This provides an important teaching moment, highlighting the importance of good design beyond simple syntactic well-formedness and behavioral correctness.
- Still other antipatterns may defy easy static analysis but can be detected through "insider knowledge". In our position as instructor, we can fine-tune our feedback to the particulars of the assignment, allowing us to give comments that would be outside the scope of a general analysis.

We begin our paper with an overview of WebTA and related work on automated grading and critique (§2). We then give examples of common antipatterns in student code and explain how we detect them and respond to them through WebTA (§3). We conclude with some ideas for future development (§4).

2 TOOLS FOR AUTOMATED GRADING AND CRITIQUE

A wide array of tools provide assistance to programmers, both experienced and novice, in the form of continuous feedback on static and dynamic properties of their code. We start with a discussion of our tool, WebTA, and compare it to related products in the domains of Integrated Development Environments (IDEs) and Automated Grading Systems.

2.1 WebTA

WebTA is a web-based tool that critiques student programs in introductory Computer Science courses. An optional Learning Tools Interoperability (LTI) Module provides services required for authentication with, and grade reporting back to, the Canvas Learning Management System (LMS). Although Canvas is our platform of choice, in principle the module can plug in to any other LMS implementing the LTI standard, including Blackboard and Moodle.

Data sources for the system include Student Code, Instructor Tests, Patterns Database, and Grade Reports. The Patterns Database contains four kinds of rules for identifying patterns and dispensing advice to the students. A basic rule contains a description of a code pattern that the instructor may recognize manually. Error rules are used to provide feedback and hints for compile-time and runtime errors. A regular expression rule can be used to identify patterns in the source code. Rules can be used to traverse the abstract syntax tree to identify more subtle patterns.

Every time a student submits code to WebTA, their code is subjected to all tests designed for the project. Students learn to develop code to pass each test and immediately discover if new code has side-effects that cause other tests to fail. Students are provided with immediate feedback on their programs, just when they need it during the development process. Faculty encode guidance and feedback into a database of common mistakes. When student code exhibits symptoms of a problem, the database guidance is triggered and students immediately receive the instructor's advice. This kind of guidance covers situations arising from compile and runtime errors, as well as more general coding style mistakes.

Listing 1: Instructor Tests

```
@Test
@CanvasTaTest( points = 5,
        name = "fibRecursive␣Edge␣Case",
        description = "Checks␣for␣n␣=␣-1" )
public void fibRecursiveEdgeCaseTest( ) {
  Fibonacci prog = new Fibonacci( );
  long result = prog.fibRecursive( -1 );
  if ( result != -1 ) {
    fail( "fibRecursive(" + -1 + ")␣=␣" + -1
      + ".␣Your␣method␣returned␣" + result);
  }
}
```

When students connect with WebTA through Canvas, a startup screen that explains the current problem and tells them which files they should upload to receive a code critique. After clicking on the *Critique My Code* button, students receive an online report which includes a Critique Summary. Under the hood, the system has compiled the student's code and run it through a series of shakedown tests. Students can scroll down from the critique summary to view details of the critique, including errors and warnings generated both at compile-time and run-time. Scrolling further down the code critique, students find a listing of each code file submitted, with advice generated via textual analysis of the code.

The instructor can configure the system to run both public and secret tests, run the student's own test code against their program, assess the student's unit test cases to determine their ability to generate edge cases, produce feedback by matching rules run against the source code, or matching rules against output text.

As an example, consider the following assignment:

> *Develop a class named Fibonacci that contains the method* `fibRecursive` *which given an integer n returns the long nth element of the Fibonacci Sequence. If n is out of range, return* `-1`.

In addition to testing common Fibonacci values, the instructor wants to ensure that the students have conformed to the range specification. The instructor sets up a secret test, with the result of the test shared but not the test inputs themselves. This test, using JUnit test conventions, is shown in Listing 1. Tests can be toggled as secret or shared dynamically through the WebTA interface.

The instructor also creates rules for the static analyzer, or reuses existing ones. Rules consist of a regular expression matching a potential problematic code snippet, coupled with appropriate advice. For example, anticipating a Knee-Jerk pattern (§3.4) where students add a vacuous base case, the instructor could set up the rule shown in Listing 2. In this way, the instructor provides the student with better feedback than the error message (stack overflow) triggered by failing a test.

Listing 2: Instructor rule capturing an empty base case.

```
if match( "if␣*\(.*\)\s*\{\s*\}" )
"It␣looks␣like␣you␣have␣an␣empty␣base␣case."
```

2.2 Related tools

We include a brief survey of tools related to WebTA, highlighting certain tools that have potential to detect and critique antipatterns for novice programmers.

2.2.1 Autograders. Autograders have a long history dating back to at least 1960 [12]. These systems often include a testing component that provides a rigorous shakedown of the student work to expose compilation and execution errors.

Some autograder systems, like *Marmoset* [18] and *JUG* [3], as well as professional analysis tools like *JExercise* [19], are entirely test-driven and do not examine source code. A sole focus on program behavior addresses our antipattern concerns only partly. First, error messages from black-box test results do not necessarily give students insight into what is wrong with their code. Second, some antipatterns may manifest themselves via improper programming practices but do not have any effect on program behavior; these "code smells" [10, 15] cannot be detected through unit testing. To address these issues, instructors need to draw on their pedagogical and domain knowledge to guide novices in a meaningful way.

The following autograder systems include facilities for analysis and feedback on source code, and therefore show promise in providing the kind of feedback on antipatterns that WebTA currently provides.

- *Web-CAT [8].* Web-CAT is highly configurable due to its modular architecture. Plugins for common IDEs allow its use while students are coding. It works with a variety of programming languages. Web-CAT grades assignments and provides feedback to the student based on both instructor and student provided test cases. Instructors can plug in their own constraints and triggers for feedback. This can be very helpful in addressing the kinds of antipatterns we are discussing in this paper.
- *BOSS [14]* is a course management system that originated as an autograder. BOSS includes among its features, a database and file-independent storage system, a submission and testing framework, and a student front-end. BOSS checks runtime behavior, code style, and detects plagiarism.

2.2.2 Critiquers. Critiquers are similar to autograders, but they focus on providing highly interactive and targeted feedback to student programmers [1]. While these systems often perform testing, they make strong use of the instructor's domain knowledge to identify patterns and formulated meaningful responses. This makes them well-suited for providing novices with the kinds of feedback we are discussing in this paper. WebTA falls into the category of automated critiquer, along with the following:

- *Test My Code (TMC) [20]* is an assessment system that enables instructors to build scaffolding and automated instructor-initiated feedback into programming exercises. TMC is integrated into the student's programming environment and provides tasks for the student to work on. The tool works within an environment of high instructor-student interaction, providing the ability for instructors to iteratively and precisely identify points of critique within student code.
- *Java Critiquer [16]* provides individualized feedback and just-in-time learning opportunities to students. It performs static assessment of programming style, programming errors, and design by using regular expressions to match snippets of code with trigger patterns in instructor created rules. Students use the tool iteratively to improve their code before submission.
- *JDeodorant [9]* is an Eclipse plugin that detects several classic code smells [15] in source code, including Feature Envy, Type/State Checking, Long Method, God Class and Duplicated Code. JDeodorant is targeted for experienced programmers rather than novices.

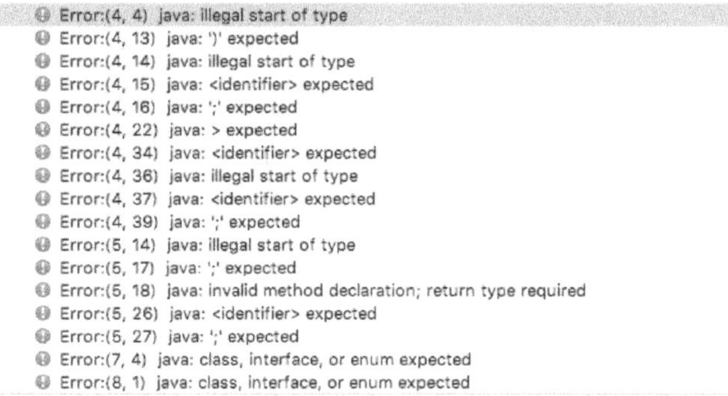

Figure 1: Errors normally associated with misplaced code.

3 ANTIPATTERNS: CHARACTERISTICS, DETECTION, AND RESPONSE

Examination of student code submitted to WebTA has helped us identify several code antipatterns, which we can then detect automatically and provide appropriate just-in-time feedback to students. The examples given here are derived from actual student submissions, slightly modified for brevity.

3.1 Misplaced Code

While learning to program in Java, beginning students are focused at the level of procedural code, working on individual expressions and statements; the larger object-oriented structures of classes and methods mean little or nothing to them, leading them to neglect the necessary enclosing "boilerplate". This leads to the *Misplaced Code* antipattern: inserting good code outside of any method or other appropriate enclosing structure. This will stop the compilation process, but the resulting error messages do not produce meaningful feedback that would assist a novice coder (Fig. 1).

We have tailored our syntactic analysis to bundle up such illegal code fragments in such a way as to allow further analysis to continue. Thus we can provide feedback about the code even if it is misplaced. For example, in Listing 3 there is a misplaced sequence of statements; the student has plunged into the details of implementing the assignment without declaring an enclosing

Listing 3: Misplaced Code

```
public class Hello {
    String s = "Hello␣World";
    String result = "";
    for(int i=0; i < s.length(); i++) {
        result = s.charAt(i) + result;
    }
    return result;
}
```

method. WebTA detects the code fragment, bundles it as a unit separate from the rest of the abstract syntax tree, and determines that if the bundled code were contained within a method it would be syntactically correct. So we can suggest to the student:

> *Your code statements follow the rules of the Java language, but they're not in the right place. In Java, all statements must belong to a method, but your statements are not inside any method declaration. (For tips on how to make a method declaration, click here.)*

3.2 Pseudo-Implementation

The *Pseudo-Implementation* antipattern occurs when students implement the methods called for by a Java interface, but neglect to use the reserved word *implements* in the class definition, thereby failing to enforce the contract of the interface type. A similar issue arises for abstract classes wherein students develop code in a new class, neglecting to extend the abstract class. In some cases, students only implement a subset of the methods contained in the abstract class. In other cases, students copy the encapsulated code into their own class and avoid inheritance.

An example is shown in Listing 4; the student has declared a class `Reverse` that implements the single method `reverseString` required by the interface `ReverseInterface`, but has failed to explicitly tag the class as implementing the interface.

This is a particularly vexing problem for students as the code will often run correctly on their machine where they create an instance of class `Reverse` and store it in a variable of the same type. However, this often breaks in instructor test cases where an instance of `Reverse` is likely to be stored in a variable of type `ReverseInterface`.

Detecting this pattern can be achieved in a couple of ways:

- Statically: By traversing the Abstract Syntax Tree, the pseudo-implemented class can be inspected to determine if it matches the method signatures declared in the interface.
- Dynamically: Instructors can include a simple `instanceof` test case in their test suite, to ensure that an instance of the class is indeed also an instance of the interface. (Listing 5).

3.3 Localized Instance Variable

In the *Localized Instance Variable* antipattern, students declare an instance variable but only use it as if it were a local variable in a single method. Often, as in Listing 6, these variables are both modified and used within the method.

Listing 4: Interface Pseudo-Implementation

```
public interface ReverseInterface {
    public String reverseString( String s );
}

// Reverse implements ReverseInterface
public class Reverse {
    // required by ReverseInterface
    public String reverseString( String s ) {
        String result = "";
        for(int i = 0; i < s.length(); i++) {
          result = s.charAt( i ) + result;
        }
        return result;
    }
}
```

Listing 5: one way to detect the Interface Pseudo-Implementation pattern.

```
    @Test
    public void testImplementsInterface( )
        ↪ throws FileNotFoundException {
        Reverse test = new Reverse( );
        if ( !(test instanceof
            ↪ ReverseInterface) ) {
            fail( "Your␣Reverse␣class␣does␣not␣
                ↪ implement␣ReverseInterface."
                ↪ );
        }
    }
```

Listing 6: Localized Instance-Variable

```
public class Reverse {
  String result = "";
  public String reverseString( String s ) {
    for(int i = 0; i < s.length(); i++) {
      result = s.charAt( i ) + result;
    }
    return result;
  }
}
```

We detect this by slicing the instance variable within the Abstract Syntax Tree. If the variable is not public and is only used in a single method, WebTA suggests that the student make the variable local to the method.

Consider, however, the case where a student defines an instance variable and only supplies a reader method, a writer method, and/or initializes the variable in a constructor (Listing 7). In such cases, where there are no defined behaviors operating on the variable, one has to question whether the data member belongs in the class or if it is perhaps a property of another class.

Listing 7: Instance Variable with no Behavior

```
public class Elephant {
   private int numberPoached;
   public int getNumberPoached() {
      return numberPoached;
   }
   public void setNumberPoached(int i) {
      numberPoached = i;
   }
}
```

Listing 8: Empty Knee-Jerk Code

```
1 public double abs( double d ) {
2    double result = d;
3    if ( d < 0 ) {
4       for( int i = 0; i < 10; i++ ) {
5       }
6       result = -d;
7    }
8    return result;
9 }
```

This case can stymie automatic detection because of notable exceptions, such as key-value pairs or the value slot in a linked-list node. This is where the instructor's knowledge of the problem domain is required to whether or not WebTA should report a problem to the student.

3.4 Knee-Jerk

Students in an introductory programming course are bombarded with new terms and programming constructs, and are asked to write code before a deep understanding of the new constructs has settled in. Consequently, it is common for first year students to utilize the *Knee-Jerk* antipattern: implementing a language construct in a vacuous way, simply because it was recently studied in class. Listing 8 shows a simplified example: working on an assignment to implement a method that returns the absolute value of a number, a student includes a for-loop (lines 4-5) because the code structure was covered recently in class.

Often, the body of such knee-jerk code is left empty. This makes it easy to detect using either a regular expression (in the case of static analysis of the code) or by walking the abstract syntax tree representing this method. Upon detecting empty knee-jerk code, we highlight the fragment and ask the student why it is included in their code.

Somewhat more challenging is the case when code is provided within the body of the knee-jerk fragment (Listing 9 lines 4-6). In the special case where the body code does not contribute to the outcome of the method, this pattern may be detected by slicing the dependency graph of the outcome of the method. If the code does not affect the result of the method, the fragment is highlighted and the student is advised that the code may be unnecessary.

Listing 9: Independent Knee-Jerk Code

```
1  public double abs( double d ) {
2     double result = d;
3     if ( d < 0 ) {
4        for( int i = 0; i < 10; i++ ) {
5           System.out.println( i );
6        }
7        result = -d;
8     }
9     return result;
10 }
```

Listing 10: Entangled Knee-Jerk Code

```
1 public double abs( double d ) {
2    double result = d;
3    for( int i = 0; i < 10; i++ ) {
4       if ( d < 0 ) {
5          result = -d;
6       }
7    }
8    return result;
9 }
```

An open problem for us, can occur when the knee-jerk code fragment includes valid code that impacts the result of the method (Listing 10 lines 3-7). In this example, the student write a for-loop around the internal logic of the method. The loop has no real effect and method still produces a valid result. A human reading this code can easily identify the loop as unnecessary. Here the instructor can use specific knowledge about the assignment to identify and flag code that matches this pattern.

In general, instructors can be mindful of knee-jerk coding behavior and anticipate places where new concepts may be used inappropriately. For instance, methods that can be easily implemented by straight-line code can be tagged so as to trigger a critique when conditional or iterative constructs appear.

3.5 Repeated Resource Instantiation

A common programming pattern is to instantiate a single resource (*e.g.*, an input or output stream) and uses that resource continually through execution. But student misunderstandings may lead to code that inadvertently instantiates multiple copies of the resource. Consider the code in Listing 11, where the variable declaration that instantiates a new `Scanner` object is inserted within the body of a loop. Execution of this loop results in multiple instantiations of `Scanner` objects, contrary to the intentions of the student. A more appropriate solution is shown in Listing 12, with the `Scanner` declaration and initialization outside of the loop.

The Repeated Resource Instantiation antipattern can be seen as a form of Knee-Jerk antipattern. Students are taught how to read keyboard input with the `Scanner` class in their first lab, before they know about conditional statements or loops. Until they encounter an example with piped input or file I/O, students have no reason to

Listing 11: Repeated Resource Instantiation

```
for (int i; i < 10; i++) {
    Scanner input = new Scanner( System.in );
    System.out.println( input.next( ) );
}
```

Listing 12: Repeated Resource Instantiation (solution)

```
Scanner input = new Scanner( System.in );
for (int i; i < 10; i++) {
    System.out.println( input.next( ) );
}
```

consider issues beyond manual keyboard input. Thus the Scanner declarations that they see in their initial straightline code becomes in essence a rote formula that they replicate without any reflection, and the consequences of the placement of the resource instantiation are not clear to them.

This example also exhibits the *Variable Declared In Loop* antipattern, shown more simply in Listing 13. Interestingly, this status of this antipattern is sensitive to the programming language in question. A Java expert would typically declare a variable in the smallest scope; this is legitimate because the JVM Specification dictates that the compiler declare stack entries prior to entering a loop; thus implying a move of the declarations outside the loop. But this is not true for all languages, and keeping the variable declaration within the loop may amount to an unnecessary repetition of resource allocation. In general, reallocation of space for declared variables upon each iteration is inefficient and wasteful—although easy for a compiler to optimize away. Since we want to teach our students the best general practices, we characterize the code in Listing 13 as an antipattern and advocate for a solution in Listing 14.

The effects of Repeated Resource Instantiation can be subtle. The code in Listing 11 is syntactically correct and, when tested with keyboard input, appears to execute as intended. Yet problems occur when the input is piped to standard input from another source. When this happens, the piped data is queued in the buffer of the instantiation of the first iteration—only to be overwritten by the instantiation of the second iteration. Thus the code only retrieves one iteration worth of data, then blocks, waiting for keyboard input.

Detecting Repeated Resource Instantiation is sometimes context dependent. An instructor can specify a particular resource to track, then WebTA looks for sequences of code containing multiple copies of code that instantiates the resource. Alternatively, WebTA can traverse the abstract syntax tree looking for instantiation of the resource within the body of a loop. Some open questions include: How deeply should we traverse the abstract syntax tree? If the resource instantiation is contained within a method and the method is called within a loop, does the code match the pattern? When do we consider the expertise of the student? A novice will be surprised by the side-effects of Repeated Resource Instantiation, whereas an expert could capitalize upon them. For now, we rely on the instructor's knowledge of the students and assignment to guide the detection of this pattern.

Listing 13: Variable Declared in Loop

```
for (int i; i < 10; i++) {
    int x = i * i;
    System.out.println( x );
}
```

Listing 14: Variable Declared in Loop (solution)

```
int x;
for (int i; i < 10; i++) {
    x = i * i;
    System.out.println( x );
}
```

4 CONCLUSION

WebTA currently detects and reports on approximately 200 antipatterns, including those described in §3. Many, such as violations of style guidelines, are relatively simple to detect, while others require more subtle analysis and in some cases knowledge of the particulars of the assignment. These antipatterns typically do not appear in professional or academic software engineering texts because they are not patterns that seasoned developers would produce. Aware of the misconceptions or practices they can fall into, we can provide students feedback through WebTA that is more focused, more appropriate to their level of understanding, and less intimidating than what they would encounter in a more traditional development environment.

Apart from the challenge of automated detection, the concept of early programming antipatterns is of interest in its own right, and we are continuing to mine student submissions for new entries in our antipatterns library. We plan to use WebTA to track the frequency of antipatterns and determine if antipattern production declines with use of WebTA, comparing to earlier work. We can then bundle our library of known antipatterns and provide instructors with instructions on how to detect and respond to them with appropriate feedback for their students. Continued and broader use of WebTA will provide us with the data needed to confirm the effectiveness of our automated critique method.

Moreover, we have designed WebTA to be extensible, so that other instructors can define their own antipatterns and means of detection and feedback. Our library of antipatterns will be made publicly available as part of our WebTA distribution. We hope that this perspective on novice programming can inspire more meaningful and appropriate critique for students in this high-risk period of their computing careers.

REFERENCES

[1] N. M. Ali, J. Hosking, and J. Grundy. 2013. A taxonomy and mapping of computer-based critiquing tools. *IEEE Transactions on Software Engineering* 39, 11 (2013), 1494–1520.

[2] Brett A. Becker, Graham Glanville, Ricardo Iwashima, Claire McDonnell, Kyle Goslin, and Catherine Mooney. 2016. Effective compiler error message enhancement for novice programming students. *Computer Science Education* 26 (2016), 148–175. Issue 2-3.

[3] Christopher Brown, Robert Pastel, Bill Siever, and John Earnest. 2012. JUG: A JUnit generation, time complexity analysis and reporting tool to streamline

grading. In *Proceedings of the 17th ACM Annual Conference on Innovation and Technology in Computer Science Education*. New York, NY, USA, 99–104.

[4] Neil Brown and Amjad Altadmri. 2017. Novice Java programming mistakes: Large-scale data vs. educator beliefs. *ACM Transactions on Computing Education* 17 (2017). Issue 2.

[5] William J. Brown, Raphael C. Malveau, Hays W. "Skip" McCormick, and Thomas J. Mowbray. 1998. *AntiPatterns: Refactoring Software, Architectures, and Projects in Crisis*. John Wiley & Sons.

[6] John DeNero, Sumukh Sridhara, Manuel Pérez-Quiñones, Aatish Nayak, and Ben Leong. 2017. Beyond autograding: Advances in student feedback platforms. In *Proceedings of the 2017 ACM SIGCSE Technical Symposium on Computer Science Education*. ACM, ACM, NY, NY, 651–652.

[7] Christopher Douce, David Livingstone, and James Orwell. 2005. Automatic test-based assessment of programming: A review. *Journal on Educational Resources in Computing (JERIC)* 5, 3 (2005), 4.

[8] Stephen H. Edwards and Manuel A. Perez-Quinones. 2008. Web-CAT: Automatically grading programming assignments. In *Proceedings of the 13th Annual Conference on Innovation and Technology in Computer Science Education*. 328–328.

[9] Marios Fokaefs, Nikolaos Tsantalis, Eleni Stroulia, and Alexander Chatzigeorgiou. 2011. JDeodorant: Identification and application of extract class refactorings. *Proceedings of the 33rd International Conference on Software Engineering* (2011).

[10] Martin Fowler. 1999. *Refactoring: Improving the Design of Existing Code*. Addison-Wesley.

[11] Luke Gusukuma, Austin Cory Bart, Dennis Kafura, and Jeremy Ernst. 2018. Misconception-driven feedback: Results from an experimental study. In *Proceedings of the ACM Conference on International Computing Education Research*. 160–168.

[12] Jack Hollingsworth. 1960. Automatic graders for programming classes. *Commun. ACM* 3, 10 (Oct 1960), 528–529.

[13] Petri Ihantola, Tuukka Ahoniemi, Ville Karavirta, and Otto Seppälä. 2010. Review of recent systems for automatic assessment of programming assignments. In *Proceedings of the 10th Koli Calling International Conference on Computing Education Research*. ACM, 86–93.

[14] M. Joy and N. Griffiths. 2004. Online submission of coursework—A technological perspective. In *Proceedings of the IEEE International Conference on Advanced Learning Technologies*. 430–434.

[15] Robert C. Martin. 2009. Smells and heuristics. In *Clean Code: A Handbook of Agile Software Craftsmanship*. Prentice Hall, Chapter 17.

[16] L. Qiu and C.K. Riesbeck. 2008. An incremental model for developing educational critiquing systems: Experiences with the Java Critiquer. *Journal of Interactive Learning Research* 19, 1 (2008), 119–145.

[17] Noa Ragonis and Mordechai Ben-Ari. 2005. A long-term investigation of the comprehension of OOP concepts by novices. *Computer Science Education* 15 (2005), 203–221. Issue 3.

[18] Jaime Spacco, David Hovemeyer, William Pugh, Fawzi Emad, Jeffrey K. Hollingsworth, and Nelson Padua-Perez. 2006. Experiences with Marmoset: Designing and Using an Advanced Submission and Testing System for Programming Courses. In *Proceedings of the 11th Annual ACM Conference on Innovation and Technology in Computer Science Education*. 13–17.

[19] Hallvard Trætteberg and Trond Aalberg. 2006. JExercise: A specification-based and test-driven exercise support plugin for Eclipse. *Proceedings of the 2006 OOPSLA Workshop on Eclipse Technology Exchange* (2006).

[20] Arto Vihavainen, Thomas Vikberg, Matti Luukkainen, and Martin Pärtel. 2013. Scaffolding students' learning using Test My Code. In *Proceedings of the 18th ACM Conference on Innovation and Technology in Computer Science Education*. 117–122.

[21] Stelios Xinogalos. 2015. Object-oriented design and programming: An investigation of novices' conceptions on objects and classes. *ACM Transactions on Computing Education* 15 (2015). Issue 3.

A K–8 Debugging Learning Trajectory Derived from Research Literature

Kathryn M. Rich
Michigan State University
richkat3@msu.edu

Carla Strickland
UChicago STEM Education
castrickland@uchicago.edu

T. Andrew Binkowski
University of Chicago
abinkowski@uchicago.edu

Diana Franklin
UChicago STEM Education
dmfranklin@uchicago.edu

ABSTRACT

Curriculum development is dependent on the following question: What are the learning goals for a specific topic, and what are reasonable ways to organize and order those goals? Learning trajectories (LTs) for computational thinking (CT) topics will help to guide emerging curriculum development efforts for computer science in elementary school. This study describes the development of an LT for Debugging. We conducted a rigorous analysis of scholarly research on K–8 computer science education to extract what concepts in debugging students should and are capable of learning. The concepts were organized into the LT presented within. In this paper, we describe the three dimensions of debugging that emerged during the creation of the trajectory: (1) strategies for finding and fixing errors, (2) types of errors, and (3) the role of errors in problem solving. In doing so, we go beyond identification of specific debugging strategies to further articulate knowledge that would help students understand *when* to use those techniques and *why* they are successful. Finally, we illustrate how the Debugging LT has guided our efforts to develop an integrated mathematics and CT curriculum for grades 3–5.

KEYWORDS

Debugging, K–8, Learning trajectory, Computational thinking

ACM Reference Format:

Kathryn M. Rich, Carla Strickland, T. Andrew Binkowski, and Diana Franklin. 2019. A K–8 Debugging Learning Trajectory Derived from Research Literature. In *Proceedings of the 50th ACM Technical Symposium on Computer Science Education (SIGCSE '19), February 27-March 2, 2019, Minneapolis, MN, USA.* ACM, New York, NY, USA, 7 pages. https://doi.org/10.1145/3287324.3287396

1 INTRODUCTION

Several school districts, including public schools in Chicago, New York City, and San Francisco, have begun CS for All initiatives that will bring computational thinking (CT) instruction to all students. The knowledge to create research-based curricula – namely what, how, and when to teach CT material – is still emerging. There exist two bodies of research literature to draw upon: one discussing what CT concepts students *should learn* [2–4, 23, 37] and the other exploring what students at different ages *did learn* through various CT-related activities [14–16, 19, 21, 22, 33] This paper brings these two bodies of work together to develop a learning trajectory (LT) for the CT practice of debugging. Our research questions are:

- What debugging concepts should children be taught?
- How could those concepts be organized?
- What are reasonable orders for addressing those concepts?

We build on prior work synthesizing existing research into guidance for practitioners and curriculum developers [10, 17, 18]. In particular, we make the following contributions:

- Identification of specific *learning goals* for debugging.
- Identification of three *dimensions* of debugging that can be used to organize those learning goals.
- Identification of literature that supports partial ordering of the debugging learning goals.

The rest of the paper is organized as follows. First, we describe related work. Next, we describe the methods we used to develop the trajectory and present our LT for Debugging. Then we share examples of how we have used the LT for curriculum development. We end with a conclusion and discussion of limitations.

2 RELATED WORK

We draw on three bodies of existing work: theory of learning trajectories; empirical research on debugging; and research and syntheses about CS in elementary school.

2.1 Learning Trajectories

The National Research Council [11] defines learning progressions as "descriptions of the successively more sophisticated ways of thinking about a topic that can follow one another as children learn about and investigate a topic" (p. 214). Typically, a learning progression starts with knowledge that students are expected to bring to a learning experience and ends with a societal norm of what students should know. Between these endpoints are intermediate stages representing progress toward the overall goal [5]. A less linear model, called Pieces of Knowledge [24], expresses independent kernels of knowledge that one could learn in any order, but that all must be learned to gain full understanding of a concept.

SIGCSE '19, February 27-March 2, 2019, Minneapolis, MN, USA

ACM ISBN 978-1-4503-5890-3/19/02...$15.00
https://doi.org/10.1145/3287324.3287396

A related construct is a *learning trajectory* (LT), which Simon [35] defines as a prediction of how learning might proceed via students' engagement in a particular activity. An LT has three parts: (1) an overall learning goal, (2) a predicted pathway to the learning goal (with periodic waypoints), and (3) instructional activities that help students move along the path [8]. A key difference between a learning progression and an LT is the latter's attention to activities [5]. This paper focuses on the first two components of our Debugging LT, goals and pathways, because full discussion of activities is beyond the scope of this paper. However, we acknowledge that the draft version of the LT presented here will both *shape* and *be shaped by* our ongoing curriculum development efforts. In the discussion, we share one activity developed through use of the LT. In future work, we will present results of tests of these activities and how we used the results of the studies to refine and elaborate the LT.

As we developed this Debugging LT, we drew, in particular, on the work of other researchers who have developed progressions for disciplinary practices in science. In Schwarz et al.'s [32] work on scientific modeling, the learning progressions are described not as a single sequence of levels of understanding, but as a set of dimensions of the practice. The dimensions of a practice are components that are related, but can develop separately. Often, dimensions separate metaknowledge of a practice from the activities of a practice. Schwarz et al.'s two dimensions of scientific modeling are *scientific models as tools for predicting and explaining* and *models change as understanding improves.* The first dimension roughly corresponds to metaknowledge about the practice, and the second to the activity of the practice. Following this work, we aimed to identify dimensions of debugging, with at least one focused on metaknowledge and at least one focused on activity . The dimensions that emerged from our analysis are presented in Section 4.

2.2 Debugging

In a seminal study, Klahr and Carver [26] identified four stages of debugging: Bug identification, or describing a discrepancy between intended and actual program outcome; Program representation, or thinking about the program structure to hypothesize possible locations for the bug; Bug location, or inspecting the program at hypothesized locations to search for errors; and Bug correction, or making the correction. In this paper, we refer to this as an Observe -> Hypothesize -> Modify -> Test cycle used to debug programs.

More recently, embodied pre-coding instruction in debugging was found to be helpful, improving students' confidence and abilities to cope with errors [1]. A debugging game, Gidget, was created for teens to learn debugging skills [27]. The environment scaffolded the process of debugging by identifying the existence of a bug.

2.3 CT Learning Trajectories

Researchers have attempted to discover what CT concepts students use successfully at different ages [14, 19, 34]. In addition, several efforts have synthesized existing knowledge and research to guide future curriculum development. The K-12 CS Framework [18] was released in spring 2016, the CSTA released standards soon afterward [17], and several states have used these documents to guide their own standards development. In addition, we recently published LTs for sequence, repetition, conditionals [31], and decomposition [30].

3 METHODS

Here we briefly describe our three phases of work, inspired by [10].

3.1 Identifying Learning Goals

We conducted a review of 108 articles [29] focused on computer-science education found in the Educational Research Information Center database, the Special Interest Group in Computer Science Education (SIGCSE) conference proceedings, and the Innovation and Technology in Computer Science Education (ITiCSE) conference proceedings using keywords such as "computational thinking," "computer science domains," and "computer science pedagogy," with the additional signifiers "K–8," "K–5," and "K–12." We focused on research published between 2006 and 2016. During this review, we extracted debugging-related learning goals (LGs) mentioned by the authors. For the purposes of this trajectory, a learning goal is defined as *any explicit statement or implicit endorsement of what students can or should **know** or be able to **do** in relation to debugging.* Attention to both knowing (metaknowledge) and doing (practice-based activity) was particularly important for learning goals related to debugging (a practice), as described in Section 2.1.

As it was extracted, each learning goal was tagged with an *evidence type:* student evidence if the goal was supported by work with students, and theoretical evidence if not.

3.2 Synthesizing Consensus Goals

We next synthesized small collections of LGs that expressed similar ideas into consensus goals (CGs). The four authors (two with computer science expertise and two with curriculum development expertise) created independent groupings, then came to collaborative agreement on the final set of CGs. Examples of groups of LGs that were synthesized into single CGs are included in Section 4.1.

A cross-check was performed on all consensus goals with relevant learning goals to ensure that the CGs aligned with the original intent of the LGs. Each CG was then coded with its strongest evidence type. That is, if at least one LG under a CG had student evidence, the CG was coded as having student evidence. Otherwise, it was coded as having theoretical evidence.

3.3 Connecting Consensus Goals

To begin organizing the CGs into pathways, we next identified dimensions of debugging by looking for threads of CGs that could be described independently of each other. Following the lead of [32], we looked, in particular, for at least one dimension focusing on metaknowledge (what students should *know*) and one focusing on activity (what students should be able to *do*). We then organized the CGs related to each dimension by increasing complexity. Ordering was based on evidence from the source articles, the theoretical assumption that trajectories should progress from knowledge familiar to the student toward formalized disciplinary knowledge, and consideration of hypothetical activities in which students might engage. Orders were represented as arrows between CGs. As part of this assembly process, we also identified suggested paths through the trajectory for beginning, intermediate, and advanced students. We acknowledge that our proposed pathways do not represent the only way a student could learn these concepts. Rather than functioning as a strict prescription, our arrows are intended to define possible learning pathways that allow students to learn gradually, building on their prior knowledge. Additionally, we note that because much of the source literature involved students using block-based (rather than text-based) languages, our ordering of goals is most appropriate for students using graphical programming languages.

4 RESULTS

We now present the results of this process. We begin by delving into the development of consensus goals. We then present the learning trajectory itself with the description, literature evidence, and rationale for the dimensions and connections between the CGs.

4.1 Consensus Goals

Eleven CGs were synthesized from 36 LGs – 25 with student support and 11 with theoretical support. Table 1 presents each CG, along with a comment placing it in context, followed by one example LG that influenced that CG and the number of LGs that were synthesized into each CG.

To illustrate the process of synthesizing several LGs into one CG, we show two examples. These two examples are chosen because they illustrate the subtleties involved in creating CGs. The source literature was consulted often to glean the context of individual learning goals and remain true to their original intent.

Table 2 shows the three LGs that were synthesized into the CG, "Errors can be caused by missing, as opposed to incorrect, information within instructions." The evidence code for each goal is given in parentheses after the goal text. This table illustrates one way in which similarities between individual LGs were identified. Most of the debugging LGs referred in some way to fixing code. To create CGs, we gathered LGs that were similar in their description of either *what* was to be fixed or *how* it was to be fixed. LG1–LG3 in Table 2 are examples of the former: they all refer in some way to incompleteness of code. The presumed omission is *what* needs to be fixed. The CG therefore refers to the idea that errors can be caused by omission. These ideas of *what needs to be fixed* and *how it should be fixed* correspond to the types of errors (D2) and strategies (D1) dimensions of the LT described in Section 4.2.

Table 3 shows the six LGs that were synthesized into the CG, "Iterative refinement can fix errors." In contrast to the focus on *what* should be fixed in the CG in Table 2, this CG focuses on *how* errors could be fixed. Table 3 includes LGs that exemplify different aspects of the Observe -> Hypothesize -> Modify -> Test cycle of debugging based on outcome. These seemingly independent learning goals are tied together by a discussion within one paper [16] that describes different methods students used to fix their code, and the skills that led to different levels of success. This discussion of the different skills as part of a single process led to the CG and the identification of other LGs that address individual aspects of this cycle.

Note that the CGs are written to capture not the specific actions or skills cited in the individual LGs, but rather the knowledge that students need to perform those actions. We chose to word CGs in this manner for two reasons. First, we felt that wording goals in terms of understanding made the big ideas in the trajectory more transparent for more audiences (e.g., teachers with varying CS/CT experience). Second, understanding goals are less prescriptive than specific action goals, and we hope this allows the trajectories to be used flexibly for curriculum development.

4.2 Debugging Trajectory and Dimensions

Figure 1 depicts the Debugging LT. The four gray boxes are offline, or "unplugged," CGs, whereas the seven white boxes are computer-based CGs. A CG is marked as offline if the concept is general enough to be applied in a setting outside of a computer program. Information on the lower right corner of each box indicates the number of LGs that were coalesced into this consensus goal and the stronger type of evidence found for a CG (S for student evidence, T for theoretical evidence). The code in the upper left corner of most boxes (D1, D2, or D3) refers to the dimension on which the CG appears. The dimensions are described later in this section.

The CGs are connected by 16 arrows, 5 of which are supported by information extracted from the literature. The type of literature support found for an arrow is also indicated as student-supported (S) or theoretically-supported (T). Arrows without a letter label are based on theoretical considerations, rather than literature evidence.

The Debugging trajectory begins with a foundational skill for independent debugging: the ability to recognize whether or not there is an error. Literature suggests that without scaffolding (Section 5.1), this is a prerequisite to successful debugging. Flannery and Bers [16] described three groups of PK-K children programming a robot to dance. One group had trouble evaluating whether current solutions had problems or not. The two other, more advanced groups recognized errors and attempted to fix them via trial-and-error strategies, but had varying success. This evidence suggests that understanding that there is an *intended* outcome for most tasks, and being able to tell whether the actual outcome matches the intended outcome, is critical to successful debugging.

From this starting point, the consensus goals were organized into three dimensions, represented roughly from top to bottom in Figure 1: (D1) strategies for finding and fixing errors, (D2) types of errors, and (D3) the role of errors in problem solving. Dimension 1 largely focuses on activity, while dimensions 2 and 3 largely focus on the metaknowledge that makes debugging activity meaningful, akin to prior work in science [32].

4.2.1 *D1: Strategies for finding and fixing errors.*

The first debugging dimension (D1), *strategies for finding and fixing errors,* consists of five debugging strategies discussed in the literature: iterative refinement by trial and error, using intermediate results, observing step-by-step execution, reproducing errors, and addressing compile errors in order of appearance.

Research evidence suggests trial and error is the first debugging strategy attempted by students. Both Flannery and Bers [16] and Fessakis, Gouli, and Mavroudi [15] found that PK-K children utilized trial and error as their debugging strategy. In addition, trial and error is the most direct use of the observed incorrect outcome, taking the recognition of a bug a step farther to acknowledge that the particular nature of the unexpected outcome can be used to theorize what the problem might be, make a change, and check if the problem is fixed. Thus, iterative refinement is placed immediately after the recognition of errors in the beginning strand, with the trial and error strategy being the simplest form of iterative refinement.

Table 1: The 11 Debugging Consensus Goals

Consensus Goal	Comments	Example Supporting LG	No. of LGs
Outcomes can be used to decide whether or not there are errors.	Realizing there is an error is the first step to fixing it, and critically analyzing the outcome is a way to do it.	"Recognize when instructions do not correspond to actions." [2]	6
Iterative refinement can help fix errors.	This is the first step toward understanding that Observe -> Hypothesize -> Modify -> Test [26] can be used to debug code.	Make a hypothesis about the cause of a problem. [6]	6
Errors play a valuable role in problem solving.	This CG is particularly useful for young children who need to manage emotions. Errors are normal and useful.	"[D]ebug understandings if their instructions produce something unexpected"	2
Small errors can change outcomes.	Students should understand that programming errors are often small (case changes, number of iterations), despite their potentially large effects.	"[U]nderstand that small errors" can change outcomes. [13]	4
Intermediate results can help find and fix errors.	This CG progresses from the idea of looking at the final result to recognize errors. Students can also examine intermediate results.	Fix nearly complete code by "inserting wait blocks" to see intermediate results. [33]	2
Step-by-step execution of instructions can help find and fix errors.	This technique builds on the usefulness of intermediate results.	"Desk-check a solution" by tracing by hand. [20]	6
Errors can be caused by missing, as opposed to incorrect, information within instructions.	Distinguishing between ordering of instructions, wrong arguments, and the absence of necessary instructions.	"[D]ebug" or complete an existing program. [15]	3
Reproducing a bug can help find and fix it.	This is advanced for K–8. The difference between reproducing a bug and rerunning a program is subtle for young learners.	Reproduce an unexpected problem. [36]	1
Compile errors should be fixed in the order the compiler reports them.	This CG is also advanced, as it is most appropriate for text-based languages.	"[F]ix a program that had errors" identified by the parser. [21]	1
Code can always be improved, but it may not be worth the effort.	This CG serves as a bridge between debugging and quality – there is a fine line between bugs and elements that could be improved (e.g., speed).	"[M]anage their programming processes" by questioning "their decisions and actions" to reflect on debugging processes. [25]	1
Debugging techniques can be chosen strategically.	This is the capstone CG for debugging. Once students understand individual techniques, they should choose between them strategically.	Correct errors in a "systematic, efficient manner" [36]	14

Table 2: Synthesis Example 1

LG1	Fix nearly complete code. [33] (S)
LG2	Identify "what [is]lacking in instructions." [14] (S)
LG3	"[D]ebug" or complete an existing program. [15] (S)
CG	Errors can be caused by missing, as opposed to incorrect, information within instructions. (S)

Research literature did not provide insight into the relationship between the remaining four debugging strategies, though there is a similarity between the use of intermediate results and step-by-step execution. Namely, the state of a program after each step is executed is, in itself, an intermediate result. Thus, these two strategies are linearly connected in the LT. Using intermediate results is located

Table 3: Synthesis Example 2

LG1	Attempt to solve a problem within a program. [16] (S)
LG2	Use "a trial and error model" to solve a problem. [15] (S)
LG3	Make a hypothesis about the cause of a problem. [16] (S)
LG4	Test a theory about what is causing a problem in a program. [27] (T)
LG5	Decide how to change a program when it does not produce the desired results. [7] (S)
LG6	"Repeatedly change and run" buggy "code to find a solution" [6] (S)
CG	Iterative refinement can help fix errors. (S)

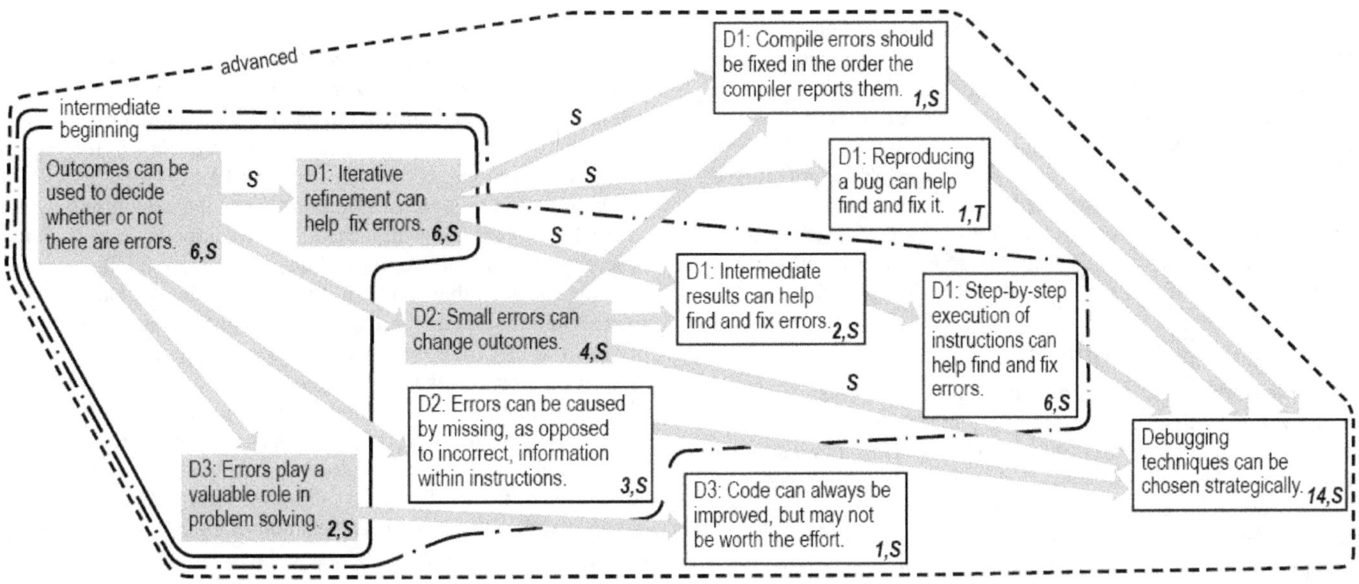

Figure 1: The Debugging Trajectory

prior to step-by-step execution because step-by-step execution is a particular strategy using intermediate results, whereas the notion of using intermediate results could lead generally to other strategies (such as removing the last half of the code and running it to see if the bug is in the first half or last half of that script or function). The other two strategies, reproducing bugs and addressing compiler errors in order, are not related and so are located on separate paths.

Using intermediate results and step-by-step execution are considered intermediate concepts because they require more deliberate thought than trial and error, but they are not considered advanced because students can use them in any non-trivial program. Reproducing an error is considered advanced because the need to reproduce an error implies that the error does not necessarily always occur, and that step-by-step execution may not be a successful strategy. This fact alone makes such bugs more difficult to identify and fix than others. Addressing compile errors is considered advanced because students are more likely to begin with languages such as Scratch [28] that are designed to avoid compile errors.

4.2.2 D2: Types of errors. The second dimension (D2), *types of errors,* contains two types of errors: small errors, which may include errors in punctuation, syntax, and case, and errors of omission, which may include missing instructions or use of instructions that lack the appropriate precision to communicate needed information. There are fundamental differences in these two ideas. For example, the cognitive act of scrutinizing existing code to find a small error is different from the cognitive act of discerning missing information or steps. However, the research we reviewed did not provide evidence of any dependence between these ideas, so they exist independent paths in the LT. These CGs are in the intermediate strand, as opposed to beginner, because the trial-and-error debugging strategies used by beginners do not suggest that novice students attend to the differences in errors. They are on the intermediate path, as opposed to advanced, because each was supported by at least one LG that stemmed from work with students in grades 3–5 [14, 21, 33].

4.2.3 Role of errors in problem solving. The third dimension (D3), *the role of errors in problem solving,* consists of only two CGs: understanding the value of errors in problem solving and assessing the worth of improvements. The former is in the beginning strand, as we consider this a powerful and pervasive idea that can be taught in elementary classrooms outside of computing instruction. Young children have trouble regulating their emotions, making it hard to persevere when they encounter failure [12], so explicitly teaching the prevalence and usefulness of errors could help young learners the most, both generally and in the context of programming.

The latter CG is in the advanced strand and meant to address the close relationship between fixing errors and making improvements in quality and how to assess whether improvements are worthwhile. Very simple programs may have a "right answer," giving a programmer a point at which to stop debugging. However, more complex programs have many design decisions that have no single, clear solution, and there becomes a subtle difference between a bug and a desire to improve (e.g., improve performance or make the interface easier to use).

The trajectory ends with the consensus goal "Debugging techniques can be chosen strategically." This nexus is intended to capture the idea that one must deliberately choose a strategy based on the problem at hand. This ability to choose between debugging strategies and approaches is a more complex skill than learning the individual ideas or strategies.

5 DISCUSSION

This trajectory is only a starting point. An LT consists of more than the one-sentence consensus goals described in this paper and suggested paths through them. Full details of our LT can be found online [9]. Each consensus goal has an understanding goal (described in this paper) and an action goal. In addition, there are example activities that move students from one consensus goal to the next, building on the prior knowledge.

LTs can be used in several ways. They can serve as the basis of experiments to verify or refute connections within the LT. However, this LT's most promising role is in curriculum development. We first discuss its use in creating scaffolding that can allow curricula to temporarily bypass specific CGs. Second, we discuss an example of how it was used to create a lesson in an integrated mathematics + CT curriculum in order to explicitly teach debugging.

5.1 Guiding Scaffolding

The ordering within the learning trajectory is not intended to be entirely prescriptive. Indeed, scaffolding and careful activity design can allow for the consensus goals to be addressed in a different order. For example, although the ability to recognize the presence an error is listed first in the Debugging LT, a system or activity in which the identification of the error is provided would allow students to learn and practice some debugging skills without requiring the ability to recognize or identify the specific errors (e.g., Gidget [27]). In this case, however, the learning trajectory is very useful in guiding what specific things must be provided by scaffolding in order to allow students to be successful in later learning goals.

5.2 Guiding Activity Development

The LT also can guide activity development. The authors are developing an integrated mathematics + CT curriculum guided by this and other LTs. This interdisciplinary endeavor began with the identification of "anchor" activities in which CT concepts can be used to support mathematics learning. The LTs were then used to identify what necessary CT skills should be developed in order to prepare students for the anchor activities. Activities were designed to build the identified skills.

Here, we describe one activity for elementary school students, developed with reference to the Debugging LT, but not yet published by the authors. This activity is designed to explicitly teach students to closely observe program execution and think critically about what happened, corresponding to the consensus goals "Outcomes can be used to decide whether or not there are errors." and "Iterative refinement can help fix errors." While the latter goal can encompass varying degrees of reasoning (from random changes to well-thought-out changes), we are explicitly teaching students to carry out the process in a methodical manner.

We designed this activity to teach debugging and repeat loops within the mathematical context of representing fractions on a number line. The primary task is to modify code in Scratch that partitions a number line, so that a number line segment is divided into four equal parts. The starting code uses move and stamp blocks to divide a number line segment covering the interval 0 to 360 into four partitions of 50 units (with 160 left over). Students run the program, observe, and record the outcome. They are asked to identify what is wrong (partitions are too small, entire interval is not partitioned), what block affected that (move), and whether the current number of steps used as an argument in the move block needs to be made smaller or bigger (bigger). They are then prompted to choose a new number for the argument and repeat the process until they find the correct number to accomplish the four equal partitions (for this age group, large-number division is not expected). Students are then asked to repeat the process of finding the proper arguments to partition the number line into 6 equal parts, adjusting both the number of iterations in the repeat loop and the number of steps in the move block.

The cognitive process of reasoning about what was wrong, shown in our Debugging LT, is discernable in this activity. Once students observe and identify the problem (the parts are too small), they then identify the block that caused it, hypothesize about what direction they should take in fixing it, and make slight modifications to the program to test their hypotheses. The process of debugging the program is broken down into discrete steps (Observe >Hypothesize->Modify->Test) that even young children can handle. In future studies, we plan to use activities such as this one to test whether, for small children, making these steps explicit can help them be successful in future debugging efforts. Preliminary field testing has shown that 3rd and 4th grade students enjoy and successfully engage with this activity in an elementary mathematics classroom setting. Students even noted similarities with hypothesizing and testing in science and suggested that they debug every time they fix a problem, not just a program.

6 CONCLUSIONS AND LIMITATIONS

Here we present a learning trajectory related to the practice of Debugging in CS/CT and present a description of the dimensions of debugging represented in the trajectory. While the current version of the Debugging trajectory includes all the particular strategies and error types that were mentioned in the reviewed literature, we do not imagine that these are a definitive list of what might be taught in elementary CT curricula. As we reviewed the existing CS/CT literature, we found the topic of debugging to be underrepresented in comparison to other topics such as loops and conditionals. As debugging is inherent to all practices of CS/CT, it is possible that it has been overlooked or unrecognized as a separate concept, especially during early introductions to CS/CT, where students may expend more effort debugging than implementing newly learned concepts. We hope that this trajectory signifies a more isolated and targeted view of debugging practices in early CS/CT education.

Limitations of this LT are rooted in our specific focus on K-8 students and the dominance of block-based languages in the reviewed literature. It is likely that the grade level and specific language and platform will influence student debugging practices. This is especially interesting as students transition from block-based languages, which are purposefully designed to prevent certain types of errors, to text-based languages that will introduce students to a new class of errors and debugging strategies. We expect that additional strategies and types of errors will prove useful and merit inclusion in this trajectory as more research is added to the field.

ACKNOWLEDGMENTS

This material is based on work supported by the National Science Foundation under Award 1542828 and Award 1742466. Any opinions, findings, and conclusions or recommendations expressed are those of the authors and do not necessarily reflect those of the National Science Foundation.

REFERENCES

[1] Jung-Hyun Ahn, Yaoli Mao, Woonhee Sung, and John B Black. 2017. Supporting Debugging Skills: Using Embodied Instructions in ChildrenâĂŹs Programming Education. In *Society for Information Technology & Teacher Education International Conference*. Association for the Advancement of Computing in Education (AACE), 19–26.

[2] Charoula Angeli, Joke Voogt, Andrew Fluck, Mary Webb, Margaret Cox, Joyce Malyn-Smith, and Jason Zagami. 2016. A K-6 computational thinking curriculum framework: Implications for teacher knowledge. *Journal of Educational Technology & Society* 19, 3 (2016).

[3] Michal Armoni and Judith Gal-Ezer. 2014. Early computing education: why? what? when? who? *ACM Inroads* 5, 4 (2014), 54–59.

[4] Valerie Barr and Chris Stephenson. 2011. Bringing computational thinking to K-12: what is Involved and what is the role of the computer science education community? *Acm Inroads* 2, 1 (2011), 48–54.

[5] Michael T Battista. 2011. Conceptualizations and issues related to learning progressions, learning trajectories, and levels of sophistication. *The Mathematics Enthusiast* 8, 3 (2011), 507–570.

[6] Matthew Berland, Taylor Martin, Tom Benton, Carmen Petrick Smith, and Don Davis. 2013. Using learning analytics to understand the learning pathways of novice programmers. *Journal of the Learning Sciences* 22, 4 (2013), 564–599.

[7] Douglas H Clements. 2002. Computers in early childhood mathematics. *Contemporary issues in early childhood* 3, 2 (2002), 160–181.

[8] Douglas H Clements and Julie Sarama. 2004. Learning trajectories in mathematics education. *Mathematical thinking and learning* 6, 2 (2004), 81–89.

[9] Everyday Computing. 2019. Trajectory Visualizations. Retrieved February 27, 2019 from http://everydaycomputing.org/public/visualization/

[10] Jere Confrey, Alan P Maloney, and Andrew K Corley. 2014. Learning trajectories: a framework for connecting standards with curriculum. *ZDM* 46, 5 (2014), 719–733.

[11] National Research Council et al. 2007. *Taking science to school: Learning and teaching science in grades K-8*. National Academies Press.

[12] Adele Diamond and Kathleen Lee. 2011. Interventions shown to aid executive function development in children 4 to 12 years old. *Science* 333, 6045 (2011), 959–964.

[13] Hilary Dwyer, Bryce Boe, Charlotte Hill, Diana Franklin, and Danielle Harlow. 2013. Computational Thinking for Physics: Programming Models of Physics Phenomenon in Elementary School. *Engelhardt, Churukian, & Jones (Eds.) 2013 PERC Proceedings* (2013), 133–136.

[14] Hilary Dwyer, Charlotte Hill, Stacey Carpenter, Danielle Harlow, and Diana Franklin. 2014. Identifying elementary students' pre-instructional ability to develop algorithms and step-by-step instructions. In *Proceedings of the 45th ACM technical symposium on Computer science education*. ACM, 511–516.

[15] Georgios Fessakis, Evangelia Gouli, and E Mavroudi. 2013. Problem solving by 5–6 years old kindergarten children in a computer programming environment: A case study. *Computers & Education* 63 (2013), 87–97.

[16] Louise P Flannery and Marina Umaschi Bers. 2013. LetâĂŹs dance the âĂIJrobot hokey-pokey!âĂİ ChildrenâĂŹs programming approaches and achievement throughout early cognitive development. *Journal of research on technology in education* 46, 1 (2013), 81–101.

[17] CSTA Standards Task Force. 2011. *CSTA K–12 Computer Science Standards*. Technical Report. Computer Science Teacher's Association, New York.

[18] K-12 Computer Science Framework. 2016. K–12 Computer Science Framework. Retrieved October 10, 2018 from http://k12cs.org

[19] Diana Franklin, Gabriela Skifstad, Reiny Rolock, Isha Mehrotra, Valerie Ding, Alexandria Hansen, David Weintrop, and Danielle Harlow. 2017. Using upper-elementary student performance to understand conceptual sequencing in a blocks-based curriculum. In *Proceedings of the 2017 ACM SIGCSE Technical Symposium on Computer Science Education*. ACM, 231–236.

[20] Ursula Fuller, Colin G Johnson, Tuukka Ahoniemi, Diana Cukierman, Isidoro Hernán-Losada, Jana Jackova, Essi Lahtinen, Tracy L Lewis, Donna McGee Thompson, Charles Riedesel, et al. 2007. Developing a computer science-specific learning taxonomy. *ACM SIGCSE Bulletin* 39, 4 (2007), 152–170.

[21] Chris Gregg, Luther Tychonievich, James Cohoon, and Kim Hazelwood. 2012. EcoSim: a language and experience teaching parallel programming in elementary school. In *Proceedings of the 43rd ACM technical symposium on Computer Science Education*. ACM, 51–56.

[22] Shuchi Grover and Satabdi Basu. 2017. Measuring student learning in introductory block-based programming: Examining misconceptions of loops, variables, and boolean logic. In *Proceedings of the 2017 ACM SIGCSE Technical Symposium on Computer Science Education*. ACM, 267–272.

[23] Shuchi Grover and Roy Pea. 2013. Computational thinking in K–12: A review of the state of the field. *Educational Researcher* 42, 1 (2013), 38–43.

[24] David Hammer and Tiffany-Rose Sikorski. 2015. Implications of complexity for research on learning progressions. *Science Education* 99, 3 (2015), 424–431.

[25] Filiz Kalelioğlu. 2015. A new way of teaching programming skills to K-12 students: Code. org. *Computers in Human Behavior* 52 (2015), 200–210.

[26] David Klahr and Sharon McCoy Carver. 1988. Cognitive objectives in a LOGO debugging curriculum: Instruction, learning, and transfer. *Cognitive Psychology* 20, 3 (1988), 362–404.

[27] Michael J Lee, Faezeh Bahmani, Irwin Kwan, Jilian LaFerte, Polina Charters, Amber Horvath, Fanny Luor, Jill Cao, Catherine Law, Michael Beswetherick, et al. 2014. Principles of a debugging-first puzzle game for computing education. In *Visual Languages and Human-Centric Computing (VL/HCC), 2014 IEEE Symposium on*. IEEE, 57–64.

[28] John Maloney, Mitchel Resnick, Natalie Rusk, Brian Silverman, and Evelyn Eastmond. 2010. The scratch programming language and environment. *ACM Transactions on Computing Education (TOCE)* 10, 4 (2010), 16.

[29] Kathryn Rich, Carla Strickland, and Diana Franklin. 2017. A Literature Review through the Lens of Computer Science Learning Goals Theorized and Explored in Research. In *Proceedings of the 2017 ACM SIGCSE Technical Symposium on Computer Science Education*. ACM, 495–500.

[30] Kathryn M Rich, T Andrew Binkowski, Carla Strickland, and Diana Franklin. 2018. Decomposition: A K-8 Computational Thinking Learning Trajectory. In *Proceedings of the 2018 ACM Conference on International Computing Education Research*. ACM, 124–132.

[31] Kathryn M Rich, Carla Strickland, T Andrew Binkowski, Cheryl Moran, and Diana Franklin. 2018. K–8 learning trajectories derived from research literature: sequence, repetition, conditionals. *ACM Inroads* 9, 1 (2018), 46–55.

[32] Christina V. Schwarz, Brian J. Reiser, Elizabeth A. Davis, Lisa Kenyon, Andres Acher, David Fortus, Yael Shwartz, Barbara Hug, and Joe Krajcik. 2009. Developing a learning progression for scientific modeling: Making scientific modeling accessible and meaningful for learners. *Journal of Research in Science Teaching* 46, 6 (2009), 632–645.

[33] Linda Seiter. 2015. Using SOLO to classify the programming responses of primary grade students. In *Proceedings of the 46th ACM Technical Symposium on Computer Science Education*. ACM, 540–545.

[34] Linda Seiter and B. Foreman. 2013. Modeling the learning progressions of computational thinking of primary grade students. In *Proceedings of the Ninth Annual International ACM Conference on International Computing Education Research*. ACM, 59–66.

[35] Martin A. Simon. 1995. Reconstructing mathematics pedagogy from a constructivist perspective. *Journal for Research in Mathematics Education* 1995 (1995), 114–145.

[36] David Weintrop, Elham Beheshti, Michael Horn, Kai Orton, Kemi Jona, Laura Trouille, and Uri Wilensky. 2016. Defining computational thinking for mathematics and science classrooms. *Journal of Science Education and Technology* 25, 1 (2016), 127–147.

[37] Jeannette M. Wing. 2006. Computational thinking. *Commun. ACM* 49, 3 (2006), 33–36.

Learning to use Functions: The Relationship Between Misconceptions and Self-Efficacy*

Maria Kallia
King's College London
London
maria.kallia@kcl.ac.uk

Sue Sentance
King's College London
London
sue.sentance@kcl.ac.uk

ABSTRACT

Computer programming is one of the most researched subjects within computer science education; within this much attention has been focused on exploring the difficulties and common misconceptions that students experience when learning to program. The study reported here has two aims: firstly, to investigate students' misconceptions around functions by setting up a programming test of advancing difficulty and complexity based on the Bloom and Solo taxonomies, and secondly, to explore the impact that misconceptions have on students' self-efficacy in programming, along with students' self-evaluation and self-efficacy in computer science. Our study revealed seven misconceptions in the area of functions, three of which have never before been reported in the literature, to our knowledge. Additionally, the results suggest that misconceptions do not only prohibit students' progress and learning but have a significant impact on students' self-efficacy in programming.

CCS CONCEPTS

• **Social and professional topics → CS1; K-12 education;**

KEYWORDS

misconceptions in programming, functions, self-efficacy

ACM Reference Format:
Maria Kallia and Sue Sentance. 2019. Learning to use Functions: The Relationship Between Misconceptions and Self-Efficacy. In *SIGCSE '19: 50th ACM Technical Symposium on Computer Science Education, February 27–March 2, 2019, Minneapolis, MN, USA.* ACM, New York, NY, USA, 7 pages. https://doi.org/10.1145/3287324.3287377

1 INTRODUCTION

Increasingly, computer programming is becoming integrated into secondary schools across the world, playing a central role in the computer science curriculum. This specific aspect of computer science has attracted much research attention due to the acknowledged and multifaceted difficulties that it causes students, some of which are known as misconceptions, false conceptions or misunderstandings [27]. Undoubtedly, identifying, understanding and addressing students' misunderstandings and misconceptions in programming is vital and imperative for helping students to reach a more precise conceptualisation [15]. Particularly in computer programming this needs to be conducted as early as possible, as misconceptions that are left unresolved can render a student unable to further continue with this subject and may also have an impact on students' self-efficacy in programming and in computer science.

In this study we were particularly interested in exploring students' misconceptions by creating assessment tasks of graded complexity, enabling us to capture a wide range of students' errors. In comparison with most existing studies, we decided to limit our research to one specific area in programming to uncover as many misconceptions as possible. Therefore, we have chosen to investigate misconceptions in the area of *functions* as the literature indicates that this is one of the most difficult parts of programming [16, 20, 32] and because from our teaching experience we felt that there are more misconceptions in these area than the ones that have already been reported. Secondly, we were also interested in investigating the potential impact that misconceptions may have on students' self-efficacy in computer programming by taking into consideration students' self-evaluation on the programming test and students' perceived ability in computer science.

The study endeavours to provide answers to the following research questions:

- RQ1: What are the misconceptions of 16 year old (11th Grade) students in the area of functions?
- RQ2: Do students' misconceptions impact students' self-efficacy in programming and how does the self-evaluation and efficacy in computer science may contribute to this?

To answer these questions, we employed a mixed methods research design. We first collected and qualitatively analysed students' responses in six different programming tasks with increased complexity. The analysis of this phase resulted in the identification of 7 misconceptions in functions, of which 3 have never before been reported as misconceptions in the literature, to the authors' knowledge. In the second phase, we quantitatively analysed students' performance and their responses on self-efficacy in programming and computer science with the SPSS software package. To this end, a correlation and a causal comparative group design were employed. In total, 83 students participated in the study.

*Produces the permission block, and copyright information

SIGCSE '19, February 27–March 2, 2019, Minneapolis, MN, USA

ACM ISBN 978-1-4503-5890-3/19/02.
https://doi.org/10.1145/3287324.3287377

2 BACKGROUND

2.1 Misconceptions in Sciences

Children, according to Piaget [24], search for understanding by interacting with the surrounding environment; learning comes as a combination of previous experience and present mental schemata which are developed through assimilation and accommodation. However, experiences do not always develop correct interpretations [38] and thus, the problem is that once misconceptions take seed in a child's mind, it is very difficult for them to be altered [11]. In fact, Longfield[19] asserts that humans have the tendency to hold on to information that lines up with their existing theories or understanding while they reject or abandon those that will put them to disequilibrium. Cognitive disequilibrium is a distressing state where humans try to remain in equilibrium and to achieve this, they discard information that does not align with their views [24]. Ben-Ari[5] postulates that the conceptual distance between students' own version of understanding and the scientific view determines students' existing misconceptions. Misconceptions, therefore, are developed by a person's experience [21] and represent an incorrect understanding of an idea which the literature has characterised as a misconception, preconception, naive belief, alternative conceptions or misunderstandings [35].

Most of the research work conducted around students' misconceptions is concentrated in the sciences where misconceptions have been separated into five distinct categories: *Preconceived Notions, Nonscientific Beliefs, Conceptual Misunderstandings, Vernacular Misconceptions, Factual Misconceptions* [9]. In computer programming, identifying students' errors or misunderstandings and misconceptions started early in around 80s. For example, one of the first studies conducted in this area was conducted by Perkins and Martin [23] who identified four types of fragile knowledge: *Partial knowledge, Inert knowledge, Misplaced knowledge* and *conglomerated knowledge.* Du Boulay [10] has also contributed significantly in this research area and emphasised concrete sources of students' misconceptions in programming: *Misapplication of analogy, Overgeneralisations* and *Interactions.* Du Boulay also referred to specific problematic areas in programming which he categorises into *Orientation, Notional machine, Notation, Structures,* and *Pragmatics.*

To identify students' misconceptions, several methodologies have been proposed. Kaczmarczyk et al. [15] used semi-structured interviews with a modified think-aloud protocol in which students discussed a subset of Java problems and the analysis of students' transcripts was based on grounded theory and qualitative analysis. Based on this work, qualitative analysis was also used by Veerasamy et al. [40] to reveal misconceptions in introductory programming in Python. Fleury [12] used interviews with students and a collection of Java programs while Sirkiä [32] studied students' errors in python by examining the log files from students' solution to visual program simulation exercises.

2.2 Bloom's and SOLO Taxonomies

In designing assessment tools for programming, many researchers have turned their attention to the Bloom and Solo taxonomies. Bloom's taxonomy is centered around the planning of educational objectives in a hierarchical manner, starting from less complex levels to more advanced ones. Specifically, in the revised Bloom's taxonomy, proposed by Anderson et al. [1], the taxonomy levels are *Remembering, Understanding, Applying, Analysing, Evaluating,* and *Creating.* Bloom's taxonomy has been used in computer science as an assessment method to categorise the assessment questions. Some of the studies adapted Bloom's taxonomy include Lister and Leaney[17], Starr et al.[36] and Thompson et al.[37].

The SOLO taxonomy, suggested by Biggs and Collis[6], is another way of evaluating students' performance. The specific taxonomy is also hierarchical and is mostly used to classify students' levels of understanding in the following levels: *Prestructural, Unistructural, Multistructural, Relational,* and *Extended abstract.* In computer science, the taxonomy has been successfully used for categorizing students' responses on examination (e.g. [13, 18]).

2.3 Self-Efficacy in learning

Self-efficacy is a construct rooted in the social cognitive theory of Albert Bandura [3]. As such, Bandura and Schunk [4, p. 31] define self-efficacy beliefs as *"people's judgment of their capabilities to organize and execute courses of action required to attain designated types of performances".* In other words, self-efficacy is a construct referring to an individual's perceived capabilities in a specific task.

In academic and school settings, self-efficacy has attracted tremendous attention, especially in research that focuses mostly on the affective-emotional aspects of learning. There is generally a common agreement among these studies that students that have high perceptions of their capabilities engaged more, are better motivated and perform better than students that have low feelings of competence [4, 45]. Zimmerman [43] also highlighted the importance of self-efficacy on students' self-regulation learning. For example, students with high self-efficacy arrange their working schedule in a more efficient way than the students who demonstrate lower levels of efficacy [7] while also use learning strategies and self-evaluation processes that promote learning and evaluate the outcome of their self-monitoring correspondingly [44, 46].

Therefore, monitoring students' level of self-efficacy is a process that is critical and necessary for educators who are interested in investigating not only their students' actual performance but also factors that may contribute to this performance. To our knowledge, there are no studies that have investigated students' levels of self-efficacy in programming and how these levels differ from students who demonstrate misconceptions and students that do not. This is the gap that this study endeavors to address.

3 METHODOLOGY

3.1 Students' misconceptions

To explore students' misconceptions in functions, qualitative analysis, and specifically content analysis, was employed. Content analysis is a systematic coding and categorizing approach which is employed to investigate trends and patterns, their frequency and relationships in textual information [39].

Incorporating content analysis in computer programming is not a direct process. Shah et al. [30] presented a qualitative content analysis approach for programming errors which includes four steps: paraphrasing, generalization, categorization and check. Paraphrasing is a process that removes the code components not related with the error (not content-bearing). Generalisation involves the description of the error in natural language and categorisation includes the process of producing more abstract versions of the generalisations made previously to produce categories that include similar errors. Finally, the check refers to the validation process of the errors and the category to which they have been assigned.

Based on the aforementioned approach described, we explored and categorised students' misconceptions in functions.

3.2 Students' misconceptions and self-efficacy in programming and computer science

For the second phase of the study, we employed a correlation and a causal comparative research design. To explore the relationship between misconceptions and students' self-efficacy, we employed an independent t test in which we compare the self-efficacy levels of students that showed evidence of misconceptions and students that did not. Additionally, to explore the relationship between self-efficacy in programming, self-evaluation on the programming test and computer science, correlation analysis was used. In particular Spearman's rho correlation was used since the data for all the examined variables, except efficacy in programming, were not normally distributed.

3.3 Participants

To answer the research questions of the study, we considered a homogeneous purposive sample. We were very careful to select students that had sufficient experience in programming and also in functions. Students' previous experience in functions was particular important to our study as the literature suggests that misconceptions are extremely tenacious and resistant to change. Therefore, we wanted the students to have the time to develop misconceptions in functions and hold onto these. Thus, we first contacted computer science teachers and explicitly asked them to participate in our study with their computing class only if the latter fulfilled the aforementioned criteria.

In total, 83 students (11th Grade/Year 12) participated in the study from 4 different schools, of which 18 were girls and 65 were boys. The test was written in Python as students had been exposed to this language mostly.

3.4 Instruments and Data collection

To investigate misconceptions in functions, we created 6 programming tasks that captured different levels of complexity. On designing our assessment tool, we took into consideration Scott's [29] argument that assessment tests should include questions from all six levels of Bloom's taxonomy as most of the students are able to respond to low-level questions and few students can answer the most complex questions. In this way, we had a more objective way to determine what each student had understood or not. The most influential study, however, was Shuhidan et al.'s [31], in which Bloom's taxonomy was used to classify the multiple-choice questions and SOLO taxonomy to evaluate students' responses. In the same vein, in our assessment test, Bloom's taxonomy was employed to categorise the questions to Bloom's different levels and SOLO taxonomy was used to evaluate students' level of understanding. Extra consideration was given to Whalley and Kasto's [41] paper in which they categorise different types of programming tasks into Bloom's and SOLO taxonomy. Building on these studies, we created 6 programming tasks of advancing difficulty which are presented in the end of this paper.

The first task asked the students to match the concepts of parameters, arguments, return statement, function definition, calling a function and print statement with the appropriate annotated text in the given code. The aim here was to see if the students had a basic understanding of the concepts that are included in this part of the curriculum. The second task included a short program in Python which included two functions and asked the students to identify and correct the errors (both syntax and logic). This task was a little more advanced than the first one as it included logical errors in addition to syntactical and, thus, a deeper understanding of functions was required by the students. The third task asked the students to read a program written in Python and answer two reading comprehension questions: *"What is the purpose of the program"* and *"What will be the output of that program"*. The fourth task was a Parson's Puzzle: the students were asked to put in the correct order a group of code statements in order for the program to succeed its purpose (it was given in written form). The fifth task was a fill-in-the-blanks exercise focusing on parameters, arguments and return variables, and the sixth task asked the students to write from scratch a program that creates and calls a function that calculates the area of a triangle.

When the students finished the programming tasks, they continued with the self-evaluation and self-efficacy questions. Specifically, the students responded to two 11-point(0-10) Likert-scale questions about how they evaluate themselves on the test (How do you think you did on the test from 0 to 10?) and their general efficacy in computer science (How do you think you get on with computer science course from 0 to 10?). These two questions were employed from Román-González et al.'s study [28]. Additionally, to measure the self-efficacy in computer programming we employed the Pintrich et al.'s [25] self-efficacy scale which was adapted to reflect the computer programming course and has a Cronbach's alpha of .93. We should note here that this self-efficacy scale (for programming) was given first before students move on to the programming tasks. The reason we distributed this questionnaire first was because we didn't want students' self-efficacy in programming to be influenced by their specific performance on the programming tasks.

The data were collected through an online survey tool and the link to the test was given to teachers. Each teacher dedicated an hour of to the test and the accompanied questionnaire.

3.5 Validity and Reliability

To ensure the validity and reliability of the interpretation of the misconceptions, two researchers were involved in the process: the first researcher produced the coder manual with the categories (misconceptions) which was used by the second researcher to categorise again the students' errors. The inter-rater reliability of Cohen's kappa was calculated and a substantial agreement was found: k=0.675, $p < .001$ (approximate 95% confidence interval on Kappa: 0.612 - 0.737). Only categories that both researchers agreed upon are presented in this paper.

Table 1: Students' misconceptions

Misconceptions	Percentage of students	Task
1: Students think that return statements should be used after the call to the function to return and print the function's output	48.19%	Task: 4 and 6
2: Students think that return value should have the same name with the function	24%	Task: 6
3: Students think that parameters should be explicitly defined to be used inside the function	19.27%	Task: 2
4: Students think that parameters and arguments should have the same name	15.6%	Task: 5 and 2
5: Students think that arguments should include the return variable	12%	Task: 5
6: Students think that local variables can be accessed from a function to another	10.8%	Task: 6
7: Students think that calling a function prints the result	8.4%	Task: 6

Figure 1: Examples: Students' misconceptions

Example – Misconception 1 (Task 4)

```
def output (grade):
  if grade > 12:
    result = "pass"
  else:
    result = "fail"

def main ():
    mark = int (input("insert grade:"))
    print (output(mark))
    return result
```

Example – Misconception 2 (Task 6)

```
def area (a, b):
  area = a*b
  return area

def main ():
  height = int (input("Enter the rectangle's height:"))
  width = int (input("Enter the rectangle's width: "))
  print (area (height, width))
```

4 DATA ANALYSIS AND RESULTS

4.1 Students' Misconceptions in Functions

The aim of the programming tasks analysis was to discover common errors that students make in programming and to uncover misconceptions that may held by the students in the area of functions. Table 1 summarises the misconceptions that the study uncovered, the percentage of students that demonstrated the misconception and the task that illustrated the misconception. Figure 1 depicts examples from students' code that demonstrate misconception 1 and 2.

4.2 Students' performance and self-efficacy on task and computer science

Table 2 shows the descriptive statistics of students' performance, self-evaluation, self-efficacy in computer science and self-efficacy in computer programming. The sample is split in two groups: students that demonstrated the misconceptions and students that did not.

To examine whether students' level of self-efficacy in computer programming differ between students that hold misconceptions and students that do not we employed the independent t test to compare the levels of self-efficacy between the two groups.

The results suggest that the self-efficacy levels in programming of students that hold misconceptions are significantly lower than students that did not show evidence of misconceptions ($t=3.614$, $p<.05$, $r=.41$) .

Additionally, to examine whether students' levels of self-efficacy in computer science differ between students that hold misconceptions and students that do not we employed the Mann-Whitney test since some of the data were not normally distributed.

The results suggest that the self-efficacy levels in computer science of students that hold misconceptions are significantly lower than students that did not show evidence of misconceptions ($U=386.0$, $z=-3.415$, $d=0.374$).

5 DISCUSSION

In this section we will discuss the research findings by answering the research questions addressed in the first part of this paper.

5.1 Students' misconceptions in Functions

The first research question related to students' misconceptions in functions. As table 1 illustrates, our study revealed seven misconceptions students demonstrate in this part of the curriculum. The first misconception that was made by a large number of students (48.19%) points out to a very specific error: students put the return statement under the calling statement in order to print and return the result of the function. Our interpretation is that students regard that putting the calling statement first and then putting the return statement is the way to return and print the result of a function. Another error that students made quite often in the tasks – and it relates again to the return value – is that students named the

Table 2: Descriptive Statistics

Misconceptions				Performance	Self-Evaluation	EfficacyCS	EfficacyProgramming
No	N	Valid	25				
		Missing	0				
	Mean			91.2	7.44	7.40	5.366
	Median			90.0	8.00	7.00	5.25
	Mode			88.0	8	7	6.0
	Std. Deviation			5.375	1.873	1.472	.8623
Yes	N	Valid	58				
		Missing	0				
	Mean			43.0	5.16	5.93	4.39
	Median			41.0	5.0	6.0	4.43
	Mode			29.5	5	6	3.5
	Std, Deviation			17.74	2.033	1.746	1.216

Table 3: Independent t test

						95% Confidence Interval of the Difference
	t	df	Sig. (2-tailed)	Mean Difference	Std. Error Difference	Lower|Upper
efficacyProgramming	3.614	81	.001	.971110	.268728	.436426|1.505794

Table 4: Mann-Whitney U test

	performance	efficacyCS	self-evaluation
Mann-Whitney U	.000	386.000	287.5
Wilcoxon W	1711.000	2097.0	1998.5
Z	-7.198	-3.415	-4.386
Asymp. Sig. (2-tailed)	.000	.001	.000

return variable the same as their function. Although it is not clear to us if this error happened by mistake, the fact that 24% of students demonstrated this in their code led us to believe that some students erroneously believe that the name of the variable that must be returned should be the same as the name of the function. Finally, our study found one more misconception regarding return values: some students put the return variable to the arguments list (misconception 5). Our interpretation is that the students thought that in order to return a value back, the variable holding this value must be placed in the arguments. Although previous researchers [33, 34] have reported errors that students make with return values, this is the first time, to our knowledge, that these specific ways of handling return values are reported in the literature.

A comparison of the findings with those of other studies confirms that misconceptions 3, 4, 6 have been reported again in the literature. Specifically, misconception 3 refers to students' erroneous understanding that parameters must be assigned a value inside the function's body in order to be used. The same misconception was reported by Sirkiä and Sorva[33]. Additionally, misconception 6 which refers to students' erroneous belief that local variables in the function can be accessed outside the function was also reported by Sirkiä and Sorva [34]. Misconception 4 is about students' misunderstandings and confusion about naming parameters and arguments. Chen et al. [8] referred to students' misunderstandings about formal and actual parameters and therefore we categorise these error to a general confusion that students have with these concepts. Finally, our study found one other misconception: few students thought that calling a function will also print the result. Although we have included this misconception in the list, we are reluctant to support that this error stems from a misconception as only a few students demonstrated this error.

5.2 Do students' misconceptions impact students' self-efficacy in programming? What is the role of self-evaluation and efficacy in computer science?

Very little can be found in the literature on the question of if and how students' misconceptions can impact students' self-efficacy beliefs in programming. To this end, this study's second aim was to explore this relationship by comparing the self-efficacy levels between students that showed evidence of possessing the aforementioned misconceptions and students that did not. The results depicted in table 2 and 3 suggest that students who hold misconceptions in programming demonstrate significant lower levels of self-efficacy in programming than do students that do not hold misconceptions (r=0.41). The results are not surprising as students that demonstrated these misconceptions scored lower than the other students and there are many studies that correlate performance with self-efficacy beliefs [26, 42]. Nevertheless, the results highlight an important and often neglected factor that accompanied students to the journey from false beliefs to accurate conceptualizations.

Previous studies have noted the importance of previous experience in computing and students' self-efficacy in programming [2, 22]. In our study it is evident that students' efficacy beliefs in computer science are significantly different between the two groups with the group demonstrating misconceptions achieving lower levels of efficacy. This was somehow expected as the correlation between efficacy in computer science and efficacy in computer

Table 5: Correlations

			efficacyProgramming	Performance	self-evaluation	efficacyCS
Spearman's rho	efficacyProgramming	Correlation Coefficient	.1000	.546**	.639**	.714**
		Sig. (2 tailed)	.	.000	.000	.000
		N	83	83	83	83

**Correlation is significant at the 0.01 level (2-tailed).

programming is strong as table 5 depicts. On similar grounds, the study of Wiedenbeck et al. [42] showed that previous experience in programming affects self-efficacy which in turn impacts students' success in this course. The role of previous performance in programming and how this is contributing to students' self-efficacy in programming was also highlighted in the study conducted by Jegede [14] who found that students' performance in programming courses significantly predicts students' self-efficacy in programming.

Another interesting finding stems from students' self-evaluations. It seems that students who didn't have misconceptions tend to underestimate their performance while students with misconceptions tend to overestimate their performance. This is interesting indeed as it may suggest that students with misconceptions hold on to these mistaken ideas strongly and therefore they cannot accurately estimate their performance.

6 CONCLUSION

The current study set out to explore misconceptions that 11th Grade (Year 12) students hold with regards to functions, and secondly to investigate if students that demonstrate misconceptions experience statistically significant lower levels of self-efficacy in programming than students that do not. We also included two other variables that the literature suggests as potential factors impacting students' self-efficacy in programming: students' capability beliefs in computer science and their self-evaluations on the specific programming test.

One of the most significant findings to emerge from this study is the identification of 7 misconceptions, of which 3 have never before been identified in the literature to our knowledge. These misconceptions reflect the fact that the return variable seems to be confusing to students at this age and stage. The second major finding was that misconceptions in programming may have an impact on students' self-efficacy in programming. The results indicated that students who do not demonstrate these misconceptions had statistically significant higher levels of self-efficacy in programming and self-efficacy in computer science.

From a methodological point of view, we believe that our approach – which included a specific part of the computing curriculum along with an assessment tool based on the Blooms and SOLO taxonomies – is an effective approach for capturing the complexity of a programming area and depicting students' misunderstandings at multiple levels. From a pedagogical point of view, our study contributes to the research field of misconceptions and identified three new misconceptions in functions. As a final point, by linking misconceptions and other factors with self-efficacy in programming we have highlighted affective aspects of programming. These are often neglected and we recommend that more research focuses on the relationship between affective and cognitive factors within the learning and teaching of programming.

A APPENDICES

Programming Tasks

Task 4

The purpose of the following program is to print the result of a test (fail or pass). To pass the test the grade should be higher than 12. The code statements are numbered but are misplaced. Can you put the statements in the right order in order for the program to achieve its goal?

```
mark = int(input(" insert grade: "))
result = "fail"
result = "pass"
print (output(mark))
else:
if(grade>12):
def main ():
return result
def output (grade):
```

Task 5

The following program takes as an input two numbers and calculates their sum by calling a function. Fill in the blanks in order for the program to achieve its purpose.

```
def sum (____A______):
   ___B___ = n1 + n2
 return result

def main ():
 number1 = int(input("type the first number"))
 number2 = int(input("type the second number"))
 print sum (____C____)
```

REFERENCES

[1] Lorin W Anderson, David R Krathwohl, Peter W Airasian, Kathleen A Cruikshank, Richard E Mayer, Paul R Pintrich, James Raths, and Merlin C Wittrock. 2001. A taxonomy for learning, teaching, and assessing: A revision of BloomâĂŹs taxonomy of educational objectives, abridged edition. *White Plains, NY: Longman* (2001).

[2] Petek Askar and David Davenport. 2009. An Investigation of Factors Related to Self-Efficacy for Java Programming among Engineering Students. *Online Submission* 8, 1 (2009).

[3] Albert Bandura. 1977. Self-efficacy: toward a unifying theory of behavioral change. *Psychological review* 84, 2 (1977), 191.

[4] Albert Bandura and Dale H Schunk. 1981. Cultivating competence, self-efficacy, and intrinsic interest through proximal self-motivation. *Journal of personality and social psychology* 41, 3 (1981), 586.

[5] Mordechai Ben-Ari. 2001. Constructivism in computer science education. *Journal of Computers in Mathematics and Science Teaching* 20, 1 (2001), 45–73.

[6] JB Biggs and KF Collis. [n. d.]. Evaluating the Quality of Learning: The SOLO Taxonomy, 1982.

[7] Therese Bouffard-Bouchard, Sophie Parent, and Serge Larivee. 1991. Influence of self-efficacy on self-regulation and performance among junior and senior high-school age students. *International Journal of Behavioral Development* 14, 2 (1991), 153–164.

[8] C.L. Chen, S.Y. Cheng, and J.M.C. Lin. 2010. A study of misconceptions and missing conceptions of novice Java programmers. In *Proceedings of the International Conference on Frontiers in Education: Computer Science and Computer Engineering (FECS' 12)*. The Steering Committee of The World Congress in Computer Science, Computer Engineering and Applied Computing (WorldComp), 84–89.

[9] National Research Council, Division of Behavioral, Social Sciences, and Board on Science Education; Committee on Undergraduate Science Education Education. 1997. *Science teaching reconsidered: A handbook*. National Academies Press.

[10] Benedict Du Boulay. 1986. Some difficulties of learning to program. *Journal of Educational Computing Research* 2, 1 (1986), 57–73.

[11] Paul Eggen and Don Kauchak. 2001. *Educational Psycology: Windows on Classrooms. 8th.* Upper Saddle River, NJ: Pearson.

[12] Ann E Fleury. 2000. Programming in Java: student-constructed rules. In *ACM SIGCSE Bulletin*, Vol. 32. ACM, 197–201.

[13] Cruz Izu, Amali Weerasinghe, and Cheryl Pope. 2016. A study of code design skills in novice programmers using the SOLO taxonomy. In *Proceedings of the 2016 ACM Conference on International Computing Education Research*. ACM, 251–259.

[14] Philip Olu Jegede. 2009. Predictors of java programming self efficacy among engineering students in a Nigerian University. *arXiv preprint arXiv:0909.0074* (2009).

[15] Lisa C Kaczmarczyk, Elizabeth R Petrick, J Philip East, and Geoffrey L Herman. 2010. Identifying student misconceptions of programming. In *Proceedings of the 41st ACM technical symposium on Computer science education*. ACM, 107–111.

[16] Maria Kallia and Sue Sentance. 2017. Computing Teachers' Perspectives on Threshold Concepts: Functions and Procedural Abstraction. In *Proceedings of the 12th Workshop on Primary and Secondary Computing Education*. ACM, 15–24.

[17] Raymond Lister and John Leaney. 2003. Introductory programming, criterion-referencing, and bloom. *ACM SIGCSE Bulletin* 35, 1 (2003), 143–147.

[18] Raymond Lister, Beth Simon, Errol Thompson, Jacqueline L Whalley, and Christine Prasad. 2006. Not seeing the forest for the trees: novice programmers and the SOLO taxonomy. *ACM SIGCSE Bulletin* 38, 3 (2006), 118–122.

[19] Judith Longfield. 2009. Discrepant teaching events: Using an inquiry stance to address students' misconceptions. *International Journal of Teaching and Learning in Higher Education* 21, 2 (2009), 266.

[20] S. Madison and J. Gifford. 1997. *Parameter passing: The conceptions novices construct*. Technical Report. https://eric.ed.gov/?id=ED406211

[21] Ralph E Martin, Colleen M Sexton, and Jack A Gerlovich. 2002. *Teaching science for all children: Methods for constructing understanding*. Allyn and Bacon.

[22] J Owolabi and BA Adegoke. 2014. Multilevel Analysis of Factors Predicting Self Efficacy in Computer Programming. *International Journal on Integrating Technology in Education (IJITE)* 3, 2 (2014).

[23] DN Perkins and Fay Martin. 1986. Fragile knowledge and neglected strategies in novice programmers. In *first workshop on empirical studies of programmers on Empirical studies of programmers*. 213–229.

[24] Jean Piaget. 1971. Biology and knowledge: An essay on the relations between organic regulations and cognitive processes. (1971).

[25] P.R. Pintrich, D.A.F. Smith, T. Garcia, and W.J McKeachie. 1991. A manual for the use of the Motivated Strategies for Learning Questionnaire (MSLQ). (1991).

[26] Sarantos Psycharis and Maria Kallia. 2017. The effects of computer programming on high school students' reasoning skills and mathematical self-efficacy and problem solving. *Instructional Science* 45, 5 (2017), 583–602.

[27] Yizhou Qian and James Lehman. 2017. Students' misconceptions and other difficulties in introductory programming: a literature review. *ACM Transactions on Computing Education (TOCE)* 18, 1 (2017), 1.

[28] Marcos Román-González, Juan-Carlos Pérez-González, Jesús Moreno-León, and Gregorio Robles. 2017. Extending the nomological network of computational thinking with non-cognitive factors. *Computers in Human Behavior* 80, 2018 (2017), 441e459.

[29] Terry Scott. 2003. Bloom's taxonomy applied to testing in computer science classes. *Journal of Computing Sciences in Colleges* 19, 1 (2003), 267–274.

[30] Philipp Shah, Marc Berges, and Peter Hubwieser. 2017. Qualitative content analysis of programming errors. In *Proceedings of the 5th International Conference on Information and Education Technology*. ACM, 161–166.

[31] Shuhaida Shuhidan, Margaret Hamilton, and Daryl D'Souza. 2009. A taxonomic study of novice programming summative assessment. In *Proceedings of the Eleventh Australasian Conference on Computing Education-Volume 95*. Australian Computer Society, Inc., 147–156.

[32] T Sirkiä. 2012. *Recognizing Programming Misconceptions–An Analysis of the Data Collected from the UUhistle Program Simulation Tool*. Department of Computer Science and Engineering, Aalto University. Master Thesis.

[33] Teemu Sirkiä and Juha Sorva. 2012. Exploring programming misconceptions: an analysis of student mistakes in visual program simulation exercises. In *Proceedings of the 12th Koli Calling International Conference on Computing Education Research*. ACM, 19–28.

[34] Teemu Sirkiä and J Sorva. 2012. Recognizing Programming Misconceptions: An Analysis of the Data Collected from the UUhistle Program Simulation Tool. *Master's thesis, Department of Computer Science and Engineering, Aalto University* (2012).

[35] John P Smith III, Andrea A DiSessa, and Jeremy Roschelle. 1994. Misconceptions reconceived: A constructivist analysis of knowledge in transition. *The journal of the learning sciences* 3, 2 (1994), 115–163.

[36] Christopher W Starr, Bill Manaris, and RoxAnn H Stalvey. 2008. Bloom's taxonomy revisited: specifying assessable learning objectives in computer science. In *ACM SIGCSE Bulletin*, Vol. 40. ACM, 261–265.

[37] Errol Thompson, Andrew Luxton-Reilly, Jacqueline L Whalley, Minjie Hu, and Phil Robbins. 2008. Bloom's taxonomy for CS assessment. In *Proceedings of the tenth conference on Australasian computing education-Volume 78*. Australian Computer Society, Inc., 155–161.

[38] Fiona Thompson and Sue Logue. 2006. An exploration of common student misconceptions in science. *International Education Journal* 7, 4 (2006), 553–559.

[39] Mojtaba Vaismoradi, Hannele Turunen, and Terese Bondas. 2013. Content analysis and thematic analysis: Implications for conducting a qualitative descriptive study. *Nursing & health sciences* 15, 3 (2013), 398–405.

[40] Ashok Kumar Veerasamy, Daryl D'Souza, and Mikko-Jussi Laakso. 2016. Identifying novice student programming misconceptions and errors from summative assessments. *Journal of Educational Technology Systems* 45, 1 (2016), 50–73.

[41] Jacqueline Whalley and Nadia Kasto. 2013. Revisiting models of human conceptualisation in the context of a programming examination. In *Proceedings of the Fifteenth Australasian Computing Education Conference-Volume 136*. Australian Computer Society, Inc., 67–76.

[42] Susan Wiedenbeck, Deborah Labelle, and Vennila NR Kain. 2004. Factors affecting course outcomes in introductory programming. In *16th Annual Workshop of the Psychology of Programming Interest Group*. 97–109.

[43] Barry J Zimmerman. 2000. Attaining self-regulation: A social cognitive perspective. In *Handbook of self-regulation*. Elsevier, 13–39.

[44] Barry J Zimmerman and Albert Bandura. 1994. Impact of self-regulatory influences on writing course attainment. *American educational research journal* 31, 4 (1994), 845–862.

[45] Barry J Zimmerman and Anastasia Kitsantas. 1997. Developmental phases in self-regulation: Shifting from process goals to outcome goals. *Journal of educational psychology* 89, 1 (1997), 29.

[46] Barry J Zimmerman and Manuel Martinez-Pons. 1990. Student differences in self-regulated learning: Relating grade, sex, and giftedness to self-efficacy and strategy use. *Journal of educational Psychology* 82, 1 (1990), 51.

Educational Experiences of Blind Programmers

Catherine M. Baker
Journalism, Media & Computing
Creighton University
Omaha, NE, USA
catherinebaker@creighton.edu

Cynthia L. Bennett
Human Centered Design & Engineering
University of Washington
Seattle, WA, USA
bennec3@uw.edu

Richard E. Ladner
Computer Science & Engineering
University of Washington
Seattle, WA, USA
ladner@cs.washington.edu

ABSTRACT

As diversity efforts in computer science begin to recognize disabled programmers as an underrepresented group, we step back to chronicle the experiences of blind programmers in higher education. Through a survey and follow-up interviews with 10 blind programmers, we share reflections and barriers important for the computing education community to understand as we attempt to welcoming cultures for disabled programmers. Our findings illuminated a variety of barriers blind programmers faced in college and the impact that they had on their ability to succeed in the field. We found that barriers permeate all parts of these blind student's' education from accessing the materials and doing the homework to working with professors. These barriers increased feelings of the isolation, decreased motivation especially when tasks were inaccessible, and prevented them from learning all the concepts covered in their degree program.

CCS CONCEPTS

• Human-centered computing → Accessibility → Empirical studies in accessibility

KEYWORDS

Computer science; education; blind programmers; accessibility

ACM Reference format:

Catherine M. Baker, Cynthia L. Bennett, Richard E. Ladner. 2019. Educational Experiences of Blind Programmers. In *Proceedings of 50th ACM Technical Symposium on Computer Science Education (SIGCSE '19), February 27-Mar. 2, 2019, Minneapolis, MN, USA.* ACM, NY, NY, USA, 7 pages . DOI: https://doi.org/10.1145/3287324.3287410

1 Introduction

Diverse teams benefit companies, however computer science is not a very diverse field [8]. In reaction, several diversity efforts have sprung up to raise participation. While necessary, most have focused on increasing the participation of women and minorities, but few have considered disability. Notably, AccessComputing [19] has attempted to increase the participation of people with disabilities in computer science by cultivating mentorships with students and professionals with disabilities, and financially supporting conference attendance and internships. But AccessComputing does not penetrate day-to-day classroom environments. In order to widen diversity efforts to support computer science professionals with disabilities, it is important to understand the challenges they must overcome. Our work focuses on a subset of this concern, challenges faced by blind students during postsecondary computer science coursework.

As much of the academic literature thus far has focused on either introduction to computer science [3,9,17] or the experiences of these engineers once in the industry [11], we focus our research on the period between the two, computer science degree acquisition. We know that students with disabilities are less likely to study STEM fields and more likely to drop out of STEM programs than their non-disabled peers [5]. Based on this, we would like to understand the barriers that blind students face in computer science in hopes of increasing the number that persist in their degree. Some preliminary work suggests some of these challenges. Mealin and Murphy-Hill [2] found that many blind software engineers were not using many of the tools built in to integrated development environments (IDEs) and hypothesized it was due to the students not learning them in school. Additionally, in a blog post [6], Doustdar mentioned he chose to continue his education outside of a university as his computer science coursework was highly visual. We wish to discover a more nuanced and comprehensive view of the challenges these students face during their studies.

SIGCSE '19, February 27-March 2, 2019, Minneapolis, MN, USA

ACM 978-1-4503-5890-3/19/02…$15.00
https://doi.org/10.1145/3287324.3287410

2 Related Work

While little research chronicles the experiences of blind programmers while acquiring their degree, some work has focused on the curricular changes and accommodations made by instructors of blind students [6, 8]. But this work lacks student perspective. The afore-mentioned interview study by Mealin and Murphy-Hill [11] comprises the only glimpse of educational experiences by blind computer science professionals with the aim to raise awareness to computing researchers. While this work introduces how blind programmers navigate code, became interested in computer science and navigated misperceptions about their disability in professional settings, our study follows this to elucidate more specific challenges encountered across the entire computer science degree requirements and social experiences with professors and peers.

The accessibility challenges with IDEs and code editors have been studied and a few have been designed with a blind developer in mind. Some have focused on making specific existing environments more accessible. Emacspeak [13] is a spoken interface for Emacs. Sodbeans [17], which is built into NetBeans, and EdSharp [20] augment the information that is provided by the screen reader. Other tools increase access to individual aspects of coding, including IDE enhancements. Potluri et al. [12] started by categorizing the accessibility issues in IDEs and then created CodeTalk, a Visual Studio plugin, to address a subset of the issues discussed. Baker et al [1] created StructJumper, an Eclipse plug-in to help blind students navigate in the code. Smith et al. [15] created a plug-in to make the program hierarchy more accessible. Stefik et al. [16] used audio cues to highlight a change in scope as a program executed. Vickers et al. [18]'s system plays audio cues upon entry and exit of program structures. Finally, Balik et al. [2] created GSK, a tool to help blind students create and share graphs crucial for participating in many computer science classes. These tools importantly remove barriers to inaccessible aspects of computer science. Our study steps back to quantify these barriers in hopes of better understanding how they impact learning.

Finally, introducing blind students to computer science has gained recent attention since many beginner coding tutorials remain inaccessible. Stefik et al. [17] created an educational infrastructure with accessible programming activities and a supplementary curriculum for teachers. Others introduce programming concepts with robotics [10], Twitter data [9], chat bots [3] and audio output [14] to enhance nonvisual interactivity. These approaches aim to recruit blind students in to computer science. In this study, we instead focus on barriers encountered after our participants decided to pursue a career in computing.

3 Methods

3.1 Survey and Interviews

We conducted a survey and follow-up semi-structured interviews. The survey was conducted to gain a broad overview of the problems blind programmers encountered during their degree. The interview questions were gleaned from survey results as we hoped to gain a deeper understanding of participants' responses and experiences. The interviews took 30-60 minutes and were transcribed for open coding and analysis afterwards.

3.2 Participants

Survey participants were recruited using mailing lists, research contacts and snowball sampling. On the survey, participants were asked if they would be willing to participate in the follow up interview. Inclusion criteria for study participation were that they completed a degree in computer science or a related field, they used a screen reader while completing the degree, and be 18 or older. After closing the survey, we removed responses that were likely spam (i.e. had multiple responses that did not make sense for the question) and concluded with 15 responses to the survey. All 15 survey respondents were male with an average age of 31.7 (SD = 6.9). Six participants had a graduate degree. Ten participants did their degree in North America, the other five in Europe. The median graduation year was 2009 (range 1995-2014). Participants averaged 12 years of computer science experience (SD = 7.5).

We conducted the interviews with 10 of the survey respondents (referred to as i1-i10). Interviewees were selected to represent a range of experiences including reported barriers, when they attended school, and whether they completed a graduate degree. The average age of the interview participants was 29.2 (S.D. = 5.1). Four of the participants had received a graduate degree. Six of the participants did their degree in North America, the other four in Europe. The median graduation year was 2009.5 (range 1995-2014). Participants had an average of 12.3 years of computer science experience (S.D. = 7.8).

3.3 Analysis

Interviews were audio recorded and transcribed. After reviewing all of the transcripts, the authors used open coding with two researchers initially coding together to establish the code book. Once the code book was established, the authors coded the remaining interviews independently. Once all interviews were coded, the researchers reviewed the interviews coded by the other, added any codes that were missed, and arbitrated any disagreement regarding the application of codes.

4. Results

Survey and interview results revealed a variety of issues that students face while completing their degree. These barriers came in the form of inaccessible materials and assignments, and from faculty misperceptions about capabilities of blind programmers. In the survey, 8 of the 15 respondents reported at least half their classes had inaccessible portions. In the following sections, we will describe these challenges in detail.

4.1 Technology

This section details the current state of IDEs and other technologies commonly used by our participants. On the survey, participants were asked to detail their preferred set-up(s) for coding. The four most common IDEs were Visual Studio (7 participants), Eclipse (6 participants), Notepad (3 participants), and Notepad++ (3 participants). Though IDEs and editors designed with blind programmers in mind have been created ([20], [13], [17]) only 4 participants indicated they used one of these IDEs. Eleven participants indicated which screen reader they use most often. JAWS was the most common screen reader listed (8 participants), followed by NVDA (3 participants), Window Eyes (2 participants), and Voiceover (2 participants). Finally, 5 participants used a Braille display, while 3 did not. The other 7 participants did not indicate explicitly whether or not they used a Braille display.

We found that many participants encountered issues with IDEs. The accessibility challenges ranged from completely unusable to advanced features proving inaccessible. All but three respondents to the survey had accessibility challenges with the IDEs that they used most often. Common problems indicated on the survey were interface builders (6 participants), debuggers (3 participants), syntax highlighting (2 participants), and diagrams (2 participants).

Additionally, participants clarified that while an IDE may be accessible, learning to use it was much more complex. Most guides for IDEs that participants attempted to use were geared toward sighted users, often littered with directions like "click here" which made them irrelevant to a blind programmer. Determining keyboard equivalents was complex, often leading participants away from assignments in search alternatives. Unsurprisingly, we learned that participants like i9 with prior knowledge of the IDEs found it essential for setting them up to succeed.

Attempting to, and failing to, use inaccessible IDEs deterred some participants from trying new ones. One participant said:

> *And like my confidence was pretty low that these programs would even work if I had the time to spend. So I was kind of going under this assumption that they wouldn't anyway. And I think I would have been right in most cases, but I don't know. ... So I didn't have time to spend and you know, put like 40 hours into Eclipse and then learn, oh ok cool, you know, it's not accessible. - i1*

The burden of spending so much extra time to no avail stuck with i1 to the point that potentially wrongfully assuming an IDE would be inaccessible was a more efficient use of his time.

For some of our participants like i8, choosing to avoid learning new IDEs during university was a purposeful choice that, in the short term, mitigated some of the overhead skill acquisition in order to keep up with his classes. However, such choices came with tradeoffs. I8 is now learning how to use a debugger as he never used one in college. He learned that his previous strategies were ineffective in comparison.

Another barrier came when participants were asked to complete assignments with unique software downloaded onto specific machines. Often, this software was built for beginner students meant to direct their attention from IT to learning programming concepts. But these computers remained restrictive disallowing some of our participants from downloading important assistive technologies onto them.:

> *But the problem was that you could only access that server from the lab machines and the lab machines didn't have any speech on them. So I couldn't use it all. So I actually – I ended up having to set up my own machine and you know set-up Oracle, set up PHP, Apache, and all things like that. But I had to get the assignment in, you know, to the same deadline that everyone else did. – i6*

Participants were burdened when they had to configure separate machinery. This often required extra work which distracted them from coursework. Additionally, lab spaces serve additional purposes other than just access to the technology. Lab spaces can serve as a communal space for students and without access to the machines in these spaces may be less inviting to blind students.

4.2 Accommodations

One of the factors that affected a student's experience was the quality of the accommodations that were provided. In this section, we will discuss their experiences related to these accommodations in regard to accessing lectures, materials, and assignments.

4.2.1 Lecture. One of the major problems blind students face in lecture is missing context, as what is spoken does not replicates visual content:

> *The professor would say something like 'sizeof int,' right? So he would leave out that it was actually 'sizeof left parenthesis int right parenthesis semi-colon. ...' So you miss all that. So when I first started learning C in college, I would actually write 'sizeof space int semi-colon' on my exams. –i2*

Issues such as this were compounded when the lecturer handwrote and gestured to content rather than speaking it out. I2 acknowledged that requesting content be read out loud presented a new experience for the lecturer and would sit at the front of the room as a physical reminder of the accommodation. When the professor did not verbalize their handwriting and did not provide the same information in accessible course materials, participants relied on friends in the class whose notes were likely also inaccessible; for i1, this meant receiving unreadable notes in MathType or Microsoft Word's Equation Editor.

4.2.2 Materials. Our participants had difficulty obtaining course materials such as textbooks and handouts in an accessible format on time. Participants tended to prefer one of a few different mediums: Braille, audio, or electronic but each format had its pros and cons.

Producing Braille textbooks is time consuming, requires specialized equipment and expertise, and is expensive to create. Those who received Braille textbooks cited large delays interfering with their learning. I2 ordered braille transcription 2 months in advance to receive them when classes started. I1 would sometimes not get the braille book until over half way through the term, if at all. In order to have access to the book for the entire term, he would sometimes drop and retake a course. To mitigate the cost and time factors, i4 ordered books from a Braille library. However, they often were not the same book assigned, but the faculty would look them over and determine if they adequately covered the topics.

Multiple (i2, i4, i7, i8) participants used audiobooks from sites like Learning Ally [21]. Books from Learning Ally were appreciated because they recruited readers versed in the subject.

This had two benefits. The first was that they could read the subject material in a way that made sense. For things like code, they would know what needed to be read, such as punctuation. Additionally, they would often describe the diagrams by prioritizing the pertinent information. But they also had a downside. One participant found the spoken code very hard to listen too:

> *So, books and audio when it comes to programming is very inefficient. Some of the readers, what they would do, is they would actually spell the entire code. So they would say f-u-n-c-t-i-o-n. Space... - i2*

Since there is no established standard for verbalizing code, audio book readers sometimes omitted information. For example, participants indicated readers would fail to communicate indentations which can be consequential for certain programming language. Additionally, it is not possible to search audiobooks, which can make them less useful for looking up information.

Participants loved obtaining an electronic format of the textbook as they were versatile and searchable. For example, participants could read content with a screen reader or refreshable braille display, and write notes and highlight important content. However, electronic formats were difficult to obtain. Three of the interview participants (i1, i5, i6) contacted the textbook publishers directly to obtain a premade electronic version, but only one actually received a textbook. Those unable to get the electronic version directly from the publisher scanned the hardcopy book and used Optical Character Recognition (OCR) software to extract text. However, OCR works best with prose and stem-related content including computer code is often interpreted incorrectly. Since correct syntax is imperative in computer science, even intermittent errors could confuse students as to whether they did not understand the material or whether their OCR version of the textbook was inaccurate. One participant's office providing accommodations for students with disabilities hired workers with knowledge of computer science and were therefore able to correct OCR-produced errors. However, if the student was unable to get the OCR corrected, explicitly mentioned by (i3, i5, i6), then they received the textbook with the afore-mentioned errors. One participant described the effect as:

> *Then scan was always the last scenario because that would have a drastic effect on my mark. You know, to the point where I was ... getting First [highest grade] for the things where I had electronic copies of books readily available to me, but I was barely passing modules where I had to get the book scanned. - i6*

Textbook formats varied but all had pros and cons. Students experimented with different types but never completely succeeded in obtaining their course materials on time in an accessible format.

Another common resource students needed access to were diagrams. In general, they were either provided in a tactile form or a verbal/textual description. Sometimes students would only get a small subset of the diagrams made accessible because conversion took time, special equipment in the case of tactile graphics, and expertise. Additionally, the source of descriptions varied. For one student, the professor included descriptions on his slides. Others relied on friends or family members to describe the images. We discovered that who provided the descriptions largely impacted their accuracy. Our participants reiterated that diagram describers need to be knowledgeable of the material:

> *And it's kind of like well, ok, I need to know where the switches are and stuff like that. ... But, you know, if you don't know about computers, you can't just look at some of these diagrams and give an accurate description of them. - i6*

Participants encountered similar miscommunication when someone served as their go-between during exams. A common scenario consisted of a reader describing questions on the exam and transcribing answers as participants dictated. Multiple participants lamented these experiences negatively. i4 described one of his tests:

> *And the problem was the person they got to actually do the writing for me was a chemistry post graduate - had never done this part of mathematics before. So he didn't know what the hell he was writing. - i4*

Timely and accessible textbooks and diagrams proved important but rarely-available components to participant success. It was important that description authors were aware of the field Second, since participants were still learning the content, they were unqualified to provide the reader instructions on what and how to communicate. However, services like Learning Ally which recruited subject matter experts to read computer science textbooks did not mitigate this barrier given the limits of audio books on searching and inconsistent descriptions given no universal reading standard. Finally, exams represented negative experiences for our participants when nonexperts not only could not describe content but when they could not transcribe answers as intended.

4.2.3 Assignments. Some participants were provided alternate assignments or exemptions during their computer science degree programs. These examples spanned using different technologies to complete coursework, building a different system, leveraging human assistance, receiving grades based on the accessible components, and being excused altogether.

One of the most common issues occurred when assignments steered students toward an inaccessible IDE. This was often not consequential as assignment requirements could be fulfilled regardless of the IDE, but it did mean that they undertook extra work to learn the IDE on their own and they may not have had access to the same tools (i.e. debugging).

Another common alteration was changing the form factor of the assignment, resulting in different output with similar application of programming concepts. Participants sometimes wrote text descriptions of non-textual answers (i5 and i9) or doing a console based application instead of GUI application (i3, i6, i10).

However, other participant scenarios exemplified two very different assignments. I9 built a chat application once when the rest of his class built a visual game. This application *"covered some common concepts and others which the game did not. So it was equal but not the same."*

The second major assignment change occurred when the participant was assigned a sighted partner to relay visual information, or when a reader completed visual aspects under the participant's direction. I6 was asked to create a drawing application. He had a sighted peer help him by watching him run his code to communicate if it succeeded, but he wasn't very motivated by the assignment:

> *And to be completely honest, I didn't put a huge amount of effort into that assignment. Because I just hated the idea of kind of spending hours and hours of making something I'd just never be able to use. –i6*

The student's motivation was decreased by having an assignment that he did not find exciting as he would be unable to actually use (and debug) the output. The low effort meant that he later realized that he did not know those topics as well, which is a challenge when topics build upon those earlier topics they did not learn well.

Some professors did not adapt assignments but ambiguously communicated they would consider the extra challenges when grading. I2, described just one of a few similar experiences:

> *He said, you know, as long as your code is written to the best of your ability. ... So he said double check the logic and stuff and you know, we will realize that you were never actually able to compile and run this program. – i2*

I2 was okay with this outcome as he felt confident about the content. However, it likely is not a good option in general. The process of understanding errors and figuring out how to fix them was part of the assignment that he was not able to do and thus he may not have learned as much as if he had been able to read the output and properly debug errors.

Finally, although rare, some participants were excused from individual assignments, portions of courses, and courses altogether. Participants cited professor disbelief in a blind student. For I6, this meant he was talked out of taking an elective. Most exempt courses consisted primarily of graphical or electronics content. Participants had to advocate strongly to enroll when the professor or department would have waived the requirement. I1 took an independent study version of a course in lieu of the established version which was inaccessible, but his attempts to adapt course content with the instructor were unsuccessful, defeating the purpose of the specialized course opportunity. Several participants relayed faculty were forthcoming about not knowing how to teach them, imagining exemption from visually-based content and assignments over constructing accessible alternatives. Common in these stories is that participants were not interested in missing out on any assignments or courses. Instead, they had to assert their right to complete all degree requirements.

Adapted or removed assignments altogether carried repercussions. Differences in assignments could be ambiguous as to whether they were scaffolding a similar learning experience or whether they would be evaluated objectively. Participants further had to rely on peers or readers, decreasing their engagement with the content. Finally, inaccessible assignments increased workload and interfere with concept mastery, deficiencies that some participants did not realize for years.

4.3 Social Impacts

We found in our interviews that social factors also impacted participant experiences. I4 summarized social support as paramount:

> *You need both individual buy-in and you also need organizational buy-in from the university. Otherwise you can actually have the best and brightest student in the class who happens to be blind and if they can't get the requisite support, then they've got a huge, huge, huge problem. - i4*

As such, we briefly overview the impact of faculty and other students on participants' educational experience.

Faculty were often responsible for accommodating students directly, most commonly by sending course materials even when they did not typically distribute them to motivate class attendance. Participants reported incidents when faculty would refuse to send these materials and i4 had to enroll the assistance of university compliance personnel when advocating for himself did not work. When faculty were unwilling to work with the students, it made it difficult for students. Five participants (i1, i2, i3, i4, i5) mentioned having push back from the faculty or dropping courses to have a more accommodating faculty member. In particular, i2 had faculty that encouraged him to change his major and he nearly dropped his degree because he was frustrated with having to fight to gain access to materials. However, participants also praised supportive faculty; i1 remembered one faculty member who sent slides before each lecture, complete with text descriptions of diagrams.

Accessibility barriers also manifested during group projects. Several projects required students submit diagrams of how the software will work. I6 recounted his team leaving him out since he couldn't discern diagram drawings based on conversation alone

> *But even so, it wasn't ideal. I mean they were understanding, but, you know, there were lots of sessions where they'd all be talking and I wouldn't be able to say anything at all. Not because I didn't want to, but just because I couldn't really follow what they were talking about. - i6*

Participants had difficulty following real-time creation of inaccessible materials to be submitted for their group projects. This had further consequences than just their participation in the work the group was doing. I6 continued, *"But it's also a social thing, you know. Cause if you're the one person in the group that doesn't talk, you know, guess who the one person who doesn't get invited for drinks afterwards is.* "Being unable to participate in parts of the group projects was isolating for some participants. As other students can be help one another study and navigate computer science altogether, participants who did not contribute equally during group projects experienced isolation.

5. Discussion

We uncovered numerous barriers that characterize computer science education for blind students. Our participants recalled exploring numerous alternative technologies, textbooks, and assignment formats which added extra work. Further, accessibility barriers fostered disbelief that new technologies would be accessible, decreasing motivation to engage with important tools and concepts they would later need in their careers. Finally, social factors were hugely important but under addressed. We'll now highlight three areas for collaboration among educators and researchers toward removing these barriers.

5.1 Enforce Accessible Course Materials

First, we believe that enforcing the use of accessible course materials will alleviate pressure for blind students to explore accessible alternatives. Throughout our interviews, it was clear accommodations often remediated tools that could have been designed more accessibly. To enforce use of high quality accessible materials and tools, it will require partnerships with faculty, curriculum developers, education technology researchers and companies, university IT, and offices for students with disabilities. Faculty will need to be involved to provide subject matter expertise, university personal who prepare and implement accommodations for students with disabilities will provide more expertise on specific issues faced by students with disabilities and the creation of the alternative materials. Additionally, if curriculum developers and educational technology research consider the needs of students with disabilities from the beginning, then it can decrease the need for accommodations.

Further research is needed to improve the process of creating accessible materials. Currently, the central challenges include time, expertise, and specialized equipment needed to provide accessible alternatives. This not only burdens students but requires faculty to have their materials ready far in advance. Alternative materials production then rests on the few experts, removing agency from blind students and faculty until accessible materials are sent back in return. There has been some work starting in this area to help improve the process of creating tactile formats of the images in a textbook using the Tactile Graphics Assistant [7]. However, this is just one piece and we need to continue improving alternative materials production to be expedient and producible by non-experts. This work can uplift everyone involved in providing accommodations by allowing students and faculty to be able to play a more active role.

5.2 Support Faculty Learning

Second, we found that faculty need more support. Blind participants were largely the only information source for faculty. Yet blind students are not experts in accessible education, and when left to retool inaccessible curriculum, faculty can be further burdened or even suggest damaging alternatives like exempting assignments. AccessComputing [4] aims to equip instructors with Universal Design for Learning techniques such that students with disabilities can engage with few accommodations. Faculty and disability service professionals can also participate in communities of practice to create networks that can help identify steps to make classrooms and programs more accessible and inclusive and recruit more students with disabilities [22]. Researchers must consider how to scale these trainings and approach departments and universities for greater buy-in so faculty participation is expected and rewarded.

5.3 Foster Social Integration of Blind Students

Finally, blind students should be intentionally socially integrated. Accommodations to functionally be able to complete assignments are viewed as the means for disabled students to access their education. Yet we found these modifications were insufficient and could even increase isolation when, for example, an alternative assignment meant a participant was the only person working with a partner or building a different system altogether. First, blind students should have access to the spaces, machinery, and events hosted by departments. Recruitment events to improve diversity should explicitly include disability as an underrepresented group. Finally, adapted coursework should minimize social isolation and assignments deemed too visual for blind students should be replaced for the entire class with more inclusive alternatives.

Further research on creating more accessible technologies, such as collaborative accessible graph creation, could increase engagement from blind students during group work and other assignments. As technologies become more accessible, there will be less burden on students to find good accommodations.

6. Conclusion

This study shows that blind students encounter numerous barriers to obtain a computer science degree, and current research and efforts are only scratching the surface. Existing programs must be amplified and supplemented with more direct support from educational technology researchers and universities to remove barriers. In this paper, we revealed specific obstacles blind students faced and posited three overlapping areas for collaboration among educators and researchers to foster more fair and welcoming programs. By implementing accessible course materials and tools, supporting faculty accessibility education, and prioritizing integrating blind students, we hope to provide some steps forward toward a more diverse computing field.

ACKNOWLEDGMENTS

This material is based upon work supported by the National Science Foundation Graduate Research Fellowship Program under Grant No. (DGE-1256082).

REFERENCES

[1] Catherine M. Baker, Lauren R. Milne, and Richard E. Ladner. 2015. StructJumper: A Tool to Help Blind Programmers Navigate and Understand the Structure of Code. In *Proceedings of the 33rd Annual ACM Conference on Human Factors in Computing Systems - CHI '15*, 3043–3052. https://doi.org/10.1145/2702123.2702589

[2] Suzanne P. Balik, Sean P. Mealin, Matthias F. Stallmann, Robert D. Rodman, Michelle L. Glatz, and Veronica J. Sigler. 2014. Including Blind People in Computing Through Access to Graphs. In *Proceedings of the 16th International ACM SIGACCESS Conference on Computers & Accessibility - ASSETS '14*, 91–98. https://doi.org/10.1145/2661334.2661364

[3] Jeffrey P. Bigham, Maxwell B. Aller, Jeremy T. Brudvik, Jessica O. Leung, Lindsay A. Yazzolino, and Richard E. Ladner. 2008. Inspiring Blind High School Students to Pursue Computer Science with Instant Messaging Chatbots. In *Proceedings of the 39th SIGCSE Technical Symposium on Computer Science Education - SIGCSE '08*, 449. https://doi.org/10.1145/1352322.1352287

[4] Sheryl Burgstahler. 2008. *Equal access: {Universal} design of instruction.* Retrieved November 13, 2018 from https://www.washington.edu/accesscomputing/sites/default/files/doit-sync/files/Equal-Access-Universal-Design-of-Instruction.pdf

[5] Sheryl Burgstahler and Richard Ladner. 2006. AccessComputing: From Research to Practice | The Alliance for Access to Computing Careers. Retrieved May 3, 2016 from http://www.washington.edu/accesscomputing/resources/accesscomputing-research-practice

[6] Parham Doustdar. 2016. The Tools of a Blind Programmer – Parham Doustdar's Blog. Retrieved April 21, 2016 from https://www.parhamdoustdar.com/2016/04/03/tools-of-blind-programmer/

[7] Chandrika Jayant, Matt Renzelmann, Dana Wen, Satria Krisnandi, Richard Ladner, and Dan Comden. 2007. Automated Tactile Graphics Translation: In the Field. *Proceedings of the 9th International ACM SIGACCESS Conference on Computers and Accessibility - Assets '07*. 75. https://doi.org/10.1145/1296843.1296858

[8] Maggie Johnson. 2015. The Computer Science Pipeline and Diversity: Part 1 - How did we get here? Retrieved May 7, 2016 from http://googleresearch.blogspot.com/2015/07/the-computer-science-pipeline-and.html

[9] Shaun K. Kane and Jeffrey P. Bigham. 2014. Tracking @stemxcomet: Teaching Programming to Blind Students via 3D Printing, Crisis Management, and Twitter. In *Proceedings of the 45th ACM Technical Symposium on Computer Science Education - SIGCSE '14*, 247–252. https://doi.org/10.1145/2538862.2538975

[10] Stephanie Ludi. 2013. Robotics Programming Tools for Blind Students. In *28th Annual International Technology and Persons with Disabilities Conference Scientific/Research Proceedings.* Retrieved May 26, 2016 from http://scholarworks.calstate.edu/handle/10211.3/121968

[11] Sean Mealin and E Murphy-Hill. 2012. An Exploratory Study of Blind Software Developers. In *Proceedings of 2012 IEEE Symposium on Visual Languages and Human-Centric Computing - VL/HCC '12.* Retrieved February 27, 2014 from http://ieeexplore.ieee.org/xpls/abs_all.jsp?arnumber=6344485

[12] Venkatesh Potluri, Priyan Vaithilingam, Suresh Iyengar, Y. Vidya, Manohar Swaminathan, and Gopal Srinivasa. 2018. CodeTalk. In *Proceedings of the 2018 CHI Conference on Human Factors in Computing Systems - CHI '18*, 1–11. https://doi.org/10.1145/3173574.3174192

[13] T. V. Raman. 1996. Emacspeak---Direct Speech Access. In *Proceedings of the Second Annual ACM Conference on Assistive Technologies - Assets '96*, 32–36. https://doi.org/10.1145/228347.228354

[14] Jaime Sánchez and Fernando Aguayo. 2005. Blind Learners Programming Through Audio. *Extended Abstracts on Human Factors in Computing Systems - CHI '05*. 1769–1772. Retrieved February 27, 2014 from http://dl.acm.org/citation.cfm?id=1057018

[15] Ann C. Smith, Joan M. Francioni, Mohd Anwar, Justin S. Cook, Asif Hossain, and M. Fayezur Rahman. 2003. Nonvisual Tool for Navigating Hierarchical Structures. In *Proceedings of the 6th International ACM SIGACCESS Conference on Computers and Accessibility - ASSETS '04*, 133. https://doi.org/10.1145/1029014.1028654

[16] Andreas Stefik, Christopher Hundhausen, and Robert Patterson. 2011. An empirical investigation into the design of auditory cues to enhance computer program comprehension. *International Journal of Human-Computer Studies* 69, 12: 820–838. https://doi.org/10.1016/j.ijhcs.2011.07.002

[17] Andreas M. Stefik, Christopher Hundhausen, and Derrick Smith. 2011. On the Design of an Educational Infrastructure for the Blind and Visually Impaired in Computer Science. In *Proceedings of the 42nd ACM Technical Symposium on Computer Science Education - SIGCSE '11*, 571. https://doi.org/10.1145/1953163.1953323

[18] Paul Vickers and James L Alty. 2002. When bugs sing. *Interacting with Computers* 14, 6: 793–819. https://doi.org/10.1016/S0953-5438(02)00026-7

[19] About | The Alliance for Access to Computing Careers. Retrieved April 21, 2016 from http://www.washington.edu/accesscomputing/about

[20] EdSharp. Retrieved November 8, 2017 from https://github.com/EmpowermentZone/EdSharp

[21] Learning Ally - Support for Dyslexia and Learning Disabilities. Retrieved May 7, 2016 from https://www.learningally.org/

[22] Communities of Practice | AccessComputing. Retrieved December 1, 2018 from https://www.washington.edu/accesscomputing/get-involved/educators-employers/communities-practice

Computer Science Principles for Teachers of Blind and Visually Impaired Students

Andreas Stefik
University of Nevada, Las Vegas
Las Vegas, NV
stefika@gmail.com

Richard E. Ladner
University of Washington
Seattle, WA
ladner@cs.washington.edu

William Allee
University of Nevada, Las Vegas
Las Vegas, NV
wallee777@hotmail.com

Sean Mealin
North Carolina State University
Raleigh, NC
spmealin@ncsu.edu

ABSTRACT

The College Board's AP Computer Science Principles (CSP) content has become a major new course for introducing K-12 students to the discipline. The course was designed for many reasons, but one major goal was to broaden participation. While significant work has been completed toward equity by many research groups, we know of no systematic analysis of CSP content created by major vendors in relation to accessibility for students with disabilities, especially those who are blind or visually impaired. In this experience report, we discuss two major actions by our team to make CSP more accessible. First, with the help of accessibility experts and teachers, we modified the entire Code.org CSP course to make it accessible. Second, we conducted a one-week professional development workshop in the summer of 2018 for teachers of blind or visually impaired students in order to help them prepare to teach CSP or support those who do. We report here on lessons learned that are useful to teachers who have blind or visually impaired students in their classes, to AP CSP curriculum providers, and to the College Board.

CCS CONCEPTS

• **Human-centered computing → Accessibility systems and tools**; • **Social and professional topics → K-12 education**;

KEYWORDS

Blind and Visually Impaired, Accessibility, Computer Science Principles, Professional Development, The College Board, Code.org

ACM Reference Format:
Andreas Stefik, Richard E. Ladner, William Allee, and Sean Mealin. 2019. Computer Science Principles for Teachers of Blind and Visually Impaired Students. In *Proceedings of the 50th ACM Technical Symposium on Computer Science Education (SIGCSE '19), February 27-March 2, 2019, Minneapolis, MN, USA.* ACM, New York, NY, USA, 7 pages. https://doi.org/10.1145/3287324.3287453

SIGCSE '19, February 27-March 2, 2019, Minneapolis, MN, USA

ACM ISBN 978-1-4503-5890-3/19/02...$15.00
https://doi.org/10.1145/3287324.3287453

1 INTRODUCTION

After years of curriculum development and piloting, the College Board has created a new AP course for high school aged students to learn computer science and potentially earn college placement or credit. Unlike AP Computer Science A, a course exclusively in Java with a traditional CS1 design, Computer Science Principles (CSP) was designed from the ground up to teach big ideas and computational practices while also being engaging to a wide spectrum of students.

One of the claimed benefits of the CSP course is its appeal to equity, meaning it should be inclusive toward all students. In this regard, data released by the College Board reports that approximately 76,000 students took the AP CSP Exam in 2018 [11]. Of these, they categorize 5,082 (6.7%) as Black/African American, 14,020 (18.5%) as Latino/Hispanic, and 22,721 (29.9%) as Female. Change can be slow, but current data appears to be in a positive direction.

While CSP is making solid progress toward equity in regard to women and minorities, we know of no systematic work evaluating its impact on students with disabilities. After researching what the College Board makes public and asking them, they do not keep reliable data on participation by students with disabilities. This experience report focuses on the impact of the CSP curriculum on blind or visually impaired students.

To begin thinking about this group, we gathered 11 teachers of diverse backgrounds for a one-week professional development workshop for the purpose of familiarizing them with the CSP framework [10], the Code.org CSP curriculum and pedagogy [12], and the modifications made to a Code.org curriculum that we created in collaboration with accessibility experts and teachers of blind and visually impaired students. Participants in the workshop prepared lessons and taught them as a way of honing their teaching pedagogy and critiquing the original and modified Code.org CSP curriculum. We recruited from teachers who teach and/or support blind and visually impaired students exclusively and general education teachers that have no direct training with blind or visually impaired students, but that nevertheless have such students in their classrooms. We did this to ensure we were listening to perspectives of teachers that have expertise in blindness and those in general education classrooms, as we suspected they might be different.

The rest of this paper is as follows. First, we discuss related work and then the teachers themselves. Second, we discuss Code.org's CSP curriculum, including their embedded online tools, and our modifications to make it more accessible. Third we describe the workshop and some of its highlights. Finally, we outline the overall lessons learned related to accessibility of the AP CSP course.

2 RELATED WORK

To our knowledge, our workshop is the first to bring in teachers from a variety of backgrounds to specifically focus on education strategies and curriculum development for blind and visually impaired students in CSP. Although working with the teachers directly seems to be relatively rare, many workshops and camps have been held for these students to increase both interest and proficiency for Computer Science and other STEM disciplines.

The data for studies focusing on teachers of blind and visually impaired students is typically obtained through interviews and observation. To understand the strategies that teachers use in mainstream classes, Lartec et al. interviewed 20 teachers with blind students [18], which uncovered several themes, such as verbalizing visual information, providing the student with additional time to understand the information, and allowing peer assistance. When interviewing instructors teaching at a STEM-focused camp for blind students [34], Villanueva et al. found that teachers needed to be aware of three main themes listed in most-to-least importance: availability of accessible resources, understanding the needs of the teacher and student, and general STEM knowledge.

Looking at Computer Science education, several studies introduced tools to increase the efficacy of students navigating code [7] and presented the results of a survey and interviews which found blind students encountered many more problems than their sighted counterparts. For example, students reported struggling with directions that relied on visual information (e.g., click on the blue button on the right) and had many accessibility problems with development environments. As a solution to this latter problem, Stefik et al. developed a programming environment designed for accessibility from the ground up, which is commonly used at residential schools for the blind [30].

As a way to provide exposure to accessible concepts and build interest, many camps have been held which focused on concepts such as data analysis and accessible visualization [17], creating interactive chatbots [9], robotics [19], and general programming [30]. Other camps have been held for general STEM disciplines, such as astronomy [8] and chemistry [37].

3 WORKSHOP STAFF AND TEACHERS

The workshop staff consisted of the four authors of this report. The author Ladner participated in a Code.org professional development workshop in the summer of 2018 several week prior to the workshop. The authors Stefik and Allee are developers of the accessible tools used in the modified curriculum, and Mealin is a very experienced blind computer scientist.

As mentioned earlier, over the course of a 1-week workshop we interacted with 11 teachers from varying backgrounds. Three were teachers at residential schools for the blind, three were itinerant teachers of the visually impaired (TVIs) working as consultants or for school districts, three were teachers at mainstream public schools that have blind or visually impaired students in their class, one, who was himself blind, taught at the college level, and one was an assistive technology specialist at a school for the blind. All had experience working with blind students either individually, in a classroom setting with only blind and visually impaired students, or in a general education classroom setting with some blind students. All but four of the teachers had experience teaching academic computer science or coding as a career and technical education (CTE) teacher. Two had experience teaching CSP to at least one blind student, trying to adapt Code.org's curriculum on their own. Table 1 shows the background of each teacher that participated.

We recruited this diverse group, working with blind students in different ways and with different levels of computer science knowledge, intentionally to learn a diversity of perspectives. As a result, we gathered varied feedback from those that were experts in blindness, but knew less about adapting computer science principles, to the opposite, with general education teachers that were intimately familiar with CSP, but did not necessarily know how to modify curriculum to blind or visually impaired students. This diversity helped us gather varied feedback on 1) the Code.org curriculum 2) The College Board's procedures in regard to blindness, and 3) our modifications for making it accessible.

4 THE CODE.ORG CSP CURRICULUM

The Code.org CSP curriculum is very much a *discovery and inquiry* curriculum, whereby in each lesson students are presented with a computing problem to solve. This is done either as an "unplugged" activity, using handouts or other offline materials, or as a "plugged" activity, using the online tools provided by Code.org. The activities are typically completed in pairs or small groups. The discovery activities are guided by the teacher, but students are not told how to solve the problem. The teaching philosophy for student activities is sometimes called *Think-Pair-Share*. This means students first work individually or in small groups thinking about a solution to a problem, perhaps using trial and error or logical thinking, while sometimes taking notes in a journal. Second, in pairs or small groups, students compare and combine solutions. Finally, students share ideas with the entire class. In this stage there is no correct answer. The goal is for students to share possible solutions.

The discovery and inquiry approach leads to the concepts that the students should be learning, but not necessarily to the technical language that is found in textbooks or on the AP CSP exam. The structure of a lesson follows the pattern "Activity - Concept - Vocabulary." The purpose of the activity is to ground a concept in a concrete way, then move to the technical vocabulary used more generally in the computer science field after. In this way, students gain a deeper understanding of the meaning of the vocabulary rather than being potentially intimidated by it at the beginning.

There are a total of 79 lessons found in 8 units in the Code.org CSP curriculum. The online curriculum covers the 7 big ideas and 6 computational thinking practices found in the College Board AP CSP framework [10]. Briefly, these big ideas are Creativity, Abstraction, Data and Information, Algorithms, Programming, the Internet, and Global Impact. Those and the computational practices embody how the College Board sees the content of a high school computer

Table 1: Background of Teachers

Job Description	School Setting	CS Teaching
CTE Teacher	School for the Blind	Coding
Computer Science Teacher	Public School	AP CSP and AP CS A
Math/CS Teacher	School for the Blind	CS
CTE Teacher	School for the Blind	Coding
Itinerant TVI	School District	None
Itinerant TVI	School District	None
Assistive Technology Specialist	School for the Blind	None
Consultant TVI	Independent	None
CS Teacher	College Level	CS
CS Teacher	Public School	CSP
CS Teacher	Public School	CS

science course. The 8 units in the Code.org CSP curriculum for 2018-2019 are titled:

- Unit 1 - The Internet
- Unit 2 - Digital Information
- Unit 3 - Intro to Programming
- Unit 4 - Big Data and Privacy
- AP Explore Performance Task Prep
- Unit 5 - Building Apps
- AP Create Performance Task Prep
- Post AP (done after taking the AP exam in early May)

The curriculum makes extensive use of online tools. They include five versions of an Internet Simulator used in Unit 1, a text compression widget and two pixelation widgets used in Unit 2, the App Lab programming environment used in Units 3 and 5, and the encryption widget used in Unit 4.

5 ACCESSIBILITY OF THE CURRICULUM

In order for an online curriculum to be accessible to blind and visually impaired students, it must be compatible with modern screen readers such as JAWS [25] and NVDA [1] on PCs and VoiceOver [6] on Mac. It must also be compatible with the magnification tools built into PCs and Macs and add-on tools such as ZoomText [27]. For an online curriculum like Code.org's, this is accomplished by adhering to the WCAG 2.1 AA guidelines [36], and by utilizing the ARIA standard [35] for interactive web pages. This is not a straightforward process, requiring a fairly high level of accessible web development expertise. In addition to technical accessibility, there can also be usability issues even when these guidelines are followed. For example, a web page might be WCAG compliant, but still difficult to use through a screen reader.

Generally speaking, Code.org's curriculum is not accessible to students who are blind and use screen readers. With their permission, we first analyzed all of the lessons and content and tracked what was and was not accessible. We provide here an overview of our findings.

To begin with, the online website for the course is often not compliant with WCAG 2.1, which means that people with disabilities may not be able to use it. Examples of this might be as simple as missing alternate descriptions for an image, to more complex minutia related to WCAG that are not crucial to describe in this report. Second, for the lessons themselves, many of the unplugged activities use visual metaphors and artifacts. To be clear, blind and visually impaired people can certainly interpret visual metaphors if the content is accessible, but that does not mean it is easy.

Because this requires some explanation, consider that some of these visual concepts in the curriculum could be made to have physical metaphors as an alternative. For example, Unit 1 Lesson 5 of Code.org's curriculum provides students with a "Flippy Do" template [13], which is used to teach binary numbers. Students are asked to cut and fold a piece of paper along printed lines and fill in blank spaces. Modifying this lesson could involve a variety of possible changes. One could remove the Flippy Do, modify a digital version for use with a screen reader, or create a Flippy Do template using Braille. In our modification, we decided to be pragmatic. We wrote changes to the text to make the Flippy Do less necessary, but also provided a Braille Flippy Do as an alternative.

So far as we could tell, all of the visual, and incredibly creative, online interactive tools in the Code.org curriculum are not screen reader accessible. In particular, the App Lab programming tool is not accessible even though there was a way to move from a blocks-based code to and from text-based JavaScript code, that could, in principle, be accessible. However, accessing that text through App Lab prevents that text from being sent to the screen reader. To put the problem plainly, a blind user using App Lab JavaScript mode through a screen reader would hear no sound, regardless of the fact that it is just text.

By blocks-based environment, we mean a programming setting where visualization and direct manipulation are used to write programs, as opposed to writing text. While the reader might assume that a highly visual blocks-based programming environment might be inaccessible to the blind or visually impaired, and this assumption is correct, there has been some progress on making blocks-based environments accessible. For example, Milne and Ladner [20] created an accessible blocks-based environment for younger children. This is possible to do, so long as appropriate accessibility standards are followed on a per platform basis.

While we point out that current blocks-based environments are not accessible, we do think it is important to mention evidence from Weintrop [38, 39], which shows that they do have some benefits to learners. Effect sizes in such studies are relatively small, with some showing no effect and others showing a small one. Our interpretation of that work is that, depending on how blocks-based programming environments are used, they overall have a limited, but real, positive impact on learning at the high-school age. However, they also exclude both our population entirely and some others with disabilities not discussed in this report (e.g., those with certain physical disabilities).

6 MAKING THE CURRICULUM ACCESSIBLE

The goal of our modified version of the Code.org CSP curriculum was to adopt the "discovery and inquiry" pedagogy and overall educational philosophy of the curriculum but convert all the online lessons to accessible formats using the WCAG 2.1 accessibility guidelines and ARIA as our initial guide. This meant finding alternative unplugged activities for the strongly visually oriented ones and developing alternative interactive tools to provide pragmatic solutions for our population.

The modified curriculum was done prior to the workshop. For nearly a year, we employed a team of three teachers of blind and visually impaired students to modify the curriculum across the board, focusing especially on the lessons and their unplugged activities to make accessible alternatives. At the same time, our development team collaborated with outside experts and developed equivalent accessible interactive tools as replacements for the inaccessible ones in the Code.org CSP online curriculum. We wrote our own accessible versions of many of them as replacements for the inaccessible tools. Our replacements work by creating similar tools in the Quorum web-based programming environment that is already WCAG 2.1 compliant. For each of these tools, the Quorum source code is available to students or teachers who can make changes to customize it or make it better in some way. The modified curriculum uses the Quorum programming language environment instead of App Lab for the programming development lessons especially in Units 3 and 5.

As one final point on Code.org's curriculum and the complexities surrounding it, we want to be very careful in stating that these past two sections of our paper were not intended to be critical of any CSP curriculum development group. In particular, Code.org actively requested our team to evaluate their curriculum for accessibility and has been overwhelmingly supportive of our explicit search for what is and is not currently accessible. We imagine many other curriculum providers are in a similar situation. We would point out that because of this collaboration, and that of our teachers and students, all of the materials and tools described in this section are available for use at the time of this writing.

7 QUORUM PROGRAMMING LANGUAGE

The Quorum programming language is a "born accessible" programming ecosystem, meaning it was accessible from its formation and has accessibility as a first-class design goal. By our own internal tracking, Quorum is used in approximately half of residential schools for the blind and visually impaired in the United States. The language is not solely for individuals with visual impairments, but it is inclusive of that group. The Quorum language has a wide number of applications, including LEGO robotics programming, digital signal processing, 2D/3D graphical, physics simulations, 3D positional audio or other programs—all of which we have made accessible.

The Quorum programming language is also classed as an "evidence-oriented" programming language [29], which means its core syntax and semantics are derived from both technical specifications and human-factors data. For those unfamiliar with evidence-oriented programming, a recent Dagstuhl was conducted on the topic [28]. Language constructs like "for", for looping, are intentionally not included, and were replaced in favor of notation choices with more obvious semantic identity, like "repeat." These choices are not arbitrary and were derived from measurements of human productivity, not just the opinions of the designers. In addition to making the language easier for programmers to understand, reducing syntactic clutter in the language (such as removing unnecessary parenthesis and end-of-line symbols) makes code easier to understand when using accessibility technologies such as screen readers.

While the core of our curriculum is online and we support accessibility in this sense through standard mechanisms, some teachers prefer offline tools because screen reading technologies on desktop are mature. For this reason, users can either program online using our editors or they can use Sodbeans, an offline plugin for the NetBeans development environment that adds Quorum and accessibility support. Our team is also creating a new environment, called Quorum Studio, that bypasses the standard Java Accessibility bridge for a custom accessibility layer. We call our approach "accessible graphics mapping."

Briefly, the way the accessible graphics mapping works, which is available today and which Quorum Studio is being built upon, is to have an accessibility intermediate layer that combines native call-downs to accessibility systems on a per-platform basis. This might sound trivial, but there is no common intermediary for accessibility without it. Every platform, to our knowledge, is incompatible with accessibility systems on every other. From there, a graphics pipeline, like OpenGL or DirectX, "maps" to the intermediate layer.

On Microsoft platforms, for example, it is easy to create an application that has "buttons" on a "form" that are accessible. However, it is significantly more difficult to make graphical applications, like those in games, accessible, even if they also have items that look and act like buttons. On Windows, Quorum tackles this problem by connecting to what Microsoft calls UI automation.

Thus for accessible graphics mapping, Quorum users first create standard events (e.g., button clicks, typed keys), which are automatically sent to the intermediate layer and translated into native accessibility events. After translation, the intermediate layer tells the operating system that graphical components are "acting like" various accessibility systems, allowing bi-directional control. This creates an operating system specific accessibility event stream.

At the native level, accessibility technologies like screen readers pick up on this event stream, which makes a graphical component appear to be a native accessible application. Thus, whether the user created a button or a complex 2D or 3D shape, the user obtains information in a similar way. The full technical details of this system are too complex to describe in this short paper. Suffice to say that while versions of the technology are available today in Quorum 6, they are complex and will evolve over time.

8 HIGHLIGHTS OF THE WORKSHOP

The workshop was modeled after the Code.org TeacherCon conference that was held in June 2018 in Atlanta, GA. A major component was the use of their Teacher-Learner-Observer (TLO) model whereby the teachers were placed into pairs who prepared and co-taught a lesson from the Code.org CSP curriculum. With 11 teachers, one teacher was paired with our blind staff member to form six pairs. Each pair was assigned one Code.org CSP lesson to prepare and teach where the resource for the lesson was a combination of a Code.org lesson plan and a modified accessible lesson plan. Each pair was asked to prepare a 40-minute accessible lesson using whatever resources they wanted from the two lesson plans, and in addition, teachers were asked to be creative in making the lesson as accessible as possible. Because so many of our teachers were experienced with blind and visually impaired students, many new ideas to improve the modified accessible lesson plans emerged.

While each pair taught a lesson, the remaining 9 participants played the role of students. Among the 9 participants there were always one or two who were blind. This forced teachers to take into account that they have blind students in their class. The remaining staff members stayed in the room as observers, helping participants remain in their roles. The observers' took notes and provided additional feedback when the lesson was completed.

At the end of each lesson, one of the observers and the pair of teachers left the room to reflect on their teaching in terms of what choices they made and why they made them, with a particular emphasis on making the lesson accessible. At the same time, the 9 "students" in the lesson reflected on what they learned and what might have been improved to make the learning experience better. After about 5 to 10 minutes, everyone joined back together to share their reflections with each other. During this final reflection period many new ideas came out about how to make the lesson more accessible and engaging for the students.

In addition to the TLO activities, there were other activities we focused on generating ideas for improving the modified curriculum, to strengthen the teachers' capacity to teach blind and visually impaired students, and to prepare the students for the AP CSP Exam. These activities included:

- Overview of the history of CSP and its framework.
- Overview of the Code.org CSP curriculum and its accessible modification.
- Overview of the Explore Performance Task and discussion of interesting topics that might interest blind and visually impaired students.
- Overview of and practice with the Quorum programming environment.
- Overview of and practice with two Quorum-based online educational tools.
- Demonstration of SAS Graphics Accelerator [24] for accessible big data analysis.
- Overview of the Create Performance Task and discussion of interesting non-visual programming tasks that blind and visually impaired students might develop.
- Discussion led by our blind staff member on highlights of his career in computer science including obstacles he has encountered and how they were overcome.
- Discussion and critique of the AP CSP Exam led by teachers who have taught CSP.
- Discussion of how to build a computer science community among teachers of blind and visually impaired students.
- Discussion of proper ways to interact with students who are blind or visually impaired, led by TVIs.

9 LESSONS LEARNED

Although the primary purpose of the workshop was professional development for teachers of blind and visually impaired students, there was much to learn from these teachers that apply to any teachers who have blind or visually impaired students in their classes, to AP CSP curriculum providers, and to the College Board. In this section, we review some of these lessons learned.

9.1 Lessons for Teachers

It is important to recognize that students who are blind or visually impaired generally have the capability of completing the AP CSP course. Including a student who is blind or visually impaired who is prepared intellectually and has facility with technologies like screen readers or magnification tools need not be an excessive burden provided the curriculum itself is accessible. Most of these students in mainstream settings have Teachers of the Visually Impaired (TVIs) who work with students to improve their access to academic subjects. AP CSP teachers should work closely with the TVI to help make their class as accessible as possible and to learn some of the best ways to interact with these students. The TVI may or may not know about accessible educational tools for computer science that are available to their students. Here is a short list of accessible educational tools that were discussed during the workshop:

- The Quorum Language for general programming [33]
- SAS Graphics Accelerator for data analysis [24]
- Instructional Material Centers as a resource to find accessible materials for any course [16]
- Flying Blind (Top Tech Tidbits in Assistive Technology) [14]
- AccessCSforAll to find a hotline for individual support for teachers [3]

Some advice that came from the workshop teachers is to be flexible. If an activity needs to be modified or replaced, just do it. Share your modification or replacement with others to save them time. If a tool can't be used by one of your students, report this to the curriculum provider so that they can improve it.

9.2 Lessons for AP CSP Providers

A major goal of AP CSP is broadening participation, which means the inclusion of all students regardless of gender, race, ethnicity, socioeconomic, or disability status. This goal cannot be achieved without attention to the accessibility of the curricula.

A first step would be to do an evaluation with regard to accessibility. This evaluation should be done by a qualified accessibility professional to be as complete as possible. After the evaluation, revisions of a curriculum should be prioritized using criteria based on the impact on students and teachers. A revision could be as simple as providing an alternative accessible unplugged activity. For the Explore Performance Task, include examples that relate to accessibility. These examples will invigorate all students, disabled or not, to think outside of the box. Examples mentioned by workshop participants included content like the Graphiti refreshable tactile graphics display [5], Orcam MyReader [23], Smart cane [4], Tap wearable keyboard [32], or Sunu Band [31].

For the Create Performance Task, it might be necessary to provide an alternative and accessible programming environment. Programming environments that only produce visual animations can be limiting for all students. Programming environments that control robots and/or audio are reasonable alternatives, but not all platforms are equally accessible. The broader point is that curriculum should not be exclusively in one sensory modality. Even if one is perceived to be engaging, like visuals genuinely can be, content providers need to be creative and engage in varying sensory modalities if they wish to be general purpose and for all students.

This is an issue of equity and the law, since students with disabilities have the legal right to participate in K-12 education through section 504 [21]. Some states have been more explicit. For example, in Nevada, SB-200 [26] requires all computer science courses at the K-12 level to be accessible. To our knowledge, this is the only state to call out this requirement for computer science explicitly as of today, although we would be unsurprised if other states followed suit given the overall goal of equity that is often discussed as part of computer science education.

9.3 Lessons for The College Board

The teachers in the workshop had three categories of advice for the College Board, which were related to practice examples, accommodations, and the AP CSP Exam. When coming to their conclusions, teachers had full access, and many knew, the College Board's existing accessibility and accommodations guidelines [2]. Generally, there is a need for more clarity and acknowledgement that students who are blind or visually impaired are included in their advice to students in their documentation. In the sample tests and questions, as it stands now, teachers found that they did not convincingly take disability status into account. Many examples were purely visual, with no alternatives, and it was unclear to them whether this might deflate a blind student's exam score without just cause.

Teachers had a number of concerns with the practice examples provided by the College Board. These centered largely around the fact that much of the content provided was purely visual. In theory, teachers recognized the College Board "might" accept non-visual alternatives, but the guidelines were vague or led to other concerns. Examples might include, would video with scrolling text or a spoken podcast be acceptable formats for the Explore Task? We would encourage the College Board to re-think such issues.

Teachers had many questions about accommodations, but they boiled down to what kind of help a blind or visually impaired student can receive while doing either of the Performance Tasks. For example, if a pertinent phrase is listed in a student's Individualized Education Program (IEP), like that the teacher is able to describe visuals to them, can they have similar accommodations in the explore/create task (e.g., a teacher verifying a camera is not pointed at the ceiling, putting a visual box or circle around lines of code specified by the student)? There is no acknowledgements for exceptions in the "musts, may, and may not" list for teachers involvement in performance tasks. Considering that about 13% of K-12 students in the United States have an IEP [15], more clarity in addressing the needs of these students in taking AP CSP and other AP courses should be addressed.

There was considerable concern by the teachers about the use of Braille math on the exam. There are currently two competing standards: Nemeth and Unified English Braille (UEB). Depending on which state the student is from, they learn one or the other, yet the College Board uses only Nemeth for CSP. Teachers urged us to make it clear that this matters a great deal. A student who knows UEB, but not Nemeth, would have a truly extraordinary barrier placed in front of them and their exam scores may not reflect their abilities. These dialects of Braille are quite different and knowing one hardly means that a student is familiar with the other. Overall, as the Braille Authority of North America points out, the situation regarding Nemeth and UEB is complicated [22].

There is also concern about whether any practice exams are available in appropriate Braille formats and how equity is achieved as certain questions are omitted from the exam for blind test takers. For example, if statistical procedures at the College Board do not take into account the "ease" of a question when dropping questions for reasons of disability, this could provide students a non-equitable advantage or disadvantage. In either case, the statistical evidence for the decisions made needs to be publicly available for scrutiny.

10 ROADMAP

As one final consideration in this work, we want to at least mention what we think needs to change for computer science to be accessible in K-12. First, the AP course aside, a great deal of the tools used by students in K-12 are not accessible to blind or visually impaired students. This includes all of the ones used commonly, like Scratch, SNAP!, Alice, and many others. This needs to change. All of Quorum's accessible output systems are open source and the ideas, or even code, can be adapted freely.

Part of the issue with accessibility is that it is a second class citizen. We regularly hear about equity for women and underrepresented minorities and we agree this is critical. However, if we are to embrace equity and computer science for all, we have to really mean it. The College Board, for example, should not endorse any curriculum, for any discipline, that is not accessible. Accessibility can be the default if we want it to be.

11 CONCLUSIONS

We held a one-week professional development workshop in the summer of 2018, the goal of which was both to train teachers of blind and visually impaired students and evaluate accessibility in CSP. This included a modification of Code.org's online curriculum for this population, in addition to analysis of it by 11 teachers. Overall, we found that while many lessons can be modified, the CSP community has significant challenges ahead. Notably, curriculum today has systemic barriers including the lack of engaging non-visual alternatives. Many tools are not compatible with web standards such as WCAG 2.1 AA. We think making progress on this will take dedicated effort, but with evidence in hand on the barriers, we think teachers, content providers, and others now have a roadmap for what challenges to consider first.

ACKNOWLEDGMENTS

The work is supported by the National Science Foundation under Grant numbers 1738259 and 1738252. We would like to especially thank Baker Franke at code.org for his kind and helpful comments throughout this project.

REFERENCES

[1] NV Access. [n. d.]. NV Access: Empowering Lives through Non-Visual Access to Technology. Retrieved August 28, 2018 from https://www.nvaccess.org/

[2] AccessCollegeBoard 2018. AP SSD Guidelines. Retrieved October 30, 2018 from https://apcentral.collegeboard.org/pdf/ap-ssd-guidelines-2017-18.pdf

[3] AccssCSforAll. [n. d.]. AccssCSforAll Website. Retrieved August 31, 2018 from https://www.washington.edu/accesscomputing/accesscsforall

[4] Access CS For All. [n. d.]. AssisTech. Retrieved August 31, 2018 from http://assistech.iitd.ernet.in/smartcane.php

[5] Inc. American Printing House for the Blind. [n. d.]. Graphiti refreshable tactile graphics display. Retrieved August 31, 2018 from https://www.aph.org/graphiti/

[6] Apple. [n. d.]. Accessibility. Retrieved August 28, 2018 from https://www.apple.com/accessibility/mac/vision/

[7] Catherine M. Baker. 2017. Increasing Access to Computer Science for Blind Students. *SIGACCESS Access. Comput.* 117 (Feb. 2017), 19–22. https://doi.org/10.1145/3051519.3051523

[8] Bernhard Beck-Winchatz and Mark A. Riccobono. 2008. Advancing participation of blind students in Science, Technology, Engineering, and Math. *Advances in Space Research* 42, 11 (2008), 1855–1858.

[9] Jeffrey P. Bigham, Maxwell B. Aller, Jeremy T. Brudvik, Jessica O. Leung, Lindsay A. Yazzolino, and Richard E. Ladner. 2008. Inspiring Blind High School Students to Pursue Computer Science with Instant Messaging Chatbots. *SIGCSE Bull.* 40, 1 (March 2008), 449–453. https://doi.org/10.1145/1352322.1352287

[10] The College Board. [n. d.]. AP Computer Science Principles. Retrieved August 28, 2018 from https://apcentral.collegeboard.org/courses/ap-computer-science-principles

[11] The College Board. [n. d.]. Number of Girls and Underrepresented Students Taking AP Computer Courses Spikes Again. Retrieved August 31, 2018 from https://www.collegeboard.org/membership/all-access/counseling-admissions-financial-aid-academic/number-girls-and-underrepresented

[12] Code.org. [n. d.]. Computer Science Principles. Retrieved August 28, 2018 from https://code.org/educate/csp

[13] Code.org. [n. d.]. Lesson 5: Binary Numbers. Retrieved August 28, 2018 from https://curriculum.code.org/csp-18/unit1/5/

[14] LLC Flying Blind. [n. d.]. Flying Blind Empowerment Through Technology. Retrieved August 31, 2018 from http://www.flying-blind.com/

[15] National Center for Education Statistics. [n. d.]. Fast Facts, Students with Disabilities. Retrieved August 28, 2018 from https://nces.ed.gov/fastfacts/display.asp?id=64

[16] American Federation for the Blind. [n. d.]. Instructional Resource Centers for the Blind and Visually Impaired. Retrieved August 31, 2018 from http://www.afb.org/info/afb-national-education-program/national-instructional-materials-accessibility-standard-nimas/instructional-resource-centers/235

[17] Shaun K. Kane and Jeffrey P. Bigham. 2014. Tracking @Stemxcomet: Teaching Programming to Blind Students via 3D Printing, Crisis Management, and Twitter. In *Proceedings of the 45th ACM Technical Symposium on Computer Science Education (SIGCSE '14)*. ACM, New York, NY, USA, 247–252. https://doi.org/10.1145/2538862.2538975

[18] Jane K. Lartec and Felina P. Espique. 2012. Communication Strategies of Teachers Educating Students Who Are Legally Blind in the General Education Setting. *Insight* 5, 2 (2012), 70.

[19] Stephanie Ludi and Tom Reichlmayr. 2011. The Use of Robotics to Promote Computing to Pre-College Students with Visual Impairments. *Trans. Comput. Educ.* 11, 3, Article 20 (Oct. 2011), 20 pages. https://doi.org/10.1145/2037276.2037284

[20] Lauren R. Milne and Richard E. Ladner. 2018. Blocks4All: Overcoming Accessibility Barriers to Blocks Programming for Children with Visual Impairments. In *Proceedings of the 2018 CHI Conference on Human Factors in Computing Systems (CHI '18)*. ACM, New York, NY, USA, Article 69, 10 pages. https://doi.org/10.1145/3173574.3173643

[21] U.S. Department of Education. [n. d.]. Protecting Students With Disabilities, Frequently Asked Questions About Section 504 and the Education of Children with Disabilities. Retrieved August 28, 2018 from https://www2.ed.gov/about/offices/list/ocr/504faq.html

[22] Braille Authority of North America. [n. d.]. Unified English Braille (UEB). Retrieved August 28, 2018 from http://brailleauthority.org/ueb.html#plans

[23] Orcam. [n. d.]. OrCam MyReader 2 Website. Retrieved August 31, 2018 from https://www.orcam.com/en/myreader2/

[24] SAS. [n. d.]. SAS Graphics Accelerator for data analysis. Retrieved August 31, 2018 from http://support.sas.com/software/products/graphics-accelerator/index.html

[25] Freedom Scientific. [n. d.]. Freedom Scientific's JAWS home page. Retrieved August 28, 2018 from https://www.freedomscientific.com/Products/Blindness/JAWS

[26] "Senators Woodhouse; Denis; Ford; Spearman; Cancela; Carlton; Frierson; Atkinson; Cannizzaro; Gansert; Manendo; Parks; Ratti; Segerblom; and Fumo". [n. d.]. Senate Bill No. 200. Retrieved August 28, 2018 from https://www.leg.state.nv.us/App/NELIS/REL/79th2017/Bill/5073/Text

[27] Ai Squared. [n. d.]. Zoom Text. Retrieved August 28, 2018 from https://www.zoomtext.com/

[28] Andreas Stefik, Bonita Sharif, Brad. A. Myers, and Stefan Hanenberg. 2018. Evidence About Programmers for Programming Language Design (Dagstuhl Seminar 18061). *Dagstuhl Reports* 8, 2 (2018), 1–25. https://doi.org/10.4230/DagRep.8.2.1

[29] Andreas Stefik and Susanna Siebert. 2013. An Empirical Investigation into Programming Language Syntax. *Trans. Comput. Educ.* 13, 4, Article 19 (Nov. 2013), 40 pages. https://doi.org/10.1145/2534973

[30] Andreas M. Stefik, Christopher Hundhausen, and Derrick Smith. 2011. On the Design of an Educational Infrastructure for the Blind and Visually Impaired in Computer Science. In *Proceedings of the 42Nd ACM Technical Symposium on Computer Science Education (SIGCSE '11)*. ACM, New York, NY, USA, 571–576. https://doi.org/10.1145/1953163.1953323

[31] Sunu. [n. d.]. The Sunu Band. Retrieved August 31, 2018 from https://www.sunu.io/index.html

[32] Tap. [n. d.]. Tap Wearable Keyboard, Mouse and Controller. Retrieved August 31, 2018 from www.tapwithus.com

[33] Quorum Development Team. [n. d.]. The Quorum Language. Retrieved August 31, 2018 from https://quorumlanguage.com/

[34] Idalis Villanueva and Marialuisa Di Stefano. 2017. Narrative Inquiry on the Teaching of STEM to Blind High School Students. *Education Sciences* 7, 4 (2017), 89.

[35] W3C. [n. d.]. Accessible Rich Internet Applications (WAI-ARIA) 1.1. Retrieved August 28, 2018 from https://www.w3.org/TR/wai-aria-1.1/

[36] W3C. [n. d.]. Web Content Accessibility Guidelines (WCAG) 2.1. Retrieved August 28, 2018 from https://www.w3.org/TR/WCAG21/

[37] Henry B. Wedler, Lee Boyes, Rebecca L. Davis, Dan Flynn, Annaliese Franz, Christian S. Hamann, Jason G. Harrison, Michael W. Lodewyk, Kristin A. Milinkevich, Jared T. Shaw, Dean J. Tantillo, and Selina C. Wang. 2014. Nobody Can See Atoms: Science Camps Highlighting Approaches for Making Chemistry Accessible to Blind and Visually Impaired Students. *Journal of Chemical Education* 91, 2 (2014), 188–194.

[38] David Weintrop. 2015. Comparing Text-based, Blocks-based, and Hybrid Blocks/Text Programming Tools. In *Proceedings of the Eleventh Annual International Conference on International Computing Education Research (ICER '15)*. ACM, New York, NY, USA, 283–284. https://doi.org/10.1145/2787622.2787752

[39] David Weintrop and Nathan Holbert. 2017. From Blocks to Text and Back: Programming Patterns in a Dual-Modality Environment. In *Proceedings of the 2017 ACM SIGCSE Technical Symposium on Computer Science Education (SIGCSE '17)*. ACM, New York, NY, USA, 633–638. https://doi.org/10.1145/3017680.3017707

Accessible AST-Based Programming for Visually-Impaired Programmers

Emmanuel Schanzer
Bootstrap / Brown University
schanzer@BootstrapWorld.org

Sina Bahram
Prime Access Consulting
sina@sinabahram.com

Shriram Krishnamurthi
Brown University
sk@cs.brown.edu

ABSTRACT

Most programmers rely on visual tools (block-based editors, auto-indentation, bracket matching, syntax highlighting, etc.), which are inaccessible to visually-impaired programmers. While prior language-specific, downloadable tools have demonstrated benefits for the visually-impaired, we lack language-independent, cloud-based tools, both of which are critically needed.

We present a new toolkit for building fully-accessible, browser-based programming environments for *multiple* languages. Given a parser that meets certain specifications, this toolkit will generate a block editor familiar to sighted users that also communicates the structure of a program using spoken descriptions, and allows for navigation using standard (accessible) keyboard shortcuts.

This paper presents the toolkit and a first evaluation of it. While the toolkit allows for full editing of code, we chose to focus strictly on navigation for this evaluation, using the navigation-only study design of Baker, Milne and Ladner. Visually-impaired programmers completed several tasks with and without our tool, and we compared their results and experience. Users had improved accuracy when completing tasks, were significantly better able to orient when reading code, and felt better about completing the tasks when using the tool. Moreover, these improvements came with no significant change in task completion time over plain text, even for experienced programmers who navigate text using screen readers set to high words-per-minutes.

CCS CONCEPTS

• Human-centered computing~Empirical studies in accessibility • Human-centered computing~Accessibility technologies • Human-centered computing~Accessibility systems and tools • Social and professional topics~People with disabilities

KEYWORDS: Accessibility; Visually Impaired/Blind Programmers; Screen Reader; Code Navigation; Code Structure; Blocks

ACM Reference format:

Emmanuel Schanzer, Sina Bahram, Shriram Krishnamurthi. 2018. Accessible AST-Based Programming for Visually-Impaired Programmers. In *Proceedings of 50th ACM Technical Symposium on Computer Science Education (SIGCSE '19), February 27-Mar. 2, 2019, Minneapolis, MN, USA.* ACM, NY, NY, USA, 7 pages. https://doi.org/10.1145/1234567890

ACM ISBN 978-1-4503-5890-3/19/02...$15.00.
DOI: https://doi.org/10.1145/1234567890

1 Introduction

Reading the textual syntax of a program can be non-trivial. Novice and expert programmers use various visual cues, such as block languages, auto-indentation, syntax highlighting, bracket-matching, and more. However, these cues are useless for the roughly 65,000 blind and visually-impaired students in the US alone [6], who must rely primarily or solely on the textual syntax of the language, as spoken aloud by a screen reader or communicated through a Braille display.

Screen readers are adept at communicating structure, and conventions for navigating tree-like structures (e.g. mailboxes, directories, etc.) are well-defined [4]. Unfortunately, screen readers do not have access to a program's structure. Tokens are read one-at-a-time, and the program is broken up into nothing more than a series of lines. Navigation suffers accordingly, with programmers forced to use arrow keys to read each line of code. Losing the visual cues on which sighted programmers rely is a significant impairment: blind programmers have been shown to have more difficulties navigating and understanding the structure of code than their sighted counterparts [5, 9, 10].

Prior work has shown significant gains when screen-readers are given access to *structure* rather than the raw text. Smith et al. [5] created a language-specific tool to allow blind programmers to navigate the tree structure of *files* in the Eclipse IDE, and Baker et al. [2] created the StructJumper plugin for Eclipse that allows programmers to navigate a Java program's structure.

However, browser-based programming environments are becoming increasingly popular in education. Environments such as Code.org's AppLab, Bootstrap's WeScheme, MIT's Scratch, and others live in the browser [13]. For schools that have adopted Chromebooks, desktop applications are not even an option. These factors limit the usefulness of prior work, and introduce an additional engineering constraint.

Our tool, CodeMirror-Blocks (CMB), expands on prior work in three significant ways. First, *it is designed to be extensible to other languages.* When provided with a parser that meets certain requirements (described in the documentation), CMB will create a fully-accessible Abstract Syntax Tree (AST) editor for that language, rendered as blocks. Second, *it is designed to run entirely in a web browser.* CMB is built atop the popular CodeMirror library, which is used by thousands of software tools worldwide

[3]. Any programming environment that uses CodeMirror can be accessibility-enabled by attaching this tool to the appropriate parser. Finally, *it decouples the textual syntax from the spoken descriptive label for that text*, allowing for plain-language description of fragments of code.

While our tool allows for navigation and editing of code, this first phase of the evaluation is strictly limited to navigation.

2 Related Work

Difficulties for blind developers to explore code efficiently as well as lack of access to advanced IDE features were qualitatively explored by Mealin et al. [5]. Baker et al. provide additional evidence for the claim that blind developers are forced to read entire source code files repeatedly and rely on their short-term memory for complex pieces of information such as a nested conditional within a loop, while also remembering their current depth in said code [2].

2.1 Audio-Based Efforts

Stefik et al.'s work on SodBeans [10] provides both speech and audio cues to notify blind developers of errors, assist in debugging, and convey scope. It lays out three rules for providing lists of information about code: lists must be browsable, short, and place important things first. CMB attempts to strictly follow these rules. To address the concern that audio cues are hard to understand [2], CMB uses audio *and* speech cues, so that users can learn audio cues over time but are never forced to remember them. Our hope is that this hybrid approach will be accessible to novices and useful for experts.

2.2 Purpose-Built Programming Languages

Stefik et al.'s work on the Quorum [12] language shows that syntactic decisions can have a positive effect on accessibility. Unfortunately, many programmers (and students) cannot choose the language they use, and anyway such a language may not be a good fit for the task in other ways (such as its features or semantic choices). Many of the observations of that work may be replicable by custom descriptions in CMB (section 3.4 and 3.5).

2.3 Enhancements to Existing IDEs

Potluri et al. explored enhancing blind developers' efficiency through their work on CodeTalk [7]. CodeTalk makes extensive use of audio cues and aims to make improvements in four areas: Discoverability, Glanceability, Navigability, and Alertability. CodeTalk is a Visual Studio plugin and, as such, it can achieve exacting control over sound effects and much tighter control over said sound effects' timing in relation to speech cues. While we do not evaluate CMB along these four categories, we agree that they are appropriate for blind developers. Evaluation along these lines is an area for future work.

2.4 Structural Information

Screen readers use hierarchical language to convey heading level, and therefore position, in many contexts. Several already-discussed works [2, 5, 7, 10] include this feature. CMB also prioritizes structural information for the blind, and goes further to provide context beyond simple location (see section 3.4).

3 Design and Implementation

CMB had several design and implementation constraints:

1. *It should not be tied to any one programming language.* The editor should be flexible enough to work with different languages (assuming they can satisfy the parser constraints).
2. *It should be easy to integrate into existing cloud-based editing environments.* The editor should not require any browser plugins or extra programs to be installed, and should not require any server-side processing.
3. *It should communicate structure.* As with StructJumper, the structure of code should be navigable via keyboard, announcing relevant information via a screen reader.
4. *It should describe code*, instead of reading syntax. This addresses the same problem as Quorum, in a different way.
5. *It should be performant.* The tool should be responsive and memory-efficient enough to run on tablets, underpowered laptops, etc.

Our editor is built around a continuously-updated AST. The editor has an internal definition of an AST structure, as well as various *ASTNode* types (such as literals, function applications, conditionals, etc.), which can be rendered as text or as a DOM tree in the browser.

3.1 Language Flexibility

The first constraint is addressed through the AST interface. An ASTNode includes `from` and `to` positions (implemented as line-character pairs), as well as a `type` field that declares whether the node represents a conditional, a literal, etc. To use our accessible editor, a language designer must provide a parser that generates the appropriate AST nodes. Additionally, language designers can provide new ASTNode types in order to express semantic elements not defined within the library itself.

3.2 Browser-Only Implementation

To address the second constraint, our editor is implemented entirely in JavaScript, as a wrapper for the widely-used CodeMirror library [3]. By implementing much of the same API as CodeMirror, any project that uses CodeMirror can integrate our editor with minimal effort beyond parsing (which it presumably already has, or must anyway build).

CodeMirror runs on all major browsers, and provides text-handling features like syntax-highlighting, bracket-matching, auto-indenting, and more. While it provides a compelling experience for sighted programmers, it is completely opaque to users who rely on screen readers. Sadly, the best web-based experience for programmers who use screen readers is essentially an unformatted `textarea`. Fortunately, CodeMirror has a notion of *widgets*, which are arbitrary DOM nodes that can replace a range of text. We exploit this mechanism in CMB, leveraging CodeMirror's robust support for undo/redo, cursor tracking, scrolling, etc.

3.3 Relationship to ARIA

ARIA [1] is a set of attributes designed to enhance accessibility, typically by providing semantic information about content. After parsing the contents of a CodeMirror editor into an AST, we render each root node as a DOM tree, embed a great deal of information via ARIA attributes, and use those trees as widgets to replace the corresponding text range in CodeMirror. These DOM trees allow us to replicate the functionality of StructJumper, expressing the underlying structure of the code entirely in the browser. When navigating a tree, a blind user orients in terms of *label* ("what am I looking at?"), *level* ("how deep am I?"), *size of the set* ("how many are there at this level?"), and *set locus* ("where am I at this level?"). CMB represents each of these — for every AST node — using `aria-label`, `aria-level`, `aria-setsize` and `aria-posinset`, respectively.

3.4 Describing Structure

One of the key insights of StructJumper was the recognition that a program can be thought of either as a list of tokens (after lexing) or as a tree structure (after parsing). Their paper demonstrates that visually-impaired programmers benefit from navigating the *structure* of the code, rather than hearing the tokens read aloud. CMB does exactly this.

Consider the following simple program:

```
(define (add a b) (+ a b)
(define (factorial n)
  (if (n < 2) 1 (* n (factorial (- n 1))))
```

A CMB user would see the first function rendered as a block:

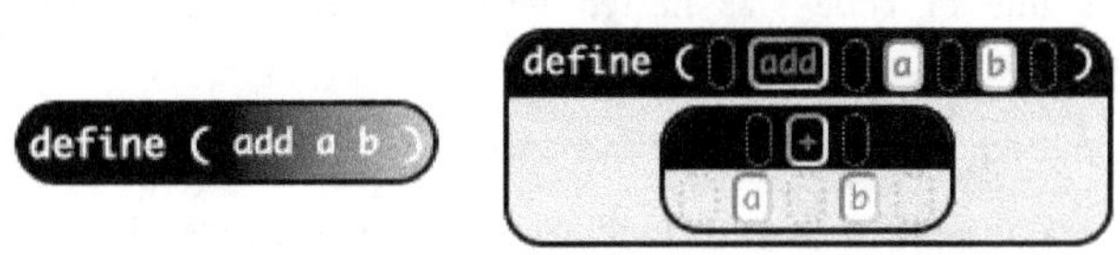

Figure 1 - Function definition block (collapsed and expanded)

When the block is focused, a V.I. user would hear "`add: a function definition with two arguments: a and b. Level 1. 1 of 2.`" Immediately, they are given a useful, descriptive label, the level, the ordinality and the size. Repeatedly hitting `down-arrow` will read the rest of the function, one part at a time:

```
add
two arguments: a and b
a
b
plus expression, two inputs
plus
a
b
```

Alternately, they can *collapse* the function definition (`left-arrow`), and move on to the next top-level expression. `Shift-left-arrow` collapses *all* nodes, allowing the user to quickly skim even very large programs, expanding only the nodes they are interested in.

At any time, the user can also convert a node into its syntax, and navigate it using normal text controls. This dual-syntax functionality allows for a "syntax when you need it, structure when you don't" approach for both sighted and V.I. users. Prior work has shown this modality to be effective [15].

CMB provides search functionality, allowing the user to search for a term and page through all the matches in the document. Instead of jumping from line to line in the document, however, the user jumps from *matching node to matching node*. A sighted user, after jumping to a random cursor location, will quickly scan the adjacent code to see where they are. For a blind user, however, hearing a line and column number is not a useful way to orient. CMB provides a keyboard shortcut that will read the labels of the ancestors of the active node. For example, instead of hearing "line 812, column 9", they hear "`inside multiply expression, 3 inputs; inside if-expression, inside foo: a value definition.`"

3.5 Describing Code

When parsing a program to generate an ASTNode, the parser may also specify a *label* for that node, which is rendered to the DOM using the `aria-label` attribute. This effectively separates the way a node is *written* in the syntax from how it is *described*. Descriptions can be pedagogical in nature ("`foo: a function definition that is public, static and produces a double`"), and can be tailored for age-level or even spoken language ("`foo: una definición de función que es pública, estática y produce un doble`"). There are many interesting implications of this feature, but space limits our ability to discuss it here.

While CMB will automatically provide location information for all nodes in the tree, it is up to the parser to provide good labels for those nodes. In short, any use of CMB is only as good as the parser with which it is used.

3.6 Performance

By relying on CodeMirror, we achieve performance essentially for free: our widgets are only rendered when they are visible. The DOM nodes rendered and tracked are proportional to the size of the *visible content* instead of the size of the program, resulting in limited memory use and computation. Using the Chrome Task Manager, we found that displaying a large program used only 277MB using this approach, and that even-larger programs never used more than 290MB to display.

4 Study Design

To evaluate CMB, thirteen blind programmers completed three tasks using two browser-based environments: CMB as the experiment and a browser `textarea` element as the control. Readers may point out that more sophisticated methods of browser-based text delivery exist (using `contentEditable` on a styled element, for example), but their support for screen-readers is so poor as to be nearly unusable. We wanted to compare our tool to the most accessible web-based option available. After participants had completed the tasks, we asked them questions about their experience.

We are aware of the challenges faced by those looking to generalize from this sample. Similar studies (including StructJumper) with single-digit sample sizes are common in this space, highlighting the urgency of making programming accessible to more users.

4.1 Participants

Using mailing lists, social media posts, and personal contacts, we recruited 13 participants with an offer of a stipend of USD 150 in exchange for two hours of their time. The number of participants compares favorably to the sizes of other similar studies: the SIGCHI paper on StructJumper, for instance, had only seven. In addition, the community of visually-impaired programmers is small — which highlights the need for work like ours.

Of the 13, three were "novice programmers" (1-5 years of experience), seven had "moderate experience" (5-10 years), and three more were "experienced" (10 or more years). One self-reported as being "somewhat comfortable" with screen-readers, and all others as being "very comfortable". 12 participants were totally blind, while one had profound visual impairment.

4.2 Configuration

Following the format of the StructJumper study, we conducted interviews remotely using screen-sharing in Skype to watch and record as the participants worked through the tasks. Participants used either NVDA or JAWS (latest version as of May 2018) with a current version of Chrome (as a preferred platform) or Firefox (as a fallback). Participants used their preferred screen-reader settings for talking speed and verbosity.

Blind programmers are comfortable hearing the syntax of their preferred language(s) spoken aloud, and typically have their speech settings turned up to several hundred words per minute (one of this paper's authors, who is blind, listens at well over 750wpm!). Programmers who can parse Java syntax into ASTs in their heads at hundreds of words per minute will mask the effects of a tool designed to communicate AST information. To mitigate this effect, we specifically chose a language, Racket, with which few of the participants were familiar.

4.3 Procedure

Participants were asked to provide information about their visual impairment, programming experience, and screen reader use before the interviews were conducted. As with StructJumper, the study was divided into three parts:

1. A short "training session" in which participants learned to use CMB.
2. A series of tasks with and without our tool, using two different code bases.
3. A short, post-session interview.

In the training session, participants explored a small, "training" code base and learned the various key commands and shortcuts needed to navigate it. Once they felt familiar with CMB, participants were asked to follow a series of directions to check if they knew each of the key commands. After this period, the experimental portion of the study began.

Participants were given two sample programs (*Space Invaders* and *Aliens vs. Cows*), each of which had similar levels of structural complexity (maximum nesting depth ~10 levels) and length (~250 lines of code). Both programs represent interactive animations, similar to those use in the widely-used Bootstrap:Algebra [8] curriculum, representing a real-world test case for CMB. Both make use of data structures, recursion, multiple function and variable definitions, `switch`-like condition statements and deeply-nested `if`-expressions. Before completing the tasks, users were given up to 15 minutes to familiarize themselves with the program. To minimize interaction effects, we counterbalanced which program was used with which tool, and which code base was encountered first.

After 15 minutes, the participants were given three tasks modeled on those used by Baker, Milne and Ladner [2]. The first two involved navigating the code to answer questions. These questions were non-trivial, requiring substantial program comprehension and testing the capabilities of the tool as a navigation aid. One was designed to be easier if the user relied on search (the *With Search* task), and the other forced the user to manually-scan the entire program (the *Without Search* task). As with Baker et al., our goal was to determine whether search is an effective modality in the context of a structured code-reader. The third task, *Conditions*, asked the user to indicate which conditions would have to be true in order for a particular line of code to execute. In both programs, this line of code was nested within multiple `if`-expressions, buried within a function definition.

The three tasks for *Space Invaders* were:

1. *Locate With Search*: Find the location in the code where a cow is removed from the list of cows.
2. *Locate Without Search*: Find the location in the code where a cow's direction is updated because it hit a wall.
3. *Conditions:* What conditions have to be true in order for the UFO to be moved left?

The three tasks for *Aliens vs Cows* were:

1. *Locate With Search*: Find the location in the code where `ALIEN-SIZE` is used to determine if an alien hits a bullet.
2. *Locate Without Search*: Find the location in the code that is evaluated when the mouse button is down.
3. *Conditions:* In what situation is the input parameter `w` returned unchanged from the mouse-handler?

Participants were timed as they completed each task, and their answers and duration of the task were recorded. Following the StructJumper protocol, the specific timing of each task's start and end were based on the moment the interviewer finished reading the question and the moment the participant stated their answer after looking at the code. Due to timing restrictions, we deviated from the StructJumper study in one significant way: participants were given a limit of 5 minutes to complete each task.

Answers were rating on a scale from 0-3 points. For the *Locate* tasks, 3 points were awarded if they found the precise location of the desired expression, 2 points for finding the location of a similar or related expression, 1 point for a loosely-related section of code, and no points if their answer was unrelated to the desired expression. For the *Conditions* tasks, 3 points were awarded for finding the precise conditions necessary for the desired expression to be evaluated, and a point was subtracted for every extraneous or missing condition (until reaching zero). If a participant did not provide an answer in the allotted time, they received a score of 0.

After completing all three tasks for the first code base, participants were asked to provide three ratings of their experience on the Likert scale established by Baker et al. The difficulty and frustration of task completion were rated 1 (not at all) to 5 (very). How well they knew where they were in the code while completing the tasks were rated 1 (no idea) to 5 (always knew where they were in the code).

Once participants completed all three tasks with one program and rated their experience, participants repeated the process with the second program. If they used CMB for the first program they were given a `textarea` for the second, and vice versa. After completing both sets of tasks and reflections, participants were asked to share their thoughts on the process, both with and without CMB.

4.4 Analysis

StructJumper's use of a desktop environment and the context of a single, fixed language make direct comparisons to CMB impossible. However, the similarities in research question allow us to borrow heavily from their analysis.

The two factors at work in our design are the program participants encountered first (*Aliens v. Cows* and *Space Invaders*) and whether or not they used CMB first. We used a 2x2 mixed factorial design, allowing us to model both within-subject and between subject variables. Participants completed a total of 6 tasks, for a total of 78 tasks completed altogether. When analyzing task completion time, we used a mixed-effects model ANOVA with Tool and Participant as model variables. For the semantically anchored scale, we used the descriptive statistics to identify the impact of the Tool. Differences between groups with and without the tool were assessed for significance using two-tailed t-tests.

5 Evaluation Results

We measured the impact of CMB using multiple dimensions, including time-to-complete, accuracy-of-answer, and the semantically-anchored self-reported scales for perceived difficulty, frustration, and orientation. For participants who did not finish the task in the time allotted, we capped their completion time at 5m and gave them an accuracy score of 0.

While the tool is intended for novice users, the difficulty in recruiting novice V.I. users led to most participants being "expert users" with years of experience reading code-as-text. As such, we might expect to see an *increase* in task time for this population.

While not significant, we found that average task completion time was slightly slower when using CMB, but also more accurate. In addition, participants' perception of task difficulty and sense of frustration when completing the task were all better when using CMB, and their sense of orientation within the code was significantly improved.

5.1 Task Completion Time

Participants were *more successful* completing the tasks in the 5m allotted when using CMB. If participants had not been capped at 5m, the average completion time would be greater for every unfinished task. This impact would be disproportionally greater for tasks done without CMB, of which far more were left unfinished (10) than with CMB (3).

	Without CMB		**With CMB**	
	Mean	***SD***	***Mean***	***SD***
Task 1 - Time	2m29s	2m3s	2m39s	1m44s
Task 2 - Time	1m55s	1m28s	2m27s	1m18s
Task 3 – Time	2m56s	1m20s	2m40s	1m30s
Avg. Time	2m28s	1m38s	2m35s	1m19s

As expected, this population was slightly (though not significantly) slower with CMB than without it. Participants completed the *Locate with Search* an average of 10 seconds slower with CMB, and *Locate without Search* wan average of 32 seconds slower. However, the *Conditions* task – the most cognitively demanding of the three - was actually completed an average of 16 seconds faster with CMB than without it.

5.2 Task Score

	Without CMB		**With CMB**	
	Mean	***SD***	***Mean***	***SD***
Task 1 – Score	2.31	1.11	2.62	0.51
Task 2 – Score	2.39	1.12	2.53	0.88
Task 3 – Score	1.85	1.34	2.23	1.17
Avg. Score	2.18	1.19	2.46	0.88

When using CMB, participants scored higher — and more consistently so — on every task. The largest difference in task score was found on the cognitively-demanding *Conditions* task. When using CMB, 9 (out of 39) tasks lost points due to inaccurate answers, compared to 6 without it. However, CMB resulted in less than one-third the number of incomplete tasks (10) than traditional text (3).

Participants lost points in the *Locate* tasks because they found a related part of the code but not the precise location. These specific mistakes involved participants searching for a particular term, finding it, and then reporting it as the answer without checking to see if this term was being used in the right place.

More participants lost points on the *Conditions* task than any other task. Of the 13 participants in the study, 8 received the full score when using CMB, compared to only 6 without. Of those who lost points but still managed to complete the task, every point lost was due to participants failing to consider the impact of nested `if`-statements.

5.3 Participant Experience

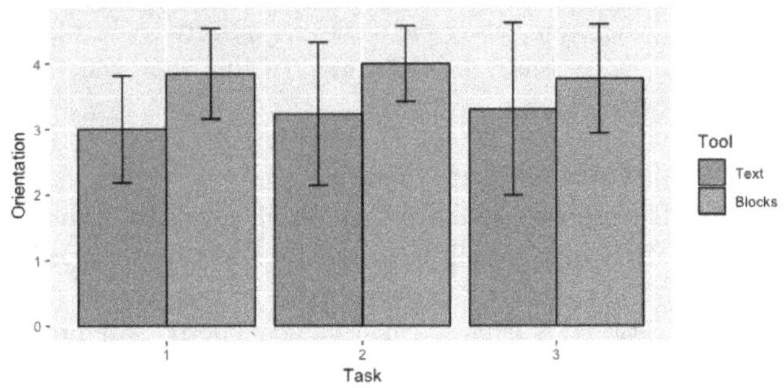

Figure 2 – Orientation was significantly improved

When describing their ability to *orient* themselves while completing the tasks, users felt that CMB was significantly better than reading raw text ($p < 0.005$). Scores of 3 or above were more far more frequent with the tool (38) than without it (29).

	Without CMB		With CMB	
	Mean	***SD***	***Mean***	***SD***
Difficulty	1.34	1.03	1.31	0.98
Frustration	1.31	1.28	0.77	1.09
Orientation**	3.18	1.07	3.85	1.07

Users also reported lower levels of *frustration* when completing tasks - as well as the perception that tasks were less difficult – when using the tool. These differences were not significant.

5.4 Qualitative Results

After completing the tasks, participants were asked a series of open-ended questions about their experiences, to get a sense for what ways (if any) they found the tool helpful, frustrating, or useful. Several common themes emerged.

5.4.1 Orienting Better. Nearly every participant commented that CMB helped them orient themselves when reading code. Some participants attributed this to the fact that browsing with CMB naturally enforced an understanding of structure (“*everything is arranged so you hear the structure just by going to the next node*”). Other participants made ample use of “orientation shortcuts” in CMB, which would read all of the ancestors of a particular node. Several pointed out that “location” in a text editor is often defined in terms of line and column numbers, and said they preferred CMB's orientation within the AST:

“*It's way more useful to hear that what I'm looking at is inside an if-expression, which is inside the definition of the hitting-wall function, rather than just hearing that I'm on line 215.*”

5.4.2 Focus on Structure, not Syntax. Reading the structure of a program is a different task than reading the syntax, and many participants remarked on how freeing it was to be able to focus on the structure: e.g., that “*The TreeView was really nice. I didn't have to think about indentation to form a tree on my own*” or “*I wish I had this tool for when I'm exploring new languages! I liked that it always gave me a consistent view of the code...I'm often a little distracted if I get different indentation, or if there are a lack of spaces I get funny line wrapping with my braille display.*”

This effect may have been enhanced by the fact that virtually none of the participants were familiar with the syntax of the language. One might expect, for example, that the syntax burden would be less of an issue for Java programmers reading Java code; on the other hand, it better reflects the experience of a novice. Indeed, allowing students to focus on structure instead of syntax is one of the goals of block languages like Scratch. Replicating that effect in in a way that is accessible for visually-impaired users is an important goal for this study.

5.4.3 Perceived Speed. Many participants indicated that things “felt faster” when using CMB. In particular, they liked the ability to collapse blocks and “skim”: “*Loved the collapsed-all! Really handy to skip over to skip over stuff I don't care about. Very quickly, I knew that the then clause of the if-expression was something I could skip. Being able to just collapse it was awesome.*”

6 Future Work

While this evaluation focused exclusively on using CMB to *navigate* code, future user studies will focus on the *editing* functionality. And given CMB's ability to let users manage their cognitive load (choosing when to work directly with syntax and when to avoid it), it would be useful to evaluate the tool when examining languages with which the users are already familiar.

The user studies described here also provided extensive feedback about areas for future development. The simple search functionality implemented for this study was clearly a limitation, and multiple users communicated that a more robust search feature would have been helpful when completing these tasks. Additionally, several users asked for a “glances” stack, which would allow them to hit a key and have their current position saved. After further exploration, they could hit a different key a quickly return to the location at the top of the stack.

Finally, it would be valuable to explore the impact of using CMB as an IDE for *sighted* users. Having the computer read a description of a block in an age-appropriate language, or different natural language, could have major implications for all learners – not just those with visual impairments.

ACKNOWLEDGMENTS

We are grateful to AccessCSforAll for their enormous efforts to recruit participants, and to the participants themselves for their time and feedback. We also thank Vint Cerf, the ESA Foundation and the US National Science Foundation for supporting this work.

REFERENCES

[1] World Wide Web Consortium. Accessible Rich Internet Applications (WAI-ARIA) 1.1 W3C Recommendation 14 December 2017. Retrieved August 29th, 2018 from https://www.w3.org/TR/wai-aria-1.1/

[2] Catherine M. Baker., Lauren R. Milne., and Richard E. Ladner. 2015. Structjumper: A Tool to Help Blind Programmers Navigate and Understand the Structure of Code. In *Conference on Human Factors in Computing Systems.*

[3] CodeMirror. Retrieved August 29th, 2018 from https://codemirror.net/

[4] Becky Gibson. 2007. Enabling an Accessible Web 2.0. In International Cross-Disciplinary Conference on Web Accessibility.

[5] Sean Mealin, Emerson Murphy-Hill. 2012. An Exploratory Study of Blind Software Developers. In *Visual Languages and Human-Centric Computing.*

[6] National Federation for the Blind, Retrieved August 29th, 2018 from https://nfb.org/blindness-statistics

[7] Venkatesh Potluri, Priyan Vaithilingam, Suresh Iyengar, Y. Vidya, Manohar Swaminathan, and Gopal Srinivasa. 2018. CodeTalk: Improving Programming Environment Accessibility for Visually Impaired Developers. In *Conference on Human Factors in Computing Systems.*

[8] Emmanuel Schanzer, Kathi Fisler, and Shriram Krishnamurthi. 2018. Assessing Bootstrap: Algebra Students on Scaffolded and Unscaffolded Word Problems. In *Symposium on Computer Science Education.*

[9] Ann C. Smith, Justin S. Cook, Joan M. Francioni, Asif Hossain, Mohd Anwar, and M. Fayezur Rahman. 2003. Nonvisual Tool for Navigating Hierarchical Structures. In *SIGACCESS Accessibility and Computing.* no 77-78, (pp. 133-139). ACM.

[10] Andreas Stefik, Andrew Haywood, Shahzada Mansoor, Brock Dunda, and Daniel Garcia. 2009. "Sodbeans." In *International Conference on Program Comprehension.* pp. 293-294.

[11] Andreas Stefik, Christopher Hundhausen, and Robert Patterson. 2011. An empirical investigation into the design of auditory cues to enhance computer program comprehension. In *International Journal of Human-Computer Studies,* no 69 (pp. 820-838).

[12] Andreas Stefik,, Susanna Siebert, Melissa Stefik, and Kim Slattery. 2011. An empirical comparison of the accuracy rates of novices using the Quorum, Perl, and Randomo programming languages. In Workshop on Evaluation and Usability of Programming Languages and Tools (pp. 3-8).

[13] Wilson, C. (2014). Hour of Code: We can solve the diversity problem in computer science. ACM Inroads, 5(4), 22-22.

[14] Anja Thieme, Cecily Morrison, Nicolas Villar, Martin Grayson, and Siân Lindley. 2017. Enabling Collaboration in Learning Computer Programing Inclusive of Children with Vision Impairments. In Proceedings of the 2017 Conference on Designing Interactive Systems (DIS '17). ACM, 739-752.

[15] Weintrop, D., & Holbert, N. (2017). From Blocks to Text and Back: Programming Patterns in a Dual-Modality Environment. In Proceedings of the 2017 ACM SIGCSE Technical Symposium on Computer Science Education (pp. 633-638). New York, NY, USA: ACM.

From Clusters to Content: Using Code Clustering for Course Improvement

David A. Joyner
College of Computing
Georgia Institute of Technology
Atlanta, GA USA
david.joyner@gatech.edu

Ryan Arrison
College of Computing
Georgia Institute of Technology
Atlanta, GA USA
rarrison@gatech.edu

Mehnaz Ruksana
College of Computing
Georgia Institute of Technology
Atlanta, GA USA
mehnazruksana@gatech.edu

Evi Salguero
College of Computing
Georgia Institute of Technology
Atlanta, GA USA
esalguero3@gatech.edu

Zida Wang
College of Computing
Georgia Institute of Technology
Atlanta, GA USA
zwang795@gatech.edu

Ben Wellington
College of Computing
Georgia Institute of Technology
Atlanta, GA USA
bwellington3@gatech.edu

Kevin Yin
College of Computing
Georgia Institute of Technology
Atlanta, GA USA
kyi@gatech.edu

ABSTRACT

Large undergraduate CS courses receive thousands of code submissions per term. To help make sense of the large quantities of submissions, projects have emerged to dynamically cluster student submissions by approach for writing scalable feedback, tailoring hints, and conducting research. However, relatively little attention has been paid to the value of these tools for informing revision to core course materials and delivery methods. In this work, we applied one such technology—Sense, the eponymous product of its company—to an online CS1 class delivered simultaneously for credit to on-campus students and for free to MOOC students. Using Sense, we clustered student submissions to around 70 problems used throughout the course. In this work, we discuss the value of such clustering, the surprising trends we discovered through this process, and the changes made or planned to the course based on the results. We also discuss broader ideas on injecting clustering results into course design.

SIGCSE '19, February 27-March 2, 2019, Minneapolis, MN, USA

ACM 978-1-4503-5890-3/19/02...$15.00
https://doi.org/10.1145/3287324.3287459

ACM Reference format
David A. Joyner, Ryan Arrison, Mehnaz Ruksana, Evi Salguero, Zida Wang, Ben Wellington, and Kevin Yin. 2019. From Clusters to Content: Using Code Clustering for Course Improvement. In *Proceedings of 50th ACM Technical Symposium on Computer Science Education (SIGCSE '19), February 27-March 2, 2019, Minneapolis, MN, USA.* ACM, New York, NY, USA, 7 pages. https://doi.org/10.1145/3287324.3287459

1 Introduction

One characteristic of large computer science courses is the presence of numerous different solutions to coding problems posed on homework assignments and tests. These solutions exist at an interesting intersection of more mathematical problems and more freeform problems: like mathematical problems, there exist objective criteria for correctness, but like essays or short-answers, there is a nearly infinite number of ways to approach the problems correctly. Many of these different approaches may have superficial differences like differing variable names, but deeper similarity in their underlying structure and behavior [9].

CS educators need to be able to understand the breadth of student answers to inform their own teaching and to deliver appropriate feedback to the right students. However, manually coding student submissions for the type of approach taken is an arduous process, and the work involved grows linearly with scale. Efforts in other areas have been made to cluster student solutions for more efficient feedback and evaluation [1][15][22], but CS education has a unique opportunity due to the simulatability and underlying objective similarity between students' answers.

To address this, multiple initiatives have arisen to perform this processing automatically (e.g. [5]). Most prior research, however, has focused on the mechanics of these systems rather than their use as a tool for researching patterns of student submissions and using those patterns to inform content revisions, tailored feedback, or new initiatives. In this research, we put one such system—Sense, the eponymous name of the company that developed it—to work in an online CS1 class. We begin by giving a brief background of the course in which the tool is used, and then provide a deeper look at some of the results that were uncovered through this analysis. We do not claim that these results reflect general trends in CS1 as we can only generalize to our instruction and delivery style, but rather they are emblematic of the kinds of analysis and results that can be generated using clustering tools such as Sense. Then, we discuss the immediate revisions made and planned for the course based on these results, as well as some more ambitious proposals for integrating content clustering more directly into the student-facing course experience. This analysis and results together demonstrate the potential power of using code clustering tools for course content improvement.

2 Related Work

Significant work has been performed on clustering student responses based on similarity, both in computer science education and in education more broadly. Tools like GradeScope [22], Powergrading [1], and Mathematical Language Processing [13] address this issue in short answer or open math problems by first clustering student submissions together, then mapping those to tailored feedback. GradeScope in particular uses these clusters for emergent rubrics where instructors can modify point deductions for individual errors and have those modifications propagate to all student assignments present in similar clusters. More commonly, work has also been done for constructing expert systems with in-built knowledge of common error types [10][11].

More specifically within computer science education, OverCode [5] and other tools [18][19] address the same need by clustering and visualizing student responses to coding problems. Other work has been performed to generate formative feedback for students based on error models [11][12][24], match prewritten code feedback to new submissions [7][14][17], or identify the differences between new submissions and working submissions for tailored feedback [6][16][21][25][26][27].

Similar work has been done with different goals as well. Much of the early work on clustering student code submissions used abstract syntax trees to evaluate the likelihood that code plagiarism had taken place [20], a technique that has since been extended to educational environments [2][8].

Notably, however, despite the massive number of initiatives in this area, the significant focus has been on delivering individual feedback to the student. While this is without question a valuable goal, it is not the only relevant application of these technologies. Rather than relying on the system to deliver content feedback directly to students, it is also possible that systems like these could instead give instructors information about student patterns of interaction to be used in modifying the content itself.

3 Course Background

This analysis took place as part of the delivery of an online CS1 class. The class is simultaneously offered as a for-credit class at a major public research university in the United States and as a set of Massive Open Online Courses (MOOCs) to the public on the edX platform. Since its inception in January 2017, 785 students have taken the class for credit, and nearly 1,673 have completed a public offering of the course as a MOOC. The class teaches Python 3 and presupposes no prior CS knowledge; it is intended as the first class that new CS majors take and also fulfills the CS requirement for all majors at the university.

The analysis here more narrowly targeted for-credit students' responses from two consecutive semesters (approximately 350 total students) as the goal was to specifically revise the course content for the patterns present among these for-credit students.

As part of the course experience, students complete approximately 350 programming problems. These problems come in three forms: exercises, which are interspersed between short video lectures; problems, which are collected into problem sets at the end of each course chapter; and tests, which are delivered as part of timed and digitally proctored assessments. In all three types of problems, students use a web-based programming interface that generates immediate feedback and evaluation on the correctness of their responses. A limited hint generation system is built in based on an expert system monitoring for the occurrence of certain code or output errors, but most evaluation takes place based on a comparison of student code output to the output of a correct answer to the same prompt.

4 Clustering Results

For this analysis, we used Sense to cluster student responses to every problem on each of six of the course's problem sets. Each problem set is topic-specific: these six sets covered functions, error handling, strings, lists, file I/O, and dictionaries. Prior to these problem sets, students learn loops, conditionals, and operators, and so those concepts exist in their responses to these questions as well. It is important to note that the goal of this work is not to demonstrate a list of common errors and misconceptions in CS1 in general, but rather to show how clustering analyses can be used to uncover such patterns within specific courses with minimal effort.

4.1 Clustering Example: The Rainfall Problem

The sections below cover the high-level trends uncovered in each problem set, but to understand these results, it is useful to first look more deeply at the analysis of a single problem. One problem outside these problem sets that we evaluated was a variation on the famous [4] Rainfall problem [23], which was offered during the third timed and proctored test in the course. Due to technical constraints, rather than have students repeatedly get another piece of user input, our variation supplied students with a list of observed rainfall values as integers, into which -1 was inserted somewhere after the first digit. Students were asked to average and return all integers before -1. Most students answered the problem correctly (184 out of 190 who attempted it in one semester), although we questioned whether the modifications made to read from a list instead of from user input fundamentally changed the difficulty of the problem.

To answer this question, we uploaded student submissions to Sense. We found first of all that the vast majority of students opted to use a for loop: only 4% of all student submissions used a while loop, which is the method that would more similarly match the traditional framing of the Rainfall problem. 67% of the submissions used a for loop, but broke the loop (either by calling `break` or by returning from within the loop) once it encountered a -1. So, while only 4% of students used a loop definition that would work for the traditional rainfall problem, 71% had a loop body that would generally work for the traditional problem.

Among the remaining 29% of responses, we observed some additional interesting variation. 8% of submissions first modified the list to remove all values after -1, either with the `del` command or by slicing the list until the first instance of -1, found through use of the `list.find()` or `list.index()` methods. They then averaged the remaining list, some with a for loop and some by calling `sum(list)/len(list)`. Interestingly, the `sum` function is not covered in the course material. An additional 8% of students took a similar approach, but without using the `find()` or `index()` method. They initially looped over the list to find the index of -1, then either sliced the list or looped over the list again until that index. While not common, this reflected to us the need to reemphasize list slicing and indexing, which previously had been relegated primarily to a callback to the chapter on strings.

Among the remaining 13% of responses, some entirely unique observations were observed; some were particularly sophisticated, while some were particularly suboptimal. On the sophisticated side, one student wrote two functions: one to average any list, and one to call that function on the list sliced up until the index of -1; another student completed the problem in a single line. These sophisticated responses were fruitful to share with students as exemplary answers. On the suboptimal side, one student generated an entirely new list and added values to it until -1 was reached; another student used nested for-loops to re-find the index of -1 for every value in the list.

This analysis was performed for every one of the 70 problems across the six problem sets. The sections below summarize the interesting trends observed across the problems that we analyzed.

4.2 Functions

The 11th chapter of the course covered functions. For this chapter, the problem set contained twelve problems. Evaluating these problems, we discovered three primary trends.

First, we found that most students' submissions contain some unnecessary structural component, such as an else statement in which nothing really happens like adding zero to a count. For example, one problem asked students to check whether or not a string contained a series of three sevens. We found that 7% of students created an else block in which they either added zero to their count or used the keyword continue. This also occurred in another problem which asked students to find the average word length from a string. 26% of students used pass or "reassigned" a variable without changing its value, or added zero to their count.

Second, we found that when using a formula, students often do their calculations in one or two long lines rather than breaking it up into parts. For example, one problem asked students to calculate the damage a Pokemon would face based on various parameters such as type and level. In this problem, though a lengthy formula was involved, only 27% of students broke their calculations into several parts. Another problem asked students to determine whether a given year was a leap year. We found that 17% of students did their calculations all in one line.

Third, we found that students would sometimes use brute force rather than built in functions or functions of their own. For example, one problem asked the students to make a countdown given the range of numbers. Instead of using Python's range function and a loop, 11% of students manually printed each number in the countdown. In another problem, students were asked to find the average word length given a string. This problem required the students to make three functions, one for word count, one for letter count, and one for average word length. To calculate letter count, students could use their word count function since this accounts for the number of characters that are not letters (spaces) but only 5% did while others recalculated the number of spaces.

4.3 Error Handling

The 12th chapter of the course covered error handling. For this chapter, the problem set contained eight coding problems. Evaluating these problems, we found two primary trends.

The first trend is that as exercises rose in complexity, students demonstrated a stronger tendency to store the result of an expression into a variable prior to printing it, even if printing it was the only remaining task to be performed with the result of the expression. One early problem asked students to attempt up to three calculations, the first two of which could cause an error. 48% of students printed the expressions' results directly, while 43% attempted the expression, stored its result in a variable, and then printed it if an error had not arisen.

Two problems later, students were asked to find pressure given other values using the expression PV = nRT. Here, 71% of students stored the result of an expression in a variable, then later returned it. Only 22% returned the result directly, even though this approach led to fewer lines of code and a more straightforward algorithm.

Secondly, in this chapter, students were able to individually formulate their own algorithms and approaches to more challenging coding prompts. In one later problem, students were asked to write a word count function that could correctly ignore consecutive spaces. 42% of students used a "forward-checking" algorithm, where when encountering a space, the function would check the next character in the string before incrementing the word count. 18% instead implemented a "backwards-check" algorithm with a boolean variable that tracked whether the previous character was a space. The following problem expanded on this prompt and saw even more significant differentiation: 57 clusters of unique solutions were observed in the next problem, which removed the assumption that the string would start with a word and required students to take special steps in the event of strings with all punctuation marks or no characters.

4.4 Strings

The 14th chapter of the course covers strings, including indexing, splicing, and their context as a data structure. This chapter included a total of fourteen coding problems, the first eight intended for all students and the last six handling more advanced concepts. Two of the most prominent patterns included the use of the `.find()` method as opposed to a range for-loop and a common tendency for the `len()` function to cause an index error, and misunderstanding the difference between strings and lists of strings.

First, as students gain more and more experience using Python and for-loops, they ought to realize that using `for i in range()` is advantageous because each iteration grants both the index and the piece of data through indexing brackets. However, many students in this chapter opted to use a for-each loop on their strings, utilizing the `.find()` method to retrieve the index of their values. This approach is suboptimal, however: even when it works, it is more complex and computationally intensive, and it also fails whenever the string has the same character multiple times.

Second, it is common in Python to use the length of a string as a parameter in the `range()` function, such as `for i in range(len(string))`. In this case, the range begins at zero and ends with `len(string)-1`, as upper bounds are exclusive. However, that upper bound is invisible to students; thus, when they attempt to use the upper bound outside of a loop, they tend to use `len(string)`. When Python encounters this, it will throw an index error because the loop tries to iterate past the length of the string.

Third, the chapter teaches students the `split()` method, which splits a string into a list of strings; however, students do not cover lists until the next chapter. Thus, there are several instances where students treat the output of splitting a string as a string itself, such as trying to call `upper()` on the entire list.

4.5 Lists

The 15th chapter of the course introduced the topic of lists in Python. For this chapter, the problem set contained seven coding problems and four advanced coding problems. Evaluating these problems, we discovered three primary trends.

The first major trend is that students very much preferred to use if statements vs if-else statements. In one question, students were asked to find names that appeared in one list but not another. Most (78%) students created an empty list, then ran a for loop through the first list of names with a nested if-conditional that checked if the name in the first list was not in second. If that was true, they append that name to the empty list, and return that list at the end of the function. A smaller subset of students (10%) used the same process, with the exception being the nested if-conditional. They instead used an if-else conditional, where the if-statement determined if the name on the first list was in the second list. If it was, then pass; else, append that name to the empty list. This method was far less common and the code was longer than it could be, but it remained valid. Notably, this countered an earlier trend where students included structurally unnecessary elements in their code; it appears that as the course moves on, students develop more of a comfort with this abbreviated representation and fewer include unnecessary components. Similarly, in another question, students were asked to write a function that takes in a list of integers and to find the average of all the integers greater than 100. The most common method (63%) was to create a variable and a counter both equal to zero, then loop through the list. A nested if-conditional would then check if the integer was greater than 100. If it was, then it was added to the sum and 1 was added to the counter; at the end, the average was returned. As before, there was a small group of students (21%) who used an `else` as well, typically with `pass` or `continue` as the only body of the else block.

The second trend is that students tended to understand, and even over-rely, on some list functions like indexing, appending, sorting, and iteration. In one problem, students were asked to find the movie with the highest sales from a list of tuples, each of which contained the movie title and the total ticket sales. Most students (51%) used a for loop to implement a typical linear search, looping through each tuple and analyzing the second index of the tuple. From there they found the maximum sale and returned the movie name. A smaller but significant group of students (19%) created an empty list, added all the sales to the new list, and then used the `sort()` method or `max()` function to get the highest gross. They then used another linear search to find which movie corresponded to that sale. In another question, students were given a list that contained integers and asked to find if three sevens in a row appeared. The largest group of students (34%) looped through the list by position, which allowed them to check the value at the corresponding index in the list and the following two values. However, the next largest group instead used a more complex reasoning structure to count the number of consecutive 7s encountered so far and reset it when a non-7 digit was encountered. This mirrored the preference for using for loops without the range function noted in the analysis of strings. Still others, interestingly, joined the list into a string and searched for "777" or took other more innovative approaches.

The third trend is that students struggled to use efficient code, particularly regarding the return in functions. In one question, students were asked to define a function which took two parameters, a list of answers, and a list of the answer key, and to compare the answers to the key. However, there was the possibility that the answer list and the key list were of different lengths; students were instructed to return -1 in that instance. Students did so correctly, but many set a variable equal to -1 then returned the variable, mirroring in part the pbservation earlier regarding a reluctance of some students to return an expression's result directly. Others even defined a variable equal to the string "-1", then converted the string to integer, then returned the integer. In another question, students were asked to write a function that found a triangle's hypotenuse and angle based on three parameters, the opposite and adjacent lengths of the triangle and a boolean that determined whether to use degrees or radians. Many students did so efficiently, but some took a longer approach, where they would set variables equal to what they wanted to return, then returned those variables.

4.6 File Input/Output

The 16th chapter of the course covered File Input and Output. For this chapter, the problem set contained ten problems. Evaluating these problems, we discovered two interesting trends.

First, while the course material covers a few different ways to read files, students appear to prefer to iterate over the open file. On a problem that requires students to simply read lines from a file and store them as tuples, 63% chose to use `for line in file` instead of methods like `read()` and `readlines()`. While there is nothing inherently wrong with that approach for this problem, it is somewhat more limiting in what can be done with it, and this limiting factor is seen arising in later problems where students need to re-read the file more than once. Upon reaching these problems, most students stick to this approach even though it demands more convoluted logic, like closing and reopening the file.

Second, regarding closing files, most students closed files at the end of the function rather than as soon as file-reading had completed. One problem, for example, had 82% of students closing a file as the last line of code, even though they only used the file at the very beginning of the code. For many of these students, closing the file actually took place *after* the return statement, meaning that the file was never actually closed.

4.7 Dictionaries

The 17th chapter of the course covered dictionaries. This chapter had twelve coding problems and three advanced coding problems in the problem set. Three trends stuck out to us in this chapter: the use of for loops and nested for loops in place of populating a dictionary more directly, the use of lists to avoid using dictionaries directly, and the use of try and except.

While most students took understandable approaches, the first trend we observed was that a non-trivial number of students took one of several approaches that effectively bypassed using dictionaries as they were constructed to be used. For example, one problem asked students to write a function to take a string and return an integer:list dictionary, where the keys were word lengths and the values were lists of words with the corresponding length. Some students took approaches like iterating through the keys to find the right key before appending to the list rather than just looking up the key directly.

Second, some students—presumably more comfortable working with lists from the previous chapter—unpacked dictionaries into lists for processing. These students appeared to believe that dictionaries were effectively two disjoined lists rather than understanding that keys actually point to values in the dictionary. These students thus did not grasp that an easier way to populate a dictionary would have been to use the key to modify the values, and instead they would create a list and then use indexing to make a key variable. Often, they would then use a two-dimensional list and nested for loops for the values.

Third, we found an interesting carry over from the chapter on error handling. On the one hand, we found a non-trivial number of students who, rather than handling edge cases deliberately, assumed the code would operate correctly and caught errors if they arose. This reflected a mature understanding of the role error handling could play. However, another non-trivial set of students appeared to use try and except blocks more haphazardly. These students included error-handling code that did not actually react to errors; they also wrapped try blocks around code that would not generate errors in the context of the problem. Still others used no error handling code and were forced to handle potential problems more deliberately by, for example, preemptively checking if values were the right types for subsequent operations.

5 Content Modifications

As noted above, most prior research using tools like Sense has focused on delivering students individualized feedback based on their answer patterns. This is a highly desirable goal and not in conflict with our approach; however, we also note that by delivering this feedback only to students who commit the error, we risk excluding students who possess the underlying misconception but never demonstrate it in their work. For example, we noted above that in the chapter on functions, many students have an unnecessary structural component of their code, like a statement merely saying `else: pass`. This suggests either a misconception that every `if` must have an `else`, or an undesirable stylistic preference to have an `else` for every `if`. To resolve this, we authored additional content deliberately exploring whether an `else` is required for every `if`, in order to ensure that a correct understanding is reinforced for every student.

A number of similar modifications have either been made or are planned for the near future based specifically on the outcomes of this analysis. These include:

- Authoring exercises on the readability of long formulas.
- Authoring exercises reinforcing the ability and desirability of returning the results of simple expressions directly.
- Authoring additional content regarding available functions like `range` and `sum`, and embedded reminders on appropriate times to use these functions.
- Authoring additional instructional material on the situations under which using `string.find()` or `string.index()` will fail, and alternatives to avoid needing those method calls in the first place.
- Moving content requiring students to process the result of calling `string.split()` into the chapter on lists.

- Revising the autograder to more intelligently assess whether a file has been closed.
- Authoring additional content regarding the scope of file reading and the benefits of closing a file as soon as its contents have been read into the program.
- Author additional content regarding the scope of variables in a function, specifically targeting inadvertently accessing variables from outside the function rather than the function's own parameters.
- Authoring additional content regarding the usefulness of dictionaries rather than just syntax for using dictionaries.
- Authoring content guiding students on how to understand whether error handling code is necessary rather than merely the structure of error handling code.

6 Conclusion

Significant work has been done, both in CS education and in education more broadly, on clustering student answers to support individualized feedback. However, most of this research has stopped there in its application of these clustering techniques. Once clustered, however, there are significant additional improvements that can be made to course content based on the knowledge gained from this analysis.

In this work, we have demonstrated one such approach to using the results of a sophisticated code-clustering algorithm to inform the revision of the course content itself. We uploaded over 14,000 student code submissions to the clustering system spanning 70 different exercises. We then used the results to inform general revisions to the content to specifically target the common misconceptions and errors observed in the results of that analysis.

We do not claim that this approach is generally superior or preferable to using clustering for tailored feedback, but we do argue that using clustering to inform more broad content revision has additional benefits. Modifying the course content itself removes the reliance that every student demonstrates every misconception they hold in their work. Tailored feedback is excellent for giving individualized and just-in-time correction, but it may miss students who for one reason or another never demonstrate the need for that correction. Revising the material more broadly targets them as well, and it reinforces the correct conception among students who may not have misconceptions but are not firm in their correct conceptions.

We have not performed a systematic analysis of the change in student behavior based on these changes, but anecdotally we have noticed significant changes. One prominent change occurred in response to new content targeting variable scope and functions: we noted a significant drop in the number of questions from students who did not realize that their functions were looking at variables defined outside the function rather than variables passed in through the parameter list. This reflected to us the value in targeting content specifically to the misconceptions and errors observed through clustering analyses like these.

6.1 Limitations

The results from our specific analyses listed in this research likely are not generalizable out to other classes as well. Student patterns in our class are driven by our own instructional material, and different approaches will lead to different patterns. This research is a demonstration of the use of code clustering in rather than a list of common errors and misconceptions in CS1.

That said, the technology used in these analyses may be used for research on common errors. If a shared set of problems is distributed and used across multiple classes, then a clustering analysis may identify what errors are specific to individual instructional styles and what errors are more inherent to the content. Such a shared corpus of exercises would be valuable in assessing what is inherently difficult about programming.

6.2 Future Work

Others have looked at using clustering for tailoring feedback or detecting plagiarism, and we have looked at using clustering for revising content. There are significant other potential applications of submission clustering that we plan to explore as well. First, this clustering may also serve as a valuable research tool, both for broader CS education research and in evaluating other improvements made to the class. The changes documented here targeted specific desired changes in the patterns of students' answers on the problem sets. Follow-up analyses of future semesters' submissions may allow us to establish the effectiveness of those changes.

Second, on our preliminary research, we have observed that there are some clusters of students that appear to group together across multiple assignments. This is unsurprising on those problems where the majority of students tend to take the same approach, but it is curious to note instances where the same small group of students takes the same unorthodox approach across multiple exercises. Are they a study group who happens to arrive at the same ideas together? Are they a group of people with a particular background that causes them to favor some answers over others? Are they a circle of people copying answers from one another? The usage of clustering to track groups of people across problems has significant potential.

Third, clustering may also be used to foster greater social connectedness in a class, an approach that could be particularly relevant for students in an asynchronous online class or MOOC. For example, one can imagine that upon submitting an answer, a clustering system finds the similar answers from previous submissions and alerts the student, "Your approach to the problem is similar to 72% of prior individuals! Would you like to see some of the approaches the other 28% take?" In addition to some of the benefits of tailoring the selection of alternate examples to the individual's own approach, this may also help the student contextualize their own meta-knowledge and establish if they are adopting common behaviors.

REFERENCES

[1] Sumit Basu, Chuck Jacobs & Lucy Vanderwende (2013). Powergrading: a clustering approach to amplify human effort for short answer grading. *Transactions of the Association for Computational Linguistics, 1*, 391-402.

[2] Sébastien Combéfis & Arnaud Schils (2016, November). Automatic programming error class identification with code plagiarism-based clustering. In *Proceedings of the 2nd International Code Hunt Workshop on Educational Software Engineering*, 1-6. ACM.

[3] Molly Q. Feldman, Ji Yong Cho, Monica Ong, Sumit Gulwani, Zoran Popović, and Erik Andersen. Automatic Diagnosis of Students' Misconceptions in K-8 Mathematics. In *Proceedings of the 2018 CHI Conference on Human Factors in Computing Systems*, 264. ACM.

[4] Kathi Fisler. (2014, July). The recurring rainfall problem. In *Proceedings of the Tenth Annual Conference on International Computing Education Research*, 35-42. ACM.

[5] Elena L. Glassman, Jeremy Scott, Rishabh Singh, Philip J. Guo, and Robert C. Miller. (2015). OverCode: Visualizing variation in student solutions to programming problems at scale. ACM Transactions on Computer-Human Interaction (TOCHI), 22(2), 7.

[6] Sumit Gulwani, Ivan Radiček, and Florian Zuleger. (2018, June). Automated clustering and program repair for introductory programming assignments. In Proceedings of the 39th ACM SIGPLAN Conference on Programming Language Design and Implementation (pp. 465-480). ACM.

[7] Andrew Head, Elena Glassman, Gustavo Soares, Ryo Suzuki, Lucas Figueredo, Loris D'Antoni, and Björn Hartmann. (2017, April). Writing reusable code feedback at scale with mixed-initiative program synthesis. In *Proceedings of the Fourth (2017) ACM Conference on Learning @ Scale*, 89-98. ACM.

[8] David Hovemeyer, Arto Hellas, Andrew Petersen, and Jaime Spacco. (2016, August). Control-flow-only abstract syntax trees for analyzing students' programming progress. In *Proceedings of the 2016 ACM Conference on International Computing Education Research*, 63-72. ACM.

[9] Jonathan Huang, Chris Piech, Andy Nguyen, and Leonidas Guibas. (2013, June). Syntactic and functional variability of a million code submissions in a machine learning MOOC. In *AIED 2013 Workshops Proceedings Volume*, 25.

[10] Magdalena Jankowska, Colin Conrad, Jabez Harris, and Vlado Keselj. (2018). N-Gram Based Approach for Automatic Prediction of Essay Rubric Marks. In *Advances in Artificial Intelligence: 31st Canadian Conference on Artificial Intelligence, Canadian AI 2018, Toronto, ON, Canada, May 8–11, 2018, Proceedings 31*, 298-303. Springer International Publishing.

[11] David A. Joyner. (2018, June). Intelligent Evaluation and Feedback in Support of a Credit-Bearing MOOC. In *Proceedings of the 19th International Conference on Artificial Intelligence in Education*, 166-170. Springer, Cham.

[12] Shalini Kaleeswaran, Anirudh Santhiar, Aditya Kanade, and Sumit Gulwani. (2016, November). Semi-supervised verified feedback generation. In *Proceedings of the 2016 24th ACM SIGSOFT International Symposium on Foundations of Software Engineering*, 739-750. ACM.

[13] Andrew S. Lan, Divyanshu Vats, Andrew E. Waters, and Richard G. Baraniuk. (2015, March). Mathematical language processing: Automatic grading and feedback for open response mathematical questions. In *Proceedings of the Second (2015) ACM Conference on Learning @ Scale*, 167-176. ACM.

[14] Victor J. Marin, Tobin Pereira, Srinivas Sridharan, and Carlos R. Rivero. (2017, April). Automated personalized feedback in introductory Java programming MOOCs. In *Proceedings of the 2017 IEEE 33rd International Conference on Data Engineering (ICDE)*, 1259-1270. IEEE.

[15] Agathe Merceron and Kalina Yacef. (2005). Clustering students to help evaluate learning. In *Technology Enhanced Learning*, 31-42. Springer, Boston, MA.

[16] Andy Nguyen, Christopher Piech, Jonathan Huang, and Leonidas Guibas. (2014, April). Codewebs: scalable homework search for massive open online programming courses. In *Proceedings of the 23rd International Conference on World Wide Web*, 491-502. ACM.

[17] Sagar Parihar, Ziyaan Dadachanji, Praveen Kumar Singh, Rajdeep Das, Amey Karkare, and Arnab Bhattacharya. (2017, June). Automatic grading and feedback using program repair for introductory programming courses. In *Proceedings of the 2017 ACM Conference on Innovation and Technology in Computer Science Education*, 92-97. ACM.

[18] Ronen Tal-Botzer (2018). U.S. Patent Application No. 15/549,179.

[19] Lina F. Rosales-Castro, Laura A. Chaparro-Gutiérrez, Andrés F. Cruz-Salinas, Felipe Restrepo-Calle, Jorge Camargo, and Fabio A. González. (2016, November). An Interactive Tool to Support Student Assessment in Programming Assignments. In *Ibero-American Conference on Artificial Intelligence*, 404-414. Springer, Cham.

[20] Saul Schleimer, Daniel S. Wilkerson, and Alex Aiken. (2003, June). Winnowing: local algorithms for document fingerprinting. In *Proceedings of the 2003 ACM SIGMOD international conference on Management of Data*, 76-85. ACM.

[21] Saksham Sharma, Pallav Agarwal, Parv Mor, and Amey Karkare. (2018, June). TipsC: tips and corrections for programming MOOCs. In *Proceedings of the 19th International Conference on Artificial Intelligence in Education*, 322-326. Springer, Cham.

[22] Arjun Singh, Sergey Karayev, Kevin Gutowski, and Pieter Abbeel. (2017, April). Gradescope: a fast, flexible, and fair system for scalable assessment of handwritten work. In *Proceedings of the Fourth (2017) ACM Conference on Learning @ Scale*, 81-88. ACM.

[23] Eliot Soloway. (1986). Learning to program = learning to construct mechanisms and explanations. *Communications of the ACM, 29*(9), 850-858.

[24] Kristin Stephens-Martinez, An Ju, Krishna Parashar, Regina Ongowarsito, Nikunj Jain, Sreesha Venkat, and Armando Fox. (2017, August). Taking Advantage of Scale by Analyzing Frequent Constructed-Response, Code Tracing Wrong Answers. In *Proceedings of the 2017 ACM Conference on International Computing Education Research*, 56-64. ACM.

[25] Ryo Suzuki, Gustavo Soares, Andrew Head, Elena Glassman, Ruan Reis, Melina Mongiovi, Loris D'Antoni, and Bjoern Hartmann. (2017, October). TraceDiff: Debugging unexpected code behavior using trace divergences. In *2017 IEEE Symposium on Visual Languages and Human-Centric Computing (VL/HCC)*, 107-115. IEEE.

[26] Ke Wang, Rishabh Singh, and Zhendong Su. (2018, June). Search, align, and repair: data-driven feedback generation for introductory programming exercises. In *Proceedings of the 39th ACM SIGPLAN Conference on Programming Language Design and Implementation*, 481-495. ACM.

[27] Jooyong Yi, Umair Z. Ahmed, Amey Karkare, Shin Hwei Tan, and Abhik Roychoudhury. (2017, August). A feasibility study of using automated program repair for introductory programming assignments. In *Proceedings of the 2017 11th Joint Meeting on Foundations of Software Engineering*, 740-751. ACM.

Applying Machine Learning to Improve Curriculum Design

Robert Ball, Linda Duhadway, Kyle Feuz, Joshua Jensen, Brian Rague and Drew Weidman
School of Computing, Weber State University, Ogden, Utah USA
{robertball, lindaduhadway, kylefeuz, joshuajensen1, brague, dweidman}@weber.edu

ABSTRACT

Creating curriculum with an ever-changing student body is difficult. Faculty members in a given department will have different perspectives on the composition and academic needs of the student body based on their personal instructional experiences. We present an approach to curriculum development that is designed to be objective by performing a comprehensive analysis of the preparation of declared majors in Computer Science (CS) BS programs at two universities. Our strategy for improving curriculum is twofold. First, we analyze the characteristics and academic needs of the student body by using a statistical, machine learning approach, which involves examining institutional data and understanding what factors specifically affect graduation. Second, we use the results of the analysis as the basis for applying necessary changes to the curriculum in order to maximize graduation rates. To validate our approach, we analyzed two four-year open enrollment universities, which share many trends that help or hinder students' progress toward graduating. Finally, we describe proposed changes to both curriculum and faculty mindsets that are a result of our findings. Although the specifics of this study are applied only to CS majors, we believe that the methods outlined in this paper can be applied to any curriculum regardless of the major.

CCS CONCEPTS

• Computer Science Education • Computational Science and Engineering Education

KEYWORDS: curriculum, machine learning, objective reasoning

ACM Reference format:
Robert Ball, Linda Duhadway, Kyle Feuz, Joshua Jensen, Brian Rague and Drew Weidman. 2019. Applying Machine Learning to Improve Curriculum Design. In *Proceedings of SIGCSE '19: The 50th ACM Technical Symp. on Computing Science Education Proceedings (SIGCSE'19).* ACM, Minneapolis, MN, USA. ACM. NY, NY, 7 pages. https://doi.org/10.1145/3287324.3287430

1. Introduction

When discussing curriculum design, faculty may be inordinately influenced by personal experience and anecdotal evidence.

ACM ISBN 978-1-4503-5890-3/19/02...$15.00
https://doi.org/10.1145/3287324.3287430

The specific academic scenarios of a few students may drive curriculum discussion in a direction in which statistics and facts about actual student performance are dismissed or ignored. Under these conditions, disagreements among faculty about which curriculum best serves the students are likely to emerge. What courses should be taught? How should these courses be sequenced? Beyond the basic requirements for ABET accreditation, what should be done to help students graduate?

This paper presents a more objective approach to refining curriculum in order to meet student needs. We recognize there are both similarities and differences among institutions, computer science (CS) programs, and the students enrolled in those programs. For the purpose of this paper we define curriculum to be the courses offered in a department, the content taught in these courses, the sequence of courses a student takes to graduate, and the instructional modality (e.g. online, traditional lecture, hybrid, etc.).

Our approach to improving curriculum is twofold. First, we analyze the characteristics and academic needs of the student body by using an objective, statistical, machine learning approach, which involves examining institutional data and understanding what factors specifically affect graduation. Second, we use the results of the analysis as the basis for applying necessary changes to the curriculum in order to maximize graduation rates.

For this analysis we specifically investigated only academic, age, and gender factors while purposely leaving out financial, marital, race, and social factors. While there are many important socioeconomic and personal factors that affect graduation (see Related Works), for this study we address only those academic factors that were readily and reliably accessible across all students. Many social factors such as pregnancy, marital status, etc. impact only some members of the student community during their academic careers while certain academic factors, such as a student's level of mathematical competence, can be consistently monitored over time for all students.

In this study we examined every course undergraduate CS majors attended during a twelve-year interval at two institutions with similar Carnegie classification profiles (Master's University; very high undergraduate; open enrollment). We analyzed our own institution's student transcript data then proceeded to identify a similar institution to determine if the trends we discovered were unique to our particular program. We found similar trends at both institutions. A total of 4,266 anonymized individual transcripts were analyzed for graduation factors from the two institutions. Transcripts were acquired only for those students who declared a CS major between 2005 – 2017 and enrolled in at least one CS course during that time period. Student course grades were not a transcript selection criterion.

The overarching question driving this study is the following: *What curriculum changes can faculty implement to help our students graduate?*

Our answer is to first understand the factors that influence student success, at which point we can then create the courses needed to help them succeed. For example, if most students struggle with math then what can faculty do to mitigate that hurdle? Our approach was to first systematically discover that such a problem exists before trying to fix it. As part of the context of this study, we also recognized that students have multiple paths available to earn the same degree and come from many academic backgrounds and as such there is no one particular path of courses that exactly maps to all students. Although the specifics of this study are applied only to CS majors, we believe that the methods outlined in this paper may be applied to any curriculum regardless of the major.

In this paper we present related work, describe statistical trends that may or may not lead to graduation, show important academic weaknesses by leveraging Machine Learning (ML) algorithms, and explain how there is no effective "one size fits all" curriculum. Finally, we detail our curriculum plans resulting from this analysis and relate these findings to the work of other researchers.

2. Related Work

The subject of institutional retention of students has been heavily studied. Many of these studies have focused primarily on the retention rate of the entire institution [4, 5, 8, 14]. Considering that many sources of governmental funding for institutions are driven by factors such as retention and student graduation rates, the abundance of studies on the topic is not a surprise.

According to the National Center for Education Statistics, open enrollment institutions have a retention rate of approximately 59% and among those who matriculate at these institutions only about 32% end up graduating within 6-years of their first institutional attendance (NCES, 2018). Studies have shown that there are many factors that may contribute to the remaining 68% of students who do not complete their degree within the 6-year timeframe, such as student-faculty relationships, institutional support services (e.g. student counseling and advisement), students developing a sense of belonging to the institution, and pre-college preparation.

Quantitative factors that affect graduation include cumulative GPA, first-semester GPA, race, and income [2, 5, 6, 11, 15, 16]. While the aforementioned studies focused on students starting and finishing at a single institution, Jones-White conducted a study of students at the University of Minnesota-Twin Cities utilizing data from the National Student Clearinghouse that considered all the institutions a student engaged with while earning a degree. They found that the factors previously discovered generally held true, even if a student transferred to different institutions to complete a degree [7].

Taken as a whole, these previous studies demonstrate the complexity of the problem facing higher education when addressing graduation rates. An information-driven approach to this issue will increase the likelihood of success. One such study was conducted at Harvey Mudd College to determine strategies to increase the recruitment and success of female CS students [1]. This study carefully considered and applied the qualitative factors previously described, encouraging social interaction among female students even before they arrived on campus for their first semester. Examples included offering students the opportunity to attend the Grace Hopper Celebration of Women in Computing and grouping students into CS1 course sections based on prior CS experience. The results of those efforts continue to validate the factors found in the studies discussed.

3. General Approach

In trying to understand student performance trends and likelihood of graduation we used two main approaches. The first approach is top-down involving creativity, insight, data visualization, and statistical inference. We classified the students into different academic categories. For example, we found that students who had taken dual or concurrent enrollment (CE) courses in high school (courses that counted towards both high school and college credit) had higher GPA's than most students that did not take CE courses. However, these same CE students often transferred to more selective institutions.

The second approach is bottom-up, identifying factors about each student from their transcripts (e.g. age, gender, concurrent enrollment credit) and entering these data into Machine Learning (ML) algorithms. We employed ML algorithms for two purposes: (1) to determine what factors were the most important in predicting graduation; and (2) to verify ML algorithm accuracy. Verification of the ML algorithms involved comparison with a baseline majority class algorithm and three-fold cross validation to determine how well the ML algorithms understood the student population and trends.

4. Statistics (Top-Down) Approach

Our first approach of evaluating the student populations from the two institutions is called Exploratory Data Analysis. The general approach is to use statistics, visualization, creativity, and intuition in order to gain insight into the data. Although each institution is different and thus might reflect unique student performance trends when compared with other institutions, the conclusions from studies such as Jones-White indicate that we should in fact expect very similar trends among open enrollment institutions. Consequently, although we began our analysis with only data from our own institution (University *Anonymous1*), interest in comparing data across institutions prompted the subsequent acquisition of anonymized transcripts from University *Anonymous2* for the same twelve-year period of time. (Internal Review Board (IRB) approval from both institutions was secured, and student identities were kept confidential.)

Although we found many unique and interesting trends that affect only our respective institutions, the most important trends that likely generalize to other institutions can be found in Table 1. Dual or concurrent enrollment (CE) courses are courses that students took in high school that also count for University credit. Advanced Placement (AP) is similar to CE but is based on taking a third-party exam to determine qualification for university credit. Math course category counts indicate the *first* math course students enrolled in at any institution of higher education and thus takes into account math courses transferred from other institutions. We define *Developmental Math* as any math course before college algebra. *Introductory Math* is any math course that includes college algebra up to any other math course before the calculus level. *Advanced Math* is calculus level and above. For instance, if a student is in the *Advanced Math* category then the first math course taken by the student at any university is calculus or higher. On the other hand, if the student is in the *Developmental Math* category then their first math course at the university was a math course at a level lower than College Algebra.

Transfer Credit means that the student took a course at another institution and transferred it to their current institution for credit. For example, CS 101 was taken elsewhere, but articulates and transfers with credit to our institution. *Transfer Credit w/o CS* means that the student transferred credit, but no CS courses. *CS Transfer Credit* means that at least one CS course was transferred. *Traditional Student* classifies a student who (a) is less than 20-years-old, (b) did not enroll in any concurrent courses, (c) did not receive AP credit, and (d) did not transfer any credits from another institution.

Table 1. Results from both institutions (number of students).

	total	GPA	average age	% female	% graduated in CS
All students:	4266	2.86	26.37	8.27%	22%
Concurrent credit	991	2.94	22.2	8.68%	22%
Advanced Placement (AP)	387	3.10	23.11	8.79%	35%
Math					
Developmental	656	2.29	26.98	9.76%	10%
Introductory	1988	2.71	24.82	7.65%	27%
Advanced	1023	3.09	26.92	6.55%	55%
Age					
< 20 years old	676	2.42	18.28	10.36%	15%
20 - 24 years old	1403	2.71	22.06	6.77%	29%
>= 25 years old	1918	2.88	32.57	8.97%	31%
Developmental math	656	2.29	26.98	9.76%	10%
Non-Developmental math	3610	2.92	26.26	8.01%	28%
Developmental English	300	2.20	27.32	8.33%	14%
Non-Developmental English	3966	2.82	26.3	8.27%	33%
Transfer Credit					
Transfer credit w/o CS	2336	2.85	27.49	8.69%	25%
CS transfer credit	998	2.91	28.93	6.71%	43%
No transfer credit	2336	2.55	27.49	8.69%	21%
Traditional Students:	148	2.28	18.31	5.41%	11%

Table 1 reveals the general trends for the different groups. We specifically show how GPA, age, gender, and graduation rate vary among the different groups. For example, the *Advanced Math* group showed the highest graduation rate (40.86%) followed by the *CS Transfer Credit* group (36.17%). In contrast, *Developmental Math* students were the least likely to graduate (9.3%). Although the graduation rate of the *Advanced Placement* group (30.49%) is relatively high, it is interesting to note this group of students were more likely to leave the open enrollment institutions examined in this study to go to more selective institutions.

Performing a one-way ANOVA on the GPA's of the different groups, we obtain statistical significance with f=123.73 p<0.01. Figure 1 shows the various GPA's of the different groups. The vertical bars show the standard error of each GPA. If the standard error bars cross then there is not statistical significance between them, otherwise there is statistical significance. For example, the *Advanced Math* and *Advanced Placement* groups overlap showing that there is not statistical significance between their GPA's, but they both have statistical significantly higher GPA's than all the other groups.

Performing a one-way ANOVA on the graduation rates of the different groups, we get the following: f=105.03 p<0.01. Figure 2 shows the various graduation rates of the different groups. Similar to Figure 1, the vertical bars show the standard error of each group.

Before comparing Figure 1 to Figure 2, the reader might expect that a high GPA would necessarily imply a high graduation rate. However, upon careful inspection of these figures, one can see that the trend of higher GPA does not always correlate with higher graduation rates in Computer Science for a given student category.

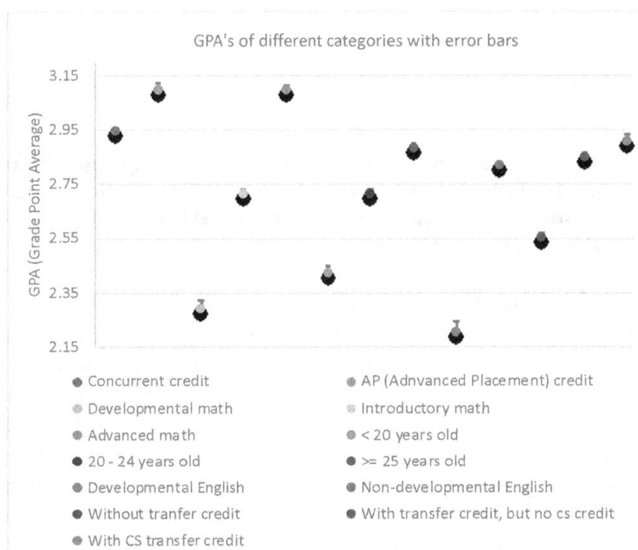

Figure 1. The average GPA's of the groups from Table 1. The legend reads from left to right. Non-overlapping standard error bars signify statistical significance between groups.

For example, the GPA of *Advanced Placement* students and students that started in *Advanced Math* is similar. However, the AP students graduate far less than the *Advanced Math* group. Why? It appears that *Advanced Placement* students and *Concurrent Credit* students may view the open enrollment institutions examined in this study as a launching pad to transfer to other, more selective universities. It is highly likely that many of these students eventually graduate, but not with their original institutions.

Another example, in this instance involving transfer credit, shows that the *CS Transfer Credit* group in Figure 1 has a slightly higher GPA compared to the *Transfer Credit w/o CS* group, but only slightly (2.9 to 2.8 respectively). However, for graduation rates, the *CS Transfer Credit* group has approximately double the graduation rate (24.6% to 11.5% respectively). In this example, it appears prior exposure to CS increases the chances of earning the degree. There are admittedly many different ways to think about and categorize students based on the data. However, the best categories are clearly those that identify features and characteristics that support and improve student graduation rates.

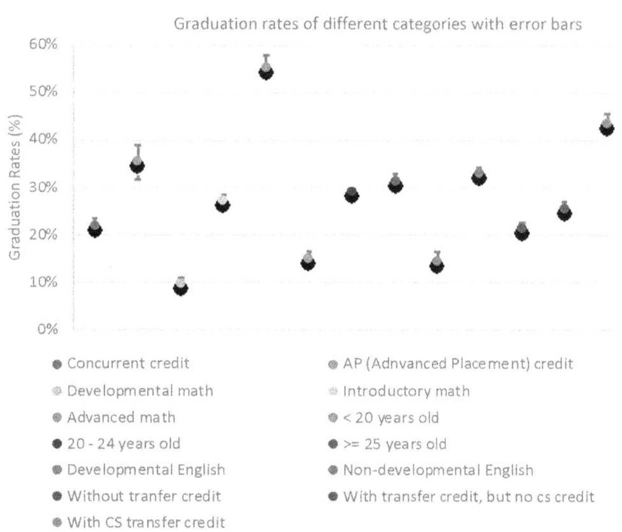

Figure 2. The average graduation rates of the groups from Table 1. The legend reads from left to right. Non-overlapping standard error bars signify statistical significance between groups.

5. Machine Learning (Bottom-Up) Approach

In contrast to the statistical approach, in which the researcher is responsible for identifying meaningful categories to perform the analysis on the student data, our machine learning approach lets the data speak for itself. In supervised machine learning the goal of the learning algorithm is to learn a mapping from a feature space X (e.g. age, gender, etc.) to a label space Y (e.g. graduation rate) [10]. In our scenario the features are extracted from the student transcripts and the label space is the binary output of whether the student graduated from the institution with a BS degree in CS.

From the student transcripts we extract the following features:

- Age (when taking their first CS program class at a university)
- Gender
- First English course
- First Math course
- International status
- Advanced Placement credit
- Transfer credit
- CS Transfer credit
- Concurrent credit
- GPA (either overall or at a particular semester)

All of above features are binary values except for Age, First English course, First Math course, and GPA. We use a one-hot encoding to convert first English course into two binary features (Developmental English and Introductory English). Similarly, First Math course is converted to three binary features (Developmental Math, Introductory Math, Advanced Math). Age and GPA are both scaled to the range [0,1] using a non-linear quantile transformation such that each feature's probability distribution function is mapped to a uniform distribution. This technique is robust to outliers so that the scale remains consistent with and without the outliers present.

The first objective of our machine learning approach is to quantify the effect each individual feature has on graduation. To do this we chose learning algorithms that allow this influence to be assessed. Decision trees are one good choice because each node in the tree uses exactly one feature to determine which branch to take next. This leads to the Gini importance factor [3] which is a measure of the importance of each feature in the overall tree.

Logistic regression is another algorithm that allows direct measuring of the effect that each feature has on the overall decision of the learning algorithm. In logistic regression, a coefficient is learned for each feature which determines how much the given feature affects the predicted value. The magnitude of the value of the coefficient is an indication of how important the feature is in determining the class label. The sign of the coefficient is an indication of whether the feature leads to the positive or negative class (graduate vs non-graduate). This coefficient is equivalent to the log-odds ratio [13].

We are specifically interested in determining which features best lead to graduation and which do not. In addition, we look at how those features change as the student progresses through the current curriculum. Do certain factors become more or less important over time in predicting graduation? Does the accuracy of the prediction improve the further a student progresses in the program?

To accomplish this objective, we look at the graduation outcomes of students enrolled in four specific courses in the program typically taken in the following sequence: CS 1, CS 2, Data Structures and Algorithms, and Operating Systems. All the extracted features remain the same during this analysis except for overall GPA. Overall GPA is replaced by the semester GPA at the time the specified course was completed.

Table 3 shows which features are influential on the Decision Tree (GR) and Logistic regression (OR) models. The relative importance of each feature at the point of each course are shown with the smaller number being more important and the higher numbers being less important. The omission of data for the Operating System course is addressed later in Section 5. Unremarkably, GPA is the most important feature for all courses across both models. In other words, the higher the GPA of the student, the more likely they graduated.

Table 3. Ranking of feature importance at different points in a student's curriculum progression. GR is a ranking based on the Gini Importance factor extracted from the decision tree model. OR is a ranking based on the log-odds ratio extracted from the Logistic Regression model. * indicates the feature is correlated with the negative class (non-graduate) in the Logistic Regression model. 'DSA' = 'Data Structures and Algorithms.'

	Overall		CS 1		CS 2		CS DSA	
Feature	GR	OR	GR	OR	GR	OR	GR	OR
Age	3	7	4	7	4	13	4	9
Gender	7	12	8	11	8	8	8	10
Dev_Engl	7	4	8	13	8	9	10	4
Intro_Engl	4	2	8	5	8	5	5	5
Dev_Math	7	9	7	8	8	7	10	11
Intro_Math	6	11	3	3	3	3	9	8
Adv_Math	2	3	2	2	2	2	2	2
Intnl	7	8	8	4	8	11	7	7
AP	7	6	5	6	5	4	6	3
Transfer (any credit)	7	13	8	12	7	12	10	13
CS Transfer	5	5	8	10	8	10	10	11
Concurrent	7	10	6	9	6	6	3	6
GPA	1	1	1	1	1	1	1	1

There are several similar outcomes from the two models. Both ML algorithms rank GPA and Advanced Math high (with Intro English being high for overall courses) while ranking gender, international status, and non-CS transfer credit low. Since GPA as well as English and Math class enrollments are gender-neutral measures, these rankings indicate that when examining measures of academic preparation alone (social factors notwithstanding), females are as likely to succeed in CS programs as their male counterparts, which validates the work by Alvarado and Dodds [1].

In table 3, the rank listed for Age indicates relatively high significance for the Gini importance factor (GR) when compared to the log-odds ratio (OR). This is likely because the effect of age is non-linear: as age increases graduation rates increase up to a certain point after which the graduation rate again decreases. The decision tree can account for this by splitting age at different points. However, Logistic Regression is forced to treat age linearly which leads to age having less influence on the predicted graduation.

The log-odds ratio rankings listed in table 3 indicate that AP and concurrent credit are both the only consistently negative predictors of graduation. This is consistent with what we deduced in Section 4 where students start at one institution in question but soon transfer to other (usually more selective) institutions to finish their degree.

The second objective of the machine learning approach is to predict which students will graduate from the institution with a BS degree in Computer Science. This objective encompasses two sub-goals: (1) to validate that the results in Table 3 are better than a baseline guess and (2) to further understand how the ML algorithms can be used for understanding the student population as they progress through the program.

Table 4. Classification Accuracy at different points in a student's curriculum progression. Each number is a percentage of accuracy. 100 would indicate perfect prediction and 0 would indicate no success at all in prediction. The bold numbers show the highest prediction rate per course.

	DT	LR	Ada	RF	MC
All	71.29	70.53	**72.69**	68.75	62.07
CS1	66.45	65.83	**66.72**	61.61	63.15
CS2	61.38	**63.87**	63.31	58.55	56.19
DSA	63.20	**64.56**	64.15	57.00	56.59
OS	75.11	76.65	**76.93**	68.08	75.46

We compare four different machine learning (ML) algorithms: Decision Tree (DT), Logistic Regression (LR), AdaBoost DT ensemble (Ada), and Random Forest (RF) [12]. We also compare against the baseline accuracy of choosing the majority class (MC). The MC algorithm simply chooses what most students do. For example, if 75% of the students do not graduate then the MC algorithm chooses 'not graduate' for every student and is, therefore, correct 75% of the time. If any given ML algorithm does not perform significantly better than the baseline MC algorithm then we conclude that the ML algorithm in that case is not effective. In addition, we use three-fold cross validation where the data is randomly split into three chunks - two chunks are used for training and the third chunk is used for testing. This training and testing process is applied a total of three times - once for each of the three chunks - and then the results are averaged. In other words, we made sure that we were predicting on data randomly ordered so that we did not bias our results.

Table 4 shows the classification accuracy for the different ML algorithms for each course compared to the baseline majority class (MC) algorithm. For example, for all courses in the dataset (first row in Table 4) the AdaBoost DT ensemble (Ada) algorithm had the best accuracy (72.69%), a 10.62% improvement over the MC baseline algorithm. There is a general improvement in predicting graduation rates from CS 1 to Data Structures and Algorithms (DSA) when compared to the MC baseline. For CS 1 there is a 3.57% improvement over the MC baseline, for CS 2 there is a 7.68% improvement, and for DSA there is a 7.97% improvement.

The astute reader may have noticed that data for the Operating System (OS) course is not shown in Table 3. It is because there is a noticeable lack of improvement between any of the classification algorithms and choosing the MC baseline for the OS course with only a 1.47% improvement. In other words, the ML algorithms are not significantly better than the baseline algorithms at predicting graduation for students in the OS course. As a result, no feature rankings were shown for the OS course in Table 3 because they would not have been valid.

These results indicate that the features extracted from the student transcript help predict which students will successfully complete the program early in a student's curriculum progression but may be less helpful by the time a student is taking upper-division courses. We suspect that if a student reaches the upper-division courses life events and circumstances not captured by a student transcript have a more significant effect on graduation than those features captured on the student's transcripts.

6. From Study to Practice

Unsurprisingly, the biggest issue regarding student graduation success appears to be academic preparation. However, the results from this study suggest a double-edged sword: if the student is underprepared, then they are less likely to graduate, but if they are over-prepared then they are more likely to transfer to a more selective institution. What makes a student 'unprepared'? We found that starting in developmental Math and English courses has a negative effect on a student's prospects for graduation. Unprepared students also have a lower GPA, which is a secondary measure of their success rate at a university. The unprepared students start off with lower GPA's than their prepared counterparts, potentially activating a downward spiral. These students begin with developmental Math and/or developmental English and end up not doing well in those courses. They may then proceed to CS1 and obtain marginally passing grades. If they continue with the program then their GPA is biased low, which becomes a fundamental indicator of their lack of success.

On the other hand, there are two main types of 'prepared' students: those students with higher GPA's that begin the program in Advanced Math and those students who earn high school credit (concurrent and AP students). The first group does well and demonstrates the highest graduation rates while the student with high school credit often transfers to other institutions. Identifying these student academic groupings is just the first step. Once the factors have been identified that contribute to or detract from graduation success we have the difficult task of effectively managing and modifying our curriculum to match our student's needs. Advocating general university policies, such as more choices for day care for older students with young children, is beyond the scope of this paper. However, there are many things that institutions can do to help different social groups succeed.

The study at Harvey Mudd College cited in Section 2 shows that changing curriculum to increase the percentage of women in CS1 can be effective [1]. Based on our analysis, we now plan to offer specific sections of CS1 to address the needs of beginning CS students who have had little or no background in programming or software design and will most likely have attended classes in developmental Math and/or developmental English. Another potential change involves offering math courses oriented to CS majors. For example, many universities across the US offer Business Calculus or Engineering Calculus. These courses are specifically designed to meet the needs of those majors, typically eschewing the proof-heavy traditional mathematics approach. Our analysis also indicates that many of our students who take Developmental Math fail to graduate in CS. Developmental Math courses designed specifically for CS majors may help these students acquire the requisite mathematical skillsets that will increase the likelihood of success in subsequent CS classes. On the other end of the student preparation spectrum, we also plan to offer CS honors-track courses targeting those students that have Advanced Placement (AP) or concurrent credit. The course content and activities in these honors-track classes will offer an academic challenge to these students in order to increase retention and reduce the number of transfers to other institutions.

To support student advising and manage the various pathways available to students as they navigate the CS program, we plan to introduce a survey website that will direct students toward the appropriate sections/courses based on their prior classes and past academic experiences. Although having many different sections of introductory courses customized to student needs may appear daunting, the results from Section 5 show that the influence of academic preparation on graduation diminishes as students progress to upper division courses. In other words, the beginning courses help all students reach a minimal level of competence that allows them to succeed in later courses. Thus, our results suggest that having multiple sections or sequences of courses later in the curriculum is not necessary to ensure student success. Lastly, since age is such a strong factor as indicated by one of the ML algorithms, what can a department do to support the scholastic needs of both older and younger students, and how do these needs differ? We have experienced success with night courses, similar to courses offered during the day, but allowing working adults the option and convenience to continue their education.

7. Conclusion

Anecdotal, emotional accounts of the experiences of a few students should not be the driving factor in curriculum development. We advocate an objective, comprehensive study of the overall student body. By looking at the data highlighting the factors that contribute to or detract from graduation success, a department can provide their students the individual attention that they need. Using statistics and machine learning algorithms, decisions can be made about curriculum modifications that will improve student success. Since starting this study, faculty discussions regarding curriculum have been less emotionally-charged and faculty as a whole have applied their logical minds towards solving curriculum issues, generating a more positive feeling about program design.

This paper centers on two important components of curriculum development. First, we have discovered a number of trends related to student graduation rates that should hold across open enrollment institutions nationwide. Such trends show that students whose first courses in Math and/or English are developmental experience a detrimental effect on their prospects for graduation, but that students who have obtained high school credit, such as concurrent credit or AP credit, often find the introductory courses not sufficiently challenging and transfer to more selective institutions.

We have identified many different characteristics about students and how these features impact their graduation. Understanding an individual student's academic background and guiding that student to an appropriate set of courses (e.g. developmental courses for CS majors, calculus for engineers, introductory computer science courses, etc.) tailored to their individual needs is a much more effective strategy when compared to a one-size-fits all approach.

Second, the related works section clearly illustrates that predicting graduation is a multi-dimensional problem that is difficult to quantify. Social issues, race, gender, financial aid, etc. are all factors to consider when trying to understand graduation rates.

However, by objectively looking at the data for a particular institution, one can use statistics and Machine Learning (ML) algorithms to determine the factors in a student's academic pathway that significantly influence successful degree completion.

8. REFERENCES

[1] Alvarado, C., & Dodds, Z. (2010). Women in CS: an evaluation of three promising practices. Proceedings of the 41st ACM tech. symposium on CS education, (pp. 57-61).

[2] Attewell, P., Heil, S., & Reisel, L. (2011). Competing explanations of undergraduate noncompletion. American Educational Research Journal, 48, 536-559.

[3] Breiman, L. (2001). Random forests. Machine learning, 45, 5-32.

[4] Crosling, G., Heagney, M., Thomas, L., & others. (2009). Improving student retention in higher education: Improving teaching and learning. Australian Universities' Review, 51, 9.

[5] Delen, D. (2010). A comparative analysis of machine learning techniques for student retention management. Decision Support Systems, 49, 498-506.

[6] Ishitani, T. T. (2006). Studying attrition and degree completion behavior among first-generation college students in the United States. The Journal of Higher Education, 77, 861-885.

[7] Jones-White, D. R., Radcliffe, P. M., Huesman, R. L., & Kellogg, J. P. (2010). Redefining student success: Applying different multinomial regression techniques for the study of student graduation across institutions of higher education. Research in Higher Education, 51, 154-174.

[8] Lykourentzou, I., Giannoukos, I., Nikolopoulos, V., Mpardis, G., & Loumos, V. (2009). Dropout prediction in e-learning courses through the combination of machine learning techniques. Computers & Education, 53, 950-965.

[9] McFarland, J., Hussar, B., Brey, C., Snyder, T., Wang, X., Wilkinson-Flicker, S., . . . others. (2017). The Condition of Education 2017. NCES 2017-144.

[10] Mitchell, T. M. (1997). Machine Learning (1 ed.). New York, NY, USA: McGraw-Hill, Inc.

[11] O'Keeffe, P. (2013). A sense of belonging: Improving student retention. College Student Journal, 47, 605-613.

[12] Pedregosa, F., Varoquaux, G., Gramfort, A., Michel, V., Thirion, B., Grisel, O., . . . Duchesnay, E. (2011). Scikit-learn: Machine Learning in Python. Journal of Machine Learning Research, 12, 2825-2830.

[13] Peng, C.-Y. J., Lee, K. L., & Ingersoll, G. M. (2002). An Introduction to Logistic Regression Analysis and Reporting. The Journal of Educational Research, 96, 3-14.

[14] Porter, K. B. (2008). Current trends in student retention: A literature review. Teaching and Learning in Nursing, 3, 3-5.

[15] Rogulkin, D. (2011). Predicting 6-Year Graduation and High-Achieving and At-Risk Students. Online Submission.

[16] Warburton, E. C., Bugarin, R., & Nunez, A.-M. (2011). Bridging the Gap: Academic Preparation and Postsecondary Success of First-Generation Students. Statistical Analysis Report. Postsecondary Education Descriptive Analysis Reports.

The Relationship between Prerequisite Proficiency and Student Performance in an Upper-Division Computing Course

Sander Valstar, William G. Griswold, Leo Porter
University of California, San Diego
{avalstar,wgg,leporter}@eng.ucsd.edu

ABSTRACT

While it is widely believed that taking a class's prerequisites is critical for success, less is known about how proficiency with the prerequisite knowledge from those courses affects performance in later courses. Specifically, it is unclear how well students understand material from prerequisite courses and whether that understanding may impact their outcomes in the subsequent course. Additionally, in subsequent courses, do students strengthen their knowledge from prerequisite courses and, if they do, does that improvement matter for the subsequent course? This study examines the prerequisite knowledge of 208 students in an upper-division data structures class at a large North American research university. Prerequisite proficiency on entry to the course was surprisingly low, with nearly a third of students demonstrating low proficiency and only a quarter high proficiency. Students modestly improved their proficiency during the term, lifting a third of those with low proficiency to at least medium proficiency. Overall, final exam performance was significantly correlated with prerequisite knowledge. For those with low initial proficiency, improvement in proficiency was significantly correlated with performance on the final. These results suggest that more attention needs to be placed on reinforcing prerequisite knowledge for those with low proficiency.

KEYWORDS

Prerequisites, data structures, student performance

ACM Reference Format:

Sander Valstar, William G. Griswold, Leo Porter. 2019. The Relationship between Prerequisite Proficiency and Student Performance in an Upper-Division Computing Course. In *Proceedings of the 50th ACM Technical Symposium on Computer Science Education (SIGCSE '19), February 27-March 2, 2019, Minneapolis, MN, USA.* ACM, New York, NY, USA, 7 pages. https://doi.org/10.1145/3287324.3287419

1 INTRODUCTION

Although prerequisites have been shown to be valuable for student outcomes outside computing [9, 18], their value has not been empirically studied in computing. Studying the importance of prerequisite success takes on greater meaning in light of institutional pressure to reduce failure rates, as well as recent discussions about reducing prerequisites to speed time to degree [19].

SIGCSE '19, February 27-March 2, 2019, Minneapolis, MN, USA

ACM ISBN 978-1-4503-5890-3/19/02...$15.00
https://doi.org/10.1145/3287324.3287419

Many instructors have a story about the student who somehow enrolled in their course without a required prerequisite, suffering dire consequences. But what happens when a student has taken the prerequisite and just did poorly in that class—does low prerequisite knowledge relate to poor performance, and if so, to what extent? What percentage of students enter courses with insufficient proficiency of required prerequisites? Do students improve on their deficiencies in prerequisite knowledge during the course?

To answer these questions, we measured the prerequisite knowledge of 208 students in an upper-division data structures class through a pre- and post- survey. From these results, we examined changes in proficiency over the term, correlated pre-term and post-term proficiency with the students' final exam scores, and analyzed which prerequisite content was most salient for student success.

We expected that proficiency with prerequisite knowledge would be generally high as the prerequisites for this course are reported to be rigorous and demanding. Yet we also had concerns that the very low rates of D's and F's (< 7% *combined*) in the prerequisites could mean that some instructors were giving passing grades to students who are not truly prepared for the next step. Other possible factors include fading knowledge for those not taking these courses back-to-back [3] and cheating in prerequisite courses [11, 15].

The results were both sobering and encouraging. Prerequisite proficiency on entry to the course was far lower than anticipated. We classified student prerequisite proficiency as low (under half of the questions correct), medium (50-70%), or high (over 70%). Nearly a third of students (29%) demonstrated low proficiency and only 27% demonstrated high proficiency. On the other hand, students improved their proficiency over the term, by 8 percentage points on average, with a number of low-proficiency students improving to at least medium proficiency by the time of the final.

Not entirely surprising is our finding that final exam performance is correlated with prerequisite proficiency, 0.366 (Pearson correlation coefficient) for the pre-term test, 0.384 for the post-term test, and 0.434 for the two taken together. Improvement in prerequisite proficiency during the term mattered: for students demonstrating low proficiency on the pre-term prerequisite test, their improvement on the post-term test was correlated (0.371) to their performance on the final. All of these correlations were statistically significant. Not all prerequisite knowledge was found to be equally important, however, nor was proficiency uniform over the subject matter. For example, a student's ability to perform a basic runtime analysis was the strongest predictor of performance on the final. We discuss which topics were of most importance in detail.

Taken together, these results show the importance of proficiency with prerequisite knowledge for future performance in computing, and highlight the possible benefits of putting more attention on the reinforcement of prerequisite knowledge.

2 BACKGROUND

Course prerequisites are commonly used in curricula to ensure students have the necessary prerequisite knowledge to succeed in subsequent courses. In computing, course prerequisites are described in the ACM curricula recommendations CS 2013 [12]. Prerequisites can play a variety of roles in the curriculum, including ensuring students have the proper background knowledge or sufficient maturity, that they display a certain degree of commitment to a program, or to convey program requirements [19]. In particular, the role of mathematics and introductory computing prerequisites have been well discussed [19]. There is pressure, however, to reduce the depth of prerequisite chains to aid with students' time to degree [19]. In view of these discussions, the role prerequisite proficiency plays in student success in computing courses deserves further study.

Outside computing, Martin found that grades in prerequisite courses, specifically statistics and mathematics, correlated with student performance in an agriculture price analysis course [9]. Expanding on the work of Martin in agriculture, Vitale et al. found that cumulative GPA and grades in prerequisite courses predict student grades in a Farm and Agribusiness Management course [18].

In computing, direct connections between prerequisite course grades or knowledge from prerequisite classes has not been similarly established. However, there has been substantial work examining a myriad of factors that determine students success in introductory programming courses. These factors include prior knowledge, gender, motivation, self-efficacy, and achievement goals [8, 13, 21, 23]. Although each of these factors have shown promise, Wilson et al. recently cautioned that these relationships may not always replicate [20], which has led to large replication efforts [22]. Our work expands on our understanding in computing by establishing a direct relationship between prerequisite course knowledge and success in upper-division computing courses.

The study most closely related to ours is that of Muralidharan et al. [10]. Muralidharan et al. examined student performance in Hindi and mathematics with 8th grade students in India, finding that a surprising majority of students are lacking prerequisite knowledge from prior grade levels. Their study goes on to show that an intervention program targeting prerequisite knowledge can significantly improve outcomes. In our study, we similarly examine student prerequisite knowledge entering an Advanced Data Structures course, finding that incoming students demonstrate a wide range of proficiency and that improvement in prerequisite proficiency during the course is correlated with improved final scores.

3 RESEARCH QUESTIONS

Our study has five primary research questions:

- RQ1. Are most students arriving with sufficient prerequisite knowledge to start subsequent courses?
- RQ2. Do students, particularly those with low preparedness, improve their proficiency in prerequisite content as they progress through subsequent courses?
- RQ3. Does incoming prerequisite proficiency impact final exam scores?
- RQ4. If there is a relationship between incoming prerequisite proficiency and final exam scores, which prerequisites are most meaningful?
- RQ5. Does improvement in prerequisite proficiency translate to improved final exam scores?

4 STUDY DESIGN

To understand the influence of prerequisite proficiency on final exam performance we chose to study an instance of the course "Advanced Data Structures" (ADS), an early upper-division course in our CS program. This is an excellent candidate for our study because it has a wide range of prerequisites including software, theory, and hardware. As we were interested in actual proficiency at the time of taking the course, not just performance in the prerequisite courses, we tested proficiency at the beginning and the end of the term. Our study has institutional Human Subjects approval.

4.1 Course Context

The ADS course we studied was taught at a large North American research university on the quarter system. This 10-week course is designed for CS majors and minors, and is one of the gateway classes to other advanced courses in the major. The goal of the class is for students to learn how to program and analyze high-performance data structures. The data structures studied include trees, hash tables, Huffmann coding, and graphs. Related topics include memory management, pointers, and recursion. Assignments are programmed in C++. The course has three principal prerequisites, all lower-division courses: introductory data structures (CS2), advanced discrete math, and computer organization.

4.2 Data Collection

In order to be able to study the relative levels of prerequisite proficiency we needed a tool to broadly examine the prerequisite knowledge of the students in this class. We chose to test the prerequisite knowledge of students by means of two surveys. In a pre-study for the present study, we ran the surveys online. However, we found a significant mismatch between student correctness in the online survey versus questions which were subsequently given in class. This suggested that students collaborated or used outside aids while completing the survey online. So, for this study, we performed the data collection with an in-class survey, on paper. The first survey was taken during the first day of class and the second survey was taken during the last week of class, before the final exam. Both surveys consisted of 15 multiple-choice questions and students were given 20 minutes for each survey. This format was chosen to balance the needs of data capture with the time taken away from the class lecture time.

4.3 Survey Content

The following courses are prerequisites for majors for the upper-division data structures class at our institution:

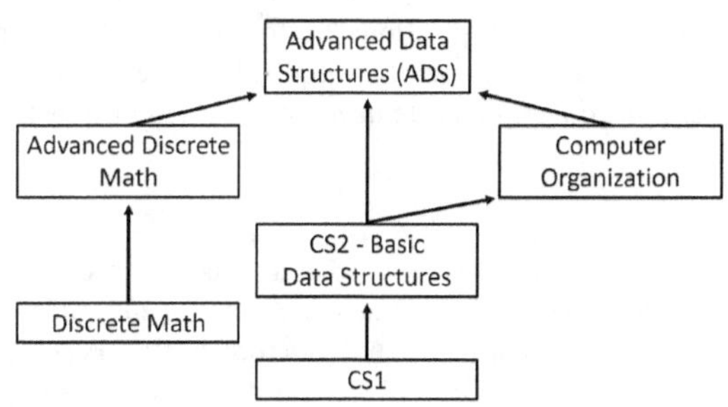

Table 1: Survey questions listed by question topic and related prerequisite courses.

Q	Topic	Related courses
1	Pass by value/reference	CS1
2	Valid Heap not BST	CS2 - Basic Data Structures
3	Valid Heap not BST	CS2 - Basic Data Structures
4	Valid BST not Heap	CS2 - Basic Data Structures
5	Neither Heap nor BST	CS2 - Basic Data Structures
6	Best List implementation	CS2 - Basic Data Structures
7	Runtime analysis	CS2 - Basic Data Structures and Adv. Discrete Math
8	Invariants	Discrete Mathematics and Adv. Discrete Math
9	Tracing recursion	CS1 and Adv. Discrete Math
10	Assembly	Computer Organization
11	Bitwise arithmetic	Computer Organization
12	Little-endian addressing	Computer Organization
13	Pointers	Computer Organization
14	Probability	Discrete Mathematics
15	Tracing recursion	CS1 and Adv. Discrete Math

Table 2: Low, medium, and high groups on Survey 1.

Group	Threshold	# students	% students
lowS1	$0 \le score\ S1 < 8$	61	29.3%
mediumS1	$8 \le score\ S1 \le 10$	90	43.3%
highS1	$10 < score\ S1 \le 15$	57	27.4%

Lacking validated assessments for direct prerequisite courses, we selected questions for our survey from those used in prior research studies on these topics [4, 6, 7, 14]. In cases where such a question was not available, we asked the instructor of the corresponding prerequisite course to supply us with two easy and two medium difficulty multiple-choice questions for us to use.

The two surveys were designed to be essentially equivalent, matched question-for-question. To limit the effects of memorization between the two surveys, small changes were made to the questions in the second survey, making sure that the changes did not make a question harder or easier. For example, on a tracing question, it was important that the number of statements that needed to be traced stayed the same. Table 1 lists the question topic and associated prerequisite courses for each survey question. Publicly hosted PDF versions of both surveys can be found online [2]. Because questions 2-5 are topically related, we reversed the order of these questions between the first and second survey. In the table (and the rest of this paper), the order of questions 2-5 for Survey 2 has thus been reversed so that they align with the equivalent questions in Survey 1. For example, question 5 on Survey 2 is treated as question 2 in the table.

4.4 Population

The first survey was taken by 365 students, the second by 236 students, and the final by 363 students. A total of 209 students took both surveys and 208 of those students took both surveys and the final exam. Unless stated otherwise, the statistics in this paper are based on these 208 students.

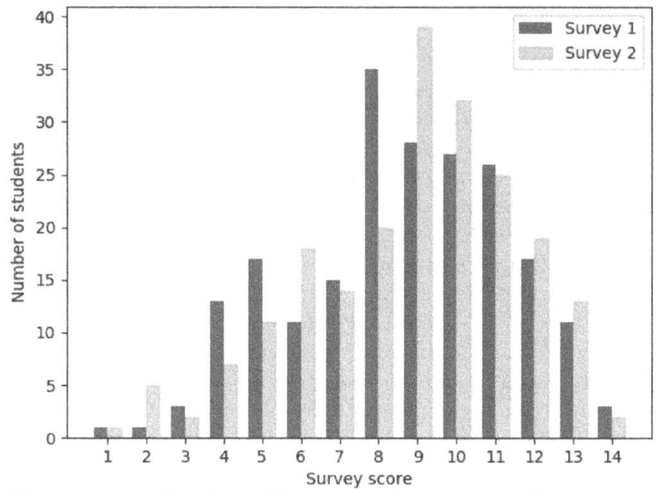

Figure 1: Distribution of Scores on Surveys 1 and 2. Respectively: avg=8.6 (57%), 9.8 (65%); median=9, 10; std dev=2.7, 2.7.

Table 3: Low, medium, and high groups on Survey 2.

Group	Threshold	# students	% students
lowS2	$0 \le score\ S2 < 8$	44	21.2%
mediumS2	$8 \le score\ S2 \le 10$	73	35.1%
highS2	$10 < score\ S2 \le 15$	91	43.8%

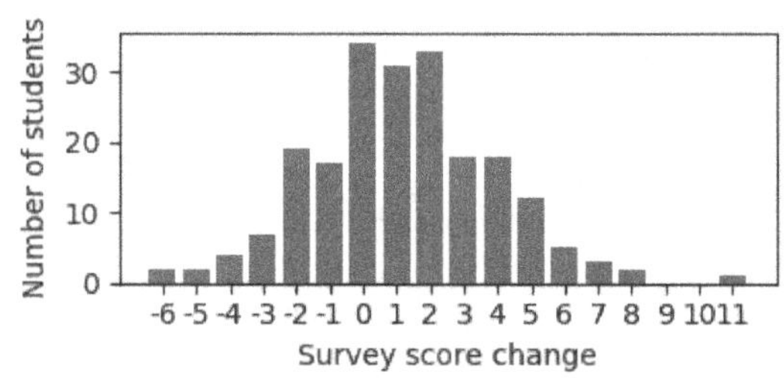

Figure 2: Distribution Score Change. The average score change was 1.2 points (8%), with a median of 1 and a standard deviation of 2.7.

5 RESULTS

5.1 RQ1: Early-Term Prerequisite Proficiency

For Survey 1 students scored an average of 8.6 out of 15 points with a median of 9 and a standard deviation of 2.7. Figure 1 shows a bar chart of the distribution.

Table 2 shows the amount of low-, medium-, and high-performing students for Survey 1. We define low performance as below 50% (below 8) and high performance as above 70% (above 10). As listed in Table 2, just over 29% of students answered fewer than 50% of the questions on prerequisite topics correctly.

In sum, the students entering a subsequent course like ADS exhibit a wide distribution of prerequisite proficiency, with about a third having considerably lower proficiency than expected.

5.2 RQ2: Change in Proficiency during Term

For Survey 2 students scored an average of 9.8 out of 15 points with a median of 10 and a standard deviation of 2.7. Figure 1 shows a bar chart of the score distribution for Survey 2. Table 3 shows the number of low-, medium-, and high-performing students for Survey 2 using the same thresholds as Survey 1.

Table 4: Low, medium, and high groups on the Final Exam.

Group	Threshold	# students	% students
lowFinal	$0 \leq score < 59$	64	30.8%
mediumFinal	$59 \leq score \leq 65.5$	76	36.5%
highFinal	$65.5 < score \leq 75$	68	32.7%

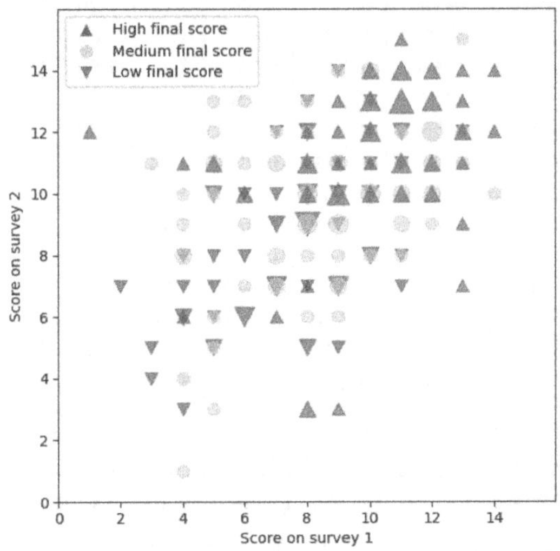

Figure 3: Comparison of Survey 1, Survey 2, and final scores. Low, medium, and high scores are defined in Table 4. A data point's size conveys the number of students under the point.

The score improvement between Surveys 1 and 2 was 1.2 (8%) on average, with a median of 1 and a standard deviation of 2.7. The scores on Survey 2 were significantly different compared to Survey 1 with a p-value less than 10^{-4}. As seen in Figure 2, most students improved their score by 0, 1, or 2 points out of 15. This resulted in over a quarter of the low performers on Survey 1 moving to medium or high proficiency. Overall, these results demonstrate that for the prerequisites in this study, as students progress in a subsequent course, they improve their prerequisite proficiency.

5.3 RQ3: Relationship between Prerequisite Proficiency and Final Exam Scores

The average score on the final exam was 61.8 points out of 75 (82%), with a median of 63 (84%) and a standard deviation of 6.9 (9%). For both surveys, the students' scores are significantly correlated to their final exam performance. For Survey 1 the correlation to final exam grades is 0.366, for Survey 2 the correlation is 0.384, and for the sum of the scores for Survey 1 and 2 the correlation is 0.434. The p-values for these Pearson correlations are all below 10^{-7}.

The same correlations are illustrated in Figure 3. We binned students based on their final exam performance as low, medium, or high performers. To obtain a balanced grouping we used the two tertile points of the score distribution as thresholds. The reason the group sizes are not perfectly in balance despite using the tertile points as thresholds is because multiple students received the same final score. Notable is that these thresholds are at 79% and 87% of a full score, so on average students did much better on the final exam than on our prerequisite surveys. Table 4 shows the groupings.

In Figure 3, each student is plotted in the scatter plot with the x axis being their score on Survey 1 and the y axis being their score on Survey 2. The color and shape of the data point indicates whether the student performed low, medium, or high on the final. The size of the data point indicates the number of students represented by it. Note that in cases when there were students from multiple performance levels in the same point, multiple data points appear (e.g., a large green triangle and a small yellow circle). Where these multiple points occur, the color may appear as combinations of others (e.g., orange is a combination of red and yellow).

Figure 3 hence visualizes the correlation between prerequisite proficiency and final exam performance. Most strikingly, it shows that most of the high performing students on the final were those who performed well on both Survey 1 and Survey 2 (upper right quadrant). Overall, we find a strong correlation between prerequisite proficiency and final exam performance.

5.4 RQ4: Which Prerequisites Relate to Final

To gain insight on whether prerequisite knowledge can be unbundled into more- and less-relevant topics, we performed a few per-question statistical analyses. Table 5 lists the correlation of the individual survey questions to the final exam scores, providing a hint as to which prerequisites might be important for performance on the final. Significantly correlated questions are listed in bold. Question 7, which concerns runtime complexity analysis, is the highest (significantly) correlated question for both Survey 1 and 2.

Some questions may be harder than others, reducing correlation at the extremes because there is little to distinguish high and low proficiency. Additional signal might be teased out of such questions by using conditional probabilities. For example, getting the right answer on a really hard survey question might be associated with high performance on the final, yet getting it wrong might say little about doing poorly on the final. Such distinctions are captured by the concepts of Sufficiency and Necessity [5]. A high likelihood of high performance when getting a survey question right is interpreted as meaning that the prerequisite knowledge is *sufficient* for success. A low likelihood of high performance when getting a survey question wrong is interpreted as meaning that the knowledge is *necessary* for success.

We express sufficiency as a likelihood ratio—the ratio that one outcome is more likely than another—specifically the positive likelihood [5]:

$$Sufficiency = \frac{P(E|H)}{P(E|{\sim}H)}$$

where the variable E stands for Evidence (in our case answering a question correctly), H stands for Hypothesis (the student falling in the top 50% of the final exam scores), and $E|H$ means E *given* H (all students that answered the survey question correctly and were in the top 50% of the final exam scores).

Necessity is the negative likelihood, that of finishing in the top half of the final if a student answers a question *incorrectly*, that is, ${\sim}E|H$. Since we are interested in the association between answering the question incorrectly and being in the *bottom* 50% on the final exam, ${\sim}E|{\sim}H$, we use inverse necessity (inverse negative likelihood):

$$Inverse\ Necessity = \frac{P({\sim}E|{\sim}H)}{P({\sim}E|H)}$$

The question most strongly associated with high final exam performance when answered correctly (sufficiency) is question 12 for both Survey 1 and 2. Its sufficiency of 2.10 on Survey 2 means

Table 5: Statistics for survey questions: percentage of correct answers and comparison to final exam scores: correlation with p-values, sufficiency, and inverse necessity. Bolded values indicate significant correlation for *alpha* = 0.05.

		Survey 1					Survey 2				
Q	Subject	correct	correl	p-val	suff	nec^{-1}	correct	correl	p-val	suff	nec^{-1}
1	Pass by value/reference	64%	0.050	0.470	1.13	1.25	71%	0.103	0.139	1.24	1.68
2	Valid Heap not BST	44%	0.006	0.937	0.99	1.00	44%	0.065	0.350	1.27	1.20
3	Valid Heap not BST	56%	**0.190**	**0.006**	1.36	1.46	75%	**0.193**	**0.005**	1.21	1.80
4	Valid BST not Heap	62%	0.055	0.434	1.04	1.07	83%	0.126	0.069	1.14	1.90
5	Neither Heap nor BST	76%	0.108	0.120	1.15	1.55	90%	0.063	0.370	1.03	1.37
6	Best List implementation	61%	0.032	0.646	1.13	1.21	65%	0.071	0.307	1.06	1.12
7	Runtime analysis	61%	**0.329**	**0.000**	1.85	2.56	69%	**0.284**	**0.000**	1.34	1.92
8	Invariants	34%	0.009	0.895	0.89	0.94	41%	0.072	0.299	1.05	1.03
9	Tracing recursion	78%	0.119	0.087	1.05	1.17	77%	**0.211**	**0.002**	1.16	1.65
10	Assembly	56%	**0.200**	**0.004**	1.43	1.57	43%	**0.235**	**0.001**	1.59	1.40
11	Bitwise arithmetic	58%	**0.155**	**0.025**	1.25	1.35	67%	**0.217**	**0.002**	1.36	1.86
12	Little-endian addressing	21%	**0.194**	**0.005**	1.91	1.18	27%	**0.252**	**0.000**	2.10	1.30
13	Pointers	69%	**0.244**	**0.000**	1.47	2.35	69%	**0.203**	**0.003**	1.32	1.87
14	Probability	55%	**0.215**	**0.002**	1.34	1.42	72%	**0.265**	**0.000**	1.36	2.19
15	Tracing recursion	70%	**0.198**	**0.004**	1.16	1.40	88%	-0.049	0.479	1.02	1.12

Table 6: Correlation between change in survey score and final exam score, broken down by the groups defined in Table 2, Significant correlations are in bold for *alpha* = 0.05 and underlined for *alpha* = 0.005.

Group	avg. impr.	med. impr.	σ	corr.	p-val
lowS1	2.90	3	2.8	**<u>0.371</u>**	**<u>0.003</u>**
mediumS1	1.01	1	2.4	0.114	0.284
highS1	-0.37	0	2.0	**0.306**	**0.020**

that students who answered it correctly had more than twice the probability of ending up in the top half of the class than in the bottom half. Question 12 was deemed difficult by the authors of this paper, and the students performed worst on it.

The question most highly associated with low final exam performance when answered incorrectly (inverse necessity) is question 7 on Survey 1 and 14 on Survey 2. Question 7 was deemed by the authors as solvable with just a basic proficiency. Question 7 stands out for being strong for sufficiency, inverse necessity, and correlation. As such, we can safely (and unsurprisingly) conclude that early-term proficiency in runtime analysis is crucial to good performance in an Advanced Data Structures class. The second highest question for inverse necessity was question 13, a basic question on pointers. As the data structures class jointly teaches C++ programming, the importance of having a background in C is unsurprising. The high necessity for question 14 on Survey 2, regarding basic probability, was a surprise, as ADS does not explicitly use probability. Question 10, regarding assembly language, inexplicably exhibits a similar pattern. The necessity of an apparently unrelated topic raises the possibility that there are dependences that remain to be understood or may be indicative of an intervening variable (e.g., study skills, mathematical reasoning, maturity, etc.).

Overall, we find that most prerequisite topics exhibit positive correlations and modest sufficiency and necessity. Some related topics that exhibit the strongest values, like runtime analysis, make sense. However, the high inverse necessities for unrelated topics leave many open questions.

5.5 RQ5 - Relationship between *Improvement* in Prerequisite Mastery and Final Score

The correlation of score change between Surveys 1 and 2 for the entire class was small and insignificant at 0.02, p-value of 0.77. Examining the course on a whole can mask effects for subpopulations, and we were curious if low performers on Survey 1 saw a significant benefit from improving their prerequisite proficiency. Examining student performance based on the groups defined in Table 2, lowS1 and highS1 have significant correlation, as shown in Table 6. We do not find significance for mediumS1, however their 1-point improvement is small. The scores of the high performers barely moved, interestingly. The movement and correlation for lowS1 is especially strong, improving a median 3 points, with a correlation of 0.371 and a p-value of 0.003. This effect can also be seen in the left half of Figure 3, which contains those students who performed poorly on Survey 1. For those students, if they continue to do poorly on Survey 2 (students in lower-left corner) they tend to have poor final exam scores, whereas students who improved on Survey 2 (students in upper-left corner) they tend to have better final exam scores.

In sum, most of the improvement in proficiency is due to the improvement of those with low entering proficiency, and that improvement had a significant correlation with their final score.

6 DISCUSSION

In this section we reflect on our research questions, results, limitations, and threats to validity.

6.1 Findings

The relatively low early-term prerequisite proficiency that we identified, combined with the correlation between proficiency and final exam performance, shows that many students will indeed be struggling. This is especially worrying as Muralidharan et al. [10] found that virtually no learning at the 8th grade math level is occurring for students who lack proficiency with the lower grade math materials. They found intervention with a focus on proficiency with lower grade math materials is required in order for students to make progress with their learning at the 8th grade math level.

In our study, we find that students do improve their prerequisite proficiency over the term, however they do so only marginally on average. But we also find that the amount of improvement in prerequisite proficiency is especially correlated to final exam performance for students with low early-term prerequisite proficiency.

One group we did not discuss was the 16 students who dropped the course (and hence are not included among our 208 participants). Their average early-term proficiency was 7 percentage points lower than those who finished the course, with 43% demonstrating low proficiency and only 12% high proficiency. While not statistically significant (likely due to the small sample size), this result suggests that prerequisite proficiency may be even lower at the start of the term than we found here. Moreover, it may indicate that lack of proficiency may be a reason for students dropping the course.

Given these findings, we suggest two possible courses of action: (1) final exams should be carefully designed to ensure that students who pass have achieved proficiency before proceeding to the next course (see discussion of course grades in the next section) and/or (2) teachers of upper-division computer science courses, especially those with many prerequisites, should consider helping students reinforce their prerequisite knowledge at the beginning of the term.

6.2 Why Students Lack Prerequisite Knowledge

Grades in Prerequisite Courses. In this study, we found that prerequisite proficiency in an upper-division Computer Science class is much lower than one might expect, given the students achieved passing grades in prerequisite courses. When we analyzed the failure rate of the prerequisite courses for Advanced Data Structures [1] we found that at our institution, on average, only 2.9% and 3.6% of students will receive a D or F (respectively) with the remainder of the students received a C or higher. (A 'D' grade presently allows students to progress at our institution). Our study highlights that not just 3.6% of students but likely 29% of students are failing in their prerequisite proficiency. We suspect there might be some form of grade inflation occurring and the consequence is that we are sending under-prepared students into subsequent classes.

Multiple Prerequisite Paths. At our institution, we offer non-majors options for prerequisite courses to provide flexibility. For example, non-majors can complete either a computer organization course that follows CS2, teaching C and assembly programming, or a non-major's CS1 course in C. Either course should teach students the necessary knowledge in C (e.g., pointers) to begin a course in C++, however one may do so in more detail. Additionally, one interdisciplinary major at our institution (with a large number of required units and few students) requires the Advanced Data Structures course but waives the Computer Organization prerequisite. As such, part of the effect seen in this study may be due to students bypassing prerequisites or due to some prerequisite courses being inferior to others as preparation for this course. Further inquiry is the topic of ongoing future work.

Unrealistic Expectations. Prior work in CS1 has shown that students often underperform instructor expectations. For example, instructors expect students completing CS1 to be able to complete the rainfall problem when, in reality, few students are so capable [16]. It is possible that this mismatch is again at play, where our survey questions on prerequisites were viewed as relatively easy by the authors when in reality, they may be difficult for students. This underscores the importance of using meaningful assessments at the end of courses (e.g., concept inventories [17]) to measure student learning in order to better understand their abilities.

6.3 Limitations and Threats to Validity

Limitations. Generalizability from our study is limited as we only studied one course (ADS) and one term. Because correlation is not causation, the correlations found might not imply that increased prerequisite proficiency causes increased performance on the final. However, the fact that increased proficiency over the term was correlated with increased final exam performance for low- and high-performing groups provides compelling complementary evidence.

Underlying Factors. Although our survey focused on prerequisite knowledge, the relationship between the survey and the final exam may not be entirely related to prerequisite content. There may be intervening variables as perhaps prerequisite proficiency is related to students' general study habits or motivation in the field. Moreover, perhaps "better" students took the survey seriously and hence did better on the survey than those who did not. However, evidence that questions on particularly critical prerequisite topics were most strongly correlated with student exam performance suggests that at least some portion of the effect found related to the content itself.

Threats to Validity. The two surveys we used as a measuring tool are not validated and the questions were drawn from many different sources. Some survey questions may have been too hard for all students, making them less useful in our study. Although most students answered all questions, students were given a relatively short amount of time to complete them. As such, students may have hurried through the last questions and hence impacted findings. In addition, those who completed the survey were those who were in class on the two days the survey was given, so the results may be biased for the population of students who frequently attend class.

7 CONCLUSION

In our study of prerequisite proficiency in an upper-division advanced data structures course, we find that students varied in their proficiency to an unexpected degree, that prerequisite proficiency correlated with higher final exam scores, and that students improve on their understanding of prerequisites in a way that correlates to improved final exam scores. In sum, these findings support more care by instructors in ensuring students have fundamental proficiency with their course content before allowing them to move on to subsequent courses. In turn, instructors who teach courses with multiple prerequisites may wish to provide students with resources to buttress their mastery of prerequisites early in the term. Additional study is needed to understand whether these findings replicate across multiple institutions and across multiple courses, however, these results offer a promising glimpse of how prerequisites relate to student success in upper-division computing courses.

8 ACKNOWLEDGEMENTS

The authors wish to thank our reviewers for their helpful suggestions and the course instructor, Hau Nguyen, for his assistance. This work was supported in part by NSF award 1712508.

REFERENCES

[1] Course and professor evaluations (cape). http://cape.ucsd.edu/. Accessed: 2018-11-05.

[2] Prerequisite surveys. https://paperdata.page.link/surveys. Accessed: 2018-11-05.

[3] A. D. Baddeley and A. D. Baddeley. *Your memory: A user's guide*. Carlton Books New York, NY, USA:, 2004.

[4] H. Danielsiek, W. Paul, and J. Vahrenhold. Detecting and understanding students' misconceptions related to algorithms and data structures. In *Proceedings of the 43rd Technical Symposium on Computer Science Education*, pages 21–26, 2012.

[5] R. O. Duda, P. E. Hart, and N. J. Nilsson. Subjective bayesian methods for rule-based inference systems. In *Proceedings of the June 7-10, 1976, National Computer Conference and Exposition*, AFIPS '76, pages 1075–1082, 1976.

[6] T. Götschi, I. Sanders, and V. Galpin. Mental models of recursion. SIGCSE '03, pages 346–350, New York, NY, USA, 2003. ACM.

[7] S. Hamouda, S. H. Edwards, H. G. Elmongui, J. V. Ernst, and C. A. Shaffer. A basic recursion concept inventory. *Computer Science Education*, 27(2):121–148, 2017.

[8] A. Lishinski, A. Yadav, J. Good, and R. Enbody. Learning to program: Gender differences and interactive effects of students' motivation, goals, and self-efficacy on performance. In *Proceedings of the 2016 Conference on International Computing Education Research*, pages 211–220, 2016.

[9] M. A. Martin. Course prerequisites and undergraduate student performance. *NACTA Journal*, 33(1):38–42, 1989.

[10] K. Muralidharan, A. Singh, and A. J. Ganimian. Disrupting education? experimental evidence on technology-aided instruction in india. Technical report, National Bureau of Economic Research, 2016.

[11] S. E. Newstead, A. Franklyn-Stokes, and P. Armstead. Individual differences in student cheating. *Journal of Educational Psychology*, 88(2):229, 1996.

[12] A.-C. J. T. F. on Computing Curricula. Computer science curricula 2013. 2013.

[13] V. Ramalingam, D. LaBelle, and S. Wiedenbeck. Self-efficacy and mental models in learning to program. *SIGCSE Bulletin*, 36:171–175, 2004.

[14] J. Sheard, A. Carbone, R. Lister, B. Simon, E. Thompson, and J. L. Whalley. Going solo to assess novice programmers. pages 209–213, 2008.

[15] Simon and J. Sheard. Academic integrity and computing assessments. In *Proceedings of the Australasian Computer Science Week Multiconference*, pages 3:1–3:8, 2016.

[16] E. Soloway. Learning to program= learning to construct mechanisms and explanations. *Communications of the ACM*, 29(9):850–858, 1986.

[17] C. Taylor, D. Zingaro, L. Porter, K. C. Webb, C. B. Lee, and M. Clancy. Computer science concept inventories: past and future. *Computer Science Education*, 24(4):253–276, 2014.

[18] J. Vitale, S. Wanger, and D. Adams. Explaining student performance in an undergraduate agricultural economics classroom. *NACTA Journal*, 54(1):2, 2010.

[19] H. M. Walker. Prerequisites: Shaping the computing curriculum. *ACM Inroads*, 1(4):14–16, Dec. 2010.

[20] C. Watson, F. W. Li, and J. L. Godwin. No tests required: Comparing traditional and dynamic predictors of programming success. In *Proceedings of the 45th Technical Symposium on Computer Science Education*, pages 469–474, 2014.

[21] B. C. Wilson and S. Shrock. Contributing to success in an introductory computer science course: a study of twelve factors. *SIGCSE Bulletin*, 33:184–188, 2001.

[22] D. Zingaro, M. Craig, L. Porter, B. A. Becker, Y. Cao, P. Conrad, D. Cukierman, A. Hellas, D. Loksa, and N. Thota. Achievement goals in CS1: Replication and extension. In *Proceedings of the 49th Technical Symposium on Computer Science Education*, pages 687–692, 2018.

[23] D. Zingaro and L. Porter. Impact of student achievement goals on cs1 outcomes. In *Proceedings of the 47th Technical Symposium on Computing Science Education*, pages 279–296, 2016.

ACM Code of Ethics: Looking Back and Forging Ahead

Marty J. Wolf
Bemidji State University
Dept of Math & Computer Science
Bemidji, MN 56601
+1-218-755-2825
mjwolf@bemidjistate.edu

Don Gotterbarn
East Tennessee State University
Computing Sciences
Johnson City, TN
+1-423-929-0660
don@gotterbarn.com

Michael S. Kirkpatrick
James Madison University
Department of Computer Science
Harrisonburg, VA
+1-540-568-3371
kirkpams@jmu.edu

ABSTRACT

This special session will involve three related components. It will begin with a history of the ACM Code of Ethics and Professional Conduct (the Code), its evolving presence in the computing curriculum guidelines over time, and its documented use outside of academe. This will lead into an overview of the major changes to the Code that occurred in the most recent update.

The third component and primary focus of the session will be to work with participants to identify ways that ACM and the ACM Committee on Professional Ethics (COPE) can help Computer Science educators integrate the Code as broadly as possible into diverse programs, ranging from Kindergarten to PhD-level. The outcome of the session would be a preliminary set of guidelines for programs and departments to adopt the Code, potential challenges to be addressed when formalizing those guidelines, and suggested approaches to resolve these difficulties. If attendance is sufficiently large, we would adopt a jigsaw model, breaking into smaller focus groups that are tasked with distinct portions of the Code. Each group reports back at the end, and members of COPE will collate the results into a document for future distribution and work.

Categories and Subject Descriptors

• **Social and professional topics~Codes of ethics** • *Social and professional topics~Model curricula* • *Social and professional topics~Socio-technical systems* • Applied computing~Computers in other domains

Keywords

ACM Code of Ethics; computing ethics; teaching computing ethics; history of computing ethics

SIGCSE'19, February 27-March 2, 2019, Minneapolis, MN, USA

ACM ISBN 978-1-4503-5890-3/19/02.
https://doi.org/10.1145/3287324.3287519

1. OBJECTIVE

In July 2018, the ACM released an update to its Code of Ethics and Professional Conduct (the Code) [1]. Concomitant with the release, the ACM and the ACM Committee on Professional Ethics (COPE) have begun an effort to support computing professionals in making ethically responsible decisions in their professional practice. This effort includes support for computing educators to integrate the Code into their courses, and potentially into the ways that programs are managed. COPE, as well as SIGCAS, has actively provided this support by hosting workshops, special sessions, and Birds of a Feather sessions at almost every recent SIGCSE. This special session is an opportunity for the SIGCSE community to work with COPE on developing ways to better help computing departments assimilate the values of the Code into their pedagogy, practice, and day-to-day operations. We want educators from all levels to take part. We recognize that the ways that COPE should understand what it means for a program to adopt the Code will differ depending on the level of the program. We want to have input from faculty at all levels: grade school, middle school, high school, community colleges, bachelor's programs, and graduate programs.

The session will begin with a report on the history of the Code and how it has been present in computing curriculum guidelines and accreditation standards. That report will be followed by a brief report on the major revisions to the Code that occurred in the update published in July 2018. The rest of the session will be a working session where participants identify specific ways that COPE might support departmental adoption of the Code. There are sure to be challenges identified as well. Ultimately, the ideas and issues generated in this session will become part of COPE's plan for supporting departmental adoption of the Code. Further, attendees' contributions will be incorporated into educational materials that the ACM plans to produce and distribute in its continued support of the Code.

The SIGCSE community's input is an essential part of this process. The SIGCSE community has a significant role in fostering ethical thinking in aspiring computing professionals. Eventually, as computing departments adopt the Code, the task of fostering ethical reasoning will become both an individual and a departmental responsibility.

2. OUTLINE

- Introduction/History of the Code (10 mins) – Gotterbarn (one the authors of the 1992 Code) will introduce the session and give a history of the Code's development and uses in industry and law.

- History of the Code in Computing Curricula (10 mins) - Kirkpatrick will review Computing Curricula since 1978, identify how the teaching of computing ethics has evolved over that time, and discuss different pedagogical techniques for making it relevant to and integrating it into mainstream computing courses (i.e., courses not devoted exclusively to societal and ethical issues).
- Small Group Brainstorming (15 mins) – Wolf will lead attendees as they break into groups based on education level to identify the practical day-to-day implications of adopting the Code for a computing department at their level of education.
- Large Group Reporting (15 mins) – Groups will report back their findings to all attendees so that commonalities and differences can be identified. Attendees will begin to identify challenges.
- Small Group Work Session (15 minutes) – Groups reconvene to generate items to incorporate into a report to be used by COPE in establishing guidelines for programs to adopt the Code. The report will include items identified in the previous sessions and additional items that are generated from the cross-fertilization of ideas.
- Wrap Up (5 minutes) – Groups report back any major new discoveries. We collect the reports.

3. EXPECTATIONS

The intended audience is a cross-section of computing educators from all levels of education from kindergarten to doctoral level. The audience will cover the history of the Code and the evolution of computing ethics in computing curricula since 1978. Most importantly, everyone, including the session leaders, will learn about the diversity and complexity of different computing programs. Each group has the opportunity to better understand the expectations with respect to the development of ethical computing that others have relative to their level in the educational structure. There is opportunity to address those expectations. Attendees will have identified ways that programs might use the Code to focus their operation in ways consistent with what the ACM expects from its members. Importantly, all will be made aware of potential challenges of doing so. The attendees will be asked to submit the ideas their groups generate. The session organizers will collate the information after the session for further analysis by COPE and be reported back to attendees and to ACM.

4. SUITABILITY FOR A SPECIAL SESSION

COPE is seeking input from a broad cross-section of the computer science education community. To get quality input, the session attendees need some background information. Most of the session then requires the generation and sharing of ideas. Since both activities are required, neither a paper or panel is consistent with these activities.

5. ABOUT THE FACILITATORS

Don Gotterbarn and Marty J. Wolf are the co-chairs of COPE. Both have extensive experience in computing ethics scholarship and the teaching of computing ethics. Michael S. Kirkpatrick is the educational coordinator for COPE and has extensive experience in developing case studies. All three were on the Executive Committee of the Code 2018 International Task Force. In addition to their work to update the Code, the three facilitators are major contributors of "The Code" [2] a forthcoming booklet being distributed to ACM members that contains the ACM Code of Ethics and Professional Conduct, case studies, and guidance for using the Code.

6. REFERENCES

[1] Gotterbarn, et al. ACM Code of Ethics and Professional Conduct. (July 2018) https://www.acm.org/code-of-ethics.

[2] The Code. (October 2018). ACM, New York, New York USA

Four Models for Including Community Colleges in Broadening Participation: A Call to Action

Amardeep Kahlon
Austin Community College|
Austin, TX USA
akahlon@austincc.edu

Deborah Boisvert
University of Massachusetts Boston
Boston, MA USA
deborah.boisvert@umb.edu

Louise Lyon
Education, Training and Research
Scotts Valley, CA USA
louann.lyon@etr.org

Melanie Williamson
Bluegrass Technical College|
Lexington, KY USA
melanie.williamson@kcts.edu

Wendy DuBow
NCWIT
University of Colorado
Boulder, CO USA
wendy.dubow@ncwit.org

1. SUMMARY

While computer science (CS) jobs are growing rapidly, universities are not producing enough CS graduates to fill a projected shortage of almost a million workers by 2020 [1]. To add to this problem, there is a striking lack of diversity in the graduates of CS programs nationwide [2]. Of the degrees awarded, the overwhelming number - 80% - were awarded to males, while only 5% went to African-Americans, 18% to Asians, and 9% to Hispanics [3, 2]. Bringing community colleges (CCs) into the fold will enable us to confront this projected workforce shortage [2]. More importantly, it will enable us to diversify one of the most important fields of our time, computer and information sciences. Over half of community college (CC) students are non- white, and more than half of all Hispanic and Black undergraduates start at community college [4].

Given that community colleges enroll minorities and women in larger numbers than four-year institutions, it is imperative for both CCs and four-year institutions to engage in collaborative efforts to broaden the participation of diverse peoples into computing and facilitate unobstructed pathways from the two-year to four-year educational programs. While CCs are rich in diversity, their students face an inordinate number of obstacles transferring to a bachelor's degree, particularly in CS.

The complexities of the CC landscape require that experts from various backgrounds come together to share knowledge and experiences to contribute to a better understanding of the role CCs can play with four-year institutions in broadening participation efforts in CS and information technology (IT). Lyon & Denner [5] argue that "we are at an inflection point where community colleges will be a vital and viable pathway for the many women and racial/ethnic minority students who are already engaged at their institutions to consider CS and successfully transfer to complete a bachelor's degree in the field."

SIGCSE'19, February 27-March 2, 2019, Minneapolis, MN, USA.

ACM ISBN 978-1-4503-5890-3/19/02
DOI: https://doi.org /10.1145/3287324.3287338

2. CONTEXT

Funded by a National Science Foundation (NSF) grant, a workshop was held at the Google headquarters in Mountain View, CA, in 2018. Stakeholders invited to this workshop were: researchers, educators and administrators from CCs and research universities, and members of think tanks. The overarching goal of this workshop was to provide a forum for sharing experiences and for brainstorming strategies/models that will empower CCs to become an integral part of the conversation on Broadening Participation in Computing (BPC) in CS and information technology (IT). The attendees at this workshop collectively identified the following models for the intentional inclusion of CCs in BPC:

CS Principles Plus (CSP+) Course: The group recommended a college and career-aligned CSP course that could be a part of the general core for existing community college students with credit earned through dual enrollment for high school students.

Changing Perceptions: The group recommended this model as a way to change perceptions about the students and faculty in, and the rigor of, community college CS coursework and also confront the negative bias about CCs in general.

Structured Pathways: This strategy examines the barriers transfer students face both in the form of coursework that will not transfer and advising structures that do not guide students or advise them into computing programs. The CSP+ course could be an integral component of this structured pathway.

National CC BPC Alliance: This model was recommended as a long-term strategy for addressing BPC. Once again the CSP+ course would be the most immediate and impactful step towards establishing this model.

3. FORMAT

In this interactive panel, the panelists will: Describe the problem and explain the goal of the workshop; Introduce each of the 4 models/strategies; Recount what has been done to move each of the models forward (this could be examples from our work, things we know others are doing, or if no progress so far, then soliciting ideas for next steps). The panelists and audience will break up into 5 groups and ask people to share what they are doing that is related to each model and/or contribute to a plan for each model.

4. PRESENTERS

This panel is comprised of organizers of this workshop. They are part of a larger group of seven educators from various levels of institutions – community colleges, research universities, and education research institutions – and researchers.

4.1 AMARDEEP KAHLON (MODERATOR) is a Professor of Computer Science and director of Fast Track to Success at Austin Community College. Compared to a four-year school, the community college population is very diverse, not just in ethnicity, race, age, and gender but also in levels of educational attainment. I have a deep understanding of the challenges and obstacles faced by community college students as they attempt transfers to a four-year school. While there are many challenges, there are also many opportunities to build pathways and bridges for these students. As director of Texas Affordable Baccalaureate Expansion grant, I have worked to create coursework, support services and an articulation agreement for a 100% online, competency-based, and affordable bachelor's degree. I have worked with colleges and universities around Texas to create accelerated pathways for students in computer science and information technology. It is imperative for community colleges and four-year schools to work together to remove the barriers to transfers thereby increasing the diversity and the numbers of CS/IT graduates.

4.2 DEBORAH BOISVERT is Director of the BATEC Center for Computing and IT at University of Massachusetts Boston focusing on professional development for K-12 educators and designing coursework and developing computing pathways from high school to community college in several urban settings. As an urban laboratory, this work has utilized shared resources (across industry, academia, and community), subject matter expertise (curricular guidance and best practices for student engagement) and financial resources (materials, supplies and funds for participant support). I believe that a holistic system of problem-based coursework and multiple touchpoints in an upward trajectory must interweave awareness, preparation and advancement throughout the academic and work-based learning components to increase the success of minority students. This belief has accentuated the need for community colleges as an integral part of the Broadening the Participation conversation.

4.3 LOUISE ANN ("LOU ANN") LYON is a Senior Research Associate at ETR and brings industry experience in the software engineering workplace as well as research knowledge from Learning Sciences and Feminist Studies to her work on diversifying technology at postsecondary institutions and in the workplace. She was Principal Investigator on a research project studying underrepresented student perspectives on transferring and completing bachelor's degrees in CS [5], and was the principal author of an upcoming ACM Community College Transfer Pathway report. Her experiences attending community colleges and talking with underrepresented students at CCs in California have convinced her of the critical role that CCs play in the postsecondary education landscape in the U.S., particularly regarding BPC.

4.4 MELANIE WILLIAMSON is Assistant Dean and Professor of Computer & Information Technologies. She is passionate about women in computing and is co-leader of the Community College Involvement Project Team at NCWIT. She has chaired and organized the Kentucky Community College Women in Computing ACM-W Celebration, the first community college centered regional women in computing conference. She believes that involvement of community colleges in broadening the participation of minority and underrepresented populations in the field of computing is important, as the CC population tends to be varied in gender, ethnicity, and age. By including community colleges you increase pathways and may create new paths that may better fit a diverse population.

4.5 WENDY DUBOW is the director of evaluation and a senior research scientist at the National Center for Women & Information Technology (NCWIT). NCWIT exists to provide members and other stakeholders with research- and evidence-based practices for increasing the meaningful participation of all girls and women in computing disciplines. She has been a Principal Investigator on two NSF grants focused on broadening participation in computing at the community college level. From these interventions, working with the NCWIT Academic Alliance community college representatives, and from her research findings, she has concluded that there is as much work to be done to recruit and retain women and other historically under-represented minorities in community college computing as at 4-year post-secondary institutions. She can share the challenges and opportunities she and her team have identified.

5. REFERENCES

[1] American Association for Community Colleges (AACC): Students at community colleges, 2016.
[2] Data USA: Computer Science - Diversity. 2015. Retrieved March 05, 2018, from https://datausa.io/profile/cip/110701/#demograp hics
[3] Jaggars, S. S., Fink, J., & Fletcher, J. (2016). A Longitudinal Analysis of Community College Pathways to Computer Science Bachelor's Degrees (Rep.). Mountainview, CA: Google.
[4] Kalil, O., & Jahanian, F. (2013, December 11). Computer Science is for Everyone! [Web log post]. Retrieved March 5, 2018, from https://obamawhitehouse.archives.gov/blog/2013 /12/11/computer-science-everyone
[5] Lyon, L. A. & Denner, J. (2016). Student Perspectives of Community College Pathways to Computer Science Bachelor's Degrees. Mountain View, CA: Google.

Leading Conversations about Microaggressions, Bias, and Other Difficult Topics

Colleen M. Lewis
Computer Science Dept.
Harvey Mudd College
Claremont, CA, USA
lewis@cs.hmc.edu

Wendy M. DuBow
NCWIT
University of Colorado, Boulder
Boulder, CO, USA
wendy.dubow@ colorado.edu

Kyla McMullen
Comp. & Info. Science & Eng.
University of Florida
Gainesville, FL USA
drkyla@ufl.edu

ABSTRACT

Many SIGCSE attendees are committed to inclusive teaching practices and creating an inclusive culture within their classrooms; yet, advocating for and sustaining these initiatives may require having difficult conversations with our colleagues and students. Understandably, many faculty are unsure about how to talk about sensitive topics such as race and gender with their colleagues and students. Research suggests that practicing some of these difficult conversations is essential to achieve the goals of inclusive teaching and culture. In our well attended session at SIGCSE in 2018, attendees learned strategies for responding to bias in academic settings. This was facilitated by playing two rounds of a research-based game developed by the NSF project CSTeachingTips.org (#1339404). This session will extend the work begun last year by helping attendees to replicate this activity with their colleagues. In this special session, attendees will first play the game to practice those strategies in small groups and will then receive facilitation tips and guidance for conducting this activity on their own. All attendees will receive a printed copy of the game and a link to download and print more copies.

CCS CONCEPTS

• Social and professional topics~Computing education

KEYWORDS

Microaggressions; bias; inclusive teaching

1 SUMMARY AND OBJECTIVE

The special session seeks to help attendees build their capacity to address and respond to bias in their academic environments. Most importantly, the special session will prepare attendees to replicate this session at their institution. Helping attendees bring learning from SIGCSE back to their colleagues is an important way to disseminate and scale strategies for creating more inclusive CS classrooms, ultimately broadening participation in computing.

ACM ISBN 978-1-4503-5890-3/19/02.
https://doi.org/10.1145/3287324.3287518

2 OUTLINE OF ACTIVITIES

As attendees arrive, they will be asked to create groups of three to six people, which was successful in our SIGCSE Special Session in 2018 that was attended by approximately 80 people.

2.1 Presentation of Session Goals (5 minutes)

The session will begin with a brief introduction by the presenters to the structure and goals of the session.

Session Goals:

- Develop and practice strategies for responding to bias or problematic statements in the classroom.
- Practice explaining the benefits of inclusive teaching strategies to faculty and students who may be skeptical.
- Create connections among SIGCSE attendees committed to inclusive teaching practices.
- Prepare attendees to facilitate these discussion about bias with their colleagues.

After reviewing the goals for the session, the presenters will explain the first interactive portion of the special session. Groups will be provided a printed copy of the instructions and these instructions will be displayed on the screen for easy reference.

2.2 Interactive Portion 1 (25 minutes)

Groups will be asked to do a quick round of introductions before beginning the first interactive portion of the game. Attendees will then participate in the activity. In addition to the instructions, each group will have a set of sixteen cards. One person draws a card and read the question to a small group. Each member of the group answers the question or passes. After 3 minutes or hearing all answers, the person who read the question reads the sample answer from the card aloud and picks their favorite answer (the "winner"). The "winner" keeps the card to tally who won the most times. The person who reads the question rotates clockwise.

The cards encourage participants to (1) identify opportunities to apply inclusive teaching practices and (2) practice strategies for responding to bias or problematic statements in the classroom. The following list is a sample of the questions, which all begin "What would you do if..."

- students never ask questions during class?

- during class a student with a lot of prior CS experience asks questions about advanced topics irrelevant to the class.
- some students did very poorly on a recent exam?
- your colleague says: "we want diversity, but we don't want to water down the content."
- your colleague says: "students should just tell me if I offend them."
- your colleague says: "women just aren't interested in CS."
- your colleague says: "there are so few Black and Latinx students in CS, it is a lot easier for them to get CS jobs."
- your colleague says: "Brenda needs to be more confident."

Groups will vary in the speed that they progress through each of the cards, and we expect few groups to get through more than seven or eight cards. The goal is to have experience with the game before discussing how to facilitate this game with their colleagues.

The attendees may all have experience with these scenarios, and they can learn from each other to better be able to promote an inclusive classroom community.

2.3 Synthesis of Strategies for Fostering Inclusion (20 minutes)

After the game, the presenters will facilitate a debrief of the game identifying the key, relevant strategies for addressing these real-life scenarios and creating inclusive cultures. This debrief is focused on a list of four strategies for fostering inclusion that are listed with the game instructions:

- **Empathize:** Assume that there is a reason for students' behavior when they seem unengaged or are pursuing ineffective learning strategies.
- **Promote belonging:** Respond to behavior that may unintentionally signal to students that they don't belong in CS. This may be particularly important for students with less experience or who do not identify with CS stereotypes.
- **Challenge stereotypes:** Stereotypes can have negative consequences. Even seemingly positive stereotypes, like "Asians are good at math," are still problematic because they ignore individual variation, create unfair expectations, and may implicitly insult another group of people.
- **Change structures:** Sometimes initiatives to promote inclusion in CS focus on strategies for how students can respond to bias that they face. While these may be helpful strategies, they may unintentionally send the message that the student is as fault. Instead, we should focus on changing the structures that lead to bias or marginalization.

After reviewing the four strategies, the presenters will answer attendee questions to wrap up the debrief.

2.4 Facilitation Tips and Discussion (25 minutes)

For the final part of this session, the presenters will share recommendations for facilitating this activity. To do so, we will draw from materials we have developed in prior work training participants to be "ambassadors" for change in their home institutions. Small groups will then brainstorm and practice how they might propose this session with their colleagues and address any challenges they might face in facilitating the session. The ultimate goal is not to prepare participants to be "experts" but rather to be the "best prepared student in the class," facilitating these conversations back home in ways where everyone is learning together.

We will bring enough sets of cards for each attendee to have a copy. This will allow everyone who wants a set to have one and some attendees to be able to take multiple sets home or request additional sets be mailed to them.

3 PRESENTERS

Colleen Lewis is an assistant professor of CS at Harvey Mudd College where typically 40% to 50% of the CS majors identify as women. Colleen Lewis researches how people learn CS and how people feel about learning CS. Her research seeks to identify effective teaching practices for creating equitable learning spaces where all students have the opportunity to learn. Lewis is the PI for CSTeachingTips.org, a NSF-sponsored project (#1339404) for disseminating effective CS teaching practices.

Wendy DuBow is Director of Evaluation and a Senior Research Scientist with the National Center for Women & Information Technology (NCWIT) at the University of Colorado Boulder. Her research focuses on issues related to gender, diversity, and technology; organizational change and curriculum reform; and the interactions of majority and minority groups. She conducts mixed methods social science research, creates practical print and multimedia resources, and evaluates the effectiveness of the various programs and materials NCWIT produces.

Kyla McMullen is an Assistant Professor of Computer and Information Science and Engineering at the University of Florida. Dr. McMullen is the leader of the SoundPAD Laboratory at the University of Florida, which focuses on the Perception, Application, and Development of 3D audio in various contexts. Dr. McMullen also researches programming self-efficacy as an effect of IDE design, paired-programming, and active learning.

4 SUITABILITY FOR A SPECIAL SESSION

This innovative and interactive format would only be possible as a special session. This special session could be particularly helpful for new attendees so that they can meet other attendees. The session provides the important opportunity for attendees to become better prepared to facilitate conversations with their colleagues about microaggressions, bias, and other nonsense.

5 ACKNOWLEDGEMENTS

The development of CSTeachingTips.org and the special session content were funded by NSF grant #1339404. These materials are based upon resources from NCWIT.org (NSF #1725018).

Wrestling with Retention in the CS Major: Report from the ACM Retention Committee

Alison Derbenwick Miller
(Moderator)
Oracle
Redwood Shores, CA USA
alison.derbenwick@oracle.com

Christine Alvarado
Computer Science & Engineering
Univ. of California, San Diego
San Diego, CA USA
cjalvarado@eng.ucsd.edu

Mehran Sahami
Computer Science Dept.
Stanford University
Stanford, CA USA
sahami@cs.stanford.edu

Elsa Villa
College of Education
University of Texas, El Paso
El Paso, TX USA
evilla@utep.edu

Stuart Zweben
Computer Science & Engineering
The Ohio State University
Columbus, OH USA
zweben.1@osu.edu

ABSTRACT

This panel focuses on the challenges of collecting and analyzing data relating to retention of students in undergraduate computer science education programs. The panelists will share learnings and recommendations from the final report of the ACM Retention Committee and share their individual perspectives on data collection challenges, promising interventions, and recommendations for actively addressing retention for all students.

KEYWORDS

Retention, computer science education, undergraduate programs.

ACM Reference format:

A. Derbenwick Miller, C. Alvarado, M. Sahami, E. Villa and S. Zweben. 2019. Wrestling with Retention in the CS Major: Report from the ACM Retention Committee. In *Proceedings of the 50th ACM Technical Symposium on Computer Science Education (SIGCSE'19). February 27-March 2, 2019, Minneapolis, MN, USA.* ACM, New York, NY, USA. 2 pages. https://doi.org/10.1145/3287324.3287326

1 Summary

Improving the representation of women and students from other underrepresented groups in higher education computer science (CS) programs remains a challenge. Despite high profile success stories at colleges like Harvey Mudd College and Carnegie Mellon University [1, 2] the percentage of women at most college and university CS programs is only about 20% [3]. Retaining students who have shown interest in studying CS is an important aspect of improving this situation.

In 2016, the ACM Education Board convened a committee of university faculty to examine factors leading to low participation of women and underrepresented minorities in CS programs. This committee has worked for two years to gather and analyze data related to retention of these groups in undergraduate CS programs in colleges and universities across the United States, including exploring the complexities of defining and identifying retention in a 2018 SIGCSE BOF [4]. The committee found that the question of retention is made more complicated than it might initially seem by factors such as the different paths that may exist to the major, and the intent of the student in the early CS courses.

This panel is based on the work the committee has done to address these and other subtle issues of measuring student retention early in undergraduate CS programs. The panel focuses on the first and second courses in a CS program, as this is the first opportunity for CS Bachelor's programs to impact retention for a large number of students. Panelists will share the learning from this committee's work, including:

- Different notions of "retention" in different contexts.
- Different types of data available for tracking and understanding students' goals and motivations.
- Challenges of data collection specific to each institution, and to creating a unified data set to help understand student retention across institutions.
- Insight that has been gained from initial data analysis at different institutions and across institutions.
- Insight that has been gained from two case studies.

Panelists also will discuss some of the interventions that are showing success in retaining students, and make recommendations for addressing the issue of retention.

2 Panel Structure

The panel content will be structured as follows:

- 15 minutes: Panel overview, panelist introductions, flow of majors at each panelist's institution.
- 30 minutes: Panel moderator seeds discussion with some or all of the following topics:
    - Barriers and solutions to data collection

ACM ISBN 978-1-4503-5890-3/19/02
https://doi.org/10.1145/3287324.3287326

    - Suggested data analysis approaches
    - Insights from data analysis
    - Data-driven retention strategies or projects
- 30 minutes: Questions and audience discussion.

3 Position Statements

3.1 Alison Derbenwick Miller

Alison Derbenwick Miller leads Oracle's international team responsible for philanthropic outreach to advance CS education with the goal of improving knowledge, skills, innovation, and diversity in technology fields. She serves on a number of computing education bodies, including currently co-chairing the ACM Retention Committee and as a member of the ACM Education Board. Diversity and retention in computer science are complex issues, especially in a global context, and Derbenwick Miller believes the best way to understand retention challenges and develop successful interventions is through data-driven analysis combined with anecdotal evidence.

3.2 Christine Alvarado

Christine Alvarado develops programs, curriculum and pedagogies to make computer science education more accessible and engaging, especially for women and other groups underrepresented in computing. As a professor at Harvey Mudd College (HMC), Alvarado helped lead efforts in curriculum and program development that led to the percentage of women in CS increasing from 13% historically to nearly 50% today. Now at UC San Diego, Alvarado founded and directs the Early Research Scholars Program (ERSP), a research apprenticeship for second-year students modeled on the research program she helped develop at HMC. In her classroom-based research, Alvarado works to understand factors that predict success in large CS courses, and to build stronger communities within these courses.

3.3 Mehran Sahami

Mehran Sahami works at the crossroads of CS education, data analytics, and machine learning. He has been involved in numerous educational projects including serving as past co-chair of the ACM Education Board and co-chair of the ACM/IEEE-CS joint task force on Computer Science Curricula 2013 (CS2013). Sahami has also worked on building statistical models to aid in the analysis and understanding of educational data. He will discuss challenges in data collection as well as models analyzing gender dynamics in introductory CS courses. These models help provide greater understanding of real versus perceived retention issues in introductory courses, especially with regard to students' intentions to pursue CS as a major.

3.4 Elsa Villa

Elsa Villa directs the Center for Education Research and Policy Studies at UTEP, having taught at numerous levels: grades 7 through 12, community college, and university in the disciplines of mathematics, science, education, engineering, and CS. Villa led a NSF-funded qualitative study investigating identity and agency in undergraduate Latina students. Since 1994, Villa has led and co-led numerous STEM grants from corporate foundations and state and federal agencies. Villa brings critical minority institution and minority student perspectives to the panel.

3.5 Stuart Zweben

Stu Zweben co-authors the annual reports of the CRA Taulbee Survey of doctoral-granting departments in the CS, CE, and Information areas, and the ACM NDC Study of non-doctoral-granting departments in computing. His many years of experience doing these surveys, his recent work with the CRA Generation-CS Report on the current enrollment surge in CS, and his more than a decade in academic administrative positions at a large public university, give him an understanding of the type of data that realistically can be obtained from most academic departments. Zweben will discuss the committee's analysis of retention-related data from NCWIT, and the prospects for a much more comprehensive study at a national level.

4 Conclusion

Successful interventions to improve the retention of women and underrepresented minority students in undergraduate CS programs require a better understanding of the extent and the nature of the problem at many different kinds of institutions. This panel will provide an understanding of the complexities of data collection and analysis across a sampling of universities and provide practical suggestions on the kinds of data that can and cannot be successfully collected, how factors such as intention to major complicate efforts to understand retention, and how data-supported interventions can help to address retention challenges.

ACKNOWLEDGMENTS

The panelists wish to thank ACM and the additional members of the ACM Retention Committee: Chris Stephenson (co-chair), Lecia Barker, Valerie Barr, Tracy Camp, Erin Mindell Cannon, Carol Frieze, Colleen Lewis, Lee Limbird, Debra Richardson, and Henry Walker.

REFERENCES

[1] B. Spice, "Women Are Almost Half of Carnegie Mellon's Incoming Computer Science Graduates," retrieved September 20, 2017 from https://www.csd.cs.cmu.edu/news/women-are-almost-half-carnegie-mellons-incoming-computer-science-undergraduates

[2] O. Stanley, "Harvey Mudd College Took on Gender Bias and Now More Than Half Its Computer Science Majors are Women," Retrieved September 20, 2017 from https://qz.com/730290/harvey-mudd-college-took-on-gender-bias-and-now-more-than-half-its-computer-science-majors-are-women/.

[3] S. Zweben and B. Bizot, "2017 Taulbee Survey: Another Year of Record Undergrad Enrollment: Doctoral Degree Production Steady While Master's Production Rises Again," Computing Research News, vol. 30(5), pp. 2–48, May 2017.

[4] Henry M. Walker, Mehran Sahami, and Christine Alvarado. 2018. Challenges and Approaches for Data Collection to Understand Student Retention: (Abstract Only). In Proceedings of the 49th ACM Technical Symposium on Computer Science Education (SIGCSE '18). ACM, New York, NY, USA, 1062-1062.

Why and How to Spend a Sabbatical in Industry

Ryan McFall
Hope College
mcfall@hope.edu

Zachary Kurmas
Grand Valley State University
kurmasz@gvsu.edu

Phillip Conrad
UC Santa Barbara
conrad@acm.org

Dennis Frailey
Raytheon Company (Retired)
University of Texas at Arlington
frailey@acm.org

CCS CONCEPTS

• **Social and professional topics → Computing education**; Employment issues;

KEYWORDS

Sabbatical

ACM Reference Format:
Ryan McFall, Zachary Kurmas, Phillip Conrad, and Dennis Frailey. 2019. Why and How to Spend a Sabbatical in Industry. In *Proceedings of the 50th ACM Technical Symposium on Computer Science Education (SIGCSE '19), February 27-March 2, 2019, Minneapolis, MN, USA.* ACM, New York, NY, USA, 2 pages. https://doi.org/10.1145/3287324.3287334

1 SUMMARY

We believe that more Computing faculty should spend some time in industry in order to experience for themselves the types of jobs their students are likely to take at graduation and throughout their careers. Each panelist has spent at least one sabbatical in industry and found the experience to be far more beneficial than anticipated. We all found that our sabbatical experiences helped us to (1) develop our skills, (2) discover and practice the skills that are currently being used in industry, (3) gain credibility with our students, (4) improve our understanding of the computing profession beyond software development, and (5) build relationships with local businesses. Many of us returned to the classroom thinking "I can't believe they let me teach college without any industry experience".

Our goal for this panel is to convince the audience that an industry sabbatical is both beneficial and accessible.[1] Specifically, we will

- clearly explain the benefits of a sabbatical in industry (for the faculty member, the employer, the students, and the university as a whole), and
- advise interested faculty how to go about organizing such a sabbatical (including pitfalls to avoid).

One panelist (Dennis) has also hired university faculty members for sabbatical positions while he was working in industry. He will share this perspective, as well as discuss the importance of using an industry sabbatical to better understand computing jobs beyond the stereotypical developer role that many students take upon graduation.

[1]By "accessible", we mean that one can be arranged with a reasonable amount of diligence and persistence. It's not easy, because preparing a good sabbatical proposal requires hard work; but, arranging a sabbatical in industry doesn't require an *undue* amount of work or luck.

SIGCSE '19, February 27-March 2, 2019, Minneapolis, MN, USA

ACM ISBN 978-1-4503-5890-3/19/02.
https://doi.org/10.1145/3287324.3287334

2 RYAN MCFALL

I spent Fall semester 2013 as a software developer at Open Systems Technologies (OST) in Grand Rapids, Michigan. OST is a consultancy with a diverse set of clients. At the time I was there, it was rapidly growing (from around 25 developers to somewhere around 60 currently). I was a member of a small team developing an internal web application for a legal services provider. I worked on both front and back end code for the system, and was able to see how database technologies such as Object-Relational Mapping frameworks such as NHibernate are used in the real world. And, while I had previously built significant web applications using perl and PHP, the sabbatical provided my first experience with a modern web framework (AngularJS in this case). As a result of my sabbatical, I enhanced the coverage of ORMs in my database course, developed a course on web development using the Angular framework, and presented a workshop at a CCSC conference on Angular development as well.

In addition to gaining experience as a software developer, I also sat in on a client acquisition meeting and several candidate interviews. The interviews in particular were very helpful as they allowed me to share what I observed with my students as they prepared for job interviews. Prior to my sabbatical, OST did not have any interns or full time employees who were Hope College graduates. In the past five years, four Hope graduates have obtained full-time employment at OST, with two other students completing internships there.

Bio: Ryan is a Professor of Computer Science at Hope College, where he has served since 2000. He recently completed his second term as department chair and is looking forward to being able to focus on teaching and scholarship again. He teaches a wide variety of courses including introductory programming for non-majors, web design, computer graphics, and database systems.

3 ZACHARY KURMAS

I have completed two year-long industry sabbaticals. The first was in 2010-2011 with Atomic Object. Atomic Object is a consultancy in Grand Rapids Michigan. The company, and my sabbatical experience there, are very similar to Ryan's experience at OST.

I spent the 2017-2018 academic year working as a software developer for Spectrum Health, a large healthcare company based in Grand Rapids, Michigan. Their IT department is almost 1500 employees, which includes about 50 developers.

This sabbatical with Spectrum Health was an ideal complement to my first sabbatical at Atomic Object. At Atomic Object, I learned how to develop software in a professional environment. In contrast, the main benefit from working at Spectrum Health was learning about the business processes that large companies use to manage very large, long-running, integrated software projects. I was particularly intrigued by (1) the way Spectrum Health integrated Agile practices into their existing, traditional planning and deployment processes, and (2) how Spectrum Health manages the complexity of maintaining a codebase and production environment that integrates several separate applications using many different data sources. I now have a much better understanding of why our students need to develop problem solving skills that can be applied more broadly than simply writing and debugging code.

I also got to personally experience the challenge of working in a codebase that has been modified by dozens of developers over the course of several years (i.e., dealing with documentation that is now missing and/or out of date).

Working at both Atomic Object and Spectrum Health and experiencing the differences in both workflow and culture will help me better direct students toward the type of company at which they will be happiest and most successful.

Bio: Zack is an Associate Professor of Computer Science at Grand Valley State University, where he has served since 2004. His main teaching interests include Computer Organization/Architecture and Web Programming. He also enjoys developing software for use in the classroom.

4 PHILLIP CONRAD

I spent the Summer of 2014 working as an "intern" for AppFolio, a Software as a Service (SaaS) startup near Santa Barbara, California. Rather than take a formal sabbatical, I asked AppFolio if they would be willing to offer me a "summer internship" in which I would have the same experience as an entry-level developer with a B.S. degree (i.e., my typical student).

During my time at AppFolio, I worked on two different teams as a Rails developer. I experienced many moments of humility as two of my first team members were former students who were now teaching me advanced concepts of agile, test design (including mocking and stubbing), continuous integration, and design patterns (to name just a few). By the sixth week, I was feeling confident in my ability to "pull my weight" in helping the team to complete each sprint. I came away with a renewed appreciation of the importance of the fundamentals we teach, but also a renewed ability to relate those fundamentals to current real world practices and career opportunities, to better motivate my students.

Bio: Phil is a Senior Lecturer at the University of California, Santa Barbara, where he has been on the Computer Science faculty since 2008. His main focus area is Computer Science Education.

5 DENNIS FRAILEY

I spent eight summers as an intern at Ford Motor Co. while a college student (graduate and undergraduate) and then for Texas Instruments in the summer during my 7 years as a full-time faculty member at SMU. I learned more about computer science and software engineering in these summer jobs than I ever did in the classroom. I took a sabbatical in 1977 from SMU to work at TI full time and ended up leaving the academic life to work in industry for the rest of my career (while teaching as an adjunct professor for the next 40 years). At TI and, later, Raytheon, I occasionally hired university faculty members during their sabbaticals so I have seen the situation from both the faculty and employer viewpoints.

I believe the most productive kind of sabbatical is where the faculty member works in a product development or support division of the company, not in a research division. Not only will they learn more about what their students are likely to experience, but they will develop an appreciation of many things not typically covered in the computer science textbooks.

Furthermore, I encourage faculty to consider sabbaticals that include non-developer roles (especially after the first sabbatical). Although software development is part of what I did, especially during my internship years, it was not the major part during my sabbatical year. I believe it is very important for CS faculty to understand that their students will not likely spend the bulk of their careers doing software development.

Bio: Dennis is a retired Principal Fellow from Raytheon company. He earned a B.S in Math from the University of Notre Dame, an MS in Computer Science from Purdue, and one of the earliest PhDs in Computer Science from Purdue in 1971. He has taught computer science and software engineering at SMU, U of Texas at Austin, and U of Texas at Arlington for almost 50 years. Dennis won the 2008 SIGCSE Lifetime Achievement Award for service to computer science education.

Punch Cards to Python: A Case Study of a CS0 Core Course

Thomas Babbitt
United States Military Academy
West Point, New York
thomas.babbitt@westpoint.edu

Charles Schooler
United States Military Academy
West Point, New York
charles.schooler@westpoint.edu

Kyle King
United States Military Academy
West Point, New York
kyle.king@westpoint.edu

ABSTRACT

There is an immense interest in teaching computer science concepts - and programming specifically - to everyone. The United States Military Academy at West Point has required every student, regardless of major, to pass a computer science zero (CS0) course for the last 50 years: From punch cards to Python. We present a history of our CS0 course and the lessons learned from the most recent redesign of the course. We review the last decade of student assessments and how they influenced the latest iteration.

We contrast the expectations of students in a CS0 course with those in a CS1 course. We discuss the national efforts to make CS accessible to all and explore the challenges unique to a CS0 course. We demonstrate similarities between our course and the Advance Placement CS Principles and show where differences are justified. We review the relevant pedagogical research for CS0 and present lessons learned over multiple iterations of the course.

Based on our current course review and implementation, we believe that Computer Science for everyone is attainable and relevant to the needs of every student.

CCS CONCEPTS

• **Social and professional topics** → **Computer science education**; *Computational thinking*; *Model curricula*; *CS1*; • **Applied computing** → *Interactive learning environments*;

KEYWORDS

Undergraduate Education, Computer Science Education, programming, programming tools, computational thinking

ACM Reference Format:
Thomas Babbitt, Charles Schooler, and Kyle King. 2019. Punch Cards to Python: A Case Study of a CS0 Core Course. In *Proceedings of the 50th ACM Technical Symposium on Computer Science Education (SIGCSE '19), February 27-March 2, 2019, Minneapolis, MN, USA.* ACM, New York, NY, USA, 7 pages. https://doi.org/10.1145/3287324.3287491

1 INTRODUCTION

Interest in computing education for *everyone* has grown rapidly in the last few years. In 2016, the White House launched the *Computer Science for All* initative [38], a large-scale effort to support pre-K through 12th graders using local and state programs. The *CS for All* initiative is maintained today through the National Science Foundation (NSF) and already has awarded over 200 grants [8]. In 2017, the first Advanced Placement Computer Science Principles (AP CSP) exams were administered. The AP CSP is a multidisciplinary computing course with seven focus areas: Creativity, Abstraction, Data and Information, Algorithms, Programming, The Internet, and Global Impact [6].

Today, most colleges offer an introduction to Computer Science course (CS0) geared toward students outside the computing discipline. There is little consensus on the role of computer programming in a CS0 course, with some courses focusing exclusively on programming but others focusing on programming concepts instead of programming itself [33]. For the last 50 years, every student at West Point has been required to learn computer programming. Since 1989, it has been as part of the school's compulsory CS0 course. We believe that programming occupies a central role in computing literacy and thus about a third of our CS0 focuses on programming instruction.

This paper discusses the history of our CS0 course, reviews the challenges in teaching computer programming to novices, explores the current best-practices in programming instruction, analyzes the last decade of student feedback for our institution's CS0 course, and enumerates the most valuable lessons learned in the most recent curricula redesign.

We assert that CS0 should be a requirement for all college students. While programming instruction is inherently challenging, we maintain that a CS0 education is attainable for everyone.

2 BACKGROUND

This section explores the challenges of teaching computer science concepts, specifically programming, to novice programmers and explores the current thinking and best practices for teaching a CS0/CS1 course.

2.1 History of CS0 at Our Institution

West Point's CS0 course has changed a number of times over the past 30 years (see Figure 1). Prior to 1989, a required course taught a number of different programming languages including FORTRAN with punch cards. Starting in 1989, with the restructuring of departments, a designated CS0/CS1 course was implemented and required for all students. The course focused exclusively on programming and problem solving and was similar to an introduction to Computer Science (CS1-level) course taught at most universities. The course was originally based on Turbo Pascal, which was popular at the time. The documentation on why the language was chosen is lost; however, it is worth noting that the AP Computer Science A/AB at that time also used Turbo Pascal.

In 1996, the programming language changed to Ada 95 in order to align with other CS courses taught at our institution. In 2001, the course switched to Java.

SIGCSE '19, February 27-March 2, 2019, Minneapolis, MN, USA
2019. ACM ISBN 978-1-4503-5890-3/19/02.
https://doi.org/10.1145/3287324.3287491

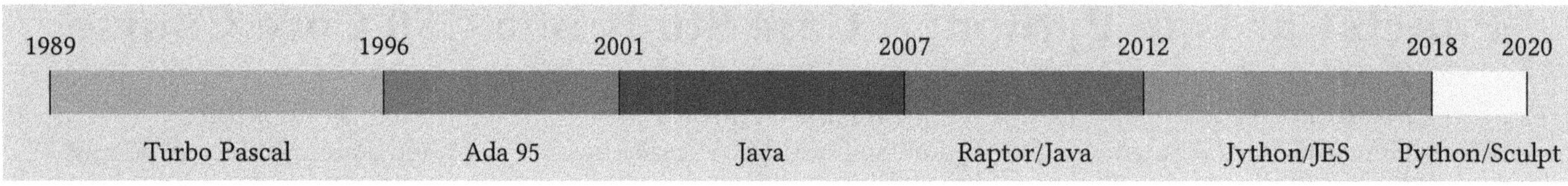

Figure 1: Course Time Line

In 2007, the course transitioned to Raptor with Java [9]. While the functionality is different from MIT's Scratch [33], many of the concepts are similar. It uses flow charts to solve a problem and generates much of the Java code for the student. The focus was on the concepts and problem-solving process which reduced the emphasis on programming.

In 2012, a pilot course using Jython [15] ran and was implemented the next year. This course used a multimedia approach [12, 14, 25]. It increased the emphasis on programming concepts, but maintained the rigor in networks, security, hardware, and ethics.

The most recent redesign, piloted in 2018, transitioned students to a Javascript (Skulpt) Python 3 implementation. The course material for the programming section borrow heavily from the *Think Like a Computer Scientist* text on Runestone Academy [26]. Section 3 provides details on the most resent course redesign.

2.2 AP CS Principles Overview

The AP Computer Science Principles (AP CSP) course covers six computational thinking practices: connecting computing, creating computational artifacts, abstracting, analyzing problems and artifacts, communicating, and collaborating. There are seven "Big Ideas": creativity, abstraction, data and information, algorithms, programming, the internet, and global impact [6, 20, 28]. Each "Big Idea," has a number of enduring understandings, learning objectives, and essential knowledge. In Section 3.1.1, we discuss how our course overlaps with AP CSP.

2.3 CS0 vs CS1 Expectations

The expectations of a CS0 course are different from those of a CS1 [10]. The AP CSP course is described as an introductory computing course [6], which we would consider a CS0. CS1 courses go into more depth on subjects that are germane to only those students who will pursue a Computer Science degree. Some examples of this include: introduction to data structures, object-oriented programming, and inheritance [7, 36].

Since programming is a "Big Idea" in AP CSP it should be in a CS0 course. Additionally, there should be an expectation of networking, cyber, and hardware lessons in a CS0 versus a CS1 course. We include all of these concepts in our redesigned course.

2.4 Relevant Pedagogical Research

Before embarking on the latest redesign of our CS0 course, we conducted a literature review. Based on the review, Problem Based Learning (PBL) [17, 37] and Worked-Out Examples [21, 30] were the best options.

The Jython Environment for Student (JES) [12, 15] version uses a PBL approach to teach programming. Students are given instruction and then directed to apply their knowledge to challenges, typically homework problems. Course scaffolding includes detailed discussion on picture objects with properties such as height, width, pixel coordinate, and color values. Students are taught basic programming constructs such as conditionals and iteration. Then students were expected to apply the programming constructs such as sequence, iteration, and selection to effect changes to a picture.

From the literature and the collective experience of the course designers, we decided to move to a worked-out examples approach in our new course in which we dedicate a large portion of the class to "walking" students through example problems. Examples give students a place to start and provide the recurring aspects of a task. Worked-out examples help novices reach early successes without cognitive overload, i.e. excessive stress [21].

Once the novice programmer has acquired a baseline set of recurring aspect knowledge and some rudimentary problem solving skills, instruction can transition from product-based to process-based worked-out examples. Product-based worked-out examples consist of only the recurring knowledge such as how to assign a variable. Process-based worked-out examples add in the *how* and the *why*, such as the realization that a variable is a location in memory with a particular value. This improves the novice programmer's problem solving skills and helps transfer these skills to high order problems and other domains.

Fading is the key to making novice programmers self-sufficient. *Forward fading* consists of removing the first part of the problem and letting the novice programmer solve the problem by providing the solution. *Backwards fading* provides the beginning of the problem and the novice programmer completes the problem [41].

There are also extraneous difficulties in learning to program, such as an Integrated Development Environment (IDE) or compiler/interpreter. These programs can be unintuitive to the novice and may contribute to the cognitive overload that novices experience in learning to program [5].

2.5 General Purpose Languages

Hiding the details of program execution makes beginner languages more accessible to novices. Beginner languages like MIT's Scratch [33] feature drag-and-drop interfaces for programming constructs like *for loops* and function declarations. There is research that suggests that using a beginner language is appropriate for a CS0 course [13]; however, some experiences suggest that beginner languages are limited in their utility for solving real-world problems [18].

2.6 Historical CS1 Failure Rates

The general consensus is that introductory programming courses are difficult [16, 39, 40]. In fact, CS1 courses have both the highest

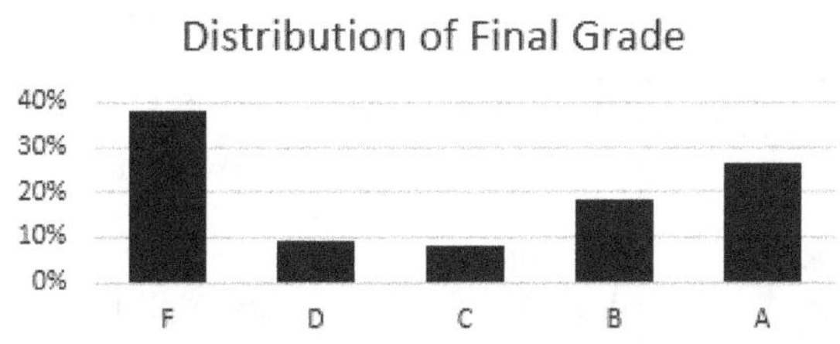

Figure 2: Historical CS1 Grades [34]

enrollment rates and the highest dropout rates at many schools [23, 24, 35]. Study after study indicates that students in introductory programming courses will generally fall into one of two groups: a highly successful group and a failing group [31, 32, 34]. Generally there are very few students in between. The most common grade in a CS1 course is an "F" followed by an "A" (Figure 2) [34].

The distribution of IQ across the general population is, by definition, a normal distribution. We asked ourselves, if student performance in an introductory programming course is a function of intelligence, why doesn't student performance exhibit the same distribution as IQ? Our research shows that student grades are not a function of cognitive capacity, development, or style; attitude or motivation; demographic factors, such as previous exposure to math or computers; or a number of aptitudes [34, 40].

Prior work argues that the highly integrated nature of the computer programming splits learners into groups that either succeed or fail [34, 40]. Computers have a multitude of components that work simultaneously to perform a single task. Programs similarly have a multitude of concepts that work simultaneously to generate the instructions for the completion of that task. The concepts must be learned serially, but no individual concept makes sense in isolation.

Since programming concepts are so integrated, a failure to understand one single concept makes it increasingly difficult to understand the next. Conversely, each idea that a student successfully grasps provides more context for reasoning about additional concepts. These students find programming concepts to be increasingly complementary and intuitive and have a greater chance of success [34, 40]. The result is one group of successful students and a second group of comprehensively confused students. This manifests in a bi-modal distribution of final grades.

Over the past seven years, the percentage of students who pass our CS0 course has been approximately 99%. Most years there are over 1,100 students taking the course. Unlike the statistics in the previous paragraphs, the AP CSP course has a passing rate of 72.7% for 2018 [4]. Passing is considered three or higher on the AP exam. The percentage to earn the lowest grade of one in 2018 is 7.6%. Because we focus on many computing topics, a student that struggles in programming does not automatically fail our course.

3 COURSE DESCRIPTION

Our redesigned CS0 course is divided into three modules: Hardware, Software, and Cyber. Table 1 enumerates the topics in each module. Each module is composed of roughly ten 75-minute lessons. The redesigned course starts with hardware then transitions to software with lessons covering operating systems, algorithms, and high level programming languages prior to programming. The course culminates with discussions on networks, data, ethics, cyber security, and cyber law & warfare.

This redesign commits much more time to hardware and cyber concepts than did previous course iterations. Over the past few years, the software module had slowly grown to give instructors more time on the topic that students struggle with the most i.e., programming. However, our direct experience from last year's pilot argues that spending more time on hardware actually does more to help students comprehend programming concepts than do additional software lessons. We believe that ordering the hardware lessons before the software lessons, and expanding the time spent on hardware, together increase student understanding of computer programming. We intend to collect the data necessary to explore that hypothesis.

Each lesson is structured so that it begins with a short quiz on the assigned reading to check knowledge and frame the discussion [3, 22]. We discuss the lesson topic for about 20-30 minutes. Every lesson concludes with a 15-20 minute in-class activity/worked out examples (Section 2.4) when students apply or explore the lesson concepts through some interactive activity. Importantly, interactivity helps to solidify concepts and make them less abstract. For example, during the robotics lesson, we watch a robot refine its stored map as it navigates obstacles in the classroom. During our web lesson, students manipulate a chat room using HTML, Javascript, and cookies.

3.1 Key Decisions

There were a number of key decisions made in redesigning the course: to keep it a CS0 instead of a CS1 course, to use a high level language instead of a beginner language, and to ensure a large overlap with the AP CS Principles course.

3.1.1 Use AP CS Principles as a model. Our course has a large overlap with the AP CSP course. We cover approximately 84% of the learning outcomes. The lesson topics to CS Principle "Big Ideas" crosswalk are found in Table 1. See Section 2.2 for an overview of AP CSP.

The major area where our course differs from the AP course is a reduced emphasis on collaborative work (a AP CSP computational thinking practice). While there are opportunities to collaborate, graded events are almost exclusively individual. Second, we also reduced emphasis in the *Data and Information* "Big Idea" in favor of other topics.

There are two concepts we think are important albeit slightly outside of the scope of the AP CSP. The first is hardware; we spend quite a bit of time discussing the hardware in a computer, then use an Arduino and robots to help solidify the concept. The second important concept is Cyber Law and warfare.

3.1.2 Follow CS0 Expectations. Trying to model our CS0 course after the typical CS1 courses is not feasible. As a compulsory course for mostly non-Computer Science majors, the design of a CS0 course is, and ought to be, different from a CS1 course. Our course trades a rigorous programming education for more breadth across IT topics [1]. However, we believe that their exposure in our CS0

Hardware		Software		Cyber	
Our Lesson Topics	AP CSP "Big Ideas"	Our Lesson Topics	AP CSP "Big Ideas"	Our Lesson Topics	AP CSP "Big Ideas"
Computers	Abstraction	OS and File Systems	Abstraction	WWW	Internet; Global Impact
Encoding data	Abstraction	Algorithms	Algorithms	The Internet	Internet
CPU	Abstraction	Languages	Abstraction	Data & Ethics	Data; Global Impact
Analog to Digital Conversion	Abstraction	Variables and Expressions	Abstraction; Programming	Threats in Cyberspace	Abstraction; Internet; Global Impact
Sensor Lab: Arduino	Creativity	Turtle Graphics & Modules	Creativity; Abstraction	Cybersecurity	Internet; Global Impact
LANs	Internet	Functions; Selection; Iteration	Programming	Cyber Law & Warfare	Global Impact
Robots & Drones	Abstraction; Global Impact	Software Development; Debugging	Programming		

Table 1: Our Lesson Topics Crosswalk the AP Computer Science "Big Ideas"

course sets a solid foundation for students that are interested in doing more in that domain.

3.1.3 Use Updated and Online Textbooks. We use three textbooks for our new course. The first is *Understanding the Digital World* [19] which covers hardware, the internet, privacy, and security. The second is *How to Think Like a Computer Scientist* online book (thinkcspy) on the Runestone Academy website [26]. The thinkcspy "book" embeds course material, videos, and knowledge checks along side executable programming challenges. This approach is well documented in [2, 27]. The third is an arduino uno that we use for labs.

The course textbook becomes stale over time (see Section 4.1). Defenses against this are readily available. Using a newer book for the non-programming portion facilitates up-to-date instruction on many of the non-programming AP CSP "Big Ideas." An on-line interactive book for programming can be modified each semester to help keep the course interactive and fresh.

3.1.4 Use of a General Purpose Language. We chose to use a general purpose language, specifically Python. Python is a popular language with a minimal syntax that is readily used to solve a variety of real-world problems. This real-world utility is limited by our choice to use a JavaScript-based Python implementation. We use JavaScript (Skulpt) so that we can integrate and assess students directly on Blackboard, our web-based LMS. Skulpt is not a complete Python implementation, it does not support C extensions, and it runs in a browser instead of a traditional operating system. Skulpt works well for our purposes, but limits students' ability to leverage external libraries and execute examples they find online.

Ideally, we want the simplicity of a beginner language, such as a simple web-based editor, with the power and utility of a general-purpose language, so that students can use their knowledge more directly to solve real-world problems.

3.1.5 Ensure Interactive Feedback. Students struggle to understand how to combine the many components of a language into a meaningful program. To reduce the amount of students' time spent on syntactic errors, we've configured our editor to detect and provide feedback on most syntactic errors. Programming challenges in the new course are accompanied by a battery of unit tests. This gives immediate and detailed feedback to the student each time the program is executed and reduces cognitive load [29]. For instance, if a student must define a function that adds two numbers together, the unit tests will verify that they've defined a function, the function is named correctly, the function takes two arguments, and the function leverages the addition operator and a return statement, and that the function returns the correct value given two numbers.

We can achieve a high-level of interactivity for programming questions through Runestone Academy's unit tests. If unit tests have been defined for a question, then students receive immediate feedback on issues with their code. A robust set of tests for code will edge students toward solving a problem on their own.

This immediate and detailed feedback has been crucial in the early programming lessons in helping students diagnose their programs' errors. We've found that these unit tests greatly reduce the time students spend randomly trying new approaches in the hope that something will work.

3.2 Transitioning to Web-Based Instruction

For the pilot course offering, we explored various web-based programming platforms. Computer programming is increasingly moving to the web. Platforms like Microsoft's Azure Notebooks, Binder, Trinket, and CodeEnvy provide programming environments and development tools through a web browser. These programming tools have the benefit of being accessible from any Internet-connected device.

An online book eliminates the need for students to install and learn a programming tool, like JES [15]. Every student is already intimately familiar with how to use a web browser, and a web-based environment is much less intimidating for a novice programmer.

3.2.1 Use an Interactive Web-Based Programming Environment (Gadget). Our *Gadget* (Figure 3) incorporates the look and feel of trinket.io's Trinket with Runestone's Python 3/Skulpt code evaluation engine. Gadgets are hosted directly within Blackboard and, like Runestone, allow students to write and execute code within the

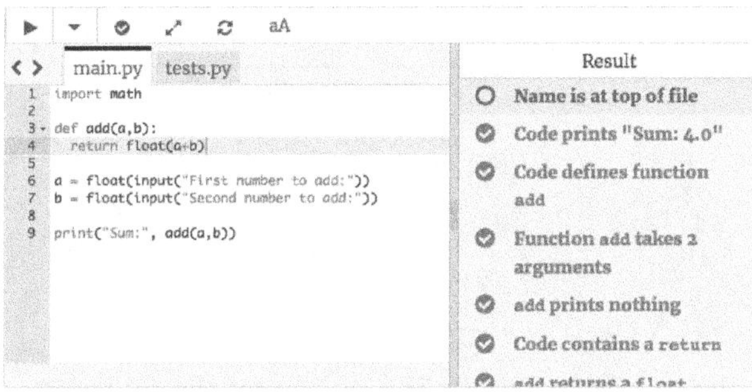

Figure 3: An IT105 Gadget incorporates the look and feel of trinket.io's Trinket with Runestone's Python 3 code evaluation engine

assigned reading webpage. Gadgets are also used for programming assessment. We are able to create programming questions alongside multiple choice, or other types of questions, when building a Blackboard assessment.

Gadgets, like Trinkets, are built on the open-source Ace editor which detects syntax errors and provides syntax highlighting. We created a robust unit-testing framework that makes it easy for instructors to incorporate a wide variety of tests in their programming questions. Gadgets also support sending code to the Python Tutor website for visual debugging [11].

3.2.2 Addressing Limitations of Web-based Programming. Our initial pilot suffered from a severe lack of integration. The hardware and cyber modules were hosted and accessed through Blackboard but the software module was hosted and accessed through Runestone. On top of requiring a second account for students, student scores had to be regularly transferred between the two systems.

In the end, we ported the relevant lessons from *How to Think Like a Computer Scientist* to Blackboard and created our own inline code execution tool (see above). Integrating with Blackboard significantly reduced the overhead of teaching programming across our nearly 30 offerings of the course. Unfortunately, the integration is not native and gadgets are slow to load and don't play well with other tools in the Blackboard ecosystem, such as the Lockdown Browser. We hope to see an LMS with a native code execution ability in the future or another more seamless plugin framework for integrating a code execution tool into a LMS.

4 STUDENT FEEDBACK ASSESSMENT

Figure 4 has three plots that show the results from the last decade of end-of-course surveys. The number of respondents per year is listed at the bottom (n). Each value statement on the end-of-course survey uses a five-value "Likert" rating scale. The scores on the rating scale, starting at one and ending at five, are: Strongly Disagree, Disagree, Neutral, Agree, and Strongly Agree. The higher the value the more a given student agrees with a particular statement. The vertical line at AY13 represents the major revision of the course from Rapter/Java to Jython depicted in Figure 1.

These results helped inform the decision to modify the course. The statement topics fall into three general categories describing: (1) textbook contribution (Figure 4a); (2) motivation (Figure 4b); and (3) confidence in being able to use programming or technology to solve future problems (Figure 4c).

The end-of-course survey value-statements are:

A6 My motivation to learn and to continue learning has increased because of this course.

C6 The textbook and readings made a major positive contribution to how much I learned.

D1 I learned to think about the implications of technology as a result of this course.

D4 If you have to learn a new piece of software that requires you to program it, how confident are you that you can use the software to solve your problem?

D5 How confident are you that you can learn and use a new piece of information technology on your own?

Our CS0 course was redesigned twice in the last decade, with pilots running in academic years 2012 and 2018. They have significantly smaller sample numbers, $n = 107$ and $n = 16$ respectively and results are annotated with *pilot.*

4.1 Textbook Utility

The statement with the largest downward trend for both the Raptor/Java and Jython version of the course is the one based on the perceived utility of the textbook (**C6**). Figure 4a illustrates the trend. Students initially enjoy a new textbook but after a year or two that level of satisfaction drastically reduces.

We cannot pinpoint the exact cause for the changes; however, there are a number of reasons students' satisfaction with the utility of a textbook could wane over time. Some possible causes includes the following: concern over the textbook cost, or the fact that all students must take this core course, so over time the key focus areas become known and free study guides replace the textbook. Additionally, slides and in-class examples are actively incorporated and the textbook is emphasized less by the instructors [3, 22]. In a CS0 course, like ours, a textbook falls behind current technologies quickly. Due to the small sample size, the significant increase in perceived utility for the online interactive textbook for the pilot in 2018 is not considered definitive.

4.2 Motivation

Proving relevance and engendering effort for a programming course, for a History or Chinese-language major who sees minimal value beyond graduation, is challenging. Table 4b shows the results for question **A6**. Enthusiasm for a new version of the course initially increases and then begins to drop. From 2008-2012 the values remain relatively consistent with a slight drop in 2012. In 2013, there is a significant drop, which corresponds to a transition year. The JES focused course shows a similar trend starting in 2013. Motivation initially increases for a few years and then shows a downward trend.

The first year is likely lower because students' older peers, who took the previous version of the course, cannot assist in study. It increases as the student body becomes more familiar with the content and then declines once the content becomes too well known. We speculate it is due to extensive familiarity with the course (as when numerous examples are available for students to cut and paste), staleness of tools, or predictability of instruction itself.

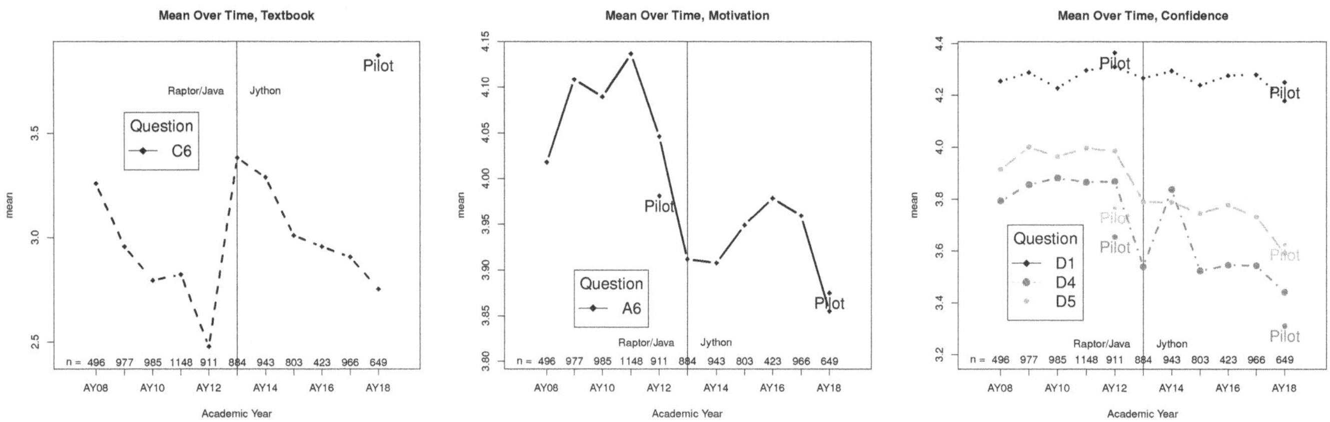

(a) Textbook (b) Motivation (c) Confidence

Figure 4: End of Course Survey Results

4.3 Problem Solving Using Programming or Technology

There are three survey statements related to problem-solving using programming and technology (Figure 4c). Response levels for **D1** remained consistently high over the past decade and focused on awareness of technology. Today's companies must take into account the moral and ethical issues, as well as second and third order effects of using technology. They must not be timid in learning or using new technology in their day-to-day lives. Most students have grown up in a ubiquitous technology world that likely contributes to this consistency.

Items **D4** and **D5** relate to students' confidence in their skills in programming or in using technology to solve a problem. Both of those statements have shown a downward trend over the past five years. Reasons may include: relevance of the material, presentation methods, scaffolding, textbook, and tools used. Many of these problems have been discussed herein previously.

5 LESSONS LEARNED

This section summarizes the most significant lessons learned through our redesign. These lessons are discussed in details in the other sections of this paper, but we enumerate them here so that it might be a handy summary for other schools that are also looking to implement or redesign their CS0 courses:

Include programming instruction in a CS0 course. There is no consensus on the role of programming in a CS0 course. We believe that programming is a central component of computer literacy.

Include computer hardware instruction. Our initial pilot results strongly indicate that students with a firmer grasp of computer hardware concepts will better absorb programming concepts.

Keep the textbook fresh. Our student assessments over the last 10 years indicate that the value of a CS0 textbook degrades over time.

Use a general purpose language Use Python or JavaScript, instead of a beginner language. While hiding the details of program execution makes beginner languages more accessible to novices, exposure to more challenging details may be necessary for the student to advance beyond trivial program designs [39].

Make the course web-based. If using an LMS, it is best to integrate programming. This reduces the context switch between the course material and code execution. Many coding platforms exist online so this approach doesn't deprive students of a realistic development environment.

Ensure there is interactive feedback. Immediate and detailed feedback is crucial, especially in early programming lessons, to help students diagnose programming errors.

Use the AP CS Principles Course as a guide. Every institution is different and its courses takes a unique approach; however, the AP CSP is a standard measure of what a CS0 course should look like. A good amount of overlap is desirable.

6 CONCLUSION

Our institution has been teaching Computer Science concepts and programming to every student for over 50 years. As computing becomes increasingly relevant to other disciplines, the need for every student to have a basic understanding of computers and computer programming will only increase. While the expectations for students in a CS0 course are lower than those in a CS1 course, we believe that CS0 is a valuable and necessary component of every college student's education. Decades of student assessment and feedback support the conclusion that a college-level CS0 course should be compulsory and grades indicate it is attainable for all.

ACKNOWLEDGMENTS

Special thanks to Dr. Suzanne Matthews for her assistance in shaping and reviewing this paper. Her efforts significantly improved the final version. The views expressed in this article are those of the authors and do not reflect the official policy or position of the Department of the Army, Department of Defense or the U.S. Government.

REFERENCES

[1] Kenneth L. Alford, Curtis A. Carter, Daniel J. Ragsdale, Eugene K. Ressler, and Charles W. Reynolds. 2004. Specification and Managed Development of Information Technology Curricula. In *Proceedings of the 5th Conference on Information Technology Education (CITC5 '04)*. ACM, New York, NY, USA, 261–266. https://doi.org/10.1145/1029533.1029598

[2] Christine Alvarado, Briana B. Morrison, Barbara Ericson, Mark Guzdial, and Brad Miller. 2012. *Performance and use evaluation of an electronic book for introductory Python programming*. Technical Report GT-IC-12-02. Georgia Institute of Technology.

[3] Thomas Berry, Lori Cook, Nancy Hill, and Kevin Stevens. 2010. An Exploratory Analysis of Textbook Usage and Study Habits: Misperceptions and Barriers to Success. *College Teaching* 59, 1 (2010), 31–39. https://doi.org/10.1080/87567555.2010.509376 arXiv:https://doi.org/10.1080/87567555.2010.509376

[4] College Board. 2018. AP Score Distributions. https://apscore.collegeboard.org/scores/about-ap-scores/score-distributions//

[5] Paul Chandler and John Sweller. 1996. Cognitive Load While Learning to Use a Computer Program. *Applied Cognitive Psychology* 10, 2 (Apr 1996), 151–170. https://doi.org/10.1002/(SICI)1099-0720(199604)10:2<151::AID-ACP380>3.0.CO;2-U

[6] CollegeBoard. 2017. AP® Computer Science Principles: Including the Curriculum Framework. https://apcentral.collegeboard.org/pdf/ap-computer-science-principles-course-and-exam-description.pdf?course=ap-computer-science-principles

[7] Nell B. Dale. 2006. Most Difficult Topics in CS1: Results of an Online Survey of Educators. *SIGCSE Bull.* 38, 2 (June 2006), 49–53. https://doi.org/10.1145/1138403.1138432

[8] National Science Foundation. 2018. Computer Science for All (CSforAll:RPP). https://www.nsf.gov/funding/pgm_summ.jsp?pims_id=505359

[9] John C. Giordano and Martin Carlisle. 2006. Toward a More Effective Visualization Tool to Teach Novice Programmers. In *Proceedings of the 7th Conference on Information Technology Education (SIGITE '06)*. ACM, New York, NY, USA, 115–122. https://doi.org/10.1145/1168812.1168841

[10] Dee Gudmundsen, Lisa Olivieri, and Namita Sarawagi. 2011. Using Visual Logic©: Three Different Approaches in Different Courses - General Education, CS0, and CS1. *J. Comput. Sci. Coll.* 26, 6 (June 2011), 23–29. http://dl.acm.org/citation.cfm?id=1968521.1968529

[11] Philip J. Guo. 2013. Online Python Tutor: Embeddable Web-based Program Visualization for Cs Education. In *Proceeding of the 44th ACM Technical Symposium on Computer Science Education (SIGCSE '13)*. ACM, New York, NY, USA, 579–584. https://doi.org/10.1145/2445196.2445368

[12] Mark Guzdial. 2003. A Media Computation Course for Non-majors. In *Proceedings of the 8th Annual Conference on Innovation and Technology in Computer Science Education (ITiCSE '03)*. ACM, New York, NY, USA, 104–108. https://doi.org/10.1145/961511.961542

[13] Mark Guzdial. 2008. Education: Paving the Way for Computational Thinking. *Commun. ACM* 51, 8 (Aug. 2008), 25–27. https://doi.org/10.1145/1378704.1378713

[14] Mark Guzdial and Elliot Soloway. 2002. Teaching the Nintendo Generation to Program. *Commun. ACM* 45, 4 (April 2002), 17–21. https://doi.org/10.1145/505248.505261

[15] Mark J. Guzdial and Barbara Ericson. 2016. *Introduction to Computing and Programming in Python, A Multimedia Approach* (4th ed.). Pearson, Hoboken, NJ, USA.

[16] Filiz KALELIOĞLU and Yasemin Gülbahar. 2014. The Effects of Teaching Programming via Scratch on Problem Solving Skills: A Discussion from Learners' Perspective. *Informatics in Education* 13, 1 (2014).

[17] Judy Kay, Michael Barg, Alan Fekete, Tony Greening, Owen Hollands, Jeffrey H. Kingston, and Kate Crawford. 2000. Problem-Based Learning for Foundation Computer Science Courses. *Computer Science Education* 10, 2 (2000), 109–128. https://doi.org/10.1076/0899-3408(200008)10:2;1-C;FT109 arXiv:https://doi.org/10.1076/0899-3408(200008)10:2;1-C;FT109

[18] Caitlin Kelleher and Randy Pausch. 2005. Lowering the Barriers to Programming: A Taxonomy of Programming Environments and Languages for Novice Programmers. *ACM Comput. Surv.* 37, 2 (June 2005), 83–137. https://doi.org/10.1145/1089733.1089734

[19] Brian W. Kernighan. 2017. *Understanding the Digital World.* Princeton University Press, 41 Williams Street, Princeton, New Jersey, 08540.

[20] Richard Kick and Frances P. Trees. 2015. AP CS Principles: Engaging, Challenging, and Rewarding. *ACM Inroads* 6, 1 (Feb. 2015), 42–45. https://doi.org/10.1145/2710672

[21] Chee Sern Lai, Kahirol Mohd Salleh, Nor Lisa Sulaiman, Mimi Mohaffyza Mohamad, and Jailani Md Yunos. 2014. The effects of worked example and problem solving on learning performance and cognitive load. In *4th Shanghai International Conference on Social Science 2014.* 131–143.

[22] James Lang. 2009. Choosing and Using Textbooks. https://www.chronicle.com/article/ChoosingUsing-Textbooks/44820

[23] Katherine Long. 2014. UW maxed out on computer-science space. *The Seattle Times* (2014). https://www.seattletimes.com/seattle-news/uw-maxed-out-on-computer-science-space/

[24] Katherine Long. 2016. Demand for computer science forces Washington colleges to ramp up. *The Seattle Times* (2016). https://www.seattletimes.com/seattle-news/education/with-surge-in-computer-science-majors-state-colleges-struggle-to-keep-pace/

[25] Tanya Markow, Eugene Ressler, and Jean Blair. 2006. Catch That Speeding Turtle: Latching Onto Fun Graphics in CS1. In *Proceedings of the 2006 Annual ACM SIGAda International Conference on Ada (SIGAda '06)*. ACM, New York, NY, USA, 29–34. https://doi.org/10.1145/1185642.1185648

[26] Brad Miller and David Ranum. 2014. Runestone Interactive: Tools for Creating Interactive Course Materials. In *Proceedings of the First ACM Conference on Learning @ Scale Conference (L@S '14)*. ACM, New York, NY, USA, 213–214. https://doi.org/10.1145/2556325.2567887

[27] Bradley N. Miller and David L. Ranum. 2012. Beyond PDF and ePub: Toward an Interactive Textbook. In *Proceedings of the 17th ACM Annual Conference on Innovation and Technology in Computer Science Education (ITiCSE '12)*. ACM, New York, NY, USA, 150–155. https://doi.org/10.1145/2325296.2325335

[28] Ralph Morelli, Chinma Uche, Pauline Lake, and Lawrence Baldwin. 2015. Analyzing Year One of a CS Principles PD Project. In *Proceedings of the 46th ACM Technical Symposium on Computer Science Education (SIGCSE '15)*. ACM, New York, NY, USA, 368–373. https://doi.org/10.1145/2676723.2677265

[29] Roxana Moreno. 2004. Decreasing Cognitive Load for Novice Students: Effects of Explanatory versus Corrective Feedback in Discovery-Based Multimedia. *Instructional Science* 32, 1 (01 Jan 2004), 99–113. https://doi.org/10.1023/B:TRUC.0000021811.66966.1d

[30] Roxana Moreno, Martin Reisslein, and Gamze Ozogul. 2009. Optimizing Worked-Example Instruction in Electrical Engineering: The Role of Fading and Feedback during Problem-Solving Practice. *Journal of Engineering Education* 98, 1 (Jan 2009), 83–92. https://doi.org/10.1002/j.2168-9830.2009.tb01007.x arXiv:https://onlinelibrary.wiley.com/doi/pdf/10.1002/j.2168-9830.2009.tb01007.x

[31] Andrew Petersen, Michelle Craig, and Daniel Zingaro. 2011. Reviewing CS1 Exam Question Content. In *Proceedings of the 42Nd ACM Technical Symposium on Computer Science Education (SIGCSE '11)*. ACM, New York, NY, USA, 631–636. https://doi.org/10.1145/1953163.1953340

[32] Leo Porter and Daniel Zingaro. 2014. Importance of Early Performance in CS1: Two Conflicting Assessment Stories. In *Proceedings of the 45th ACM Technical Symposium on Computer Science Education (SIGCSE '14)*. ACM, New York, NY, USA, 295–300. https://doi.org/10.1145/2538862.2538912

[33] Mitchel Resnick, John Maloney, Andrés Monroy-Hernández, Natalie Rusk, Evelyn Eastmond, Karen Brennan, Amon Millner, Eric Rosenbaum, Jay Silver, Brian Silverman, and Yasmin Kafai. 2009. Scratch: Programming for All. *Commun. ACM* 52, 11 (Nov. 2009), 60–67. https://doi.org/10.1145/1592761.1592779

[34] Anthony Robins. 2010. Learning edge momentum: a new account of outcomes in CS1. *Computer Science Education* 20, 1 (2010), 37–71. https://doi.org/10.1080/08993401003612167

[35] Anthony Robins, Janet Rountree, and Nathan Rountree. 2003. Learning and Teaching Programming: A Review and Discussion. *Computer Science Education* 13, 2 (2003), 137–172. https://doi.org/10.1076/csed.13.2.137.14200 arXiv:https://doi.org/10.1076/csed.13.2.137.14200

[36] Hamzeh Roumani. 2006. Practice What You Preach: Full Separation of Concerns in CS1/CS2. In *Proceedings of the 37th SIGCSE Technical Symposium on Computer Science Education (SIGCSE '06)*. ACM, New York, NY, USA, 491–494. https://doi.org/10.1145/1121341.1121495

[37] John R Savery. 2006. Overview of problem-based learning: Definitions and distinctions. *Interdisciplinary Journal of Problem-based Learning* 1, 1 (2006), 3.

[38] Megan Smith. 2016. Computer Science For All. https://goo.gl/F96bYV

[39] Elliot Soloway. 1993. Should We Teach Students to Program? *Commun. ACM* 36, 10 (Oct. 1993), 21–24. https://doi.org/10.1145/163430.164061

[40] J. Sorva. 2010. Reflections on threshold concepts in computer programming and beyond. *Proceedings of the 10th Koli Calling International Conference on Computing Education Research* (2010).

[41] Tamara Van Gog, Fred Paas, and Jeroen JG Van Merriënboer. 2004. Process-oriented worked examples: Improving transfer performance through enhanced understanding. *Instructional Science* 32, 1-2 (2004), 83–98.

Designing a Middle School Science Curriculum that Integrates Computational Thinking and Sensor Technology

Alexandra Gendreau Chakarov
University of Colorado Boulder
Boulder, CO
alexandra.gendreau@colorado.edu

Mimi Recker
Utah State University
Logan, UT
mimi.recker@usu.edu

Jennifer Jacobs
University of Colorado Boulder
Boulder, CO
jennifer.jacobs@colorado.edu

Katie Van Horne
University of Colorado Boulder
Boulder, CO
katie.vanhorne@colorado.edu

Tamara Sumner
University of Colorado Boulder
Boulder, CO
sumner@colorado.edu

ABSTRACT

This experience report describes two iterations of a curriculum development process in which middle school teachers worked with our research team to collaboratively design and enact instructional units where students used sensors to investigate scientific phenomena. In this report, we examine the affordances of using a sensor platform to support the integration of disciplinary learning and computational thinking (CT) aligned with Next Generation Science Standards [13] and the CT in STEM Taxonomy developed by Weintrop and colleagues [31]. In the first unit, students investigated the conditions for mold growth within their school using a custom sensor system. After analyzing implementation experiences and student interest data, our team engaged in another round of co-design to develop a second instructional unit. This unit uses a different sensor system (the micro:bit) which supports additional CT in STEM practices due to its block-based programming interface and its real time data display. For the second unit we selected a different phenomenon: understanding and designing maglev trains.

KEYWORDS

Computational Thinking, Middle School Science, Sensors

ACM Reference Format:

Alexandra Gendreau Chakarov, Mimi Recker, Jennifer Jacobs, Katie Van Horne, and Tamara Sumner. 2019. Designing a Middle School Science Curriculum that Integrates Computational Thinking and Sensor Technology. In *Proceedings of the 50th ACM Technical Symposium on Computer Science Education (SIGCSE '19), February 27-March 2, 2019, Minneapolis, MN, USA.* ACM, New York, NY, USA, 7 pages. https://doi.org/10.1145/3287324.3287476

1 INTRODUCTION

Computational thinking (CT) and big data practices are having profound effects in all scientific domains and are fundamentally changing the ways scientists work. Exposing students to these practices not only gives them insight into these modern scientific practices but also introduces them to applications of computer science and data science.

States across the U.S. are increasingly adopting a new approach for K-12 science education called the Next Generation Science Standards (NGSS) [13]. These standards define science education in terms of three dimensions: science and engineering practices, disciplinary core ideas, and crosscutting concepts with the goal of making science classes more inquiry-driven and similar to the work of scientists.

However, a critical gap remains in understanding how to best integrate CT into NGSS-aligned science instruction beyond simply including more and bigger datasets or adding technological instruments. Instead, the goal is to provide students with ongoing experiences to advance their CT skills and support their understanding of how those skills are a fundamental aspect of contemporary scientific inquiry.

One promising approach is through the use small, mobile sensors [3, 8, 16]. Sensors have long been used to support the learning of computer science and computational thinking through tools such as LEGO Mindstorms™ and other robotics [14, 23]. As these sensors become increasingly low-cost and widely available, they are more accessible to teachers for classroom use. They can be instrumented to provide fine grained and continuous measurements of the physical world (e.g., temperature, magnetism) in order to explore scientific phenomena such as air quality [32] or information about the local watershed [15].

Moreover, research suggests that focusing on *place* can offer a powerful tool for engaging learners from underrepresented groups in STEM [1, 11, 19, 30]. Place-based investigations focus on personally relevant scientific phenomena or activities that address issues meaningful to the local community. Students consider *why here?* and *so what?* questions that provide local context for the phenomenon they are learning about [6].

As part of our research on integrating CT and sensor technology into middle school science curriculum, our goal is to design a coherent sequence of lessons that meet all of the criteria described above and represented in Figure 1 as "design constraints." To this end, we employ a design methodology that we label the CT-Integration Cycle, which involves developing, implementing, and reflecting on CT-integrated science units. The CT-Integration Cycle draws on

SIGCSE '19, February 27-March 2, 2019, Minneapolis, MN, USA

ACM ISBN 978-1-4503-5890-3/19/02...$15.00
https://doi.org/10.1145/3287324.3287476

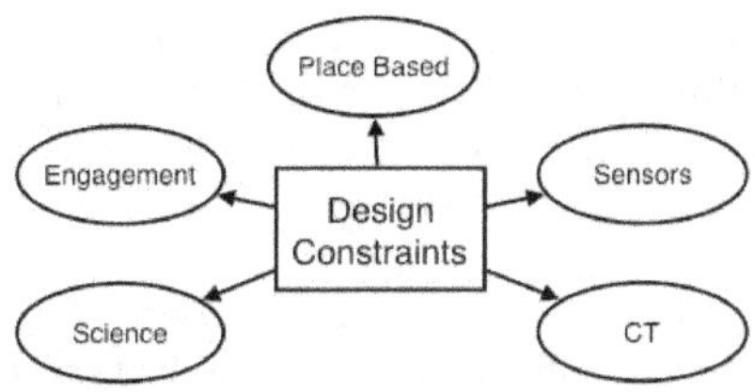

Figure 1: Set of constraints that influence our design process.

three strategies that have proven useful in developing NGSS curriculum: design based implementation research (DBIR), storylines, and collaborative design (co-design).

In DBIR, new educational interventions are developed and refined through iterative design cycles, involving field deployment and data collection [7]. DBIR emphasizes the cyclic nature of the design work where reflections from previous implementations influence the next development session. Moreover, a critical aspect of DBIR is on addressing key problems of practice in the target environment, in our case middle school science.

Storylines [20, 21] are a resource for developing science curricula that are meant to support NGSS alignment. Storylines provide an avenue for the integration of CT into science classes by explicating what science concepts students will "figure out" and which practices they will use to make sense of phenomena through a series of connected, student-generated questions. We use storylines as a central tool in our curriculum design because they encourage well-articulated learning experiences and are flexible enough to incorporate CT practices. We describe the storyline process in Section 2.1.1 .

A central tenet of our work is that the curriculum should be co-designed with teachers. Taking an active role in the generation of their own storylines and accompanying lesson materials ensures that teachers have a strong voice and sense of agency in the initiatives that affect their daily practice [12, 28]. We describe co-design in more detail in Section 2.1.2

This experience report details the first iteration of the CT-Integration Cycle in which students used a custom sensor system to investigate their school for the potential for mold growth by collecting temperature and humidity data. We reflect on the extent to which the first iteration met each of the design constraints listed in Figure 1 and on how our experiences throughout iteration one influenced a second CT-Integration Cycle with respect to the co-design process and the design constraints.

2 METHODOLOGY

Integrating CT into middle school science curriculum requires balancing a number of competing factors, such as those displayed in Figure 1. Below, we discuss the design strategies we used to meet these constraints along with the "Computational Thinking in STEM Taxonomy"[31] that heavily influences our work.

2.1 Design Strategies

We utilize two design strategies that have proven successful in developing NGSS-aligned science curriculum: storylines and co-design. We choose these strategies because they help ensure that the focal science content is addressed in a manner that provides a solid foundation for student learning. When designing curriculum that is intended to be implemented in mainstream science classes, it is especially important to demonstrate to stakeholder groups that discipline specific science learning is not sacrificed when additional components are added and ideally these additional components serve to enhance students' science learning. In addition, we utilize sensors as an entry point for CT to ground the CT integration in students' place.

2.1.1 Storylines. Storylines serve as unit guides and are created before individual lessons are written to ensure coherence as well as incremental knowledge building [20, 25, 29]. Storylines typically begin with a scientific phenomenon (e.g., how the moon affects tides) that is intended to "anchor" the unit. Students generate questions and ideas about the phenomenon and progress through a series of smaller questions, eventually leading them to be able to answer a bigger question or respond to a challenge [26]. In developing storylines, design teams strive to predict likely student questions and provide a sequencing of ideas and activities that sustains continuity and interest throughout the unit [21]. The aim is to help students feel and act like scientists or drivers of the scientific inquiry process, rather than simply as students who are learning about science [17]. Of critical importance is tying the anchoring phenomena to issues that are locally relevant and interesting for students, in order to support motivation and promote deeper levels of thinking [4].

2.1.2 Co-Design. Co-design has been used as a productive curriculum building experience [7, 28], especially for science curriculum [18], as a way to increase teachers' engagement with and investment in the curriculum. The co-design process integratlly involves the teachers' expertise when developing the storyline units, and helps ensures that the resulting storyline units are both feasible and appropriate for their local school context.

2.2 Computational Thinking Analysis Framework

While several frameworks exist for examining CT [5, 9, 22], we chose one that is designed specifically to work with integrating CT into STEM. Weintrop and colleagues [31] defined the "Computational Thinking in STEM Taxonomy" to provide a specific breakdown of what CT can look like in STEM classes. They identified four major categories of CT practices: *data practices, modeling and simulation practices, computational problem solving practices,* and *systems thinking practices.* They specifically chose the term "practices" to suggest their relatedness to the NGSS science and engineering practices. For iteration one, we focused primarily on the data practices category because it provides a familiar entry point for science teachers. For iteration two, we added several of the computational problem solving practices.

2.2.1 Data practices. Data practices describe the different ways that students should work with and understand data. Data practices involve collecting, creating, manipulating, analyzing, and visualizing data. These practices allow students to develop a deep understanding of how data can work for them to aid in their scientific investigations.

2.2.2 Computational Problem Solving Practices. Computational problem solving practices are the portion of the taxonomy most closely related to computer science. These practices involve breaking down a question into parts that can be investigated using computational tools as well as choosing the best computational tool based on the assessment of different approaches to addressing the question. These practices also involve more traditional computer science principles of programming, modularity, abstraction, and debugging but applied to problems in mathematics and science.

While this framework provides a helpful basis for determining where CT exists in different STEM units, it lacks a suggested entry point for designing new units as well as a suggested sequences of practices. During iterations of the CT-Integration Cycle, we designed different potential sequences of practices.

3 CT-INTEGRATION CYCLE ITERATION ONE

Four middle school teachers from a large urban public school district (three science teachers and one integrated STEM teacher) participated in the first iteration of the project. In this district, integrated STEM is a required elective course that meets less frequently than regular classes and focuses on topics such as civil engineering, introductory programming, and electronics.

3.1 Development

The participating teachers attended three full-day professional development workshops throughout the 2017-18 academic year. During the workshops, they co-designed an NGSS-aligned storyline unit that incorporated a custom sensor system, prepared to implement the unit, shared and discussed videoclips from their implementation, and reflected on how to improve future units as well as the sensor system.

The storyline, outlined in Figure 2, was based on the driving question *Does our school have the right conditions to support mold growth?* As part of the unit, students were encouraged to consider: *(1) why and how does mold grow, (2) can mold grow in our school,* and *(3) how can we make our school less hospitable to mold growth.*

A custom sensor system was used to examine whether particular locations in the students' schools were favorable environments for mold growth. The system measured temperature, humidity, pressure, carbon dioxide, and total volatile organic compounds. Sensors were preprogrammed to collect data every second. Students could determine where to put the sensor and when to start and stop the data collection. To access the data, students copied it from the SD card on the sensor system to their computers. They used spreadsheet software (Google Sheets) to analyze and visualize the relevant data.

3.2 Implementation

Each teacher implemented the five-lesson unit in their classroom in Spring 2018. Within each class, groups of approximately four students each received a sensor system. The three science teachers completed the unit over a one-week period, whereas the integrated STEM teacher implemented it over a three-week period (because she saw her students only one or twice a week). A researcher was present for the first and last lesson. During the use of the sensor system, a researcher was present in the classroom if the teacher requested it (three of the four teachers did). Students ranged from 5th grade to 8th grade, were evenly split between girls and boys, and over 50% self-identified as Hispanic.

3.2.1 Date Collected. We collected a variety of qualitative and quantitative data including: (1) video from the first and last lesson, (2) pre/post teacher interviews, (3) written teacher reflections, (4) student checkins from Lesson 1 and Lesson 5 (asking *What are you doing today?, Why are you doing this today?, How does what you are doing today relate to mold?*), (5) observational notes from Lesson 1 and Lesson 5, and (6) student artifacts.

As part of the curriculum, teachers collected student surveys at the end of each lesson. These brief, online surveys measured students' perceptions of the storyline, including whether they saw the lessons as coherent, relevant, and engaging.

3.3 Findings

In this section, we consider each design constraint in terms of the teachers' implementation of the storyline unit. Overall, the general impression from both the researchers and the teachers was that the mold growth storyline was sufficiently place-based and engaging to students, but that design elements related to the sensor system, science practices, and CT practices could be improved.

Place Based. Although the storyline was designed to be place-based (e.g., students explored their own schools), several teachers went even further than anticipated with their focus on place. Two teachers instructed their students to write recommendations to local stakeholders (principals, custodians) about mold growth in the school based on the data they collected. For example, one teacher prompted his students to argue for shutting down their school due to the possibility of mold growth. This teacher felt that a strong emphasis on place prompted his students to be more engaged than usual and peaked their interest in collecting data. Students of another teacher actually found mold and drew up a remediation plan, even offering to continue to monitor the affected area.

Engagement. Student survey data provides evidence that the storyline supported student engagement. Looking across the unit, 64.5% of students reported that the lessons mattered to them and 73.5% reported that the lessons mattered to their class. In addition, a majority of students (58%) felt excited about the lessons and almost half (49%) stated that they felt like scientists during the lessons.

Sensor System. The custom sensor system created for the teachers' implementation of the mold growth storyline functioned solely as a data collection mechanism. The system allowed students to collect all possible data from the embedded sensors, with a sampling rate of every second. Students simply pressed the sample button to start data collection and pressed it again to stop data collection. Thus, the system only supported the *Collecting Data* CT Practice. Furthermore, teachers reported that the sensor system was not especially user friendly and students' only feedback that data was being collected was a flashing green light.

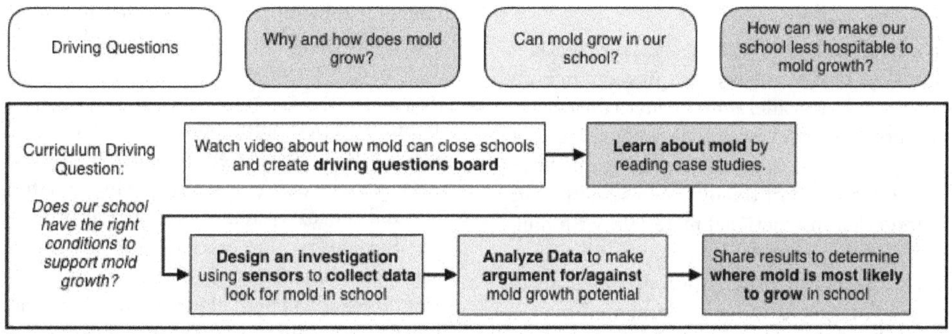

Figure 2: Storyline of the mold unit that addresses the question: Does our school have the right conditions to support mold growth? The bold text in the graphic refers to NGSS Practices and CT Practices.

NGSS Science Practices. The mold growth storyline was quite short and targeted only a portion of one disciplinary core science idea about organism growth in given environments. The storyline did include a relatively large emphasis on student engagement in science and engineering practices, such as students asking questions along with planning and carrying out an investigation to determine the potential for mold growth. Throughout the unit, students created written products that incorporated the cross cutting concepts of cause and effect as well as modeling.

Computational Thinking Practices. With respect to CT, the storyline focused mostly on data practices. Emphasizing data practices fit well with the capabilities of the existing sensor system and was a familiar entry point for the participating teachers. The students *collected* data using the sensor system and uploaded the data to their computers. Their next tasks were to *manipulate* the data to only display the relevant information (temperature and humidity), *analyze* the data to determine if the environment supported mold growth, and then create a *visualization* communicating the results of their analyses. The majority of students successfully undertook these tasks. However, we noted important differences in implementation of these practices between the Integrated STEM teacher and the science teachers. For example, the Integrated STEM teacher highlighted the appropriateness of various visualizations and helped her students learn how they could use visualizations to communicate what the data meant. The science teachers, on the other hand, placed more of an emphasis on the students' final answers rather than carefully attending to the analytic process.

3.4 Reflection

The first iteration of the CT-Integration Cycle, which included the development and implementation of the mold growth storyline unit, generated a wealth of information about how to integrate CT into science curriculum that addresses specific design constraints and culminates in a positive learning experience for students. Five lessons learned from this iteration were:

(1) More information needs to be provided to teachers about what is expected when implementing CT practices.
(2) Highlighting the place-based aspect of scientific investigations supports student engagement.
(3) A custom sensor system may support limited CT Practices.
(4) Exploring the conditions for mold growth in a dry climate over a limited timeframe may not provide variable or especially interesting data.
(5) A one week unit is likely too short to meaningfully implement many science and CT practices.

4 CT-INTEGRATION CYCLE ITERATION TWO

The second iteration of the CT-Integration Cycle is currently in progress, taking place during the 2018-2019 school year. Our project team is working with the same school district as in iteration one. For this iteration, there are six participating teachers: two returning teachers (one science and one Integrated STEM), plus four additional teachers (three science teachers and one Integrated STEM). Below, we describe a new storyline unit currently under development that focuses on understanding and designing maglev trains. We provide information about each design constraint related to this new unit, taking into account our experiences from the first iteration of the CT-Integration Cycle.

4.1 Co-Design

The first iteration of the CT-Integration Cycle began in Fall 2017 and did not include a summer component where teachers participated in the development of a storyline unit from scratch. Rather, the research team played a larger role in the initial design of the mold growth storyline, with the teachers acting as co-designers by critiquing and adapting the storyline and related instructional materials.

A critical element of the second iteration of the CT-Integration Cycle was a three-day workshop during Summer 2018 which enabled both researchers and teachers to more collaboratively develop the initial maglev train storyline. The teachers reported feeling heavily invested in this process and the two returning teachers took on larger roles as leaders in the workshop. One teacher mentioned they enjoyed the "progressive and innovative nature of what all of this [co-designing unit] with sensors offers." Overall the teachers valued the collaborative nature of the process. As one teacher expressed: "Each person in our group brings a different aspect to our team... this has allowed us to develop a much more solid storyline than any of us could have done alone."

4.2 Development

During the summer workshop, the teachers and researchers worked together to develop a storyline unit to answer the question: *how do maglev trains works?*, with careful consideration given to the design constraints shown in Figure 1. The development process led to a detailed outline with a sequence of lessons for the unit, to be later fleshed-out by the research team. Additionally, the research team will create lesson plans and other instructional materials, with multiple opportunities for the participating teachers to provide input and suggest revisions prior to their implementation, see Figure 3. The maglev storyline unit is targeted to be implemented over a three-week period and thus has significantly more depth in the coverage of the science content, CT practices, and sensor use compared to the mold growth storyline unit.

In the maglev train storyline unit (see Figure 3), students investigate the electromagnetic forces that enable a maglev train to levitate and serve as a propulsion mechanism for the train. The students build a variety of models and used the sensors on the micro:bit (described below) to investigate magnetic fields created by simple magnets, electrical circuits, and electromagnets to gather evidence that will help them explain how a maglev train functions. Students utilize CT and engineering design processes to apply the science concepts to create an efficient, fully functional scale model maglev train. Lastly, they write a proposal for why a maglev train should be built in their community using all of the information that they have learned throughout the storyline unit.

Place Based. Similar to the mold growth unit, a central goal in developing the maglev train unit was to incorporate place in a meaningful way for students. To do so, a focus throughout the unit is on how maglev trains serve local communities. For example, the unit incorporates videos and other information about the function and benefits of existing maglev trains, and students write a proposal for the installation of a maglev train in their own community.

Engagement. Whereas in the first CT-Integration Cycle, the research team selected mold growth as the focal phenomenon, there was a more collaborative and inclusive process for selecting the focal phenomenon for the second iteration. The research team and the teachers discussed multiple candidate phenomena and created an interest survey asking students which of eight phenomena they found most interesting and relevant. Results from the survey indicated that students' top two choices were maglev trains and color changing playgrounds. The teachers then engaged in a sustained exploration of both these options, and agreed that maglev trains held the most promise in terms of meeting all of the design constraints. In prior work, developing learning activities based on phenomena identified through these measures has proven an effective strategy for ensuring the engagement of diverse students in high school biology [17].

Sensor System. The design of the custom sensor did not readily support CT practices other than *Collecting Data*. Going forward, we wanted to utilize a sensor system that could support additional CT Practices and had additional benefits over the custom system. Thus, in iteration two, we elected to use the micro:bit, a microcontroller designed for educational use. Micro:bits are becoming increasingly popular as part of an introductory computing experience [24, 27]. The micro:bit contains a variety of onboard sensors including a magnetometer and an accelerometer, with additional sensors being developed by our industry partner. The micro:bit is relatively low cost (presently costing less than $20 compared to the original sensor system which was approximately $175), portable, and does not require external software installation to program (an important consideration when working with schools). It is easily programmable in both block and text based languages [2, 10], which will allow students to have more control over the data collection process and better incorporate the *CT Computational Problem Solving Practices*. Data can be collected using the micro:bit and transfered to a computer and/or displayed using the LEDs on the micro:bit, thus allowing students to see the data in real time as it is collected. For the maglev storyline unit, the students will program the magnetometer sensor on the micro:bit to measure the magnetic fields created by static and electromagnets. In addition, the accelerometer will be used when the students design a train car that meet various constraints, see the Figure 3. All of the data students collect can be displayed on the micro:bit in real time and also recorded to their computers for later analyses.

NGSS Science Standards The increased length of the maglev storyline allows for more science standards to be included and for the unit to go more deeply into these topics as compared to the mold storyline. The maglev storyline incorporates four science performance expectations involving forces, motion, and electromagnetic fields. The *Cross Cutting Concepts* include cause and effect, systems and system, and stability and change. The *Science and Engineering Practices* include asking questions and defining problems, planning and carrying out investigations, constructing explanations and designing solutions, and engaging in an argument from evidence.

Computational Thinking Practices. The increased length of the maglev train storyline unit relative to the mold growth storyline also allows for more time to be spent on CT practices. The students will *program* the magnetometer sensor on the micro:bit to *collect* information about the magnetic field strength, which will help them *visualize* the strength of magnetic field. They will also *program* the LEDs to display the data on field strength. When investigating the electromagnets, students will *analyze* the data *collected* to see how coiling copper wire creates a stronger magnet. While programming the micro:bit, the students will involve the additional computational problem solving practice of *debugging*.

4.3 Reflection

The development of the second iteration of the CT-Integration Cycle builds off lessons learned from iteration one: the design constraints listed in Figure 1 necessarily narrow the set of candidate phenomena, the robust design of a sensor system is important, an investigation of the phenomenon should involve data that is variable, and students benefit from getting real time feedback when they are collecting data.

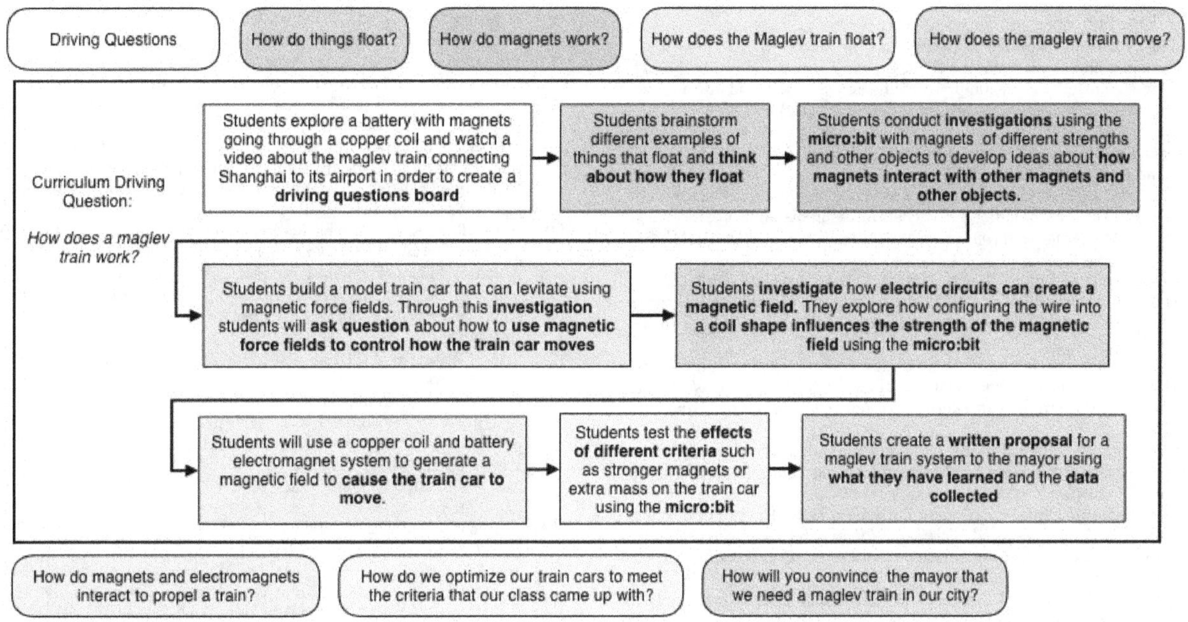

Figure 3: Draft storyline of the maglev unit: How does a maglev train work? The bold text represents NGSS and CT Practices.

The teachers who have participated in our research have been clear in their desire to deeply understand CT, to learn ways to apply CT in their classes, and to help create resources that support CT integration for the K-12 education landscape as a whole. Goals for iteration two include capturing teachers' evolving understanding of CT and ensuring that both the science teachers as well as the Integrated STEM teachers deeply integrate CT Practices with disciplinary instruction. Along these lines, some topics that we plan to address with the teachers are developing a common vocabulary for core CT concepts, explicating that CT does not simply mean coding, and articulating the vertical (between grades) and horizontal (between subjects) integration of CT in K-12 classrooms.

5 LESSONS LEARNED

Designing science curriculum that integrates CT and incorporates all of the design constraints in Figure 1 requires thoughtful design choices and collaboration. We found the utilization of storylines to be an effective tool for to developing coherent, NGSS-aligned CT integrated units. In addition, the co-design process allowed teachers to have a strong agentic voice in the direction of the storylines.

Although selecting appropriate scientific phenomenon to anchor a storyline is always a critical first step, an important lesson learned from our work is that the use of sensors means that the set of potential phenomenon is necessarily restricted. The selected phenomenon should not only match the capabilities of the available sensors, but it should allow for the collection of relevant data over time so that the analyses and sense-making from the data help move the unit forward. Furthermore, we found that CT practices can be best incorporated if the data is variable in nature and if the sensors can be programmed by the students. In this way, the sensors would support a variety of meaningful CT practices and serve as more than simply a preprogrammed data collection tool.

In addition, just like a single unit cannot support all of the science and engineering practices, it also cannot target all of the CT practices. In terms of designing curriculum to enable a trajectory of CT learning, we found it helpful to start by incorporating the CT *Data Practices*, such as collecting, manipulating, analyzing, and visualizing data. These practices provide a familiar and comfortable entry point for both science teachers and their students, both of whom often do not have much programming experience.

Finally, to effectively integrate CT and sensors into science curriculum, on-going professional development and curricular resources, like the ones we are developing, are essential components.

6 CONCLUSION

We were successful in developing storyline units that met a relatively large number of specific constraints: they had to be place-based, engaging to students, use sensor technology, align with the Next Generation Science Standards, and incorporate CT practices. The co-design process involving both researchers and teachers together with an extended reflective process helped to ensure that all of these constraints were met. Over the next year, as we engage in the second iteration of the CT-Integration Cycle, we will continue to develop and revise the maglev train storyline unit. Ultimately our goal is to generate a set of building blocks together with explicit guidance for others who are seeking to integrate CT and sensor technology into mainstream science classes.

ACKNOWLEDGMENTS

We thank the anonymous reviews for their valuable suggestions and feedback. This material is based upon work supported by the National Science Foundation under Grants No. 1742046 and 1742053. We thank the teachers, students, and administrators of the participating school district.

REFERENCES

[1] Stamatina Anastopoulou, Mike Sharples, Shaaron Ainsworth, Charles Crook, Claire O'Malley, and Michael Wright. 2012. Creating personal meaning through technology-supported science inquiry learning across formal and informal settings. *International Journal of Science Education* 34, 2 (2012), 251–273.

[2] Thomas Ball. 2017. Physical computing for everyone. In *Software Engineering: Software Engineering Education and Training Track (ICSE-SEET), 2017 IEEE/ACM 39th International Conference on.* IEEE, 3–3.

[3] Paulo Blikstein. 2012. Bifocal modeling: a study on the learning outcomes of comparing physical and computational models linked in real time. In *Proceedings of the 14th ACM international conference on Multimodal interaction.* ACM, 257–264.

[4] Phyllis C Blumenfeld, Elliot Soloway, Ronald W Marx, Joseph S Krajcik, Mark Guzdial, and Annemarie Palincsar. 1991. Motivating project-based learning: Sustaining the doing, supporting the learning. *Educational psychologist* 26, 3-4 (1991), 369–398.

[5] Karen Brennan and Mitchel Resnick. 2012. New frameworks for studying and assessing the development of computational thinking. In *Proceedings of the 2012 annual meeting of the American Educational Research Association, Vancouver, Canada*, Vol. 1. 25.

[6] Cory A Buxton. 2010. Social problem solving through science: An approach to critical, place-based, science teaching and learning. *Equity & excellence in education* 43, 1 (2010), 120–135.

[7] Barry J Fishman, William R Penuel, Anna-Ruth Allen, Britte Haugan Cheng, and NORA Sabelli. 2013. Design-based implementation research: An emerging model for transforming the relationship of research and practice. *National society for the study of education* 112, 2 (2013), 136–156.

[8] Bjørn Fjukstad, Nina Angelvik, Maria Wulff Hauglann, Joachim Sveia Knutsen, Morten Grønnesby, Hedinn Gunhildrud, and Lars Ailo Bongo. 2018. Low-Cost Programmable Air Quality Sensor Kits in Science Education. In *Proceedings of the 49th ACM Technical Symposium on Computer Science Education.* ACM, 227–232.

[9] Shuchi Grover and Roy Pea. 2013. Computational thinking in K–12: A review of the state of the field. *Educational Researcher* 42, 1 (2013), 38–43.

[10] Gareth Halfacree. 2017. The Official BBC micro: bit User Guide. (2017).

[11] J Kahn and R Hall. 2016. Getting personal with big data: Stories with multivariable models about global health and wealth. In *annual meetings of the American Educational Research Association, Washington, DC Best Paper award, SIG for Learning Sciences and Advanced Technologies.*

[12] Finn Kensing and Joan Greenbaum. 2013. Heritage: having a say. In *Routledge international handbook of participatory design.* Routledge, 21–36.

[13] NGSS Lead States. 2013. Next generation science standards: For states, by states.

[14] Irene Lee, Fred Martin, Jill Denner, Bob Coulter, Walter Allan, Jeri Erickson, Joyce Malyn-Smith, and Linda Werner. 2011. Computational thinking for youth in practice. *Acm Inroads* 2, 1 (2011), 32–37.

[15] Nanette Marcum-Dietrich, Steve Kerlin, Carolyn Staudt, and Melinda Daniels. 2018. Our Watershed: Students Use Data and Models to Make a Difference in Their Own School Yard. *The Science Teacher* 85, 2 (2018), 39.

[16] Leyla Norooz, Matthew Louis Mauriello, Anita Jorgensen, Brenna McNally, and Jon E Froehlich. 2015. BodyVis: A New Approach to Body Learning Through Wearable Sensing and Visualization. In *Proceedings of the 33rd Annual ACM Conference on Human Factors in Computing Systems.* ACM, 1025–1034.

[17] William R Penuel. 2016. Studying science and engineering learning in practice. *Cultural Studies of Science Education* 11, 1 (2016), 89–104.

[18] William R Penuel, Brian J Reiser, Michael Novak, Tara A.W. McGill, Kim Frumin, Katie Van Horne, Sumner Tamara, and Watkins Douglas Adams. 2018. Using Co-Design to Test and Refine a Model for Three-Dimensional Science Curriculum that Connects to Students' Interests and Experiences.. In *In Proceedings of the 2018 annual meeting of the American Educational Research Association, New York, New York.*

[19] Amy L Powers. 2004. An evaluation of four place-based education programs. *The Journal of Environmental Education* 35, 4 (2004), 17–32.

[20] BJ Reiser, M Novak, and M Fumagalli. 2015. NGSS storylines: How to construct coherent instructional sequences driven by phenomena and motivated by student questions. In *Illinois Science Education Conference, Tinley Park, IL. http://bit.ly/1sS1y26.*

[21] Brian J Reiser. [n. d.]. Designing coherent storylines aligned with NGSS for the K-12 classroom.

[22] Alexander Repenning, David Webb, and Andri Ioannidou. 2010. Scalable game design and the development of a checklist for getting computational thinking into public schools. In *Proceedings of the 41st ACM technical symposium on Computer science education.* ACM, 265–269.

[23] Mitchel Resnick, Stephen Ocko, et al. 1990. *LEGO/logo–learning through and about design.*

[24] Albrecht Schmidt. 2016. Increasing computer literacy with the BBC micro: bit. *IEEE Pervasive Computing* 15, 2 (2016), 5–7.

[25] Yael Schwartz, Ayelet Weizmann, David Fortus, Joe Krajcik, and Brian Reiser. [n. d.]. Middle school science curriculum: Coherence as a design principle.

[26] Christina V Schwarz, Cynthia Passmore, and Brian J Reiser. 2017. *Helping students make sense of the world using next generation science and engineering practices.* NSTA Press.

[27] Sue Sentance, Jane Waite, Steve Hodges, Emily MacLeod, and Lucy Yeomans. 2017. Creating Cool Stuff: Pupils' Experience of the BBC micro: bit. In *Proceedings of the 2017 ACM SIGCSE Technical Symposium on Computer Science Education.* ACM, 531–536.

[28] Samuel Severance, William R Penuel, Tamara Sumner, and Heather Leary. 2016. Organizing for teacher agency in curricular co-design. *Journal of the Learning Sciences* 25, 4 (2016), 531–564.

[29] Tricia Shelton. 2015. Climbing the NGSS mountain. *The Science Teacher* 82, 9 (2015), 65.

[30] Katie Headrick Taylor and Rogers Hall. 2013. Counter-mapping the neighborhood on bicycles: Mobilizing youth to reimagine the city. *Technology, Knowledge and Learning* 18, 1-2 (2013), 65–93.

[31] David Weintrop, Elham Beheshti, Michael Horn, Kai Orton, Kemi Jona, Laura Trouille, and Uri Wilensky. 2016. Defining computational thinking for mathematics and science classrooms. *Journal of Science Education and Technology* 25, 1 (2016), 127–147.

[32] Michelle Hoda Wilkerson and Michelle Fenwick. 2017. Using mathematics and computational thinking. *Helping students make sense of the world using next generation science and engineering practices* (2017), 181–204.

One Size Fits All: Designing for Socialization in Physical Computing

Gabriella Anton
School of Education and Social Policy
Northwestern University
2120 Campus Drive, Evanston, IL
gabby.anton@gmail.com

Uri Wilensky
School of Education and Social Policy
Northwestern University
2120 Campus Drive, Evanston, IL
uri@northwestern.edu

ABSTRACT

National and state educational initiatives are increasingly prioritizing computer science and computational thinking as valued sets of skills and practices. However, despite ongoing efforts to broaden participation in computing, the field faces increasing underrepresentation of women and other racial and ethnic groups. In this paper, we argue that physical computing can provide rich, varied entryways into computing practices, and that kits that support social or collaborative use may be more compelling for underrepresented groups. We present the design of a scaled-up physical computing kit, called StegaCircuits, which we created to foster more social, exploratory introductions to computing. We present preliminary data collected during user tests at a Maker Faire that suggest StegaCircuits supports social introductions to physical computing through multi-user interaction. Finally, we highlight promising facets of the design that may positively impact cognitive and emotional responses to computing fields.

KEYWORDS

Physical Computing; Socialization; Design

ACM Reference format:

Gabriella Anton and Uri Wilensky. 2018. One Size Fits All: Designing for Socialization in Physical Computing. In *Proceedings of 50th ACM Technical Symposium on Computer Science Education (SIGCSE '19), Feb. 27-Mar. 2, 2019, Minneapolis, MN, USA.* ACM, NY, NY, USA, 7 pages. https://doi.org/10.1145/3287324.3287423

1 Introduction

With increasing National support for CS initiatives, it is vital to consider how emerging tools and initiatives will support broadening participation in CS, contextualize practices, and provide support structures for young learners from diverse backgrounds who are considering a pathway into computing. In this paper, we first explore the literature on these perceptions and argue that physical computing can provide rich, varied entryways into computing. We present the design of a new physical computing kit, intended to provide more social introduction to computing. Finally, we present preliminary data collected during user tests at a Mini Maker Faire that suggest the design of *StegaCircuits* supports social introductions to physical computing through multi-user interaction with the kit.

1.1 Extending the Protean Machine

Early proponents of computer science education, notably Seymour Papert, envisioned a world in which children could readily access the "protean" nature of computers to explore powerful ideas and express their ideas through computational construction [19]. Though early work featured both virtual and physical components, innovations in technologies has made physical computing more accessible and has shifted more computing activity into the real-world, "[affording] a much wider range of experience and possibility than the box on one's desk" [10]. In the past several decades, physical computing has become an increasingly popular venture in educational settings, reflecting a broader societal movement in "making" and Do-It-Yourself (DIY) practices. While physical computing can be applied across myriad contexts, the core practice involves constructing a system between the virtual and physical world through computer software and hardware that interacts with the analog world. Educational initiatives that engage learners with physical computing support a creative acquisition of computational practices and skills in nontraditional domains [15, 8, 10]. They open the black box of computational processes so learners can engage more deeply with domain knowledge [2, 12, 6, 5]. While educational ventures in this area offer a wealth of computational benefits they also provide learners access to "objects-to-think-with", leveraging prior interests and passions to access new domains of knowledge [19]. Lastly, participation in these initiatives may increase accessibility to programming and provide sociocultural context in which students can engage and represent personal interests [10, 15].

While there are many successes in physical computing initiatives, learning physical computing can be a daunting affair. Compared to a solely virtual experience, learners are required to master more systems and concepts – interacting with the virtual system, the physical system, and the associated practices of both. Depending on the context of the physical computing project, learners may also need to master non-technical skills in addition, for example, electronic textiles require learners to understand sewing as well as circuitry and programming [15,7]. As such, the design of the physical computing kit has potential to greatly influence learners' engagement through how well it scaffolds skill building and supports early interactions.

1.2 Designing for Cognition

Aligning with the goals of use, there has been a bifurcation in the design of physical computing kits developed. Other scholars have characterized these kits as professionally-driven or child-driven, reflecting the target audience of the kits and the associated user outcomes [4].

Professionally-driven kits, like Arduino microcontrollers, support high-end construction and production. Developing with these kits necessitates a great deal of technical knowledge, as it requires users to know circuitry, programming, and design to link together electronic components with the microcontroller and program them to respond to the analog world. Child-driven kits, like OzoBots, LittleBits [1], or SnapCircuits, orient towards ease of use and playful construction. These kits primarily embed computational power in components rather than the system broadly (e.g., sensors that are programmed to automatically work when connected), in order to background technical knowledge for children. Despite the wealth of educational kits designed for youth, professionally-driven kits have become wildly popular in education, reflecting a desire to introduce authentic tools to students in preparation for careers in engineering or computer science [4]. More so, while these initiatives are shown to be successful, the shrinking size of physical computing kits currently on the market changes the structure of initial interactions with the materials. When demonstrating how to create a circuit or highlighting how to connect wires to pins on a microcontroller, hands obscure the view, making complex and technical content more challenging to learn. The small size of these components often results in a more Instructionist, or teacher-directed introduction rather than student-driven, constructionist approach [19].

Child-driven kits support easy "low floor" entries into computing, but their modularity "constrains what we build and how we think" [20]. These kits do not support high end use. There is a finite number of builds that can be made with these kits. More so, users are required to learn multiple systems if following a pathway into intermediate or more advanced physical computing practices. On the other hand, professionally-driven kits support high-end use and provide greater freedom in the forms of construction that users can take. However, these kits require an initial focus on the "technicalities of making things work – connecting together the breadboard, motor drivers, jumper wires, and resistors", which can refocus pedagogy and early learning experiences to technical content rather than big ideas in constructionism and computing [4].

1.3 Designing with a Social Lens

As many of the barriers to computer science for underrepresented groups are social in nature [15], we argue that it is imperative to consider the aspects of design that promote socialization in addition to the ease of use, technical abilities required, and the support of high end use. These negative perceptions reflect an understanding of computation as isolated or solitary, and dissociated from communal goals, among others [17], highlighting a desire for social connection during the process of learning computing and during the application of knowledge. As these are barriers to the field, these perceptions should be leveraged in the design of new computing tools. While these goals can be embedded in the social structure or in the pedagogy of the class, the tools and representations that students are introduced to shape their conceptions about computing. As such, the design of computing tools should incorporate new forms and features that reflect sociability throughout the computing process. Below, we briefly highlight the ways that existing kits aid in this goal.

Child-driven kits can facilitate collaborative building, similar to other low-tech construction kits like Legos or blocks. However, online communities related to child-driven physical computing kits are often focused around teacher or parent support. For those with child oriented spaces, associated communities range in intensity and goals of participation. Kits with greater flexibility, like LittleBits, manage age-appropriate communities that allow structured showcasing of personal projects to peers. As a consequence of the target audience, these communities are curated and often showcase artifacts that are more playful and creative than impactful for broader communities.

There are much stronger communities around professionally-driven kits, often featuring a large, active community of learners; tutorials and project/help guides; shared spaces and venues to showcase endeavors (e.g., MakerFaires) [22]; and exposure to the application of these tools as exemplary societal, real-world solutions to problems across diverse domains [11]. Despite necessitating a more complex, technical introduction, one cannot dismiss the benefits of learning authentic practices in a community of hobbyists and other real-world individuals. Authenticity has been found to be a salient, positive feature of entry level computer science classes with youth [23, 9]. Furthermore, the architecture of the materials can be more easily modified to support new forms of expression while remaining recognizable to users. Not only do users of professionally-driven tools have infinite constructions that could be made, there is active development in broadening the applications and mediums through which to express oneself with these kits. As such, we argue that the social, community structures around the professional-kits justify the challenges associated with a more technical entry, and it would be worthwhile to focus attention on the development of scaffolding for youth into these high-end kits.

2 Introducing StegaCircuits

Leveraging affordances of professionally-driven and child-driven kits, we have designed an introductory physical computing kit that supports a social entry of younger children into physical computing using microcontrollers like Arduino.

We developed the StegaCircuits physical computing kit, a set of dramatically scaled-up electronic components, ranging from 10 to 20 times the size of traditional electronic kits, designed as an introductory kit to physical computing with professionally-driven materials. The kit contains a standard set of components, including a microcontroller, single and tricolor LEDs, a button, a simplified tilt switch sensor, and wires. In the following section, we detail the construction of the kit and the design features that support our overarching principles.

2.1 Design Features

In the following section, we highlight StegaCircuits features that support our design principles, 1) lower technical thresholds commonly associated with professionally-driven kits, 2) support exploratory or user-driven learning, and 3) facilitate social introductions to computing. The first and second principles are explored together, as many design features were intended to address both.

2.1.1 Lowering Thresholds and Supporting Exploration.

As briefly referenced above, the design of most professionally-driven circuitry kits requires higher technical knowledge for use, including ideas from simple circuitry, basic programming, and soldering or knowledge of breadboards, among others. Furthermore, most kits have minimal visual cues, instead relying on user memorization. For example, the polarity of conventional LEDs is distinguished by two subtle cues: 1) the anode, or positive, lead is longer than the cathode, or negative, lead or 2) within the case, the anode is smaller than the cathode. These cues are both visually subtle and counterintuitive, with the polarity of anodes identifiable through both longer or shorter visual cues, depending on context (see figure 1).

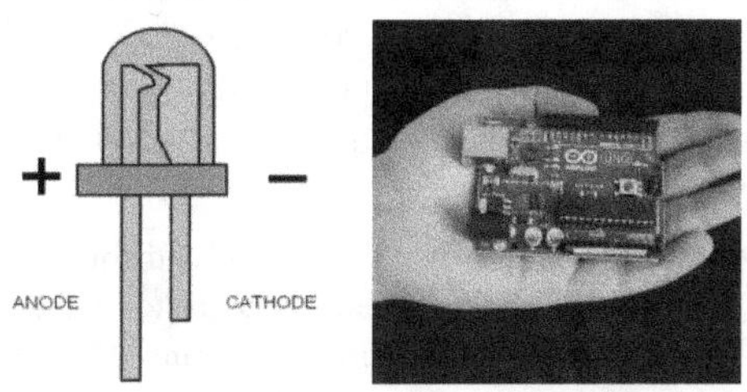

Figure 1: Left, diagram of an LED indicating positive and negative visual cues. Right, a traditional Arduino microcontroller with a hand for scale.

This technical threshold can result in two outcomes. First, learners may be discouraged by the technical aspects and lose confidence or interest in physical computing. Second, learning to overcome these technical thresholds becomes a highly instructive experience, in which the learner must procedurally follow the directions of a teacher or visual guide (e.g., blog post, YouTube video). Across either option, the learner loses agency to explore his/her own interests. Constructionist learning environments support a strong connection between design and learning, providing a rich context for learners to engage in the process of learning, shared through showcasing personally meaningful artifacts [16]. More so, the size of most physical computing components makes learning, both Instructionist and Constructionist, more challenging as hands easily obstruct visual cues or the materials themselves.

As such, the StegaCircuits kit is designed to lower the technical threshold and support exploratory introductions by increasing the size of components 10 to 20 times compared to their traditional form. The increased size is intended to reduce the cognitive load of technical skill by making components and wiring more visible. Furthermore, the increased size is intended to simplify instruction, thus lowing the ratio of instruction to exploration and making time in instruction more effective (see figure 2).

In addition to size, StegaCircuits incorporates embedded salient cues in the components themselves, designed to reduce the cognitive load traditionally required for these technical practices. There are several types of cues implemented for this goal, detailed below.

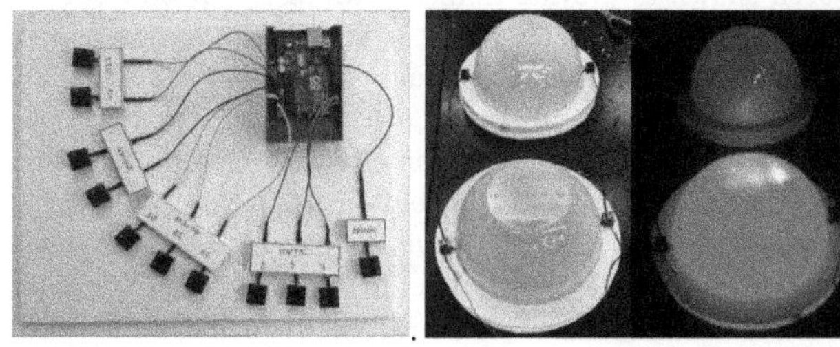

Figure 2: Left, *StegaCircuits* microcontroller, featuring simplified pin interface, conductive Lego wires, and Arduino Uno. Right, *StegaCircuits* single color LEDs.

1. Polarity is labeled across all components so that students are reminded visually that polarity is important for many components, and so that they do not need to memorize subtle cues or schematics to remember how to connect a component.

2. With the increased size of components, the labels themselves are also larger. This is designed to reduce misreading as well as supporting the labels being read from a greater distance. Compared to the text on the Arduino microcontroller, the labels on the StegaCircuits components are approximately 10 times larger. Furthermore, the spacing, placement, and structure of the labels were designed to reduce visual impediments and embed cognitive supports.

As this kit is designed to be an introductory tool, we have limited the number of pins that can be accessed, providing only three of both digital and analog pins, in order to focus the introduction on pins most commonly used in simple projects without adding the complexity of 20 input/output pins and the handful of special power pins.

3) To remove the need to learn about the breadboard and soldering, we use conductive Legos as the connectors between circuits. Conductive Legos are attached to each component, including the microcontroller. In the kit, the wires to connect these components together consist of plastic coated wires with conductive Legos at either end. As such, there is uniformity in how components should be connected across the entirety of the kit. We selected Legos for this role as they are easily recognizable cultural forms that youth know how to use immediately, which is intended to ease the entry into this new field [14].

4) The StegaCircuits button simplifies the traditional design by showcasing the mechanisms (opening or closing the circuit) embedded in the components. In addition to providing a more

interactive experience, these two inputs highlight core concepts about circuitry embedded in tools that are designed to highlight this mechanism rather than concealing it.

2.1.2 Facilitating Social Introductions to Physical Computing.

The final design principle of StegaCircuits, facilitating social introductions to physical computing, seeks to disrupt the perception held by many underrepresented groups that Computer Science is an asocial or solitary practice [15]. Physical computing has been shown to provide learners with many opportunities to express social and cultural funds of knowledge, in addition to providing common mediums through which they can be more easily shared [15, 7]. Furthermore, professionally-driven kits, like Arduino, have a strong, active community of both professional and hobbyist makers, even successful youth makers, who are applying the materials and practices to solve real-world problems, which directly opposes the perception that computer science is dissociated from communal goals [15]. As such, this space is rich in opportunity to disrupt negative perceptions while supporting a creative exploration of computing.

This goal is supported, first, by building a scaffolded introductory tool for a professionally-driven kit, despite the higher level of technical knowledge required in order to construct projects. We argue that the benefits of being able to easily access a passionate community with shared practices, language, and materials is more important than the challenges associated with technical barriers, which are lowered through design features of StegaCircuits. Finally, in support of using professionally driven kits, youth recognize and respect authentic materials or tools, with studies indicating kids find it positively impacts perceptions of computer science tools [23, 9].

As community and real-world application is already present in the Arduino community, the design features supporting social design focus on making the process of learning physical computing more social. StegaCircuits is designed to afford a more social introduction by physically allowing multiple users to interact around a single kit, without loss of visibility or disrupting the state of the project being constructed.

Connecting with the broader community, we privilege authenticity and simplicity in the design of the components. Many child-driven kits "black box" or encase computational power in components to lower technical barriers. In the design, we seek to open the black box by reducing components to a simple form. To do so, we wire normally sized electronic components into giant lightweight shells that only enlarge and protect the internal structure. In the LEDs, these shells are held together with Lego blocks so users can open them to see the traditionally sized components inside. The scaled microcontroller is designed similarly, as a lightweight shell with a real Arduino microcontroller secured on the top and then wired to the board with conductive Lego wires. With this design, users can quickly and easily remove the Arduino from the board to be used in projects when they've completed the introductory materials. As the normally sized electronic components are only fastened in shells, users can relate the technical information and design cues on the shells to these internal structures, helping the scaffold learners into use of the real projects. In the case of the microcontroller, users can literally remove the shell and transition to building normally sized projects. In this way, the design is intended to provide a scaffolded experience while maintaining authentic practices for learners.

3 User Testing

The StegaCircuits kit is designed with numerous features to support learners' entry into physical computing, addressing both cognitive and social factors. The core assumption guiding the development is that an increased size of components will support social interactions during use. To test this assumption, we conducted user testing to answer: does an increase in size of physical computing kits support social interactions during use?

3.1 Methodology

To answer this question, we conducted user testing at a Maker Faire held in a large Midwestern city in the US. This Maker Faire engaged over 1000 attendees (48% Female, 49% Male; median age of 19 years) during the daylong event.

The first author attended the Maker Faire as an exhibitor with the StegaCircuits kit. The block-based programming environment mBlock was used to control the kit throughout the duration of the day, selected over the text-based Arduino IDE to provide access to a wider audience. Users were supported in either modifying the physical components in the circuits or the computer program running on the kit.

The StegaCircuits exhibit was video recorded for the entirety of the day. The Maker Faire required attendees to sign a consent for photo release and publication prior to entering the event. Users in this study were attendees who entered the exhibit space. A total of 110 attendees (42 female, 68 male) interacted with the kit. Of these, there were 44 children and 66 adults.

Segments were identified in the video recording that corresponded to the start and end of a user testing session with an individual attendee or group of attendees. Segments could overlap, reflecting concurrent interactions across either individuals or groups. From these segments, we captured descriptive features including counts of individuals, and concurrency of group interaction. Interaction was operationalized as either physical or visual engagement with the kit, to capture broad forms of participation ranging from active collaboration to observation or intent participation [21].

Given the nature of the event, these analyses focus solely on capturing whether multi-user interaction takes place rather than defining the landscape of interaction types or the cognitive or affective impact of these interactions, a decision which will be explored further in the discussion. However, to highlight types of interactions that may be facilitated with the StegaCircuits kit, we provide two qualitative vignettes of user interactions. The first was selected to represent a typical interaction that occurred at the Maker Faire, and the second showcases a case of deep engagement.

4 Analysis

First, we will report descriptive statistics capturing multi-user interaction of the kit. Next, we will qualitatively explore two user experiences with the StegaCircuits physical computing kit.

4.1 Multi-user Interaction

Through analysis of the video, we identified a total of 31 groups of attendees, and 30 individuals who interacted with the kit. Groups ranged in size from 2 to 5 individuals with an average of 2.6 individuals per group. There was a high frequency of concurrent interactions, with 39 of the total 61 user clusters (the term cluster referring to both groups of attendees and individual attendees), or 63.9% of clusters overlapping with at least one or more. The largest concurrent session included 5 user clusters, with a total of 12 individuals (see figure 3, left). During the sessions, each cluster engaged in interaction with some aspect of the kit, including programming, documenting the output, and discussing design of materials. Reframing to highlight individual experience, 60% of users interacted with at least one other attendee that he/she did not know while exploring the kit. These descriptive statistics support the effectiveness of StegaCircuits' design in affording social engagement during use, through support of multi-user interaction.

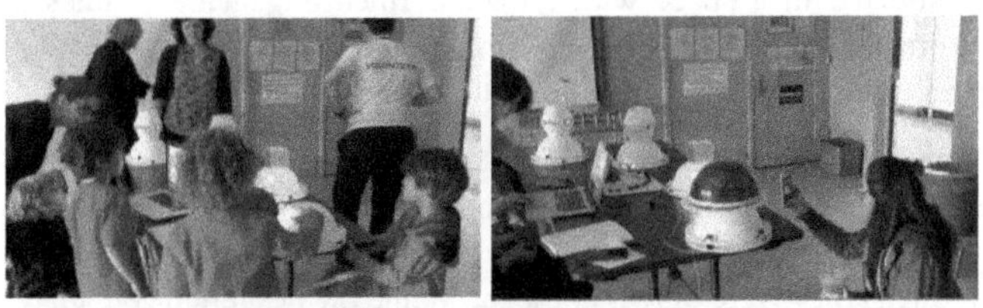

Figure 3: Left, multi-user interaction with StegaCircuits. Right, concurrent use of the kit.

4.2 Engagement with the Design

In the following section, we detail two vignettes of user interactions around StegaCircuits. The first takes place early in the day, capturing a concurrent session between two individual attendees. The second takes place near the end of the day and captures the interactions of a family triad. The former reflects a typical use case observed during the Maker Faire user testing while the latter reflects atypically prolonged engagement. Across both, the first author acts as facilitator, and will be called as such in the vignettes.

4.2.1 Concurrent, Short-term Engagement.

Attendees at the StegaCircuits exhibit tended to visit for shorter durations, most for 2-5 minutes. However, these visits were typically overlapping with others who arrived independently. The following vignette provides a description of typical concurrent, short-term engagement seen at the exhibit.

A teenage girl walks past the door, looking in as she passes. She pauses and hesitantly enters the room, in which the facilitator is sitting alone with a program running on the kit. The girl asks what the materials are and expresses delight in the flashing lights. Asked if she wants to help change the program, the girl agrees, moving from the front of the table to stand next to the facilitator. Though offered to take control of the computer, the girl opts to instruct the facilitator to modify the code. During this time, a teenage boy peeks his head into the room, pauses and begins to back away when he sees the facilitator and girl working, then slowly approaches with his hands behind his back. He walks around the front of the table, peering down at the components. He asks various questions about how the components work, making connections to his experiences with Scratch and with robotics. During this process, the girl remains standing in the same location, near the facilitator and computer. She watches the kit as the boy asks his questions but does not engage verbally in turn. The girl shifts to the front of the table, squatting down to film the output (flashing LEDs) of the program she had modified (see figure 3, right). The boy moves to the computer to modify the code. The video, focusing on the LEDs, captures the actions of the boy, who intermittently gets up to check on or connect components before returning to program. After capturing several videos, the girl thanks the facilitator then leaves the room.

This vignette includes several key moments that are suggestive of deeper social or emotional reactions to the kit. First, both individuals approached the room in a similar fashion, peering in as they walked past then pausing or doubling back to see the flashing StegaCircuits kit. Both hesitantly entered but were quick to express curiosity and interest in the materials. This reaction was reflective of many entrances to the room. Many who entered the room appeared to be overcoming hesitations to enter the space, likely because it was one of the exhibits provided a room compared to other booths and exhibits located in hallways at the Maker Faire. The StegaCircuits exhibit was provided a separate room to support the size of the materials and desire to capture audio. Secondly, these two users did not know each other but spent almost 3 minutes sharing use of a single physical computing kit. Both interacted with the kit for about 5 minutes, meaning the majority of time was shared with a stranger. Despite this, both felt comfortable exploring with their own forms of interaction. At this time, we are not assessing the quality of the interaction or the outcomes of the shared use due to the nature of the data collected during this user testing. Broadly, we see this engagement as suggestive of size supporting varying goal states for users concurrently interacting with the kit.

4.2.1 Concentrated, Prolonged Engagement.

Transitioning from concurrent use to shared use, this vignette highlights a family triad (mother, daughter, son) collaboratively using the physical computing kit. The exploration was led by the daughter, appx. 6 years old, but featured moments of inspiration from her younger brother, appx. 4 years old.

The facilitator was again alone in the room with the physical computing kit running. The family entered and both children expressed immediate excitement at the flashing lights and shapes of the components. The younger brother intermittently shouted, "that's *so* cool!" while trying to grab or hug the flashing LEDs for the entirety of their 30-minute stay. The daughter commented on the size, reflecting both verbally and physically that the components looked like giant versions of the buzzer robot she had just built (see figure 4, left). She pulled the small robot out of her pocket and began to explain how she could modify the StegaCircuits to function in the same manner. After imagining some new creations, the facilitator introduced her to the programming, asking if she wanted to change what the lights did. They worked together modifying the code, the daughter instructing the facilitator on the changes she should make. During this process, the younger brother became increasingly excited about the lights when he realized he could look inside the shells. At this, the daughter incorporated the brother's favorite color into sequence of flashing lights. Though occasionally distracted by other objects in the room, the daughter remained working with the kit for 34 minutes. During this construction, she compared the kit with other familiar objects, designed and tested a new light sequence, created a song and integrated it in the kit using the speaker, and recorded her own sounds using the computer microphones.

Figure 4: Left, a young girl compares the size of the kit to a buzzer robot. Right, a family reacts to modifying a circuit.

The interaction around the kit shows deep and prolonged engagement with physical computing concepts and skills. The daughter, who engaged most deeply and consistently out of the triad, used the kit to make connections to prior experiences in her life both with computing and general creation. The joint engagement with her brother inspired her to incorporate his interests into the program she designed. Finally, both expressed ongoing excitement about the form of the kit – suggesting an emotional response to the materials. More so, the mother's mediation between the children and the kit suggested initial concern for their interaction with the tool. The mother had originally held back the younger brother from touching the components. However, when the facilitator shared that they were constructed primarily from plastics, foam board, and Legos, the mother appeared happy and relieved to let him play with the components. This could suggest the low-cost, easy-access materials increases accessibility through a perceived normalcy of the kit. Through this type of deep engagement, characterized by at least 15-minutes interaction with the kit, only occurred two other times during this user testing, this vignette highlights promising pathways to explore further.

5 Discussion

These analyses suggest that the size of the StegaCircuits kit supports social interactions during use, as reflected in the multi-user interactions that took place. We identified ongoing multi-user interactions that often took place with a sequence of strangers. More so, the size of the kit supported the natural interaction of 12 individuals at one time. Additional study is required to more deeply understand the differences between when users engage in active participation as compared to observation or intent participation, where learners actively observe and listen in on practices in shared endeavors [21]. Through the vignettes, we highlight potential forms these multi-user interactions may take, including concurrent, observation, and collaboration.

As mentioned earlier, this paper focuses solely on identifying the existence of social interactions with the kit rather than documenting the forms and impacts of these social interactions during use. The shift away from the latter is a result of short interaction times throughout user testing. In this time, we identified a typical pattern of user engagement: observation, asking questions, picking up and modifying components or circuits, and observing others' use. We found the typical engagement time to range from 2 -5 minutes, with less time actively constructing. Similar to engagement in museums both in the variety and number of boots/exhibits, we hypothesize these shorter times result from the format of the Maker Faire rather than the design itself. More so, the separate room appeared to have caused hesitation for users as they entered and began to interact with the materials. As such, future user testing should be conducted in a space with longer normed engagement times to capture the breadth of social interactions that may take place while being more formally introduced to physical computing.

Finally, the vignettes showcase forms of social interaction around the kit that appear to evoke emotional reactions to the design. In the first vignette, both teens overcame their hesitation in entering the room as they were drawn to the kit. While the hesitation could have been contextual rather than tied to computing materials, affective responses and the impacts on engagement should be further explored. More so, shared excitement in the materials appeared to scaffold co-design, or goals sharing, during construction as reflected interactions of the family triad (see figure 4).

6 Conclusions and Implications

Initial user testing suggests that StegaCircuits can support social introductions to physical computing by allowing for multiple users to concurrently interact with components of a single kit. Future research will focus on forms that this multi-user interaction takes, and the cognitive and affective impact on users. Additionally, the construction of the components with easily accessible materials (i.e. foam board, plastic bowls, Legos, and paint) appeared to lower the perceived technical barrier to computing for some users. For others, the construction seemed to spark curiosity and imagination. Future work will explore how the materials themselves may impact perceptions of computing by disrupting the stereotypical forms.

More broadly, this work showcases the process of developing a computing tool intended to counter negative social perceptions of computing. Through the design principles and features, we identify ways to increase socialization in computing while maintaining authenticity in the application and extension. Finally, we argue that tools designed to disrupt the traditional forms may be powerful in engaging underrepresented groups in computing.

REFERENCES

[1] Ayah Bdeir. 2009. Electronics as material: LittleBits. In Proceedings of the 3rd International Conference on Tangible and Embedded Interaction, pp. 397-400. ACM.

[2] Matthew Berland. 2016. Making, tinkering, and computational literacy. Makeology: Makers as learners 2: 196-205.

[3] Paulo Blikstein. 2013. Digital fabrication and 'making' in education: The democratization of invention. FabLabs: Of machines, makers and inventors 4.

[4] Paulo Blikstein. 2015. Computationally enhanced toolkits for children: historical review and a framework for future design. Foundations and Trends in Human–Computer Interaction 9, no. 1: 1-68.

[5] Paulo Blikstein, and Uri Wilensky. 2007. Bifocal modeling: a framework for combining computer modeling, robotics and real-world sensing. In annual meeting of the American Educational Research Association (AERA), Chicago, USA.

[6] Corey Brady, Kai Orton, Weintrop, Gabriella Anton, Sebastian Rodriguez, and Uri Wilensky. 2017. All roads lead to computing: Making, participatory simulations, and social computing as pathways to computer science. IEEE Transactions on Education 60: 59-66.

[7] Leah Buechley, Mike Eisenberg, Jaime Catchen, and Ali Crockett. 2008.The LilyPad Arduino: using computational textiles to investigate engagement, aesthetics, and diversity in computer science education. In Proceedings of the SIGCHI conference on Human factors in computing systems, pp. 423-432. ACM, 2008.

[8] Leah Buechley, and Hannah Perner-Wilson. 2012. Crafting technology: Reimagining the processes, materials, and cultures of electronics. ACM Transactions on Computer-Human Interaction (TOCHI) 19, no. 3: 21.

[9] Betsy DiSalvo. 2014. Graphical qualities of educational technology: Using drag-and-drop and text-based programs for introductory computer science. IEEE computer graphics and applications34, no. 6: 12-15.

[10] Michael Eisenberg. 2003. Mindstuff: Educational technology beyond the computer. Convergence 9, no. 2: 29-53.

[11] Shuchi Grover, Stephen Cooper, and Roy Pea. 2014. Assessing computational learning in K-12. In Proceedings of the 2014 conference on Innovation & technology in computer science education, pp. 57-62. ACM, 2014.

[12] Yu Guo, Aditi Wagh, Corey Brady, Sharona T. Levy, Michael S. Horn, and Uri Wilensky. 2016. Frogs to Think with: Improving Students' Computational Thinking and Understanding of Evolution in A Code-First Learning Environment. In Proceedings of the 15th International Conference on Interaction Design and Children, pp. 246-254. ACM.

[13] Michael S. Horn. 2013. The role of cultural forms in tangible interaction design. In Proceedings of the 7th International Conference on Tangible, Embedded and Embodied Interaction, pp. 117-124. ACM.

[14] Nathan Holbert. 2016. Leveraging cultural values and "ways of knowing" to increase diversity in maker activities. International Journal of Child-Computer Interaction 9: 33-39.

[15] Yasmin B. Kafai, Eunkyoung Lee, Kristin Searle, Deborah Fields, Eliot Kaplan, and Debora Lui. 2014. A crafts-oriented approach to computing in high school: Introducing computational concepts, practices, and perspectives with electronic textiles. ACM Transactions on Computing Education (TOCE) 14, no. 1: 1.

[16] Yasmin B. Kafai, and Mitchel Resnick. 1996. eds. Constructionism in practice: Designing, thinking, and learning in a digital world. Routledge.

[17] Jane Margolis and Allan Fisher. 2003. Unlocking the clubhouse: Women in computing. MIT Press.

[18] NSF. Women, Minorities, and Persons with Disabilities in Science and Engineering. 2017. Retrieved January 05, 2018 from https://www.nsf.gov/statistics/2017/nsf17310/static/downloads/nsf17310-digest.pdf

[19] Seymour Papert. 1980. Mindstorms: Children, computers, and powerful ideas. Basic Books, Inc.

[20] Hannah Perner-Wilson, Leah Buechley, and Mika Satomi. 2011. Handcrafting textile interfaces from a kit-of-no-parts. In Proceedings of the fifth international conference on Tangible, embedded, and embodied interaction, pp. 61-68. ACM.

[21] Barbara Rogoff, Ruth Paradise, Rebeca Mejia Arauz, Maricela Correa-Chávez, and Cathy Angelillo. 2003. Firsthand learning through intent participation. Annual review of psychology 54, no. 1: 175-203.

[22] Shirin Vossoughi, and Bronwyn Bevan. 2014. Making and tinkering: A review of the literature. National Research Council Committee on Out of School Time STEM: 1-55.

[23] David Weintrop, and Uri Wilensky. 2015. To block or not to block, that is the question: students' perceptions of blocks-based programming. In Proceedings of the 14th International Conference on Interaction Design and Children, pp. 199-208. ACM.

CS0: Introducing Computing with Raspberry Pis

Brian Krupp
Baldwin Wallace University
Berea, Ohio
bkrupp@bw.edu

Andrew Watkins
Baldwin Wallace University
Berea, Ohio
anwatkin@bw.edu

ABSTRACT

This paper presents our experience implementing a newly designed introduction to computing course for first year undergraduate students. The redesigned course focuses on the use of Raspberry Pi microcomputers as a common computing platform in order to encourage student experimentation and fun in a relatively low-cost environment. The course we describe represents a departure at our university from a traditional first-semester introduction to computing which emphasized foundational technical and mathematical skills but less exploration of the field of computing in a more wholistic manner. Our new course focuses on exposure to computing through experimentation. Additionally, it emphasizes community building among the students as well as affording them the opportunity to bring their creativity to bear in a final project showcase. As a result, the course is proving to be attractive not just to traditional computing majors but to a wider swath of the university community. This paper describes the topics selected in the redesign of the course, a summary of the labs involved, a discussion of assignments, and a description of the final project process. We discuss feedback received from students and the overall perception of the course among students and faculty. We also reflect on our experiences from redesigning the course and provide advice for those wishing to adopt a similar introductory course.

CCS CONCEPTS

• **Social and professional topics → Computing education**;

KEYWORDS

CS0, Raspberry Pi, Introduction to Computing

ACM Reference Format:
Brian Krupp and Andrew Watkins. 2019. CS0: Introducing Computing with Raspberry Pis. In *Proceedings of the 50th ACM Technical Symposium on Computer Science Education (SIGCSE '19), February 27-March 2, 2019, Minneapolis, MN, USA.* ACM, New York, NY, USA, 7 pages. https://doi.org/10.1145/3287324.3287488

1 INTRODUCTION

Teaching computing at small universities and colleges offers some interesting challenges. With the need to balance an appeal to a wide range of majors found in a typical liberal-arts or small comprehensive undergraduate university setting along with providing a strong technical education for students pursuing studies in the computing disciplines, developing an appropriate introductory course is not always easy. Given the additional requirement of maximizing (sometimes limited) faculty resources, one path is to create a single course that is accessible to all while still offering appropriate technical challenges for those whose interests lie within the discipline.

This paper presents our experience implementing a newly designed introduction to computing course for first year undergraduate students. The redesigned course focuses on the use of Raspberry Pi microcomputers as a common computing platform in order to encourage student experimentation and fun in a relatively low-cost environment. Additionally, it emphasizes community building among the students as well as affording them the opportunity to bring their creativity to bear in a final project showcase. As a result, the course is proving to be attractive not just to traditional computing majors but to a wider swath of the university community.

We begin our discussion of this experience with some background of our original course and the goals for its redesign (Section 2). We then dive into to the various topics covered in this new course and offer descriptions of the course's key components including a summary of the lab experiences, a discussion of other assignments, and a description of the final project process (Section 3). This is followed by an evaluation from our first year of offering this course (Section 4), and we give some thoughts on its continued evolution (Section 5). We close this paper by providing our reflections on this experience and offering some suggestions for those wishing to adopt a similar introductory course (Section 6). We hope that by sharing the goals and design of this course, as well as our experiences teaching it, other institutions can generate ideas for their own introductory computing courses.

2 BACKGROUND

At the time of the redesign of our CS0 course, our university was offering six computing related degrees: Computer Science, Software Engineering, Computer Network Security Analyst, Information Systems Analyst, Digital Media: Interactive Design, and Digital Media: Graphic Design. These six major were being served by two different CS0 courses: one for the Software Engineering and Information Systems majors and another for the remaining computing related degrees. While the two courses had slightly different emphases, both offered a general survey of the field of computing. These courses also tended to focus fairly heavily on technical topics, such as Boolean logic, binary and other number systems, circuit design, low level machine instructions, and computing theory and algorithm analysis. They followed an approach found in texts such as Brookshear's introduction to computing[16]. While our faculty

SIGCSE '19, February 27-March 2, 2019, Minneapolis, MN, USA

ACM ISBN 978-1-4503-5890-3/19/02...$15.00
https://doi.org/10.1145/3287324.3287488

employed many active learning teaching methodologies for covering this material, the focus was still fairly traditional, with an emphasis on activities that fostered the mastery of this technical material.

When the department decided to phase out the Information Systems Analyst major, we used this as an opportunity to reconsider the role of this CS0 course in our majors. Recognizing that much of the technical content was covered in more depth across our curriculum and hoping to offer an introduction to the discipline in a manner that was more broadly appealing, we undertook a redesign of the CS0 courses. We began by reducing our offerings to only one common course with an eye toward fostering a greater sense of community among all of our computing students as well as other students across the university with an interest in computing. Taking inspiration from much in the CS Principles community [18],[19],[20], we began to focus a course around the seven "Big Ideas" of computing with content emphasis on programming, data, and the Internet. Conceptually, we found that students could be better served with a redesign of the course that focused on the following goals:

- **Learning Through Experimentation**: We wanted to remove lecturing as much as possible from the course and have students learn by doing.
- **Building Community**: We wanted to focus on students learning how to work together in groups, learn about different computing organizations on campus, and learn about different research groups.
- **Understanding Different Majors**: We wanted students to understand the different majors we offer and get exposure to topics in each major.
- **Understanding the Impact of Computing**: We wanted students to understand the different ways that computing has benefited our society and realize new issues that have surfaced due to its pervasiveness.

Related research in redesigning an introduction to computing course focused on similar goals. One approach focused on redesigning their introductory course through the incorporation of different computing themes while maintaining common goals across the sections [24]. In this course, the authors also focused on emphasizing teamwork. In another study, Bailey and Forbes emphasized the use of active leanring strategies to help students retain knowledge, particularly non-majors who might lack the motivation for the course material [15]. They reiterated that, in a CS0 course, motivation is imperative and that students may tend to focus too much on the final grade rather than acquisition of knowledge or skill. Malan focused on redesigning the introduction to computing course so that it could be more inviting to all students including those that are non-majors [21]. Through an empahsis on accessibility, among other goals, they were able to double enrollment in the course in one year. Similar efforts by Marling and Juedes focused on redesigning the course for students with little to no experience with more attention given to computational thinking and the inclusion of motivational material and activities [22].

Across these related studies, we found common themes: improving accessibility, motivating students in the field, and fostering teamwork throughout the course. By utilizing a highly accessible platform such as the Raspberry Pi and having a final project that requires significant teamwork, our hope was that students would become more motivated in the field and, through the redesign, the course would accomplish our four main goals.

3 COURSE DESIGN

In order to achieve our various goals, we designed the course around the use of Raspberry Pis as a common experimental platform. The Pi became the de facto textbook and served as the main component for in-class labs, exercises, and the final projects. With a strong community supporting various projects for the Pi [13],[12], there was not a short supply of ideas for labs and exercises in the course. By using Pis, we were able to introduce a broad range of areas in computing and give students hands-on experience in these areas, including programming, physical computing, data mining and visualization, networking, and security and privacy. With our department offering five majors ranging from computer science to interdisciplinary digital design, our goal was to ensure that all students from this wide range who may have previously only focused on their own conceptions of computing would get exposure to topical concentrations in all of our computing related majors. As an additional benefit of choosing the Raspberry Pi, the price was comparable and often less than a traditional textbook.

Using a Raspberry Pi for the final group project also contributed towards the goal of building a community. The group project (as well as pair work in the labs) required students to connect with their peers early in their academic career. The expectation was that students would also have an early opportunity to apply some basic computing skills in creating a meaningful project, which would hopefully build confidence and encourage future projects with their peers.

Throughout the course we also wanted students to develop a deeper understanding of the impact of computing. Computing has had a profound impact in society—both positively and negatively. It is critical for students to understand the impacts of the code they create, networks they implement, or graphics they design. Towards this goal, students were required to read chapters from *Blown to Bits* which provided thought-provoking views on computing and its role in society[14]. Students were also required to read selected news articles, watch selected TED Talk videos, and participated in discussions on issues of ethics in computing.

At the conclusion of the course, the following learning outcomes were expected:

- Students will understand core concepts in computing including programming, networking, data representation, and their relation to each other.
- Students will become cognizant of social issues in computing such as privacy and ethics.
- Students will gain an understanding and appreciation for the complexity in implementing the hardware and software that they consume.
- Students will learn about the computer science community both locally and globally and how they can become active participants.
- Students will learn about different careers in computing and each career's role in the field of computing.

Table 1: Course Outline

Week	Major Topic	Sub Topics	Project Milestone
1	Introduction	Course, Majors, Organizations, and Intro to Pi	
2	Programming and Algorithms	Programming in Scratch	
3	Programming and Algorithms	Big Ideas in Programming and Designing Algorithms	Project Brainstorm
4	Programming and Algorithms	Intro to Python, Comparing Python and Scratch	Project Group Formation
5	Exam	Exam #1, Project Work Day	Project Pre-proposal Due
6	Data and Information	Binary, Boolean Algebra, Automation, and Sound	
7	Data and Information	Assembly, Clocking, Colors, and Images	
8	Data and Information	Data Gathering, Privacy, and Security	
9	Data and Information	Data Representation and Analytics	
10	Exam	Exam #2, Final Project Work Day	Project Proposal Due
11	The Internet	WWW, HTTP, and Server Software	
12	The Internet	Networking, Network Security, and Web Development	
13	Project Work Week		Project Update with Instructor
14	Physical Computing	Circuitry, Embedded Computing	
15	Conclusion	Course Conclusion	Project Final Report Due
Finals	Final Project	Final Project Presentation	Project Presentation

- Students will become confident in working on computing projects and have confidence to develop their skills further.

To illustrate how these course concepts came together in practice, Table 1 presents an outline of the course by topic and demonstrates the breadth of topics we presented to the students. It also indicates how work towards the final project was incorporated throughout. For the remainder of this section, we present an overview of the design of the labs, assignments, and final project.

3.1 Labs

Labs were designed towards several of the goals that we have in the course. To foster learning through experimentation, the in-class labs encouraged both learning through trial and error as well as providing the opportunity to be creative. In designing the labs and exercises, we were intentional on introducing opportunities for students to experiment and learn on their own why a certain outcome occurred. We wanted students to feel comfortable with "breaking" software (and even hardware, at times) with the understanding that the class offered a safe, relatively low-cost, environment for these types of "mistakes." The labs also gave students an opportunity to express their creativity. Some examples of this included music composition, web page design and creation, and image filtering and manipulation.

To work towards building a community, students were asked to work on labs in pairs or small groups. Labs were also aligned with each major content area in the course so students could get practical exposure to each area. Some labs were guided, due to their complexity, where the instructor would walk students step by step through the lab. However, often students had various checkpoints within a lab that they had to work towards within their group. Most labs were also designed for the entire meeting time which was 75 minutes. Due to the nature of the Raspberry Pi being a popular device for various maker projects, we found many resources to leverage in the creation of labs for the course. We often provided supplemental instructions when needed; however, the original content of the lab was also referenced so that students knew from where we derived the lab and they could also find other activities that were available on the referenced site. During this first experience with this course, we offered the following labs:

- Gravity Simulation in Scratch (2 Labs)
- Implementing Algorithms in Scratch
- Implementing Algorithms in Python
- Generating Sound with Sonic Pi
- Image Manipulation and Representation
- Mapping the Weather
- Graphing the Weather
- Creating a Web and SSH Server
- Web Page Development

To give a sense of the experience, we describe a few the labs below in greater detail:

Implementing Algorithms in Scratch and Python In these two labs, students had the opportunity to implement an algorithm in two different programming languages: Scratch and Python. The transition from Scratch to Python allowed students to see how a visual block based programming language is translated to a traditional text based programming language. Students compared the implementation of the same algorithm in both languages and there was an in-class discussion on the differences. Our goal for the pairing of these labs was for students to gain an understanding that, despite syntax differences, most languages provide similar constructs—such as variables, loops, functions, etc.—for implementing an algorithm. In this exercise, we also emphasized the importance of resisting the temptation to immediately program, but instead encouraged our students to take time to think about the algorithm and how they would translate it into executable code.

Mapping and Graphing the Weather These two separate but related labs focused on collecting data using a REST based API and representing data in different formats. Part of the goal of this series of labs was to provide students an understanding of how data can be represented and visualized. Additionally, it offered students an opportunity to understand how data is retrieved through one API and displayed through another API. The lab also demonstrated how data is formatted in a widely adopted format such as JSON. To visualize temperature data, students used colored map markers to represent the current temperature based on readings from world-wide weather stations. Students also implemented data validation techniques to ensure the data they received was in an acceptable range. While labs were derived from existing labs available on the Raspberry Pi Foundation's website [10] [11], we provided supplemental notes to enrich the student experience and tailor the labs for our classroom environment.

Twitter Posting and Scraping This lab provided students a way of understanding the ethical implications of being able to create a Twitter client that could collect data about any given topic and subsequently post data about that topic. Given the timing of the US elections in 2016 and concerns of Twitter accounts that may have impacted the election [23] [8], the lab raised the awareness of students as to how easy it is to create a Twitter bot. The lab also helped students learn a bit about mining and analyzing user data and the ethical implications surrounding this technology.

3.2 Assignments

Assignments were designed to require students to read a chapter from *Blown to Bits* [14], read a computing article, watch a video, or perform their own research. Often they were designed to also ask the student questions on computing's role in society, ethical concerns, or how to become involved in the CS community. Students were permitted to work on assignments in pairs to help promote working together and building a community. Below is a sample of assignments used in the course with a brief description.

Computing History and Careers In this first assignment, students watched a YouTube video on Alan Turing [3] and then describe the impact of his team's work on World War II. They also investigated the computing majors offered at our university and found a career related to each one. Based on the the career they chose, they researched what the job responsibilities and the potential salary are for that position using information from the Bureau of Labor Statistics. This assignment allowed them to learn more about the different computing majors they could choose from and careers related to each major.

Algorithms In this assignment, our goal was for students to reflect on the role of computing in society where it focused on algorithms and their impact. Students watched a TED talk video on Algorithms [2] and responded to questions such as: How have algorithms changed the way financial services operate? What effects have algorithms had on financial jobs? What ways can algorithms conflict with each other without human oversight and how do algorithms affect your life today? Students also were asked to identify a good use and bad use of technology from the first chapter in *Blown to Bits* [14] Our goal with this assignment was for students to understand that algorithms are not without flaws and while they can have serious benefits to society, they are ultimately created by humans and can be prone to human failure.

Security and Privacy In this assignment, students described the difference between authentication and authorization and provided an analogy with a popular application they use. They researched the OWASP Top 10 [9] and identified the top three threats. They were asked to describe two factor authentication and why it is stronger than single factor authentication. Lastly, they investigated the mobile permissions on their device and how those permissions can grant access to the data without limitation. The goal of this assignment was not only for students to learn more about security and privacy, but also how these topics tie into their daily use of devices and applications.

Web and Internet In this assignment, students watched a TED Talk given by Tim Berners-Lee [7]. They summarized the talk and responded to questions that asked them to discuss how the video affected what they would want in a the future world-wide web (WWW). They also researched Gopher, as an an example of an early Internet application, where they provided an opinion on why Gopher failed when the WWW became more prominent. We also asked the students to decide if Berners-Lee would have been wealthy had he decide to charge for access to the web. The goal of this assignment was for students to learn more about the history of one of the applications they interact with daily, the world wide web, and to learn its original intent.

Additional Readings and Discussion Students were required to complete additional readings throughout the course and reflect on the readings or contribute to discussions. Examples of these readings included a perspective on how computer science is not a science in the traditional sense and how it is not about computers [4] as well as one which discussed why Python is a preferred first language to learn [17]. Students were also asked to watch several additional TED talk videos for discussion in class or to post on discussion boards [6] [1] [5].

3.3 Final Project

With the class designed around the extensive use of a Raspberry Pi, the final project required students to explore in groups how they could use this particular technology to produce something of interest. The topic for the project was left to the students to decide; however, we required they get approval and meet several other milestones for their proposed project before the second exam in the course. This approval process ensured that the complexity of the project was appropriate for a final project, that it was well understood what would be delivered by the end of the semester, and that the groups had been given a chance to work out their dynamics as well as how they would divide the labor on the project. By exposing students to various labs and resources early in in the course, our goal was for students to have ideas for suitable projects and know of additional resources they could use in the execution of their designs.

With the goal of building a community, students were required to work in a team of two to four students. We emphasized that students would rank each other's contribution on a Likert scale at the end of the semester, stressing the importance of making a significant contribution to their group.

Since the course provided a broad survey of computing topics and students took exams throughout the semester, a traditional final exam was replaced in favor of having the class to presenting their final projects. The final project was graded on the following criteria:

- Relative Complexity and Effort to Complete Project
- Project Completion from the Original Proposal
- Application to Area in Computing
- Presentation of Project
- Individual Reflection

For presenting the project, students were required to describe their project, provide a demonstration, and explain what they learned, what challenges they faced, both technically and collaboratively, and how they overcame those challenges. In the individual reflection students were asked to describe their contribution to the project, discuss their personal challenges and how they overcame them, and explain how they would approach the project differently after having gone through the experience.

4 EVALUATION

To evaluate the success of achieving the desired outcomes of the course, we performed both a qualitative and quantitative assessment. Given the goals of the course, we found that a qualitative assessment was more valuable in measuring the desired outcomes. In this section, we provide an assessment of the final projects and student evaluations from the course.

4.1 Final Projects

With a high degree of freedom for the final project topic and with the students being primarily first year undergraduates, we were concerned that the final projects would lack substance and creativity. Additionally, with not having a collection of reference projects from past semesters to provide, students did not have a baseline of what was the appropriate difficulty and scope of the final project. However, the students exceeded expectations and several groups completed advanced projects that one could expect from much more experienced students.

Not unexpectedly, gaming and game development was popular among our students. Students used the basic programming skills they developed in Scratch and Python. An example of one such project was a Scratch based side scrolling game where the player had to control the sprite to avoid obstacles. This game incorporated multiple levels and the user had a set amount of lives (see Figure 1). Although several projects involved game creation, students chose to explore a large variety of computing topics for their final projects—demonstrating how their exposure to these topics throughout the class encouraged them to learn more about the computing field as a whole. One such example included extending the Sonic Pi lab and combining physical computing to produce an application that would allow a user to record a song using the computer's keyboard, and then end the recording and allow it to be played back. While notes were recorded, visual feedback was provided using LEDs as well as audio feedback of the actual note (See Figure 2). Another project included the creation of a chat application that allowed students to communicate from one Pi to another. This involved some more advanced programming concepts and using sockets in Python; however students were able to work from examples they found online to create a working solution.

While some groups chose to extend work that they completed as part of the in-class labs for their final project, this was not always the case. For example, students often invested their time in exploring

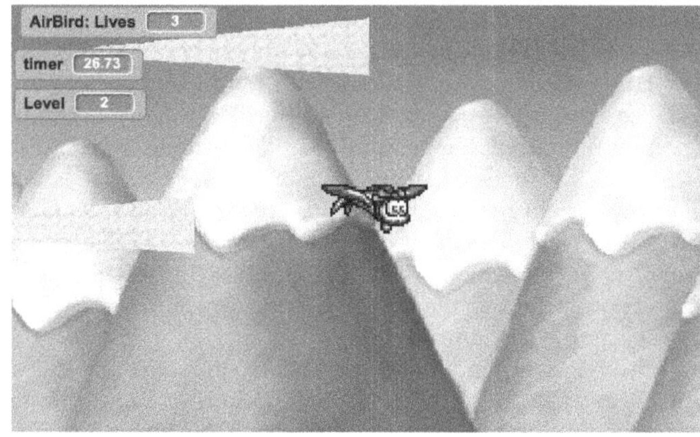

Figure 1: Final Project Game Side Scroller

Figure 2: Final Project Incorporating Multimedia

a variety of robotic kits available for the Pis. Some students built web interfaces that were able to capture statistics about their Pi-based robots. Another project of note in this vein was a group that used two Pis–one to power a Google-glass style interface to drive a second Pi-based robotic vehicle.

Overall, we were amazed at the ingenuity and creativity of many of the final projects. It seems that the students often surprised themselves in the amount they were able to accomplish.

4.2 Student Evaluations

At the end of the semester, students had the opportunity to provide feedback on the course and instruction. Here, we focus on the scores that are relevant to the desired outcomes in the redesign of the course. In reviewing the quantitative feedback that students provided, using a scale of 1 to 4 with 1 being "Strongly Disagree" and 4 being "Strongly Agree," we found the following: 1) With an average score of 3.3, students found that the course made real world connections to the concepts covered in the course. 2) With an average score of 3.4, students found technology tools utilized were appropriate to the course.

Comments from students reiterated the findings above. From the feedback from students, we learned that the course was very informative and introduced big ideas that were interesting and helpful. Students suggested that the environment allowed them to easily learn new concepts, work well with their peers, and feel valued in the classroom. Students also expressed that they enjoyed the freedom they had in the course and that they had fun while learning. Below are some comments that support the findings:

- "My professor was extremely helpful and created an environment where I was easily and naturally able to learn new concepts that I genuinely was interested in."
- "I really liked how much my professor valued his student's opinions and responses to current topics and situations significant to today's technology world."
- "I like this course a lot because I feel it is not a lecture more doing than listen"
- "I really enjoyed the freedom in this class. The partner work helped me understand how to work better as a team player."

Another important theme that emerged in the student comments was the accessibility and value the students found in this course. Several comments that support this are the following:

- "Very informative and introduced big ideas that were very interesting and helpful to what we were doing."
- "This was a great intro course with not coming in with any previous knowledge."
- "It's good that the class takes into consideration all of the different levels of computing/programming knowledge the students have."
- "I enjoyed the course.... It helped me decide my major.
- "This class is very broad and eye opening so I think it could be a requirement for all majors."

In general, students also shared overall positive feedback on the instructors including availability, responsiveness, and pedagogy. This is important to note as we believe it has an impact on accomplishing the desired outcomes in redesigning the course.

5 FUTURE WORK

While we believe the first year of offering the course was very successful, there are several changes we would like to include. With robotics playing a larger role in computing and the capability for students to create wireless sensors and incorporate physical computing, we would like to include labs centered around these two aspects. We piloted two labs with our department's community outreach group that utilized "self-driving" robots and created a reaction game using Pis, buttons, passive buzzers, and other components and believe these would make a good addition to the course. Another change would be to offer even more time for student and research groups to present to the class towards the end of the semester. While we were deliberate in discussing different student organizations and research groups at the beginning of the semester, we believe it could be more valuable to bring these groups in towards the end as well to be a segue into joining the groups. Finally, we are planning on creating a department-wide computing showcase at the end of the semester featuring project work from classes across the majors, including the CS0 class. This will allow students to demonstrate their projects to the rest of our computer science students as well as non-majors. The event should also give the students ideas of the types off projects the upper class students are engaged in and to potentially get involved in their efforts. This kind of event also works towards the goal of building a community of computing students.

6 DISCUSSION

Given the feedback from students, the projects and labs that they produced, and the reflections they provided in assignments and discussions, we believe that the redesign of this course was successful in meeting the desired outcomes and goals. There were other patterns we observed throughout the semester as a result of the redesign. One is that by students having the opportunity to be creative in labs and on their final project, we noticed they seemed more willing to share their work with their peers and had a sense of pride in the work they completed. In some cases, we noticed friendly competitiveness between students on achieving a desired outcome in a lab or doing something that was not required but added new features.

Throughout the semester, we found that the number of labs was a good balance for students and allowed lecture periods where we needed to dive deeper into a concept to be more engaging where students were more active participants. While a good number of articles, videos, and lecture content was shared among the instructors, it is important to note that each brought their own flavor to the course.

Although most of the labs and course content content could be completed on other Linux-based computing platforms, there are several advantages to choosing the Raspberry Pi. From an economic perspective, Raspberry Pis are less expensive than most course textbooks and provide an inexpensive means of guaranteeing a common computing platform. This frees the instructor from having to manage different platforms and different configurations in the class and reduces the issues that could arise in the labs. This also ensures that students who do not have a technical background in installing and configuring their own Linux environment are still able to participate and be successful in the course, which makes the course more accessible. The Pi also allows students to perform projects that require a physical computing aspect by using the GPIO headers on the Pi. In the first offerings of the course, students took advantage of this capability by, for example, controlling a remote control car, capturing video through the PI's camera interface, and creating a musical instrument. By utilizing the Pi, students can also take advantage of numerous on-line resources they can reference for potential projects. Additionally, by computing majors purchasing a Pi in this course, they have a common platform for future project work. We believe these advantages make the use of the Raspberry Pi a key component of this course.

Our experience and our students' experiences with this redesigned introduction to computing class have been largely positive. Given the number of non-computing majors we are seeing in the course during its second year, we are also having a wider reach across our university community. The incorporation of Raspberry Pis into this level of course has added to student engagement and enthusiasm and produced exciting results—both in terms of students' technical development as well as their development as participants in the wider computing community. It is an approach we wholeheartedly recommend others explore as they look to redesign or retool their CS0 courses.

REFERENCES

[1] 2010. The year open data went worldwide. https://www.ted.com/talks/tim_berners_lee_the_year_open_data_went_worldwide

[2] 2011. How Algorithms Shapre Our World. https://www.ted.com/talks/kevin_slavin_how_algorithms_shape_our_world

[3] 2012. Alan Turing - Celebrating the life of a genius. https://www.youtube.com/watch?v=gtRLmL70TH0

[4] 2012. Computer science isn't a science and it isn't about computers - Jonah Kagan. http://www.jonahkagan.me/projects/writing/cs-essay.html

[5] 2012. Discover the physical side of the internet. https://www.ted.com/talks/andrew_blum_what_is_the_internet_really?language=en

[6] 2014. The DIY orchestra of the future. https://www.ted.com/talks/ge_wang_the_diy_orchestra_of_the_future

[7] 2014. A Magna Carta for the Web. https://www.ted.com/talks/tim_berners_lee_a_magna_carta_for_the_web

[8] 2017. How Russian Twitter Bots Pumped Out Fake News During The 2016 Election. https://www.npr.org/sections/alltechconsidered/2017/04/03/522503844/how-russian-twitter-bots-pumped-out-fake-news-during-the-2016-election

[9] 2018. Category:OWASP Top Ten Project - OWASP. https://www.owasp.org/index.php/Category:OWASP_Top_Ten_Project

[10] 2018. Graphing the Weather. https://projects.raspberrypi.org/en/projects/graphing-the-weather/

[11] 2018. Mapping the Weather. https://projects.raspberrypi.org/en/projects/mapping-the-weather

[12] 2018. Raspberry Pi Projects. https://www.instructables.com/id/Raspberry-Pi-Projects/

[13] 2018. Raspberry Pi Projects - Projects to Make with Raspberry Pi. https://www.raspberrypi.org/resources/make/

[14] Harold Abelson, Ken Ledeen, and Harry R. Lewis. 2008. *Blown to Bits: Your Life, Liberty, and Happiness After the Digital Explosion.* Addison-Wesley, Upper Saddle River, NJ.

[15] Tammy Bailey and Jeffrey Forbes. 2005. Just-in-time Teaching for CS0. In *Proceedings of the 36th SIGCSE Technical Symposium on Computer Science Education (SIGCSE '05).* ACM, New York, NY, USA, 366–370. https://doi.org/10.1145/1047344.1047469

[16] J. Glenn Brookshear and Dennis Brylow. 2015. *Computer Science: An Overview* (12th ed.). Pearson, Boston, MA.

[17] Elliott Hauser Website CEO and cofounder of trinket io Python instructor at UNC Chapel Hill Duke grad Ally. 2014. Why Python is a Great First Language. https://blog.trinket.io/why-python/

[18] Marie desJardins. 2015. Creating AP&Reg; CS Principles: Let Many Flowers Bloom. *ACM Inroads* 6, 4 (Nov. 2015), 60–66. https://doi.org/10.1145/2835852

[19] Dan Garcia, Brian Harvey, and Tiffany Barnes. 2015. The Beauty and Joy of Computing. *ACM Inroads* 6, 4 (Nov. 2015), 71–79. https://doi.org/10.1145/2835184

[20] Jeff Gray, Michele Roberts, and Jonathan Corley. 2017. Getting Principled: Reflections on Teaching CS Principles at Two College Board University Pilots. In *Proceedings of the 2017 ACM SIGCSE Technical Symposium on Computer Science Education (SIGCSE '17).* ACM, New York, NY, USA, 249–254. https://doi.org/10.1145/3017680.3017758

[21] David J. Malan. 2010. Reinventing CS50. In *Proceedings of the 41st ACM Technical Symposium on Computer Science Education (SIGCSE '10).* ACM, New York, NY, USA, 152–156. https://doi.org/10.1145/1734263.1734316

[22] Cindy Marling and David Juedes. 2016. CS0 for Computer Science Majors at Ohio University. In *Proceedings of the 47th ACM Technical Symposium on Computing Science Education (SIGCSE '16).* ACM, New York, NY, USA, 138–143. https://doi.org/10.1145/2839509.2844624

[23] Daisuke Wakabayashi and Scott Shane. 2017. Twitter, With Accounts Linked to Russia, to Face Congress Over Role in Election. https://www.nytimes.com/2017/09/27/technology/twitter-russia-election.html

[24] Zoë J. Wood, John Clements, Zachary Peterson, David Janzen, Hugh Smith, Michael Haungs, Julie Workman, John Bellardo, and Bruce DeBruhl. 2018. Mixed Approaches to CS0: Exploring Topic and Pedagogy Variance After Six Years of CS0. In *Proceedings of the 49th ACM Technical Symposium on Computer Science Education (SIGCSE '18).* ACM, New York, NY, USA, 20–25. https://doi.org/10.1145/3159450.3159592

Usage of Hints on Coding-Based Summative Assessments

Jennifer K. Olsen
CHILI Lab
École Polytechnique Fédérale de Lausanne
Lausanne, Switzerland
jennifer.olsen@epfl.ch

Armando Fox
Computer Science Division, EECS Department
University of California, Berkeley
Berkeley, CA, USA
fox@berkeley.edu

ABSTRACT

A recent in-class exam in a software engineering course included a section in which students had to write code and/or tests under conditions they might face on real software engineering projects, including complex, multi-part coding questions in which later parts of the question build on earlier parts. To avoid "cascading penalties" on later questions that build on earlier ones, students could reveal the answer for any question during the exam for a "reveal penalty": If the student identified the correct place in the code to copy and paste the revealed answer, they would get 20% of the question points. That is, by simply revealing every answer and copy-pasting it correctly, even the weakest student should be able to achieve 20% of the points for the coding portion of the exam. In this paper, we study how students used this mechanism. Surprisingly, some students chose to take zero points for certain questions rather than revealing the answer, and some who asked for an answer to be revealed were unable to correctly incorporate it to get the question correct. We also find a correlation between student scores on the non-coding multiple-choice section of the exam, which had no hints/reveals available, and the coding section, even though students who performed poorly on the non-coding first half of the exam should have been able to score well on the coding part by using the reveal mechanism. That is, weak students did not benefit as much as would be expected from revealable answers. Pedagogical interpretation of these results informs our future use of the "buy a hint" format for coding-based exams.

CCS CONCEPTS

• **Social and professional topics → Computing education**;

KEYWORDS

Hints, Summative Assessment

ACM Reference Format:

Jennifer K. Olsen and Armando Fox. 2019. Usage of Hints on Coding-Based Summative Assessments. In *Proceedings of the 50th ACM Technical Symposium on Computer Science Education (SIGCSE '19), February 27-March 2, 2019, Minneapolis, MN, USA.* ACM, New York, NY, USA, 6 pages. https://doi.org/10.1145/3287324.3287472

SIGCSE '19, February 27-March 2, 2019, Minneapolis, MN, USA

ACM ISBN 978-1-4503-5890-3/19/02...$15.00
https://doi.org/10.1145/3287324.3287472

1 INTRODUCTION

If exams in large-enrollment programming courses elicit handwritten responses to coding questions, the questions must be heavily constrained both because students are "flying blind" without the ability to try out their code and because freeform code is time-consuming to grade. As a result, some students have evolved partial-credit strategies [9] for such questions that allow them to pass the exam without producing working code: "...you usually get the marks for making the answer look correct. Like if it's a searching problem, you put down a loop, and you have an array and an if-statement. That usually gets...not all of [the marks], but definitely a pass."

One mitigation for this unfortunate state of affairs is to administer exams in which students must produce code under realistic conditions [3, 7]. In our upper-division software engineering course, for both technical and policy reasons, we created an in-class proctored exam in which one-half consists of multiple-choice conceptual questions and one-half consists of writing code and tests. The coding portion of the exam features complex, multi-part questions in which later parts of a question build on the code required for earlier parts [6]; to avoid a "cascading penalty" for students who get stuck on an earlier part of such questions, the exam environment allows a student to reveal the answer to a subpart of any coding question at a penalty of 80% of the points associated with that subpart[1], thereby allowing the student to proceed to subsequent parts of the question. No such "reveal" facility is provided for the non-coding multiple-choice part of the exam. We report here on the experience with the first deployment of this exam environment to 121 students in this course. In particular, we are interested in the behaviors of students requesting hints and how these behaviors differed across students. We examine the aggregate exam data to answer the following questions:

RQ1. Does a student's coding knowledge (as assessed by their score on the multiple-choice part of the exam) predict their score on the coding part of the exam?

RQ2. Following from RQ1, do weaker-performing students (as measured by scores on the multiple-choice part of the exam) ask for more answers? Are weaker-performing students less able to correctly use the answers they do reveal?

RQ3. When a student cannot get a coding question correct without revealing the answer, does the student's performance on the multiple-choice part predict how often they will request a hint/answer, or predict which answers are requested?

[1] While the design of the exam software is more general, and allows (for example) the instructor to provide a gradient of hints at a variety of "costs" in exam points, our initial usage of this exam format was under the duress typical of fast-paced large-enrollment CS courses, hence the simplified exam design.

RQ4. What changes, if any, should be made to exam design, administration, or scoring policies in light of the findings?

2 EXAM DESCRIPTION

2.1 2.1 Two-Part Exam Content

The exam consisted of two parts.[2] **Part 1** consisted of 29 multiple-choice questions, primarily conceptual, worth a total of 50 points. **Part 2** consisted of five major coding questions, with a total of 16 sub-parts, worth a total of 60 points. The exams were extensively dry-run by course alumni and teaching assistants and calibrated to approximately "1 point per minute", as students were allowed two hours to complete the entire exam and could move back and forth between the two parts during that period.

The coding questions all involved either adding features (code) to a full-stack Web application written in Ruby on Rails, or writing tests for existing code in that application. The application on the exam had previously been the subject of several homework assignments, so it was assumed that students who had attempted the assignments were familiar with the application's structure.

The exam software was such that students were allowed full read-only access to the Internet during Part 2 of the exam, including Google search, via Google's cache. Students could therefore find and search documentation, example code, programmer bulletin boards such as StackOverflow, and so on, but could not initiate messages in such a way as to solicit answers to exam questions. The software that facilitates the exam environment is described in [6].

2.2 Questions and Hints

Each of the five coding questions in Part 2 consisted of multiple parts that built cumulatively on each other, for a total of 16 subparts. Every subpart was accompanied by an instructor-provided test case the student could use to immediately evaluate their own solution, an unlimited number of times and with no penalty, as in a real software engineering setting. A student unable to answer a question correctly had two choices:

(1) Leave that part of the question and very probably all remaining parts of the question blank, receiving 0 points

(2) Request to reveal the answer to that part, at a "cost" of 80% of the points for that specific part.

If the student chose (2), the revealed answer consisted of one or more lines of code accompanied by a pointed hint suggesting where that code should be copy-pasted. For example, one of the reveals reads as follows:

"Since the movie ID is captured by the :id parameter in the route, somewhere in the stream controller method should be a call to Movie.find(params[:id])"

Thus, for a subquestion worth N points, the student's performance on that question can be classified into one of four mutually exclusive categories, as Table 1 shows.

The **IN** category includes answers that were left blank and answers consisting of incorrect or incomplete code. The self-check tests provided to the students (and used by the autograder) will fail for either reason and cannot generally distinguish the two

[2]The exam questions and data files necessary to replicate are results can be downloaded at http://bit.ly/2QnnvFi

Table 1: Four mutually exclusive ways a student can answer a question on Part 2.

Points	Description
N points (full credit)	**CN:** student answered the question Correctly with No hint
$0.2N$ points	**CH:** student got question Correct by revealing the Hint and correctly incorporating it into the code
0 points	**IH:** student got question Incorrect because despite revealing the Hint, they were unable to incorporate it correctly into the code
0 points	**IN:** student got question Incorrect but chose Not to reveal the hint. The question may have been left blank, or the student may have given an incorrect answer. (See text for clarification.)

cases. Inspecting the specific files where students would have had to insert code is difficult to do in an automated way, because the starter code provided to the students did not include explicit "your code here" guidance–part of the assessment is whether the student knows which file(s) to modify and where. Nonetheless, in either case, the student knows their answer is incorrect and worth zero points, so numerically there should be *no downside* to requesting the hint/answer that might get them $0.2N$ points. Indeed, a student who revealed the answers for *all 16 subquestions* in Part 2 could receive $0.2(60) = 12$ points, simply by incorporating (i.e. copy-pasting) the revealed code snippet in the correct place.

For the purpose of this analysis, we took into account the students' Part 2 *raw scores, before* the hint penalty was subtracted; that is, the total number of correct question points regardless of whether hints were revealed to get the answers. In other words, students who asked for *all* hints and used them properly would be able to achieve the same raw score as a student who asked for no hints and answered all of the questions correctly. All students had an equal opportunity to earn a perfect raw score on Part 2 of the exam independent of their knowledge (modulo the ability to identify where in their code to copy-paste the revealed hints/answers). We chose to use the raw score because it provides a better comparison of the correctness on Part 2 of the exam, although it does not reflect the students' final grade.

2.3 Study Subjects

Participants consisted of 121 students (79M, 40F, 2 unstated gender) of which 45 are declared CS majors or double majors, 5 are Cognitive Science majors, and 69 are undeclared or unknown. (At our institution, declaration can occur quite late. Historically, students who choose this restricted-elective course are majors or likely intended majors.) In addition to lecture, each student regularly attends one of six TA-led sections. We found no statistically significant differences related to section attendance, so we do not consider that data. Because the exam required students to use preconfigured laboratory computers that were in limited supply, the exam was administered in two sessions on consecutive days of two hours each. We found no statistically significant differences in the score distributions between the two sessions, therefore no evidence of information leakage.

3 ANALYSIS

To better understand the impact and use of hints within the exam, we omit from our analysis those students who scored 60 points (100%) on Part 2 of the exam without requesting any hints (i.e. for whom all Part 2 questions were "CN" using the categorization of Table 1). Of the 121 students in the data set, 73 students (60.33%) meet this criterion, suggesting that the exam was not too easy since we do not see a ceiling effect. To understand if the hints were useful to students, we also investigated if students were able to successfully apply the hint provided. Out of the 244 questions in which a hint was requested across the students, in 206 of the questions (84.4%), the students were able to correctly apply the hint to get the question correct. This result indicates that the hints were not too hard for students as there was no floor effect. For the 73 students included in the analysis, the Part 1 scores ranged from 12.17/50 to 41.34/50 ($M = 27.73, SD = 6.12$). The Part 2 test scores ranged from 0/60 to 60/60 ($M = 44.53, SD = 14.21$). Finally, the range of hint reveals went from 0/16 to 14/16 ($M = 3.29, SD = 3.04$).

3.1 RQ1 Correlation of Test Scores

Does students' performance on Part 1 of the exam predict their score on Part 2? We chose to use the raw score because it reflects the students' abilities to use the hints. With use of the hints, we would not expect to find a correlation between Part 1 and Part 2 scores. If there is a correlation, it indicates that there is something more interesting occurring with the use of hints that would not be seen if the score after the hint penalty was put into place was used since this would mask the ability to use the hints with their coding knowledge. Surprisingly, we found a significant positive (Pearson) correlation between Part 1 scores and Part 2 *raw scores* ($r = 0.29, p < .05$, see Figure 1). This result surprises us because we expect that the availability of a hint that could provide a student with full points on a question should serve to "equalize" raw scores. What we find instead is that students with lower scores on Part 1 of the exam still had lower performance on the coding (Part 2) of the exam, suggesting that they either have trouble incorporating the revealed answer into the right place in the code or chose not to request the revealed answer for reasons we are unsure of.

3.2 RQ2 Hint Usage

To help explain the correlation between the Part 1 and Part 2 test scores, we investigated the difference between hint use on Part 2 of the exam. We first ask: Does the Part 1 score correlate with the number of revealed hints in Part 2? We found a significant negative Pearson correlation between the Part 1 test scores and the number of subquestions that had hints revealed ($r = -0.25, p < .05$, see Figure 2), indicating that students with lower test scores on Part 1 of the exam requested more hints during Part 2 of the exam, as one would expect.

To understand the relationship between the results of the previous two figures, recall that a student's answer to any given subquestion can be categorized into one of the four mutually exclusive categories CN, CH, IN, IH, as Table 1 showed. We ran a multivariate

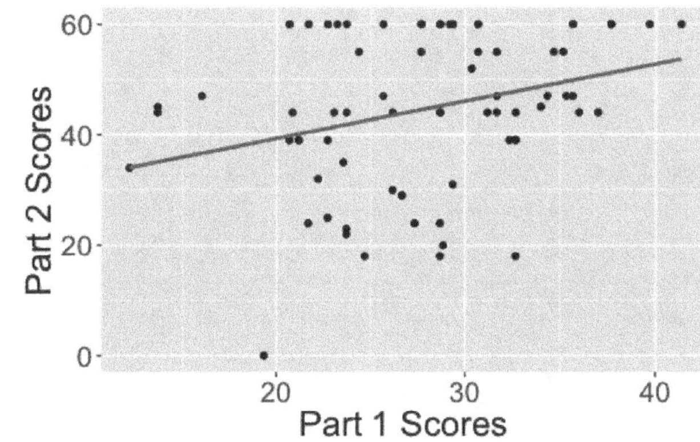

Figure 1: Correlation between Part 1 and 2 scores for students who did not get perfect scores without hints.

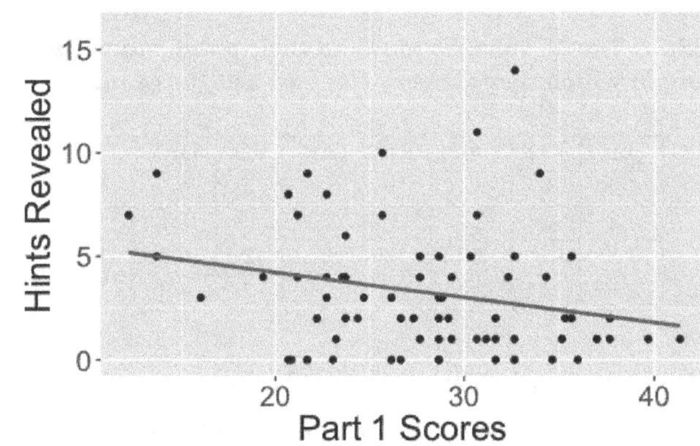

Figure 2: Correlation between Part 1 scores and number of hint reveals during Part 2.

regression to understand how Part 1 scores correlate with subquestion classification. We found that Part 1 scores were a significant predictor of subquestion classification ($F(3, 69) = 3.92, p < .05$, see Figure 3).

Figure 3 shows the results of our post-hoc analysis, which we summarize here. We found the following:

- A significant positive correlation between Part 1 scores and CN questions ($r = 0.37, p < .05$). Students with higher Part 1 scores were able to answer more Part 2 questions correctly without help.
- A significant negative correlation between Part 1 scores and IN questions ($r = -0.27, p < .05$). Students with lower Part 1 scores had more Part 2 questions incorrect without seeking help on those questions. We return to this result later.
- A marginally significant negative correlation between Part 1 scores and CH questions ($r = -0.20, p = .09$).
- No significant correlation between Part 1 scores and IH questions ($r = -0.17, p = .14$). This and the previous bullet suggest that there is no difference in stronger vs. weaker students' ability to use the hints once revealed.

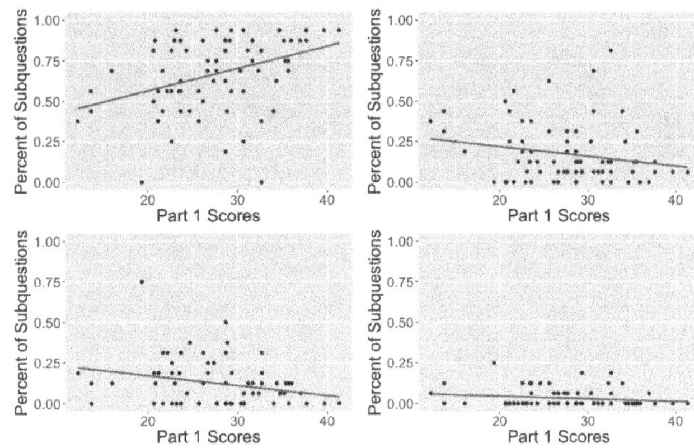

Figure 3: Correlations between Part 1 scores and subquestion categorization with correct subquestions on the top and without hints on the left.

Table 2: The 16 subquestions and their point values, in the order in which they appeared on Part 2 of the exam.

Qn#	Pts	Qn#	Pts	Qn#	Pts	Qn#	Pts
1.1	2	2.1	3	3.1	2	4.1	5
1.2	2	2.2	3	3.2	10	5.1	8
1.3	1	2.3	3	3.3	2	5.2	8
1.4	1	2.4	3	3.4	2	5.3	5

3.3 RQ3 Hint Behaviors

Does a student's Part 1 score tell us anything about their hint strategy in Part 2, that is, whether they are more or less likely to ask for a hint when they need one? We consider that a student "needs a hint" if they asked for the hint and got the question right (CH), asked for the hint but got the question wrong (IH), or got the question wrong and asked for no hint (IN).

We found no significant correlation between Part 1 test scores and hint requests when needed ($r = 0.07, p = .58$). This result indicates that students with lower Part 1 scores were neither more nor less likely to request a hint when it would have been useful than students with higher Part 1 scores. Across all students, the mean rate of hint requests when it would be useful was 60.75% of the questions. But this hint rate has more of an impact on the lower scoring students, as they have more questions on which they need help. By requesting help at the same rate as higher scoring students, they have more questions that they get incorrect without a hint, as seen in the results in section 3.2.

Were specific questions more likely to have their hints revealed in cases where the hint would have been useful, and if so, was there any interaction between those questions' features and Part 1 test scores? To answer this question, we ran a generalized logistic regression to find the likelihood that a hint would be revealed. As question features, we included the placement of the subquestion within the exam (1-16), the placement of the subquestion within its broader question (1-4), and the point value assigned to that question (1-10) in the model along with the Part 1 test scores. Table 2 summarizes these features.

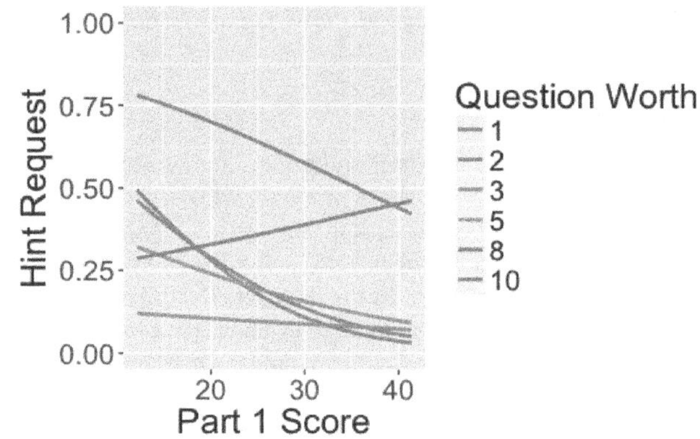

Figure 4: Slopes of likelihood of hint requests based on Part 1 test score by question worth.

We found that there was a main effect of Part 1 test scores on the likelihood of revealing a hint ($z = -2.83, p < .05$). There were no main effects of the features exam order ($z = -0.05, p = -.96$), question order ($z = -0.24, p = .81$), or question points ($z = -1.04, p = .30$). There was a significant interaction between question points and Part 1 test scores with the effect of lower Part 1 scores being more pronounced in the lower point subquestions ($z = 2.69, p < .05$). There was no significant interaction between exam order or question order and Part 1 test score ($z = 0.05, p = .96$ and $z = 0.11, p = .91$), respectively. These results indicate that students with lower Part 1 test scores are more likely to request hints on lower point questions than higher scoring students (see Figure 4).

Because students with lower Part 1 scores, tended to have more IN questions than stronger students, we wanted to understand if this result was due to the hints being too difficult or because they may have run out of time. After a student requested a hint and it was not able to help them to get a question correct, they may have no longer bothered to ask for a hint when it could be useful. To test this hypothesis, we compared the percentage of questions where a student could not answer the question on their own (i.e., CH, IH, IN) and asked for a hint between students who never had an IH to students who did. Using a Wilcoxon Rank Sum test to control for the non-normality of the data, we found that there was not a significant difference between students that never had an IH event ($M = 60.7\%$) and how often they asked for a hint when it would be useful and students that had an IH event ($M = 63.4\%$), $W = 618, p = .88$. When we analyzed only the questions that occurred after an IH event ($M = 37.9\%$), there was still no significant difference, $W = 394, p = .053$, indicating that the inability to use a hint did not discourage students from trying. However, this result is marginally significant and the timing of the event may have had an impact. Investigating when CN, CH, IN, and IH occur in the problem sequence using a Kruskal-Wallis test indicates that there is a difference in when the categories occur, $\chi^2(3) = 268.24, p < .05$. With a post-hoc analysis using a Bonferroni correction, we find that CN questions ($M = 7.1$) occur before CH questions ($M = 9.5, p < .05$), CN and CH questions occur before IN ($M = 13.1$) or IH questions ($M = 12.2, p < .05$ for all four comparisons), and there is no significant difference in when IH and IN questions occur ($p = .21$). Given these results together, it is likely that students who had an IH event, ran out of time before they could apply the hint and subsequent questions were not answered. However, it may also be that the questions later in the exam were just more difficult.

4 DISCUSSION AND LESSONS

To summarize the observations of the previous section, and describing students as "stronger" or "weaker" based on their Part 1 (conceptual multiple-choice questions) test scores:

(1) Stronger students are able to answer more coding questions correctly without help.
(2) Weaker students got more Part 2 questions wrong without seeking help when it would have been useful, because they requested help at the same rate as stronger students rather than at a higher rate. This may have been due to them running out of time.
(3) Stronger and weaker students are equally well able to use the hints once provided.
(4) Weaker students are more likely to request hints on lower-scoring coding questions than higher-scoring ones.

4.1 Future Exams

As we have described elsewhere [6], there are major pedagogical and logistical benefits to this course in having coding-based, autograded exams with "cascading" multi-part questions, so it is likely we will continue to use this format. The findings here suggest some possible improvements:

Hint gradient. Future exams will likely feature a gradient of multiple hints per question, where less-explicit hints incur a lower penalty, possibly encouraging lower-performing students to at least try answering using hints.

Make hint availability more explicit. We will also emphasize that both in terms of a higher numerical score and with respect to being able to complete more of the exam, there is no reason to leave a question blank without revealing a hint about it, and we will incorporate machinery into the test-submission system that warns the student of this. ("You didn't answer question 4.1 and you didn't ask for a hint about it. If you answer it correctly with a hint, you can still get 20% of the points. Are you sure you don't want to ask for a hint?")

Better instrumentation to understand finer-grained effects of hint usage. The exam infrastructure was developed under a time crunch, and the main goal was to allow a limited hint system while ensuring the integrity of the exam. A casualty of this prioritization is that while the exam system allowed students to submit answers to any question multiple times, counting only the final submission toward the official score, few students used this feature. Since students could run the autograder locally to check their score, few students made more than two submissions total (submitting the entire exam after checking their work locally). Since we only see the intermediate state of student work when they submit, we have limited visibility into (e.g.) how a specific student answer changed as the result of revealing a particular hint. We will modify the exam environment to capture student code snapshots each time they run local checks or reveal a hint. Tracking these changes will also allow us to find which questions were not attempted.

Understanding interaction between hints and other information sources. As mentioned in the introduction, our exam system also gives students read-only access to the Internet only during Part 2 of the exam. While we checked that the specific answers to exam questions were not readily available via straightforward searches, considerable information exists in the form of similar code examples, tutorials, and so on that students could take advantage of to answer test questions. This is an intentional pedagogical choice, as we wanted the exam to resemble the atmosphere in which students would be doing professional programming. Do students consult those vast resources before revealing the targeted hints created by the instructor? How much time do students invest searching and trying to adapt/use Internet resources in answering exam questions (thereby mimicking the very process we want to test) before giving up or revealing a hint? We have some instrumentation in place that would allow limited analysis of this question, and we will instrument student use of the Internet much more systematically on future exams with a view towards investigating this question.

4.2 Threats to Validity

We used performance on Part 1 as a proxy for student ability, but the questions on that part have not been formally calibrated for reliability, so our interpretations distinguishing "stronger" and "weaker" students may be at risk.

The point values of Part 2 questions were derived from the time it took for experienced teaching assistants to answer the exam questions correctly. We believe time taken is a proxy for conceptual question difficulty since the actual amounts of code required were modest, but this might be wrong.

This exam format was new for the students in our course and, as far as we are aware, other programming-centric courses in our department. One previous study introducing a similar new format as part of an exam [5] found that students reported higher levels of "exam anxiety" for the new-format coding section of the exam than for the traditional paper-and-pencil (non-coding) section; that international students and those with less prior programming experience tended to be more anxious; and that numerous students commented that the exam was less realistic (and more anxiety-inducing) than the lab or homework assignments on coding, as the latter were not tightly time-constrained as the exam was. However, it also found positive correlations ($r = 0.664, df = 76, p < 0.05$) between performance on the two parts of the exam.

Finally, we are sympathetic to the authors of a system for automatically generating programming hints by eliding code from a reference solution [2]: when they deployed this system in a large course, they reported that "apparently advertising the hint system via email, in the lecture, and in the exercise sessions was not sufficient" for all students to be aware of how it worked. While we publicized the details of our exam-hint mechanism and scoring policy over a week before the exam, and even provided a "practice exam" several days before the exam so that students could become familiar with the hint system (using questions similar in format but unrelated to those on the real exam), few students tried the practice environment. It is therefore possible that student hint usage was affected by an incomplete understanding of either how to reveal the hints or how doing so would affect their scores.

5 RELATED WORK

Students and instructors in the University of Aarhus' introductory programming course reacted positively to the use of coding-based exams [3], albeit without a hint system. Daly and Waldron [4] enforce "closed book" coding-based exams because "weaker students... are likely to waste time looking for the solution in the book"; because our more complex questions are open-ended and had never appeared on an exam or lab before, we judged that allowing Internet searches would de-emphasize memorization of detailed language syntax or library calls while still requiring that the student be able to code.

Most work on giving hints for programming-related problems has focused on either formative rather than summative assessment [8] or on self-regulation in intelligent tutoring systems [1]. While other computer-based testing facilities have used correctness of student answers as a way to do adaptive testing [10], we are unaware of other work in which exam-takers can elect whether to receive a hint in exchange for a point penalty. The closest analogue of which we are aware occurs in competitions such as the ACM Programming Contest, in which precompiled stub libraries are sometimes available for students to test partially-completed code.

6 CONCLUSIONS

The ability to "buy a hint" on a programming exam was born of necessity: We wanted complex "cascading" coding questions on the exam in which later parts depend on earlier parts, without having to penalize students repeatedly for failing to answer an earlier part. We were surprised that our analysis suggests that weaker students did not appear to take as much advantage of the hints as we expected, and that when they did so, it was often on lower-points questions. This may be due to how students allocated their time causing them not to reach the end of the exam, which was worth more points. To better understand how these behaviors affect the measurements that summative assessments are intended to provide, future exams in this format will include finer-grained instrumentation, including timestamping of when students attempt to run test cases (a proxy for trying to check their response before submitting) and for which question parts (to isolate ordering and timing effects in our analyses).

REFERENCES

[1] Vincent Aleven, Ido Roll, Bruce M McLaren, and Kenneth R Koedinger. 2016. Help helps, but only so much: research on help seeking with intelligent tutoring systems. *International Journal of Artificial Intelligence in Education* 26, 1 (2016), 205–223.

[2] Paolo Antonucci, Christian Estler, Durica Nikolić, Marco Piccioni, and Bertrand Meyer. 2015. An incremental hint system for automated programming assignments. In *Proceedings of the 2015 ACM Conference on Innovation and Technology in Computer Science Education*. ACM, 320–325.

[3] Jens Bennedsen and Michael E Caspersen. 2007. Assessing process and product: a practical lab exam for an introductory programming course. *Innovation in Teaching and Learning in Information and Computer Sciences* 6, 4 (2007), 183–202.

[4] Charlie Daly and John Waldron. 2004. Assessing the assessment of programming ability. In *ACM SIGCSE Bulletin*, Vol. 36. ACM, 210–213.

[5] Pari Delir Haghighi, Judy Sheard, Chee-Kit Looi, David Jonassen, and Mitsuru Ikeda. 2005. Summative Computer Programming Assessment Using Both Paper and Computer.. In *ICCE*. 67–75.

[6] An Ju, Ben Mehne, Andrew Halle, and Armando Fox. 2018. In-class coding-based summative assessments: tools, challenges, and experience. In *Proceedings of the 23rd Annual ACM Conference on Innovation and Technology in Computer Science Education*. ACM, 75–80.

[7] Chris Piech and Chris Gregg. 2018. BlueBook: A computerized replacement for paper tests in computer science. In *Proceedings of the 49th ACM Technical Symposium on Computer Science Education*. ACM, 562–567.

[8] Kristin Stephens-Martinez and Armando Fox. 2018. Giving hints is complicated: understanding the challenges of an automated hint system based on frequent wrong answers. In *Proceedings of the 23rd Annual ACM Conference on Innovation and Technology in Computer Science Education*. ACM, 45–50.

[9] Des Traynor, Susan Bergin, and J Paul Gibson. 2006. Automated assessment in CS1. In *Proceedings of the 8th Australasian Conference on Computing Education-Volume 52*. Australian Computer Society, Inc., 223–228.

[10] Wim J Van der Linden, Cees AW Glas, et al. 2000. *Computerized adaptive testing: Theory and practice*. Springer.

A Collaborative Practicum Targeting Communication Skills for Computer Science Researchers

Lori Pollock
Computer and Information Sciences
University of Delaware
Newark, DE
pollock@udel.edu

ABSTRACT

Computer science researchers spend significant time writing and presenting their research ideas to conference audiences, reviewers, funding agencies, collaborators, and other technical and general audiences. Good communication skills can increase a researcher's effectiveness and efficiency, while currently most students rely on their PhD mentor, technical writing courses, tutors, or self-teaching to improve their communication skills. This paper details a graduate level course to provide graduate students with a collaborative practicum in building strong communication skills for a technical research career in computer science. Each class meeting is activity-based, using collaborative small-group analysis of writing and presentation samples and peer reviewing with rubrics created by the students and refined by the instructor. Assignments require students to stretch their thinking and practice their communication skills. Students write weekly reflect blog entries guided by prompts to promote reflection about their communication experiences, challenges and successes. We summarize and reflect on initial outcomes from two instantiations of the course.

CCS CONCEPTS

• **Social and professional topics → Computing education**;

KEYWORDS

CS education, communication skills, CS researchers

ACM Reference Format:
Lori Pollock. 2019. A Collaborative Practicum Targeting Communication Skills, for Computer Science Researchers. In *Proceedings of the 50th ACM Technical Symposium on Computer Science Education (SIGCSE '19), February 27-March 2, 2019, Minneapolis, MN, USA.* ACM, New York, NY, USA, 7 pages. https://doi.org/10.1145/3287324.3287454

1 INTRODUCTION

Beyond their actual research work, researchers devote considerable time to writing technical papers, proposals for funding or promoting their projects, and technical reviews. Additionally, they spend time creating and giving presentations of varying lengths and forms (e.g., talks, posters) to various audiences. Computer science researchers who are good communicators can more effectively share their ideas, make a stronger impact, procure more opportunities including funding and jobs, and enjoy more fruitful research collaborations. However, the communication skills that benefit a computer science researcher go beyond communication skills typically taught in an English technical writing or oral communications course or even a communication skills for computer scientist course [4, 6]. Like any research community, there is a culture that includes expectations and tradition for the content and writing and presentation styles of each type of document or presentation. For instance, paper reviewers in computer science research areas expect certain components and writing style, such as the organization and content of the experimental evaluation sections.

Most computer science researchers hone their communication skills as part of the apprenticeship training of their PhD studies. Advisors review, mark up, and discuss the areas for improvement as the student writes about their research contributions for each technical paper submission. Students hopefully generalize from the comments and change how they write the next technical paper. Students give practice presentations to their peers and professors in preparation for conference presentations, and revise and learn from the feedback. This apprenticeship process can work well for students with advisors who take the time for this revision and teaching process and students who easily recognize the patterns of poor writing and work to change their writing. However, the apprenticeship approach of iterative writing, feedback, and revision on the part of the mentor can significantly lengthen the time needed for writing prior to paper deadlines, and can lack consistency among advisor-advisee partnerships.

In this paper, we seek to tackle the inefficiency and potential inconsistency of the apprenticeship model to building computer science researchers' communication skills through a collaborative practicum approach. This paper describes the details of a graduate level course created to provide first-to-second year graduate students with a collaborative practicum in building strong communication skills for a technical research career in computer science. The course is a practicum in that each class meeting is activitiy-based, and assignments require students to stretch their thinking and practice their communication skills. The practicum is collaborative as the class meeting activities involve considerable peer review and collaborative small-group work.

After presenting an overview of the course, we describe the classroom activities and assignments that comprise the collaborative practicum, organized by the types of communications that computer science researchers typically need to master. We conclude

SIGCSE '19, February 27-March 2, 2019, Minneapolis, MN, USA

ACM ISBN 978-1-4503-5890-3/19/02...$15.00
https://doi.org/10.1145/3287324.3287454

with some initial outcomes and reflections from the student participants' journals, last day of class conversation, and evaluations.

2 RELATED WORK

To our knowledge, this is the first paper describing a collaborative practicum approach to teaching communication skills to graduate students in computer science research. Through a web search of curricula for CS graduate students, we identified a few courses in technical communication for computer science researchers; however they do not appear to be collaborative practicums [9]. Graduate students can also learn about communication skills at mentoring workshops at conferences such as the Grace Hopper Celebration, Tapia Conference, CRA-W Mentoring Workshops, and PhD symposiums in conjunction with major research conferences.

Many CS departments incorporate oral communication components in their undergraduate program, to prepare students for the workforce. Some integrete early in the undergraduate degree program such as the CS1 level [3, 6] or sophomore level [7]. At University of Toronto, the department develops students' oral, writing and interpersonal communications skills as part of teaching interactive multimedia web technology [4]. Presentation skills are commonly included as key components of undergraduate seminar or colloquium courses [2]. Other schools integrate communication skills throughout the undergraduate curriculum [1]. These courses are primarily not specific to a research career.

3 COURSE OVERVIEW

The collaborative practicum course in communication skills for Computer Science (CS) researchers is a 3-credit course at the graduate level, targeted at first and second-year graduate students, but also open to undergraduate researchers. To register for the course, students must have one semester of computer science research experience with an advisor and a current research project. Interested students complete an application that includes their advisor, stage of their career in terms of degree milestones, and short description of the research project that they would be using as their topic of writing and presentation. The course is limited to 12 students so the instructor can get to know the students' communication challenges and provide individual feedback. Students are selected from the applicant pool based on supporting students from a wide range of advisors and advisor input on students' who they deem will benefit most among their students' applications.

The course is a one-semester (15 week) course. The class meets in person on campus twice a week for 75 minutes each class period. Twice during the semester, the class period is replaced by an individual conference meeting with the instructor for 30-45 minutes.

3.1 Learning Objectives

The course was designed with learning objectives that align primarily with the communication skills that PhD students need to hone during their PhD training to be successful computer science researchers. Specifically, (as listed on the course syllabus), at the end of this course, the students should be able to:

- Critically analyze a computer science research paper for writing quality
- Organize and write a detailed outline of a well organized computer science research paper that follows expected standards of technical papers
- Organize and write a well structured technical conference or journal paper in computer science
- Develop and present a clear, concise elevator talk for their own research topic
- Critically analyze and provide quality feedback to other CS researchers on elevator talk, research presentation, and research writing
- Present strong arguments to justify their research decisions in a proposal or thesis defense and research paper
- Develop and present clear, interesting research talks that tell the story of their research, enticing others to read their papers
- Develop a clear, concise resume and cover letter that market their best qualities and experiences

Table 1: Communication Skills by Week

Week	Topic
1	Dissecting a research paper
2	Writing an abstract
3	Writing an introduction
4	Writing about state of the art
5	Organizing the guts of a research paper
6	Presenting the approach
7	Writing about the evaluation study
8	Elevator talks
9	Conference vs journal paper; Titles, conclusions and future work
10	Creating & giving conference presentations
11	Proposal and proposal defense
12	Creating & presenting a research poster
13	Research CV/cover letter writing
14	Writing/responding to technical reviews

3.2 Course Activity Schedule

To achieve the learning objectives, the topics and timeline were established as shown in Table 1. The first half of the semester is dedicated to writing a technical paper, with each week devoted to a major section of the paper. During the second half of the semester, we focus on oral presentations and other kinds of documents that researchers need to create, present, and defend effectively.

3.3 A Collaborative Practicum Approach

As a collaborative practicum, students actively engage in activities that promote writing, reading, presenting, feedback, and strong argument to justify their research decisions. These activities occur both during whole class and small group discussions face-to-face and online. To increase collaborative learning, early on, we establish the class as a fun, safe learning environment where students all feel comfortable to participate actively in informal peer review to strengthen everyone's communication skills. The classroom is set up as round tables of 4-6 people.

The writing assignments are distributed as small homeworks throughout the semester, with iterative refinement. During Thursday class time, we introduce the next section to learn how to write, discuss the major content, organization and style using examples of good writing from highly respected conferences, make generalizations sometimes through collaboratively creating rubrics, and assign writing homework focused on that section for the following Tuesday. In Tuesday's class, we provide feedback through various peer review activities and assign revisions and reflective journaling.

3.4 Student Assessments

Students are assessed based on the quality of their contribution in the following areas, with the indicated weights for their final grade:

- 35% Writing assignments
- 15% Peer reviews
- 10% In-class contributions through active participation
- 30% Oral presentations
- 10% Weekly reflective blog and final reflection interview

The student assessments of the writing and oral presentation assignments are based on rubrics created by the students and refined by the instructor. To help guide students in their writing content and style, students collaboratively create a rubric, given an established rubric structure and examples, before they embark on each specific writing assignment. Sometimes, for time sake, the students complete a partially completed rubric that already includes the criteria. The instructor refines the rubric before the students use it as a guide to insure good coverage and quality. Peer reviews are graded periodically using a simple rubric to insure that students are getting valuable feedback from their peers. Each class period, students are assessed on their active participation in their small group and whole group discussions, on a check plus, check, check minus, absent scale. Students write a weekly online blog that is only visible to them and the instructor. Their entries are reflective answers to prompts provided by the instructor to promote reflection about their communication experiences, challenges and successes.

4 COLLABORATIVE PRACTICUM DETAILS

Here, we describe in more detail the in-class activities, assignments, and reflective journaling prompts for each of the major communication skills targeted by this course.

Getting started. The first day of class starts with an icebreaker where students find three people they do not already know and have a individual conversation to identify at least one commonality between them beyond appearance and computer science. Students then introduce each other to the whole class. As a whole group, the class determines the research areas represented by the class and which students share research areas. This partitioning is used for peer reviewing later in the course. Next, students are given 20 minutes to write a paragraph abstract that summarizes their current research topic to an audience of computer scientists that they want to excite about their research. The restrictions are no more than 300 words, no copying from previous writings, and upload at the end of the 20 minutes to the course management system. This in-class writing activity serves as a base writing sample.

The first student reflection blog entry pertains to this experience, where students are given the prompts: *What was challenging about the in-class writing experience? How did you go about your writing?* For the next class, students must identify three conferences and the top two journals in their research area (in consultation with their advisor), locate two conference papers and two journal papers from the past year's top venues in their field that they believe are well-written and easy to understand. They develop a list of features that these papers have that make them well written, and bring a hardcopy of the two conference papers to next class.

Dissecting a research paper. Sitting by common (or closely related) research areas, student share and discuss their features of good technical papers, using the example conference papers they bring to class. Groups report out on dissecting the content of computer science technical papers, including the main sectioning, titles of sections and subsections, orderings, lengths, and styles. Students note the similarities and differences among research areas and different types of papers - presentation of new techniques, experimental studies, literature surveys, etc. This provides an overview of computer science technical papers at a meta level.

Writing an abstract. Students begin in class by analyzing each sentence of the abstracts of their sample good conference papers, in a small group format, looking for commonalities and making generalizations. They work together to develop a template for the sentence ordering of a technical abstract, focusing on what questions are being answered by each sentence. Using shared space, the whole class collaboratively creates a rubric for writing/assessing a technical abstract during class. The rubric structure is set up as columns for criteria/element to be assessed, characteristics for excellent/good quality (almost full to full points), characteristics for poor quality (0-few points). Initial criteria given to the students include *Content: Introduce context of research problem, Jargon and abbreviations, Concise and succinct, Spelling/grammar, Sentence Flow.* Homework consists of writing an abstract for their current research problem as if they had the work done. After writing the initial abstract, they use the instructor-refined rubric to guide them in a second version and upload revised abstract to shared space.

During the next class, students work in pairs dissect each others' abstracts together labeling what each sentence is describing and discussing the flow between sentences. In 10-minute intervals, students in the same research area use a hardcopy rubric to evaluate others' abstracts, circling the most appropriate characteristics regarding each criteria and adding comments to provide feedback. After markup, they have 5 minutes to discuss each others' comments and then move to the next abstract peer review. The student reflection blog entry answers the prompts: *What is the biggest thing you learned today? Has your confidence in writing a good abstract changed in any way? How?* For homework, students use the peer review feedback to again revise their abstract and submit for instructor feedback and assessment.

Writing an introduction. In class, students work in small groups examining example good papers with a focus on the introduction. Their goal is to answer the questions: (1) How is the introduction related to the abstract? (b) Reverse engineer the sequence of questions that the Introduction is answering. (c) Using the examples you have seen so far, what is the typical length of an introduction to a conference paper? (d) How should the contributions listing be phrased? Then, the whole class uses the answers from small group analysis to summarize and generalize the content, format, length, level of writing, and comparison of the introduction to the abstract. For homework, students use their abstract as a skeleton and the sequence of questions as an outline to write a first draft of an introduction. The reflection blog entry focuses on *How helpful was the peer review of your abstract? What are the most prominent changes you are going to make to your abstract? How do you plan to go about writing your introduction?*

The next class is devoted to peer review of introductions, with students reading the introductions in shared space and writing comments and questions in the margins using the introduction rubric provided by the instructor. Students then discuss their comments/questions with the author of the evaluated introduction. With an instructor-provided checklist of some, but not all good writing tips, each student examines their own introduction and then their partner's introduction looking for issues and highlighting them. Again, students discuss their findings. Instead of a reflective blog entry, students are invited to write anonymously in a shared file any remaining questions they have for the instructor in regard to introductions and abstracts and the checklist of good writing tips. For homework, students revise their introduction based on the peer review and good writing tips review.

Writing about state of the art. Using their examples of good conference and journal papers, students work in small groups to complete an initial partial rubric in shared space for the state of the art/related work section of a paper. They are also tasked with creating a list of good phrases to use when commenting on limitations of others' research contributions and bad words and phrases to use when commenting on limitations as they make the case for their own paper's research contributions in filling an open gap in the field. Also, during class, students begin an outline of what topics and key papers should be covered in a state of the art section for their own research contributions. For their reflective blog entry, students are asked to comment on *which checklist items of good writing tips were new to them, what they learned today about writing state of the art sections, and other new writing tips they gained in the past week.* For homework, they are assigned to write a first draft of a state of the art section and place in the shared space.

In the following class period, the students are given two example state of the art sections and an instructor-refined rubric and charged with evaluating the two sample writings with focus on what the authors do well and anything they could do better. A whole class discussion ensues to share critiques with safety of the writings not being from the students. Next, students peer review in pairs by research area, writing comments and questions in the margins and using the state of the art rubric. After peer reviews and peer discussions of reviews, the whole class discusses any remaining questions and concerns. Homework consists of revising their state of the art sections based on peer review and uploading for instructor assessment and feedback. The reflective blog entry focuses on *describing any challenges they are having with writing a state of the art section, and answering: How did the related work rubric work for you? Would you use it in the future in paper writing? Any parts that were unclear/not useful?*

Organizing the guts of a research paper. Organizing the guts (paper minus abstract, introduction, related work, evaluation and conclusions) seems to be one of the most challenging for students; everyone's technical sections are differentdue to unique research contributions. Prior to the class on organizing a research paper, students are tasked with learning about concept maps - What are they? How can they create one, on paper or with a tool? Their homework includes identifying the concepts in their own research, identifying their relationships, and creating an initial concept map towards organizing an approach section of a paper.

The next class focuses on: How do I tell MY story? How do I organize the actual guts of my paper? What should the sections/subsections be? What figures/charts will help tell my story? We discuss the process of first determining what story they want to tell - What are the pieces of their story, the contributions and the concepts involved in those contributions, and then how do the pieces fit together? Second, we discuss how to tell their story so someone not in their research group can understand and appreciate its awesomeness. We talk about what pictures might bring the story to life. The first step is done through concept mapping. The second step is done through outlining and figure design.

To get students started, we again begin with analysis. Given a sample good conference research paper, the students work in small groups to reverse engineer the guts of the paper into a concept map. They are guided to examine section and subsection titles, how they are related to the concepts, how they are ordered and how they flow, and why they believe they included that section in that order. They also analyze the choice of figures/charts in terms of what they are clarifying or expanding upon and why they were most likely included.

The students then focus on their own concept maps particularly using the dependencies between concepts and relative importance of each concept to create a draft of a table of contents, which consists of their main sections and subsections with informative titles. They share with peers, peers ask probing questions and provide feedback, and students revise. The next step is to add in captions for each potential figure/chart that they believe should be included in each section to increase readability. For homework, students fill out their table of contents into a more detailed outline, with a phrase or sentence for almost every paragraph they intend to write. At the start of each (sub)section, they are to write one sentence that states what that (sub)section is intended to describe so peer reviewers know what the intent is for that (sub)section. The detailed outline constitutes the beginnings of the approach section(s). For reflectiive blog entry, students answer the questions: *How did the concept mapping and table of contents exercise work for you? What challenges did you face? What did you find easier to do?*

Presenting the approach. After students have created their concept maps and detailed outlines for organizing the guts of the research paper, students take turns reading them, asking clarifying questions, and trying to tell the story back to the author. Based on where the interpretations go wrong, the peers suggest revisions to the titles and subtitles to increase clarity. Simultaneously, each student takes turns getting feedback on the detailed outline from the instructor during this class period.

In the interest of not having students get too bogged down in a single paper section and the typical longer length of the approach sections, students are not required to write an entire draft of the approach sections. Instead, homework on presenting the approach consists of choosing the two approach subsections that they are more comfortable with the detailed outline and writing those two subsections to completion. During the next class, students peer review the approach writings using a rubric for good writing style for an approach subsection created by the instructor. Student reflective blog entry focuses on answering the questions: *What part of the Approach rubric criteria do you believe you struggle with the most? How do you think you could make that criteria easier to achieve?*

Writing about the evaluation study. Students are asked to think about how they would evaluate their research, answering the questions: (1) What questions would you answer by your evaluation? (2) For each question, what would you measure? How would you get that measurement? (3) What would you use for your subjects/data source for evaluation? Justify that choice. (4) What would be possible threats to the validity of your study? (5) How would you reduce those threats in your evaluation design?

During the next class, students work in small groups examining two examples of evaluation sections along with a rubric for writing an evaluation section. The small groups report out their questions and comments on the content, organization, and writing style, comparing the two writing samples, which do not follow the same style. The class also discusses similarities and differences between evaluation section writing expectations between different computer science research subareas, using the sample conference papers gathered at the start of the course. Collaboratively, students complete a partially complete rubric for an evaluation section.

The next phase of working on evaluation sections is presentation of the findings as an interesting story. Discussion centers around how to present the data quantitatively, the big stories that are revealed from the data, the side stories, and qualitative analysis that indicates where the approach does well and where it does not do so well. Students write a first draft detailed outline of their evaluation section with as much information as they have about their topic. Some students have not yet completed an evaluation of their research. Their outline is expected to include the evaluation study design details with section and subsection titles, and evaluation results and disucssion and a description of the graphs/figures that they would include. In the next class, students peer review the evaluation outline with the instructor-refined evaluation rubric.

Elevator talks. To get started, students are assigned to write a 3-minute elevator talk in a shared space. The talk should include introducing themselves, their general research problem area, specific research problem they are working on, why the problem is important, what makes it non-trivial, and their proposed overall strategy and intuitively why it is a promising strategy. During class, each student slowly reads their elevator talk to other students, getting feedback on which components are missing, unclear, or seemed out of order and whether any content should be removed and any terminology that needs to be defined. Students then rewrite their elevator talk and show it to at least one peer for feedback on the revision. The last stage of feedback is from the research advisor; students are directed to show their written elevator talk to their advisor and get feedback.

Once students have the content in writing, they are tasked with practicing their elevator talk and creating a videotape of themselves giving their elevator talk and sharing the videotape with the instructor. In the next few class periods, students give their elevator talks to the instructor as their classroom exit ticket. We also discuss personal personna related to appearance, behavior, competencies, and how to stand out, including in person and online. In the student reflective blog, students answer the question: *How comfortable do you feel with your elevator talk? Why/why not?*

Titles, conclusions and future work. Students often struggle with creating descriptive, concise titles for papers. For homework, students scan the titles of papers from the past year's top conference in their field, and write a list of characteristics that they think make a good title for a technical paper. In class, we discuss the characteristics and merge the lists. Students are challenged to create a good title for their research, and other students critique. Since the conclusions and future work section is typically only two paragraphs and follows a simple template, we do not spend much time on this. The main activity is to examine 3 good and slightly different writing samples and discuss the following questions as a whole class: How long is the conclusions? Future work? What is the main content/flow of conclusion? How many different future work ideas are presented? Long term or short term, what order?

The final assignment with respect to writing a research paper is to merge their title, abstract, introduction, state of the art, detailed approach section outline, detailed evaluation section outlines, written conclusions and future work. Students download the ACM conference style for latex and format their "almost complete" research paper, and finally write a section at the end called "My Open Questions on Writing this Paper." This almost complete paper is discussed at the individual student-instructor conference meeting.

Conference vs journal paper. To gather examples to contrast, students are assigned to ask their advisor for a conference paper and corresponding journal paper that was based on the conference paper. It could be theirs or another research group. Class activity consists of discussion of the reasons to publish a journal paper versus a conference paper, journal first versus extended conference papers as journal papers, and then working in small groups which report on the differences and similarities between the sample conference and associated journal papers that the students gathered.

Creating and giving conference presentations. In preparation for class, students are given a technical paper to read. Class begins with the instructor giving an example short research presentation for the research paper. Students write observations of how the paper and talk differ - what content is included or excluded and how is included content presented orally versus in writing? Considerable time is devoted to analyzing the "hook" slides, the slides which hook the audience into wanting to hear about the presenter's research in more detail. Students prepare a set of 2-4 hook slides and practice them for the next class. Each student presents their hook slides while the audience writes anonymous feedback on what went well and what could be improved. Students write in their reflective blogs about: *How did it go for you? What feedback was most useful? How did you respond to the feedback?*

Proposal and proposal defense. Students are assigned to obtain two example dissertation research proposals from their advisor. Class discussion begins with a discussion of 1. What is the purpose of the proposal? For the committee/advisor? For you? 2. Who is the audience? We review the NSF intellectual merit review criteria and discuss the similarities in the criteria applied to a PhD research proposal. In small groups, students collaboratively analyze the sample PhD proposals focusing on the questions: What are the key components of a research proposal? How is it different from a research paper? Audience? Scope? Length? Writing style?

Given two example research proposals along with the proposal presentation slides, students in small groups compare the documents and create a list of suggestions for going from proposal to presentation slides. Building on the hook presentation, students are assigned to create a research proposal presentation for their current research. They are encouraged to reuse the content from their writing of the abstract, introduction, state of the art, approach detailed outline, and evaluation design. The research proposal presentation is to be geared to a PhD committee audience and about 10-15 minutes maximum. In addition to a proposal presentation by each student in class with audience feedback, one class is devoted to how to prepare for a proposal defense questioning, developing lists of typical questions in small groups, merging those lists, and discussing how to interact with the committee through role play of good and bad behavior. We discuss the differences between proposal and final dissertation, and proposal defense and thesis defense.

Creating and presenting a research poster. Students are provided links to several good online resources on how to create awesome research posters and a template for a vertical poster. They are tasked with creating a layout with subtitles on each mini-box for a draft poster on some aspect of their research, putting it in the shared space. During the next class, small groups use a research poster rubric to evaluate two sample computer science research posters. After using the rubric on full posters, students peer review each others' poster layouts/drafts. Students are given a week to use their feedback and the rubric to create a first full poster draft.

We discuss how presenting a poster is different than a presentation, and role play presenting a poster to illustrate do's and don'ts. Students participate in a practice run of poster presentations with peer feedback with an evaluation form. They then participate in a department-wide public poster presentation reception.

Research CV/cover letter writing. In small groups, students analyze two example CVs and develop a shared list of good characteristics of a strong CV and a list of content/style that should not be included. The whole class uses the examples and lists to discuss good and bad qualities of the content and style of a good CV. Students must bring two copies of their current CV to class. After the discussion, students use the good characteristics document as a guide to analyze their own CV, making a list of changes they plan to make to their CV. They are assigned to revise their CV by next class, In 5-minute rounds, students peer review each others' CVs. The same process is used for cover letters.

Writing/responding to technical reviews. For homework, students read advice on writing technical reviews [5, 8]. We start class with reading two sample technical reviews, each with some negative and positive feedback, and some bad review behavior. Students identify the bad behavior, and rewrite how the same feedback could be given more effectively. Students guess which paper was accepted, and discussion about the acceptance process ensues. After discussing reactions to paper reviews and learning from reviews, students conduct a mark up process with a sample review by highlighting negative comments and suggestions, and then inserting a comment that states how they could handle that feedback if it were their paper. The review analysis leads to how to write a good, fair technical review, and how to present different kinds of feedback, with a checklist of do's and don'ts created by the students.

5 INITIAL OUTCOMES AND REFLECTION

To date, we have offered this course two times, spring 2017 and spring 2018, each with 12 students. Reflections on the course are derived from an in-class feedback session, anonymous course evaluations, students' reflective blogs, and observations of students' changes in artifacts and presentations through the semester.

Several themes arose in the student feedback and classroom observations from the first two instantiations. Students became much more confident about their ability to write after the key content and style components of each section were dissected using sample writings, and they began to see the patterns in technical writing for each section. They initially thought that since they were writers and presenters in training that they would not be able to give valuable feedback and they would not trust their peers' feedback. However, the creation and use of rubrics on content, structure and style gave them the confidence to analyze others' writing with focus on specific criteria; their revisions demonstrated their trust in their peer's observations using the rubrics. Thus, breaking down each section with a rubric seems key to their confidence and ability to produce good technical writing and provide valuable peer feedback. The instructor has to minimize the amount of individual feedback they are expected to provide as the instructor. This is why it is important that the students build trust in peer reviews.

Students were well engaged in the active classroom as a collaborative practicum in writing/presentation analysis, writing, and peer feedback with goals and time restrictions to keep them on task. Attendance and promptness to class was critical, and students who showed up late quickly realized the negative impact.

There is always room for improvement. While the rubrics were very useful, students suggested the instructor provide rubrics for later sections, as creating them was tedious and they felt they learned enough from creating the initial ones. Some students commented that they would rather cover less kinds of communication and dive deeper into more practice in either writing or oral communication, or leave more room for more oral presentation practice.

After both instantiations, several students emailed the department chair to suggest that the course be required of all early PhD students. They found that the analysis, write, peer review, revision process was hugely helpful. They enjoyed getting to know about the research being done by students outside their research area, through the peer review and oral presentation processes.

REFERENCES

[1] Karen Anewalt and Jennifer Polack. 2017. A Curriculum Model Featuring Oral Communication Instruction and Practice. In *Proceedings of the 2017 ACM SIGCSE Technical Symposium on Computer Science Education (SIGCSE '17)*. ACM, New York, NY, USA, 33–37. https://doi.org/10.1145/3017680.3017775

[2] Barbara M. Anthony. 2014. Offering an Undergraduate Computer Science Colloquium. *J. Comput. Sci. Coll.* 29, 4 (April 2014), 6–12. http://dl.acm.org/citation.cfm?id=2591468.2591471

[3] Chris Bennett and Timothy Urness. 2009. Using Daily Student Presentations to Address Attitudes and Communication Skills in CS1. In *Proceedings of the 40th ACM Technical Symposium on Computer Science Education (SIGCSE '09)*. ACM, New York, NY, USA, 76–80. https://doi.org/10.1145/1508865.1508896

[4] Lil Blume, Ron Baecker, Christopher Collins, and Aran Donohue. 2009. A "Communication Skills for Computer Scientists" Course. In *Proceedings of the 14th Annual ACM SIGCSE Conference on Innovation and Technology in Computer Science Education (ITiCSE '09)*. ACM, New York, NY, USA, 65–69. https://doi.org/10.1145/1562877.1562903

[5] Michael Ernst. 2005. Reviewing a Technical Paper. https://homes.cs.washington.edu/~mernst/advice/review-technical-paper.html.

[6] Jean H. French. 2012. Implementing a Communication-intensive Core Course in a CS Curriculum: A Survey of Methods (Abstract Only). In *Proceedings of the 43rd ACM Technical Symposium on Computer Science Education (SIGCSE '12)*. ACM, New York, NY, USA, 672–672. https://doi.org/10.1145/2157136.2157398

[7] Jessen T. Havill and Lewis D. Ludwig. 2007. Technically Speaking: Fostering the Communication Skills of Computer Science and Mathematics Students. In *Proceedings of the 38th SIGCSE Technical Symposium on Computer Science Education (SIGCSE '07)*. ACM, New York, NY, USA, 185–189. https://doi.org/10.1145/1227310.1227375

[8] Shriram Krishnamurthi. 2009. How to Write Technical Paper Reviews. https://cs.brown.edu/~sk/Memos/Paper-Reviews.

[9] University of Utah Computer Science. 2014. CS 6030 – Technical Communications in Computer Science. http://www.cs.utah.edu/~thompson/cs6030/.

Understanding CS Undergraduate Students' Professional Development through the Lens of Internship Experiences

Amanpreet Kapoor
Computer & Info. Science & Engineering
University of Florida, Gainesville, FL, USA 32611
kapooramanpreet@ufl.edu

Christina Gardner-McCune
Computer & Info. Science & Engineering
University of Florida, Gainesville, FL, USA 32611
gmccune@ufl.edu

ABSTRACT

Professional development is critical for preparing undergraduate CS students for their future careers. Industry internships offer students pathways for professional development. However, little is empirically known about the impact industry-based internships have on CS students' career paths as well as the effectiveness of CS degree programs in preparing students for these professional development opportunities. In this paper, we present a thematic analysis of open-ended survey responses of 40 CS undergraduate students in the US who participated in an internship. This study aimed to understand the impact that professional internships have on: CS students' career goals, students' perceptions of the gaps between academia and industry, and students' strategies for professional success. We found four themes that describe the impact of internships on CS students. Internships (1) strengthened students' commitment to CS degrees and careers; (2) encouraged exploration of CS careers and industries; (3) promoted personal/professional growth; and (4) developed awareness of professional expectations. We also analyzed students' perception of the curriculum's effectiveness and found that students were strategically working to improve their technical skills outside of coursework to secure employment. These findings have the potential to retain students in computing and reduce the gaps between academia and industry, thereby increasing CS students' competitiveness in the workforce.

KEYWORDS

Internship; Professional development; Curricula improvement; Computing careers; Industry; Retention

ACM Reference format:

Amanpreet Kapoor and Christina Gardner-McCune. 2019. Understanding CS Undergraduate Students' Professional Development through the Lens of Internship Experiences. In *Proceedings of 50th ACM Technical Symposium on Computer Science Education (SIGCSE '19), February 27-March 2, 2019, Minneapolis, MN, USA.* ACM, New York, NY, USA, 7 pages. https://doi.org/10.1145/3287324.3287408

SIGCSE '19, February 27-March 2, 2019, Minneapolis, MN, USA

ACM ISBN 978-1-4503-5890-3/19/02...$15.00
https://doi.org/10.1145/3287324.3287408

1 INTRODUCTION

The US Bureau of Labor Statistics projects that by 2020 there will be 1.4 million computer science (CS) related jobs available and 400,000 CS graduates with the skills to apply for those jobs [5]. In addition, CS jobs are projected to grow at 13% over the next decade [12]. While academic institutions are working to keep up with surging enrollments to educate students to address the increasing industry demand [3], 26% of the recent CS major graduates are underemployed in the United States according to a 2018 report by the Federal Reserve Bank of New York [26]. This suggests that current CS graduates may be underprepared to secure computing jobs, thus exacerbating the current challenge the US educational system is facing in preparing enough CS students to satisfy this demand. In addition, employers report that CS graduates often lack technical abilities, personal skills, and professional qualities [2, 22, 23].

As academic institutions, our role is to create pathways for career preparation through our degree programs to help students gain entry into computing communities of practice (CoP) [29] and to make their transition from college to the industry as effective as possible. One way that students access these CoPs is through internships. Internships allow students an opportunity to undergo experiential learning thereby enhancing an undergraduate's intellectual, personal, and ethical growth [9].

In this paper, we focus on understanding the impact that internships have on: CS students' career goals, students' perceptions of the gaps between academia and industry, and students' strategies for professional success. This research is a part of a larger study aimed at understanding students' computing professional identity through the development of their technical competency in CS degree programs, professional experiences, and independent skill development [13].

2 BACKGROUND

2.1 Role of Internships in Future Employment

Internships have become an integral part of employers' recruitment process as they provide them the ability to evaluate potential candidates over an extended period of time in a working environment [19, 27]. Studies have shown that pursuing an internship is positively correlated with an improved chance of getting a full-time job offer and a higher starting salary [19, 27]. A 2017 National Association of Colleges and Employers (NACE) survey reported a staggering 91% of employers considered candidate experience when making hiring decisions and half of the employers sought new graduates to be hired from an internship or a co-op program [4, 7]. In addition, NACE also surveyed 44,000 students in 2014 and found that 52.1% of students with an internship or co-op who applied for jobs received at least one offer of a full-time position compared with 38.6% of applicants without the internship or co-op—a difference of 13.5% [19]. Thus, it is evident that internships are playing a key role in preparing students for their professional careers and in obtaining full-time positions. However, little is empirically known about the impact these internships have on CS students' career goals and the students' perceptions of the effectiveness of CS degree programs in preparing them for these opportunities.

2.2 Situated Learning, Communities of Practice

In the context of undergraduate degree programs, internships are one avenue for students to initially participate in computing communities of practice (CoP). Lave and Wenger's Situated Learning theory describes how individuals acquire professional skills through co-construction of knowledge when interacting in a social context, apprenticeship, or CoP [16]. Further, Wenger states that "Communities of practice are groups of people who share a concern or a passion for something they do and learn how to do it better as they interact regularly" [29]. Wenger's CoP research extends research on apprenticeship, Situated Learning theory, and legitimate peripheral participation (LPP).

The theory of legitimate peripheral participation describes how members of CoP start off on the periphery of the community as a newcomer. As newcomers gradually gain understanding and mastery of key skills and practices valued by the community, they become more central to the functioning of the community and are eventually recognized as old timers within the community [16]. Throughout this process of participation in the community, members' identities are reconstructed and transformed as they seek to become full practitioners within the community. While there are official pathways to earning credentials to become part of professional CoPs, participation in the community is essential for recognition, acceptance, and membership within the community [29].

In the context of computing CoP, internships offer students, who are newcomers to the computing industry, a way to become members of a community by allowing them to participate in simple tasks that further the goals of the community/ organization. Through these peripheral activities, CS students become acquainted with the tasks, vocabulary, and organizing principles of the computing community and its practitioners.

2.3 Existing Research in CS Undergraduate Professional Development

Research in professional development described the lack of technical abilities, personal skills, and professional qualities in recent CS graduates [2, 22, 23], and the strategies for CS departments to prepare their students for their future careers using experiential learning [17]. Other research in professional development for CS undergraduate students has focused on the professional development of students through participation in capstone courses [21], project-based courses [6] or experience in internship programs developed through industry-academia partnerships [8]. This research includes Parker's study that found that software engineering capstone courses influenced CS students' professional identity formation, and aided them in exploring CS career options [21]. In another study, Fryling et al. found that a department-scaffolded internship program at Siena College had a positive impact on CS students' retention [8]. Research on CS industry internships is limited. However, Tomer and Mishra found CS students at an Indian university identified a gap between their academic training and their internship experience which led them to have mixed satisfaction with their CS degree program [28]. Further, Kapoor found that CS students at a US university who had industry internship experiences were more likely to have definitive career goals and were involved in student clubs and research experiences when compared with students who had not interned [14].

Overall several gaps exist in CS professional development literature (1) lack of extensive literature or qualitative studies that empirically gauge the impact of internships on CS students' professional goals; (2) studies on real-world internships as most prior studies focused on students' professional development through programs crafted by the university, or students' supervision in industry-academia collaboration by an academic supervisor [6, 8, 21]; and (3) studies gauging CS students' perceptions of gaps between industry and CS degree programs in the US as most prior studies focused on the gaps in industry-academia through the viewpoint of employers [2, 22, 23]. Therefore, in this study, we focus on understanding the role of internships on CS students' career goals and their perceptions on the effectiveness of CS degree programs in preparing them for their professional careers.

3 METHODS

3.1 Study Design

We designed a cross-sectional survey-based study focused on understanding the impact that professional internships have on CS students' career goals, students' perceptions of the gaps between academia and industry, and students' strategies for professional success. 97 students enrolled at the University of Florida in the United States participated and completed the survey in Spring 2016. The university had a population of 1519 undergraduate CS majors in 2016. The CS undergraduate degree program offered at our university allows students to major in CS, or Computer Engineering (CE). The students can choose a major when they start college but can change it at any time. For this paper, we report on the data of 40 CS undergraduate students who had an internship experience. In this study, we focused on exploring the following research questions:

RQ1. How do professional internships impact CS undergraduate students?

RQ2. What lessons can we learn from CS undergraduate students' professional experiences that can strengthen our academic curriculum?

RQ3. What lessons can students learn from CS undergraduate students' professional experiences that can aid to their professional success?

3.2 Participants Recruitment

Students were recruited from our university's CS1, data structures, software engineering, senior design courses, and several CS technical electives. The survey participants were given no more than 1% extra credit towards their final grade for participating based on pre-approval by the course instructors.

3.3 Participants

The age range of the participants was 18 to 23 based on the enrolled CS undergraduate population at our university. The details of the survey respondents are as follows: 148 students responded to our survey, 102 students completed more than 94% of the survey (Completion Rate: 68.9%). Out of the 102 students, 5 students did not major or minor in CS or CE. Thus, we were left with 97 CS/CE undergraduate students (see Table 1). Out of these 97 CS/CE students,

(a) 41.2% of 97 students interned (n=40);

(b) 48.2% of 81 students interned (n=39), excluding freshmen;

(c) equal proportion of males and females interned (Table 1).

For this paper, we exclude the data for students who did not have a prior internship experience. Thus, we report data on 40 CS undergraduates (41.24% of 97) who completed more than 94% of the survey and had an internship experience.

Table 1: Demographics of Study Participants (N=97)

Intern Experience	Academic Standing (By Year)					Gender*	
	1	2	3	4	5-6	M	F
Yes	6.7% n=1	57.1% n=8	44.8% n=13	42.4% n=14	80.0% n=4	40.5% n=30	40.9% n=9
No	93.3% n=14	42.9% n=6	55.2% n=16	57.6% n=19	20.0% n=1	59.5% n=44	59.1% n=13

*Note: One student did not specify gender and interned.

3.4 Data Collection

We gained consent from the Institutional Review Board at our university and used Qualtrics to administer the survey. The participants were asked to complete a consent form prior to the survey. The survey consisted of 3 demographic, 36 multiple choice, and 16 open-ended questions and was completed on average within 32 minutes. For this paper, we focus on 6 open-ended questions that are relevant to answer our research questions (see Table 2). We also use three demographic questions on gender, major and academic standing; and one multiple choice question on whether they participated in an internship.

3.5 Data Analysis

We analyzed student responses to six open-ended questions using inductive content analysis and thematic analysis in Microsoft Excel. We were following a grounded theory process of inductive coding [25]. We started with the raw data and created codes inductively using words from participants responses. The first author created primary codes which were then clustered to form categories, and these categories formed the basis of our codebook. We coded 129 student responses into 150 unique primary codes, which were clustered to form 78 categories. We then combined these categories into themes. 11 themes emerged to answer our three research questions: 4 for RQ1, 4 for RQ2, and 3 for RQ3.

To verify the reliability of the first author's coding scheme, the second author performed the inter-rater reliability at theme level on 36% of the dataset chosen at random. The Cohen's Kappa was an average of 0.72 for the coding scheme which qualifies as a substantial agreement [15]. The authors discussed the themes in which there was a disagreement until a consensus was reached about the theme accuracy and reliability. Then the data was recoded. Table 3 highlights an example of our inductive content and thematic analysis. This was followed by a frequency analysis of responses within each theme. We counted unique participants when computing these frequencies, to avoid counting multiple responses from the same participant within any theme. Some participants' responses belonged to more than one theme and thus the percentages don't add up to 100%.

Table 2: Survey Questions to Answer Our Research Questions

Research Question	Survey Questions
RQ1. How do professional internships impact CS undergraduate students?	Describe the impact of internship experiences on your career goals and interests.
RQ2. What lessons can we learn from CS undergraduate students' professional experiences that can strengthen our academic curriculum?	* How well has the CS curriculum here at the university prepared you for industry and/or research professional experiences? * Can you think of a course whose use/ application was way different in the industry than as taught here at the university? * Describe your experience in the CS/CE degree program? Reflect on the quality of your academic experience. * Please provide additional comments or suggestions for improving the degree program and experience at the university.
RQ3. What lessons can students learn from CS undergraduate students' professional experiences that can aid to their professional success?	Reflecting on your degree experience, what advice would give to students enrolled in this program to improve their experience in the program and their professional success?

Table 3: Example of Inductive Content and Thematic Analysis

Survey Question: Have you participated in any internships? If yes, how did it affect your career goals and interests?			
Raw Data	It made me *like my career* even more	It made me *not want to change my CS major* anymore	Helped me to *decide on CEN*[Computer Engineering]
Primary Code	Like a CS career	Not change a CS major	Choosing Computer Engineering
Category	Strengthened to pursue a CS career	Strengthened to pursue a CS major	
Theme	Strengthened students' commitment to CS		

4 FINDINGS

4.1 Impact of professional internships

We analyzed student responses to an open-ended survey question: *Have you participated in any internships? If yes, how did it affect your career goals and interests?* 34 students who interned responded to this question. Four themes emerged from our data on the impact of professional internships on CS undergraduate students' career goals (RQ1). These themes and their respective frequencies are shown in Table 4.

Table 4: Themes for Impact of Internships on Career Goals

Themes for Impact on Career Goals	n (N=34)	%
strengthened students' commitment to CS	14	41.1%
encouraged exploration of CS careers and industries	12	35.3%
promoted personal/professional growth	6	17.6%
developed awareness of professional expectations	5	14.7%

4.1.1 Strengthened students' commitment to CS

We found that internships played a crucial role in strengthening CS students' commitment to pursue a CS major or CS careers. 41.1% of 34 students (n=14) mentioned that the internship had a positive impact on their career goals: strengthened their career goals, increased their interest in CS, or increased their determination to pursue a CS major. The two most prominent categories in this theme included: strengthened their commitment to pursue a CS career and strengthened their commitment to pursue a computing major. The three students who belonged to "strengthened to pursue a CS major" category were either sophomores or juniors. Representative quotes from students belonging to this theme include:

It has given me experience as well as encourage me to stay with computer science - Male, Senior

It made me not want to change my CS major anymore - Female, Sophomore

It made me more determined to get my degree in CSE - Male, Junior

4.1.2 Encouraged exploration of CS careers and industries

Within this theme, we found that internships were allowing CS undergraduates to explore areas within CS as well as industries or work cultures of different types of companies. This exploration led 35.3% of 34 students (n=12) to determine their interests and dislikes. 58% of 12 students (n=7) whose responses were coded in this theme had a negative experience and wanted to avoid a CS area such as Information Technology or Web Development or a certain type of company or industry like military or an established corporation after their internship. On the other hand, 33% of 12 students (n=4) had a positive impact and wanted to work for the same company or a CS area. One student had both a positive impact to work in an area as well as a negative impact to avoid a different area. Those who had a negative experience were willing to explore a different area in the future. Some representative quotes from this theme include:

It significantly affected my career goals. It made me more interested in simulation and in working for government contracted companies - Male, Senior

I know more about what interests me and which fields of study to avoid - Female, Sophomore

I have interned as an IT tech for a construction company. It made me not want to work in IT ever again - Male, Junior

4.1.3 Promoted personal/professional growth

In this theme, students explained that internships helped them to grow personally as well as professionally. The personal growth was not only limited to an increase in their knowledge and skills, but the student's responses also pointed out evidence of growth in dispositional temperament including confidence and responsibility. This growth had an agentic influence on students' behavior helping them to pick future courses or decide CS specialization areas. The internship also provided them with an opportunity to get subsequent job offers.

Taught me to teach myself things - Male, Junior

I loved my internship. It finally made me confident about my abilities in computer science - Female, Senior

Lead to the acquisition of a post graduate job - Female, Senior

4.1.4 Developed awareness of professional expectations

CS students who participated in internships indicated that internships shaped their outlook on the tech industry, and they gained awareness about professional expectations in industry. Students explained that internships provides them with a new perspective on working in the industry and their CS degree.

It allowed me to see what it was like working in a professional environment and how working in a company would be – No gender specified, Sophomore

It helped me understand how the industry works actually. I did realize that I might not want to do the work I was doing in my internship but look at something else - Female, Senior

4.2 Students' perceptions of the effectiveness of their CS degree program

To gauge students' perception of their curriculum's strength in preparing them for the professional experiences, we asked them: *How well has the CS curriculum at the university prepared you for industry and/or research professional experiences?* We found two primary themes: Effective and Needs improvement. In addition, 8.6% of 38 students (n=3) who responded to this question were not sure about the program's effectiveness.

47.4% of 38 students (n=18), considered the curriculum to be "Effective". These students felt that the curriculum prepared them exceptionally or adequately for their professional development including for getting jobs or for interviews. Students also pointed out that the curriculum has prepared them to learn new topics, as well as advanced classes were effective in preparing them for the industry.

Pretty well I'd say. It has taught me to teach myself how to code in new languages at least - Male, Senior

It has prepared me enough to land me a job [internship] at Lockheed - Female, Freshman

Decently well, judging from interviews - Male, Junior

44.74% of 38 students' responses (n=17) were categorized into "Needs improvement" theme. In this theme, students reported that the curriculum fairly or poorly prepared them for their professional careers. In addition, students found the curriculum to be more geared towards preparing them for graduate school or research, and several other students perceived their prior knowledge or self-initiatives to learn new languages and tools were necessary for preparing them for their future careers.

The curriculum is more geared towards students pursuing graduate school or research - Male, Junior

Only somewhat. It's been mostly personal investment in different technologies. [University] only provides the "paper" that allows you to get in the door. The rest is on you - Male, Sophomore

For my internship, I taught myself two languages and used little of what I learned in school - Female, Senior

It gave me some good base knowledge of things, which is helpful. But all of the tangible skills that I have that actually earned me a job, were self-taught or taught to me by another entity - Male, Junior

To better understand the CS students who reported that the curriculum needs improvement, we used their comments from several questions in the survey where they explained how academia was different from the industry (see Table 1). 13 students provided feedback on the distinction. We found two themes which answered RQ2. These themes included the need for a broader curriculum; and better alignment between languages, tools, and frameworks used in industry and academia.

4.2.1. Need for a broader curriculum

Six CS students mentioned that the CS academic degree programs need more industry or job-related courses, and holistic improvement of pedagogical practices. The key issues students emphasized in this theme included offering more tech electives, fewer general education credits, optional hardware courses, and including practical applications in theory heavy courses.

Better balance of theoretical and skill driven CS skill and more app development classes - Male, Junior

For my internship, I taught myself two languages and used little of what I learned in school. I wish the CS department would teach more real-world applications of code and teach both coding and concepts in lecture rather than deeply relying on concepts and letting you figure out the rest on your own - Female, Senior

4.2.2. Better alignment between languages, tools, and frameworks used in industry and academia

Seven CS students stated that a programming language, framework, tool, or methodology used in academia was not used in the industry. They commented on the ubiquity of the agile software development model in the industry, and less usage of languages like C++ and Java in the industry.

Another thing I think should be changed is the focus on C++. In my first couple years here, I thought C++ was this great language and it would come in handy to know it well since I was using it in multiple classes. Then, when I went to interview with companies, not a single one even touches the language. I think it's important to teach a C-based language to have that experience, but it should be limited to one class. There are so many other languages in which knowledge of them will actually benefit us, that we should be using - Male, Junior

4.3 Student Strategies for Professional Success

Our third research question focused on the lesson's students can learn from professional and academic experiences that can help other students for their professional success. 37 students responded to a question: *Reflecting on your degree experience, what advice would give to students enrolled in this program to improve their experience in the program and their professional success?* We found 28 unique categories from 37 student responses. Three themes emerged from these categories: Work outside curriculum, Be strategic in coursework, and Have social supports and network.

4.3.1 Work outside curriculum

In this theme, 54.1% of 37 students (n=20) recommended that their peers do work/learn outside the CS curriculum. Prominent strategies in this category included: Learning outside school (8), Getting involved with student organizations (7), Doing side projects (6), Learning to program for interviews and industry (5) and Doing internships (4).

Do a lot of practice in your free time by visiting programming contest websites (SPOJ *and the likes), watch YouTube videos, but most importantly GET INVOLVED* - Male, Junior

Sign up for the right professors, get an internship early, get really good at learning outside the classroom - Male, Senior

I would encourage other students to get internships to experience what the computing field is actually like. The classes at university don't give a good indication of what it's like to work in the professional field at all - Female, Sophomore

School is not enough to be successful in this field, you must learn a lot on your own and topics that are being discussed/introduced in the industry - Male, Junior

4.3.2 Be strategic in coursework

In this theme, 54.1 % of 37 CS students (n=20) suggested strategies to follow during the CS degree program. Prominent strategies in this category included: Taking courses offered by specific professors (6), Working hard and not procrastinating (6), Taking courses with projects and working hard in them (3), Teaching yourself before classes (2), Taking courses to determine interests (2) and Taking electives in areas of interest (2).

Take a wide variety of courses early to find out what does and does not interest you. Don't seek electives that are easy, but rather interesting - Male, Senior

Work hard on your projects and make sure to do a good job, as opposed to just doing what you need to do to get by. If you slack off you will have a lot of catching up to do before attending and interview or actually going to a job - Male, Junior

4.3.3 Have social supports and network

In this theme, 24.3% of 37 students (n=9) advised other students to make friends in CS/classes, talk to TA's and Professors, attend office hours, do networking, and take advice from seniors for professional success or a better CS degree program experience.

Make lots of connections. Make friends with your TAs, professors, and classmates. It makes the course so much more enjoyable and easier - Female, Freshman

I would suggest them to talk to professors and their seniors and try various things in their initial years to figure out what they like and then focus on that field in the later years - Female, Senior

5 DISCUSSION AND CONCLUSION

Our paper contributes to the CS professional development literature in the following ways:

Explaining the impact of internships on students' career goals. Our findings suggest that industry-based internships are playing a crucial role in retaining CS students in computing programs, promoting exploration of different areas of computing and computing careers, and developing awareness of professional expectations. Thus, these industry internship avenues serve as pathways for CS students to become members of professional CS communities of practice (CoP). Further, these internship experiences are influencing CS students' to either continue pursuing a specific CS area or to explore another CS area in the future based on their experiences as they explore different professional CS CoPs. These findings are crucial as prior research has shown that that CS students have misconceptions about computing or its specializations [1, 10, 11, 18]. Our findings also suggest that CS students may like or dislike a certain CS area after their internship and this experience may lead them to avoid or lean towards a specialized CS area after their internship. This finding extends prior research on CS students' selection of CS specialization which states that CS students' pick specializations based on their enjoyment in individual classes [10]. In addition, our findings on students' retention/commitment to a CS major after industry-based internships extend prior results from Siena College [8] who found that a department-based CS internship program had a positive impact on student retention for upperclassmen.

Despite the benefits students found from participating in internships, finding from our study give cause for alarm as only 48% of CS students in our sample had at least one internship experience during their 2nd-5th year. We have found that these numbers are similar across junior (44%) and senior years (42%). Results from a Gallup-Purdue Index revealed that 61% undergraduate students use career centers for internship search assistance [19, 20]. Thus, further research is needed to better understand (1) the characteristics that differentiate successful internship applicants from unsuccessful applicants and (2) why students especially juniors and seniors have not had at least one internship experience, given that companies give preference to students who have had internship experiences [7, 19, 27].

Analyzing students' perception of the effectiveness of CS degree programs in preparing them for their careers. Overall, we found mixed responses from students completing at least one industry experience: 48% of the students felt that the curriculum is effective, and 47% CS students felt that the curriculum needs improvement in preparing them for the internships. Nationally, one-third recent U.S. college graduates strongly agreed that their internship allowed them to apply what they were learning in the classroom [24]. Internationally, Tomar and Mishra found CS students' reporting similar patterns of mixed satisfaction and dissatisfaction with CS degree program's preparation for industry experiences [28].

Students in our study recommended that the CS curriculum needs to be broadened to include more courses in web or app development, more practicality and project-based learning coursework, and inclusion of relevant programming languages that are used in the industry. These findings support prior work on the perceptions of employers reporting recent graduates to be struggling with software tools, and lacking project experiences [3, 22]. These issues prevent students from gaining employment.

Thus, degree programs need to ensure that these gaps are minimized by updating their curriculum frequently including programming languages, tools, frameworks, and new CS courses to better align the coursework with demands in the industry, ensuring there is a balance of practice and computing theory. These practices will better prepare our students for jobs in the industry and thereby satisfy the demand for CS graduates.

Identifying CS students' strategies for professional success. Overall, we found that students were working outside academia to gain additional skills needed to secure an internship or a full-time job. Moreover, they were recommending this strategy to other students. Thus, there is a need to understand what skills students are gaining outside of our curriculum that are helpful for their participation in industry internships. Further, we need to evaluate which skills we can integrate into our coursework so that all students can benefit from it and are provided with access to such resources in every university.

6 RECOMMENDATIONS

We highly recommend that students pursue at least one CS internship prior to completing their CS degree program. We also suggest that departments make internships mandatory for CS students given the role they play in students' professional development as well as the industry's predilection towards applicant's prior experience in the new graduates' recruitment process. Further, we recommend that departments ensure that their CS curriculum is effective in balancing theoretical and practical applications in computing, thereby preparing students for industry jobs, and reducing demand for lack of CS graduates.

7 OUR DEPARTMENTAL RESPONSE

In light of the findings from this study and engagement with the undergraduate student body and industrial advisory board, our department has reviewed its curriculum over the last two years. We have begun making significant changes in course structure and quality control to ensure our CS degree program and support programs are effectively preparing our students for jobs in the industry as well as providing the fundamental CS knowledge needed by computing professionals. We have also begun offering internship workshops and seminars for freshmen and sophomores in collaboration with student organizations.

8 LIMITATIONS

The findings presented in this paper represent a snapshot of the internship experiences taken from a small sample of CS students at a large US-based university. Hence, the findings may not generalize to large populations of students at similar or different institutions or experiences of CS students in other countries. Further, in the future, additional data on the type of internship, area and type of company might help to better characterize the population. Lastly, given that this study gave students extra credit at the end of semester, the study population could be skewed towards high performing students that wanted to take every opportunity to secure a good grade in their course or low performing students that wanted an extra grade boost.

REFERENCES

[1] Biggers, M., Brauer, A., and Yilmaz, T. 2008. Student perceptions of computer science. *Proceedings of the 39th SIGCSE technical symposium on Computer science education - SIGCSE '08* (New York, New York, USA, 2008), 402.

[2] Brechner, E. 2003. Things they would not teach me of in college. *Companion of the 18th annual ACM SIGPLAN conference on Object-oriented programming, systems, languages, and applications - OOPSLA '03* (New York, New York, USA, 2003), 134.

[3] Camp, T., Zweben, S., Stout, J. and Buell, D. 2016. Booming enrollments: a panel summary from SIGCSE 2016. *ACM Inroads*. 7, 2 (May 2016), 12–14. DOI:https://doi.org/10.1145/2915920.

[4] College Students: You Simply Must Do an Internship | LiveCareer: *https://www.livecareer.com/career/advice/jobs/internship-importance*. Accessed: 2018-08-31

[5] Computer Science is for Everyone! | whitehouse.gov: *https://obamawhitehouse.archives.gov/blog/2013/12/11/computer-science-everyone*. Accessed: 2018-01-21.

[6] Dean, C., Lynch, T.D. and Ramnath, R. 2011. Student perspectives on learning through developing software for the real world. *2011 Frontiers in Education Conference (FIE)* (Oct. 2011).

[7] Employers Prefer Candidates With Work Experience: *http://www.naceweb.org/talent-acquisition/candidate-selection/employers-prefer-candidates-with-work-experience/*. Accessed: 2018-08-31.

[8] Fryling, M., Egan, M., Flatland, R.Y., Vandenberg, S. and Small, S. 2018. Catch 'em Early: Internship and Assistantship CS Mentoring Programs for Underclassmen. *Proceedings of the 49th ACM Technical Symposium on Computer Science Education - SIGCSE '18* (New York, New York, USA, 2018), 658–663.

[9] Gardner, J. and Veer, G. Van der 1998. *The Senior Year Experience. Facilitating Integration, Reflection, Closure, and Transition.* (p. 81-94). San Fransisco, CA: Jossey-Bass Publishers. Retrieved August 31, 2018, from https://eric.ed.gov/?id=ED412890

[10] Hewner, M. and Guzdial, M. 2011. How CS majors select aspecialization. *Proceedings of the seventh international workshop on Computing education research (ICER '11)*. ACM, New York, NY, USA, 11-18.

[11] Hewner, M. 2013. Undergraduate conceptions of the field of computer science. *Proceedings of the ninth annual international ACM conference on International computing education research - ICER '13* (New York, New York, USA, 2013), 107.

[12] Hogan, A. and Roberts, B. 2015. Occupational employment projections to 2024. *Monthly Labor Review*, U.S. Bureau of Labor Statistics. (Dec. 2015). DOI:https://doi.org/10.21916 /mlr.2015.49.

[13] Kapoor, A. and Gardner-McCune, C. 2018. Understanding Professional Identities and Goals of Computer Science Undergraduate Students. *Proceedings of the 49th ACM Technical Symposium on Computer Science Education - SIGCSE '18* (New York, New York, USA, 2018), 191–196.

[14] Kapoor, A. 2019. Deconstructing Successful and Unsuccessful Computer Science Undergraduate Interns. *Proceedings of the 50th ACM Technical Symposium on Computer Science Education - SIGCSE '19* (New York, New York, USA, 2018).

[15] Landis, J.R. and Koch, G.G. 1977. The Measurement of Observer Agreement for Categorical Data. *Biometrics*. 33, 1 (Mar. 1977), 159. DOI:https://doi.org/10.2307/2529310.

[16] Lave, J. and Wenger, E. 1991. Situated learning: Legitimate peripheral participation. *Learning in doing*. 95, (1991), 138. DOI:https://doi.org /10.2307/2804509.

[17] Lawrence-Fowler, W.A., Grabowski, L.M. and Reilly, C.F. 2015. Bridging the divide: Strategies for college to career readiness in computer science. *2015 IEEE Frontiers in Education Conference (FIE)* (Oct. 2015), 1–8.

[18] McGuffee, J.W. 2000. Defining computer science. *ACM SIGCSE Bulletin*. 32, 2 (Jun. 2000), 74–76. DOI:https://doi.org/10.1145 /355354.355379.

[19] National Association of Colleges and Employers. 2014. *The Class of 2014 Student Survey Report*. Retrieved August 31, 2018, from www.naceweb. org

[20] Looking for Career Help: *https://www.insidehighered.com/news/2016/12/13/only-17-percent-recent-graduates-say-career-centers-are-very-helpful*. Accessed: 2018-08-31.

[21] Parker, R. 2018. Developing Software Engineers. *Proceedings of the 49th ACM Technical Symposium on Computer Science Education - SIGCSE '18* (New York, New York, USA, 2018), 276–276.

[22] Radermacher, A. and Walia, G. 2013. Gaps between industry expectations and the abilities of graduates. *Proceeding of the 44th ACM technical symposium on Computer science education - SIGCSE '13* (New York, New York, USA, 2013), 525.

[23] Radermacher, A., Walia, G. and Knudson, D. 2014. Investigating the skill gap between graduating students and industry expectations. *Companion Proceedings of the 36th International Conference on Software Engineering - ICSE Companion 2014* (New York, New York, USA, 2014), 291–300.

[24] Recent Grads More Likely to Have Had Useful Internships: *https://news.gallup.com/poll/179201/recent-grads-likely-useful-internships.aspx*. Accessed: 2018-08-31.

[25] Strauss, A. and Corbin, J. 2008. *Basics of Qualitative Research: Techniques and procedures for developing grounded theory*. DOI:https://doi.org/ 10.4135/9781452230153

[26] The Labor Market for Recent College Graduates: *https://www.newyorkfed.org/research/college-labor-market/college-labor-market_compare-majors.html*. Accessed: 2018-08-31.

[27] The Positive Implications of Internships on Early Career Outcomes: *http://www.naceweb.org/job-market/internships/the-positive-implications-of-internships-on-early-career-outcomes/*. Accessed: 2018-08-31.

[28] Tomer, G. and Mishra, S.K. 2016. Professional identity construction among software engineering students. *Information Technology & People*. 29, 1 (Mar. 2016), 146–172. DOI:https://doi.org/10.1108/ITP-10-2013-0181.

[29] Wenger, E. 1998. *Communities of Practice: Learning, Meaning, and Identity*. Cambridge university press. DOI:https://doi.org/10.1017/CBO9780511803932

[30] Why Colleges Should Make Internships a Requirement: *https://news.gallup.com/opinion/gallup/222497/why-colleges-internships-requirement. aspx*. Accessed: 2018-08-31.

Assessing the Attitudes Towards Computing Scale: A Survey Validation Study

Dana Wanzer
The Findings Group
2646 Woodridge Drive
Decatur, Georgia USA
dana@thefindingsgroup.org

Tom McKlin
The Findings Group
2646 Woodridge Drive
Decatur, Georgia USA
tom@thefindingsgroup.org

Doug Edwards
Center for Education Integrating
Science Mathematics and Computing
Georgia Institute of Technology
Atlanta, Georgia USA
doug.edwards@ceismc.gatech.edu

Jason Freeman
Center for Music Technology
Georgia Institute of Technology
840 McMillan Street
Atlanta, Georgia USA
jason.freeman@gatech.edu

Brian Magerko
Digital Media Program
Georgia Institute of Technology
85 Fifth Street NW
Atlanta, Georgia USA
magerko@gatech.edu

ABSTRACT

Students who have positive attitudes towards computing are more likely to intend to persist in computing and ultimately persist in computing. Thus, this study describes the development and assessment of the Attitudes Towards Computing Scale, which was developed based on Williams et al. [20] Computer Science Attitude Survey. Assessment of the survey involved testing its reliability, dimensionality, and validity. Internal consistency reliability of the subscales and the total scale were strong. However, dimensionality tests using factor analysis did not support a five-factor structure; rather, the factor analyses suggested either using one item per subscale or mean composites of the subscales to form a total score of attitudes towards computing. This suggests there may not be meaningful differences among subscales. Tests of criterion validity show that the short-form of the scale, using a mean composite score of either one item per subscale or the composites of the subscales themselves, predict students' computing knowledge and intentions to persist just as well as using the subscales. Furthermore, an example is shown why using the subscales may be problematic due to multicollinearity issues. Recommendations for improving scales, such as not using reverse-coded items and having a sufficient number of items that differentiate between subscales, are provided. Ultimately, this study provides the computer science field with a scale of attitudes towards computing that demonstrates moderate validity and offers an example of how to assess other scales used in computer science education.

SIGCSE '19, February 27-March 2, 2019, Minneapolis, MN, USA

ACM ISBN 978-1-4503-5890-3/19/02.
https://doi.org/10.1145/3287324.3287369

KEYWORDS

Computing Attitudes; Survey Development; Survey Validation; Reliability; Validity; Factor Analysis

ACM Reference format:

D. Wanzer, T. McKlin, B. Magerko, D. Edwards, and J. Freeman. 2019. Assessing the Attitudes Towards Computing Scale: A Survey Validation Study. In *Proceedings of ACM SIGCSE Technical Symposium, Minneapolis, Minnesota, USA (SIGCSE 2019),* ACM, NY, NY, USA, 7 pages. https://doi.org/10.1145/3287324.3287369

1 Introduction

Many researchers in the computer science community are focusing on ways to increase persistence in computing that will broaden participation in the field and help meet a growing demand for computing skills in the workforce. According to the theory of planned behavior, the most important precursor to behavior, such as persistence in the workforce, is behavioral intention, such as intentions to persist [1, 2]. There are three determinants of intentions to persist: perceived control over the behavior, subjective norms associated with the behavior, and attitudes towards the behavior (see Figure 1).

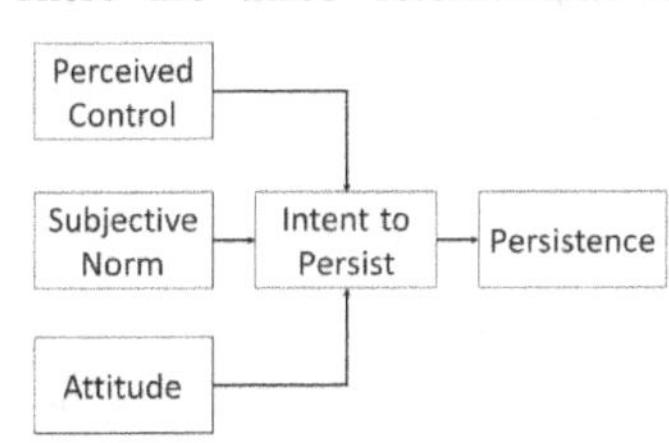

Figure 1. Theory of Planned Behavior for Predicting Persistence in Computing

Research on students' attitudes towards computer science suggest that some students, particularly female students, may have neutral or negative attitudes towards computing, which can detract from their likelihood of pursuing computing as a major or career [6, 17]. Thus, computer science education programs that target student attitudes towards computing are likely to improve students' likelihood of persisting in computing. First, an adequate measure of attitudes towards computer science is needed.

Over a decade ago, Williams and colleagues [20] developed the Computer Science Attitude Survey (CSAS) to measure attitudes towards computer programming and computer science in general. This instrument was derived from the Fennema-Sherman Mathematics Attitude Scale [5], which was based on the premise that students' attitudes affect the way they view, pursue, and achieve within a given field.

The CSAS includes 57 items across five dimensions: (a) Confidence in Learning Computer Science and Programming, (b) Attitudes Towards Success in Computer Science, (c) Computer Science as a Male Domain, (d) Usefulness of Computer Science and Programming, and (e) Effective Motivation in Computer Science. The reliability of the subscales of the CSAS ranged from α = .82 to .91 [20].

Researchers and evaluators have adapted the CSAS to respond to shifts in computer science education and the immediate needs of programs they work with. Researchers working with the EarSketch program have adapted the CSAS to form the *Attitudes Towards Computing* scale of the EarSketch Student Survey. The EarSketch Student Survey also includes a measure of intentions to persist and measures of creativity at both the person level and place level [10]. The Attitudes Towards Computing scale of the EarSketch Student Survey is based on the CSAS but is much shorter in length, consisting of only 19 items instead of 57. It does not include the *Computer Science as a Male Domain* and *Attitudes Towards Success* dimensions of the CSAS; rather, it includes two scales of *Computing Enjoyment* and *Computing Identity and Belongingness* which were created by the researchers. The subscales and items are shown in Table 1.

To date, no research has been conducted on the validity of the Attitudes Towards Success scale of the EarSketch Student Survey. Thus, this study examines the validity of the Attitudes Towards Success scale by examining its reliability, dimensionality, and content validity, which are commonly used techniques for assessing scale validity [18]. This study also aims to provide computer science researchers with an example of survey validation techniques that can be used with other scales in computer science.

2 Methods

2.1 Samples

Two samples of high school students were used in this study. Both samples came from a larger research and evaluation study on EarSketch [10]. The first sample consisted of students participating in the 2016-17 year of EarSketch (n = 439) and the second sample consisted of students participating in the 2017-18 year of EarSketch (n = 423). The 2016-17 year of EarSketch was a quasi-experimental design and included treatment, quasi-comparison, and comparison group students; for the purposes of this study, we examine all students who participated in the study and not just those who were in the treatment group because we believe the construct would have similar reliability and dimensionality across all students.

Table 1. The Attitudes Towards Computing scale items

Computing Confidence
1. I have a lot of self-confidence when it comes to computing.
2. I am sure I could do advanced work in computing.
3. I think I could handle difficult computing problems.
4. I'm not good at computing. (R)
Computing Enjoyment
1. I enjoy computing.
2. Computing makes me nervous. (R)
3. Computing is difficult. (R)
4. I feel comfortable computing.
Computing Importance and Perceived Usefulness
1. I will be able to get a good job if I learn computing.
2. I will use computing in many ways throughout my life.
3. Computing is of no relevance to my life. (R)
4. Taking computing classes is a waste of time. (R)
Motivation to Succeed in Computing
1. I like solving computing problems.
2. When a computing problem arises that I can't immediately solve, I stick with it until I have the solution.
3. When I am working on a computing problem that I can't immediately understand, I want to work harder to get it.
4. Figuring out computing problems does not interest me. (R)
Computing Identity and Belongingness
1. I feel like I "belong" in computer science.
2. I consider myself as a scientist, technologist, engineer, or mathematician.
3. I take pride in my computing abilities.

Note: Items marked with an (R) are reverse-coded items.

2.2 Procedures and Measures

At the beginning and the end of the EarSketch program, students took a test of their computing knowledge and the EarSketch Student Survey. Items on the EarSketch Student Survey were rated on a 5-point Likert scale ranging from 1 = *strongly disagree* to 5 = *strongly agree*, with a 3 = *neutral*.

3 Results: Reliability

Reliability was measured with internal consistency, which is the general agreement between multiple items that comprise one larger construct. Internal consistency reliability was conducted using the Omega Total instead of Cronbach's alpha because many of the assumptions of Cronbach's alpha like tau equivalence were violated (see [11] for more information on why Cronbach's alpha may not be an acceptable measure of internal consistency). Omega Total is conceptually related to Cronbach's alpha and interpreted in much the same fashion, though it is slightly more conservative in its estimates. Coefficients range in value from 0 to 1; the higher the score, the more reliable the generated scale. Nunally [13] indicates that between .65-70 is an acceptable reliability coefficient. Omega Total was calculated using the ci.reliability function in the MBESS package [8].

The Omega Totals for the five constructs and the overall mean composite of the Attitudes Towards Computing Scale ranged from .648 to .931 (see Table 2). Reliability was lowest for the enjoyment sub-scale, indicating that this sub-scale may need to be supplemented by other items or items may need to be improved. Not surprisingly, the Omega Total for the total scale outperformed the reliability for each of the sub-scales; this is likely due to the number of items in the total scale (n = 19) versus the number of items in each of the sub-scales (n = 3 or 4 items per subscale).

Table 2. Omega Total (ω) for Both Samples Across Sub-Scales and the Total Scale

Sample	1		2	
Reliability Measure	ω	*r*	ω	*r*
Confidence	.815	.58	.834	.47
Enjoyment	.667	.54	.648	.42
Importance	.807	.53	.775	.54
Motivation	.822	.61	.796	.58
Identity	.815	.73	.822	.62
Total	.931	.73	.927	.62

Note: Omega Total (ω) and inter-item correlations (r) are shown.

4 Results: Dimensionality

Dimensionality refers to how many dimensions or sub-constructs there are to the data. It is measured using factor analysis techniques. Dimensionality was first explored using exploratory factor analysis (EFA) with the first sample and then confirmed with confirmatory factor analysis (CFA) using the second sample. Recommended resources for factor analysis include [12, 19], both of which have guides for conducting analyses in SPSS.

4.1 Exploratory Factor Analysis

EFAs were performed with the psych package [14] in R to determine how many dimensions or factors comprised the Attitudes Towards Computing Scale and how the items aligned to each factor. EFAs were performed using maximum likelihood estimation with an oblique (direct oblimin) rotation because subscales in the Attitudes Towards Computing Scale were likely to be correlated with one another. Initial tests to determine whether EFAs could be performed (i.e., Bartlett's test, Kaiser-Meyer-Olkin [KMO] test of sampling adequacy, and determinant of the matrix) were all satisfactory.

EFAs were evaluated based on extracted communalities and factor loadings [3]. Extracted communalities were assessed to see whether items in a factor are sufficiently related to one another; guidelines suggest that extracted communalities should be above .30. Factor loadings determine how strongly items are related to that factor; guidelines suggest that items should be at minimum above .30 but it is desirable that they are above .50. Furthermore, items should only have factor loadings above .30 on one factor, otherwise they are crossloading across multiple factors and should be removed.

4.1.1 EFA 1: Two Factors with 19 Items. Parallel analysis was performed with the hornpa package [7] to determine how many factors to retain; results indicated retaining two factors, which does not align with the theoretical model suggesting five factors. Thus, a two-factor EFA was performed with all 19 items. Results were not favorable (see Table 3): one item did not load onto any factor greater than .30, two items were crossloading, and three items had extracted communalities less than .30 suggesting either the item is not related to the other items or there needs to be another factor. The two factors explained a total 48% of the variance of all the items, indicating that the set of items explains a large percentage of the variance in the latent variable of attitudes towards computing. Although the crossloading items are problematic, we first removed the three items with low extracted communalities to see if that is enough to improve the model.

Table 3. Results from EFA 1– Two Factors with All 19 Items

Item	F1	F2	EC	Issues
Confidence2	.856		.623	
Confidence1	.835		.632	
Confidence3	.822		.606	
Identity3	.632		.583	
Enjoyment4	.595		.609	
Identity1	.584		.648	
Identity2	.482		.392	
Enjoyment1	.456	.423	.629	Crossloading
Motivation1	.443	.430	.619	Crossloading
Enjoyment3_R	.395			Low EC
Confidence4_R	.385		.336	
Importance4_R		.806	.598	
Importance3_R		.784	.520	
Importance2		.569	.520	
Motivation4_R		.526	.497	
Motivation2		.443	.424	
Importance1		.418		Low EC
Motivation3		.400	.398	
Enjoyment2_R				Low FL; Low EC

Note: Items correspond to the numbers and factors in Table 1; items with a "R" at the end are reverse-coded items. F1 and F2 refer to the factor loadings for factors 1 and 2, respectively. EC = extracted communality, FL = factor loading

4.1.2 EFA 2: One Factor with 16 Items. The three problematic items from EFA1 were removed and a new parallel analysis performed with the remaining 16 items, which indicated retaining one factor. Thus, a second EFA was performed using one factor with the 16 items, which resulted in an acceptable solution (see Table 4): all items had extracted communalities and factor loadings above .30 and the factor explained a total 48% of the total variance of all the items.

4.1.3 EFA 3: One Factor with Best Item Per Subscale. An alternative EFA was tested with just the best-performing item (i.e., the one with the highest factor loading in EFA2) from each of subscale of the Attitudes Towards Computing Scale. This EFA resulted in an acceptable solution (see Table 5): all items had extracted communalities above the minimum of .30, factor loadings all exceeded .60, and the factor explained a total 59% of the variance of all the items.

Table 4. Results from EFA 2 – One Factor with 16 Items

Item	Factor Loading	Extracted Communality
Identity1	.811	.658
Enjoyment1	.798	.636
Motivation1	.797	.635
Enjoyment 4	.775	.601
Identity3	.755	.570
Confidence1	.717	.514
Confidence3	.695	.483
Confidence2	.692	.479
Importance2	.683	.467
Motivation4_R	.680	.462
Motivation2	.633	.400
Motivation3	.629	.395
Identity2	.629	.395
Importance4_R	.619	.383
Confidence4_R	.576	.332
Importance3_ R	.548	.300

4.1.4 EFA 4: One Factor with Subscale Composites. An alternative EFA was also tested with mean composites of each of the five subscales of the Attitudes Towards Computing Scale. This was performed because factor analyses often use parcels (i.e., means) of items to reduce the overall number of items analyzed and improve analyses [9]. This EFA resulted in an acceptable solution (see Table 5): all items had extracted communalities above the minimum of .30, factor loadings all exceeded .70, and the factor explained a total 64% of the variance of all the composite items.

4.1.5 EFA Conclusions. Overall, the theoretical 5-factor model of the Attitudes Towards Computing Scale was not supported; parallel analysis suggested only one or two factors underlying the data. Removing poorly performing items (see Table 3) improved the model, but the third and fourth EFAs—consisting of one item per subscale and the mean composites for each subscale, respectively—performed the best of all models with extracted communalities factor loadings far exceeding the minimum of .30. Ultimately, there may be too few items to result in five subscales or there may be a more dominant higher-order construct of attitudes towards computing, as evidenced in the 1-factor EFAs. These results also suggest that revisions of items may be needed as the subscales are not being perceived as sufficiently distinct by participants. However, although a longer scale may provide five clear subscales, it will also be more burdensome on participants.

Table 5. Results from EFAs 3 and 4

	Best Item (EFA3)		Composites (EFA4)	
Construct	FL	EC	FL	EC
Identity	.826	.682	.851	.724
Motivation	.815	.664	.828	.686
Confidence	.813	.661	.819	.671
Enjoyment	.722	.521	.767	.588
Importance	.662	.438	.715	.511

4.2 Confirmatory Factor Analysis

CFAs were performed using maximum likelihood estimation using the lavaan package [15, 16] in R; each of the four models tested from the EFAs were tested again using CFA with the second sample. See Table 6 for the results of the CFAs.

The first CFA tested the theoretical model with all 19 items loading onto their respective subscale factor and the subscale factors loading onto a global computing attitudes factor. This model did not fit the data well, with none of the fit indices reaching goal values. The Beta factor loadings suggested the reverse-coded items had much lower factor loadings onto their respective factors compared to the non-reverse-coded items. Removing the reverse-coded items greatly improved the model fit (see Table 6, Model 1b). However, there were then too few items in two of the factors that had two reverse-coded items. Furthermore, the attitudinal factors were also extremely highly related to one another, with Beta factor loadings to the global attitudinal factor ranging from .815 to .927.

Table 6. CFA Results for All Four Models Tested

Model	X^2 (df)	CFI	RMSEA	SRMR
Goal Values	**Smaller**	**> .9**	**< .08**	**< .06**
1: Theoretical Model	530.5 (147)	.889	.087	.065
1b: Theoretical minus reverse-coded items	137.5 (60)	.971	.061	.032
2: 16 items (EFA2)	555.4 (104)	.853	.112	.065
3: Best Item per Subscale (EFA3)	9.7 (5)	.994	.052	.017
4: Composites of subscales (EFA4)	20.3 (5)	.983	.094	.022

Note: X^2 = chi-square; df = degrees of freedom; CFI = Comparative Fit Index; RMSEA = Root Mean Square Error of Approximation; SRMR = Standardized Root Mean Square Residual.

The second CFA tested the results from EFA2 with all 16 items loading onto the general computing attitudes factor. This model did not fit the data well, with none of the fit indices reaching goal values. Examination of the modification indices suggested that similar items (e.g., Confidence2 and Confidence3, Importance3_R and Importance4_R, Motivation2 and Motivation3) were more highly correlated to one another than to the other items. Allowing these items to correlate, or removing one from each pair of items, greatly improved model fit but suggests that participants are not perceiving these items as sufficiently different from one another.

Similar to the EFA results, the third and fourth models were the best performing CFA models; however, the third model consisting of only the best performing item from each subscale performed best with all fit indices exceeding goal values.

5 Results: Criterion Validity

Criterion validity, which assesses how well our survey predicts the outcomes of other scales (i.e., intent to persist in computing and computing knowledge), was analyzed with the both samples together. Mean composites were created based on the four models tested. For the first model, subscales were created based on the averages of each of the three or four items (see Table 1). For the second model, scores for all 16 items from EFA2 were averaged. For the third model, scores for the best item from each subscale (EFA3) were averaged. For the fourth model, scores for each sub-construct from the first model were averaged and then the average of those five sub-constructs was computed. Correlations among all the composite scores are shown in Table 7. Correlations among the subscale composites (top left box) range from r = .51 to .71, which are very high and would be problematic in regression analyses due to multicollinearity. Correlations among the three composites from the three EFA models (bottom right box) range from r = .93 to .99, suggesting scores across models are nearly identical.

Table 7. Correlation Among All Subscales and Total Scales

	1	2	3	4	5	6	7	8
1. Confidence								
2. Enjoyment	.66							
3. Importance	.56	.51						
4. Motivation	.65	.62	.65					
5. Identity	.71	.61	.61	.70				
6. EFA2	.86	.74	.79	.88	.87			
7. EFA3	.78	.70	.73	.81	.85	.94		
8. EFA4	.85	.80	.79	.87	.88	.99	.93	

Note: Values in the top left box are the correlations among the subscales. Values in the bottom right box are correlations among the composites created from the three EFA models.

However, the mean composite of the best item from each subscale (EFA3) is not a perfectly continuous variable. Whereas EFA2 and 4 are more continuous (Figure 2a), EFA3 has small gaps between values across the x-axis (Figure 2b).

To test the criterion validity of the four models on outcome variables of interest, a series of regressions were performed such that the outcome variable was predicted by the mean composite(s) from each model while controlling for retrospective pre-test scores of the outcome variable. For instance, the independent variables in the regression for model 1 consisted of the retrospective pre-test score of the outcome variable (e.g., Intent to Persist or computing knowledge at pretest) and the mean composites for each of the five subscales of the Attitudes Towards Computing Scale. This was repeated for each model across both outcome variables of interest. The R-squared values were compared to see if any model had greater predictive validity than other models.

Table 8 shows the resulting R-squared values. Overall, there were very minor differences in the criterion validity across models. This suggests that there is no real loss of information in the Attitudes Towards Computing scale when only a handful of items are used compared to using composites comprised of all or most items.

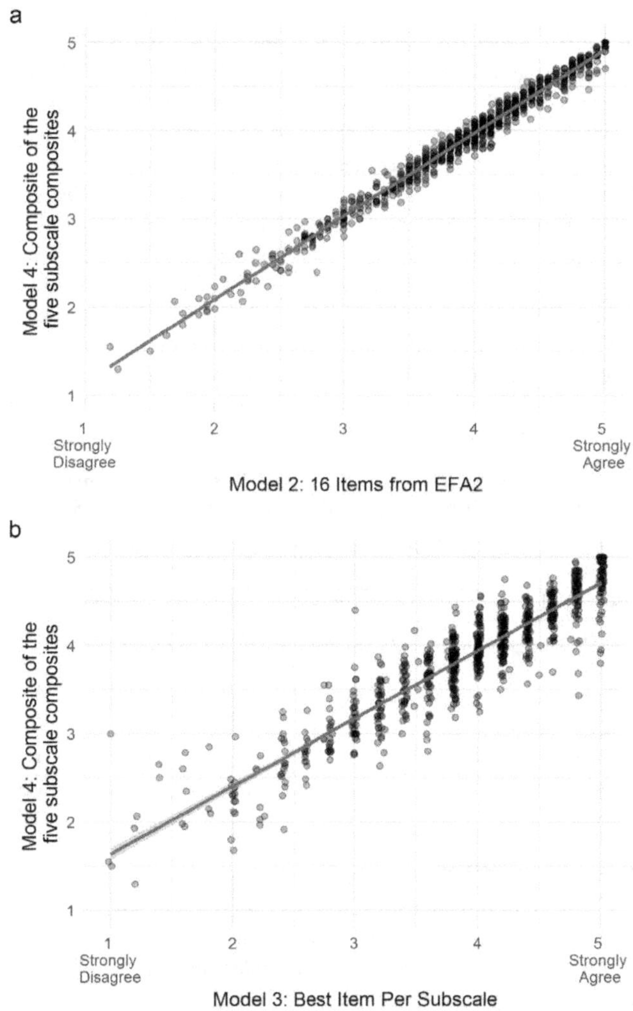

Figure 2. Correlations Between EFA 4 with EFAs 2 and 3

Table 8. R-Squared Values for Regressions Predicting Computing Knowledge and Intent to Persist

Model	Computin g Knowledge	Intent to Persist
1: Five subscale composites	46.5%	71.8%
2: 16 items (EFA2)	45.7%	70.4%
3: Best Item per Subscale (EFA3)	45.2%	72.0%
4: Composite of the Composites of each subscale (EFA4)	45.8%	69.8%

5.1 Multicollinearity: An Example

When independent variables are strongly correlated, it may cause issues in statistical inference such that regression coefficients are unstable. To demonstrate how the strong correlations of the subscales of the Attitudes Towards Computing Scale can be problematic, another regression was performed predicting computing knowledge and intent to persist with retrospective pre-test scores of computing knowledge or intention to persist and all five subscales of the Attitudes Towards Computing Scale. Table 9 shows the simple correlations and regression coefficients for the first model examined in Table 8. Despite having moderate to strong positive correlations between each of the subscales and the two outcome variables, one of the standardized regression coefficients (Betas) was negative which is an example of suppression. The multicollinearity results in unstable Beta weights that fluctuate widely depending on which subscales are included in the regression. Therefore, it would be more advisable to use a mean composite of either one item per subscale (e.g., Model 3 in Table 8) or a mean composite of all the items (e.g., Model 2 or 4 in Table 8).

Table 9. Simple Correlations and Beta Coefficients for Computing Knowledge and Intent to Persist Post Scores

	Computing Knowledge		Intent to Persist	
Subscale	**r**	**Beta**	**r**	**Beta**
Pretest Score	.70	.597	.74	.429
Confidence	.27	.007	.57	.021
Enjoyment	.24	.078	.54	.001
Motivation	.40	.135	.61	.121
Importance	.32	.028	.65	.174
Identity	.24	-.076	.72	.285

6 Conclusions

The purpose of this study was to examine the reliability, dimensionality, and validity of the Attitudes Towards Computing Scale. Overall, reliability of the subscales and the total scale of Attitudes Towards Computing was high. However, tests of dimensionality did not support the theorized 5-factor solution; rather, the items and subscales were so highly correlated that a 1-factor solution fit the data best. Both EFAs and CFAs supported using either one item per subscale or mean composites of each subscale. Furthermore, there was no loss of information in using a total composite or composite of just one item per subscale when predicting Intent to Persist or Computing Knowledge.

7 Discussion

This research sheds light on some issues with common practices in survey development, including reverse-coded items, survey fatigue, and pretesting.

First, many scales contain reverse-coded items, but people interpret reverse-coded items differently than non-reverse-coded items, which can result in factor analysis issues [15]. Reverse-coded items tend to either not perform well with non-reverse-coded items or to load onto their own separate factor.

Second, researchers often have to balance having enough items to have meaningful subscales and having too many items that introduce survey fatigue in participants. Though the Attitudes Towards Computing scale did not provide meaningful subscales, we believe the total scale is still useful in measuring attitudes towards computing globally. This study resulted in both a long (16 items, or 13 items if reverse-coded items are removed) and short (5-items) form of the Attitudes Towards Computing scale.

Third, this study's failure to find support for the 5-factor solution highlights the importance of thoroughly pretesting surveys. Pretesting surveys can involve expert review, testing the survey through the Quality Appraisal System [21], and cognitive interview techniques [4]. If pretesting had been done with the items of the Attitudes Towards Computing Scale, many of the issues highlighted in this paper may have been identified prior to costly data collection efforts. Importantly, this study focused on criterion validity, but there are many other types of validity that were not discussed. For example, pretesting can be useful for construct validity (i.e., the extent to which a test measures the construct it claims it measures) and content validity (i.e., the extent to which a test covers the full range of the concept's meaning).

Ultimately, we believe this study highlights the need for researchers to rigorously test the scales they use. It is our hope that this study can serve as a guide for researchers in testing their own scales to determine whether they are reliable and valid for the populations they are using it with.

ACKNOWLEDGMENTS

This material is based upon work supported by the National Science Foundation under Grant No. 1504293. The curriculum described in this paper is available at http://earsketch.gatech.edu/itec2120/book.html.

REFERENCES

[1] Ajzen, I. 2001. Nature and operation of attitudes. *Annual Review of Psychology.* 52, 1 (Feb. 2001), 27–58. DOI:https://doi.org/10.1146/annurev.psych.52.1.27.

[2] Ajzen, I. 1991. The theory of planned behavior. *Organizational Behavior and Human Decision Processes.* 50, 2 (Dec. 1991), 179–211. DOI:https://doi.org/10.1016/0749-5978(91)90020-T.

[3] Costello, A.B. and Osborne, J.W. 2005. Best practices in exploratory factor analysis: Four recommendations for getting the most from your analysis. *Practical Assessment, Research & Evaluation.* 10, 7 (2005), 1–9.

[4] De Leeuw, E., Borgers, N. and Smits, A. 2004. Pretesting questionnaires for children and adolescents. *Methods for testing and evaluating survey questionnaires.* S. Presser, J.M. Rothgeb, M.P. Couper, J.T. Lessler, E. Martin, J. Martin, and E. Singer, eds. John Wiley & Sons, Inc. 409–429.

[5] Fennema, E. and Sherman, J.A. 1976. Fennema-sherman mathematics attitudes scales: Instruments designed to measure attitudes toward the learning of mathematics by females and males. *Journal for Research in Mathematics Education.* 7, 5 (Nov. 1976), 324. DOI:https://doi.org/10.2307/748467.

[6] Funke, A., Berges, M. and Hubwieser, P. 2016. Different perceptions of computer science. *2016 International Conference on Learning and Teaching in Computing and Engineering (LaTICE)* (Mumbai, India, Mar. 2016), 14–18.

[7] Huang, F. 2015. *hornpa: Horn's (1965) Test to Determine the Number of Components/Factors.*

[8] Kelley, K. 2007. Methods for the Behavioral, Educational, and Social Sciences: A R package. *Behavior Research Methods.* 39, 4 (Nov. 2007), 979–984. DOI:https://doi.org/10.3758/BF03192993.

[9] Little, T.D., Cunningham, W.A., Shahar, G. and Widaman, K.F. 2002. To parcel or not to parcel: Exploring the question, weighing the merits. *Structural Equation Modeling: A Multidisciplinary Journal.* 9, 2 (Apr. 2002), 151–173. DOI:https://doi.org/10.1207/S15328007SEM0902_1.

[10] Magerko, B., Freeman, J., Mcklin, T., Reilly, M., Livingston, E., Mccoid, S. and Crews-Brown, A. 2016. EarSketch: A STEAM-based approach for underrepresented populations in high school computer science education. *Trans. Comput. Educ.* 16, 4 (Sep. 2016), 14:1–14:25. DOI:https://doi.org/10.1145/2886418.

[11] McNeish, D. 2017. Thanks coefficient alpha, we'll take it from here. *Psychological Methods.* Online First, (May 2017). DOI:https://doi.org/10.1037/met0000144.

[12] Meyers, L.S., Gamst, G. and Guarino, A.J. 2017. *Applied multivariate research: Design and interpretation.* SAGE.

[13] Nunnally, J.C. 1978. *Psychometric theory.* McGraw-Hill.

[14] Revelle, W. 2018. *psych: Procedures for Psychological, Psychometric, and Personality Research.*

[15] Rosseel, Y. 2012. lavaan: An R package for structural equation modeling. *Journal of Statistical Software.* 48, 2 (2012), 1–36. DOI:https://doi.org/10.18637/jss.v048.i02.

[16] Rosseel, Y., Oberski, D., Byrnes, J., Vanbrabant, L., Savalei, V., Merkle, E., Hallquist, M., Rhemtulla, M., Katsikatsou, M., Barendse, M., Chow, M. and Jorgensen, T.D. 2018. *lavaan: Latent Variable Analysis.*

[17] Schulte, C. and Knobelsdorf, M. Attitudes towards computer science-computing experiences as a starting point and barrier to computer science. *Third International Workshop on Computing Education Research* (Atlanta, GA, USA).

[18] Slavec, A. and Drnovšek, M. 2012. A perspective on scale development in entrepreneurship research. *Economic and Business Review.* 14, 1 (2012), 39–62.

[19] Tabachnick, B.G. and Fidell, L.S. 2013. *Using multivariate statistics.* Pearson Education.

[20] Williams, L., Wiebe, E., Yang, K., Ferzli, M. and Miller, C. 2002. In support of pair programming in the introductory computer science course. *Computer Science Education.* 12, 3 (Sep. 2002), 197–212. DOI:https://doi.org/10.1076/csed.12.3.197.8618.

[21] Willis, G.B. and Lessler, J.T. 1999. Question Appraisal System - QAS-99. (1999), 84.

Are You Game?

Assessing Students' Perception of Learning, Instructors' Perspective, and Learning Attitude

Hadi Hosseini
Rochester Institute of Technology
Rochester, NY, USA
hhvcs@rit.edu

Laurel Perweiler
Rochester Institute of Technology
Rochester, NY, USA
lmp2265@rit.edu

ABSTRACT

The use of gameful activities in education has been widely celebrated in recent years as an effective pedagogical method in engaging students, exciting cognitive abilities, and promoting mastery. Despite the popularity of game-based learning, to date, little has been done to analyze the impacts of introducing such interventions on students and instructors alike. We focus on hybrid teaching strategies that blend educational games with instructional scaffolding in introductory computer science teaching. We assess the effectiveness of incorporating these teaching strategies by leveraging various empirical evaluation techniques and study their impacts from three different dimensions: students' point of view, instructors' perspective, and students' performance. In addition, we establish correlations between students' approaches to learning and game-based learning, and further discuss how learning concentration and curiosity relate to students' perception of game-based activities.

CCS CONCEPTS

• **Social and professional topics → Computer science education**; *Computational thinking*.

KEYWORDS

Game-based learning; Learning Styles; Scaffolding; Introductory Computer Science

ACM Reference Format:
Hadi Hosseini and Laurel Perweiler. 2019. Are You Game?: Assessing Students' Perception of Learning, Instructors' Perspective, and Learning Attitude. In *Proceedings of the 50th ACM Technical Symposium on Computer Science Education (SIGCSE '19), February 27-March 2, 2019, Minneapolis, MN, USA.* ACM, New York, NY, USA, 7 pages. https://doi.org/10.1145/3287324.3287411

1 INTRODUCTION

One of the most fundamental, and yet simple, structured educational activities is learning through game play. Games often engage cognitive reasoning, physical and gesture coordination, and psychological arousal. In the past few decades, games have been the center of attention in higher education as a means to teaching new concepts, fostering student interactions, and promoting critical thinking. The use of games in education to teach concepts is arguably motivated by its connection to the learning theory, and primarily, the *self determination theory* [6]. Gameful activities that target learners' intrinsic motivation by making activities "enjoyable" and fun also engage the learners emotionally, and as a result, improve cognition and critical thinking [23, 24].

In this paper, we focus on a particular type of game-based learning (GBL) activities. Our approach is to blend gameful activities with lesson planning to improve instructional scaffolding and promote a deeper level of learning. The goal is to use GBL activities as initial compelling tasks that not only engage students but also cultivate a challenging platform to raise student curiosity. Adopting a *modular* game design paradigm [11, 12], we develop game-based interventions in teaching introductory computer science courses that help improve student engagement. In particular, we focus on designing GBL activities for teaching the concept of 'graph traversal' to first year computer science (CS) students.

We assess the effectiveness of incorporating these teaching strategies by leveraging various empirical evaluation techniques and study their impacts from three different dimensions: students' point of view, instructors' perspective, and students' performance. The goal is to paint a wholesome picture on the impacts of gameful activities, particularly in computer science teaching. Formally, we are interested in answering the following questions about the impact of GBL in teaching introductory CS courses:

(1) Does GBL improve students' perception of learning, team work, and critical thinking? Do students perceive GBL as potential chaos and threat to the clarity of instruction?
(2) Is there any relationship between student learning traits and the perception of GBL activities?
(3) How do instructors perceive GBL in teaching introductory CS courses?

In addition, we are interested in establishing whether and to what degree students' perception of the GBL activities influence their responses to the core survey questions and whether students' approaches to learning and their attitude towards learning affect their perception of GBL methods in the classroom.

1.1 Our Results

This empirical study was conducted on first-year students in a large-scale institution involving ten sections and eight instructors. Sections were randomly assigned to the control and the study groups. We collected anonymous post-activity survey data, conducted semi-structured interviews with instructors, and analyzed students' grading performance.

ACM ISBN 978-1-4503-5890-3/19/02...$15.00
https://doi.org/10.1145/3287324.3287411

Our statistical analysis suggests that 1) students significantly perceived GBL positively with respect to learning, working in groups, and cultivating critical thinking, 2) there was no substantial correlation between students' attitude towards learning and GBL activities, 3) there was no significant difference between the study and the control group with respect to organization and clarity of instruction, and 4) students attitude towards concentration and critical thinking positively correlates to their perception of GBL activities and their acceptance of such methods.

1.2 Related Work

Game-based learning has been the center of attention among the educators and practitioners in higher education pedagogy [3, 7, 27] and K-12 education [5, 17, 26]. It has been seen as an effective way of improving students' motivation and engagement in the learning process through relevant gameful activities [9, 28]. There has been significant effort in the gamification domain to utilize digital or computer games for education purposes [4, 8, 16, 19, 21, 22, 26, 30]. Most of these works are inspired by the popularity of video games or computer games to improve learner engagement: teaching cybersecurity through computer games [18, 25], educational games for K-12 computing [15, 32], improving active learning for teaching data structure or algorithm concepts [8, 10], and developing game engines for entry-level classes in gaming [21, 31].

In contrast to computer-based approaches, traditional games tend to utilize the elements of games and gameful design for delivering CS concepts or improving assessments. The use of traditional games to teach concepts in computer science has been popularized in recent years, as a way to reconnect to fundamental notions of play. These approaches range from designing board games, puzzles, or other game modules with the objective of teaching concepts. For example, pencil puzzles (e.g. Sudoku) were proposed to encourage computational thinking in computer science assessments, which were shown to improve students' enjoyment and their perception of coding skills [1] while being gender- and experience-neutral [2].

We focus on the use of traditional gameful activities without the use of computers in classroom delivery as a means to promoting active learning and instructional scaffolding.

2 STUDY DESIGN

One of the preliminary, yet fundamental, concepts in teaching data structures in the first year sequence is graph traversal or graph search algorithms such as Breadth First Search (BFS) or Depth First Search (DFS). These algorithms are arguably the first techniques that students have to learn, and may be confusing at times for first time students. In particular, instructors reported several issues when teaching concepts (e.g. backtracking), making graph traversal a suitable topic for our study.

Going into the activity, students had a basic introduction and understanding of the fundamental concepts of graphs but were not yet introduced to traversal algorithms. The intended learning outcome of this topic are that students expected to 1) apply the steps of traversal on graphs, 2) distinguish between BFS and DFS and their applications, 3) apply and comprehend backtracking.

The lectures in the control group were usual standard lectures with occasional active learning methods such as question-answering, pair work, etc. The lesson planning in the study group started with an introduction about graphs, basic terminology, and a reminder of the past session followed by an interactive GBL activity (see details below). After the GBL activity, instructors explained the main concepts by making connections to the GBL activity. Finally, students partake in a post-assessment activity using Kahoot.

In order to introduce these concepts we introduced a game-based activity with the intention of studying the effectiveness of such interventions on students and instructors alike.

Table 1: A sample assignment of numbers to letters in COMPILE.

C	O	M	P	I	L	E
7	6	5	9	8	1	4

2.1 COMPILE

We designed an activity, called "COMPILE" that reflects various elements of games and gameplay for teaching graph traversal and backtracking, and includes elements such as randomization, props, team play, competition, and creative development. In designing our activity, we were inspired by a popular video game Fallout [29] in which players are tasked with unlocking certain "SPECIAL" powers. Each letter in "SPECIAL" has different levels to unlock, and depending on these values the next paths will be unlocked.

We designed a constrained graph with nodes corresponding to words and edges corresponding to paths between the nodes. The words can be chosen freely depending on the context. We chose the nodes with words that would foster creativity and students can relate to in a fun way. These words contained different CS-related terms and random instructor names. Figure 1 illustrates a sample version of the COMPILE graph. The actual graph contains about 75 nodes and more than 120 edges. Students were first tasked to assign numbers to each of the seven letters in "COMPILE", which in turn will act as constraints on the given graph (Table 1). Then students were asked to traverse the graph following these constraints. For example, when visiting the node 'M8', if the initial chosen value for the letter 'M' is less than 8, you are not allowed to collect that word and should either continue at a neighbor node or backtrack to find an alternate path. Below are the detailed steps of COMPILE:

(1) Assign a value (or level), between one and ten, to each letter in COMPILE, such that all seven letters sum up to forty. You are free to use a number more than once or not at all.
(2) Traverse the tree starting at the top node. You can only hit the node if you have a number greater than or equal to the associated letter. You may go back one level if you do not have the correct number associated with the letter.
(3) Collect words on your final traversal, i.e. the nodes from the path found from the start node to the end node.
(4) Create a story with collected words attached to the final nodes. This is equivalent to filling in the edges of a graph.

Once the (pre-identified) end node in the graph is reached, students in each group collect the words they hit on their final traversal and create a story. This is where freedom and creativity are granted. Students were able to utilize the words in any possible order to

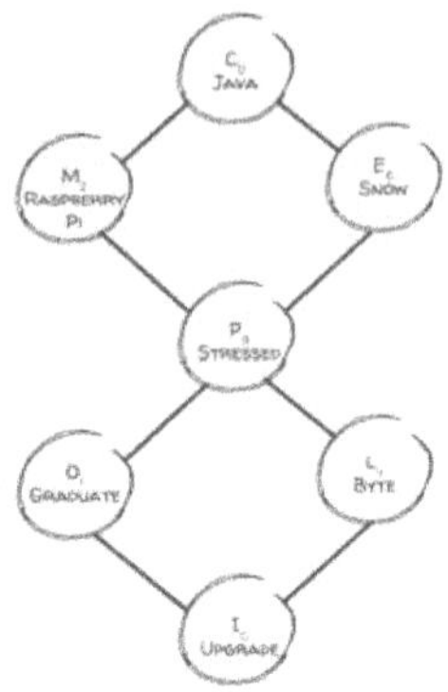

Figure 1: A sample version of the COMPILE graph. The actual graph contains about 75 nodes and more than 120 edges.

come up with a story to present to the class. The whole activity was completed in pairs of two, and the best (funniest) stories (by student votes) won candy prizes. Predictably, students in all participating sections were comfortable sharing their unique stories to the class due to a friendly and encouraging environment that was created through interaction, with several funny and engaging stories. For instance, one group created the following story:

"*It was a dark and stormy night at [X] institution. The evil professor [SMITH] was stuck inside finishing his next evil assignment. [SMITH] found that when he made students fail, it gave him a MAGIC feeling inside. After taking a swig of some JAVA, he proceeded to email his finished creation to Professor [DOE] and the rest of the CS department. Little did they know he know, that [DOE] and the rest of the department would STUDY his evil ways and also create their own evil exams and labs to destroy the hopes and dreams of the CS/SE student body. These new evil accomplices proved to be a big upgrade to his evil plot. After the evil [SMITH] puts forth his plan, he will make sure that no student ever GRADUATES.*"[1]

2.2 Post Assessment

The post-assessment activity was designed as a game module and was presented towards the end of the lecture as a fun approach to gauge students' knowledge of the covered content. In this post-assessment activity, students participated in a short ungraded quiz using Kahoot.it platform. Kahoot provides a fun gamified platform for online quizzes where students move up the ladder board by correctly and quickly answering the questions. Students participated by answering five multiple-choice questions, and the top 10 students received candy prizes. We would like to note that the participation was completely anonymous and students were given a chance to choose any nickname to enter the game using their computer devices (e.g. cellphones, laptops, tablets).

2.3 Evaluation Methods

We used a combination of questionnaires, grades, and semi-structured interviews with educators to investigate the effectiveness of the proposed GBL interventions.

[1]Names have been changed due to confidentiality.

Table 2: Descriptive statistics of students' responses grouped by category.

	Study		Control	
	μ	σ	μ	σ
About the lecture	5.24	1.38	3.88	1.68
Working together	5.05	1.35	3.90	1.30
Lecture opportunities	4.96	1.36	3.98	1.468
About you	5.14	1.39	4.73	1.4

We used post-activity online questionnaires to gauge students' perception of the proposed interventions. The set of questions were selected from the Experiences of Teaching and Learning Questionnaire (ETLQ) [14] into four main categories: About the lecture (9 questions), Working Together (7 questions), Lecture Options (6 questions), About You (7 questions), and an open-ended question for any additional comments or feedback. To ensure the reliability of the measure over the responses, we chose a 7-point Likert scale from strongly disagree to strongly agree.

3 EMPIRICAL EVALUATION

We conducted our study in a computer science course on data structure and design with an object-oriented perspective – the second course in an introductory CS sequence. The students were generally first-year computer science or software engineering students with basic knowledge about programming in Python and elementary data types and structures (e.g. stacks, queues).

We randomly selected 5 sections (out of 10) with 4 distinct instructors as our study (test) group, and the rest with 4 instructors as the control group. Each section of this course on average has about 44 enrolled students. The total of 57 ($\approx$ 28%) students from the study group and 25 ($\approx$ 12%) from the control group completed the voluntary and anonymous online questionnaire after the study. The low response rate is generally attributed to voluntary participation and not assigning any additional incentives (e.g. grades) for participating in the survey after the lecture. Table 2 illustrates the descriptive statistics of the responses in each category.

3.1 Statistical Significance Analysis

Since our data set contained several possibly correlated variables, we ran a Principle Component Analysis (PCA) between the responses to all 29 questions to find meaningful correlations between the responses. Only the first PCA (PC-1) provided meaningful explanation of the variance and explains about 50.9% of variables. Figure 3 illustrates the first and second components. Other principle components are more or less equal (and unsubstantial), implying that there is only one group of questions which correlate with each other, and it includes all but the 'About You' questions.

Although the control and study groups are not strictly divided by PC-1, their means are statistically different (Figure 3). The two samples have unequal variances and sample sizes (Figure 2), hence, we conducted a Welch two sample t-test. There was significant difference in the scores between the study group (μ = 5.42) and the control group (μ = 2.065); $t(45.05) = 4.488, p = 4.942e - 05$. These

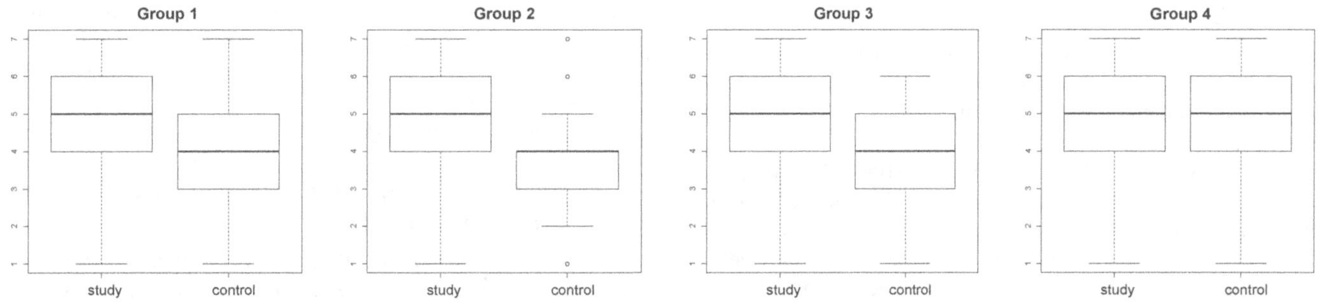

(a) About the lecture (b) Working together (c) Lecture opportunities (d) About you

Figure 2: Box plots visualizing the statistical distribution of responses in every category.

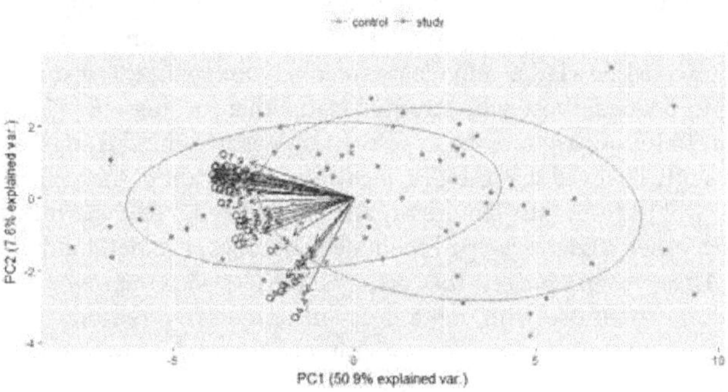

Figure 3: Principle component analysis for study and control groups. Only PC-1 and PC-2 are drawn.

results imply the study group had statistically significant positive perception of the game-based interventions with respect to lecture style, working with peers, and enjoyment of the lecture.

Although our initial analysis showed significant difference between the groups, it does not provide sufficient justification as to what factors influence these results. In the next section we further dissect the various parameters by relating to the learning theory and psychology of learning to paint a more vivid picture on the impacts of GBL interventions on students' perception of learning.

3.2 Detailed Analysis

In this section, we delve deeper into the pedagogical aspects of employing GBL in CS lesson planning and discuss the ramifications of our findings on a variety of key classroom dynamics.

With multiple comparisons (29 variables), we conducted unpaired two-sample t-test with Bonferroni correction. After this correction, the responses to most questions were statistically significant between the two groups except a few questions about communicating knowledge and ideas effectively, making relevant connections between topics, and discussing important ideas. One check question was included in the 'About You' section to ensure the accuracy of the collected data against *response bias* and remained significantly correlated to two other questions in previous sections. This means that students generally were sincere about their responses and completed questions accurately on average.

3.3 Enjoyment and Students' Interest

The students found the game-based interventions successful in creating a fun and enjoyable environment. There was a significant difference between the two groups (after Bonferroni correction) on all questions related to enjoyment and students' interest in the GBL activities. Students in the study group reported that the lecture helped them stay interested, was better than a typical class, provided plenty of opportunities to gain interest in the topic, and overall enjoyed the lecture. In fact, the probability values were among the strongest for all questions in this category ($p < 2.39e-05$). These results are consistent with previous research on positive impacts of GBL in educational context [4, 13], further confirming that play and games can raise cognitive arousal and improve students' motivation.

3.4 Working Together and Critical Thinking

Working with fellow classmates in university classrooms can sometimes be intimidating, particularly for first-year students. They are often scared or hesitant to work with others or may find group activities absurd without meaningful contribution to the learning process. Interestingly, we find out that working together towards a reasonable educational game can boost students' sense of group work while showing the benefits of working together. In particular, our analysis shows that students were generally comfortable with working with other students, felt that their views were valued among their peers, and in general during the lecture (statistical significance after Bonferroni correction $p < 0.0002$). Moreover, the lecture provided plenty of opportunities to work with others and develop the concept with the instructor and other students.

With respect to cultivating thinking and learning, students perceived the GBL lecture as a lecture that helped them improve their learning performance; encouraging them to focus on the topic. This stands in sharp contrast with a belief that incorporating game-based activities often distracts students from learning [20].

A few students commented about positive aspects of these activities in their critical thinking process. One student commented "*I believe this lecture generally helped me understand the topic of DFS and BFS. Visualizing the topic / using unique examples, in my opinion, help me to pay more attention and be more active in the lecture*".

3.5 GBL $\stackrel{?}{=}$ Chaos

Even though the empirical evaluations suggest that students strongly support the use of games and game-based activities, our further detailed analysis on responses suggests interesting revelations about students' perception of classroom dynamics.

First, there was no significant difference between the groups on the *clarity of instructions* and *clear linkage to the intended learning outcomes*. This finding suggests that both groups perceived the lectures similarly, implying that the GBL lecture did not introduce chaos or any confusion with respect to instructions and connections to the subject matter. Nevertheless, students reported that the GBL lecture did not provide plenty of 'opportunity for problem solving and discussing important ideas' nor 'working on technical procedures specific to the subject'. These findings suggest that students do not find GBL activities significantly different from regular lectures when it comes to technical details and procedures.

We should also note that all significance testing was done with Bonferroni correction. Interestingly, the responses to *all* of these questions (except the 'About You' section) were statistically significant without Bonferroni correction. The only response with statistically significant difference in this category (Lecture Option) was about motivation and gaining interest, i.e. "This lecture provided plenty of opportunities for me to gain interest in the topic.", with the study group ($\mu = 5.37, \sigma = 1.20$) and the control group ($\mu = 3.76, \sigma = 1.42$), $p = 1.49E - 05$. Thus, we postulate that, perhaps, the collected data does not have sufficient statistical power, motivating further studies to truly capture such relationships.

4 LEARNING STYLES AND ATTITUDES

Figure 4 illustrates the pairwise Pearson correlation for the study and the control groups. The horizontal and vertical lines denote the four groups of questions. These figures further confirm the significant correlation between groups 1 and 3, although the rest of the correlations are insignificant. Moreover, the correlations between group 4 (About You) responses and the rest of the responses is insignificant, which further confirms our initial PCA analysis.

4.1 Between-Group Analysis

A common natural question in the context of teaching strategies is to investigate whether students' perception of the new intervention is correlated to their learning styles and attitudes. To answer this question, we analyzed the correlation between the responses to the 'About You' questions. This section included explicit questions about students' (self reported) attitude towards learning: 'ideas in my academic reading often send me off on long chains of thoughts', 'it is important for me to follow arguments, or to see the reason behind things', 'when I communicate ideas, I reflect on how well I've gotten my points across', 'concentration is not usually a problem for me, unless I've been really tired', and 'on the whole, I am systematic and organized in my studying'. These standardized questions where directly adopted from ETLQ questionnaire [14].

The PCA analysis between the responses did not show any strong correlations between those answers, and a following t-test confirms that there is no statistical difference in these questions between the study and the control group. Moreover, no statistically meaningful correlation between these questions and other questions exists, implying that we cannot attribute students' perception of GBL or team work to their learning styles or personal factors. It is worth noting that there was also no significant correlation between any of the questions about the lecture or working together with whether students perceived to be doing well in this course in general.

4.2 Within-Group Analysis: Concentration and Critical Thinking

Our analysis showed that both groups had statistically similar attitude toward learning. The next interesting question is to draw the relationships between students' perception of GBL activities and their learning style and attitude towards information processing.

Our analysis reveals two strong correlations about students information processing and their responses to the questions about lecture style. First, students who responded strongly about their ability to concentrate and focus on topics also strongly supported that the GBL activities provided plenty of opportunities to communicate knowledge and ideas effectively and gain interest in the topic. Second, those who strongly stated that for them 'it is important to follow arguments, or to see the reason behind things' also strongly believed that the GBL lecture was relevant to the topic and enjoyable, found the lecture organized, and believed that working with other students helped them develop deeper understanding.

These results suggest that perhaps learners with improved focus abilities or those who value deep argumentative reasoning and critical thinking are more welcoming to gameful activities due to the inherent discover-and-advance feature of GBL activities.

4.3 Examining Student Comments

We also examined the open-ended comments to provide a more wholesome picture of students' experiences in the study group.

Overall, students generally enjoyed the GBL activities and enjoyed engaging with other students in the class; it helped them stay more focused on the material at hand. Most students, formally and informally, indicated that they were able to visualize the material that instructors were explaining afterwards. One student mentioned "*I thought the game was a fun break from the usual lecture. I really enjoyed the mini quiz at the end where everyone could participate. It not only engaged the class, but it would probably help the professor to tackle any misconceptions that students may have about the material right there. It was nice it was anonymous because I feel like people are too shy to ask questions*". Another student mentioned "*I believe this lecture generally help me to understand the topic of DFS and BFS. Visualizing the topic / using unique examples in my opinion help me to pay more attention and be more active in the lecture*".

As our statistical analysis showed, certain students connect with particular learning and delivery styles better than others. Few students reported that they could not relate the activities to the topic. One student commented "*I don't feel like I gained much knowledge from the lecture, but I think that had the game not been a component of the class I would have been able to learn more*". Another commented that "*There is already so much material to go over each lecture that the activity that didn't help us learn or review*". Even though these were not substantial, they convey a key message: there needs to be a serious attempt from instructors to harness the gameful activities and put effort in making meaningful connections to the concepts.

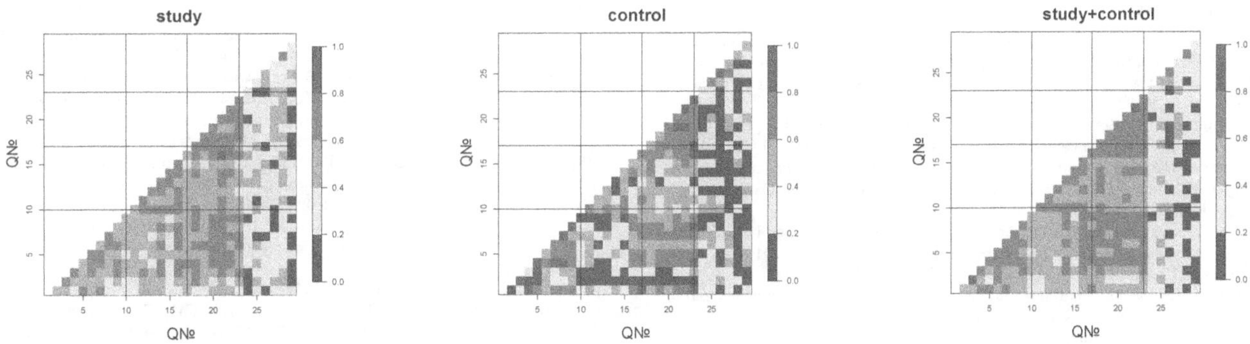

(a) Study group (b) Control group (c) Study+Control group

Figure 4: The pairwise Pearson correlation between 29 questions: colors indicate the absolute value of the Pearson coefficient.

4.4 Impact on Grades

To gain more insights into learning performance of students, we analyzed students' summative performance on the final exam as secondary data. The final exam questions were designed independently from this study. In fact, to avoid any type of bias, instructors were not informed about the possible collection of grades for further analysis. We did a post analysis of the questions in the final exam and identified six questions out of 23 total questions that were related to graph traversal algorithms. These questions ranged from multiple choice questions to comprehensive question.

We ran a two sample unpaired t-test between the total grades of students on the selected six questions about graph traversal. With respect to students' grades, there was significant difference between the students in the study group ($\mu = 25.52, \sigma = 26.12$) and the control group ($\mu = 23.67, \sigma = 27.37$); $t(131) = 2.10, p = 0.03$.

Despite this statistical confirmation, we refrain from making any immediate conclusions about learning performance and believe that these findings should be interpreted solely as encouragement for future studies on the impact of GBL on learning performance.

5 INSTRUCTORS' POINT OF VIEW

One of the pillars of any successful intervention in teaching strategies is educators' view point and tendency to adopt the newly proposed teaching methods. Therefore, we analyzed this dimension by conducting a series of semi-structured interviews.

A total of four instructors (out of 8) adopted the interventions in their classes (study group). The instructors who participated in the presentation of this experiment had generally positive feedback. They thought the lecture was way more interactive than any other previous lectures. One instructor stated how he had students in his class who had never spoken during in-class activities, who finally participated and spoke for the first time during the GBL lecture.

Another instructor stated that this form of lecture was like "*a breath of fresh air*" and that he would love to do more activities like this one, where "*rules can be taught quickly*". This instructor was quickly inspired by the game-based techniques he observed in "COMPILE" and started implementing short activities into the beginning and the end of his higher-level CS lectures.

While the presentation of this activity created a lot of excitement by trying a new teaching-style, it also led to some instructors being hesitant and nervous. One instructor spoke up by admitting his biggest fear was time management and not having sufficient time for the lecture, particularly because these lectures are heavily coordinated. However, he turned out to be "*pleasantly surprised at the end of the lecture-block when he did not run into that issue*".

These instructors mentioned that they are determined to adopt similar strategies in other CS courses. In fact, at the time of writing this article, three of the instructors have been revamping the first course in the introductory CS sequence by incorporating similar gameful activities into the recitation sections of these courses.

6 DISCUSSION

We investigated the effectiveness of incorporating GBL strategies from students' point of view, instructors' perspective, and students' performance. Our results suggest that i) students' significantly perceived GBL positively with respect to learning, working in groups, and cultivating critical thinking, ii) there was no substantial correlation between students' attitude towards learning and GBL activities, iii) students considered both lectures similar with respect to organization and clarity of instruction, and iv) students attitude towards concentration and critical thinking positively correlates to their perception of GBL activities.

Although there was a significant difference between the performance of the two groups, it is difficult to wholeheartedly count this as a success story. Several other parameters throughout the semester, such as instructors' teaching style, delivery of other topics, and the feedback on assigned homeworks, may impact the performance of students. As such, measuring the effectiveness of GBL interventions on learning outcomes requires a thorough controlled study over a long period of time and across various groups. We think that this is an extremely exciting, and yet challenging, future direction.

Finally, the choice of activity and game design, is heavily dependent on the subject matter, and even the topic at hand. Thus, a hybrid teaching method perhaps is superior to any single teaching strategy. Certain type of topics are naturally more suitable for such interventions; a point that was confirmed by the participating instructors.

REFERENCES

[1] Zack Butler, Ivona Bezáková, and Kimberly Fluet. 2017. Pencil Puzzles for Introductory Computer Science: an Experience-and Gender-Neutral Context. In *Proceedings of the 2017 ACM SIGCSE Technical Symposium on Computer Science Education*. ACM, 93–98.

[2] Zack Butler, Ivona Bezáková, and Kimberly Fluet. 2018. Analyzing Rich Qualitative Data to Study Pencil-puzzle-based Assignments in CS1 and CS2. In *Proceedings of the 23rd Annual ACM Conference on Innovation and Technology in Computer Science Education (ITiCSE 2018)*. ACM, New York, NY, USA, 212–217. https://doi.org/10.1145/3197091.3197109

[3] Jeff Cain and Peggy Piascik. 2015. Are serious games a good strategy for pharmacy education? *American Journal of Pharmaceutical Education* 79, 4 (2015), 47.

[4] Thomas M Connolly, Mark Stansfield, and Thomas Hainey. 2007. An application of games-based learning within software engineering. *British Journal of Educational Technology* 38, 3 (2007), 416–428.

[5] Sara Corbett. 2010. Learning by playing: Video games in the classroom. *New York Times* 15 (2010).

[6] Edward Deci and Richard M Ryan. 1985. *Intrinsic motivation and self-determination in human behavior.* Springer Science & Business Media.

[7] Richard Dennis. 2016. Hooked on Games: A Guide to Game-Based Learning.

[8] Darina Dicheva and Austin Hodge. 2018. Active Learning Through Game Play in a Data Structures Course. In *Proceedings of the 49th ACM Technical Symposium on Computer Science Education (SIGCSE '18)*. ACM, New York, NY, USA, 834–839. https://doi.org/10.1145/3159450.3159605

[9] Martin Ebner and Andreas Holzinger. 2007. Successful implementation of user-centered game based learning in higher education: An example from civil engineering. *Computers & education* 49, 3 (2007), 873–890.

[10] Britton Horn, Christopher Clark, Oskar Strom, Hilery Chao, Amy J. Stahl, Casper Harteveld, and Gillian Smith. 2016. Design Insights into the Creation and Evaluation of a Computer Science Educational Game. In *Proceedings of the 47th ACM Technical Symposium on Computing Science Education (SIGCSE '16)*. ACM, New York, NY, USA, 576–581. https://doi.org/10.1145/2839509.2844656

[11] Hadi Hosseini and Maxwell Hartt. 2016. Game-based Learning in the University Classroom. *Teaching Innovation Projects* 6, 1 (2016), 4.

[12] Hadi Hosseini and Maxwell Hartt. 2018. From the Players Point of View. In *The Power of Play in Higher Eeducation*. Palgrave Macmillan. (forthcoming).

[13] Hadi Hosseini, Maxwell Hartt, and Mehrnaz Mostafapour. 2019. Learning IS Child's Play: Game-Based Learning in Computer Science Education. *Journal of Planning Education and Research, ACM Transactions on Computing Education (TOCE)* forthcoming (2019).

[14] Dai Hounsell, Noel Entwistle, C Anderson, A Bromage, K Day, J Hounsell, R Land, J Litjens, V McCune, E Meyer, et al. 2005. Enhancing teaching-learning environments in undergraduate courses. *Final Report to the Economic and Social Research Council on TLRP Project L* 139251099 (2005).

[15] Joh D. Huff. 2016. A Simple Line Game With Real-Time Visualization of the Internal Data Structure (Abstract Only). In *Proceedings of the 47th ACM Technical Symposium on Computing Science Education (SIGCSE '16)*. ACM, New York, NY, USA, 726–726. https://doi.org/10.1145/2839509.2851063

[16] Daiki Isayama, Masaki Ishiyama, Raissa Relator, and Koichi Yamazaki. 2017. Computer Science Education for Primary and Lower Secondary School Students: Teaching the Concept of Automata. *ACM Transactions on Computing Education (TOCE)* 17, 1 (2017), 2.

[17] Ge Jin, Manghui Tu, Tae-Hoon Kim, Justin Heffron, and Jonathan White. 2018. Game Based Cybersecurity Training for High School Students. In *Proceedings of the 49th ACM Technical Symposium on Computer Science Education (SIGCSE '18)*. ACM, New York, NY, USA, 68–73. https://doi.org/10.1145/3159450.3159591

[18] Ge Jin, Manghui Tu, Tae-Hoon Kim, Justin Heffron, and Jonathan White. 2018. Game based Cybersecurity Training for High School Students. In *Proceedings of the 49th ACM Technical Symposium on Computer Science Education*. ACM, 68–73.

[19] Bokyeong Kim, Hyungsung Park, and Youngkyun Baek. 2009. Not just fun, but serious strategies: Using meta-cognitive strategies in game-based learning. *Computers & Education* 52, 4 (2009), 800–810.

[20] Meaghan C Lister. [n. d.]. Gamification: The effect on student motivation and performance at the post-secondary level. *Issues and Trends in Educational Technology* 3, 2 ([n. d.]).

[21] Yin Pan, Sumita Mishra, and David Schwartz. 2017. Gamifying Course Modules for Entry Level Students. In *Proceedings of the 2017 ACM SIGCSE Technical Symposium on Computer Science Education (SIGCSE '17)*. ACM, New York, NY, USA, 435–440. https://doi.org/10.1145/3017680.3017709

[22] Marina Papastergiou. 2009. Digital game-based learning in high school computer science education: Impact on educational effectiveness and student motivation. *Computers & Education* 52, 1 (2009), 1–12.

[23] Jan L Plass, Bruce D Homer, and Charles K Kinzer. 2015. Foundations of game-based learning. *Educational Psychologist* 50, 4 (2015), 258–283.

[24] Elizabeth Simpson. 1971. Educational objectives in the psychomotor domain. *Behavioral Objectives in Curriculum Development: Selected Readings and Bibliography* 60, 2 (1971).

[25] Valdemar Švábenský and Jan Vykopal. 2018. Challenges Arising from Prerequisite Testing in Cybersecurity Games. In *Proceedings of the 49th ACM Technical Symposium on Computer Science Education*. ACM, 56–61.

[26] Anastasios Theodoropoulos, Angeliki Antoniou, and George Lepouras. 2017. How do different cognitive styles affect learning programming? Insights from a game-based approach in Greek schools. *ACM Transactions on Computing Education (TOCE)* 17, 1 (2017), 3.

[27] Sigmund Tobias, J Dexter Fletcher, and Alexander P Wind. 2014. Game-based learning. In *Handbook of Research on Educational Communications and Technology*. Springer, 485–503.

[28] Nicola Jane Whitton. 2007. *An investigation into the potential of collaborative computer game-based learning in higher education*. Ph.D. Dissertation. Edinburgh Napier University.

[29] Wikipedia. 2018. Fallout (Video Game). https://en.wikipedia.org/wiki/Fallout_(series).

[30] Michael F Young, Stephen Slota, Andrew B Cutter, Gerard Jalette, Greg Mullin, Benedict Lai, Zeus Simeoni, Matthew Tran, and Mariya Yukhymenko. 2012. Our princess is in another castle: A review of trends in serious gaming for education. *Review of Educational Research* 82, 1 (2012), 61–89.

[31] Chang Yun, Hesam Panahi, and Zhigang Deng. 2016. A Multidisciplinary, Multifaceted Approach to Improve the Computer Science Based Game Design Education: Methodology and Assessment. In *Proceedings of the 47th ACM Technical Symposium on Computing Science Education (SIGCSE '16)*. ACM, New York, NY, USA, 570–575. https://doi.org/10.1145/2839509.2844582

[32] Rui Zhi. 2018. Exploring Data-driven Worked Examples for Block-based Programming. In *Proceedings of the 2018 ACM Conference on International Computing Education Research*. ACM, 294–295.

Factors That Influence Students' Motivation and Perception of Studying Computer Science

Merilin Säde
Institute of Computer Science
University of Tartu
Tartu, Estonia
merilin.sade@ut.ee

Reelika Suviste
Institute of Computer Science
University of Tartu
Tartu, Estonia
reelika.suviste@ut.ee

Piret Luik
Institute of Computer Science
University of Tartu
Tartu, Estonia
piret.luik@ut.ee

Eno Tõnisson
Institute of Computer Science
University of Tartu
Tartu, Estonia
eno.tonisson@ut.ee

Marina Lepp
Institute of Computer Science
University of Tartu
Tartu, Estonia
marina.lepp@ut.ee

ABSTRACT

A large number of students drop out in the first year of their Bachelor's studies in Computer Science (CS). It is a problem in many countries worldwide. The aim of this study was to develop a scale for measuring the motivation and perception factors that influence students' decision to start studying Computer Science (CS), and to find the differences between these factors. A questionnaire was conducted based on expectancy-value theory to measure students' motivation and perception. Data were collected from 140 students who started their Bachelor studies in CS at a university in Estonia. The scale, named FICSS (Factors Influencing Computer Science Studies), was conducted and validated using exploratory and confirmatory factor analyses. Two models were identified: a four-factor model describing students' motivation ("Intrinsic value", "Utility value", "Social influences" and "Time for family") and a five-factor model ("Satisfaction with choice of specialty", "Social dissuasion", "Demanding work", "Salary and job security" and "Social status") that describes students' perception. "Intrinsic value" and "Utility value" were the highest-rated motivational factors. The lowest-rated factor was "Social influences". Among the perception factors, the factors with the highest means were "Satisfaction with choice of specialty" and "Salary and job security" while "Social dissuasion" was rated lowest.

CCS CONCEPTS

• **Social and professional topics** → *Computer science education*;

KEYWORDS

Computer Science Students; Expectancy-Value Theory; Motivation

ACM ISBN 978-1-4503-5890-3/19/02...$15.00
https://doi.org/10.1145/3287324.3287395

ACM Reference Format:
Merilin Säde, Reelika Suviste, Piret Luik, Eno Tõnisson, and Marina Lepp. 2019. Factors That Influence Students' Motivation and Perception of Studying Computer Science. In *Proceedings of the 50th ACM Technical Symposium on Computer Science Education (SIGCSE '19), February 27-March 2, 2019, Minneapolis, MN, USA.* ACM, New York, NY, USA, 6 pages. https://doi.org/10.1145/3287324.3287395

1 INTRODUCTION

Information and Communication Technology (ICT) plays an important role in the development of today's society. Skilled ICT professionals are essential in all fields of the economy. However, an expanding need for more qualified ICT professionals is still a worldwide problem. The European Commission estimated that there will be around 500,000 vacant positions for ICT specialists by 2020 [8]. Unfortunately, since 2006 the number of computer science graduates in the European Union has been rapidly dropping [11]. The main problem is the high dropout rate among the first-year Bachelor's students [5, 18, 30]. This is also an issue in Asia [34], USA [26] and in many countries in Europe [14, 19]. It has been found that an important factor for leaving the studies was a loss of interest in the field of, and career in, Computer Science (CS) which is directly related to motivation [4]. Several researchers have also reported that intrinsic and extrinsic factors of motivation are key factors that influence career choice in higher education [18, 28]. Based on these studies' findings there may be potential misjudgment in students' motivation and perception of studying CS. Our study considers the importance to understand students' reasons for choosing CS as a career. Understanding students' academic choices and behaviors would help us to improve methods to recruit motivated CS students who are unlikely to drop out and also help us support their studies by preparing them for the CS major.

Universities are looking for different ways to increase the number of enrollments in CS [25] and one reason why universities are providing MOOCs (Massive Open Online Courses) is to attract and retain students [10]. At the researched university in Estonia the conditions for admission to CS Bachelor's studies have changed in a way that a candidate who has passed the final evaluation in MOOC "Introduction to Programming" provided in Estonian by the university will be guaranteed admission to the CS curriculum.

During the programming MOOC the students realize if CS is the field they want to study. Using MOOC as an entrance-exam shows us and to the students if CS is suitable for them. In Estonia teaching programming is not common in schools, but prior experience in programming can influence students' choice to study CS [16]. We wanted to see if this strategy that we use to recruit students to study computer science is effective method to accept motivated students. Therefore, we wanted to know if the reasons to study CS differ between students who graduated the MOOC and who did not.

The aim of this study was to develop a scale for measuring the motivation and perception factors that influence students' decision to start studying Computer Science (CS), to find the differences between these factors, and to compare motivation of MOOC graduates and non-graduates. We seek answers to three research questions:

(1) Is the developed scale a valid and reliable instrument to measure motivation and perception among first-year CS students?
(2) What are the highest and the lowest rated factors influencing students' choice to start studying CS?
(3) What are the differences in these factors between MOOC graduates and non-graduates among CS students?

2 THEORETICAL BACKGROUND

2.1 Motivation

"A driving force or forces responsible for the initiation, persistence, direction, and vigor of goal-directed behavior" is the definition of motivation given in the Oxford's Dictionary of Psychology [7]. Motivation is a complex concept consisting of different factors related to interest, achievement goals, value beliefs, self-efficacy and control beliefs [20]. Overall, there is no general definition of motivation, but it usually consists of either intrinsic or extrinsic factors [21]. Several researchers have claimed that motivation is an important factor that affects students' career choice [18, 19] and not only in the field of CS but in other disciplines too.

Career choice in computer science can be investigated with various methods based on different motivation theories. For example Social Cognitive Career Theory have been used to identify factors that influence career choice in CS [2] or self-determination theory has been used to study first-year students' motivation to start studying in IT-related curricula [15].

Our research is based on modern Expectancy-Value Theory (EVT). This theory explains that students' effort, choices, and performance are related to their expectancy and task value beliefs [35]. Expectancies present beliefs of students that they have the possibility of success in that task and value describes the evaluation of the potential benefits associated with the academic task [35]. Task value is a key term of this theory and is defined by four components: attainment value or importance, intrinsic value or interest, utility value or usefulness, and cost [35]. Attainment value describes the importance of doing well on a given task, while intrinsic value indicates the enjoyment that one gains from performing an academic task. Utility value or usefulness refers to how a task fits into an individual's future plans, for example, studying CS for a further career path. Cost describes the assessment of the effort that will be needed to accomplish the activity (including emotional cost) and how it will limit access to other activities (e.g., spending time with family) [35]. Expectancy and task value beliefs are directly influenced by perceptions of competence, perceptions of the difficulty of different tasks, and individuals' goals [9]. Our study is based on EVT because choosing a career is voluntary and especially relevant for research trying to explain people's engagement in learning [35]. This framework is widely used to investigate motivations why individuals choose teaching as a career and perceptions about teacher profession [32, 33], and it is also adapted for different IT disciplines [3], bus not often used in CS. We argue that it would be also innovative and useful to investigate CS students' motivation and perception based on a different theory, which is used in other disciplines [23, 24, 25] and not used widely to investigate why students choose to study CS.

2.2 Factors influencing individuals' choice to start CS studies

Reasons, why students choose their career, are different and complex. A factor that has been found influencing students' decision to start studies in CS is interest in ICT [13, 15, 16]. This factor is part of the intrinsic motivation defined by Deci and others [21] and is similar to intrinsic value construct because both of these factors concern doing a task out of interest and gaining enjoyment.

Another factor that can influence students' motivation is the reputation of CS-related fields in society. Kori et al [17] investigated the reasons why IT students choose an IT-related curriculum and distinguished reasons that are related to reputation and opportunity of CS in society: IT labour market (many jobs or career opportunities), importance in the future career (the field, in general, is important for the future), field development (the IT field is constantly developing) and salary in IT. Alshahrani et al. [2] examined the factors why students choose to study computer science and found that salary and job security were considered important motivators among students. Tillberg and Cohoon [27] examined the undergraduate computer science female and male students' career choices and found out that good career prospects are an motivator (e.g., decent salary) to study CS. These various authors conclude that job-related factors can influence students' decision to choose CS studies.

Personal social influences and dissuasions can also affect students' motivation and perception of studying CS. Research in career choices has indicated that parents' expectation and encouragement in the academic process play an important role in child's career choice in CS [2, 6] and overall in STEM fields [29]. Alexander et al. [1] point out that parents and friends who worked in a computer-related career were one of the most important sources for advice on career choice.

Another factor that can influence students' motivation and perception of studying is time for family. Students may have to combine their studies with family responsibilities [23].

Furthermore, students' prior experience in the field can influence their career choice [2]. Many IT students have learned to program before starting their studies in higher education and differences were found in the motivation of students who had and those who did not have experience in programming [16]. It has been found that students' experience in CS and IT may lead them to study the discipline [13].

3 METHODOLOGY

3.1 Sample and procedure

The participants in this study were first-year students who started their Bachelor studies in CS at the university in September 2017. Data were collected via an online questionnaire in September 2017 during a lecture. The students who were absent from the lecture received a link to the questionnaire by email. Submitting the questionnaire did not affect completion of the course in which the survey was carried out and answering was voluntary. The sample included 140 students (77% male and 23% female), which was 74% of the students matriculated. The average age was 23 years, with the maximum age of 49 years and a minimum age of 19 years. The number of MOOC graduates was 38, which was 27% of the students.

3.2 Instrument

To measure students' motivation and perception of studying CS at the university, a questionnaire was designed by the authors based on expectancy-value theory [9, 35]. The developed questionnaire was based on the FIT-choice scale [31] that was used to investigate Estonian preservice teachers' motivation and perception about their career choice [24]. We adapted this scale to the CS discipline by rephrasing the items and considering motivation aspects from previous studies about career choice in CS [13, 15]. For example, we replaced the item "I am interested in teaching" with "I am interested in computer science"; the item "Teachers make a worthwhile social contribution" was changed to "I want to contribute to the development of the IT field", etc. We left out items describing work with children/adolescents and enhancement of social equity. We added items "I like to work in a rapidly developing field", "I want to work in a technology-rich environment" and "Work in the IT field allows me to work in different countries". The questionnaire was compiled with experts from the university in the field of computer science and educational theory.

The composed scale consisted of 23 items about motivation and 24 items about perception. All the items were on a 7-point Likert scale. The questionnaire was divided into three sections. In the first section, students were asked to indicate the degree of importance of each of the motivation items (e.g., "I have always wanted to learn computer science", "Studying computer science suits my abilities") for choosing the CS curriculum. Items were on a scale ranging from 1 (not at all important) to 7 (very important). The second and third sections included items about students' perception. The second part contained 6 items about students' satisfaction with choosing the CS curriculum (e.g., "I am satisfied with my choice to learn computer science", "I have been encouraged to choose another specialty") and the scale was from 1 (not true at all) to 7 (completely true). In the third section, students were asked to evaluate the statements based on the extent to which they agreed that this statement was true in the IT field. This question contained 18 items (e.g., "Work in the field of IT requires high professional knowledge", "IT sector jobs are well paid"), which were on a scale from 1 (strongly disagree) to 7 (completely agree). The questionnaire ended with the background data.

3.3 Data analysis

The data were analyzed using both exploratory and confirmatory factor analyses. Exploratory factor analysis (EFA) by principal axis method with varimax rotation was performed to identify a suitable structure for confirmatory factor analysis (CFA). The analyses were carried out using SPSS version 25.0 and AMOS version 21.0. The following five indicators for the goodness-of-fit of the models were evaluated: (a) chi-square test; (b) comparative fit index (CFI); (c) Tucker-Lewis index (TLI); (d) root mean square error of approximation (RMSEA); and (e) standardized root mean square residual (SRMR). Two CFAs were performed to test motivation and perception factors. The following cut-off points were used for the goodness-of-fit of the models: for CFI $\geqslant 0.95$ [22], TLI $\geqslant 0.90$ [12], RMSEA $\leqslant 0.06$ to 0.08 [22] and SRMR $\leqslant 0.08$ [22].

Linear mixed models were used. Multivariate analysis of variance with the Bonferroni adjustment for multiple comparisons was used to identify differences between the factors. Multivariate test between subjects effects with Bonferroni adjustment was used for identifying differences in factors between in group of MOOC graduates and in the group of non-graduates.

4 RESULTS

The first EFA determined a structure of four-factor model about students' motivation. Seven items were excluded due to a low commonality, which was less than 0.35 and final model consisted 16 items about motivation. The total variance explained by these factors was 62.61%. The CFA was performed to examine the factor structure reached by the EFA and the four-factor model was estimated. The model showed acceptable results after taking into account several modification indices. The fit indices for the motivation model were: χ^2 = 145.77, df = 91, CFI = 0.96, TLI = 0.94, RMSEA = 0.07 and SRMR = 0.07. The factors were named "Intrinsic value" (IV), "Utility value" (UV), "Social influences" (SI) and "Time for family" (TF) (Fig. 1)

Two EFAs were performed to determine underlying constructs for students' perception. The first EFA determined a structure of two-factor and the second EFA a structure of three-factor model. Three items were excluded due to a low commonality (less than 0.35) and final model consisted 21 items. The total variance explained by these factors was 74.93% and 63.63%. At first, the model showed lack of fit but, after taking into account of several modification indices, the model fit respective data. The fit indices for the perception model were: χ^2 = 255.02, df = 171, CFI = 0.96, TLI = 0.95, RMSEA = 0.06 and SRMR = 0.06. The factors were named "Satisfaction with choice of specialty" (SWCS), "Social dissuasion" (SD), "Demanding work" (DW), "Salary and job security" (SJS) and "Social status" (SS) (Fig. 2). Both models fit data sufficiently well.

The standardized factor loadings (ranging from 0.65 to 0.88 in the motivation model and from 0.54 to 1.02 in the perception model) and item reliabilities (ranging from 0.42 to 0.77 in the motivation model and from 0.29 to 1.03 in the perception model) of FICSS scale were high or moderate and thus all the items in both models are good indicators of latent factors. The Cronbach's alpha measures (ranging from 0.81 to 0.90 in the motivation model and from 0.80 to 0.92 in the perception model) of internal consistency were acceptable for all factors. Mauchly's Test of Sphericity indicated that the

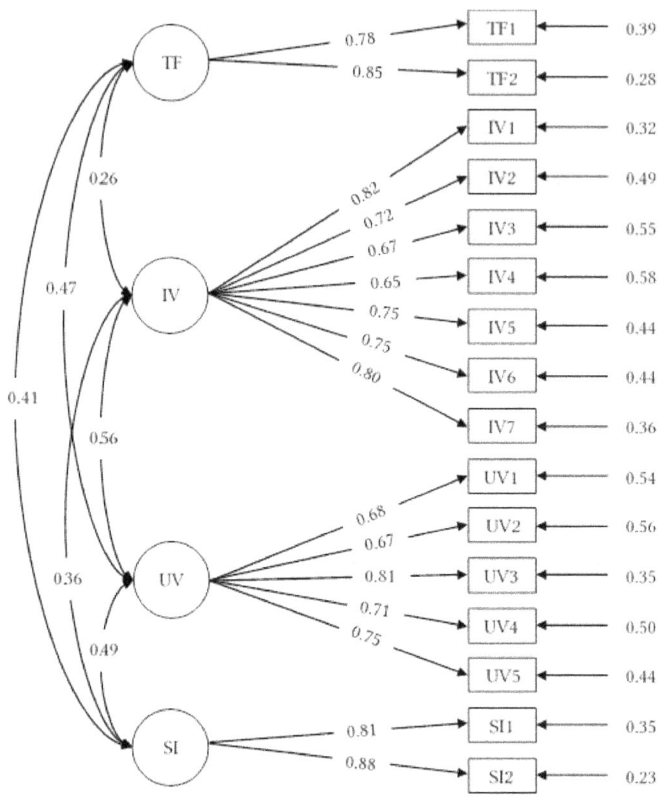

Figure 1: CFA model for the FICSS scale motivation factors

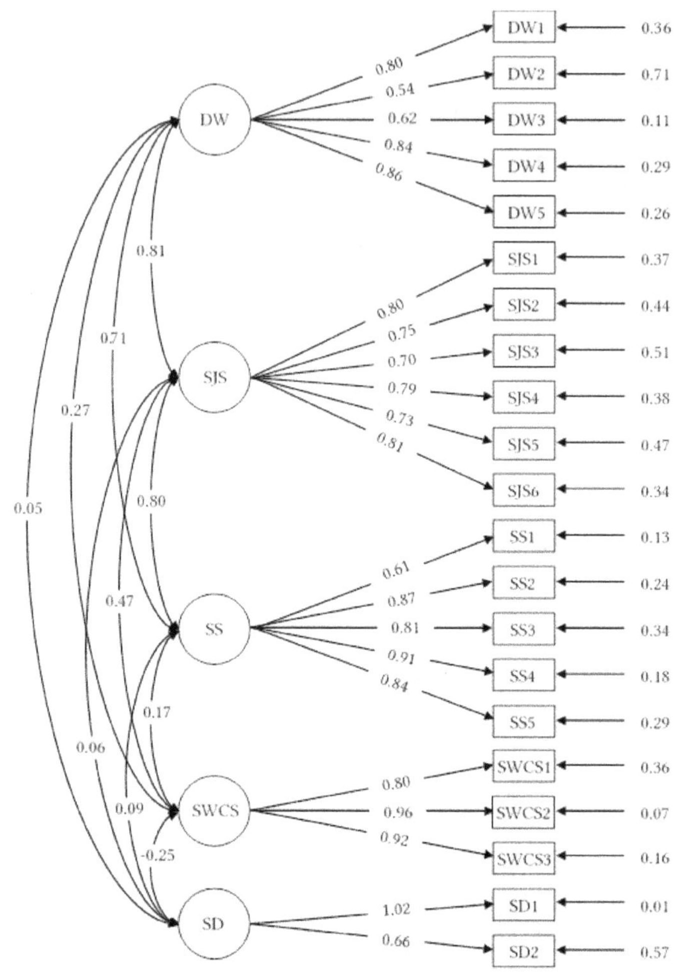

Figure 2: CFA model for the FICSS scale perception factors

assumption of sphericity has been violated in case of motivation, $\chi^2(3) = 37.34$, $p < 0.01$, therefore degrees of freedom were corrected using Greenhouse-Geisser estimates of sphericity. Repeated measures ANOVA determined that there were statistically significant differences between the factors ($F(2.64, 366.27) = 72.66$, $p < 0.01$). Pairwise comparison with Bonferroni correction revealed that there was no statistically significant difference between the factors "Intrinsic value" and "Utility value" ($p = 1.00$) (Table 1). However, these factors were statistically significantly higher from all other factors (in all cases $p < 0.05$). "Social influence" indicated significantly lower evaluations compared to all other factors (in all cases $p < 0.01$). For perception, Mauchly's Test of Sphericity also indicated that the assumption of sphericity has been violated, $\chi^2(9) = 242.48$, $p < 0.01$ and degrees of freedom were corrected using Greenhouse-Geisser estimates of sphericity. Repeated measures ANOVA determined that there were statistically significant differences between the factors ($F(2.22, 308.23) = 164.76$, $p < 0.01$). Pairwise comparison with Bonferroni correction revealed that there was no statistically significant difference between the factors "Satisfaction with choice of specialty" and "Salary and job security" ($p = 1.00$). However, these factors were statistically significantly higher from all other factors (in all cases $p < 0.05$). The lowest rating was for "Social dissuasion", which indicated significantly lower evaluations compared with all other factors (in all cases $p < .01$).

Table 1: Factor descriptive statistics (in ranking order) for motivation and perception factors (n = 140)

Factor	Min	Max	Mean	Std. deviation
Motivation				
Intrinsic value	1.71	6.86	5.11	1.14
Utility value	1.60	7.00	5.11	1.26
Time for family	1.00	7.00	3.93	1.72
Social influence	1.00	7.00	3.38	1.76
Perception				
Choice of specialty	1.67	7.00	6.81	1.17
Salary and job security	2.00	7.00	5.74	0.96
Demanding work	1.60	7.00	5.53	1.05
Social status	1.60	6.80	4.96	1.13
Social dissuasion	1.00	7.00	2.94	1.66

In this study, to compare means between MOOC graduates and non-graduates, a multivariate analysis of variance with the Bonferroni adjustment for multiple comparisons was used. The results showed that there were no significant differences between MOOC graduates and non-graduates in motivation to start studying CS with means 4.64 and 4.28, std. errors 0.17 and 0.10 $F(1, 138) = 3.12$, $p = 0.08$). The ranking order of motivation factors in both groups was also the same. The factors "Intrinsic value" and "Utility value" had the highest means in both groups. Both factors were rated 5 or over 5. In perception, there were no significant differences between MOOC graduates and non-graduates with means 4.97 and 4.92, std. errors 0.12 and 0.07 $F(1, 138) = 0.13$, $p = 0.711$), the ranking order of factors in both groups was the same. The factor "Satisfaction with choice of specialty" had "Salary and job security" the highest mean rating, in both groups.

5 DISCUSSION

The aim of the study was to develop a scale for measuring motivation and perception factors that influence students' decision to start studying Computer Science and also to find the differences between these factors and to compare motivation of MOOC graduates and non-graduates.

First, we examine the extent to which the developed scale is a valid and reliable instrument to measure motivation and perception among first-year CS students. A four-factor model describing students' motivation ("Intrinsic value", "Utility value", "Social influences" and "Time for Family") and a five-factor model ("Satisfaction with choice of specialty", "Social dissuasion", "Demanding work", "Salary and job security" and "Social status") that describes students' perception showed a relatively good fit between the hypothesized model and the observed data according to the following cut-off points: CFI $\geqslant 0.95$ [22], TLI $\geqslant 0.90$ [12], RMSEA $\leqslant 0.06$ to 0.08 [22] and SRMR $\leqslant 0.08$ [22]. Some motivation constructs of the developed FICSS scale merged into one factor compared to the FIT-Choice scale and was named "Intrinsic value". These factors were "Perceived abilities", "Positive prior experiences" and "Intrinsic value". Perception factors "Expert career" and "High demand" formed one factor in FICSS and was named "Demanding work". "Salary" and "Job security" fused into one construct and was named "Salary and job security". Motivation factors "Time for family" and "Social influences" from FIT-Choice emerged as well. Perception factors "Social status", "Social dissuasion" and "Satisfaction" arose in the FICSS scale as well.

This showed that FIT-Choice scale can be adapted to study students' motivation and perception of studying CS. This can also mean that FIT-Choice scale could be easily used in other disciplines as well.

We also investigated the highest and the lowest rated factors in motivation and perception that influence students' choice to start studying CS. We found out that "Intrinsic value" which represent interest in a topic (e.g., "I like computer science") with perceived abilities in CS (e.g., "I have good IT skills") and "Utility value" or usefulness in the future (e.g., "I want to contribute to the development of the IT field") were the main motivators for choosing CS studies. In previous studies interest in the field was the most important reason why students chose CS [10, 27, 28], but usefulness in the future was less emphasized. Another finding was that "Social influence" including items like "My family thinks that I should study CS" was the least rated motivational factor. It seems that that significant others (e.g., friends and family) do not play a critical role in motivation with regard to CS, which is controversial to previous studies [6]. We found that "Satisfaction with choice of specialty" (e.g., "I have carefully thought about wanting to learn computer science") and "Salary and job security" (e.g., "Work in IT field provides a stable income") were the most relevant factors regarding perception. It was expected that stability in an IT job and salary affect students' perception the most, because salaries are higher and job opportunities are better in the IT. However, students' satisfaction with their specialty has not previously been described in studies about students' career choices in CS [4, 13, 15, 17] and is novel. We found that "Social dissuasion" (e.g., "I have been encouraged to choose another specialty") was the least rated factor of perception. Like "social influence" factor, which has little effect on the students' motivation, others have little impact on perceptions too.

Finally, the results indicated that there were no significant differences in the identified factors in motivation and perception between MOOC graduates and non-graduates among CS students. These results need to be interpreted with caution. Due to a small number of MOOC graduates ($n = 38$), which was 27% of the students, there might be meaningful difference in case of motivation. Previous findings support that prior experience in the CS field has a significant impact on student motivation [2, 16].

6 CONCLUSIONS

We have developed a FICSS scale for measuring the motivation and perception factors that influence students' decision to start studying CS with two models. We suggest that the FIT-Choice scale could be easily used in other disciplines as well. Our results suggest that "Utility value" and the novel factor "Satisfaction with choice of specialty" should be given more attention in research regarding students' motivation to start their studies in CS.

Our findings show that students believe that studying CS is useful for them in the future. Therefore, we also advise that cooperation with IT companies should be addressed more when designing computer science curricula. This could show students that they can contribute to the development of the IT field while studying and retain students. Our results do not explain that using MOOC as an entrance-exam had influence on students' motivation who graduated MOOC and who did not. This issue should be investigated more deeply in future research.

The study has some limitations that have to be taken into account when generalizing the findings. First, as sample included small number of MOOC graduates compared to non-graduates, therefore these results need to be interpreted with caution. Second, when we compared MOOC graduates and non-graduates among CS students, we did not consider other previous experiences related to CS. For example, students could have participated in different CS related MOOCs or worked in the IT field before their CS studies. Third, we studied motivation and perception of choosing CS studies only in the context of one particular university and therefore the results may not be generalizable to other universities and countries. Fourth, we adapted the survey from an instrument that was developed for teachers. Although, we considered motivation aspects from previous studies about career choice in CS, there might have been some motivational aspects specific to computer science that were left out from research.

We believe that more research would be useful to find out what motivational factors influence students during their studies. In addition, we propose further work in longitudinal research about CS students' motivation in higher education to examine changes in their motivation. We think that further research should be done to investigate students' motivation and perception in CS also in high school.

REFERENCES

[1] Patricia Margaret Alexander, M Holmner, Hugo Hendrik Lotriet, Machdel C Matthee, HV Pieterse, Saloshana Naidoo, Hossana Twinomurinzi, and Danie Jordaan. 2011. Factors affecting career choice: Comparison between students from computer and other disciplines. *Journal of Science Education and Technology* 20, 3 (2011), 300–315.

[2] Amnah Alshahrani, Isla Ross, and Murray Wood. 2018. Using social cognitive career theory to understand why students choose to study computer science. In *Proceedings of the 2018 ACM Conference on International Computing Education Research*. ACM, 205–214.

[3] Joseph Appianing and Richard N Van Eck. 2015. Gender differences in college students' perceptions of technology-related jobs in computer science. *International Journal of Gender, Science and Technology* 7, 1 (2015), 28–56.

[4] Maureen Biggers, Anne Brauer, and Tuba Yilmaz. 2008. Student perceptions of computer science: a retention study comparing graduating seniors with cs leavers. In *ACM SIGCSE Bulletin*, Vol. 40. ACM, 402–406.

[5] Juris Borzovs, Laila Niedrite, and Darja Solodovnikova. 2015. Factors affecting attrition among first year computer science students: the case of University of Latvia. (2015).

[6] Jody Clarke-Midura, Frederick J Poole, Katarina Pantic, Chongning Sun, and Vicki Allan. 2018. How Mother and Father Support Affect Youths' Interest in Computer Science. In *Proceedings of the 2018 ACM Conference on International Computing Education Research*. ACM, 215–222.

[7] Andrew M. Colman. 2015. A Dictionary of Psychology. http://www.oxfordreference.com/view/10.1093/acref/9780199657681.001.0001/acref-9780199657681-e-5239

[8] European Commission. 2018. Digital Skills & Jobs. https://ec.europa.eu/digital-single-market/en/policies/digital-skills

[9] Jacquelynne S Eccles and Allan Wigfield. 2002. Motivational beliefs, values, and goals. *Annual review of psychology* 53, 1 (2002), 109–132.

[10] Fiona M Hollands and Devayani Tirthali. 2014. Why Do Institutions Offer MOOCs?. *Online Learning* 18, 3 (2014), n3.

[11] Tobias Hüsing, Werner B Korte, Nils Fonstad, Bruno Lanvin, Gabriella Cattaneo, Marianne Kolding, and Desirée van Welsum. 2013. E-leadership: E-skills for Competitiveness and Innovation–Vision, Roadmap and Foresight Scenarios. *prepared for European Commission* (2013).

[12] Karl G Jöreskog and Dag Sörbom. 2006. LISREL 8.80 for Windows [Computer software].

[13] Päivi Kinnunen, Matthew Butler, Michael Morgan, Aletta Nylen, Anne-Kathrin Peters, Jane Sinclair, Sara Kalvala, and Erkki Pesonen. 2016. Understanding initial undergraduate expectations and identity in computing studies. *European Journal of Engineering Education* 43, 2 (2016), 201–218.

[14] Päivi Kinnunen and Lauri Malmi. 2006. Why students drop out CS1 course?. In *Proceedings of the second international workshop on Computing education research*. ACM, 97–108.

[15] Külli Kori, Margus Pedaste, Heilo Altin, Eno Tõnisson, and Tauno Palts. 2016. Factors That Influence Students' Motivation to Start and to Continue Studying Information Technology in Estonia. *IEEE Transactions on Education* 59, 4 (2016), 255–262.

[16] Külli Kori, Margus Pedaste, Äli Leijen, and Eno Tõnisson. 2016. The role of programming experience in ICT students' learning motivation and academic achievement. *International Journal of Information and Education Technology* 6, 5 (2016), 331.

[17] Külli Kori, Margus Pedaste, Margus Niitsoo, Rein Kuusik, Heilo Altin, Eno Tõnisson, Inga Vau, Äli Leijen, Mario Mäeots, Leo Siiman, et al. 2014. Why do students choose to study Information and Communications Technology? *The European Procedia Social and Behavioral Sciences* 191 (2014), 2867–2872.

[18] Külli Kori, Margus Pedaste, Eno Tõnisson, Tauno Palts, Heilo Altin, Ramon Rantsus, Raivo Sell, Kristina Murtazin, and Tiia Rüütmann. 2015. First-year dropout in ICT studies. In *Global Engineering Education Conference (EDUCON), 2015 IEEE*. IEEE, 437–445.

[19] Ilias O Pappas, Michail N Giannakos, and Letizia Jaccheri. 2016. Investigating factors influencing students' intention to dropout computer science studies. In *Proceedings of the 2016 ACM Conference on Innovation and Technology in Computer Science Education*. ACM, 198–203.

[20] Paul R Pintrich. 2003. A motivational science perspective on the role of student motivation in learning and teaching contexts. *Journal of educational Psychology* 95, 4 (2003), 667.

[21] Richard M Ryan and Edward L Deci. 2000. Self-determination theory and the facilitation of intrinsic motivation, social development, and well-being. *American psychologist* 55, 1 (2000), 68.

[22] James B Schreiber, Amaury Nora, Frances K Stage, Elizabeth A Barlow, and Jamie King. 2006. Reporting structural equation modeling and confirmatory factor analysis results: A review. *The Journal of educational research* 99, 6 (2006), 323–338.

[23] Leslie S Stratton, Dennis M O'Toole, and James N Wetzel. 2008. A multinomial logit model of college stopout and dropout behavior. *Economics of education review* 27, 3 (2008), 319–331.

[24] M Taimalu, P Luik, and K Täht. 2017. Teaching motivations and perceptions during the first year of teacher education in Estonia. *Global perspectives on teacher motivation* (2017), 189–219.

[25] Manar Abu Talib and Ashraf Elnagar. 2015. A new computer science student recruitment strategy University of Sharjah (UOS) case study. *Journal of Computer Science* 11, 1 (2015), 145.

[26] Jerry O Talton, Daniel L Peterson, Sam Kamin, Deborah Israel, and Jalal Al-Muhtadi. 2006. Scavenger hunt: computer science retention through orientation. In *ACM SIGCSE Bulletin*, Vol. 38. ACM, 443–447.

[27] Heather K Tillberg and J McGrath Cohoon. 2005. Attracting women to the CS major. *Frontiers: A Journal of Women Studies* (2005), 126–140.

[28] Sarah Theres Völkel, Wiktoria Wilkowska, and Martina Ziefle. 2018. Gender-specific motivation and expectations toward computer science. In *Proceedings of the 4th Conference on Gender & IT*. ACM, 123–134.

[29] Ming-Te Wang, Jessica Degol, and Feifei Ye. 2015. Math achievement is important, but task values are critical, too: examining the intellectual and motivational factors leading to gender disparities in STEM careers. *Frontiers in psychology* 6 (2015), 36.

[30] Christopher Watson and Frederick WB Li. 2014. Failure rates in introductory programming revisited. In *Proceedings of the 2014 conference on Innovation & technology in computer science education*. ACM, 39–44.

[31] Helen MG Watt and Paul W Richardson. 2007. Motivational factors influencing teaching as a career choice: Development and validation of the FIT-Choice Scale. *The Journal of experimental education* 75, 3 (2007), 167–202.

[32] Helen MG Watt, Paul W Richardson, Uta Klusmann, Mareike Kunter, Beate Beyer, Ulrich Trautwein, and Jürgen Baumert. 2012. Motivations for choosing teaching as a career: An international comparison using the FIT-Choice scale. *Teaching and teacher education* 28, 6 (2012), 791–805.

[33] Helen MG Watt, Paul W Richardson, and Kari Smith. 2017. *Global perspectives on teacher motivation*. Cambridge University Press.

[34] Fumei Weng, France Cheong, and Christopher Cheong. 2010. The combined effect of self-efficacy and academic integration on higher education students studying IT majors in Taiwan. *Education and Information Technologies* 15, 4 (2010), 333–353.

[35] Allan Wigfield and Jacquelynne S Eccles. 2000. Expectancy–value theory of achievement motivation. *Contemporary educational psychology* 25, 1 (2000), 68–81.

Introducing Practical SHA-1 Collisions to the Classroom

Monique Mezher
Department of Computer Science
University of Virginia
Charlottesville, Virginia
mmm5fd@virginia.edu

Ahmed Ibrahim
Department of Computer Science
University of Virginia
Charlottesville, Virginia
a.i@virginia.edu

ABSTRACT

There is a lack of hands-on exercises in cryptanalysis offered at the university level for a variety of reasons. One reason is the high amount of computations needed to complete cryptanalysis attacks. However, enabling students to perform fixed prefix SHA-1 collision attacks on PDFs does not require any advanced computation power. This paper presents a hands-on exercise for university students and professionals to generate SHA-1 collisions. The exercise shows how SHA-1 is vulnerable to fixed-prefix collisions, and how students are able to leverage existing tools to create their own SHA-1 collisions between arbitrary PDF files. In our two classroom runs of the exercise, over 90% of the students who performed the exercise found it to be a useful tool to reinforce their knowledge of SHA-1 collisions. The exercise increases awareness about hash collisions and urges caution when dealing with digitally signed PDFs that utilize SHA-1 as their hashing mechanism. To our knowledge, this is the first exercise designed to introduce practical SHA-1 collisions for students in the classroom.

ACM Reference format:
Monique Mezher and Ahmed Ibrahim. 2019. Introducing Practical SHA-1 Collisions to the Classroom. In *Proceedings of the 50th ACM Technical Symposium on Computer Science Education, Minneapolis, MN, USA, February 27-March 2, 2019 (SIGCSE '19)*, 6 pages.
https://doi.org/10.1145/3287324.3287446

1 INTRODUCTION

Cryptographic hash functions are an important building block used in digital certificates and network protocols such as SSL/TLS and SSH that require data integrity. The requirements, properties, and applications of cryptographic hash functions are usually discussed in security courses. Student understanding of the usage, benefits, and weaknesses of cryptographic hash functions is therefore essential to prepare them for industrial or academic environments where they may be asked to assess protocol acceptability or suggest improvements on designs requiring assured data integrity. Students need to know the specific definition of security which pertains to cryptographic hash functions.

Computational security is fulfilled when cryptographic hash functions meet several levels of resistance. They must assure preimage resistance, in that it is not computationally feasible to find a plaintext message m that hashes to a known hash h. They must assure second preimage resistance, in that it is not computationally feasible to choose plaintext messages n and m, $n!=m$, where the hashed output $H(n)$ is identical to the hashed output $H(m)$. Finally, they must assure collision resistance, in that it is not computationally feasible to find any pair of messages, (n,m), such that their hashed outputs are identical [11]. Only under the assurance that all three levels of resistance are met is it said that a cryptographic hash function is computationally secure. Once a hash function does not meet one of these criteria, it is no longer considered computationally secure; this is the case of SHA-1, whose collision resistance has been disproven.

Although the SHA-1 hash function has been theoretically attacked since 2005 [13], there had been little exposure of the insecurity of SHA-1 until Steven et. al. [7] provided a proof-of-concept collision in 2017 on two unique PDFs. Forty-eight hours after the release of their paper, code was released on Github enabling their fixed prefix to be leveraged to create arbitrary PDF collisions. When these attacks were released, major browsers like Chrome and Mozilla Firefox deprecated their support for SHA-1 signed certificates.

Yet students still have little attachment to this attack or its repercussions. Explaining the hash function compression functions requires familiarity with discrete mathematics and some formality of cryptanalysis. Therefore, a gap exists between getting students to acknowledge a cryptographic hash function is insecure and proving its insecurity in practice. This gap is further widened by the difficulty of abstracting complex bit operations while explaining compression functions to students without prior cryptography experience and the high amounts of computation necessary for cryptanalysis attacks to complete. To help bridge the gap, more hands-on exercises in cryptanalysis should be offered at the university level which are easy to perform with minimal setup time. To our knowledge, there have been no known classroom exercises creating SHA-1 collisions offered to date.

In this paper, an exercise is presented which allows for students to enhance their understanding of practical hash functions collisions by allowing them to create their own SHA-1 fixed-prefix collisions from two distinct PDFs. The exercise is useful for students to realize how potent hash collisions can be, while allowing them to learn more about the SHA-1 hash function and the fixed-prefix attack limitations. Due to the targeted fixed-prefix near-collision blocks being precomputed before the attack begins, the SHA-1 exercise works well on students' laptops and performs in minutes. The exercise also gets rid of the pre-exposure barrier for complex cryptanalysis; one does not need to be an expert in cryptography to perform an attack on SHA-1. The exercise was developed in the Fall of 2017, offered at the University of Virginia in the Spring 2018 and Fall 2018 Network Security course, and performed by 80 students.

SIGCSE '19, February 27-March 2, 2019, Minneapolis, MN, USA

ACM ISBN 978-1-4503-5890-3/19/02...$15.00
https://doi.org/10.1145/3287324.3287446

The rest of the paper is organized in six additional sections. Section 2 will discuss notable collision attacks on MD5 and SHA-1 within the past twenty years. Section 3 will discuss prior work on SHA-1 collisions and the exercises derived from past educational tools, as well as how others are providing exercises to students in security and our prior attempts. Section 4 introduces the exercise and the procedure followed by the students to perform it. Section 5 presents the design of our SHA-1 exercise and the goals which it aims to accomplish. Section 6 displays how the exercise's utility was tested and the results of its offering. Section 7 explains intended future work on the exercise. Finally, Section 8 concludes with final thoughts on this exercise and its implications.

2 HISTORY OF COLLISION ATTACKS

Over time, many hash functions are cracked through cryptanalysis and no longer hold collision resistance. For instance, MD5 was theoretically broken by Wang and Yu in 2005 [14] by a modular differential attack and leveraging bit conditions found in the rolled out MD5 compression function. This attacked allowed for certain colliding properties to be met and for the creation of two colliding messages in about 2^{39} operations - a significantly faster approach than brute force guessing. Based off of this attack, in 2007, Stevens et al. [9] were able to construct two X.509 certificates [3] with different name fields but identical digital signatures. This was the first practical proof-of-concept for MD5 showing that its insecurity could be dangerous for users and companies to continue to validate certificates which were signed using MD5.

Similarly, SHA-1 had the first attack on its construction function in early 2005 which explained a theoretical attack to find collisions in 2^{80} operations [5]. That same year, collisions were witnessed in 2^{69} operations [12]. Though not shown to be insecure in practical application, Microsoft announced in 2013 that they would not accept SSL certificates using SHA-1 after January 1st, 2017 [1] [10]. This announcement came after the Flame attack in 2012, where a rogue X.509 certificate had been successfully signed to appear to be trusted by a Microsoft Root Authority. This certificate had been used to download malicious software during Windows updates to computers with the certificate installed [4]. The SHA-1 algorithm was fully broken in 2016 after researchers concluded that they had found collisions in the full algorithmic design [8].

3 RELATED WORK

Our prior work on MD5 serves as an example of an exercise dedicated to collision education. An exercise created in the Fall of 2017 allowed students to create MD5 collisions on any two images using an Amazon t2.large EC2 server within 24-99 hours. The exercise also served the purpose of introducing them to the process of collision generation.

However, this exercise lacked scalability and did not prove to be cost-effective for an academic setting. Each student's collision required a large amount of computation power and over 1 GB of RAM for the collision process, and could not be parallelized on the server. Due to these constraints, a class of 50 students would require 50 EC2 servers to create one collision per student, running at a cost of 11.55 USD per student.

We decided that this was too high a cost for students to pay, and unreasonable for universities to cover for the end result. Despite its drawbacks, the design of the collision creation exercise and the format of the information presented to students did serve as references on how to build the SHA-1 exercise documentation.

Since the SHA-1 break, we have not found any classroom exercises created focused on introducing SHA-1 to students. However, there have been programs released allowing users to create and test SHA-1 collisions. Marc Stevens, one of the key researchers involved with the SHA-1 fixed-prefix attack, released a SHA-1 collision detection library and command line tool which allows for the detection of collisions in files using cryptanalytic tools [6]. Although this library's documentation has some detail about the SHA-1 hash function, the detection program and command line tool are mainly for protective measures rather than for education.

Erling Ellingsen created an online tool that allowed users to make PDF collisions using the fixed-prefix attack with files under 64 kB in size [2]. This tool, while taking advantage of the collision, restricted the size of both files as a result of the JPEG comments they were embedded in requiring they be 64 kB or less. The tool also failed to inform the user of what was happening in the collision creation.

Robert Xiao, a researcher at Carnegie Mellon University, created a tool on Github called *sha1collider* [15] which permitted users to generate PDF files greater than 64 KB with colliding SHA-1 checksums by introducing restarts within the JPEG comments. Currently, not all PDF viewers support comment restarts, so collisions created with restarts embedded cannot always be opened in generic PDF viewers like Adobe Reader.

Xiao also implemented a specific "progressive" JPEG feature in which users could format images into progressive JPEGS, allowing some with lower resolution to forego the restart markers and render normally on PDF viewers. Due to its simple commands and reliability under the progressive marking for small, lower resolution PDFs, the *sha1collider* tool is what we ultimately decided to use for our exercise creation.

Since the SHA-1 break, we have not found any classroom exercises created focused on introducing SHA-1 to students. However, there have been programs released allowing users to create and test SHA-1 collisions. Marc Stevens, one of the key researchers involved with SHA-1's fixed-prefix attack, released a SHA-1 collision detection library and command line tool which allows for the detection of collisions in files using cryptanalytic tools [6]. Although this library's documentation has some detail about the SHA-1 hash function, the detection program and command line tool are mainly for protective measures rather than for education. Erling Ellingsen created an online tool allowing for users to make PDF collisions using the fixed-prefix attack with files under 64 kB in size[2]. This tool, while taking advantage of the collision, restricted the size of both files as a result of the JPEG comments they were embedded in requiring they be 64 kB or less. The tool also failed to inform the user of what was happening in the collision creation. Robert Xiao, a researcher at Carnegie Mellon University, created a tool on GitHub called *sha1collider*, permitted users to collide files greater than 64 KB in size by introducing restarts within the JPEG comments. Currently, not all PDF viewers support comment restarts, so collisions created with restarts embedded cannot always be opened in generic

PDF viewers like Adobe Reader [15]. Xiao also implemented a specific "progressive" JPEG feature in which users could format images into progressive JPEGS, allowing some with lower resolution to forego the restart markers and render normally on PDF viewers. Due to its simple commands and reliability under the progressive marking for small, lower resolution PDFs, the *sha1collider* tool is what we ultimately decided to use for our exercise creation.

4 THE SHA-1 COLLISION EXERCISE

In order to enable students to generate their own PDFs with colliding SHA-1 checksums, we introduced the concept and theory in class, assigned them a hands-on exercise which we designed, and asked them questions about what they learned in the exercise and on paper exams.

In class, we explained cryptographic hash functions, the SHA-1 fixed-prefix collision, and how this collision was leveraged to create the program used in the exercise. In the hands-on exercise, the students were introduced to checksums and were asked to perform checksums on two pre-downloaded files, as well as run the program on the files and assure their output SHA-1 sums were equivalent. In addition, students were asked to download their own files, manipulate them, run the colliding program on them, and attempt to email them to an instructor and record what happens.

The hands-on exercise is contained in a preconfigured Kali virtual machine with all necessary scripts and dependencies required to run the *sha1collider* software. It also comes preloaded with two PDFs called *realsylabus.pdf* and *fakesyllabus.pdf*, shown in Figure 1, to be used for their first SHA-1 collision generation.

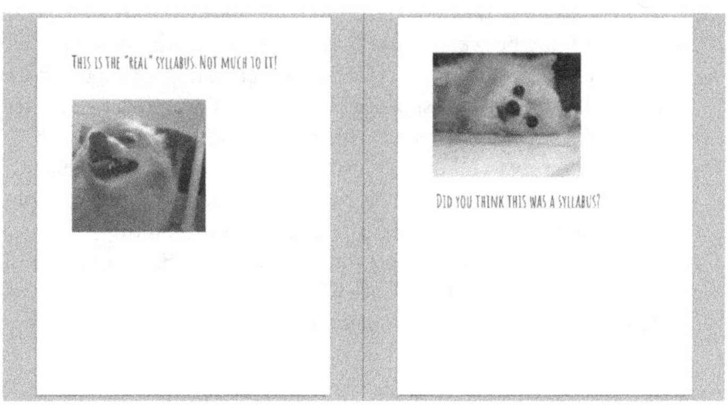

Figure 1: The two preloaded PDFs

Students are asked to compute the files' SHA-1 checksums and confirm that they are different, explicitly asking the first major question of "Are the sha1sum values different?". After confirming their unique checksums, they are asked to check and record the individual file sizes using a given command. They are then told to run the *sha1collider* program on the two files, which produces output files *out-realsyllabus.pdf* and *out-fakesyllabus.pdf*. With these files, students are asked to repeat previous measurements of their file sizes and checksums. Students should find that both the file sizes and checksums appear the same.

It is assured that the key point in this exercise is known by asking them if the PDFs' contents are visibly different and ask them to open both files. With all other instructions followed properly, the content of both output files should be distinctly different. It is expected that students have understood, using evidence-based practice, that the *sha1collider* tool has taken the fixed-prefix collision prefix and appended it to their new, combined suffixed PDFs.

After students complete the first portion of the exercise, the concepts learned are reinforced and they are given a document template which includes undefined lease terms, as shown in Figure 2. Students are asked to complete the agreement by filling out their own custom terms and names twice, thereby creating two different PDFs. At this point, we ask them to generate the corresponding colliding files using the *sha1collider* tool. Thus, students not only learn about the collision, perform it on given, known-to-work files, but also create arbitrary files of their own to collide.

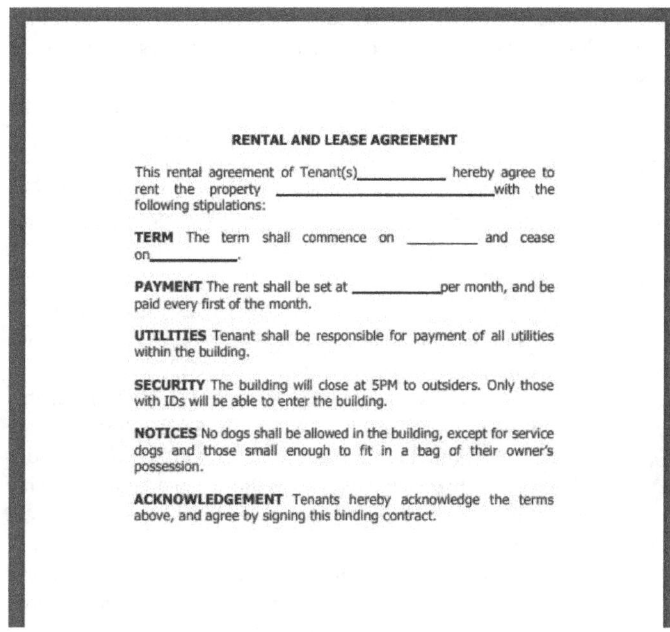

RENTAL AND LEASE AGREEMENT

This rental agreement of Tenant(s)__________ hereby agree to rent the property ______________________with the following stipulations:

TERM The term shall commence on ________ and cease on__________.

PAYMENT The rent shall be set at __________per month, and be paid every first of the month.

UTILITIES Tenant shall be responsible for payment of all utilities within the building.

SECURITY The building will close at 5PM to outsiders. Only those with IDs will be able to enter the building.

NOTICES No dogs shall be allowed in the building, except for service dogs and those small enough to fit in a bag of their owner's possession.

ACKNOWLEDGEMENT Tenants hereby acknowledge the terms above, and agree by signing this binding contract.

Figure 2: The rental agreement given for students to fill out

5 EXERCISE DESIGN

This exercise design focused on three major goals: (a) the exercise must be easy to complete, (b) it must be useful for students to perform, and (c) it must reinforce their prior knowledge about SHA-1 hash collisions. These three goals guided our exercise development and will be individually discussed at length.

In order to establish these goals, we gave the students a document with step-by-step instructions to guide them to their first collision creation, followed by instructions to perform their own document and collision creations. In addition, the document included screenshots allowing students to follow along with commands and supplement their understanding of the material. The remainder of this section explains the goals we had in mind while designing this exercises.

5.1 Easy Completion

Students in computer science courses at universities are often asked to download multiple virtual machines and software packages, while also making multiple manipulations of their system settings in order to begin different exercises. Our goal was to ensure that the exercise was simple to run with the least amount of downloading and system reconfiguration on the student's end. Therefore, we ended up designing this exercise to be pre-downloaded on a virtual machine used for multiple other labs and projects during the semester.

The Kali virtual machine came with the *sha1collider* package installed, as well as two previously-tested PDFs which could be used in the collision generation. Furthermore, the lab instructions came with a link to a document to be edited and used as another PDF candidate for collisions. This document was guaranteed to fit within the restricted JPEG size limit during progressive JPEG creation. By giving students the pre-downloaded package on their virtual machines, they had virtually no setup time, so long as they downloaded the original virtual machine at the beginning of the semester.

Alternatively, one could have decided to put these files and software packages on a cloud-computing instance, as the generation of the PDFs is not computationally heavy. However, since students must download two files from the Internet during the exercise and must keep their files for the duration of the lab, a single cloud instance would be cumbersome for small classes, and nearly impossible to manage for larger classes.

The lack of security of shared cloud instances was a major concern; The private and public keys would have to be shared classroom-wide and the possibility of cost-surges during exercise performance meant that data was not guaranteed to be saved. Therefore, this alternative proved infeasible. The possibility of handing students instructions for downloading using the command line was also discussed but ultimately rejected in favor of the use of a virtual machine in hopes that it would be a more uniform procedure between different operating systems.

The final exercise format included step-by-step instructions, plus screenshots of each step being performed. This visual aid assured that students would not get lost during the exercise or have syntax-related issues during the exercise, allowing them to focus on the conceptual material.

5.2 Utility of Exercise

In order to assure that our exercise would be useful for students' understanding of the danger of hash collisions, we took the commonly-used rent contract abstraction to the next level. Students downloaded two rental lease agreements and were asked to fill each out with different terms. These two agreements were then used to create two different, colliding PDFs using the fixed-prefix and near collision blocks with the *sha1collider* tool.

This portion of the exercise gave students a tangible example which they created themselves in which they were able to see the original and output colliding files' new SHA-1 checksums. Then, students were asked to attempt to send these files to their teaching assistant or instructor. When students tried to do so using their university email accounts, they were stopped and a "Virus detected" notification was shown, informing the student of the prefix-collision being recognized by the email server.

5.3 Knowledge Reinforcement

Finally, the exercise was required to enforce the curriculum covered in a cybersecurity course about cryptographic hash functions and known collisions for it to be considered useful in facilitating student's learning. In order to do this, an overview of cryptographic hash functions was included, as well as a high-level, detailed section about the fixed-prefix attack performed on SHA-1.

There were also multiple steps included at the beginning of the exercise to walk students through how to check SHA-1 checksums via the command line *openSSL* tools, and gave an explanation of what the *sha1collider* tool changes in PDFs.

6 ANALYSIS AND RESULTS

The exercise, given in the form of a PDF document distributed online, was performed by 45 students at the University of Virginia in the Spring 2018 Network Security course. The exercise was then performed in the Fall 2018 Network Security course by 35 students.

All three of these goals were evaluated in a series of survey questions given to students after they performed the exercises. These questions and corresponding goals were as follows:

(1) How easy was it to follow directions? (Ease of Completion)
(2) How much do you think what you learned in this lab was useful? (Utility of Exercise)
(3) How much do you think this lab reinforced your SHA-1 collision's knowledge? (Knowledge Reinforcement)

For each survey question, students were asked to give a rating on an integer scale between 1 and 5, with 5 being the highest positive score. For our exercise to be considered successful, we expected the majority of students to respond with a rating of 4 or 5, and expected $\geq 80\%$ of students to respond with a rating of 3, 4, or 5.

The responses to all question were positive and met our success criteria. When asked to rate the ease of following the instructions given to them, 91% of students responded with a rating of 4 or 5 and 98% of students responded with 3, 4, or 5, as shown in Figure 3. However, of the 2% of students who responded with a 1 or 2, all were successfully able to complete the exercise in its entirety.

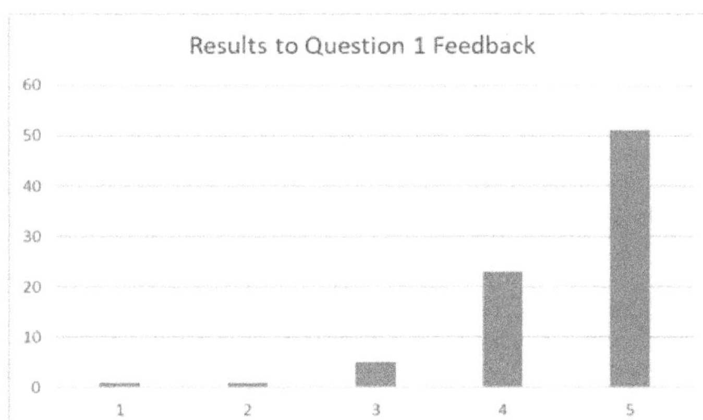

Figure 3: How easy was it to follow directions?

When asked to respond about the utility of the information presented, as displayed in Figure 4, also fit our specified success criteria. Seventy-two percent of students gave utility a 4 or 5 rating, and 93% of all student responses were 3, 4, or 5 ratings. There was only one 1-rating given, indicating there was some utility presented to nearly all students who completed the survey.

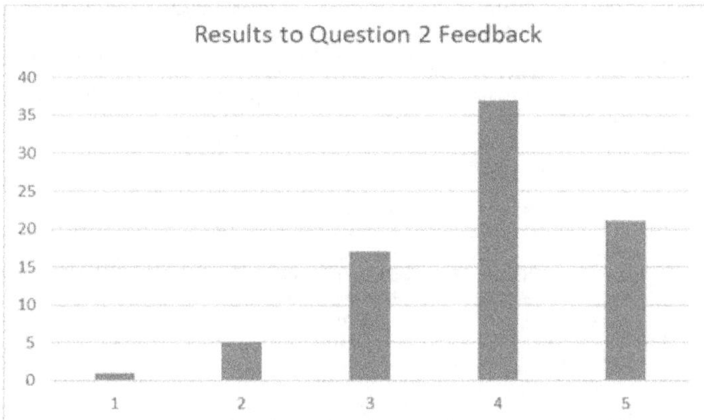

Figure 4: How much do you think what you learned in this lab was useful?

In regards to the reinforcement of their knowledge, shown in Figure 5, the results met our criteria and were similar to the responses given when questioned about the utility of the exercise. Of the students who completed the survey, 67% expressed high levels of with a 4 or 5 rating and 90% of students responded with a 3, 4, or 5 rating. Only 7% of students gave a low reinforcement rating of 2; only one student reported a 1 on their feedback. These results served as positive motivation for continuing to give this exercise to teach students about SHA-1 collisions.

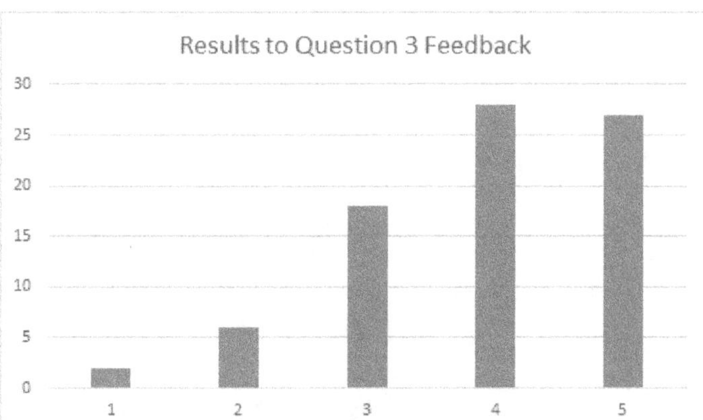

Figure 5: How much do you think this lab reinforced your SHA-1 collision's knowledge?

Students in the Network Security class during the both the Fall and Spring 2018 semesters had an exam a few days after they performed the exercise that included questions about MD5 and SHA-1 collisions. In this exam, they were asked to answer two questions about the SHA-1 hash function which had been discussed previously during class lectures. These questions were:

(1) Is it feasible to generate 2 different PDF files with the same SHA-1 checksum?
(2) Does SHA-1 maintain the second pre-image resistance hash function requirement?

Of the 53 students who took the exam in the Spring 2018 semester, 49 students responded correctly to question 1. However, only 25 students answered question 2 correctly. Similar results were recorded for students in the Fall 2018 semester; Of the 38 students who took the exam, 32 students responded correctly to question 1, while only 18 students responded correctly to question 2. Our exercise, though containing material about cryptographic hash functions and SHA-1's fixed-prefix collision attack, did not cover the difference between pre-image, second pre-image, and collision resistance. Therefore, we speculate that the first question may have been answered with a much higher positive score rate due to the hands-on exercise that students performed prior to examination. This speculation is supported by the results of the students who did not perform the exercise; of the students known to not perform the exercise who also took the exam, one answered question 1 correctly and none answered question 2 correctly. Regardless, this information suggests that, to further reinforce concepts to students, we should take care to address the different levels of resistance which a cryptographic hash function is required to meet for security within the exercise.

7 FUTURE WORK

It was incredibly useful for us to gain feedback immediately following the release of our exercise from our students. While we did take quantitative measurements of their satisfaction with the aforementioned goals on a 1-5 scale, we also allowed students to share their opinions and thoughts on how to improve the exercise. Therefore, the premise of our future work is based mainly on student and peer suggestion on how to better engage the primary audience's learning.

Notable feedback indicated that some students wanted more intense, in-depth work to understand the lower-level collision creation. Other students noted that they were shocked at how easy generating colliding PDFs was by using the fixed-prefix collision. The majority of students had positive comments and suggested that the exercise was both fun and a unique learning experience.

Our future plan is to include the suggestions received from students about how to better serve their interests. We will start by requiring students to construct their own colliding PDFs from building blocks given through the fixed-prefix PDF, progressive JPEG images, and PDF footers. This will allow the students to understand the formation of PDFs and where the collision is occurring, while reducing the amount of work needed for to generate colliding files. This change would help students feel in control, see the low-level framework of PDFs, and further enforce their understanding of the limitations of this collision attack.

Furthermore, although our attempted exercise to introduce MD5 collisions to students was infeasible in a classroom setting, we plan on making an instructional video showing the differential path search process and providing an explanation on what this process intends to achieve. We hope that with the additional classroom instruction, students will become comfortable with more advanced cryptography attacks on hash functions.

8 CONCLUSIONS

In this paper, we presented how we designed and offered a hands-on exercise on SHA-1 collisions in the classroom. The exercise was easy for the students to perform, useful, and assured reinforcement of theory taught in the classroom.

With over 90% of students having a positive experience with the exercise's utility and knowledge reinforcement, we are motivated to continue to refine the SHA-1 hands-on exercise.

The feedback we received shows that the exercise has been a valuable experience to the students. Our exercise is available online here: https://github.com/aicsuva/Hands-on-SHA1-Collisions-Using-sha1collider. Our future plan includes adding a PDF building block section, students will be able to further understand the attack and remember the vulnerability in their future work in the cybersecurity field.

9 ACKNOWLEDGEMENTS

We would like to give our thanks and appreciation to Elie Bursztein for helping analyze the SHA-1 collisions attack and to Simranjit Bhatia for helping analyze the feedback surveys.

REFERENCES

[1] Amerk. [n. d.]. SHA1 Deprecation Policy. ([n. d.]). https://web.archive.org/web/20131113032317/http://blogs.technet.com/b/pki/archive/2013/11/12/sha1-deprecation-policy.aspx
[2] Erling Ellingsen. 2017. Sha1 Collider. (2017).
[3] Russell Housley, W Polk, Warwick Ford, and David Solo. 2002. *Internet X.509 Public Key Infrastructure Certificate and Certificate Revocation List (CRL) Profile.* Technical Report.
[4] Microsoft. [n. d.]. Flame Malware Colision Attack Explained. ([n. d.]). https://blogs.technet.microsoft.com/srd/2012/06/06/flame-malware-collision-attack-explained/
[5] Vincent Rijmen and Elisabeth Oswald. 2005. *Topics in Cryptology – CT-RSA 2005: The Cryptographers' Track at the RSA Conference 2005, San Francisco, CA, USA, February 14-18, 2005. Proceedings.* Springer Berlin Heidelberg, Berlin, Heidelberg, Chapter Update on SHA-1, 58–71. https://doi.org/10.1007/978-3-540-30574-3_6
[6] Marc Stevens. 2017. sha1collisiondetection. "https://github.com/cr-marcstevens/sha1collisiondetection". (2017).
[7] Marc Stevens, Elie Bursztein, Pierre Karpman, Ange Albertini, and Yarik Markov. 2017. The first collision for full SHA-1. (2017).
[8] Marc Stevens, Pierre Karpman, and Thomas Peyrin. 2016. Freestart Collision for Full SHA-1. (2016).
[9] Marc Stevens, Arjen Lenstra, and Benne de Weger. 2007. Chosen-Prefix Collisions for MD5 and Colliding X.509 Certificates for Different Identities. In *Advances in Cryptology - EUROCRYPT*, Moni Naor (Ed.). Lecture Notes in Computer Science, Vol. 4515. Springer Berlin Heidelberg, 1–22.
[10] KODUMURI SUSENA and K KISHORE KUMAR. 2015. Implementation of SHA-1 HMAC-SHA-1 Proof of Ownership Protocol on a Mixed-Breed Cloud Resemble for Unharmed Licensed Deduplication. *International Journal of Scientific Engineering and Technology Research* 4, 28 (July 2015), 5329–5332.
[11] Asawa Tiwari. 2012. *Egyptian Informatics Journal* 13 (2012), 199–208.
[12] Xiaoyun Wang, Yiqun Lisa Yin, and Hongbo Yu. 2005. *Advances in Cryptology – CRYPTO 2005: 25th Annual International Cryptology Conference, Santa Barbara, California, USA, August 14-18, 2005. Proceedings.* Springer Berlin Heidelberg, Berlin, Heidelberg, Chapter Finding Collisions in the Full SHA-1, 17–36. https://doi.org/10.1007/11535218_2
[13] Xiaoyun Wang and Hongbo Yu. 2005. How to Break MD5 and Other Hash Functions. *Shandong University* (2005).
[14] Xiaoyun Wang and Hongbo Yu. 2005. How to Break MD5 and Other Hash Functions. In *Advances in Cryptology – EUROCRYPT*, Ronald Cramer (Ed.). Lecture Notes in Computer Science, Vol. 3494. Springer Berlin Heidelberg, 19–35.
[15] Robert Xiao. 2017. sha1collider. "https://github.com/nneonneo/sha1collider/". (2017).

Teaching Cybersecurity with Networked Robots

Ákos Lédeczi, Miklós Maróti, Hamid Zare, Bernard Yett, Nicole Hutchins, Brian Broll, Péter Völgyesi, Michael B. Smith, Timothy Darrah, Mary Metelko, Xenofon Koutsoukos, Gautam Biswas
Vanderbilt University
Nashville, TN, USA
akos.ledeczi@vanderbilt.edu

ABSTRACT

The paper presents RoboScape, a collaborative, networked robotics environment that makes key ideas in computer science accessible to groups of learners in informal learning spaces and K-12 classrooms. RoboScape is built on top of NetsBlox, an open-source, networked, visual programming environment based on Snap! that is specifically designed to introduce students to distributed computation and computer networking. RoboScape provides a twist on the state of the art of robotics learning platforms. First, a user's program controlling the robot runs in the browser and not on the robot. There is no need to download the program to the robot and hence, development and debugging become much easier. Second, the wireless communication between a student's program and the robot can be overheard by the programs of the other students. This makes cybersecurity an immediate need that students realize and can work to address. We have designed and delivered a cybersecurity summer camp to 24 students in grades between 7 and 12. The paper summarizes the technology behind RoboScape, the hands-on curriculum of the camp and the lessons learned.

CCS CONCEPTS

• **Applied computing → Interactive learning environments**; *Collaborative learning*; • **Computing methodologies →** Distributed programming languages.

KEYWORDS

visual programming, robotics, cybersecurity, computer science education, Snap!, NetsBlox

ACM Reference Format:

Ákos Lédeczi, Miklós Maróti, Hamid Zare, Bernard Yett, Nicole Hutchins, Brian Broll,, Péter Völgyesi, Michael B. Smith, Timothy Darrah, Mary Metelko, Xenofon Koutsoukos,, Gautam Biswas, Vanderbilt University, Nashville, TN, USA . 2019. Teaching Cybersecurity with Networked Robots. In *SIGCSE '19: 50th ACM Technical Symposium on Computer Science Education, February 27–March 2, 2019, Minneapolis, MN, USA.* ACM, New York, NY, USA, 7 pages. https://doi.org/10.1145/3287324.3287450

SIGCSE'19, February 27–March 2, 2019, Minneapolis, MN, USA

ACM ISBN 978-1-4503-5890-3/19/2...$15.00
https://doi.org/10.1145/3287324.3287450

1 INTRODUCTION

Educational robotics is widely used to introduce K-12 students to computer science and engineering [1, 8, 11]. Building and controlling robots have broad appeal for young learners. The typical means of programming robots is writing the program in either a block-based or a simple text-based language, connecting the robot to the computer via USB, and then downloading the program to the robot. In turn, the program executes on the microcontroller of the robot. While there is nothing wrong with this approach, this paper presents an alternative that has certain advantages.

RoboScape relies on WiFi-enabled robots. Each robot has a fixed program that accepts commands transmitted wirelessly and can send back sensor readings over WiFi as well. The robot program that a user of RoboScape is expected to write is, in essence, a smart remote controller. The program runs locally in the browser, enabling a rapid development cycle and making debugging easier. It also makes it possible to control multiple robots from the same program that, in turn, can carry out a task in a collaborative manner.

The programming interface of RoboScape is implemented as a NetsBlox service. NetsBlox is an open-source, networked, visual programming environment based on Snap! [15] that is specifically designed to introduce students to distributed computation and computer networking [2, 3, 12]. RoboScape introduces another unique feature: wireless commands from the users' programs and sensor messages from the robots can be overheard by the other users' programs in the room. Hence, students can eavesdrop on and even take control of others' robots. This provides an excellent opportunity to illustrate the need for cybersecurity and to teach it in a hands-on manner.

The rest of the paper is organized as follows. First we present a brief overview of NetsBlox and then describe the technical details of RoboScape. Section 4 outlines curricular opportunities Roboscape enables that we have used to teach cybersecurity to K-12 students during a week-long summer camp. We conclude by presenting the lessons learned in delivering the material to 24 students and a brief summary of related work.

2 NETSBLOX OVERVIEW

NetsBlox adds a few carefully selected abstractions to Snap! that enable users to create distributed applications. Remote Procedure Calls (RPC) provide access to a set of online data sources such as maps, weather, seismic information, astronomy imagery, etc. and provide useful utilities such as plotting or cloud variables. An RPC is just like a function, i.e., a custom block in Snap!, but it runs remotely on the NetsBlox server. Note that an RPC is more than just a call to a web API. Related RPCs are grouped together into services that can have state information, can cache data, and optionally can send messages to the caller. For example, the map service returns an image from Google Maps but maintains information for subsequent coordinate transformations from screen coordinates to latitude and longitude and vice versa. It also caches maps to avoid unnecessary API calls.

Figure 1 shows a sample RPC calling block. The first pull down menu lets the user select the service. Picking a service automatically populates the second menu with the available RPCs of the given service. Once an RPC is selected, the block re-configures to show the required input arguments.

Figure 1: A sample RPC call block

NetsBlox also incorporates message passing. Messages are similar to events already present in Snap!, but they also contain data fields and can be sent across the network to other NetsBlox programs running on different computers. A message has a type associated with it specifying its name and data fields. A pair of corresponding send and receive blocks are shown below. Notice the last field of the send block specifying the address the message is to be sent to. There are a number of ways NetsBlox supports message addressing that is beyond the scope of this paper. The interested reader is referred to [3]. Note that NetsBlox simulates peer to peer messaging, but in reality every message goes through the NetsBlox server.

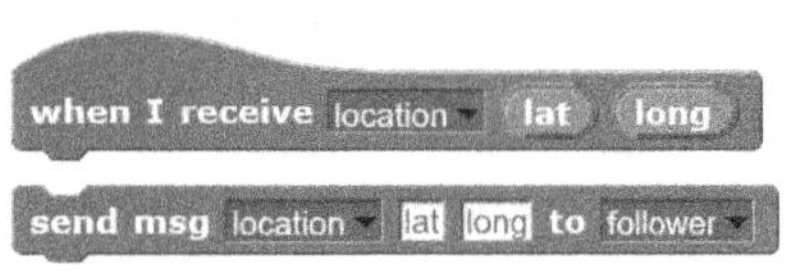

Figure 2: Message sending and receiving blocks

RPCs and messages enable the creation of a wide range of distributed applications and consequently, they open the door to teaching some of the fundamental concepts of distributed computing.

3 ROBOSCAPE

RoboScape is implemented as a NetsBlox service. Robot commands are RPCs. The robot's responses are messages. There are two versions of RoboScape. The first one defines a separate RPC for each different type of command, e.g., *set speed*, *get range*, etc. It also uses different message types for different sensors. The second one was designed specifically for cybersecurity education. It has a generic *send* RPC with two fields: robot and command. The command is a text field where the user needs to provide the command and its arguments as text, e.g., *"set speed 50 50"*. There are only two message types: *robot command* and *robot message*. The *robot command* is for eavesdropping on other users' commands. The NetsBlox server sends this message to every client who has registered to listen on the given robot. Similarly, the *robot message* is sent by the server to each registered client upon receiving a message from a robot. The payload of these messages is also text. Making the communication text-based makes it easy to motivate and implement encryption. The rest of the paper covers this text based communication version of RoboScape only.

The architecture of RoboScape is shown in Figure 3. All clients running in a web browser are connected to the NetsBlox server via the internet. Similarly, the WiFi enabled robots are connected to the NetsBlox server as well. In other words, all communication goes through the server. The communication between the clients and the server is the standard NetsBlox method: http requests for RPCs and WebSockets for messaging. The robots and the server use UDP for communication. The robots run a custom C program that receives the commands, executes them, and sends messages back to the server. The NetsBlox server code was not modified. RoboScape was added as an additional service akin to any other service NetsBlox supports.

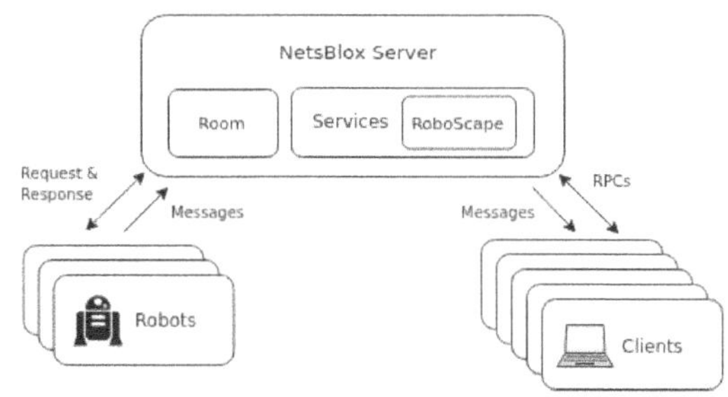

Figure 3: RoboScape architecture

The RoboScape prototype has been implemented with Parallax ActivityBot 360 robots. The cost of the robot is $250. The platform has two main wheels driven by motors with optical encoders, an ultrasonic range sensor, a couple of touch sensors ("whiskers"), a buzzer, a custom button, two LEDs, and an XBee WiFi module. See Figure 4.

Figure 4: Parallax ActivityBot 360

The basic commands are shown in Table 1. The commands can be overheard as *robot command* messages. Furthermore, when the robot receives the given command, it replies with an acknowledgement containing a time stamp. These, in turn, are sent to the registered clients as *robot messages*. So, if a user registers to receive communication from a given robot and it calls the *send* RPC, it will receive a *robot command* message from the server (simulating overhearing a command) and a *robot message* from the server simulating overhearing the robot's acknowledgement. If the command

Table 1: Basic RoboScape commands

Command	Arguments
is alive	RID (Robot ID)
set speed	RID, left, right
beep	RID, duration, pitch
get range	RID
get ticks	RID
set led	RID, A/B, on/off/toggle
listen	RID

requested a sensor reading, e.g., "*get range*", a third message will be sent with the actual sensor values. The following *robot messages* are supported:

Table 2: Robot messages

Message	Fields
alive	RID (Robot ID), time
beep	RID, time, duration, pitch
speed	RID, time, left, right
range	RID, time, range
ticks	RID, time, left, right
whiskers	RID, time, left, right
button	RID, time, isPressed

To illustrate how easy it is to use RoboScape, consider the simple but fully functional project shown in Figure 5. The program enables the user to drive the robot using the arrow keys on the keyboard. When the green flag is clicked (the standard way to start a program in Scratch, Snap! and NetsBlox), we call the listen RPC of the RoboScape service that registers the client with the server that it wants to listen to the specified robot. Note that the robot ID used is the last few digits of its MAC address.

The arrow key handlers simply use the *set speed* command to specify the speed of the left and right wheels, respectively. The space key serves as the emergency stop button. Finally, there is the handler of the *robot message* message. We parse the message and if its first word is *whiskers*, we stop the robot. That is, if the robot encounters an obstacle, it stops.

From a technical point of view, an interesting question is how network latency effects the performance of the robot programs. A robot command travels from the web browser of the user to the NetsBlox server running in the cloud and then down to the robot. The acknowledgement and/or any sensor values travel back the same way. From a user experience point of view, this delay is not noticeable. When running a program like the one depicted in Figure 5, hitting a the arrow keys starts the robot within a fraction of a second.

To quantify the latency, we carried out an experiment. We issued a command in a loop as fast as possible. Since send is a blocking call returning either a sensor value (*get range* or *get ticks*) or a true or false whether the command succeeded or not (*set speed* or *beep*), the time between two such commands includes the latency of the full round trip. We tried different commands and two different local WiFi networks: a relatively slow mobile personal hotspot and a

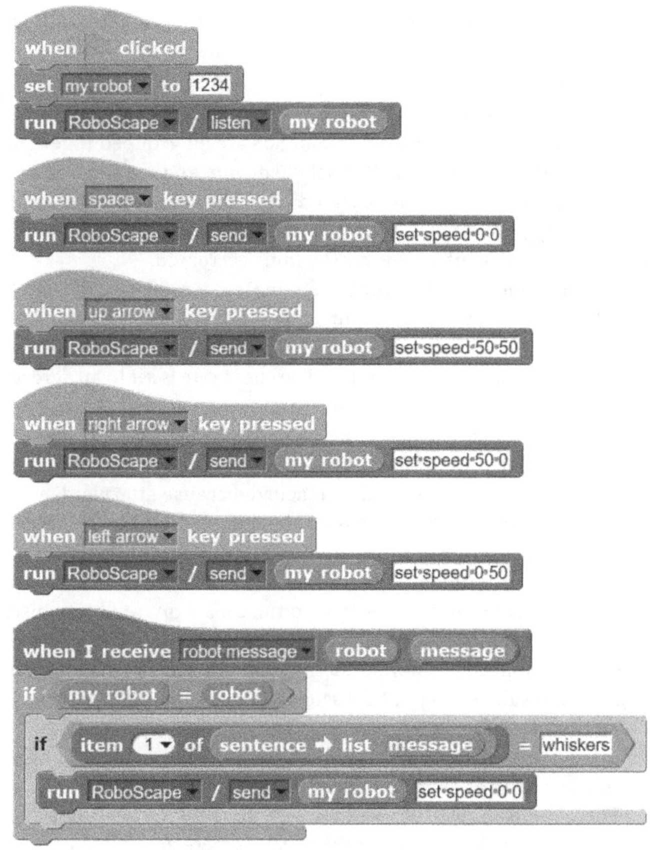

Figure 5: A simple RoboScape project implementing driving the robot with keyboard commands

fast WiFi router. The average latency across all experiments came to between 100 and 120 milliseconds. That is faster than human response time. Interestingly, if we measure the time when a message arrives in response to a command (as opposed to a return value), the delay doubles. Since the network latency should be about the same, this added delay must be due to extra processing on the server and the client dealing with message passing. While this performance is more than satisfactory, the system can be sped up significantly by running a copy of the NetsBlox server on the local network as opposed to the Amazon cloud.

4 CYBERSECURITY

This section briefly summarizes which cybersecurity concepts can be taught using RoboScape.

DDoS. Since all one needs to know is the robot ID in order to issue commands to it, it is really easy to mount a (Distributed) Denial of Service (DDoS) attack. Instead of taking control of a robot overtly by issuing *set speed* commands, we show the students how to issue *set led* or short *beep* commands rapidly in a loop. As more and more students start doing this, the robot starts to lose real messages and its behavior becomes erratic. The first task we assign the students is to modify their driving program to detect if there is an attack occurring. The simplest way is counting the number of commands issued and comparing it to the number of commands overheard. Then we introduce two new commands. The *set total rate* command limits the number of commands (per second) the robot accepts to a specified number. This is of course not effective since the real commands and the attackers' commands are all grouped together. The second command is called *set client rate* and it specifies the maximum rate commands accepted from the same client as well as a penalty period when the robot does not accept any command from the given client whenever the limit is crossed.

The challenge problem for the students is a race we call tug of war. Two students control the same robot. The robot is placed in the middle of the room and the objective for each student is to drive the robot to his or her side of the room. The client rate is set to an agreed upon fixed number. The students can use manual driving, that is, they can use the keyboard of their laptops for various commands. The challenge comes from the fact that you want to issue the last command before the rate limit is reached, because afterwards you cannot issue any new commands for the duration left of the current second.

Encryption. Students quickly realize that it would be much better if the robot did not accept commands from anybody else. This presents an opportunity to introduce the concept of encryption. The robots support a simple Caesar's cipher. The corresponding command is called *set key* and it sends the shift amount to the robot. Once the robot receives a new key (the default is 0 at startup), it decrypts every message using the key before sending it and it only accepts commands encrypted with the very same key.

There are two obvious weaknesses with this scheme. Some students figure out the first one quickly: since there are only a limited number of commands and, for example, if you want to drive your robot, you must use *set speed*, one can relatively easily break the encryption by brute force even using a relatively slow, blocks-based language. The second weakness is that the very first *set key* command is not encrypted.

Figure 6 shows the code that listens to *set key* commands sent to a robot and steals the key. It uses the last stolen key to decrypt the command and extract the new key. Since the initial key is zero, if the attacker intercepts the very first *set key* command, the program will be able to eavesdrop on the robot indefinitely, no matter how many times the key is changed. This simple example introduces the students to the need of secure key exchange.

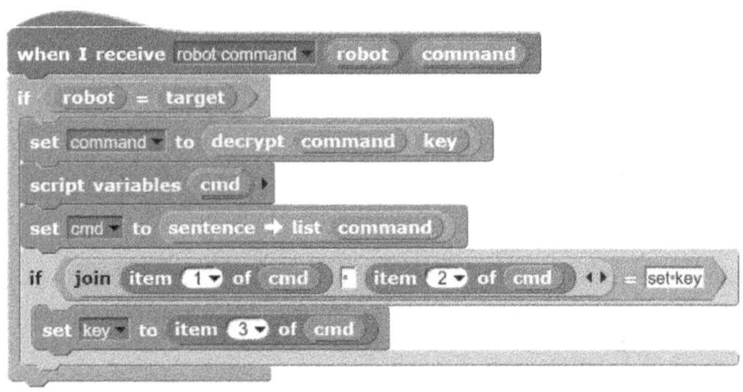

Figure 6: Eavesdropping on a robot and stealing the key when a *set key* command is overheard

Hardware key/secure key exchange. A simple way for secure key exchange in RoboScape is to have the robot generate the key and never send it across the wireless network. When the user pushes the button on the robot for two seconds, the robot generates a new key and "plays it" on two LEDs. There is one LED for bit 0 and another for 1. The robot blinks one or the other for half a second from the most significant bit to the least. The student writes this number down, converts it from binary to decimal, and types it in their program. Once they do this, the key thief program of Figure 6 will no longer work.

The brute force code breaking can also be made much harder: instead of a single shift value for the Caesar's cipher, RoboScape supports using a list of shift values. The encryption then proceeds by shifting the first character of the message by the first shift value, the second by the second and so on in a circular fashion. The robot itself generates four 4-bit shift values. Knowing this, brute forcing a *set speed* command may still be possible (even though the number of possible combinations are over 64,000 as opposed to fewer than 100), but if the first thing the user's program does is change the key to a new list of more than 4 values, and then continue to change it frequently, the attackers will not be able to keep up.

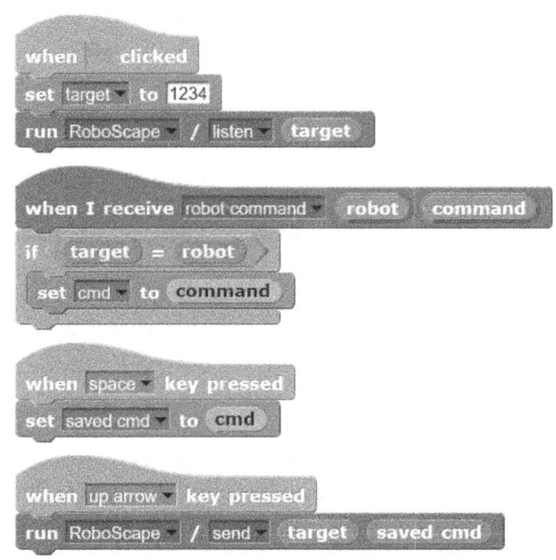

Figure 7: Capturing encrypted commands and replaying them on demand

Replay attacks. At this point of the curriculum, students should have secured their robots via the aforementioned, scaffolded tasks. Instruction on additional robot interference then takes form in the application of replay attacks. Even though the attackers cannot break the encryption, they can still overhear messages and reissue them themselves. The program in Figure 7 allows the attacker to capture any commands the user sends to the robot and even though they cannot decrypt it, the person can observe the robot's behavior, and issue the saved command at a later time. For example, they can wait until the robot turns, press the space button to save the last command overheard (presumably the turn command), and then they can cause the robot to turn any time they choose to by pressing the up arrow.

There is a simple fix to this problem with RoboScape: each command can be prepended by a sequence number. If a robot receives a command that starts with a number, it will only allow commands that also start with a number from then on. Furthermore, it will only accept numbers that are strictly greater than the last received sequence number. To allow for lost messages, it accepts numbers in the range $[seq + 1, seq + 100]$ where seq is the last received valid sequence number.

Table 3 lists the cybersecurity related commands.

Table 3: Cybersecurity specific commands

Command	Arguments
set key	RID (Robot ID), key
set total rate	RID, rate
set client rate	RID, rate, penalty
reset rates	RID
reset seq	RID

5 LESSONS LEARNED

We conducted two one-week long camps with a total of 24 students from grades 7-12. The students were split approximately evenly between male and female. A high school teacher also participated in one of the camps. Based on the curricular affordances provided by our environment, we completed a domain unpacking of key CS concepts and practices available in the K-12 CS Framework [7] to support the design of a scaffolded introduction to cybersecurity and a prepost assessment to evaluate learning gains. Key concepts include computational thinking (CT), algorithms and programming, networks and the internet, and the impact of computing, with a focus on the practice of creating computational artifacts. We could not assume prior computer programming experience, so we started with an introduction to NetsBlox programming that included increasingly difficult tasks designed to target the CT and programming concepts of control structures, variables, and modularity. The second day was dedicated to learning RoboScape by creating simple robot driving programs. This day not only allowed for additional programming practice, but it also provided for a preliminary introduction to key networking concepts to support the more advanced cybersecurity tasks to come. The final three days targeted our cybersecurity-specific material through scaffolded tasks introducing DDoS, encryption, and other concepts. We additionally emphasized the framework concept of impacts of computing through cybersecurity guest lectures applying curriculum content to real world applications. The hands-on portion of the curriculum is summarized in Table 4.

Our prepost assessment was designed based on the concepts and practices implemented in our curriculum and was sectioned into CT, networking, and cybersecurity. For instance, given the assumption of little to no prior programming experience and the introduction to control structures on Day 1 of the camp, the CT section of our assessment included a question on the use of conditional statements to better assess prior knowledge and to evaluate student understanding post-camp. In addition to learning gains, we implemented a prepost survey targeting students' self efficacy in programming, attitudes towards technology, and task values placed upon robotics and cybersecurity to evaluate student attitudes toward the curriculum content and their abilities.

Table 4: Daily schedule

Day	Topics
1	Intro to NetsBlox programming
2	Intro to RoboScape programming
3	Attack detection, DDoS, its mitigation
4	Encryption, secure key exchange
5	Replay attack, its mitigation, final project

Table 5 reflects our results, showing that most categories improved significantly (p-score < 0.05) from pre-test to post-test. This is reflected in the average scores from the assessment (on a 0-1 scale) and survey (on a 1-6 scale). Also included is the effect size experienced in each area; effect size is simply the average of post-test scores minus the average of pre-test scores, which is then divided by the standard deviation of the full sample. As shown here, students experienced remarkably significant improvements in all sections of the questionnaire; they were specifically addressed during the camp in the form of robotics applications and throughout several guest lectures, so it is reassuring to see the results. Additionally, students expressed improvement in two sections of the motivational survey, showing that they feel more comfortable in completing programming tasks related to robotics and cybersecurity while also appreciating the value of technology. This makes sense considering the topics of the camp as well as its elective nature. In addition, students could be heard saying the following during post camp interviews that nicely supports our results: "The robots really helped because we got to apply what we've learned to an actual situation where we can see the results." "It's interesting and I really like coding now... before I kind of viewed it [coding] as something that could spark my interest, but now it [the camp] has heightened my love for coding and I want to explore more."

Table 5: Survey Results

Category	Pre Avg.	Post Avg.	P-Score	Eff. Size
CT	0.70	0.91	0.001	0.833
Networking	0.58	0.80	0.001	0.845
Cybersecurity	0.61	0.81	0.002	0.674
Self-Efficacy	4.81	5.42	<0.001	0.627
Tech Att.	5.39	5.65	0.011	0.368
Task Values	5.27	5.55	0.176	0.159

We would next like to briefly address the result which did not experience significant improvement. While there was some amount of improvement in the value students place on robotics, cybersecurity, and programming tasks, it was not enough to be significant. The main issue here seems to be that students already valued those areas highly, so there was not as much room for improvement as in the other areas.

There is plenty of anecdotal evidence of the success of the camps as well. Student engagement in both camps was very high. After the second day, that is, after the students started programming the robots, they regularly arrived half an hourly early and took very short lunch breaks. One could hardly see any mobile phones even though we did not ban them. None of the students went on social media or played online games during the camp. The participating high school teacher remarked how unusual this was with teenagers, saying "I did not see them on cell phones, they were engaged with programming their robot."

The anonymous survey at the end of the camp also showed very positive attitudes toward the camp. Most students expressed how much fun they had and how much they learned. The few negative comments were from students who had no previous programming experience (and were probably the younger learners) who had a somewhat harder time keeping up with the fast-paced camp. To illustrate students' attitudes about the camp, here are some answers to the question, "What was your favorite part of the camp?": "Writing brute-force programs for 4-key encryption." "...being able to apply new and exciting features to the robots that I never thought I would be able to do. It really makes we want to get more engaged in computer science as well as networking." "...hacking people's robots and watching them become confused and making them think their robots are broken." "... racing other teams' robots and fighting with others to get the robot to go a certain direction."

Several students identified encryption as the most difficult concept they learned. Others listed various aspects: "Everything I tried that didn't work made sense once I broke it down and really thought about it except for maybe the command to stop and turn around the robot when its whiskers hit an obstacle." "For a day or two I couldn't wrap my head around lists for some reason but it clicked. Everything else was also a challenge but I eventually got the hang of most of the content!" "The geometry killed me, and some of the robot programming was hard..." The students' engagement is nicely illustrated by this comment: "Lots of complex subjects were taught in the GPS presentation that I studied more when I got home, but it did take me a while to try and fully understand some of the concepts taught."

6 RELATED WORK

The most similar camp to the one we put on seems to be Cyber Discovery and its offshoot, Junior Cyber Discovery (JCD), which covered the same general topic areas of robotics and cyberspace and used a Parallax Boe-Bot for hands-on activities to teach the students about code security, wireless signal transmission, and programming [16]. The use of the Boe-Bot was very prominent during the one reported year of JCD, though those students also designed and build the robots [5]. Another series of camps that has seen rapid growth is GenCyber [13],[10]. One example occurred at Purdue University Northwest [6], where cybersecurity ideas were integrated with game-based learning, using a pair of 3D VR games to teach social engineering, information security, and secure online behavior. Another example built around the GenCyber model was CyberPDX [4]. The GenCyber programming section involved two tools for teaching new programmers - Blockly, which is a graphical, block-based language similar to NetsBlox, and Turtle Graphics in Python. CyberPDX students move on to writing their own encryption program (given a decryption one) or to creating a brute-force attack program. Both camps demonstrated significant learning gains.

Our camp mainly differs from these examples in that attendees were able to focus entirely on how to best program the robots. On the cyber side, our camp was focused on cybersecurity instead of general cyber ideas, as students were tasked with defending their robots while attempting to hack the robots of other groups. These examples also tend to be aimed at different age or experience groups instead of using robotics as a teaching tool for programming and cybersecurity aimed at predominantly high school students.

The Cozmo robot from Anki [14] is a sophisticated yet inexpensive platform. It is being used in introductory robotics course at Georgia Tech (CS 3630), and supports remote control through an SDK. However, it requires a direct Bluetooth connection to a mobile device, and only one robot per device is allowed. As such, it would not be an ideal platform for our purposes. Finally, Sphero is a small robotic ball that is suitable for a robotics and mobile computing course [9]. Students can learn and use simple programming tools on a smart-phone app to send commands or other information to the robots. It is also set up to allow for growth in programming knowledge, from simple block languages up to JavaScript. We plan to provide support for additional robot platforms in the future.

7 CONCLUSIONS AND FUTURE WORK

While both RoboScape and the curriculum of the camp are first prototypes, and the participants were self selected and not representative of the general K-12 student population, we can draw some preliminary conclusions. The apparent success of the summer camps shows the promise of teaching robotics and cybersecurity together in a hands-on manner. The fact that students with no previous programming experience were able to mount cyber attacks and implement simple cyber defense techniques by the end of the week seems to validate the value of the RoboScape approach. Implementing and running the code in the browser made understanding the concepts and designing and debugging the robot control programs easier. One lesson for the future is that we need to create two versions of the curriculum: one with students who have not programmed before and a more advanced version for students who have. Next year, we will develop and deliver two such variants. We also plan to develop a PD week for interested teachers so that they can take the material and implement it in their schools as an after school club. Finally, we'll evaluate additional robotic platforms with different sensors and actuators for potential support by RoboScape and the cybersecurity curriculum.

8 ACKNOWLEDGEMENTS

This material is based in part upon work supported by the National Security Agency Science of Security Lablet, the Air Force Research Laboratory under Award FA 8750-14-2-0180 and the National Science Foundation under grants CNS-1644848, CNS-1238959, CNS-1739328, and DRL-1640199. Any opinions, findings, and conclusions or recommendations expressed in this material are those of the author(s) and do not necessarily reflect the views of the US Government.

REFERENCES

[1] F. B. V. Benitti. Exploring the educational potential of robotics in schools: A systematic review. *Computers & Education*, 58(3):978–988, 2012.

[2] B. Broll, A. Lédeczi, P. Volgyesi, J. Sallai, M. Maroti, A. Carrillo, S. L. Weeden-Wright, C. Vanags, J. D. Swartz, and M. Lu. A visual programming environment for learning distributed programming. In *Proceedings of the 2017 ACM SIGCSE Technical Symposium on Computer Science Education*, pages 81–86. ACM, 2017.

[3] B. Broll, Á. Lédeczi, H. Zare, D. N. Do, J. Sallai, P. Völgyesi, M. Maróti, L. Brown, and C. Vanags. A visual programming environment for introducing distributed computing to secondary education. *Journal of Parallel and Distributed Computing*, 118:189–200, 2018.

[4] W. chang Feng, R. Liebman, L. Delcambre, M. Lupro, T. Sheard, S. Britell, and G. Recktenwald. Cyberpdx: A camp for broadening participation in cybersecurity. In *2017 USENIX Workshop on Advances in Security Education (ASE 17)*, Vancouver, BC, 2017. USENIX Association.

[5] J. Holcomb, M. Nelson, H. Tims, G. Cazes, and G. Turner. Junior cyber discovery: Creating a vertically integrated middle school cyber camp. In *Proceedings of the American Society for Engineering Education*, June 2012.

[6] G. Jin, M. Tu, T.-H. Kim, J. Heffron, and J. White. Game based cybersecurity training for high school students. In *Proceedings of the 49th ACM Technical Symposium on Computer Science Education*, SIGCSE '18, pages 68–73, New York, NY, USA, 2018. ACM.

[7] K12 Computer Science Framework. http://www.k12cs.org, 2016. Cited 2018 August 31.

[8] F. Klassner and S. D. Anderson. Lego mindstorms: Not just for k-12 anymore. *IEEE Robotics & Automation Magazine*, 10(2):12–18, 2003.

[9] S. Kurkovsky. Mobile computing and robotics in one course: Why not? In *Proceedings of the 18th ACM Conference on Innovation and Technology in Computer Science Education*, ITiCSE '13, pages 64–69, New York, NY, USA, 2013. ACM.

[10] T. Ladabouche and S. Lafountain. Gencyber: Inspiring the next generation of cyber stars. *IEEE Security & Privacy*, 14(5):84–86, 2016.

[11] M. J. Mataric. Robotics education for all ages. In *Proc. AAAI Spring Symposium on Accessible, Hands-on AI and Robotics Education*, 2004.

[12] NetsBlox website. https://netsblox.org. Cited 2018 August 31.

[13] B. R. Payne, T. Abegaz, and K. Antonia. Planning and implementing a successful nsa-nsf gencyber summer cyber academy. *Journal of Cybersecurity Education, Research and Practice*, 2016(2), 2016.

[14] J. Skågeby. "Well-Behaved Robots Rarely Make History": Coactive Technologies and Partner Relations. *Design and Culture*, 10(2):187–207, 2018.

[15] Snap!: a visual, drag-and-drop programming language. http://snap.berkeley.edu/snapsource/snap.html. Cited 2018 August 31.

[16] H. Tims, G. Turner, C. Duncan, and B. Etheridge. Work in progress - cyber discovery camp - integrated approach to cyber studies. In *2009 39th IEEE Frontiers in Education Conference*, pages 1–2, Oct 2009.

Fakesbook

A social networking platform for teaching security and privacy concepts to secondary school students

Maximilian Zinkus, Oliver Curry, Marina Moore, Zachary Peterson, Zoë J. Wood
Computer Science - California Polytechnic State University
San Luis, Obispo, CA
mzinkus,owcurry,mmoore32,znjp,zwood@calpoly.edu

ABSTRACT

As frequent users of social networking applications, middle and high school students are well-suited for curricular interventions that leverage these technologies. Allowing students to see "behind the curtain" of these applications provides them with a unique opportunity to better understand the discipline of computer science upon which these technologies are built and influences their perceptions of computer security and privacy. We present a novel social networking simulation that allows students to create a social network account, including profile data and images, and to manage privacy settings and friend connections. The platform, named Fakesbook, presents students with a visualization of the social network as a graph, enabling them to observe the spread of profile data (theirs and others') depending on friend connections and choices of privacy settings. We additionally present our lab curriculum which uses Fakesbook to enable active learning and adversarial thinking to engage students and build agency with regard to privacy and computing concepts. We deployed and, over several years, evaluated our platform and curriculum with hundreds of students from a diverse set of backgrounds at educational events designed to introduce these populations to computer science, cybersecurity, and privacy. Survey results indicate that students gained or deepened their understanding of online privacy and security and that 86% of participants found that Fakesbook helped them "think about privacy and computer security."

KEYWORDS

security and privacy, computer science education, privacy and social networking applications

ACM Reference Format:
Maximilian Zinkus, Oliver Curry, Marina Moore, Zachary Peterson, Zoë J. Wood. 2019. Fakesbook: A social networking platform for teaching security and privacy concepts to secondary school students . In *Proceedings of the 50th ACM Technical Symposium on Computer Science Education (SIGCSE '19), February 27-March 2, 2019, Minneapolis, MN, USA.* ACM, New York, NY, USA, 7 pages. https://doi.org/10.1145/3287324.3287486

SIGCSE '19, February 27-March 2, 2019, Minneapolis, MN, USA

ACM ISBN 978-1-4503-5890-3/19/02...$15.00
https://doi.org/10.1145/3287324.3287486

1 INTRODUCTION

Social networking has become ubiquitous for people of many backgrounds and ages, including a large percentage of minors and young adults. Facebook alone has self-reported over two billion monthly active users [3], and recent literature estimates around 75% of all children ages 12-17 interact with some form of social networking regularly [7, 14]. Concerningly, teenagers with fully public profiles are more likely to experience online cruelty or harassment [7].

Our work stems from the notion that by fostering understanding of online privacy and risk management we can encourage students to adopt safer privacy practices. Additionally, as computer science educators, we aim to build a platform that allows students to see "behind the curtain" to enable deeper understanding of social networking applications. We do this in two ways. First, we provide a platform that visualizes a graph with all users, within a small classroom setting, as nodes, and "friend" relationships as edges. Using the graph visualization, we enable students to see how privacy settings and social connections translate into their data being accessible to a wider and wider group of people. Second, we create a lab experience that highlights the power of programming and contextually introduces computer science as a discipline. Specifically, we want students to understand that data privacy and access control can be controlled programmatically, and thus we include an introductory encryption exercise using the Python programming language. This exercise provides a context-based (privacy and security) introduction to basic programming concepts (variables, loops, arrays and arithmetic operators).

We present the development of our social networking application, Fakesbook, our curriculum, and evaluation through instructional use of the platform over multiple years and with hundreds of students. Fakesbook was used in one-time lab experiences of up to two hours with diverse groups of 20-25 secondary school students of various ages. For each lab experience, we ran Fakesbook on a local network to avoid sharing student information on a public system, while providing students freedom to explore the consequences of various privacy settings. These lab experiences, guided by our curriculum of exercises on the Fakesbook platform and introductory encryption programming lessons, allow secondary school students to gain insight into social networking. Post-lab surveys indicate that the activities and platform were successful in enhancing students' understanding and value of privacy and computer security. Our platform is made available via GitHub for interested educators at *https://github.com/Fakesbook/Fakesbook.*

2 RELATED WORK

Content posted on social networking sites can have real consequences, evidenced by many who report regretting posts they have made [21]. However, users of social networks often have little understanding of the connection between privacy settings and their data, and education about the differences even at the college level is lacking [8, 10]. Using our platform and a pedagogical approach which draws on strategies of visualization and adversarial analysis, we seek to encourage safer privacy practices in social network users at an early stage. Visualization, when paired with active learning [5] and adversarial analysis [11], has been shown to benefit computer science and cybersecurity education. Specific examples include cryptography [13, 17], network security [1, 22], phishing [15], password security [23], and software security [12]. Some of these visualizations are highly detailed, at the expense of accessibility. Tao et. al. [17] and Schweitzer [12] provide visualizations in cryptography and software security respectively, both of which are information-dense. However, they are likely inaccessible to our target audience. Atwater et. al. [1] provide visualization in network security, using a graph-like format to describe a communication network. We employ a similar visual pattern to describe a social network. Zhang-Kennedy et. al. [23] employ a generated interactive narrative along with visualization to convey password security and found that the narrative was helpful for impact and memorability. Our associated lab curriculum overlays a narrative on the Fakesbook application with the goal of similarly improving outcomes. Ours is the first work that we are aware of to use visualization for communicating privacy concepts.

Regarding privacy pedagogy in general, the U.S. National Security Agency and Department of Homeland Security (NSA/DHS) jointly provide certification for institutions of higher education of program content including privacy [20]. They provide associated Knowledge Units [19] which document baseline topic coverage. Our lab experience, consisting of the Fakesbook application and associated curriculum, addresses the first two of the four listed outcomes in the Privacy Knowledge Unit, and additional curricula can expand it to address the other two more fully. As these certifications are usually applied to tertiary educational programs, we consider this to be strong support for our curricular content.

3 OVERVIEW

Our aim with this work is to communicate the importance of privacy and security in social networking applications and to encourage students to engage with these concepts and disciplines. To provide students the opportunity to explore privacy settings in a social networking platform, we developed Fakesbook, a web application that mimics the basic behavior of a typical social networking application. However, unlike a typical social networking application, we visualize the network graph and highlight the sets of users who can see each element of a user's profile data. This software can be used to introduce privacy concepts to a general audience, and to encourage them to make proactive decisions on what to share on these kinds of platforms. We leverage our platform through our associated curriculum comprised of lab activities.

4 THE FAKESBOOK PLATFORM

Platform overview: Fakesbook is a simplified version of commercial social networking applications designed to run privately, on a local network, and intended only for educational use. Our platform allows students to create mock social networking accounts, including basic information about themselves and a profile image. After a brief registration and profile data population process, students are directed to a single view containing the remaining features of the platform. This view displays the user population graph with 'friend' connectivity, a profile information panel, and a privacy settings panel. An example of the complete view is shown in Figure 3.

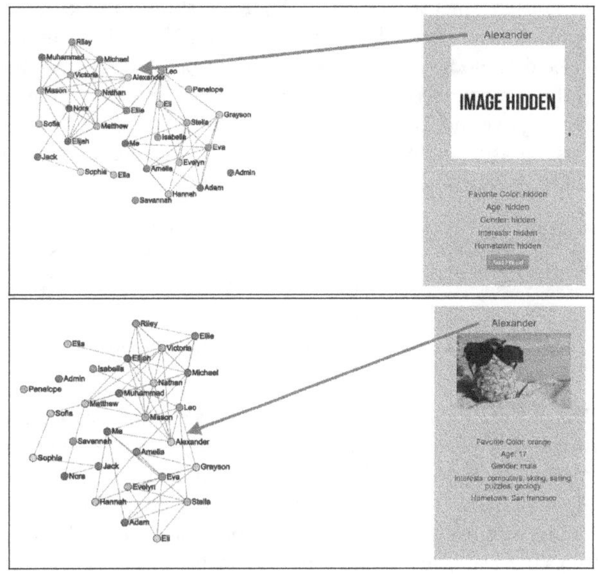

Figure 1: Top image: the current user's view of another user's profile. The other user, 'Alexander', has set their privacy settings to only *friends* and the current user, 'Me', is not yet their friend. Bottom image: view of Alexander's profile, (profile image from public domain), after friending the current user. Graph shows updated edge between users and modified layout per the change.

Steps for platform use: The Fakesbook platform is intended to be used in a directed lab setting. In our curriculum, students are guided through the following steps:

- **Create a user account (profile):** Supported profile data fields include name, favorite color, age, gender, interests, hometown, and an image. The data population screen step compromises its own screen in the platform. In addition, users may edit their profile data fields when viewed/selected in the main screen.
- **Create the social network ('friending'):** Once a user has created an account, their main view is a large screen that shows all other users who have created an account on Fakesbook. The platform allows for 'friending,' where students can connect with their peers by selecting a target user in the network view and clicking 'Add Friend.' The request is pending until the target user accepts, emulating popular social networks and somewhat mitigating excessive friending which may distract from the exercise.
- **Modify privacy settings:** Students can control the visibility of their data by editing the relevant privacy settings for their

profiles, as shown in Figure 2. Privacy settings determine if the data is visible to *everyone*, *friends of friends*, or just *friends*.

Social Network Graph Visualization: Visualizations are designed to highlight graph connectivity and the effect of privacy settings on the propagation of profile data. Students can select (click on) any node in the graph to view that user's profile (as determined by that user's privacy settings). Figure 1 shows an example of viewing another user's data before and after "friending". Students can also drag nodes around to move the graph, which allows them to better see connections, as highly-connected graphs can lead to obscuring overlap. D3.js and additional JavaScript is used to give the visualization basic physical interactivity, through features such as collision resistance of nodes and elasticity of edges.

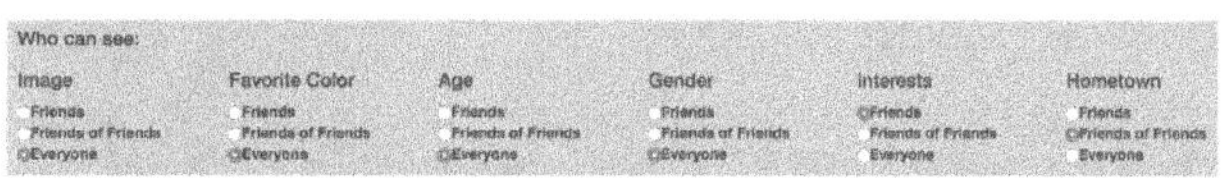

Figure 2: Fakesbook privacy settings panel.

Profile Data Visualization: When students edit their data privacy settings, they can see exactly who else has access to view each element of their profile. This is a core component of Fakesbook as it allows students to see how easily their data can be made visible to others and especially the result of permissive default privacy settings (i.e. *everyone*). When a user interacts (clicks or hovers their mouse) with their account privacy settings, Fakesbook displays a visualization that highlights the users with access to the profile item related to that privacy setting. Color coding (green, yellow, orange) is used to help key the user into the meaning of having their data more widely available. In this regard, we quietly exploit common associations of green with "good" and orange with "warning." We justify these associations upon the observation that teenagers with fully public profiles are more likely to experience online cruelty or harassment [7]. However, to mitigate concern, we don't include this in the student discussion. Figure 3 illustrates sets of users in the social network graph who can see various elements of a profile with each privacy setting option. The top image in Figure 3 is set to *friends* only, whereas the middle image is set to *friends of friends*, and the bottom image is set to *everyone*. In addition, when a user interacts with their own profile data, the same graph visualization appears to strongly associate profile data with other user's access. These visualizations and immediate visual feedback when changing privacy settings encourages students to realize their agency in controlling data access to others.

User Profile Data Storage: During the use of the Fakesbook platform, an SQLite [16] database is used to store profile data. This data can be exported as an ASCII text file as shown in Figure 4. This text data can then be shown to students and used in additional curricular exercises as described in Section 5. The instructor can export the current database at any time and load new databases onto the platform. Additionally, Fakesbook includes a secondary tool which can be used to populate the database with a network of generated users, which is intended to be used if example user profiles or graphs with specific shape are required.

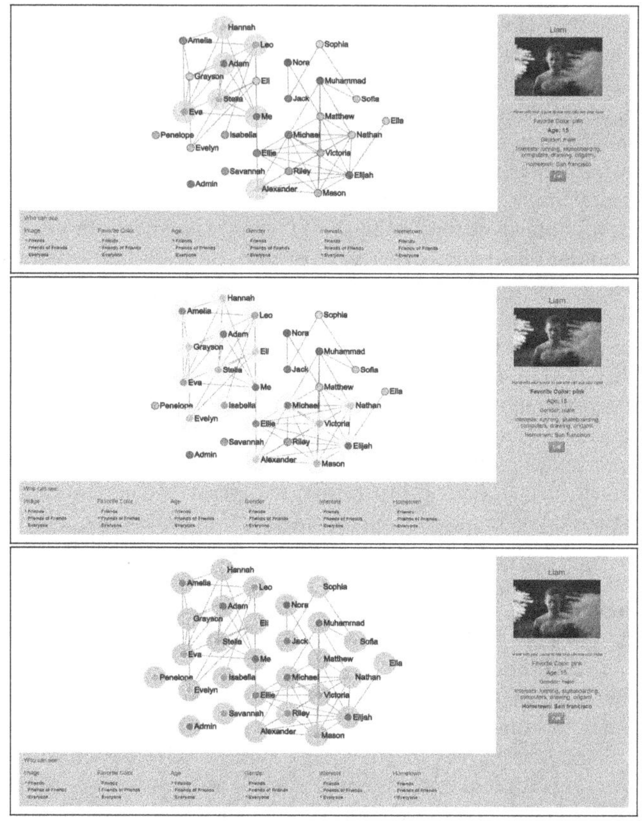

Figure 3: Top: example Fakesbook graph with the *friends* of the currently logged in user highlighted in green. Middle: example Fakesbook graph with the *friends of friends* and *friends* of the currently logged in user highlighted in yellow. Bottom: example Fakesbook graph with *everyone* highlighted in orange (profile image from public domain).

```
('Grayson', 'female', '19.jpg', 'red', 'board games, body building, mountain biking, juggling, coin collecting, ', 'San Jose')
('Harper', 'female', '22.jpg', 'blue', 'stamp collecting, painting, snowboarding, bird watching, frogs, ', 'San Francisco')
('Chloe', 'female', '10.jpg', 'blue', 'computers, skateboarding, hiking, football, sewing, ', 'Los Angeles')
('Michael', 'female', '23.jpg', 'blue', 'robotics, rock climbing, body building, writing, cosplaying, ', 'Los Angeles')
('Nova', 'female', '24.jpg', 'pink', 'sewing, coin collecting, astronomy, yoga, ', 'San Francisco')
('Evelyn', 'male', '13.jpg', 'blue', 'knitting, snowboarding, stamp collecting, cars, hiking, ', 'San Diego')
('Daniel', 'male', '1.jpg', 'blue', 'football, snowboarding, chess, origami, sewing, ', 'San Francisco')
('Natalie', 'male', '18.jpg', 'green', 'rugby, computers, drawing, cooking, ', 'San Francisco')
('Oliver', 'male', '0.jpg', 'purple', 'botany, snowboarding, painting, sculpture, running, ', 'San Jose')
('Emma', 'female', '8.jpg', 'purple', 'video games, running, coin collecting, computers, skiing, ', 'San Jose')
('Bella', 'female', '9.jpg', 'red', 'sculpture, writing, painting, archaeology, magic tricks, ', 'San Diego')
('Levi', 'female', '26.jpg', 'red', 'basketball, skiing, frisbee, rockets, painting, ', 'Los Angeles')
('Joseph', 'female', '3.jpg', 'yellow', 'yoga, chess, archaeology, skateboarding, robotics, ', 'San Diego')
('Zoey', 'male', '17.jpg', 'green', 'puzzles, cosplaying, robotics, rockets, juggling, ', 'San Jose')
('Julian', 'female', '12.jpg', 'orange', 'computers, painting, space, cooking, ', 'San Diego')
('Scarlett', 'female', '5.jpg', 'pink', 'astronomy, board games, chess, origami, bird watching, ', 'Los Angeles')
('Elena', 'female', '15.jpg', 'orange', 'writing, body building, puzzles, origami, snowboarding, ', 'San Jose')
('Asher', 'male', '14.jpg', 'purple', 'snakes, stamp collecting, frogs, sailing, space, ', 'Fresno')
```

Figure 4: An example of Fakesbook user data saved and stored as an ASCII text file. Such a file can be used to start a lab without the need for user registration and can also be shown to students and used in subsequent exercises.

Implementation: Fakesbook is backed by a Python/Flask [4] webserver, uses the Twisted [18] module for parallelization, an SQLite [16] relational database, and an extensive D3.js [2] frontend. The Flask webserver communicates with the database to store and update user data, and to serve that user data upon request over HTTP. The Twisted layer wraps the Flask webserver in order to parallelize the application through multi-threading to maintain responsiveness under load. The D3.js frontend runs in the user's browser, rendering the user interface and visualizations while requesting the latest social network graph data from the server, and forwarding user inputs such as registration to Flask for storage. See Figure 5 for an overview of the platform architecture.

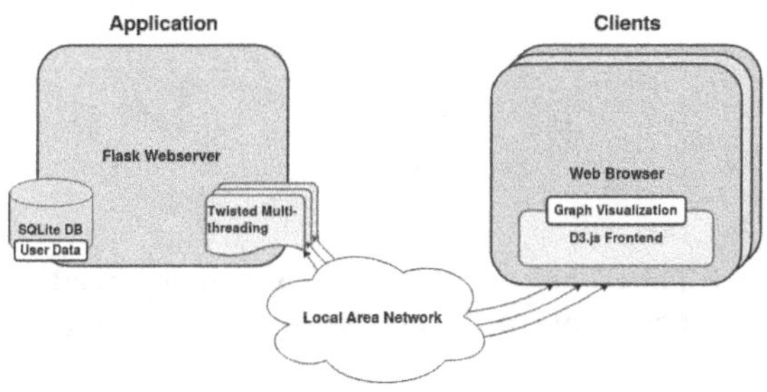

Figure 5: Fakesbook platform architecture.

This lightweight client-side rendering architecture, paired with relatively small class sizes (~25 students), allows us to instantiate the platform in constrained environments, such as on a laptop in a classroom, while providing near real-time updates to graph structure visualizations. The user interface provides immediate feedback for user actions where possible by allowing the visualization to update asynchronously with the backend.

Keeping to information security principles, privacy settings are evaluated in Flask rather than in the frontend, and the data sent to each client is replaced with *Hidden* where appropriate.

5 PEDAGOGICAL APPROACH

Instructional setting: Fakesbook is meant to be used in a lab setting under direction from an instructor, and our curriculum is intended for small classes with access to workstations with web browsers that can be directed to a local server running the platform. Instructor presence is critical in that reflection and active learning activities are central to our curriculum, and these participation-based activities are challenging when class sizes grow larger. However, the platform is not restricted to a particular curriculum and we hope can be extended to support additional learning outcomes.

Warm-up: To motivate students to start thinking about social networks and how people and data might be connected, the lab starts by asking students to use pen and paper to draw out their own immediate social network. Figure 6 shows an example network created by a participating student. This warm-up guides students to start thinking about graphs, social networks, and privacy in a way that is inclusive and scaffolded, supporting students with perhaps little interest or familiarity with the technologies that implement social networking. We then transition to a discussion about social networking companies and applications to set our context.

Building a social network (organic): Next, we direct students to create a profile on Fakesbook, leading them through profile creation and encouraging realistic inputs for "interests," while allowing them to withhold other information they may feel uncomfortable sharing. Once accounts are made, we allow for the evolution of an organic graph structure as students 'add friends' with their in-class peers and discover Fakesbook features. An example of an organic graph is shown in Figure 7. We ask students to observe graph

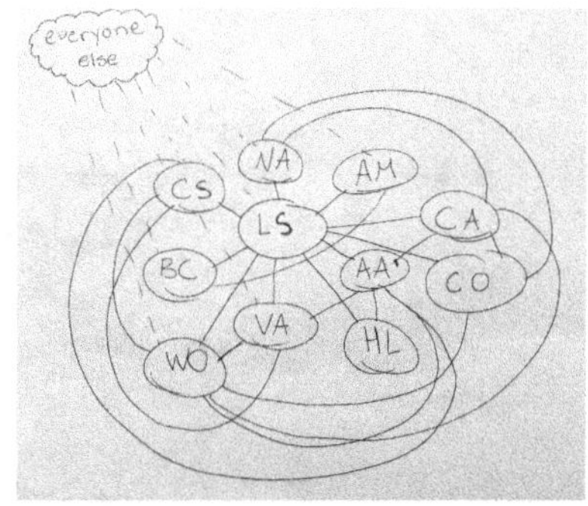

Figure 6: A participants hand drawn social network.

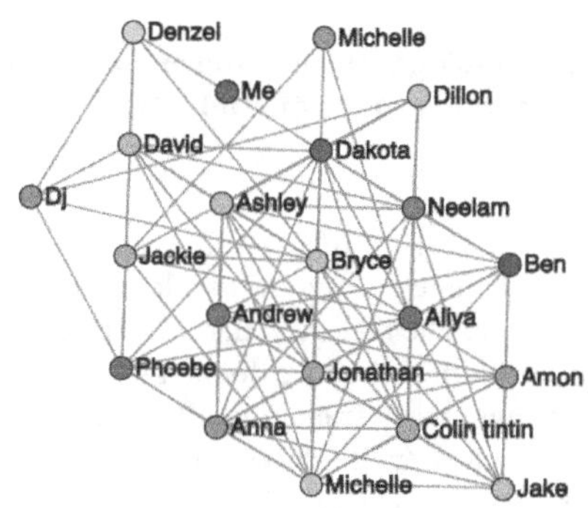

Figure 7: Example of an organically generated Fakesbook graph.

structure and discuss how they went about creating connections. Then we encourage the students to check who else can access their profile data, and change their privacy settings and observe the effects of the changes. Through this interaction we leverage the studied benefits of visualization paired with active learning to impart familiarity with and encourage critical analysis of privacy settings [5, 9]. Reflection questions at this stage include:

- How connected is the graph?
- Are any friend-of-a-friend connections surprising?

Building a social network (guided): In our experience, we have found that the majority of the student groups tend to create atypical social networking graphs (i.e. overly inclusive to all, with everyone friending everyone else, or overly reticent with few connections between those present). Essentially, creating a social network constrained to the fellow participants of the lab setting, which might include many unfamiliar peers, is abnormal to normal social networks with much larger sets of users. As we want our subsequent exercises to be applied to a more typical social network [6] (with clusters of highly connected groups and few edges between these groups), we then lead the students to create a new graph. As before, students create a 'realistic' profile, however, they are required to

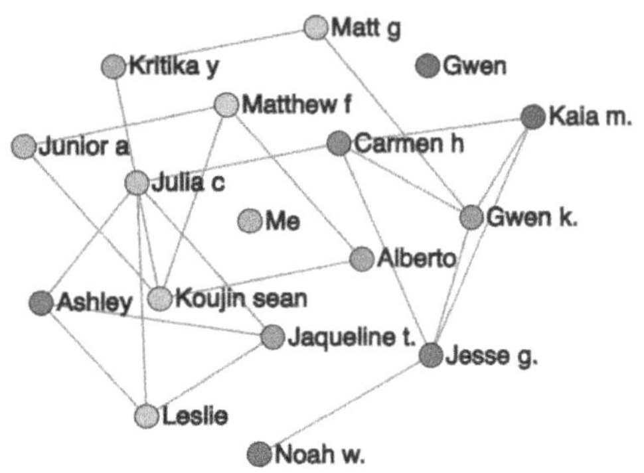

Figure 8: A Fakesbook graph showing an example of a graph generated by separate groups of students.

list at least three interests in their profiles and to use the 'hometown' field to simulate 'checking in' to a location (i.e. Starbucks Cafe, school, etc., to mimic the 'checking in' feature of many social networking applications). Then we divide the students into small groups and task them with 'friending' all other members within their group. Once each group is fully connected we select one or two students from each group and ask them to friend another student in a different group, continuing in this manner until links between all the groups are created. Figure 8 shows an example of one of these graphs. Students are asked to review and update their privacy settings as they might typically set them, with the requirement that everyone have their profile image be visible to everyone.

Finally, we ask students to perform an adversarial analysis of profile data use. Students are asked to use the platform to discover useful marketing or identifying information about students in the other groups. For example, students are asked to identify where each member of other group is located and potential products to advertise to the other group members. Students usually exhibit a high level of engagement as they figure out how to exploit the graph and connections to learn about one another. Participants commonly express surprise at how easy it was to find information about one another, either directly or via friends (and friends of friends). We conclude this lesson by discussing results and strategies and revisiting social networking applications motivations with regards to data collection and security.

Context-based introduction to programming: To further help students see behind the curtain, we show students the text file that demonstrates how profile data can be digitally stored. Using this as a starting point, we transition to an exercise focused on data and encryption. We lead students through an introductory programming exercise to encrypt and decrypt this text data using Python and a Caesar cipher. We provide and carefully discuss base code to introduce variables, loops, characters, arrays, and the necessary mathematical operators. This final lab exercise is meant to empower students to see that computer programming is accessible and that

```
for k in perms:
    if perms[k] == 0:
        if is_friend:
            show[k] = usermap[k]
        else:
            show[k] = "hidden"
    elif perms[k] == 1:
        if is_friend or is_fof:
            show[k] = usermap[k]
        else:
            show[k] = "hidden"
    elif perms[k] == 2:
        show[k] = usermap[k]
```

Figure 9: Fakesbook code shown to students relating programming concepts to the platform.

they can control how data might be stored and communicated between computers. At this point, we also show students a key segment of code from the Fakesbook platform, shown in Figure 9.

This code segment is associated with privacy control and sharing it allows us to emphasize the connection between the platform itself, programming, and privacy and security concepts.

6 RESULTS

Fakesbook has been used over a two-year period to expose hundreds of secondary school students to concepts related to cybersecurity and privacy. In our experience, the platform generates a good deal of student excitement, engagement, and ultimately learning for the lab participants.

Fakesbook was first used in Spring 2017 during an event designed to introduce secondary school students to computer science. Four sections of ~25 students used the platform in its alpha state for a short lab of 30 minutes and provided feedback.

Fakesbook was then used in Summer 2017 in the 'cyber track' for three separate week-long summer camps targeted at introducing secondary school students to engineering. Specifically, the lab was used in Cal Poly, EPIC: Engineering Possibilities in College, which is a unique summer program for middle- and high-school students. The camp aims to include 50% underrepresented groups in engineering including female, first-generation, and low-income students. Each Fakesbook lab was a two-hour experience using our curriculum with three groups of ~20 students participating. Anecdotally, students were positively engaged in the exercises, and particularly enjoyed the adversarial mining of other students' data. Based on observations, further revisions to the lab were made, including adding more instructor direction on friending to produce more typical social network graphs. A desired attribute is fewer friend connections per node, as excessive connectivity blurs the distinction between the *friends of friends* and *everyone* groups and is atypical in real social network graphs [6].

Fakesbook was used again in Summer 2018 in both a designated 'cyber' track and a general 'engineering' track over a three-week period for EPIC. Six groups of ~20 students participated in the lab. Students completed pre- and post-lab surveys assessing their attitudes on online privacy and security and their thoughts on the Fakesbook platform. Pre-lab questions included:

(1) "Have you ever changed the privacy settings from the default on any of your social media accounts?" (yes: 91.7% No: 6.6%)

(2) "Overall, how important is it to you to keep your online data private? (images, status updates, location)?" (5-point Likert scale; ≥4: 81%, 3: 2.4%, 4: 30.6%, 5: 50.4%)
(3) "What data do you think would be useful for social media companies to collect from users?" (free response not coded)

Post-lab questions included:

(1) "Overall, how important is it to you to keep your online data private? (images, status updates, location)?" (5-point Likert scale; ≥4: 91.6%, 3: 5.6%, 4: 23.1%, 5: 68.5%)
(2) "How likely to talk to your parents or your friends about data and privacy online?" (5-point Likert scale; ≥4: 50%, 3: 27.8%, 4: 27.8%, 5: 22.2%)
(3) "Did working with the 'fakesbook' application and seeing a graph of a social network help you think about privacy and computer security?" (yes: 86.1%, maybe: 11.1% no: 2.8%)
(4) "Any comments or final thoughts?" (free response, see below)

The pre-lab surveys indicate that students were already thinking about privacy and social media prior to the lab, while post-lab surveys indicate they deepened their knowledge and engagement from participating in the lab. When asked in the pre-lab survey, "Have you ever changed the privacy settings from the default on any of your social media accounts?", eight of the 121 students indicated that they had never changed their privacy settings, two indicated 'N/A' (likely students without social media accounts), while the remaining 111 students responded with 'yes'. This indicates that participants started their lab experience with some engagement with social networking privacy settings.

When asked in the pre-lab survey, "Overall, how important is it to you to keep your online data private? (images, status updates, location)?" on a five-point scale, prior to the lab, the average score was 4.22 (with a standard deviation of 0.98). After the lab, students increased their self-evaluation of the importance of online privacy, responding to the same question with an average score of 4.57 (standard deviation of 0.72). This increase in the importance of online privacy indicates that the students gained respect for the importance of privacy and security due to the lab activities.

We also asked in the post-lab survey about the utility of the Fakesbook platform. Specifically, "Did working with the 'fakesbook' application and seeing a graph of a social network help you think about privacy and computer security?" Participants responded very positively, with 86% responding that it was helpful, and 11% responding that 'maybe' it was helpful.

In addition, the post-lab survey allowed for students to voluntarily add "Any comments or final thoughts." Out of the 55 voluntary written comments about the lab, 45 (80%) were very positive, along the lines of "this was my favorite lab" or "The 'fakesbook' application was extremely helpful in visualizing online connections!". The remaining 10 comments primarily related feedback about the 'friending' process in Fakesbook or the challenges of the Caesar cipher python coding portion of the lab, which we are taking into consideration for future work. The fact that close to 40% of all participants voluntarily wrote very positive comments attests to their enthusiasm for the lab activity.

Another way to measure the impact of the lab experience is to examine student's plans for reflecting on the lab and sharing the information with others. In the post-lab survey we asked students about the likelihood of them talking to their parents and friends about privacy. The majority, 77.8%, of students rated that they were likely or very likely to speak to others about the topic, which indicates the positive impact of the lab experience for participants.

7 CONCLUSION & FUTURE WORK

Minors and young adults today are creating data-rich online presences on social networks. Through a combination of our platform and curriculum, we seek to convey familiarity with the concepts of online privacy and risk management and to promote student understanding of their agency in these regards. We devise our approach to leverage the well-studied pedagogical efficacy of interactive visualization and adversarial thinking. Through this combination, we seek to promote online safety for young users who might put their personal data at risk before fully understanding the implications of their actions. It is our goal that this exercise will empower students to control their data and the context-based programming assignment might encourage them to consider learning more programming. Fakesbook is available on GitHub, https://github.com/Fakesbook/Fakesbook and interested educators can contribute to the project via use and software development.

Future work includes supporting self-guided student exercises, e.g. "You just changed your privacy settings, how many people do you think can see your hometown now", which would enable the platform to support embedded assessments and more independent student exploration.

In addition, to validate our progress toward privacy education, future work includes following up with students after their experience with the platform. The majority of students indicated that they were likely to speak to others about the topic, however, the addition of follow-up interviews would allow us to better measure the impact of our tool on short- and long-term behavior.

Finally, we envision that this platform could be extended as an educational tool. For example, further work on the graph visualization could help students see the relationships between sub-groups in the graph. In addition, we are interested in extending the visualizations on the platform to communicate graph theory concepts which are central to common algorithms in computer science.

ACKNOWLEDGMENT

The authors would like to thank the organizers and volunteers of Expanding Engineering and of EPIC. This paper is based on research supported by the National Science Foundation under Grant No. 1628726. Any opinions, findings, and conclusions or recommendations expressed in this material are those of the authors and do not necessarily reflect the views of the National Science Foundation.

REFERENCES

[1] Erinn Atwater, Cecylia Bocovich, Urs Hengartner, and Ian Goldberg. 2017. Live Lesson: Netsim: Network simulation and hacking for high schoolers. In *2017 USENIX Workshop on Advances in Security Education, ASE 2017, Vancouver, BC, Canada, August 15, 2017.* https://www.usenix.org/conference/ase17/workshop-program/presentation/atwater
[2] D3. 2017. D3.js - Data-Driven Documents. (2017). https://d3js.org/
[3] Facebook. 2017. Company info - stats. (2017). https://newsroom.fb.com/company-info/ [Online, accessed 26-Jan-2018].
[4] Flask. 2017. Flask (A Python Microframework). (2017). http://flask.pocoo.org/
[5] Scott Grissom, Myles F. McNally, and Tom Naps. 2003. Algorithm Visualization in CS Education: Comparing Levels of Student Engagement. In *Proceedings of the*

2003 ACM Symposium on Software Visualization (SoftVis '03). ACM, New York, NY, USA, 87–94. https://doi.org/10.1145/774833.774846
[6] A. Hashmi, F. Zaidi, A. Sallaberry, and T. Mehmood. 2012. Are All Social Networks Structurally Similar?. In *2012 IEEE/ACM International Conference on Advances in Social Networks Analysis and Mining*. 310–314. https://doi.org/10.1109/ASONAM.2012.59
[7] A. Lenhart, M. Madden, A. Smith, K. Purcell, K. Zickuhr, and L. Rainie. 2011. *Teens, Kindness and Cruelty on Social Network Sites*. Technical Report. PewResearch-Center. http://www.pewinternet.org/~/media//Files/Reports/2011/PIP_Teens_Kindness_Cruelty_SNS_Report_Nov_2011_FINAL_110711.pdf
[8] Marina Moore, Maximilian Zinkus, Nathan Lemay, Zachary Peterson, and Bruce DeBruhl. 2018. Introducing privacy to undergraduate computing students. *Journal of Computing Sciences in Colleges* 33, 4 (2018), 157–164.
[9] Thomas L. Naps, Guido Rössling, Vicki Almstrum, Wanda Dann, Rudolf Fleischer, Chris Hundhausen, Ari Korhonen, Lauri Malmi, Myles McNally, Susan Rodger, and J. Ángel Velázquez-Iturbide. 2002. Exploring the Role of Visualization and Engagement in Computer Science Education. *SIGCSE Bull.* 35, 2 (June 2002), 131–152. https://doi.org/10.1145/782941.782998
[10] Gregory L. Orgill, Gordon W. Romney, Michael G. Bailey, and Paul M. Orgill. 2004. The Urgency for Effective User Privacy-education to Counter Social Engineering Attacks on Secure Computer Systems. In *Proceedings of the 5th Conference on Information Technology Education (CITC5 '04)*. ACM, New York, NY, USA, 177–181. https://doi.org/10.1145/1029533.1029577
[11] T. Scheponik, A. T. Sherman, D. DeLatte, D. Phatak, L. Oliva, J. Thompson, and G. L. Herman. 2016. How students reason about Cybersecurity concepts. In *2016 IEEE Frontiers in Education Conference (FIE)*. 1–5. https://doi.org/10.1109/FIE.2016.7757363
[12] Dino Schweitzer and Jeff Boleng. 2009. Designing Web Labs for Teaching Security Concepts. *J. Comput. Sci. Coll.* 25, 2 (Dec. 2009), 39–45. http://dl.acm.org/citation.cfm?id=1629036.1629042
[13] Dino Schweitzer and Wayne Brown. 2009. Using Visualization to Teach Security. *J. Comput. Sci. Coll.* 24, 5 (May 2009), 143–150. http://dl.acm.org/citation.cfm?id=1516595.1516626
[14] M. Sharples, R. Graber, C. Harrison, and K. Logan. 2009. E-safety and Web 2.0 for children aged 11-16. *Journal of Computer Assisted Learning* 25, 1 (2009), 70–84. https://doi.org/10.1111/j.1365-2729.2008.00304.x
[15] Steve Sheng, Bryant Magnien, Ponnurangam Kumaraguru, Alessandro Acquisti, Lorrie Faith Cranor, Jason Hong, and Elizabeth Nunge. 2007. Anti-Phishing Phil: The Design and Evaluation of a Game That Teaches People Not to Fall for Phish. In *Proceedings of the 3rd Symposium on Usable Privacy and Security (SOUPS '07)*. ACM, New York, NY, USA, 88–99. https://doi.org/10.1145/1280680.1280692
[16] SQLite. 2017. SQLite. (2017). https://sqlite.org/
[17] Jun Tao, Jun Ma, Melissa Keranen, Jean Mayo, and Ching-Kuang Shene. 2012. ECvisual: A Visualization Tool for Elliptic Curve Based Ciphers. In *Proceedings of the 43rd ACM Technical Symposium on Computer Science Education (SIGCSE '12)*. ACM, New York, NY, USA, 571–576. https://doi.org/10.1145/2157136.2157298
[18] Twisted. 2017. Twisted. (2017). https://twistedmatrix.com/trac/
[19] U.S. Department of Homeland Security (DHS) U.S. National Security Agency (NSA). 2018. 2019 Knowledge Units. (2018). https://www.iad.gov/NIETP/documents/Requirements/CAE-CD_2019_Knowledge_Units.pdf
[20] U.S. Department of Homeland Security (DHS) U.S. National Security Agency (NSA). 2018. National Centers of Academic Excellence in Cyber Defense (CAE-CD) Designation Program Guidance. (2018). https://www.iad.gov/NIETP/documents/Requirements/CAE_Program_Guidance.pdf
[21] A. Wang, S. Komanduri, P.G. Leon, G. Norcie, A Acquisti, and L.F. Cranor. 2011. "I regretted the minute I pressed share": A Qualitative Study of Regrets on Facebook. *Symposium on Usable Privacy and Security* (2011), 16. http://cups.cs.cmu.edu/soups/2011/proceedings/a10_Wang.pdf
[22] Xiaohong Yuan, Percy Vega, Yaseen Qadah, Ricky Archer, Huiming Yu, and Jinsheng Xu. 2010. Visualization Tools for Teaching Computer Security. *ACM Trans. Comput. Educ.* 9, 4, Article 20 (Jan. 2010), 28 pages. https://doi.org/10.1145/1656255.1656258
[23] L. Zhang-Kennedy, S. Chiasson, and R. Biddle. 2013. Password advice shouldn't be boring: Visualizing password guessing attacks. In *2013 APWG eCrime Researchers Summit*. 1–11. https://doi.org/10.1109/eCRS.2013.6805770

Primary School Teachers' Conceptions of Computational Thinking

Megean Garvin
University of Maryland, Baltimore County
Baltimore, MD
mgarvin@umbc.edu

Heather Killen
University of Maryland
College Park, MD
hkillen@umd.edu

Jan Plane
University of Maryland
College Park, MD
jplane@cs.umd.edu

David Weintrop
University of Maryland
College Park, MD
weintrop@umd.edu

ABSTRACT

Computational thinking (CT) is increasingly becoming a part of the K-12 educational landscape. While high schools with computer science teachers or technology coaches on staff are well positioned to help teachers integrate computational thinking into instruction, early childhood through middle schools (grades p-8) are often less well equipped. Further, the concept of CT is often poorly defined, especially as it relates to younger learners. Despite these challenges, teachers are being asked to integrate CT into other content lessons. To understand if and how this is happening, we conducted a statewide survey of primary (early childhood through middle school) Maryland teachers. The survey asked the teachers about their conceptualization of CT, CT resources they rely on, and their comfort levels to provide effective CT instruction for their students. The results of our survey demonstrate that teachers hold diverse views of the concept of CT and use a varied set of instructional resources in their classrooms. The contribution of this work is in helping advance our understanding of the current state of CT in primary classrooms.

CCS CONCEPTS

• **Social and professional topics → Computational thinking**;

KEYWORDS

Computational Thinking, K-8, Teacher Perceptions; Computing across the curriculum, ACM proceedings

ACM Reference Format:

Megean Garvin, Heather Killen, Jan Plane, and David Weintrop. 2019. Primary School Teachers' Conceptions of Computational Thinking. In *Proceedings of the 50th ACM Technical Symposium on Computer Science Education (SIGCSE '19), February 27-March 2, 2019, Minneapolis, MN, USA.* ACM, New York, NY, USA, 7 pages. https://doi.org/10.1145/3287324.3287376

SIGCSE '19, February 27-March 2, 2019, Minneapolis, MN, USA

ACM ISBN 978-1-4503-5890-3/19/02...$15.00
https://doi.org/10.1145/3287324.3287376

1 INTRODUCTION

Computational thinking (CT) was first described as valuable for children to learn and assimilate into their everyday lives by Seymour Papert[1]. Later, CT reemerged in the early twenty first century with the work of Jeannette Wing[2],[3]. Researchers and educators now agree that computational thinking (CT) should be embedded within curricula from early childhood through high school[4],[5],[6],[7]. However, CT encompasses numerous skills, practices, and processes, and an ongoing debate persists as to which are essential to include in a comprehensive CT definition. Levels of complexity from the novice to expert and across the early childhood to high school levels of instruction further complicate defining CT. Globally, attempts to further delineate a definition in the United States[8], Canada[9], England[10], Ireland[11], Greece[12], Turkey[13], and India[14] have resulted in multiple lists defining what CT does and does not include. Literature reviews[13],[11], [15] and various CT pedagogical frameworks and guides [16], [10], [9]provide varying views of CT.

CT is fundamentally needed to study computer science, but it is also useful for understanding concepts within other content disciplines beyond computing[17]. Spurred by policy calls for change and integration within other content disciplines[18], more studies have shown how CT can be successfully integrated in early childhood classrooms[19], within mathematics and science at all levels[20], in social studies and music classes[18] and art classes[21]. Yet, CT integration from early childhood through middle school lags behind the advancements at the high school level. Primary teachers do not always identify themselves as CT integration specialists[22].

In order to gauge and establish a baseline of primary teachers' understanding of CT, a survey was created and distributed across Maryland. In particular, we were interested in the following research questions:

(1) How do primary school teachers (pre-K-8) define computational thinking, and how does their definition inform their classroom resource choices?
(2) How comfortable are primary school teachers to integrate and teach computational thinking?

This study focuses on four constructs to understand primary teachers' conceptualization of CT. First, we ask each teacher to provide a definition of CT. Next, we ask teachers to list resources that they use in their classrooms. We are also interested in determining which subjects teachers currently teach, which lessons they currently integrate CT, and which subjects they believe CT should be integrated. Finally, we had a series of questions to gauge the teachers' comfort with teaching CT.

2 PRIOR WORK

Expert definitions of CT range from a few lines to several pages of complex text. For example, Steve Furber[23]provided a brief definition while referring to CT being applied and integrated into other disciplines. "Computational thinking is the process of recognizing aspects of computation in the world that surrounds us, and applying tools and techniques from Computer Science to understand and reason about both natural and artificial systems and processes (pg.29)." As for the lengthy definitions, CSTA and ISTE (2011) created a one page operational definition including two lists of problem solving processes and skills, and NRC (2010) provides over two pages listing various aspects of definitions from leading experts within the 114 page workshop report on the scope and nature of computational thinking. This lack of a consistent and clear CT definition at the expert level is problematic when attempting to convince teachers to integrate and implement CT in the primary classrooms.

For our purposes, we know that there are two particular documents in the United States that teachers might have at least heard of, if not read. The Next Generation Science Standards[6] includes computational thinking within the science and engineering practice as using mathematics and computational thinking. The more recent K-12 Computer Science Framework (2016) provides the following definition in the glossary: "The human ability to formulate problems so that their solutions can be represented as computational steps or algorithms to be executed by a computer (pg. 260)." However, the framework also provides six pages of text delineating CT practices and how CT is not simply the use of computers. CT "extends beyond the general use of computers or technology in education to include specific skills such as designing algorithms, decomposing problems, and modeling phenomena (pg. 70)." We suspect that teachers might draw upon language from either one of these documents when they provide us with a CT definition.

2.1 Primary Subject Integration Models

Local education agencies (LEAs) in the United States have begun to align themselves to standards and include CT in early childhood through middle school curricula. The two standard models of subject integration include the specialization class and integration within other core content disciplines. The debate over specialization and generalization at these levels has persisted for over 50 years[24]. Even though LEAs have moved away from one classroom teacher who is a generalist and teaches all of the subjects (mathematics, science, English language arts, social studies, music, and art), generalists are still expected to master the core subjects. What has been found is a series of trade-offs between the generalist who would integrate across all subjects within the same classroom, and the specialist who would only focus on one or two subjects to teach across many classes of students[25]. Specialists are able to spend less time planning and typically have deeper content knowledge about the subject that they teach, but in return, they teach a larger number of students and have less time to fully get to know individual students[24]. This particular trade-off is seen as detrimental at the elementary level. For example, a recent study found that teacher specialization at the elementary level led to decreased student achievement and attendance and increased behavioral issues[26]. Fryer argues that the trade-off of less human interaction (between teacher and student) for content driven specialist instruction results in less customization of instruction for students' needs. The concern is that formative classroom assessment which attends to student thinking[27] and feeds back into lesson planning might not occur with the elementary specialists; however, with more time to focus on one or two subjects, specialists report making more meaningful adjustments to their classroom instruction for their students[25].

The subjects that first were migrated from the generalist to a specialist included art and music. Art elementary specialists emerged in most schools through the end of the 20th century only to fear losing their programs due to budget cuts and a focus on the emerging high stakes testing[28]. Art specialist are often the only art teacher in the school, and this led to less professional development opportunities and isolationism at the elementary level[29]. Issues with the lack of professional development and isolationism have also been reported with K-12 computer science teachers[30]. Regardless of the subject and even when given the same amount of planning time during the school day, the isolated specialist is forced to connect to colleagues who are external to their school and who may not have the same school norms or constraints. This particular trade-off is problematic for individual specialists but can be overcome with school and LEA support. Careful consideration of these trade-offs needs to be evaluated by LEAs as they move forward with CT integration.

3 METHODS

For this work, we are using the state of Maryland as a case study to understand how primary teachers conceptualize CT. LEAs must provide students with access to well-rounded curricula and demonstrate that a percentage of "8th grade students (are) enrolled in fine arts, physical education, health, and computational learning." The way that the state has written this implies a preference for CT to be taught by a specialist as it is listed with other disciples which are typically taught by specialists, but in Maryland, LEAs have local control over curricula and teaching assignments. CT might be taught by specialists and/or generalists.

The 2018 Maryland Computing Education Landscape survey was sent electronically via email to public teachers in all of the 24 Maryland LEAs. The primary teacher subsection of questions yielded 130 responses. These teachers were employed by 20 of the 24 Maryland LEAs. For this study, primary teachers with varying professional development experiences were surveyed from across the state of Maryland. Maryland contains urban, suburban, and rural communities from the Appalachian Mountains to the Chesapeake Bay and Atlantic Ocean. Each teacher provided responses to four survey constructs: CT concept, resources, integration, and comfort. (See Figure 1.)

The first construct is the teachers' conceptualization of CT. Teachers were asked to provide their own CT definition. Following the

Primary Teacher CT Survey Items		
Constructs	Items	Response Formats
CT Concept	Please provide your definition of computational thinking.	Open Ended
Resources	I have used the following resources in my classroom.	Check all that apply and other open ended
	Whom within your school do you seek out for computing education assistance?	Check all that apply and other open ended
	Outside of your school, where do you go for additional ideas, resources, or help to improve your computing education instruction?	Check all that apply and other open ended
Integration	I currently teach the following subjects.	Check all that apply and other open ended
	For which subjects are you currently integrating computational thinking?	Check all that apply and other open ended
	For which subjects do you believe that computational thinking should be integrated into lessons?	Check all that apply and other open ended
Comfort	I have received adequate training for the computing education material I teach.	Likert Scale
	I am comfortable integrating computational thinking into my lessons.	Likert Scale
	I am comfortable creating my own computing integrated classroom materials.	Likert Scale
	I am comfortable teaching computer programming.	Likert Scale

Figure 1: The 2018 Maryland Computing Education Landscape Survey subsection of the primary teacher survey constructs, items, and response formats.

Glaser and Strauss[31] constant comparative method, each CT definition response was categorized by content based on known CT expert definitions and additional themes that emerged within the teachers' responses. Ultimately, 10 categories were coded across all 130 responses: algorithm, abstraction, decomposition, problem solving, programming or coding, using mathematics, using a computer or technology, digital citizenship, critical thinking, and do not know. An IRR analysis was performed to assess the degree that coders consistently assigned categorical themes to the respondents' definitions of CT. Cohen's kappa[32] was computed and indicates almost perfect agreement, kappa = 0.984[33]. The IRR analysis suggested that coders had a high degree of agreement in assigning categorical themes to respondents' definitions of CT and therefore, statistical power for subsequent analysis is not substantially reduced.

In addition to the definitions, teachers provided resource information that they use within their classroom. The classroom resources resulted in 89 total resources which were further categorized into resource types including: application or game (18), device (15), device with lessons (6), learning management software (2), lessons (1), programming software (19), programming software with lessons (27), and videos or learning support resources (1). Teachers also indicated internal and external school resources that they use to help improve their computing education instruction. The integration construct asked teachers which subjects they currently teach, in which subjects they currently integrate CT, and which subjects they believe CT should be integrated.

Finally, the primary teachers rated their comfort level on Likert scales by providing the extent to which they agreed with 4 statements. Chronbach's alpha[34] reliability test was conducted on the comfort results for four comfort level measures (adequate training, CT integration into lessons, creating their own CT integrated classroom materials, and teaching computer programming). The Chronbach's alpha level is .84 indicating that there is inter-term survey reliability between these four items. Furthermore, deleting any of the comfort level items would not significantly increase the alpha level.

4 RESULTS

The data was analyzed within and between constructs. Here, we provide the data within each construct, and then, we provide a limited analysis between constructs.

4.1 CT Conceptualization

As expected, the teachers provided an assortment of CT definitions, varying in content and length. Figure 2 contains example definitions and the codes that were applied to each definition. For example, one teacher defined CT as "knowing how to use computers" and another teacher submitted "computer's way of solving problems." Both of these definitions were coded for using a computer and both are insufficient CT definitions. Some teachers used expert terminology such as "computational thinking is made up of 4 components that do not all need to be present for it to be considered CT. The components (decomposition, abstraction, patterns, and algorithm) are used to solve problems." Other teachers used phrases like "break the problem up into smaller steps" which was coded as decomposition. Teachers most frequently included problem solving in their definitions followed by algorithms and using a computer or technology. Ten total teachers (1 early childhood, 4 elementary, and 5 middle school) did not provide a definition. (See Figure 3.) Only 4 teachers mention problem solving, algorithm, and abstraction in their definition, and only 2 teachers mention algorithm, abstraction, and decomposition. There were 85 teachers who never mention algorithm, abstraction, and decomposition together, and 55 teachers mention problem solving but not algorithm, abstraction, and decomposition together.

Primary Teachers' CT Definitions	
Please provide your definition of computational thinking.	**Codes**
Knowing how to use computers	Using a computer/Technology
Being able to solve a problem by looking at all the possible solutions- by using technology or no technology	Problem Solving Using a computer/Technology
Computational thinking is a students' development of digital citizenship and ability to solve problems using the formulas and accessible technological platforms readily available.	Problem Solving, Using Mathematics, Using a computer/Technology
Computational thinking is being able to identify the problem, break the problem up into smaller steps, make abstractions as needed, and then solve the problem.	Algorithm, Abstraction, Decomposition, Problem Solving, Digital citizenship
computer's way of solving problems	Problem Solving, Using a computer/Technology
Thinking like a computer to follow a set of operations/algorithms to complete a project	Algorithm
pretty much learning to think like a computer. pattern matching, analyzing data and creating solutions using step by step solutions such as algorithms.	Algorithm, Abstraction, Problem Solving
Computational thinking is made up of 4 components that do not all need to be present for it to be considered CT. The components (decomposition, abstraction, patterns, and algorithm) are used to solve problems.	Algorithm, Abstraction, Decomposition, Problem Solving
Using trial and error and persistence to work out a series of steps to solve a problem.	Algorithm, Problem Solving,
Using problem solving skills (debug, decompose etc.) to systemically solve problems and/or design or create solutions to real world problems.	Algorithm, Decomposition, Problem Solving

Figure 2: The primary teachers' CT definitions and the codes that were applied to each definition.

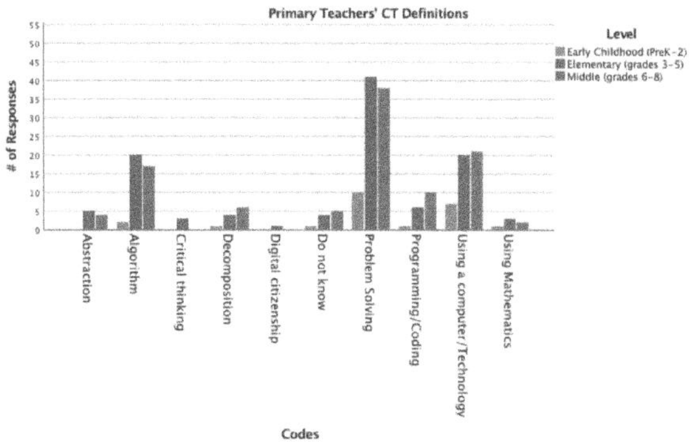

Figure 3: The frequency of primary teachers' CT definition coded responses.

4.2 Resources

Teachers have multiple resources including classroom materials and colleagues to assist them as they teach CT. The 89 classroom resource materials available and listed by primary teachers were coded and placed into 9 broader categories. The teachers prefer resources that contain *programming software and lessons* and *devices and lessons* more often than all other types of resources. Both of these resources provide the teacher with curricula support, which enables the teacher to easily integrate and adapt the provided lessons into their daily lesson plans. Teachers also reported *using games, applications, learning management systems,* and *videos or learning support resources*; however, these resources do not necessarily promote CT. The inclusion of these classroom resources might in part be due to the confusion some teachers demonstrated in their CT definition. Simply using technology does not suggest that students are engaged in CT. (See Figure 4.) Respondents provided

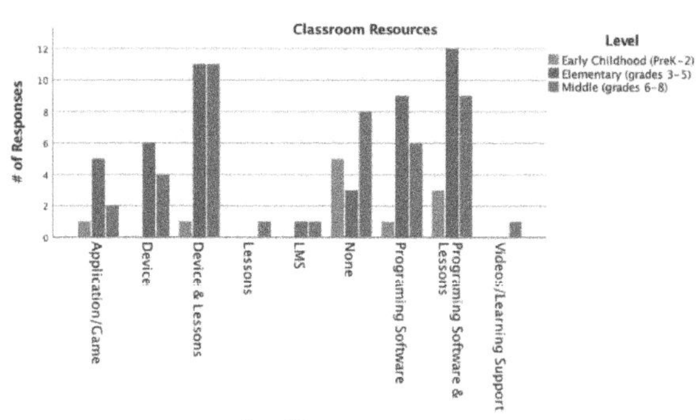

Figure 4: The frequency of responses for the types of classroom resources reported by primary teachers.

additional insight into where they turn for lesson and classroom support when integrating CT. The majority of teachers responded that they seek the assistance of a *fellow teacher in their school* (53) or *a fellow teacher in another school* (51). *Media center specialists* (34) and *technology teachers* (38) within primary schools provide support to their colleagues. (See Figure 5). There were 6 teachers who responded that they rely on themselves and 32 who claim that they do not have any resource support, pointing to possible isolationism. Further analysis through a crosstabulation of teachers

Primary Teacher CT Resource Support			
Within the School	Fellow Teacher	53	31.5%
	Technology Teacher	38	22.6%
	Media Center Specialist	34	20.2%
	Do not have	32	19.0%
	Myself	6	3.6%
	IT Support	2	1.2%
	STAT Teacher	1	0.6%
	School Administrator	1	0.6%
	Paraprofessional	1	0.6%
	SUBTOTAL	168	100.0%
External to School	Websites	105	44.5%
	Fellow Teacher in another school	51	21.6%
	Supervisor/Central Office Personnel	33	14.0%
	Community meet ups	8	3.4%
	Media Center Specialist in another school	7	3.0%
	Local Library	7	3.0%
	Conferences/Workshops	6	2.5%
	Local Nonprofit	6	2.5%
	Professional Development	4	1.7%
	Family/Friend	4	1.7%
	Technology department	2	0.8%
	College Professor	1	0.4%
	None	2	0.8%
	SUBTOTAL	236	100.0%

Figure 5: The primary teachers' responses listing the internal and external supports that they use while integrating CT into their classrooms.

by level and subjects taught layered with internal school resources revealed that of the 6 respondents who indicated themselves, there were 5 technology teachers (2 elementary and 3 middle school) and 1 teacher who teaches elementary science. The respondents who claim to have no support in their school included teachers who teach technology at each level (1 early childhood, 12 elementary, and 9 middle school). Other than turning to another teacher or media center specialist in another school, teachers rely on assistance from *websites* (105) and *supervisors or central office personnel* (33). There were not many teachers who attended *community meet ups* (8), *conferences or workshops* (6), or *professional development* (4). Family, friends, and even a college professor are also listed by respondents as resources.

4.3 Integration

Approximately, half of the respondents (67) indicated that they were not currently teaching technology in their classrooms. The other respondents who indicated that they currently taught technology were teaching within the primary level (5 early childhood, 27 elementary, and 31 middle school). The teachers who teach technology, mathematics, science, and English language arts were more likely to integrate CT into their lessons.

All but 2 teachers believed that CT should be integrated into primary lessons. Most teachers responded that CT should be integrated in technology (117), science (115), and mathematics (117)lessons. English language arts (83), social studies (77), art (78), and music (81) are not far behind with teachers acknowledging that CT should be integrated in these subjects areas as well. The higher responses to integrate CT across these subject areas is promising, but the previous issues among CT definitions and classroom resource selection raises our concerns that there is a disconnection between teachers' willingness to integrate CT and their CT conceptualizations. This potentially increases the margin of error for CT integration.

Primary Teacher CT Integration Responses						
Subject	**Currently Teaching**	**% Currently Teaching**	**Currently Integrating**	**% Currently Integrating**	**Believe Should Integrate CT**	**% Believe Should Integrate CT**
Mathematics	42	14.2%	37	16.4%	117	17.5%
Science	45	15.2%	35	15.6%	115	17.2%
English Language Arts	44	14.9%	34	15.1%	83	12.4%
Phonics	20	6.8%	0	0	0	0
Spelling	25	8.4%	0	0	0	0
Social Studies	37	12.5%	22	9.8%	77	11.5%
Art	0	0	4	1.8%	78	11.6%
Music	3	1.0%	3	1.3%	81	12.1%
Technology/CS	63	21.3%	58	25.8%	117	17.5%
Media	5	1.7%	3	1.3%	0	0
STEM	5	1.7%	0	0	0	0
Engineering	2	0.7%	1	0.4%	0	0
PLTW	3	1.0%	2	0.9%	0	0
ELL	2	0.7%	0	0	0	0
None	0	0	0	0	2	0.3%
Total	**296**	**100.0%**	**225**	**100.0%**	**670**	**100.0%**

Figure 6: Primary teachers indicated which subjects they currently teach, which subjects they currently integrate CT, and which subjects they believe CT should be integrated.

4.4 Comfort Levels

Teacher comfort was reported by answering Likert scale questions. The majority of primary teachers who responded to the survey reported being comfortable teaching programming (51.5%), creating integrated CT classroom materials (52.3%), and integrating CT into lessons (66.2%). Despite the higher comfort levels in these areas, only 43.8% of the teachers agreed that they had received adequate training. (See Figure 7.) An average of 26 teachers (20%) chose to remain neutral and not provide their opinion on all four measures. The 10 teachers who did not know a CT definition answered these questions in interesting patterns. There were 3 teachers who indicated that they were comfortable integrating CT into lessons and 5 teachers who believed that they can create CT classroom materials.

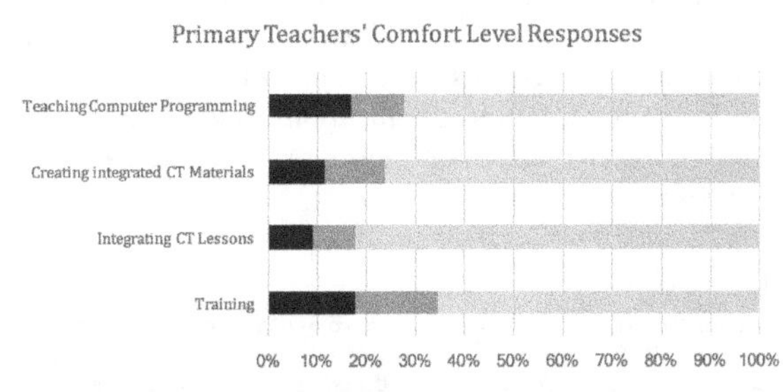

Figure 7: Primary teachers indicate their level of comfort teaching programming, creating integrated CT classroom materials, integrating CT into lessons, and receiving adequate training.

4.5 Between Constructs

The patterns between the four constructs provide additional insight into primary teachers' understanding of and support for teaching CT. By crosstabulating CT definition codes with the types of classroom resources teachers report using, we can determine the frequency of teachers who indicate using programming software with and without lessons and those that most frequently includes *problem solving*, *using a computer*, and *algorithms* in their CT definition. A similar pattern is seen with teachers who indicated using devices with or without lessons. The *using a computer* CT definition code was the only one which was indicated within each type of classroom resource. We are also interested in determining which

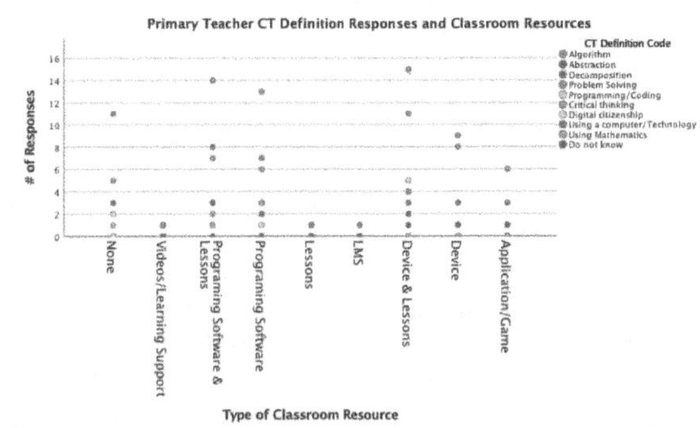

Figure 8: The frequency of primary teachers' CT definition codes by the types of classroom resources.

classroom resource type is most frequently indicated by frequency of internal school support. Teachers who indicated that they relied on colleagues (fellow teacher, media center specialist, or technology teacher) for support also list most frequently that they use *programming software with lessons* followed by *using a device with lessons.* (See Figure 9.) This is promising to see that these teachers have in school support and are comfortable seeking out their colleagues for this support. In fact, seeking a fellow teacher in their school for support occurred in all classroom resource types even when a teacher indicated no classroom resources. Unfortunately, the overall total of 36 (28%) of the teacher respondents who indicated that they rely on a fellow teacher for support was still too low.

5 DISCUSSION

The 2018 Maryland Computing Education Landscape Survey was extended to primary teachers for the first time in order to establish a baseline of teachers' conceptualizations of CT. The primary teachers who responded to the survey provided valuable information. The constructs that we studied each provided a glimpse into how CT is being integrated by teachers in the primary classrooms across the state.

With the CT definition complexities at the expert level, we expected to see variation among the teachers' CT definitions. As previously shown, elementary pre-service teachers struggle to adequately define CT without CT instruction integrated within undergraduate coursework[35]. With teachers remaining neutral or

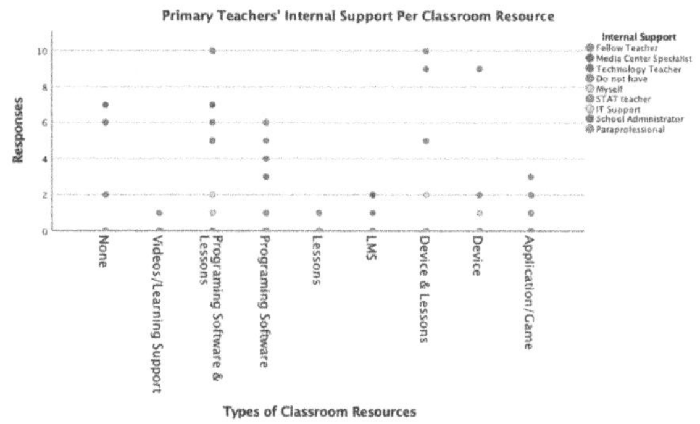

Figure 9: The frequency of primary teachers' responses by the types of classroom resources and the type of internal school support.

disagreeing that they had received adequate training, more professional development is needed for primary teachers. Some of the primary teachers' definitions contained expert level terminology while others described terms in lay language without stating the term. Perhaps, primary teachers answered in similar ways in which they might attempt to explain CT to their students. Regardless, there were clearly CT conceptualizations which better aligned to the varied expert definitions and those which did not. Surprisingly, only 6 definitions include *using mathematics* which aligns with the placement of CT in NGSS. The majority of responses include describing CT as *problem solving*. While this aspect is promising, our concern is that the next frequent code is using a computer or technology often paired with solve problems. Simply using a device or even "thinking like a computer" does not directly provide students with opportunities to develop CT. Another potential transfer of teacher knowledge might be from the digital literacy standards that were adopted by the state in the past. Digital literacy has been defined as "the assortment of cognitive-thinking strategies that consumers of digital information utilized (pg. 6)[36]." Media center specialist were often tasked to create and deliver these learning materials for teachers and students. Teachers might be equating CT with these standards as a "repackaging" without truly understanding the differences between them.

The resources that primary teachers report using help us understand what additional support structures need to be put into place. LEAs should invest in high quality programming software and devices which come with lessons plans. Preferably, LEAs will provide these classroom resources with companion professional development opportunities for teachers to work with materials while they collaboratively build learning communities. Primary teachers who teach technology rely on themselves or report that they do not have any school support. More school and LEA level support is needed to combat the isolationism for these teachers. At the same time, careful consideration needs to be taken when teachers who are teaching technology are considered a primary support for colleagues within their building. It is helpful to have someone with which to assist and brainstorm lesson ideas, but this teacher should not be seen as a computing troubleshooter and be relied upon to help with technology difficulties. This may overburden the teachers who are teaching technology.

Most of the teachers who responded agreed that CT integration should occur within the core content areas (science, mathematics, English language arts, and social studies. The path to be able to achieve this lofty goal needs to be carefully planned within each of the 24 LEAs for the in-service teachers, and the higher education institutions in the sate need to integrate CT within the undergraduate teacher preparation programs. Through each avenue, the public school teachers with higher comfort levels will integrate CT into daily lesson plans.

In Maryland, LEAs need to determine if they will hire and support a computing teacher specialist or provide professional development for the generalist primary teachers. Ultimately, it would be wise to invest in support for both generalists and specialists for each primary school. Having at least one well-trained CT specialist on staff will benefit the entire school. This might be the media center specialist who receives CT-focused professional development, or a computing specialist teacher who is certified in computer science and teaches computing classes. With the proper curricula materials and adjustments, all of the primary teachers, regardless of what subjects they teach, can in time, integrate CT daily into their classrooms and across the core disciplines.

6 CONCLUSION

Many states, including Maryland, began computing education reform efforts at the high school level and recently shifted focus to place more emphasis on computing education initiatives at earlier levels of instruction with a particular focus on CT. The Maryland ESSA plan provides the policy catalyst for LEAs to provide primary students high quality CT instruction. However, there is much work to be done to help prepare our primary teachers to integrate CT into every classroom and across all subject areas. Professional development needs to be differentiated for generalist and specialist primary teachers. This baseline study provides us with the current status of CT integration at the primary level. Our intention is to use this information to provide guidance and professional development support to the 24 Maryland LEAs as they work toward ESSA compliance. Our hope is that when we survey Maryland public school primary teachers again in 2020, we will have more primary teachers who identify themselves as teachers who teach CT, develop more sophisticated CT conceptualizations, select high quality CT classroom resources, and attend more professional development, workshops, or conferences.

REFERENCES

[1] Seymour Papert. *Mindstorms: Children, computers, and powerful ideas.* Basic Books, Inc., 1980.

[2] Jeannette M Wing. Computational thinking. *Communications of the ACM*, 49(3):33–35, 2006.

[3] Jeannette M Wing. Computational thinking and thinking about computing. *Philosophical transactions of the royal society of London A: mathematical, physical and engineering sciences*, 366(1881):3717–3725, 2008.

[4] National Research Council et al. *Report of a workshop on the scope and nature of computational thinking.* National Academies Press, 2010.

[5] National Research Council et al. *Report of a workshop on the pedagogical aspects of computational thinking.* National Academies Press, 2011.

[6] NGSS Lead States. Next generation science standards: For states, by states. 2013.

[7] K-12 Computer Science Framework Steering Committee et al. K-12 computer science framework. 2016.

[8] Shuchi Grover and Roy Pea. Computational thinking in k–12: A review of the state of the field. *Educational Researcher*, 42(1):38–43, 2013.
[9] Donna Kotsopoulos, Lisa Floyd, Steven Khan, Immaculate Kizito Namukasa, Sowmya Somanath, Jessica Weber, and Chris Yiu. A pedagogical framework for computational thinking. *Digital Experiences in Mathematics Education*, 3(2):154–171, 2017.
[10] A Csizmadia, P Curzon, M Dorling, S Humphreys, Th Ng, C Selby, and J Woollard. Computational thinking: A guide for teachers. *Computing at Schools*, 2015.
[11] James Lockwood and Aidan Mooney. Computational thinking in secondary education: Where does it fit? a systematic literary review. *Online Submission*, 2(1):41–60, 2018.
[12] Emmanuel Fokides and Pinelopi Atsikpasi. Redefining the framework for teaching programming to primary school students: Results from three pilot projects. *British Journal of Education, Society & Behavioural Science*, 20:1–11, 2017.
[13] Filiz Kalelioglu, Yasemin Gülbahar, and Volkan Kukul. A framework for computational thinking based on a systematic research review. *Baltic Journal of Modern Computing*, 4(3):583, 2016.
[14] J Shailaja and R Sridaran. Computational thinking the intellectual thinking for the 21st century. *International Journal of Advanced Networking & Applications, May 2015 Special Issue*, pages 39–46, 2015.
[15] Cynthia Selby and John Woollard. Computational thinking: the developing definition. 2013.
[16] Charoula Angeli, Joke Voogt, Andrew Fluck, Mary Webb, Margaret Cox, Joyce Malyn-Smith, and Jason Zagami. A k-6 computational thinking curriculum framework: Implications for teacher knowledge. *Journal of Educational Technology & Society*, 19(3), 2016.
[17] Mark Guzdial. Education paving the way for computational thinking. *Communications of the ACM*, 51(8):25–27, 2008.
[18] David Barr, John Harrison, and Leslie Conery. Computational thinking: A digital age skill for everyone. *Learning & Leading with Technology*, 38(6):20–23, 2011.
[19] Marina Umaschi Bers, Louise Flannery, Elizabeth R Kazakoff, and Amanda Sullivan. Computational thinking and tinkering: Exploration of an early childhood robotics curriculum. *Computers & Education*, 72:145–157, 2014.
[20] David Weintrop, Elham Beheshti, Michael Horn, Kai Orton, Kemi Jona, Laura Trouille, and Uri Wilensky. Defining computational thinking for mathematics and science classrooms. *Journal of Science Education and Technology*, 25(1):127–147, 2016.
[21] Aaron D Knochel and Ryan M Patton. If art education then critical digital making: Computational thinking and creative code. *Studies in Art Education*, 57(1):21–38, 2015.
[22] Joyce MALYN-SMITH, Irene A LEE, and Joseph IPPOLITO. Profile of a ct integration specialist. *Siu-cheung KONG The Education University of Hong Kong, Hong Kong*, page 60, 2017.
[23] Steve Furber et al. Shut down or restart? the way forward for computing in uk schools. *The Royal Society, London*, 2012.
[24] Richard C Anderson. The case for teacher specialization in the elementary school. *The Elementary School Journal*, 62(5):253–260, 1962.
[25] Kimberly A Markworth, Joseph Brobst, Chris Ohana, and Ruth Parker. Elementary content specialization: models, affordances, and constraints. *International Journal of STEM Education*, 3(1):16, 2016.
[26] Roland G Fryer Jr. The" pupil" factory: Specialization and the production of human capital in schools. *American Economic Review*, 108(3):616–56, 2018.
[27] Daniel M Levin, David Hammer, and Janet E Coffey. Novice teachers' attention to student thinking. *Journal of Teacher Education*, 60(2):142–154, 2009.
[28] Laura H Chapman. Status of elementary art education: 1997–2004. *Studies in Art Education*, 46(2):118–137, 2005.
[29] Leslie Gates. Professional development through collaborative inquiry for an art education archipelago. *Studies in Art Education*, 52(1):6–17, 2010.
[30] Aman Yadav, Sarah Gretter, Jon Good, and Tamika McLean. Computational thinking in teacher education. In *Emerging Research, Practice, and Policy on Computational Thinking*, pages 205–220. Springer, 2017.
[31] Barney G Glaser and Anselm L Strauss. The discovery of grounded theory: strategies for qualitative theory. *New Brunswick: Aldine Transaction*, 1967.
[32] Jacob Cohen. A coefficient of agreement for nominal scales. *Educational and psychological measurement*, 20(1):37–46, 1960.
[33] J Richard Landis and Gary G Koch. The measurement of observer agreement for categorical data. *biometrics*, pages 159–174, 1977.
[34] Lee J Cronbach. Coefficient alpha and the internal structure of tests. *psychometrika*, 16(3):297–334, 1951.
[35] Aman Yadav, Chris Mayfield, Ninger Zhou, Susanne Hambrusch, and John T Korb. Computational thinking in elementary and secondary teacher education. *ACM Transactions on Computing Education (TOCE)*, 14(1):5, 2014.
[36] Barbara Jones and Suzanne L Flannigan. Connecting the digital dots: Literacy of the 21st century. *Educause Quarterly*, 29(2):8–10, 2006.

PRADA: A Practical Model for Integrating Computational Thinking in K-12 Education

Yihuan Dong[1], Veronica Catete[1], Robin Jocius[2], Nicholas Lytle[1], Tiffany Barnes[1], Jennifer Albert[2], Deepti Joshi[2], Richard Robinson[2], Ashley Andrews[2]
[1]North Carolina State University, Raleigh, North Carolina
[2]The Citadel, Charleston, South Carolina
{ydong2,vmcatete,nalytle,tmbarnes}@ncsu.edu
{rjocius,jalbert,djoshi,rjmr,ashley.andrews}@citadel.edu

ABSTRACT

One way to increase access to education on computing is to integrate computational thinking (CT) into K12 disciplinary courses. However, this challenges teachers to both learn CT and decide how to best integrate CT into their classes. In this position paper, we present PRADA, an acronym for Pattern Recognition, Abstraction, Decomposition, and Algorithms, as a practical and understandable way of introducing the core ideas of CT to non-computing teachers. We piloted the PRADA model in two, separate, week-long professional development workshops designed for in-service middle and high school teachers and found that the PRADA model supported teachers in making connections between CT and their current course material. Initial findings, which emerged from the analysis of teacher-created learning materials, survey responses, and focus group interviews, indicate that the PRADA model supported core content teachers in successfully infusing CT into their existing curricula and increased their self-efficacy in CT integration.

CCS CONCEPTS

• **Social and professional topics → Computational thinking**; *K-12 education*;

KEYWORDS

Professional Development; Computational Thinking

ACM Reference Format:
Yihuan Dong, Veronica CatetÃĺ, Robin Jocius, Nicholas Lytle, Tiffany Barnes, Jennifer Albert, Deepti Joshi, Richard Robinson, Ashley Andrews. 2019. PRADA: A Practical Model for Integrating Computational Thinking in K-12 Education. In Proceedings of the 50th ACM Technical Symposium on Computer Science Education (SIGCSE '19), Feb. 27–Mar. 2, 2019, Minneapolis, MN, USA. ACM, NY, NY. 7 pages. https://doi.org/10.1145/3287324.3287431

SIGCSE '19, February 27-March 2, 2019, Minneapolis, MN, USA

ACM ISBN 978-1-4503-5890-3/19/02...$15.00
https://doi.org/10.1145/3287324.3287431

1 INTRODUCTION

Computational Thinking (CT) is the thought processes involved in formulating problems so their solutions can be represented as computational steps and algorithms [1], which often include problem decomposition and abstract reasoning. As computational technologies are becoming a more integral part of our lives and workforce, it is important for students to develop these CT skills early and with equal opportunity in order to prepare them for their future careers. Teaching CT in core classes has the advantage to avert the selection bias present in elective or after school programs [21]. However, this challenges us to effectively train teachers to be able to understand CT concepts, identify CT components in their lessons, and foster a CT mindset among their students.

After Wing re-introduced the concept of CT in 2006 [25], a number of attempts have been made to define what CT is at various granularities [2, 9, 22, 24]. However, many definitions include Computer Science terms (automation, parallelization, etc.) that are not only hard to explain in any K-12 classroom, but are also difficult to understand without actual "coding" activities, which not all teachers have the resources or knowledge to facilitate. Furthermore, CT professional development (PD) without intentional content contextualization fails to offer affordances for how teachers can utilize CT to support disciplinary learning goals. There is a need for a CT definition that teachers can effectively use to communicate CT to students in core classroom settings. Such a CT definition needs to be:

(1) understandable by K-12 teachers, the majority of whom have limited Computer Science knowledge
(2) integratable into existing curricula, and
(3) generalizable to any discipline

In this paper, we present PRADA (an acronym for Pattern Recognition, Abstraction, Decomposition, and Algorithms) as a practical and understandable way of introducing the core ideas of CT to non-computing teachers in order to support them in infusing CT into their curricula. We piloted PRADA as part of a summer PD on infusing CT into middle and high school content area courses. During the PD, we taught and encouraged teachers to both recognize the PRADA elements that already exist in their courses, and also helped them to create digital artifacts in a block-based programming language to facilitate teaching PRADA. We approached the professional development with the following preliminary questions:

(1) Were the teachers able to create computational artifacts?
(2) Were the teachers able to correctly identify the PRADA components in their artifacts?

(3) Did teachers show an increase in self-efficacy towards understanding and teaching PRADA?
(4) Were there any interesting trends in teacher created artifacts and feedback?

This paper presents our preliminary results which emerged from interpretations of daily teacher feedback, semi-structured interviews, and summative PD surveys, but focused primarily on the teachers' products: lesson plans and block-based programs. We begin with an overview of CT frameworks and pedagogical strategies for CT PD. Then, we make the case for the use of PRADA as an understandable way of introducing CT to non-computing K-12 teachers. The next part presents the methodology used for this investigation and continues on to show evidence from the teacher artifacts indicating exemplars of successful implementations of PRADA. We conclude with a discussion of our findings and recommendations for future CT teacher professional development.

2 LITERATURE REVIEW

In the last decade, the concept of Computational Thinking has undergone several reformations. Wing has moved CT from the concepts fundamental to computer science (solving problems, designing systems and understanding human behavior [25]), to the "thought processes involved in formulating problems and their solutions so that the solutions are represented in a form that can be effectively carried out by an information-processing agent" [24]. The important distinction here is that the solutions can be carried out by another agent effectively.

In 2011, the International Society for Technology in Education (ISTE) and Computer Science Teachers Association (CSTA) came together to create an operational definition of CT that could provide a framework and set of vocabulary terms for all K-12 teachers [9]. They describe CT as a problem-solving process that includes formulating problems, logically organizing data, representing data through abstractions, automating solutions, reflecting on the efficiencies of possible solutions, and generalizing and transferring this process to a variety of problems. However, while these ideas are general enough to apply to any discipline, there remains a lack of clarity with regard to how teachers can use CT to support content learning and a need for more concrete models and supports for classroom integration.

Several attempts have been made to map CT specifically to other subject areas. Weintrop et al. have developed a taxonomy of CT practices for both Math and Science disciplines drawing on major connections to modeling and abstraction [21, 22]. Each of the four CT skill sets identified by Weintrop and his team evolved from reviews of literature and common coursework, as well as interviews and discussions with K-12 educators and researchers. Both Data and Information skills, as well as Modeling and Simulation skills, map directly to STEM practices. The new skills, Computational Problem Solving and Systems Thinking, focus more directly on practices deliberately expressed in Computer Science, such as debugging, assessment of solution effectiveness, and thinking in levels, which might be difficult for K-12 teachers to easily recognize within their own curricula or unpack for students.

Similarly, the vocabulary terms used in the early CT framework identified by the National Research Council [4, 7] present definitional challenges for teachers. In this framework, in addition to data manipulation and simulations, both parallelization and automation are used as high level concepts. Although these last two skills are useful for software engineers, these may be difficult or impractical to integrate into middle and high school courses.

In order to demystify the terminology around CT [4], a simplified skill set and vocabulary has been defined by k12cs.org and further modified by Google Education [10, 16]. K12cs.org focuses on: Defining problems; developing and using Abstractions; Creating computational artifacts; and Testing and refining artifacts. Although simplified, not all classrooms have ready access to computing technology, so the latter half of the CT skills can be difficult for teachers to implement. Instead, Google focuses on Problem decomposition, Pattern recognition, Abstraction, and Algorithm design [10]. As stand-alone or intermixed concepts, these can be implemented into other subjects by simply modifying existing lesson plans instead of needing to create something entirely new. An example of each concept is listed below [4]:

Pattern Recognition in Social Studies - identify trends in data from historical or social statistics
Abstraction in Science - simplify models of Newtonian mechanics or solar systems
Decomposition in English/Language Arts - write outlines, identify arguments
Algorithms in Math - list steps for doing long division or integral calculus

Although the historical trend in CT literature has been on identifying key concepts and a core definition [12], there is a new trend exploring how to teach these concepts to in-service teachers [5, 19, 26]. As noted by Margolis [17] and Yadav [26, 27], teachers will not be able to provide their students with quality CT instruction until the teachers themselves understand the construct and feel confident about its integration in their curriculum. If teachers do not feel confident in their abilities to teach computational thinking, students may have negative experiences in learning the concept [13].

Teachers' thinking and practice are understood to be shaped in large part by continued professional learning [3, 8]. Recent research by Bower et al. indicates that "teacher's computational thinking capabilities are relatively malleable" and professional development may sufficiently impact teachers' understanding of CT. According to Bower's study, teachers can learn CT concepts in a short amount of time, building self-efficacy [5]. Furthermore, a 2018 survey by Sands et al. found that there were no differences on teachers' conceptions of computational thinking based upon either the content area (STEM vs. non-STEM) or grade level (primary vs. secondary) [19], making CT PD a level learning field for in-service teachers.

However, there were some limitations to Bower's study: CT was taught in a stand-alone context not situated in the teachers' own domains. While teachers' self-efficacy and conceptual understandings of CT increased after the PD, teachers expressed concern over how to integrate CT into their classrooms [5]. Sands' study suggests that in order to successfully teach CT, training needs to be content-specific and focused on how to integrate computational thinking ideas into existing curricula. Specifically, teachers need to be introduced to computational thinking in a way that meets their disciplinary learning goals and fits within their pedagogical practices [19] rather than being an "instructional add-on in the K-12 curriculum" [11].

3 DEFINING CT AND PRADA

3.1 What is PRADA

Google's "Computational Thinking for Educators" course identifies Decomposition, Pattern Recognition, Abstraction, and Algorithm design as the key elements that make up Computational Thinking [10]. Even though CT is essential to programming, it can be used to facilitate problem solving across all disciplines, not strictly Computer Science. There is no strict ordering of these elements, and each element can be taught separately. We reordered these elements into PRADA as a mnemonic device to help teachers and students remember the terms. We also revised Google's CT definition, as shown in italics, to make it more adaptable to different disciplines:

Pattern Recognition observing and identifying patterns, trends, and regularities in data, *processes, or problems*

Abstraction identifying the general principles *and properties that are important and relevant to the problem*

Decomposition breaking down data, processes, or problems into *meaningful* smaller, manageable parts

Algorithms developing step by step instructions for solving [a problem] and similar problems

3.2 Why PRADA

There are several advantages in using PRADA as a way of introducing CT. The four elements are detailed enough to capture the essence of CT defined in previous frameworks. We emphasize PRADA as a mindset, not bounded by content area or tools, that helps people solve problems in a systematic and generalizable way. We consider coding to be an important activity that can facilitate the understanding of PRADA, but teaching PRADA does not require teachers to create coding activities or artifacts for their students. PRADA can also be taught with various unplugged activities. Figure 1 shows a mapping of PRADA compared to other popular CT components. PRADA strips out the Computer Science/coding specific components described elsewhere and retains the parts that can be easily generalized and integrated into different disciplines within K-12. Non-CS/coding specific components that are left out, namely Data & Information and Modeling & Simulations, can still be explained with PRADA, as analyzing data generally involves abstracting useful information from recognized patterns, and simulation generally involves decomposing a phenomenon into parts/abstractions, and creating algorithms to mimic observed or hypothesized processes. Additionally, PRADA maintains a meaningful difference between elements such that each element in the PRADA model represents a distinguishable process during problem-solving and can be taught and explained in separate class activities.

PRADA also gives teachers a set of memorable keywords to convey to their students when teaching CT. A previous research study that involved implementing CT in middle school science classrooms shows that the teachers had trouble mapping CT concepts to their teaching material. As a result, the teachers requested a concrete set of names of the key concepts so they could teach and reinforce the terms in each day's activity [6]. PRADA serves as a manageable and memorizable set of keywords that teachers can explicitly introduce and reinforce in their daily classes.

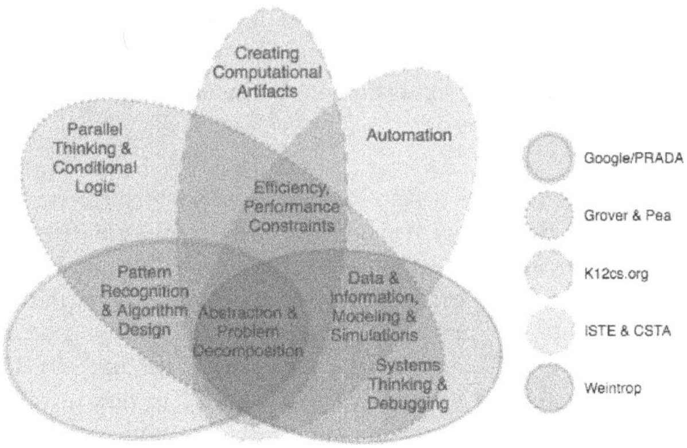

Figure 1: A mapping of popular CT components

In this paper, we argue that the PRADA model can support K-12 teachers' exploration of how to integrate CT into disciplinary classrooms. Our goal is to help teachers realize that many of the pedagogical practices and materials that they already use within their classrooms can address or provide distinct affordances for integrating the PRADA model. However, to do this, teachers need practice and support to recognize and apply CT elements to their own disciplinary content (see examples in section 2). It is with this in mind that we organized our Infusing Computing professional development program to provide opportunities for teachers to work together both within and across disciplines and to learn to create programs with extensive support from computer scientists.

4 METHODS

During two intensive, 5-day Infusing Computing PD workshops in North and South Carolina in Summer 2018, we engaged 116 middle and high school teachers in designing plans to integrate computational thinking into their classrooms. We designed each day of the workshop to include: Snap*!* programming bootcamps, content area focused PRADA sessions, and collaborative development sessions, which culminated in the development of a learning segment that integrates CT into each teacher's disciplinary classroom instruction. Specifically, the PRADA session began with a whole-group discussion of the PRADA element of the day in which teachers discussed concrete examples of how their existing teaching practices included PRADA elements, followed by examining and analyzing, in small groups, the sample classroom artifacts created by the research group. In the development sessions, teachers worked collaboratively in either school or content teams to make their projects. Although teachers were encouraged to create learning segments that allowed students to practice coding, this was not a requirement. Instead, teachers had the flexibility to build lessons around CT using the resources available in their classrooms. Typical learning segment components included a Snap*!*-like prototype, a learning plan that explicitly identified how PRADA elements were addressed, and supplemental pedagogical materials (e.g., graphic organizers, templates, slideshow presentations, coding guides).

We recruited Math, Science, Social Studies, and English/Language Arts (ELA) content area teachers for grades 6-12 in both states to attend individually or to bring teams from their schools. There were 58 teachers in each of our two workshops, PD1 and PD2, with teachers from several content areas as shown in Table 1. Although many teachers attended in teams, teachers could choose to work individually or with other self-selected teams within the workshop to create learning segments that would be meaningful in their own classrooms. Overall, there were 116 people in 40 teams across the two weeks, with teams ranging in size from one to as many as 6 teachers.

Table 1: Teacher participants and project by discipline

	Math	Science	Humanities	Interdisciplinary
PD1 Teachers	21	24	13	
PD1 # Projects	4	11	4	2
PD2 Teachers	20	19	17	
PD2 # Projects	7	7	3	2

PD sessions were led by members of the research team with support from local area teacher leaders with experience in integrating computing into their curricula. Taking on the roles of participant-observers [23] gave members of the research team the opportunity to interact with participants on a regular basis and to work systematically to understand the teachers' developing understandings of the PRADA model, as well as their beliefs and expectations regarding integrating CT into their classrooms. We believe that these roles allowed us important insights into the data analyzed in this paper, particularly given that the goal of this work is the evaluation of teachers' understanding and implementation of PRADA, rather than their perceptions of the PD or facilitators.

4.1 Data Collection & Analysis

Primary sources of data for this analysis included teacher products (block-based programming prototypes, learning segment plans, and related artifacts), pre- and post-PD surveys, daily reflections, feedback forms for teacher presentations, and audio-recorded teacher interviews. Data analysis proceeded in three overlapping and recursive phases: systematic review and coding of learning segment artifacts, purposive sampling and analysis of focal learning segments, and triangulation of data sources.

During the first phase of analysis, the first author, an expert who participated in the design and the implementation of the PD, reviewed the learning segments and the block-based programming project files of all the collaborative teacher submissions (n = 40). While many of the products have interdisciplinary connections, of the 40 products, 11 were primarily designed for math, 18 for Science, 7 for Humanities (Social Studies and English Language Arts), and 4 were purposefully designed for all disciplines. Products included a form where teachers were to elaborate how their planned lessons would target each PRADA concept. Each submission was reviewed to determine whether or not the interpretation of PRADA in the context of the lesson plan agreed with what we intended the teachers to learn. Based on our expert review, most teams successfully implemented PRADA as 32.5% of the projects had a correct explanation and implementation for all 4 of the PRADA elements, and 32.5% of the projects had a correct explanation and implementation for two or more elements of PRADA. Of the remaining 13 projects, 6 identified PRADA elements by name, 4 incorrectly identified PRADA elements, and 3 made no mention of PRADA.

In the second phase, we used purposive sampling to select four case studies representing math, science, humanities, and interdisciplinary products to analyze evidence of teachers' understandings of the PRADA model within their learning segments. Purposive sampling is "based on the assumption that one wants to discover, understand, or gain insight; therefore one needs to select a sample from which one can learn the most" [18]. The case studies selected were based on the following criteria: the lesson plan is complete, the learning segment or supporting document clearly describes how each of the four elements of PRADA is identified and used in the lessons, and the block-based coding prototypes were completed with a clear indication of the presence of some PRADA elements (e.g. proper use of the repeat block demonstrating understanding of pattern recognition).

During the third and final phase of analysis, we focus on participant feedback. The project team examined feedback from presentations, survey results, and teacher interviews to triangulate findings across sources using the constant comparative method [20].

5 CASE STUDIES

We report our preliminary findings from the PRADA themed Infusing Computing PD using four exemplary projects. We intend these case studies to demonstrate how teachers successfully identified and infused CT into their own domains, as well as to highlight how teachers were able to bridge domains using PRADA. After we present a description of each product, we list the teacher explanations for integrating PRADA in quotes, and we offer our own interpretations of the product's relation to each PRADA element in italics. We also discuss how these exemplars illustrate opportunities for additional support that may be needed for teachers struggling with some elements of CT.

5.1 Interdisciplinary Exemplar: Life in the Middle Ages

One interdisciplinary group of high school teachers made a historical puzzle game for students to explore life in the Middle Ages through puzzles and quizzes. Table 2 shows how the teachers explained the PRADA elements, providing good examples and activities in all cases except for abstraction.

5.2 English/Language Arts Exemplar: Historical Game

In our second exemplar for 6th grade English Language Arts, teachers created a historical role-playing game to provide context for students' reading of narrative and expository texts. Table 3 shows how this team was able to identify and apply all four PRADA elements in their learning segment and identified student learning for patterns, abstraction, and decomposition.

Table 2: PRADA in the interdisciplinary product

Pattern Rec.: "Students should identify the repetition in games, the progression of the timeline, characters, puzzle patterns, and the patterns in graph plotting".
Abstraction: Students would demonstrate abstraction through "overarching knowledge of the middle ages." *This suggests that the teachers either consider the knowledge to be abstractions, or they did not understand abstraction enough to provide concrete examples.*
Decomposition: Students should "research events and note dates in the timeline, discover specific characteristics from the prologue of the game, break down the logical components in the puzzle games, and so forth".
Algorithms: Students would design algorithms to "code the different parts of the game and create a storyboard".

Table 3: PRADA in the humanities product

Pattern Rec.: During their explorations of the world, the teachers task students with recognizing the "repetition in history, storytelling, coding" when clicking on similar items.
Abstraction: "Understand history inspiring fiction" *This demonstrates a good disciplinary use of the concept of abstraction, drawing parallels between history and stories.*
Decomposition: Students should "break down plot diagrams into subcategories and look further into what blocks go into a specific abstraction". *This implies a good understanding of our CT definitions of decomposition and abstraction (naming a functional group of blocks) and the attempt to connect decomposition to abstraction.*
Algorithms: In their Snap*!* file, teachers used multiple sprites to handle different functionalities, reused code in different sprite objects, and correctly coordinated the logic and timing between the sprites, demonstrating impressive understanding. *Teachers did not specify student activities for algorithms.*

5.3 Science Exemplar: Rock & Mineral Quiz

The science exemplar, Rock & Mineral Quiz, was developed for students in 6th - 10th grade science classes to review and practice knowledge learned about the components of rocks and minerals in rock cycles. The first Snap*!* project created by the teachers was designed to monitor and evaluate students' ability to respond to questions related to rocks and minerals throughout a class period. The other project is intended to be used in a exploratory lab activity, where the students measure different properties of rock specimens and input the measurements into the Snap*!* project to check whether they made correct inferences. The project files demonstrate a clear understanding of pattern recognition and decomposition through the reuse of code segments and use of multiple sprites and control structures to handle different logic. There is no clear indicator of abstraction in either of the project files. Table 4 shows the breakdown of PRADA elements listed for this group. We felt that the listed elements for Decomposition and Algorithms may need to be reversed, but they could be appropriate depending on how they are carried out and discussed in classrooms.

Table 4: PRADA in the science product

Pattern Rec.: Students should "recognize the composition of rocks throughout the rock cycle" (science) and "recognize patterns in the coding language and how to incorporate loops" (coding).
Abstraction: Students should identify global and local properties (science) and code them as global and local variables in Snap*!* (coding).
Decomposition: Students should "break down the composition of minerals by characterizing density, hardness, and strength" (science) and "will complete sorting activities to learn where command blocks are located" (coding).
Algorithms: Students investigate "the rock cycle in a series of labs and activities" (science) and "break down the previously written code for a review game in Snap*!* by replacing lines of code with different questions" (coding).

5.4 Math Exemplar: ACT Football

Our exemplar math product is an ACT practice quiz football game. Each question is associated with a number of yards that will advance their team if answered correctly, or penalize their team if answered incorrectly. The teachers described two ways of using the game: as a practice for the ACT test and as a way of having the students learn CT and coding skills. Table 5 demonstrates the use of PRADA by this team.

Table 5: PRADA in the math product

Pattern Rec.: Students will be "questioned on pattern recognition as they play, such as:'what does the game do when a correct answer is given? A wrong answer?'" They expect the students to be able to notice the repetitive patterns in the game and familiarize themselves with the game mechanics.
Abstraction: Teachers will "display a [custom] block and explain [how it is] considered an abstraction" that is "composed of an algorithm".
Decomposition: In the Snap! project, teachers demonstrated understanding of decomposition by creating custom blocks named "coin toss", "initial possession", and "play" *Teachers did not specify how students would practice or demonstrate decomposition.*
Algorithms: Students will "use an algorithm to decide what level of questions they want to answer which will determine their advancement in the football game". Later, the students will be asked to "use an algorithm to create a block of code that will ask a question and respond to the answer as to whether correct or incorrect", which is an algorithm the teachers crafted in the "play" block in their Snap! project.

6 ANALYSIS OF TEACHER FEEDBACK

The analysis of teacher post-PD surveys demonstrates tha PRADA was warmly received. In both PDs, respondents showed a high level of willingness to adopt PRADA and high self-efficacy in being able to design and teach using PRADA. Table 6 shows the average response for Likert-style questions participants received.

Table 6: Average rating for teacher Self-Efficacy (1 strongly disagree to 5 strongly agree)

	PD1	PD2
I am more likely to incorporate PRADA activities in my classroom.	4.59	4.55
I can more effectively design PRADA activities.	4.43	4.40
I can better engage students in making sense of PRADA and designing solutions to problems.	4.46	4.40

Our analysis of teachers' daily reflections and interviews reveals that PRADA seemed to be well-received because its elements connected easily with already established concepts in the teachers' disciplines. For example, as one teacher notes, "Abstraction for math is basically modeling - I do it every day!". As they established connections between CT and existing curricula, teachers began to understand that they already engage in computational thinking ("in math, we use abstractions all the time"), but they now had the toolkit to be able to express these ideas using CT language. As one teacher put it, "The introduction of the terminology of PRADA was helpful, as teachers realized that they are already doing this." Another said, "... I really do this within my teaching already. I just need to share with students this terminology in science class."

Teachers were also able to identify CT in their colleagues' learning segments. For instance, as one teacher noted in their feedback to a colleague, "I love that [students] can do a creative model of their physical quilt that models computational thinking." Another teacher focused specifically on the disciplinary elements of calculus that mirrored PRADA: "It is interesting that calculus in and of itself is representative of computational thinking. It's very "meta" that the students are creating a program to better understand multiple representations while they are simultaneously gaining a deeper understanding of PRADA concepts that are mirrored in calculus concepts."

However, while teachers had success in both identifying and creating connections with PRADA elements, some confusion existed in how to teach these elements within a classroom. As one teacher put it: "HOW do you teach abstraction? I can recognize it, but what are ways that I can emphasize it, and have my students value abstraction?" This was further compounded with some teachers still having confusion over to what degree they needed to incorporate programming into their teaching of CT ("Are we expected to have the students code, or, is that just an option?").

A few teacher products did not explicitly relate PRADA elements to their disciplines, but only indicated how PRADA relates to coding. This may reflect a potential lack of understanding of PRADA as a connector between CT and disciplines; as one teacher said, "PRADA helps me work in coding in my classroom". However, this may also simply be a limitation of our data collection instrument which only provided small text boxes for explaining how their products related to PRADA. In our 3C model of Code, Connect, Create [15] for integrated CT professional development, teachers attended sessions on learning to code, to connect PRADA to their disciplines, and to create their learning segments for the classroom. Teachers may have been eager to demonstrate their understanding of PRADA in the context of coding, rather than in their own disciplines.

7 DISCUSSION & CONCLUSIONS

Unlike other coding-focused CT models, PRADA is an abstraction of the mindset that is commonly used by computer scientists and programmers when solving problems. We emphasize the word mindset because PRADA is a thinking process, not bounded by content area or tools, to help people solve problems in a systematic and generalizable way. When helping teachers make connections to their disciplinary areas, we have found that while STEM areas have natural connections to CT through activities like modeling, simulations and experimental methods (e.g., NGSS), other areas like English Language Arts can also benefit from applying and recognizing CT. However, before a teacher can map the PRADA elements to their curriculum, they need to learn to recognize PRADA elements within their discipline and see examples of how PRADA elements can be introduced. We believe that our approach to helping teachers learn about CT and how to integrate it into their classrooms provided them with opportunities to discover and elaborate on PRADA elements and to design their own learning segments with the assistance of computing experts. Teachers could enforce a long-term conversation about CT by identifying places in their existing curriculum where students are struggling and looking for opportunities to integrate CT and coding to help students learning.

Furthermore, we hypothesize that the PRADA model could also help teachers realize how the CT mindset can be used across disciplines to develop generalized problem-solving skills and dispositions. Research shows that interdisciplinary lessons give students the opportunity to apply knowledge from different areas in problem solving [14]. As our findings demonstrate, interdisciplinary teacher teams can mix and match PRADA elements from different content areas, which mitigates the concern that some PRADA elements might be hard to identify or explain in certain content areas. In addition, PRADA can help generalize CT across disciplines, providing students with a more tangible model with which to make sense of the problem-solving process and other CT approaches. While we have shown that teachers are successful at developing interdisciplinary lessons through PRADA, research into their pedagogical effects in classroom environments is still needed. Though our research team has developed and helped teachers implement CT lesson using the PRADA model[6], the broader potential impact of PRADA can only be fully realized when teachers can understand CT and implement effective CT-integrated lesson plans themselves.

In conclusion, this paper proposed and demonstrated how PRADA can be used to help K-12 teachers develop an understanding of Computational Thinking and how to integrate it into their disciplinary courses. We argue that PRADA is a CT model that can be easily understood by teachers, even those with little to no experience with programming or computer science. While the elements of CT are not novel, the way in which they were integrated into the teacher PD and the way teachers were asked to integrate them into their classrooms is novel. In the future, we will further investigate the impact of this promising PRADA model for supporting teachers in integrating CT into K12 classrooms.

ACKNOWLEDGMENTS

This material is based upon work supported by the National Science Foundation under grant numbers 1742351 and 1742332.

REFERENCES

[1] Alfred V Aho. 2011. Ubiquity symposium: Computation and computational thinking. *Ubiquity* 2011, January (2011), 1.

[2] Charoula Angeli, Joke Voogt, Andrew Fluck, Mary Webb, Margaret Cox, Joyce Malyn-Smith, and Jason Zagami. 2016. A K-6 computational thinking curriculum framework: Implications for teacher knowledge. *Journal of Educational Technology & Society* 19, 3 (2016).

[3] Deborah Loewenberg Ball. 2000. Bridging practices: Intertwining content and pedagogy in teaching and learning to teach. *Journal of teacher education* 51, 3 (2000), 241–247.

[4] Valerie Barr and Chris Stephenson. 2011. Bringing Computational Thinking to K-12: What is Involved and What is the Role of the Computer Science Education Community? *ACM Inroads* 2, 1 (Feb. 2011), 48–54. https://doi.org/10.1145/1929887.1929905

[5] Matt Bower, Leigh N Wood, Jennifer WM Lai, Cathie Howe, Raymond Lister, Raina Mason, Kate Highfield, and Jennifer Veal. 2017. Improving the computational thinking pedagogical capabilities of school teachers. *Australian Journal of Teacher Education* 42, 3 (2017), 4.

[6] Veronica Cateté, Nicholas Lytle, Yihuan Dong, Danielle Boulden, Bita Akram, Jennifer Houchins, Tiffany Barnes, Eric Wiebe, James Lester, Bradford Mott, and Kristy Boyer. 2018. Infusing Computational Thinking into Middle Grade Science Classrooms: Lessons Learned. In *Proceedings of the 13th Workshop on Primary and Secondary Computing Education (WiPSCE '18)*. ACM, New York, NY, USA. https://doi.org/10.1145/3265757.3265778

[7] National Research Council et al. 2010. *Report of a workshop on the scope and nature of computational thinking*. National Academies Press.

[8] Barbara A Crawford. 2007. Learning to teach science as inquiry in the rough and tumble of practice. *Journal of research in science teaching* 44, 4 (2007), 613–642.

[9] International Society for Technology in Education (ISTE), Computer Science Teachers Association CSTA), et al. 2011. Operational definition of computational thinking for K-12 Education. online.

[10] Google. 2018. What is Computational Thinking? https://computationalthinkingcourse.withgoogle.com/unit?lesson=8&unit=1

[11] Cynthia L Greenleaf, Cindy Litman, Thomas L Hanson, Rachel Rosen, Christy K Boscardin, Joan Herman, Steven A Schneider, Sarah Madden, and Barbara Jones. 2011. Integrating literacy and science in biology: Teaching and learning impacts of reading apprenticeship professional development. *American Educational Research Journal* 48, 3 (2011), 647–717.

[12] Shuchi Grover and Roy Pea. 2013. Computational thinking in K–12: A review of the state of the field. *Educational Researcher* 42, 1 (2013), 38–43.

[13] Maya Israel, Jamie N Pearson, Tanya Tapia, Quentin M Wherfel, and George Reese. 2015. Supporting all learners in school-wide computational thinking: A cross-case qualitative analysis. *Computers & Education* 82 (2015), 263–279.

[14] Leslie Jarmon, Tomoko Traphagan, Michael Mayrath, and Avani Trivedi. 2009. Virtual world teaching, experiential learning, and assessment: An interdisciplinary communication course in Second Life. *Computers & Education* 53, 1 (2009), 169–182.

[15] Robin Jocius, Yihuan Dong, Deepti Joshi, Richard Robinson, Tiffany Barnes, Veronica Catete, Jennifer Albert, Ashley Andrews, and Nick Lytle. under review. Code, Connect, Create: The 3C Professional Development Model to Support Computational Thinking Infusion. *Computer Science Education* (under review).

[16] K12cs.org. 2018. Computational Thinking. https://k12cs.org/computational-thinking/

[17] Jane Margolis. 2010. *Stuck in the shallow end: Education, race, and computing*. MIT Press.

[18] Sharan B Merriam. 1988. *Case study research in education: A qualitative approach.* Jossey-Bass.

[19] Phil Sands, Aman Yadav, and Jon Good. 2018. Computational Thinking in K-12: In-service Teacher Perceptions of Computational Thinking. In *Computational Thinking in the STEM Disciplines*. Springer, 151–164.

[20] Anselm Strauss and Juliet M Corbin. 1990. *Basics of qualitative research: Grounded theory procedures and techniques*. Sage Publications, Inc.

[21] David Weintrop, Elham Beheshti, Michael Horn, Kai Orton, Kemi Jona, Laura Trouille, and Uri Wilensky. 2014. Defining computational thinking for science, technology, engineering, and math. In *American Educational Research Association Annual Meeting, Philadelphia, Pennsylvania.*

[22] David Weintrop, Elham Beheshti, Michael Horn, Kai Orton, Kemi Jona, Laura Trouille, and Uri Wilensky. 2016. Defining computational thinking for mathematics and science classrooms. *Journal of Science Education and Technology* 25, 1 (2016), 127–147.

[23] Stephen Wilson. 1977. The use of ethnographic techniques in educational research. *Review of educational research* 47, 2 (1977), 245–265.

[24] J Wing. 2011. Research notebook: Computational thinkingâĂŤWhat and why? The Link Magazine, Spring.

[25] Jeannette M Wing. 2006. Computational thinking. *Commun. ACM* 49, 3 (2006), 33–35.

[26] Aman Yadav, Sarah Gretter, Susanne Hambrusch, and Phil Sands. 2016. Expanding computer science education in schools: understanding teacher experiences and challenges. *Computer Science Education* 26, 4 (2016), 235–254.

[27] Aman Yadav, Hai Hong, and Chris Stephenson. 2016. Computational thinking for all: pedagogical approaches to embedding 21st century problem solving in K-12 classrooms. *TechTrends* 60, 6 (2016), 565–568.

Computational Thinking in the Danish High School: Learning Coding, Modeling, and Content Knowledge with NetLogo

Line Have Musaeus[†]
Center for Computational Thinking and Design
Aarhus University
Denmark
lh@cc.au.dk

Peter Musaeus
Centre for Health Sciences Education
Aarhus University
Denmark
peter@cesu.au.dk

ABSTRACT

Computational thinking (CT) is emerging as an important theme in computer science and high school education. However, research is needed to inform high-school teachers how to foster students' development of CT in computer science and other subjects. Evidence suggests that agent-based modeling is a valuable way for students to learn CT in different subjects. This paper reports a teaching experiment where researchers, developers, and high school teachers collaborated to develop six NetLogo models. The models were used in nine Danish High Schools in the following four subjects: Biotechnology, chemistry, biology, and social science. Teachers and students had no or very limited experience with programming. Students build CT and content knowledge by using, modifying, and creating code in the models. This paper provides details for others to adopt the models and the underlying CMC framework, which integrates: Coding, Modeling, and Content. The paper evaluates the results from an open-ended questionnaire with all participating students (n=210) and semi-structured interviews with all teachers (n=15). Thematic analysis was applied to categorize the qualitative data. Results showed that students were able to use, modify, and create code in NetLogo that enabled them to develop CT and content knowledge. The CMC framework represents a fruitful way for teachers to design and teach and for students to tinker with learning CT.

CCS CONCEPTS

• Social and professional topics → Computing education; K-12 education; Computational thinking;

KEYWORDS

Computational thinking; K-12 education; Educational intervention; Computer models, Teacher professional development.

ACM Reference format:

Line Have Musaeus and Peter Musaeus. 2019.Computational Thinking in the Danish High School: Learning Coding, Modeling and Content Knowledge with NetLogo. In SIGCSE '19: SIGCSE '19: The 50th ACM Technical Symposium on Computer Science Education, *Feb. 27–March 2, 2019, Minneapolis, MN, USA*. ACM, NY, NY, USA, 6 pages. https://doi.org/10.1145/3287324.3287452

[†] Corresponding author

ACM ISBN 978-1-4503-5890-3/19/02...$15.00
https://doi.org/10.1145/3287324.3287452

1 INTRODUCTION

Seymour Papert [1] coined the notion of Computational Thinking (CT) in 1980 to describe the inquiry necessary to solve problems by means of computational ideas or computers. He applied the notion to make formal geometry more accessible to children by means of computational models. In 2006, Wing [2] referred to CT as the competence to think like a computer-scientist. Wing argued that CT represented a universally applicable attitude and skill set everyone, not just computer scientists, would be eager to learn and use [2 p. p. 33]. This definition referred back to Papert's [1] original insight that CT was an inquiry process in any subject, not only say computer science. Papert emphasized that the essence of the computer was its universality that gave power to the computational thinker with the computer to simulate real-world phenomena [1 p.VIII].

CT can be a way of teaching high school students modelling and coding [22] but to what extent does such activities lead high-school students to build content knowledge in other subjects than computer science such as biology, chemistry, English etc.? According to Papert [1] and Wing [2], CT stimulates students' understanding or construction of content knowledge. Although CT is being introduced into the subject of high school computer science [4, 11, 12, 13] and other subjects [10], it is still unclear how CT should be taught in high-school, whether learning CT helps learning another subject and finally whether CT should be taught in most or any subject.

CT can be said to have two meanings in the high school curricula. First, CT can be a learning goal in computer science (or Informatics as high school computer science is mostly called in Europe). In this case, CT is a means towards learning skills or knowledge relating to computer science such as learning programming. Second, CT can be a means towards learning content knowledge (in math, social science, biology etc.) by using CT to close the students' gaps in understanding between representing a phenomenon and the phenomenon itself. It follows from this second approach that CT is a competence that should be taught in high-school in order for the students to learn to grasp content in a subject (not just computer science) by means of computational ideas or the computer.

Researchers have demonstrated that agent-based modeling can be an effective way of teaching CT in relation to content knowledge [6, 7, 8]. We therefore choose to use NetLogo, which is an agent-based modeling tool that has been used in both biology teaching [16, 18] social sciences [17] chemistry [10] and mathematics [22].

In this paper, we report a design-based research study focusing on high-school students (n=210) and teachers (n=15) using NetLogo to develop CT and content knowledge. We used a sequential transformative design with quantitative data (from students) and qualitative data (from students and teachers). The research was conducted in four Danish high school subjects: Biotechnology, chemistry, biology and social/political science in nine different schools. The research aim was to develop teachers and students' integration of Coding, Modeling and Content construction (CMC see figure 1):

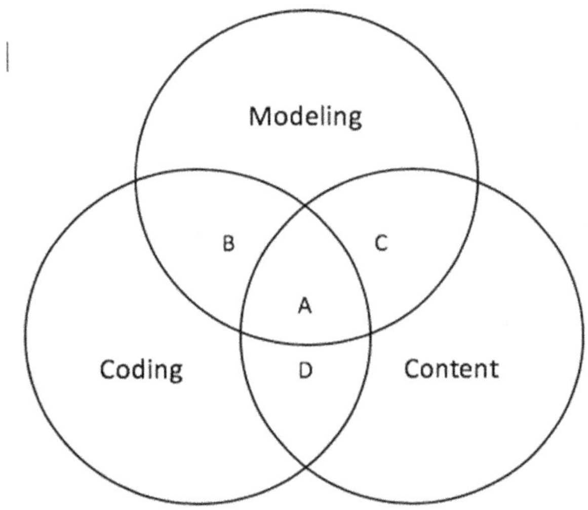

Figure 1: The CMC approach. A: Taking both modeling, coding as well as content into consideration when designing the models. B: Altering sections of code to modify the model. C: Comparing and modifying the model to fit the content matter. D: Concepts from content matter are illustrated in the code to facilitate students work with coding.

1.1 Research question

The objective of this teaching development project was to provide models and code with interface elements that students could tinker with and hereby develop CT. In particular we wanted to evaluate whether the CMC (coding, modelling, and content) approach can aid researchers, developers, and teachers to produce learning environments for students' acquisition of CT and content knowledge?

2 METHOD

Participants: Fifteen high school teachers (nine males and six females) in fifteen high school classes (in nine different high schools) employed the models in their classes. Altogether, 210 students participated.

NetLogo: NetLogo is an agent-based modeling environment. A NetLogo model includes the Interface tab, the Info tab, and the Code tab. The model is displayed in the Interface and students can manipulate its accompanying plots and parameters. The Info tab describes both the model as well as its structure, properties, and rules (i.e. rules assigned to the entities in the model). It also gives suggestions as to what to explore and extend in the model. The Code tab includes the code for the model with comments. Any changes made in the Code tab will result in changes to the model and the interface [15].

Step 1: Developing NetLogo models. Three researchers and two developers constructed six NetLogo models with five high school teachers as collaborators.

The aim was that students could tinker with the models and examine how patterns at a macro level, e.g. of ion transport across a cell membrane, arise from simple rules and interactions at the micro level, such as atoms and molecules, in a system (see figure 2).

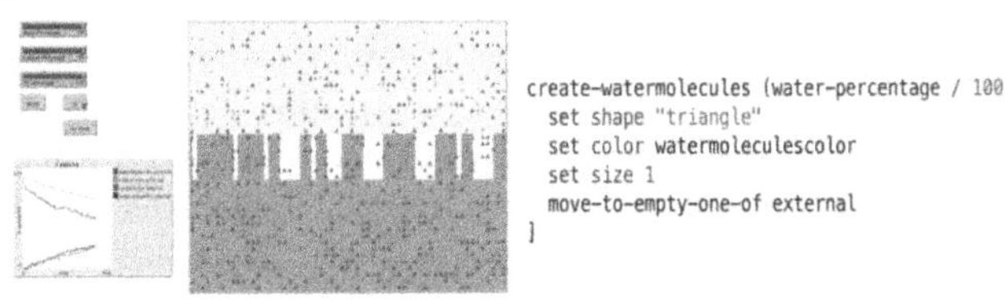

Figure 2: NetLogo model of cell membrane, showing both the 'Interface' and 'Code'.

On running the model, students could explore how these simple rules resulted in complex and unpredictable patterns.

Step 2: Designing learning activities. In designing the models, we used procedures and functions in the code to ensure that students worked at the appropriate level of abstraction (see figure 2).

Abstraction refers here to understanding a representation, identifying, and analyzing the elements that makes up the model of the represented phenomenon. All students were given the same one-minute video introduction to NetLogo.

The CMC approach (figure 1) served both as a framework in the design phase/step of the models and the pedagogy around using these models in teaching. Thus researchers, developers, and high school teachers used the approach throughout the study, to simultaneously design the computational models and plan the learning activities. The team designed the models primarily to serve as initial starting points or idea generators for students to tinker with, use and modify. Students could interact with models built as half-baked microworlds. A microworld is defined as a less developed representation of a phenomenon [14, 15].

Subsequently, we used structured learning activities to take the students through tasks such as creating a new set of agents in NetLogo, e.g. potassium ions, with specific structures and rules, in the model of a cell membrane that already contained sodium ions (figure 2). The students worked in pairs to support peer-to-peer collaboration, using an online questionnaire describing the tasks and related questions they needed to answer. The learning activities lasted for a total of 90 minutes.

Teachers were able to gain support from researchers and developers online or in short prerecorded guiding videos before and during classroom sessions.

Step 3: Students working with the models. We used a constructionist approach to learning [20, 21] that involved students tinkering with the model interface and code. This involved students playfully manipulating the code of a computational model to generate and pursue questions in relation to the model, much as described in Wagh et al. [15]. This is especially important for students who are novices in computing and programming [23].

We encouraged students to use, modify, and create the model and code by giving them specific tasks to perform. Thus, the model was what Vygotsky [21] conceived of as a semiotic sign meaning a representation for someone that could become a mediated activity for the student. Hereby the model, when appropriated by the student, resulted in a regulatory change in the students' behavior, understanding etc. In the interest of time and because both teachers and students had limited or no experience with computer programming, we chose to let students work with pre-designed computer models rather than have them develop models from scratch. But students were encouraged to modify models and ponder to what extent they furthered the construction of their understanding of content knowledge or CT.

The underlying code in NetLogo consisted of variables and rules such as for molecules in a system. Our aim was that the code should represent a phenomenon as well as the structure and rules of the agents and the dynamic relations between the agents that we wanted to investigate [1]. Hence, the interface should illustrate these relations with accuracy. Furthermore, the code and the interface were designed in order to facilitate the intended learning activities we wanted to achieve. In summary, our aim was to provide students with models and code with interface elements that were easy to tinker with.

Step 4: Collection of data. We conducted design-based research with a sequential transformative design, in which we collected quantitative and qualitative data from students and qualitative data from teachers. Students filled out online questionnaires, while working with the model. In order to analyze data, we employed a description of CT competences and learning goals from the literature [19, 3] as shown below in table 1.

CT category	CT sub-category
CT baseline	CT baseline Perspective development
Subject progress	Subject baseline Subject progress
Understanding the model	Using the model Analyzing the model Understanding the model Decomposing the model Levels of thinking Scaling the phenomenon Pattern recognition Sorting relevant from irrelevant information
Model/subject	Representation of the model Representation of the subject Transferring subject knowledge to the model and back
Interface/code	Analyzing macroscopic syntax Formulating macroscopic syntax with elements of microscopic syntax
Working with code	Creating solutions Defining problems in the model Generalize solutions by algorithmic thinking Capture essential properties common to a set of agents Motivation for working with computational models

Table 1: Categories used for classification in data analysis

The online questionnaire covered the 22 sub-categories of CT (see table 1). The questionnaires all contained the same pre-post question regarding the students' perspective on using a computer model in the subject. Approximately 10% of the questions were multiple-choice questions, the rest required the students to formulate their own answers. Students answers were scored by two independent researchers and pooled into six categories (see table 1) and the percentage of students able to accommodate the learning goals described were calculated (figure 3).

Three independent researchers coded qualitative and quantitative data separately.

Each of the teachers participated in a semi-structured group interview. The interviews were conducted between one and three weeks after the learning activities had taken place. Each interview consisted of three parts: Firstly, teachers were asked if there were any challenges when using the model. Secondly, teachers were asked to elaborate on the advantages for both students and teachers on using the CMC approach. Finally, in the third and last part of the interviews, teachers were asked to consider if they would use the CMC approach when working with other phenomena or even with other subjects. The interviews were audio-recorded and analyzed by two independent researchers who gathered, analyzed, and discussed relevant quotes.

3 RESULTS

3.1 Quantitative data: Students

We examined how students were able to use and understand the model they worked with, analyze and evaluate the model in regard to the subject, if the students were able to draw connections between the code and the interface, and finally if the students were able to successfully modify the code in order to improve the model.

As shown in figure 3, almost all of the students were able to perform the tasks related to these learning goals, with successfully performing students ranging from 74 to 90%. However, 79% of the students were able to perform tasks such as modifying the properties of an agent or adding a new type of agent (figure 3, last category "working with code"). This is suggestive of a highly positive effect in light of the fact that 93% of all students reported that they had no or very little experience with programming.

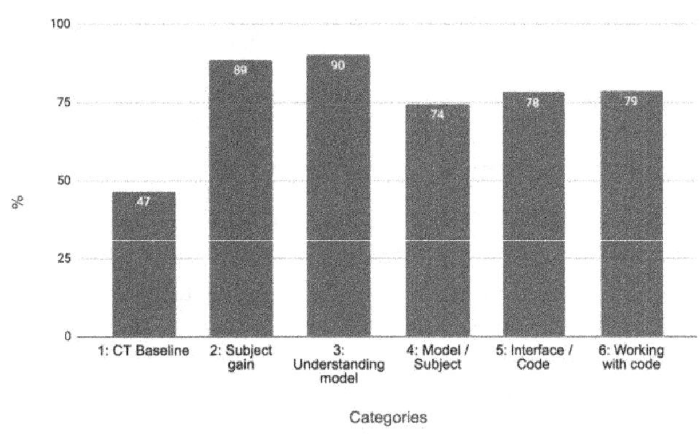

Figure 3: Percentage of students that successfully solved tasks in category

With a pre- and post-test in the form of a questionnaire we probed what students perceived they could learn from models in the subject (e.g. chemistry) as shown in figure 4.

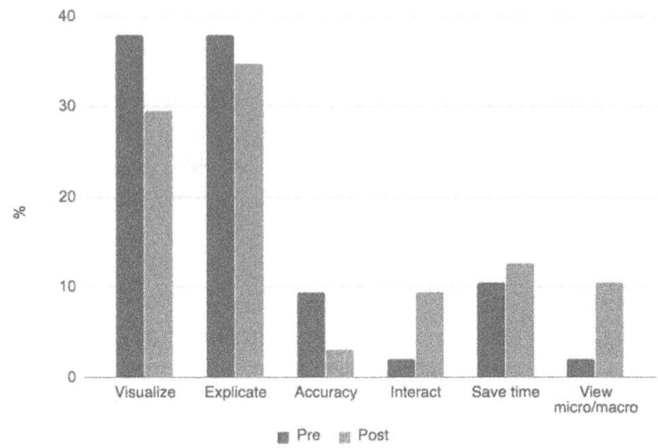

Figure 4: Students' perception of learning objectives acquired after working with computer models.

Interestingly, before having worked with a model, more students reported that computer models helped them visualize and explicate a phenomenon better as opposed to after. One explanation for this finding could be that a pictorial understanding of something is not a deeper conceptual understanding. Thus, students might realize that a visualization (e.g. a picture) does not have adequate information or does not adequately represent the more complex representations that a computer model is capable of. This might be the case in dynamic phenomena (e.g. transport across cell membrane osmosis) where a simple visualization carries less dynamic information that a NetLogo model.

After having worked with a model there was an increase in students who described being able to interact with the model, to save time as oppose to conducting an experiment in real life, and to see micro- and macro-levels of the phenomenon as important purposes of computer models.

3.2 Qualitative data: Teachers

In the semi-structured interviews teachers were asked to elaborate on their experiences with the CMC approach and how NetLogo worked as a learning environment in their class. Of the 15 teachers, only two had prior programming experience in NetLogo. Nevertheless, teachers found that using NetLogo, as a programming environment, made them confident enough to conduct the learning activities without any prior experience in programming or in NetLogo.

"When they [the students] see that the computational model does not match with their own perception of the phenomenon, they can change the code until it fit with what's in their head. That is what the program [NetLogo] can really give me. I can simply check, or see visually, what the students thinks. I have not been able to do that in any other way."

Figure 5: Quotation from a biotechnology teacher

Four teachers mentioned that when students use and modify the code in a model and interact with the teacher while doing so, the students reveal their perception of the phenomenon to the teacher, expressed by a male science teacher in figure 5. Some teachers mentioned that the activities activated other groups of students (such as quiet girls or poor students) than would normally be the most active in class. However, some teachers expressed concern over the fact that a small group of students persistently over the project period lacked motivation for working with code (see quotation in figure 6). More than half of the teachers expressed a wish for more models of other phenomena relevant to their subject and with more complex content knowledge embedded in the models.

"All students started tinkering with the model and most of the students worked very concentrated with the tasks given in the questionnaire. However, a few students didn't seem to be motivated by the tasks, and I found it difficult to engage them."

Figure 6: Quotation from a social science teacher

4 DISCUSSION

4.1 Quantitative data: Students

The finding (figure 3) that a majority of students were able to use, understanding, analyze, and evaluate the models and modify the code behind the models to improve them needs explanation. We take it to mean two things. First, the CMC approach can be used to design meaningful learning activities in which students obtain CT learning goals. Second, NetLogo is an appropriate programming environment for high school students in any of the four subjects tested.

Pre- and post-questions suggested that students change their perspective on what computer models can be used for in subjects when working with a model, see figure 4. Especially interesting is the finding, that students become increasingly aware of levels in phenomena after working with a model. Students emphasized the importance of levels thinking by pointing out how the interface of a NetLogo model can visualize the macro-level described by the micro-level in the code behind. This touch on a point that other researchers have made about affordances of interacting with code to engage in inquiry that help students think through and learn about mechanism [27].

4.2 Qualitative data: Teachers

An interesting quotation is from a male teacher (see figure 5). He elaborates how the application of the CMC approach enabled him as a teacher to elicit the students' perception of the phenomenon. Hence, the quotation demonstrates how powerful a tool computer models can be to teachers, as it helps them to scaffold and evaluate the student' progress in regards to both CT and the content knowledge. However, we must also be aware of the concern illustrated in figure 6 that not all students become motivated by the CMC approach.

Teachers asked for the project team of developers to develop more models in all subjects. Given the teachers enthusiasm about the models, this in no way suggests laziness on their behalf, but rather that teachers wanted to experiment with more models as learning activities. However, we did not adequately provide more models due to lack of resources.

The tinkering approach produced both eureka moments for students (when a representation was especially informative and thus an aha-experience) as well as moments of frustration when students were uncertain about how the model worked and what it represented. Other researchers have concluded when working with NetLogo models that a minimally structured activity followed by a highly structured activity (e.g. the use of worksheets) might lead to longer-term learning gains [24, 25]. The second design principle is to apply three steps: Use, modify, and create as a progression in learning tasks leading the students down a path of working with and learning code and acquiring aspects of CT [5, 26]. By applying these principles, we believe that the students become more motivated, engaged and less intimidated by working with computer models and with code. Thereby rendering the measurement of students' modeling skills and CT [9].

Keeping in mind that this design-based research study focused on developing CT and modeling in high school subjects, our study suggests that it is possible to plan short interventions of CT sequences and obtain student learning in CT in other subjects than computer science. However, future research is needed to examine how students with a limited computer coding proficiency learn to work with increasingly more complex code. As students refine the models and build the code to represent more and more complex phenomena it would be relevant to investigate student experiences: What do students perceive as complex code and why? This has ramifications for how the model should be designed in order to be adequately complex and accommodate relevant learning goals in CT. In particular, we would, based on this study, suggest that future design-based research use agent-based modeling in order to develop models of teaching CT in different high-school subjects.

5 CONCLUSION

In this work, we have focused on developing teaching activities around computer models that represent phenomena in both biotechnology, chemistry, biology, and social sciences. The modeling approach helped students tinker with both models and content knowledge. Although this teaching experiment found that students gained knowledge in both CT and content knowledge through working with computer models of phenomena in four different subjects more work should be conducted on extending the models into new subjects and domains. Four issues should be of concern here. First, to make sure we are not just describing a Pygmalion effect where anything new (e.g. a new NetLogo model) will have a short-term positive effect but not a long-term positive effect on performance. Second, we need to conceive of abstraction in terms of not only student understanding of content in a given high school subject but abstraction as a concrete manifestation or a computational solution that can be used in subjects for problem solving. Third, students problem solving should be measured using a continuous variable and not a Boolean variable. For instance, a limitation of this study leading to measurement bias was the use of a methodology where we rated poor performance as zero and successful performance as one. CT is hardly a dichotomous variable that students either have or do not have, but a set pf complex problem solving skills. Thus CT should be tested with dynamic (cognitive and computational) models in terms of whether students are successful in using, modifying and creating code over time. Fourth, more comparative research should be conducted in terms of how well different subjects might facilitate students' development of CT. We found biotechnology, social science and chemistry equally amenable to model phenomena whereby students could learn CT. All participating teachers were able to collaborate with researchers and developers in this project to produce models that generated CT in students regardless of their subjects.

CT helps raise fundamental ontological questions in high-school teaching about what is biology, social science etc.? This was originally pointed out by Papert [1 p.140] who asked: What is the potential influence of computation on students' understanding of physics? Will CT bring student nearer to grasping what a subject is or merely confuse them about phenomena, representations, codes and models? Our teaching experiment showed that by letting students tinker with models they were able to integrate both coding, modelling and content knowledge.

ACKNOWLEDGMENTS

We are grateful to PhD Palle Nowack for engaging in fruitful discussions leading to the CMC approach. We thank professors: Michael E. Caspersen, Deborah Tatar, Keld Nielsen, Arthur Hjort, and research assistant Nick Nielsen for discussions about CT. We thank the anonymous reviewers for constructive and relevant feedback. We are grateful for financial support from Region Midt and It-vest. Last, we extend our thanks to the 15 teachers and 210 students participating in the study.

REFERENCES

[1] Papert, S. (1980). *Mindstorms: Children, computers, and powerful ideas.* Basic Books, Inc.

[2] Wing, J. M. (2006). Computational thinking. *Communications of the ACM, 49*(3), 33-35.

[3] Brennan, K., & Resnick, M. (2012, April). New frameworks for studying and assessing the development of computational thinking. In *Proceedings of the 2012 annual meeting of the American Educational Research Association, Vancouver, Canada* (Vol. 1, p. 25).

[4] Bocconi, S., Chioccariello, A., Dettori, G., Ferrari, A., Engelhardt, K., Kampylis, P., & Punie, Y. (2016, July). Exploring the field of computational thinking as a 21st century skill. In *Proceedings of the International Conference on Education and New Learning TechnologiesJuly 2016Barcelona, Spain Page* (pp. 4725-4733).

[5] Lee, I., Martin, F., Denner, J., Coulter, B., Allan, W., Erickson, J., ... & Werner, L. (2011). Computational thinking for youth in practice. *Acm Inroads, 2*(1), 32-37.

[6] Centola, D., Wilensky, U., & McKenzie, E. (2013, April). A hands-on modeling approach to evolution: Learning about the evolution of cooperation and altruism through multi-agent modeling-The EACH Project. In *International Conference of the Learning Sciences: Facing the Challenges of Complex Real-world Settings* (p. 166). Psychology Press.

[7] Machluf, Y., & Yarden, A. (2013). Integrating bioinformatics into senior high school: design principles and implications. *Briefings in bioinformatics, 14*(5), 648-660.

[8] Ioannidou, A., Repenning, A., Lewis, C., Cherry, G., & Rader, C. (2003). Making constructionism work in the classroom. *International Journal of Computers for Mathematical Learning, 8*(1), 63-108.

[9] Weintrop, D., Beheshti, E., Horn, M. S., Orton, K., Trouille, L., Jona, K., & Wilensky, U. (2014, July). Interactive assessment tools for computational thinking in High School STEM classrooms. In *International Conference on Intelligent Technologies for Interactive Entertainment* (pp. 22-25). Springer, Cham.

[10] Tatar, D., Harrison, S., Stewart, M., Frisina, C., & Musaeus, P. (2017). Proto-computational thinking: The uncomfortable underpinnings. In *Emerging research, practice, and policy on computational thinking* (pp. 63-81). Springer, Cham.

[11] Lockwood, J., & Mooney, A. (2017). Computational Thinking in Education: Where does it fit? A systematic literary review. *arXiv preprint arXiv:1703.07659.*

[12] Grover, S., & Pea, R. (2013). Computational thinking in K–12: A review of the state of the field. *Educational Researcher, 42*(1), 38-43.

[13] Caspersen, M. E., Gal-Ezer, J., Nardelli, E., Vahrenhold, J., & Westermeier, M. (2018, February). The CECE Report: Creating a Map of Informatics in European Schools. In *Proceedings of the 49th ACM Technical Symposium on Computer Science Education* (pp. 916-917). ACM.

[14] Kynigos, C. (2007). Using half-baked microworlds to challenge teacher educators' knowing. *International journal of computers for mathematical learning, 12*(2), 87-111.

[15] Wagh, A., Cook-Whitt, K., & Wilensky, U. (2017). Bridging inquiry-based science and constructionism: Exploring the alignment between students tinkering with code of computational models and goals of inquiry. *Journal of Research in Science Teaching, 54*(5), 615-641.

[16] Wilensky, U. (1999). NetLogo (and NetLogo User Manual), Center for Connected Learning and Computer-Based Modeling, Northwestern University. http://ccl.northwestern.edu/netlogo/.

[17] Hjorth, A., & Wilensky, U. (2014). Re-grow Your City: A NetLogo Curriculum Unit on Regional Development. Boulder, CO: International Society of the Learning Sciences.

[18] Wilensky, U., & Reisman, K. (2006). Thinking like a wolf, a sheep, or a firefly: Learning biology through constructing and testing computational theories—an embodied modeling approach. *Cognition and instruction, 24*(2), 171-209.

[19] Wing, J. 2011. Research notebook: Computational thinking "What and why? ". In *TheLink Magazine, Spring. Carnegie Mellon University, Pittsburgh.*

[20] Papert, S., & Harel, I. (1991). Situating constructionism. *Constructionism,* 36(2), 1-11.

[21] Vygotsky, L. S. (1980). *Mind in society: The development of higher psychological processes.* Harvard university press.

[22] Weintrop, D., Beheshti, E., Horn, M., Orton, K., Jona, K., Trouille, L., & Wilensky, U. (2016). Defining computational thinking for mathematics and science classrooms. *Journal of Science Education and Technology, 25*(1), 127-147.

[23] Nowack, P., & Caspersen, M. E. (2014, November). Model-based thinking and practice: A top-down approach to computational thinking. In *Proceedings of the 14th Koli Calling International Conference on Computing Education Research* (pp. 147-151). ACM.

[24] Berland, M., Martin, T., Benton, T., Petrick Smith, C., & Davis, D. (2013). Using learning analytics to understand the learning pathways of novice programmers. *Journal of the Learning Sciences, 22*(4), 564-599.

[25] Jang, H., Reeve, J., & Deci, E. L. (2010). Engaging students in learning activities: It is not autonomy support or structure but autonomy support and structure. *Journal of educational psychology, 102*(3), 588.

[26] Sentance, S., & Waite, J. (2017, November). PRIMM: Exploring pedagogical approaches for teaching text-based programming in school. In *Proceedings of the 12th Workshop on Primary and Secondary Computing Education* (pp. 113-114). ACM.

[27] Sherin, B. L. (2001). A comparison of programming languages and algebraic notation as expressive languages for physics. *International Journal of Computers for Mathematical Learning,* 6, 1-61.

WatDFS: A Project for Understanding Distributed Systems in the Undergraduate Curriculum

Michael Abebe, Brad Glasbergen, Khuzaima Daudjee
Cheriton School of Computer Science, University of Waterloo
{mtabebe,bjglasbe,kdaudjee}@uwaterloo.ca

ABSTRACT

The ubiquity of distributed computing systems has led to an increased focus on distributed systems in the undergraduate curriculum. In this paper, we describe the design of, and our experiences with, a new distributed systems project where students implement the core components of a distributed file system called WatDFS. The WatDFS project enables students to meet learning objectives from across the distributed systems curriculum and interact with real systems, while providing a high-quality testing environment that yields actionable feedback to students on their submissions.

ACM Reference Format:
Michael Abebe, Brad Glasbergen, Khuzaima Daudjee. 2019. WatDFS: A Project for Understanding Distributed Systems, in the Undergraduate Curriculum. In *Proceedings of the 50th ACM Technical Symposium on Computer Science Education (SIGCSE '19), February 27-March 2, 2019, Minneapolis, MN, USA.* ACM, New York, NY, USA, 7 pages. https://doi.org/10.1145/3287324.3287473

1 INTRODUCTION

The collection of vast amounts of data in domains such as science, commerce and health has outstripped the computing and storage capacity of a single, centralized machine, fueling the need to store and access these data on clusters of machines that together provide enhanced storage and compute capacities [30, 33]. Many everyday services that users interact with, such as Netflix, Gmail and Facebook are all backed by such clusters. These clusters are popularly called *distributed systems* and have become ubiquitous, providing the view of a single coherent system with appropriate transparencies for storing and managing user data. Due to their ubiquity, from the perspective of both individual users and the design and development of large-scale industrial applications, there is a need to focus on distributed systems in the undergraduate curriculum [4, 24].

At our university, distributed systems is a semestered course taught at the 4th-year level to approximately 120 undergraduate students, with an operating systems course being a pre-requisite. The course focuses on the fundamentals of distributed systems [34], covering the following topics: architectures of distributed systems, a brief overview of computer networks, communication paradigms including remote procedure calls (RPCs), distributed file systems, coordination/synchronization, replication, consistency, and fault tolerance. A primary focus of the course is understanding the trade-offs made as a consequence of design decisions in distributed systems [3, 8, 23]. We evaluate a student's understanding of these fundamental concepts and their trade-offs via four assignments throughout the semester and a final written exam. Two written assignments focus on assessing the students' understanding of the principles of distributed systems. The other two assignments together form a programming project that enables students to apply the fundamental course concepts through their *implementation and use.* These programming assignments, and our experiences with them, are the focus of this experience report.

Previously, a distributed systems programming project in our course required students to implement the functionality of an RPC library using socket primitives [7, 16] to support client-server computing. To allow students to learn the basics of socket programming, students first implemented an `echo` server that would respond to client requests with the contents of each request. For the second programming assignment, they developed an RPC library that allowed applications to invoke function calls on a remote server. This second assignment required locating a server that could satisfy client requests via a directory server, serializing the request, and sending it to the remote server. The server deserializes the request, executes it, and then serializes and sends back the result.

Reflecting on the previous assignments that comprised the programming project, we observed that the assignments covered topics from only the first few course modules. Furthermore, the product of the assignments was an RPC library that necessitates integration into a software project from its inception. Consequently, students lacked the opportunity to use their library with real-world system software and applications that use RPCs. Finally, some students made small mistakes in their assignments which stymied communication between client and server, hindering the implementation and testing of the rest of the assignment's functionality. Based on these reflections, we decided to develop an entirely new set of programming assignments that encompass material from the whole course, allow students to interact with existing systems and applications seamlessly, and support a testing environment that gives students high-quality and timely feedback on their submissions.

Towards this goal, we created a programming project that comprised a pair of assignments in which students develop a distributed file system, **WatDFS**, which acts as a *real* file system in a Unix environment. Consequently, students can interact with their file system using standard tools and Unix commands such as `cat`, `echo` and `cp` to access and manage their files, or edit them with a text editor.

Students implement WatDFS using the Filesystem in Userspace (FUSE) library [2, 35, 36], which is supported by the Virtual File System (VFS) layer of most popular operating systems. A key advantage

SIGCSE '19, February 27-March 2, 2019, Minneapolis, MN, USA

ACM ISBN 978-1-4503-5890-3/19/02...$15.00
https://doi.org/10.1145/3287324.3287473

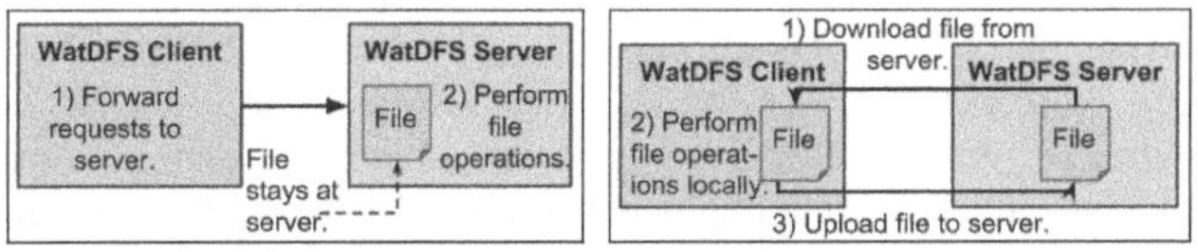

(a) Remote-Access Model (b) Upload-Download Model

Figure 1: Two models of distributed file systems: the remote-access model, which sends all requests to the server, and the upload-download model, which operates on files locally.

of using FUSE is that it precludes the need to write kernel-space code that is often complex and difficult to comprehend [26, 31] for students who want to learn the core concepts of distributed systems. Over the course of the two assignments, students implement WatDFS using two standard distributed file system models: the remote-access model, and the upload-download model [34].

In this paper, we share our experiences of rolling out the WatDFS assignments in the hope that our explanations and reflections will be useful pedagogically for other educators who design similar assignments or build upon our work in their classes. Importantly, our analysis focuses on how the WatDFS project serves to bridge the gap between the theory and practice of distributed systems, which is otherwise difficult to achieve in the classroom [5, 9, 11, 16, 25, 38].

2 DESIGN OF THE WATDFS ASSIGNMENTS

In the WatDFS assignments, students implement the core components of a distributed file system. Completed, WatDFS supports creating, opening, reading, writing and closing files on local or remote machines. WatDFS follows the typical client-server architecture: an application interacts via standard I/O system calls with a WatDFS client, which in turn communicates with a WatDFS server.

Students implement WatDFS using two common models in distributed file systems: remote-access and upload-download (Figure 1). In the remote-access model, the client forwards all requests to the server, which then performs the file system operations on behalf of the client. The remote-access model performs poorly if the latency between the client and server is high because every request must be sent to the remote (and potentially distant) server. By contrast, in the upload-download model, the client downloads a copy of the file from the server, performs operations locally and — when the client is done with the file — uploads the file back to the server. Consequently, the upload-download model reduces latency when repeatedly operating on a remote file by performing operations locally and avoiding excess communication with the remote server. More generally, the remote-access and upload-download models represent two common design choices in client-server architectures: moving computation to the server (in this case, file operations), or moving data (transferring files), and therefore computation, closer to the client. As students implement these models, they are directly presented with the algorithmic tasks and ensuing performance trade-offs discussed in the course.

2.1 Architecture of WatDFS

As mentioned in Section 1, we designed the assignments such that students can use and test their code using real systems and applications. In the course, students learn that popular distributed file systems are implemented such that applications can interact with them

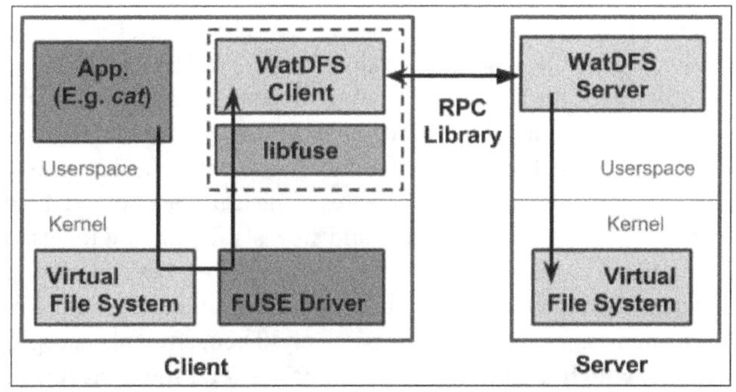

Figure 2: The architecture of WatDFS: requests from an application arrive at the WatDFS client through `libfuse`. If necessary, the WatDFS client communicates with the WatDFS server on a remote machine using an RPC library which performs file system operations on the server. Students implement the WatDFS client and server.

transparently. That is, applications operate without knowledge that the file they are accessing may reside on a remote machine [18]. In implementing the assignments, students directly observe the value of access transparency in file systems because they can use their assignment solution as a real file system without modifying existing applications. Although access transparency simplifies the integration between a distributed file system and applications, the file system may return errors, for example network errors, that applications do not expect. Thus, the WatDFS assignments also expose students to transparency challenges.

Traditionally, distributed file systems such as Sun's Network File System (NFS) achieve access transparency by integrating directly into the kernel. However, we preferred that students did not have to modify kernel code because of the challenges associated with the lack of memory protection, standard libraries, debugging tools, and complex dependencies [26, 31]. Instead, WatDFS uses FUSE to allow students to create their own file systems entirely in user-space in C or C++ (Figure 2). Applications issue system calls to manipulate files, which are passed through the kernel into the VFS and the FUSE driver. The FUSE driver issues the corresponding `libfuse` calls to a user-space client library, which the students implement. To manage files, the client library issues remote procedure calls (RPCs) to the WatDFS server that students implement. The WatDFS server handles client requests and supports ten `libfuse` calls for both assignments [2]. The semantics for the `libfuse` calls varies per assignment; we describe their behavior in the following sections.

We provide students with a custom RPC library, which supports registering functions at the server that the client can then call. The RPC library is provided to students to reduce implementation time and enables them to focus on distributed file-system concepts.

2.2 Remote-Access Model

The WatDFS assignments require students to support distributed file-system functionality using `libfuse` and an RPC library, both of which are new technologies for students. With that in mind, we designed the remote-access assignment to familiarize students with these technologies and the basics of WatDFS before beginning the more challenging upload-download assignment.

In the remote-access model, the WatDFS client handles `libfuse` calls by issuing file-system operations to the WatDFS server, which executes them on the client's behalf and sends back the results. We suggest that students first implement the `getattr` `libfuse` call, which is used to retrieve file metadata. Afterwards, students support the `mknod` call, which creates a file if it does not exist, and the `open` call, which opens a file and stores a file handle for use in subsequent `libfuse` calls. The `read` and `write` `libfuse` calls are considered next, which read data from a file into a buffer and write data from a buffer into a file, respectively. Then, students complete `release`, which is called asynchronously after a file is closed and signals that the file system can close the file and free any associated metadata. Finally, students implement the remaining calls: `utime`, which changes the file modification time; `fsync`, which flushes the file to disk; and `truncate`, which adjusts the file's size.

Students are provided with detailed descriptions of the `libfuse` calls in the assignment specification, and must decide which file-system operations the WatDFS server should perform when it receives a request from a client. To assist students with this task, we provide an instrumented `libfuse` library that logs the name and arguments of received calls to a debugging file. With the logged information, students can write or use existing applications to interact with their WatDFS client and observe how, and when, different `libfuse` calls are issued. Students are encouraged to use the `strace` tool [1] on existing applications (e.g., `cat`) to observe the system calls that they make and how they are translated to `libfuse` calls.

We simplified design and debugging for this first assignment by requiring students to follow a specific RPC protocol, which allows automated tests (Section 2.4) to quickly point out communication errors before students work on the higher-level functionality.

2.3 Upload-Download Model

In the second assignment, students implement WatDFS using the upload-download model. In the upload-download model, the WatDFS client downloads and locally caches a copy of the file from the WatDFS server, performs file operations on the cached copy and uploads the file copy back to the server when the client is done using it. Students build on their remote-access model solution, adding support for file transfer, cache consistency, and mutual exclusion.

WatDFS uses a timeout-based caching scheme similar to that of NFS, which allows stale reads, as covered in class. In this timeout-based caching scheme, a file is periodically re-downloaded from the server, or re-uploaded to the server, when a *freshness condition* F no longer holds. WatDFS defines the freshness condition for a file as follows.

Let T_{client} be the time the file was last modified by the client, and T_{server} the time the file was last modified at the server. Let $T_{validate}$ be the time the client last validated the freshness of the file, where $T_{validate}$ is the time the client downloaded the file if it has not yet been validated. Then the freshness condition for time T is $F = [(T - T_{validate}) < T_{fresh}] \vee [T_{client} == T_{server}]$, where T_{fresh} is a configurable interval that defines the amount of time that can elapse between file validation checks. When F is false, the client must synchronize its copy of the file with the server.

In words, the freshness condition is true, if the file has been recently validated, or if the file has not been modified locally at the client or the server since the time the file was last downloaded. At the end of freshness check, $T_{validate}$ is updated to the current time. Note that the first clause of the freshness condition can be evaluated without contacting the server and the second clause requires retrieving only file metadata from the server. Students are expected to include these optimizations in their solution.

Students are required to perform all file operations locally at the client, which means that a copy of the file must be downloaded first. Before every read operation, the freshness condition must be checked; if it fails, then the file is downloaded from the server. After write operations, the freshness condition is checked; if it fails, then the file is uploaded to the server. In WatDFS, three `libfuse` calls have special semantics: `open` should always fetch the file from the server, `release` should upload the file to the server if it was open for writes, and `fsync` forces an upload of the file to the server.

Students must prevent concurrent file modification by ensuring that a file is open in write mode by only one client at a time. The WatDFS server enforces this requirement by returning an error (`-EACCES`) if it receives a request to open a file in write-mode that has already been opened in write mode by another client. To prevent partial file updates, students implement atomic uploads and downloads of files, while allowing multiple simultaneous downloads. To assist students with these mutual-exclusion requirements, we provide them with an implementation of a reader-writer lock.

2.4 Assessment of WatDFS Assignments

Student submissions are primarily assessed through automated test cases. Students may submit their assignments any number of times before the deadline to a Marmoset server [29], which has two classes of test cases. A student can immediately view the results of all *public tests* for their submission, but must pass all of the public tests before they can run the *release tests*. For a given submission, a student can see at most two failed release test cases and can release test their submission at most five times in a 24-hour window. The limited availability of release tests encourages students to re-examine their code when they fail a test, develop their own system tests and to start their assignments early [29].

In the remote-access model assignment, the public tests issue simple file operations and verify that the RPC requests and responses are correct. These basic tests account for 30% of the assignment's mark. This assignment's release tests are end-to-end system tests, verifying that applications using I/O system calls perform correctly. The most difficult tests involve reading and writing large files, which necessitates invoking multiple RPCs to ensure that entire buffers of data are read or written. The release tests account for 65% of the assignment's mark, and 5% is awarded for a short README.

All tests in the upload-download model assignment are end-to-end system tests. The public tests are similar to the remote-access model's release tests, but also ensure that files are correctly uploaded and downloaded from the server, and account for 40% of the assignment's mark. The release tests are worth 35% of the assignment's mark and test the cache consistency and mutual exclusion requirements of the assignment. For example, one test ensures that when the freshness interval expires, a client re-downloads the file from the server and sees any updates. Finally, we allocate 25% of the assignment's marks to a system manual, where students describe the architecture and design decisions of their WatDFS solution.

3 OUTCOMES AND EXPERIENCES

The WatDFS assignments are designed with a number of learning goals and objectives in mind. In this section, we discuss these goals, share our experiences from the deployment of the assignments in our course, and describe extensions to WatDFS.

3.1 Learning Goals and Objectives

The WatDFS assignments give students the opportunity to *use* and *apply* concepts from distributed systems by implementing the core components of a distributed file system. We highlight the relevant curricular content that students are exposed to when doing the WatDFS assignments, based on learning objectives in the distributed systems course and from the relevant curricula [4, 24].

3.1.1 Relevance to Course Material. The course introduces distributed system *models* and the *trade-offs* associated with them. In WatDFS, students implement a client-server model: the WatDFS client initiates a request on behalf of the application, and the WatDFS server satisfies the request. The remote-access model features a stateless client, while the upload-download model uses a stateful client. When implementing the upload-download model, students must manage *distributed state* and *replicas* using the timeout-based cache *consistency* scheme. A complete solution also uses *mutual-exclusion* primitives to ensure that there is at most a single-writer to a file, and to provide *atomic* file transfers during the file upload or download. Finally, for the WatDFS client to communicate with the WatDFS server, students must make *RPCs*. In summary, by implementing the two common models of distributed file systems, students are directly exposed to the trade-offs between the two models, which are representative of choices faced by distributed systems developers.

Given the nature of the WatDFS assignments, students also focus on *systems-related* learning objectives such as using file systems. While completing the WatDFS client, students must implement `libfuse` calls, which have similar behavior and interfaces to VFS calls. Students were also exposed to *access transparency* since the WatDFS client enables applications to access local and remote resources using the same file system interface.

3.1.2 Use of Real Systems and Applications. FUSE enables students to develop a distributed file system that supports access transparency. This design choice has two important consequences: (i) it exposes students to key systems and software development practices, and (ii) it makes it easier for students to test and reason about correctness (Section 3.1.3).

As WatDFS is a programming assignment, it requires students to apply many fundamental concepts in *system and software development*. We provide students with starter code and libraries to complete the WatDFS assignments. To successfully use this code, students must read and understand the documentation and examples, building on their experience from doing so in their prerequisite operating systems course. As WatDFS executes entirely in user-space, students had to perform system calls. Doing so requires understanding system call functionality, arguments, and return values. The ability to read and understand documentation and follow examples is an essential skill when working with systems/technologies [14]. In fact, it is a common requirement for students who are asked to work on system design and development on a work (co-op) term or when they start full-time employment as software developers. [1]

3.1.3 High Quality Testing Environment. WatDFS acts as a real file system, allowing students to test their code easily: any existing application that performs file creation, reads, or writes can be used to test functionality. Students are required to discuss their testing strategy in their documentation, which encourages students to design and write their own tests. Many students reported using existing command line tools (`echo`, `cat`, `less`, `tail`) to manipulate files. Students also wrote their own test cases using programming languages such as `C++` and `python` to edit files in WatDFS using language-specific features.

To provide students with feedback, we used Marmoset [29] as an automated test-server. As described in Section 2.4, we used a combination of public and release tests. However, for each failed test we also provided guidance on how students could alter their system. For example, in the case of the RPC protocol tests for the remote-access model, a test asserted that the WatDFS client issued the correct RPC and handled the return correctly. If the test fails, we configured Marmoset to print any called `libfuse` functions and their expected argument types to help students reproduce the test locally. For the end-to-end system tests, we provided a brief description of the failed test which a student can use to construct a similar test case as well as a general description of the cause of failure. For example, a test description in the upload-download model is "Testing error handling when a file is opened multiple times"; on a test failure a student would receive: "Expected to get `EACCES` on second file open, but got no errors". Such guided statements helped students correct their own code, and as we discuss next, resulted in a positive experience with the assignment.

3.2 Experiences with WatDFS

We now share our experiences with the WatDFS assignments, highlighting their effectiveness and providing insight into our plans to iteratively improve the teaching and learning environment for students. We base our discussion on analyses of 115 student grades, questions posed by students on the class discussion forum, and conversations with students both during office hours and in class.

Figure 3a displays a cumulative distribution function (CDF) of student grades for the remote-access model assignment. The x-axis of the graph corresponds to the percentage of students that achieved at least the grade on the y-axis. We show three plots, one for each of the three sub-components of the assignment. The figure shows that almost all students (95%) achieved full marks for the RPC protocol portion of the assignment, indicating that students understood how to use the RPC library and `libfuse`. Students who lost marks on the assignment tended to do so on a test of handling reads and writes from/to large files, which was worth 10% of the (total) assignment mark. Submissions that failed this test did not loop within `libfuse` `read` and `write` calls until the requested amount of data was read/written, as noted in the assignment specification.

To better understand how students worked through the assignment, we examined 221 student questions on the class discussion

[1] Our university has a large co-operative education program, and many students work at software/systems companies such as Google, Facebook, Amazon or start-ups.

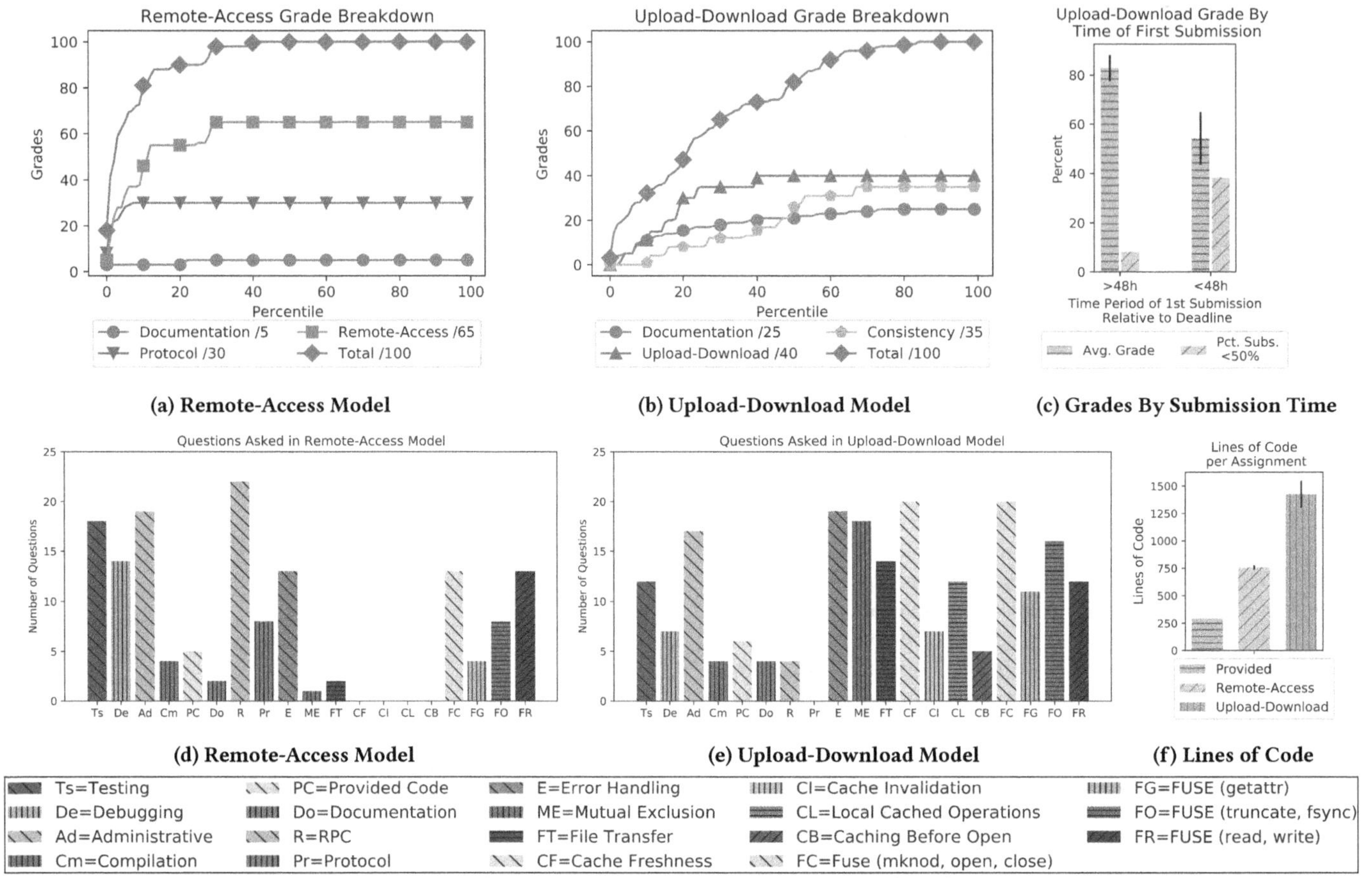

Figure 3: Metrics for student assesment in the WatDFS assignments. Student grades, displayed as a cumulative distribution function (CDF), for WatDFS assignments, and average lines of code. A break down of the number of questions asked in each assignment that relate to a particular topic. Sub-topics share a color, and a short description of each topic is offered as a legend.

forum. We selected 19 different categories and subcategories relating to the assignment specification/requirements and labeled each question according to which of the categories and subcategories it belonged. In Figure 3d, we display the number of questions that were asked in each category for the remote-access model assignment. Subcategories share a common color, and the first letter of their abbreviation, with their parent category. For example, questions about FUSE (purple color — FC, FG, FO, FR) were further categorized based on the specific function in question.

As noted in Section 2.2, the remote-access model assignment is designed to familiarize students with the RPC library, `libfuse`, and programming/debugging in WatDFS. Consequently, student questions for this assignment (Figure 3d) were primarily focused on testing and debugging (e.g. "Why am I failing this test?", "How do I trace the calls '`cat`' makes?"), the usage of the provided code (e.g. "Why am I getting this RPC error?"), or `libfuse` calls, specifically those related to file creation, reading and writing. Based on the types of questions that students asked and the grades that students attained, we can infer that the remote-access model was successful in helping students familiarize themselves with WatDFS.

In contrast to the remote-access model, the upload-download assignment generated questions that were mostly related to error handling, cache consistency, mutual exclusion and how these topics applied to operations supported by `libfuse`. Error handling was more important in the upload-download assignment than in the remote-access model because the remote-access model simply reported errors back to the application. In the upload-download model, students had to decide what to do when an error occurred in the middle of an operation, such as during file transfer.

Given the objectives of the upload-download assignment, many of the questions related to cache consistency: clarifying the freshness condition or when a file should be considered invalid. These questions focused on the semantics of caching in the context of `libfuse` operations that are outside the boundaries of file open and close operations. The crux of these questions is the gap between the theory and practice of the upload-download model. Specifically, standard textbooks [34] state that the upload-download model performs all operations locally, and that the file is first downloaded to the client on the file open call. However, downloading a copy of the file only on `libfuse` `open` while performing all file operations locally is not possible because some `libfuse` calls (e.g. `getattr`, `truncate`, `mknod`) can occur before `open`. Consequently, some students were unsure of the semantics because not all operations can be applied locally if the file is downloaded only on `open`. In future versions of the WatDFS assignments, we plan to be clearer that all operations are to be performed locally, even if that necessitates downloading the file first to support the upload-download model semantics. We say this while keeping in mind that practice can deviate from theory where system design and development is concerned.

While reviewing student grades for the upload-download model (Figure 3b), we observed more variation compared to the remote-access model. A majority of students (60%) passed all of the basic upload-download model tests, with 33% of students passing all of the cache consistency tests. Overall, more than 80% of students passed the majority of the programming tests. Inspection of submissions that passed all of the upload-download tests, but did not pass all of the cache consistency tests (27% of students) revealed that these submissions either did not check the freshness condition and/or enforce mutual exclusion, or had errors in implementing these requirements. We gave students three weeks to work on the upload-download model and through weekly reminders emphasized the importance of beginning the assignment early. Indeed, we observed a significant difference in the average grade between students who had at least one submission to the Marmoset test servers 48 hours before the assignment deadline and those who did not (Figure 3c). 70% of students who received less than half of the programming marks had no submissions until within 48 hours of the assignment deadline, indicating that they may have run out of time. Moreover, 45% (8%) of students who had their first submission within (prior to) 48 hours of the deadline did not pass the majority of tests.[2] Figure 3f displays the average lines of code in student submissions for the remote-access (758 lines) and upload-download (1425 lines) assignments, including provided code (294 lines).

Finally, as noted in Section 2.4, 25% of the marks in the upload-download model were allocated for a system manual describing design choices. We encouraged students who did not complete the full functionality of the assignment to describe how they would have implemented the functionality in WatDFS. Importantly, this requirement allows students to express their understanding of the concepts even if they had a partial implementation.

Overall, our experience has been that the WatDFS assignments exposed students to the core aspects of distributed systems and key systems technologies. Although anecdotal, a student summarized their experience as: "*This assignment was probably my favorite part of the course and the most fun I've had programming for any assignment [...] FUSE was a brilliant way to integrate the course concepts into something very practical and I was really happy that I could actually test my work by trying to edit the remote files in Vim.*"

3.3 Extensions to WatDFS

There are several opportunities for extending the WatDFS assignments. Both the remote-access model and the upload-download model could be extended to include operations on file system directories, which students were not required to support. To do so in the upload-download model would require managing a cache of different object types with different rules for files and directories. The WatDFS assignment currently operates with all clients interacting with a single server. Students could be tasked with managing multiple WatDFS servers or using a quorum protocol to keep server state consistent while supporting file replicas.

With the exception of the `libfuse release` call, WatDFS operations are synchronous. Consequently, in the upload-download model, the entire file must be downloaded before any operations can take place. Students could implement asynchronous features in WatDFS to support downloading a file in the background, or predictively prefetching a file. Alternatively, WatDFS could support Coda file system style callbacks that indicate a file has been modified, and allow the application to force a new download of the file [27].

Finally, although WatDFS follows a design similar to NFS, there exist a wide variety of distributed file systems including those that provide varying consistency models [32], fault tolerance schemes [17, 37], metadata management [13], or interfaces [22]. The WatDFS assignments could be modified to incorporate these ideas.

4 RELATED WORK

The WatDFS assignments are most closely related to the user-level distributed file systems projects described by McDonald [20]. However, any application can use WatDFS as a file system because FUSE maintains standard file system interfaces. Thus, students use standard tools and language features to interact with WatDFS, as opposed to a limited number of rewritten applications [20]. Furthermore, WatDFS focuses on the consistency of distributed file systems and allows students to examine the differences between the remote-access model and the upload-download model. McDonald's assignment is in the context of a computer-networks class, so it focuses on the implementation of specific networking protocols [10]. Although there has been discussion on using `libfuse` for educational systems [12, 19, 21], WatDFS focuses on the different models of distributed file systems and core distributed systems concepts.

A typical operating systems course assignment is to develop file system functionality inside an educational operating system. Such assignments may implement an alternative file system design, ensure crash-consistency, or extend file system functionality with key-value stores [6, 15]. WatDFS differs by focusing on file access and management in distributed systems and the challenges that arise in a distributed environment. Finally other user-space systems assignments [28] for tasks traditionally done in kernel-space (e.g., memory management), share our experience that it is easier for students to debug and develop outside of the kernel while learning the core concepts and challenges associated with the task.

5 CONCLUSION

In this paper, we described our experiences with a new pair of programming assignments for a distributed systems class where students develop a distributed file system called WatDFS. The WatDFS assignments provide students with the opportunity to compare two popular models of distributed file systems, and importantly, use and apply concepts from the entire course. Our early analysis found that the first assignment successfully introduced students to the new technologies used in the assignment, and over 80% of students passed the majority of the test cases in the second, more challenging, assignment. We plan to use our experiences to continue to improve the teaching and learning environment for students. We hope that by sharing our experiences, other educators will be motivated to pursue similar projects and benefit from our insights.

[2] 65% of students had at least one submission more than 48 hours prior to the deadline.

ACKNOWLEDGMENTS

We thank Byron Weber Becker and Heather Root for their helpful comments on this paper, as well as Mikhail Kazhamiaka, Siddhartha Sahu and Zhiwei Shang who supported the deployment of the assignment as teaching assistants. The University of Waterloo provided funding for this project.

REFERENCES

[1] 2017. strace. https://www.cs.hmc.edu/~geoff/classes/hmc.cs135.201109/homework/fuse/.

[2] 2018. libfuse. https://github.com/libfuse/libfuse.

[3] Daniel J Abadi. 2012. Consistency tradeoffs in modern distributed database system design: CAP is only part of the story. *Computer* 2 (2012), 37–42.

[4] ACM/IEEE-CS Joint Task Force on Computing Curricula. 2013. *Computer Science Curricula 2013.* Technical Report. ACM Press and IEEE Computer Society Press. https://doi.org/10.1145/2534860

[5] Jeannie R Albrecht. 2009. Bringing big systems to small schools: Distributed systems for undergraduates. In *ACM SIGCSE Bulletin*, Vol. 41. ACM, 101–105.

[6] Jeremy Andrus and Jason Nieh. 2012. Teaching operating systems using android. In *Proceedings of the 43rd ACM technical symposium on Computer Science Education.* ACM, 613–618.

[7] Andrew D Birrell and Bruce Jay Nelson. 1984. Implementing remote procedure calls. *ACM Transactions on Computer Systems (TOCS)* 2, 1 (1984), 39–59.

[8] Navin Budhiraja and Keith Marzullo. 1992. *Tradeoffs in Implementing Primary-Backup Protocols.* Technical Report. CORNELL UNIV ITHACA NY DEPT OF COMPUTER SCIENCE.

[9] Justin Cappos, Ivan Beschastnikh, Arvind Krishnamurthy, and Tom Anderson. 2009. Seattle: a platform for educational cloud computing. *Acm sigcse bulletin* 41, 1 (2009), 111–115.

[10] Martin Casado and Nick McKeown. 2005. The virtual network system. In *ACM SIGCSE Bulletin*, Vol. 37. ACM, 76–80.

[11] Henrik Bærbak Christensen. 2016. Teaching DevOps and cloud computing using a cognitive apprenticeship and story-telling approach. In *Proceedings of the 2016 ACM Conference on Innovation and Technology in Computer Science Education.* ACM, 174–179.

[12] Jeffery Forrester. 2015. Platforms for Teaching Distributed Computing Concepts to Undergraduate Students. (2015).

[13] Sanjay Ghemawat, Howard Gobioff, and Shun-Tak Leung. 2003. *The Google file system.* Vol. 37. ACM.

[14] Sarah Heckman, Kathryn T Stolee, and Christopher Parnin. 2018. 10+ years of teaching software engineering with itrust: the good, the bad, and the ugly. In *Proceedings of the 40th International Conference on Software Engineering: Software Engineering Education and Training.* ACM, 1–4.

[15] David A Holland, Ada T Lim, and Margo I Seltzer. 2002. A new instructional operating system. In *ACM SIGCSE Bulletin*, Vol. 34. ACM, 111–115.

[16] Mark A Holliday, J Traynham Houston, and E Matthew Jones. 2008. From sockets and RMI to web services. In *ACM SIGCSE Bulletin*, Vol. 40. ACM, 236–240.

[17] Cheng Huang, Huseyin Simitci, Yikang Xu, Aaron Ogus, Brad Calder, Parikshit Gopalan, Jin Li, Sergey Yekhanin, et al. 2012. Erasure Coding in Windows Azure Storage.. In *Usenix annual technical conference.* Boston, MA, 15–26.

[18] Steve R Kleiman et al. 1986. Vnodes: An Architecture for Multiple File System Types in Sun UNIX.. In *USENIX Summer*, Vol. 86. 238–247.

[19] Geoff Kuenning. 2011. CS 135 FUSE Homework Assignments, Fall 2011. https://www.cs.hmc.edu/~geoff/classes/hmc.cs135.201109/homework/fuse/.

[20] Chris McDonald. 1996. User-level distributed file systems projects. In *ACM SIGCSE Bulletin*, Vol. 28. ACM, 333–337.

[21] Halli Elaine Meth. 2014. Decafs: A modular distributed file system to facilitate distributed systems education. (2014).

[22] Subramanian Muralidhar, Wyatt Lloyd, Sabyasachi Roy, Cory Hill, Ernest Lin, Weiwen Liu, Satadru Pan, Shiva Shankar, Viswanath Sivakumar, Linpeng Tang, et al. 2014. f4: FacebookâĂŹs warm blob storage system. In *Proceedings of the 11th USENIX conference on Operating Systems Design and Implementation.* USENIX Association, 383–398.

[23] David Oppenheimer, Jeannie Albrecht, David Patterson, and Amin Vahdat. 2005. Design and implementation tradeoffs for wide-area resource discovery. In *High Performance Distributed Computing, 2005. HPDC-14. Proceedings. 14th IEEE International Symposium on.* IEEE, 113–124.

[24] Sushil K Prasad, Almadena Yu Chtchelkanova, et al. 2011. NSF/IEEE-TCPP curriculum initiative on parallel and distributed computing: core topics for undergraduates.

[25] Ariel S Rabkin, Charles Reiss, Randy Katz, and David Patterson. 2012. Experiences teaching MapReduce in the cloud. In *Proceedings of the 43rd ACM technical symposium on Computer Science Education.* ACM, 601–606.

[26] Aditya Rajgarhia and Ashish Gehani. 2010. Performance and extension of user space file systems. In *Proceedings of the 2010 ACM Symposium on Applied Computing.* ACM, 206–213.

[27] Mahadev Satyanarayanan, James J. Kistler, Puneet Kumar, Maria E. Okasaki, Ellen H. Siegel, and David C. Steere. 1990. Coda: A highly available file system for a distributed workstation environment. *IEEE Transactions on computers* 39, 4 (1990), 447–459.

[28] Sam Silvestro, Timothy T Yuen, Corey Crosser, Dakai Zhu, Turgay Korkmaz, and Tongping Liu. 2018. A User Space-based Project for Practicing Core Memory Management Concepts. In *Proceedings of the 49th ACM Technical Symposium on Computer Science Education.* ACM, 98–103.

[29] Jaime Spacco, David Hovemeyer, William Pugh, Fawzi Emad, Jeffrey K Hollingsworth, and Nelson Padua-Perez. 2006. Experiences with marmoset: designing and using an advanced submission and testing system for programming courses. *ACM Sigcse Bulletin* 38, 3 (2006), 13–17.

[30] Michael Stonebraker, Sam Madden, and Pradeep Dubey. 2013. Intel big data science and technology center vision and execution plan. *ACM SIGMOD Record* 42, 1 (2013), 44–49.

[31] Red Hat Storage. 2011. Linus Torvalds doesn't understand user-space filesystems. https://redhatstorage.redhat.com/2011/06/28/linus-torvalds-doesnt-understand-user-space-storage/.

[32] Douglas B Terry, Marvin M Theimer, Karin Petersen, Alan J Demers, Mike J Spreitzer, and Carl H Hauser. 1995. Managing update conflicts in Bayou, a weakly connected replicated storage system. In *ACM SIGOPS Operating Systems Review*, Vol. 29. ACM, 172–182.

[33] Maarten van Steen and Andrew S Tanenbaum. 2016. A brief introduction to distributed systems. *Computing* 98, 10 (2016), 967–1009.

[34] Maarten Van Steen and Andrew S Tanenbaum. 2017. *Distributed Systems.* Pearson Education.

[35] Bharath Kumar Reddy Vangoor, Vasily Tarasov, and Erez Zadok. 2017. To FUSE or Not to FUSE: Performance of User-Space File Systems. In *Proceedings of FAST'17: 15th USENIX Conference on File and Storage Technologies.* 59.

[36] Ivan Voras and Mario Zagar. 2006. Network distributed file system in user space. In *Information Technology Interfaces, 2006. 28th International Conference on.* IEEE, 669–674.

[37] Sage A Weil, Scott A Brandt, Ethan L Miller, Darrell DE Long, and Carlos Maltzahn. 2006. Ceph: A scalable, high-performance distributed file system. In *Proceedings of the 7th symposium on Operating systems design and implementation.* USENIX Association, 307–320.

[38] Joel Wein, Kirill Kourtchikov, Yan Cheng, Ron Gutierez, Roman Khmelichek, Matthew Topol, and Chris Sherman. 2009. Virtualized games for teaching about distributed systems. *ACM SIGCSE Bulletin* 41, 1 (2009), 246–250.

Computer Organization and Design Course with FPGA Cloud

Ke Zhang, Yisong Chang, Mingyu Chen, Yungang Bao, Zhiwei Xu
State Key Laboratory of Computer Architecture, ICT, CAS
University of Chinese Academy of Sciences (UCAS)
Beijing, China
{zhangke,changyisong,cmy,baoyg,zxu}@ict.ac.cn

ABSTRACT

Computer Organization and Design (COD) is a fundamentally required early-stage undergraduate course in most computer science and engineering curricula. During the two sessions (lecture and project part) of one COD course, educational platforms play an important role in cultivating students' computational thinking, especially the ability of viewing the hardware and software in a computer system as a whole (computer system thinking ability for short in this paper). In order to improve teaching quality, in this paper, we discuss the deployment of an inexpensive in-house Field Programmable Gate Array (FPGA) cloud platform, which can provide students with hardware-software co-design methodology and practice. The platform includes 32 FPGA nodes and the scale can be dynamically changed. Each cloud node is heterogeneously composed of an ARM processor and a tightly-coupled reconfigurable fabric to provide students with hands-on hardware and software programming experiences. We illustrate our efforts to make the FPGA cloud as an easy-to-use resource pool to elastically support a class with 92 undergrads via Internet access and to monitor students' experimental behaviors. We also present key insights in our teaching activities that indicate such appliance is feasible to provide practice of both basic principles and emerging co-design techniques for students. We believe that our cost-effective FPGA cloud is of significant interests to educators looking forward to improving computer system-related courses.

CCS CONCEPTS

• Applied computing → Education; • Computer systems organization; • Hardware → Reconfigurable logic and FPGAs; Hardware-software codesign; • Networks → Cloud computing;

KEYWORDS

FPGA Cloud, Computer Organization and Design, Computer System Education, Hardware-Software Co-design

ACM Reference Format:
Ke Zhang, Yisong Chang, Mingyu Chen, Yungang Bao, Zhiwei Xu. 2019. Computer Organization and Design Course with FPGA Cloud. In *SIGCSE'19: 50th ACM Technical Symposium on Computer Science Education, February 27–March 2, 2019, Minneapolis, MN, USA.* ACM, New York, NY, USA, 7 pages. https://doi.org/10.1145/3287324.3287475

ACM ISBN 978-1-4503-5890-3/19/2...$15.00
https://doi.org/10.1145/3287324.3287475

1 INTRODUCTION

Computer Organization and Design (COD) is an early-taught undergraduate course that typically covers fundamental CPU design principles, instruction set architecture (ISA), assembly language and input/output interfacing in both lecture and project sessions. As a key component in ACM computer engineering curriculum [1], COD is essentially required to teach students the concepts of hardware and software as well as the synergy of both parts in a computer system. Moreover, COD gradually attracts attention in computer science undergraduate programs (e.g., ACM's 2013 curriculum guidelines [2]) as either a required course or an elective to show an abstraction of hardware from a programmer's perspective.

In the COD lab course, students are required to fully understand and carefully apply abstract concepts they learnt in lectures to practicing ordinary low-level software programming in assembly and C language or even advanced hardware logic design. Therefore, compared with other traditional lecture-centric courses, the COD course largely depends on educational platforms to provide real and interactive engineering environments for students to conduct hands-on experiments. As a result, it is crucial for educators and instructors to elaborately design and massively use educational platforms in both lecture and project sessions of a COD course in order to cultivate students' computational thinking [34], especially ability of viewing the hardware and software in a computer system as a whole (*computer system thinking ability* for short).

A) Using new hardware in COD platforms

The evolution of modern computer systems has been widely inspired by emerging heterogeneous acceleration and domain-specific architecture [14]. This trend emphasizes the key importance of *hardware-software co-design* to all participants in the field of computer system [3]. Therefore, besides basic software programming, students are strongly recommended to study hardware design principles and the co-design concepts as early as possible in computer system-related courses and especially in the early-stage COD class, improving their *computer system thinking ability.* Given the state-of-the-art heterogeneous computing systems, we argue that the key challenge to further improve teaching effects by manifesting system-level *hardware-software co-design* in COD courses lies in the exploitation of an appropriate educational platform that provides heterogeneous co-design capability for students.

In traditional COD courses, software ISA simulators [7, 17, 22, 32] are widely used as experimental environments for students' writing

[1]First authors Zhang and Chang have made equal contributions to this work.

and executing low-level programs. However, such virtual platform not only inherently restricts execution time and flexibility, but also exhibits an incomplete system view to students due to the shortage of real hardware components. The avant-grade single-board computers based on System-on-Chip (SoC) [28, 31] provide software execution environment on real hardware platforms but lack capability to integrate additional hardware accelerators. Similarly, despite suitability for hardware-related experiments, Field Programmable Gate Array (FPGA)-based development boards [9, 26] fail to support complicated software development.

Fortunately, a heterogeneous FPGA (e.g., Xilinx's Zynq UltraScale+ MPSoC [36]) which has been just commercially available can overcome all the above-mentioned shortcomings. This hybrid device tightly couples a high-performance, software-programmable hard core SoC (commonly based on ARM processor) with a reconfigurable logic fabric on the same chip die. Such configuration has been confirmed in setting up a feasible experimental platform for embedded system-related courses [25, 33]. We believe that heterogeneous FPGAs are more appropriate and cost-effective as educational platforms to demonstrate the concept of hardware-software co-design and deliver related experimental environment in COD courses.

B) Introducing cloud computing to COD platforms

Instructors of COD courses used to hand out each student one hardware experimental kit that would be connected to his or her laptop during projects. Due to different progresses of students' experimental projects, 1) status of dozens of kits are diverse, and 2) the number of simultaneously in-use kits is frequently changed. These two factors lead to a low utilization rate of the experimental kits. In addition, each student conducts projects privately in the laptop with an attached hardware kit, making his or her experimental behaviors entirely invisible to instructors. Motivated by emerging cloud computing technology, we believe that these situations would be improved if we could make experimental kits as a pool of remotely accessed resources that can be unilaterally provisioned and automatically monitored. Some preliminary cloud-based experimental platforms [10, 24, 37, 38] were established to provide remotely accessed development kits for students.

C) Why not commercial public FPGA cloud?

Cloud vendors have provided FPGAs as public acceleration resources for users to rent (e.g., Amazon's AWS F1 instance [4]). From our perspective, such public FPGA cloud exhibits several drawbacks in COD teaching:

1) Expensive economic costs to deploy the same number of FPGAs as in our in-house FPGA cloud within a semester. Note that the purpose of public FPGA cloud is mostly for accelerating web services, so the FPGA devices used in public cloud are always high-end and costly products,

2) Complicated FPGA development and configuration flow in public cloud that requires students to learn additional skills non-related to the COD course,

3) The execution environment of FPGA cloud is mainly based on virtual machines (VMs) running on the remote server, introducing unpredictable penalties and inter-VM contentions for various users.

D) Putting it all together

In this paper, we propose an in-house heterogeneous FPGA-enabled cloud platform with multiple nodes (32 for our current implementation) connected via Gigabit Ethernet for teaching COD courses in both lecture and project. Each node is an inexpensive custom circuit board based on Xilinx Zynq UltraScale+ MPSoC which provides both hardware and software programmability in a single board for students with the cost of only \$950. We make each physical node with a fully-fledged Linux kernel and related environment atop the ARM SoC as a general cloud resource in which students can configure FPGA fabric, interact with logic modules in FPGA and launch software applications. All available resources are managed and scheduled via Ethernet by a commercial-grade cloud computing framework on a front-end x86 server. A pre-configured user-end VM running on each student's laptop provides standard toolchains of both hardware and software development. Unlike the server-end VMs for execution in public FPGA cloud, in such user-end VM, students use a simple script-based design flow to compile their FPGA designs and software programs offline, request an experimental cloud resource, and transparently upload the generated FPGA configuration files as well as executable binaries to the requested resource for execution via campus network. In order to fully achieve teaching objectives in both computer science and engineering curricula and comprehensively demonstrate the concepts of *hardware-software co-design* on our FPGA cloud, we propose an exploratory assignment on ISAs and a live demo about details of network packets processing in our COD lectures, as well as experimental projects that cover both fundamental principles and emerging techniques. Some key advantages our FPGA cloud provides for teaching COD course include:

Ease of use and maintenances. The cloud platform allows students to conduct projects as using local experimental kits without resource contention between each other, making it possible to carry out performance-related studies on remote hardware. Moreover, our FPGA cloud platform can be simply managed by teaching assistants of the COD course, without additional engineering efforts.

Elasticity and low cost. Resource pooling dynamically adjusts the number of available resources as per students' demands to afford a class of 92 students to conduct projects within the scope of only 32 nodes, significantly saving the infrastructural budget.

Teaching Assistance. Detailed execution behaviors of each student are monitored and logged in the cloud. Such information indicates learning outcomes of one student, helping instructors make individual teaching policies for different students.

2 BACKGROUND

Conventional COD courses mainly concentrate on how to teach students hardware abstraction from a software programmer's point of view, thus emphasizing the importance of ISAs and relevant assembly programming in experimental projects. With the minimum economic cost and educators' efforts, the software ISA simulator is a good choice for students to use, which is even leveraged today in some representative COD-like courses [29, 30]. As the rise of inexpensive hardware single-board computers such as Raspberry Pi, some educators have asked their students to conduct experiments on such platforms [21, 27].

On the other hand, emphasizing hardware design in COD course offers a new bottom-up perspective to students to fully understand computer systems instead of pure ISAs. In experimental projects of such class, students are required to implement their preliminary

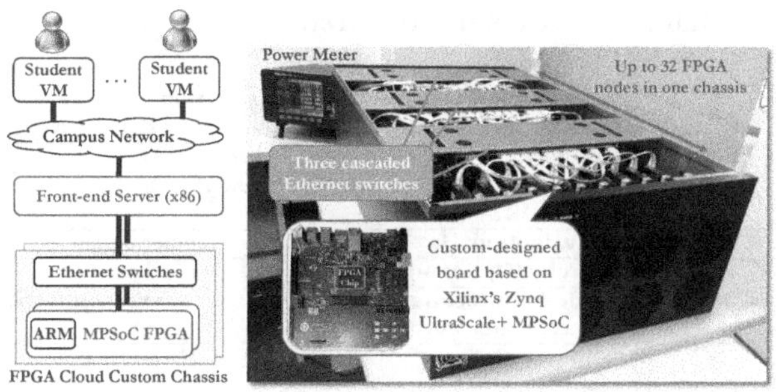

Figure 1: Our proposed FPGA cloud architecture and one prototype chassis with 32 individual physical FPGA nodes that is large enough to support our COD class with 92 students.

CPU cores using a hardware description language (HDL) such as Verilog HDL. However, these CPU cores are always verified just in HDL behavioral simulation and logic synthesis rather than implemented to run on real hardware [18, 29, 30]. Although real-world FPGAs are involved in some classes [5, 6, 8, 11, 13, 15, 16, 23], it is still extremely difficult for early undergrads to independently afford the task of organizing a minimum runnable system that wraps their CPU cores to various I/O components (e.g., memory, UART, etc.) with standard interfaces. This task always requires a significant amount of FPGA-specific knowledge and sufficient hardware design experiences that are out of the range of COD course.

In summary, existing experimental platforms in COD-related courses rarely offer students a real-world executable system-level environment with an easy-to-use interface to help them fully understand computer systems.

3 FPGA CLOUD IN COD COURSE

In this section, we introduce our proposed FPGA cloud architecture as well as one prototype chassis, and related methods to provide an easy-to-use interface for students. Based on the FPGA cloud, we discuss improvements in both lectures and projects of our COD course to emphasize *hardware-software co-design.*

3.1 Architectural and Technical Overview

Figure. 1 depicts our proposed FPGA cloud architecture and one in-house chassis in which at maximum 32 nodes based on custom circuit boards using Xilinx's Zynq UltraScale+ MPSoC FPGAs are interconnected via three cascaded Ethernet switches. More chassis can be cascaded for larger class. The design objective of our FPGA cloud is to effectively abstract platform details and agilely help students to leverage the FPGA cloud in campus via an user-friendly Ethernet-accessible interface, avoiding unnecessary efforts that negate students' concentration on the COD course.

First, we leverage and modify a commercial-grade cloud resource management framework—OpenStack [20] to provision each physical node in the custom chassis as a general cloud resource. As shown in the left part of Figure. 2, the modified OpenStack controller runs on the front-end x86 server to communicate with hardware control planes in FPGA chassis and provides APIs to allow students to request and release resources on-demand using either webpage or command line via Ethernet. OpenStack maintains a database of

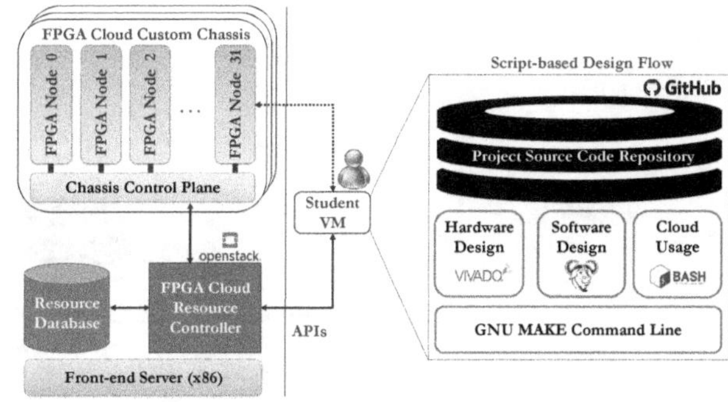

Figure 2: Efforts to provide an easy-to-use FPGA cloud service. An OpenStack-enabled resource manager (left part) allows students' remote access to the allocated FPGA node (arrowed dash line). A scripted design flow on each student's VM (right part) simplifies FPGA development and usage.

information of all physical nodes in the FPGA cloud, both in use and available for elastic allocation and release.

Second, in order to remove numerous FPGA design complexities for students, we implement a bunch of pre-built scripts that runs inside the commercial FPGA design tool (i.e., Xilinx's Vivado [35] in our current COD course) in the VM to automatically setup an FPGA project with static logic of complex I/O components surrounding students' synthesizable HDL designs and to strictly execute key design flow steps, making students purely concentrate on their HDL design that are strongly related to the contents of COD course. We further spread such script-based design flow via standard GNU `MAKE` command line to uniformly cover FPGA hardware development, software compilation and FPGA cloud usage (right part of Figure. 2). By this means, complicated experimental procedures are abstracted into one single and simple `MAKE` command, saving a large amount of efforts for students to carry out projects via the FPGA cloud. Moreover, all relevant source files and scripts in an experimental project are organized into a repository hosted on GitHub Classroom [12]. Therefore, all students' behaviors are committed in the repository to trace variations of one student's ability in different phase of COD course and make just-in-time guidance.

3.2 Usage in Lectures

Rigid oral explanations in conventional COD lectures leave students far away from real systems, making it difficult to understand some knowledge units that requires hardware-software collaboration. Although hands-on experiments relieve such situation to some extent, they are still unable to cover all relevant key points mentioned in the lecture class. In order to fill such gap, we attempt to propose an exploratory assignment as well as a live demo based on our FPGA cloud as supplementaries in lectures of our COD course.

Exploratory Assignment. As a fundamental interface between hardware and software, ISA is a strongly required knowledge unit in COD courses. This point is especially important to computer science students to understand hardware and computer system, as they have rare opportunities to engage in hardware-related courses.

Consequently, we push students to make a comprehensive comparison among ISAs of x86, ARM, MIPS and the emerging RISC-V

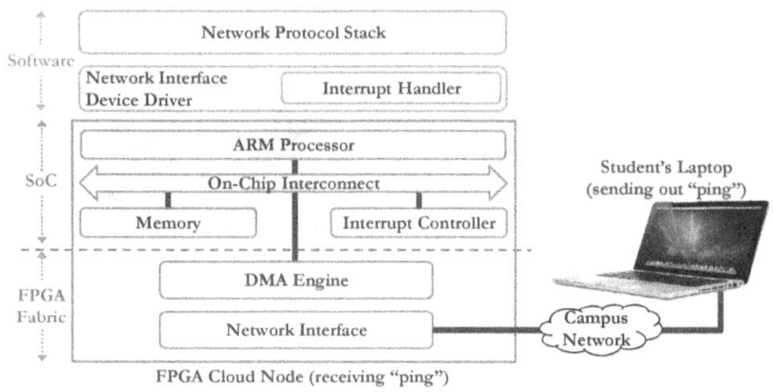

Figure 3: Full system stack on an FPGA cloud node to demonstrate system-level details when processing a "ping" network packet as a live demo in lectures of our COD course.

in basic assembly blocks, segmentations in binary object and executable files, endianness, application binary interface (ABI) and stack management based on practical compilation as well as analysis of binary files. Students use the standard GCC compilers and related `binutils` for x86 and ARM ISAs in the operating systems on each student's VM and the requested cloud resource respectively, as well as GCC cross-compiling environments for MIPS and RISC-V pre-deployed in the VMs. We provide a series of standard micro-benchmarks written in C language and encourage students to custom-design some other programs for comparison.

Live Demo. Advanced input/output interfacing, mainly including direct memory access (DMA) and interrupt, is an essential system concept that deeply relies on hardware-software collaboration. Due to shortage in real application scenario, it is very difficult for students to understand this key concept just according to descriptions in COD textbook. Moreover, such knowledge unit is rarely involved in a COD experimental project since students are required to learn a huge amount of additional knowledge out of the range of COD course. As a result, in our lecture in COD course, we build a live demo about details of network packet processing on real-world hardware-software full system stack inside our FPGA cloud platform, which is interactively visible to students for observation of system-level I/O processing behaviors. To make the demo easily to understand, we select `ping`, a common networking utility students are familiar to use in daily life as an illustrative example. We also abstractly introduce some easy-to-understand concepts of network protocol stack and device driver in our COD course in advance.

Figure. 3 briefly describes the full system stack in one FPGA cloud node and the hardware network processing path in a student's laptop with the VM. For students' hardware visibility, we implement a network interface and its related DMA engine in the FPGA fabric of each physical cloud node. System-level information of this newly-involved network interface is configured during resource allocation. Meanwhile, students are enabled to observe operations in ARM-end operating system via traces logged by pre-modifications in kernel-level network device driver and protocol stack.

After obtaining the IP address of an allocated FPGA cloud resource, one student executes a GNU MAKE command in the VM to launch the FPGA development tool GUI that automatically prepares the environment for remote signal probing of key hardware ports from network interface and DMA engine. The student then sends

Table 1: FPGA cloud-inspired COD lab projects

#	Project name and brief description
1	**Basis of Assembly Language:** Function call routine and stack management
2	**Basic CPU Design:** Register file, ALU and single-cycle CPU
3	**Advanced CPU Design:** Multi-cycle CPU with interface to DDR memory and UART
4	**Performance Evaluation:** Hardware performance counter design
5	**Memory Hierarchy (Optional):** Instruction and data cache
6	**Domain-Specific Architecture (Optional):** Custom deep convolutional neural network accelerator with DMA interface

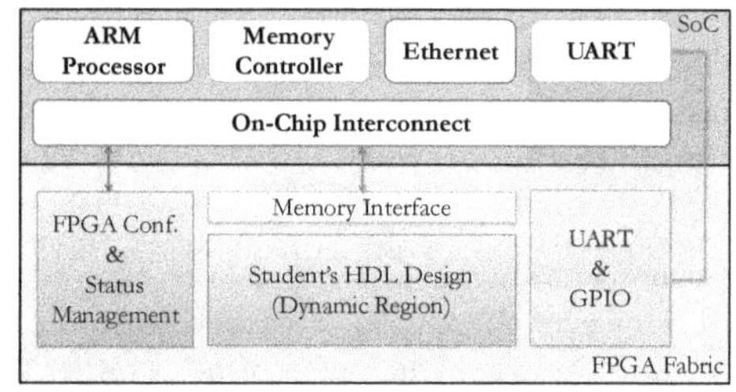

Figure 4: A template architecture in FPGA cloud node to facilitate easy integration of students' HDL design into a minimum runnable system.

out a "ping" packet to the obtained IP address. When the "ping" packet is injected into the network interface of the cloud node, variations of hardware signals are displayed in the GUI in time, allowing students to observe packet movements in hardware data path. Traces in the operating system allow students to clearly understand life cycles of network packets and motivate students to obtain insights in the approaches of hardware-software interactions.

3.3 Usage in Labs

Based on our FPGA cloud, we redesign the projects in our COD labs as shown in Table. 1. The main target is to push students to make their outcomes in these projects executable in an actual hardware-software environment, instead of a pure simulation.

In the first experimental project, students are disciplined in software programming abilities within hybrid assembly and C language on the ARM processors of cloud nodes, which emphasizes the most fundamental concepts of function call routine and runtime stack management. In this manner, students are driven to deeply understand the hardware interface from a programmer's perspective. If educators would like to extend such project arrangement with more software-oriented experiments, existing projects based on conventional platforms like Raspberry Pi or x86 are also inherently supported in our FPGA cloud without modifications to run atop the high-performance ARM processor. Moreover, exclusive occupancy of one physical cloud node guarantees students to conduct further software performance studies.

In the following projects, students are guided to implement synthesizable hardware components in the FPGA fabrics and make it executable with software collaborations. In order to simplify students' design efforts in such hardware-centric projects, we propose a template architecture in our FPGA cloud node as shown in Figure. 4. Based on such template, students are encouraged to

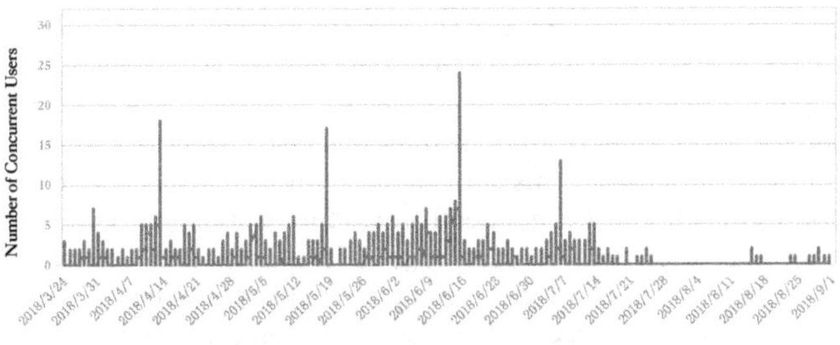

Figure 5: The number of in-use nodes in the FPGA cloud measured every 20 seconds during the 2018 Spring semester in which our COD course carried on, and short Summer semester to conduct students' research projects, respectively. The X-axis is cataloged into each day during both semester.

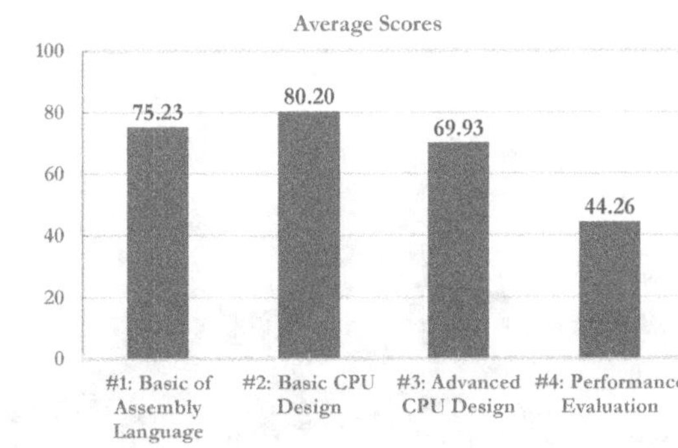

Figure 6: Average score (100-point grading system) of each required project in our class as declared in Table. 1.

implement custom CPU cores in the dynamic region based on either conventional MIPS or emerging RISC-V ISA to practice fundamental CPU design principles. Custom cores share the same address space of DDR4 memory populated on the FPGA circuit board with the ARM processor. In this manner, ARM processor is leveraged as an auxiliary engine that is easily driven by students in their VM-based development environment, taking charge of FPGA configuration, data and program loading, UART communication, status management and hardware debugging of students' cores. Undergrads are also required to implement a C language-based software framework running atop custom CPU cores to allow applications access memory-mapped hardware UART and GPIO interfaces.

Students are cultivated with the quantitative approach via a project towards design of hardware performance counters. Based on performance evaluation results, students optionally optimize the memory hierarchy of their CPU cores via instruction and data cache. Students also electively involve in design of deep convolutional neural network accelerators in the dynamic region of template architecture as well as implement an ARM-end full software stack incorporating with accelerators. By this means, students acquire preliminary skills in heterogeneous acceleration and domain-specific architecture design.

After disciplined with these experimental projects in a full semester, outstanding students in our COD course afford to further conduct research projects independently on our FPGA cloud in the short terms during summer vacations, some of which were highlighted in one tutorial [19] we held in ISCA 2018 (one of the flagship annual academia conferences in computer architecture).

4 TEACHING PRACTICE AND DISCUSSION

In this section, we mainly discuss some key observations we acquire from teaching practice in our COD course with the FPGA cloud in the Spring and Summer semester of 2018 to illustrate the efficiency and feasibility of our FPGA cloud as an easy-to-use infrastructure in motivating students to study computer system-related courses.

The number of concurrent users (Y-axis) monitored in our cloud appliance is chronologically plotted in Figure. 5. We used Linux shell scripts persistently running on the front-end server with our OpenStack-based resource controller to acquire how many students were using this platform every 20 seconds and log the data for the whole 2018 Spring and Summer semester (160 days, 690K log entries in total). In this figure, several spikes can be recognized around 2018/3/31, 4/14, 5/19, 6/16 and 7/7, which are due dates for each project. The maximum number in this plot is 24, which means 24 FPGAs in the cloud were simultaneously occupied and utilized by 24 students. Therefore, in the case of a COD class with 92 students, one 32-node FPGA cloud chassis can meet our course requirement. One more thing to be noticed is that several single-digit numbers were recorded from 8/11 to 8/31 in the Summer semester. The reason is that after the COD course, three outstanding students volunteered to join our research group and were actively involved in one of our research projects. Therefore, utilizing the FPGA cloud to teach in our computer system course can successfully help some early undergrads engage in computer system-related research.

Figure. 6 shows the average score of each required experimental project in the class of 2018 Spring semester. With the help of our easy-to-use design flow and user interface of the FPGA cloud, all experimental projects are feasibly carried out. In the beginning of this course, students started to be acquainted with this cloud platform in Project #1 and #2 that target programming in assembly as well as basic CPU design respectively and got good scores. In Project #3, students' average grade decreased as the integration of their custom CPUs into real-world environment increases difficulties in CPU design and HDL implementation compared with the previous projects. This situation was even worse in Project #4 since more sophisticated benchmarks were involved for performance evaluation exposing more design defects in students' CPU design and implementations. Another reason causes the lowest average grade in Project #4 lies in that existing debugging environment in our FPGA cloud is not efficient enough for students to fix complex bugs of their CPU cores in a four-week period. Moreover, grades of optional projects are ignored as there were few students to engage in such projects as important dates of these two projects were much close to final exams of other courses.

We asked our students to complete two surveys respectively in the middle and end of spring semester. The survey results from Table. 2 show that the students' satisfaction with the usage of remote FPGA cloud platform (72/82=87.80%) was much higher than using FPGA cards located in our computer lab (22/82=26.83%). As demonstrated in Figure. 7, most of students preferred to use cloud rather than local hardware kits due to the ease-of-use of our FPGA cloud

Figure 7: An instructor and a teaching assistant are leading the 92 students in our COD course to conduct experimental projects in a computer lab.

Table 2: Survey results of satisfaction to the FPGA cloud in our COD course. Note that 10 students who are minor in computer science are not required to conduct lab projects.

# of students	Remote FPGA Cloud Platform	Local FPGA Development Kits
who were fond of using	72	22
who never used	2	19
who completed lab projects	82	82
in the class (lectures + labs)	92	92

Table 3: Student engagement in three academic fields represented by student counts, which shows that how the degree of learners' interest in these areas changes during the semester ("+": favor, "++": strong interest, "–": dislike).

	Computer Science Major	Computer Architecture and System	Research in Computer Science
+ → ++	21	24	16
++ → ++	51	18	36
– → +	8	32	16
+ → –	10	10	11
– → –	2	8	13

platform. In terms of teaching effectiveness for both lecture and lab part of our COD course, as shown in Table. 3 we can notice that 55.43% (51/92) of the students have been sustainably interested in the major of computer science and 45.66% ((24+18)/92) for computer architecture & system throughout this course. More importantly, by leveraging the FPGA cloud platform in both lectures and labs, our teaching approach gradually changes additional 34.78% (32/92) students' attitude towards computer system-related knowledge from dislike to favor. Therefore, over 80% sophomore undergrads would like to take more computer system-related courses in the following semesters. Last but not least, in the third column of this table, an increasing number (16+16) of these early undergraduates are willing to conduct computer system-related research in the future and 3 people joined our research lab during this summer. As instructors, we should also pay attention to the 10 or 11 students who became unfriendly to CS in the end of our course. One student replied "Coding in HDL was terrible and hardware debugging was also tedious". Although this phenomenon exists for certain learners, we need to mitigate this side effect in following terms in order to improve the teaching effectiveness for all students. There are several possible solutions, such as adding HDL introduction and practice in the beginning or before the class, improving our FPGA cloud with an advanced debugging framework, and so on.

5 LIMITATIONS AND FUTURE WORK

Debugging and Simulation. As discussed in Section 4, debugging FPGA design in a remote manner currently exhibits inefficiency, especially for hardware-software co-debugging to find design defects of a custom CPU core. We plan to further boost our simulation framework which would be nearly the same as the hardware-software execution environment in our cloud FPGA node to allow students conduct local co-debugging in their VMs.

Project Schedule. We would like to rearrange the time slot of each project and coordinate with other courses to meet learning diversity of various students, making each of them possible to participate in all experimental projects.

Grading Method. Currently, the FPGA cloud platform can only return a result log file to each student after he or she completes a test case online. Therefore, the student could not see his or her score for this project instantly. Moreover, this also increases instructors' and teaching assistants' workloads due to the tedious and manual updates of project scores for each student. To tackle this problem, we would like to integrate an advanced auto-grading feature in our next-version FPGA cloud.

6 CONCLUSIONS

In this paper, we describe an in-house FPGA cloud platform for a COD course which can be effectively used to introduce the essential concept of hardware-software co-design for next-generation computer system design to early undergrads. Our proposed FPGA cloud provides an easy-to-use interface as well as a simple script-based design flow to cultivate students' *computer system thinking ability* with the minimum additional cost. We believe that our FPGA cloud and relevant ecosystem would be also appropriate to service students and instructors in many other computer system-related courses such as operating system, computer architecture, embedded system design, and so on.

7 ACKNOWLEDGMENTS

This work is supported by the National Key Technologies Research and Development Program of China under Grant No. 2017YFB1001602, by the National Natural Science Foundation of China under Grant No. 61702485, 61420106013, 61521092 and 61702480, and by the Youth Innovation Promotion Association of CAS under Grant No. 2017143 and 2013073. We appreciate Prof. Xiufeng Sui for his teaching in one of the two lecture classes of COD course at UCAS. We thank Zihao Yu, Bowen Huang, Sha Liu, Huizhe Wang, Xu Zhang, Lei Yu, Ran Zhao and Zhiwei Lai for their teaching and engineering assistance in our COD lab projects. We also thank anonymous reviewers' valuable feedbacks.

REFERENCES

[1] ACM. 2004. Computer Engineering Curricula 2004: Curriculum Guidelines for Undergraduate Degree Programs in Computer Engineering. https://www.acm.org/binaries/content/assets/education/curricula-recommendations/ce-final-report.pdf.

[2] ACM. 2013. Computer Science Curricula 2013: Curriculum Guidelines for Undergraduate Degree Programs in Computer Science. https://www.acm.org/binaries/content/assets/education/cs2013_web_final.pdf.

[3] ACM. 2016. Computer Engineering Curricula 2016: Curriculum Guidelines for Undergraduate Degree Programs in Computer Engineering. https://www.acm.org/binaries/content/assets/education/ce2016_web_final.pdf.

[4] Amazon Web Services. 2017. Amazon EC2 F1 Instances. https://aws.amazon.com/ec2/instance-types/f1/.

[5] Arizona State University. 2018. Progressive Learning Platform. https://plp.asu.edu/.

[6] D. Baldwin, P. Sanderson, R. McCartney, S. Ludi, N. T. Ramachandran, and C. Taylor. 2011. SIGCSE Special Project Showcase. In *Proc. 42nd SIGCSE Technical Symposium on Computer Science Education.* 5–6.

[7] Bochs. 2018. The Cross Platform IA-32 Emulator. https://bochs.sourceforge.net/.

[8] E. Brunvand. 2011. Games as Motivation in Computer Design Courses: I/O is the Key. In *Proc. 42nd SIGCSE Technical Symposium on Computer Science Education.* 33–38.

[9] P. Bulic, V. Gustin, D. Sonc, and A. Strancar. 2013. An FPGA-based Integrated Environment for Computer Architecture. *Computer Applications in Engineering Education* 21, 1 (March 2013), 26–35.

[10] Z. Chai, Z. Wang, W. Yang, S. Ding, and Y. Zhang. 2014. OpenHEC: A Framework for Application Programmers to Design FPGA-based Systems. In *Proc. 1st International Workshop on FPGAs for Software Programmers.* 59–64.

[11] M. L. Corliss and M. Melara. 2011. VIREOS: An Integrated, Bottom-up, Educational Operating Systems Project with FPGA Support. In *Proc. 42nd SIGCSE Technical Symposium on Computer Science Education.* 39–44.

[12] Github. 2018. Github Classroom: Your Course Assignments on GitHub. https://classroom.github.com/.

[13] M. Gschwind. 1994. Reprogrammable Hardware for Educational Purpose. In *Proc. 25th SIGCSE Technical Symposium on Computer Science Education.* 183–187.

[14] J. Hennessy and D. Patterson. 2018. A New Golden Age for Computer Architecture: Domain-Specific Hardware/Software Co-Design, Enanced Security, Open Instruction Sets, and Agile Chip Development. In *Turing Lecture of ACM/IEEE International Symposium on Computer Architecture (ISCA).*

[15] M. J. Jipping, S. Henry, K. Ludewig, and L. Tableman. 2006. How To Integrate FPGAs Into a Computer Organization Course. In *Proc. 37th SIGCSE Technical Symposium on Computer Science Education.* 234–238.

[16] D. B. Larkins, W. M. Jones, and H. E. Rickard. 2013. Using FPGAs as a Reconfigurable Teaching Tool Throughout CS Systems Curriculum. In *Proc. 44th SIGCSE Technical Symposium on Computer Science Education.* 397–402.

[17] LC3Help.com. 2018. LC-3 Simulator. http://www.lc3help.com/.

[18] MIT Computation Structure Group. 2017. 6.175: Constructive Computer Architecture. https://csg.csail.mit.edu/6.175/.

[19] ICT of CAS. 2018. The Case for Labeled Von Noeumann Architecture (LvNA). https://sdc.ict.ac.cn/isca2018-tutorial/.

[20] OpenStack. 2018. OpenStack. http://www.openstack.com/.

[21] R. Ord. 2018. CSE 30: Computer Organization and System Programming. https://cseweb.ucsd.edu/~ricko/CSE30/.

[22] D. Patti, A. Spadaccini, M. Palesi, F. Fazzino, and V. Catania. 2012. Supporting Undergraduate Computer Architecture Students Using a Visual MIPS64 CPU Simulator. *IEEE Transactions on Education* 55, 3 (Aug. 2012), 406–411.

[23] Penn Engineering. 2016. Computer Organization (Course: ESE534). https://www.seas.upenn.edu/~ese534/.

[24] C. Quan, Y. Chen, S. Li, and Y. Zhao. 2016. Exploration of the Computer Hardware Experiment Teaching Method based on the Cloud Platform. In *Proc. IEEE Frontiers in Education Conference (FIE).* 1–5.

[25] D. Roggow, P. Uhing, P. Jones, and J. Zambreno. 2015. A Project-based Embedded Systems Design Course Using a Reconfigurable SoC Platform. In *Proc. IEEE International Conference on Microelectronics Systems Education (MSE).* 9–12.

[26] S. Sohoni, S. D. Craig, and S. Lu. 2017. Impact of Prior Exposure to the PLP Instruction Set Architecture in a Computer Architecture Course. In *Proc. 48th SIGCSE Technical Symposium on Computer Science Education.* 555–560.

[27] Stanford University. 2017. CS107E Computer Systems From the Ground Up. https://web.stanford.edu/class/cs107e/.

[28] D. Tarnoff. 2015. Integrating the ARM-based Raspberry Pi into an Architectural Course. *Journal of Computing Sciences in Colleges* 30, 5 (May 2015), 67–73.

[29] UC Berkeley EECS. 2018. CS61C: Machine Structures. https://inst.eecs.berkeley.edu/~cs617.

[30] UIUC ECE. 2018. ECE 411: Computer Organization and Design. https://courses.engr.illinois.edu/ece411/fa2018/.

[31] E. Upton, J. Duntemann, R. Roters, T. Mamtora, and B. Everard. 2016. *Learning Computer Architecture with Raspberry Pi* (1st ed.). Wiley Publishing.

[32] K. Vollmar and P. Sanderson. 2006. MARS: An Education-Oriented MIPS Assembly Language Simulator. In *Proc. 37th SIGCSE Technical Symposium on Computer Science Education.* 239–243.

[33] K. L. Wang, C. S. Cole, T. Wang, and J. Harris. 2013. An Effective Project-based Embedded System Design Teaching Method. In *the 120th American Society for Engineering Education (ASEE) Annual Conference and Exposition.* 6849:1–6849:9.

[34] J. M. Wing. 2006. Computational Thinking. *Communication of the ACM* 49, 3 (March 2006), 33–35.

[35] Xilinx. 2018. Vivado Design Suite – HLx Editions. https://www.xilinx.com/products/design-tools/vivado.html/.

[36] Xilinx. 2018. Zynq UltraScale+ MPSoC. https://www.xilinx.com/products/silicon-devices/soc/zynq-ultrascale-mpsoc.html/.

[37] K. Zhang, M. Chen, and Y Bao. 2018. ZyForce: An FPGA-based Cloud Platform for Experimental Curriculum of Computer System in University of Chinese Academy of Sciences (Abstract Only). In *Proc. 49th SIGCSE Technical Symposium on Computer Science Education.* 1091.

[38] Y. Zhang, Y. Chen, X. Ma, Y. Tang, Y. Niu, S. Li, and W. Liu. 2017. Remote FPGA Lab Platform for Computer System Curriculum. In *Proc. ACM Turing 50th Celebration Conference - China (TUR-C).* 3:1–3:6.

Visualizing Classic Synchronization Problems

Dining Philosophers, Producers-Consumers, and Readers-Writers

Joel C. Adams
Department of Computer Science
Calvin College
Grand Rapids, MI USA 49546
adams@calvin.edu

Elizabeth R. Koning
Department of Computer Science
Calvin College
Grand Rapids, MI USA 49546
erk24@students.calvin.edu

Christiaan D. Hazlett
Department of Computer Science
University of Illinois, Urbana-Champaign
Champaign, IL USA
christiaanhazlett@gmail.com

ABSTRACT

Classic synchronization problems are often used to introduce students to the subtleties of concurrency and synchronization mechanisms, such as semaphores, monitors, locks, and condition variables. The Dining Philosophers, Producers-Consumers, and Readers-Writers are all classic problems in which a correct solution requires the actions of multiple processes or threads to be synchronized. In this paper, we present visualizations for these three problems and describe their use as pedagogical tools to help students build accurate mental models of concurrency abstractions such as starvation, deadlock, livelock, and correct execution. We also present the results of an experiment that indicate students find using these visualizations to be significantly more engaging than reading a textbook, with no significant difference in learning. We do not claim that our visualizations should replace a course text; rather we present them as engaging pedagogical tools to complement the textbook in courses on *Operating Systems*, *Programming Languages*, and other courses where concurrency and synchronization are covered.

CCS CONCEPTS

• Computing methodologies~Shared memory algorithms • Social and professional topics~Computer science education • Software and its engineering~Synchronization

KEYWORDS

Dining Philosophers; Graphics; Parallel; Producers; Consumers; Readers; Writers; Synchronization; Threads; Visualization

ACM Reference format:

Joel Adams, Elizabeth Koning and Christiaan Hazlett. 2018. Visualizing Classic Synchronization Problems: Dining Philosophers, Producers-Consumers, and Readers-Writers. In *Proceedings of the 2019 ACM SIGCSE Technical Symposium on Computer Science Education (SIGCSE'19). ACM, New York, NY, USA, 7 pages.* https://doi.org/10.1145/3287324.3287467

ACM ISBN 978-1-4503-5890-3/19/02...$15.00
https://doi.org/10.1145/3287324.3287467

1 INTRODUCTION

Classic synchronization problems, such as the Cigarette Smokers, the Dining Philosophers, the Producers-Consumers (also known as the Bounded Buffer problem), the Readers-Writers, and the Sleeping Barber Problems are commonly used to introduce CS students to the subtleties of concurrency.

Operating Systems textbooks (e.g., [14-16]) commonly cover a subset of these problems and use solutions to these problems to illustrate the use of semaphores, locks, condition variables, monitors, and related mutual exclusion and synchronization mechanisms. For example, [14] uses the Dining Philosophers, Producers-Consumers, and Readers-Writers Problems to illustrate the use of semaphores; and revisits the Dining Philosophers Problem to illustrate the use of a monitor.

Programming Languages textbooks may also use these problems to illustrate programming languages' concurrency features. For example, [9] uses the Producers-Consumers Problem to illustrate semaphores and monitors; [13] uses the same problem to explain Ada's Task-rendezvous mechanism, Java's semaphores, and Java's monitor mechanism.

Some of these problems involve real-world entities (cigarette smokers, philosophers, barbers) and have a concrete, non-abstract scenario that may be relatively easy for students to understand. Other problems deal with more abstract entities (producers, consumers, readers, writers) that may make it more challenging for students to build accurate mental models. To help students understand these problems, traditional textbooks often include figures, but static figures and diagrams are necessarily limited in their abilities to depict the dynamic interactions of the entities. These limitations stem from publisher economics and the static nature of the paper on which such books are printed. By contrast, software is a more flexible medium that can be used to create dynamic, interactive visualizations of these problems.

In this paper, we present software visualizations of the Dining Philosophers, Producers-Consumers, and Readers-Writers problems and explore their use. We also present the results of an assessment activity whose results indicate (i) that students learn as much from interacting with these visualizations as they do from reading a textbook, and (ii) that students find the visualizations to be significantly more engaging than a textbook.

2 RELATED WORK

Our project adds to an extensive literature on visualization. In this section, we present a very brief overview of that literature.

In recognition of the limitations of paper-technology textbooks at communicating how an algorithm solves its problem, computer science (CS) educators have created a wide variety of algorithmic visualizations over the years. For example, [4, 7, 11, 12] present dynamic visualizations of various sequential algorithms and report that such visualizations help students understand those algorithms. [16] reports that students who explore a visualization *interactively* learn significantly more than those who view it passively. Our project differs from these in its focus on concurrent algorithms.

CS educators also have a long history of looking for ways to help students visualize concurrent and/or parallel algorithms. For example, [17] presents a visualization of the Readers-Writers Problem, using specialized hardware and a vintage-1988 Modula-like language called Portal. [8] provides an overview of efforts in this area, circa 1993. [6] presents a visualization of the Dining Philosophers Problem using a 1994 sequential animation library called XTANGO and the SR programming language, with each philosopher represented as an SR process. Likewise, [10] presents three parallel algorithm visualizations using a 1999 parallel simulator called MultiPascal and a visualization tool called JSAMBA. These projects generally use a "post-mortem" approach: a concurrent program's behavior is traced during its execution (e.g. saved to a file), that trace is then used to drive the visualization after the program has terminated. Our project differs from these in (i) providing a visualization of the concurrent program's behavior in real-time, during program execution; (ii) using multithreading instead of multiprocessing; and (iii) using an object-oriented language (C++) and approach.

A project whose aims align with ours is ThreadMentor [2, 3], which provides a C++/GTK class library of GUI widgets for real-time visualization of specific multithreading synchronization constructs—threads, semaphores, monitors, locks, etc.—and demonstrates their use using the Cigarette Smokers, Dining Philosophers, and Readers-Writers Problems. However, the current version of GTK is not thread-safe [5]; neither [2] nor [3] describes the architecture in sufficient detail to indicate how ThreadMentor resolves this issue. Our project differs from ThreadMentor by (i) using the Thread Safe Graphics Library (TSGL) [1] instead of GTK; (ii) using TSGL to create real-time graphical visualizations of the actual concurrent entities—philosophers, producers, consumers, readers, writers, etc. (vs. ThreadMentor's lower-level synchronization primitives)—and how they interact to solve a given problem; and (iii) including the results of an assessment exercise that indicates students find interacting with these visualizations to be more engaging than reading a textbook. We chose TSGL because it is a native C++ (in which parallel applications are commonly written), thread-safe, general library for real-time graphical drawing. It also provides platform independence by being built atop OpenGL. [1] presents results of an experiment in which the use of a TSGL visualization improved student understanding of the parallel loop construct.

3 THE VISUALIZATIONS

The Dining Philosophers, Producers-Consumers, and Readers-Writers Problems seem to be the "classic" problems that are most commonly-used by textbook authors. In this section, we present our visualizations for these three problems.

3.1 The Dining Philosophers Problem

In the Dining Philosophers Problem, $N > 1$ philosophers sit around a circular table. Each philosopher goes through an endless cycle of thinking, getting hungry, eating, thinking, getting hungry, eating, and so on. Between each pair of philosophers is a single fork, and a philosopher must acquire both forks in order to eat. Since each philosopher is a perfect logician, the problem is to devise a single protocol for each philosopher to follow in sharing the forks, that will ensure no one starves.

Our visualization of this problem can be run from the command-line as follows:

```
$ ./DiningPhilosophers [N] [speed] [protocol]
```

If no command-line arguments are specified, parameter *N* defaults to 5 philosophers, the *speed* defaults to 5 (on a scale of 1-60), and the *protocol* defaults to odd-even check (see Section 3.1.3 below). Figure 1 shows our visualization at the outset:

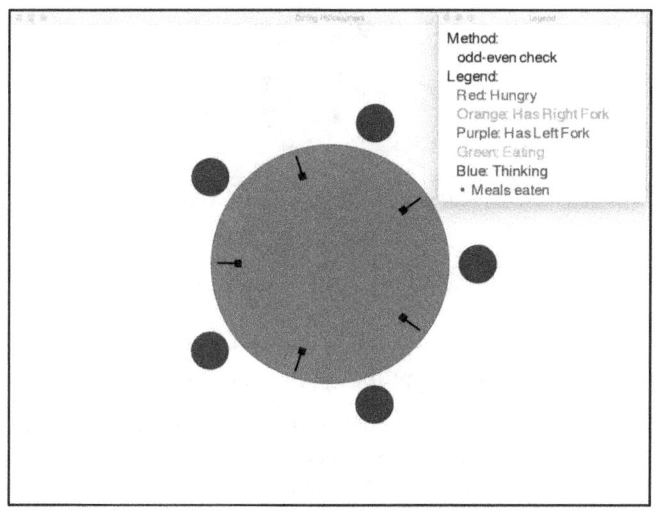

Figure 1: The Dining Philosophers, Initial State

As can be seen, our visualization draws a circular gray table with *N* equidistant forks around it. A philosopher, represented by a circle that is color-coded to indicate her current state, sits between each pair of forks. A separate legend-window indicates the state corresponding to each color; each philosopher begins in the blue 'thinking' state.

3.1.1 Deadlock. A deadlock occurs if each process or thread in a group is holding a resource that is needed by another member of the group, in a circular-waiting pattern. Operating Systems textbooks frequently use the Dining Philosophers problem to illustrate the topic of deadlock. For example, [14-16] all illustrate deadlock by presenting a "first attempt" Dining Philosophers protocol like the following for each philosopher to follow:

```
Semaphore fork[N];
right = getID();
left = (right+1) % N;
while (true) {
   /* think for a while */
   fork[right].acquire();
   fork[left].acquire();
   /* eat for a while */
   fork[right].release();
   fork[left].release();
}
```

This protocol has a philosopher pick up her right fork when it is available and then pick up her left fork when it becomes available. If all philosophers happen to get hungry at the same time, a deadlock ensues. Our visualization uses this protocol if 'w' (for wait-when-blocked) is given as the command-line *protocol*:

```
$ ./DiningPhilosophers 5 5 w
```

Since each philosopher starts out by thinking for a random length of time, the protocol will seem to work correctly for a while, but eventually the philosophers deadlock, as shown in Figure 2:

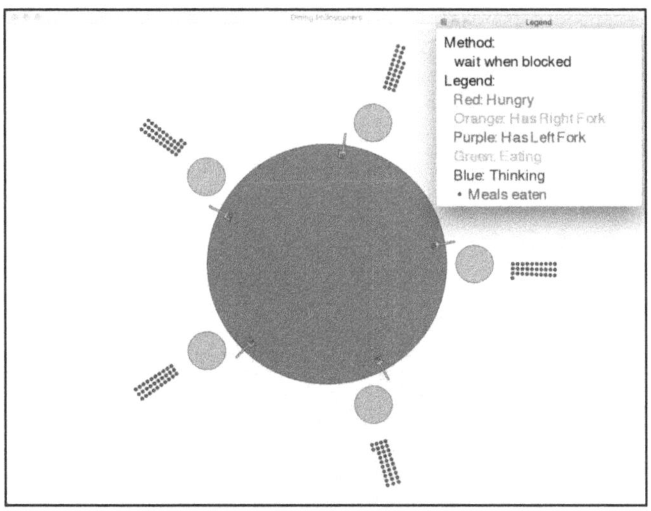

Figure 2: The Dining Philosophers, Deadlocked

Each brown dot "behind" a philosopher represents a meal she has eaten. The number of these dots varies because a philosopher thinks and eats for random lengths of time. When these dots stop appearing behind a hungry philosopher, she begins to starve.

3.1.2 Livelock. In an attempt to fix the deadlock problem, a protocol like the one below might be presented to students:

```
/* same variables as before */
while (true) {
   /* think for a while */
   fork[right].acquire();
   do {
     if (fork[left] is in use) fork[right].release();
     else fork[left].acquire();
   } while (I have less then 2 forks);
   /* eat for a while */
   fork[right].release();
   fork[left].release();
}
```

Seeking to avoid a deadlock, this protocol has a philosopher pick up her right fork when it is available, but if her left fork is not available, put down her right fork. While this does avoid a deadlock, it can unfortunately lead to *livelock*: if all of the philosophers become hungry at the same time, they will all pick up their left forks, all put down their left forks, all pick up their left forks, all put down their left forks, ... forever. Since no philosopher gets to eat, a livelock also leads to starvation. Our visualization uses this protocol if 'f' (for forfeit when blocked) is given as the command-line *protocol*:

```
$ ./DiningPhilosophers 5 5 f
```

Using this protocol, our philosophers will endlessly oscillate between the "hungry" and "has right fork" states. Figure 3 shows the two views this protocol will alternately produce:

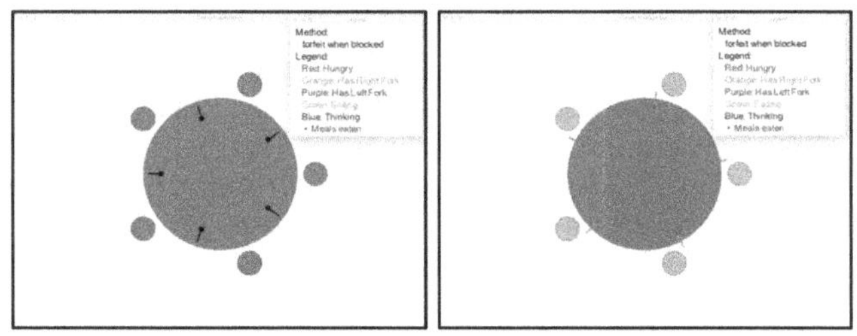

Figure 3: The Dining Philosophers, Livelocked

In Figure 3, the philosophers following this protocol endlessly cycle between the two states. Our visualization thus lets students see and experience the difference between livelock and deadlock.

3.1.3 A Correct Solution. One way to solve the Dining Philosophers Problem is to use a protocol like the one below:

```
/* same as before */
id = getID();
while (true) {
   /* think for a while */
   if ( odd(id) ) {
        fork[right].acquire();
        fork[left].acquire();
   } else {
        fork[left].acquire();
        fork[right].acquire();
   }
   /* eat for a while */
   fork[right].release();
   fork[left].release();
}
```

By having odd-numbered philosophers pick up their forks in a right-then-left ordering and even-numbered philosophers pick them up in a left-then-right ordering, this protocol prevents any circular-wait from developing, and thus avoids the deadlock issue. Since a philosopher only releases her fork after she is finished eating, it also avoids the livelock issue. Our visualization uses this protocol by default, if no command-line protocol is given:

```
$ ./DiningPhilosophers 7
```

Figure 4 shows our visualization using 7 philosophers after it has run for a few minutes:

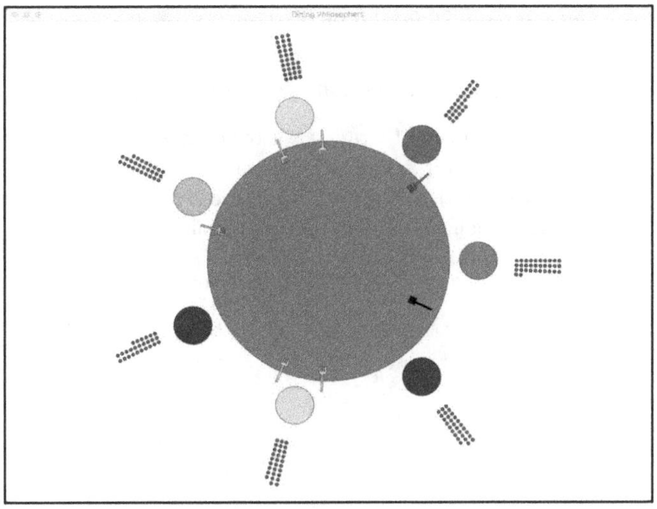

Figure 4: The Dining Philosophers, Working Correctly

At the moment captured in Figure 4, philosopher 0 is at the "one o-clock position", is even-numbered, is hungry, and has acquired her left fork but cannot yet acquire her right fork; her left neighbor (1) is odd-numbered, hungry, and cannot yet acquire her right fork because 0 has it; 1's left neighbor (2) is thinking; 2's left neighbor (3) has acquired both forks and is eating; 3's left neighbor (4) is thinking; 4's left neighbor (5) is odd-numbered, has acquired her right fork, but cannot yet acquire her left fork because it is in use; 5's left-neighbor (6) is even-numbered, has acquired both forks, and is eating. The brown "meals eaten" dots behind each philosopher provide a visual indicator that no one is starving. As before, different philosophers have eaten different numbers of meals because each thinks and eats for slightly different random lengths of time.

Our Dining Philosophers visualization thus allows a student to specify the number of philosophers, the speed of execution, the philosophers' protocol, and to view the resulting behavior. Students can also view/modify the program's source code, letting them explore the protocol-code that produces a given behavior.

3.2 The Producers-Consumers Problem

In the Producers-Consumers Problem, $M > 0$ producer entities produce items and $N > 0$ consumer entities consume the items produced by the producers, ideally in the order they were produced. The problem is to come up with a scheme ensuring that:

- Each item produced by a producer is consumed by some consumer (i.e., no item gets lost).
- No item produced by a producer is consumed by more than one consumer (i.e., no item gets duplicated).
- No producer or consumer waits forever (i.e., no starvation).

The usual approach to solving this problem is to introduce an intermediate FIFO data structure called a *buffer*, into which the producers deposit their items, and from which the consumers retrieve the items. When this buffer has a fixed capacity, the problem is often called the *Bounded Buffer Problem.*

Textbooks often use this problem to introduce the topic of monitors, since building the buffer as a monitor provides the conditions needed to solve the problem. (A monitor has self-synchronizing methods that use a lock to ensure mutually exclusive access and condition variables for synchronization.) Given a shared buffer implemented as a monitor, the producer and consumer entities can be easily coded as follows:

```
/* declaration of shared buffer */
```

```
void producer() {
  while (true) {
    /* produce item it */
    buffer.put(it);
  }
}
```

```
void consumer() {
  while (true) {
    it = buffer.get();
    /* consume it */
  }
}
```

Our visualization can be run from the command-line as follows:

```
$ ./ProducerConsumer [M] [N]
```

where M and N are the numbers of producers and consumers, respectively. M and N both default to 5, as shown in Figure 5:

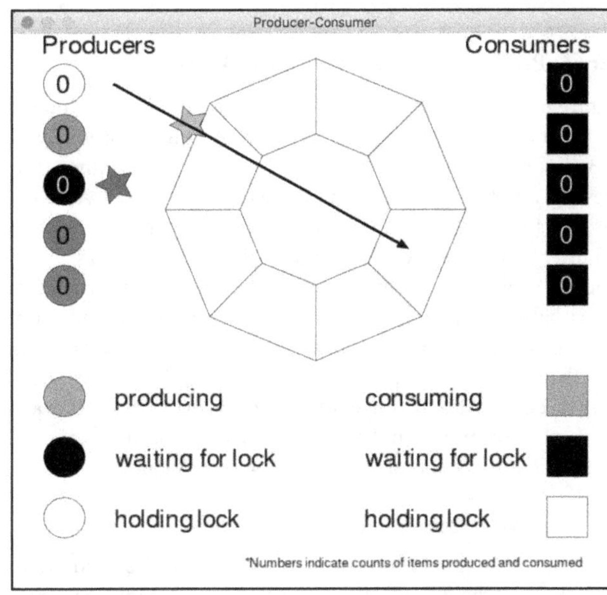

Figure 5: Producers-Consumers, Initial View

On the left is a column of producers, represented by circles; on the right, a column of consumers, shown as squares. The numbers inside a producer or consumer indicates the number of items it has produced and deposited, or has retrieved and consumed, respectively. In the middle is a circular buffer with room for 8 items. An item is represented by a star that appears next to its producer. In Figure 5, the topmost producer (0) has produced an item, has acquired the buffer's lock, and is depositing its item into the buffer; producers 1, 3, and 4 are in the process of producing items, producer 2 has produced an item and is waiting to acquire the buffer's lock. Since the buffer is empty, all of the consumers are also waiting to acquire the buffer's lock.

Note this visualization's color-coding: an entity waiting for the lock is colored black, one that has acquired the lock is colored white, and an item is colored with the color of its producer.

Figure 6 shows the same visualization later in the run:

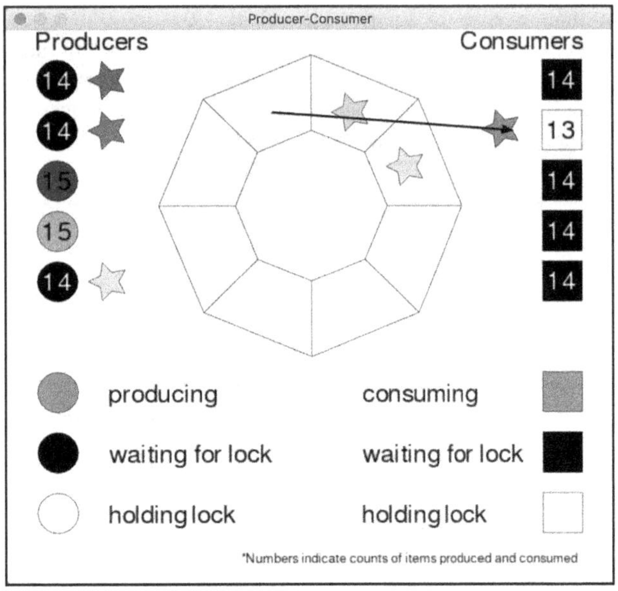

Figure 6: Producers-Consumers, Later View

In Figure 6, producers 0, 1, and 4 have all produced items and are awaiting their chance to deposit them into the buffer; producers 2 and 3 are in the process of producing items. Consumer 1 is retrieving an item from the buffer, which contains two other items; consumers 0, 2, 3, and 4 are all waiting to get items from the buffer but must wait (along with the producers) until consumer 1 releases the buffer's lock. Note that the production of items is balanced among the producers and the consumption of items is balanced among the consumers. As before, students can access the source to see the code that is driving the visualization.

By seeing that only one entity can ever access the buffer at a time, a visualization can help students build accurate mental models of a monitor and its mutually exclusive behavior.

3.3 The Readers-Writers Problem

In the Readers-Writers Problem, $M > 0$ writer entities write items to a shared database, and $N > 0$ reader entities read items from that database. While writers must write in a mutually exclusive fashion, all readers can read simultaneously because reading does not alter the database. The problem is to devise such a system and ensure that no reader or writer starves. The Producers-Consumers Problem would be similar to this problem, if multiple consumers could retrieve items from the buffer simultaneously.

Since a write must be performed mutually exclusively but a read need not, a key question is: When a writer is finished writing and both readers and writers are waiting, who gets to proceed? There are at least two ways to answer this question:

- In the *writer-priority protocol*, a waiting writer gets to proceed before any waiting readers.
- In the *reader-priority protocol*, waiting readers get to proceed before any waiting writers.

Textbooks [14, 16] present solutions using the reader-priority protocol; [15] presents solutions using both protocols.

Our visualization for this problem supports both protocols; it can be invoked as follows:

```
$ ./ReadersWriters [M] [N] [protocol]
```

where M is the number of writers, N is the number of readers, and *protocol* can be 'r' for reader-priority, or 'w' for writer-priority (which is the default). If omitted, both M and N default to 6. Figure 7 shows this visualization using all default values:

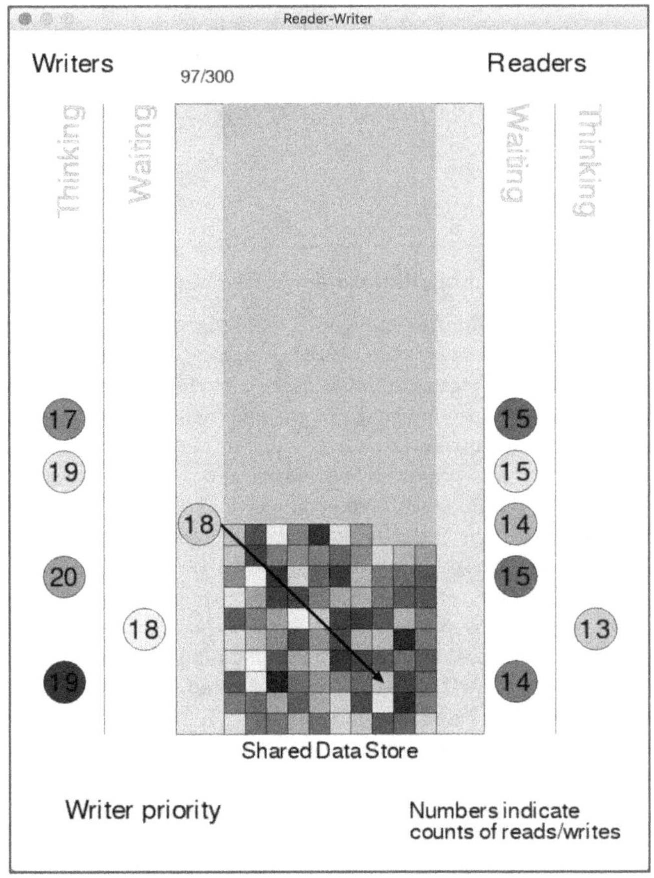

Figure 7: Readers-Writers, Early View

Readers and writers may be in any of three states: "thinking" about their next action, "waiting" to perform their next action, or performing their action. Our visualization provides six columns—one for each kind of entity's three states—plus a seventh central column for the database. This visualization thus uses spatial-positioning to show an entity's state, rather than color-coding.

When it writes, a writer may either create a new database entry or update an existing entry. In Figure 7, the writers have filled roughly a third of the database with new entries. Writer 2 has entered the database and is updating an entry; writers 0, 1, 3, and 5 are all "thinking" about their next write; writer 4 is ready and waiting to write; readers 0-3 and reader 5 are all waiting to read; and reader 4 is "thinking" about the last item it read. Since this is the writer-priority version, writer 4 will get to go next.

Figure 8 shows this same run a bit later in the execution:

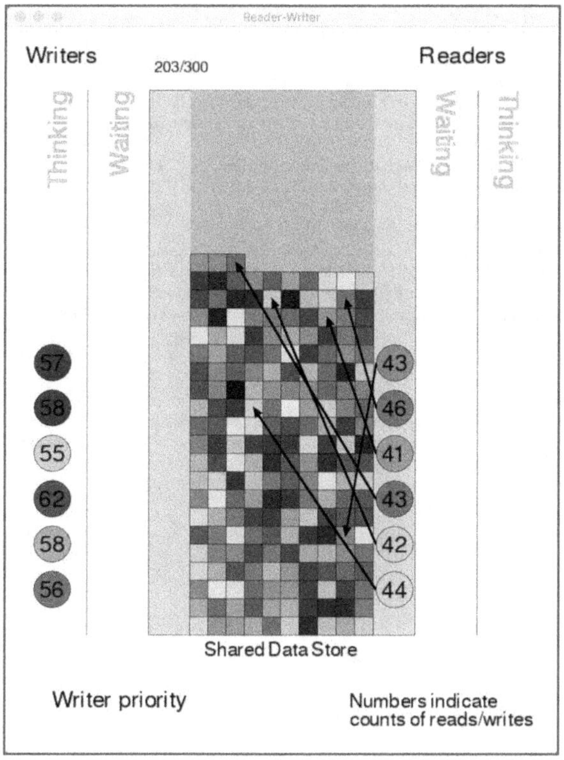

Figure 8: Readers-Writers, Later View

Unlike a writer, all of the readers can access the database and read different items simultaneously, as Figure 8 shows. By seeing the behaviors and the source code (which they may modify), students can see how these behaviors are produced. Space limitations prevent us from showing the reader-priority protocol, but it lets students see and experience how that protocol's behavior differs.

4 ASSESSMENT

To evaluate this work, we identified two research questions:

RQ1: Does interacting with our visualizations improve long-term recall of these problems, compared to reading a textbook?

RQ2: Do students find our visualizations to be a more engaging way to explore these problems, compared to reading a textbook?

To answer these questions, we devised the following experiment:

1. 34 volunteer subjects were recruited from our CS2 course (*Data Structures*, to ensure students had not seen these topics before), using extra course-credit as an incentive.
2. The subjects were randomly divided between a control group and a treatment group.
3. Simultaneously, and in identical computer labs:
   a. Both groups watched a short (~15 minute) video that introduced multithreading, concurrency, synchronization, and the Dining Philosophers Problem.
   b. For 10 minutes, the control group studied a textbook's discussion of that problem and its solutions, while the treatment group interacted with our visualization for it.
   c. Both groups watched a short (~10 minute) video that introduced the Producers-Consumers Problem.
   d. For 10 minutes, the control group studied a textbook's discussion of that problem and its solutions, while the treatment group interacted with our visualization for it.
   e. Both groups watched a short (~10 minute) video that introduced the Readers-Writers Problem.
   f. For 10 minutes, the control group studied a textbook's discussion of that problem and its solutions, while the treatment group interacted with our visualization for it.
4. Two weeks later, all subjects were emailed a link to a 14-question online quiz. Twelve questions covered details of the three classic problems; one question covered race conditions; the final question had subjects rate how engaging they found the post-video activities on a 1-5 scale.

22 of our volunteers showed up for the experiment and completed the quiz, so our sample size was limited. Our null hypothesis for RQ1 was that there would be no significant difference in quiz performance between the control and treatment groups. The treatment group's mean score was 9.9 compared to 10.5 for the control group; this difference was not significant ($p=0.3387$), so we were unable to reject the null hypothesis for RQ1. The control group outperforming the treatment group stems from our use of randomized groups: our control group's median CS2 final exam score was 84.5 compared to 80.5 for our treatment group.

For RQ2, our null hypothesis was that there would be no significant difference in the two groups' engagement-ratings of the post-video activities. The treatment group's mean rating was 4.2 compared to 2.8 for the control group; this difference was significant ($p=0.0090$), so we reject the null hypothesis for RQ2.

Thus, we found no significant difference in learning between our textbook-readers and our visualization-users, but the latter group measured their experience as significantly more engaging, despite our small sample size. The similarity of the two groups in learning is interesting, given that the students in our treatment group were measurably weaker than those in our control group.

Our experimental materials (videos, quizzes, visualizations, etc.) are all available upon request.

5 CONCLUSIONS

We have presented interactive visualizations for three "classic" synchronization problems: The Dining Philosophers, Producers-Consumers, and Readers-Writers Problems. By controlling the number of concurrent entities and the protocol, students can *see* abstractions like deadlock, livelock, and starvation in real-time, as well as the behaviors of correct solutions to these problems.

We have also presented experimental results that indicate: (i) students using our visualizations achieved levels of learning that were statistically similar to students reading textbook materials, and (ii) students found our visualizations to be significantly more engaging than traditional textbook treatments of the same topics. By letting students see and dynamically experience concurrent protocols in action, our visualization tools can supplement a course textbook by "bringing to life" the text's static figures and descriptions, and thus help students build more accurate mental models of concurrency abstractions.

Our thanks to NSF (DUE#1225739) and to the Calvin College Science Division, whose support made this work possible.

REFERENCES

[1] J. Adams, P. Crain, C. Dilley, S. Nelesen, J. Unger, M. Vander Stel, Seeing Is Believing: Helping Students Visualize Multithreaded Behavior, *Proc. of 47th ACM Technical Symposium on Computer Science Education* (SIGCSE'16), March 2016, 473-478. DOI= 10.1145/2839509.2844557.

[2] M. Beady, S. Carr, X. Huang, C.K. Shene, A Visualization System for Multithreaded Programming, *Proc. of 31st SIGCSE Technical Symposium on Computer Science Education* (SIGCSE'00), March 2000, 1-5.

[3] S. Carr, J. Mayo, and C.K. Shene, ThreadMentor: a Pedagogical Tool for Multithreaded Programming, Journal on Educational Resources in Computing (JERIC), 3(1), March 2003, Article 1. DOI= 10.1145/958795.958796.

[4] E. Fouh, M. Akbar, C. Shaffer. The Role of Visualization in Computer Science Education. *Computers in the Schools: Interdisciplinary Journal of Practice, Theory, and Applied Research*, Vol. 29, 2012, 95-117. DOI=10.1080/07380569.2012.651422.

[5] Gnome Developer, GNOME Threads, Online, Accessed 2018-08-04: https://developer.gnome.org/gdk3/stable/gdk3-Threads.html.

[6] S. Hartley, Animating operating systems algorithms with XTANGO, *Proc. of 25th SIGCSE Technical Symposium on Computer Science Education* (SIGCSE'94), March 1994, 344-348.

[7] C. Kehoe, J. Stasko, A. Taylor. Rethinking the evaluation of algorithm animations as learning aids. *International Journal of Human Computer Studies*, (54)2, Feb 2001, p. 265-284. DOI=10.1006/ijhc.2000.0409.

[8] E. Kraemer and J. Stasko, The Visualization of Parallel Systems: an overview, *Journal of Parallel and Distributed Computing*, 18(2), June 1993, p. 105-117.

[9] K. Louden and K. Lambert, *Programming Languages: Principles and Practice* (3e), Cengage, 2011.

[10] T. Naps and E. Chan, Using Visualization to Teach Parallel Algorithms, *Proc. of 30th SIGCSE Technical Symposium on Computer Science Education* (SIGCSE'99), March 1999, 232-236.

[11] S. Roger, Integrating Animations into Courses, *Proc. of 1st Conference on Integrating Technology into Computer Science Education* (ITiCSE'96), June 1996, 72-74.

[12] C. Shaffer, M. Cooper, A. Alon, M. Akbar, M. Stewart, S. Ponce, S. Edwards. Algorithm Visualization: The State of the Field. *ACM Transactions on Computing Education*, 10(3), August 2010. Article no. 9. DOI=10.1145/1821996.1821997.

[13] R. Sebasta, *Concepts of Programming Languages* (10e), Pearson, 2012.

[14] A. Silberschatz, P. Galvin, and G. Gagne, *Operating Systems Concepts* (9e), Wylie, 2012.

[15] W. Stallings, *Operating Systems: Internals and Design Principles* (8e), Pearson, 2014.

[16] A. Tanenbaum, H. Bos, *Modern Operating Systems* (4e), Pearson, 2015.

[17] M. Zimmerman, F. Perrenoud, and A. Schipper, Understanding Concurrent Programming Through Program Animation, *Proc. of 19th SIGCSE Technical Symposium on Computer Science Education* (SIGCSE'88), Feb 1988, 27-31.

Up or Down? An Insight into Programmer's Acquisition of Iteration Skills

Cruz Izu
School of Computer Science,
The University of Adelaide
Adelaide, Australia
cruz.izu@adelaide.edu.au

Cheryl Pope
School of Computer Science,
The University of Adelaide
Adelaide, Australia
cheryl.pope@adelaide.edu.au

Amali Weerasinghe
School of Computer Science,
The University of Adelaide
Adelaide, Australia
amali.weerasinghe@adelaide.edu.au

ABSTRACT

Iteration is one of the basic programming constructs taught in a CS1 course. Students learn to use loops by being exposed to a range of loop examples, initially with scalar values and then over composite data such as vectors. When writing a finite loop to iterate over a vector, we can iterate upwards or downwards. In many cases, the order does not change the outcome; however, for some tasks it is important to consider which direction is most suitable before writing a solution. For example, if we want to shift the elements of a vector one position to the right (left), we should choose a downward (upward) loop. However, when we asked undergraduate students to implement the shift right task, most of them used an upward loop. This outcome indicates the students didn't consider the loop direction before coding the iterative task.

We hypothesise that this was in part due to course materials favouring upward loops. To confirm this hypothesis, we have analysed the examples presented in our local CS0/CS1 courses as well as four popular MOOCs. This analysis has corroborated an overwhelming bias towards upward loops. We have also found a lack of instruction regarding the possible impact of direction on code efficiency. Thus, in order to improve novice programmers' iteration skills, we propose CS1 examples that expose students to a more balanced mix of up/down loops and the explicit choice of direction.

CCS CONCEPTS

• **Social and professional topics** → **CS1**; *Computing education*;

KEYWORDS

iteration, down loops, program design, novice programmers

ACM Reference Format:
Cruz Izu, Cheryl Pope, and Amali Weerasinghe. 2019. Up or Down? An Insight into Programmer's Acquisition of Iteration Skills. In *Proceedings of the 50th ACM Technical Symposium on Computer Science Education (SIGCSE '19), February 27-March 2, 2019, Minneapolis, MN, USA.* ACM, New York, NY, USA, 7 pages. https://doi.org/10.1145/3287324.3287350

ACM ISBN 978-1-4503-5890-3/19/02...$15.00
https://doi.org/10.1145/3287324.3287350

1 INTRODUCTION

Learning to code is a complex task, starting with the syntax and semantics of core language features (variable declaration, assignment, iteration, selection), in conjunction with understanding of the computer model [19], I/O analysis [11] algorithmic design [16], and problem solving [4]. Novice programmers demonstrate difficulties with all these elements, as illustrated in [5, 9, 13, 18].

Iteration is one of the basic programming constructs to build both small and large programs. Iteration is comprised of *for* loops, *while* loops and its variants (do-while, repeat-until etc). When teaching iteration, the focus is generally on when to choose a *for* or a *while* loop, how to express complex conditions and how to avoid common errors such as writing an infinite or empty loop, or having off-by-one errors [1, 8]. As off-by-one errors are commonplace, students are instructed to pay attention to the loop range. However, direction, whether the loop should go up or down, has been hardly discussed in the literature. While working on our previous paper [7] we discovered most students will always write an up loop, even when the solution will be easier using a down loop. Thus, we decided to investigate the impact of loop direction in code design. In particular, this study addresses the following research questions:

- RQ1 – Will students who have completed introductory programming courses consider the direction of the loop when writing code to shift a vector to the right?
- RQ2 – Do CS1 course materials expose students to up and down loops? Is the impact of choice of direction clearly demonstrated?

The main contributions of this work are: (1) a think-loud study observing students solving the shift-right vector problem, which highlighted the fact most students are inclined to *always* use upwards loop, and (2) the identification of a lack of materials that demonstrate loop direction as an explicit part of design.

The rest of the paper is organised as follows: section 2 introduces a literature review of iteration, section 3 describes the think-aloud investigation for a simple iterative task that highlighted the issue of loop direction as part of the design space. This insight triggered an analysis of the loop examples used in a range of CS1 courses which is presented in section 4 and discussed in section 5 with implications and recommendations for educators. Finally, section 6 summarises our findings.

2 BACKGROUND

Cherenkova et al [3] explored the difficulties of CS1 students when learning to program by analysing error rates on the first submission to weekly code-writing problems; their analysis showed *loops* and *conditionals* were the most challenging topics.

To master iteration, students should both understand how loops work and how to write them. Several approaches have been used to assess loop comprehension. Students have been asked to describe the output or explain in their own words the outcome of an operation such as calculating the sum [10] or the average [12] of an array, or printing a multiplication table [1]. Alternatively, multiple-choice questions have been used to test code comprehension. For example, Shihudan et al. [17] used 20 MCQ, which included a range of simple and nested loop examples. Cetin [1] explored how well students understood the concept of a loop by asking a range of comprehension questions. He noted some students need to trace each iteration, while others were able to apply chunking and see the loop as one step; he also reported the case of nested loops been seen as running in parallel, this misconception was also found in [8].

Moving from comprehension to writing skills, Whalley et al [20] analysed students' performance in coding two iterative tasks: a simple loop to calculate average and a more challenging nested loop to print a box of asterisks. Note that in order to write good iterative solutions, students need to use two inter-related skills: design skills and coding skills. To ease the learning in a CS1 course, most problems provide explicit information of what to implement, so that design is minimal. Hence students can acquire the core coding skills first. As problem descriptions get more complex, students start to make design choices and then code them.

Cherenkova's study[3] showed students did better with looping based on data structures compared to problems that contain loops over ranges of integers. Examples of loops iterating over a data structure follow a given pattern (i.e. from 0 to length). However, they were unable to apply that knowledge to problems that had a wider choice of range values. Ginat [6] focused on the ability of CS2 students to write nested loops to generate a range of tuples. Both studies focused only on the range.

To the best of our knowledge, there are no published studies that have considered loop direction as part of loop design. The works cited in this section use only loops that iterate upwards; the only exception is 2 MCQs in [17] that showed code iterating concurrently from both the first element and the last element towards the center of the array by using 2 indexes (one going up and the other going down). In summary, not only are there no studies that consider direction, none of the other studies have included downward loop examples as exercises.

3 THINK-ALOUD STUDY

This section introduces an iterative task that was part of a think-aloud study that combined program comprehension and programming skills. The case analysis of that task provided the motivation for exploring loop direction.

3.1 Data Collection

We approached students during CS1 and CS2 teaching sessions. The students that volunteered had programming knowledge equivalent to CS0, plus 8-weeks of instruction in their current CS1 or CS2 course. The CS1 course teaches object oriented programing in C++, while the CS2 covers algorithm design and data structures.

Task 2

Write code that moves all elements of an array one place to the right, with the rightmost element being moved to the leftmost position.

Figure 1: Shift right coding exercise.

We recorded 20 think-aloud cases: 9 students were studying CS2 (the Data Structures course), with a CS1 average mark of 68% (standard deviation of 13%) and 11 students were taking CS1 (the OOP course). Note that this set was not aimed to be representative of the entire CS1/CS2 student cohort.

Each student met one-on-one with one of the authors. After being welcomed, they were given a short description of a new concept, followed by 3 tasks, and asked to think aloud as they complete them[2]. The first task has been analysed and reported in previous work [7]. The second task, shown in Figure 1, which we analysed in this study, focuses on programming skills, in particular in using iteration to shift an array one position to the right. The third task is a combination of both reasoning and programming skills, omitted in this work due to space limitations.

Each student solved this problem task on paper while they were recorded verbalising their thoughts. These recordings were transcribed and paired with their paper solution. We should note this coding task favours the use of a down loop to update the array values from the right (top) value to the left (bottom) value as will be explained in section 3.3.

3.2 Methodology

We first classified each paper solution both by its correctness and by its approach. Four students misinterpreted the task description in some way; for example, they did not update the array but instead made a copy, or they misread the direction of the shift. These students were excluded from the analysis. The solutions were coded by one author into three different approaches as shown in Figure 2. A second author checked and confirmed the classification. Both coders were in agreement for all cases.

We then read through the transcriptions in order to find the different patterns of thought that led to the same design. When students with the same paper solution followed a similar thought pattern, we selected one case as representative of that subgroup.

Table 1: Iterative strategies used for *shift right* exercise

Case	Description	Works?	Count
Case 1(a,c)	Down loop	Yes	3
Case 1b	Down loop	No	1
		Total Loop downwards	4
Case 2	Up self-corrected loop	Yes	3
Case 2b	Up loop (failed correction)	No	2
Case 3	Up incorrect loop	No	7
		Total Loop upwards	12

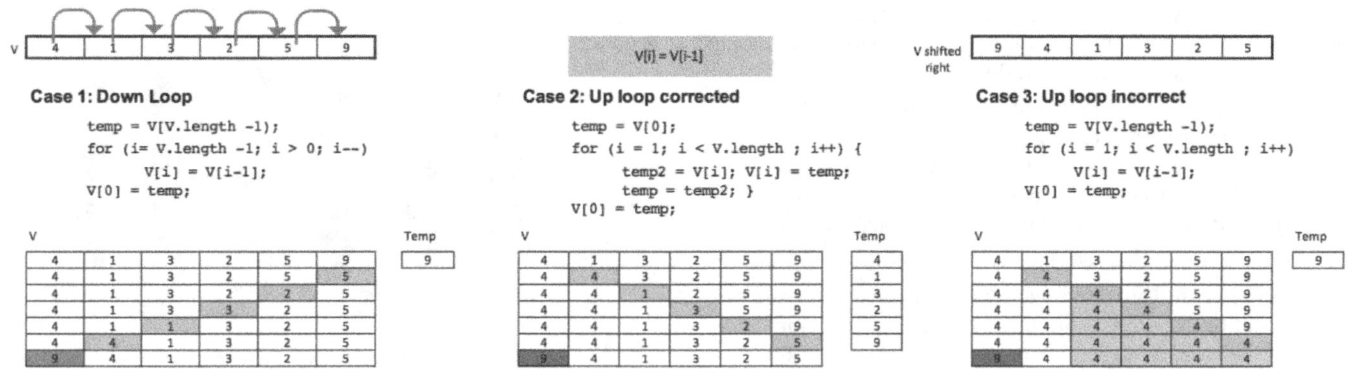

Figure 2: Three iterative approaches to shift right.

3.3 Case Analysis

Table 1 shows a summary of the code approaches used by students while completing the task. Only 25% of students wrote a downward loop when coding; furthermore, half of those started with an upward loop and on realizing it wouldn't work, changed the loop direction. Thus, only 2 out of 16 students made a deliberate down loop choice to start with.

Figure 2 shows a diagram to explain these three general approaches. The leftmost diagram shows the use of a down loop, storing the last array element value into a "temp" variable and then copying all array elements to the right (starting from the end and working towards the start of the array). Finally, "temp" is copied into the first element. Case1 is the simplest and most efficient code. Case 3 shows a similar shift step placed inside an *up* loop. As before, the last element is stored into "temp" and the elements are all shifted to the right inside the loop, and finally V[0] set to the "temp" value. We can see by looking at the rightmost diagram that Case 3 is incorrect as it copies the value of V[0] into all other locations. Lastly, Case 2 (middle diagram) shows how students self-corrected the upward loop by performing three steps for each iteration through the array elements from smallest to largest: 1) copy the value at the next array location to a temporary variable 2) copy the current value to the next array location 3) write the temporary value to the current value. Case 2 is functionally correct, but requires two additional copies in each loop iteration.

In the rest of this section we will explore the student's design thoughts behind each case.

3.3.1 Case 1: Downward loop. There were only 2 students that chose the down loop before coding. As they produce different solutions, we will examine them separately as case 1a and case 1b.

Case 1a: *plan for downward loop* The first case student traced the problem on paper with initial values {1,2,3,4} and target values {4,1,2,3}. He thought about the process of moving the data to the right prior to writing any code. Then reflected on writing the down loop as follows:

> So I want to start with that 3, to shift that to the right, and then I want to count..count down. [inaudible]....equal to 0 I think....So it's got to start at 3, move that 3 to the right .... What I hope this does, is it's gonna take this element here, and set that equal to this element there.. and then that's gonna keep going until it reaches the zero element.

We should note this was the only student that fully articulated their design before writing the code.

Case 1b: *chose down loop first on the fly*

This student also chose the loop direction to be down *prior* to writing any code for a different reason as per transcript:

> OK, so from previous work I remember that it's kind of best to work backwards. So, hum, so we want to try to make sure we don't lose any numbers in the process. . . . So we'd start from the end so "i" equals the end of the array minus 1. And then we want to go to the first part of the array which would be 0, or generally in programming the first one would be 0

Thus, the student explicitly recalls the fact they have seen a backward loop problem before. Unfortunately, the paper solution shows a coding mistake, as the student wrote "i<=0" as the loop condition instead of "i>0". Thus, he wrote an empty loop.

Case 1c: *Start with upward, then changed to downward loop*

Case 1c (representative of 2 students) went straight to write a *standard* up loop without fully working through the design first. Let's briefly see the thought process of this case:

> For loop int i = 0. I just ahh need to scan the, all the elements in the value. Size....i++. Mm I also need a variable to store the rightmost element.

The student then writes inside the loop the statement "array[i] = array[i-1]", but quickly realised that the code won't work, as verbalised below

> If I go this way...the previous one will be always changing. So, maybe I should go from the rightmost side ... go left to right.

Then, the student reverses the loop correctly to complete the task.

3.3.2 Case 2: Upward self-corrected loop. In the previous case, the student reversed the loop to preserve the values as they are shifted. An alternative, more convoluted, approach is to preserve the next value with an additional variable *temp2*.

Case 2 is representative of this approach; the student chooses an upward loop and straight away realises they need to be careful not to lose any values as verbalised in their think-aloud:

> so we have a for loop that runs from i=0, i<n, i++. OK, so what we want to do is we want to take the i'th value of array and we want to store it somewhere. We don't want to loose the next value so we can't just paste it over the next value because that will be lost.

Then, the student verbalised the way to correct the loop body:

> So what we want to do, we want to set that value, we want to store that value, put it in temp, define temp. .... we need to do something with temp. We need to put that in, i+2, so we need to give temp .... so we make....that's frustrating....dug myself into a hole.

Eventually, after some struggle and some tracing on an example with values {5, 6, 7, 8}, the student works out how to use two variables to implement a swap and writes correct but complicated code. When this student is shown the downward loop approach in the next task, their reaction is to quip "they did it much more eloquently than I did."

Note we had three students that used the same correction, while another 2 students (not listed due to space limitations) attempted but failed to correct the loop block.

3.3.3 Case 3: Upward incorrect loop. Similarly to cases 1c and 2, case 3 started writing an upward loop.

> OK, so I'm going to make a for loop that goes through the whole list and then when it gets to the end it will put that value at the start. So ... we're going to increment it each time. ... we might make that less one and do the last thing at the end outside of the for loop .... we need to put the value to the right to the value at the current position. So, i + 1 would be the value to the right. We need to assign that to the value at i. And then outside of the for loop we're going to say, the first value is equal to value at value(size-1) because it's indexed differently.

The main difference for students that follow this approach compared with case 2 is that they wrote the code assuming it will work. They did not do any tracing to see they will lose the original values.

3.4 Think-aloud conclusions

The analysis of the think-aloud transcripts have shown that students will rarely consider using a down loop when needed. Most students produced either complicated code or incorrect code. Cases 2 and 3 seem to indicate they are using a top-down design [15], doing a local expansion of the *Loop plan schema* over the shift operation. Tracing was a key step for students using the upward loop (cases 1c and 2) to identify the potential data dependencies when updating data elements within the array.

Why didn't students consider a down loop solution more often, either as an initial possibility or after initial difficulties with the up loop? Case 1b offers some insight by mentioning they have seen a similar example from previous work. Following the learning framework described by Pirolli and Recker [14], it appears most students have not integrated down loops into their declarative knowledge of iteration. In other words, they have not been instructed or shown enough down loop examples to consider their use on a novel situation that will favour down loops.

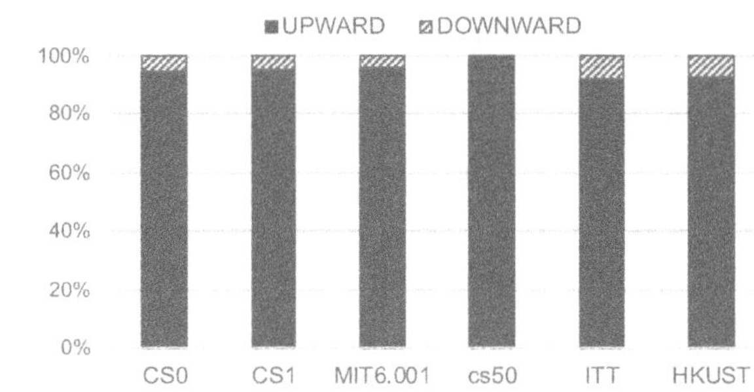

Figure 3: Relative frequency of upward/downward loops.

4 STUDENTS' EXPOSURE TO LOOPS

To confirm that their design approach could be due to lack of down loop examples during instruction, we measured the range and type of loop examples that an average CS1 student will see. This section presents the result of that analysis.

4.1 Sample Course Selection

We evaluated a total of six courses, including our local courses CS0 and CS1, plus 4 MOOCs: HarvardX: cs50, HKUST: Intro to Java Prog Pt 1 (Java programming), IIT BombayX: cs101.x (C programming) and MITx: 6.001 Introduction to Computer Science and Programming Using Python (Python programming).

Our local courses reflect the loop exposure of the students who completed the think-aloud task. The 4 MOOCs were chosen to benchmark across different world regions and using different languages to verify that the range of loop examples is similar across differing institutions and languages.

For each course, we counted any instances of loops (for, while, do..while) appearing in the course materials (i.e. lecture recordings, examples, worksheets, etc) provided to students. We included both the materials used to teach iteration as well as any other course materials on other topics that contained loops. Each item was classified as having an up-loop or a down-loop based on whether the loop index was incremented or decremented respectively. In addition, for the CS0 and CS1 course we analysed whether the students were guided to make design decisions on whether the loop should go up or down.

4.2 Analysis of Loop Exposure

There was wide variation in the *number* of loop examples students see in the courses we reviewed (ranging from 15 to 92). Figure 3 shows a summary of the up/down distribution. Although we expected a direction bias, the results were an eye-opener: in our own courses, down loops are only 5% of examples, compared with 95% for up loops. Our courses are not an exception; the relative down frequency across the 6 courses ranged from 0% to 8% with a median, mean and mode of 5%.

Are problems better solved with up loops? or it just the preferred (unconscious) choice? To further explore this bias, we extended the analysis for our local courses to classify them by the following categories:

- **optimal**: problems where the direction used in the example led to code that is more efficient (fewer operations and/or less memory) and/or more readable
- **neutral**: problems where the direction of the loop does not change the efficiency or readability of the solution.

An example of an *optimal* direction problem is a task to print the values of the array, which by convention is from first to last so it should use an up loop. Shifting the elements one position to the right, or calculating the cumulative sum of an array are also array operations that have an implied direction. In these cases, code is simpler if we follow the direction we want to print or update.

Neutral problems, for example finding the maximum value of an unsorted number array, have no design advantage in terms of loop direction, i.e. we could do the search going up or going down, although by habit we will tend to iterate upwards.

Our students have solved the countdown problem (see Table 2) so they have written at least one optimal down loop. Thus, how does our think-aloud problem differ from these previous examples, such that students could not make the connection? Our study's task is an *optimal* down problem, like the count down example which they have solved. However, unlike the countdown example, the direction is not explicitly indicated by the problem description. We speculate students will use down loops for problems in which the direction is given as part of their description. On the other hand, *implicit* examples do not give any indication from their description that a specific direction should be used, and this may cause students to use the upward direction by default.

For students to choose a direction for an optimal implicit problem, they need to have been exposed to a similar type in their prior learning. To investigate how frequently students see these different categories of problems, we further classified the loop examples across our CS0/CS1 courses into four subgroups: (neutral,implicit), (neutral,explicit), (optimal,implicit) and (optimal,explicit) An example of each type of problem is shown in Table 2 [1]

97% of the problems were classified as neutral with regards to loop direction. Over two semesters our students have seen **six** problems that have an optimal loop direction; 4 of them have the direction explicitly given in the problem description; the remaining 2 were implicit, one going up and one going down. In short, they have seen only one problem similar in design to the shift right task.

5 DISCUSSION

Firstly, our analysis of the students' approach to loop design reveals two issues that are common to code design in general: (1) most students code on the fly with minimal design before writing the first line of code and (2) being able to trace the code, either in their head as they write it, or tracing it on paper afterwards is critical to get a correct working solution for non-trivial problems.

Secondly, the analysis has shown that both answers to our research questions are negative. In regards to *RQ1*, students **did not** consider the direction of the loop when solving to shift right coding task. Most students attempted to write a solution using an up loop. This non-optimal choice of direction introduces additional complexity into the program structure, increasing opportunities for errors as well as decreasing code readability. Thus, only 3 out of the 5 students that attempted to self correct their upward loop were able to create a successfully working solution. More worrying are the seven students (43%) that could not see the flaw in their solution. The transcripts do not reveal the exact source of their mistake. It could be a superficial learning of loops due to relying on code execution to verify their solutions work - note none of them did attempt to test their solution on paper. It may also be possible their mental model of loop execution could be parallel instead of sequential, which could be corrected by explaining the concept of data dependencies with an example; such as the incorrect loop from Figure 2 and make them trace it to why it fails. But whatever the cause, it is clear that loop direction was not explicitly part of their design consideration.

The down loop solution is not only more efficient, it is also easier to code. Optimal down loop problems, such as the one presented to students in our think aloud study, are not necessarily obvious on first inspection and if the students do not normally consider the direction as part of their design process, they may choose to use a contrived up loop rather than the more elegant down loop solution.

In regards to *RQ2*, the secondary analysis of the iteration examples given to students reveals an overwhelming bias of course materials towards up examples. Upward is more commonplace that downward, so it is reasonable that they have more coverage and we are not advocating for a specific ratio of up and down loops. It is not just a question of asking students to write more down loops. Our students exhibited what Perkins called *inert knowledge* [13] where they know the syntax for writing down loops, but do not have the ability to determine when to apply them. Therefore, novice programmers should be exposed to both alternatives (up/down), but importantly they should be exposed to cases where the design does or does not affect efficiency/readability (optimal/neutral) and cases where the direction is not obvious from surface cues (explicit/implicit). We should emphasize these different categories so that students have the scaffolding to make correct design decisions.

5.1 Implication for Educators

This study should increase educators' awareness of the innate bias in most course materials towards upward iteration examples. It would be simple to reduce this bias by showing more down examples as well as asking students to solve iterative neutral problems in one or both loop directions. This is useful coding practice that reinforces loop semantics and demonstrates that in those cases the direction makes no difference to the outcome.

More importantly, educators should explicitly demonstrate the differences between optimal and neutral problems so that students can *identify* when loop direction *is* going to have an impact on their solution. We should model, using one or two optimal problems, the need to analyse if the loop direction is important or not. There are multiple ways to introduce this concept when discussing algorithmic design and problem solving, two examples are given hereunder.

[1] as there was no (neutral, explicit) problem, we created a possible example by making the direction explicit (shown in italics) to a neutral problem

neutral,implicit	neutral,explicit

Problem: Calculate the Factorial of 6
Solution:
`for(int i = 6; i >= 0; --i) {`
`    FACT *= i;`
`}`
// could be equally calculated as 1*2*3*4*5*6
	Problem: Find the largest value in arr *starting from the last element.* **Solution**:
	`int maxV = arr[arr.length-1];`
	`for(int i = arr.length -2; i > 0; i--)`
	`   maxV = max(maxV, arr[i]);`
	// Down loop used as the problem dictates search from last to first.

optimal,implicit	**optimal,explicit**

Problem: Concatenate letters from two strings
Solution:
`result = "";`
`for(int i=0; i< a.length; i++) {`
` result=result+a.charAt(i)+b.charAt(i);`
`}`
// concatenate builds the string from left (first) to right (last).
	Problem: Print a countdown from 10 to 0 and then Blastoff.
	Solution:
	`for(int i = 10; i > 0; i--) {`
	`  printf("%d\n", i);`
	`}`
	`printf("Blastoff");`
	// direction indicated by start & end values

Table 2: Loop classification examples

5.1.1 Iteration Task sample 1. Implement the 4 subtasks listed below. For each task, consider if the iteration order, up or down, makes any difference to the design.

(1) find if an array Ar contains value *v*.
(2) count how many times value *v* appears in array Ar
(3) find the first appearance of value *v* in array Ar
(4) find the last appearance of value *v* in array Ar

They should work out up/down is neutral for (1) and (2), but it is optimal to use an up loop for (3) and a down loop for (4).

5.1.2 Iteration Task sample 2. An array's values are stored in consecutive memory locations. Thus, if we want to remove an element from a sorted array, we need to shift the remaining elements of the array to remove the gap. Similarly, if we need insert a new element and keep the array sorted, we should shift zero or more elements to create a gap. Sketch the steps to do these two operations and then write the code for the following two methods:

```
void remove(int value, int* array);
void insert(int value, int* array);
```

Note this task implements a shift left/right respectively of the remaining elements of the array. Apart from being a clear example of the impact of loop direction in its function, it will also help students to revise their mental model of array storage in memory.

5.1.3 Other considerations. The potential impact of language choice on student mental models of iteration should also be considered. Languages like Java, C and C++ always require *explicit* specification of both loop direction and range. The availability of other iterative constructs, such as the Python "`for X in Y`" construct, can hide these decisions from students by implying a predominant or default direction and range.

In a crowded curriculum, it is possible to reduce the bias towards upward iteration examples without requiring additional time or costly resources. Minor changes on examples and exercises plus a brief discussion on whether a given problem is neutral or optimal in terms of loop direction will be sufficient to expose students to the need to consider loop direction when is not explicit in the problem. In addition, the changes should improve students' design skills in general by learning to look for *any* implicit factors.

5.2 Threats to Validity

There are two threats to validity: (1) our observation is based on the limited sample of 16 students, although this is a large number for a think-aloud study, and (2) there is only a small number of problems that require loop direction analysis. However, modeling an infrequent case is still relevant as it will help students to consider other unusual scenarios.

6 CONCLUSIONS

Students learn to iterate through a range of examples and exercises. This study has shown the dominance of upward loops in teaching materials predisposing students to directly write an upward loop, as they did when solving the "shift right" task.

Students in our CS0/CS1 courses have had some exposure to down loops and should be able to write a simple down loop. However, we did not modeled for them the need to consider the direction of the loop for those problems, such as the shift right task, in which one direction is optimal is terms of code simplicity and readability.

We propose CS1 courses increase their limited exposure to down loops, for example by asking student to write the same problem in either direction. CS1 courses should incorporate a few simple problems with an optimal loop direction. Deciding whether the problem is optimal or neutral should be made explicit through instruction.

These changes have minimal overhead in terms of instruction and will help novice programmers programming skills by (1) improving their semantic knowledge of loops, (2) showing potential data dependencies that need to be considered due to sequential execution of the loop, and (3) developing their ability to identify when a down (or up) is the best direction to iterate over the loop.

REFERENCES

[1] Ibrahim Cetin. 2015. Student's Understanding of Loops and Nested Loops in Computer Programming: An APOS Theory Perspective. *Canadian Journal of Science, Mathematics and Technology Education* 15, 2 (Feb. 2015), 155–170. https://doi.org/10.1080/14926156.2015.1014075

[2] Elizabeth Charters. 2003. The Use of Think-aloud Methods in Qualitative Research An Introduction to Think-aloud Methods. *Brock Educ. J.* 12, 2 (2003), 68–82.

[3] Yuliya Cherenkova, Daniel Zingaro, and Andrew Petersen. 2014. Identifying Challenging CS1 Concepts in a Large Problem Dataset. In *Proceedings of the 45th ACM Technical Symposium on Computer Science Education (SIGCSE '14)*. ACM, New York, USA, 695–700. https://doi.org/10.1145/2538862.2538966

[4] Michael de Raadt. 2007. A Review of Australasian Investigations into Problem Solving and the Novice Programmer. *Computer Science Education* 17, 3 (2007), 201–213. https://doi.org/10.1080/08993400701538104 arXiv:https://doi.org/10.1080/08993400701538104

[5] Sandy Garner, Patricia Haden, and Anthony Robins. 2005. My Program is Correct but It Doesn'T Run: A Preliminary Investigation of Novice Programmers' Problems. In *Proceedings of the 7th Australasian Conference on Computing Education - Volume 42 (ACE '05)*. Australian Computer Society, Inc., Darlinghurst, Australia, Australia, 173–180. http://dl.acm.org/citation.cfm?id=1082424.1082446

[6] David Ginat. 2004. On Novice Loop Boundaries and Range Conceptions. *Computer Science Education* 14, 3 (Sept. 2004), 165–181. https://doi.org/10.1080/0899340042000302709

[7] Cruz Izu, Cheryl Pope, and Amali Weerasinghe. 2017. On the Ability to Reason About Program Behaviour: A Think-Aloud Study. In *Proceedings of the 2017 ACM Conference on Innovation and Technology in Computer Science Education (ITiCSE '17)*. ACM, New York, NY, USA, 305–310. https://doi.org/10.1145/3059009.3059036

[8] Cruz Izu, Amali Weerasinghe, and Cheryl Pope. 2016. A Study of Code Design Skills in Novice Programmers Using the SOLO Taxonomy. In *Proceedings of the 2016 ACM Conference on International Computing Education Research (ICER '16)*. ACM, New York, NY, USA, 251–259. https://doi.org/10.1145/2960310.2960324

[9] Lisa C. Kaczmarczyk, Elizabeth R. Petrick, J. Philip East, and Geoffrey L. Herman. 2010. Identifying Student Misconceptions of Programming. In *Proceedings of the 41st ACM Technical Symposium on Computer Science Education (SIGCSE '10)*. ACM, New York, NY, USA, 107–111. https://doi.org/10.1145/1734263.1734299

[10] Mike Lopez, Jacqueline Whalley, Phil Robbins, and Raymond Lister. 2008. Relationships Between Reading, Tracing and Writing Skills in Introductory Programming. In *Proc. 4th Int. Workshop on Computing Education Research (ICER '08)*. ACM, New York, NY, USA, 101–112. https://doi.org/10.1145/1404520.1404531

[11] Jeroen J. G. Van MerriÃńnboer and Marcel B. M. De Croock. 1992. Strategies for Computer-Based Programming Instruction: Program Completion vs. Program Generation. *Educational Computing Research* 8, 3 (1992), 365–394. https://doi.org/10.2190/MJDX-9PP4-KFMT-09PM arXiv:https://doi.org/10.2190/MJDX-9PP4-KFMT-09PM

[12] Roy D. Pea. 1986. Language-Independent Conceptual "Bugs" in Novice Programming. *Journal of Educational Computing Research* 2, 1 (1986), 25–36. https://doi.org/10.2190/689T-1R2A-X4W4-29J2 arXiv:https://doi.org/10.2190/689T-1R2A-X4W4-29J2

[13] David. Perkins, Fay Martin, and MA. Educational Technology Center, Cambridge. 1985. *Fragile Knowledge and Neglected Strategies in Novice Programmers. IR85-22 [microform] / David Perkins and Fay Martin.* Distributed by ERIC Clearinghouse [Washington, D.C.]. 35 p. pages. http://www.eric.ed.gov/contentdelivery/servlet/ERICServlet?accno=ED295618

[14] Peter Pirolli and Margaret Recker. 1994. Learning Strategies and Transfer in the Domain of Programming. *Cognition and Instruction* 12, 3 (1994), 235–275.

[15] Robert S. Rist. 1991. Knowledge Creation and Retrieval in Program Design: A Comparison of Novice and Intermediate Student Programmers. *Hum.-Comput. Interact.* 6, 1 (March 1991), 1–46. https://doi.org/10.1207/s15327051hci0601_1

[16] Anthony Robins, Janet Rountree, and Nathan Rountree. 2003. Learning and Teaching Programming: A Review and Discussion. *Computer Science Education* 13, 2 (2003), 137–172. https://doi.org/10.1076/csed.13.2.137.14200 arXiv:https://doi.org/10.1076/csed.13.2.137.14200

[17] Shuhaida Shuhidan, Margaret Hamilton, and Daryl D'Souza. 2009. A Taxonomic Study of Novice Programming Summative Assessment. In *Proc. 11th Australasian Conf. on Computing Education - Volume 95 (ACE '09)*. Australian Computer Society, Inc., 147–156. http://dl.acm.org/citation.cfm?id=1862712.1862734

[18] Elliot Soloway, Jeffrey Bonar, and Kate Ehrlich. 1983. Cognitive Strategies and Looping Constructs: An Empirical Study. *Commun. ACM* 26, 11 (Nov. 1983), 853–860. https://doi.org/10.1145/182.358436

[19] Juha Sorva. 2013. Notional Machines and Introductory Programming Education. *Trans. Comput. Educ.* 13, 2, Article 8 (July 2013), 31 pages. https://doi.org/10.1145/2483710.2483713

[20] Jacqueline Whalley, Tony Clear, Phil Robbins, and Errol Thompson. 2011. Salient elements in novice solutions to code writing problems. *Conferences in Research and Practice in Information Technology Series* 114 (2011), 37–45.

Can You Teach Me To Machine Learn?

An Exploration of Pedagogical Content Knowledge for Teaching Machine Learning to Non-Majors

Elisabeth Sulmont
Centre for Intelligent Machines
McGill University
Montreal, Canada
elisabeth.sulmont@mail.mcgill.ca

Elizabeth Patitsas
Integrated Studies in Education
McGill University
Montreal, Canada
elizabeth.patitsas@mcgill.ca

Jeremy R. Cooperstock
Centre for Intelligent Machines
McGill University
Montreal, Canada
jer@cim.mcgill.ca

ABSTRACT

Machine learning (ML) has become an important topic for students across disciplines to understand because of its useful applications and its societal impacts. At the same time, there is little existing work on ML education, particularly about teaching ML to non-majors. This paper presents an exploration of the pedagogical content knowledge (PCK) for teaching ML to non-majors. Through ten interviews with instructors of ML courses for non-majors, we inquired about student preconceptions as well as what students find easy or difficult about learning ML. We identified PCK in the form of three preconceptions and five barriers faced by students, and six pedagogical tactics adopted by instructors. The preconceptions were found to concern themselves more with ML's reputation rather than its inner workings. Student barriers included underestimating human decision in ML and conflating human thinking with computer processing. Pedagogical tactics for teaching ML included strategically choosing datasets, walking through problems by hand, and customizing to the domain(s) of students. As we consider the lessons from these findings, we hope that this will serve as a first step toward improving the teaching of ML to non-majors.

CCS CONCEPTS

• **Social and professional topics** → **Computing education**; • **Computing methodologies** → *Machine learning*;

KEYWORDS

Machine learning; computer science education

ACM Reference Format:

Elisabeth Sulmont, Elizabeth Patitsas, and Jeremy R. Cooperstock. 2019. Can You Teach Me To Machine Learn?: An Exploration of Pedagogical Content Knowledge for Teaching Machine Learning to Non-Majors. In *Proceedings of the 50th ACM Technical Symposium on Computer Science Education (SIGCSE '19), February 27-March 2, 2019, Minneapolis, MN, USA.* ACM, New York, NY, USA, 7 pages. https://doi.org/10.1145/3287324.3287392

ACM ISBN 978-1-4503-5890-3/19/02…$15.00
https://doi.org/10.1145/3287324.3287392

1 INTRODUCTION

Not long ago, machine learning (ML) was a topic of interest limited largely to computer science (CS) and statistics. But with the steady increase of accessible computing power and large data sets, ML has been applied to a wide range of domains. With its increasing use, ML has become relevant to a much broader community, and with it a need to understand how we can teach ML to non-major students.

Furthermore, when we consider the implications of ML, such as, job automation [6, 10], privacy concerns [4, 28], and algorithmic bias perpetuating discrimination [9, 25], ML is a critical issue in today's society. Yet, the inner workings of ML remain a mystery to most people [26]. Given the ubiquity and increasingly important role of ML in consequential decision-making, we suggest that rectifying this lack of understanding is of high value to society.

Research in education has identified *pedagogical content knowledge* (PCK) as an important component of effective pedagogy [33]. PCK refers to the knowledge needed by an educator to teach a particular subject matter. Common types of PCK include an educator's knowledge about student misconceptions, preconceptions, barriers to learning, and tactics for assisting student learning.

1.1 Research Questions and Goals

In this paper, we explore examples of PCK for teaching ML to non-majors. For the purposes of this paper, we define "non-majors" as students without a background in CS or statistics.

Specifically, we wanted to know what preconceptions instructors can identify non-major students as having about ML, what misconceptions these students have, what barriers students face, and what pedagogical tactics are used to assist the students.

This is an exploratory work. The motivation for our project is to widen the literature on ML education for non-majors, specifically in how to teach the topic, which we believe is essential for ML education to develop.

Our contributions include identifying common preconceptions and barriers of students, as well as tactics of instructors. In our interviews with ten experienced ML instructors, our participants noted that students were generally unaffected by *mis*conceptions, but rather a lack of conception to begin with.

In previous work, using the same interview data, we identified and classified learning goals for non-majors using the Structure of Observed Learning Outcomes taxonomy (SOLO) [2].

Building on our previous work, in writing this paper we found it useful to organize the reported student barriers and instructor tactics around the SOLO taxonomy. What barriers did students face at each SOLO stage, and what tactics do educators use to target students at that stage?

Table 1: Interview Participants

ID	Position	Setting	Teaching
P1	Information Professor	Public Research University	Introductory information science
P2	Psychology Professor	Public Research University	Computational psychology
P3	Psychology Professor	Public Research University	Computational psychology and neuroscience
P4	Statistics Teaching Fellow	Public Research University	Intro ML for professional master's in data science
P5	Business Management Professor	European Private Catholic University	Introduction to business analytics for law students
P6	Biology Professor	Public Research University	Quantitative methods for biology
P7	Journalism Professor	Private Research University	Data and computational journalism
P8	Cognitive Science & CS Professor	Private Liberal Arts College	Topics in AI
P9	Data Scientist and Instructor	AI Research Center	Workshops for upper-level business people
P10	Data Scientist and Instructor	Online Learning Platform	ML courses for research scientists

2 RELATED WORKS

2.1 Pedagogical Content Knowledge

2.1.1 Origin. In 1986, Shulman argued that there was too strong of a separation between content and pedagogy in education research and policy, arguing that for a teacher to be effective, one was useless without the other. He proposed "pedagogical content knowledge" as a type of content knowledge specifically for teaching in an effort to emphasize and explain how a teacher transforms subject matter to be more amenable to students [33].

Shulman offered that PCK consisted of the following: "the most useful forms of representation of those ideas, the most powerful analogies, illustrations, examples, explanations, and demonstrations -in a word, the ways of representing and formulating the subject that make it comprehensible to others...also includes an understanding of what makes the learning of specific topics easy or difficult: the conceptions and preconceptions that students of different ages and backgrounds bring with them to the learning of those most frequently taught topics and lessons."[33, 6-7]. Although the concept of PCK was subsequently embraced by the research community, Shulman did not give a clear way to capture PCK with its broad definition. Difficulties in articulating and documenting PCK have been found since its introduction [1, 20, 23].

2.1.2 In Computer Science. Saeli et al. [31] conducted a review of PCK for programming. To define PCK-content, it was driven by four questions: why teach programming, what should be taught, what are the student difficulties, and how should the topic be taught. Hubbard's [17] review analyzed how computing PCK is conceptualized and investigated. Yadav et al. [37] measured PCK through teachers' responses to teaching vignettes about student's understanding of programming constructs, to which they found improvements needed in how teachers address students' programming errors. Other PCK research has focused on K-12 teacher education (e.g. [18, 24]). CS PCK education literature is limited, but there is work on student misconceptions for topics such as, programming (e.g. [7, 19, 30]), and algorithms and data structures (e.g. [8, 29, 32]).

2.1.3 In Statistics. Groth [12] sketched a hypothetical descriptive framework of statistical knowledge for teaching based off of research on mathematical knowledge for teaching [14–16], while maintaining the separation between statistics and mathematics. Groth cites building data and designing a study as examples of non-mathematical statistical knowledge. Lee and Hollebrands's [22] work on effectively engaging students in learning statistics with technology resulted in a framework for a specialized knowledge called technological pedagogical statistical knowledge (TPSK). There are three components in TPSK and each depend on the one before it: statistical knowledge, technological statistical knowledge, and technological pedagogical statistical knowledge.

2.2 Machine Learning Education Research

This area of research is still growing, as ML is such a new subject in university curricula. There has been work in AI education; notably the Symposium on Educational Advances in Artificial Intelligence, which first met in 2010. Research on ML education has been present through that venue, including assignment designs [13, 34].

Of relevance to our study is Lavesson's [21] case study of a master's level ML course (30 students). In the course evaluation results, Lavesson reports that students found the evaluation and comparison of learning algorithms (through statistical tests and different evaluation metrics) to be difficult. Students felt more comfortable comparing algorithms theoretically than comparing them empirically with statistical tests and experiments. The implementation of ML algorithms using programming was found to be easiest out of all learning outcomes. Our present work extends his findings by a more in-depth analysis of why certain topics are more difficult and with a focus on non-majors. Additionally, as opposed to sampling only a single course, our work contributes an analysis of data sampled over multiple courses within different disciplines.

2.2.1 Teaching Machine Learning to Non-Majors. Literature on teaching ML to non-majors is even more sparse than the already minimal literature on ML education, comprising of papers on curricula for non-majors. Way et al. [35] [36] presented their findings from a multi-year project called "Broader and Earlier Access to Machine Learning" to which resulted in an online repository of flexible module materials. Gil [11] designed a data science course with ML topics for non-programmers, through a workflow paradigm and a visual interface called WINGS. Pre-tested on non-majors, Gil proposes that learning basic ML concepts without programming is more approachable due to less time investment (e.g., required CS courses, lessons spent on programming).

3 METHODS

With no prior work focused on ML PCK, our goal for this study was to begin this line of investigation. We chose to speak to instructors who have taught non-majors to uncover the breadth of ML PCK.

3.1 Interviews

3.1.1 Participants. Participants were recruited through cold emails and mailing lists related to CS and data science education. The only requirement for participation was experience teaching ML concepts to non-majors. All of the participants' institutions reside in Canada or the USA, with the exception of P5 (Europe). All are professors, except for three instructors (P4, P9, P10) who all have their PhDs. Table 1 provides an overview of the participants.

3.1.2 Structured Interview. The development of the interview questions was informed by PCK literature. This affected questions intended both to probe for, and address, the difficulties and misconceptions faced by instructors and students. Appendix A contains the interview questions. All interviews were conducted over voice-call, except for P2 who answered by email. The average length of voice-call interviews was 21 minutes. Interviews took place between June and July 2018. Transcripts contained mostly paraphrased content of what the interviewees said, with some direct quotations. The first author conducted all the interviews and transcription.

3.2 Qualitative Analysis

Transcripts were coded iteratively for content, and were coded through consensus by four people. Two of the coders are authors of the paper; the other two are members of the same research group. All coders have a strong CS background, although one coder had no experience with ML. Two coders have strong education background and the other two have intermediate education backgrounds.

First, all four coders read the transcripts in their entirety and based on first impressions created four initial categories. These were preconceptions, easy for students, difficult for students, and tactics. Early in the coding process, we recognized the need for two more categories: hard to teach, and teacher goals. We free coded the transcripts in order of the questions (i.e., code all the transcripts for Question 2, then all the transcripts for Question 3, etc.).

3.2.1 Grouping Codes. Next, we clustered the codes that were repetitions of the same concept or very close to being repetitions. Through consensus, we then formed groups of codes that naturally fit together, regardless of the category under which they were originally coded, which resulted in 38 groups. Groups titled "Math", "Visual", "Human vs. Computer", and "Related to Domain" were the most populated groups. In addition, there were groups related to pedagogy ("Tools", "Techniques") and groups about preconceptions about ML. "Math" and "Programming" were unique groups because they encapsulated difficulties within their disciplines that did not exclusively occur while learning ML (e.g., debugging).

In examining our groupings, we noticed that the group titled "Design Decisions" was mostly full of "difficult for students" codes, whereas the group on teaching students a given ML algorithm was dominated by the "easy for students" codes. On further examination of the codes that represented some learning goal/objective, we observed a pattern that the easy to teach learning goals were aligned with the lower levels of the SOLO taxonomy and the hard to teach learning goals were grouped along with issues that correspond to higher levels of the SOLO taxonomy.

3.2.2 Regrouping Codes. Once we realized that the SOLO taxonomy could help us re-cluster our codes, we grouped our codes into nine categories: one for each SOLO stage as well as one for each transition between stages. Unlike the other SOLO stages, the pre-structural group did not have learning goals — it consisted entirely of preconception-related codes.

In our prior work, we described our observations about what learning goals fell into which SOLO stage. In this paper, we will focus on the clusters that corresponded to the transitions between SOLO stages — the barriers that students faced in development, and the tactics that instructors used to facilitate student development.

We will also describe the codes which did not neatly fit into our SOLO-inspired organization of codes: the difficulties students faced surrounding math and programming, as well as the instructional tactics which spanned multiple SOLO levels.

4 PRIOR WORK: LEARNING GOALS CLASSIFIED BY THE SOLO TAXONOMY

While this paper focuses on the PCK needed to transition students from one SOLO stage from another, it is first worth describing the learning goals that we classified into each SOLO stage.

The SOLO taxonomy has been found useful for classifying learning objectives and designing curricula and course materials [3, 5]. We found that learning goals described as easy to teach were consistently at the lower end of the SOLO taxonomy, while harder goals were found consistently at the higher end. Table 2 provides a broad overview of the learning goals found in our data.

Table 2: Instructor-Based Taxonomy of ML Learning Goals for Non-Majors using SOLO Stages

Unistructural Stage
(Describe, Trace, Interpret, Identify) simpler ML algorithms that do not require a high-level of prerequisite math knowledge.
Multistructural Stage
Compute a baseline. *Implement* an algorithm with black box. *Plan* for training and testing phase by splitting data. *Convert* raw data into computer input.
Relational Stage
Relating between real life and computer input/output. *Evaluate* performance with consideration to the bias-variance tradeoff. *Apply* evaluation to tune parameters to improve performance.
Extended Abstract Stage
Develop a model from scratch to solve a problem. *Communicate* performance and limitations of model.

After establishing what students learn at each SOLO stage, we turned to PCK for supporting development. We will describe preconceptions students have (which affects the transition to the unistructural stage) and then the student barriers and pedagogical tactics corresponding to the transitions between the other SOLO stages.

5 PRECONCEPTIONS

Preconceptions are an important element of PCK. It is important for educators to know where students are beginning from, particularly to support them reaching a unistructural stage of learning.

When asked for student preconceptions, P10 responded that students have asked, "Can you teach me to machine learn?" It is important to note the marked difference in the ML exposure that non-majors may have vs. those with a CS/math background, seen in something as simple as using the term "machine learning" correctly. In the interviews, we found three recurrent preconceptions:

- **ML is Important:** students believe that ML is extremely powerful and conclude that it is the "next big thing" and will "get you a job". According to participants, this reflects a common student motive for taking an ML course. P10 spoke to this saying that research scientists, as students, express a need to use ML because more publications are coming out using ML techniques.
- **Heard of ML from Popular Media:** Students have heard of ML technology through popular media, such as news articles on AlphaGo and autonomous cars. P9 offered repercussions of this; students read sensationalized media on ML and they[1] have to repeatedly debunk the limits of ML during the duration of the course.
- **Implementing ML is not accessible:** Some participants noted their students often feel that they are unfit to implement ML, perceiving that they need a strong CS/math background. This has been debunked in the literature [11, 35].

These preconceptions concern themselves with the reputation of ML rather than how ML works. This reputation can cause students to view ML as an intimidating subject to learn and/or to overestimate ML's abilities.

6 FACILITATING STUDENT DEVELOPMENT ALONG THE SOLO STAGES

The barriers that students face in learning ML change as the students develop in their understanding of the topic. Anticipating and appreciating student difficulties is an important component of PCK, as is having instructional tactics for these various barriers.

Here we describe the different barriers students face as they progress along the SOLO taxonomy, alongside the tactics reported by participants that were targeted at particular SOLO stages.

6.1 Getting Students to a *Unistructural Stage*

In the SOLO taxonomy, students first begin at a prestructural stage where they do not understand the topic at hand. This corresponds to the preconceptions we discussed in Section 5. The prestructural stage is aptly described by P3 as a *lack* of understanding rather than *mis*understanding.

The next stage of the SOLO taxonomy is the unistructural stage, wherein students can understand a single element of the topic. What PCK do ML educators have about facilitating the transition from prestructural to unistructural understanding of ML?

Participants noted two tactics for facilitating this transition, and one barrier that students encounter.

[1]We refer to all participants with gender neutral pronouns throughout this paper.

6.1.1 Barrier: Human Thinking vs. Computer Processing. It was mentioned frequently that students attribute human qualities to computers, for example, that computers have intuition or common sense that will influence their decision. Or that computers can take in data (e.g., language, images) and process it similar to humans. Psychology students specifically want to map ML to the the brain and models of learning previously encountered during their psychology studies. This barrier is possibly due to a lack of exposure to algorithmic thinking, considering their non-major background. P8, who teaches to both CS and non-majors, explicitly noted that this was an issue with only the non-major students.

6.1.2 Tactic: Working through Simple Problems by Hand. Participants described working through simple problems by hand to promote student understanding of ML algorithms. The key to these problems is that they are low dimensional, so students can trace the steps of the algorithm sequentially.

6.1.3 Tactic: Simulating an Algorithm. Along the same line of understanding algorithms, participants promoted simulation of algorithms, which can come in different forms. Two participants described activities where their class simulates an algorithm as a whole. For example, P3 turns the class into a multi-level perceptron where every student acts as a function within the network. Students pass a note as input and output, following the network structure, with each student altering the note to their function. The goal is to demystify the black box by having students experience an algorithm's sequential logic. Other forms include interactive visualizations of algorithms (e.g., pyLDAvis [2] for Topic Modeling).

6.2 Getting Students to a *Multistructural* Stage

When at a multistructural stage, students learn the individual steps needed to transform an algorithm into model (e.g., data cleaning, creating features, using Sckit-learn), but cannot yet see how the individual steps all come together.

In the context of machine learning, we define an *algorithm* to be a set of instructions. A *model* is the result of training data being inputted into an algorithm to make predictions on unseen data.

There are no overarching themes in the data for transitioning to the multistructural stage. Participants had comments for this stage that were not expressed by others. This indicates future work needed to further investigate these two stages and their progression.

6.3 Getting Students to a *Relational* Stage

At a relational stage, students can combine their skills learned in previous stages to build and tune a model, as well as students making design decisions about features and parameters. Participants noted these were difficult for students to learn.

6.3.1 Barrier: Underestimating Decision-Making in ML. According to participants, students believe that ML requires little human decision. It is more difficult to design a model (i.e., choosing algorithm, features, and parameters) than to implement a model. P6 described that students were surprised that humans are responsible for deciding when to stop tuning a model, expecting more automation and less decision-making.

[2]Available at https://github.com/bmabey/pyLDAvis

6.3.2 *Tactic: Strategically Choosing Data Set(s).* Participants reported using low-dimensional data sets throughout a course, whether in assignments or in-class examples. Students can grasp more easily what is happening to the input and analyze the output without getting lost in a large number of features. For example, P6 described using the IRIS data set[3] because of its low-dimension (four attributes). Even with its low-dimensionality, effective models can be trained on it. There are other benefits to low-dimensions, including faster run time and less data cleaning.

In addition, participants described minimizing the data sets they use throughout the courses. As P10 stressed, every new data set is a cognitive barrier for students because students need to get acquainted with its unique format and in addition, will probably need to clean it, which takes time. P6 uses the IRIS data set for every new algorithm they introduce. By using it on each algorithm taught, they aim to show that the same question can be addressed using different tools. They concluded that it helps students build confidence, noting that students often try their unrelated final project models on the IRIS data set as a reference point.

6.4 Getting Students to an *Extended Abstract* Stage

Students at a extended abstract stage are able to develop a model to solve a specific problem using their model building skills from the previous stage to compare different models and select the best solution. At this stage, students also evaluate whether ML methods are suitable for a problem. Participants noted one barrier and tactic in facilitating student development to this stage.

6.4.1 *Barrier: Perceiving the Limits of ML Applications.* When given a problem, students lack the immediate inclination to identify the constraints of applying ML as a solution. This may be related to students' over-estimation of the capabilities of ML. P9 says that they have to re-iterate that a model is only as good as the data, i.e., ML applications depend heavily on quality and quantity of data.

6.4.2 *Tactic: Open-Ended Problems.* Participants described teaching their students through open-ended problems for assignments, class activities, and final projects, which would involve developing a new model from scratch.

7 GENERAL PEDAGOGICAL TACTICS

Whereas the tactics from Section 6 were targeted to particular learning goals or transitions, participants additionally described tactics that they used generally. By "generally" we mean they used this tactic for numerous transitions, or they mentioned the tactic without a reference to a specific learning goal. These were generally used throughout a course, and are sufficiently flexible that they can be used for a variety of learning goals.

7.1 Visualization

When answering Question 3 or 6 (see Appendix A), participants overwhelmingly mentioned "visualization" broadly. This term encapsulates a wide range, including some of the tactics that were presented in previous sections. In response to Question 3, participants expressed that visualized concepts are easier. This could be because a concept lends itself to visualization (e.g., could be drawn on a blackboard) or because a concept has an existing visualization (e.g., online interactive demos). This was especially cited for explaining algorithms.

There was no consensus on a type of visualization; each participants had their own methods. One participant who did not include programming, advocated for drag-and-drop type interfaces for building ML processes, such as Microsoft Azure Machine Learning Studio. Another created demos on Jupyter notebooks that his class could follow along to. Finally, a few mentioned data plotting.

7.2 Relating to the Real World

Using real world applications was strongly promoted by participants. This can come in the form of showing how certain models solve common problems, such as Naive Bayes for effective spam filtering. Or, students solving socially significant issues using public data sets (e.g., predicting benign or malignant tumors using the Breast Cancer Wisconsin Data Set[4]).

It may not even have to do with solving a problem, but the context. Two participants described using data related to their school; school newspaper archives and the course catalog as a subject of topic modeling and NLP respectively. As a final example of diverse applications, one participant has students read O'Neil's *Weapons of Math Destruction* [27], which concerns itself more with how ML causes problems within society. This real world relation contextualizes ML's importance by highlighting to students its increasing relevance in solving and, even, creating contemporary problems.

7.3 Domain Specificity

The majority of our participants teach ML to a specific discipline, to which they expressed the importance of teaching to the discipline of the students. P6's final comment on teaching non-majors was that having an instructor from the students' domain is more effective than sending students to the CS department. P9 agreed with this saying if an instructor approaches teaching ML to non-majors as a CS instructor, they will lose students in the math and programming.

Being domain specific helps with student motivation. P2 noted that their students are "eager to finally combine psychology and computation". In addition, P7 made an interesting comment in answering question 4 that student difficulty depends on disciplinary norms, citing difference in math and programming exposure across disciplines. This may be another reason to support domain-specificity.

According to the participants' answers, being domain specific can look like focusing course content to relevant ML methods to the students' field, showing domain-specific examples, or giving domain-specific problems or data sets to solve.

8 GENERAL STUDENT BARRIERS

Math and programming arose as difficult topics for students. These topics were broadly mentioned and our interview questions did not aim to capture their details. From the participants' comments, student difficulty with math and programming is independent from learning ML, yet necessary to address in order to teach ML.

[3] Available at https://archive.ics.uci.edu/ml/datasets/iris

[4] https://archive.ics.uci.edu/ml/datasets/Breast+Cancer+Wisconsin+(Diagnostic)

8.1 Math as a Barrier for Students

Math was consistently brought up by participants, with probability and linear algebra noted as subtopics. P2 sums up the participants' thoughts on math when they say "anything mathematical seems to elicit some concern in many students". P7 describes their students as "self-identified as not able to do math". This reflects that a source of difficulty is that math itself causes anxiety, rather than its application. Additionally, there were comments on the lack of prerequisite(s) in math or retainment of prerequisite(s) math course(s) as a source of the difficulty.

Some instructors actively avoided teaching with math as a way around this barrier. As much as there were comments on math difficulties, only one participant offered a way to deal with math difficulties that did not require omitting math. P7 purposefully speaks of students as "not being good at math yet" and empowers their journalism students by saying that because they are good at learning, they will be able to learn the necessary math concepts.

8.2 Programming as a Barrier for Students

Programming did not come up as consistently as math, but not all participants include programming in their courses. Non-major students usually have at most one programming course done, which is one of the sources of student difficulty. This is also a reason why some participants do not include programming and opt to use visual interfaces for implementing ML (e.g., Microsoft Azure).

Although programming was broadly mentioned, the most agreed difficulty on programming was debugging. P3 had an interesting comment that "if students had a bug, they saw it more as a problem with programming than understanding of ML concepts so they don't get demotivated", which may be a helpful re-framing.

9 DISCUSSION

Through our interviews with ten participants, we uncovered a range of themes that begin to explore ML PCK for non-majors. We suspect that some of the results presented here are not specific to non-majors, but may be transferable to CS and statistics students. For example, there is overlap between our results and Lavesson's [21] course evaluation findings on easier and more difficult topics in ML (see Section 2.2). This is especially notable because Lavesson presents the perspectives of CS students.

9.1 Limitations

Our short interview format helped us recruit more participants and gain breadth. However, as the interviews lasted on average of 21 minutes to accommodate our uncompensated participants' busy schedules, this affected the depth of conversation. We did not interview any students nor observe any classrooms, thus limiting our study to the perspectives of instructors.

There were considerable differences in the ML course content taught by our participants and the motivation of their students for learning the subject. While this helps survey a broad scope of course content, it may have reduced consensus on the themes since the participants were often describing different topics and student populations, unique to their respective courses. However, given that ML is a new subject to be taught to non-majors, these issues arise naturally with the subject of study.

9.2 Future Work

To the best of the authors' knowledge, this is the first work on ML PCK. We hope to provide a foundation for future PCK studies in ML. Our interview format did not focus on specific ML concepts because we did not know which concepts, across disciplines, would be consistently relevant. Having identified several learning goals as well as common barriers, more specific questions can be developed to capture more detailed PCK.

Although "visualization" was a frequently mentioned tactic, participants lacked specificity as to what it meant. There is opportunity to more clearly define what constitutes visualization of ML and best practices for doing so.

More work is needed on the role of math and programming while learning ML. How do these subjects facilitate understanding while teaching/learning ML? Is math development and programming development separate from ML development? And in terms of course design for non-majors with little prerequisites: how much math needs to be included? Is programming necessary?

10 CONCLUSION

We identified examples of pedagogical content knowledge (PCK) for teaching machine learning, namely in the forms of preconceptions and barriers faced by students along with instructional tactics.

Student preconceptions include ideas that ML is important, but also not accessible. The data from our participants are evidence that it is possible to teach ML to those with little to no math/CS background. Instructors reported students having difficulty appreciating the human decision-making aspects of ML, and overestimating the power of ML to solve real-world problems. Visualization was a popular tactic for teaching ML; it appears that more visualization tools would be useful for ML educators.

PCK is important to building a teacher's competence. Our results highlight opportunities for innovation in teaching ML as well as the relationships ML has with math and programming.

A INTERVIEW QUESTIONS

(1) Could you briefly describe the context in which you teach machine learning? (i.e. what background do your students have and what are the motivations?)
(2) What are some common ML preconceptions that students have before taking your course?
(3) What ML concepts do students have the easiest time with?
(4) What ML concepts do students have most difficulty grasping?
(5) What are the most common mistakes students make?
(6) Are there any examples, analogies, or other methods of explaining concepts that you find particularly effective?
(7) Any other comments on teaching non-technical students machine learning?
(8) Do you have any formal education in teaching? If so, when?

ACKNOWLEDGMENTS

We thank the participants for their time and insights. We also acknowledge Horatiu Halmaghi and Jessica Quynh Tran for partaking in the qualitative analysis. This work was supported with funding from NSERC.

REFERENCES

[1] Deborah Loewenberg Ball, Mark Hoover Thames, and Geoffrey Phelps. 2008. Content Knowledge for Teaching: What Makes It Special? *Journal of Teacher Education* 59, 5 (2008), 389–407. https://doi.org/10.1177/0022487108324554 arXiv:https://doi.org/10.1177/0022487108324554

[2] John B Biggs and Kevin F Collis. 1982. *Evaluating the quality of learning: The SOLO taxonomy (Structure of the Observed Learning Outcome).* Academic Press.

[3] Gillian M Boulton-Lewis. 1995. The SOLO taxonomy as a means of shaping and assessing learning in higher education. *Higher Education Research and Development* 14, 2 (1995), 143–154.

[4] Danah Boyd and Kate Crawford. 2012. Critical questions for big data: Provocations for a cultural, technological, and scholarly phenomenon. *Information, communication & society* 15, 5 (2012), 662–679.

[5] Claus Brabrand and Bettina Dahl. 2009. Using the SOLO taxonomy to analyze competence progression of university science curricula. *Higher Education* 58, 4 (2009), 531–549.

[6] Erik Brynjolfsson and Andrew McAfee. 2012. *Race against the machine: How the digital revolution is accelerating innovation, driving productivity, and irreversibly transforming employment and the economy.* Brynjolfsson and McAfee.

[7] Michael Clancy. 2004. Misconceptions and attitudes that interfere with learning to program. *Computer science education research* (2004), 85–100.

[8] Holger Danielsiek, Wolfgang Paul, and Jan Vahrenhold. 2012. Detecting and understanding students' misconceptions related to algorithms and data structures. In *Proceedings of the 43rd ACM technical symposium on Computer Science Education.* ACM, 21–26.

[9] Virginia Eubanks. 2018. *Automating inequality: How high-tech tools profile, police, and punish the poor.* St. Martin's Press.

[10] Carl Benedikt Frey and Michael A Osborne. 2017. The future of employment: how susceptible are jobs to computerisation? *Technological forecasting and social change* 114 (2017), 254–280.

[11] Yolanda Gil. 2016. Teaching Big Data Analytics Skills with Intelligent Workflow Systems.. In *AAAI.* 3997–4088.

[12] Randall E Groth. 2007. Toward a conceptualization of statistical knowledge for teaching. *Journal for research in Mathematics Education* (2007), 427–437.

[13] Michael Guerzhoy and Renjie Liao. 2018. Understanding How Recurrent Neural Networks Model Text. http://modelai.gettysburg.edu/2018/rnntext/index.html

[14] Heather C Hill and Deborah Loewenberg Ball. 2004. Learning mathematics for teaching: Results from California's mathematics professional development institutes. *Journal for research in mathematics education* (2004), 330–351.

[15] Heather C Hill, Brian Rowan, and Deborah Loewenberg Ball. 2005. Effects of teachers' mathematical knowledge for teaching on student achievement. *American educational research journal* 42, 2 (2005), 371–406.

[16] Heather C Hill, Stephen G Schilling, and Deborah Loewenberg Ball. 2004. Developing measures of teachers' mathematics knowledge for teaching. *The elementary school journal* 105, 1 (2004), 11–30.

[17] Aleata Hubbard. 2018. Pedagogical content knowledge in computing education: a review of the research literature. *Computer Science Education* (2018), 1–19.

[18] Peter Hubwieser, Marc Berges, Johannes Magenheim, Niclas Schaper, Kathrin Bröker, Melanie Margaritis, Sigrid Schubert, and Laura Ohrndorf. 2013. Pedagogical content knowledge for computer science in German teacher education curricula. In *Proceedings of the 8th Workshop in Primary and Secondary Computing Education.* ACM, 95–103.

[19] Lisa C Kaczmarczyk, Elizabeth R Petrick, J Philip East, and Geoffrey L Herman. 2010. Identifying student misconceptions of programming. In *Proceedings of the 41st ACM technical symposium on Computer science education.* ACM, 107–111.

[20] Dona M. Kagan. 1990. Ways of Evaluating Teacher Cognition: Inferences Concerning the Goldilocks Principle. *Review of Educational Research* 60, 3 (1990), 419–469. https://doi.org/10.3102/00346543060003419 arXiv:https://doi.org/10.3102/00346543060003419

[21] Niklas Lavesson. 2010. Learning machine learning: a case study. *IEEE Transactions on Education* 53, 4 (2010), 672–676.

[22] Hollylynne S Lee and Karen F Hollebrands. 2011. Characterising and developing teachersâĂŹ knowledge for teaching statistics with technology. In *Teaching statistics in school mathematics-challenges for teaching and teacher education.* Springer, 359–369.

[23] John Loughran, Pamela Mulhall, and Amanda Berry. 2004. In search of pedagogical content knowledge in science: Developing ways of articulating and documenting professional practice. *Journal of research in science teaching* 41, 4 (2004), 370–391.

[24] Melanie Margaritis, Johannes Magenheim, Peter Hubwieser, Marc Berges, Laura Ohrndorf, and Sigrid Schubert. 2015. Development of a competency model for computer science teachers at secondary school level. In *2015 IEEE Global Engineering Education Conference (EDUCON).* IEEE, 211–220.

[25] Safiya Umoja Noble. 2018. *Algorithms of Oppression: How search engines reinforce racism.* NYU Press.

[26] Cathy O'Neil. 2016. *Weapons of Math Destruction: How Big Data Increases Inequality and Threatens Democracy.* Crown Publishing Group, New York, NY, USA.

[27] Cathy O'Neil. 2016. *Weapons of math destruction: How big data increases inequality and threatens democracy.* Broadway Books.

[28] Nicolas Papernot, Patrick McDaniel, Arunesh Sinha, and Michael Wellman. 2016. Towards the science of security and privacy in machine learning. *arXiv preprint arXiv:1611.03814* (2016).

[29] Elizabeth Patitsas, Michelle Craig, and Steve Easterbrook. 2013. On the countably many misconceptions about #hashtables. In *Proceeding of the 44th ACM technical symposium on Computer science education.* ACM, 739–739.

[30] Yizhou Qian and James Lehman. 2017. StudentsâĂŹ misconceptions and other difficulties in introductory programming: a literature review. *ACM Transactions on Computing Education (TOCE)* 18, 1 (2017), 1.

[31] Mara Saeli, Jacob Perrenet, Wim M. G. Jochems, and Bert Zwaneveld. 2011. Programming in Secondary School : A Pedagogical Content Knowledge Perspective.

[32] Otto Seppälä, Lauri Malmi, and Ari Korhonen. 2006. Observations on student misconceptions: A case study of the Build–Heap Algorithm. *Computer Science Education* 16, 3 (2006), 241–255.

[33] Lee S. Shulman. 1986. Those Who Understand: Knowledge Growth in Teaching. *Educational Researcher* 15, 2 (1986), 4–14. https://doi.org/10.3102/0013189X015002004 arXiv:https://doi.org/10.3102/0013189X015002004

[34] Douglas Turnbull. 2012. Music Genre Classification. http://modelai.gettysburg.edu/2012/music/

[35] Thomas Way, Lillian Cassel, Paula Matuszek, Mary-Angela Papalaskari, Divya Bonagiri, and Aravinda Gaddam. 2016. Broader and Earlier Access to Machine Learning. In *Proceedings of the 2016 ACM Conference on Innovation and Technology in Computer Science Education.* ACM, 362–362.

[36] Thomas Way, Mary-Angela Papalaskari, Lillian Cassel, Paula Matuszek, Carol Weiss, and Yamini Praveena Tella. 2017. Machine Learning Modules for All Disciplines. In *Proceedings of the 2017 ACM Conference on Innovation and Technology in Computer Science Education.* ACM, 84–85.

[37] Aman Yadav, Marc Berges, Phil Sands, and Jon Good. 2016. Measuring computer science pedagogical content knowledge: An exploratory analysis of teaching vignettes to measure teacher knowledge. In *Proceedings of the 11th Workshop in Primary and Secondary Computing Education.* ACM, 92–95.

Self-paced Mastery Learning CS1

Jennifer Campbell
University of Toronto
Toronto, ON, Canada
campbell@cs.toronto.edu

Andrew Petersen
University of Toronto Mississauga
Mississauga, ON, Canada
andrew.petersen@utoronto.ca

Jacqueline Smith
University of Toronto
Toronto, ON, Canada
jsmith@cs.toronto.edu

ABSTRACT

This report documents the implementation of a self-paced, mastery learning inspired CS1 course. The course was designed to increase the completion rates observed in flipped and online CS1 formats already offered at our institution. We explore the experience of students in the course and evaluate performance outcomes using grade data from all three CS1 formats, student survey responses, and exit interviews. Our evaluation identifies three main challenges in our implementation. First, the course requires significant resources and administering it is significantly more time consuming for instructors than a regular course. Second, students hesitated to treat mastery quizzes as formative. Finally, the flexibility that the course provided, with little structure and few incentives to help students stay on track, led to considerable procrastination.

These factors combined to lead students to delay coursework until the end of the semester – and beyond. As a result, while our data shows an increase in completion relative to the online format, we saw no change in completion relative to the flipped CS1 offering and saw no change in student performance as evaluated by a final exam. However, students reported more deep engagement with and understanding of the material, which encourages us to further develop the course.

KEYWORDS

self-paced; mastery learning; cs1; novice programming

ACM Reference Format:
Jennifer Campbell, Andrew Petersen, and Jacqueline Smith. 2019. Self-paced Mastery Learning CS1. In *Proceedings of the 50th ACM Technical Symposium on Computer Science Education (SIGCSE '19), February 27-March 2, 2019, Minneapolis, MN, USA.* ACM, New York, NY, USA, 7 pages. https://doi.org/10.1145/3287324.3287481

1 INTRODUCTION

CS1 courses are challenging to teach for several reasons. First, students enter the course with a wide range of prior programming experience [22]. Some students have never programmed before, while others have taken high school courses or are self-taught. Second, the students enrolled have vastly different goals and motivation, with some intending to major in Computer Science and others taking the course as a program requirement or elective. As a result, CS1 courses generally have high drop and failure rates [3, 25].

At our institution, we use research-informed pedagogical methods to enhance student success in CS1: we use a flipped teaching model in the face-to-face offerings and student-student and student-tutor interactions in the online offerings. However, many of our students still find the course difficult. In fall 2014, of the 1110 students enrolled at the beginning of CS1, 245 (22%) appeared in a class list for a subsequent term. Since they re-enrolled, it's clear that our students want to complete CS1, but many end up dropping and repeating the course. Drop rates are worse in our online CS1 [10], which is not surprising since courses delivered using an online format generally have lower completion rates than face-to-face courses [2, 17].

In previous work, we investigated why our students chose to drop out of a CS1 offering. The decision to leave a course is complex, but many students reported falling behind, being unable to recover or consciously choosing to prioritize other courses to manage workload, and eventually dropping the course [21].

In response to these findings, we implemented a self-paced, mastery learning based version of our CS1 course. Self-paced offerings provide students with opportunities to manage their own workload in a flexible manner and, ideally, to catch up on topics that were not initially well understood. To help students understand where they need to spend their effort, we introduced mastery learning to the self-paced structure. Mastery learning requires students to demonstrate high levels of learning on each of a series of checkpoints through a course with group learning, diagnostic formative tests, and support for individualized instruction.

In this paper, we describe our experience implementing this course and report on the outcomes. We begin, in Section 2, with a discussion of the basis of self-paced and mastery learning, and then describe the course and students at our institution in Section 3. We provide quantitative and qualitative descriptions of the course outcomes in Section 4 and then present lessons learned in Sections 5 and 6.

2 RELATED WORK

Other institutions have implemented self-paced computer science courses, with the earliest efforts occurring in the 1970's [1, 5]. Most of these efforts were truly independent study aimed at increasing capacity. More recent efforts have focused on replacing lectures with more effective learning environments. When a self-paced CS1 was introduced at the University of Southern Florida, the failure rate decreased from 19% to 13% and the drop rate decreased from 31% to 18% [8]. In their version, the end date of the course was fixed, but the coursework dates were flexible, with two fixed test dates serving as checkpoints during the semester. Rochester Institute of Technology used streaming as a mechanism for introducing flexible pacing in their introductory programming courses [26]. After completing the first programming course, students were streamed

SIGCSE '19, February 27-March 2, 2019, Minneapolis, MN, USA

ACM ISBN 978-1-4503-5890-3/19/02...$15.00
https://doi.org/10.1145/3287324.3287481

into one of two follow-on sequences: a single course or a two-course sequence. The two-course sequence covered the same material as the single course, plus reviewed topics from the first programming course. They reported that retention improved and grades increased.

Why might self-pacing improve retention? In studies of recall, allowing students to distribute how they allocate their study time is beneficial – but only if the students regulate themselves to spend more time on more challenging items [24]. The instructor may be able to influence how much time a learner spends on a task by providing incentives (marks) or emphasizing the importance of mastery [6], but the effective use of these techniques hinges on the learner accurately identifying the value the instructor ascribes to a piece of work and the instructor identifying which concepts are most difficult. Furthermore, it's unclear whether the extra time will be spent effectively; Nelson and Leonesio found that simply spending more time did not yield an increase in recall in most cases [20]. Spaced repetition of study, rather than simply spending more time, is more effective [19].

These lessons also apply to self-regulated study of more complex tasks. Successful self-regulation requires that learners make effective decisions about where to allocate time [15]. Inexperienced learners may not have developed the ability to identify when they need to allocate more time and how to use that time effectively, so scaffolding may be required. One frequently utilized strategy is to put students into frequent, low-stakes testing situations. Asking the learner to recall information in a test situation highlights gaps in knowledge, which encourage more study on unmastered (hopefully, difficult) concepts [14], and frequent tests encourage spaced repetition.

To provide structure to our self-paced offering, we used ideas from mastery learning. Mastery learning, which relies on frequent, often formative assessments to evaluate whether students have mastered prerequisite topics before allowing them to move on to later content, has been shown to be effective, especially in the sciences [9, 13]. Mastery learning has also been used in CS [7, 12, 16, 18]. Robins proposed Learning Edge Momentum, a theory that students fall behind because they fail to master prerequisite topics [23], and this work lead directly to their implementation of a mastery-based CS1 course [18]. Their student completion rates remained static, but students were found to have learned the material more thoroughly. However, students were concerned about a perceived lack of organization of the course and time management. Some also disengaged once they had achieved a passing course mark, rather than striving for mastery over all of the course material [18].

3 DESCRIPTION

3.1 The Course

We report on our CS1 course, taught in Python, offered concurrently in three different formats at a research-intensive North American public university. Since 2013, we have delivered our face-to-face CS1 course using a flipped classroom format [4, 11] and in 2014 we began offering additional sections in an online format [10]. In 2018, we piloted a new face-to-face, self-paced, mastery learning format. Students enrolled themselves in the format of the course they preferred.

In all three course formats, the course concepts are introduced through instructional videos and online exercises. For flipped and self-paced formats, the online instruction is followed by additional exercises and instruction in class, and for the online format, it is followed by additional online materials.

Work	Weight
Surveys	1%
Attendance	5%
Mastery quizzes	28% (4% each)
Assignments 1, 2, 3	21% (5%, 8%, and 8% respectively)
Final exam	45%

Table 1: Marking Scheme for Mastery format

In the self-paced, mastery learning format, we divided the course material into seven modules, which we called *quests*. Each quest culminated in a mastery quiz on which students were required to earn 80% in order to proceed with the subsequent course material. If that mark was not achieved, students had to retake another version of the mastery quiz at a later date. There were three quiz sessions each week and students signed up for quizzes in advance.

There were three hours of class each week and students were required to attend at least two. In class, students were given worksheets to complete, and the instructors and TAs circulated the room answering questions. Frequently, small study groups formed, and the teaching staff would lead a discussion on the topic they were working on.

Besides quizzes, students also completed three assignments, a final exam, and were given credit for completing the surveys associated with this evaluation (see Table 1). Attendance was worth 5%.

The course is self-paced with no deadlines for assignments, although assignments must be submitted before the final exam is written. The course instructors made a highly unusual arrangement with the university administration to allows students to write the final exam not only at the usual time, but also two or four months later. This allows students who take longer to master the course material to defer taking the final exam. The class lectures ended at the end of the end of the regular 12-week semester, but some TA and instructor help was still available.

3.2 The Students

Our CS1 course is offered three times each year, and we report on a semester in which students intending to major in CS are the minority. The majority of students enrolled were required, or had the option, to take CS1 to fulfill a requirement for their non-CS programs. Table 2 shows the reasons for enrolling by course format.

The proportion of women enrolled in the course ranged from 59% in flipped to 69% in self-paced. The high proportion of female students is typical of this course in this semester and a Pearson's Chi-squared test shows the difference in gender balance across course formats is not significantly different (χ^2=2.08, df=2, p=0.353). A Kruskal-Wallis test showed no significant difference in self-reported prior experience for students enrolled in the three different course formats (χ^2=0.7233, df=2, p=0.697). We used Pearson's Chi-squared for gender since the data is categorical, and Kruskal-Wallis for prior experience since it was based on a 7-point Likert-type scale with non-normally distributed data (Shapiro-Wilk normality test, p<.001).

Section	CS Program	Required for non-CS program	An option for non-CS program	Elective
Self-paced (n=32)	28%	44%	22%	6%
Flipped (n=331)	14%	46%	19%	19%
Online (n=67)	12%	36%	27%	37%

Table 2: Reason for enrolling in CS1

3.3 The Evaluation

To evaluate the effectiveness of the mastery format, we assessed course outcomes (pass, fail, and drop rates) and conducted surveys of students from all three course formats. An initial survey was conducted at the beginning of the course and asked students for demographic information and for their reasons for enrolling in the course. The final survey, conducted near the end of the standard 12 week semester, asked students to report on their experience in the course and their satisfaction with the course format.

705 students (52 self-paced, 476 flipped, and 177 online) gave informed consent and completed at least one of the two surveys. Students earned 1% towards their final course grade for completing both the initial and final surveys, regardless of whether they consented to be included in any published results.

We invited all students who completed the self-paced course to participate in an exit interview and two students did. We also gathered student feedback from institutionally mandated end-of-term student opinion surveys for all course formats.

In the analysis that follows, we set a p-value of .05 for statistical significance. We report exact values for p to three decimal places, unless the value is less than .001.

4 RESULTS

To assess students' overall impressions of the course, we reviewed the free response comments students provided in the end-of-term surveys, coding them as positive, neutral, or negative and clustering them into themes. Overall, the feedback was positive, with 87% of the students in the self-paced section, 95% in flipped , and 78% in online indicating that the course was a positive experience. Feedback on specific themes is included in the following sections.

4.1 Outcomes: pass, fail, or drop

Table 3 shows the pass, fail, and drop rates by section, as well as the number of students who have yet to write the final exam (we cannot conclude yet if these students will pass, fail, or drop). The table includes all students who enrolled in the course, not just study participants.

Through the self-paced, mastery learning format, we aimed to give students more flexibility with the course timeline and exam date in order to help them successfully complete the course. In the past, students have fallen behind and dropped the course, only to re-enroll and successfully complete it during a subsequent semester.

Section	Pass	Fail	Drop	Did not write exam
Self-paced (n=60)	42 (70%)	2 (3%)	9 (15%)	7 (12%)
Flipped (n=588)	413 (70%)	40 (7%)	102 (17%)	33 (6%)
Online (n=225)	125 (56%)	21 (9%)	51 (23%)	28 (12%)

Table 3: Pass, fail, and drop rates

We hoped that the added flexibility would decrease the drop rate and result in more students passing the first time they enroll. Unfortunately, the drop rate for the self-paced format was not significantly different from flipped (Pearson's Chi-squared test: χ^2=.004, df=1, p=.948), nor online (Pearson's Chi-squared test: χ^2=1.3611, df=1, p=.243), which has a notoriously high drop rate [10].

4.2 Exam grades

The coursework varied by course format, but all students wrote a common final exam. To compare performance in the course, we examined final exam grades of all enrolled students (not just study participants). Students in the self-paced section had a mean exam grade of 72%, while the average was 71% for flipped and 70% for online.

While there was no statistically significant difference in exam grades between formats (Kruskal-Wallis: χ^2=.073, df=2, p=.964), we saw variation within the self-paced section. Self-paced students had the option of writing the final exam during the standard exam period (April), 2 months later (June), or 4 months later (August). At the time of writing, students intending to write the exam in August have not yet done so. Table 4 shows the course outcomes for self-paced students who wrote the exam in April and June. The same exam was written by all students, but the June exam average was over 13% lower. A Shapiro-Wilk normality test confirms each set of exam grades is normally distributed (April p=.162, June p=.164), and a Welch two sample t-test shows that the April and June exam grades are significantly different (t=2.500, df=35.443, p=.017).

Section	Pass	Fail	Exam Average	Course Average	Term Average (w/o exam)
April (n=24)	24 (100%)	0 (0%)	77.8%	81.0%	83.7%
June (n=20)	18 (90%)	2 (10%)	64.7%	69.5%	73.4%

Table 4: Self-paced outcomes by exam writing date

Shapiro-Wilk normality tests confirm the set of course grades for each exam date are normally distributed (April p=.077, June p=.232). The mean course grade for the students who wrote in June was 11.5% lower than for those who wrote in April, which a Welch two sample t-test shows is a significant difference (t=2.856, df=36.802, $p < .001$).

Section	Yes	No	Prefer not to answer
Self-paced (n=36)	32 (88%)	2 (6%)	2 (6%)
Flipped (n=332)	130 (39%)	156 (47%)	46 (14%)
Online (n=106)	53 (50%)	37 (35%)	16 (15%)

Table 5: Responses to "Did you fall behind?"

Assignment	A1	A2	A3
Minimum	1	10	6
Maximum	89	108	80
Mean	23.7	41.7	42.2
Median	13.5	24	27

Table 6: Mastery assignment submissions by the number of days past the flipped/online deadlines

4.3 Falling behind

With no assignment deadlines and flexible exam scheduling, we reviewed when students completed their coursework and whether they kept up with the course. Table 5 shows a summary of self-reported responses to the question "Did you fall behind?" Students in the self-paced section report falling behind significantly more than students in the other two sections (Pearson's Chi-squared test: χ^2=26.24, df=2, $p<.001$).

If students reported falling behind, they were asked how difficult they found it to recover on a 7-point Likert-type scale from 1 (not at all) to 7 (very difficult). The mean scores were approximately 5 for all three formats.

Students in the self-paced section fell behind students from the other sections early in the course. Table 6 shows self-paced student assignment submissions by the number of days past the standard deadlines for flipped and online. On average, self-paced students submitted Assignment 1 over three weeks past the regular deadline, with a median of nearly two weeks later. One student submitted A1 on time and 12 (39%) submitted within one week of the standard deadline.

The lateness of the Assignment 1 submissions carried over to Assignment 2, with the first submission coming 10 days after the regular deadline. The mean days late for Assignments 2 and 3 are similar, in part due to the requirement that assignments be submitted before writing the exam which limited the lateness of A3 submissions. For those who wrote in April (n=24), there was a spike in submissions in the week leading up to the exam (four A1s, fours A2s, and 11 A3s). Similarly, for those who wrote in June (n=20), four submitted A2 and 10 submitted A3 in the week before the exam. There were 10 students who submitted two or more assignments within a single week and two students who submitted all three assignments within a three day period before the April exam. Some students are falling behind in the self-paced course and cramming to catch up.

4.3.1 Student comments on time management and pacing. Students in all sections reported feeling overwhelmed by the pace of the course, with some students identifying portions of the the course that they felt moved too quickly:

> The course was taught very well overall, but the pacing sped up a lot for the final few weeks, allowing less time to grasp more complicated topics.

With the cumulative nature of the course material, minor misunderstandings or gaps in knowledge from early in the course can cause difficulty with learning later concepts. Students sometimes view this as a pacing issue with the course, but we believe that the self-paced mastery learning format can help to address this issue.

Students in both the online and self-paced sections noted that they had been given significant freedom to work as it fit into their schedules. In one case, a student from the online section framed this positively:

> It gave me the flexibility to work around my schedule to learn concepts of this course. Although there were set deadlines, the videos are fairly straightforward to follow and make notes to learn the material.

However, most students in the self-paced section found that they had been given too much freedom and understood that they did not know how to handle that flexibility:

> We have to rush our class content at the end of the semester due to the reason that we did not know how to pace ourselves.

> The only issue I had was with how difficult it was to pace oneself so that they don't fall too far behind.

As a result, many students called on the instructors to provide more structure:

> Next time, I hope the instructors do provide more structure to keep everyone on track, even if this does mean more rigid deadlines (and therefore less freedom to work at our own speed).

> Even though the instructor did remind students a few times, I think it would be better if there is a weekly reminder of where the regular lectures are at, so students can get a sense of how much ahead or behind they are in the course.

Our feeling, from the feedback we reviewed, is that students in the self-paced section fell behind partly because there was insufficient structure to motivate them to push ahead and partly because they felt uncertain about the material. They appreciated the opportunity to learn topics thoroughly, but they did not always feel the pressure necessary to work on topics in a timely manner. The online students, in contrast, were required to keep pace with a schedule and felt that they did not have as solid a grasp of the material as a result.

4.4 Attendance and interaction

In the exit survey, we asked a set of 7-point Likert-type questions (with labels only on 1 and 7) about attendance, interaction, and community:

Q1 How often did you attend lecture? (1: never, 7: always)
Q2 How much did you interact (both online and face-to-face) with your instructor? (1: not at all, 7: a significant amount)

Q3 How satisfied were you with your sense of connection to your instructor? (1: very dissatisfied, 7: very satisfied)
Q4 How much did you interact (both online and face-to-face) with your classmates? (1: not at all, 7: a significant amount)
Q5 How satisfied were you with your sense of community with your classmates? (1: very dissatisfied, 7: very satisfied)

Since some attendance in the self-paced section was required, we expected self-paced students would report attending more lectures than flipped students. The mean scores on Q1 were higher in mastery (6.033) than flipped (5.52), but they were not significantly different as measured by a Wilcoxon rank-sum test (Z=-.901, $p = .184$).

For Q2 through Q5, we used a Kruskal-Wallis test to examine the difference between the distribution of answers for students from each course format. On Q2, students from all three formats reported significantly different amounts of interaction with their instructor (χ^2=58.762, df=2, $p < .001$). Self-paced students reported more interactions with their instructor than flipped students, who reported more than online students (self-paced mean 5.71 vs. flipped mean 4.287 vs. online mean 2.949). Self-paced students were also more satisfied with their sense of connection to their instructor than students from the other formats (χ^2=32.427, df=2, p<.001).

Unsurprisingly, students in the self-paced and flipped sections report interacting significantly more with their classmates than students in the online section ($p < .001$ and $p < .001$). Self-paced students reported significantly more interaction with classmates than flipped students (means 5.567 vs. 4.571, Wilcoxon rank-sum test: Z=-2.648, p=.004). Students from all three formats were fairly satisfied with the sense of community with their classmates (self-paced mean 5.516, flipped mean 4.88, online mean 4.062), but self-paced students were significantly more satisfied than the flipped (Wilcoxon rank-sum test, Z=-1.994, $p = .023$) and online (Z=-3.540, $p < .001$).

4.4.1 Student comments on interaction. Students in all sections mentioned the value of office hours and interaction with the instructors and TAs. However, they varied in their opinions about how much interaction was occurring. In the flipped section, students generally felt there was sufficient faculty and TA support outside of class:

> I didn't interact much with the professors, but when i did they were very helpful and also there were alot of TA help during office hours. This course had way more help as compared to the other courses i am taking and i really liked that!

Despite having faculty participating in relatively small lectures, and the availability of several course-wide TA and instructor office hours each weekday, students in the self-paced section perceived a need for more support outside of the class meetings:

> ... wish to have more time to meet with either TAs or instructors out of the classroom.

No students in the flipped section discussed interactions with other students, despite the encouragement to work in groups on worksheets in class. Although self-paced students reported the most interaction with classmates and the greatest satisfaction with the sense of community with classmates, students from self-paced and online expressed a desire for more interaction. We were surprised to get this feedback from the self-paced section, as students were encouraged to work closely together in groups:

> I did make a few great friends in this course, but because we were all at different stages of the course, we didn't work together as much as I would have hoped. I did not have much interaction beyond the four or five people I sat with every class, and I think the instructors could have done more to promote problem solving and communication in the whole classroom.

4.5 Course Structure

Students in the three sections mentioned different aspects of the course when speaking about structure. Students in both the online and the flipped sections generally found the tightly defined structure, which required that they complete work throughout each week[1], to be helpful, and they linked the structure to difficulties they overcame:

> I found it extremely confusing and difficult at the beginning, but with the help of the weekly Prepare and Perform assignments and professor/TA office hours help, I was able to gain a better understanding of the material.

> [online resources] were quite helpful in testing whether or not I understood the basics of the weekly concepts. Rehearse exercises were the most helpful resource since they provided examples that would require a deeper understanding of the concepts as well as provide a solution to the problems presented.

Students in the self-paced section highlighted that the course structure encouraged them to learn more deeply:

> I love self-paced classes. I think this was a great opportunity for me to be able to think deeply about every element of the course content.

> ... because the lecture was self-paced, I felt that I can learn materials in the course thoroughly.

One student in the self-paced section also cited the content structure of the course as being beneficial, though we believe this comment applies equally well to all sections, since they used similar "quests" to organize content:

> The quests broke the course content down into manageable chunks, and it was much easier to identify the topics I had trouble with and find ways to improve. I think the "quest" approach also allowed me to dedicate my learning to long-term memory. In many other courses, I am frustrated when I forget everything I learned before - yet this mastery-based course helped me develop a lasting skill.

5 LESSONS LEARNED

5.1 Course administration is challenging

Our self-paced section was rather resource intensive. It had a 30:1 student to instructor teaching credit ratio, with two instructors working together on the course, each receiving credit for one teaching unit. The other formats had an average student to instructor ratio of 163:1. The increase in instructors was in part because the self-paced format has more administrative overhead. Tracking student progress

[1] Prepare, Rehearse, and Perform work was completed at the beginning, middle, and end of each week. Rehearse work was done face-to-face in class for flipped and self-paced students, but all other work was completed online for students in all course formats.

and managing the writing of mastery quizzes is a significant task. Quizzes must be marked in a timely fashion, but students are writing different versions of the quizzes each week. Since there are no formal assignment deadlines, organizing assignment marking and getting TA help with it can prove challenging. The instructor's duties extend beyond the end of a standard semester. For future self-paced offerings, we must find ways to reduce the instructor resources required, and credit the teaching workload that extends past the end of term.

Beyond the instructor, the course is also a challenge to administer for the academic unit. It does not have a standard duration and students can write the exam at different times. Some course grades are submitted months earlier than others and for those who are writing later, their transcripts need to reflect that the course is ongoing.

In addition to the workload of running the course, there was significant work in preparing the course materials and software is being developed to administer online mastery quizzes. While this work is front-loaded in preparing the course, maintenance is ongoing work.

5.2 Mastery quizzes are unfamiliar assessments

Most of the students in the self-paced format had never taken a self-paced, mastery learning course before, and thus were not likely to have encountered assessment tools like mastery quizzes before.

Students had varying levels of willingness to attempt the mastery quizzes. The "try early, fail early" approach worked well for some students, while others were very cautious to only write the quiz when they were sure they were ready. Some students struggled with failure, either after they failed a mastery quiz, or by putting off writing a quiz because they worried they might fail. We will need to be more explicit about the objectives of these quizzes, and about the importance of failure as part of the process.

Students are very interested in finding out which questions they failed on the mastery quizzes, which can help them identify the gaps in their understanding. Studying from similar assessment materials, such as past exams, is something students are often do. However, we could not give students access to the quizzes without compromising them for future use. Quite a lot of work goes into creating and maintaining a few versions of each quiz. We allowed students to view the quizzes while supervised (i.e., without phones, etc), but this was resource intensive. To scale up this course format, we would need to have another way to give students feedback on where they went wrong. We may provide testing objectives for each part of the quiz, however we need to limit students' ability to overfit their studying to the quiz questions.

5.3 More flexibility, more procrastination

Keeping students on track was a major challenge in the self-paced course. None of the students in the self-paced section kept up with the pace of the regular sections - and most of the students in the regular section are keeping up, with similar pass rates. While students were given some feedback on where they should be each week with the course material, they may need more regular, clear, and individualized feedback on their pacing.

Despite our expectations that students would welcome a flexible schedule and the ability to work at their own pace, many students wanted clear deadlines for their coursework. We need to explore further what exactly deadlines mean in a self-paced course.

6 CONCLUSION AND FUTURE WORK

We did not see any significant difference in student outcomes (course outcome or exam grade) in the self-paced mastery learning format of the course, compared to our other formats. However, we did see that students in the self-paced format who opted to write their final exam later did not do as well as those who wrote on the regular schedule.

We plan to offer the self-paced format of the course again in the coming year. We will include more explicit discussion of how we expect students to use the self-paced mastery learning format to increase their learning, and about the role that failure plays in a successful learning, and programming, experience. We will especially focus on how we can structure the course to support students to avoid falling behind.

REFERENCES

[1] John O Aikin. 1981. A Self-Paced First Course in Computer Science. *ACM SIGCSE Bulletin* 13, 1 (Feb. 1981), 78–85.

[2] Radwan Ali and Elke M Leeds. 2009. *The Impact of Face-to-Face Orientation on Online Retention: A Pilot Study.* DigitalCommons @ Kennesaw State University.

[3] Jens Bennedsen and Michael E Caspersen. 2007. Failure Rates in Introductory Programming. *ACM SIGCSE Bulletin* 39, 2 (Jun 2007), 32.

[4] Jennifer Campbell, Diane Horton, Michelle Craig, and Paul Gries. 2014. Evaluating an Inverted CS1. In *Proceedings of the 45th ACM Technical Symposium on Computer Science Education (SIGCSE '14).* 307–312.

[5] Curtis R. Cook. 1976. A Self-Paced Introductory Fortran Programming Course. In *Proceedings of the Sixth SIGCSE Technical Symposium on Computer Science Education (SIGCSE '76).* 78–79.

[6] John Dunlosky and Keith W Thiede. 1998. What Makes People Study More? An Evaluation of Factors that Affect Self-Paced Study. *Acta psychologica* 98, 1 (1998), 37–56.

[7] Sophie Engle and Sami Rollins. 2013. Expert Code Review and Mastery Learning in a Software Development Course. *Journal of Computing Sciences in Colleges* 28, 4 (2013), 139–147.

[8] Grandon Gill and Carolyn F Holton. 2006. A Self-Paced Introductory Programming Course. *Journal of Information Technology Education: Research* 5 (2006), 095–105.

[9] Thomas R Guskey and Therese D Pigott. 1988. Research on Group-based Mastery Learning Programs: A Meta-Analysis. *The Journal of Educational Research* 81, 4 (1988), 197–216.

[10] Diane Horton, Jennifer Campbell, and Michelle Craig. 2016. Online CS1: Who Enrols, Why, and How Do They Do?. In *Proceedings of the 47th ACM Technical Symposium on Computing Science Education (SIGCSE '16).* 323–328.

[11] Diane Horton, Michelle Craig, Jennifer Campbell, Paul Gries, and Daniel Zingaro. 2014. Comparing Outcomes in Inverted and Traditional CS1. In *Proceedings of the 2014 Conference on Innovation & Technology in Computer Science Education (ITiCSE '14).* 261–266.

[12] Mehdi Jazayeri. 2015. Combining Mastery Learning with Project-based Learning in a First Programming Course: An Experience Report. In *Proceedings of the 37th International Conference on Software Engineering - Volume 2 (ICSE '15).* 315–318.

[13] Fred S Keller. 2017. Engineering Personalized Instruction in the Classroom. *Revista Interamericana de Psicologia/Interamerican Journal of Psychology* 1, 3 (2017).

[14] Asher Koriat and Robert A Bjork. 2006. Illusions of Competence during Study Can Be Remedied by Manipulations that Enhance Learners' Sensitivity to Retrieval Conditions at Test. *Memory & Cognition* 34, 5 (2006), 959–972.

[15] Nate Kornell and Robert A Bjork. 2007. The Promise and Perils of Self-regulated Study. *Psychonomic Bulletin & Review* 14, 2 (2007), 219–224.

[16] Noel LeJeune. 2010. Contract Grading with Mastery Learning in CS 1. *Journal of Computing Sciences in Colleges* 26, 2 (2010), 149–156.

[17] Yair Levy. 2007. Comparing Dropouts and Persistence in E-learning Courses. *Computers & Education* 48, 2 (Feb 2007), 185–204.

[18] Brendan McCane, Claudia Ott, Nick Meek, and Anthony Robins. 2017. Mastery Learning in Introductory Programming. In *Proceedings of the Nineteenth Australasian Computing Education Conference (ACE '17).* 1–10.

[19] Arthur W Melton. 1970. The Situation with Respect to the Spacing of Repetitions and Memory. (1970).

[20] Thomas O Nelson and R Jacob Leonesio. 1988. Allocation of Self-Paced Study Time and the "Labor-in-Vain Effect". *Journal of Experimental Psychology: Learning, Memory, and Cognition* 14, 4 (1988), 676.

[21] Andrew Petersen, Michelle Craig, Jennifer Campbell, and Anya Tafliovich. 2016. Revisiting Why Students Drop CS1. In *Proceedings of the 16th Koli Calling International Conference on Computing Education Research - Koli Calling '16.*

[22] Eric Roberts. 2000. Strategies for Encouraging Individual Achievement in Introductory Computer Science Courses. In *Proceedings of the Thirty-first SIGCSE*

Technical Symposium on Computer Science Education - SIGCSE '00.
[23] Anthony Robins. 2010. Learning Edge Momentum: A New Account of Outcomes in CS1. *Computer Science Education* 20, 1 (2010), 37–71.
[24] Jonathan G Tullis and Aaron S Benjamin. 2011. On the Effectiveness of Self-Paced Learning. *Journal of Memory and Language* 64, 2 (2011), 109–118.
[25] Christopher Watson and Frederick WB Li. 2014. Failure Rates in Introductory Programming Revisited. In *Proceedings of the 2014 Conference on Innovation & Technology in Computer Science Education - ITiCSE '14.*
[26] Keith J Whittington, Dianne P Bills, and Lawrence W Hill. 2003. Implementation of Alternative Pacing in an Introductory Programming Sequence. In *Proceedings of the 4th Conference on Information Technology Curriculum.* 47–53.

Microteaching: Recursion, Coding Style, Creative Coding, Inheritance and Polymorphism, Loops, and the Internet

Colleen M. Lewis
Computer Science Dept.
Harvey Mudd College
Claremont, CA, USA
lewis@cs.hmc.edu

Daniel D. Garcia
EECS Department
UC Berkeley
Berkeley, CA, USA
ddgarcia@berkeley.edu

Helen H. Hu
Computer Science Dept.
Westminster College
Salt Lake City, UT USA
hhu@westminstercollege.edu

Saber Khan
Packer Collegiate Inst. &
Processing Fdn
Brooklyn, NY, USA
mrkhanatndv@gmail.com

Nigamanth Sridhar
Department of EE and CS
Cleveland State University
Cleveland, OH, USA
n.sridhar1@csuohio.edu

Bryan Twarek
San Francisco Unified
School District
San Francisco, CA, USA
twarekb@sfusd.edu

Chinma Uche
Academy of Aerospace and
Engineering
Windsor, CT, USA
cuche@crec.org

ABSTRACT

SIGCSE is packed with teaching insights and inspiration. However, we get these insights and inspiration from hearing our colleagues talk about their teaching. Why not just watch them teach? This session does exactly that. Six exceptional educators will present their favorite piece of innovative lecture content just as they would their students. The moderator, Colleen Lewis, will describe the central pedagogical move within the innovation and how this connects to education research. The goal of the session is to inspire SIGCSE attendees by highlighting innovative instruction by exceptional educators. The specific content of the innovative instruction may be applicable for some attendees, and the discussion of the underlying pedagogical move within each innovation can be applied across the attendees' teaching.

1 SUMMARY AND STRUCTURE

Each of six exceptional educators will be given ten minutes to teach the audience something. After this, the moderator will draw the attention of the audience to particular pedagogical moves that the instruction included. Attendees can see a new approach to introducing a topic or a new pedagogical move. No matter what, we expect attendees will be taking ideas from this session directly back to their teaching!

A Special Session of this style was first run at SIGCSE in 2018, and it was well attended and received. The format is based upon a practice in chemistry of sharing "Five Slides About," which introduce a topic in a novel or concise way (https://www.ionicviper.org/types/five_slides_about). Resources from each of the presenters will be shared on CSTeachingTips.org.

SIGCSE '19, February 27-March 2, 2019, Minneapolis, MN, USA

ACM ISBN 978-1-4503-5890-3/19/02.
https://doi.org/10.1145/3287324.3287514

4 EXCEPTIONAL EDUCATORS

4.1 Recursion with "Vee" - Dan Garcia

In our Beauty and Joy of Computing (BJC) CS0 class at UC Berkeley, we introduce recursion using E. Paul Goldenberg's "Vee" project. It starts innocently enough...a sprite is positioned at the bottom of the stage and told to draw a "V" shape picture by running the vee command. vee has the sprite turn left, move out, and run a random shape command (square, circle or triangle) from the shapes list, which draws a random embellishment on the end of the left branch. Then it backs up and does the same thing on the right side. We run the program together a few times in class; the result is mostly yawns. Then (and here's the magic), we add vee itself to the shapes list. Students are asked to sketch what they think will happen and share their sketches with their neighbors. We then re-run vee (and cross our fingers). When vee generates a beautiful and flowering tree (especially if it happens on the first try), there is often a collective gasp from the hundreds of students. We emphasize that the vee command didn't change, but now vee can call vee, which can call vee, and so on. We go on to show that the same ideas behind vee can be used to create an arbitrarily long English sentence.

Dan is a Teaching Professor in the EECS department at the University of California, Berkeley.

4.2 Coding Style with POGIL - Helen Hu

POGIL (Process Oriented Guided Inquiry Learning) engages students by grouping them in teams to work collaboratively through activities and construct their own understanding of CS content. POGIL activities are carefully designed to foster student

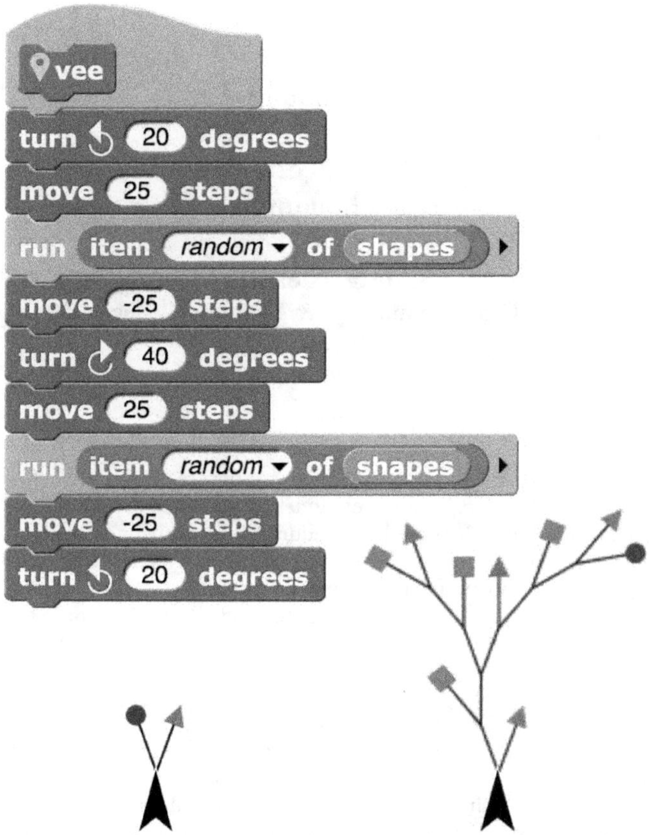

Figure 1: The vee command in Snap (above) and resulting images before (left) and after (right) vee is added to the list of shapes.

learning by guiding students through a learning cycle of exploration, concept invention, and application. In this short lesson, I will demonstrate how a POGIL activity would lead students to discover and invent programming style rules in an introductory programming class.

Helen Hu is a Professor and Chair of Computer Science (CS) at Westminster College.

4.3 Creative Coding with p5.js - Saber Khan

p5.js is creative coding library that evolved from Processing, the popular Java library used by visual artists. With built-in functions and variables p5.js provides an exciting avenue to learn coding. I will show how to create simple shapes using the library, how to move the shapes, and finally how to make them interactive. The lesson will involve variables, loops, conditional statements and formatting. This introductory lesson, one I give at the start of the semester for students who only know block-based code, provides students with a new paradigm for using text to create interesting sketches based on their creativity. The lesson ends with an assignment for students to create their own original design.

Saber Khan is a middle and high school CS teacher at Packer Collegiate Institute in Brooklyn, NY, and a Processing Foundation Fellow for K12 Outreach.

4.4 Inheritance & Polymorphism - Nigamanth Sridhar

Students in a CS1 course learning about object-oriented programming have to get a strong understanding of inheritance and polymorphism. These topics form the foundation for students in a CS major to be able to build skills and understanding of later topics and courses. Yet, students often view inheritance and polymorphism in a high "syntax-specific" manner, which promulgates a large number of misconceptions that later manifest in serious misuse of object-oriented features in a language such as Java or Python. This lesson is focused on decoupling the concepts of inheritance and polymorphism from the syntax that is used to establish these relationships.

Nigamanth Sridhar is a Professor of CS at Cleveland State University. He also serves as the Dean of the College of Graduate Studies.

4.5 Loops through Dance! - Bryan Twarek

Unplugged activities are intentionally designed kinesthetic lessons that help students digest complicated concepts in ways that relate to their own lives. Something that is done in an unplugged environment can often set the stage for or review a concept done in a plugged environment. Both are vital pieces of the curriculum as they build student knowledge and understanding in different ways. In this lesson, I will show how we explore the concept of loops through an unplugged dance activity. I designed the lesson for an introductory middle grades course, but it can be adapted across K-12+ grade levels.

Bryan Twarek (BT) is CS Program Administrator at the San Francisco Unified School District (SFUSD), where he oversees policy, curriculum, and professional development for PK-12 CS education.

4.6 The Internet – Chinma Uche

The growth of CS has led to diversity in AP CSP classrooms where students come in with different backgrounds and levels of preparation. To provide opportunities for success, teachers have begun to develop dynamic classrooms that use student centered activities and cooperative learning structures to engage all students. An effective tool for getting a diverse classroom to learn well is questioning. Questioning creates the opportunity for students to ask questions that they have to each other and then think through the material together. Questioning proves useful when approaching the CSP big idea, "the Internet." Through unplugged activities and student developed questions, students can more successfully grapple with key concepts. Questioning can also be useful for teacher professional development.

Chinma Uche is a high school Math and CS teacher in a school that started offering AP CSP to all 9th grade students in 2017 as a way of broadening participation in computing.

Community College Transfer Pathways

Jumee Song (moderator)
Siegel Family Foundation
New York, NY
Jumee.song@siegelendowment.org

Jeffrey Forbes
Duke University
Durham, NC
forbes@cs.duke.edu

Louise Ann Lyon
ETR
Scotts Valley, CA
Louann.lyon@etr.org

Leslie Maxwell
California State University, Monterey Bay
Seaside, CA
lkern@csumb.edu

Cindy Tucker
Blue Grass Community & Technical College
Lexington, KY
Cindy.tucker@kctcs.edu

ABSTRACT

As traditional tech talent pools are being been tapped out and unable to meet the growing workforce demand, matriculation at a community college and transfer to a four-year institution for completion of a bachelor's degree plays a crucial role in diversifying the tech workforce. However, the important role of community colleges in the computer science education pipeline is often overlooked [1]. This panel will provide an overview of the computing workforce landscape, discuss the role of community colleges to increase the diversity of students in computer science, and share case studies that highlight promising practices for the inclusion of community colleges in the CS educational pathway.

CCS CONCEPTS

• Social and professional topics~Computing education programs
• Social and professional topics~Model curricula

Keywords

Community College; Transfer; Pathway; Two-Year College; Computer Science; Postsecondary

1. SUMMARY

Effective education pathways to computer science related occupations are critical for the modern technology-driven workforce. For most computing technology companies, a bachelor's degree is the minimum qualification required to be considered for a software engineering, or similarly compensated computer science related job. Bachelor's degree earners make up about 43% of the computing workforce, while Associates' degree earners only make up about 10% [1]. This creates a distinct barrier for most minority students, as less than 10% of Black and Hispanic students attend a four-year university [2]. Alternatively, about 36% of students at community college are Black and Hispanic, 14% and 22% respectively [3]. To address this barrier, it is important to closely explore 2-year to 4-year transfers in computing fields [4]. This panel addresses the question of why community college transfer pathways are critical, and how to create effective transfer programs and relationships between educational institutions. Panelists will also address the challenges students face navigating confusing transfer processes, which often do not allow credits to transfer between institutions, resulting in only 1% of community college students to graduate with a computer science bachelor's degree within 4 years through a 2+2 pathway [5].

ACM ISBN 978-1-4503-5890-3/19/02.
https://doi.org/10.1145/3287324.3287336

2. PANEL STRUCTURE

Each panelist will be given 10 minutes to introduce themselves and present their respective positions prompted by the moderator, 40 minutes total. The moderator will then facilitate a discussion by soliciting questions from the audience, 35 minutes total.

3. JEFFREY FORBES

Jeff Forbes is an Associate Professor of the Practice of Computer Science at Duke University, and the Chair of the ACM Education Policy Committee. Prof. Forbes is engaged in a number of leading efforts to address to critical and complex issues of education and broadening participation in computing via organizations such as ACM, NSF, CMD-IT, and CRA. Prof. Forbes will provide context on why the ACM Education Policy Committee focused on Community Colleges, and give an overview of their Community College Transfer Pathway Report.

4. LOUISE ANN LYON

Louise Ann ("Lou Ann") Lyon, PhD, is a Senior Research Associate at ETR and brings industry experience in the software engineering workplace as well as research knowledge from Learning Sciences and Feminist Studies to her work on diversifying technology at postsecondary institutions and in the workplace. As the principal author of the ACM's Community College Transfer Pathway Report [1], Dr. Lyon will share an overview of the postsecondary and workforce landscape and promising practices from the report. Additionally, Dr. Lyon will discuss the supports and challenges underrepresented community college students face when attempting to transfer and complete bachelor's degrees in CS drawn from her findings in an earlier study [6].

5. LESLIE MAXWELL

Leslie Maxwell, Assistant Program Director in Computer Science at California State University Monterey Bay, has played a key role in the development of a cohort-based CS pathway model that addresses the capacity, quality, and diversity challenges facing computer science by building partnerships between community colleges, university, and technology companies. CSin3, the first cohort program launched in 2013, is a collaboration between Cal State Monterey Bay and Hartnell College, where students are placed into highly supported learning communities, take classes at both schools, and earn a Bachelor's degree in 3 years. Leslie was one of the co-authors of SIGCSE 2017's Best Paper for New Curricula, Programs, Degrees, and Position Paper track. Leslie will share insights on how her team successfully implemented CSin3 and a similar 4-year program, and provide an update on their outcomes and new initiatives, including replicating the cohort model at another community college and CSU.

6. CINDY TUCKER

Cindy Tucker is a Professor of Computer and Information Technologies at Bluegrass Community and Technical College (BCTC) in Lexington, KY. She is Vice Chair of the ACM Committee for Computing Education in Community Colleges (CCECC) and co-coordinator of the ACM Kentucky Community Colleges Women in Computing (KYCC-WiC) celebration. She is faculty sponsor for BCTC's local ACM-W student chapter. She is currently serving as the Chair of the ACM-W Community College Committee. As one of the case study contributor to the ACM's Community College Transfer Pathway Report, Cindy will discuss seamless transfer between Kentucky's two-year and four-year public institutions enabled by a Kentucky statute which declares "Each community college of the Kentucky Community and Technical College System may offer within the two (2) year academic curriculum of the college, any and all lower division academic courses offered for undergraduate credit at any and all of the four (4) year public colleges and universities. All lower division academic courses offered by the community colleges shall be transferable for academic credit to any and all four (4) year public colleges and universities, regardless of the number of academic credits earned by any student at one (1) or more community college." [7].

7. JUMEE SONG (MODERATOR)

Jumee Song is a Director at Siegel Family Endowment (SFE). SFE is a foundation focused on understanding and shaping learning in our technology driven world. Through its Workforce portfolio, SFE is interested in learning about and supporting programs that equip young people with future-relevant skills and access to career pathways, as well as initiatives that drive system-level change to make it possible for everyone to participate in the future economy. Prior to joining SFE, Jumee was the Director of Strategic Programs at CSforALL, a hub and central resource for people interested in computer science education to find providers, schools, funders, and researchers focused on the goal of providing quality CS education to every child in the U.S.

8. REFERENCES

[1] Lyon, L.A. et al (2018). Lighting the Path: From Community College to Computing Careers. Association for Computing Machinery (ACM), New York, NY. https://www.acm.org/binaries/content/assets/education/lighting-the-path-from-community-college-to-computing-careers.pdf

[2] National Center for Education Statistics (NCES). Table 322.30. Retrieved 4/30/18 from: https://nces.ed.gov/programs/digest/d16/tables/dt16_322.30.asp.

[3] College Board Research. "Research Brief." Retrieved 5/2/18 from https://trends.collegeboard.org/sites/default/files/trends-in-community-colleges-research-brief.pdf.

[4] Tang, C., Tucker, C., Servin, C., and Geissler, M. (2018) Computer Science Curricular Guidance for Associate-Degree Transfer Programs. In *Proceedings of the 49th ACM Technical Symposium on Computer Science Education* (SIGCSE '18). ACM, New York, NY, USA, 435-440.

[5] Jaggars, S. S., Fink, J., Fletcher, J., & Dundar, A. (2016). A Longitudinal Analysis of Community College Pathways to Computer Science Bachelor's Degrees. Mountain View, CA: Google Inc. Retrieved from http://goo.gl/Eiz33G.

[6] Lyon, L. A. & Denner, J. (2016). Student Perspectives of Community College Pathways to Computer Science Bachelor's Degrees. Mountain View, CA: Google Inc. Retrieved from https://goo.gl/Q0wJJv.

[7] KRS 164.583. Retrieved 8/29/18 from http://www.lrc.ky.gov/statutes/statute.aspx?id=4331

Curious about Student Participation in Humanitarian Open Source Software?

Darci Burdge
Nassau Community College
Garden City, NY, USA
darci.burdge@ncc.edu

Gregory W. Hislop
Drexel University
Philadelphia, PA, USA
hislop@drexel.edu

Grant Braught
Dickinson College
Carlisle, PA, USA
braught@dickinson.edu

Josh Dehlinger
Towson University
Towson, MD, USA
JDehlinger@towson.edu

Christian Murphy
University of Pennsylvania
Philadelphia, PA, USA
cdmurphy@seas.upenn.edu

Joanna Klukowska
Courant Institute, NYU
New York, NY, USA
joannakl@cs.nyu.edu

Lynn Lambert
Christopher Newport University
Newport News, VA, USA
llambert@cnu.edu

Patricia Ordonez
University of Puerto Rico Rio Piedras
San Juan, PR, USA
pattiordonez@gmail.com

Karl R. Wurst
Worcester State University
Worcester, MA, USA
kwurst@worcester.edu

ABSTRACT

This special session is intended for people who are curious about integrating Humanitarian Free and Open Source Software (HFOSS) into their courses and involving students in HFOSS projects. HFOSS participation provides an excellent vehicle to introduce students to computing for social good while also giving them experience with real-world software development. The session will begin with a series of lightning talks by faculty who have incorporated HFOSS participation into one or more of their courses. This will be followed by a small group activity to allow attendees to ask questions and discuss individual interests in integrating HFOSS activities and to become familiar with HFOSS educational resources available for instructors. The session will conclude with some closing comments on current and planned activities of instructors who are teaching with HFOSS and suggestions for faculty who would like to pursue this teaching approach themselves.

CCS CONCEPTS

• **Social and professional topics → Computing education**;

KEYWORDS

HFOSS, Humanitarian Free and Open Source Software, Computing for Social Good, Real-world projects

ACM Reference Format:

Darci Burdge, Gregory W. Hislop, Grant Braught, Josh Dehlinger, Christian Murphy, Joanna Klukowska, Lynn Lambert, Patricia Ordonez, and Karl R. Wurst. 2019. Curious about Student Participation in Humanitarian Open Source Software?. In *Proceedings of the 50th ACM Technical Symposium on Computer Science Education (SIGCSE '19), February 27-March 2, 2019, Minneapolis, MN, USA.* ACM, New York, NY, USA, 2 pages. https://doi.org/10.1145/3287324.3287521

ACM ISBN 978-1-4503-5890-3/19/02.
https://doi.org/10.1145/3287324.3287521

1 OBJECTIVE

Free and Open Source Software (FOSS) is important for computing education for two primary reasons. First, openness means that students have access to code and other artifacts and have the potential to participate in large-scale software projects to an extent not available with proprietary software. Second, FOSS has become an important part of the software industry and a fertile source of innovation in software engineering. Every computing student should become familiar with FOSS tools and processes as part of preparation for professional practice. A variety of research studies and experience reports document faculty use of open source in computing education including [1, 3, 8, 9].

Humanitarian Free and Open Source Software (HFOSS) is open source software that exists to better the human condition by addressing some societal issue. Existing projects address issues such as health care, education, economic development, and the environment. HFOSS provides an excellent vehicle to introduce computing for social good to computing students.

There is a growing community of faculty who are employing HFOSS projects in their classes including [2, 4–7, 10, 11]. This activity centers on students participating in HFOSS projects by making various types of contributions to the project. The effort also extends to instructor interest in helping students learn about open source culture, processes, and tools through learning activities in a wide range of classes. This special session will provide a window on the work of this community with the objective of introducing the educational potential of HFOSS to a broader group of faculty within the SIGCSE community.

The session will be interactive and allow time for hands-on exploration and small group discussion. The first part of the session will consist of a series of lightning talks by faculty who are helping students participate in HFOSS projects. Most of the presenting faculty started with little or no open source experience themselves, and understand the instructor learning needed to become effective as instructors for HFOSS.

The second part of the session will be a small group activity that will introduce attendees to resources available for instructors interested in teaching HFOSS such as foss2serve.org. The small groups will also allow more informal time for questions and discussion of particular interests and considerations of individual attendees. The session will conclude with some final comments on planned activities in this area and information on how faculty can become more involved in the community of HFOSS educators.

2 OUTLINE

The schedule for the Special Session will be as follows:

- Opening Remarks (5 minutes, Darci Burdge)
- Lightning talks (35 minutes,Grant Braught, Josh Delhinger, Joanna Klukowska, Lynn Lambert, Chris Murphy, Patti Ordonez, Karl Wurst)
- Small Group Activity (30 minutes, All organizers)
- Closing remarks (5 minutes, Gregory Hislop)

3 EXPECTATIONS

This special session is intended for any computing instructor interested in learning about the educational opportunities presented by Humanitarian Free and Open Source Software. No prior knowledge of open source is expected. Faculty from any area of computing are welcome. The HFOSS community tends to appeal particularly to instructors interested in teaching software development and programming, but other areas are also represented. HFOSS has been applied in upper level courses in software engineering, in capstone courses, and other project-oriented courses. It has also been applied in introductory courses including CS1, CS2 and Data Structures. Courses in other computing areas such as cybersecurity have also made use of HFOSS learning opportunities.

Attendees will learn about the range and nature of HFOSS use in higher education via vignettes and comments provided in short, lightning talk style presentations. This will be followed by an opportunity for attendees to discuss in small groups ideas that they might have to involve their students in HFOSS. This discussion will include an opportunity to receive suggestions about existing learning resources that might be relevant to individual interests.

4 SUITABILITY FOR A SPECIAL SESSION

The community of faculty working with student participation in HFOSS is growing and faculty who hear of the idea are often interested in learning more about it. Although there have been longer workshops offered on the topic, having a short session like this that will allow people to satisfy their curiosity without need to make a major commitment seems like a useful offering for the SIGCSE community. A panel session would not allow as many HFOSS faculty as participants, and would not allow the high level of interactivity that this special session will support. Having more participants will allow us to illustrate the breadth of courses and types of learning activities where faculty are using HFOSS. Having the interactivity will provide a means to deliver much more individualized information to attendees.

ACKNOWLEDGMENTS

This material is based on work supported by the National Science Foundation under Grant Nos. DUE-1525039, DUE-1524877, and DUE-1524898. Any opinions, findings and conclusions or recommendations expressed in this material are those of the author(s) and do not necessarily reflect the views of the National Science Foundation (NSF).

REFERENCES

[1] Judith Bishop, Carlos Jensen, Walt Scacchi, and Arfon Smith. 2016. How to Use Open Source Software in Education. In *Proceedings of the 47th ACM Technical Symposium on Computing Science Education (SIGCSE '16)*. ACM, New York, NY, USA, 321–322. https://doi.org/10.1145/2839509.2844665

[2] Grant Braught, John Maccormick, James Bowring, Quinn Burke, Barbara Cutler, David Goldschmidt, Mukkai Krishnamoorthy, Wesley Turner, Steven Huss-Lederman, Bonnie Mackellar, and Allen Tucker. 2018. A Multi-Institutional Perspective on H/FOSS Projects in the Computing Curriculum. *ACM Trans. Comput. Educ.* 18, 2, Article 7 (July 2018), 31 pages. https://doi.org/10.1145/3145476

[3] Moara Sousa Brito, Fernanda Gomes Silva, Christina von Flach G. Chavez, Debora C. Nascimento, and Roberto A Bittencourt. 2018. FLOSS in Software Engineering Education An Update of a Systematic Mapping Study. *SBES '2018, Brazilian Symposium on Software Engineering - Education Track* (2018).

[4] Heidi J.C. Ellis, Gregory W. Hislop, Monisha S. Pulimood, Becka Morgan, and Ben Coleman. 2015. Software Engineering Learning in HFOSS: A Multi-Institutional Study. *122nd Association for Engineering Education Annual Conference and Exposition* (2015).

[5] Heidi J.C. Ellis, Gregory W. Hislop, Josephine Rodriguez, and Ralph A. Morelli. 2012. Student Software Engineering Learning via Participation in Humanitarian FOSS Projects. *119th Annual ASEE Conference and Exhibition* (2012).

[6] Heidi J. C. Ellis, Gregory W. Hislop, Stoney Jackson, and Lori Postner. 2015. Team Project Experiences in Humanitarian Free and Open Source Software (HFOSS). *Trans. Comput. Educ.* 15, 4, Article 18 (Dec. 2015), 23 pages. https://doi.org/10.1145/2684812

[7] Gregory W. Hislop, Heidi J.C. Ellis, S. Monisha Pulimood, Becka Morgan, Suzanne Mello-Stark, Ben Coleman, and Cam Macdonell. 2015. A Multi-Institutional Study of Learning via Student Involvement in Humanitarian Free and Open Source Software Projects. In *Proceedings of the Eleventh Annual International Conference on International Computing Education Research (ICER '15)*. ACM, New York, NY, USA, 199–206. https://doi.org/10.1145/2787622.2787726

[8] Debora M. C. Nascimento, Roberto Almeida Bittencourt, and Christina Chavez. 2015. Open source projects in software engineering education: a mapping study. *Computer Science Education* 25, 1 (2015), 67–114. https://doi.org/10.1080/08993408.2015.1033159 arXiv:https://doi.org/10.1080/08993408.2015.1033159

[9] G. H. L. Pinto, F. F. Filho, I. Steinmacher, and M. A. Gerosa. 2017. Training Software Engineers Using Open-Source Software: The Professors' Perspective. In *2017 IEEE 30th Conference on Software Engineering Education and Training (CSEE T)*. 117–121. https://doi.org/10.1109/CSEET.2017.27

[10] Lori Postner, Heidi J.C. Ellis, and Gregory W. Hislop. 2018. A Survey of Instructors' Experiences Supporting Student Learning Using HFOSS Projects. In *Proceedings of the 49th ACM Technical Symposium on Computer Science Education (SIGCSE '18)*. ACM, New York, NY, USA, 203–208. https://doi.org/10.1145/3159450.3159524

[11] Samuel A. Rebelsky. 2015. HFOSS-Lite in CS2: Incorporating the Ushahidi Crowdmapping Program in a Data Structures and Algorithms Course (Abstract Only). In *Proceedings of the 46th ACM Technical Symposium on Computer Science Education (SIGCSE '15)*. ACM, New York, NY, USA, 514–514. https://doi.org/10.1145/2676723.2691885

"You don't have to be a white male that was learning how to program since he was five:" Computer Use and Interest From Childhood to a Computing Degree

Mathilde Collain
University of Oklahoma
Norman, Oklahoma
mathilde.collain@gmail.com

Deborah Trytten
University of Oklahoma
Norman, Oklahoma
dtrytten@ou.edu

ABSTRACT

Margolis and Fisher's book, Unlocking the Clubhouse (UTC), has long been regarded as seminal to the understanding of the lack of gender diversity in computing. This book found that boys and girls had different experiences with computers in the home and school environment, and that these different experiences had a direct impact on the desire of students to study computing. We wanted to know if the explanations Margolis and Fisher found were applicable for students in a more typical CS program in 2017, so we conducted a study to investigate the home and pre-college experiences of students who are currently majoring in CS or Computer Engineering (CE), and these students' pathway into computing majors. We recruited 11 participants from a large public institution in the Midwest U.S., and conducted interviews of these students using a protocol adapted from UTC. We performed a qualitative iterative and inductive analysis of these interviews and found that while technology access had greatly improved, views and attitudes were much slower to change. We discovered that fathers preferentially teaching sons about computing, while less prevalent than it was in UTC, still occurs. We also found that the participants, including the women, had more diverse pathways into computing than what Margolis and Fisher found. This suggests that UTC needs to be fully replicated at broad range of institutions to get a more complete picture of the multitude of pathways women use to enter into computing careers.

CCS CONCEPTS

• **Social and professional topics** → **Computer science education**; **Computer engineering education**; **Women**; *Children*; Race and ethnicity;

KEYWORDS

Women in computing, Children and computers, Computer Science Education, Computer Engineering Education, Race/ethnicity diversity in computing

SIGCSE '19, February 27-March 2, 2019, Minneapolis, MN, USA

ACM ISBN 978-1-4503-5890-3/19/02...$15.00
https://doi.org/10.1145/3287324.3287383

ACM Reference Format:
Mathilde Collain and Deborah Trytten. 2019. "You don't have to be a white male that was learning how to program since he was five:" Computer Use and Interest From Childhood to a Computing Degree. In *Proceedings of the 50th ACM Technical Symposium on Computer Science Education (SIGCSE '19), February 27-March 2, 2019, Minneapolis, MN, USA.* ACM, New York, NY, USA, 7 pages. https://doi.org/10.1145/3287324.3287383

1 INTRODUCTION

In 2017 women represented 57% of all bachelor degrees' holders, however women earn only 18% of computer science (CS) bachelor degrees [21]. Numerous researchers have studied the reasons for the unbalanced gender proportions in this field *e.g.* [2, 4, 10, 15, 22]. The impact of the absence of women from computing is well understood, from being unable to educate enough computer scientists to fulfill society's needs to having technology designed and implemented in ways that can disinterest or disenfranchise half of the population. Margolis and Fisher conducted a remarkable study at Carnegie Mellon University (CMU) between 1995 and 1999: *Unlocking the Clubhouse (UTC)*[16] where they examined how women were excluded from computing, from their childhood to their college experiences.

While UTC was a seminal study for understanding the role of gender in computing, it has limitations. One of its limitations was that the study was done at an exceptional institution: CMU. It is not clear that the factors that influence major selection and the personal experiences of students attending this top tier computer science program would be similar to those attending more typical but less prestigious institutions. In addition, nearly twenty years have passed since the study was performed. During this time, access to computers has radically changed. The internet has become ubiquitous. Wireless networking has flourished. There is much more technology available to many more people. It seems as if these massive societal changes regarding computing should have produced a more equitable environment for women to pursue computing. And yet female participation in computing remains shockingly low.

Margolis and Fisher's study inspired us to answer the following research questions: In what ways did current computing majors experience computing as children, both at home and at school? What pathways into computing majors did our participants follow, and were any of these pathways gendered? Inspired by the protocol of the original study, we decided to recruit and interview Computer Science (CS) and Computer Engineering (CE) students to collect their stories about finding their interest in computing. For this replication, we chose to host our study at Midwestern University (MU): a large, public, state flagship institution in the Midwest. This institution has B.S., M.S. and doctoral programs and a modest national ranking in computer science. This institution has few of the extraordinary attributes of CMU, however it is a research intensive university. The results from our replication should be transferable to other large public institutions with similar attributes.

As qualitative researchers, we acknowledge that our backgrounds and experiences can impact our conclusions. Collain is an international CS master student who arrived in the U.S. in 2017. Trytten is a faculty member in Computer Science and an adjuct in Womens' and Gender Studies. As women working in computing, we have experienced and observed gender-based discrimination. These experiences can influence our interpretation of the events we study, even though we aspire to represent faithfully the stories that participants trust us with. As a researcher, Trytten tends to look for systemic institutional and social causes for gender-based discrimination (*e.g.* computing is presented in ways that are uninteresting to women) instead of looking to individual behavior as a root cause (*e.g.* women aren't interested in computing).

2 *UNLOCKING THE CLUBHOUSE*

Our research corresponds to the first three chapters of UTC: *The Magnetic Attraction* which explains the early childhood experiences of their participants with computing, *Middle and High-School: A Room of His Own* which describes the participants' computing experiences in middle and high-school, and *Computing with a Purpose* which focuses on the choice to major in computing.

Margolis and Fisher found that early childhood experiences were different for boys and girls. Young boys had a "magnetic attraction" towards computers. From the moment someone (usually the father) introduced them to computers and programming, boys were fascinated, almost obsessed. Young girls experienced computers differently: only a quarter of them had a passionate relationship with computers. Young girls liked computers, but had other interests; Girls tended to learn how to program later. The identification of computing as a masculine discipline was reinforced by the parents' computing background and knowledge: 43% of the participants' fathers and only 8% of the mothers were considered the family expert on computers. Computers were primarily found in the boy's room even when it was a shared family computer [16]

Margolis and Fisher showed that gender differences widened with age. In middle and high-school, boys dominated computing clubs, computer labs and computing classes. Girls missed early opportunities to discover computing and thus had little interest in it. Girls needed encouragement from teachers, friends or family to enter the computing world. Girls tended to experience chilly climates in computing classes and doubt their abilities in this masculine field. Yet, introductory classes in high-school were important milestones along the girls' pathways to CS: one third of the women in the study cited a high-school computing course as an entry point to CS [16].

Students' interest in computing and the factors that led them to study CS in college were also examined. Again, men and women differed. Men tended to pursue CS mainly because they were passionate about computing–which they enjoyed throughout their childhood. Women were excited about computing and its context: the career, the applications, the possibilities. Many women talked about what Margolis and Fisher coined as "computing with a purpose": how they can use their computing abilities outside the field. They were also pulled into computing by people from their family or school environment. [16]

3 METHODS

Qualitative research has been widely and successfully used to analyze inequity in STEM disciplines [11, 17, 23, 24]. A qualitative study does not aim for statistical significance or generalizability [5]. On the contrary, a qualitative approach allows researchers to discover new and unknown patterns. That is why we chose to use qualitative methods in our study.

Margolis and Fisher conducted interviews with 263 participants, including 97 computer science students, over 4 years. We had to reduce this number to one manageable by only one interviewer in a single semester. We decided to interview 10 to 20 students majoring in CS or CE. While this sample size is small by statistical standards, it is reasonable for a qualitative study [5, 12].

We included CE students in our participant pool, even though they were absent from the previous study, because we were having difficulty recruiting due to IRB-imposed restrictions on recruitment. CE is similar in many ways to CS, although the increased emphasis on computer hardware and non-programming related laboratory classes is different. We chose to recruit students in their third and fourth year because they are better established in their respective majors and identities than first and second year students.

Since our research questions examine the differences between male and female students, we over-sampled females in the participant pool. In the end, 54% of the participants identified as female and 46% identified as male, while females are about 18% of the computer science and computer engineering undergraduate student populations (taken from an uncited institutional FactBook to protect the anonimity of MU).

Our initial recruitment efforts were through email. About twenty students responded to one of the emails we sent, although not all were recruited. We also posted a flyer in several MU buildings frequented by CS/CE students. Finally, one author (MC) assisted with an event organized by a local organization promoting the inclusion of women in computing, in order to recruit more female participants. There she gave an informal talk presenting the research concept. At least one woman was recruited from this event. In the end, eleven participants were recruited, included six females and five males.

Participants first completed a five minute online questionnaire. The first part of this questionnaire explained the minimal risks and absence of personal benefits of the study, informed participants about the utilization of their personal data, and asked for their consent. The second part of the questionnaire asked participants about a their social identities (gender, race/ethnicity, etc.). We asked them which high-school they graduated from, which allowed us to gain limited socio-economic background data [19] without asking intrusive questions. Finally, we asked them about their parents' educational level and occupation(s).

We chose to use interviews as the main source of data for our research. We constructed a semi-structured protocol for the interviews similar to those asked in UTC. We asked about childhood experiences of the students with computing, their experiences with computing in primary and secondary schools, and their pathway to a CS/CE major. We also included questions that were relevant in the context of our research, which did not appear in UTC. For instance, we asked participants about their first personal computer. Interviews were typically around a half hour. Each participant was interviewed once.

We first transcribed all interviews. Although transcription is a time-consuming process, it helped us develop a deep understanding of participants' pathways. The transcripts were then thematically coded using NVivo software. We created coding nodes as we were reading using an iterative and inductive methodology. We changed the organization of the coding tree several times, to adapt to new nodes and ideas. We then checked all of the coding, restarting the process from the nodes this time. We then systematically used text queries on node contents to locate additional snippets that might be related. Once everything was categorized, we compared our results to themes and results that were or were not present in UTC.

In this article, the quotes extracted from the personal interviews include the following formatting: ... denotes that some words were removed from the quote (usually for brevity or clarity), [*some text*] is an addition from us to clarify the participant's meaning in the larger context of the interview. After some statements we have numerical counts of the number of participants whose stories supported the observation. Some of the numerical counts are given as (A/B) where A is the number of participants who supported the observation and B is the total number of participants who spoke to the issue under discussion.

4 RESULTS AND DISCUSSION

4.1 Participants

Table 1 shows the results from our survey. The majority of the participants are women by design. Our sample is not very diverse in terms of race/ethnicity or socio-economic status. Most of the participants are white and attended school districts with a relatively small number of students who received free and reduced price lunches. We infer from this that most of the participants were middle class or above. We collected the race/ethnicity of the participants but the small size of our sample prevented us from finding meaningful patterns related to racial and ethnic social identities??.

4.2 Computers At Home

From a very young age, the participants had access to one or more computers at home. In fact, they only remember growing up with computers. Amy[1] remembers using a computer for the first time at four years old, but notes: "I don't remember a time when we didn't have it, you know?"

This experience is very different from the ones found in UTC. During the childhood of UTC participants, the percentage of American households owning a computer was below 20%. During the childhood of these participants, the percentage grew from 40% to 80% [26]. Technology access has greatly increased over the years and the participants in our study were more likely to have a computer at home than those in UTC. But access remains unequal on a societal level: Black and Hispanic children, and poor children are less likely to have access to a computer at home, even today [14, 25]. The digital divide also impacts computing skills [1].

The home computer was shared most of the time by the participant's family. We also found examples of computers reserved for the children or the parents. Daniel, for instance, could only use the computer sparingly: "At first, it was the computer that my parents would use. ... it was a special treat to the use the computer at that time."

Table 1: Participants Characteristics

	Number
Gender	
Women	6
Men	5
Major	
Computer Science	8
Computer Engineering	3
Race/ethnicity [a]	
White	6
Hispanic or Latino/a	4
Asian or American-Asian	2
Black or African-American	1
Parents' Education [b]	
Graduate or Professional School	6
Undergraduate	4
High-school	1
High-school Poverty [c] [d]	
Mid-low	5
Low	2

[a] The total is above 11 because several participants indicated multiple race/ethnicities.
[b] Maximum of the two parents' education.
[c] Low: less than 25% free and reduced-priced lunch, mid-low : between 25.1 et 50% [20]
[d] The total number is below 11 because some participants did not provide this information.

Computers were often located in a common room, accessible to the entire family (5/7). This is a difference from UTC, where the boy's bedroom was the preferred place for a computer. This change is probably due to the centrality of computers to twenty-first century life. This location can also be linked with the parent's control over the computer (7/11 parents). Most parents wanted to keep an eye on the time their children spent on the computer or what they did with it. Hannah describes that kind of control in her house: "Our computer was downstairs, in an open area [...] Anyone in the house would know you're on it, on the computer. So, if you've been on it for too long, "Get off of it!"" and after: "In starting high-school, we really, really liked to play online, but we would get in trouble because it wasn't educational at that point". Valcke et al. also found that parents actively controlled their childrens' use of computers, particularly the Internet, impacting the time children spent online [27].

Some parents trusted their children more and exercised little to no control over computing time or content. Diane's mother said for

[1] All names, including MU, are pseudonyms.

example: "As long as you're not searching for dangerous things or downloading malware, we're fine." And Barbara's parents left her with no supervision: "They trusted me enough, and I was already so stressed out by school, they knew all I was doing was schoolwork!"

At the time of the study, all participants had a personal computer but they acquired them at different moments. Most of the participants had a computer before the end of high-school: three during middle-school, and five during high-school. The three last participants obtained their computer at the beginning of college–one of them, Hannah, explains the reasons why she had her computer this late: "In high-school, we had computer labs anyways and... it was expensive."

The circumstances in which the participants acquired their own computers also differed. The parents (particularly the fathers) bought the computer for their children almost half of the time (4/10). Amy tells us a common story: "And so, my dad got me my own, because I was using it a lot for school."

Sometimes the participants bought their computer themselves (2/10) or built them (2/10). Some also did research before choosing a computer, like Barbara who "did a lot of research on the type that I wanted, ... and I wanted a specific laptop with custom specs", reflecting her knowledge of computers. Eleanor had a completely different perspective:

> I didn't do any research, or anything before ... I looked at them all and I found one that –I wasn't paying for it, my mom and dad did– I found the one that had –it was like really cool, it had red under the keyboard.

We did not find a pattern of gendered differences in terms of computer ownership. Boys and girls obtained a personal computers at some point. This is different than what Margolis and Fisher found. In UTC, 17% of women and 40% of men had a personal computer during their childhood. The fact that more equitable access to computing during childhood has not produced gender parity in computing disciplines is indicative of bigger societal problems with equity in computing.

The expert in the house was defined as the person who could fix issues with the computer, with varying degrees of abilities: from basic fixing tricks such as power cycling the computer and removing dust to more complex tasks such as deleting a virus or taking apart the computer. In most cases, the dad was the family expert (7/11). Almost half of the participants reported themselves to be the expert (5/11), improving their skills until becoming better than their parents. Amy shared this path: "When I was small, my dad usually fixed it [the computer], ... but it got to a point where I was 10 and I was fixing all the problems."

On the contrary, nearly half of the participants labeled their mother as a novice. Justin for instance described his mom as "clueless" and Hannah relates a similar story: "She [mom] is not that great. She barely understands how to use her phone!" This is similar to the results found by Margolis and Fisher. Few mothers were and are the family experts on computing.

4.3 Computers in School

In school, all of the participants had access to computers, most of the time in a specific room (the library or a computer lab) and less often in classrooms. The students used computers for various tasks, but primarily for office-related tasks (typing a report, using spreadsheets, using a presentation tool) (11/11) and online research (5/11). Other tasks included games (4/11), artistic activities (3/11), reading activities (3/11), scientific activities (2/11). Some of these tasks were done as homework, as Justin explains: "Yeah [we would use computers in regular classes], but not during the class. It would be required for most of our writing classes and stuff, like 'Hey, make sure this is typed.'" We found the use at school to be similar than what Becker reported in 2000: "Most computer use at school falls short of helping students reach a high-level of mastery."[3]

Many of the participants' high-schools did not offer a computing class. In our sample, fewer girls than boys took a programming class in high-school. However, in the case of these participants, the critical factor appears to be whether the participant's high school had such a class available, rather than a gender-related choice to not pursue computing. Instead of advanced technical classes, the students had basic courses in which they learned various simple information processing tasks, such as web browsing, keyboarding, and word processing. Sometimes the "computer class" was a catch-all class: Eleanor, for instance, learned how to write a check there.

Most of basic classes happened in elementary and middle school, but Hannah recalls that she had to take a keyboarding class in high-school: "[It] was really kind of silly because at that point everyone knew how to do it [keyboarding]."

Even when participants had more advanced classes, or technical clubs, available the experience could still be disappointing. Daniel for instance tells us about his programming club:

> [It was] definitely not... a good learning environment, cause the teacher didn't know anything about writing programming in C. So, actually I had to go to my Dad for most of help with that, because no one else had any background knowledge on how to work with that. ... It was really hard at the beginning; my Dad is not a great teacher. He's good at programming, but he's really bad at explaining things. It was kind of overwhelming.

Advanced computing classes and clubs were and, in the experience of these participants, are dominated by boys. Sam tells us about the situation in his programming class: "There was definitely more males which is sad. ... When I was there, there ... maybe were 3 or 4 girls, in the class of 20." For Lucy, the dominance of boys is what prevented her from participating in the computing club at her high-school:

> It was always completely dominated by males and I just didn't feel comfortable. ... Being in an environment of males who... all they do is play video games and I didn't do that, so I didn't feel like I could connect with them very well.

These stories align with the number of girls taking the AP test in Computer Science: in 1999 17% of test takers were female, in 2012 19% and in 2017[2] 26% [8, 9]. Despite the progress that has been made, especially in the last couple years, the same stereotypes and

[2]For this last date, the percentage include the AP CS A (24% women) and AP CS Principles (30% women) tests. This breakdown comes from an email distributed on the CS Matters mailing list by Maureen Reyes of The College Board from Tuesday, July 11, 2017.

mechanisms that kept girls away twenty years earlier can still be observed [6, 13, 18].

4.4 Major in CS and CE

Not all of the participants began college with a major in CS or CE. In fact, only four of them did. The other seven participants' pathways to CS/CE had a detour. We distinguished 4 different paths to a major in CS/CE: the *early bird*, the *late bird*, the *second-time-around* and the *legacy*.

The early bird is the person who catches the CS/CE train from high-school and stays on it until graduation in college. They typically took a programming class in high-school and decided to study CS/CE in college, naturally. Lucy is an early bird: she started computing with HTML as a child, she took that AP CS class in high-school and explains why:

> Since I started doing the web stuff when I was young, I've been constantly thinking about how much we can change and improve, using computers in everyday life and so by high-school and having done a little more research and seeing more news articles, I was already pretty sure I wanted to go into computer science in college, so... It also counted as a foreign language. [laugh]

After this class, she indeed started a computer science degree, as she had planned.

The late bird is the person who did not experience CS/CE in high-school, but discovered computing in college. In high-school, they may have felt that CS/CE was not for them, and had no class or club available to show them otherwise. In college, they initially studied something else, sometimes even outside of STEM. These participants discovered programming through a introductory class for non-majors and became committed to computing. Amy is the typical late bird: during all her childhood, she mainly used her computer for typing and wanted to major in English. Her brother was very interested by technology and video games, but she was not: "At that time I wasn't really interested in doing computer science, I don't know... I was just like "It's not my thing!"" During her interview, she mentioned her brother multiple times: he was the tech-savvy one, he got a very nice and expensive computer in high-school, he took a programming class; "that's just been [laughs] his thing." In college, Amy decided to try a introductory class to computer science to fill her schedule and she got a revelation: "So I enrolled in that and it went great, it went so great. It was amazing, I was doing so well in that class –like everything he said to me, I understood perfectly for some reason.".

The second-time-around is the person who discovered their interest in computing in high-school, but stepped away and rediscovered CS/CE in college. Some of these participants took a programming class or participated in a technical club (robotics). But then something make them retreat from CS, e.g. poor teaching, lack of programming experience, or self-doubt. Luckily, they experienced CS/CE again in college, in the form of a programming for non-majors class (or other exposure) and decided to return to CS/CE. Chris, for instance, is a second-time-around: he started web development at the age of nine, then was introduced to programming by a colleague of his Dad, but the experience was disappointing:

> By the time I got into eighth grade I wanted to do computer science, and I had an interview with one of Dad's coworkers at his company, and he introduced me to programming and ... He didn't really introduce it in the right way, so I kinda got distracted.

So, he majored in aerospace engineering. He describes later his second attempt at computing in college: "I was an aerospace engineering major and while I was there I took programming for non-major and I fell in love with programming for real."

The legacy is the person who wants to follow their parents' steps and draws their confidence to jump late in the CS/CE train from this. They did not experience computing in any high school class or club and did not learn on their own. Eleanor is the participant who belongs to this group. Although other participants had parents in the CS/CE field (as a job or a hobby), she was most impressed by her mom's success in the field, as she describes when answering the question "Why did you decide to study CS/CE?":

> Because my mom did. ... She looked at all the degrees that Emerald University[3] offered and she found out that this one was the one that made the most money, outside of college so she –that's when she decided to go, she had no computer experience at all. And so I figured I was at least half as smart as my mom, so if she would go through it and embrace, then surely I could do it too.

and earlier

> When I was little, at three o'clock in the morning maybe, so if you'd wake up you go see her, doing the magic [smiling] –that's what I thought it was. And, hum, that's what made me want to be a computer engineer in the first place.

In UTC, we do not hear the stories of late birds and second-time-around people. We think this likely to be related to the highly competitive environment of CMU, although there are other possibilities. For example, if we interviewed students at CMU now, we might find these patterns represented.

Our results show the importance of introductory programming classes to recruiting computing majors: all of the participants except one took an introductory class in high-school or college that motivated them to pursue a degree in CS/CE. Several participants were recruited into computing fields from programming classes designed for non-computing majors. High quality and engaging computing classes for non-majors are one way to increase the number of computing majors, as previously recognized ??.

4.5 Challenges

The participants also shared with us some of the challenges they faced during their pathway to CS/CE. The most common challenge found was doubt: self-doubt, and doubt about the career itself. Hannah explains it this way:

> So, that's when it gets really hard and feels really frustrating: it's like, sometimes, there's this huge learning curve, it feels like everybody knows everything before. ... I try to tell myself: You know, these people

[3]Pseudonym

> have been doing this for years, and I just started and they're really familiar with this system and I'm just, you know, a little puppy trying to learn how to swim.

Some female participants were also intimidated by a male expert in their family, like Barbara:

> I was really nervous, because my cousin is extremely smart in this, in this aspect, like that's what he does for the Navy –he codes and does hardware on aircraft for the Navy. ... So, my cousin is extremely intelligent, so I was very intimated because when he would talk about it [computer science], I would have no idea what he was talking about, which is probably why I was apprehensive, to go in right away –it's because I was intimidated by him.

And there is also the fear not to match some unspoken CS/CE criteria. Sam struggled a lot with this issue, comparing himself unfavorably with friends in the field:

> I was kind of intimidated, because I was like "Maybe, you have to fit these certain criteria before you can be good." Hum, and so there was like this beginner barrier that I was like "Man, I don't think I can do it."

But after a long battle with himself, and after succeeding in internships, he finally realized he could do it and now tries to encourage other beginners:

> And you don't have to be a white man that was learning how to program since they were five –anybody can program! Like, you can be non-engineer, you can be engineer, you can be anything and learn how to code!

These doubts are the main source of difficulty that the participants shared. This particularly resonate with a 2011 study who searched for the factors influencing the decision to stay in CS after the first introductory class in college and found that: "Comparisons with peers with respect to prior programming experience and speed caused some students to question whether they should pursue their interest in CS." ([7]) In chapter 5 of UTC, we also found a similar phenomenon: women are overwhelmed by the knowledge of their male peers and lack confidence in their own abilities. We discovered that those who succeed enough in CS to stay still have the same fears and doubts.

5 LIMITATIONS

The biggest limitation of this study is the small number of participants. It is not clear that we reached data saturation. Our participants also lacked diversity, especially in socio-economic status. In addition, all of these participants came from only one institution. While this institution is more typical than CMU, every institution has unique features and histories that make it unable to representative the college experience as a whole.

The coding of the data was done by one researcher (MC). It would have been preferable to have two independent coders and perform inter-rater reliability tests to verify that coding was done consistently.

6 CONCLUSIONS AND FUTURE WORK

Our first research question examined the childhood and school experiences with computing of current computing majors. We found that the technology advancement has impacted childrens' experiences with computers, and thus their desire to learn computer science. Therefore, it seems that children today have many more and more equitable opportunities to engage with technology. As an example, now many children have their own computers instead of having to share a computer with a sibling.

Social constraints in computing have been much slower to evolve. We heard stories of fathers still being the family experts in computing, and fathers teaching their sons how to program or take apart a computer. We heard stories of girls who thought programming was not for them because they were standing in the shadow of their brother or male cousin. We also heard stories about fathers teaching their girls how to reboot a computer (a far cry from taking apart a computer). It is clear that many of these participants experienced computing being transmitted in families through a father/son connection that continues to preferentially advantage male children.

Our second research question examined the pathways into computing that current computing majors found. We heard more diverse profiles of students: students who discovered programming late, students who discovered CS by chance, students who had no experience in computing prior to college. This suggests that replicating the remainder of Unlocking the Clubhouse at other institutions is likely to be fruitful. It would be especially useful to see if institutions such as community colleges, institutions with comprehensive online programs, institutions with a primary teaching mission, primarily minority-serving institutions, would give a more complete picture of where women in computing came from.

The choice to implement UTC at CMU can now be seen as hegemonic. The book was widely read and is well respected (it currently has more than 2000 citations listed on Google Scholar), in part because it came from this premiere institution. However, performing this analysis at this institution focused on the needs of atypical women–women who were pursuing computing degrees at one of the most competitive and prestigious institutions in the U.S. The fact that this work has been seen as a definitive source for encouraging women in computing is problematic. The needs of women who were not academic superstars, who came from more varied social identities and backgrounds, or who were not sufficiently competitive to seek education at CMU were not considered. This is not an indictment of UTC itself, but rather of the willingness of the computing community to generalize inappropriately from qualitative work, when they should have asked first how similar their institution is to CMU. Our work has the same unavoidable limitation, as all qualitative work must. Only continuing to reproduce this study at a wide range of institutions will remedy this limitation.

ACKNOWLEDGMENTS

The authors would like to thank Susan Walden for her help during the interview process. The authors would also like to thank the students who participated in this study.

REFERENCES

[1] Harouna Ba, William Tally, and Kallen Tsikalas. 2002. Investigating Children's Emerging Digital Literacies. *Assessment* 4, 1 (2002), 4–48.

[2] Theresa Beaubouef and Wendy Zhang. 2011. Where Are the Women Computer Science Students? *J. Comput. Sci. Coll.* 26, 4 (April 2011), 14–20. http://dl.acm.org/citation.cfm?id=1953573.1953576

[3] Henry Jay Becker. 2000. Who's Wired and Who's Not: Children's Access to Technology. *The Future of Children* 10, 2 (2000), 44–75. https://doi.org/10.2307/1602689

[4] Sylvia Beyer. 2014. Why are women underrepresented in Computer Science? Gender differences in stereotypes, self-efficacy, values, and interests and predictors of future CS course-taking and grades. *Computer Science Education* 24, 2-3 (2014), 153–192. https://doi.org/10.1080/08993408.2014.963363

[5] Maura Borrego, Elliot P. Douglas, and Catherine T. Amelink. 2009. Quantitative, Qualitative, and Mixed Research Methods in Engineering Education. *Journal of Engineering Education* 98, 1 (January 2009), 53–66.

[6] Sapna Cheryan, Allison Master, and Andrew N. Meltzoff. 2015. Cultural stereotypes as gatekeepers: increasing girls' interest in computer science and engineering by diversifying stereotypes. *Frontiers in Psychology* 6, FEB (feb 2015). https://doi.org/10.3389/fpsyg.2015.00049

[7] Ruth E. Anderson Colleen M. Lewis, Ken Yasuhara. 2011. Deciding to Major in Computer Science: A Grounded Theory of Students' Self-Assessment of Ability. In *ICER '11 Proceedings of the seventh international workshop on computing education research.* https://doi.org/10.1145/2016911.2016915

[8] College Board. 2012. AP Data - Archived Data 2012. https://research.collegeboard.org/programs/ap/data/archived/2012.

[9] College Board. 2017. AP Program Participation and Performance Data 2017. https://research.collegeboard.org/programs/ap/data/participation/ap-2017.

[10] Jacquelynne S. Eccles and Ming-Te Wang. 2016. What motivates females and males to pursue careers in mathematics and science? *International Journal of Behavioral Development* 40, 2 (mar 2016), 100–106. https://doi.org/10.1177/0165025415616201

[11] Cynthia E. Foor, Susan E. Walden, and Deborah A. Trytten. 2007. "I Wish that I Belonged More in this Whole Engineering Group:" Achieving Individual Diversity. *Journal of Engineering Education* 96, 2 (2007), 103–115. https://doi.org/10.1002/j.2168-9830.2007.tb00921.x

[12] Greg Guest, Arwen Bunce, and Laura Johnson. 2006. How Many Interviews Are Enough? *Field Methods* 18, 1 (2006), 59–82. https://doi.org/10.1177/1525822X05279903 arXiv:arXiv:1011.1669v3

[13] Catherine Hill, Christianne Corbett, and Andresse St. Rose. 2010. Why So Few? Women in Science, Technology, Engineering, and Mathematics. https://files.eric.ed.gov/fulltext/ED509653.pdf.

[14] Sharon Judge, Kathleen Puckett, and Sherry Mee Bell. 2006. Closing the digital divide: Update from the early childhood longitudinal study. *The Journal of Educational Research* 100, 1 (2006), 52–60. http://www.tandfonline.com/doi/abs/10.3200/JOER.100.1.52-60

[15] Kathleen J. Lehman, Linda J. Sax, and Hilary B. Zimmerman. 2017. Women planning to major in computer science: Who are they and what makes them unique? *Computer Science Education* 26, 4 (2017), 277–298. https://doi.org/10.1080/08993408.2016.1271536

[16] Jane Margolis and Allan Fisher. 2001. *Unlocking the Clubhouse: Women in Computing.* MIT Press, Cambridge, Massachusetts.

[17] Jane Margolis, Estrella Rachel, Joanna Goode, Jennifer Jellison Holme, and Kim Nao. 2008. *Stuck in the Shallow End: Education, Race and Computing.* MIT Press, Cambridge, Massachusetts. 216 pages.

[18] Allison Master, Sapna Cheryan, and Andrew N. Meltzoff. 2016. Computing whether she belongs: Stereotypes undermine girls' interest and sense of belonging in computer science. *Journal of Educational Psychology* 108, 3 (2016), 424–437. https://doi.org/10.1037/edu0000061

[19] National Center for Education Statistics. 2016. Search for Public Schools. https://nces.ed.gov/ccd/schoolsearch/index.asp.

[20] National Center for Education Statistics (NCES). 2018. Concentration of Public School Students Eligible for Free or Reduced-Price Lunch. The Condition of Education, https://nces.ed.gov/programs/coe/indicator_clb.asp.

[21] National Center for Science and Engineering Statistics National Science Foundation. 2017. Women, Minorities, and Persons with Disabilities in Science and Engineering: 2017. https://www.nsf.gov/statistics/wmpd/. Special Report NSF 17-310. Arlington, VA.

[22] Scott Ragsdale. 2015. Pursuing and Finishing an Undergraduate Computing Degree: Insights from Women Computing Graduates. *J. Comput. Sci. Coll.* 30, 5 (May 2015), 52–59. http://dl.acm.org/citation.cfm?id=2752981.2752995

[23] Elaine Seymour and Nancy M. Hewitt. 2000. *Talking About Leaving: Why Undergraduates Leave the Sciences.* Westview Press. 444 pages.

[24] Deborah A. Trytten, Anna Wong Lowe, and Susan E. Walden. 2012. "Asians are Good at Math. What an Awful Stereotype" The Model Minority Stereotype's Impact on Asian American Engineering Students. *Journal of Engineering Education* 101, 3 (2012), 439–468. https://doi.org/10.1002/j.2168-9830.2012.tb00057.x

[25] US Census Bureau. 2017. The Digital Divide: Percentage of Households by Broadband Internet Subscription, Computer Type, Race and Hispanic Origin. https://www.census.gov/library/visualizations/2017/comm/internet.html.

[26] US Census Bureau. 2018. American Community Survey, Computer and Internet Use. https://www.census.gov/topics/population/computer-internet.html, https://www.census.gov/content/dam/Census/library/publications/2018/acs/ACS-39.pdf.

[27] M Valcke, S Bonte, B De Wever, and I Rots. 2010. Internet parenting styles and the impact on Internet use of primary school children. *Computers & Education* 55 (2010), 454–464. Issue 2.

Cybersecurity is Not a Fad: Why Cyber is a Game Changer for Computer Science Education

Blair Taylor
Clinical Associate Professor of Computer and Information Sciences
Towson University
Towson, MD, USA
btaylor@towson.edu

ABSTRACT

First, the bad news – Cybersecurity is here to stay. Threats are escalating and organizations are increasingly vulnerable. Hackers are smarter, there are more of them, and they continue to wreak havoc across critical infrastructure systems. There is a huge, growing shortfall of cyber talent. All students, and especially computer science students, need to learn cyber, but there is an acute shortage of cybersecurity faculty.

The good news – Cybersecurity is here to stay. We continue to need skilled cyber workers. Students like cyber. Cyber can draw more students to Computer Science and create opportunities for Computer Science faculty.

Dr. Blair Taylor will share her experiences building cyber curriculum from the classroom perspective and from her experience working with NSA to build a National Cybersecurity Curriculum Program.

KEYWORDS: Cybersecurity, Computer Science Education

ACM Reference format:

Blair Taylor. 2019. Cybersecurity is Not a Fad: Why Cyber is a Game Changer for Computer Science Education. In *SIGCSE'19: The 50th ACM Technical Symposium on Computer Science Education, Feb 27-Mar 2, 2019, Minneapolis, MN, USA.* ACM, New York, NY, USA, 1 pages. https://doi.org/10.1145/3287324.3290954

BIOGRAPHY

Dr. Blair Taylor is an award-winning educator with 20+ years' experience in academia. She is a national expert in cybersecurity education and curriculum development. As a Clinical Associate Professor in the Department of Computer and Information Sciences at Towson University, she has received over $5 million of external funding. Her projects include Security Injections @ Towson, which provides security modules for integrating security across the curriculum and is a national model for teaching secure coding to introductory programming students, and SPLASH, which offers Secure Programming Logic for college credit to high school girls.

Dr. Taylor also works with NSA's College of Cyber as a Subject Matter Expert on long-term strategies to increase the pipeline of qualified students and build the nations' cyber workforce. These programs include the National Cybersecurity Curriculum Program and the Cyber Cube.

Dr. Taylor has received the University System of Maryland Regents Award for Teaching, the Fisher College of Science and Mathematics Outstanding Faculty Award and the Business Outreach Award. She has been recognized as one of 50 Women to Watch by the Baltimore Sun Magazine and one of Maryland's top female tech leaders by MDBIZNews. She holds a B.A. in Mathematical Science and an M.S. in Computer Science from Johns Hopkins University and a doctorate in Applied Information Technology from Towson University.

ACM ISBN 978-1-4503-5890-3/19/02.
https://doi.org/10.1145/3287324.3290954

Assessing In-service Teachers' Development of Computational Thinking Practices in Teacher Development Courses

Siu-Cheung Kong
Department of Mathematics and Information Technology
The Education University of Hong Kong
Hong Kong
sckong@eduhk.hk

Andrew Chan-Chio Lao
Henry Fok Pearl Jubilee College
University of Macau
Macau
andrewlao@umac.mo

ABSTRACT

To promote computational thinking (CT) education in primary schools, in-service teachers need to attend CT teacher development programmes. One of the intended learning outcomes of the programme is to improve CT practices of teachers, which is one of the three key elements in the CT framework proposed by Brennan and Resnick. Assessing one's CT practices is challenging because there is no universally agreed-upon assessment method on CT practices in the existing literature. This study adopted the Evidence-centered Assessment Design (ECD) method to design test questions to evaluate teachers' development of CT practices. This study provided two Teacher Development Courses (TDCs) to enable teachers to teach CT through programming. TDC 1 focused on developing CT concepts, practices and perspectives of teachers, while TDC 2 put emphasis on pedagogies of teaching CT. 80 teachers participated in the two courses. The CT practices tests were administered before the courses, between the two courses and after the courses respectively. Results indicated that CT practices were improved progressively when the in-service teachers attended the two courses. It indicated that it is useful for teachers to experience programming practices in their initial learning as well as during their pedagogical development.

CCS CONCEPTS

• **General and reference~Empirical studies** • **General and reference~Measurement** • **General and reference~Evaluation** • Applied computing~Education

ACM Reference format:

Siu-Cheung Kong and Andrew Chan-Chio Lao. 2019. Assessing In-service Teachers' Development of Computational Thinking Practices in Teacher Development Courses. In *Proceedings of 50th ACM Technical Symposium on Computer Science Education (SIGCSE '19), February 27-Mar. 2, 2019, Minneapolis, MN, USA.* ACM, New York, NY, USA, 7 pages. https://doi.org/10.1145/3287324.3287470

KEYWORDS

Assessment, Computational Thinking (CT), Computational Thinking practices (CT practices), In-service teacher, Teacher development

1 INTRODUCTION

According to Wing [1], CT is a fundamental ability for everyone, and it should be introduced to everyone. Students are encouraged to equip themselves with this ability in the digital era, such that they could become a problem solver, innovative creator, and critical thinker in the digital era. As programming knowledge and skills can stimulate CT development [2], past studies suggested that students could learn and foster CT through programming courses [3, 4]. Many CT programmes pop up at national scale such as the UK and Australia. Therefore, teaching CT is becoming a global initiative.

To better promote CT education, in-service teachers at K-12 level should receive the related teacher development for teaching preparation. Scholars emphasized the necessity of teacher development programmes for the strategic goals to successfully embed CT into K-12 education [3].

According to literature, there were few studies explored CT development of teachers. For example, Yadav and colleagues [5] explored the impact of CT modules on pre-service teachers in an educational psychological course. This study attempted to address CT development of in-service teachers and tried to understand how in-service teachers develop their CT practices through teacher development programme. This study attempted to develop an instrument to evaluate one of the key components of CT, that is CT practices, for K-12 school teachers.

2 BACKGROUND

2.1 Computational Thinking Framework

At K-12 level, past studies reported that the educators usually taught CT through programming education [6], STEM education [7] or tangible coding environment [8]. Programming is suggested to be an effective way to immerse learners in CT environment, through which problem-solving tasks can be completed using CT practices like algorithmic thinking [4]. Additionally, previous studies argued that visual programming languages (i.e. block-based programming) are better than traditional programming languages (i.e. text-based programming) in K-12 context because of its simplified syntax [2, 4]. Hence, teaching CT through block-based programming such as Scratch and App Inventor is an effective way for beginners [6]. This study deployed the CT framework proposed by Brennan and Resnick [6], which considers block-based programming as an effective means to develop CT.

Brennan and Resnick [6] proposed three key components of CT, namely CT concepts, CT practices, and CT perspectives. They refer CT practices as problem-solving practices that people practice in the programming processes. Brennan and Resnick consider being incremental and iterative, testing and debugging, reusing and remixing, and abstracting and modularizing as important practices of CT when young learners start to learn programming. Being incremental and iterative means the "iterative cycles of imagining and building (p.7)" [6]. Students work out the solutions step-by-step and then further develop the solutions after they try them out. Testing and debugging means the process of anticipating and solving problems through "trial and error, transfer from other activities, or support from knowledgeable others (p.7)" [6]. Reusing and remixing means that students build on their own or others' work to "create things much more complex than they could have created on their own (p.8)" [6]. Abstracting and modularizing means that students "build something large by putting together collections of smaller parts (p.9)" [6]. Specifically, abstraction is always applied in "defining patterns, generalizing from specific instances, and parameterization (p.1)" [9], which helps students handle complexity. Apart from the CT practices proposed by Brennan and Resnick, algorithmic thinking is added and considered as one of the key CT practices. It refers to "formulate computational problems and systematically process information and gain a deeper understanding of symbol systems and representations, algorithmic notions of flow of control, and conditional logic (p.384)" [10]. These five CT practices are therefore included in this study for evaluation.

2.2 Teacher Development Courses

CT could enhance students' problem-solving ability when they start to think computationally. Thus, to equip students in K-12 schools with CT, teachers should learn first so they can inspire students when they start practicing their teaching. Previous studies argued that "it is important to provide teachers with an adequate knowledge about CT and how to corporate it into their teaching (p.1)" to nurture students with CT at K-12 level [5]. However, the major challenge of promoting CT education is that there are few experienced teachers to teach CT in schools [11]. For attempts to implement CT education successfully in K-12 level, it is critical to organize Teacher Development Courses (TDCs) for in-service teachers to enhance their CT knowledge and block-based programming skills.

A teacher development programme for promoting CT education in primary schools was implemented in this study. In the academic year of 2017/2018, teachers from 20 schools attended the related TDCs. This study investigated the learning improvements in terms of CT practices of the courses. The teacher development programme comprised of two courses, namely Teacher Development Course 1 (TDC 1) and Teacher Development Course 2 (TDC 2). The two courses were taken in progression. Teachers were required to complete TDC 1 before they participated in TDC 2. Each TDC lasted for 39 hours (i.e. three hours per session and there were 13 sessions). For TDC 1, it had a focus on building teachers' CT concepts, practices and perspectives. The course went through the CT curriculum in grade four of primary school, which helped the teachers understand the basic CT concepts and practices such as reusing and remixing, and testing and debugging that they are expected to deliver in their classrooms. At the end of TDC 1, they needed to develop a mobile app to solve problems that occur in their classrooms. The course provided review and presentation sessions for teachers to recap what they had learnt in TDC 1 and received feedback from the instructors of the course. In sum, TDC 1 provided practical hands-on experiences of teachers as well as opportunities to solve real-life problems through programming. TDC 2 put emphasis on pedagogies of teaching CT in general such as pair programming and addressing individual differences in programming activities. The teachers were also guided to discuss pedagogies of fostering CT in primary school classrooms and ways to evaluate students' work in the programming course. TDC 2 also taught CT concepts, practices and perspectives when examples of teaching programming in the primary curriculum were used in deliberating pedagogy of CT education. The course put more effort on CT practices like abstraction and algorithmic thinking. The teachers were required to work in groups to design a scheme of work on a unit of the CT curriculum in the primary school programming course in their final projects. It facilitated teachers to think about how to deliver CT concepts, practices and perspectives in primary school classroom in the best way.

2.3 Evidence-centered Assessment Design

Evidence-centered assessment Design (ECD) can be applied as an educational assessment method from the perspective of evidentiary argument. Messick [12] described ECD with two steps: (1) firstly illuminating a construct for complicated knowledge, skills or other attributes, (2) then exploring what behaviors or performances under which tasks or online performances can reflect this construct. ECD builds explicit assessment arguments and designed tools to help with both developing new assessment design and evaluating familiar ones [13]. This method has a core feature of providing evidences of desired outcomes to support the argument. One important advantage for using ECD is the validity of inferences made upon scores from tests [14], especially for some hard-to-measure variables. Therefore, there were more and more researchers turned to use evidence-centered design to develop assessments [15, 16]. ECD can be used in a large scale of assessment [17].

3 METHODOLOGY

There are few standardized CT assessment methods in the current literature due to a wide variety of CT definitions and conceptualizations put forward in the recent decade. Therefore, it is challenging to measure the effectiveness of the interventions of CT education [18]. Scholars generally tend to design assessment test to address different operationalization definition of CT [18, 19]. In this study, we intended to use the ECD approach to identify measurement constructs of CT practices and propose tasks as test items to capture the performance of teachers so that we can measure the improvements of CT practices in the TDCs. This study intended to design paper-and-pencil tests in which real-life problems were put up for teachers to write down the pseudocodes to solve the problems. This study attempted to use the test to explore whether teacher's CT practices were improved after attending the two TDCs.

3.1 Participants and Procedures

A total of 80 in-service primary school teachers attended the two TDCs. Among these participants, 46 (57.5%) were male and 34 (42.5%) were female. The average years of teaching was 11.7. Nearly all teachers taught more than one subject. There were 64 (80%) taught computer/information technology, 43 (53.8%) taught mathematics, 28 (35%) taught general studies, 14 (17.5%) taught English, and 13 (16.3%) taught Chinese. Of these teachers, 20 of them (25%) stated that they had a degree in computer science.

In general, three to four teachers from each of the 20 schools were recruited to join the TDCs. Based on the current CT framework, learning and teaching materials together with the evaluation tests were designed and reviewed by a research team. Two researchers with background of computer science and education reviewed the questions of the test and set the test duration as 30 minutes. Marking rubrics were designed to assess participants' responses. During the TDCs, in-service teachers were asked to do three CT practices tests at different time points to examine their development. The first test was conducted before the start of the first TDC. The second test was conducted after participants handed in the final project of TDC 1, that was after four months of the first test. The third test was conducted after the end of the second TDC, that was after five months of the second test. All the three tests were identical, and all questions were collected after the tests without discussing answers of any questions. After receiving all test outcomes, two researchers were trained to familiarize with the rubrics and started to mark all scripts independently. The two researchers were required to refine their scores for those disagreed markings. The reliability of the instruments was calculated using the Cronbach Alpha in SPSS 21. To carefully control other factors that might impact the learning outcomes, same teachers were assigned to both classes, same teaching materials were used, and the two classes started and ended nearly at the same time.

3.2 Assessment Design

This study adopted the ECD approach [16, 20, 21] for assessment design. The same method was employed in a large-scale pilot assessment program by Snow and his colleagues [22], in assessing CT practices. In line with the steps of ECD, the major process of assessment design in this study was to develop a set of testing questions to collect evidences that could make proper inferences about CT practices. Specifically, regarding the five components proposed in this study under the framework of CT practices, which were also called the constructs in ECD, a set of Focal Knowledge, Skill, and Ability (FKSAs) was formulated. These FKSAs formed the goals of current assessment, and the in-service teachers needed to acquire these abilities. The evaluators assess the in-service teachers' CT practices development based on the FKSAs. A set of test items corresponding to the FKSAs of the five CT practices components were designed to meet those goals. The research team reviewed all designed items to ensure strong inferential relations between each CT practice construct with the evaluation items.

A total of five questions were designed using the above design method. We referred to the Baseline Report [22] during the design process to determine the crucial abilities in CT practices and developed the test questions accordingly. The questions were examined by CT experts of the research team to ensure they reflect the FKSA's contents and be able to test CT practices. For example, the FKSAs of testing and debugging include the "ability to efficiently identify the source of error(s)" and the "ability to explain the cause of errors and fix them" (p.43) [22]. For abstracting, its FKSAs comprises the "ability to identify abstractions" and the "ability to design an abstraction to represent a problem or solution" (p.44) [22]. Based on the framework of CT practices reviewed and selected in this study, five constructs were included. Table 1 shows the mapping of the five questions aligning with the five selected constructs of CT practices.

Table 1: Mappings of CT Practices and Test Questions

Constructs of CT Practices	Q1	Q2	Q3	Q4	Q5
Being Incremental and Iterative					v
Testing and Debugging	v				
Reusing and Remixing		v			v
Abstracting and Modularizing				v	v
Algorithmic Thinking			v	v	v

The five questions were set up using task-based design, in which each question depicted a scenario and then asked the teachers to solve the tasks on the described problems by answering questions or writing pseudocodes. The scenarios in the tasks help to trigger the problem-solving processes.

3.3 Assessment Rubrics

Corresponding to the design of test questions, a set of assessment rubrics were designed for collecting evidences on CT practices of participants from their answers. The assessment rubrics had two types. The first type was the correctness of the answer (applied to all five questions), in which the evaluators simply gave full score for the right answer and gave no score for the wrong answer. The second type was collecting evidences from the written answer (applied to Q1, Q4, and Q5), in which the evaluators assessed whether the targeted CT practices were reflected through their writing scripts and pseudocodes. The scores of these two types of the assessment rubrics were added up for calculating the scores of the test. Q1 and Q4 were taken as examples for illustrating the assessment of the test.

Q1 (see Figure 1) was a task on identifying and correcting the two incorrect parts made by a wheat processing factory worker - firstly, the wrong indication of factory “#1” to factory “#3” (the scenario have set up with two factories only); and secondly, the wrong setting of factory temperature for processing soft wheat (the scenario set when the factory temperature is higher than 40°C, the factory should switch on fans to lower the temperature to below 40°C and dry the wheat). This question aimed to test participants’ ability of debugging in CT practices - to find and correct wrong parts of the pseudocodes of the scenario depicted in the stem of the question.

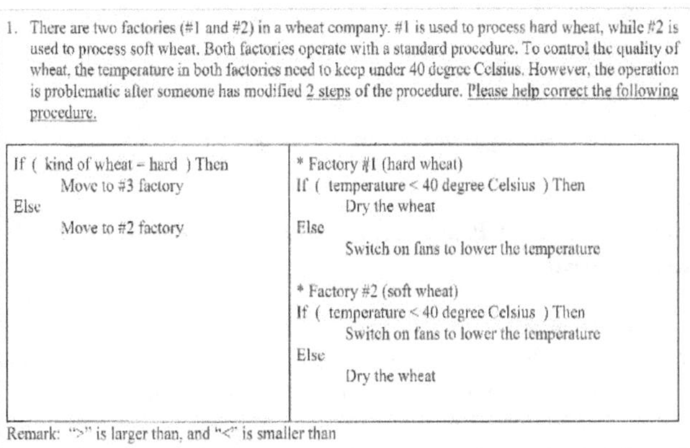
1. There are two factories (#1 and #2) in a wheat company. #1 is used to process hard wheat, while #2 is used to process soft wheat. Both factories operate with a standard procedure. To control the quality of wheat, the temperature in both factories need to keep under 40 degree Celsius. However, the operation is problematic after someone has modified 2 steps of the procedure. Please help correct the following procedure.

If (kind of wheat = hard) Then
Move to #3 factory
Else
Move to #2 factory
	* Factory #1 (hard wheat)
	If (temperature < 40 degree Celsius) Then
	Dry the wheat
	Else
	Switch on fans to lower the temperature
	
	* Factory #2 (soft wheat)
	If (temperature < 40 degree Celsius) Then
	Switch on fans to lower the temperature
	Else
	Dry the wheat

Remark: “>” is larger than, and “<” is smaller than

Figure 1: Question 1 Testing Debugging Ability of Participants in CT Practices

The assessment for Q1 had two parts. One part was the correctness of the answer, two scores were given when participants identified the above two errors; and one score was given when participants only identified one errors. Otherwise, no score was given. The other part was the correctness of the written answer, one score was awarded when participants changed factory number from “#3” to “#1”; and another one score was awarded when participants changed the operator from “<” to “>” in the pseudocode to set factory temperature higher than 40°C. The total score of Q1 was four.

Q4 (see Figure 2) was a task on choosing the counter for a faster cashier service in a supermarket. The question scenario was inspired by Wing’s [1] example on modeling of multi-server systems in computer science. The scenario of Q4 gave the information on the length of queuing time and the number of customers queuing in two different cashier counters. This question attempted to test the ability of abstracting and the ability of algorithmic thinking in CT practices.

The first part of Q4 asked participants to determine the cashier counter, based on the information given in the scenario, for a faster cashier service. Participants needed to demonstrate the ability of algorithmic thinking to calculate the total queuing time in each cashier counter (i.e. by multiplying the length of queuing time and the number of customers queuing) to make comparison and then the correct choice of queue. The assessment for this part was at the level for the correctness of final answer: one score for the correct answer (i.e. counter 1) and no score for the incorrect answer.

The second part asked participants to provide an algorithm to help customers to determine the counter for a faster cashier service. Regarding the ability of algorithmic thinking, participants had to use operators of “<” or “>” for comparing the total queuing time in two cashier counters. In addition, participants needed to demonstrate their ability of abstracting in setting up an expression using variables for the number of customers queuing in each counter (such as N_1 and N_2), to calculate the total queuing time in two cashier counters (such as the product of N_1 x 5 minutes and the product of N_2 x 7 minutes). Participants also needed to use an algorithm (such as if...then...else...) for finding a faster cashier counter.

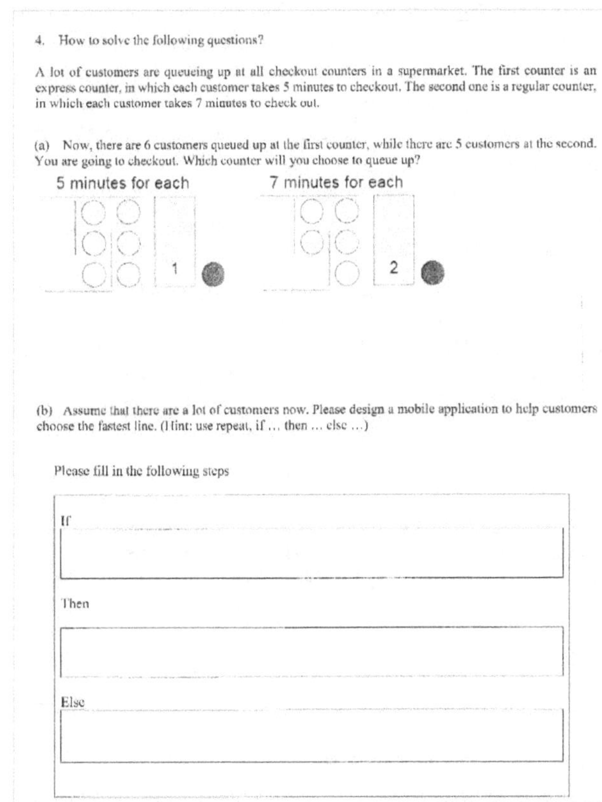
4. How to solve the following questions?

A lot of customers are queueing up at all checkout counters in a supermarket. The first counter is an express counter, in which each customer takes 5 minutes to checkout. The second one is a regular counter, in which each customer takes 7 minutes to check out.

(a) Now, there are 6 customers queued up at the first counter, while there are 5 customers at the second. You are going to checkout. Which counter will you choose to queue up?

(b) Assume that there are a lot of customers now. Please design a mobile application to help customers choose the fastest line. (Hint: use repeat, if ... then ... else ...)

Please fill in the following steps

If

Then

Else

Figure 2: Question 4 Testing Ability of Participants in Algorithmic Thinking and Abstracting in CT Practices

The assessment for this part was the correctness of written answer. Regarding the ability of algorithmic thinking, one score was given when participants used operators of “<” or “>” to compare the expressions on the total queuing time of the two cashier counters. Regarding the ability of abstracting, one score was given when participants used suitable variables to represent the number of customers in each counter; and one score was given when participants used an algorithm (if...then...else...) correctly for the computation to suggest the cashier counter for faster service. Thus, the total score of Q4 was four. The maximum score of the whole test with the five questions were 21.

4 RESULTS AND DISCUSSION

The inter-rater reliability values were 0.98 for the 1st test, 0.97 for the 2nd test, and 0.99 for the 3rd test, indicating that coders had a high degree of agreement and suggesting that CT practices was graded similarly between two coders. Moreover, Cronbach alpha value was 0.79, showing that the current test is reliable with acceptable internal consistency. Result of one-way ANOVA was F (2, 228) = 4.60, p = 0.011, suggesting that there were significant differences among three tests. Figure 3 shows a line graph indicating uprising average scores of all teachers in the three tests.

Before the test-by-test comparisons were carried out, we checked whether each data set was normally distributed. Both Skewness and Kurtosis were ranged from -1 to +1, meaning that the data was fairly normal. Paired two samples t-tests were then carried out to compare the CT practices achievement of all teachers. Table 2 shows the t-tests results of all teachers in the three tests. They showed consistent improvement across the three tests. Significant increase in the means of the scores of the first and the second tests was found, t (74) = -2.54, p = 0.013, indicating that the CT practices of teachers improved after attending TDC 1. There was significant increase again in the means of the scores of the second and third tests, t (74) = -2.62, p = 0.011, indicating that the CT practices of teachers also improved after attending TDC 2. Finally, the means of the scores of the third test was significantly higher than that of the first test, t (74) = -4.32, p = 0.000, indicating that the CT practices of all the teachers were improved after attending both TDCs. In other words, the provision of these two courses were able to support teachers to gain CT practices progressively.

Table 2: Paired Two Samples T-Test Examining CT Practices Development of All teachers

	Pre-test (Total score = 21)	Post-test (Total score = 21)	*t*
	M (SD)	M (SD)	
Test 1-Test 2	16.84 (3.31)	17.67 (2.87)	-2.54*
Test 2-Test 3	17.67 (2.87)	18.32 (2.55)	-2.62*
Test 1-Test 3	16.84 (3.31)	18.32 (2.55)	-4.32***

Note. **p* <.05; ***p* <.01; ****p* < .001

Because there were 20 teachers stated that they had computer science degrees, this study attempted to analyze the data again by excluding the scores of these teachers. Three teachers did not reveal their educational background. In this regard, 57 teachers were used for all the paired two samples t-tests again. Similarly, there were significant differences among the results of the three tests, F (2, 172) = 5.44, p. = 0.005. Figure 3 also shows the mean scores of the three tests of teachers without Computer Science (CS) degrees. Paired two samples t-tests results indicated that these teachers had significant improvement of CT practices after taking each TDC course. The mean of the third test was also significantly higher than that of the first test, t (56) = -4.86, p = 0.000, indicating that teachers without CS degrees also gain CT practices through the two teacher development courses. It should be noted that their mean scores were consistently lower than the mean scores of all in-service teachers in the three tests.

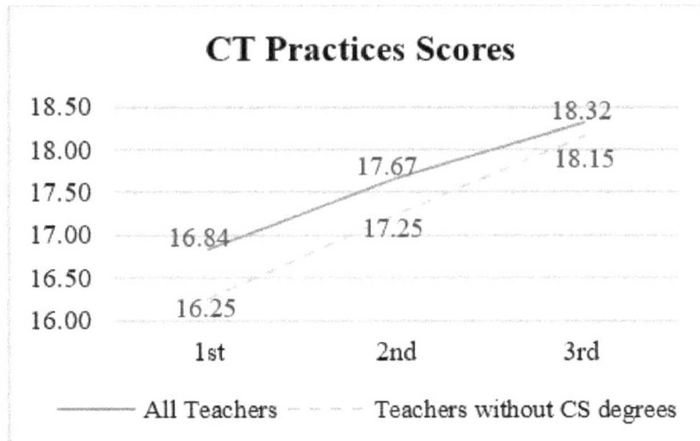

Figure 3: The CT Practices Scores of Learners in the 1st, 2nd and 3rd Tests

Further analysis was carried out to evaluate the in-service teachers' CT development in each construct of the CT practice. Since the assumption of normality for parametric test had been violated, a non-parametric Friedman test of differences among repeated measures was conducted. The results showed that there were statistically significant differences in four constructs of the CT practices among the three tests, namely being incremental and iterative ($\chi^2(2)$ = 9.41, p = 0.009), reusing and remixing ($\chi^2(2)$ = 6.66, p = 0.036), abstracting and modularizing ($\chi^2(2)$ = 9.14, p = 0.010), and algorithmic thinking ($\chi^2(2)$ = 8.89, p = 0.012). However, there was no significant difference in the construct of testing and debugging ($\chi^2(2)$ = 2.06, p = 0.357). Post hoc analysis using the Wilcoxon signed ranks test was then conducted to explore the differences between each test (see table 3). Significant differences were found in the above four construct of CT practices after the teachers attending the two TDCs. The results confirmed that the courses could improve CT practices of teachers in four constructs. Further analysis need to be conducted to investigate why the construct of testing and debugging was not improved in the two TDC courses.

Table 3: Wilcoxon Signed Ranks Test Examining Each CT Practice Development of All Teachers

	Test 1	Test 2	Test 3		Z	
	M (SD)	M (SD)	M (SD)	Test1-Test2	Test2-Test3	Test1-Test3
II (Sub-score = 1)	0.23 (0.41)	0.38 (0.46)	0.39 (0.48)	-2.97**	-0.90	-2.70**
TD (Sub-score = 4)	3.29 (1.06)	3.43 (1.05)	3.51 (0.95)	-1.13	-0.62	-1.83
RR (Sub-score = 5)	4.20 (1.02)	4.48 (0.84)	4.56 (0.79)	-2.38*	-0.75	-2.88**
AM(Sub-score = 3)	2.29 (0.87)	2.45 (0.76)	2.55 (0.74)	-1.73	-1.22	-2.48*
AT (Sub-score = 8)	6.83 (1.35)	6.94 (1.27)	7.31 (1.07)	-0.49	-2.62**	-3.06**

Note. II means being incremental and iterative, TD means testing and debugging, RR means reusing and remixing, AM means abstracting and modularizing, and AT means algorithmic thinking.

$^{*}p<.05$; $^{**}p<.01$; $^{***}p<.001$

5 CONCLUSION

In conclusion, the teacher development programme of this study was proved to be effective in developing CT practices of in-service teachers. They demonstrated continuous improvement in their ability of CT practices after attending TDC1 and TDC2. These results indicated that it is important for teachers to experience the programming processes in both their initial learning as well as during their pedagogical development. It is also important in asking teachers to solve real world problem in the teacher development programme. This study reported an empirical study that offers evidence on CT practices development of teachers and provide insight into assessment of CT practices using the ECD approach.

For future TDCs on developing CT practices of teachers, we should provide opportunities for participants to experience the programming processes in the early stage of the programme as well as create openings for participants using programming to solve real world problems. Since there was no significant improvement in the testing and debugging construct after attending the two TDCs, it is recommended to investigate further from two perspectives. One is to revise the test with more items related to testing and debugging. Another way is to put more effort in the TDCs for teachers to practice testing and debugging during the courses. The results of the study indicated that it is important to provide chances for teachers to practice reuse and remix codes and build their programs incrementally embedding testing and debugging in the process of completing the programming tasks. Abstraction and algorithmic thinking are indispensable abilities in the solution design process when teachers are delegated to solve programming problems like the task discussed in question 4 of the evaluation item of this study. This is also the reason why it is necessary for teachers to complete programming project at the end of the first course. It is an opportunity for them to gain hands-on experiences to solve real-life problem and therefore has chance to design solution practicing their abilities of abstraction and algorithmic thinking. It is useful for teachers to practice the programming process when they are involved in discussion about pedagogies of delivering CT in classrooms. It enables teachers to recap and organize what they have learnt in CT practices, which can foster their CT practices development. In the future, it is crucial to observe how in-service teachers' development influence students' CT learning. It is interesting to see whether there are differences in CT development of students whose teachers have attended TDCs and whose have not.

ACKNOWLEDGEMENTS

The authors would like to acknowledge the funding support of this Coolthink@JC project from the Hong Kong Jockey Club Charities Trust.

REFERENCES

[1] Jeannette M. Wing. 2006. Computational thinking. *Communication of the ACM* 49, 3 (March 2006), 33-35. DOI: https://doi.org/10.1145/1118178.1118215

[2] Ana Liz Souto O. de Araujo, Wilkerson L. Andrade, Dalton D. Serey Guerrero. 2016. A systematic mapping study on assessing computational thinking abilities. In *Proceedings of the IEEE Frontiers in Education Conference.* Erie, PA. 9 pages.

[3] Valerie Barr and Chris Stephenson. 2011. Bringing computational thinking to K-12: What is involved and what is the role of the computer science education community?. *ACM Inroads* 2, 1 (February 2011), 48-54. DOI: http://dx.doi.org/10.1145/1929887.1929905

[4] Sze-Yee Lye, and Joyce Hwee-Ling Koh. 2014. Review on teaching and learning of computational thinking through programming: What is next for K-12? *Computers in Human Behavior* 41 (Dec 2014), 51-61. DOI: https://doi.org/10.1016/j.chb.2014.09.012

[5] Aman Yadav, Chris Mayfield, Ninger Zhou, Susanne Hambrusch, and John T. Korb. 2014. Computational thinking in elementary and secondary teacher education. *ACM Transactions on Computing Education* 14, 1, Article 5 (March 2014), 16 pages. DOI: https://doi.org/10.1145/2576872

[6] Karen Brennan and Mitchel Resnick. 2012. New frameworks for studying and assessing the development of computational thinking. In *Proceedings of the 2012 Annual Meeting of the American Educational Research Association, Vancouver, Canada.* 25 pages.

[7] Florence R. Sullivan, and John Heffernan. 2016. Robotic construction kits as computational manipulatives for learning in the STEM disciplines. *Journal of Research on Technology in Education* 48, 2 (Feb 2016), 105-128. DOI: https://doi.org/10.1080/15391523.2016.1146563

[8] David Barr, John Harrison, and Leslie Conery. 2011. Computational thinking: A digital age skill for everyone. *Learning & Leading with Technology* 38, 6 (Mar-Apr 2011), 20-23.

[9] Jeannette M. Wing. 2010. Computational thinking: What and why?. (November 2010). Retrieved August 30, 2018 from https://www.cs.cmu.edu/~CompThink/resources/TheLinkWing.pdf

[10] Siu-Cheung Kong. 2016. A framework of curriculum design for computational thinking development in K-12 education. *Journal of Computers in Education* 3, 4 (December 2016), 377-394. DOI: https://doi.org/10.1007/s40692-016-0076-z

[11] Shuchi Grover, and Roy Pea. 2013. Computational thinking in K–12: A review of the state of the field. *Educational Researcher* 42, 1 (Jan 2013), 38-43. DOI: https://doi.org/10.3102/0013189x12463051

[12] Samuel Messick. 1994. The interplay of evidence and consequences in the validation of performance assessments. *Educational Researcher* 23, 2 (Mar 1994), 13-23. DOI: https://doi.org/10.2307/1176219

[13] Robert J. Mislevy, Geneva Haertel, Michelle Riconscente, Daisy Wise Rutstein, and Cindy Ziker. 2017. *Assessing Model-Based Reasoning using Evidence-Centered Design.* Springer, Cham. DOI: https://doi.org/10.1007/978-3-319-52246-3

[14] Michael J. Zieky, 2014. An introduction to the use of evidence-centered design in test development. *Psicología Educativa* 20, 2 (Dec 2014), 79-87. DOI: https://doi.org/10.1016/j.pse.2014.11.003

[15] Robert J. Mislevy, Russell G. Almond, and Janice F. Lukas. 2003. A brief introduction to evidence-centered design. *ETS Research Report Series, 1* (Jun 2003), i-29. DOI: https://doi.org/10.1002/j.2333-8504.2003.tb01908.x

[16] Robert J. Mislevy and Geneva D. Haertel. 2006. Implications of evidence-centered design for educational testing. *Educational Measurement: Issues and Practice 25*, 4 (April 2007), 6-20. DOI: https://doi.org/10.1111/j.1745-3992.2006.00075.x

[17] Kristen, Huff, Linda Steinberg, and Thomas Matts. 2010. The promises and challenges of implementing evidence-centered design in large-scale assessment. *Applied Measurement in Education* 23, 4 (Sep 2010), 310-324. DOI: https://doi.org/10.1080/08957347.2010.510956

[18] Valerie J. Shute, Chen Sun, and Jodi Asbell-Clarke. 2017. Demystifying computational thinking. *Educational Research Review* 22 (Nov 2017), 142-158. DOI: https://doi.org/10.1016/j.edurev.2017.09.003

[19] Byeongsu Kim, Taehun Kim, and Jonghoon Kim. 2013. Paper-and-Pencil programming strategy toward computational thinking for non-majors: Design your solution. *Journal of Educational Computing Research* 49, 4 (Dec 2013), 437-459.

[20] Robert J. Mislevy. 2007. Validity by design. *Educational Researcher* 36, 8 (Nov 2007), 463-469. DOI: https://doi.org/10.3102/0013189x07311660

[21] Thomas M. Haladyna (Ed.) and Steven M. Downing (Ed.). 2006. *Handbook of Test Development* (1st ed.). Evidence-centered assessment design. Chapter 4. New York, Routledge. DOI: https://doi.org/10.4324/9780203874776.ch4

[22] Eric Snow, Linda Shear, Daisy Rutstein, Haiwen Wang, Emi Iwatani, Yuning Xu, Satabdi Basu, and Carol Tate. 2017. Baseline Report (Sept., 2017). Retrieved August 15, 2018 from https://www.sri.com/sites/default/files/brochures/coolthink_baseline_report_final_1.pdf

Teaching Accessibility: A Design Exploration of Faculty Professional Development at Scale

Saba Kawas
The Information School | DUB Group
University of Washington
Seattle, Washington
skawas@uw.edu

Laura Vonessen
Paul G. Allen School of Computer Science | DUB Group
University of Washington
Seattle, Washington
laurav4@cs.washington.edu

Andrew J. Ko
The Information School | DUB Group
University of Washington
Seattle, Washington
ajko@uw.edu

ABSTRACT

Most CS students learn little about accessibility in higher education; this is partly because most CS faculty know little about accessibility. Unfortunately, higher education CS faculty lack a model of professional development for learning to teach new topics. Therefore, we investigated the feasibility of a "micro" professional development model for teaching accessibility in CS courses that could be used at scale. We conducted 18 semi-structured interviews with U.S. CS faculty, asking them to explore a prototype of a web-based professional development tool that linked accessibility topics to CS topics. We found that many organizational factors limited faculty's autonomy to integrate accessibility in many of their courses. We also found that individual values and knowledge constrained faculty's ability and willingness to both learn and integrate accessibility topics into their courses. However, many faculty expressed desire to teach accessibility in their courses if they had access to even basic accessibility content and materials to use in their courses.

CCS CONCEPTS

• **Social and professional topics → Computing education programs**; • **Human-centered computing** → *Accessibility theory, concepts and paradigms*;

KEYWORDS

Accessibility; professional development; higher education

ACM Reference Format:
Saba Kawas, Laura Vonessen, and Andrew J. Ko. 2019. Teaching Accessibility: A Design Exploration of Faculty Professional Development at Scale. In *Proceedings of the 50th ACM Technical Symposium on Computer Science Education (SIGCSE '19), February 27-March 2, 2019, Minneapolis, MN, USA.* ACM, New York, NY, USA, 7 pages. https://doi.org/10.1145/3287324.3287399

1 INTRODUCTION

Many companies want to provide accessible products and services, reaching people with a wide range of abilities. To achieve this, companies need software engineers to have knowledge of how to build accessible software. Unfortunately, most software designers and engineers are not taught about accessibility in courses [19], and so many software designers and engineers overlook the accessibility of software products and services.

Fortunately, many CS faculty are open to learning. A recent national survey of higher education CS faculty in the U.S. showed that faculty across most areas of CS are interested in learning how accessibility topics might be integrated into their specific courses [18]. Faculty report three things to teach accessibility part of CS courses: sufficient expertise on accessibility to teach these topics, concrete ideas about how to integrate accessibility into their specific sub-disciplines of CS, and time.

Some efforts have begun to provide these, but not in scalable ways. For example, the Teach Access consortium (teachaccess.org), including Facebook, Microsoft, Google, Adobe, and others, formed in 2016 to advocate for the teaching of accessibility in CS in higher education. It encourages faculty to teach more about accessibility, develops accessibility learning materials, has begun offering professional development workshops for faculty, and has offered small grants to individual faculty willing to update their course materials with accessibility content. And for the small number of earlier adopters, there is a lot of content already. For example, there are resources on accessibility in general [6], materials on accessibility in the context of CS from organizations such as AccessComputing [8] and TeachAccess, and a range of published research ideas on how to integrate accessibility into specific subjects, such as software engineering [9–11], HCI courses [16, 17], and web development [4, 8].

Unfortunately, finding scalable ways to encourage these integrations, and scalable ways to train faculty on the pedagogy required to succeed at teaching them [2, 14, 15], is not straightforward [13, 20]. This problem is not specific to teaching accessibility in CS. In K-12 education, for example, teachers are required to pursue professional development, including evening, weekend, and summer classes to learn new teaching methods, content areas, and techniques for managing classrooms [3]. These mechanisms scale teacher learning by incentivizing or even requiring teachers to improve their practice and learn new content knowledge. And with good reason: high quality professional development can have measurable improvements on both teacher and student learning, and can lead to concrete change in what and how teachers teach [12].

Most higher education faculty have no such external incentive to learn. This means that most change in higher education must come

SIGCSE '19, February 27-March 2, 2019, Minneapolis, MN, USA

ACM ISBN 978-1-4503-5890-3/19/02...$15.00
https://doi.org/10.1145/3287324.3287399

Figure 1: The three stages of interaction in screenshots of our accessibility micro-PD prototype: 1) choosing courses from broad areas, 2) selecting an accessibility learning objective, and 3) learning the accessibility concept and how to teach it.

in small, incremental, well-timed, and individually-led interventions [5]. Administrators have found that incentives and resources are key, but only work when faculty find time to learn and change what they teach [1]. This suggests that even if CS faculty are willing to learn and teach about accessibility, they need resources that are closely integrated with what they already teach, easy to learn, and require no major time commitments. We ask the following research question: how might we provide such professional development about accessibility to higher education CS faculty, in the absence of time and incentives?

In this paper, we explore the feasibility of an idea we call "micro" professional development (micro-PD): a personalized, integrated, and low-commitment approach to teaching accessibility. We describe the micro-PD concept, the content it would require, and the results of an evaluation study of an early prototype of micro-PD prototype at the 2018 SIGCSE Technical Symposium.

2 MICRO PROFESSIONAL DEVELOPMENT

Our vision of accessibility micro-PD is for it to reduce the amount of time it takes for CS faculty to learn about accessibility and integrate concepts into their courses. Our approach was to create a new genre of web-based instruction, in which faculty would visit a website, select courses relevant to their CS teaching expertise, learn accessibility concepts that are specifically relevant to the courses they teach, and then obtain relevant materials to adapt and integrate into their course. The key idea underlying this approach is to create a *mapping* from CS learning objectives to accessibility learning objectives and offer materials that teach these specific links. This approach deviates from conventional forms of teacher professional development, which require faculty to sign up for entire classes or complete online training [3].

Figure 1 portrays our prototype for micro-PD, showing three stages of interaction. The first stage is to identify which learning objectives a teacher has expertise to teach. To streamline this, our prototype used courses as collections of learning objectives, asking faculty to identify which courses they have expertise to teach. While showing individual learning objectives would provide the most granularity, it would pose a high burden, since there are hundreds of learning objectives in CS curricular frameworks like the ACM Computing Curricula. Figure 1 shows the first few of the 19 courses in our list.

The second stage in the prototype is to identify accessibility learning objectives that are relevant to the selected CS learning objectives. Table 1 shows examples of CS learning objectives in specific CS courses that can be mapped to accessibility learning objects for different courses they could teach. For example, in NLP, one can talk about applications of NLP to problems of speech and hearing, and even pose challenges such as recognizing the speech of deaf speakers. Or, in data structures courses, one can use problems that involve representation and translation of Braille characters to Unicode characters.

CS faculty should be expected to know or identify these relevant links independently. We identified them by mining AccessComputing's knowledge base and W3C standards. We also found links from the other direction, examining CS learning objectives from the ACM Computing Curriculum Guidelines and using our accessibility knowledge to identify links that weren't clear in other sources. We interviewed two Computer Science accessibility faculty experts for any additional links and asked them to review the micro-PD content. This resulted in 72 accessibility learning objectives mapped to CS learning objectives.

Through this process, we discovered four types of links between CS and accessibility:

- **Equivalent objectives.** Some accessibility concepts are *equivalent* to CS learning objectives. For example, HCI is about designing computer systems while taking the people who will use them into account; these people will have varying abilities.
- **Accessibility as examples.** Some accessibility topics can be used as examples to illustrate CS concepts. For example, a database course might discuss data modeling problems through disability, which is a good example of a complex, nuanced data type that schemas often oversimplify (is disability binary, enumerated?).

Table 1: Sample of Mapping Accessibility Topics to Learning Objectives in CS Courses

Computer Science Course	Learning Objective Example
Computer Vision	Students should know how (1) optical character recognition (OCR) can recover textual information from scanned text, which is useful for blind and people with low vision, and that (2) object recognition can help automatically generate ALT text for existing images on the Internet.
Programming Languages	Students should know that people who are blind can read and write code using screen readers because screen readers navigate hierarchies, and program's abstract syntax trees are inherently hierarchical.
Networks	Students should know that many communication technologies were motivated by the needs of people with disabilities. For example, the modem was invented to transmit text over phone lines for people who are deaf [7].
Natural Language Processing (NLP)	Students should know that the quality of speech recognition algorithms depends on the quality of the data used to train them, and that such data should include people who are deaf, hard of hearing, or include speech impediments.
Visualization	Students should know that nearly 8.5% of people are color blind, and therefore color choices in visualizations can impact what is perceptible.
Robotics	Students should know that many of the primary applications of robotics are in assistive contexts for people with motor impairments, such as robotic walkers, intelligent artificial limbs, and autonomous vehicles.
Data structures	Students should know that text can be represented in many different ways, including popular encodings such as ASCII and Unicode, but also Braille and sign language.
Algorithms	Students should know that accessibility poses many grand challenges in algorithms, such as efficiently transmitting high frame rate of sign language video and finding walking routes for people with mobility issues.
Introduction to programming	Students should know that the syntax of a language is different than its semantics, and can learn this by learning how programmers who are blind read and comprehend code independent of its syntax.
Software engineering	Students should know that accessibility frameworks are an exemplar of *code reuse*, since they can take care of many of the accessibility concerns for you when used properly. For example, default buttons in an Android application can expose information to the android screen reader without you having to write your own screen reader.
Human Computer Interaction	Students should know what accessibility is, how it relates to user interface design, how to design and implement accessible interfaces, and how different disabilities can be supported through universal and ability-based design principles.

- **Accessibility as context**. Some accessibility knowledge serves as historical context for CS. For example, text messaging has its origins in TTY, a way deaf people used to transmit text over phone lines, which was made possible by a modem that deaf physicist Robert H. Weitbrecht invented [7].
- **Accessibility as motivating problems**. Accessibility problems can prompt interesting applications of core CS topics. For example, people who are deaf can benefit greatly from real-time captioning, which is a grand challenge for real-time natural language processing.

After stage two identifies relevant accessibility learning objectives, the last step is teaching the instructor the accessibility concepts and providing examples for how to integrate them into the teaching of the CS learning objective. Figure 1 shows an example of a mapping that results from choosing Algorithms course, linking the learning objective of understanding data compression to the accessibility problem of achieving high fidelity video for streaming sign language. Our vision is for the micro-PD to include all the links we identified and course materials such as slides to teach the concept to students in class. For this paper, our prototype contained 36 mappings distributed across 19 courses, but no course materials.

3 FEASIBILITY EVALUATION

To investigate whether the micro-PD content we described in the previous section is sufficient to support faculty learning and integration of accessibility concepts. We designed a feasibility study in which we would simulate a cold outreach to random CS faculty and observe their response to our prototype and its content. While distributing emails would have most closely mimicked our intended deployment at scale, this would have made it difficult to richly capture faculty's in situ responses. Therefore, we instead planned a study at the 2018 ACM SIGCSE Technical Symposium on Computer Science Education, where many CS faculty go to learn about new insights from the research on and practice of CS teaching and learning. Our approach was to find faculty during breaks and meals, ask them for 10-15 minutes of their time to learn about teaching accessibility, and elicit their reactions. In the rest of this section, we detail our method and describe our results.

3.1 Method

Of the 1,753 attendees at SIGCSE 2018, we approached 40, either between sessions, or at the end of three sessions about accessibility,

Table 2: Participant demographics

Gender	Male (12), Female (6)
Department	Computer Science (14), Department of Electrical and Computer Engineering (2) College of Cyber (1), Creative and Applied Computing/Math (1)
Title (some w/ multiple roles)	Professor (3), Associate Professor (6), Assistant Professor (3), Instructional Assistant Professor (1), Instructor (3), Associate Dean (1), Chair (1), Research Scientist (2), Sr. Software engineer (1)
Years of teaching experience	1-5 (3), 6-10 (5), 11-15 (4), 16-20 (3), 21-25 (2), 26+ (1)
Knowledge of accessibility (self-reported)	Not knowledgeable (4), Some knowledge (10), Knowledgeable (4), Expert (0)
Main Role	Teaching (15), Research (9), Administration (6), Software development (1)
Expertise areas (some with multiple)	HCI (4), CS education (3), Software engineering (2), Web development (2), AI and machine learning (2), Networks (2), Intro programming (2), Systems (2), Programming languages(1), Algorithms (1), Cybersecurity (1), GIS (1), Project management (1), Computational Science and Engineering (1), Computational optimization (1), Databases (1), Computer organization (1), Bio-informatics (1), Operating systems (1), Honey bee technology (1), Embedded systems (1), Complexity (1)
Class size	1-10 (1), 11-20 (2), 21-30 (8), 31-40 (2), 80 (1), 100 (1), 120 (1), 200 (1), 500 (1)
Course level	Lower-level undergraduate (9), Upper-level undergraduate (7), Masters (1), Ph.D. (1)

which attracted attendees interested in learning to teach about accessibility and teaching inclusively. Of the 40, 12 declined (due to lack of time, interest, or perceived relevance of accessibility), or did not attend our scheduled time, and 10 did not meet our inclusion criteria, having never served as a CS instructor in higher education. This left 18 faculty participants, of which 6 were women. We stopped recruiting when the issues that faculty raised were no longer new, as our goal was to identify the range of reactions, but not their prevalence.

Faculty had 2 to 49 years of teaching experience (median 12) and ranged from lecturers to full professors, including an associate dean and a department chair. Their main duties included teaching (15), research (9), administration (6), and software development (1). Only 4 reported being knowledgeable about accessibility. Faculty had expertise in 22 distinct CS areas, from theoretical areas such as complexity theory to applied areas such as web development and software engineering. Class sizes and levels varied (11 with 30 students or less, four with 100 or more). The resulting sample therefore captured a diversity of contexts, topics, and expertise of CS faculty. Table 2 has detailed participants' information.

When an instructor agreed to participate, we began by asking them to think of the next course they are or would prepare for in the next couple of months. We had them imagine they just received an email from their department chair encouraging them to take a look at our micro-PD web-based tool to decide whether it would be useful to them. We encouraged faculty to start with that specific course in mind, but if our prototype did not include that course, to explore the course closest to their expertise. While they used the micro-PD site, we audio- and video-recorded their interactions and prompted them to think aloud about their reactions to the content, and asking clarifying questions. If faculty were silent for too long, we asked them what they were thinking, or to elaborate on interactions we could not interpret. After they were done exploring, we performed a semi-structured interview asking about the potential barriers and support needed to use this tool, as well as to explore issues that came up during the think-aloud while using the micro-PD prototype. We also asked about the broader issues of motivation, expectations, and constraints that might prevent them from using this tool and any ideas to improve it. After the interview was complete, we had instructors fill out a demographic survey. Interactions with faculty ranged from 13 to 26 minutes.

3.2 Results

To analyze the transcripts, field notes, and video, primary and secondary researchers used deductive coding with continuous comparative analysis, developing a codebook to identify feasibility issues with our accessibility micro-PD. The researchers independently coded statements from the transcripts against these codes and then discussed disagreements with the themes to further refine them. We followed Hammer and Berland's [5] best practices on qualitative coding, not treating the coding results as data but as an organization of claims about the data. Therefore, we focused more on deeply discussing and resolving disagreements between codes than achieving inter-rater reliability of coding.

Overall, faculty's reaction to the concept of micro-PD was positive. They liked the idea of having access to teaching materials that would be easily integrated into their current courses. That said, there were numerous barriers they saw before such a vision would be viable. At the high level, these ranged from extrinsic factors such as institutional context and policy, the curricular factors that constrained course changes, individual faculty constraints, and perspectives on the micro-PD content itself.

3.2.1 Organizational constraints. Several of the reactions that faculty expressed concerned organizational factors that constrained or influenced their course preparation decisions. For example, as faculty viewed the content, one point of tension some faculty surfaced were the ACM curricula recommendations, and how they constrained adoption. There were varying degrees to which faculty felt the standard constrained them or was relevant when preparing their courses:

> When we revise our curriculum, we go to the ACM guidelines and make sure that we're matching that. When I'm designing a course I don't do that, but when you're revising a curriculum you do.

In at least some cases, this distinction was because courses simply were not included in the ACM curricula recommendations, such as "Intelligent game-based learning environments" or "Accessibility."

The lack of visibility of accessibility in the ACM curricula (only mentioned in the two knowledge areas HCI and Social Issues and Professional Practice [19]), was also mentioned as problematic. In particular, this instructor was discussing her technique of mentioning accessibility at a high-level in introductory courses and whether this was part of the ACM recommendations:

> There's ACM guidelines that sort of tell you what you should be covering... I've not looked at those guidelines in a while, but...I doubt that [it is].

Even when faculty could see how accessibility fit, many instructors commented that courses were already full of required topics, with no room to add on anything extra without having to take something else out:

> [This material] would have to embed without adding extra time because all of us have courses that are already crammed in there.

Even when faculty saw ways of integrating accessibility content without adding content, and they personally wanted to integrate it, many shared that department policies constrained them. For example, some of the content suggested discussing more accessible languages such as the Quorum programming language [17]:

> We use C++ and I don 't have any control over...that

Other faculty perceived more intellectual freedom in their choices of what and how to teach CS learning objectives:

> There's nothing at an institutional level—I'm not being handcuffed by..some kind of departmental restrictions on what I teach in the course.

Some faculty felt they had freedom but feared they would not have support. In one case, an accessibility topic was even a required topic in a course, but the instructor felt he did not have enough support in how to teach it and so did not. In some cases, department, university, and student values interacted with faculty's willingness to integrate content:

> The...university has an objective what that class needs to cover, but then the students [also] have an objective of what they want to get out of the class ... To what extent, of that limited time, would it be appropriate to spend discussing these [accessibility] topics?

Some instructors mentioned that being able to show students concrete examples that companies are interested in accessibility can be a way of catching their interest.

> If I were to show this and say, "Hey, you know even Microsoft thinks this is important," and they see the little logo on that...they can get excited about that.

3.2.2 Individual constraints. While faculty viewed organizational and course constraints as unavoidable, they also lamented their own personal values, knowledge and resources constraints.

Not surprisingly, many of the faculty said that they were far too limited in their own time to prepare for teaching, research, and other academic and service duties to have time to innovate in teaching:

> Time would be an issue ... you're fighting fires all the time.

More surprisingly, however, was that some faculty were simply worried that they would forget that such a resource exists or never find it. Some faculty suggested needing multiple reminders about the content or having multiple broadcasts on the SIGCSE mailing list for lists of resources. One instructor mentioned that while in the process of preparing for an algorithms course it wouldn't occur to him to look for a resource on accessibility, but if it were part of a collected list of resources on teaching algorithms he would be more likely to stumble across it.

While most reported needing time, and most faculty reported having little knowledge about accessibility, many were enthusiastic about the potential of the micro-PD tool to provide them sufficient expertise. One faculty, for example, who had only 5 years of teaching experience, and no knowledge of accessibility, started generating ideas for an accessibility assignment after learning some of the basic concepts in accessibility:

> Our CS 2 is where we do like object-oriented stuff, so you could say, "Here's a generic compression thing," and then, "Okay, now what about specialized kinds of compressions?" And then also highlight [to] them that accessibility portion, too... Use it as an introduction to a new topic slash introduction to an assignment for them...I think it would make a cool assignment.

The value faculty saw in teaching accessibility varied. For example, one instructor was interested in learning more about accessibility for a course which included web development topics, but skeptical about its relevance to the operating systems course he taught. Others were more enthusiastic or even already taught accessibility courses or were in the process of putting one together. When faculty did not see or agree with a link between their topic and accessibility, some saw this as a sign that accessibility wasn't relevant to their version of the course, while others enjoyed the serendipity of seeing new ideas.

> I hadn't thought about this... I would definitely incorporate it...that's what I use these things for, sparking ideas.

3.2.3 Reactions to content. One clear pattern that emerged when faculty engaged in the content was that they would likely not use it without modification. Some faculty mentioned that they often get materials from their faculty colleagues, and so getting recommendations with links to examples from our micro-PD would be ideal. All faculty said that even when borrowing content, they would adapt it to their own use. In reference to the content in our micro-PD tool:

> [Slides] would have to be customized a little bit, but that would be fine.

Some faculty noted that many courses with the same titles have dramatically different content, and so organizing accessibility topics by courses often led to misalignments. For example, a course on programming languages might be about a specific programming language, language theory in general, or it could be about the design of new programming languages. Some faculty recommended adding faceted browsing features to help them narrow down to the set of learning objectives most relevant to their course:

> You might consider ... helping them filter into what their area is to get that set of things versus trying to come at the course level where you may have missed something.

Faculty also wanted significantly more motivation for why accessibility was relevant to the course, and why it was relevant to students:

> How do I naturally bring up those topics so it doesn't feel like it's forced or artificial?

Most instructors felt a need for more information on where these accessibility topics came from, although not always for the same reasons. Some wanted to verify licensing issues, asking about Creative Commons licenses for the content. Others wanted to verify that the content was developed by a legitimate, credible source of expertise. One wanted to be able to learn more about accessibility topics to be prepared for student questions, and a few wanted to share links with students so they could find out more on their own.

> It may be something that they fall back on... Say they present the slides, a student asks an annoying but actually really good question [and] I'm stumped—I'm going to go back and dig into the deeper stuff.

Nearly all faculty desired for course materials provided by the tool to go beyond just slides. Faculty mentioned many possibilities, such as activities, assignments, homework or exam problems, projects, videos, simulations, examples, and data sets.

Some faculty expressed confusion about the audience of the tool. For example, one at first interpreted the content being presented to the instructor as a handout for students, and others wanted to be able to direct students directly to the tool for flipped classroom activities.

> Since I usually use a flipped classroom, I would like to know if this would be suitable for the students to view on their own and then if there are activities that I can use in the classroom.

Other faculty thought this tool would be a way to make their courses accessible for students with disabilities. This repeats a fundamental confusion that Shinohara et al. also discussed [18], which one instructor articulated in the following way:

> Maybe at the high level there's two branches of, "How do you make your own content accessible?" and, "How do you teach accessibility to others?" Having that be clear—that's where I got confused, but ... both of those things are of interest.

4 DISCUSSION

While our data show that the faculty in our sample viewed the idea of micro-PD as promising and valuable, many complex factors constrained their willingness and ability to change course content. These exist at many different levels: curricular frameworks narrow their choices, departmental values create fear of change, and faculty's own busy schedules limit the time they are willing to engage with even small amounts of professional development. We also observed divergent reactions to our preliminary content, with some faculty finding it highly useful and informative, while others could not imagine how to adapt it to their needs.

Some limitations in our prototype and evaluation hinder our ability to interpret the results. One factor is in who we were able to recruit. SIGCSE attendees may be more open to learning about teaching and changing their instruction. Some of the faculty we approached declined to participate due to lack of interest or doubt that accessibility topics could be relevant to the courses they teach. Additionally, faculty we recruited at the accessibility sessions were more motivated about accessibility. Another factor is that some courses had more accessibility content than others. We also didn't evaluate the tool at scale and whether faculty would be motivated to use it. While one of the main micro-PD goals is to provide accessibility materials that are delivered on-line in an organized and small chunks to make it digestible and easy to access by faculty who don't have time. We did not quite mimic someone receiving an email with a link to the content, so some faculty may not have explored independently as much as they did in our face-to-face interactions.

Although there are limitations on our interpretation, our results do show the range of reactions to the concept of micro-PD for teaching accessibility, and the flexibility it would require to serve this range. Micro-PD would need both more content and a range of course material formats for integration to support the diversity of teaching styles that exist. Additionally, because most faculty were likely more motivated to engage because of the conference and the face-to-face interactions in our study, the bar for polished, highly personalized, and highly adaptable web-based content is likely higher than our results might suggest.

These interpretations suggest several avenues for future research. First, we need further investigation into precisely how to structure and present content so it is easy to integrate and appropriate. A more detailed case study of faculty use of content could elicit these requirements. Second, with enough content ready for adoption, a pilot deployment to CS faculty would also reveal to what extent the findings in this study would also occur in the even more complex reality of daily faculty life.

While more research is needed, our data does show that there are already faculty who are motivated to teach accessibility, and would find even basic materials such as the ones we shared more than adequate to get started. If we can come together as a community to develop this content, building a community of accessibility experts to fully express the micro-PD vision in this paper, we may be able to reach an order of magnitude more CS faculty than currently teach accessibility. And with this effort, we can reach more students, and therefore more end users, with more accessible software.

ACKNOWLEDGMENTS

The authors would like to thank all the faculty who participated in our evaluative study at SIGCSE 2018. The project was approved by the Institutional Review Board IRB ID STUDY00004124. This work is supported by National Science Foundation Grants 1539179, 1314399, 1240786, 1153625, and Microsoft, Google, Adobe.

REFERENCES

[1] M. Besterfield-Sacre, M. B. Monica F Cox, K. Beddoes, and J. Zhu. 2014. Changing engineering education: Views of US faculty, chairs, and deans. *Journal of Engineering Education* 103, 2 (2014), 193–219. https://doi.org/10.1002/jee.20043

[2] K. E. Bigelow. 2012. Designing for success: Developing engineers who consider universal design principles. *Journal of Postsecondary Education and Disability* 25, 3 (2012), 211–225.

[3] H. Borko. 2004. Professional development and teacher learning: Mapping the terrain. *Educational Researcher* 33, 8 (2004), 3–15. https://doi.org/10.3102/0013189X033008003

[4] J.Rosmaita Brian. [n. d.]. Accessibility first!: a new approach to web design. ACM SIGCSE Bulletin.

[5] W. Dennis. 2001. Teaching science in higher education: Faculty professional development and barriers to change. *School Science and Mathematics* 101, 5 (2001), 246–257. https://doi.org/10.1111/j.1949-8594.2001.tb18027.x

[6] E. A. Draffan, M. Wald, K. Dickens, G. Zimmermann, S. Kelle, K. Miesenberger, and A. Petz. 2015. Stepwise approach to accessible MOOC development. *Studies in Health Technology and Informatics* 217 (2015), 227–234.

[7] ITU News-Accessibility for all. June,2011. How the deaf developed a phone of their own. International Telecommunication Union News. https://www.itu.int/net/itunews/issues/2011/05/36.aspx Last accessed 16 April 2018.

[8] A. J. Ko, R. E. Ladner, Andrew J Ko, and Richard E Ladner. 2016. AccessComputing Promotes Teaching Accessibility. *ACM Inroads* 7, 4 (2016), 65–68. https://doi.org/10.1145/2968453

[9] Stephanie Ludi. 2002. Access for everyone: introducing accessibility issues to students in Internet programming courses. https://doi.org/10.1109/FIE.2002.1158617

[10] Stephanie Ludi. 2007. Introducing accessibility requirements through external stakeholder utilization in an undergraduate requirements engineering course.. In *Proceedings of the 29th International Conference on Software Engineering*. 736–743. https://doi.org/10.1109/ICSE.2007.46

[11] Israel Martin-Escalona, Francisco Barcelo-Arroyo, and Enrica Zola. 2013. The introduction of a topic on accessibility in several engineering degrees.. In *Global Engineering Education Conference (EDUCON)*. 656–663. https://doi.org/10.1109/EduCon.2013.6530177

[12] C. Mouza. 2009. Does research-based professional development make a difference? A longitudinal investigation of teacher learning in technology integration. *Teachers College Record* 111, 5 (2009), 1195–1241.

[13] Bohma Paul. [n. d.]. Teaching accessibility and design-for-all in the information and communication technology curriculum: Three case studies of universities in the United States, England, and Austria.

[14] Cynthia Putnam, Maria Dahman, Emma Rose, Jinghui Cheng, and Glenn Bradford. 2015. Teaching Accessibility, Learning Empathy.. In *Proceedings of the 17th International ACM SIGACCESS Conference on Computers & Accessibility*. 333–334. https://doi.org/10.1145/2700648.2811365

[15] Cynthia Putnam, Maria Dahman, Emma Rose, Jinghui Cheng, and Glenn Bradford. 2016. https://doi.org/10.1145/2831424

[16] Kristen Shinohara. 2016. Cynthia L Bennett, and Jacob O Wobbrock.. In *Proceedings of the 18th International ACM SIGACCESS Conference on Computers and Accessibility*. 229–237. https://doi.org/10.1145/2982142.2982158

[17] Kristen Shinohara. 2017. Teaching Accessibility in a Technology Design Course.. In *12th International Conference on Computer Supported Collaborative Learning (CSCL)*. International Society of the Learning Sciences, Philadelphia, PA.

[18] Kristen Shinohara, Saba Kawas, Andrew J. Ko, and Richard E. Ladner. 2018.

[19] C. Velasco et al. 2004. IDCnet: inclusive design curriculum network – first results. https://doi.org/10.1007/978-3-540-27817-7{_}16

[20] Annalu Waller. 2009. Vicki L Hanson, and David Sloan.. In *Proceedings of the 11th international ACM SIGACCESS conference on Computers and accessibility*. 155–162.

Utilizing the Affinity Research Group Model in a Summer Research Experience for Undergraduates Program

Ben Jelen
Indiana University
Bloomington, Indiana
bcjelen@indiana.edu

Julia Dunbar
University of Washington
Seattle, Washington
jcd17@uw.edu

Susan Monsey
Indiana University
Bloomington, Indiana
skmonsey@iu.edu

Olivia K. Richards
Pennsylvania State University
University Park, Pennsylvania
orichards@psu.edu

Katie A. Siek
Indiana University
Bloomington, Indiana
ksiek@indiana.edu

ABSTRACT

In this paper, we describe how we integrated the Affinity Research Group (ARG) model into a 10-week summer research experience for undergraduates (REU) over the last three years. Each summer, ten REU students participated in: an annual two-day team-building orientation; a four day long ramp-up session to learn about REU projects and the skill sets they would need to master; weekly meetings with graduate and faculty mentors to define objectives, deliverables, and progress; and weekly skill development workshops to learn how to conduct research, prepare for future endeavors, and present oneself in professional settings. A total of seven faculty and twelve graduate students participated in ARG model process meetings to ensure students received comparable experiences and facilitated professional development activities. We provide an overview of our REU ARG model experience and reflect on improvements based on faculty mentor, graduate mentor, and undergraduate researchers' experiences.

CCS CONCEPTS

• **Social and professional topics → Computing education; Computing education programs;** • **Applied computing → Health informatics;**

KEYWORDS

Research Experience for Undergraduates (REU); Affinity Research Group (ARG) model; mentoring

ACM Reference Format:

Ben Jelen, Julia Dunbar, Susan Monsey, Olivia K. Richards, and Katie A. Siek. 2019. Utilizing the Affinity Research Group Model in a Summer Research Experience for Undergraduates Program. In *Proceedings of the 50th ACM Technical Symposium on Computer Science Education (SIGCSE '19), February 27-March 2, 2019, Minneapolis, MN, USA.* ACM, New York, NY, USA, 7 pages. https://doi.org/10.1145/3287324.3287501

SIGCSE '19, February 27-March 2, 2019, Minneapolis, MN, USA

ACM ISBN 978-1-4503-5890-3/19/02...$15.00
https://doi.org/10.1145/3287324.3287501

1 INTRODUCTION

Research experiences for undergraduates (REUs) are valuable from a student, faculty, and university perspective [23]. More recently, REUs have been recognized as a valuable graduate student opportunity [1, 11]. REUs can improve undergraduate retention in STEM – especially in underrepresented and first generation college student groups [4, 13]. Undergraduate researchers learn about critical thinking, communication skills, grit, and comfort with uncertainty [23, 29] – although the uncertainty must be appropriately scaffolded within a well planned research experience [8, 30]. Faculty can improve their teaching, mentoring, and provide applied learning experiences to students while building on their own research agendas [23] by iteratively collaborating with graduate student mentors to provide a personalized undergraduate research experience [30]. In addition, faculty learn to mentor students from diverse backgrounds while possibly addressing their own biases [4] if gender equity programming is available [14]. Graduate students, who are being trained as near-future scholars and major contributors to scientific knowledge, are not well investigated in their role as REU mentors [1] – despite faculty reporting that they learned on their own how to mentor researchers [4]. Finally, universities improve scientific contributions [23], student engagement [4], and community outreach through REUs.

Undergraduate researcher experiences are dependent on how the undergraduate is immersed in an organized program with a developed social, scholarly group culture [4, 8]. In addition, undergraduate researchers must feel they are contributing in a well scaffolded research project that will make contributions to a scientific community [4] while also aligning with their cultural, contextual, political, and desires to serve the broader community [15, 29]. In this experience report, we contribute: (1) an overview of how the Affinity Research Group (ARG) model was applied to Indiana University's 10-week summer ProHealth REU site and (2) qualitative experiences of undergraduate researchers, faculty mentors [4], and the less studied, but integral graduate student mentor perspectives.

The ProHealth REU site provided a diverse cohort of 30 undergraduate scholars with opportunities to contribute to health and computing communities through research dissemination and continue on in their academic pursuits with dedicated mentorship by seven faculty and twelve graduate student mentors.

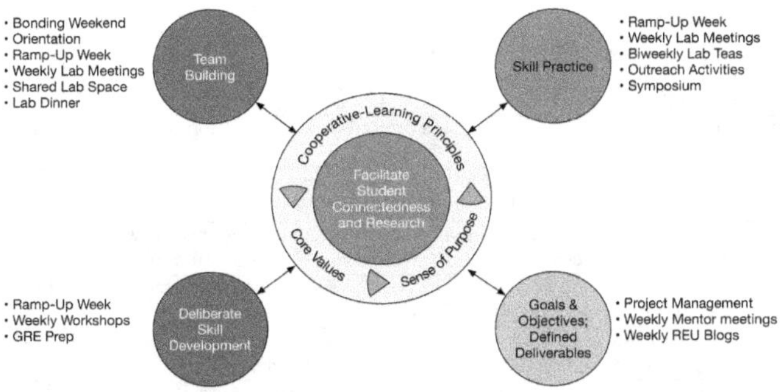

Figure 1: Affinity Research Group Model elements adapted from [8, 32] with our REU site activities listed near each element.

2 BACKGROUND

Since the ProHealth REU site engages undergraduates in interdisciplinary research, we aimed to extend project-based learning, which has been successfully applied to interdisciplinary undergraduate research endeavors [9], so that students could transition from practitioner to apprentice to researcher. Dahlberg et al. successfully applied situated learning theory to fully immerse undergraduates in a community of practice and integrate them into a research community [6], however we were unsure how to integrate the theory. Villa et al. mapped how situated learning theory elements relate to ARG model experiences [32] which has been shown to successfully develop a cooperative computing research experience [8, 31, 32].

Thus, we we utilized the Affinity Research Group model where faculty and graduate student mentors share their *affinity* for their research to undergraduate students. The mentors guide undergraduate researchers in developing new skills so that each research team member – including the undergraduate researcher with a diverse background – becomes a subject-matter expert. With their new expertise, undergraduate researchers become equal contributors to the research group [8]. The ARG model is composed of four main elements: team building; deliberate skill development; skill practice; and goals and objectives with accompanying defined deliverables [32]. These elements are often accompanied with close mentor-student interactions, professional development, and communication skills. When all of these elements become routine, they become part of the lab culture that empowers research team members to implement what they have learned into research progress [8].

3 REU SITE OVERVIEW

The main intellectual pursuit for the ProHealth REU site at Indiana University was to develop undergraduates from diverse backgrounds into scholars who can contribute to the design, development, and evaluation of pervasive systems that empower lay people to proactively manage their health and wellness. Students were fully engaged in cross-cutting computing research that can solve real world health problems and make an impact on people's lives – two factors that have been shown to attract underrepresented groups in computing [19, 20]. The ProHealth REU provided students with a unique opportunity to learn techniques in the areas of human computer interaction (HCI), health informatics, pervasive computing (mobile or wearable), environmental sensing (ambient and on-body), machine learning, and the social and legal implications of these technologies.

3.1 Administration

Our REU site was led by a principal investigator (PI) who coordinated with a school-level assistant dean and external evaluator. The assistant dean assisted with recruitment, coordinating with university-level undergraduate research summer programs, and logistics including student travel, social activities, orientation, room and board, and university-level accounts (e.g., building access cards, stipend payments, and email). The experienced external evaluator assessed the REU site by facilitating interviews at the start and end of the REU, administering the CISE Common REU Evaluation Toolkit [28], administering site-specific surveys pre, mid, and post experience, and coordinating with our service-learning collaborators to assess the impact of the REU site's service activities. The PI also recruited and trained faculty and graduate student mentors, recruited and coordinated training for the undergraduate researchers, and followed up with all REU site stakeholders. Faculty and graduate student mentors utilized materials from the ARG model [8, 31, 32] to become effective mentors who engendered a supportive, collaborative research community that provided students with diverse abilities the opportunity to learn research skills while making scientific, research contributions.

3.2 Site Demographics

Since 2016, the REU site has trained and funded 30 undergraduate researchers, trained 10 research group affiliated undergraduate researchers funded through federal and internal programs, and trained 47 school-affiliated undergraduate researchers who were funded similarly. All affiliated undergraduate researchers participated in the same training workshops led by our REU site mentors and social experiences led by the assistant dean. Thus, our REU site benefited our school by providing training, social, and administrative programming resources.

The ProHealth REU site was committed to diversifying computing research experiences for traditionally underserved groups where 87% (26/30) of participants were from groups traditionally underrepresented in computing (73% (22/30) women, 37% (11/30) underrepresented minority (URM) groups, and 33% (10/30) first generation college students). The ProHealth REU site's participants were more diverse than 30 REU sites reported in 2016 where 42% were women and 34% were from URM groups [29]. In the ProHealth REU, 56% (17/30) were from liberal arts or commuter universities.

3.3 Experience

The ProHealth REU site experience immersed five pairs of undergraduates in a 10-week research community with collective mentoring from graduate students and faculty following the ARG model as shown in Figure 1 with accompanying activities in Table 1. In this section, we bolded ***ARG model elements*** and italicized our *REU site activities* that fulfilled these elements.

Each summer, we kicked off the REU site with a leadership and team development weekend for ***team building*** at a local adventure education facility. After the *bonding weekend*, undergraduate

W	Activities	Deliverables
1	Leadership and Team Dev. Bonding Weekend(TB); Orientation(TB); Ramp-up Week sessions(TB, SD, SP); ARG review; Tea: Elevator Pitches(SP); LM(TB, SP)	Ramp-up Assignments; Blog posts
2	WW: Reading papers and documenting(SD); LM(TB, SP)	Paper: Related Work and Methods outlines; Blog post
3	WW: Writing Research Papers(SD); Tea: Improv Communication(SP);Mentor Update Meeting; GRE Prep(SD); LM(TB, SP)	Paper: Related Work and Methods drafted and Introduction outline; Blog post
4	WW: Online Presence(SD); Outreach Activity(SP); GRE Prep(SD); LM(TB)	Paper: Related Work and Methods peer review, Introduction draft, Abstract outline; Web Presence: drafted; Blog post
5	WW: Graduate Admissions(SD); Tea: Inclusion and Diversity(SP); Lab dinner(TB); GRE Prep(SD); LM(TB, SP)	Paper: Related Work and Methods final, Introduction peer review, Abstract draft, Findings and Discussion outlines; Web presence: Iterate on draft; Blog post
6	WW: Presenting Research(SD); Evaluator Update to Mentors; GRE Prep(SD); LM(TB, SP)	Paper: Introduction draft, Abstract peer review, Findings and Discussion drafts; Web Presence: final; Lightning Talk: draft; Blog post
7	WW: Networking and Imposter Syndrome(SD); Tea: Lightning Talks(SP); Outreach Activity(SP); GRE Prep(SD); LM(TB, SP)	Paper: Introduction final, Abstract draft, Findings and Discussion peer reviews; Project Video: storyboard; Poster: sketch; Blog post
8	WW: Poster Review(SD, SP); GRE Prep(SD); LM(TB, SP)	Paper: Abstract peer review, Findings and Discussion drafts; Project Video: draft; Poster: draft; Blog post
9	WW: Researching Remotely(SD); Tea: Future Plans(SD); GRE Prep(SD); LM(TB, SP)	Paper: Abstract final, Findings and Discussion final; Project Video: final; Poster: iterate on draft; Blog post
10	WW: Industry Research Careers(SD); Poster Symposium(SP); Mentor debrief	Paper: final; Web Presence: final; Poster: final; Blog post

Table 1: Week by week schedule of our REU site. The ARG activity categories are team building (TB), skill development (SD), and skill practice (SP). The fourth ARG category – deliverables – is separated out into its own column. WW indicates weekly workshop professional development topics. LM indicates weekly lab meetings.

researchers moved into a *shared living space.* Mentors regularly met in preparation for the REU by iteratively developing research summaries for students based on ARG model activities [31]. Summaries included research project goals, student profile, tasks, deliverables, and benefits for the student, researchers, and research community.

For undergraduates, the first week started with *orientation* where they learned about the university and research group before starting ramp-up week. Since students were from diverse backgrounds with varying skill sets and research experience, undergraduates were not assigned to research projects before arriving. Instead, we gave them a glimpse into the different projects and skill sets they would master for each project during a week-long intensive session. This "ramp-up week" gave students the opportunity to decide if they wanted to dive deeper into statistics to be proficient at machine learning or work with older adults in a user study. *Ramp-up week* consisted of short, 30-90 minute sessions that provided students with basic research training (e.g., ethics training, finding related work), lab expectations, program aims, short academic presentations highlighting research projects, and project-specific skill training workshops. Students received short assignments to ***practice skills*** each night and blog about. Meanwhile, faculty and graduate student mentors taught the workshops and had an opportunity to work with the undergraduate researchers. At the end of the week, the undergraduates submitted their top three research project choices. Mentors met to assign undergraduates in pairs to projects based on their preferences and how the undergraduates did on their assignments. The week culminated in our first of five *lab working teas* where undergraduates gave elevator pitches about their research project.

Undergraduates worked together in a *shared lab space* near the faculty and graduate student mentors' offices, but with the flexibility to work in reserved breakout rooms or nearby research smart homes. Faculty and graduate student mentors collaboratively worked with REU students in at least *weekly meetings* on *project management* to ***define research goals***, outline specific tasks, and develop a timeline that was iterated on throughout the summer. Students became familiar with the project through scholarly readings, continued tutorials, and guided task-based learning during the first few weeks. Once students developed a deeper understanding of the problem space and began to master skills, students continued working on their research tasks to help them mature into *independent scholars* who contributed to the larger projects. Mentors coordinated with interested undergraduates on how to continue the research at their home institution through independent studies after the REU.

Undergraduates ***developed skills*** at mentor-taught *weekly workshops* where students learned research and professional development skills. Weekly workshops were scheduled so that students learned each skill within a week of applying it to their deliverables.

Research teams created a mix of ***deliverables*** that provided students the opportunity to ***practice their professional oral, written, and multi-media-based communication skills***. Students iteratively wrote a conference-quality paper. The papers were peer-reviewed by mentors and fellow undergraduate researchers so that undergraduates not only received feedback on their own paper, but they could learn from their colleagues' papers. Students developed a professional web presence via a website with a C.V., social media, and video that summarized their research contributions. Students learned to professionally present their research via presentations at *weekly lab meetings and lab teas* and posters at an end-of-summer symposium. Students documented their experience in their *weekly blog posts* to reflect on how they developed as a researcher and to assist the mentors and leadership team identify how to better support the developing scholars.

Undergraduates and mentors *practiced their computing skills* and gave back to the public by leading two two-hour long *outreach activities* during the summer. Activities included teaching middle school and high school campers and older adults at an adult-education event about circuitry via a paper circuit activity [25].

3.4 Site Results

The ProHealth REU site external evaluator administered pre- and post-program Computer and Informatics Sciences and Engineering (CISE) REU Toolkit assessments for the purpose of evaluating the effectiveness of the CISE REU program [28]. The evaluation team matched most of the REU site's pre-program and post-program assessment data (2016, N=9; 2017, N=8) based on those who provided identifying information and then ran a non-parametric Wilcoxon analysis test to assess for significant differences among assessment categories. ProHealth REUs improvement in research self-efficacy (M=4.56) was statistically significant than pre-program values (M=3.82), Z=-3.30, p=.001. In addition, the mean post-program values for Research Skills (M=4.412) were statistically significantly higher than mean pre-program values (M=3.39), Z=-2.55, p=.011. ProHealth REUs had better mean gains than the 2017 cohort of 38 REU sites in research self-efficacy, grit, and leadership [26]. During pre- and post-interviews with ProHealth REUs, we found that their experience helped them: (1) learn about new fields in computing that they otherwise had not been exposed to (e.g., HCI, machine learning, and health informatics); (2) mature in their understanding of research from a "solve a problem" mentality to research as a collaborative, iterative process; and (3) become enthusiastic about conducting research to improve the lives of others.

We surveyed mentors[1] over the 3 years (N=27) to assess the load of advising REUs and mutual benefits since our program has engaged four junior faculty to lead six projects during the first three years. During a "normal week," most mentors spent over 3 hours advising REU students and 1-2 hours prepping for these meetings. Faculty mentors spent 1-2 hours a week mentoring graduate students on how to advise undergraduates. All mentors said that their time was well spent and 60% (N=16) of mentors thought that their research with REUs would result in a publication. All mentors taught students skills and engaged socially with REUs (e.g., lunch).

Seven out of eight REUs who have graduated have gone on to graduate school – twenty-two are still working on their undergraduate degrees in various fields – from computer science to mathematics to health policy and political science. Of those still working on their degrees, nine reported obtaining research experiences in subsequent summers. One REU completed her MS and recently started a PhD Program – for a total of four REU students currently enrolled in PhD programs.

Site REUs and research group affiliated REUs have contributed to seven full conference papers [3, 10, 12, 16, 18, 22, 24] - including 3 highly competitive conferences [3, 16, 18] and a best paper award [24]. In addition, they have presented 3 workshop papers [2, 7, 21] and placed in the ACM Undergraduate Research Competition at SIGCHI [5, 27]).

4 EXPERIENCES

We briefly provide stakeholder insights from our REU site to understand their roles and challenges they faced.

4.1 Faculty Experiences – PI to Mentor

As the **Principle Investigator (PI)**, I was responsible for coordinating all of the site experiences in Table1 and working closely with faculty, graduate students, administrators, staff, external collaborators, and the undergraduate researchers.

I started planning the following year's REU site in the spring a few weeks before the current year's REU participants arrived to secure housing and team building activities. In the late summer and early fall, we recruited and interviewed undergraduates. In the fall, I followed-up with all REU stakeholders to reflect on the past REU site and their current academic plans. These follow-ups often prompt mentors to reach out to the undergraduate researchers – thus continuing their mentoring relationships. In the winter, I finalized our REU site participants and worked with administrators, staff, and the evaluator on university-level logistics. In late winter, I coordinated with faculty and graduate student mentors to identify who had a research project that could benefit their own research and undergraduate researchers. After we identified projects, we started our ARG model informed mentor training meetings. In the spring, I iterated on the schedule and recruited mentors to teach workshops and host teas throughout the 10-weeks to fulfill each element of the ARG model. During the REU site, I was the point person for anything related to our school's summer undergraduate research program. Throughout the year, I answered questions from REU participants and alumni; connected undergraduates with researchers in areas of interest; and coordinated travel for them to present their REU site research at conferences.

As a **faculty mentor**, my aim was to support the success of the undergraduate researchers and graduate student mentors. I worked with graduate student mentors to compartmentalize and identify tasks for the undergraduates. We typically iterated on the projects, research questions, tasks, and skills in the winter knowing that we most likely would iterate again once we saw the undergraduates' progress during ramp-up week. During weekly meetings with graduate mentors, we discussed how to keep students motivated for the parts of research that may not appeal to them, how authorship should be addressed, and how to adapt the project and time line based on current progress. I saw how these conversations translated into our research mentoring relationship – especially with respect to their dissertation progress.

I met weekly with undergraduate researchers. In most cases, the undergraduates we collaborated with met with a mentor 3-5 times a week. The graduate student mentors focused on teaching technical skills, whereas I worked on professional skills. We included undergraduate researchers in our collaborative meetings with researchers across the university and world. In each meeting, we ensured undergraduates could make contributions. Early in the summer, students introduced themselves and were prepared to ask about what related work and methods they should be researching. These interactions provided students with the opportunity to learn from other research collaborators. As the summer progressed, undergraduate researchers were responsible for presenting parts of the research and, by the end of the summer, showed confidence as they led longer discussions about their work.

Near the end of the REU, graduate student mentors and I worked with undergraduate collaborators to identify publication venues and discuss how we could continue supporting each other. In most cases, we decided to collaborate on a publication due within the next year and follow-up with each other about funding and collaboration opportunities. Indeed, two projects from this REU site were integral in showing the prior work necessary for a federal agency and internal university group to fund more of my research in this area.

4.2 Graduate Mentor Perspective

I was a Ph.D. student mentor in the REU for all three years. Prior to the start of each 10-week REU site, I met with my Ph.D. advisor to

[1] mentors may serve multiple years

develop long-term goals for the summer. We discussed how to make the summer valuable for both my research and the REU students, including how to compartmentalize tasks to give the students a chance to grow their research skills. I met weekly with my advisor to discuss the students' progress and ask for advice as a PhD student interested in mentoring students as a future faculty member.

During the ramp-up session, I participated as a knowledge area expert and mentor. I presented on topics that were relevant to that years' projects, such as hardware with Arduino microcontrollers and finding related work. I presented my research to give students an idea of what they would work on if they chose to work with us.

I regularly met with my REU students – typically every other day – to answer questions and support them as they progressed. We started meetings with a recap of what they had accomplished since the last meeting and how to address any roadblocks they faced. I also summarized what I was working on that week to complement their efforts. I explicitly included time to talk about graduate studies, such as, "What should I include in my graduate school applications?", or "Should I aim for an M.S. or a Ph.D.?" We concluded with setting new goals for the next time we met. New goals included different tasks, so in case they ran into a roadblock, they could continue making progress on another task. Later in the REU, I encouraged mentees to choose their own goals to foster independence. I also check-in daily, informally with mentees. Occasionally we ate lunch as another opportunity for less formal interaction.

In addition to supporting the REU students I directly mentored, I supported the REU site's students. I joined the biweekly lab teas to contribute to the group culture. I met with several REU pairs when they were working on aspects of their projects where I am an expert. For example, I met with a pair to talk about running a design workshop with older adults. I also helped other students by connecting them to graduate students and prior REUs who work in their interest area, so they could get a feel for what graduate studies in that area might be like.

Lastly, I continued mentoring previous students long after the REU experience. I exchanged several emails with REU students checking in with them, offering advice, or coordinating a meeting at an upcoming conference. For both pairs I directly mentored in 2016 and 2017, I also worked with them on submitting papers based on the work we did together (e.g., [12]).

Reflecting on my experience, our REU informed by the ARG model made both practical progress on my research as well as developed my mentoring skills. The REU students helped move my dissertation research forward in one area, while I concurrently worked on another. Their help was valuable in completing a project in a short amount of time and turning it into a publication submission. As a PhD student interested in contributing to academia, I valued the opportunity to develop my mentoring skills. I also enjoyed that I was supporting underrepresented groups in computing to build up their research skills and become contributing members of an inclusive research community.

4.3 Undergraduate Researcher Experience

4.3.1 Year 1: 1st Year Undergraduate Experience. As a freshman from an R1 university majoring in math with little knowledge of informatics, but excitement as to what technology can do for good, the REU faculty gave me a chance as a participant in the 2016 REU program. That chance turned into an international research award, numerous poster presentations, graduate school preview weekends, and several other research experiences. The doors that my REU experience has opened for me and other bright undergraduate researchers, is inspiring.

I never thought I would have had the opportunity to attend a major ACM conference as a sophomore undergraduate, let alone publish my work as part of the Student Research Competition [27]. Without the foundation of research skills that I learned as part of the REU, it simply would not have been possible. Encouragement and support from my faculty and graduate mentors solidified my interest in pursuing a Ph.D. in human-computer interaction and helped to prepare me to excel as an independent researcher.

The REU created an atmosphere that I will strive to create in my own lab, one day. Our weekly lab social meetings and workshops provided the skills necessary to navigate professional and social dynamics within a research lab. The gatherings and daily routine created a culture of camaraderie. At times throughout the first few weeks of the REU, I was lost, but I learned to fail on my own often, rely on peers, and search for answers. The group culture taught me that I could ask anyone in the larger lab group for support. Through constant iteration working on my electronically enhanced textile prototype, I failed enough and learned enough to be the lab expert in e-textiles and sewing.

Educational workshops on topics from Tableau to qualitative research methods and the inherent structure of my REU experience taught foundational skills needed to develop my own research questions and craft a plan to realistically achieve my goals over ten short weeks. As a result of thriving with the structured deliverables of the REU, I also became skilled at creating independent research plans with goals and deadlines that I applied successfully to two large projects at the University of Washington, this past summer, as a CRA-W DREU student.

As a result of my REU experience, I gained a much deeper understanding of what research truly means as well as the diverse avenues that I can take to combine my varied interests of math, human-computer interaction, and innovation - which I did not know was possible. Our mentors' genuine combination of passion, connections, and expertise allowed our "basic undergraduate ideas" to flourish. The REU showed me the power that I have to work with others to make a difference in the STEM community.

4.3.2 Year 2: Senior Undergraduate Experience. Going into the summer 2017 REU, I was a rising senior who was unsure about what she wanted to do with her life. Coming out of the REU I was a rising senior who had a plan to apply straight into PhD programs related to the fields of Health Informatics and Human Computer Interaction (HCI). This REU made me fall in love with two fields, that quite frankly I did not even know existed until I did this REU.

Beyond discovering my next steps, I also learned a multitude of other lessons from this REU experience, such as current research skills related to my field, what to expect while completing my PhD, and how to maintain a good work/life balance. During my experience I had the opportunity to be published alongside my mentors [7, 18], establishing myself as a researcher and expert regarding the interweaving and connections throughout the Asynchronous

Remote Communities [17] method that my graduate mentor was just learning about. I learned a lot from both my mentors and also from the other students participating in the REU. It was great to be surrounded by students from different backgrounds that were equally as motivated as me about research.

I can go on and on about my good experiences from this REU, but there were also a few things that I wish would have been brought more into the experience as well. Such as, more feedback from my summer mentors (specifically about writing), time scheduled to talk to any mentor in or outside of the lab, and showing more of the difference and benefits of both academia and industry.

The overall experience was very hands on and for a beginning researcher, I found this to be mostly to my benefit. However, knowing how a PhD is very independent and you have to find a lot of self-motivation, I think at times there could have been more independence during the research process. Especially, creating our own goals and writing schedule. In comparison, these are small add-ons to my net gain from the REU experience. During this REU, I not only gained knowledge, but also a strong working relationship with the lab that I hope to keep in the future, because without this experience I would not be where I am today. Which is about to embark on my PhD at the University of Washington.

4.3.3 Year 3: Non-traditional Student Experience. I came to the REU with a different perspective than the rest of my undergraduate counterparts in the summer of 2018. As a non-traditional student in the midst of a career change (student affairs to computer science), I was looking to the REU as an opportunity to start re-building my resume and to expand my professional network. The program certainly met my goals.

As a second degree student, the REU was not my first experience with research, as I was heavily involved in research in the social sciences at my previous university. However, the REU introduced me to the field of Informatics and broadened my research skills in relation to computing, technology, and data analysis. A wonderful part of the REU research experience was the interaction with the rest of the research team, whether it was my fellow undergraduate researchers, the graduate student mentors, or the faculty mentors. While there was certainly several distinct research projects going on, everyone seemed willing to help out and share their own particular skills and expertise. This was particularly helpful to me, as the graduate student that was scheduled to serve as my mentor had to cancel at the last minute and was not replaced. While the lack of a graduate student mentor was certainly a frustration at times, in retrospect, it may have ended up being a blessing in disguise. I was able to develop a sense of independence in my research that might not have been possible otherwise.

An interesting aspect of the research that I was involved in was the fact that it was the pilot study for a brand-new research project with a new faculty member. Starting from ground zero, writing a portion of the IRB, and having the opportunity to have a significant voice in the selection of the equipment used for the study helped me become an expert in many aspects of environmental sensing.

The communication and research skills taught by our mentors during the program are some of the most valuable assets of the REU program. Learning how to manage the writing, editing, and peer review process for academic research papers will be helpful as I pursue my graduate studies. While the "deliverables" expected by the end of the 10-week REU seemed daunting at the outset, the faculty encouraged us to reach higher than we might have attempted without their encouragement.

5 REFLECTIONS AND FUTURE ITERATIONS

We utilized the ARG model based on past successes for creating a research experience in computing for undergraduates [8, 32]. Fortunately, the *ARG model provided us with a base to conceptualize and implement our REU site.* The undergraduate experiences noted here and in our evaluation reports discuss how undergraduates felt they were part of a research team (team building) and learned skills that they ordinarily would not have acquired in their academic programs (skill development and practice). They also noted how, although stressful at times, the deliverables prepared them to make contributions to science. In addition, faculty and graduate students appreciated the structured materials we adapted [8, 32].

In terms of what worked, our REU site undergraduates developed a strong sense of community - which we plan to study more to see if it is ARG related, research area, or the diverse, inclusive cohort that was selected. Students appreciated being introduced to informatics and other areas of computing that, although recognized by the ACM, are not in all computing degree programs. The ramp-up week was beneficial for all stakeholders – undergraduates were able to make informed decisions on what projects they wanted to do; graduate students practiced teaching and mentoring; and faculty optimized their time with respect to teaching about their research and shared responsibility for research skill training by teaching 1-2 workshops instead of teaching all of the research skills to each undergraduate. Graduate student mentors were integral in the successful experiences of the undergraduates because there was always someone who was passionate about their research project.

We plan to iterate on two key areas - mentoring and schedule flexibility. Undergraduate researchers appreciated having a pair of mentors, however sometimes mentors travel (undergraduate experience in year 2) or cannot come because of emergencies (undergraduate experience in year 3). We will explore having a "contingency mentor" for each project where in addition to the faculty-graduate mentor pair, the contingency mentor will be aware of the research and available for events when other mentors cannot be reached. Since undergraduates present at weekly meetings and teas, the contingency mentor should be able to quickly learn about project updates and advise students. Although in most cases, we provided personalized mentoring [30], we need to work on personalizing our schedule in Table 1 to accommodate typical research roadblocks (e.g., electronic parts come in late) and assist in helping undergraduate researchers develop into independent scholars. We will investigate having a weekly workshop in week 4, after students have drafted the methods section of their research paper, to discuss how to adapt the schedule and deliverables. We can revisit this schedule at each weekly workshop.

6 ACKNOWLEDGEMENTS

The REU site is supported by the National Science Foundation Award CNS-1560276. Ben Jelen was supported by National Science Foundation Award DGE-1342962.

REFERENCES

[1] Benjamin Ahn and Monica F. Cox. 2016. Knowledge, Skills, and Attributes of Graduate Student and Postdoctoral Mentors in Undergraduate Research Settings. *Journal of Engineering Education* (2016). https://doi.org/10.1002/jee.20129

[2] Anna N. Baglione, Maxine M. Girard, Meagan Price, James Clawson, and Patrick C. Shih. 2017. Mobile Technologies for Grief Support: Prototyping an Application to Support the Bereaved. In *Workshop on Interactive Systems in Health Care (AMIA '17)*. American Medical Informatics Association.

[3] Anna N. Baglione, Maxine M. Girard, Meagan Price, James Clawson, and Patrick C. Shih. 2018. Modern Bereavement: A Model for Grief and Loss in the Digital Age. In *Proceedings of the SIGCHI Conference on Human Factors in Computing Systems (CHI '18)*. ACM, New York, NY, USA.

[4] Lecia Barker. 2009. Student and Faculty Perceptions of Undergraduate Research Experiences in Computing. *ACM Transactions on Computing Education* 9, 1 (3 2009), 1–28. https://doi.org/10.1145/1513593.1513598

[5] Gabrielle S. Cantor. 2018. Designing Technological Interventions for Patients with Discordant Chronic Comorbidities and Type-2 Diabetes. In *Extended Abstracts of the 2018 CHI Conference on Human Factors in Computing Systems (CHI EA '18)*. ACM, New York, NY, USA, Article SRC04, 6 pages. https://doi.org/10.1145/3170427.3180304

[6] Teresa Dahlberg, Tiffany Barnes, Audrey Rorrer, Eve Powell, and Lauren Cairco. 2008. Improving Retention and Graduate Recruitment Through Immersive Research Experiences for Undergraduates. In *Proceedings of the 39th SIGCSE Technical Symposium on Computer Science Education (SIGCSE '08)*. ACM, New York, NY, USA, 466–470. https://doi.org/10.1145/1352135.1352293

[7] Julia C. Dunbar, Ciabhan L. Connelly, Juan F. Maestre, Haley MacLeod, Katie Siek, and Patrick C. Shih. 2017. Considerations for Using the Asynchronous Remote Communities (ARC) Method in Health Informatics Research. In *Workshop on Interactive Systems in Healthcare 2017 at the American Medical Informatics Association Fall Symposium*.

[8] Ann Q. Gates. 2008. *The Affinity Research Group model : creating and maintaining effective research teams*. IEEE Computer Society. 104 pages. https://www.computer.org/web/cspress/arg

[9] Maria Gorlatova, John Sarik, Peter Kinget, Ioannis Kymissis, and Gil Zussman. 2013. Project-based Learning Within a Large-scale Interdisciplinary Research Effort. In *Proceedings of the 18th ACM Conference on Innovation and Technology in Computer Science Education (ITiCSE '13)*. ACM, New York, NY, USA, 207–212. https://doi.org/10.1145/2462476.2465588

[10] Alexander L. Hayes, Mayukh Das, Phillip Odom, and Sriraam Natarajan. 2017. User Friendly Automatic Construction of Background Knowledge: Mode Construction from ER Diagrams. In *Knowledge Capture (KCAP) 2017*.

[11] Jessica Horowitz and Kelly B. Christopher. 2013. The Research Mentoring Program: Serving the Needs of Graduate and Undergraduate Researchers. *Innovative Higher Education* 38, 2 (4 2013), 105–116. https://doi.org/10.1007/s10755-012-9230-3

[12] Ben Jelen, Anne Freeman, Mina Narayanan, Kate M. Sanders, James Clawson, and Katie Siek. 2019. Craftec: Engaging Older Adults in Making through a Craft-Based Toolkit System. In *Proceedings of the Thirteenth International Conference on Tangible, Embedded, and Embodied Interaction (TEI '19)*, ACM (Ed.). ACM, New York, NY, USA, 331–340.

[13] Jolene Kay Jesse. 2006. The Poverty of the Pipeline Metaphor: The AAAS/CPST Study of Nontraditional Pathways into IT/CS Education and the Workforce. In *Women and Information Technology*. The MIT Press, 238–278. https://doi.org/10.7551/mitpress/9780262033459.003.0008

[14] Karen A. Kim, Amy J. Fann, and Kimberly O. Misa-Escalante. 2011. Engaging Women in Computer Science and Engineering. *ACM Transactions on Computing Education* 11, 2 (7 2011), 1–19. https://doi.org/10.1145/1993069.1993072

[15] Gloria Ladson-Billings. 2014. Culturally Relevant Pedagogy 2.0: a.k.a. the Remix. *Harvard Educational Review* (2014). https://doi.org/10.17763/haer.84.1.p2rj131485484751

[16] Haley MacLeod, Grace Bastin, Leslie S. Liu, Katie Siek, and Kay Connelly. 2017. "Be Grateful You Don'T Have a Real Disease": Understanding Rare Disease Relationships. In *Proceedings of the 2017 CHI Conference on Human Factors in Computing Systems (CHI '17)*. ACM, New York, NY, USA, 1660–1673. https://doi.org/10.1145/3025453.3025796

[17] Haley MacLeod, Ben Jelen, Annu Prabhakar, Lora Oehlberg, Katie Siek, and Kay Connelly. 2017. A Guide to Using Asynchronous Remote Communities (ARC) for Researching Distributed Populations. *EAI Endorsed Transactions, Special Issue on Pervasive Health 2016* (2017).

[18] Juan F. Maestre, Haley MacLeod, Ciabhan L. Connelly, Julia C. Dunbar, Jordan Beck, Katie A. Siek, and Patrick C. Shih. 2018. Defining Through Expansion: Conducting Asynchronous Remote Communities (ARC) Research with Stigmatized Groups. In *Proceedings of the 2018 CHI Conference on Human Factors in Computing Systems (CHI '18)*. ACM, New York, NY, USA, Article 557, 13 pages. https://doi.org/10.1145/3173574.3174131

[19] Jane. Margolis. 2008. *Stuck in the shallow end : education, race, and computing.* MIT Press. 201 pages.

[20] Jane. Margolis and Allan Fisher. 2002. *Unlocking the clubhouse : women in computing.* MIT Press. 172 pages.

[21] Tom Ongwere, Gabrielle Cantor, Sergio Ramirez Martin, Patrick C Shih, James Clawson, and Kay Connelly. 2017. Too many conditions, too little time: designing technological intervention for patients with type-2 diabetes and discordant chronic comorbidities. In *Workshop on Interactive Systems in Health Care.*

[22] Tom Ongwere, Gabrielle Cantor, Ramirez Sergio, Patrick C Shih, James Clawson, and Kay Connelly. 2018. Design Hotspots for Care of Discordant Chronic Comorbidities: Patients' Perspectives. In *Proceedings of the Nordic Conference on Human-Computer Interaction*. ACM.

[23] John K. Petrella and Alan P. Jung. 2008. Undergraduate Research: Importance, Benefits, and Challenges. *International Journal of Exercise Science* 1, 3 (2008), 91. https://www.ncbi.nlm.nih.gov/pmc/articles/PMC4739295/

[24] Annu Sible Prabhakar, Lucia Guerra-Reyes, Anne Effron, Vanessa M. Kleinschmidt, Maggie Driscoll, Charles Peters, Vanessa Pereira, Majdah Alshehri, Tom Ongwere, and Katie A. Siek. 2017. "Let Me Know if You Need Anything": Support Realities of New Mothers. In *Proceedings of the 11th EAI International Conference on Pervasive Computing Technologies for Healthcare (PervasiveHealth '17)*. ACM, New York, NY, USA, 31–40. https://doi.org/10.1145/3154862.3154863

[25] Jie Qi, Andrew "bunnie" Huang, and Joseph Paradiso. 2015. Crafting technology with circuit stickers. In *Proceedings of the 14th International Conference on Interaction Design and Children - IDC '15*. ACM Press, New York, New York, USA, 438–441. https://doi.org/10.1145/2771839.2771873

[26] Daniela Raicu, Audrey Rorrer, and Jamie Payton. 2018. Recruitment, Evaluation, and Tracking. 2018 CISE REU PI Meeting: https://reu.uncc.edu/cise-reu-toolkit/results-cise-reu-toolkit.

[27] Olivia K. Richards. 2017. Exploring the Empowerment of Older Adult Creative Groups Using Maker Technology. In *Proceedings of the 2017 CHI Conference Extended Abstracts on Human Factors in Computing Systems (CHI EA '17)*. ACM, New York, NY, USA, 166–171. https://doi.org/10.1145/3027063.3048425

[28] Audrey Rorrer. [n. d.]. Evaluation Plans: Reserach Experience for Undergraduates: Socially Relevant Computing. http://reu.uncc.edu/toolkit/assessment/evaluation-plans.

[29] Audrey Smith Rorrer, Joseph Allen, and Huifang Zuo. 2018. A National Study of Undergraduate Research Experiences in Computing. In *Proceedings of the 49th ACM Technical Symposium on Computer Science Education - SIGCSE '18*. ACM Press, New York, New York, USA, 604–609. https://doi.org/10.1145/3159450.3159510

[30] Jeffery R. Schultz. 2001. The Transformational Process of Mentoring. In *Council on Undergraduate Research Quarterly*. Vol. 22. Council on Undergraduate Research, 72–73.

[31] Patricia J. Teller and Ann Q. Gates. 2001. Using the Affinity Research Group Model to Involve Undergraduate Students in Computer Science Research*. *Journal of Engineering Education* 90, 4 (10 2001), 549–555. https://doi.org/10.1002/j.2168-9830.2001.tb00638.x

[32] Elsa Q. Villa, Kerrie Kephart, Ann Q. Gates, Heather Thiry, and Sarah Hug. 2013. Affinity Research Groups in Practice: Apprenticing Students in Research. *Journal of Engineering Education* 102, 3 (7 2013), 444–466. https://doi.org/10.1002/jee.20016

Hello Research! Developing an Intensive Research Experience for Undergraduate Women

Suzanne Menzel
menzel@iu.edu
Indiana University Bloomington

Katie A. Siek
ksiek@iu.edu
Indiana University Bloomington

David Crandall
djcran@iu.edu
Indiana University Bloomington

ABSTRACT

This paper describes the design and implementation of a three-day intensive research experience (IRE) workshop for undergraduate women in Computer Science. Expanding on a model pioneered at Carnegie Mellon University, we developed and piloted a regional variant called HelloResearch at Indiana University. Participants were actively recruited from our own and neighboring states. Industry partners provided travel scholarships for low-income and first-generation college students, people with disabilities, and students at Historically Black Colleges and Universities (HBCUs) across the country. The primary goal of HelloResearch was to encourage the pursuit of research careers, enabling participants to reach the highest levels of leadership in their fields. In this paper, we report on the demographics of our 92 participants, outline best practices to ensure an authentic short-term research experience for the students, describe our assessment plans, and share our survey instruments to assist others in jump-starting their own regional workshops.

KEYWORDS

Accessibility, Gender and Diversity, Teamwork and Collaboration, Undergraduate Research

ACM Reference Format:
Suzanne Menzel, Katie A. Siek, and David Crandall. 2019. Hello Research! Developing an Intensive Research Experience for Undergraduate Women. In *Proceedings of the 50th ACM Technical Symposium on Computer Science Education (SIGCSE '19), February 27-March 2, 2019, Minneapolis, MN, USA.* ACM, New York, NY, USA, 7 pages. https://doi.org/10.1145/3287324.3287493

1 INTRODUCTION

Just 21% of new doctoral degrees in Computer Science are awarded to women — a percentage that has remained unchanged over the last decade [9]. Providing hands-on, meaningful research experiences to undergraduates is known to increase their interest in pursuing an advanced degree [23]. Among the various types of programs that have been proposed and conducted, *Intensive Research Experiences* (IREs) are ones that are measured in days, not weeks or years, and involve students diving into open-ended, yet narrowly-focused problems under the direct guidance of practicing researchers. The experiences culminate in the students giving brief oral presentations of their work and discussing next steps. An IRE allows students to learn about and try doing research without the uncertainty and risks associated with committing a full semester or summer to a completely unknown endeavor. It also can create ongoing mentoring relationships and be a stepping stone to longer and more sustained involvement in research.

The idea for an IRE specifically tailored for women originated at Carnegie Mellon University in 2006 with "OurCS: Opportunities for Undergraduate Research in Computer Science." They repeated the workshop four times, each time larger than the last, with the most recent in 2017 [1]. The popularity of this workshop suggests that demand for such an IRE can no longer be met by one institution in one geographical location. CMU's model has matured to the point that it is ready for export to other regions of the country to reach more diverse populations [20].

We conducted the first regional IRE, called HelloResearch [6], in October 2018 at Indiana University. Undergraduate students (91 women and 1 trans-male) worked in small teams of 6-13 scholars on carefully scaffolded research projects. Teams convened for eight research working sessions (totaling 12+ hours) over the course of three days, with some teams opting to meet for an additional evening research session. Students selected from a menu of twelve different research projects spanning areas such as Algorithms, Health Informatics, and Machine Learning. The projects were led by researchers from five different schools and one company. HelloResearch culminated with the teams presenting to an audience of research professionals, industry leaders, and peers.

In this paper, we describe the design and implementation of HelloResearch. We provide concrete advice for those considering developing an IRE at their own institution, based on our experience. The growing interest in IREs, evidenced by Google's recently-launched exploreCSR program [4] (which funded 15 research-oriented workshops for female undergraduates in 2018-19), portends an impending need to share experiences and establish best practices for IREs.

2 MOTIVATION

IREs offer an alternative for advanced undergraduates who may be exploring different career paths. Conferences, such as the Grace Hopper Celebration of Women in Computing (GHC) or Small Regional Celebrations [28] (e.g., MicWIC and InWIC), focus on networking, exploring industry careers, providing role models, and supporting students in computing. In this vein, HelloResearch included a keynote speech by a highly successful technical woman (Dr. Timnit Gebru, Google AI), a student panel about graduate school, and an undergraduate research poster session. But an IRE is more than *learning about* research; it involves *doing* real research.

We were motivated by our experiences creating the first Small Regional Celebration of Women in Computing conference based on

SIGCSE '19, February 27-March 2, 2019, Minneapolis, MN, USA

ACM ISBN 978-1-4503-5890-3/19/02...$15.00
https://doi.org/10.1145/3287324.3287493

GHC [28], which has now morphed and spread across the world [30]. Our previous experiences adapting and disseminating CMU's roadshow idea [25, 26] to HBCUs [24] prompted us to actively target this population. Our prior work designing intensive CS1 experiences for women undergraduates provided a foundation for creating compressed, authentic research experiences [29]. These three past successes combined to inspire us to try expanding CMU's OurCS into a regional IRE model that could be adapted by us and others.

In a pre-survey, we asked accepted participants what motivated them to apply to our IRE workshop. One student captured the essence of HelloResearch by responding, "I want to use computer science to change the world, and for that, research is key!"

3 GOALS

Undergraduate research opportunities can improve undergraduate retention in STEM – especially for underrepresented and first generation college students [17, 19] – by increasing their research skills and self efficacy [22]. However, to increase underrepresented groups' interests in continuing on to graduate school, researchers suggest integrating "culturally relevant pedagogy" [22] that integrates undergraduates' cultural, contextual, and political identities, and desire to serve [18] through their research activities. In addition, faculty must be trained to address their own biases that could adversely impact diverse students' academic and research success [10, 19]. By creating inclusive research experiences based on societally relevant problems, we aim to increase students' interest in joining the next generation of scholars, to develop a pipeline of role models and foster continued diversity in computing research [11]. To this end, we expect HelloResearch participants to:

- Gain an understanding/appreciation of the research process;
- Develop specific research skills;
- Increase self-efficacy and sense of belonging in computing;
- Network with peers/faculty from diverse groups and allies;
- Develop a burgeoning mentoring relationship; and
- Learn about graduate student life.

4 JUMP-STARTING AN IRE

We suggest several steps for those considering a regional IRE:

- *Learn about the model,* potentially by attending an IRE workshop and gaining first-hand experience. CMU graciously invited us to their 2017 OurCS workshop [1], which gave us the courage to embark on HelloResearch.
- *Build enthusiasm from colleagues and obtain commitment from school administrators.* We first decided on our target population, and then identified a small number of specific research areas that would appeal as culturally relevant [22].
- *Apply for funding.* HelloResearch is a partnership between academia and industry. Our major industry partners are Google and Oracle Academy. We recommend applying for exploreCRS [4] funding, for example, and then supplementing with smaller grants from local companies.
- *Identify researchers to design and lead projects.* We met face-to-face with individuals whom we thought were especially well-suited to the program. Once we had secured a few projects as examples, it was easier to solicit involvement from the larger faculty community at our own and nearby institutions. Including industry-led research projects broadened appeal and strengthened connections with the industry partner.
- *Reserve date and space.* Reserving a large block of hotel rooms on our campus had to be done a year in advance, avoiding major athletic and parent events. Due to the small-team nature of the working sessions, many small conference rooms or classrooms were needed, and some projects required a computer lab or a maker space. CMU schedules their OurCS workshop over a long weekend (e.g., fall break) when rooms are more readily available.
- *Assemble an organizing committee.* We involved researchers, staff, and students from the very beginning. We tried to avoid organizer fatigue by assigning specific tasks to individuals and giving them plenty of lead time. Although the organization of HelloResearch spanned a full year, we only met face-to-face as a large group two times.

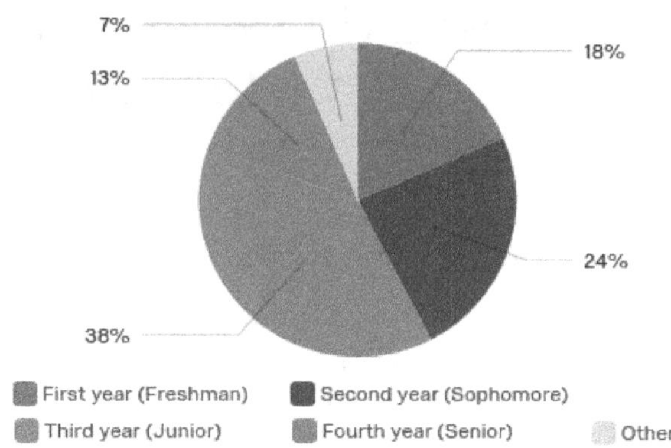

Figure 1: Participants' Current Year in School

5 ABOUT THE PARTICIPANTS

A total of 92 students from 47 different schools in 21 different states participated in HelloResearch; 44.6% came from Indiana schools and another 16.3% came from neighboring states. Figure 1 shows students' year in school, as reported in our application survey [5], where the Other category includes older students returning for a second degree, and two students in their first semester of a Masters program. We asked participants to estimate the availability of research opportunities at their institution: 18% reported "lots of opportunities" and 66% perceived having "some."

5.1 Recruitment Emphasis

Efforts to recruit diverse talent to leadership positions in industry and academia have resulted in small gains [10, 11]. HelloResearch focused on inviting a cohort of diverse women with potential for admission into graduate programs in computing-related fields. We asked faculty to encourage one to three students they knew and believed in to apply to the workshop. We anticipated that faculty could see qualifications in students that went beyond grades, and that students would respond to positive reinforcement from their professors. We urged faculty to also consider students early in their studies who would benefit from a broader vision of computing.

This snowball recruiting identified qualified, diverse participants: 23.9% (22/92) were Black and 7.6% Hispanic or Latino; 36% came from lower socioeconomic status families; 32% were first generation college students. Various institutions were represented: 54% came from public schools (including 3 from community colleges) and 46% from private, of which 7 were HBCUs and 2 were all women. Despite these positive efforts, we encountered some *resistance against diversity efforts* from faculty who voiced concerns about investing in these populations, as past research has found [19].

5.2 Access Matters

Five participants were people with disabilities, whom we contacted immediately after accepting to understand how to accommodate their needs. We applied for AccessComputing funding [2] to secure resources and travel funds, ensuring that all qualified participants could attend and share their rich and unique experiences. We accommodated deaf participants by arranging for two American Sign Language (ASL) interpreters to be present at all sessions. Although we did not anticipate this significant and worthwhile cost in our original budget, AccessComputing funding covered the costs. Assistive listening systems (ALS) were used to broadcast audio directly to special receivers and hearing aids, reducing background noise for people with hearing impairments. In addition, we provided vocabulary lists of technical terms to ASL interpreters and requested presenters to add presentation notes to their slides and share them with participants.

Our institution's Disability Services Office performed a mobility orientation for a participant who was blind. The specialist walked with the blind person between locations, explaining the terrain and street crossings, so she could later navigate independently. Since a person with visual impairments may use a cane or service animal and thus move more slowly than others, we arranged a van service for longer travel distances. People with autism may become overwhelmed and require breaks in a quiet place, so we arranged for a wellness space in the workshop venue.

We learned how to create more inclusive digital experiences through the Accessible By Design conference [3]. We provided pictures of the hotel entrance, meeting spaces, location of elevators, restrooms, and water fountains in advance, as well as approximate step counts to help participants plan their experience. We found that integrating inclusive practices improved everyone's experience.

6 BENEFITS

6.1 For the Institution

In addition to our own faculty, we invited researchers from nearby institutions to lead projects, which we found helped strengthen connections between schools. Much of this was done by involving current and past students. The Programming Languages project was led by a former undergraduate who is now finishing his Ph.D. at CMU. The Wireless Privacy project was led by a former Ph.D. student who is now faculty at Rose-Hulman Institute of Technology. The student panel included a current senior undergraduate with vast research experience (including CMU's 2017 OurCS workshop and a subsequent summer REU at CMU), a former undergraduate (now a second-year Ph.D. student at CMU), and a former M.S. student (now a Ph.D. student at the University of Notre Dame).

Access to a large number of talented undergraduates from diverse institutions is an obvious recruitment windfall for our university: these students are from underrepresented populations, have been vetted by faculty members at their schools, are already considering graduate school, are visiting the campus for several days, and have begun to establish mentoring relationships with faculty.

6.2 For Faculty Researchers

Our IRE encouraged collaboration among our own faculty that went beyond the workshop itself. One pair of faculty who co-led a HelloResearch project, for example, commented that they had always wanted to work together and HelloResearch provided an intense, but low-risk opportunity to "audition" a collaboration. The program also allowed graduate students to take an active role in designing and running research projects, giving valuable experience in teaching and mentoring.

We believe mentoring undergraduates is an educational activity that should be rewarded in merit, tenure, and promotion evaluations. For faculty who are writing grant applications, leading an IRE can be significant evidence of broader impact. On a more personal level, many faculty enjoy working with highly-motivated students and an IRE provides an excellent opportunity to recruit directly into the researcher's lab. One of our leaders was just starting to acclimate a new undergraduate into her research group, and found that the IRE project accelerated that process. Different perspectives, such as a deaf student working on an audio project, presented opportunities for the student to influence the faculty's long-term research directions.

6.3 For Industry Partners

Diverse teams can solve problems better than more homogeneous teams of greater objective ability [16]. Women of color are especially underrepresented in industry. In 2017, black women held only 3% of computing jobs, and Latinas just 1% [8]. Addressing accessibility issues in products during the design phase means *including* skilled deaf and blind people on design teams.

We found that many companies were interested in supporting our IRE, including giving money, resources, and sending speakers and project leaders. Much of this interest was driven by recruitment: industry partners with the vision and patience to allow research talent to develop will have access to a larger, better educated, and more diverse pool of researchers entering the workforce. The opportunity to lead a research project at an IRE also allows the industry partner to showcase how research is conducted in industry.

6.4 For Students

The potential benefits to students are, of course, many. Participants broadened their perspective by working together with students from other schools who share their academic interests and aspirations, including comparing and contrasting their educational trajectory and progress with others. Participants worked with researchers outside their home institution, with the possibility of developing a long-term mentoring relationship, potentially even into graduate school. They learned about the graduate school application process, and potentially increased their competitiveness for research awards, fellowships, and scholarships, and graduate school admissions (e.g., by obtaining a letter of recommendation from a team leader).

7 LOGISTICS

7.1 When and Where

Among our first actions was to choose a date and reserve a block of hotel and meeting rooms. We chose October, when seniors are thinking seriously about their next steps such as applying to graduate school. Because we intentionally targeted students from low socioeconomic status families, we arranged to waive the graduate application fees at Indiana University, IUPUI, and Notre Dame, effectively removing the financial barrier while encouraging applications to these specific schools. Identifying and reserving suitable meeting space for twelve separate research teams was a challenge.

7.2 Who

Research experience is the ultimate objective of an IRE and obtaining early commitments from researchers to design and lead research projects is critical. We took care to *represent the undertaking accurately* so that researchers understood the scope of the commitment: a multi-day workshop with many hours of research sessions constitutes a significant obligation.

We created a Facebook page and a website about ten months before the workshop, beginning with a skeleton site that described the application process and included a "Notify me" button to sign up for updates. We began accepting applications [5] in early April and filled 100 spots in six weeks. We advertised to faculty contacts from regional GHC conferences and outreach workshops, and on larger mailing lists (SIGCSE, Professhers, Systers), and by word of mouth. We kept our own faculty informed with regular updates at department meetings, seminar presentations, and local conferences. After registration closed, we continued to accept applications on a waitlist; 18 students canceled and we replaced them with waitlisted students on a rolling basis. We had 6 additional cancellations in the 4 days leading up to the workshop and 2 no-shows — those slots went unfilled. About 17% of participants were from our institution.

Once we closed registration in mid-May, we created a distribution list to communicate with participants. Three months before the workshop, we sent another survey [7] to collect roommate preferences, dietary restrictions, and travel plans. We asked their permission to be included in a public directory of attendees, to be photographed and recorded during the workshop, and to participate in an on-site interview to study the workshop's effectiveness. Some participants were unable to bring a laptop, so we arranged to provide loaners. We assisted students with travel difficulties, gathered accommodation requirements, and initiated the reimbursement process for scholarship recipients.

7.3 What

We assigned participants to projects systematically: each participant listed her top three choices, which we put into a Simplex Linear Programming problem in Excel with #participants × #projects binary variables. We used the OpenSolver Excel Add-in from opensolver.org since the number of variables was over 200. Every student received either her first or second choice. We notified students of their project assignment about a month in advance by creating a Slack workspace and inviting each participant to join the private channel for their specific project. We created individual computer accounts for each participant so that they could access our wireless network and lab machines. For some projects, we installed specialized software and hardware in our labs.

7.4 Behind-the-Scenes Roles

7.4.1 Administrative Assistant. Organizing our workshop required significant help from a staff member knowledgeable about school policies and procedures for travel, purchasing, catering, and reimbursement. We involved the administrative assistant from the beginning of the planning process, and also arranged for overtime pay so they could attend the entire workshop.

7.4.2 Project Manager. We hired an undergraduate part-time (5 hrs/wk) to maintain the website, distribute survey instruments, organize volunteers, coordinate with leaders to determine space/material needs, schedule meetings, and communicate with participants.

7.4.3 Instructional Design Coach. An experienced teaching professor on our faculty volunteered to coach the team leaders during the design phase and share ideas for promising practices. During the workshop, the coach circulated around all sessions, and was the point of contact in case anything went awry. The coach was particularly valuable for researchers from industry who are unaccustomed to working with undergraduates, as well as for faculty from other institutions who were unfamiliar with our school's facilities. But even faculty from our institution benefited from the advice of a dispassionate observer with a global view of all projects.

8 PREPARING THE MENTORS

The choice and design of research projects are key to the success of the workshop: projects need well-defined goals that can be understood by undergraduates. Projects had to be challenging and interesting, but not frustrating or overwhelming - especially given the short three-day time frame. We tried to select faculty who would enjoy the challenge of scaffolding their research for undergraduates while still ensuring a research contribution at the end. One month before the workshop, we held a mentor meeting where we provided demographic data about our participants, introduced our Instructional Design Coach, outlined two project designs, and had a Q&A with an experienced project leader from CMU's OurCS.

It was important for mentors to understand that many of our participants had little prior experience with or understanding of the research process. In our application survey, we asked students to explain what they thought research entailed. Many responses exhibited a lyrical, but marginal understanding of the process; one wrote, "Research is about discovery. Research is about learning. Research is about applying what I learn to better understand why something happens. I expect to have to write alot [sic] — something that I need to improve upon. I also expect to use my problem solving and analytical skills." Responses tended to abstract the research process, as in "Research entails tackling the problems that people do not yet have answers to. It involves thinking critically and creatively and persevering when faced with difficulty. I am not sure what day-to-day research is like, but that is what I hope to find out through this experience." Also, "The process of doing

ARG Element	IRE Activities
team building	community meals; networking breaks; interactive workshops; lab tours
skill development	4-5 hours of research workshops; panels and talks
skill practice	6-8 hours of research workshops; poster session; team presentations
goals & objectives with deliverables	project leader preparation; research workshops

Table 1: Adapting the Affinity Research Group (ARG) Model to an Intensive Research Experience (IRE)

research is to formalize curiosity into a tangible problem that can be further broken down into small pieces of steps and to eventually find insights from completing these steps."

We recommended that project leaders describe research as an iterative process that builds on prior research: review the literature, formulate a problem, try a solution, make mistakes, iterate. To save time, leaders summarized related work in the project area and showcase at least one relevant academic paper, highlighting the important sections for later close reading [13].

8.1 Affinity Research Group Model

Our IRE was informed by the Affinity Research Group (ARG) model, a structured team approach to involving students with diverse backgrounds in scholarly research [14] by having project leaders share their *affinity* for their research. Project leaders guide undergraduate researchers in developing skills so that each team member — including the undergraduate researcher with a diverse background — becomes a subject-matter expert. With their new expertise, undergraduates become equal contributors to the research group [14]. The ARG model is composed of four main elements: team building, deliberate skill development, skill practice, and goals and objectives with accompanying defined deliverables [31]. We adapted the ARG model to an IRE as shown in Table 1.

8.2 The Author Audit

We encouraged leaders to conduct an *author audit* of papers selected for study so that authors were (at least) representative of computing, and include pictures, names, and schools to show diversity (especially women and people of color). Author audits are important because although women increasingly publish in computing conferences [12], women are less likely to be cited [15]. If leaders were unable to identify related work by underrepresented groups, we suggested showcasing efforts to increase diversity (e.g., the Computing Research Association's Discipline Specific Workshops).

8.3 Research Questions

Team leaders either prepared research questions in advance to give to the students, or they planned to guide students in generating their own questions. If the latter, we recommended that leaders provide sufficient information about the problem space and instruction on formulating research questions (e.g., avoid "yes/no" questions).

9 PROJECT EXEMPLARS

HelloResearch included twelve projects representing a wide range of computer science research, from autonomous vehicle navigation, to programming language design, to augmented and virtual reality. As examples, we briefly describe two of the projects, how they fit into the IRE-adapted ARG model, and the accommodations we made for students with disabilities.

9.1 Creating Custom Technology to Improve One's Quality of Life

The undergraduate researchers reflected on personas of underserved communities in technology — from rural older adults to pregnant teens to low socioeconomic status children — to develop custom, interactive technology to assist these underserved groups improve their quality of life. The lead faculty member started her workshop with an overview of the nascent sociotechnical research to improve the health of underserved populations [27]. She also provided a brief synopsis of her own research and how her research group developed personas and scenarios based on qualitative research to seed the undergraduate researchers' ideas. The faculty leader interleaved research skill teaching with brainstorming and prototyping sessions so that undergraduate researchers could experience iteration cycles as they explored barriers that target populations faced and designed sociotechnical solutions. Research skill sessions included developing design guidelines from qualitative data, physical prototyping via 3D printing and laser cutting, and programming embedded systems.

Students identified a target population, developed a research question to address a barrier that their selected persona and scenario experienced (e.g., how can a community know what types of clothing low-income children need?), iterated on 2-3 sociotechnical solutions, built an interactive system to explore the research question (e.g., a clothing box that can sense how full it is and send notifications to donors about needs), and documented their solution for presentation and future publication.

The faculty leader was able to adapt most of the tasks for a blind undergraduate researcher by providing digital materials that the student read on her laptop with assistive software. One challenge for her was connecting alligator clips to small electrical pins during embedded system programming. To address this, we utilized pair programming so that groups of two worked together and switched off between hardware and software. The project leaders modified the way they taught electronic circuitry based on the Blind Arduino Project [21] by instructing students how to orient components based on feel — which benefited all students. In addition, all students discussed how to make their projects more accessible — from adding lights, sounds, and vibration to laser cutting braille signs.

9.2 Activity Recognition Through Deep Learning with Sound and Video

This project sought to give students experience with cutting-edge artificial intelligence and machine learning technologies and research methodologies. The project was framed in terms of next-generation home devices that could respond based on an awareness of what is going on around them — e.g., a smart home assistant might call for help if an older person falls, or might turn off the television if everyone falls asleep. To do this, devices would have to capture and analyze the sights and sounds of the household to recognize and understand what is going on around them.

The two project leaders were an expert in computer vision and an expert in audio understanding. They began by each giving brief overviews of their respective fields, concentrating on research directions, techniques, and open questions. Participants brainstormed perception abilities that they thought both could be useful for home devices. To help properly scope project goals, the team was asked to narrow the list to three: an "easy" task that they thought was easily within the capabilities of current technology, a moderate task that they thought could probably be solved, and a difficult task that would be challenging. After discussion, the team voted and decided to focus on recognizing the identity of speaking people based on both their physical appearance and their voice.

After a discussion of IRB, the team designed and carried out a methodology for collecting a (small-scale) dataset for training and testing. The team of 9 students was split into two groups to investigate visual recognition and audio recognition in parallel. Each team had access to a machine learning cloud service donated by Google. Mentors helped each team follow an iterative process typical of AI research: start with a simple algorithm, train it on part of the data, test on the rest, identify failure modes, make improvements to the algorithm based on the failures, and repeat. This iterative process meant that even if some of the recognition tasks were very difficult, participants would still have results to show during their presentation. The mentors emphasized that the goal was not to create a working system, but to better understand what work would need to be done in order to create such a system. In the end, the team developed a prototype algorithm written in Python to identify among 10 different speakers. The prototype achieved an accuracy of about 60%, compared to a random baseline of 10%, and the team analyzed the failure cases to recommend future research directions.

Decisions had to be made at various points in the project — e.g., which problem to pursue, which technical approach to try, etc. The team leaders gave their input but left the decisions themselves to the team through discussion and voting. Notes on the discussion were kept by one of the team leaders on a shared Google Doc, and participants were encouraged to also contribute to the document in real-time. Besides helping to keep the team on track, we found that this shared real-time note-taking helped allow our participant who was deaf to more actively engage in the discussion without relying on the sign language interpreters (who often struggled to interpret technical terms). To create the team presentation, the group defined nine key topics that needed to be covered (e.g., problem statement, dataset collection, approach, etc.), and assigned each topic to a participant, who created a slide for the topic and added it to a shared Google Slides presentation.

10 ASSESSMENT PLAN

Our primary objective is to measure the impact of HelloResearch on participants' intention to attend graduate school and to see if changes are sustained over time. We asked applicants to indicate where they saw themselves in 2-4 years. We repeated the question in the post-survey to assess if and how their future intentions changed

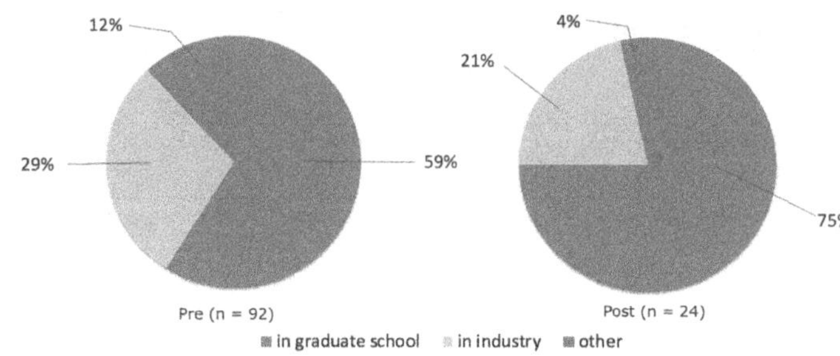

Figure 2: Where Participants See Themselves in 2-4 Years

(Figure 2). We will follow up with attendees at 6-month intervals to determine how many apply and enroll in graduate school.

During the workshop, we encouraged participants to build their LinkedIn professional identities. We invited them to a HelloResearch group so we could keep in touch. Photographers took free professional headshots for their profiles. LinkedIn provides a stable way for us to connect with the participants, over the long term, to disseminate opportunities and invitations to future studies.

We hired an external evaluator to develop ethics board approval materials, facilitate two focus group interviews during the workshop, and analyze the data to measure the utility and impact of the workshop. The evaluator is experienced in pairing quantitative with qualitative data so we can better understand not only where changes are happening, but also why the changes occurred.

Further quantitative and qualitative assessment services were provided through exploreCSR: pre-post surveys of participants, an on-site ethnographic study, and follow-up interviews with students and team leaders. One week post, we surveyed our mentors. One team leader listed the mentor benefits as "Having fun! Identifying promising students to potentially recruit as graduate students. Helping form collaborations with other faculty. Getting to know other faculty better." Conclusions drawn from analyzing the data collected from all sources will be reported in a future paper.

11 FORWARD MOMENTUM

At the end of the workshop, we provided information and resources to aid participants in taking the next step, e.g., a summer or year-long REU program. We offered to provide feedback on students' statements for graduate school applications. At least two teams have continued work on their research projects with an eye towards publication. Six students from our institution reprised their presentations in our Teaching & Learning seminar series.

We expect to repeat HelloResearch in 2020 and conduct further studies of those participants to see how they compare with the 2018 cohort. We plan to organize IRE Infrastructure workshops to aid others in designing a regional IRE based on HelloResearch.

ACKNOWLEDGMENTS

The authors thank Carol Frieze and Gloria Townsend for lighting our way. Support for HelloResearch was provided by Google, Oracle Academy, AccessComputing, Beckman-Coulter, IU's School of Informatics, Computing, and Engineering, and IU's Office of the Vice President for Diversity, Equity & Multicultural Affairs.

REFERENCES

[1] 2017. OurCS at Carnegie Mellon University. Retrieved November 2018 from http://www.cs.cmu.edu/ourcs

[2] 2018. AccessComputing Mini-Grant. Retrieved November 2018 from https://www.washington.edu/accesscomputing/apply-accesscomputing-minigrant

[3] 2018. Accessible By Design website. Retrieved November 2018 from https://accessiblebydesign.org/2018

[4] 2018. Explore Computer Science Research. http://services.google.com/fh/files/misc/2018_rfp_explorecsr.pdf

[5] 2018. HelloResearch Application Survey. Retrieved November 2018 from https://iu.box.com/s/75yxecin6mh387ceb8wqibz1i4tt0g1c

[6] 2018. HelloResearch at Indiana University. Retrieved November 2018 from http://helloresearch.sice.indiana.edu

[7] 2018. HelloResearch Summer Survey. Retrieved November 2018 from https://iu.box.com/s/o7zohr2qq19gysc1wsp4hx3l7ao0mhyl

[8] 2018. National Center for Women & Information Technology. Retrieved November 2018 from https://www.ncwit.org/

[9] NSC Research Center. 2017. Science and Engineering Degree Attainment. https://nscresearchcenter.org/wp-content/uploads/SnapshotReport27r.pdf

[10] Lavar J Charleston, Phillis L. George, Jerlando F. L. Jackson, Jonathan Berhanu, and Mauriell Amechi. 2014. Navigating Underrepresented STEM Spaces: Experiences of Black Women in U.S. Computing Science Higher Education Programs Who Actualize Success. *Journal of Diversity in Higher Education* 7, 3 (September 2014), 166–176.

[11] LaVar J. Charleston, Juan E. Gilbert, Barbara Escobar, and Jerlando F.L. Jackson. 2014. Creating a Pipeline for African American Computing Science Faculty: An Innovative Faculty/Research Mentoring Program Model. *The Journal of Faculty Development* 28, 1 (January 2014), 85–92(8).

[12] J. McGrath Cohoon, Sergey Nigai, and Joseph "Jofish" Kaye. 2011. Gender and Computing Conference Papers. *Commun. ACM* 54, 8 (Aug. 2011), 72–80. https://doi.org/10.1145/1978542.1978561

[13] Philip W.L. Fong and Philip W.L. 2009. Reading a computer science research paper. *ACM SIGCSE Bulletin* 41, 2 (6 2009), 138. https://doi.org/10.1145/1595453.1595493

[14] Ann Q. Gates. 2008. *The Affinity Research Group model : creating and maintaining effective research teams.* IEEE Computer Society. 104 pages.

[15] Gita Ghiasi, Philippe Mongeon, C Sugimoto, and Vincent LariviÃÍre. 2018. Gender homophily in citations. *23rd International Conference on Science and Technology Indicators (STI 2018)* (September 2018), 1519–1525.

[16] Lu Hong and Scott E. Page. 2004. Groups of diverse problem solvers can outperform groups of high-ability problem solvers. *Proceedings of the National Academy of Sciences* 101, 46 (2004), 16385–16389. https://doi.org/10.1073/pnas.0403723101 arXiv:http://www.pnas.org/content/101/46/16385.full.pdf

[17] Jolene Kay Jesse. 2006. The Poverty of the Pipeline Metaphor: The AAAS/CPST Study of Nontraditional Pathways into IT/CS Education and the Workforce. In *Women and Information Technology.* The MIT Press, 238–278. https://doi.org/10.7551/mitpress/9780262033459.003.0008

[18] Gloria Ladson-Billings. 2014. Culturally Relevant Pedagogy 2.0: a.k.a. the Remix. *Harvard Educational Review* (2014). https://doi.org/10.17763/haer.84.1.p2rj131485484751

[19] Lecia Barker. 2009. Student and Faculty Perceptions of Undergraduate Research Experiences in Computing. *ACM Transactions on Computing Education* 9, 1 (3 2009), 1–28. https://doi.org/10.1145/1513593.1513598

[20] Suzanne Menzel and Carol Frieze. 2018. Experiencing Research Through OurCS: Opportunities for Undergraduate Research in Computer Science. In *2018 Research on Equity and Sustained Participation in Engineering, Computing, and Technology (RESPECT).* IEEE, 1–4. https://doi.org/10.1109/RESPECT.2018.8491693

[21] Joshua Miele. [n. d.]. Blind Arduino Project. https://www.ski.org/project/blind-arduino-project.

[22] Audrey Smith Rorrer, Joseph Allen, and Huifang Zuo. 2018. A National Study of Undergraduate Research Experiences in Computing. In *Proceedings of the 49th ACM Technical Symposium on Computer Science Education - SIGCSE '18.* ACM Press, New York, New York, USA, 604–609. https://doi.org/10.1145/3159450.3159510

[23] Susan H. Russell, Mary P. Hancock, and James McCullough. 2007. Benefits of Undergraduate Research Experiences. *Science* 316, 5824 (2007), 548–549. https://doi.org/10.1126/science.1140384 arXiv:http://science.sciencemag.org/content/316/5824/548.full.pdf

[24] Katie A. Siek, Kay Connelly, Suzanne Menzel, and Laura Hopkins. 2007. Propagating diversity through active dissemination. *Computer* 40, 2 (2 2007), 89–92. https://doi.org/10.1109/MC.2007.71

[25] Katie A. Siek, Kay Connelly, Amanda Stephano, Suzanne Menzel, Jacki Bauer, and Beth Plale. 2006. Breaking the geek myth: Addressing young women's misperceptions about technology careers. *Learning & Leading with Technology* 33, 7 (2006), 19–22. https://eric.ed.gov/?id=EJ779805

[26] Katie A. Siek, Amanda Stephano, Diane Cessna, Kay Connelly, and Beth Plale. 2005. Work In Progress: Just Be An Interactive Experience for K-12 Students. In *Proceedings Frontiers in Education 35th Annual Conference.* IEEE, F3H–15–F3H–16. https://doi.org/10.1109/FIE.2005.1612119

[27] Elizabeth Stowell, Mercedes C. Lyson, Herman Saksono, Reneé C. Wurth, Holly Jimison, Misha Pavel, and Andrea G. Parker. 2018. Designing and Evaluating mHealth Interventions for Vulnerable Populations: A Systematic Review. In *Proceedings of the 2018 CHI Conference on Human Factors in Computing Systems (CHI '18).* ACM, New York, NY, USA, Article 15, 17 pages. https://doi.org/10.1145/3173574.3173589

[28] Gloria Childress Townsend, Lecia Barker, Suzanne Menzel, and J. McGrath Cohoon. 2008. Grace Hopper Visits the Neighborhood. In *Proceedings of the 39th SIGCSE Technical Symposium on Computer Science Education (SIGCSE '08).* ACM, New York, NY, USA, 513–517. https://doi.org/10.1145/1352135.1352307

[29] Gloria Childress Townsend, Suzanne Menzel, and Katie A. Siek. 2007. Leveling the CS1 playing field. *ACM SIGCSE Bulletin* 39, 1 (3 2007), 331. https://doi.org/10.1145/1227504.1227428

[30] Gloria Childress Townsend and Kay Sloan. 2015. An Effective Alternative to the Grace Hopper Celebration. In *Proceedings of the 46th ACM Technical Symposium on Computer Science Education (SIGCSE '15).* ACM, New York, NY, USA, 197–202. https://doi.org/10.1145/2676723.2677233

[31] Elsa Q. Villa, Kerrie Kephart, Ann Q. Gates, Heather Thiry, and Sarah Hug. 2013. Affinity Research Groups in Practice: Apprenticing Students in Research. *Journal of Engineering Education* 102, 3 (7 2013), 444–466. https://doi.org/10.1002/jee.20016

Collaboration Versus Cheating

Reducing Code Plagiarism in an Online MS Computer Science Program

Tony Mason*
Georgia Institute of Technology
fsgeek@gatech.edu

Ada Gavrilovska
Georgia Institute of Technology
ada@cc.gatech.edu

David A. Joyner
Georgia Institute of Technology
david.joyner@gatech.edu

ABSTRACT

We outline how we detected programming plagiarism in an introductory online course for a master's of science in computer science program, how we achieved a statistically significant reduction in programming plagiarism by combining a clear explanation of university and class policy on academic honesty reinforced with a short but formal assessment, and how we evaluated plagiarism rates before and after implementing our policy and assessment.

CCS CONCEPTS

• **Social and professional topics** → *Computer science education; CS1; Student assessment;*

KEYWORDS

MOSS, Academic Honesty, Honor Codes, Plagiarism, MOOC, Online, OMSCS

ACM Reference Format:

Tony Mason, Ada Gavrilovska, and David A. Joyner. 2019. Collaboration Versus Cheating: Reducing Code Plagiarism in an Online MS Computer Science Program. In *Proceedings of the 50th ACM Technical Symposium on Computer Science Education (SIGCSE '19), February 27-March 2, 2019, Minneapolis, MN, USA.* ACM, New York, NY, USA, 7 pages. https://doi.org/10.1145/3287324.3287443

1 INTRODUCTION

Academic honesty is critical for those engaged in research. Because we build upon the work of others, we must be able to rely on the integrity of work done by others:

> *As a society, we rely on the academic and journalistic integrity of other people's work. The whole point of academic research is to share knowledge with others and learn from one another. Since knowledge and ideas are the primary product produced by academic communities, it is essential that this knowledge is accurate and gives credit to those who created it [42].*

*Also affiliated with the University of British Columbia (fsgeek@cs.ubc.ca)

SIGCSE '19, February 27-March 2, 2019, Minneapolis, MN, USA

ACM ISBN 978-1-4503-5890-3/19/02...$15.00
https://doi.org/10.1145/3287324.3287443

The concept of intellectual integrity is not restricted to academic work; dishonest behavior spills over into the non-academic world. Cheating is a difficult habit to break, and forms of cheating (such as plagiarism) spread easily when left unchallenged [12].

While instructors for complex technical classes focus on promoting mastery, students often focus on achieving the highest possible marks. When they have not achieved mastery of the material, they may submit the work of others as their own. The issue of academic honesty in programming classes is not a new problem, having been reported early in the history of computer science education[24]. The problem of plagiarism is complicated by the fact that the division between collaboration and cheating for programming is not clear; modern work practice is often to modify existing code to fit the current need.

Plagiarism in which students copied the work of those who took the same course in earlier semesters was problematic in our online program, which grants a master of science degree in computer science to students who complete it. The program began in 2014, and all courses and student interactions are conducted online [23]. As of Spring 2018 there were 6,365 students enrolled, with most (70.2%) being US citizens or permanent residents; 85.1% were men, and 14.8% were from under-represented minorities. Most students were enrolled in a single class, in which total course enrollments reached 8,737.[1]

One challenge in delivering computer science classes at this scale is implementing an effective formative analysis of students' comprehension without unduly burdening the instructional team. Some classes in our program create unique projects each term, but this is not practical for our class, as we provide automated feedback via a "black box" testing mechanism, which requires considerable effort to modify, let alone rewrite from scratch each semester. Similarly, we found that a strict enforcement mechanism was effective in suppressing the repeated instances of academic dishonesty from the same students, but substantial effort was required to follow the *due process* requirements of the university; we observed that some instructors ignored problems rather than dedicate the considerable effort required to vigorously pursue them.

We were motivated to conduct this research because we observed that plagiarism in our course was an increasing problem. We discussed this situation internally, reviewed techniques for mitigating the issue, and even implemented several suggested mechanisms. While we found that rapid response and enforcement was effective for *subsequent* projects, we sought a mechanism that would discourage plagiarism *before* it became a burden on the instructional team. In addition, fewer cases up front would make it easier to enforce the class policy simply because there would be fewer such cases to report to the university.

[1] https://www.omscs.gatech.edu/prospective-students/numbers

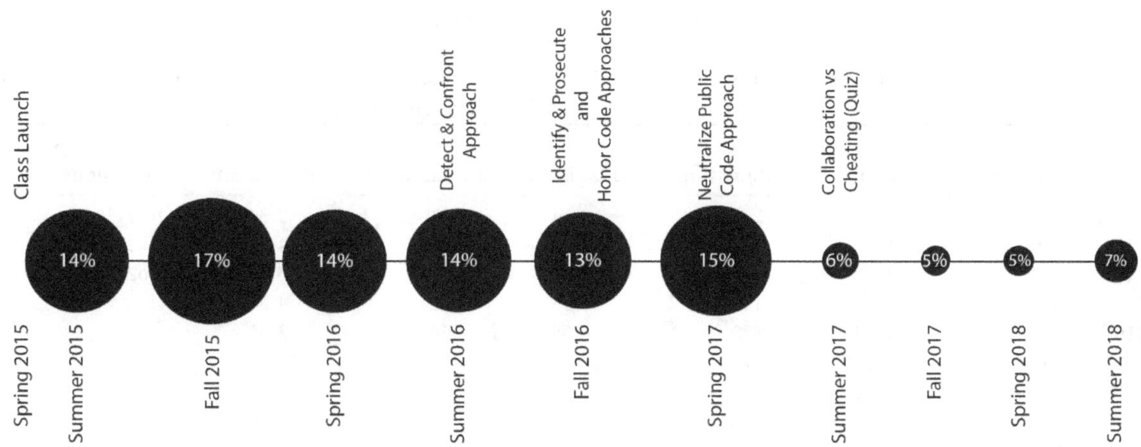

Figure 1: Course timeline

Course timeline and percentage of unique students detected via automatic plagiarism checks. See Table 5 for detailed data. A student flagged multiple times is only counted *once.*

In Summer 2017 we introduced a single change: a formal assessment, given via our learning management system (LMS), that spelled out the expected behavior from students in our class, why we viewed it as an important aspect of the course, and the potential ramifications for students that violated the policy. We observed a substantial drop in the number of detected cases. At that point we decided to perform a more rigorous evaluation of our results. This led to a thorough review of our historical data, as well as an ongoing review of subsequent classes, which allowed us to determine whether we were, in fact, observing a valid trend. We now have four semesters of data since we first implemented the formal assessment. We have observed a statistically significant decrease in the rates of plagiarism in the courses based upon our approach of using a quiz. Figure 1 shows our measured rate of plagiarism over time and the effect of our change beginning in Summer 2017. Table 4 demonstrates our claim this represents a statistically significant decrease in plagiarism.

Our approach combines a clear definition of the course expectations and the university's honor code. This is explained in detail to the students in the form of a formal assessment exercise.[2] This approach, a low-effort mechanism for clearly communicating expectations in an instructional setting, decreased our objectively measured plagiarism rate. It also represents a novel "middle ground" between prior work that showed honor codes were **not** effective in online classes and one that showed that a comprehensive course in academic honesty, with evaluation, *was* effective. We suggest this approach can be applied successfully to other, similar courses.

2 BACKGROUND

Our course includes two substantial programming projects, which are generally reused each semester with only minor revisions. While some classes in the program do change their projects from semester to semester, it is not feasible for our class to change our course projects.

[2]https://github.com/fsgeek/collaboration-versus-cheating

Students are given initial "starter" code with instructions on the project requirements. They are encouraged to *collaborate* with one another, but to complete and submit their own work. Programs are submitted to a test framework that provides feedback but not final grades. Students are required to submit a README file with the project, explaining their understanding of the project, the challenges they experienced, and *the external sources they used.*

2.1 Plagiarism

For the purposes of our evaluation, we determined the presence of plagiarism using the results of MOSS[2], which is a standard tool used in plagiarism detection for programming courses in our programs. We invoked MOSS using -l c -n 1000 -d -c ''<project name>'' -b <template> ... -b <template>. This set of options tells MOSS that the language (-l) is C[32], requests the top 1000 "hits" (-n), designates files in the same directory (-d) as part of the same program, adds a unique name to the top of the MOSS output (-c), and ensures that the starter code (-b) is not itself assessed for plagiarism.

In a normal class execution, we manually assess each case of suspected plagiarism. MOSS is a *tool* to identify *potential* cases; results are suggestive of plagiarism, but not definitive. To make a referral to the university, we must be sure that the reported offense is defensible.

In evaluating the effectiveness of our instructional approach for plagiarism reduction, we rejected using the manual evaluation method in order to avoid injecting additional bias into our analysis. Instead, we chose a definitive cut-off of 30% MOSS similarity. We chose this value because, in reviewing the cases considered by the instructional team, we noted that all instances at or above 30% had been referred by the instructional staff, no cases below 20% were referred, and some cases between 20% and 30% were referred. We were confident that a demonstrable decrease in the plagiarism rate at this level was strongly supportive of an effective reduction scheme, even if there were a small number of false positive results.

Table 1: Project 1 Submission & Plagiarism Data

Project 1 submissions consist of four distinct units; each unit is independently analyzed. Per semester, we report the total number of submissions and the percentage flagged for plagiarism (as defined in §2.1).

Semester	PR1-A		PR1-B		PR1-C		PR1-D	
	Submissions	% Plagiarism	Submissions	% Plagiarism	Submissions	% Plagiarism	Submissions	% Plagiarism
Summer 2015	152	3.95	145	4.14	121	3.31	129	5.43
Fall 2015	200	9.50	194	7.73	190	4.74	191	6.81
Spring 2016	174	5.75	170	7.06	167	3.59	162	4.94
Summer 2016	150	1.33	153	4.58	124	4.84	123	4.07
Fall 2016	183	6.01	183	6.56	156	3.85	155	5.77
Spring 2017	140	7.86	140	10.71	119	10.08	121	12.40
Summer 2017	77	1.30	70	0.00	67	2.99	68	0.00
Fall 2017	224	2.68	225	1.78	203	2.46	209	1.44
Spring 2018	274	4.01	281	4.27	235	1.70	245	2.45
Summer 2018	172	3.49	171	5.26	160	1.88	166	1.81

Although our initial choice of 30% was based on our *ad hoc* analysis of the cases that we had reviewed, prior work suggests this was a reasonable approach, based upon the low likelihood of a false positive over a large number of MOSS tokens[55]. The projects in our class typically include several hundred lines of C code written by students. As a result, the total number of unique tokens evaluated by MOSS is quite substantial, and false positives are less likely.

The original class practice involved evaluating plagiarism using only *intra*-semester data, but we observed that incorporating inter-semester data revealed 20% more cases of plagiarism. With this in mind, we converted to using a full cross-semester analysis: we compared all student submissions between Summer 2015 and Summer 2018 (10 semesters). In cases where trying to evaluate all submissions over time did not work — MOSS simply never returned results — we compared the current semester's submissions against individual prior years' submissions, combining the results at the end for the current semester. We found this result consistent with prior work [44].

2.2 Course Messaging (Pre–Summer 2017)

The inaugural semester of the course was Spring 2015; there was no prior body of work from which students could draw. Beyond making students aware of the existing university honor code, we did not raise the issue of plagiarism to the class during that semester.

In Spring 2016 we noticed indications of plagiarism and began to investigate. Our first course of action was to augment the syllabus to more clearly explain the course standards for plagiarism. We also offered amnesty to students who came forward to admit their plagiarism, but found amnesty completely ineffective; *none* of the students from the suspected cases came forward. Instead, students who had used small online examples of code came forward.

In Spring 2017 we took aggressive action by quickly completing a review of the code submissions shortly after students completed each project. When we identified specific cases of suspected plagiarism, we scheduled meetings to discuss our findings with the students. We made contact via the online student forum system (Piazza) and conducted online meetings (via WebEx or BlueJeans). Many students ignored our requests to discuss their assignments. Of those who spoke with us, some admitted to plagiarism and some denied it. All cases were submitted to the university under its process for handling the issue. The plagiarism rate between the first and second project plummeted. However, we estimate that each case we prosecuted required more than five hours of instructional team time. This approach, while effective, was too labor intensive to scale for a large class.

2.3 Collaboration versus Cheating

Beginning in Summer 2017, we augmented the existing information about course expectations, the academic honesty policy, and penalties for violating this policy with an additional reinforcement mechanism: a quiz, administered using the university's LMS, that required the students' active acknowledgement that they understood and agreed to the policy. The initial results for Summer 2017 were encouraging: the number of cases of plagiarism noticeably decreased. However, the class size for that semester was the smallest to date. While we were optimistic, we decided it was premature to declare victory.

Subsequent semesters supported our finding that there was a statistically significant decrease in the rate of plagiarism in Summer 2017. We discuss our findings in §3 and our analysis in §4.

3 EVALUATION

Each project in our course consists of discrete parts: Project 1 has four and Project 2 has two. Each component is individually submitted for grading, and we evaluate each distinct component using MOSS. Table 1 reports our results for Project 1 from Summer 2015 through Summer 2018. Table 2 reports our results for Project 2 from Summer 2015 through Fall 2017, excluding Spring 2017, as that semester we implemented a different, aggressive-prosecution model. Table 3 summarizes our results for all presentations of the course. Table 5 summarizes our results for all *unique* students identified as plagiarizing assignments in a given semester.

Table 2: Project 2 Submission & Plagiarism Data

Project 2 consists of two separate submission units. Per semester, we report the total number of submissions and the percentage flagged for plagiarism (as defined in §2.1).

Semester	Part 1		Part 2	
	Submissions	%Plagiarism	Submissions	%Plagiarism
Summer 2015	136	7.35	132	7.58
Fall 2015	147	8.16	132	8.33
Spring 2016	142	1.41	140	2.86
Summer 2016	135	8.11	126	7.94
Fall 2016	155	6.45	146	8.90
Spring 2017	122	4.10	122	3.28
Summer 2017	71	0.00	68	2.94
Fall 2017	203	0.99	196	0.00
Spring 2018	251	0.00	238	0.84
Summer 2018	164	0.00	159	3.14

3.1 Effectiveness

To evaluate our "Collaboration versus Cheating" approach, we analyze each separate part of a submitted project by performing a one-tailed two-sample t-test, assuming unequal variances. This approach is appropriate for this evaluation because we are interested only in interventions that yield lower plagiarism rates. We are testing distinct groups of students, but with similar backgrounds (see §4.2 for further discussion). We tested against the null hypothesis with a 95% confidence ($p < 0.05$).

In evaluating Project 1 cases, we use data from Summer 2015 through Summer 2018. Data from Summer 2015 through Spring 2017 represent the data prior to the introduction of this approach, while those from Summer 2017 through Summer 2018 represent the data since the implementation of this approach. We omit Spring 2017 Project 3 data, as it relates to the strong success of a rapid response scheme, where the instructional team reached out to Project 1 students. No other semester used this approach; it does not surprise us that aggressive enforcement is generally successful.

Our interpretation of these results is that the samples in question are unlikely to come from the same population ($p < 0.05$). We conclude that our intervention in this case was significant. However, we acknowledge the possibility that some other differences account for these changes (this is further discussed in §4).

Independently, we examine the number of *unique* students identified per semester. These data are shown in Table 5. The change is clearly visible from the table. We perform a comparable t-test on these results, comparing the Summer 2015 through Spring 2016 results against the Summer 2016 through Summer 2018 results, and once again note that these results are unlikely to come from the same population ($p < 0.05$).

3.2 Resource Requirements

An important consideration for us regarding the role of course instructors is the level of resources required for implementing anti-plagiarism techniques. The time required to add the quiz to the LMS is nominal, and the material can be copied from one semester to another. The post we add to our student engagement forum (Piazza) is also copied from the prior semester. The total effort required for this is less than one hour and is independent of the number

Table 3: Aggregate Plagiarism Results

MOSS-reported similarity across all semesters: breakdown by project/sub-project, reporting number of flagged submissions, percentage (of total), plus average similarity % and average line count similarity (with standard deviation).

Project	Total Submissions	Plagiarism		MOSS			
		Detected	Percent	Average %	Standard Deviation	Average Lines	Standard Deviation
PR1-A	1647	83	5.04	13.01	15.47	44.33	50.30
PR1-B	1623	92	5.67	13.11	16.96	31.19	35.23
PR1-C	1409	57	4.05	15.77	11.51	38.04	36.75
PR1-D	1475	69	4.68	18.10	15.01	41.81	59.94
PR2-A	1509	52	3.45	10.76	11.16	30.82	25.00
PR2-B	1453	61	4.20	8.21	15.41	62.77	100.14

of students in the class. Responses to follow-up questions from students and clarification of the policy require approximately an additional hour of time. Fewer than a dozen students asked follow-up questions on average; most questions consisted only of one or two paragraphs and were asked via Piazza[43] so that the answers were visible to the entire class.

The time required for the students to complete the evaluation was generally less than 15 minutes.

In addition, our work for evaluating the plagiarism activity has led us to automate much of the process involved. This is done using a set of scripts that invoke MOSS with all of the current and prior semesters' code as well as any starter code provided to the students. The scripts then collect the results from MOSS, download and "scrape" the HTML pages that MOSS provides, and generate output data files in a format that is amenable to further processing. This step can take up to three hours for a class with approximately 300 student submissions. One interesting complication is that one of the project parts is now so large that we must break up the submission process incrementally and submit the current semester submissions against prior submissions grouped by year — otherwise, MOSS fails to provide results — a frustrating type of error.

Once a case is identified, we review each of the suspect cases to eliminate those that do not appear to be genuine acts of plagiarism. This involves a review of the code and the student's README file. If these indicate a likely case of plagiarism, either a meeting is scheduled with the student — if this is the first time we have observed an issue for this student — or we refer the student to the university. Since the entire program is online, student meetings in this context are via an online video conferencing service. At least two members of the instructional team are present and, with the student's permission, the meeting is recorded. The information from MOSS is presented to them, and we discuss the similarity. If they admit to plagiarism, we give them a grade of zero points on the suspected sections of the project. The outcome is reported to the university, which tracks the issue so that repeated offenses can be handled appropriately while safeguarding the students' privacy rights.

In cases where students ignore our request for a meeting (which frequently happens), tell us they have withdrawn from the course, or do not admit to the plagiarism, we process a formal referral to the university. The referral includes a copy of the plagiarism quiz, the syllabus explaining the course policy, and the code identified by

Table 4: "Collaboration versus Cheating" Assessment T-Test Results

See §2.3. One-tailed two-sample t-test, assuming unequal variances: demonstrates statistical significance of intervention with respect to pre-intervention classes.

Project	T-crit	T-stat	P(≤**0.05**)
PR1-A	2.23	0.03	**0.032**
PR1-B	2.90	1.89	**0.011**
PR1-C	2.83	1.94	**0.015**
PR1-D	3.93	1.94	**0.004**
PR2-A	4.70	2.13	**0.002**
PR2-B	4.09	1.89	**0.004**

MOSS. Once a decision is made, the instructional team is notified. If a grade change is required, a paper form must be completed and signed by various members of the department. Overall, we estimate that prosecuting a case requires more than five hours of instructional team time.

Even the most superficial analysis indicates that any approach that minimizes plagiarism is an improvement over the simple enforcement model. Thus, we defer an actual cost calculation for this improvement.

4 ANALYSIS

We are aware of several open questions that relate directly to the veracity of our results.

4.1 Hidden Plagiarism

One possible explanation for the observed decrease in the plagiarism rate is that students became better at hiding their plagiarism. In an attempt to look for more subtle forms of plagiarism, we have supplemented our work with MOSS by adding a number of other mechanisms, including code watermarks and SHA-2 checksums, which detect tampering with the code testing environment. We have investigated several suspicious cases, but we found no new cases of plagiarism using these mechanisms. A student brilliant enough to spoof SHA-2 checksums is unlikely to need to plagiarize the code for an introductory graduate operating systems course [45].

In the unlikely case that students develop the level of insight necessary to circumvent the various plagiarism checks in the system, they must do so independently of other students, since MOSS detects collaborative plagiarism. Thus, to circumvent MOSS, a student must find a candidate code base and then substantially alter its structure to avoid detection. Even if a student were to actively use MOSS to confirm that their code no longer appeared structurally similar to the original code they plagiarized, they would then need to also make sure that their modified code *worked*, which in turn means fixing it and debugging problems that arose due to the substantive changes. Our pedagogical goal is to ensure that students understand the underlying mechanisms; this goal is achieved if the student must understand their now modified code base sufficiently well to pass the tests of their code. This effect has been separately noted, particularly with respect to MOSS and programming classes [20].

Table 5: Unique number of students detected per semester

Summer 2015	21	13.8
Fall 2015	27	16.8
Spring 2016	21	14.2
Summer 2016	20	14.1
Fall 2016	23	13.1
Spring 2017	20	14.6
Summer 2017	4	5.6
Fall 2017	11	5.1
Spring 2018	15	5.9
Summer 2018	12	7.0

One intriguing approach to detect such cases is to perform a more substantive analysis of the student submissions. Our testing mechanism saves all student submissions, which would permit us to evaluate the *history* of student code submissions more thoroughly using existing techniques [55].

4.2 Demographic Shifts

One insightful reviewer of our research suggested that our results might be due to shifting demographics. We do not have demographics for the class, but we do have them for the program (see §1). While there has been a small change in demographics, it seems unlikely that the effectiveness of our approach is due to a modest (10%) change in program demographics.

4.3 Work for Hire

A reviewer of our research indicated we did not address work-for-hire-style cheating solutions. We agree that this is a weakness of our work. We are encouraged by work being conducted by our colleagues within the program to build tools for identifying such code. It also occurs to us that their work might be combined with the analysis-over-time approach suggested in §4.1 on the theory that a student who contracts out that work would likely only submit it a few times on their own. We can also track the IP address used to submit student work to detect cases where the work-for-hire is given access to the student's account for the purposes of submitting their work to our automatic grading system.

However, we argue that our own work is a valuable tool for decreasing the rate of plagiarism, even if it does not completely eliminate plagiarism.

4.4 Strict Enforcement

One possible alternative explanation for the efficacy of our approach is the more rigorous enforcement model. While we have not formally proven this is not a factor, from Summer 2017 through Summer 2018 our enforcement was not as rigorous as it was in Spring 2017. Since Summer 2018 we have made significant strides in automating the process of generating detailed descriptions of our findings, which has made contacting students and preparing referrals to the university less time-consuming. Our scripts anonymize the MOSS output by replacing student names with unique identifiers, convert the HTML pages to PDF documents, and construct one directory per current-semester student with all the relevant information. Our hope is this will further reduce our plagiarism rate.

5 PRIOR WORK

The basic concepts around plagiarism are hardly new and have been extensively reviewed [27, 28, 37]. Indeed, the literature contains clear discussions on this problem *with respect to programming courses* decades ago [24]. While we still do not fully understand online-instruction dynamics, the available evidence suggests that plagiarism occurs in both online and in-person programs [4, 15, 25, 34, 41, 46, 54, 57]. While much of the prior work focused on *undergraduate* academic dishonesty, we did not find any prior work suggesting that these findings do not apply to course-based graduate programs as well.

Similarly, the idea of clarifying the expectations for students in programming classes is not new [21, 49]. Our research augments this prior work by evaluating these techniques in an actual classroom setting over a period of 10 semesters.

Motivating students to adhere to academic honesty policies and the instructional strategies that effectively achieve this goal, particularly with respect to plagiarism in computer science classes, remains an open area of research and practice [14]. Although some previous studies have explored the root-cause analysis for plagiarism, our goal is not to understand *why* students plagiarize, but rather to understand how to discourage it through a combination of detection and education mechanisms [18]. Our approach is consistent with prior studies suggesting a move away from a moralistic view of plagiarism, instead reframing discussion on plagiarism as an integral part of the learning process. In other words, *even if* students do not understand what plagiarism is when starting the program, educating them about it is important and beneficial, albeit a secondary goal to the instructors' [1]. That said, our research also supports the prior observation that simply informing students about an honor code *does not* lead to a decrease in plagiarism in online programs [36]. Active education on academic honesty through formal training, however, *may be* effective [13].

We admit that we do not know the optimal mechanism for motivating students to adhere to academic honesty policies. We have not explored the specific issue of motivations behind plagiarism (which the literature suggests can be cultural, economic, or perception-based), but we do note that our successful interventions are consistent with educating students, regardless of their cultural background [3, 7, 11].

There is a strong body of research describing techniques for reducing plagiarism, but there is a much smaller pool of evaluations regarding the application of these techniques [19, 35, 51]. One side-effect of this paucity of research is that the most common strategy for combating plagiarism is to shift responsibility to individual instructors, which results in haphazard enforcement and poor knowledge-sharing. By providing a rigorous review of techniques applied over time to the same class, with similar student populations, we contribute solid evidence of techniques that work. We hope that universities can incorporate this evidence into a broader initiative toward improving *all* courses, rather than relying on anecdotal knowledge shared haphazardly between individual instructors [40, 50].

6 FUTURE WORK

Besides the obvious possibilities raised during our analysis (see §4), we can see several areas of future work:

- We can augment the mechanisms available for detecting plagiarism. While MOSS is an excellent tool, it is not necessarily applicable to all programming classes. Evaluating new mechanisms for detecting code plagiarism will be useful and is an active area of research [5, 6, 16, 17, 26, 30, 33, 38, 39, 53, 56].
- We can work on identifying new ways to modify the behavior of students to achieve our goals of further improving academic honesty.
- We can improve our own analysis of the output using our existing tools. Our work on this project has already encouraged us to develop several tools we can use to ease the evaluation of student code in the future, and we suspect there is further work to be done in this area, particularly with an eye toward simplifying the process for others. Similar augmentations over MOSS have been implemented by others as well [47, 55]
- We could explore *why* this approach works. We speculate that it is because of the context in which students are presented with the information — it is presented as a formal quiz, which underscores its importance to students, whereas posts in Piazza are more likely to be viewed as background noise. Studying different ways of presenting this information to the class and measuring the outcome might be possible, but it may also raise ethical research considerations.

We also realize that future classes may learn of the techniques that the course instructors use to detect plagiarism. As a result, course instructors will need to find ways to further improve their detection abilities. At some point, the work required to circumvent these checks becomes greater than the effort of simply doing the assignment — and hopefully achieves the instructors' pedagogical goal [20].

7 CONCLUSION

Prior work demonstrates that honor codes alone are not an effective mechanism for reducing code plagiarism; this research demonstrates that explaining and reinforcing lessons in academic honesty results in statistically significant ($p < 0.05$) decreases in plagiarism rates across all of the distinctive programming submissions in a large online graduate computer science course. In addition, this technique requires minimal effort from the instructors — in contrast to a strict enforcement policy, which substantially increases the burden on the instructional staff.

REFERENCES

[1] Lee Adam, Vivienne Anderson, and Rachel Spronken-Smith. 2017. "It's not fair": policy discourses and students' understandings of plagiarism in a New Zealand university. *Higher Education* 74, 1 (2017), 17–32.

[2] Alex Aiken. 1994. MOSS: A System for Detecting Software Similarity. http://theory.stanford.edu/~aiken/moss/ (Accessed January 6, 2018).

[3] Ruth Baker-Gardner and Cherry-Ann Smart. 2017. Ignorance or Intent?: A Case Study of Plagiarism in Higher Education among LIS Students in the Caribbean. In *Handbook of Research on Academic Misconduct in Higher Education*. IGI Global, 182–205.

[4] Russell Boyatt, Mike Joy, Claire Rocks, and Jane Sinclair. 2014. What (Use) is a MOOC?. In *The 2nd international workshop on learning technology for education in cloud*. Springer, 133–145.

[5] Aylin Caliskan-Islam, Richard Harang, Andrew Liu, Arvind Narayanan, Clare Voss, Fabian Yamaguchi, and Rachel Greenstadt. 2015. De-anonymizing programmers via code stylometry. In *24th USENIX Security Symposium (USENIX Security), Washington, DC.*

[6] Aylin Caliskan-Islam, Fabian Yamaguchi, Edwin Dauber, Richard Harang, Konrad Rieck, Rachel Greenstadt, and Arvind Narayanan. 2015. When coding style survives compilation: De-anonymizing programmers from executable binaries. *arXiv preprint arXiv:1512.08546* (2015).

[7] Shih-Chieh Chien. 2017. Taiwanese College Students? Perceptions of Plagiarism: Cultural and Educational Considerations. *Ethics & Behavior* 27, 2 (2017), 118–139.

[8] Beth Cook, Judy Sheard, Angela Carbone, Chris Johnson, et al. 2014. Student perceptions of the acceptability of various code-writing practices. In *Proceedings of the 2014 conference on Innovation & technology in computer science education.* ACM, 105–110.

[9] Henry Corrigan-Gibbs, Nakull Gupta, Curtis Northcutt, Edward Cutrell, and William Thies. 2015. Deterring cheating in online environments. *ACM Transactions on Computer-Human Interaction (TOCHI)* 22, 6 (2015), 28.

[10] Henry Corrigan-Gibbs, Nakull Gupta, Curtis Northcutt, Edward Cutrell, and William Thies. 2015. Measuring and maximizing the effectiveness of honor codes in online courses. In *Proceedings of the Second (2015) ACM Conference on Learning@ Scale.* ACM, 223–228.

[11] Georgina Cosma, Mike Joy, Jane Sinclair, Margarita Andreou, Dongyong Zhang, Beverley Cook, and Russell Boyatt. 2017. Perceptual comparison of source-code plagiarism within students from UK, China, and South Cyprus higher education institutions. *ACM Transactions on Computing Education (TOCE)* 17, 2 (2017), 8.

[12] Victoria L Crittenden, Richard C Hanna, and Robert A Peterson. 2009. The cheating culture: A global societal phenomenon. *Business Horizons* 52, 4 (2009), 337–346.

[13] Guy J Curtis, Bethanie Gouldthorp, Emma F Thomas, Geraldine M O'Brien, and Helen M Correia. 2013. Online academic-integrity mastery training may improve students' awareness of, and attitudes toward, plagiarism. *Psychology Learning & Teaching* 12, 3 (2013), 282–289.

[14] Cesur Dagli. 2017. *Relationships of first principles of instruction and student mastery: A MOOC on how to recognize plagiarism.* Ph.D. Dissertation. Indiana University.

[15] Charlie Daly and Jane Horgan. 2005. Patterns of plagiarism. In *ACM SIGCSE Bulletin*, Vol. 37. ACM, 383–387.

[16] Tomche Delev and Dejan Gjorgjevikj. 2017. Comparison of string matching based algorithms for plagiarism detection of source code. (2017).

[17] Xuliang Duan, Mantao Wang, and Jiong Mu. 2017. A Plagiarism Detection Algorithm based on Extended Winnowing. In *MATEC Web of Conferences*, Vol. 128. EDP Sciences, 02019.

[18] Sarah E Eaton, Melanie Guglielmin, and Benedict Otoo. 2017. Plagiarism: Moving from punitive to pro-active approaches. (2017).

[19] Helen Ewing, Ade Anast, and Tamara Roehling. 2016. Addressing plagiarism in online programmes at a health sciences university: a case study. *Assessment & Evaluation in Higher Education* 41, 4 (2016), 575–585.

[20] genchang1234. 2015. genchang1234/How-to-cheat-in-computer-science-101. https://github.com/genchang1234/How-to-cheat-in-computer-science-101 (accessed January 6, 2018).

[21] J Paul Gibson. 2009. Software reuse and plagiarism: A code of practice. In *In 14th ACM SIGCSE Annual Conference on Innovation and Technology in Computer Science Education(ITiCSE 2009.* ACM, 55–59.

[22] Inc. GitHub. 2018. Guide to Submitting a DMCA Takedown Notice. https://help.github.com/articles/guide-to-submitting-a-dmca-takedown-notice/ (Accessed January 20, 2018).

[23] Joshua Goodman, Julia Melkers, and Amanda Pallais. 2017. Can Online Delivery Increase Access to Education? (2017).

[24] Sam Grier. 1981. A Tool That Detects Plagiarism in Pascal Programs. In *Proceedings of the Twelfth SIGCSE Technical Symposium on Computer Science Education (SIGCSE '81).* ACM, New York, NY, USA, 15–20. https://doi.org/10.1145/800037.800954

[25] Therese C Grijalva, Clifford Nowell, and Joe Kerkvliet. 2006. Academic honesty and online courses. *College Student Journal* 40, 1 (2006).

[26] Daniël Heres. 2017. *Source Code Plagiarism Detection using Machine Learning.* Master's thesis.

[27] Rebecca Moore Howard. 1995. Plagiarisms, authorships, and the academic death penalty. *College English* 57, 7 (1995), 788–806.

[28] Rebecca Moore Howard. 1999. *Standing in the shadow of giants: Plagiarists, authors, collaborators.* Number 2. Greenwood Publishing Group.

[29] Stack Exchange Inc. 2018. Stack Overflow - Where Developers Learn, Share, & Build Careers. stackoverflow.com (Accessed January 21, 2018).

[30] Hasan M Jamil. 2017. Automated personalized assessment of computational thinking MOOC assignments. In *Advanced Learning Technologies (ICALT), 2017 IEEE 17th International Conference on.* IEEE, 261–263.

[31] David A Joyner, Ashok K Goel, and Charles Isbell. 2016. The Unexpected Pedagogical Benefits of Making Higher Education Accessible. In *Proceedings of the Third (2016) ACM Conference on Learning@ Scale.* ACM, 117–120.

[32] Brian W Kernighan and Dennis M Ritchie. 2006. *The C programming language.*

[33] Hiroshi Kikuchi, Takaaki Goto, Mitsuo Wakatsuki, and Tetsuro Nishino. 2015. A source code plagiarism detecting method using sequence alignment with abstract syntax tree elements. *International Journal of Software Innovation (IJSI)* 3, 3 (2015), 41–56.

[34] Lisa M. Krieger. 2016. Stanford finds cheating – especially among computer science students – on the rise. https://tinyurl.com/yan2sull (accessed January 6, 2017) originally published February 6, 2010.

[35] Bruce Macfarlane, Jingjing Zhang, and Annie Pun. 2014. Academic integrity: a review of the literature. *Studies in Higher Education* 39, 2 (2014), 339–358.

[36] David F Mastin, Jennifer Peszka, and Deborah R Lilly. 2009. Online academic integrity. *Teaching of Psychology* 36, 3 (2009), 174–178.

[37] Hermann A Maurer, Frank Kappe, and Bilal Zaka. 2006. Plagiarism-a survey. (2006).

[38] Xiaozhu Meng. 2016. Fine-grained binary code authorship identification. In *Proceedings of the 2016 24th ACM SIGSOFT International Symposium on Foundations of Software Engineering.* ACM, 1097–1099.

[39] Xiaozhu Meng, Barton P Miller, and Kwang-Sung Jun. 2017. Identifying multiple authors in a binary program. In *European Symposium on Research in Computer Security.* Springer, 286–304.

[40] Holmes Miss and J Evelyn. 2017. Development and Leadership of a Faculty-led Academic Integrity Education Program at an Ontario College. (2017).

[41] Hannah Natanson. 2017. More than 60 Fall CS50 Enrollees Faced Academic Dishonesty Charges. http://www.thecrimson.com/article/2017/5/3/cs50-cheating-cases-2017/ (Accessed January 6, 2018).

[42] University of Ontario. 2016. Why is Academic Integrity and Honesty Important? https://secure.apa.uoit.ca/academic_integrity/module1/Module13.html

[43] Inc. Piazza. 2017. Why Piazza Works. https://piazza.com/product/overview Accessed December 31, 2017.

[44] Jonathan Pierce and Craig Zilles. 2017. Investigating Student Plagiarism Patterns and Correlations to Grades. In *Proceedings of the 2017 ACM SIGCSE Technical Symposium on Computer Science Education (SIGCSE '17).* ACM, New York, NY, USA, 471–476. https://doi.org/10.1145/3017680.3017797

[45] Zulfany Erlisa Rasjid, Benfano Soewito, Gunawan Witjaksono, and Edi Abdurachman. 2017. A review of collisions in cryptographic hash function used in digital forensic tools. *Procedia Computer Science* 116 (2017), 381–392.

[46] Heather B Shapiro, Clara H Lee, Noelle E Wyman Roth, Kun Li, Mine Çetinkaya-Rundel, and Dorian A Canelas. 2017. Understanding the massive open online course (MOOC) student experience: An examination of attitudes, motivations, and barriers. *Computers & Education* 110 (2017), 35–50.

[47] Dana Sheahen and David Joyner. 2016. TAPS: A MOSS Extension for Detecting Software Plagiarism at Scale. In *Proceedings of the Third (2016) ACM Conference on Learning@ Scale.* ACM, 285–288.

[48] Judy Sheard, Michael Morgan, Andrew Petersen, Amber Settle, Jane Sinclair, Gerry Cross, Charles Riedesel, et al. 2016. Negotiating the Maze of Academic Integrity in Computing Education. In *Proceedings of the 2016 ITiCSE Working Group Reports.* ACM, 57–80.

[49] Simon, Judy Sheard, Michael Morgan, Andrew Petersen, Amber Settle, and Jane Sinclair. 2018. Informing Students About Academic Integrity in Programming. In *Proceedings of the 20th Australasian Computing Education Conference (ACE '18).* ACM, New York, NY, USA, 113–122. https://doi.org/10.1145/3160489.3160502

[50] Raghu Naath Singh and David Hurley. 2017. The Effectiveness of Teaching and Learning Process in Online Education as Perceived by University Faculty and Instructional Technology Professionals. *Journal of Teaching and Learning with Technology* 6, 1 (2017), 65–75.

[51] Alison Smedley, Tonia Crawford, and Linda Cloete. 2015. An intervention aimed at reducing plagiarism in undergraduate nursing students. *Nurse education in practice* 15, 3 (2015), 168–173.

[52] Sami W Tabsh, Hany A El-Kadi, and A Abdelfatah. 2015. Past and present engineering students' views on academic dishonesty at a middle-eastern university. *International Journal of Engineering Education* 31, 5 (2015), 1334–1342.

[53] RL Victor and Farica P PUTRI. 2016. A Code Plagiarism Detection System Based on Abstract Syntax Tree and a High Level Fuzzy Petri Net. *DEStech Transactions on Materials Science and Engineering* mmme (2016).

[54] Yoav Yair. 2014. I saw you cheating. *ACM Inroads* 5, 3 (2014), 36–37.

[55] Lisa Yan, Nick McKeown, Mehran Sahami, and Chris Piech. 2018. TMOSS: Using Intermediate Assignment Work to Understand Excessive Collaboration in Large Classes. In *Proceedings of the 49th ACM Technical Symposium on Computer Science Education (SIGCSE '18).* ACM, New York, NY, USA, 110–115. https://doi.org/10.1145/3159450.3159490

[56] Xinyu Yang, Guoai Xu, Qi Li, Yanhui Guo, and Miao Zhang. 2017. Authorship attribution of source code by using back propagation neural network based on particle swarm optimization. *PloS one* 12, 11 (2017), e0187204.

[57] Youdan Zhang. 2013. Benefiting from MOOC. In *EdMedia: World Conference on Educational Media and Technology.* Association for the Advancement of Computing in Education (AACE), 1372–1377.

What Do CS1 Syllabi Reveal About Our Expectations of Introductory Programming Students?

Brett A. Becker
University College Dublin
Belfield, Dublin 4, Ireland
brett.becker@ucd.ie

Thomas Fitzpatrick
University College Dublin
Belfield, Dublin 4, Ireland
thomas.fitzpatrick.1@ucdconnect.ie

ABSTRACT

A well-received ITiCSE 2016 paper challenged the orthodox view that programming is hard to learn. It contended that CS1 educators' expectations are too high, which can result in poor teaching and learning, and could impact negatively on diversity and equity. The author posed a challenge to the community to collect research-based evidence of what novice programmers can achieve, and use evidence to derive realistic expectations for achievement.

We argue that before rising to this challenge we must determine: *What exactly do educators expect of introductory programming students?* This paper presents our efforts toward answering this question. We manually curated hundreds of CS1 syllabi, providing a fresh perspective of expectation in CS1 courses. We analyzed learning outcomes and their concepts, in addition to languages utilized and other useful CS1 design and delivery information.

This work contributes to a current picture of what is expected of introductory programming students, and provides an interactive online tool linked to all collected syllabi and containing all learning outcomes and other associated information. We hope this will aid the community in deciding whether or not we have unrealistic expectations of our CS1 students and if so, our contributions provide a starting point for the community to adjust them.

CCS CONCEPTS

• **Social and professional topics → Computer science education; CS1.**

KEYWORDS

CS1; CS1 languages; curriculum design; introductory programming; language choice; learning objectives; learning outcomes; novice programmers; syllabi; syllabus; teaching languages

ACM Reference Format:

Brett A. Becker and Thomas Fitzpatrick. 2019. What Do CS1 Syllabi Reveal About Our Expectations of Introductory Programming Students?. In *Proceedings of the 50th ACM Technical Symposium on Computer Science Education (SIGCSE '19), February 27-March 2, 2019, Minneapolis, MN, USA.* ACM, New York, NY, USA, 7 pages. https://doi.org/10.1145/3287324.3287485

ACM ISBN 978-1-4503-5890-3/19/02...$15.00
https://doi.org/10.1145/3287324.3287485

1 INTRODUCTION

A central focus of computing education research is the teaching and learning of a first programming language [21]. Despite this, a well-cited ITiCSE working group found that "Three decades of active research on the teaching of introductory programming has had limited effect on classroom practice" [19, p. 204]. It is also frequently stated that programming is hard to learn [1, 21], a claim that regularly goes back to the McCracken working group that found "many students do not know how to program at the conclusion of their introductory courses" [15, p. 125]. The reasons for this are believed to be multifaceted, and that difficulties in learning to program contribute to low motivation and high dropout rates [2].

At ITiCSE 2016, Andrew Luxton-Reilly presented a paper titled 'Learning to Program is Easy' [12]. The paper was well-received, earning a commendation from the program committee, and quickly generating discussion in the community [8]. Luxton-Reilly's paper challenged the orthodox view that programming is hard to learn, and claimed that this view results in uncritical teaching practices, poor student learning, and may also impact negatively on diversity and equity in computing. The paper also presented substantial evidence that this view has deeply permeated the computing education community's culture, literature and psyche. Luxton-Reilly claimed that computing educators make introductory courses difficult by establishing unrealistic expectations for novice programmers. He proposed that by revisiting the expected norms for introductory programming we may be able to substantially improve the learning of novice programmers, address negative impressions of disciplinary practices, and create a more equitable environment.

Specifically, Luxton-Reilly showed that the literature on failure rates and novice programmer ability represents a substantial body of evidence supporting the claim that students are not able to program at the level expected by instructors. He argued that it is not clear that this means that programming is inherently difficult. Instead he proposed that the computing education community should view our learning outcomes for CS1 courses as being unrealistic. He concluded with a challenge to the community: *Collect research-based evidence of what novice programmers can achieve in CS1, and use evidence to derive realistic expectations for achievement.*

Intrigued by this challenge, we realized that addressing it would most likely be complex and time consuming. It would likely require at least one large-scale, multi-institutional, multi-national study, involving significant resources and time-frames. We argue that before rising to this challenge, the community must be able to answer the question: *What exactly do we expect our introductory programming students to achieve?* This paper presents our efforts toward answering this question. We view this as a first step towards meeting Luxton-Reilly's challenge.

1.1 Overview and Motivating Questions

We manually curated CS1 syllabi by searching the websites of all 916 institutions making up the 2016-2017 QS World University Rankings® [1]. We analyzed these syllabi, seeking to answer our questions below. We also provide a web front-end to our database including learning outcome information and links to syllabi, and offer it to the computing education community as a tool, as described in Section 5. To move toward answering our overarching question *What exactly do we expect our introductory programming students to achieve?* we formulated four questions specific to CS1 learning outcomes, as these are central to Luxton-Reilly's challenge (Q1-4). To dive deeper into current CS1 teaching practices we formulated two additional questions on languages and syllabi (Q5-6):

Q1: What percentage of CS1 courses have explicit learning outcomes?

Q2: What concepts do explicit CS1 learning outcomes cover?

Q3: How do These Concepts Align With CS2013?

Q4: What do explicit CS1 learning outcomes look like?

Q5: What is the current CS1 teaching language distribution?

Q6: What are the most common computing terms found in CS1 syllabi?

In forming these questions, we aimed to provide information from three vantage-points:

(1) That of other educators, by presenting information such as their explicit CS1 learning outcomes *word for word*, for further analysis/use by the community.
(2) That of our tool, by presenting *derived* information such as a list of concepts included in learning outcomes.
(3) A somewhat agnostic view, by including information such as full-syllabus word frequency counts.

Our contributions are the beginnings of a current, multi-faceted, picture of what is expected of CS1 students, and an online tool where educators can utilize and contribute to our dataset. It is our intention that these results and the tool that we provide will better position the community to decide if we, as a community, have unrealistic expectations of our CS1 students, as proposed by Luxton-Reilly, and to move towards addressing his challenge.

Before continuing, we comment on terminology. We use the term *learning outcome* to mean an explicit statement expressing something that students are expected to know, or be able to do, upon successful completion of a course. These are sometimes called "learning objectives". We do not include as learning outcomes any consequences of learning such as student grades. It is important to recognize that it is through learning outcomes that we *tell* our students what we expect of them. This is important, as what we tell students can be adjusted, as Luxton-Reilly noted.

This paper is organized as follows. In Section 2 we review related work. In Section 3 we present our methodology, followed by our results and discussions in Section 4. In Section 5 we provide an overview of the tool that presents our data. We discuss threats to validity in Section 6 before concluding in Section 7.

[1] www.topuniversities.com/university-rankings/world-university-rankings/2016

2 RELATED WORK

What is taught in CS1 has been the subject of numerous studies over several decades [3, 13]. Although many computing degrees have similar structures, and CS1 often fills a common place in them, there are many approaches. Reflecting this, CS2013 [11] discusses various trade-offs between design decisions in first year courses, but is generally non-prescriptive with respect to first year curricula [12]. Additionally, most CS1 research does not focus on explicit learning outcomes, instead focusing on course content, material, assessment, and other practical aspects of delivery. Thus, most of these studies do not directly investigate what is expected of CS1 students.

In their 2001 ITiCSE working group, McCracken et al. [15] (mentioned in Section 1) developed a set of learning outcomes that described the expected level of skill for students at the end of their first year of study. Students were expected to be able to complete the following steps: (1) Abstract the problem from its description; (2) Generate sub-problems; (3) Transform sub-problems into sub-solutions; (4) Re-compose the sub-solutions into a working program; and (5) Evaluate and iterate. These were formulated in response to the question "What should be assessed [in CS1]" [15, p. 126]. The authors state that this is an ideal and generalized situation, and do note some problems with their abstraction.

In 2006, Schulte and Bennedsen sought to create a general, world-wide picture of teachers' opinions about what should be taught in introductory programming courses [22]. They specifically studied what educators believe to be important to teach, what they actually teach, and what they believe students find most difficult. They culled 28 topics from the literature and used these in a survey where instructors were asked to rate the difficulty and relevance of each.

Goldman et al. [6] constructed a list of 32 CS1 topics in 2010, using a structured multi-step (Delphi) process that uses a group of experts to achieve a consensus opinion. Specifically, they sought a set of key topics for which if a student fails to demonstrate a conceptual understanding of, then confidence could be given to the conclusion that the student had not mastered the course content.

In 2011, Petersen et al. [20] noted that final exams are a useful proxy for deriving curricular expectations and determining what instructors understand to be important. They presented the analysis of nine experienced CS1 instructors who reviewed final examinations from a variety of North American institutions. Their instrument drew concepts from [22] and [6] discussed above. Their final instrument contained 28 CS1 topics.

Around the same time, Elliott Tew and Guzdial were working towards developing a validated assessment of CS1 topics known as the FCS1 (Foundational CS1) assessment instrument [26]. In [25] they sought to identify concepts that a wide variety of introductory courses and approaches had in common. They chose textbooks as the external artifact representing the content of a course, because they deemed other measures such as course syllabi or assignments as not feasible to analyze at a large scale. They conducted a document analysis of the table of contents of the two most widely adopted CS1 textbooks from each of the six major publishers of computing textbooks (a total of 12 books). Using a bottom-up approach, they aggregated topics listed in the tables of contents, noting which concepts were covered by which texts. However their list became unwieldy with over 400 concepts, ranging from low-level topics such as byte code and computer architecture details to advanced topics traditionally covered later in the curriculum. They used the framework of the Computer Science volume of Computing Curricula 2001 [17] to revise their initial list of topics, resulting in 188 topics. They further refined this list by analyzing the content of canonical texts representing each of the common introductory approaches (objects-first, functional-first, and imperative-first). A concept was included in this step of revision if it was covered by all texts, or excluded by any one of the canonical texts. This resulted in a final list of 29 fundamental computing concepts common across languages and pedagogical approaches. As this list was only one step toward developing an assessment instrument, they further refined it to arrive at a list of 10 constructs amenable to testing.

The studies mentioned above involve investigating what is taught in CS1, commonly involving constructing CS1 concept lists, and often with an extra dimension such as the difficulty students have with the concepts. Also related to the present work at a different angle is the CITIDEL (Computing and Information Technology Interactive Digital Educational Library) Syllabus Collection [27], now a part of Ensemble [10]. This work aimed to provide a syllabus information tool to the computer science education community, which is also an aim of the present work.

The CITIDEL Syllabus Collection currently contains 5,083 computing syllabi, organized into 14 subjects. The subject 'Programming Fundamentals' has 406 syllabi from 67 institutions. An inspection of filenames revealed syllabi dating as far back as 1994, with possibly older syllabi also included. We decided that we wanted to compile a current collection representing more institutions, resulting in our present approach. Nonetheless we completed a preliminary analysis of the CITIDEL syllabi and plan on using this for a historic comparison with the collection we curated.

3 METHODOLOGY

Our methodology was shaped by several factors. First, we aim to provide a foundation for the community to answer the question *What exactly do we expect our introductory programming students to achieve?* We view this as a first step toward enabling the community to move towards addressing Luxton-Reilly's challenge of collecting research-based evidence of what novice programmers can achieve in CS1, and using evidence to derive realistic expectations for achievement. We felt that the core of this foundation should be *explicit* which led us to the decision to examine learning outcomes from as many up-to-date CS1 syllabi as possible. In this way we are getting to the root of what we as a community are *expecting* of our CS1 students. In addition to the analysis presented in this paper, we make these learning outcomes available word for word, in one place, as described in Section 5.

Second, as reviewed earlier, many efforts to identify CS1 concepts focus on what concepts are most important, or most difficult. This is problematic, as noted by [6, p. 5:9]: "Finding consensus on the most important and difficult concepts for a CS1 course is inherently challenging given the diversity of approaches in languages ..., pedagogical paradigms ..., and programming environments used. These factors influence the perceptions of the importance and difficulty of the topics." Thus we did not want to focus on 'important' or 'difficult' learning outcomes, but a large and representative sample of all types of CS1 learning outcomes.

Third, we noted the difficulty identified by Elliott Tew and Guzdial in analyzing course syllabi on a large scale. Facing this difficulty, we decided to curate the learning outcomes of CS1 courses on a meaningful scale, by hand. We view learning outcomes as a fundamental starting point to answer our overarching question. We believe that although it may be possible to attempt to answer this question by analyzing proxy instruments such as assessments, these would need to validly assess the learning outcomes, which is not a guarantee. Additionally, computing education lags other discipline-based education research in the number and range of validated assessments available to the research community [18]. Further, it has been suggested that the assessments we currently use to evaluate learning are simply too difficult in the first place [12], which brings into question their suitability for purposes such as ours.

3.1 Syllabus and Learning Outcome Curation

We began by randomizing the 916 institutions making up the QS World University Rankings® 2016-2017. We then procedurally searched for CS1 syllabi by following the below steps:

(1) Navigate to institution website
(2) Navigate to Computer Science / Information Technology / Computer Engineering faculty or program page
(3) Search module lists or lists of major requirements for likely CS1 courses - allowing for multiple courses per institution
(4) If at this point a syllabus was not found, we often had a course name (but it did not link to a syllabus). We then performed a Google search for <course title + university name + "syllabus">.

We populated a database with the details of these syllabi including: URL, learning outcomes, if the learning outcomes were explicitly stated, programming language, prerequisites, and other details. If the learning outcomes were explicitly stated, we saved these (verbatim) for later analysis. By explicitly stated, we mean if the syllabus had a set of statements of student expectations, often under a heading of 'learning outcomes', 'learning objectives' or similar, often appearing before any other material such as 'course content', etc. These frequently begin with wording such as 'At the end of this course the student will be able to...' or similar.

We used Guo's methodology [7] and Hertz [9] as guides in identifying CS1 courses. Where a course slightly deviated from these requirements (for instance having prerequisites), or if it was possibly a CS2 course) we tagged it so that in the future these courses could be removed from analysis if desired.

3.2 Learning Outcome Concepts

We manually analyzed the learning outcome statements to derive a list of concepts they cover. For instance if a learning outcome mentioned recursion, we added recursion to our list of learning outcome concepts. If we later found another course that mentioned recursion in a learning outcome, we marked that syllabus as such, and updated our total 'recursion count'. For syllabi that did not specifically include learning outcomes, we used the 'course content' or similar sections to continue populating our concept list. We also marked that syllabus entry with the tag '!Explicit' indicating that there were no explicit learning outcomes, and that we 'scraped' concepts from other syllabus content. This allows these syllabi to be excluded from future analysis when required, for instance, allowing researchers and educators to use our tool to only analyze those syllabi that contained explicit learning outcomes.

We decided to generate a concept list instead of using an existing one from the literature as we wanted the resulting list to represent the concepts explicitly involved in what educators expect of CS1 students, without bias inherent in lists derived from assessments, or those that focus on 'important'/'difficult' concepts, etc.

4 RESULTS AND DISCUSSION

From the 916 institutional websites we searched, we found 234 CS1 syllabi from 207 institutions. Table 1 shows the 30 countries represented in this collection and the number of syllabi, institutions, and the percent of all syllabi.

Table 1: Number of syllabi (#*S*) and institutions (#*I*) per country, and percent of total syllabi (%*T*), n = 234.

Country	#*S*	#*I*	%*T*	Country	#*S*	#*I*	%*T*
USA	118	114	50	India	4	4	2
England	33	31	14	South Africa	3	3	1
Australia	15	15	6	Turkey	3	3	1
Scotland	9	8	4	Portugal	2	1	1
Ireland	8	5	3	Sweden	2	2	1
Canada	7	7	3	Netherlands	2	2	1
New Zealand	6	5	3	Lebanon	2	2	1
Wales	5	5	2				
China, Czech Republic, Denmark, Egypt, Ghana, Hungary, Jordan, Kenya, Pakistan, Philippines, Qatar, Singapore, South Korea, Switzerland and United Arab Emirates have 1 syllabus each (<1%).							

We note that this seems biased towards Anglophone countries. We did expect some bias, particularly as we can only process English-language material. However the bias seems to not be coming so much from the list we searched, but possibly from what we are looking for. In total our list had universities from 81 countries, 72 of them not English speaking, representing 65 percent of institutions. However Table 1 shows that most syllabi found are from Anglophone countries. Nonetheless, we note that almost all websites we visited were in English, even those of institutions in non-Anglophone countries. Additionally we only saw a handful of what we believe might be syllabi in languages other than English. It is also possible that other educational systems are not strongly based on learning outcomes as countries like the USA, and EU countries. As our tool is available for researchers to contribute to (see Section 5), we would welcome syllabi from a more diverse set of countries.

4.1 Q1-4: Explicit Learning Outcomes in CS1

4.1.1 Q1: What percentage of CS1 courses have explicit learning outcomes? 154 (65.8%) of the 234 CS1 syllabi we curated have explicitly stated learning outcome or learning objective statements. We believe this is important, as explicit learning outcomes provide a direct mechanism to gauge the expectations we have for students, and are therefore central to Luxton-Reilly's challenge.

4.1.2 Q2: What concepts do explicit CS1 learning outcomes cover? Table 2 shows the learning outcome concepts we identified along with the percentage of: explicit learning outcomes containing these concepts (column Explicit); syllabi without explicit learning outcomes that contain these concepts elsewhere in the syllabus (column !Explicit); and percentage of syllabi containing each concept either in explicit learning outcomes or otherwise (column All).

Table 2: Most frequent syllabus concepts. 'Explicit' is the percentage of CS1 courses with explicit learning outcomes addressing the given concept. '!Explicit' is the percentage of CS1 courses without explicit learning outcomes where the given concept was featured somewhere else in the syllabus. 'All' is the percentage of all CS1 courses where the given concept appeared either in an explicit learning outcome, or elsewhere. $n_{Explicit} = 154, n_{!Explicit} = 80, n_{All} = 234$. Concepts are in descending order of column 'Explicit'.

Concept	Percentage of Courses		
	Explicit	!Explicit	All
Testing & debugging	56	28	45
Writing programs	55	30	46
Selection statements (if/else,etc.)	46	43	44
Problem solving (including computational thinking terms)	45	47	45
Arrays, lists, vectors, etc.	41	37	39
Basic OOP	40	32	36
Variables, assignment, arithmetic operators, declarations, data types	40	35	38
Functions, methods, procedures	38	25	33
Repetition & loops	37	29	34
Designing algorithms	29	37	31
Classes & objects	25	18	22
File handling & I/O	23	28	24
Documentation	21	11	17
Recursion	20	16	18
Data structures (general or specific - e.g. stacks)	19	30	23

The following concepts occur in < 19% of Explicit LOs, < 16% of !Explicit, and < 16% of All (presented in decreasing order of column *Explicit LOs*): Program design methodology & style, Abstraction, How computers work & history of computing, Inheritance, IDE use, Strings, Searching algorithms, program comprehension, Sorting algorithms, Exception handling, "Fundamentals of programming", Evaluating time & space complexity, Basic graphics & GUIs, Teamwork skills & communication; Encapsulation; Polymorphism; Pointers; Abstract classes & interfaces; Scope; Memory allocation; Tracing program execution; Detecting syntax errors; Detecting semantic errors; Information representation; Command prompt use; UML; Code manipulation; Functional programming; Web development; Pseudocode; Induction; Security; IT & Data; Scientific skills; Version control; Boolean logic; Multithreading & concurrency

Many interesting observations and discussions could come from Table 2, and a full discussion is limited here by space and participants. This is one of the reasons that we decided to make our data available, so that others can perform their own analyses. First, it should be noted that Table 2 is not *the* answer to Q2 – it is one of several possible, many of which can be found with the tool we have made available. Second, Table 2 provides evidence that CS1 syllabi that include explicit learning outcomes may be quite different to those that don't. This is an interesting topic for further study. Finally, we note the high rank of 'testing & debugging' (which we decided to group together) which occurs more frequently than 'writing programs'. We are confident that when 'debugging' and 'testing' are considered separately, the most frequent concept would be quite fittingly, 'writing programs'. This is something that a user of our website could determine readily.

4.1.3 Q3: How do These Concepts Align With CS2013? A full comparison of the results of this study and CS2013 [11] is a direction for future work, but we wondered how many of the concepts in Table 2 are covered by the *Software Development Fundamentals* (SDF) Knowledge Area (KA) in CS2013 [11], and specifically the Knowledge Unit (KU) *Fundamental Programming Concepts* (FPC) in that KA. Eight of the top 15 concepts presented in Table 2 are covered by the FPC KU, and 13 are covered when including the other three KUs within the SDF KA (with some overlap). The only two concepts not covered by SDF are *Basic OOP* and *Classes & objects*, which are covered by the KU *Object-Oriented Programming* under the KA *Programming Languages*. This is not surprising, given the fact that FPC "identifies only those concepts that are common to all programming paradigms" [11, p. 167].

4.1.4 Q4: What do Current CS1 Learning Outcomes Look Like? Of the 154 CS1 syllabi with explicit learning outcomes, we found a total of 1,029 learning outcome statements, an average of 6.68 learning outcomes per syllabus. All of these learning outcomes are available, word for word, on the website we describe in Section 5.

4.2 Q5: Current CS1 Language Distribution

Our fifth question was: *What is the current CS1 teaching language distribution?* Table 3 shows the languages we encountered as sole teaching languages (152 syllabi). To compare our list to [23] (a large 2012 survey of teaching languages) we omitted the 65 syllabi with no language specified (as [23] utilized more information than just syllabi, at times directly contacting instructors, they recorded a much lower number of no-language courses). To keep the comparison simple we also omitted the 17 syllabi reporting multiple languages. By this count, Java is by a good margin the most frequent CS1 language, used in 74 (49%) of the 152 syllabi. The second most frequent is Python at 36 (24%). C++ comes next at 30 (20%) followed by C at 8 (5%). Neither column adds to 100% as we do not report several languages with < 5% share. These results broadly align with those of Simon et al. [24] who conducted parallel surveys of introductory programming courses in Australasia [14] and the UK [16] (both in 2016), with a view to examining the programming languages being used.

These studies, compared to those we discuss now, provide evidence that the distribution of the top CS1 languages hasn't changed too dramatically in 20 years. In 2007, Pears et al. [19] noted that Java, C, and C++ 'topped the list'. This was also the case for surveys conducted in 1998, 2001, 2003, and 2005 (see [19]). Also in 2007, Giangrande corroborated the dominance of Java, C, and C++, notably not mentioning Python at all [5].

The most obvious shift has been the rise of Python, evidenced by comparison with Siegfried et al. [23], whose 2012 list of CS1 languages comprised of data from 404 US institutions (356 reporting single languages). Unsurprisingly, the biggest changes are Java (down from 55 to 49%) and Python (up from 12 to 24%). This shows that the rise of Python has likely come at the expense of Java, and to a lesser degree C++. Nonetheless, Python's rise was not as dramatic as anticipated given that in 2014 Guo reported that Python had overtaken Java as the teaching language of choice at the top CS schools in the United States [7]. This could be explained to some extent by the fact that Guo only examined the top 39 PhD-granting institutions, and considered CS0 courses as well as CS1.

For a comprehensive review of publications on teaching languages, the reader is guided to [13], a 2018 review of the introductory programming literature that processed more than 5,000 papers.

Table 3: Current CS1 teaching language distribution. n **= 152. The final column is data from 2012 [23],** n **= 356.**

Language	This study (2016-17 data) Number of Courses	%	From [23] (2012) %
Java	74	**49**	55
Python	36	**24**	12
C++	30	**20**	23
C	8	**5**	5

Haskell, JavaScript and R appeared ≤ 1% in both studies. We do not report languages appearing in [23] but not in our data such as Alice.

4.3 Q6: CS1 Syllabus Terms

Our final question was: *What are the most common computing terms in CS1 syllabi?* We analyzed the frequency of all words in each of the HTML syllabi (n = 185). We are currently working on PDF and other file types (n = 49). Table 4 shows the 14 most frequent computing terms overall. For the sake of presentation, and as an example of the kind of analysis our tool enables, we excluded what we deemed to be non-computing terms.

Table 4: Most frequent computing terms in 185 CS1 syllabi.

Term	Count	Term	Count
Programming	1,384	Class/es	275
Design	627	Assignment	227
Data	520	Object/s	207
Algorithm/ic/s	410	Web	196
Test/ing/s	356	Control	181
Method/s	330	Array/s	175
Function/s	317	Security	175

We intended this data to be agnostic, but for a meaningful analysis we realized that certain terms were problematic and needed some human intervention. This started with removing non-computing words. Other more specific words were also problematic. For instance, the third most frequent term in Table 4 is *Data*, but many of these occurrences probably came from the two-word term *Data Type/s*. Similarly, the ninth most frequent word is *Assignment* –

some of these probably come from the term *Assignment operator*, but many could refer to assessment tasks. On the other hand we excluded the plural word *Assignments* which came up 407 times, because this term quite likely refers to assessment tasks almost exclusively. Nonetheless, these word frequency lists could be regenerated by others with a different methodology if desired as the sources are all available on our website. This, for example, would allow a researcher to quickly locate the syllabi that contain a specific word or combination of words, allowing them to query what languages these courses use, what their learning outcomes are, etc.

5 A TOOL FOR THE COMMUNITY

We have made available a tool at csed.ucd.ie/sigcse2019/ containing all of the data used to generate our results. It allows all 234 syllabi we curated to be searched and sorted by language, location, if the learning outcomes are explicit, learning outcome concepts (including their counts from matching linked syllabi), and more. Researchers and educators are encouraged to add their own syllabi to the collection through a submissions page. Future enhancements will be geared towards making it more useful for the computing education community, and feedback is welcomed.

As a very brief example of the kind of analysis that can be done with this tool, Table 5 shows the countries (with 4 or more syllabi) with the highest percentages of syllabi containing explicit learning outcomes. The fact that European countries rank so highly is most likely due to the fact that explicit learning outcomes are an integral part of the Bologna Process [4].

Table 5: Countries with 4 or more syllabi with the highest percentages of explicit learning outcomes (%ELOs), $n = 234$.

Country	%ELOs	Country	%ELOs	Country	%ELOs
Ireland	100	Scotland	89	Canada	71
New Zealand	100	England	82	USA	58
Wales	100	Australia	73	India	25

6 THREATS TO VALIDITY

Our results have some threats to their validity. First, all of our syllabi are from institutions on the 2016/2017 QS World University Rankings®. Using rankings for similar purposes has been done by other studies (e.g. [7]), but any biases in the rankings may bias the results. We know that the ranking we used biases results towards research universities. We also noted a likely language bias discussed in Section 4. We chose to use this ranking as it included nearly 1,000 institutions which we felt fit the time and resources we had available. Future work directions include adding institutions from other rankings and sources. We also hope that members of the community avail of the opportunity to add syllabi to the collection.

We could have missed some courses. We aimed for a processing time of 5 minutes per website, amounting to one researcher working full-time for over three weeks on data collection only. We also could have incorrectly included non-CS1 courses although we found Guo's methodology [7] and Hertz's description [9] helpful.

The learning outcome concepts presented in Section 4.1 are affected by our concept of 'explicit', and our methodology in developing our concept list. However, as all of our data is available, it would be easy for these results to be replicated or the query modified to suit individual requirements. Our results on language frequency in Section 4.2 are similarly affected by the sample of syllabi. Additionally, the syllabus word frequency results are, as discussed in section 4.3, subject to some judgment calls—for example in dealing with singular and plural versions of the same word. However as above, these results could be easily reproduced, or the queries modified. Finally, it is also important to recognize that as we are looking at learning outcomes, we are analyzing what we *tell* our students we expect of them. This is important, as what we tell students can be adjusted, but also, what we tell students of our expectations may not correlate perfectly with what we actually expect.

Additionally, we acknowledge that our analysis of the curated learning outcomes focus on concepts, and not the depth to which these concepts are covered. We note however that an analysis of the depth to which these concepts are covered is possible as we provide the full wording of all learning outcomes on our website, in addition to links to the original syllabi. Finally, we do not address the possibility of reinforcement bias among syllabi. For example, it is probable that many syllabi are designed either by consulting model curricula or are inspired from other, more established syllabi at other universities. Such a possibility aligns with Luxton-Reilly's claim that certain views have deeply permeated the computing education community's culture, literature and psyche.

7 CONCLUSIONS AND FUTURE WORK

We presented a tool that allows researchers to access hundreds of current CS1 syllabi and associated data. We also present initial insights based on these syllabi, focusing on CS1 learning outcomes, languages, and syllabus keywords. These results paint a picture of what we expect CS1 students to achieve. We view this as a first step in allowing the community to answer the question: *What exactly do we expect our introductory programming students to achieve?* Answering this question, in turn, will put the community in a better position to rise to the challenge proposed by Luxton-Reilly in 2016 [12]: *Collect research-based evidence of what novice programmers can achieve in CS1, and use evidence to derive realistic expectations for achievement.*

Future work involves adding more syllabi (particularly from more diverse countries) to the collection, and conducting further analysis on the data the community now has at its fingertips. As a public tool, this work could be useful for those who are conducting CS1 research, and for educators who are designing or modifying courses.

Finally, we note that there is limited evidence on what we expect of our students on a large scale. This work demonstrates that gaining a representative picture of what we expect of our students fraught with biases and details that make gathering such evidence difficult. Nonetheless we think that the information we provide may be useful to the community.

8 ACKNOWLEDGEMENTS

The authors would like to thank the SIGCSE Board for supporting this work with a SIGCSE Special Project Grant (December, 2016).

REFERENCES

[1] Brett A. Becker, Graham Glanville, Ricardo Iwashima, Claire McDonnell, Kyle Goslin, and Catherine Mooney. 2016. Effective Compiler Error Message Enhancement for Novice Programming Students. *Computer Science Education* 26, 2-3 (2016), 148–175. https://doi.org/10.1080/08993408.2016.1225464

[2] Brett A. Becker, Cormac Murray, Tianyi Tao, Changheng Song, Robert McCartney, and Kate Sanders. 2018. Fix the First, Ignore the Rest: Dealing with Multiple Compiler Error Messages. In *Proceedings of the 49th ACM Technical Symposium on Computer Science Education (SIGCSE '18)*. ACM, New York, NY, USA, 634–639. https://doi.org/10.1145/3159450.3159453

[3] Brett A. Becker and Keith Quille. 2019. 50 Years of CS1 at SIGCSE: A Review of the Evolution of Introductory Programming Education Research. In *Proceedings of the 50th ACM Technical Symposium on Computer Science Education (SIGCSE '19)*. ACM, New York, NY, USA. https://doi.org/10.1145/3287324.3287432 *in press.*

[4] Ursula Fuller, Arnold Pears, June Amillo, Chris Avram, and Linda Mannila. 2006. A Computing Perspective on the Bologna Process. In *Working Group Reports on ITiCSE on Innovation and Technology in Computer Science Education (ITiCSE-WGR '06)*. ACM, New York, NY, USA, 115–131. https://doi.org/10.1145/1189215.1189181

[5] Ernie Giangrande, Jr. 2007. CS1 Programming Language Options. *J. Comput. Sci. Coll.* 22, 3 (Jan. 2007), 153–160. http://dl.acm.org/citation.cfm?id=1181849.1181881

[6] Ken Goldman, Paul Gross, Cinda Heeren, Geoffrey L. Herman, Lisa Kaczmarczyk, Michael C. Loui, and Craig Zilles. 2010. Setting the Scope of Concept Inventories for Introductory Computing Subjects. *Trans. Comput. Educ.* 10, 2, Article 5 (June 2010), 29 pages. https://doi.org/10.1145/1789934.1789935

[7] Philip Guo. 2014. Python is Now the Most Popular Introductory Teaching Language at Top US Universities. *Communications of the ACM Blog (BLOG@CACM), July* (2014).

[8] Mark Guzdial. September 30, 2016 (accessed August 18, 2017). *No, Really - Programming is Hard and CS Flipped Classrooms are Complicated: ITICSE 2016 Award-winning Papers.* https://computinged.wordpress.com/2016/09/30/no-really-programming-is-hard-and-cs-flipped-classrooms-are-complicated-iticse-2016-award-winning-papers/

[9] Matthew Hertz. 2010. What Do "CS1" and "CS2" Mean?: Investigating Differences in the Early Courses. In *Proceedings of the 41st ACM Technical Symposium on Computer Science Education (SIGCSE '10)*. ACM, New York, NY, USA, 199–203. https://doi.org/10.1145/1734263.1734335

[10] Gregory W. Hislop, Lillian Cassel, Lois Delcambre, Edward Fox, Rick Furuta, and Peter Brusilovsky. 2009. Ensemble: Creating a National Digital Library for Computing Education. In *Proceedings of the 10th ACM Conference on SIG-information Technology Education (SIGITE '09)*. ACM, New York, NY, USA, 200–200. https://doi.org/10.1145/1631728.1631783

[11] Association for Computing Machinery (ACM) Joint Task Force on Computing Curricula and IEEE Computer Society. 2013. *Computer Science Curricula 2013: Curriculum Guidelines for Undergraduate Degree Programs in Computer Science.* Technical Report. New York, NY, USA. 999133.

[12] Andrew Luxton-Reilly. 2016. Learning to Program is Easy. In *Proceedings of the 2016 ACM Conference on Innovation and Technology in Computer Science Education (ITiCSE '16)*. ACM, New York, NY, USA, 284–289. https://doi.org/10.1145/2899415.2899432

[13] Andrew Luxton-Reilly, Simon, Ibrihim Albluwi, Brett A. Becker, Michail Giannakos, Amruth N. Kumar, Linda Ott, James Paterson, Michael James Scott, Judy Sheard, and Claudia Szabo. 2018. Introductory Programming: A Systematic Literature Review. In *Proceedings of the 2018 ITiCSE Conference on Working Group Reports (ITiCSE-WGR '18)*. ACM, New York, NY, USA. https://doi.org/10.1145/3293881.3295779 *in press.*

[14] Raina Mason and Simon. 2017. Introductory Programming Courses in Australasia in 2016. In *Proceedings of the Nineteenth Australasian Computing Education Conference (ACE '17)*. ACM, New York, NY, USA, 81–89. https://doi.org/10.1145/3013499.3013512

[15] Michael McCracken, Vicki Almstrum, Danny Diaz, Mark Guzdial, Dianne Hagan, Yifat Ben-David Kolikant, Cary Laxer, Lynda Thomas, Ian Utting, and Tadeusz Wilusz. 2001. A Multi-national, Multi-institutional Study of Assessment of Programming Skills of First-year CS Students. *SIGCSE Bull.* 33, 4 (Dec. 2001), 125–180. https://doi.org/10.1145/572139.572181

[16] Ellen Murphy, Tom Crick, and James H Davenport. 2017. An Analysis of Introductory Programming Courses at UK Universities. *The Art, Science, and Engineering of Programming* 1, 2 (2017).

[17] The IEEE CS / ACM Joint Task Force on Computing Curricula. 2001. Computing Curricula 2001, Computer Science. (2001). https://www.acm.org/binaries/content/assets/education/curricula-recommendations/cc2001.pdf

[18] Miranda C. Parker, Mark Guzdial, and Shelly Engleman. 2016. Replication, Validation, and Use of a Language Independent CS1 Knowledge Assessment. In *Proceedings of the 2016 ACM Conference on International Computing Education Research (ICER '16)*. ACM, New York, NY, USA, 93–101. https://doi.org/10.1145/2960310.2960316

[19] Arnold Pears, Stephen Seidman, Lauri Malmi, Linda Mannila, Elizabeth Adams, Jens Bennedsen, Marie Devlin, and James Paterson. 2007. A Survey of Literature on the Teaching of Introductory Programming. In *Working Group Reports on ITiCSE on Innovation and Technology in Computer Science Education (ITiCSE-WGR '07)*. ACM, New York, NY, USA, 204–223. https://doi.org/10.1145/1345443.1345441

[20] Andrew Petersen, Michelle Craig, and Daniel Zingaro. 2011. Reviewing CS1 Exam Question Content. In *Proceedings of the 42Nd ACM Technical Symposium on Computer Science Education (SIGCSE '11)*. ACM, New York, NY, USA, 631–636. https://doi.org/10.1145/1953163.1953340

[21] Anthony Robins. 2010. Learning Edge Momentum: A New Account of Outcomes in CS1. *Computer Science Education* 20, 1 (2010), 37–71. https://doi.org/10.1080/08993401003612167

[22] Carsten Schulte and Jens Bennedsen. 2006. What Do Teachers Teach in Introductory Programming?. In *Proceedings of the Second International Workshop on Computing Education Research (ICER '06)*. ACM, New York, NY, USA, 17–28. https://doi.org/10.1145/1151588.1151593

[23] Robert Michael Siegfried, Daniel Greco, Nicholas Miceli, and Jason Siegfried. 2012. Whatever happened to Richard Reid's list of first programming languages? *Information Systems Education Journal* 10, 4 (2012), 24.

[24] Simon, Raina Mason, Tom Crick, James H. Davenport, and Ellen Murphy. 2018. Language Choice in Introductory Programming Courses at Australasian and UK Universities. In *Proceedings of the 49th ACM Technical Symposium on Computer Science Education (SIGCSE '18)*. ACM, New York, NY, USA, 852–857. https://doi.org/10.1145/3159450.3159547

[25] Allison Elliott Tew and Mark Guzdial. 2010. Developing a Validated Assessment of Fundamental CS1 Concepts. In *Proceedings of the 41st ACM Technical Symposium on Computer Science Education (SIGCSE '10)*. ACM, New York, NY, USA, 97–101. https://doi.org/10.1145/1734263.1734297

[26] Allison Elliott Tew and Mark Guzdial. 2011. The FCS1: A Language Independent Assessment of CS1 Knowledge. In *Proceedings of the 42Nd ACM Technical Symposium on Computer Science Education (SIGCSE '11)*. ACM, New York, NY, USA, 111–116. https://doi.org/10.1145/1953163.1953200

[27] Manas Tungare, Xiaoyan Yu, William Cameron, GuoFang Teng, Manuel A. Pérez-Quiñones, Lillian Cassel, Weiguo Fan, and Edward A. Fox. 2007. Towards a Syllabus Repository for Computer Science Courses. *SIGCSE Bull.* 39, 1 (March 2007), 55–59. https://doi.org/10.1145/1227504.1227331

Computational Thinking Bins: Outreach and More

Briana B. Morrison
University of Nebraska Omaha
Omaha, Nebraska
bbmorrison@unomaha.edu

Brian Dorn
University of Nebraska Omaha
Omaha, Nebraska
bdorn@unomaha.edu

Michelle Friend
University of Nebraska Omaha
Omaha, Nebraska
mfriend@unomaha.edu

ABSTRACT

Computational Thinking Bins are stand alone, individual boxes, each containing an activity for groups of students that teaches a computing concept. We have a devised a system that has allowed us to create an initial set, test the set, continually improve and add to our set. We currently use these bins in outreach events for middle and high school students. As we have shared this resource with K-12 teachers, many have expressed an interest in acquiring their own set. In this paper we will share our experience throughout the process, introduce the bins, and explain how you can create your own set.

CCS CONCEPTS

• **Computer systems organization** → **Embedded systems**; *Redundancy*; Robotics; • **Networks** → Network reliability;

KEYWORDS

Computational Thinking, Outreach, Unplugged

ACM Reference Format:
Briana B. Morrison, Brian Dorn, and Michelle Friend. 2019. Computational Thinking Bins: Outreach and More. In *Proceedings of the 50th ACM Technical Symposium on Computer Science Education (SIGCSE '19), February 27-March 2, 2019, Minneapolis, MN, USA.* ACM, New York, NY, USA, 7 pages. https://doi.org/10.1145/3287324.3287497

1 INTRODUCTION

Computational Thinking (CT) Bins were created in response to the many requests we received for outreach activities for middle and high school (secondary) students. Almost every week of the semester, some school would have a field trip to the University and we would be asked to "entertain" them for approximately an hour. Rather than just talk to them about our computing degrees, facilities, and research, we decided to actually *teach* them some computing concepts in addition to informing them about the school.

While we were familiar with CS Unplugged activities, we wanted something that required little to no explanation and that the students could do on their own. We wanted collaborative activities that could be completed in 10 to 15 minutes, or expanded for longer if needed. We based our model on the existing STEM Bins from our College of Education.

SIGCSE '19, February 27-March 2, 2019, Minneapolis, MN, USA

ACM ISBN 978-1-4503-5890-3/19/02.
https://doi.org/10.1145/3287324.3287497

Faculty in Computer Science and Teacher Education Development worked together to create a sample CT Bin and a template for all the required information we desired. We then developed a plan to allow the creation and testing of additional CT Bins. In this paper we report on our process.

2 BACKGROUND

There is a history in computer science education of utilizing computer-free "unplugged" activities which engage students in kinesthetic exercises that make computing concepts concrete. CS Unplugged [3], kinesthetic learning activities [2], and role plays in CS education [1] have been introduced at SIGCSE. In addition to use in primary and secondary computer science classrooms, these activities have been used extensively in out-of-school informal education settings such as camps, after-school clubs, and outreach. Most of these activities require a teacher or adult to lead the lesson, in order to provide instructions and guidance and to ensure that learning goals are met. For example, the "Card Flip Magic Trick"[1] requires a knowledgeable leader who can do the magic trick before explaining the underlying mathematics and computational connection to the audience.

Separately, at University of Nebraska Omaha, professors in the College of Education developed "STEM Bins." Each STEM Bin is a stand-alone activity housed in a shoebox. In order to enable use in a wide variety of contexts, these STEM Bins were designed to be used independently by small groups of students without direct leadership or intervention by a teacher. Each bin contains all the instructions and materials to complete the activity, as well as an answer key if needed. Example STEM Bin activities include: "Geometric Models for Multiplication" in which colored popsicle sticks allow students to engage in inquiry about polynomials, "Building and Flying a Paper Boomerang," and "Perspective Drawings" in which students create a three-dimensional shape with blocks and then create two-dimensional engineering drawings of different views of the shape.

The STEM bins have been useful in a broader range of settings than traditional outreach settings. They are useful for outreach in settings where participants vastly outnumber leaders, especially where participants are encouraged to move around freely, such as whole-school "STEM family nights" popular at local elementary schools and STEM celebrations at the university. They have also been used by teachers not only during formal instruction as hands-on activities, but also to provide independent extension activities for students who finish work early during class.

In the face of increased interest in outreach activities for CS Education Week and throughout the academic year, we were inspired to create computer-science themed "Computational Thinking (CT) Bins" beginning in the fall of 2016. Similar to the process described

[1] https://classic.csunplugged.org/error-detection/

by Carroll in creating STEM kits [4], we determined that rather than creating all the bins ourselves, a professor of education would create a unique assessment opportunity by assigning bin creation in the computer science teaching methods course. Students experienced the existing STEM Bins as a model, then individually or in pairs created their own CT Bins according to the requirements of the assignment, as described in the following section.

3 ORIGINATION ASSIGNMENT

The assignment to create a CT Bin is given in the CS Teaching Methods course, as a summative assessment at the end of the semester. Students may work independently or in pairs, but each pair must complete two bins to receive full credit. The students are asked to utilize the knowledge they have gained in the teaching methods course to prepare an interactive, meaningful, collaborative instructional experience. It must teach a computing concept and be accessible for middle school or high school students with no prior computing experience.

3.1 Bin Authors

The students in the CS Teaching Methods course are pursuing an endorsement to teach computer science. Most of the students are enrolled as graduate students and are in-service teachers who are pursuing an additional teaching endorsement for computer science/information technology. Some of the students are undergraduate pre-service teachers who are pursuing multiple endorsements (computer science/information technology and at least one other). For the undergraduates, the CS Methods course occurs in their final semester before student teaching, and includes a practicum experience where they spend six weeks co-teaching in classrooms of their endorsement areas.

3.2 Bin Requirements

Students are given a template to complete in creating the bin so that the bins are standardized in their appearance. Because the bins are created for multiple purposes, they are required to have both Student Materials and Teacher Materials.

The student materials include a title, instructions written in age-appropriate, kid-friendly non-technical language, and any handouts, materials, etc. This may also include an answer key, if one is needed, which should be on a separate page so that it can be easily kept hidden while the students work through the activity. The instructions include a background section that gives a motivating introduction to the computing concept being covered. For example, a bin about computer art, in which students color in a picture encoded in hexadecimal, begins by briefly describing that the screen consists of dots called pixels which have a specific color, which are made up of differing amounts of red, green, and blue.

The teacher materials are designed to give the background and information a teacher would need both to use the bin and to understand its place in the curriculum. Each begins with an overview that describes the activity broadly. The recommended grade levels and estimated time the activity will take is included. There is also a recommendation for the ideal group size to work on the bin, and the number of groups the bin supports (e.g., students work in pairs, materials for 4 pairs). There is a connection to standards section which identifies both the CSTA [5] and NE state standards that are addressed by the bin. There is a list of materials for the bin and any new vocabulary words with definitions that may be introduced in the CT Bin. A more complete description of how the activity should run and what students should do is also included. Finally, there is a "Connection to Computing" section which explains the underlying computer science concept(s). Because we assume that the teacher presenting the CT Bin may have little or no computing knowledge, a simple explanation of the purpose of the CT Bin and how it is related to computing is included. There is also a "Related Resources" section with links to more information. These last sections are particularly intended for substitute teachers or novice teachers who need more information to be able to support students in learning meaningfully from the activity. This information also helps a teacher use the bin as part of a larger topical unit, if desired.

Note that the teacher information is given to allow classroom teachers with no computing experience to use these and have the necessary information to answer questions or expand the activity if so desired. The activities do not require teachers to instruct or lead the students during the exploration process. The teacher information is provided to allow the teachers to also learn and discover the computing concepts along with their students and have the confidence to answer questions that may arise.

3.3 Assessment

The bins are assessed using a rubric, shown in Table 1. Student teachers receive feedback on how well their CT Bins meet the defined criteria. They are allowed to refine their CT Bins before the bins are then tested with outreach participants. Generally we invite those enrolled in the CS Methods course to participate in one outreach event during the semester (a STEM night, CS Ed Week event, or celebration of computing event) where they can see their CT Bins in action. This also serves as the initial testing of the CT Bin. Many teachers choose to update the CT Bin on their own after seeing it used by students.

3.4 Assignment Challenges

We have identified two major challenges with this CT Bins assignment in our CS teaching methods course: diversity of ideas, and originality of materials creation. These two challenges are connected—it is extremely difficult for teachers to create unique materials unlike those they have seen before. Teachers in our pre-service and in-service programs are exposed to a wide variety of materials, including those that are popular in national, breadth-first computing curricula like Exploring CS and CS Principles. Thus, the materials created were often similar to (or adaptations of) other materials available on the internet, such as CS Unplugged and NCWIT materials. In these cases, teachers adapted the existing instructions. The adaptations were for this independent context and elaborated on their connections to local standards. These bins typically scored quite well on the assessment rubric. However, when students did create unique materials for entirely new activities, the instructions were often less clear and robust compared to those adapted from professionally-developed and widely-tested materials. It was, therefore, a challenge to assess unique materials, since they were of lower quality than adapted materials but potentially were more

Table 1: Rubric for CT Bin Assignment

Criteria	Target	Approaching Target	Below Target	Points
Topic	The bin has a single purpose that is clearly communicated and straightforward to understand. The purpose or topic is strongly connected to computing. The bin topic is unique; there is not already a bin with this topic	The topic or purpose is unclear. There are multiple topics or purposes. There is a weak connection to computing. The bin is on a topic that is similar to other existing bins.	The topic or purpose is completely unclear. There is no connection to computing. The bin copies the activity of an existing bin	30
Usability	Students can complete the activity without oversight or instruction from a teacher. The activity is appropriately challenging for students of the identified grade level - not too childish nor too hard. The name is descriptive of the activity	Students can engage with the bin independently but may need teacher support to complete the activity. The bin is developmentally inappropriate for students of the identified grade level.	Students cannot reasonably complete the activity independently. The activity is likely to be impossibly difficult or so easy as to be boring for students of the identified grades.	50
Teacher Instructions	The teacher instructions are clear and complete. The computing concept(s) is/are fully explained for a novice teacher. The appropriate CSTA & state standards aligned with the activity are enumerated. There is a clear description of the working of the activity from a teacher point of view.	The teacher instructions are hard to follow. The concept is explained, but a novice teacher would find it challenging to understand the concept from the explanation. Some standards aligned with the activity are identified. There is a description of the activity, but it skips parts or is hard to follow.	The teacher instructions are missing or incoherent. The concept is not explained. Standards are not identified. There is no description of the activity.	20
Complete	There is a full materials list, license, authorship, and citation if needed.	The materials list is vague or incomplete. The license or authorship are missing. The activity appears to be a replication of another resource but no citation is given.	There is no materials list. The license and authorship are missing. There is evidence of intellectual property duplication from another resource. (Note: plagiarism is cause for failure and academic sanctions.)	10

creative and individualized than the adaptations. This remains an ongoing point of consideration in the design of this assessment task for our methods students.

Additionally, as we continue with this assignment, the current students now have access to the previously created bins. They are able to see what has been done before. Students have gravitated toward some particular bins, such as the cipher bins. It appears to be relatively simple to come up with a new cipher or encryption scheme and create a new bin. While we encourage students to be unique and creative in the assignment, many choose to take the easier path to completion.

4 CT BIN DESCRIPTIONS

As described above, all curated bins have a common look and feel and contain consistently structured details. Currently eleven different activities have been fully curated and are available for use, while an additional set of more recently submitted bins is still undergoing beta testing (see Section 5). Bins range in topics from searching/sorting algorithms to cryptography to image representation to computing history. Below, we briefly describe the nature of each presently available curated bin.

Robotic Buddies This activity engages students in basic notions of algorithms related to ordering and specificity. Students must use a restricted symbol language to instruct their partner how to "play robot" and assemble a given configuration of cups (see Figure 1a).

Beat the Clock Inspired by classic game shows, students are challenged with guessing the price of everyday items at various price points (e.g., a can of RedBull, a Bluetooth speaker) while counting the number of guesses needed. They consider different strategies to arrive quickest at the answer and in so doing discover binary search.

Computer Art Introduced earlier, this bin presents students with grids of decimal and hexadecimal numbers which students must identify as RGB colors. They then are asked to fill in the square regions (i.e., pixels) using colored pencils to discover the image being represented (see Figure 1b).

Card Sort In this bin, students find envelopes containing a single suit of playing cards along with some straws and English descriptions of various sorting algorithms (insertion, bubble, and merge). The goal is to explore each process and consider how they are similar or different (see Figure 1c).

Data Storage Timeline Here students explore the history of consumer data storage devices by trying to line up actual devices from oldest to newest based on their timeline of introduction to the marketplace. They also try to match description cards to the corresponding device (see Figure 2a).

Enigma Machine This bin contains a pair of "crisp tube Enigma machines"[2] along with some basic instructions about Enigma's history and how the tubes work. A series of both easy (single rotor) and hard (multi rotor) messages challenge students to practice their decoding skills and explore Enigma's complexity (see Figure 2b).

Balance it Out This activity challenges students to invent a comparison sorting algorithm and write it down as a sequence of steps. A classroom balance and a series of variably weighted containers is provided (see Figure 2c) for students to practice their steps while reinforcing that only one comparison can be made at a time.

Caesar Cipher Shown in Figure 3a, this activity allows students to practice encoding and decoding message written using a simple alphabetic shift substitution cipher.

[2] http://wiki.franklinheath.co.uk/index.php/Enigma/Paper_Enigma

Scytale Cipher For this activity, students are given a series of paper strips containing messages that can be decoded when wrapped around the correct diameter wooden dowel (see Figure 3c). They learn the history of the Scytale Cipher and are tasked with encoding their own messages.

Computers Thru History Like the data storage activity, this bin explores computing history (see Figure 4a). Students are given cards containing photos of significant computational devices ranging from an abacus to the Hollerith machine to the ENIAC. The challenge is to arrange them in chronological order and match them to descriptions of each.

Vigenère Cipher This two dimensional cipher challenge introduces students to the Vigenère square (see Figure 4c) and asks them to decode messages using different keywords. The bin also explores the relationship to Caesar Cipher in the event that students have completed multiple activities.

5 TESTING AND REFINEMENT

Following the conclusion of the CS teaching methods course, the newly created set of bins is pilot tested with students and teachers in a wide variety of contexts at our university. These events range from campus-wide STEM open houses, summer camps sessions, teacher PD workshops, to current classes. The primary goal of these pilot tests is to collect feedback about the clarity of the instructions in the bin, while also informally gauging the length of time learners take to successfully complete the activity. Every bin is pilot tested at least twice before being included into the final vetted set of bins.

Feedback cards are placed in each of the bins so that learners can report any difficulties with the activity or errors in the instructions, instructional materials, or answer keys. This feedback is then used to refine the original content of the student-created CT bin. If a major update to the materials or instructions is required, the bin undergoes another round of pilot testing. Once a bin receives positive feedback with minimal errors, the errors are corrected and the bin is promoted into a curated version. The curated version is once again reviewed by our university faculty. The supporting documentation is produced and the bin is then added to our publicly available list of bins.

5.0.1 Supporting Materials. Once the bins have been tested and refined, the documentation created in the assignments is transferred into a LaTeX template. We have utilized high school interns and undergraduate students to help in this process. Faculty review the standards mapping and the content describing the activity's relationship to computing. Curators also a check to ensure that the material is not plagiarized from another source. Because all the CT Bins are licensed under Creative Commons, we only use material that can be freely used with attribution and allows derivation. All the documentation for the student, teacher, answer keys, and any reproducible materials (such as pictures, diagrams, codes, etc.) are bundled together into a single PDF document.

In addition to the individual instructions for each bin, we also maintain a *purchase list* that contains a supply list for creating an entire set of CT Bins. The contents of all the bins are included in a spreadsheet and tallied across all bins. For example, many bins require extra paper and pencils. A complete count of the number of pencils and pads of paper (or small stacks) is given with a mapping to all the bins that require that supply. By having an entire purchase list available, any teacher that wished to make an entire set or large subset of CT Bins would have a single supply list.

We also supply designed labels which can be printed and placed on the bins to help identify them. The files containing the labels are additionally updated and made available.

6 BOX PREPARATION

Preparing a set of CT Bins from the curated materials is a fairly straightforward process. After procuring the needed items from the purchase list and the desired containers, the bins can be assembled. All of the PDF files should be printed. Copies of student materials need to be made along with copies of the necessary instructional materials. The purchase list indicates which bins require copies and exactly what must be copied. Once these copies have been made, the first step is to separate the student instructions, the answer key, and the teacher materials into separate, clearly labeled folders and envelopes as shown in Figure 3a. Some materials, like the cipher wheel or the storage device description cards shown in Figure 2a, can be laminated to increase their durability over time. Lamination can also enable use of a dry-erase marker for repeated student use without restocking the bin with additional photocopies. This is often helpful with the cryptography related bins.

Some bins require assembly of the instructional material. Instructions for assembly, often accompanied by links to YouTube videos, are provided. For example, we have provided links to Thinkiverse sites with files for 3D printing Caesar cipher wheels (see Figure 3b). We also provide links to YouTube videos for constructing the Engima machine.

Once these materials are prepared, assembly of the box is a simple matter of placing the folders into the bin along with copies of any handouts and/or special materials for the activity, like the scale and bottles in Figure 2c. Any such needed materials are described in the teacher materials for the associated bin. The folder containing teacher materials can optionally be included at the bottom of the bin, or simply excluded to avoid any potential for confusion by the students completing the activity. Finally, the labels for the bins should be printed and attached to each bin.

7 AVAILABILITY

We have made all of the information related to our CT Bins publicly available through a Creative Commons license. All the information needed to create your own set, including a purchase list, labels, and the instructional materials can be found at https://bit.ly/UNOCSED. Scroll down to the Unplugged Materials and select the Computational Thinking Bins link. A link to a zipped file containing all the materials needed can be found on the resulting page.

8 USAGE

We currently have multiple sets of the CT Bins which we continue to use for outreach activities. Additionally, we have added the bins to our "lending library". Local area teachers may complete a request form on the internet to borrow one, two, or up to an entire set of CT Bins for a period of one week. We arrange a time for pick up and we have the requested bins ready for transport. When the bins are returned, a high school intern or undergraduate student worker

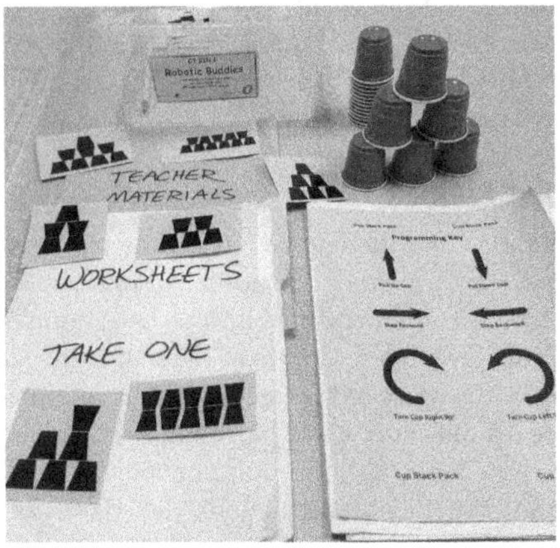

(a) Robotic Buddies

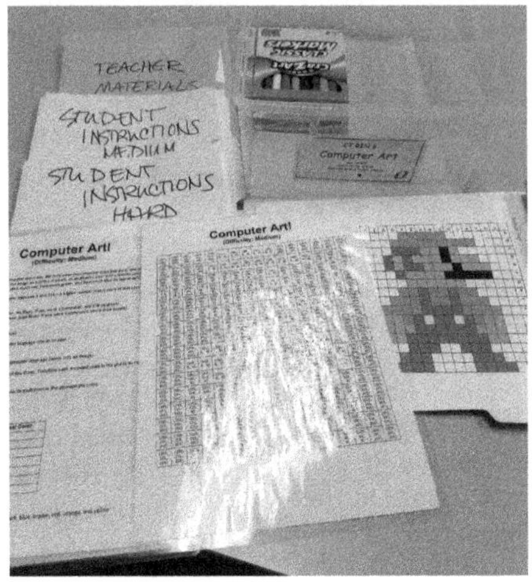

(b) Computer Art

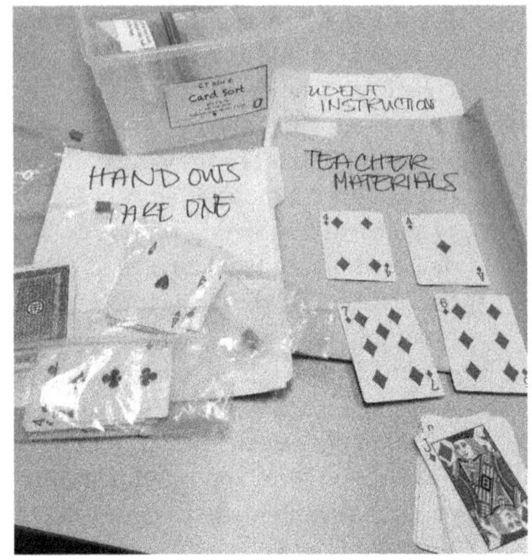

(c) Card Sort

Figure 1: First 3 CT Bins

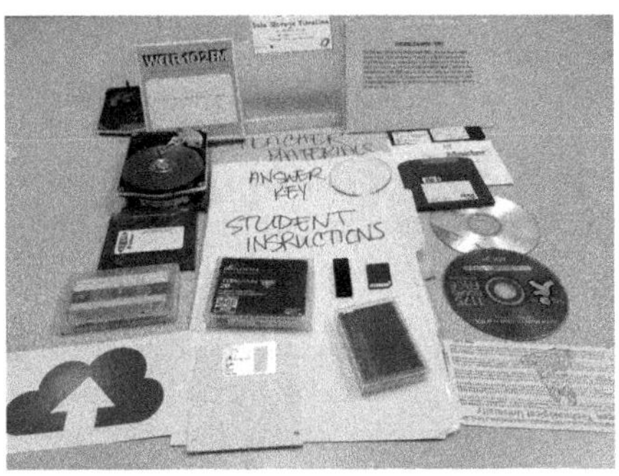

(a) Data Storage Timeline

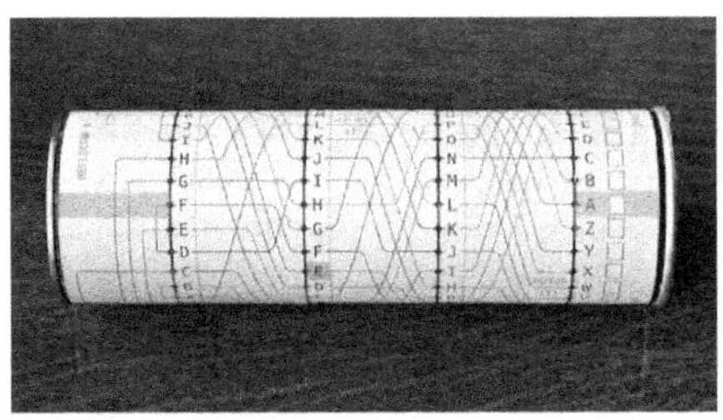

(b) Enigma Machine

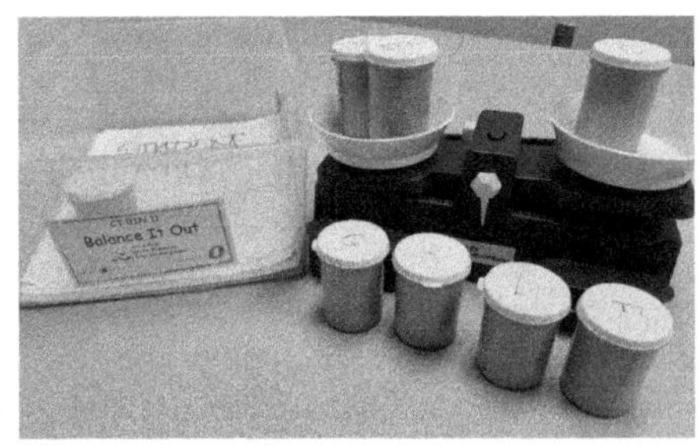

(c) Balance It Out

Figure 2: 3 More CT Bins

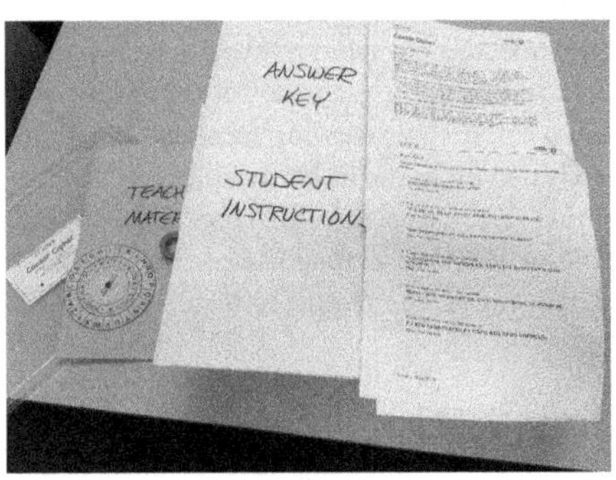

(a) Caesar Cipher

(b) 3D Cipher

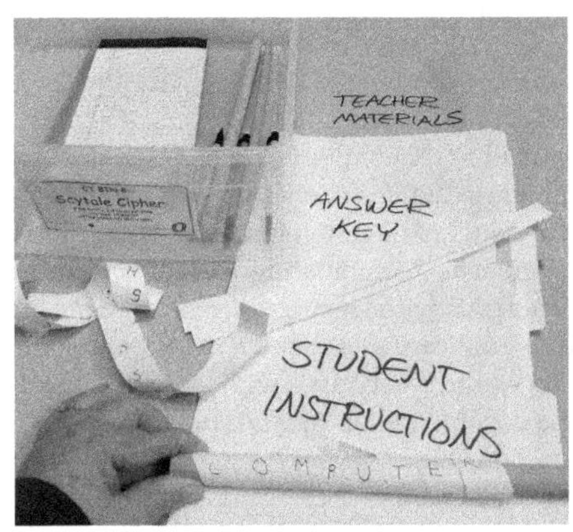

(c) Scytale Cipher

Figure 3: Cryptography CT Bins

(a) Computers Thur History

(b) Vigenère Cipher

(c) Vigenère Cipher Worksheet

Figure 4: Final 3 CT Bins

to restocks the bins and ensures that all materials are included in the returned bins. This is also when we resupply any necessary instructions, worksheets, or other consumables.

In addition to our lending library, thanks to a Google grant, we have been able to create sets of the bins for use by our Educational Service Units (ESUs). ESUs serve as intermediate level education service agencies for member school districts. There are currently 17 ESUs providing services to 261 public school districts in Nebraska. ESUs provide core services for school districts, which include staff development, technology, and instructional materials. x

Through the Google grant, we created sets of CT Bins for several ESUs and held a Professional Development session at the ESU. Teachers from the school districts served by the ESU were invited to attend along with up to five students for a day of learning about computing. The students and teachers experienced the CT Bins together. The bins were placed on tables and the students were allowed to choose which bin to work on. After 15 minutes, students were encouraged to move to a different bin. After 90 minutes, the students were asked to gather and listen to the explanations behind each of the bins along with their connections to computing. After student exploration, the researchers lead a discussion with the students on what they had learned. Students were able to define and explain algorithms, explain the concept of cryptography, and discuss computing storage devices. Additional educational resources were presented for students who wanted to continue to explore a specific topic. The goal of the CT Bins is to allow for student engagement with computing concepts without the need for an instructor or lead. While we certainly expected that students would learn while engaged with the bins, we were not explicitly trying to achieve deep learning of computing concepts, merely an introduction to spark additional interest. The CT Bins certainly met this goal. A set of CT Bins created specifically for each ESU was left there for further outreach activities after the Professional Development Day.

The CT Bins were also presented at the 2018 CSTA National Convention to over 300 attendees. Attendees were allowed to "play" with the bins and examine their contents, and some even completed the activities. The attendees were provided business cards with a URL to access a zip file containing all the materials for creating their own sets of CT Bins. The comments received from the attendees expressed their appreciation for the materials and how many were looking forward to using the bins in their classrooms. Many expressed interest in having their library obtain a set for maximum exposure. Many teachers wanted a set for use when students finished their assigned work early, as an extension activity. Other expressed interest in having a set for substitutes to be able to use during the year.

9 CONCLUSIONS

In this paper we presented the guiding philosophy and design of Computational Thinking Bins. These self-guided activities are unique from other existing curricular resources in that they enable individual and small group interaction within a self-contained activity that requires little-to-no teacher preparation.

Not only have the CT Bins described here been a well-used activity during local university-sponsored outreach events, they have also proved popular among area teachers and are regularly borrowed for classroom use. Over the 2017–2018 school year, our CT Bins effort expanded with a series of professional development workshops hosted across the state. Sets of ten curated bins were left at multiple regional educational service centers with the support of a Google grant. By physically distributing sets of these bins across the state, we increase availability and convenience for teachers and schools outside the immediate region around our university.

Through the CSTA National Convention, the CT Bins received national exposure and were well regarded. By publishing this work, we hope to expose even more potential users to the benefits and advantages of CT Bins.

ACKNOWLEDGMENTS

The authors would like to thank all the students of TED 8006 who helped to create the original Bins and all the high school and middle school students who tested various versions of the Bins. We would also like to thank Michaela S. for helping produce all the original documentation for the bins. We graciously thank Google for the grant allowing us to create sets of CT Bins for our ESUs.

REFERENCES

[1] Steven K. Andrianoff and David B. Levine. 2002. Role Playing in an Object-oriented World. In *Proceedings of the 33rd SIGCSE Technical Symposium on Computer Science Education (SIGCSE '02)*. ACM, New York, NY, USA, 121–125. https://doi.org/10.1145/563340.563386

[2] Andrew Begel, Daniel D. Garcia, and Steven A. Wolfman. 2004. Kinesthetic Learning in the Classroom. In *Proceedings of the 35th SIGCSE Technical Symposium on Computer Science Education (SIGCSE '04)*. ACM, New York, NY, USA, 183–184. https://doi.org/10.1145/971300.971367

[3] Tim Bell, Lynn Lambert, and Daniela Marghitu. 2012. CS Unplugged, Outreach and CS Kinesthetic Activities (Abstract Only). In *Proceedings of the 43rd ACM Technical Symposium on Computer Science Education (SIGCSE '12)*. ACM, New York, NY, USA, 676–676. https://doi.org/10.1145/2157136.2157410

[4] Kimberly Carroll and Katherine Scott. 2017. Creating STEM Kits for the Classroom: Preservice teachers design developmentally appropriate science lessons and gain STEM experience. *Science and Children* 55 (2017), 36–41. Issue 1.

[5] CSTA 2017. CSTA K-12 Computer Science Standards. Retrieved August, 31, 2018 from http://www.csteachers.org/page/standards

Applying Self-Determination Theory towards Motivating Young Women in Computer Science

Allison Mishkin
Oxford Internet Institute
University of Oxford
Oxford, United Kingdom

ABSTRACT

This paper applies self-determination theory (SDT), a macro-psychological theory of human motivation to explore what gets young women interested in computer science. SDT argues that when students feel equally competent, autonomous, and related to others, they will be intrinsically motivated to study. This paper applies SDT to young women in computer science to identify the best ways to motivate them towards intrinsic motivation to study computer science. Using a survey administered at Bit by Bit, a conference for young women in computer science, this paper identifies that relatedness is significantly more important for girls than either competency or autonomy. Additionally, it determines the psychological pathway through which feeling related to others influences students' motivation. Specifically, it determines that feeling related to others influences young women's sense of self-efficacy, which improves their computer science motivation. These findings contribute to our understanding of SDT and of how to motivate young women to study computer science.

KEYWORDS

Gender; psychology; belonging; self-determination theory

ACM Reference Format:
Allison Mishkin. 2019. Applying Self-Determination Theory towards Motivating Young Women in Computer Science. In *SIGCSE '19: The 50th ACM Technical Symposium on Computing Science Education, February 27– March 2, 2019, Minneapolis, MN, USA.* ACM, NY, NY, USA, 7 pages. https://doi.org/10.1145/3287324.3287389

1 INTRODUCTION

While girls report early interest in STEM careers, this declines as they mature [1]. Although girls outperform or perform as well as boys on achievement and social tests before adolescence [2], as puberty hits, young women begin to underperform and question their own ability [3]. As such, educators must identify how to sustain girls' interest and motivation in computer science.

Self-determination theory (SDT), a macro-psychological theory of human motivation, contends that to effectively sustain motivation and persistence in a discipline (such as computer science), students' need to feel competent, autonomous, and related to others [4]. According to SDT, the self-regulated learning that emerges may also predispose students towards positive developmental outcomes. An extensive literature review identified that SDT has not yet been applied to computer science education. This study remedies this by surveying attendees at a conference for high school women in technology on their experiences and motivations for studying computer science. This paper questions whether traditional computer science education satisfies girls' needs for competency, autonomy, and relatedness, and therefore develops their intrinsic motivation to continue studying computer science.

2 PREVIOUS RESEARCH

While girls and boys show similar levels of interest in computing at young ages, as they mature, young women leave computing at higher rates than their male counterparts. In 1997, Tracy Camp coined the phrase "leaky pipeline" to describe the comparative rates at which women leave the computing track, relative to men [5]. Women "leak" from the pipeline when entering high school, at the undergraduate level, and again at both the graduate education and career levels [6]. Over the past twenty years, advocacy groups, politicians, educators, and researchers have transitioned from trying to encourage more women to enter the pipeline towards plugging its holes. While Camp identified when individuals leave the pipeline, emerging research identifies why they leak or may never even enter it [7], [8]. However, most research and policy recommendations for women in technology focus on structural and not internal factors. Indeed, most interventions still focus on expanding access to computing education or on offering role models, instead of focusing on the psychological experience of being a minority in computing. However, a psychological focus is necessary in order to develop interventions that change behaviour [6]. In what follows, I explore these psychological experiences. I begin by outlining the importance of belonging, particularly for minorities in educational settings, and finally I connect belonging to motivation through the lens of self-determination theory.

2.1 The Importance of Belonging

As a minority in computing, women face a lesser sense of social fit, at best, and direct hostility and exclusion, at worst. When an individual identifies as a minority within an educational setting, she may question her belonging and therefore choose not to pursue certain educational realms or underperform within them. This phenomenon has been observed in practice when underrepresented races enter higher education [9], individuals of low socioeconomic status enter private schools [10], or when women enter STEM fields [11]. The impacts that minority-status may have on an individual's psyche are exacerbated when the individual is fighting against or within stereotypes about him or herself. Perceptions of minority status may subtly dissuade minorities from opting-into or persisting in the minority setting [12], [13]. However, fostering a sense of belonging can improve motivation and performance for stigmatized minorities.

Belonging uncertainty emerges when students doubt their sense of social fit or the likelihood of having friends in a domain. When students do not have connections or fear being alone, academic performance decreases and the importance of belonging is heightened for minority communities [14]. In one series of experiments, women who were led to believe they would have few friends in a class underperformed relative to their peers who were lead to believe they might belong in engineering courses [15]. Sensing social fit produces a state of belonging which increases motivation, persistence, and achievement in settings where individuals might feel unwelcome or underrepresented [16].

While student belonging appears linked with subsequent motivation, it develops from developmental, social, and interpersonal clues.

2.2 Developing Belonging

A student's sense of belonging emerges from signs within her socio-cultural environment. Parents, friends, teachers, and the media set expectations for what girls can achieve. Within school, students pick up clues from teachers, comments from peers, presence of friends, extra-curricular activities, and other sources to construct a sense of belonging [17]. Yet, given the persistent masculine stereotypes of computer science and limited access to computer science instruction before college, there exist few places for girls to create a sense of belonging within computer science or technical communities [18].

The lack of female role models in computer science has been offered as an explanation for the gender gap in computing since the 1980s. Early research recognized the role that gendered stereotypes and expectations from teachers and peers played in decreasing women's interest. Within American culture, engineering and computing are stereotyped as male-dominated and jobs are perceived to be largely anti-social, require innate ability, and focus on minute technical details – traits that typically alienate women [19]. Indeed, by the time they enter university, students' stereotypes of computer science are largely incompatible with female gender roles and interests [20], [21]. These cultural expectations around computing not only influence young women, but also their role models, parents, and teachers.

While little research documents how parents and teachers' expectations influence girls' study of computing, existing work on how social support systems gender career paths and the way that girls develop expectations of math and science suggests that adult figures can strongly impact girls' motivation. Roles become gendered across the lifespan. Parents' gendered attitudes towards computers impact their children's gender perceptions, and, troublingly, the lower the individual's socio-economic status, the stronger the gender stereotypes [22]. Children develop early expectations of their STEM potential and competencies from their parents [23]. These attitudes and subsequent performance may later be influenced by teachers [24]. Particularly because math and science are considered related to computer science, it appears likely that young girls might develop early expectations that they do not belong in computing. Indeed, while 46% of young boys are told by a parent they might be good at computer science, only 27% of girls are told the same [25]. Therefore, as girls develop, much of their social environment may be offering subtle clues that they do not belong in computing.

Just as social environments set belonging cues, girls pick up cues about STEM from their physical environments. The ambient belonging, or "feeling of fit in the environment and similarity to the people imagined to occupy it," is a necessary predictor of young women's motivation and decision to study or pursue computing [26, p. 1049]. In a series of experiments, researchers demonstrated how by filling classrooms with neutral objects instead of masculine objects, girls' interest in computer science became equal to their male peers. This demonstrates the power that belonging can have in predicting motivation and the extent to which masculine stereotypes can undermine this belonging.

The stereotypes and beliefs that students hold influence their career choices. A sense of computer self-efficacy is highly correlated with later decisions to pursue computer science. Early computing research found large differences between boys' and girls' self-efficacy but that, when self-efficacy was held constant, they were equally likely to be interested in computing [27]. Yet, while boys are much more likely to report and believe in their ability, in practice, boys and girls often have the same ability [28]. While boys have higher perceived self-efficacy, they are also much more likely to report support and encouragement from parents and friends [29]. There exists a continued and non-decreasing difference between boys' and girls' senses of self-efficacy. In fact, the stronger the identification with a gender role, the stronger the self-efficacy belief [30]. This awareness and young women's beliefs that boys are "abler" continues to keep girls from computing, but self-efficacy is necessary for motivation. Additionally, self-efficacy can be spread through classrooms. Peers and friends may give clues to a learner that she is capable of achieving and this effect is stronger for same gender peers [31]. Peers signal that achievement is possible and when one expects she is capable of success, her self-efficacy grows [32]. This suggests that young women need to be surrounded by others or feel that they belong and to develop self-efficacy. Yet, the gender divide in computing limits young women's ability to see what they are trying to be. It is therefore likely that environments limit young women's self-efficacy in computing.

Adults, schools, stereotypes, and role models all undermine girls' sense of social fit within technical domains. A critical problem thus emerges. If girls struggle to create a sense of belonging, but feelings of fit are inextricably linked to motivation, how can girls enter the technical fields?

2.3 Self-Determination Theory

Self-determination theory, a macro theory of human motivation, links the need for belonging and its motivational outcomes into a unified framework. It establishes a difference between extrinsic motivation – or doing things for tangible rewards or punishment – and intrinsic motivation – performing based on an internal drive. It argues that intrinsic motivation is necessary to sustain interest and positive outcomes from a given task [4]. Emerging research posits that intrinsic motivation for academics increases persistence and performance [33]. One review of self-determination theory within education found that intrinsic motivation for learning may also lead to affective, creative, and challenge-oriented outcomes [34]. Thus, intrinsic motivation may act a buffer by allowing teenagers to overcome difficult situations and to take advantage of the opportunities technology offers. This finding is particularly important as it suggests that to reduce pipeline leaks, rather than focusing efforts on increasing the number of women entering technology, one should identify strategies to teach and instill intrinsic motivation in them.

Levels of persistence and performance are tied to one's motivation when performing a task. Just as they shape gendered beliefs, parents, teachers, and social circumstances can shape motivation. SDT posits that personal and contextual factors facilitate intrinsic motivation. According to SDT, all individuals desire to feel in control of their behaviour and choices (autonomous), effective at acting on these choices (competent), and connected to others (relatedness) [4]. When these basic needs are satisfied, individuals pursue constructive engagement across settings [6]. When children and adolescents feel warmth from their social environment, they develop the intrinsic motivation necessary to seize opportunities available to them [35]. Similarly, when education systems promote learner autonomy and student engagement, students increase their self-regulation [36]. Thus, social support and motivating educational systems have the potential to produce resilient children capable of persisting in technology settings.

Needs satisfaction leads to intrinsic motivation, which then influences persistence. Much research establishes how needs satisfaction supports intrinsic motivation for and performance within learning settings across academic subjects [4]. Intrinsic motivation prepares students for optimal engagement in learning contexts. Two foundational studies establish this theoretical connection between needs satisfaction and persistence within educational domains. When teachers and learning environments support students' needs for competency, autonomy, and relatedness, students can self-regulate their learning and be intrinsically motivated to develop knowledge [34]. When students create internal goals, they are more likely to persist in educational settings [33]. While neither study focused exclusively on women, they establish a theoretical relationship between needs satisfaction and motivation within academic domains and this theoretical relationship has since been demonstrated through experimental studies. Longitudinal analyses demonstrated that intrinsic motivation was the only form of motivation that could consistently predict academic achievement [37]. Looking more specifically at needs satisfaction, for both genders, when science teachers supported students' autonomy for learning, the students perceived greater autonomy and competency, which then increased their interest in studying and working within scientific domains [38]. Despite deep documentation of the roles that autonomy support and perceived competency play in supporting intrinsic motivation [6], [39], little SDT research focuses on relatedness and education. However, interviews with engineering students and discovered that relatedness was a more salient predictor of intrinsic motivation and persistence in engineering than was autonomy support [40]. As such, it becomes necessary to explore how relatedness may support motivation.

Drawing on self-determination theory's links between relatedness and resulting motivation, researchers found that cohort programs can create supportive environments that produce feelings of relatedness in teenagers and that this relatedness supported learning outcomes [41]. They argue that institutions must create learning environments that are conducive to relatedness-development. Meanwhile, psychologists coined the term belonging uncertainty to demonstrate how, by increasing a sense of belonging, they could improve intellectual achievement and motivation [42]. When students hypothesize that they might not belong, clues supporting that belief lead to higher dropout rates and underachievement. Yet, the greater the belonging felt, the greater students' motivation to succeed and persist in the before-questioned path [42]. Belonging acts as a psychological barrier that, when supported, reduced racial minorities' achievement and health gaps and allowed them to frame adversity as a common experience, not a reflection on their worthiness [16]. Therefore, it becomes critical to focus on sources of belonging uncertainty and resolving this state to equip gender-minority students with the resilience to persist within the pipeline.

3 PRESENT STUDY

The present study looks at the relationship between needs satisfaction and motivation for women in computer science to explore the impact of basic psychological needs unto subsequent motivation.

4 METHODS

4.1 Recruitment Strategy and Eligibility

High school girls from across the New York City area were invited to participate in a women in computing event where data was collected. Participants were contacted through schools and professional education networks. The Computer Science Teachers Association, New York City Department of Education, and other professional organizations contacted their members and asked them to encourage their students to attend the event. Additionally, students were contacted directly at the New York City Computer Science Opportunity Fair. It was estimated that a total of 2,500 students were contacted.

Any student enrolled in high school who identified as female was deemed eligible for the study. As the hypotheses were directly concerned with the feeling of being an underrepresented gender in computing, it was deemed important to limit participation in the event and, by extension, the research study to those who identified as an underrepresented minority. As such, organizers could isolate a key independent variable. 500 students registered for the event and 191 attended. The study received ethical clearance from the University of Oxford Central University Research Ethics Committee (CUREC reference: SSH OII C1A 17 049).

4.2 Hypotheses

Findings from self-determination theory and its sub-theory on basic needs satisfaction suggest that both relatedness and, particularly sense of relatedness within scientific communities, can influence motivation and persistence within technical fields. This study extended SDT and findings on minority groups' motivation to female technology communities to determine its relevance for women in technical communities. Based on the importance of belonging and social support within technology communities, initial analyses extended the principles of needs satisfaction towards this academic domain and hypothesized:

1. Sense of belonging predicts intrinsic motivation towards and interest in technology.
2. It is more important to have a sense of social connection and have general non-domain relatedness satisfied for minority communities in technology.

As discussed above, there exist large gender differences in young women and men's senses of computing self-efficacy. Women cannot be what they cannot see, but seeing peers succeed in academics contributes to a feeling of self-efficacy in that domain [31]. Self-efficacy in turn leads to motivation [43], [44]. Therefore, this study hypothesizes that:

3. Sense of belonging improves motivation by increasing the student's self-efficacy.

4.2 Survey Design

On the day of the event, students were given a paper survey. All questions were on a uniform 7-point Likert scale, with relevant anchors, to simplify questioning. Subscales are explained below.

Autonomy. To assess the level of autonomy students felt in their technical education, students were given a 6-item index of the Perceived Autonomy for Learning Scale [45]. Items included "I feel understood by my instructor" and "My instructor listens to how I would like to do things." Items were averaged to create a composite score ($\alpha = .879$).

Competency. To assess how competent students felt learning technical material, students completed the 4-item Perceived Competency for Learning scale [46] with items such as "I feel confident in my ability to learn the material" and "I am able to achieve my goals in these classes." Items were averaged to create a composite score ($\alpha = .931$).

Relatedness. The Basic Psychological Needs Satisfaction and Frustration Scale [47] assessed relatedness. Measures including "I feel that the people I care about also care about me" and "I experience a warm feeling with the people I spend time with" were averaged to create a composite score ($\alpha = .773$).

Sense of Social Fit. Students' sense of social fit in computer science was assessed with items including "I feel like an outsider in technology-related settings and "Compared to most other students, I fit in computer science." [42] ($\alpha = .780$).

Motivation. Motivation was assessed along one intrinsic and three extrinsic domains: grades, careers, and parents/teachers. Intrinsic, grade, and career motivation were assessed with 5-item subscales adapted from the Science Motivation Questionnaire [48]. Items included: "Learning computer science makes my life more meaningful" and "My career will involve computer science or technology." Items were averaged to create composite items ($\alpha_{intrinsic} = .837$, $\alpha_{career} = .851$, $\alpha_{grade} = .810$).

Self-Efficacy. Five items assessed students' self-efficacy using items such as "I believe I can master technology knowledge & skills" and "I am sure I can understand computer science" [55]. Results were averaged to create a final score ($\alpha = .858$).

Students were also queried on demographic information including grade in school, computer science background, race, and school type.

4.2 Analytical Strategy

To test hypotheses 1 and 2, a series of regressions queried the connection between a subset of 138 subjects to explore how principles of self-determination theory interact with computer science. An exploratory demographic regression model queried the relationship between student experience, background, and motivation. Following these tests, regression analyses controlling for demographic variability explored how perceived autonomy support, competency, and relatedness influenced motivation for and interest in studying computer science. This model evaluated the connection between needs satisfaction and intrinsic motivation, drawing on [6]. Similar regression models explored the direct effects of relatedness constructs on motivation.

To test hypothesis 3, the indirect effects of self-efficacy, a mediation analysis looked at the mediating role self-efficacy holds for feelings of connection. Guided by [49], self-efficacy was treated as a mediator that explained the relationship between social connection and motivation.

5 RESULTS

5.1 Demographics and Motivation

A regression model including predictors for CS experience, race and school type explored the influence of demographic factors onto intrinsic motivation. Model predictors reflected a student's race (coded = 0 for white; 1 = for non-white) and school (coded = 0 for private school; = 1 for public school). Both school type and racial minority status predicted intrinsic motivation for computer science. Non-white students and public school students were less likely than were white private school students to be intrinsically motivated in computer science ($R^2 = .084$; $F = 3.408$; $p = .02$). Computer science experience showed no effect on interest. No statistically significant relationship was observed between demographics and any other dependent or independent variable.

Table 1: Demographic Predictors Influence unto Intrinsic Motivation

	β	SE	95% CI	p
Intrinsic Motivation				
Race	-.212	.233	-1.004 to -.083	.021
School Type	-.193	.189	-.777 to -.027	.036
CS Experience	.007	.203	-.388 to .417	.942

5.2 Social Connection and Motivation

Controlling for demographics, a young woman's sense of social fit predicted intrinsic motivation, while her feelings of general relatedness had a much smaller effect (R^2=.487; F=20.482; p < .001). This relationship was stronger for public school students. Similar regressions were run for career (R^2=.335; F = 10.894; p < .001) and grade motivations (R^2=.134; F = 3.406; p = .007). Sense of social fit also showed a stronger influence than relatedness onto career motivations. Sense of social fit also predicted grade motivations, but school type was non-significant in this analysis. Predictor results for intrinsic motivation are summarized in Table 2.

Table 2: Relatedness' Influence unto Intrinsic Motivation

	β	SE	95% CI	p
Intrinsic Motivation				
Sense of Social Fit	.518	.114	.591 to 1.042	.000
Relatedness	.275	.077	.141 to .446	.000
Race	-.175	.177	-.796 to -.094	.013
School Type	-.183	.147	-.672 to -.091	.011
CS Experience	.018	0.156	-.271 to .349	.804

5.2 Needs Satisfaction and Motivation

Sense of social fit significantly predicts all forms of motivation, but neither competency nor perceived autonomy support predicted motivation subtypes. Controlling for demographics, a linear regression model regressing intrinsic motivation onto basic needs was statistically significant, although sense of social fit's predictive relationship accounted for the relationship ($R^2 = .426$; F = 12.89; p < .001). Similar results were observed for both career motivations ($R^2 = .353$; F = 9.476; p < .001) and grade motivations ($R^2 = .119$; F = 2.318; p = .039). Results for motivational predictors are summarised in Table 3.

Table 3: **Needs Satisfaction and Motivation**

	β	SE	95% CI	p
Intrinsic Motivation				
Sense of Social Fit	.482	.145	.460 to 1.037	.000
Autonomy	.167	.081	-.003 to .319	.054
Competency	.074	.093	-.110 to .260	.422
	β	SE	95% CI	p
Job Motives				
Sense of Social Fit	.547	.139	.488 to 1.038	.000
Autonomy	.190	.077	.000 to .306	.050
Competency	-.151	.089	-.314 to .039	.125
	β	SE	95% CI	p
Grade Motives				
Sense of Social Fit	.305	.169	.104 to .774	.011
Autonomy	-.072	.094	-.248 to .123	.504
Competency	.049	.108	-.167 to .259	.670

5.3 The Mediating Role of Self-Efficacy

Given the effect that the presence of same-sex peers has on feelings of self-efficacy [31], Hypothesis 3 tested whether self-efficacy acts as a mediator between an individual's basic needs and later self-efficacy. Results indicate that self-efficacy mediates the relationship between sense of social fit and intrinsic motivation. As Figure 1 illustrates, sense of social fit was a significant predictor of self-efficacy (b =1.08; SE =.09; p < .001) and self-efficacy significantly predicted intrinsic motivation (b =.40; SE =.09; p < .001). There still exists a significant direct relationship between sense of social fit and intrinsic motivation (b = .52; SE=.141; p < .001). A bootstrapped approach with 5000 samples was used to test the indirect effect and it indicated that the indirect effect was significant (b = .43; SE = .16; CI (.14, .78)).

A smaller but similar effect was observed between relatedness and intrinsic motivation. Relatedness predicts self-efficacy (b= .20; SE = .09; p =.02) and, in turn, self-efficacy predicts intrinsic motivation (b = .62; SE = .07; p < .001). Relatedness' effect on intrinsic motivation is nearly significant (b = .13; SE=.07; p = .06) with an indirect effect of .13 (SE=.05; CI (.03, .24)).

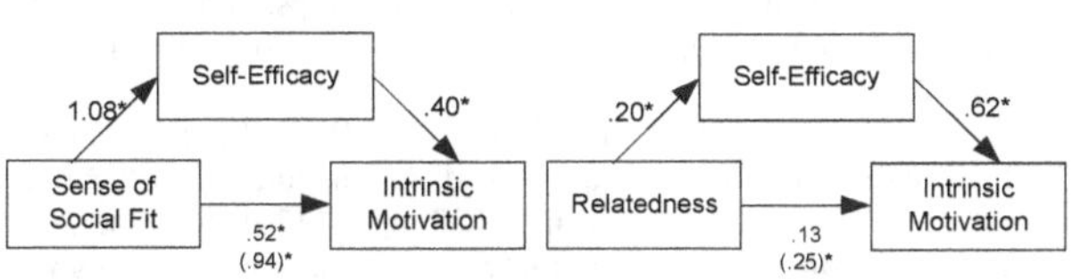

A similar relationship was observed between competency, self-efficacy, and intrinsic motivation. There exists a statistically significant relationship between perceived competency support (PCS) and self-efficacy (b = .49; SE = .07; p < .001) and between self-efficacy and intrinsic motivation (b = .64; SE = .08; p < .001). There was no direct relationship between PCS and Intrinsic Motivation (b = -.01; SE = .07; p = .88). I performed bootstrapped analysis with 5000 samples and observed an effect of .32 (SE=.09; CI=.17, p=.52. Similarly, a statistically significant relationship emerges between perceived autonomy support (PAS) and self-efficacy (b =.32; SE = .08; p < .001) and between self-efficacy and intrinsic motivation (b = .62; SE = .07; p < .001). There was no direct relationship between PAS and intrinsic motivation (b = .04; SE = .06; p=.58). The same bootstrapped analysis demonstrated an effect of .2 (SE = .20; CI=(.09, .32)). Results from both competency support and autonomy support are summarized in Figure 2.

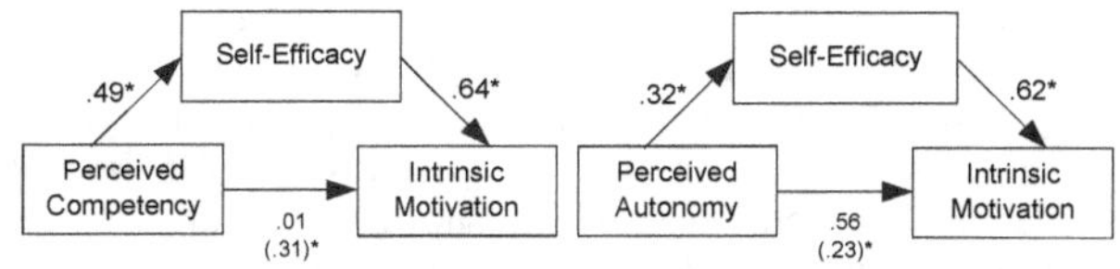

5 DISCUSSION

This paper makes two principal contributions to our understanding of how to facilitate the take-up of computer science study by young women. Firstly, it explores how basic needs support influences women's motivation. Secondly, it explicates the mechanism through which needs support leads to motivation.

While the role that autonomy and competency play in supporting motivation for learning is well established [36], relatedness and sense of inclusion have been under-emphasized in SDT literature. However, findings from Hypothesis 1 suggest that, for young women in technology, an educational minority, sense of belonging is both a necessary condition for motivation and is a significantly stronger predictor of motivation than is autonomy or competency. This contrasts with SDT findings that suggest that all needs are equally predictive or that autonomy is uniquely important [4]. However, it aligns with general findings around minorities in educational settings. When minorities feel a sense of belonging, they are motivated to persist [42]. These results are consistent with the belief that belonging, above all, is necessary to promote motivation.

In establishing the importance of belonging for young women in technology, and by extension, minorities in educational settings, hypothesis 3 investigated the mechanism by which belonging influences motivation. Mediation analyses of belonging, self-efficacy, and intrinsic motivation suggest that belonging produces a sense of self-efficacy, which in turn influences motivation.

The mediating role of self-efficacy supports earlier findings that establish self-efficacy as a correlate and predictor of interest in studying computing [27], [28]. Boys and those who identify as male have higher perceived self-efficacy in technology and computer science [18], [30]. Results from hypothesis 3 may partially explain these higher rates since girls receive less encouragement to pursue technology and this research suggests that without this support, they may have fewer places to develop the crucial sense of self-efficacy. When young women's sense of belonging is fostered, they develop a sense that they are not an "other" and are capable of achieving their goals.

Such findings do underscore a paradox – to feel efficacious enough to pursue computing, women need to feel a sense of belonging. Sense of belonging is supported when women view people like them in the field. Yet, without an existing base of women in computing, it may be difficult to establish the critical mass necessary for widespread belonging – a paradox observed in other scientific contexts [50]. This suggests that families, schools, and media must shift to appear more welcoming to women, as these may act as other sources of belonging and self-efficacy. Future research should evaluate the role that these other sources may play in promoting belonging. Additionally, the study focused on women and, in doing so, assumes that all attendees identify with the experience of being female and that it is their experience being female that potentially dissuades them from pursuing technical fields. Despite a history of exclusionary practices relating to women [51], I acknowledge that issues of race, sexual orientation, socio-economic status, and other minorities may also perceive feelings of exclusion from technology-based settings [52]. Further research should include measures directly related to gender identity, to measure the strength of gender's impacts. However, this study chooses to focus on gender, regardless of an individual's identified feelings both because it has shown the most resistance to similar targeted interventions and because feelings of relatedness, regardless of what identity it is related to, have been shown to improve persistence for intersectional feminists [53], [54].

This research highlights that psychological predictors are as significantly related to computer science study as demographic factors. At present, while much research focuses on structural factors influencing entry and exit, this research suggests that psychological factors play a significant role in motivating computer science study. Future research should closely explore how to create psychologically-supportive educational environments and outreach programmes as well as on their evaluation.

6 CONCLUSION

Amidst growing demand for computer science-trained workers and decreasing numbers of women in computer science, identifying the psychological factors that predict success in this field appears as an urgent research need. Yet, despite literature on the importance of belonging for minorities in educational settings, few studies explore how sense of belonging influences intrinsic motivation for learning. Identifying the factors that support intrinsic motivation is crucial. Only when learning is intrinsically motivated and self-regulated do individuals persist amidst obstacles. By applying self-determination theory to the experience of women in computing, this study used post positivist methods to explore motivational correlates for women in computer science. This study utilized cross-sectional surveys to identify the psychological factors that predispose one to computer science motivation. The analysis contained three parts. The first and second analyses identified that sense of social fit, more than autonomy or competency, predicts intrinsic motivation for computer science study. Finally, the third analysis identified that sense of social fit improves a young woman's sense of self-efficacy which then influences feelings of intrinsic motivation.

These results identify the mechanisms that can improve intrinsic motivation. Identifying motivational correlates for young women contributes to our understanding of how to support women in technology because it identifies the most important factor that supports learning. While SDT suggests that autonomy, competency, and relatedness equally predict motivation, this study shows how, for minorities, relatedness is uniquely important for supporting motivation. By showcasing how psychological theories differentially impact young female communities this research makes important strides in our understanding of how to best support young women's technology study.

REFERENCES

[1] N. Dasgupta and J. G. Stout, "Girls and Women in Science, Technology, Engineering, and Mathematics: STEMing the Tide and Broadening Participation in STEM Careers," *Policy Insights Behav. Brain Sci.*, vol. 1, no. 1, pp. 21–29, Oct. 2014.

[2] J. Herbert and D. Stipek, "The Emergence of Gender Differences in Children's Perceptions of Their Academic Competence," *J. Appl. Dev. Psychol. Int. Lifesp. J.*, vol. 26, no. 3, pp. 276–295, May 2005.

[3] C. Good, J. Aronson, and M. Inzlicht, "Improving adolescents' standardized test performance: An intervention to reduce the effects of stereotype threat," *J. Appl. Dev. Psychol.*, vol. 24, no. 6, pp. 645–662, Dec. 2003.

[4] E. L. Deci and R. M. Ryan, "The 'What' and 'Why' of Goal Pursuits: Human Needs and the Self-Determination of Behavior," *Psychol. Inq.*, vol. 11, no. 4, pp. 227–268, Oct. 2000.

[5] T. Camp, "The Incredible Shrinking Pipeline," *Commun ACM*, vol. 40, no. 10, pp. 103–110, Oct. 1997.

[6] J. C. Blickenstaff, "Women and science careers: leaky pipeline or gender filter?," *Gend. Educ.*, vol. 17, no. 4, pp. 369–386, Oct. 2005.

[7] L. J. Barker, C. McDowell, and K. Kalahar, "Exploring Factors That Influence Computer Science Introductory Course Students to Persist in the Major," in *Proceedings of the 40th ACM Technical Symposium on Computer Science Education*, New York, NY, USA, 2009, pp. 153–157.

[8] S. Cheryan, A. Master, and A. N. Meltzoff, "Cultural stereotypes as gatekeepers: increasing girls' interest in computer science and engineering by diversifying stereotypes," *Front. Psychol.*, vol. 6, Feb. 2015.

[9] S. L. Fries-Britt and B. Turner, "Facing Stereotypes: A Case Study of Black Students on a White Campus," *J. Coll. Stud. Dev.*, vol. 42, no. 5, pp. 420–29, 2001.

[10] R. Kramer, "Diversifiers at Elite Schools," *Bois Rev. Soc. Sci. Res. Race*, vol. 5, no. 2, pp. 287–307, Oct. 2008.

[11] M. A. Beasley and M. J. Fischer, "Why they leave: the impact of stereotype threat on the attrition of women and minorities from science, math and engineering majors," *Soc. Psychol. Educ.*, vol. 15, no. 4, pp. 427–448, Dec. 2012.

[12] A. Fisher, J. Margolis, and F. Miller, "Undergraduate Women in Computer Science: Experience, Motivation and Culture," in *Proceedings of the Twenty-eighth SIGCSE Technical Symposium on Computer Science Education*, New York, NY, USA, 1997, pp. 106–110.

[13] A. Powell, A. Dainty, and B. Bagilhole, "Gender stereotypes among women engineering and technology students in the UK: lessons from career choice narratives," *Eur. J. Eng. Educ.*, vol. 37, no. 6, pp. 541–556, 2012.

[14] R. F. Baumeister, J. M. Twenge, and C. K. Nuss, "Effects of social exclusion on cognitive processes: Anticipated aloneness reduces intelligent thought," *J. Pers. Soc. Psychol.*, vol. 83, no. 4, pp. 817–827, 2002.

[15] G. M. Walton, C. Logel, J. M. Peach, S. J. Spencer, and M. P. Zanna, "Two Brief Interventions to Mitigate a 'Chilly Climate' Transform Women's Experience, Relationships, and Achievement in Engineering," *J. Educ. Psychol.*, vol. 107, no. 2, pp. 468–485, May 2015.

[16] G. M. Walton and G. L. Cohen, "A Brief Social-Belonging Intervention Improves Academic and Health Outcomes of Minority Students," *Science*, vol. 331, no. 6023, pp. 1447–1451, Mar. 2011.

[17] B. S. Faircloth and J. V. Hamm, "Sense of Belonging Among High School Students Representing 4 Ethnic Groups," *J. Youth Adolesc.*, vol. 34, no. 4, pp. 293–309, Aug. 2005.

[18] S. Beyer, "Why are women underrepresented in Computer Science? Gender differences in stereotypes, self-efficacy, values, and interests and predictors of future CS course-taking and grades," *Comput. Sci. Educ.*, vol. 24, no. 2–3, pp. 153–192, Jul. 2014.

[19] C. M. Lewis, R. E. Anderson, and K. Yasuhara, "'I Don'T Code All Day': Fitting in Computer Science When the Stereotypes Don'T Fit," in *Proceedings of the 2016 ACM Conference on International Computing Education Research*, New York, NY, USA, 2016, pp. 23–32.

[20] S. Cheryan, B. J. Drury, and M. Vichayapai, "Enduring Influence of Stereotypical Computer Science Role Models on Women's Academic Aspirations," *Psychol. Women Q.*, vol. 37, no. 1, pp. 72–79, Mar. 2013.

[21] S. Cheryan, V. C. Plaut, C. Handron, and L. Hudson, "The Stereotypical Computer Scientist: Gendered Media Representations as a Barrier to Inclusion for Women," *Sex Roles*, vol. 69, no. 1–2, pp. 58–71, Jul. 2013.

[22] L. Shashaani, "Gender-Differences in Computer Experience and its Influence on Computer Attitudes," *J. Educ. Comput. Res.*, vol. 11, no. 4, pp. 347–367, Dec. 1994.

[23] H. R. Tenenbaum and C. Leaper, "Are parents' gender schemas related to their children's gender-related cognitions? A meta-analysis," *Dev. Psychol.*, vol. 38, no. 4, pp. 615–630, 2002.

[24] S. L. Beilock, E. A. Gunderson, G. Ramirez, and S. C. Levine, "Female teachers' math anxiety affects girls' math achievement," *Proc. Natl. Acad. Sci.*, vol. 107, no. 5, pp. 1860–1863, Feb. 2010.

[25] "Google (Firm) Gallup (Firm). (2016). Diversity gaps in computer science: exploring the underrepresentation of girls, Blacks and Hispanics."

[26] S. Cheryan, V. C. Plaut, P. G. Davies, and C. M. Steele, "Ambient Belonging," *J. Pers. Soc. Psychol.*, vol. 97, no. 6, pp. 1045–1060, Dec. 2009.

[27] I. T. Miura, "The relationship of computer self-efficacy expectations to computer interest and course enrollment in college," *Sex Roles*, vol. 16, no. 5–6, pp. 303–311, Mar. 1987.

[28] E. Hargittai and S. Shafer, "Differences in Actual and Perceived Online Skills: The Role of Gender*," *Soc. Sci. Q.*, vol. 87, no. 2, pp. 432–448, Jun. 2006.

[29] T. Busch, "Gender Differences in Self-Efficacy and Attitudes toward Computers," *J. Educ. Comput. Res.*, vol. 12, no. 2, pp. 147–158, Mar. 1995.

[30] A. H. Huffman, J. Whetten, and W. H. Huffman, "Using technology in higher education: The influence of gender roles on technology self-efficacy," *Comput. Hum. Behav.*, vol. 29, no. 4, pp. 1779–1786, Jul. 2013.

[31] D. H. Schunk and A. R. Hanson, "Peer Models: Influence on Children's Self-Efficacy and Achievement," *J. Educ. Psychol.*, vol. 77, no. 3, pp. 313–22, 1985.

[32] D. H. Schunk and F. Pajares, "The Development of Academic Self-Efficacy," in *Development of Achievement Motivation*, A. Wigfield and J. S. Eccles, Eds. San Diego: Academic Press, 2002, pp. 15–31.

[33] M. Vansteenkiste, W. Lens, and E. L. Deci, "Intrinsic Versus Extrinsic Goal Contents in Self-Determination Theory: Another Look at the Quality of Academic Motivation," *Educ. Psychol.*, vol. 41, no. 1, pp. 19–31, Mar. 2006.

[34] C. P. Niemiec and R. M. Ryan, "Autonomy, competence, and relatedness in the classroom: Applying self-determination theory to educational practice," *Sch. Field*, vol. 7, no. 2, pp. 133–144, Jul. 2009.

[35] G. Roth, A. Assor, C. Niemiec, E. L. Deci, and R. M. Ryan, "The Emotional and Academic Consequences of Parental Conditional Regard: Comparing Conditional Positive Regard, Conditional Negative Regard, and Autonomy Support as Parenting Practices," *Dev. Psychol.*, vol. 45, no. 4, pp. 1119–1142, 2009.

[36] J. Reeve and W. Lee, "Students' classroom engagement produces longitudinal changes in classroom motivation," *J. Educ. Psychol.*, vol. 106, no. 2, pp. 527–540, 2014.

[37] G. Taylor *et al.*, "A self-determination theory approach to predicting school achievement over time: the unique role of intrinsic motivation," *Contemp. Educ. Psychol.*, vol. 39, no. 4, pp. 342–358, Oct. 2014.

[38] G. L. Lavigne, R. J. Vallerand, and P. Miquelon, "A motivational model of persistence in science education: A self-determination theory approach," *Eur. J. Psychol. Educ.*, vol. 22, no. 3, p. 351, Sep. 2007.

[39] N. Ntoumanis, "A self-determination approach to the understanding of motivation in physical education," *Br. J. Educ. Psychol.*, vol. 71, no. 2, pp. 225–242, Jun. 2001.

[40] K. Trenshaw, R. Revelo, K. Earl, and G. Herman, "Using Self Determination Theory Principles to Promote Engineering Students' Intrinsic Motivation to Learn," *Int. J. Eng. Educ.*, vol. 32, no. 3(A), pp. 1194–1207, 2016.

[41] M. R. Beachboard, J. C. Beachboard, W. Li, and S. R. Adkison, "Cohorts and Relatedness: Self-Determination Theory as an Explanation of How Learning Communities Affect Educational Outcomes," *Res. High. Educ.*, vol. 52, no. 8, pp. 853–874, Dec. 2011.

[42] G. M. Walton and G. L. Cohen, "A question of belonging: race, social fit, and achievement," *J. Pers. Soc. Psychol.*, vol. 92, no. 1, pp. 82–96, Jan. 2007.

[43] A. Bandura and D. H. Schunk, "Cultivating competence, self-efficacy, and intrinsic interest through proximal self-motivation," *J. Pers. Soc. Psychol.*, vol. 41, no. 3, pp. 586–598, Sep. 1981.

[44] B. J. Zimmerman, A. Bandura, and M. Martinez-Pons, "Self-Motivation for Academic Attainment: The Role of Self-Efficacy Beliefs and Personal Goal Setting," *Am. Educ. Res. J.*, vol. 29, no. 3, pp. 663–676, Jan. 1992.

[45] A. E. Black and E. L. Deci, "The effects of instructors' autonomy support and students' autonomous motivation on learning organic chemistry: A self-determination theory perspective," *Sci. Educ.*, vol. 84, no. 6, pp. 740–756, Nov. 2000.

[46] G. C. Williams and E. L. Deci, "Internalization of biopsychosocial values by medical students: A test of self-determination theory," *J. Pers. Soc. Psychol.*, vol. 70, no. 4, pp. 767–779, 1996.

[47] B. Chen *et al.*, "Basic psychological need satisfaction, need frustration, and need strength across four cultures," *Motiv. Emot.*, vol. 39, no. 2, pp. 216–236, Apr. 2015.

[48] S. M. Glynn, P. Brickman, N. Armstrong, and G. Taasoobshirazi, "Science motivation questionnaire II: Validation with science majors and nonscience majors," *J. Res. Sci. Teach.*, vol. 48, no. 10, pp. 1159–1176, Dec. 2011.

[49] A. Hayes, "Introduction to Mediation," in *Moderation and Conditional Process Analysis: A Regression-Based Approach*, New York: Guilford Press, 2013.

[50] H. Etzkowitz, C. Kemelgor, M. Neuschatz, B. Uzzi, and J. Alonzo, "The Paradox of Critical Mass for Women in Science," *Science*, vol. 266, no. 5182, pp. 51–54, 1994.

[51] N. L. Ensmenger, *The Computer Boys Take Over: Computers, Programmers, and the Politics of Technical Expertise*. The MIT Press, 2012.

[52] C. Riegle-Crumb and B. King, "Questioning a White Male Advantage in STEM: Examining Disparities in College Major by Gender and Race/Ethnicity," *Educ. Res.*, vol. 39, no. 9, pp. 656–664, 2010.

[53] L. Espinosa, "Pipelines and Pathways: Women of Color in Undergraduate STEM Majors and the College Experiences That Contribute to Persistence," *Harv. Educ. Rev.*, vol. 81, no. 2, pp. 209–241, Jun. 2011.

[54] J. Price, "The effect of instructor race and gender on student persistence in STEM fields," *Econ. Educ. Rev.*, vol. 29, no. 6, pp. 901–910, Dec. 2010.

A Survey-based Exploration of Computer Science Student Perspectives on Mathematics

Nikki Sigurdson
University of Toronto Mississauga
Mississauga, Canada
n.sigurdson@mail.utoronto.ca

Andrew Petersen
University of Toronto Mississauga
Mississauga, Canada
petersen@cs.toronto.edu

ABSTRACT

Experts and practitioners have long published reflections on how mathematics connects with computer science and how best to integrate mathematics within computing education. However, little literature exists that investigates this area empirically. One recent study used in-depth interviews to generate a theory of the relationship between student perceptions of mathematics and their attitude toward computer science. However, this theory is based on interactions with a limited number of students. Our study tests this theory in a larger population. We present a survey-based exploration of the attitudes 218 undergraduate computer science students hold on mathematics. We present quantitative evidence that supports the theory that student career inclinations are correlated with beliefs about mathematics. We also present additional qualitative data, obtained from free-response sections of the survey, that support the idea that student inclinations affect both their perception of the value of mathematics and academic decisions such as course selection.

CCS CONCEPTS

• **Social and professional topics** → *Computer science education.*

KEYWORDS

mathematics; identity

ACM Reference Format:

Nikki Sigurdson and Andrew Petersen. 2019. A Survey-based Exploration of Computer Science Student Perspectives on Mathematics. In *Proceedings of the 50th ACM Technical Symposium on Computer Science Education (SIGCSE '19), February 27-March 2, 2019, Minneapolis, MN, USA.* ACM, New York, NY, USA, 7 pages. https://doi.org/10.1145/3287324.3287416

1 INTRODUCTION

In previous work based on student interviews, we presented evidence suggesting a relationship between the perceptions that undergraduate computer science students hold about mathematics and computer science [24]. That work focused on a small number of student stories and, considering the situation of each participant, found that students' identities as computer scientists were connected to their perspectives on mathematics. This study also suggested that student perceptions of mathematics and their program of study are intertwined, with each influencing the other.

Understanding how a program's emphasis on mathematical education, especially early on in a CS education, can affect a student's beliefs and identities is crucially connected to a major contemporary challenge in computing education: diversity. The outline for mathematical education in the current ACM undergraduate computer science curriculum guideline [1] is broad in its mathematical requirements, and many CS programs are intentionally structured with a mathematical component early in the course of study. These requirements may undermine efforts to improve diversity [4].

This paper seeks to expand on past efforts to understand students' perceptions of mathematics from their experience with computing education and to establish future directions of study by validating the findings from the previous, interview-based study. The following research questions are addressed:

(1) Does a student's career inclination affect their perception of the mathematics in computer science?
(2) Do the decisions students make about courses reflect their perceptions towards the mathematics in computer science?

In the next section, we briefly summarize the existing literature on mathematics in computing and then discuss how Hewner's theories about student conceptions of computer science [15] and their reasons for selecting courses [16] can be extended by a focus on their conception of mathematics. In Section 3, we describe our method and the context of the study. Sections 4 and 5 present the results of our survey-based study, and we summarize our findings in Section 6.

2 RELATED WORK

For several decades, the computing community has debated the mathematics necessary and sufficient for a CS program [2, 3, 7, 8, 12–14, 18–22]. These conversations have included topics such as the types of mathematics to include, the general benefits of education in mathematics – such as problem-solving skills and abstraction ability – and drawbacks to including mathematics, which include critical ties to diversity and the accessibility of CS education. However, these conversations have primarily presented the viewpoints of faculty. Little research empirically studies the perceptions students themselves hold or the impacts decisions related to mathematics have on CS students.

Recent conversations surrounding mathematics in computer science education have been recast in terms of Computational Thinking (CT) [5, 17, 26], a principle that "indicates a mental orientation to formulate problems as conversions of some input to an output and looking for algorithms to perform the conversions." CT is considered an asset for computer science students and is often-times described

SIGCSE '19, February 27-March 2, 2019, Minneapolis, MN, USA

ACM ISBN 978-1-4503-5890-3/19/02...$15.00
https://doi.org/10.1145/3287324.3287416

as strongly tied to mathematical thinking and the use of mathematics in problem solving [25]. "The term also includes thinking with many levels of abstraction, use of mathematics to develop algorithms, and examining a solution" [5]. But the scope of CT seems to be broad and multidisciplinary [6], and an explicit education in mathematics is still considered an essential part of an education in computer science [1].

Mathematical course requirements may negatively affect diversity and accessibility of computing education and other STEM (science, technology, engineering, and mathematics) fields [4]. Baldwin argues that mathematical content like applied calculus is pervasive but superfluous, and the mathematical maturity needed by CS students could be obtained through alternative means [2]. Others suggest mathematics requirements may deter some potential students; the traditional first year calculus requirement has been shown to dissuade women from continuing with a program at a rate of 1.5 more times than men [9].

Michael Hewner has published studies on a range of topics related to computer science students' perceptions, including their experiences with course choices [16] and how they broadly understand computer science [15]. However, Hewner's studies do not explicitly address choices related to mathematical courses in particular or how structures of mathematical exposure through program requirements and options affect these perceptions.

Our recent interview study [24] aimed to fill these gaps in the literature. This study looked at computer science students and their perceptions related to the mathematics in their program, and theorized that two broad groups of students exist. The first were industry-inclined, tended to be interested in software and programming, and often had a specific career goal in mind which was related to the computing industry. The second group, called theoretical-focused, either did not have a specific career path in mind or were interested in academia. Students who were industry-inclined tended to see less value in learning mathematics, and conversely, students who were theoretical-focused tended to value education in mathematics more.

The students interviewed for the aforementioned study were in a mathematically heavy program, and they often admitted that as first years they were confused about the nature and meaning in the mathematical course requirements in the context of their CS education [24]. Seymour and Hewitt [23] recognized this feeling as a broader trend in science, mathematics, and engineering education. They also found that, like the students in [24], some of their students felt their courses left them with little time to absorb and contextualize what they were learning and that the courses themselves did little to aid students in this bridging process.

3 METHODOLOGY

Our intention in this study is to test, extend, and explore the findings in [24] on a larger scale. That study involved a small number of students in interviews. We use a survey instrument administered to students in all years of study in our computer science program. Findings from the interview study helped to shape the structure and content of the survey instrument. The survey questions were designed to validate the preliminary categorizations presented in that interview study and to further refine these categories using data from a broader sample of students.

The instrument itself had three major components: a demographics section, a Likert questions section, and a short answer section. The demographics section served to collect information about the participants' years of study, gender, campus, and which CS and math courses they had completed or were currently enrolled in at the time of the survey. The Likert questions section consisted of two consecutive pages of questions, and students responded with five options ranging from strongly disagree to strongly agree. The Likert questions are presented in Table 2. The final section was a short answer segment consisting of a series of three open ended prompts to allow participants to expand on their preceding responses. The prompts were:

(1) How should the university change the mathematics in the computer science program?
(2) What is the relationship between mathematics and computer science?
(3) What are any other thoughts you have about mathematics in computer science education?

The first two prompts were designed based on data from the previous study [24]. The first was intended to probe students about how their program either satisfies or does not satisfy their understanding of the needs of the overall student population. Students could also interpret this question to mean how the program should change to suit their own personal desires/plans; either interpretation provides valuable data for the purpose of this study. The second was an open ended question intended to offer students a space to expand on their answers from the Likert scale sections. The third was meant to provide a space for any additional remarks.

3.1 Institutional Context

The design of the Likert questions section was motivated by both the results of the previous study and our specific institutional context. Students at our institution must enroll in either two majors (or a single double-major), or a major and two minors. They are admitted into programs at the end of their first year through a competitive application process based on grades in individual first year courses and overall grade point average. As a result, some students who intended to major in computer science graduate with a minor instead. As a result, whether a student is in a major or a minor is not a reliable indicator of the strength of their identity within the discipline.

At our institution, students get some choice in how they satisfy certain mathematics requirements for their program. Students entering our computer science program make a choice about which of three first year calculus options to select: an applied version, a theoretical version, and an enriched version intended for students interested in pure mathematics. Since admissions are competitive, students may have an incentive to select a path through the first year that will maximize grades, so many choose to take the applied version of calculus as it is perceived as being less difficult.

In addition to calculus, students intending to major or minor in computer science are expected to complete an introduction to computer science that includes basic data structure work and a first year mathematical reasoning course. Both of these courses are offered by the computer science department as CS courses rather than as mathematics courses. Once students are admitted to a computer science

Year of Study	1	2	3, 4+
Total Pop.	135	43	40
Took Applied First-Year Calculus	60	52	26
Took Theoretical First-Year Calculus	52	34	20
Took Enriched First-Year Calculus	10	0	5
Female	38	14	12
Male	89	26	25
Alternative or no Response for Gender	8	3	3
Math. Minor	24	18	7
Math. Major	31	10	7
Math. D. Major	9	2	2

Table 1: Demographics of Participants

program, they must complete additional mathematics and theory courses in the second year, as well as a second year statistics course.

3.2 Data Collection

The survey was administered to undergraduate computer science students at a large, research-intensive North American university. The survey was implemented using a locally hosted LimeSurvey [11] server. It was made publicly available through an access link, and participants provided consent on the first page of the instrument. Advertisement was done within courses, and the courses used were chosen specifically because they either were program requirements or targeted a certain student population based on results from the interview study [24]. These courses include the first year CS courses, the first year mathematical requirements for CS students, and mandatory or highly recommended upper year courses like advanced algorithms and operating systems. Students were encouraged to participate by the opportunity to opt-in to a draw for one of four $50 dollar gift cards after completing the survey. The draw took place after the survey was closed. All students completing the survey provided consent for the data to be used.

3.3 Data Analysis

Overall, there 312 survey responses in total, and 221 of them were fully completed. Three responses contained the same choice selected for all Likert questions, and these were removed. After this, 218 responses were used in the rest of the analysis.

As shown in Table 1, 135 were self-identified first years, 43 were second years, and 40 were upper years (3rd year and above). Like the interview study, upper years are grouped together, partially due to the lower number of responses and partially because upper year students have typically completed the foundational years of the program and are completing electives. 64 participants identified themselves as female, 140 as male, and 14 either offered an alternate response or chose not to answer.

3.3.1 Free Response Data. The free response data was analyzed separately by a single researcher who coded all of the data. Each student's responses to all three free response prompts were considered as a single submission for coding purposes.

While the interview study [24] used a full grounded theory approach to code the results that adjusted the interview question set as the interviews continued to be held and probed students for particular information which they might not have commented on without solicitation, our free response section offered students three open-ended prompts with no option for us to further question them. This means that the data obtained from our qualitative results are not directly comparable to the results in [24].

Student responses were given labels which evolved over the coding process. The initial labels were drawn from [24] and included course choice (and specifically the institution's role in communicating recommendations to students about courses), career inclinations, relationships between mathematics and computer science, and other factors of students' lives.

3.3.2 Factor Analysis of Likert Scale Questions. A factor analysis was performed on the Likert data to identify empirical factors and compare them to the ones hypothesized to exist in the interview study. We used promax rotation and explored the models created through multiple number of factors.

4 DATA

In this section, we present data from the free response sections first, to provide context, and then present a factor analysis to provide empirical support for the theory proposed by the interview study.

4.1 Free Response

4.1.1 Students' thoughts on the mathematical requirements. 16 students (17.58 % of coded responses) wrote they felt the mathematical requirements in the CS program should be more geared to computer science students. This remark was usually additionally accompanied by the feeling that when something in math is taught, its relevance to computer science should be made clear. These students disagreed about the amount of mathematics that is reasonable, ranging from believing that there should be less mathematical requirements to believing the amount of requirements are alright as they are. The distinction between these two groups often hinged on their view of theoretical (proof-based) mathematics. Some students stated that proof-based mathematics courses are beneficial because they taught problem-solving skills advantageous to computer scientists, while others thought proof-based math was not useful to computer scientists in any way. Some examples of the students' thoughts are illustrated with examples below:

`The math courses we take should have a stronger relationship to computer science, there should be courses offered that show students the connections between math and computer science, and that also show how a person who has a strong grasp in math can solve plenty of problems in computer science. There should be math and computer science courses that teach how to think logically, that teach the basics of logic and problem solving before throwing students into a math/computer science course that is excessively hard.`

`They should make the program more broad and more available to students and should not require such high CGPA for [the CS program] because an individual can do amazing in computer science but not as good in` math courses which brings their CGPA down and due to that a person who is really great and passionate about programming might not get an opportunity to pursue that career.

The university should better communicate the benefits of each mathematics course so students better understand "what they are signing up for.

I think math in CS education is good but only up to a certain point. We're not going to need to know how to use the Taylor Series to learn C#. But the way to answer problems and the thinking and logic that is applied is always useful. Thinking about a problem in different ways and knowing how to solve it is the primary job of a good CS student.

4.1.2 Mathematics and GPA. Some wrote that students were dissuaded from taking theoretical mathematics courses because of GPA considerations. They said mathematical requirements already deter students from pursuing CS, and the theoretical versions of mathematical courses are more challenging than the applied ones, and prioritizing good grades is a more important goal than learning theoretical math, even for students who personally see a value in learning theoretical math.

Those who enjoy maths will not ... take [theoretical first year calculus] due to the impact to their GPA. Unfortunately, GPA and cutoffs do affect a student's choice in which courses they take and as a result, many people have dropped courses like [theoretical first year calculus] and [theoretical intro. linear algebra] not due to lack of interest but due to the fact that it's easier and makes you more of a competitive candidate for admissions when the time comes as their is no benefit to taking [the more theoretical courses] thus why bother.

Some of these students in particular criticized the marking schemes in proof-based math courses, which they felt were unfair or too harsh, and said if they were more forgiving to students, then more would choose them.

As a first year student, the specific only thing that I strongly believe should be changed, is that the [theoretical and enriched first year calculus] courses should take some marking attributes from [applied first year calculus] and [intro to mathematical proofs]. For example, in both [these courses], a student's worst test is not counted towards their final mark. This is super important as [theoretical and enriched first year calculus] introduce a lot of new content to students. The content is so diverse and different to what most high school students are used to, that the first test in [intro to proofs], almost requires that the worst test is dropped from a students mark. The content in [theoretical first year calculus] is teaching a whole new way to think, and most professors explain this as something your brain has to get used to, making the first test a largely failed test in both courses. [...] the number of students that drop from [theoretical] to [applied first year calculus] after the first test to be incredibly high.

I would think a more effective way to take first year calculus would be 2 half-term courses, similar to [CS1] and [CS2]. This way the students' CGPA's would not suffer as much, and the concepts would be more thoroughly covered.

4.1.3 Benefits of Mathematics. Despite the large number of students who were dissatisfied with some aspect of the current program, many students (even ones with dissatisfactions) found some math requirement enlightening and beneficial. It is valuable to note that most students who advocated for more theoretical mathematics education for CS students tended to be students in math programs as well.

The [intro. to mathematical proofs] course opened my mind to a new way of thinking, and I would like to take more courses like this one in my computer science program.

My opinion is that if someone does not like mathematics, then certainly a computer science program is not appropriate for them.

I think first year computer science students should be pushed to the advanced calculus courses. Theoretical computer science is intimately tied to discrete mathematics, so developing mathematical maturity early on can really help.

The same participant additionally provided a viewpoint on the benefit of mathematics to CS students which many educators also hold:

Also, the way of thinking in mathematics and computer science are similar--it is about constructing generalized theorems/algorithms through insights about the objects you're working with. It is also about the translation of ideas into mathematical language. Students taking [theoretical or enriched first year calculus] will have the opportunity to practice these skills. It's not about the content, but the development of these abilities--if the only thing you're taking away from a calculus course is how to use formulas and add numbers, then you're wasting your time and money.

4.2 Factor Analysis

We chose to use promax rotation so that we could explore any potential correlations that existed between our factors [10]. The other common option is varimax, which does not permit measurements of correlations between factors. As seen in Table 3, the correlation matrix,

	Likert Scale Questions	Factor 1	Factor 2
A01	I am passionate about computer science.		0.45
A02	I liked mathematics before university.	0.41	0.36
A03	It is important for computer science students to learn mathematics.	0.75	
A04	I feel like the mathematics I have learned will be directly applicable in my career.	0.75	
A05	The fewer mathematics courses that I must take in university, the better.	-0.75	
A06	I chose to study computer science primarily because the industry opportunities are attractive.		0.41
A07	The computer science program should incorporate more mathematics into computer science courses.	0.71	
A08	The ability to write proofs, and use proof techniques is an important skill for computer science students.	0.61	
A09	I feel like I will use calculus tools in my future.	0.64	
A10	I would like to work for a major technology company such as Apple, Google, Microsoft, or Amazon.		0.62
A11	I like the idea of creating my own start-up.		0.46
B01	Studying computer science is more useful than studying mathematics.	-0.43	0.34
B02	Mathematics problems are fun, but only when they are easy to understand.	-0.43	
B03	All first year calculus course options are equally as good for computer science students.		
B04	If a student is successful in [first year intro. to proofs], then they should be equally as successful in first year calculus.		
B05	I avoid courses that are not directly relevant to my future.		0.38
B06	To be successful in mathematics courses means being able to know which formula to use to solve each type of problem.		0.31
B07	When I entered university I felt confident about my mathematical skills.		
B08	There are ideas in computer science which are not connected to mathematics in any way.	-0.35	
B09	I choose to take some math courses that are not mandatory.	0.67	
B10	I can be a good computer science student without being good at mathematics.	-0.48	
B11	I did better in [first year intro. to proofs] than I did in first year calculus.		
B12	Most ideas in computer science are strongly connected to mathematics.	0.61	

Table 2: Factor Analysis on Likert Scale Questions

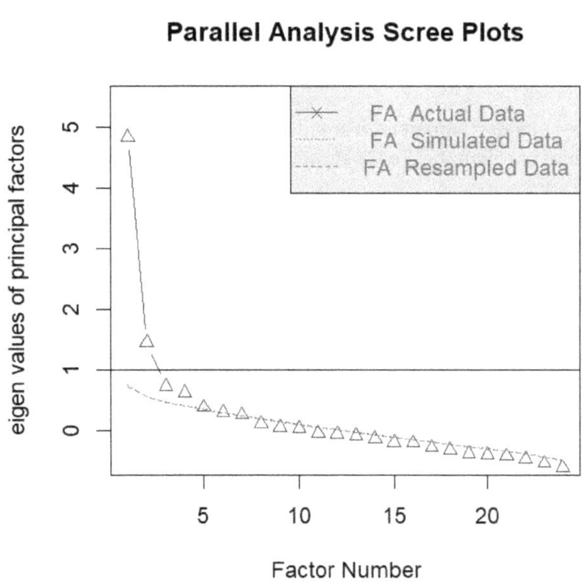

Figure 1: Scree Plot Used to Identify the Number of Factors

	Factor 1	Factor 2
Factor 1	1.0	-0.2
Factor 2	-0.2	1.0

Table 3: Correlation Matrix of Factors

the factors are weakly correlated. Based on the interview study, we expected to see at least two groups. The scree plot in Figure 1 suggested two or, more weakly, four factor models. We explored these options to see if some useful results would arise and settled on the two factor model presented in Table 2, which matches the expected theory.

In the three-factor model, a small set of questions break out to compose the third factor. These questions were A02: "I liked mathematics before university" and B07: "When I entered university I felt confident about my mathematical skills." These appear to reflect some sense of efficacy regarding mathematics. We anticipated these questions being correlated, since both addressed feelings about mathematics prior to university. With a 2 factor model, the question A02 weakly loaded to both factors, and B07 did not load above 0.3 to either factor.

In the four-factor model, our two primary factors also emerged in a similar manner to the two-factor model. The additional factors expressed data consistency. For example, one of the non-primary factors indicated our data possessed a consistent inverse relationship between the responses to B08: "There are ideas in computer science which are not related to mathematics in any way", and B012: "Most ideas in computer science are strongly connected to mathematics." We expected these questions to be correlated.

5 DISCUSSION

5.1 Career Inclination and Mathematics

The results of the factor analysis provided our results on the relationship between students' career inclinations and mathematics. Factor 1 appears to be the category of "theoretically-inclined" students, a previously observed group from the interview study. These students felt that most ideas in computer science are connected to mathematics, and that it was important for computer science students to learn mathematics. They also felt that the mathematics they had learned would be directly applicable to their careers, and they felt they would to choose to take math courses which were not mandatory.

Factor 2 is the "industry-inclined" category from the interview study. This factor represents a category of students who tend to be interested in career goals with technology companies (A10), starting their own businesses (A11), who think studying computer science is a more useful pursuit than studying mathematics (based on their own definition of useful) (B01), and these students tends to avoid courses that they see as not directly useful to their futures (B05).

Only one question loaded to both factors with a value above 0.3: "I liked mathematics before university" (A02). It is possible this is a reflection of our advertisement methods. The survey was advertised to students as being about mathematics in computer science, which could have drawn more participation from students interested in or confident about mathematics. Therefore, both factors are likely to be categories within the population of students with some degree of interest in mathematics.

5.2 Course Choices and Mathematics

From the Free Response section data, it is clear there are deep connections between students' course choices and the structure of our program's mathematical course requirements. Students frequently spoke about the importance of their grades and of maintaining them for the program entrance at the end of the first year. In the interview study, [24] where a similar program entrance system existed, this behavior was also seen. It is possible that at other institutions where programs are direct-entrance, students would be less focused on getting very high grades in their first year. As a result of this, more might attempt to take the theoretical mathematics options which so many students in the Free Response section said they might attempt if only the barriers like harsh grading and lack of a grace period were different. There was clear evidence that many students who did feel like these barriers were too high held the perspective that training in more theoretical mathematics would beneficial to them. With alternative options available, some of these students might have chosen a different route than to take applied first year calculus.

Our results and Hewner's work on students' course choices are related [16]. Hewner found that students tended to believe that any course in the curriculum had useful content, even if they had difficulty in some cases explaining why, and we see this trend in our Free Response data as well. Many of our students wrote they believed mathematics was important to CS, but their additional supporting phrases suggested they felt this way in part due to the large amount of mathematical requirements in the early years of our program. For example, the student quoted below felt that the mathematical requirements, and especially proof-components to CS theory courses at the university served to distinguish CS from simply programming.

`I think that there is strong misconception that math is not a part of CS education. I feel like this is because students entering university have a preconceived notion that CS is only programming and little to none of it is mathematical approaches to problem solving, which is what it is. I think that [the institution] is doing a good job in fighting this notion, a good example of this is how we are required to take [first year intro to proofs] and some calculus course for the CS programs. Another way [our institution] is fighting this notion is introducing proofs in CS courses such as [theoretical computer science courses].`

Overall, the results from the Free Response data aligned with the findings in [24]. However our findings are difficult to compare directly, since each respondent is only providing a brief snapshot of their perspective. In the previous study, each student's experiences and perspectives could be assessed as a integral whole, but in this work, we are limited to (usually) a single paragraph of information from each student. Our Free Response question prompts were intentionally open-ended in order to solicit more responses from students (as this section was optional.

5.3 Threats to Validity

The study did not consider students who initially entered computer science and left, or students who considered studying computer science but never tried. For both these groups of students, mathematics and mathematical requirements may have been a factor in their decisions about computer science.

6 CONCLUSION

Overall, this work provides support for the theory proposed in the original, interview-based study. The factor analysis supported the previously suggested two-component model about undergraduate computer science students' relationship with mathematics and their identities and career inclinations, while also suggesting a third, weaker factor relating to perceived efficacy.

We have also presented an overview of the perspectives students hold about the mathematics in their CS education, with the hope that these beliefs may contribute to the on-going conversation about mathematical requirements in CS. From our data it seems that a sizable fraction of students agree that mathematics has a significant relationship with the discipline. However, theoretical math courses are perceived as barriers, and they disproportionately affect some students more than others. Mathematical course requirements have already been recognized as potential threats to diversity in computing, and we present new evidence to support that students may feel dissuaded from studying computer science due to mathematics requirements and, furthermore, that CS students who see value in studying theoretical math may also be dissuaded from doing so due to curricular choices. Unfortunately, our sample contained too little diversity for separate analysis, so further work is necessary to confirm the effects of these pressures on diversity in the program.

REFERENCES

[1] 2013. Joint Task Force on Computing Curricula, Association for Computing Machinery (ACM) and IEEE Computer Society. *Computer Science Curricula 2013: Curriculum Guidelines for Undergraduate Degree Programs in Computer Science* (2013).

[2] Douglas Baldwin, Henry M. Walker, and Peter B. Henderson. 2013. The Roles of Mathematics in Computer Science. *ACM Inroads* 4, 4 (Dec. 2013), 74–80. https://doi.org/10.1145/2537753.2537777

[3] Jens Bennedsen and Michael E. Caspersen. 2008. Abstraction Ability As an Indicator of Success for Learning Computing Science?. In *Proceedings of the 4th International Workshop on Computing Education Research*. 15–26. https://doi.org/10.1145/1404520.1404523

[4] Sapna Cheryan. 2012. Understanding the Paradox in Math-Related Fields : Why Do Some Gender Gaps Remain While Others Do Not ?

[5] Peter J. Denning. 2009. The Profession of IT: Beyond Computational Thinking. *Commun. ACM* 52, 6 (June 2009), 28–30. https://doi.org/10.1145/1516046.1516054

[6] Peter J. Denning. 2017. Remaining Trouble Spots with Computational Thinking. *Commun. ACM* 60, 6 (May 2017), 33–39. https://doi.org/10.1145/2998438

[7] K. Devlin. 2003. Why CS students need math. *Commun. ACM* 46 (9), 9 (2003).

[8] John P. Dougherty. 2016. MATH COUNTS: Inside CS2013. *ACM Inroads* 7, 1 (Feb. 2016), 28–29. https://doi.org/10.1145/2876510

[9] Jessica M Ellis, Bailey K. Fosdick, and Chris Rasmussen. 2016. Women 1.5 Times More Likely to Leave STEM Pipeline after Calculus Compared to Men: Lack of Mathematical Confidence a Potential Culprit. In *PloS one*.

[10] Holmes Finch. [n. d.]. Comparison of the Performance of Varimax and Promax Rotations: Factor Structure Recovery for Dichotomous Items. *Journal of Educational Measurement* 43, 1 ([n. d.]), 39–52. https://doi.org/10.1111/j.1745-3984.2006.00003.x arXiv:https://onlinelibrary.wiley.com/doi/pdf/10.1111/j.1745-3984.2006.00003.x

[11] Limesurvey GmbH. [n. d.]. LimeSurvey: An Open Source survey tool. http://www.limesurvey.org Accessed 2018/08/31.

[12] David Gries, Bill Marion, Peter Henderson, and Diane Schwartz. 2001. How Mathematical Thinking Enchances Computer Science Problem Solving. In *Proceedings of the Thirty-second SIGCSE Technical Symposium on Computer Science Education (SIGCSE '01)*. ACM, New York, NY, USA, 390–391. https://doi.org/10.1145/364447.364754

[13] Peter B. Henderson. 2011. MATH COUNTS: Mathematical Reasoning in Computing Education. *ACM Inroads* 1, 3 (Sept. 2011), 22–23. https://doi.org/10.1145/1835428.1835438

[14] Peter B. Henderson. 2013. CS2013. *ACM Inroads* 4, 3 (Sept. 2013), 48–49. https://doi.org/10.1145/2505990.2506000

[15] Michael Hewner. 2013. Undergraduate Conceptions of the Field of Computer Science. In *Proceedings of the 9th Annual International ACM Conference on International Computing Education Research*. 107–114. https://doi.org/10.1145/2493394.2493414

[16] Michael Hewner. 2014. How CS Undergraduates Make Course Choices. In *Procs of the 10th International Conference on Computing Education Research*. 115–122. https://doi.org/10.1145/2632320.2632345

[17] James J. Lu and George H.L. Fletcher. 2009. Thinking About Computational Thinking. In *Proceedings of the 40th Technical Symposium on Computer Science Education*. 260–264. https://doi.org/10.1145/1508865.1508959

[18] Bill Marion. 2000. Discrete Mathematics: Support of and Preparation for the Study of Computer Science. In *Proceedings of the 7th Annual Midwestern Conference on Small Colleges*. 190–199. http://dl.acm.org/citation.cfm?id=369272.357730

[19] William Marion. 1989. Discrete Mathematics for Computer Science Majors – Where Are We? How Do We Proceed?. In *Proceedings of the 20th Technical Symposium on Computer Science Education*. 273–277. https://doi.org/10.1145/65293.65314

[20] Anthony Ralston. 1984. The First Course in Computer Science Needs a Mathematics Corequisite. *Commun. ACM* 27, 10 (Oct. 1984), 1002–1005. https://doi.org/10.1145/358274.358280

[21] Anthony Ralston. 2005. Do We Need ANY Mathematics in Computer Science Curricula? *SIGCSE Bull.* 37, 2 (June 2005), 6–9. https://doi.org/10.1145/1083431.1083433

[22] Anthony Ralston and Mary Shaw. 1980. Curriculum '78 – is Computer Science Really That Unmathematical? *Commun. ACM* 23, 2 (Feb. 1980), 67–70. https://doi.org/10.1145/358818.358820

[23] E. Seymour and N. Hewitt. 1997. *Talking about leaving: Why undergraduates leave the sciences.* Boulder, CO: Westview Press.

[24] Nikki Sigurdson and Andrew Petersen. 2017. Student Perspectives on Mathematics in Computer Science. In *Proceedings of the 17th Koli Calling Conference on Computing Education Research (Koli Calling '17)*. ACM, New York, NY, USA, 108–117. https://doi.org/10.1145/3141880.3141888

[25] Matti Tedre and Peter J. Denning. 2016. The Long Quest for Computational Thinking. In *Proceedings of the 16th Koli Calling International Conference on Computing Education Research*. 120–129. https://doi.org/10.1145/2999541.2999542

[26] Jeannette M. Wing. 2006. Computational Thinking. *Commun. ACM* 49, 3 (March 2006), 33–35. https://doi.org/10.1145/1118178.1118215

Impact of Steps, Instruction, and Motivation on Learning Symbolic Reasoning Using an Online Tool

Megan Fowler, Michelle Cook, Kevin Plis,
Tim Schwab, Yu-Shan Sun, Murali Sitaraman
School of Computing
Clemson University, Clemson, SC USA
mefowle@clemson.edu

Jason O. Hallstrom
Engineering & Computer Science
FAU,
Boca Raton, FL USA
jhallstrom@fau.edu

Joseph E. Hollingsworth
Computer Science
IU Southeast,
New Albany, IN USA
jholly@ius.edu

ABSTRACT

Several research studies have shown the benefits of code tracing to promote student understanding of program behavior. While code tracing on specific input values is a useful starting point, students ultimately need to be able to reason rigorously and logically about the correctness of their code on all (i.e., arbitrary) inputs. Otherwise, they may make false generalizations and may achieve only a shallow understanding. Results of a multi-semester experiment to answer the following research questions: (1) With or without steps, can students learn the basics of tracing code on symbolic input values using an online tool? And how important is classroom instruction? (2) What is the impact of motivation on student attitudes in learning to reason with such a tool? Data was obtained from 297 subjects who used the online reasoning tool in a second-year software development course for CS majors. Analysis indicates that students can do symbolic reasoning to trace code and that instruction and motivation have significant impact.

CCS CONCEPTS

• Applied computing ~ Computer-assisted instruction
• Theory of computation ~ Program reasoning

KEYWORDS

Attitudes, correctness, symbolic reasoning, motivation, online tool

ACM Reference Format: M. Fowler, et al. 2018. Impact of Steps, Instruction, and Motivation on Learning Symbolic Reasoning Using an Online Tool. In *Proceedings of 50th ACM Technical Symposium on Computer Science Education (SIGCSE '19), February 27-March 2, 2019, Minneapolis, MN, USA.* ACM, New York, NY, USA, 7 pages. DOI: https://doi.org/10.1145/3287324.3287401

ACM ISBN 978-1-4503-5890-3/19/02□$15.00
https://doi.org/10.1145/3287324.3287401

1 Introduction

To learn to develop correct software, students need a firm foundation in precise analytical reasoning skills. Analytical reasoning is the bedrock of a good computer science education, but it is difficult to learn. Running programs on select inputs and studying the outputs gives students only limited understanding, yet more thorough symbolic reasoning using paper-and-pencil methods relies on labor-intensive manual checking. The objective of this research is to understand whether we can effectively teach a vast majority of computer science students the basics of reasoning about code on all input values using a symbolic approach with the (non-exclusive) aid of a reasoning tool. The tool has already been shown to be effective in pinpointing specific difficulties for individual students and subgroups [[9]].

This research is motivated in part by the documented benefits of learning to trace code and reason [[5], [17], [20], [24]]. For example, whereas the tool discussed in [[18], [30]] lets students visualize values of variables in their code after each step, the findings in [[44]] note the benefits for learners even within a limited context without the aid of any tools. Consider the following piece of code, where `i` and `j` are two integers.

```
i = i + j;
j = i - j;
i = i - j;
```

Testing relies on running the code on specific inputs for `i` and `j`, such as 3 and 5, and checking the answers, while tracing relies on analyzing the values of `i` and `j` after each step on these inputs. A symbolic approach aims for students to learn to generalize the reasoning and understand the general purpose of the code. Here, the goal is for students to learn to reason about the effect of the code supposing the initial values of `i` and `j`, respectively are some abstract inputs, `#i` and `#j`, and to determine the values of `i` and `j` at the end of the code in terms of the abstract input values.

Beyond our own collective experiences in teaching students over multiple decades at diverse institutions, both in person and using online systems, two observations motivate the central objectives and approach of the research project underlying this paper. The first of these is a study of novice programmers at Yale [[39]], where Spohrer and Soloway note the difficulties students face in reasoning about compositions of statements, though they seem to understand the individual programming constructs. At public institutions like ours, such problems are apparent even in later CS courses, in spite of our efforts to employ best practices. The second one is a debate in learning theory about the depth of understanding students achieve after abstract versus concrete introductions [[6], [14], [22], [27]], though the setting there is not computing. The findings in [[22]] suggest that "...giving college students multiple concrete examples may not be the most efficient means of promoting transfer of knowledge" and that "because the difficulty of transferring knowledge acquired from concrete instantiations may stem from extraneous information diverting attention from the relevant mathematical structure, concrete instantiations are also likely to hinder transfer for young learners who are less able than adults to control their attentional focus." However, following a replication of the original studies and analysis, [[14]] notes that "...results confirm Kaminski et al.'s findings, but the accompanying qualitative data raise serious questions about their interpretation of what students actually learned from the abstract concept exemplification. Moreover, whereas Kaminski et al. showed that abstract learners transferred what they had learned to a similar abstract context, this study shows also that students who learned from concrete examples transferred their knowledge into a similar concrete context."

The aim of our research project is *not* to replicate the concrete versus abstract study in the programming context, yet it is closely related: Just in the way that learning algebra beyond arithmetic is useful, there is reason to believe that enhancing traditional instruction with materials and tools to help students reason about arbitrary inputs using a symbolic approach—an analysis that requires some minimal level of abstraction and generalization—will help students become more proficient programmers. So our goal is to study what it takes to learn the more abstract approach of reasoning with symbolic values, not using just one or the other.

The hope is that students learn to reason about code correctly, and see the benefits in other computing courses such as discrete mathematics, algorithm analysis, programming languages, and software engineering that demand analytical reasoning or writing formal assertions, contracts and invariants.

1.1 Educational Research Questions

The research project underlying the topics discussed in this paper considers code involving loops and recursion as well as object-based code designed with contracts, involving pre- and post-conditions. Significant data has been collected and is being analyzed. However, we focus this paper on narrower educational research questions and consider only symbolic reasoning about simple code with abstract values so that the overall presentation is meaningful. Given the growing importance of online education for the benefits to reach a diverse audience, and the role of online tools to ensure that at least a part of the CS education can happen outside a classroom, this research involves understanding the role of a reasoning tool we have built.

ERQ #1—Learning: With or without intermediate steps, can a majority of students learn the basics of tracing code using symbolic input values, instead of specific input values (1) strictly with the help of an online reasoning tool and (2) with instruction in addition to the tool?

The hypothesis here is that a significant majority of students will indeed be able to learn to reason with symbolic values; after all, students learn algebra in high schools. But such learning will require classroom instruction in conjunction with a tool. We address the role of a step-by-step approach in reasoning correctly about code compositions and whether students will follow such an approach if learnt. We also consider if students perform as well on the reasoning questions as other topics in a CS course.

We used modified questions from the NASA TLX survey to evaluate student attitudes toward the online tool. Since the online tool was the first introduction to symbolic reasoning, it became clear (through think-alouds) that the purpose of such reasoning was not obvious to students. Since we are following a developmental evaluation[1] technique (that allows new research questions to emanate), we decided to introduce the tool with a 5-minute presentation explaining that the tool's purpose is to aid in reasoning about all inputs (which the better programmers can do) and raise a second question. This question concerns motivation.

Since the idea of reasoning over abstract values is a concept that is not often taught in computer science, motivation is critical. The importance of motivation is well documented in the cognitive psychology literature. In [[31]], it is noted that motivation directs behavior toward particular goals and that individuals set goals for themselves and direct their behavior accordingly. Motivation increases the amount of effort and energy that learners expend in activities directly related to their needs and goals [[13], [26], [34]]. It determines whether they pursue a task enthusiastically and wholeheartedly or apathetically and lackadaisically.

Motivation also affects what learners pay attention to and how effectively they process the information they receive [[16], [35], [37]]. For instance, motivated learners often make a concerted effort to understand classroom material—to learn it meaningfully—and consider how they might use it in their own lives. This leads to the second question.

ERQ #2—Motivation and Attitudes: Will explaining the purpose of symbolic reasoning with an online tool impact (1) student attitudes and (2) their perception of learning?

The hypothesis based on expectancy theory here is that providing students with the tool's purpose would impact attitude towards the activity and therefore improve their motivation to complete the task successfully. Since the tool is unchanged, student learning experience should not necessarily be impacted.

We also did a demographic aggregation of data, but due to space limitations, we only make some observations without including supporting evidence.

1.2 Summary of Research Methods

To answer the research questions, we have experimented with a reasoning tool with and without associated instruction over three semesters in a required second-year course for CS majors on software development foundations in Java. We have varied when intermediate steps are provided in the tool activities. We have included a symbolic reasoning question on the exam to determine student learning. We have varied exam questions asking for steps, not asking for steps, and providing scaffolding. We have assessed student attitudes toward the reasoning tool and changes to the attitudes associated with providing a motivation for learning. [1]

2 Reasoning Tool Design

Online tutoring of programming concepts has received much attention in the CS literature (e.g., [[1], [4], [18], [23], [25], [30], [36], [42]]). There are several IDEs that provide compile-time error feedback and numerous useful capabilities (e.g., finding the declaration or all uses of a method). The novel online reasoning tool that we have developed, unlike other tutors and IDEs, is backed by the RESOLVE software verification engine [[10], [38]]. This allows it to facilitate reasoning over abstract input values. It has a strong theoretical basis and has been used for nearly a decade at multiple institutions. Thousands of undergraduate students have employed the ideas in CS courses [[12], [15], [19], [21]] and in software engineering projects [[11], [33]]. It suffices to say that the engine is far more powerful than demanded by the reasoning activities discussed here. The engine can enhance learning through a variety of logical "what if" questions. Since answers are verified automatically, answer keys are not stored or used.

2.1 Cognitive Load Considerations

In any learning environment, a learner can be easily frustrated by a plethora of uncontrolled possibilities of options. The goal is to tease out the role of "contextualization" in learning and prevent the cognitive capacity of a learner from being overloaded. This challenge is informed by cognitive learning theories. Specifically, cognitive load theory is concerned with the ease with which information can be processed in working memory [[32], [40]]. To solve problems, students must be able to hold multiple pieces of information in working memory at the same time. Therefore, working memory load, also known as cognitive load, is implicated as a major impediment to constructivist learning [[8]]. Interactive learning guides have the potential to decrease intrinsic and extrinsic cognitive load and help promote germane cognitive load and our tool has benefited from the excellent set of design guidelines for automated agents in [[43]] and the survey in [[2]].

2.2 Interface Design and Reasoning Activities

The tool has been designed with scaffolding to reduce cognitive load, as seen from the screen shot in Figure 1. The activity is at the top left with reference material below it showing only what is relevant to reason about the code on the right.

The activities begin with ones to trace code on specific input values, such as in Figure 2. The use of the tool is the first introduction to all the constructs. In the Pascal-like code shown (with which most of our students learning Java apparently have no trouble and need no introduction), we use `:=` to denote assignments to distinguish it from the mathematical equality used in assertions. The student's task is to trace the given code and replace `/* expression */` with the answer in the *Confirm* assertion (where "=" means equals, as in logic). The student can only change in the assertion. Unlike an assert statement; nothing is executed.

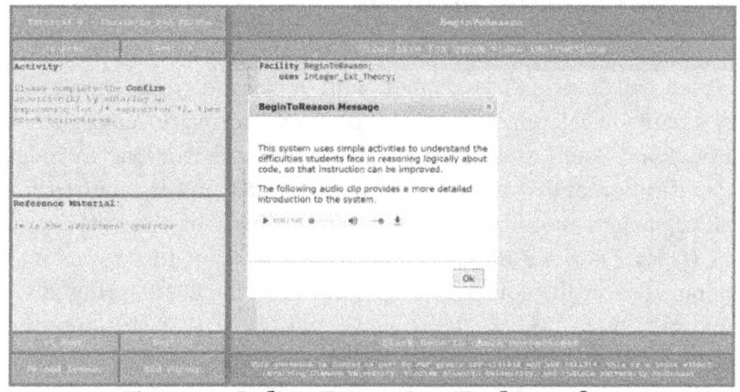

Figure 1: Online Reasoning Tool Interface

```
Facility BeginToReason;
    uses Integer_Ext_Theory;

    Operation Main();
    Procedure
        Var I, J, K: Integer;

        I := 2;
        J := 3;

        K := I;
        If (J > I) then
            K := J;
        end;

        Confirm K = /*expression*/;
    end Main;
end BeginToReason;
```

Figure 2: A Beginning Tracing Activity

An example of symbolic reasoning is shown in Figure 3.

```
6          Var I, J: Integer;
7          Read(I);
8          Read(J);
9
10         Remember;
11
12         I := I + J;
13         Confirm I = #I;
14
15         J := I - J;
16         Confirm J = #I;
```

Figure 3: Example Symbolic Reasoning & Visual Feedback

The activity asks students to state the values of `I` and `J` in terms of the input values, remembered to be `#I` and `#J`, respectively, at the line marked `Remember`. The tool has been designed to provide visual feedback that is immediate [[3]] and reduces cognitive load [[7], [28]]. An example of this feedback can be seen in Figure 3. Since `I` has changed, it is no longer true that `I = #I`, and hence, line 13 is wrong (and is in red).

When the students input their answer, it could be any number of logically equivalent answers. While all answers are verified, the system expects reasonable answers, rejecting trivial answers such as `Confirm I = I`. When a student's answer is wrong, the

[1] Parkhurst, M., Preskill, H., Lynn, J., & Moore, M. (2016, March 1). The Case for Developmental Evaluation. https://www.fsg.org/blog/case-developmental-evaluation

activity may be repeated, or a follow-on activity is given. Though not a focus of the current paper, a key benefit of this tool is that it can pinpoint obstacles specific for subsets of learners [[9]].

3 Experimental Methods

The reasoning system and the activities were administered in closed lab sessions associated with a second year course on software development that emphasizes software engineering principles and uses Java. The course description includes specification and reasoning among the topics and is required for all CS majors at our institution. Details of this course are discussed in [[19]]. Data for the experiments discussed in this paper was obtained over the course of three semesters; fall 2016, spring 2017, and fall 2017. When there were multiple lecture sections, the students were intermingled in the lab sections.

3.1 Teaching Using Only the Tool

For the fall 2016 experiment, 114 students participated in the study across 5 sections of the lab. Students did not receive any formal instruction regarding symbolic reasoning before tool use. This tool served as their first introduction to symbolic reasoning about code. Though TA help was available, few students asked for any help. Students were not time constrained and took between 20 minutes to an hour to complete all the activities.

About six weeks after working with the tool in the lab, students were asked to complete a symbolic reasoning question on a regular final exam. The question was worth a total of five points, which was 20% of the exam. There were four versions of the reasoning question and the versions were randomly distributed at testing. Two versions involved reasoning about a piece of swapping code (similar, but not identical to the one given in the introduction). The other two questions had to do with the sum of two variables. These two types of questions were then further separated by one version of the question asking students to show their work, while the other did not.

3.2 Variants and Perceptions, Without Motivation

The spring 2017 experiment consisted of 5 lab sections with a total of 91 students. Each section was provided with one of two versions of activities embedded within the tool, which served to be their only introduction to symbolic reasoning.

Version A of the activities presented students with code to trace, and one or more `Confirm` assertions to complete at the bottom of the code. If students entered an incorrect answer, they were then presented with the task again, but this time provided with intermediate `Confirm` assertions to be established.

Version B presented students with the same code to trace, but instead gave them the intermediate `Confirm` assertions right away at the beginning (similar to the example seen in Figure 3). If a student entered an incorrect answer, the tool would highlight the incorrect answer and provide them with the same code and layout.

For both versions, the tool reported how many attempts each individual student made on each lesson and sub-lesson, if applicable. Students then completed a survey regarding their opinions on the tool using a Likert scale indicating how strongly they agreed or disagreed with each survey question.

Students then completed a symbolic reasoning question on their exam. The question was worth 5 points, which was 12.5% of the exam. There were four versions of the question randomly distributed. As with the previous experiment, two questions asked students to show their work, while the other two did not. These questions were then further split to where one set only used symbols `I` and `J` as in the lessons above, while the other incorporated a third symbol, `K`. After completing the exam, twenty students (diverse in demographics and grades) were invited to participate in a retrospective think-aloud protocol.

3.3 Aided with Motivation and Instruction

The fall 2017 experiment had a total of 92 students in 5 lab sections. All students used the activities in Version B, whereby intermediate steps were given up front. The number of attempts for each lesson was collected once again, as well as the student opinion survey. Before students interacted with the online reasoning system, the instructor gave a brief introduction explaining the purpose of the reasoning activities they were to complete during the lab. Specifically, the students were told that the best programmers were able to generalize reasoning about code on all inputs, and the goal for the research was to understand what difficulties students had in doing such reasoning, and how to develop better instructional material to communicate the ideas to all students. They were also asked to be deliberate in their effort.

Students received an hour lecture on symbolic reasoning before the exam. As part of the exam, students had to answer a symbolic reasoning question. All students received the same question, which required them to state the values of `x`, `y`, and `z`, after each line of code in terms of `#x`, `#y`, and `#z`. The questions were worth 15 points, which was 15% of the exam grade.

4 Results

Some of our initial hypotheses held, while others did not. For some findings, the results are statistically significant, and in others, they are not. We have also collected information on student answers during the online activities. For example, it is easy to mine for common wrong answers and provide guided tutoring. We have done screen captures of student work from fall 2017 to supplement other collected information. Though we do not include a detailed analysis of the think-alouds in this paper, we note that they have guided one of our design decisions.

4.1 ERQ #1: Ability to Learn Symbolic Reasoning

Across all versions of the questions in fall 2016, students received an average of at least 4 points, which translates into completing approximately 80% of the question correctly. It would appear the online tool can successfully introduce all students to the basics of symbolic reasoning. At the same time, it is equally possible that the question was too easy. This is a useful, but not definitive result. Subsequent exam questions were more demanding (in terms of the number of variables and statements).

Role of Intermediate Steps

Figures 6a and 6b are based on spring 2017 data, where half the students used Version A activities, where intermediate steps were given only to students who were having difficulties, and half the students were given Version B activities, with intermediate steps from the beginning. It would appear that Version A of the activities were more successful at assisting students with symbolic reasoning. 37% of students were able to successfully trace the code for Version A on the first try, while only 24% were able to do so on Version B. Are intermediate steps not helpful?

There are several confounding factors. There were more assertions to complete in Version B, because of intermediate steps. There were four for one activity in Version B compared to two for version A, so fewer students got through the activity in one try.

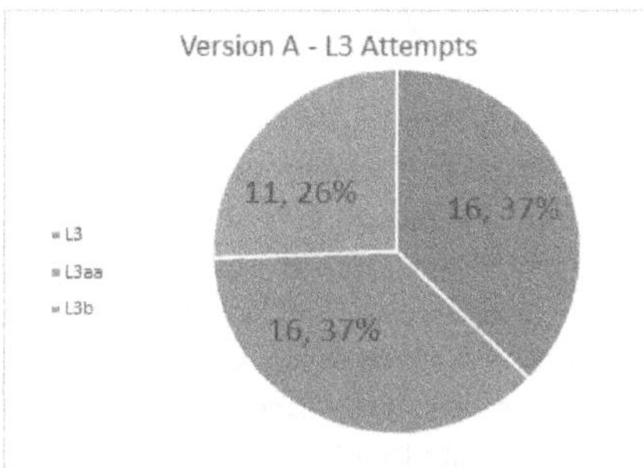

Figure 6a: Activity Version A with Steps Given As Needed

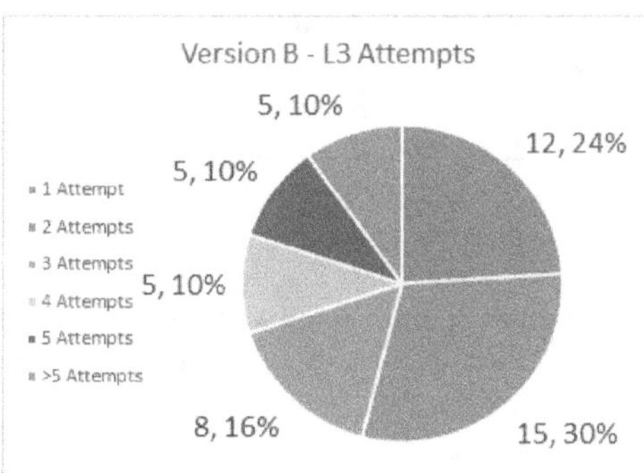

Figure 6b: Activity Version B with Steps Given Initially

In addition, in Version A, when a student provided an incorrect response, they were provided with a version with intermediate steps (similar to B), and when students failed that, it shortened the problem (L3b in the figure). By the time a student reached this lesson, she had seen a version of this problem 4 times. A detailed discussion of this particular analysis to pinpoint specific student learning obstacles is the topic of [[12]].

Another source of complication was the inability to account for submissions where student work had not been completed. Version B may have required 4 `Confirm` statements, and if one were left blank when the student submitted to check progress, it would be considered an incorrect attempt to solve the problem.

In the think-alouds, we noticed that a subset of students who made errors on Activity 3 did seem to understand the reasoning process, but made algebraic errors only because they insisted on doing it "in their heads." While we offered a sheet of paper to help with the process, only a small fraction of the students took up the offer. For this group, a step-by-step process would have been exactly what would be helpful. Though the sample size is limited, we also noticed that female and African-American students did as well as others with Version B. These observations along with observations on exam answers convinced us to switch to version B activities with intermediate steps for all subsequent sections.

Learning Reasoning w/wo Classroom Instruction

The fall 2016 course was taught in a single large lecture section (which was not repeated). To keep the comparison meaningful, we compare only spring 2017 and fall 2017 data. We used a Mann-Whitney U-test because it is more suitable to compare performance of different groups of students across semesters and because it does not require that the two independent samples are normally distributed.

In fall 2017, tool-based instruction was supplemented with a one-hour classroom lecture. The difference in scores for the exam reasoning question between the semesters as seen in Figure 7(a) was found to be statistically significant with a p value less than 0.05. In the spring, only 59.1% of students completed at least 80% of the question correctly, while in the fall, 74.2% did. A similar pattern is observed between the overall exam scores, where fall students performed significantly better, with a p value of 0.0005. While this would point directly to the benefit of classroom instruction, the topic of motivation detailed in the next subsection is a confounding factor. Regardless the important point is that symbolic reasoning can be learned by a majority of students.

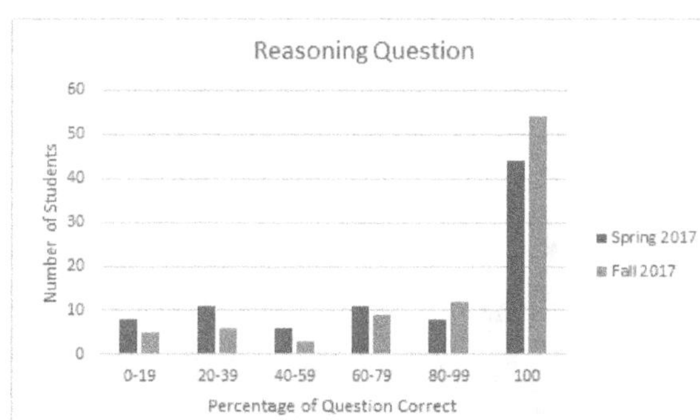

Figure 7a: Performance, w/wo Supplemental Instruction

4.2 ERQ #2: Motivation and Attitudes

To evaluate students' attitudes towards the tool, we used questions from the NASA TLX survey [[29]], with minor variations to the questions, and a major variation in using a 5-point Likert scale, instead of a continuous scale (due to limitations of our course management system.) There were two background questions and our analysis showed there was no statistically significant difference between the two semesters.

Q1 My prior preparation in CS is good
Q2 My performance in the current course is good

There were ten other questions. *Agree* or *strongly agree* are the desired outcomes for the first eight.

Q3 The interface was easy to use
Q4 I was able to understand what I needed to do
Q5 I found this to be a useful learning experience
Q6 The feedback from the system was helpful
Q7 I found the activities engaging
Q8 The task was mentally demanding
Q9 I was successful in accomplishing what I was asked to do
Q10 I had to work hard to accomplish my level of performance

Disagree or *strongly disagree* are the desired outcomes for the last two:

Q11 The pace of the task was hurried or rushed
Q12 I was insecure, discouraged, irritated, stressed, and annoyed

Each answer was assigned a numerical value according to the desired outcome. For example whereas for the question "The interface was easy to use" a response of Strongly Agree is coded as a 5, for the question "The pace of the task was hurried or rushed" Strongly Disagree is coded as a 5.

When comparing the subset of students who used version B from the spring of 2017 with the students from the fall of 2017 (who also used an identical version B), there is an observable difference in student attitudes regarding use of the online tool. This is seen in Figure 8.

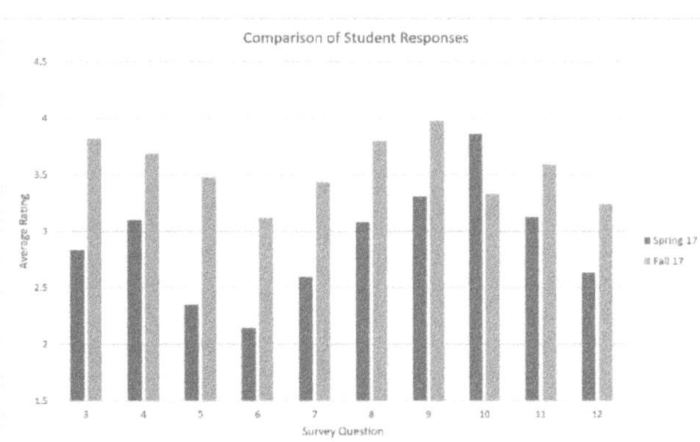

Figure 8: Impact of Motivation on Attitudes, Q3 to Q12

For questions 3 through 12, excluding question 8, student answers were more favorable in the range of 0.47 to 1.12. The response for question 8 is also favorable because it shows that students felt like they did not have to work as hard to achieve the same level of success. A Mann-Whitney U-test indicated that questions 3 through 12 had a statistically significant difference in answers when using an alpha value of 0.05.

This evidence indicates that student attitudes towards the reasoning tool and use of the tool are altered when presented with a brief introduction that provides students with a purpose and motivation to complete the task. Important to note is the significance of the response to the agreement of the statements "I found this to be a useful learning experience," and "The feedback from the system was helpful," and the disagreement to the statement "I was insecure, discouraged, irritated, stressed, and annoyed"—even though the activities were identical across groups. So our hypothesis to part (1) of ERQ #2 was correct, but part (2) about their perception of learning from the tool was wrong. Motivation was important on both counts. The positive results from motivation held across all demographics.

5 Discussion and Conclusions

Our research has shown it is possible to teach symbolic reasoning to a majority of students (at the 80% or a B-grade level). Classroom instruction and providing a motivational purpose for the tool have a statistically significant impact. Intermediate steps have been found to be useful especially for underrepresented students.

One potential threat to validity of the results is that each semester had slight variations in the experimental conditions. Using Mann-Whitney U-test on the incoming student GPA, we found that the spring and fall student populations were comparable. While both semesters were taught by the same instructor, spring was the first time this instructor taught this course. This could indicate that the instructor was better equipped to teach these concepts, and why students performed well on this particular exam. Upon further examination, overall average course grade for the fall semester is actually worse than the spring semester indicating that students did not receive an advantage due to teacher experience.

We have conducted extensive think-alouds to learn more about student thinking though we do not report the results here. Without prompting, some students explained to us how they might use symbolic reasoning in other programming and algorithms courses, suggesting that benefits might be more far reaching. Some others had difficulty with the basics of algebra, so exploring deficiencies in prior learning is a possible research direction.

ACKNOWLEDGMENTS

We acknowledge the contributions of several members of our research groups at Clemson, Florida Atlantic University, and Ohio State University. Special thanks are due to Bruce Weide. This work is funded in part by US National Science Foundation grants CCF-1161916, DUE-1611714, DUE-1609718, and DUE-1610957.

REFERENCES

[1] V. Aleven, B. M. McLaren, and J. Sewall. 2009. Scaling Up Programming by Demonstration for Intelligent Tutoring Systems Development: An Open-Access Web Site for Middle School Mathematics Learning. IEEE Trans. on Learning Technologies 2, 64-78.

[2] J. R. Anderson, A. T. Corbett, K. R. Koedinger, and R. Pelletier. 1995. Cognitive Tutors: Lessons Learned, The Journal of the Learning Sciences 4, 167-207.

[3] R. Azevedo and R. M. Bernard. 1995. A Meta-Analysis of the Effects of Feedback in Computer-Based Instruction. Journal of Educational Computing Research 13, 2, 111 – 127.

[4] P. Bhattacharya, L. Tao, B. W. Kai Qian, and E. K. Palmer. 2011. A Cloud-based Cyberlearning Environment for Introductory Computing Programming Education. In Procs. 11th ICALT, 12-13.

[5] P. Bucci, T. Long, and B. Weidi. 2001. Do We Really Teach Abstraction?, In Proceedings of the 32nd SIGCSE Technical Symposium on Computer Science Education, ACM, 26-30.

[6] K. J. Carbonneau, S. C. Marley, J. P. Selig. 2013. A meta-analysis of the efficacy of teaching mathematics with concrete manipulatives, Journal of Educational Psychology 105, No. 2, 380-400. http://dx.doi.org/10.1037/a0031084

[7] C. Chen, S. Pedersen, and K. L. Murphy. 2011. Learners' perceived information overload in online learning via computer-mediated communication. Research in Learning Technology, 19, 1, 101-116.

[8] M. P. Cook, "Visual representations in science education: The influence of prior knowledge and cognitive load theory on instructional design principles," Science Education 90, 6, 2006, 1073-1091.

[9] M. P. Cook, M. Fowler, J. O. Hallstrom, J. E. Hollingsworth, T. Schwab, Y. S. Sun, & M. Sitaraman, 2018. Where Exactly are the Difficulties in Reasoning Logically about Code? Experimentation with an Online System. In Proceedings of the 23rd Annual ACM Conference on Innovation and Technology in Computer Science Education (pp. 39-44). ACM.

[10] C. T. Cook, H. Harton, H., Smith, and M. Sitaraman, 2012. Specification Engineering and Modular Verification Using a Web-Integrated Verifying Compiler, In 2012 34th International Conference on Software Engineering (ICSE), 2012, 1379-1382.

[11] C. T. Cook, S. Drachova-Strang, Y-S. Sun, M. Sitaraman, J. C. Carver, and J. E. Hollingsworth, 2013. Specification and Reasoning in SE Projects Using a Web IDE, In Proceedings Conference on Software Engineering Education & Training (CSSE&T), 2013

[12] Cook, C. T., Drachova, S., Hallstrom, J. O., Hollingsworth, J. E., Jacobs, D. P., Krone, J., & Sitaraman, M. 2012. A Systematic Approach to Teaching Abstraction and Mathematical Modeling, In Proceedings of the 17th ACM Annual Conference on Innovation and Technology in Computer Science Education (ITiCSE '12), ACM, New York, NY, USA, 357-362.

[13] M. Csikszentmihalyi, and J. Nakamura. 1989. The dynamics of intrinsic motivation: A study of adolescents. In R. Ames & C. Ames (Eds.), Research on motivation in education: Goals and cognitions (pp. 45—71). New York: Academic Press.

[14] D. De Bock, J. Deprej, W. van Duren, M. Roelens, and L. Verschaffel. 2011. Abstract or Concrete Examples in Learning Mathematics? A Replication an Elaboration of Kaminsky, Stoutsky, and Heckler's Study. Journal for Research in Mathematics Education 42, 2, 109-126.

[15] S. Drachova-Strang, J. O. Hallstrom, J. E. Hollingsworth, J. Krone, R. Pak, and M. Sitaraman, "Teaching Mathematical Reasoning Principles for Software Correctness and Its Assessment," ACM Transactions on Computing Education 15, 3, Article 15 (August 2015), 22 pages.

[16] J. S. Eccles, and A. Wigfield. 2002. Motivational beliefs, values, and goals. Annual Review of Psychology, 53, 109–132.

[17] S. Fitzgerald, B. Simon, and L. Thomas. 2005. Strategies that students use to trace code: an analysis based in grounded theory. In Procs. ICER '05 ACM, NY, USA, 69-80.

[18] P. Guo. 2018. http://www.pythontutor.com/java.html#mode=edit

[19] J. O. Hallstrom, C. Hochrine, J. Sorber, & M. Sitaraman, 2014. An ACM 2013 exemplar course integrating fundamentals, languages, and software engineering. In Proceedings of the 45th ACM technical symposium on Computer science education (pp. 211-216). SIGCSE '14, ACM, New York, NY, USA.

[20] P. B. Henderson. 2003. Mathematical Reasoning in Software Engineering Education. Communications of the ACM 46, 9, 45-50.

[21] W. Heym, P. A. Sivilotti, P. Bucci, M. Sitaraman, K. Plis, J. E. Hollingsworth, & N. Sridhar, (2017, November). Integrating Components, Contracts, and Reasoning in CS Curricula with RESOLVE: Experiences at Multiple Institutions. In Software Engineering Education and Training (CSEE&T), 2017 IEEE 30th Conference on (pp. 202-211). IEEE.. 2017. CSEE&T, IEEE, NY, USA.

[22] J. A. Kaminsky, V. M. Stoutsky, A. F. Heckler. 2008. The Advantage of Abstract Examples in Learning Math, Learning Theory, Science 320, 454-455.

[23] R. Kumar, C. P. Rose, Y. Wang, M. Joshi, and A. Robinson. 2007. Tutorial Dialog as Adaptive Collaborative Learning Support. In Procs. Conference on Artificial Intelligence in Education: Building Technology Rich Contexts That Work, IOS Press, 383-390.

[24] C. M. Lewis. 2014. Exploring variation in students' correct traces of linear recursion. In Procs. ICER '14. ACM, NY, USA, 67-74.

[25] C. Li, Z. Dong, R. Untch, Chasteen, and N. Reale. 2011. PeerSpace—An Online Collaborative Learning Environment for Computer Science Students. In Procs. 11th ICALT, 409-411.

[26] M. L. Maehr. 1984. Meaning and Motivation: Toward a Theory of Personal Investment. Research on Motivation in Education, 1, 115-144.

[27] W. McCallum. 2008. Commentary on Kaminsky, et al, The Advantages of Abstract Examples in Learning Math, Science.

[28] R. Moreno. 2004. Decreasing Cognitive Load for Novice Students: Effects of Explanatory versus Corrective Feedback in Discovery-Based Multimedia. Instructional Science 32, 99-113.

[29] NASA, 1986. NASA Task Load Index (TLX) v. 1.0 Manual.

[30] C. O'Brien, M. Goldman, and R. C. Miller. 2014. Java tutor: bootstrapping with python to learn Java. Proceedings of the first ACM conference on Learning. ACM, New York, NY, USA. 185-186. 10.1145/2556325.2567873.

[31] J. E. Ormond. 2014. Educational Psychology: Developing Learners. Upper Saddle River, NJ: Pearson.

[32] F. Paas, T. van Gog, and J. Sweller. 2010. Cognitive load theory: New conceptualizations, specifications, and integrated research perspectives. Educational Psychology Review, 22, 2, 115-121.

[33] C. Priester, Y-S. Sun, and M. Sitaraman, "Tool-Assisted Loop Invariant Development and Analysis", In Proceedings of the 29th Conference on Software Engineering Education and Training (CSEE&T 2016), IEEE, NY, USA, 66-70

[34] P. R. Pintrich, D. Smith, T. Garcia, and W. McKeachie. 1993. Predictive validity and reliability of the Motivated Strategies for Learning Questionnaire (MSLQ). Educational and Psychological Measurement, 5, 801-813.

[35] P. R. Pintrich, and D. H. Schunk. 2002. Motivation in education: Theory, research, and applications (2nd ed.). Upper Saddle River, NJ: Prentice Hall.

[36] T. W. Price, Y. Dong, and D. Lipovac. 2017. iSnap: Towards Intelligent Tutoring in Novice Programming Environments. In Procs. SIGCSE '17, ACM, NY, USA, 483-488.

[37] K. J. Pugh, and D. A. Bergin. 2006. Motivational influences on transfer. Educational Psychologist, 41, 147 – 160.

[38] M. Sitaraman, B. Adcock, J. Avigad, D. Bronish, P. Bucci, D. Frazier, H. M. Friedman, H. Harton, W., Heym, J., Kirschenbaum, J., Krone, H. Smith, and B. W. Weide., "Building a Push button RESOLVE Verifier: Progress and Challenges," In Formal Aspects of Computing, Springer, 2011, 607-626.

[39] J. C. Spohrer, and E. Soloway. 1986. Novice mistakes: are the folk wisdoms correct? Communications of the ACM 29, 7, 624-632.

[40] J. Sweller, P. Ayres, and S. Kalyuga, 2011. Cognitive load theory. Springer, NY.

[41] Web-CAT is an advanced automated grading system that can grade students on how well they test their own code. http://web-cat.org/home

[42] J. B. Wiggins, et al. 2015. JavaTutor: An Intelligent Tutoring System that Adapts to Cognitive and Affective States during Computer Programming. In Procs. SIGCSE '15, ACM, NY, USA, 599-599.

[43] P. Wouters, F. Paas, and J. J. G. van Merriënboer. 2008. How to Optimize Learning from Animated Models: A Review of Guidelines Based on Cognitive Load. Review of Educational Research.

[44] B. Xie, G. L. Nelson, and A. J. Ko. 2018. An Explicit Strategy to Scaffold Novice Program Tracing. In Proceedings of the 49th ACM Technical Symposium on Computer Science Education (SIGCSE '18). ACM, New York, NY, USA, 344-349. DOI: https://doi.org/10.1145/3159450.3159527

Hybrid Pair Programming - A Promising Alternative to Standard Pair Programming

Hans Yuan
University of California, San Diego
h3yuan@eng.ucsd.edu

Yingjun Cao
University of California, San Diego
yic242@eng.ucsd.edu

ABSTRACT

Pair programming has been widely adopted as an effective pedagogical tool in CS1/2. The successful execution of pair programming depends on each partner contributing similar amounts of work. However, anecdotes from past research observed that some student pairs can contribute a drastically unequal amount towards their assignments. We address this through a pilot of a hybrid pair programming model. Here, students complete two halves of the assignment as independent programmers and then in partnerships. We conducted a randomized experiment on this model in a CS1 class and found that while pairs generally performed better than solo students in the checkpoint, pairs in the second stage who had worked independently during the checkpoint portion tend to be more resistant to sudden increases in difficulty. We found no significant difference on selected exam problems between the control and experiment groups. We identified lower contributors within pairs and these students showed improved scores on most exam questions directly related to their independent checkpoint work. Survey feedback on hybrid pair programming is positive. The hybrid model is easily adopted in CS classes and positions students to better face the obstacles presented by the assignment while allowing them to benefit from pair programming.

CCS CONCEPTS

• **Social and professional topics** → **Computing Education**;

KEYWORDS

Pair Programming; Hybrid Pair Programming; Assessment

ACM Reference Format:
Hans Yuan and Yingjun Cao. 2019. Hybrid Pair Programming - A Promising Alternative to Standard Pair Programming. In *Proceedings of the 50th ACM Technical Symposium on Computer Science Education (SIGCSE '19), February 27-March 2, 2019, Minneapolis, MN, USA.* ACM, New York, NY, USA, 7 pages. https://doi.org/10.1145/3287324.3287352

1 INTRODUCTION

Learning to program can be difficult for beginners. Pair programming has been shown to improve programming performance in and outside the academic environment [8, 16]. The periodic role switch between the navigator and the driver allows both students to share their ideas and collaboratively produce higher quality programs. Though pair programming benefits students at multiple levels, instructors have observed scenarios where one partner contributes vastly more than the other partner whether it was intentional [19]. In this study, we measured that 56 of the 265 students had free-rode at least 3 out of 9 assignments. The breakdown of the pair dynamics can lead to diminished benefits from pair programming [25]. Researchers have started to examine if variations of pair programming can improve student learning by reducing the pair's sensitivity to team dynamics [1, 6].

We propose a hybrid two-stage model where a programming project is divided into two stages: the checkpoint stage (stage one) and the final submission stage (stage two). The checkpoint stage initiates the project through tasks such as writing a few important helper functions or creating pseudo-code to solve the entire project. Students complete this stage independently. The final submission stage builds upon the checkpoint and leads to the completion of the whole project in the second stage. Students complete this stage using pair programming and peer review each other's independent work from the checkpoint. The act of reviewing others' code has been shown to improve student learning [22].

To measure differences between the standard pair programming and the hybrid two-stage model, we conducted a randomized experiment where half of the class completed an assignment in standard pair programming for both stages while the other half completes the assignment using the hybrid model. Groups alternate which model they used in each subsequent assignment. We designed 9 exam questions, each of which is conceptually similar to a programming assignment (PA) in either the checkpoint or final submission. At the end of the course, qualitative surveys were used to examine students' experience with the hybrid model. A pragmatic metric is proposed to identify "free-riding" or "freeloading" students and to study the impact of the soloing for the free-riders.

To summarize, this study intends to answer the following related research questions on hybrid two-stage pair programming model:

- **RQ1**: What is the effect of the hybrid pair programming model on student performance measured by programming assignment scores and exam scores?
- **RQ2**: What is the impact of hybrid pair programming model on potential free-riders?

RQ1 focuses on the effectiveness of hybrid pair programming in contrast to standard pair programming. As hybrid pair programming was proposed as a potential tool to alleviate the free-riding issue, RQ2 measures if the opportunity of individual work helps the identified free-riders.

SIGCSE '19, February 27-March 2, 2019, Minneapolis, MN, USA

ACM ISBN 978-1-4503-5890-3/19/02...$15.00
https://doi.org/10.1145/3287324.3287352

2 BACKGROUND

Pair programming in the classroom has been extensively studied since its inception [30]. The use of pair programming in introductory CS resulted in strongly favorable feedback from students [26], better quality homework code [15, 16], and stronger confidence in students' own programming ability [17]. Adoption of pair programming was associated with increased retention rates [5, 21]. Recent research also attempted to incorporate collaborative programming with an intelligent tutoring system [10] and a version-control IDE [29].

The effectiveness of pair programming depends on the team dynamics of the pair, which is influenced by individual metrics such as prior programming experience and perceived expertise [13, 26]. The cause of incompatibility was further investigated in recent research. Perceived and actual skill ability impact the pair's performance because of one's lower or higher perception of the other [25]. A student who perceives the partner as an expert would be affected by the perception, even if the perception is misinformed [28]. A study on pairing by similar skill level found that it helped the lowest quartile of the class regardless of actual skill level [2]. Studies on the impact of personality on pair programming have been inconclusive [24]. The success of pair programming also hinges on the partners sharing a single computer and working on the same piece of code together. One study tested a different "hybrid pair-programming" model where the pair collaborates as partners but submit individual project code written on separate computers [6]. This dynamic broke down the partner interactions, strengthening support for the continued use of standard pair programming.

Recently, researchers have begun to investigate through video and audio analysis whether all students did pair programming faithfully [23]. The free-riding phenomenon, where group members don't make similar levels of contribution to the programming project, has been reported in computer science classes [11, 19]. Though these observations are concerning to instructors, studies on the effects of or the remedy to free-riding are scarce. One solution to reduce free-riding is to pair students based on their skill level [2]. However, the measurement of skill level is often inaccurate and time-consuming, especially for large classes. The work presented in this paper proposes a lightweight method to identify potential "free-riders" and studies the effect of hybrid pair-programming projects on these students. We want to be clear that "free-riders" is not meant to be negative: there are instances where one partner may prefer to do the assignment rather than explain prerequisite concepts to the other partner or the weaker student may feel intimidated and allow the stronger student to take over the work [26]. The unequal contributions therefore may not be a result of unanimous intent.

Assessments, summative and formative alike, play an important role in student learning [27]. The impact of peer collaborations on student learning has been studied in education research [9]. In computer science, in-class active learning pedagogies [12, 20], two-stage exams [3, 4, 31], and two-stage programming projects [1] have been proposed to create additional opportunities to facilitate learning. In particular, the two-stage programming model [1] provides repeated opportunities for students to attempt the same project, once done in solo and once done in pairs. The study observed a positive trend on improved post-test performance. However, the time requirement of completing the same project twice might slow down the progress of a course or make lecture contents unsynchronized with assignments. Thus, the implementation of two-stage project format [1] may increase curricular development overhead.

The hybrid pair-programming model proposed in this paper solves this implementation issue. Many CS1/2 programming projects can be divided into stages without warping the progress of the class. Bypassing the implementation time constraints, the hybrid model as presented in this paper maintains the benefits of both independent and collaborative work while improving the previously proposed hybrid pair programming and two-stage models. To the best of our knowledge, this paper is the first experimental study of the proposed hybrid project format.

3 METHOD

We first introduce the experimental design of this study, followed by sample exam/programming assignment (PA) mappings and the metric to identify free-riders.

3.1 Experimental Design

Two sections of CS1 (Java) in Spring 2018 were selected for this study. The course uses media computation and topics include variables, conditionals, loops, arrays, methods, and class/objects. At our institution, students who have no prior programming experience usually take this class as their first computer science class. These two sections are back to back on MWF morning. The instructor of both sections has taught this class multiple times and is one of the authors of this paper.

For the purpose of this experiment, the two sections are treated as one big section. The total enrollment was 313 at the beginning of class and 265 by the time of the final exam. There are 9 programming assignments (PA0 to PA8), two midterms, and one comprehensive final exam. To measure the effectiveness of the hybrid pair programming model in contrast to standard pair programming, students in the class were randomly assigned into groups A and B. The group assignment is fixed for each student for the entire course. Students in group A completed odd-numbered assignments (PA1, PA3, PA5, and PA7) in hybrid pair programming format and the remaining PAs in standard pair programming format. Students in group B completed even-numbered assignments (PA2, PA4, PA6, and PA8) in hybrid pair programming and the remaining PAs in standard pair programming. Students could pair with any other student within the same group (A with A and B with B) an unlimited number of times. For each PA, students have about 3 days to complete a checkpoint and another 3-4 days to finish the final submission. The checkpoint and final submission were graded separately, and the sum of the their scores with equal weights is the final score a student received for a project. We define students who completed an assignment in hybrid pair-programming to be in the experimental group while standard pair-programming students are in the control group. Figure 1 summarizes the experimental design.

This experimental design allows an even division on the number of students in the control group (standard pair programming) and the experimental group (hybrid pair programming) for each assignment. It also ensures that a student is exposed to both conditions for an equal number of assignments. PA0 is excluded from this study because it is an extremely basic first assignment used as an introduction for students to familiarize with pair programming requirements. Based on feedback from students in previous iterations of the course, PA6, PA7, and PA8 are considerably more challenging than the first 5 assignments.

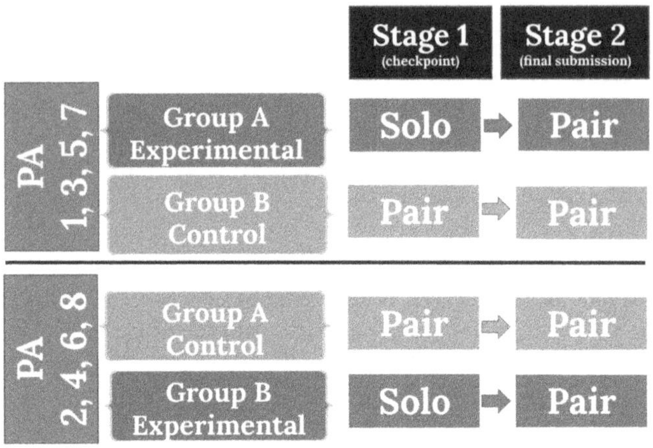

Figure 1: Experimental design to compare hybrid pair programming and standard pair programming.

3.2 Exam and PA Mapping

9 questions in the midterms and the final exam were designed to measure student understanding of respective PA's checkpoint or final submission. Table 1 shows an example of such mapping. Due to the flow of the course, not every PA's checkpoint or final submission was mapped to a certain exam question. 5 checkpoints (PA1, 2, 5, 6, and 8) and 4 final submissions (PA2, 4, 6, and 7) have a mapped exam question.

Programming Assignment Task (Part of PA6 checkpoint)	**Exam Question (Final exam, problem 7)**
Write the following method in Picture.java: *public static int embedDigits2(int contextVal, int messageVal)* This method will use shift operators (and addition) to replace the two least significant digits in *contextVal* with the value of *messageVal*. You can assume that *contextVal* will always be an integer between 0 and 255 inclusive (i.e. an 8-bit integer) and *messageVal* will always be an integer between 0 and 3 inclusive (i.e. a 2-bit integer). *Picture.embedDigits2(182,2)* returns 182. *Picture.embedDigits2(166,1)* returns 165. *Picture.embedDigits2(12,1)* returns 13	Complete the following static method, *embedDigits3*, which is in Sound.java. It takes two int parameters *contextVal* and *messageVal*. This method will replace the three least significant digits in *contextVal* with the value of *messageVal*. It returns the new value back as its return value. You can assume that *contextVal* will always be an integer between 0 and 255 inclusive (i.e. an 8-bit integer) and *messageVal* will always be an integer between 0 and 7 inclusive (i.e. a 3-bit integer). For example, *embedDigits3(180,7)* will return 183.

Table 1: Sample PA instruction and mapped exam question.

3.3 Identifying Free-riders

We designed the following procedure to identify students who might have free-rode on a certain part of an assignment. Free-riding can only occur when a student programmed in pairs (either final submission for both control and experimental groups, or checkpoint in the control group only). We make no assumptions about whether students are more or less likely to free-ride between stages and between the control and experimental groups.

Every student's PA score and exam question scores were first converted into percentiles to avoid scaling effect. We only calculate these percentiles for students who completed both the PA and the mapped exam question. We then calculate the difference between a student's PA percentile and the exam question's percentile. A larger positive difference indicates that a student received a high PA score but received a low exam score for the same conceptual topic. This suggests a disconnect in understanding between the assignment and the exam; the student is thus suspected of free-riding the paired stages without fully understanding the assignment. The threshold to determine the percentile difference is set as 20% for 7 mappings. For the remaining two mappings, we adjusted the threshold due to the granularity of attainable student scores on the exam after converting to percentiles. We identify a list of students for each of the 9 PA-exam mappings. Table 2 shows the number of times that students appeared in the searches.

Number of Occurrences	1	2	3	4	5	6
Number of Unique Students	98	72	34	13	8	1

Table 2: Number of students identified at least once in free-rider searches. No student appeared more than 6 times.

We picked 3 occurrences as a cut off because it shows a sharp decrease in the number of students from those marked twice. 56 students appeared 3 or more times out of the 9 searches and were identified as likely free-riders. Once the free-riders are identified, we focus on this subgroup of students with all their PAs and exam data in Section 4.2.

4 RESULTS

Each of the following sets of results attempts to answer the research questions of how the hybrid two-stage model, compared with standard pair programming, affects programming assignment scores, exam scores, and the impact on free-riding students.

4.1 RQ1: Hybrid vs Standard Pair Programming

4.1.1 Score difference on programming assignments. We first compare the difference between the experimental and control groups on checkpoint and final submission for all 8 PAs.

As shown in Figure 2, the checkpoint scores of the experimental group are lower on average than that of the control group throughout all the 8 PAs. Checkpoint differences on PA2, PA3, PA5, and PA7 also show statistical difference (2-sample t-test). The difference between control and experimental groups for checkpoint ranges from 0.6% to 13.5%. This result is expected as the control group's work is done by pair programming while students in the experimental group complete the checkpoint individually. Therefore the quality of the work from the control group is expected to be better at checkpoint.

For the final submission, the performance difference between the control and experimental groups are generally small and not statistically significant. The only exceptions are PA1 and PA6. For PA1, the control group outperformed the experimental group in the final submission (2-sample t-test, t=2.19, df=144, p=.02). For PA6, the

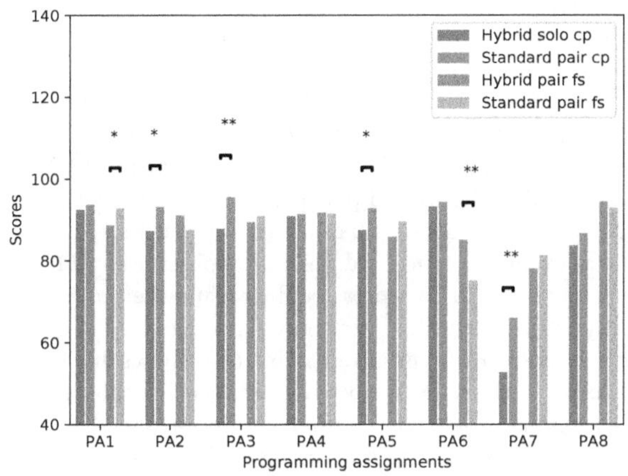

Figure 2: Scores on checkpoints (cp) and final submissions (fs) in each PA between experimental (hybrid) and control (standard) groups. * indicates $p < .05$, ** indicates $p < .001$.

experimental group outperformed the control group significantly (t=3.35, df=134, p=.0009).

We also examined the transition from the checkpoint to the final submission for the control and experimental groups. The score difference between the two stages is shown in Table 3. "$ctrl\ fs - cp$" means that we calculated the score difference between the final submission and the checkpoint for the control group. Similar calculations are performed for the experimental group. In general, the control group score difference is negative which suggests that they tend to do worse in the final submission than the checkpoint. However, the experimental group change is mostly positive. For 5 out of 8 assignments, the changes have statistical significance. The last three PAs, which are generally more challenging, showed that the experimental group tend to improve more in the final submission.

PA	$\mu(ctrl\ fs{-}cp)$	$\mu(exp\ fs{-}cp)$	t	p	sig
1	-0.78	-4.23	-1.42	0.16	no
2	-5.54	3.95	3.28	0.0	yes
3	-4.46	2.23	2.8	0.01	yes
4	-1.22	1.44	1.18	0.24	no
5	-4.28	-1.21	1.13	0.26	no
6	-18.8	-8.15	3.66	0.0	yes
7	15.16	25.41	2.35	0.02	yes
8	6.22	11.35	2.22	0.03	yes

Table 3: Performance difference between final submission (fs) and checkpoint (cp).

4.1.2 Performance on selected exam questions. Next, we examined if there is a difference on selected exam questions between the control group and experimental group. Figure 3 shows the result. Students from the control and the experimental groups perform very similarly on all 9 mapped midterm/final exam questions. No statistical significance was found (2-sample t-test).

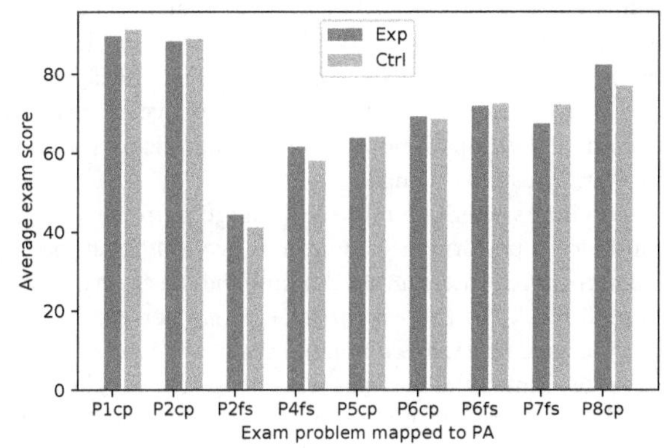

Figure 3: Exam scores on 9 selected exam questions across the control and experimental groups.

4.2 RQ2: Impact on Free-riders

All 56 identified free-riders (see Section 3 for identification criteria) have at least 3 large performance gaps between pair programming assignments (checkpoint or final submission) and their mapped exam questions. We singled out these identified students to examine whether having the solo checkpoint stage helped free-riders, we compared the performance of these students on the checkpoints that have an exam mapping. Note that although the 56 students are identified as free-riders, a student don't necessarily free-ride on every assignment.

Figure 4 visualizes the difference between checkpoint scores and exam scores between the the identified students who were in the control group and those in the experimental group. For all five checkpoints, identified students in the control group performed better in the programming assignments compared with those in the experimental group. This finding is consistent with the pattern shown in Figure 2.

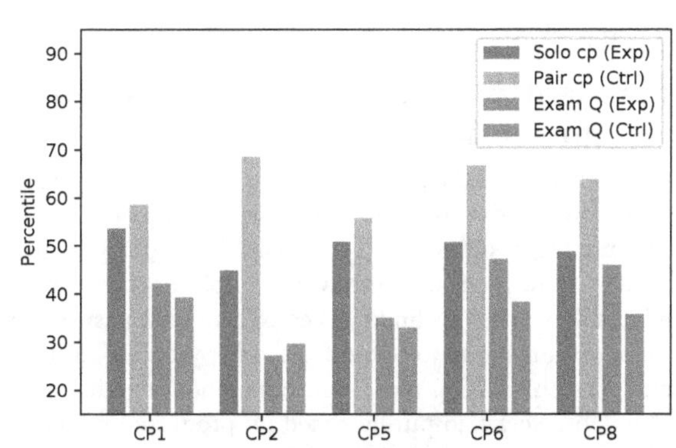

Figure 4: Free-rider performance between the experimental and control groups. Checkpoint percentiles and mapped exam question percentiles are shown.

As shown in Figure 4, although the checkpoint scores of pairs were higher than that of soloers, the pattern is reversed for exam performance. The free-riding students who completed the checkpoint solo tend to rank better than those who completed the checkpoint in pairs. The difference on exam performance between the control and experimental groups is not statistically significant for all five mapped exam questions though.

As free-riding students tend to have large performance gaps between their PA performance and exams, we examined the gaps for the identified free-riders on checkpoints and the exam questions. As seen in Table 4, the *PA percentile – Exam percentile* metric is smaller for students who completed the checkpoint solo. n_1 is the number of identified free-riders who completed the checkpoint solo. The difference between the control and experimental groups is statistically significant for PA6 and PA8 checkpoints which are among the most difficult assignments for the class. Note that the table only contains the individual free-riders' score differences even if they completed the checkpoints in pairs. This is why n_2 is not necessarily an even number.

We also examined the individual performance of the 56 identified students to see whether they performed better in solo and in pairs. The possibility of free-riding exists only when the student completes the assignment in pairs, which means in soloing, no free-riding is possible. Of the 56 students, 14 students or 25% had performed more poorly on the exams for which their mapped PA checkpoint was done in solo.

CP	$\mu(solo\ diff)$	n_1	$\mu(pair\ diff)$	n_2	t	p
1	11.48	24	19.31	29	-0.94	0.35
2	17.6	15	38.83	11	-1.63	0.12
5	15.72	25	22.79	31	-0.83	0.41
6	3.49	30	28.32	25	-2.76	0.01
8	2.71	29	27.92	24	-2.5	0.02

Table 4: Difference in performance of identified free-riders completing the checkpoints (CP) in solo or pairs. For CP2, the mapped exam question is from one out of four versions of the exam; therefore its sample sizes are smaller compared with other mapped checkpoints.

5 DISCUSSION

5.1 Standard vs Hybrid in Pair Programming Assignments

Within the first stage of the programming assignments, the primary difference between the standard and hybrid groups is the mode of completing the assignments: soloing against pairing. Figure 2 shows that the pair programmers always outperform the students performing solo work. This finding is consistent with past research in which pair scores tend to outperform soloer scores [15, 16, 18]. Pairs tend to catch mistakes more easily and produce higher quality code. Thus, in a scenario purely based on program quality, pair programming is clearly superior.

However, in the second stage where all students programmed in pairs, the scores generally did not show a difference across the two groups. The only exception is PA6 where there was a drastic difference in the final submission but not the checkpoint. Though the solo checkpoint stage tends to produce lower quality programs, these students can quickly catch up when pair programming is adopted in the final submission. Therefore, a later collaborative stage in an assignment does not seem to have interfered with the quality of pair programming for students in the experimental group. Additionally, the significant difference between the experimental and control groups for the difficult assignments (PA6 to PA8, Table 3) may indicate that the hybrid pair-programming model tends to make students better cope with difficult assignments.

As far as exams are concerned, we did not observe any difference or correlation between PA scores and their mapped exam questions, especially on the 5 checkpoints shown in Figure 3. Though this finding is consistent with prior research [16], it shows that working on a problem independently does not necessarily enable students to solve a similar problem in an exam environment.

Overall, the hybrid pair programming model produces programs at a similar quality compared with standard pair programming at the final submission stage. The solo stage enables students to work independently and introducing this stage does not affect exam performance for the general student body. As most assignments in CS1/2 require students to program a set of functions or classes, constructing the checkpoint stage is fairly straightforward. In this study, helper functions and simple functional programs in a normal assignment were selected and assigned to the checkpoint. The final submission in general requires students to build upon their work in the checkpoint and also to review each other's independent work from the checkpoint. They are expected to reconcile the differences from two independently completed checkpoint codes. This peer review process is useful as studies have shown that the learning outcomes are greater when students have the opportunity to review other students' assignments [14, 22]. This peer review opportunity is naturally available in the hybrid pair programming model, but not necessarily from standard pair programming.

5.2 Impact on Free-Riding

The team dynamics of the pair, the requirement to be physically in front of a computer, and the ability to adhere to the driver/navigator switch may all impact the effectiveness of pair programming [7, 26]. From anecdotal evidence, there are consistently groups of students who wish they programmed solo and independently. In the few pairs where one student might tackle the vast majority of the assignment, the other student is left out of the challenge whether the said student had done this intentionally or not. Therefore the free-rider intentionally or unintentionally lost the opportunity to learn from doing a programming assignment due to this imbalance in the pair. The proposed hybrid model positions every student to produce independent work, eliminating the free-riding phenomenon from the first stage. As the checkpoint is in general easier to complete and leads to the more complicated final submission, students missing necessary conceptual knowledge have the opportunity to practice and improve before pair programming starts. This in return may reduce the negative impact to student learning from free-riding.

In addition to reducing the chance of free-riding, we also observed that the performance of free-riders on exams tend to be better if a student completed the checkpoint individually. As shown in Figure 4, the 56 identified free-riding students have an average

PA score below 70% and average exam score below 60%. Therefore, free-riders tend to be students with lower academic performance. If working in pairs, the speed of writing the program with a stronger partner may force the weaker student to progress without truly understanding. The solo work seems to have enabled them to understand concepts in order to progress through the assignment, which in turn reflected in better exam performance. The reduced gap between the PA and exam scores indicated that the solo stage produced positive effects.

Another important observation is the significantly reduced PA and exam performance gap on difficult assignments (PA6 and PA8 in Table 4). The solo work seems to significantly benefit students who otherwise will most likely free-ride due to the difficulty level of the assignments. Therefore, the solo checkpoint stage in the proposed hybrid pair programming model is useful to alleviate the negative effect of free-riding, especially on harder assignments.

5.3 Student Perception of Hybrid Pair Programming

To gauge students' experience with hybrid pair programming, a short 6-question multiple-choice survey was distributed to the class at the end of the course.

The first three questions are Likert-scale questions whose choices range from strongly disagree to strongly agree.

–**Q1**: For PA checkpoints, I would prefer to work solo compared with working in pairs.

–**Q2**: Working solo on the checkpoint helps us to collaborate better for the final submission.

–**Q3**: Working solo on the checkpoint gives me the opportunity to learn independently.

The next three questions examine student preference between hybrid pair programming and the standard pair programming.

–**Q4**: What is your take on hybrid pair programming? *Answers include (A) It's an excellent way for me, (B) It's a nice idea but I have some minor concerns, (C) I am neutral, and (D) I don't like the idea at all.*

–**Q5**: What is your take on standard pair programming? *Answers provided to this question are similar to Q4.*

–**Q6**: If given a choice to complete a PA, I would strongly prefer to work on the PA using the following approach. *Answers include (A) Hybrid pair programming, (B) Standard pair programming, and (C) Work solo for the entire PA.*

The survey results from Table 5 indicate that students in general prefer to work on the checkpoint individually (Q1) as they like the opportunity to perform some independent work (Q3). However, students do not seem to indicate that working solo on the checkpoint helped them collaborate better in the final submission. This response is consistent with the similar final submission scores shown in Figure 2.

For the comparisons between hybrid pair programming and standard pair programming, students' opinions are fairly similar. A majority of students favored or had slight concerns on both programming formats but the preference of collaborative programming formats (hybrid or standard) is strong compared with pure solo work (Q6).

Question	Strongly disagree	Disagree	Neutral	Agree	Strongly agree
Q1	15.6%	20.5%	18%	21.3%	24.6%
Q2	16.4%	16.8%	29.5%	17.6%	19.7%
Q3	4.5%	4.1%	9.8%	31.1%	50.4%

	Like	Nice idea	Neutral	Don't like
Q4	38.9%	34%	18.4%	8.6%
Q5	38.1%	30.3%	19.3%	12.3%

	Hybrid PP	Standard PP	Solo
Q6	42.6%	33.6%	23.8%

Table 5: Survey on student perception of hybrid pair programming. $n = 224$.

5.4 Threats to Validity

We identify the following threats to validity for this study:

–**1.** To identify free-riders, we used a subjective threshold of 20% which may have distorted the selection process. The granularity of raw exam scores also complicated the identification process. The variety of scores of the exam problems may be limited students can earn. Therefore, many students could have an identical percentile. This caused us to change the threshold for 2 particular mapped exam questions to identify possible free-riders before filtering out unlikely free-riders with low frequency of being identified.

–**2.** Not all PA checkpoints or final submissions were mapped. Though it is possible that unmapped PA stages yield a different result, we believe the pre-selected PA to exam mappings are representative of course materials.

–**3.** Each programming assignment was treated independently. In introductory courses, each assignment likely builds its concepts on the previous assignment. A course that teaches independent concepts may be better equipped to test the local effects of hybrid pair programming at each assignment.

6 CONCLUSION

Pair programming is effective when students faithfully execute its ideas as intended. However, enforcing "true" pair programming for several hundred students is impractical. Some students might use only part of pair programming's guidelines while others might prefer a chance for independent work. Our study on this hybrid two-stage model addresses these concerns to provide students an otherwise lost opportunity to face challenges in assignments. The first stage helps increase the likelihood that all students attempt the assignments and think about their concepts, thus reducing the chance that free-riding occurs. The hybrid model improves student performance as much as standard pair programming while providing a lightweight solution reducing free-riding. With minimal curricular adjustments, the hybrid model is a promising alternative to standard pair programming.

REFERENCES

[1] L. Battestilli, A. Awasthi, and Y. Cao. Two-stage programming projects: Individual work followed by peer collaboration. In *SIGCSE*, pages 479–484, 2018.

[2] G. Braught, J. MacCormick, and T. Wahls. The benefits of pairing by ability. In *SIGCSE*, pages 249–253, 2010.

[3] Y. Cao and L. Porter. Evaluating student learning from collaborative group tests in introductory computing. In *SIGCSE*, pages 99–104, 2017.

[4] Y. Cao and L. Porter. Impact of performance level and group composition on student learning during collaborative exams. In *ITiCSE*, pages 152–157, 2017.

[5] J. C. Carver, L. Henderson, L. He, J. Hodges, and D. Reese. Increased retention of early computer science and software engineering students using pair programming. In *CSEET*, pages 115–122, 2007.

[6] M. Celepkolu and K. E. Boyer. The importance of producing shared code through pair programming. In *SIGCSE*, pages 765–770, 2018.

[7] M. Celepkolu and K. E. Boyer. Thematic analysis of students' reflections on pair programming in cs1. In *SIGCSE*, pages 771–776, 2018.

[8] A. Cockburn and L. Williams. Extreme programming examined. chapter The Costs and Benefits of Pair Programming, pages 223–243. Addison-Wesley Longman Publishing Co., Inc., Boston, MA, USA, 2001.

[9] S. Freeman, S. L. Eddy, M. McDonough, M. K. Smith, N. Okoroafor, H. Jordt, and M. P. Wenderoth. Active learning increases student performance in science, engineering, and mathematics. *PNAS*, 111(23):8410–8415, 2014.

[10] R. Harsley, D. Fossati, B. Di Eugenio, and N. Green. Interactions of individual and pair programmers with an intelligent tutoring system for computer science. In *SIGCSE*, pages 285–290, 2017.

[11] N. Herbert. Quantitative peer assessment: Can students be objective? In *ACE*, pages 63–71, 2007.

[12] H. H. Hu, B. Knaeble, and C. Mayfield. Results from a survey of faculty adoption of process oriented guided inquiry learning (POGIL) in computer science. In *SIGCSE*, pages 186–191, 2016.

[13] N. Katira, L. Williams, E. Wiebe, C. Miller, S. Balik, and E. Gehringer. On understanding compatibility of student pair programmers. In *SIGCSE*, pages 7–11, 2004.

[14] X. Li. Using peer review to assess coding standards - a case study. In *Frontiers in Education*, 2006.

[15] C. McDowell, B. Hanks, and L. Werner. Experimenting with pair programming in the classroom. In *ITiCSE*, pages 60–64, 2003.

[16] C. McDowell, L. Werner, H. Bullock, and J. Fernald. The effects of pair-programming on performance in an introductory programming course. In *SIGCSE*, pages 38–42, 2002.

[17] C. McDowell, L. Werner, H. E. Bullock, and J. Fernald. Pair programming improves student retention, confidence, and program quality. *Communications of the ACM*, 49(8):90–95, 2006.

[18] N. Nagappan, L. Williams, M. Ferzli, E. Wiebe, K. Yang, C. Miller, and S. Balik. Improving the cs1 experience with pair programming. *SIGCSE Bull.*, 35(1):359–362, Jan 2003.

[19] J. K. L. Poon. Students' perceptions of peer evaluation in project work. In *ACE*, pages 87–94, 2011.

[20] L. Porter, C. Bailey Lee, B. Simon, and D. Zingaro. Peer instruction: do students really learn from peer discussion in computing? In *ICER*, pages 45–52, 2011.

[21] L. Porter, C. B. Lee, and B. Simon. Halving fail rates using peer instruction: A study of four computer science courses. In *SIGCSE*, pages 177–182, 2013.

[22] K. Reily, P. L. Finnerty, and L. Terveen. Two peers are better than one: Aggregating peer reviews for computing assignments is surprisingly accurate. In *GROUP*, pages 115–124, 2009.

[23] O. Ruvalcaba, L. Werner, and J. Denner. Observations of pair programming: Variations in collaboration across demographic groups. In *SIGCSE*, pages 90–95, 2016.

[24] N. Salleh, E. Mendes, and J. Grundy. Empirical studies of pair programming for cs/se teaching in higher education: A systematic literature review. *IEEE Trans. Softw. Eng.*, 37(4):509–525, July 2011.

[25] J. Sennett and M. Sherriff. Compatibility of partnered students in computer science education. In *SIGCSE*, pages 244–248, 2010.

[26] B. Simon and B. Hanks. First-year students' impressions of pair programming in cs1. *J. Educ. Resour. Comput.*, 7(4):5:1–5:28.

[27] B. R. Snyder. *The hidden curriculum*. New York: Knopf, 1970.

[28] A. Tafliovich, J. Campbell, and A. Petersen. A student perspective on prior experience in cs1. In *SIGCSE*, pages 239–244, 2013.

[29] J. Warner and P. J. Guo. Codepilot: Scaffolding end-to-end collaborative software development for novice programmers. In *CHI*, pages 1136–1141, 2017.

[30] B. C. Wilson and S. Shrock. Contributing to success in an introductory computer science course: A study of twelve factors. In *SIGCSE*, pages 184–188, 2001.

[31] B. Yu, G. Tsiknis, and M. Allen. Turning exams into a learning experience. In *SIGCSE*, pages 336–340, 2010.

In Their Own Words: Gender Differences in Student Perceptions of Pair Programming

Kimberly Michelle Ying
University of Florida
Gainesville, Florida
kimying@ufl.edu

Lydia G. Pezzullo
University of Florida
Gainesville, Florida
lpezzullo@ufl.edu

Mohona Ahmed
University of Florida
Gainesville, Florida
mohonaahmed@ufl.edu

Kassandra Crompton
University of Florida
Gainesville, Florida
kcrompton@ufl.edu

Jeremiah Blanchard
University of Florida
Gainesville, Florida
jblanch@cise.ufl.edu

Kristy Elizabeth Boyer
University of Florida
Gainesville, Florida
keboyer@ufl.edu

ABSTRACT

Women continue to be underrepresented in computer science. Previous research has identified factors that contribute to women's decisions to pursue computing-related majors, but in order to truly address the problem of underrepresentation, we need to develop a deeper understanding of women's experiences within computer science courses. Pair programming is demonstrably beneficial in many ways, and we hypothesize that there are gender differences in student perceptions of this widely used collaboration framework. To explore these differences and move toward a thorough understanding of students' experiences, this paper investigates students' written responses about their experiences with pair programming in a university-level introductory computer science course. Using thematic analysis, we identified overarching themes and distinguished between what men and women reported. Both women and men wrote about their overwhelmingly positive perceptions of pair programming. Women often mentioned that pair programming helps with engagement, feeling less frustrated, building confidence, and making friends. Women also noted that it is easier to learn from peers. These findings shed light on how pair programming may lower barriers to women's participation and retention in computing and inform ongoing efforts to create more inclusive spaces in computing education.

CCS CONCEPTS

• **Social and professional topics → Computing education**; **CS1**; **Adult education**;

KEYWORDS

Gender; Pair programming; Undergraduate education

SIGCSE '19, February 27-March 2, 2019, Minneapolis, MN, USA

ACM ISBN 978-1-4503-5890-3/19/02...$15.00
https://doi.org/10.1145/3287324.3287380

ACM Reference Format:
Kimberly Michelle Ying, Lydia G. Pezzullo, Mohona Ahmed, Kassandra Crompton, Jeremiah Blanchard, and Kristy Elizabeth Boyer. 2019. In Their Own Words: Gender Differences in Student Perceptions of Pair Programming. In *Proceedings of the 50th ACM Technical Symposium on Computer Science Education (SIGCSE '19), February 27-March 2, 2019, Minneapolis, MN, USA.* ACM, New York, NY, USA, 7 pages. https://doi.org/10.1145/3287324.3287380

1 INTRODUCTION

The need for qualified talent in STEM is high and projected to increase [22]; yet women continue to be underrepresented in these fields [23]. While some areas in STEM have shown good response to efforts toward gender equity, computing lags behind, with women representing just 26% of the computer and information sciences workforce and African American and Latina women representing less than 16% [23]. This disparity is in place by the time prospective professionals graduate: Of all graduates from computer science and computer engineering bachelor's programs in the United States, just 18% are women [24].

Many women are discouraged from pursuing education and careers in computing for social reasons: they may not feel a sense of belonging and identification with the field [9], or they may desire more social support from peers than the class style allows [6]. Promising work has already identified practices that address these roadblocks and improve women's interest and persistence, such as group learning [10, 12] and pair programming [15]. The pair programming paradigm, where two programmers work together on the same code, not only produces higher quality code and promotes a more efficient work process [8, 13, 18], it also offers structured collaboration with peers [16, 17] and improves interest and retention for undergraduates, including women [14, 15].

As a matter of equity in opportunity, research is needed to understand and address the causes of the gender gap in computing. Quantitative research has been used to evaluate pedagogical approaches [10, 12] and investigate hypotheses about students' attitudes, beliefs, and traits [19, 20] as they pertain to this issue. Qualitative work offers a human-focused perspective into the unique experiences of individuals: for example, it has characterized the social contexts of computer science learning [11] and contrasted the attitudes and opportunities of women both in CS and who have left the field [9, 21]. Thematic analysis of written data is a promising qualitative approach because it captures details of individuals' unique reflections and uses these to identify important factors in the phenomenon of interest. The technique has been used to characterize perceptions of pair programming in general [4], but has not yet been used to contrast the firsthand accounts of male and female students in pair programming activities.

This paper advances the field by identifying potential factors influencing gendered perceptions of computer science coursework at the undergraduate level. It does so through a qualitative analysis of 104 open-ended survey responses from students in an introductory course for computer science majors. The central question asked is, **what differences do we observe in men's and women's perceptions of pair programming?** By identifying themes in students' perceived advantages and disadvantages of pair programming and examining which students reported these themes, this study supports hypothesis-forming for future work on advancing equal representation in computing fields.

2 RELATED WORK

The factors impacting women's interest [5, 19] and persistence [9, 21] in computing-related majors are predominantly cultural and societal. In an interdisciplinary critical review, Cheryan and colleagues [7] point to the intersection of a masculine culture and a lack of opportunities for early exposure as the key roadblocks to girls' and women's interest in pursuing computer science. Qualitative research indicates that a supportive peer community plays an important role in persistence and identity formation in computing [9, 21]. Cultural perceptions of computer science frame the field as solitary work, leading learners to believe that they will not find sufficient support from their peers in the classroom [6]. Moreover, underrepresentation perpetuates itself by leaving women who do choose computing careers feeling alienated and vulnerable to stereotype threat and impostor syndrome [21].

Pedagogical strategies have the potential to mitigate these problems. Pair programming, a widely-implemented practice in both classrooms and professional environments, is one such intervention. In pair programming, two coders share one computer: they take turns in the role of driver, who operates the computer, or navigator, who is free to read the code and suggest actions. Students working in the pair programming paradigm demonstrate improved code quality, and they work more efficiently [8, 13, 18]. The structured collaboration that pair programming offers may be the reason it can lead to better course retention than individual programming work alone [16, 17]. Prior research has evaluated excerpts related to pair programming from CS1 students' open-ended, end-of-semester reflection papers and found themes of a cognitive, affective, and social nature [4], but to our knowledge has not taken a qualitative approach to understanding the unique experiences of men and women in CS1 pair programming. This study, which takes as data student responses to open-ended questions directly inquiring about pair programming, expands on previous work by comparing the themes that predominated among female versus male respondents. It could be expected that women might appreciate pair programming in more or different ways than men. Our work explores this possibility by looking at patterns in the advantages and disadvantages of pair programming that men and women reported during an introductory computer science course.

Table 1: Prompts included as part of the students' quiz.

(1)	How does your experience in the class so far compare to what you were expecting?
(2)	Describe your relationship with the partner you had for labs 3-5 (Selection, Hex Decoder, Debugging Version Control).
(3)	In what ways do you think pair programming impacted your learning?

3 DATA AND METHODS

3.1 Course Context and Participants

This study was conducted within an introductory computer science class at a large public university in the Southeastern United States in Spring 2018. The course was taught using the Java programming language and was a required course for majors in computer science and computer engineering. Students had lecture twice a week for a total of 150 minutes of instruction. Labs, each administered by a teaching assistant (TA), were held once each week for two hours in classes of 25 or fewer students. There were 411 students enrolled in the course, 29.7% of whom were women. 187 students consented to the collection of their course data for research purposes. Consenting students did not receive any incentives for their participation, and there were no penalties for students who did not participate in the study. The demographic survey included the question, "I identify my gender as", with the options of "Female", "Male", "Other", and "Prefer not to answer". 129 of the consenting students reported their gender in the demographic survey, and 106 of those students submitted responses to the prompts regarding pair programming.

After removing two blank prompt responses, there were 104 prompt responses analyzed in total. The authors of those responses were 38 women (36.5%) and 66 men (63.5%). None of the participants selected "Other" or "Prefer not to answer" for the gender identity question. The race/ethnicities of the participants were White/Caucasian (40.4%), Asian/Pacific Islander (18.3%), Multiracial (16.3%), Hispanic/Latino (14.4%), Black/African-American (7.7%) and unspecified (2.9%). The students' majors were Computer Science (34.6%), Computer Engineering (19.2%), other Engineering (25%), and other (21.2%). Levels of prior experience differed markedly by gender, with 59.1% of male participants reporting prior experience programming and only 18.4% of female participants reporting programming experience before the course.

3.2 Procedure

At the beginning of the third lab session, students were introduced to pair programming and assigned partners with whom they would work for the next three lab sessions. Students were paired based on consent to the study and based on gender (to ensure there were some female-female pairs, male-male pairs, and mixed pairs). Due to student absences, some students may have had more than one partner throughout the three lab sessions. Additionally, if lab sections had an odd number of students, a trio was formed so that no student worked alone. Assignments for labs 3 and 4 involved writing a program and were conducive to pair programming. Lab 5 was a tutorial and did not involve submitting any code. For this lab, students worked on their own computers but referred to their partners if they needed help. After completing their fifth lab, students were given three short-answer prompts (Table 1) to complete at home as part of their weekly quiz grade. A minimum of 100 words was required for each prompt, and students were informed they would be graded only for completion. This paper reports on responses to prompts 2 and 3, which inquire about the students' feelings towards pair programming and their partners during lab sessions.

3.3 Data

There were 106 submissions for the prompts from consenting students who reported their gender in a demographic survey. From those submissions, two were removed: one whose responses to prompts 2 and 3 were blank, and the other whose response to prompt 3 was blank. The remaining 104 responses had an average word count of 114 for prompt 2 and 118 for prompt 3, with an aggregate average of 232 words. The minimum response length for prompt 2 was 11 words, while the maximum length was 232 words. Prompt 3 had a minimum response of 14 words and a maximum response of 305 words. In aggregate, the shortest response was 25 words long and the longest response was 485 words long.

3.4 Methods

Following the qualitative research methodology of thematic analysis, three researchers collaboratively coded the positives and negatives of pair programming mentioned in each student's aggregate response. Thematic analysis is a method used for organizing qualitative data into themes which relate back to the research question [2]. We used a bottom-up approach, allowing our data to directly inform the themes based on codes which were created to summarize the students' main points. The process was as follows: (1) Researchers independently read the student's response and recorded every positive and negative aspect of pair programming mentioned; (2) Researchers discussed the positives and negatives they recorded for that student until reaching a consensus; (3) Any positives and negatives not previously mentioned were added to a spreadsheet as a new code. To perform the thematic analysis, the codes were grouped by similarity and then themes were determined by summarizing the codes within each grouping. Any themes which overlapped extensively were combined, and grouping was complete once the three researchers agreed that the remaining themes were distinct from each other.

4 RESULTS

Thematic analysis resulted in 52 codes, of which 31 were positive and 21 were negative. These codes were organized into 16 themes: seven positive themes and nine negative themes, as shown in Tables 2 and 3, respectively. Due to the interrelated nature of the topics and phenomena discussed in the responses, there is some overlap between the themes reported. Similarly, some codes may fit within more than one theme but are reported under the theme which the researchers felt was most relevant.

4.1 Positive Perceptions of Pair Programming

From the 104 student responses, 98 students expressed at least one positive sentiment about pair programming, for a total of 334 positive sentiments. Seven themes emerged from these reported benefits, as shown in Table 2: *improve learning experience, career skills, positive atmosphere, networking, efficient/productive, more engaged,* and *personal gain.*

Table 2: Reported positives and their corresponding theme with counts and percentages of men and women who mentioned each code within their response.

Positives		Count (Percent)	
Theme	Original Code	Men	Women
IMPROVE LEARNING EXPERIENCE	*Improves understanding and learned new things*	24 (36.4%)	20 (52.6%)
	Broadens problem-solving techniques / Different approaches	18 (27.3%)	12 (31.6%)
	Someone to ask questions and discuss ideas	37 (56.1%)	19 (50.0%)
	Receive feedback	2 (3.0%)	0 (0.0%)
	Reinforce knowledge by explaining to partner	8 (12.1%)	2 (5.3%)
	Better recollection of material for the future	2 (3.0%)	0 (0.0%)
	Easier to learn from peers	0 (0.0%)	2 (5.3%)
	Introduced to new resources	1 (1.5%)	0 (0.0%)
CAREER SKILLS	*Improves coding*	8 (12.1%)	3 (7.9%)
	Developing workplace skills	11 (16.7%)	5 (13.2%)
	Learn to work together / Working with others	15 (22.7%)	8 (21.1%)
	Open to new suggestions	0 (0.0%)	1 (2.6%)
POSITIVE ATMOSPHERE	*More enjoyable*	5 (7.6%)	4 (10.5%)
	More comfortable	0 (0.0%)	1 (2.6%)
	Helps not feel discouraged / Less frustrating / Less stressful	4 (6.1%)	9 (23.7%)
	Friendlier atmosphere	1 (1.5%)	0 (0.0%)
	Comforting / Reassuring / Supportive	4 (6.1%)	5 (13.2%)
NETWORKING	*Help from classmates outside of class*	3 (4.5%)	1 (2.6%)
	Meet new people / Make friends	1 (1.5%)	4 (10.5%)
	Improve social/communication skills	9 (13.6%)	3 (7.9%)
EFFICIENT / PRODUCTIVE	*Efficient*	24 (36.4%)	7 (18.4%)
	Identifying errors	14 (21.2%)	5 (13.2%)
	Easier to seek help from TA	2 (3.0%)	1 (2.6%)
	Easier	7 (10.6%)	3 (7.9%)
	Require less help from TA	1 (1.5%)	1 (2.6%)
MORE ENGAGED	*Motivated by partner*	3 (4.5%)	3 (7.9%)
	Greater responsibility	1 (1.5%)	2 (5.3%)
	More engaged/focused with work	1 (1.5%)	1 (2.6%)
PERSONAL GAIN	*Feels good to help someone*	2 (3.0%)	0 (0.0%)
	Builds confidence	0 (0.0%)	3 (7.9%)
	More rewarding	1 (1.5%)	0 (0.0%)

4.1.1 Improve Learning Experience. The most common theme observed was improving the learning experience, with 86 student responses mentioning at least once that pair programming improved their learning experience. Note that this theme may have been primed by the wording of prompt 3, resulting in the high number of student responses under this theme. Specifically, the most common codes from this theme (and overall) were *someone to ask questions and discuss ideas*, with over 50% of both men and women mentioning this benefit, and *improves understanding and learned new things*, with over 40% of students mentioning this benefit and over 50% of women in particular. On more occasions than women, men reported the benefit of reinforcing their knowledge by explaining to their partner. *Receive feedback, better recollection of material for the future*, and *introduced to new resources* were codes derived exclusively from male students' responses. On the other hand, women exclusively wrote that it was easier to learn from peers, with 5.3% reporting this perception. One woman wrote:

> "...it's always been intimidating or embarrassing for me to ask for help from people that have much more experience than myself. It's nice having someone at my level to brainstorm with, and they're quickly accessible in comparison with a TA that is responsible for the entire lab..."[1]

Another woman wrote:

> "Having someone closer to my age than a TA makes it less scary to ask questions and also provides me with a constant form of encouragement."

4.1.2 Career Skills. Men and women reported improvements to career skills at similar rates, with over 20% citing the benefits of learning to work together, and 15.4% specifically mentioning developing their workplace skills. One woman wrote:

> "I think paired programming is a great idea because it helps people learn how to work together on a program. All of these skills are needed in the work place and will definitely impact our future careers."

4.1.3 Positive Atmosphere. Women attributed pair programming leading to a positive atmosphere, specifically by reducing negative emotions like discouragement, frustration, and stress and by creating an environment that was comforting, reassuring, and supportive. Men did not report this positive aspect of pair programming as much as the women in this study. These women described the relief they felt from pair programming:

> " Without a partner I am not sure if I would have been able to complete the labs at all. Perhaps, it wouldn't have been impossible, but it would have definitely been stressful and maybe so much that I don't learn at all because I'd be focused on trying to complete the lab only instead of understanding what is going on."
>
> "I would feel incredibly overwhelmed if I had to complete every lab alone. Having a friend by me to lean on when I have a question is very comforting and makes me feel as though I can program better. [...] I really hope we continue to do pair programming as it has been a huge stress reliever as opposed to doing them separately."

4.1.4 Networking. Women reported meeting new people and making friends as a benefit of pair programming more often than men, which points to its potential for mitigating the feelings of isolation many women experience.

[1]All quotes are taken directly from the students' responses and preserve any typos or grammatical errors.

> "It is also very nice to have conversation with someone during the lab and makes it more enjoyable. I also like meeting people in the class because without the pair programming, I would probably not have branched out to converse with others."

4.1.5 Efficient / Productive. Men commented on improvements to the quality of their code and coding process, citing greater efficiency and better identification of errors more often than did women. One man wrote:

> "At first when the students in my lab were all paired with each other, I thought it might slow our learning. After a few lab projects I started to realize that it was actually the exact opposite."

Another man wrote:

> "I would much rather have a partner than not have a partner because I don't have to ask the TA for help as often and can get the work done faster."

4.1.6 More Engaged. While engagement was not referenced frequently by any students, women mentioned the theme of engagement more often than men. One woman described being more motivated during lab:

> "His own motivation to successfully complete the lab helps me become more motivated to get the job done."

Another woman described how her motivation to do well in the course extends past the actual time spent pair programming:

> "I also feel the need to study more which is a good thing because I don't want to be looked at as the 'weak link' of the pair so it definitely motivates me to try and understand more and prepare for the labs more."

4.1.7 Personal Gain. Interestingly, while few students commented on personal gain, three women (7.9%) said specifically that pair programming boosted their confidence while zero men reported this.

> "I think pair programming has provided me with everything I need to gain a little bit of confidence and not give up or get frustrated so easily when I can't get my code to run properly."

4.2 Negative Perceptions of Pair Programming

From the 104 student responses, 31 students expressed at least one negative sentiment about pair programming, for a total of 56 negative sentiments. While student perceptions were positive overall, it is important to investigate the negative perceptions to determine how we might prevent these feelings in the future. Nine themes emerged from these reported disadvantages as shown in Table 3: *unequal workload, inefficient, learn more alone, incompatible partner, less hands on, less convenient, frustrating, one person's style takes over*, and *relying on someone else*. Among these negative themes, a few patterns were noticeable.

4.2.1 Predominantly female sentiments. Both men and women discussed an incompatible partner as a detriment to their pair programming experience, with women reporting it more frequently. This was most often cited as simply "incompatibility", but two women specifically said they felt they were burdening their partner, while

Table 3: Reported negatives and their corresponding theme with counts and percentages of men and women who mentioned each code within their response.

Negatives		Count (Percent)	
Theme	**Original Code**	**Men**	**Women**
UNEQUAL WORKLOAD	*Unequal workload (partner taking over)*	1 (1.5%)	1 (2.6%)
	Unequal workload (partner freeloading)	3 (4.5%)	0 (0.0%)
	Slowed learning	1 (1.5%)	0 (0.0%)
	Inefficient/Slower	5 (7.6%)	3 (7.9%)
	Work better/faster alone	4 (6.1%)	1 (2.6%)
LEARN MORE ALONE	*Hinders independent learning*	0 (0.0%)	1 (2.6%)
	Harder to complete later on your own	0 (0.0%)	1 (2.6%)
	Learn better alone	4 (6.1%)	2 (5.3%)
	Only learns part of material	2 (3.0%)	1 (2.6%)
	Difficult to focus	0 (0.0%)	1 (2.6%)
	Learning is more difficult	0 (0.0%)	1 (2.6%)
INCOMPATIBLE PARTNER	*Incompatible partner*	1 (1.5%)	2 (5.3%)
	Discouraged by partner	0 (0.0%)	1 (2.6%)
	I am burdening partner	0 (0.0%)	2 (5.3%)
	Partner is burdening me	1 (1.5%)	0 (0.0%)
	Partners are not obligated to teach	0 (0.0%)	1 (2.6%)
LESS HANDS-ON	*Less hands-on*	3 (4.5%)	2 (5.3%)
LESS CONVENIENT	*Less convenient*	3 (4.5%)	0 (0.0%)
FRUSTRATING	*Frustrating*	2 (3%)	2 (5.3%)
ONE PERSON'S STYLE TAKES OVER	*One person's style takes over*	1 (1.5%)	1 (2.6%)
RELYING ON SOMEONE ELSE	*Relying on someone else / Responsibility*	2 (3.0%)	0 (0.0%)

no men reported this sentiment. One woman expressed her frustrations with having a partner that did not care to explain things to her:

> "But, in my experience, is also frustrating to work with someone who is at a different level of understanding of the subject matter than you are. I understand how they may not feel obligated to try to explain things but it also does not help those that are behind to work with someone further along and who is unwilling to explain anything. And of course our partners are just students so it isn't really their responsibility to teach."

Men and women both reported they felt they learned more alone, but men gave almost no additional reasons for this, while a few women elaborated on this point, citing difficulty focusing and challenges in transferring skills to independent work.

4.2.2 Predominantly male sentiments. A few men perceived pair programming to be less convenient or that their partner was freeloading, but no women reported these issues. One student expressed the freeloading as only hindering his experience when the labs were more difficult:

> "I think for the easier labs, paired programming has helped me learn easier because I can do the coding for part of the lab and then give the computer to my partner and watch and learn from him. However, during the harder labs, it feels as if paired programming is pointless in my case because my partner is worse at coding then I am and thus whenever it is his turn to code, it is still just me telling him what to write."

One of these students had only negative things to say about pair programming:

> "I honestly think pair programming is stupid. I am always more prepared than my partner, and I end up teaching them the concepts. It is annoying and kind of a waste of my time. If this class was curved, I would act stupid in front of my partner and the do the lab at home. If I did the lab at home it probably wouldn't even take an hour, but instead I am forced to work with someone and it takes 2 hours. I do not think that pair programming has led to a positive impact in my education. It has only led to the resentment of my lab partner."

5 DISCUSSION

Students' perceptions of pair programming seem overwhelmingly positive. Many men and women said that pair programming improved their learning experiences overall and that it led to a more efficient and productive coding process while supporting the development of career skills. Students discussed negatives rarely. Some gender patterns do appear in the themes reported that point to relationships between the benefits and disadvantages of pair programming in relation to the challenges women face in CS1 classrooms. It is critical to note that women are not a homogeneous group with one set of experiences (and neither are men). Each student brings a unique set of past experiences, attitudes, skills, and personality traits to the classroom. This analysis does not purport to generalize about all women in CS or all women in this sample, but rather to describe and discuss the diverse perspectives in our data in a systematic manner.

Partners as Social Supports. Many men, but few women, cited reinforcing their knowledge through explaining to their partner as a benefit of pair programming (Table 2). This aligns with social cognitive learning research, which has shown that explanation and discussion helps to advance a student's understanding. When students feel positive about explaining to less experienced partners, this is likely to come across in their interactions. Some women's reflections link this dynamic to a positive atmosphere, mentioning that working with a more experienced partner who "helps me understand" helped to build confidence and that a knowledgeable partner is "less scary" to ask for help compared to a TA. Many women also said that sharing the experience of difficulty and confusion with a partner helped them feel more comfortable, less like "the only one who does not understand something." Prior research has found that women tend to have lower self-confidence than men when it comes to computer science ability, even when controlling for quantitative ability [1]. Providing a positive atmosphere where women feel less discouraged, frustrated, and stressed is a particularly important benefit for this reason.

Career Skills and Perceptions. While it is promising that some students saw pair programming as a means to develop career skills, many students did not make this connection or choose to mention it. Misconceptions about computer science abound from popular culture, including that programming is a solo activity and that computer scientists lack interpersonal skills [6]. Pair programming is an authentic way to battle this misconception. Prior research has shown that women value careers that are people-oriented and view computer science as lacking in that area [3]. In order to retain women in the field, we need to ensure they are aware of the collaboration that occurs in industry and highlight the opportunities within computer science that are more people-oriented.

Burden and Resentment. Among the few negatives that students reported, women and men largely focused on similar threads: they felt the process was inefficient, slow, and less hands-on (Table 4). However, there was one gender difference. Two women, but no men, reported the feeling of burdening their partner, while three men, but no women, said their partner was leaving them to carry the weight of the work. The dynamics of the freeloading phenomenon are worthy of further study: it may be that some students are in fact just taking advantage of their partner; others could be less-experienced students who might stay quiet due to feelings of low confidence or intimidation, or students who feel socially alienated from their partners. The feelings of burdening a partner may be entirely self-reflective or could be responses to a partner's behavior; this phenomenon could also be investigated as a window into students' affective experiences.

Implications for Instructors. It is critical that students, especially those that are underrepresented, feel welcome in the community. Given that women reported social and affective benefits to pair programming more often than men, instructional methods should encourage social interactions which can aid in reducing negative emotions. Several women valued having a peer to ask questions to, saying it was not as intimidating as asking questions to a superior. Lowering the barrier to receiving help has the potential to help all students. Instructors should emphasize that asking questions is part of the learning process to make students feel more comfortable when reaching out for help. Providing multiple ways to receive help, such as via an anonymous discussion board or through an assigned study group, could lessen the intimidation some women feel. Additionally, we need to ensure that students are able to see the value in working with others, regardless of their partner's aptitude or prior experience. Instructors should preface pair programming with a discussion on how both parties can benefit from pair programming, citing how students can reinforce their knowledge and improve their communication skills.

Table 4: Six most common negative codes mentioned by women versus six most common negative codes mentioned by men.

Rank	Women's code	Rank	Men's code
1	Inefficient/Slower	1	Inefficient/Slower
2	Learn better alone	2	Learn better alone
2	Incompatible partner	2	Work better/faster alone
2	I am burdening partner	3	Unequal workload (partner freeloading)
2	Less hands-on	3	Less hands-on
2	Frustrating	3	Less convenient

Limitations. As is the case in all qualitative research, the individual lenses through which researchers view the data influence the themes that emerge. However, the methodology of collaborative coding and discussion to consensus is designed to produce a reliable labeling of the data that can be used for further analysis. Additionally, this class was made up of 20 in-class lab sections run by 13 teaching assistants. The variability in instructors and the number of lab sections is a potential source for variability in the enforcement of the pair programming paradigm.

6 CONCLUSION AND FUTURE WORK

Our goal for this study was to understand how men and women perceive pair programming in an introductory computer science course. We analyzed 104 student responses about pair programming and identified overarching themes as well as gender differences within those themes. Both men and women had predominantly positive sentiments about their experience with their partners and with pair programming. They cited benefits of improved learning experience, gaining career skills, and networking at nearly equal rates. Benefits to social and affective well-being were reported more by women, while benefits to the overall process of completing the lab assignments were reported more by men. Only women felt they were burdening their partner, and only men felt their partner was burdening them or was freeloading.

Having assigned partners gives women the opportunity to ask questions in a safe space. This is important not just for learning, but for mitigating feelings of isolation, which are common for women in CS courses. Future research should investigate other ways to encourage students to use each other as resources. These experiences may positively impact the culture in the classroom and increase students' sense of belonging.

The disadvantages of pair programming reported by students stemmed largely from incompatible partners and preference by some to work alone. Future studies should investigate voluntary pair programming and methods for matching students. In their responses, many students describe times when they might prefer to work alone instead of with a partner. By understanding these situational preferences, we can scaffold pair programming experiences to fit within these preferences.

Future work using additional data sources, such as video recordings, students' discussion board or chat conversations, and project and assignment artifacts are also needed to better understand and support women's interest, persistence, and success in computer science. Prior research has analyzed dialogue between students engaging in pair programming, and future studies should expand on this work to look specifically at how student pairs collaborate with respect to their gender composition.

7 ACKNOWLEDGEMENTS

The authors are grateful to the members of the LearnDialogue Group for their help and encouragement. This material is based upon work supported by the National Science Foundation under grant CNS-1622438. Any opinions, findings, and conclusions or recommendations expressed in this material are those of the author(s) and do not necessarily reflect the views of the National Science Foundation.

REFERENCES

[1] Sylvia Beyer, Kristina Rynes, Julie Perrault, Kelly Hay, and Susan Haller. 2003. Gender differences in computer science students. *SIGCSE Bulletin* 35, 1 (2003), 49–53. https://doi.org/10.1145/792548.611930

[2] Virginia Braun and Victoria Clarke. 2006. Using thematic analysis in psychology. *Qualitative Research in Psychology* 3, 2 (2006), 77–101. https://doi.org/10.1191/1478088706qp063oa

[3] Lori Carter. 2006. Why students with an apparent aptitude for computer science don't choose to major in computer science. *ACM SIGCSE Bulletin* 38, 1 (2006), 27. https://doi.org/10.1145/1124706.1121352

[4] Mehmet Celepkolu and Kristy Elizabeth Boyer. 2018. Thematic Analysis of Students' Reflections on Pair Programming in CS1. *Proceedings of the 49th ACM Technical Symposium on Computer Science Education - SIGCSE '18* (2018), 771–776. https://doi.org/10.1145/3159450.3159516

[5] Sapna Cheryan, Victoria C. Plaut, Paul G. Davies, and Claude M. Steele. 2009. Ambient Belonging: How Stereotypical Cues Impact Gender Participation in Computer Science. *Journal of Personality and Social Psychology* 97, 6 (2009), 1045–1060. https://doi.org/10.1037/a0016239

[6] Sapna Cheryan, Victoria C. Plaut, Caitlin Handron, and Lauren Hudson. 2013. The Stereotypical Computer Scientist: Gendered Media Representations as a Barrier to Inclusion for Women. *Sex Roles* 69, 1-2 (2013), 58–71. https://doi.org/10.1007/s11199-013-0296-x

[7] Sapna Cheryan, Sianna A. Ziegler, Amanda Montoya, and Lily Jiang. 2017. Why are some STEM fields more gender balanced than others? *Psychological Bulletin* 143, 1 (2017), 1–35. https://doi.org/10.1037/bul0000052

[8] Alistair Cockburn and Laurie Williams. 2001. The Costs and Benefits of Pair Programming. In *Extreme Programming Examined*, Giancarlo Succi and Michele Marchesi (Eds.). Addison-Wesley Longman Publishing Co., Inc., Boston, MA, USA, 223–243. http://dl.acm.org/citation.cfm?id=377517.377531

[9] Wendy DuBow, Joanna Weidler-Lewis, and Alexis Kaminsky. 2016. Multiple Factors Converge to Influence Women's Persistence in Computing: A Qualitative Analysis of Persisters and Nonpersisters. In *2016 Research on Equity and Sustained Participation in Engineering, Computing, and Technology (RESPECT)*, Adrienne Decker, Kurt Eiselt, Jamie Payton, Tiffany Barnes, and George K. Thiruvathukal (Eds.). Atlanta, GA, USA, 1–7. https://doi.org/10.1109/RESPECT.2016.7836161

[10] Susan Horwitz, Barbara Ryder, Monica Sweat, Susan H. Rodger, Maureen Biggers, David Binkley, C. Kolin Frantz, Dawn Gundermann, Susanne Hambrusch, Steven Huss-Lederman, and Ethan Munson. 2009. Using peer-led team learning to increase participation and success of under-represented groups in introductory computer science. *ACM SIGCSE Bulletin* 41, 1 (2009), 163. https://doi.org/10.1145/1539024.1508925

[11] Jennifer Jenson, Suzanne De Castell, and Mary Bryson. 2003. "Girl talk": Gender, equity, and identity discourses in a school-based computer culture. *Women's Studies International Forum* 26, 6 (2003), 561–573. https://doi.org/10.1016/j.wsif.2003.09.010

[12] Julie Krause, Irene Polycarpou, and Keith Hellman. 2012. Exploring formal learning groups and their impact on recruitment of women in undergraduate CS. *Proceedings of the 43rd ACM Technical Symposium on Computer Science Education (SIGCSE '12)* (2012), 179. https://doi.org/10.1145/2157136.2157192

[13] Charlie McDowell, Linda Werner, Heather Bullock, and Julian Fernald. 2002. The Effects of Pair-programming on Performance in an Introductory Programming Course. In *Proceedings of the 33rd SIGCSE Technical Symposium on Computer Science Education (SIGCSE '02)*. ACM, New York, NY, USA, 38–42. https://doi.org/10.1145/563340.563353

[14] Charlie McDowell, Linda Werner, Heather E Bullock, and Julian Fernald. 2006. Pair programming improves student retention, confidence and program quality. *Commun. ACM* 49, 8 (2006), 90–95.

[15] Nachiappan Nagappan, Laurie Williams, Miriam Ferzli, Eric Wiebe, Carol Miller, Suzanne Balik, and Kai Yang. 2003. Improving the CS1 Experience with Pair Programming. In *Proceedings of the 34th SIGCSE Technical Symposium on Computer Science Education*. 359–362.

[16] Clem O'Donnell, Jim Buckley, Abdulhussain Mahdi, John Nelson, and Michael English. 2015. Evaluating Pair-Programming for Non-Computer Science Major Students. In *Proceedings of the 46th ACM Technical Symposium on Computer Science Education*. 569–574.

[17] Leo Porter and Beth Simon. 2013. Retaining Nearly One-Third more Majors with a Trio of Instructional Best Practices in CS1. In *Proceeding of the 44th ACM Technical Symposium on Computer Science Education*. Denver, CO, 165–170.

[18] Alex D. Radermacher and Gursimran S. Walia. 2011. Investigating the Effective Implementation of Pair Programming: An Empirical Investigation. In *Proceedings of the 42nd ACM Technical Symposium on Computer Science Education (SIGCSE '11)*. ACM, New York, NY, USA, 655–660. https://doi.org/10.1145/1953163.1953346

[19] Rachael D. Robnett and Campbell Leaper. 2012. Friendship Groups, Personal Motivation, and Gender in Relation to High School Students' STEM Career Interest. *Journal of Research on Adolescence* 23, 4 (2012), 652–664. https://doi.org/10.1111/jora.12013

[20] Mary Beth Rosson, John M. Carroll, and Hansa Sinha. 2011. Orientation of Undergraduates Toward Careers in the Computer and Information Sciences. *ACM Transactions on Computing Education* 11, 3 (2011), 1–14. https://doi.org/10.1145/2037276.2037278

[21] Heather Thiry and Sarah Hug. 2014. "We Should All Help Each Other": Latina Undergraduates' Practices And Identities In The Figured World Of Computing. *International Conference of the Learning Sciences* (2014), 214–221.

[22] United States Department of Labor: Bureau of Labor Statistics. 2018. Employment Projections: Employment by detailed occupation, 2016 and projected 2026.

[23] United States Department of Labor: Bureau of Labor Statistics. 2018. Labor Force Statistics from the Current Population Survey: Employed persons by detailed occupation, sex, race, and Hispanic or Latino ethnicity.

[24] Stuart Zweben and Betsy Bizot. 2017. 2016 Taulbee Survey: Generation CS Continues to Produce Record Undergrad Enrollment; Graduate Degree Production Rises at both Master's and Doctoral Levels. *Computing Research News* 29, 5 (2017), 3–51.

AP Computer Science Principles' Impact on the Landscape of High School Computer Science using Maryland as a Model

Heather Killen
University of Maryland
College Park, Md, USA
hkillen@umd.edu

David Weintrop
University of Maryland
College Park, Md, USA
weintrop@umd.edu

Megean Garvin
University of Maryland, Baltimore Co.
Baltimore, Md, USA
mgarvin@umbc.edu

ABSTRACT

The introduction of the Advanced Placement (AP) Computer Science Principles course changed the high school computer science (CS) landscape in the United States. For the first time an AP course was designed to broaden participation in computing and attract all students as opposed to being designed to challenge the highest performing students. The goal was to design a rigorous and comprehensive CS high school course that highlighted the breadth of the field of CS beyond just programming. With the course first offered for AP credit in the 2016-2017 school year, this study explores how this "introductory advanced" CS course impacted high school CS class offerings. Using data from a state-wide survey and the Maryland Longitudinal Data System Center (MLDSC), we found inconsistent impacts with the AP Computer Science Principles introduction. Some schools increased the number of CS courses while other schools decreased CS course offerings. This was counter to our expectation of an increase in CS classes at the high school level across the state. Responses from a teacher survey yielded insight into this unexpected outcome and informed explanations for these changes.

ACM Reference format:

H. Killen, D. Weintrop, and M. Garvin. 2019. AP Computer Science Principles' Impact on the Landscape of High School Computer Science using Maryland as a Model. In Proceedings of the 50th ACM Technical Symposium on Computer Science Education (SIGCSE '19). Feburary27-March 2, 2019, Minneapolis, MN, USA, ACM, NY, NY, USA, 7 pages. https://doi.org/10.1145/3287324.3287356

KEYWORDS

High School Computer Science Education; Computer Science Principles; Access; ACM Proceedings

1. INTRODUCTION

In 2012 the College Board, with the help of the National Science Foundation, developed a new Advanced Placement (AP) computer science (CS) course. This course, called Computer Sciences Principles (CSP), was specifically designed to be a broader, more welcoming introduction to the discipline than the programming-focused AP CS courses that have been offered since the early 1980's [2]. While programming is part of the curriculum, CSP also emphasizes creativity and problem solving while placing the discipline of CS in context, discussing the role of CS in global society. This broader framing is intended to encourage student populations that have been historically underrepresented (girls, minorities, lower socioeconomic status, English language learners and students with a disability status) to take CS in high school. The hope was that this introduction would be broadly useful and serve as an entry point for learners to pursue further CS instruction as a college major or career, thereby broadening participation in computing.

A number of AP CSP curricula were designed by different organizations to support the new AP CSP offering. These were first made broadly available to schools in the 2012-13 school year [2]. States and schools were therefore given some time to pilot curriculum before the AP CSP course was officially offered for college credit in the 2016-17 school year.

Using the AP program as a means to broadening participation in a field had never before been attempted. This study tries to understand if and how this effort succeeded by investigating how the AP CSP course impacted the CS high school landscape using the State of Maryland as its focus. More concretely, this paper seeks to answer the following research questions:

> *How did the introduction of a new AP CS course designed to provide an introductory advanced CS option affect the CS courses offered at the high school level?*
>
> *How do teachers explain the role of the AP CSP course in the landscape of their school?*

The data for this study comes from three distinct sources: state data from the College Board and the Maryland Longitudinal Data System Center (MLDSC) to determine which CS courses were offered by high schools across the state, and a state-wide survey of CS teachers asking about changes to CS courses at their schools and their understanding of why the changes occurred. These data give us two perspectives on how the introduction of the AP CSP course impacted the landscape of high school CS. We chose these sources to understand how the rollout and adoption of the new AP CSP course, with its unique positioning as an introductory advanced course, is affecting all CS course offerings in the first years of AP CSP exam availability. The goal is to highlight early indications of affordances and unexpected hindrances this new AP course may generate in the overall state landscape of CS education. This understanding can inform educators, administrators and policy makers across the nation tasked with making decisions about what CS courses to offer and if and how to incorporate the AP CSP into existing course offerings. Ultimately, this work will help shed light on one part of the national effort focused on broadening participation in computing.

2. PRIOR WORK

2.1 Computer Science for All

The last decade has seen a significant push to bring computer science to all learners. In the United States, a great deal of progress is due to a concerted funding effort from public and private agencies (e.g. [5, 11]), as well as non-profit organizations (e.g. [14]) focused on giving all learners the opportunity to learn foundational CS ideas. These efforts generally have widespread support from politicians, district leaders, school administration, teachers, students and parents [12]. While much progress has been made, there is still significant work that remains to be done [18, 19]. Initiatives focusing on achieving this lofty goal exist at all levels of the American educational system. This includes countless classroom and school-level initiatives, often led by small groups of committed teachers with the help of local organizations. There are also a growing number of district-level initiatives seeking to bring meaningful CS learning to students across the district, such as those in large urban districts including New York City [8] and Chicago [13], as well as non-urban districts, like the work happening in Broward and Clark Counties [14]. There are also state-wide efforts happening around the United States (e.g. [1, 6]) including an organization sharing best practices [7].

Most recently we are seeing national efforts in the United States that are working towards the goal of CS for all. While there are large scale funding efforts coordinated at the national level, only recently have specific curricular initiatives started looking beyond local and regional impacts toward national roll outs. One example of this can be seen with the Exploring Computer Science (ECS) curriculum [10, 16], which was initially developed and piloted in Southern California, but has since spread to schools across the county (e.g. [15]). A second notable example that our research investigates is the AP CSP course introduced for college credit in the 2016-17 school year. While not a specific course in the same way ECS is a course, AP CSP shares features of a single curricula in that the organization overseeing the program (the College Board) approved and endorsed only ten curricula providers.

This work builds on the growing body of literature investigating how work at the state level can bring CS to all learners (e.g. [1, 4, 7]). This research is similar to work that has looked at the impact of rolling out new CS curricula, in particular, [3]'s investigation of the introduction of the Exploring Computer Science course in Wisconsin. This work differs in that it is looking at an AP curriculum, which has its own set of features and challenges, while also seeking to gain insight into mechanisms behind the adoption (or avoidance) of the new curriculum.

3. STUDY CONTEXT AND METHODOLOGY

3.1 Computer Science in Maryland

This study focuses on the state of Maryland as a model of the changing CS landscape in the United States. We begin this section by reviewing the state of CS in Maryland before discussing the data sources used in the study. The number of Maryland students taking a CS course has been increasing annually, although the rate of increase is not consistent across gender, race and ethnic subgroups [9]. In the spring of 2018 the Maryland state government pledged 5 million dollars to computing education. This was the culmination of almost a decade of efforts by advocates of CS education, starting in 2011 with grassroots support for addressing problems in Maryland high school computing. These efforts led to an NSF funded statewide assessment of Maryland high school CS teachers in 2012 [6]. The following year NSF funded work led to the development of CS Matters, one of ten CSP curricula endorsed by the College Board. In 2015, Maryland representatives joined the 17 state alliance, Expanding Computing Education Pathways [7].

The State of Maryland has 242 public high schools that are organized into 24 local education agencies (LEAs). Each LEA has curricular discretion allowing them to independently decide which courses are offered and which curriculum will be used for each course. This creates multiple places across the state where decisions are made regarding what CS courses are offered in schools, creating a dynamic environment statewide for computing education. This organizational structure means there is no centralized body that decides what CS courses will be taught across the state, making Maryland a particularly good state to study how a new AP CS course impacts the landscape of CS education as there 24 independent LEAs make decisions about what to teach.

3.2 Data Sources and Methodology

Through partnerships with the college Board and the Maryland Longitudinal Data System Center (MLDSC) we obtained two data sets. The College Board provided data including how many public Maryland high schools offered AP CS A (the pre-existing AP CS course), AP CSP or both during the 2016/17 and 2017/18 school years. In addition, we queried the MLDSC to determine how many high schools had offered the CSP course in the previous three years (2012-13 to 2015-16 school years). This allowed us to identify schools that were piloting the course before the College Board offered the CSP AP exam.

In addition to College Board and MLDSC data, this paper analyzed data collected through a statewide landscape survey of Maryland public high school teachers. Beginning in 2012, the Maryland Center for Computing Education (MCCE) has conducted an electronic survey in alternating years of teachers and school administrators interested in computing education. The survey is based on the CSTA National Secondary School CS Survey and is distributed to the 1000+ person MCCE Contact Database of CS educators and advocates across the state.

To determine CS teachers' perceptions of CS offerings at their schools two questions were added to the 2018 landscape survey. The questions were designed to inquire about changes in course offerings at teachers' schools in the years just before and just after the AP CSP was officially offered for college credit. The exact wording of the questions was as follows:

Last school year (i.e., between the 2015/16 and 2016/17 school years), did your school make any changes to the computer science courses at your school? (Please indicate if your school had no changes, altered a computer science graduation pathway, added a new course, removed a course, changed the curriculum for a course, etc., and then, describe why you believe the changes occurred.)

This school year (i.e., between the 2016/17 and 2017/18 school years), did your school make any changes to the computer science courses at your school? (Please indicate if your school had no changes, altered a computer science graduation pathway, added a new course, removed a course, changed the curriculum for a course, etc., and then, describe why you believe the changes occurred.)

The 2018 landscape survey collected a total of 94 responses. Respondents represented 69 of the 242 Maryland public high schools and 22 of the 24 Maryland LEAs. Responses were open coded using a grounded theory approach to identify the patterns in changes of school computer science offerings [17]. This produced a set of insights complementary to the MLDSC data, allowing us to understand the changes observed at the system level and provide insight into teachers' overall perceptions of how CS at their school changed during the first two years of the AP CSP course being offered. Five codes related to perceptions regarding the increase of CS offerings in schools were determined.

4. FINDINGS

4.1 Dynamism in State-wide CS

At first glance, the introduction of AP CSP had a negligible impact on the statewide CS landscape. MLDSC data recorded a 3% decrease in Maryland high schools offering any AP CS courses from 2013 to 2018 (Table 1). This result is misleading. When the data is differentiated by course (AP CSP, AP CS A and both AP CSP and AP CS A) a more dynamic picture of a changing CS landscape emerges. AP CSP was rarely taught before the 2016-17 school year. Only 24 high schools in the state (10%) offered an AP CSP course before fall of 2016. This is not surprising, as these were the piloting years before the formal launch of AP CSP. In the 2016-17 school year, the number of schools that taught only AP CSP and schools that were teaching both AP CSP and AP CS A increased to 12% and 30% respectively. Meanwhile, schools that were only teaching AP CS A decreased from 43% to 9%. Taken together, this demonstrates a high-level impact that the AP CSP course introduction had on schools, and thus students, across a large, decentralized state.

Table 1. Number of AP CS ***classes*** taught in Maryland high schools and the number of Maryland ***high schools*** offering those classes from 2013 to 2018.

	Classes in % of total high schools		
	2013-14 to 2015-16	2016-17	2017-18
AP CSP only	7 in 3%	28 in 12%	28 in 12%
AP CSA only	104 in 43%	21 in 9%	15 in 6%
Both AP CSA and AP CSP	34 in 7%	150 in 30%	152 in 31%
All AP CS classes taught	145 in 52%	199 in 51%	195 in 49%
All AP CSP taught	24 in 10%	103 in 43%	104 in 43%

These data also reveal that AP CSP has been adopted quickly. College Board data record a 433% increase in high schools that offered the AP CSP course from 2013 to 2018, growing from 10% of MD high schools to 43% during that time. By the 2017-18 school year, the first year the College Board offered the CSP AP exam, the number of Maryland high schools offering AP CSP had increased to 43% of total schools. In the same period the number of Maryland high schools offering AP CS A decreased from 50% to 38%. Maryland high schools offering any kind of AP CS course decreased slightly (from 52% to 49%) during that same time, likely reflecting schools dropping AP CS A from their annual course offerings. Collectively, this reveals a pattern of schools replacing AP CS A with AP CSP, a pattern with potential implications that we turn to later in this paper.

4. 2 An Increase in CS Courses State-wide

We were also interested in understanding how the introduction of AP CSP changed the CS landscape within schools at the course level. To get some understanding of this, we used the MLDSC and College Board data to extrapolate a minimum number of CS **classes** offered in Maryland schools. We calculated a **minimum estimate** because we have no information on how many sections of a particular course a school might be offering. There are Maryland high schools in which more than one class of AP CSP or AP CS A is offered, which our data do not capture. There are also schools that are offering CS A and CSP courses as non-AP courses, which we have not captured. Working within these limitations (assuming that only one section of every course was taught at every school and every CS A and CSP course was taught as an AP course), we determined that the introduction of

AP CSP increased the overall number of individual AP CS courses offered by Maryland public high schools by at least 27%, from 145 to 195 courses (Table 1). Table one also demonstrates how quickly AP CSP has been adopted in the state, as 104 of the total 195 CS classes offered state-wide (53%) in 2017-18 were AP CSP.

4.3 Dynamism within individual LEAs

Having looked at the state as a whole, we then looked at individual LEA data to get as clear a picture as the data allowed to determine where exactly these changes were occurring and to see if we could identify a pattern, specific characteristics or potential explanations for this dynamism. The MLDSC data demonstrates that the complex and dynamic landscape at the state level is also found within LEAs. Between the 2016-17 and 2017-18 school years, this dynamism resulted in a variety of outcomes regarding the number of high schools offering CS courses LEA-wide (Figure 1). The most prevalent situation, found in 11 LEAs, was an equal number of AP CS course additions and subtractions in schools, resulting in no net gain or loss of schools that offered AP CS.

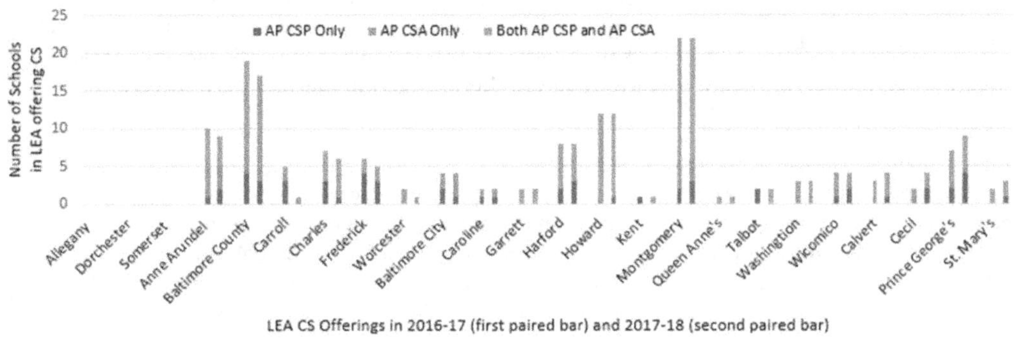

Figure 1. Number of schools offering AP CS courses by Maryland LEA

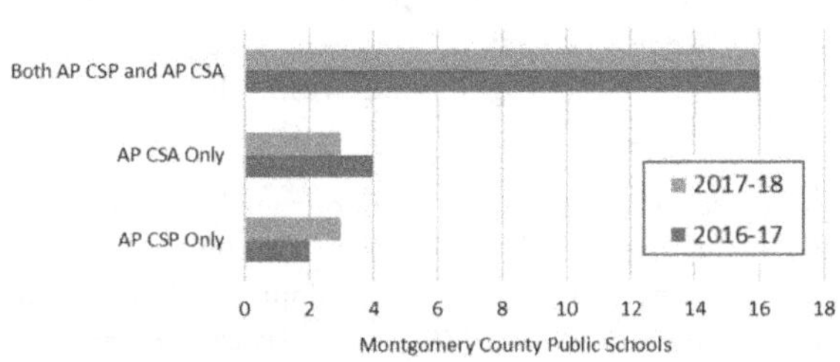

Figure 2. Schools in Montgomery LEA offering AP CS courses.

For example, Montgomery LEA had 22 schools that offered some sort of CS course in 2016-17 and 22 schools that offered some sort of CS course in 2017-18. This stasis masks a drop in the number of schools offering AP CS A and an increase in the number of schools offering AP CSP (Figure 2).

The next most common situation, represented by 6 LEAs, was a combination of school level AP CS course additions and subtractions that resulted in a net decrease in schools offering AP CS courses. These schools also show a dynamic landscape. Anne Arundel LEA increased the number of schools offering only AP CSP while losing schools that offered just AP CS A or both (Figure 3). Four LEAs had a combination of AP CS course additions and subtractions that resulted in a net increase in schools offering AP CS courses. Three LEAs had no AP CS offerings for either year (Figure 1).

It was hoped that the introduction of AP CSP would enable schools that had not been offering AP CS courses to start doing so. Our analysis indicates that this has generally not been the pattern. Seven LEAs distributed throughout the state had at least one high school that was not offering any AP CS courses add AP CSP over the 2016-17 and 2017-18 school years. We determined that only 11 of the 242 public high schools in the state offered AP CSP as their first ever CS offering. Five LEAs had at least one high school offer a single AP CS course and then added the other course, so that they offered both AP CSP and AP CSA. This was the case for six high schools in the state.

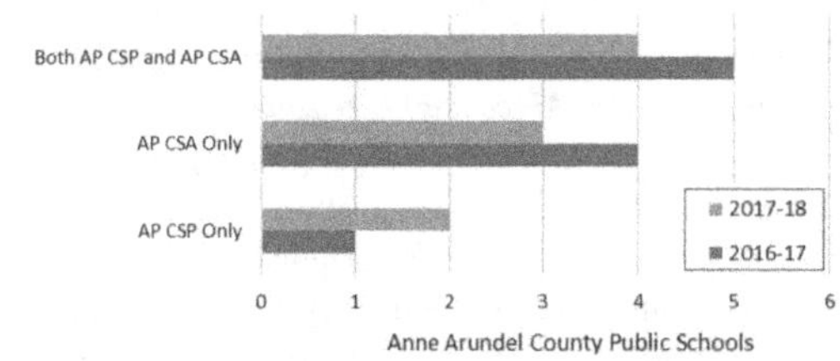

Figure 3. Schools in Anne Arundel LEA offering AP CS courses.

Our analysis also determined that LEAs were dropping CS courses between the 2016-17 and the 2017-18 school years. In four LEAs, a high school offered both AP CSP and AP CS A in the 2016-17 school year but then dropped a CS course in the 2017-18 school year. Three LEAs had high schools that had offered only AP CSP in the 2016-17 school year and dropped the course in the 2017-18 school year, offering no AP CS course. It is possible that this was the case for other schools as well, but because the data we have are aggregated by LEA the situation could be masked by what other schools in the district had done. From our data it is also not possible to determine which AP CS course was dropped when a school stopped teaching both AP CS courses.

4.4 Teacher Perceptions of Changes

To start to understand the mechanisms behind the observed dynamism, we next looked to the MCCE landscape survey data for further insight into changes observed due to the introduction of the AP CSP course. Fifty-five of the ninety-four respondents reported expanding CS programs in their schools. Expansion includes increasing course offerings or recruiting students and increasing enrollment. This is related in the following two teachers' responses: *"I heavily recruited for next year and will have 3 times the foundations students and a second AP course (AP Computer Science A)"* and *"Began teaching Foundations of Computer Science in 2016-17 with one course. 2017-18 we had two sections of FoCS!"*.

Our analysis identified five reasons AP CSP was adopted in Maryland public high schools.

Reason 1: AP CSP is being used as a (often intermediate) stage in a CS track/pathway

Most commonly in the survey, teachers mention existing introductory CS curricula (e.g. Foundations of CS and Exploring CS) as acting as a lead into AP CSP. In such cases, AP CSP can then serve as a way to prepare learners for AP CS A and a possible capstone project. A feature of this design is this four-course sequence can act as a complete high school CS pathway that covers all four years. Twelve of the 94 respondents mentioned adding a CS course to build a CS pathway of this nature. Ten of these discuss AP CSP as an intermediate course with another respondent framing AP CSP as first in a potential pathways sequence. One respondent described Foundations of CS leading to AP CSA, with no mention of AP CSP.

We can see how the new course shaped emerging CS pathways by looking at year-over-year changes within the same school For example, one teacher gave the following response for the 2016-17 question: "*Yes, added a new course 2016-17 AP CSP for first time was turned into a full-year AP level course (had been offered as semester, non-AP course); - reason: offered nationwide as AP in that year for the first time, school growing a new pathway.*" In the subsequent question, asking about the following school year, the teacher wrote: "*yes, added a new course 2017-18 AP CSA offered for first time; - reason: pathway just started, adding one course at a time; also switched curriculum for Foundations of CS course from Exploring CS to CS Discoveries at prompting of district & professional development offered*"

Reason 2: External requirements / CSP now fulfills a graduation requirement

Ten respondents discussed changes in their schools' course offerings during the years surrounding the introduction of AP CSP in terms of graduation requirement. Three specifically mention CSP, 6 discuss Foundations of CS (one person discussed both CSP and Foundations) and 2 discuss general CS. "*We added more foundations of cs and AP CS P courses. This was due to increased enrollment. I believe that the two courses now counting as the tech ed graduation requirement has greatly increased enrollment.*" A second, more direct example of this can be seen in the response: "*We added 'AP Computer Science Principles' to align ourselves with county course requirements and to offer an AP course to meet the technology education graduation requirement.*"

Reason 3: Content beyond programming more appealing

There were four respondents that discussed the shift from CS courses focusing on programming to a broader view of CS as part of the motivation for introducing AP CSP at their schools. "*Principles of Programming was changed to Foundations of Computer Science to align with curriculum promoted by code.org and professional development. It also added more emphasis on a greater range of topics in CS other than just programming.*" It is important to note that this shift to a broader view of CS was not always viewed positively. "*Programming classes were eliminated (pure code writing which many of my students wish they could do as a CS course) - not as much interest without courses now that are code driven. Students want to learn how to program and those courses are gone.*" This latter quote is interesting as it is counter to the larger narrative in CS education circles and the desire to downplay programming and its centrality to the field. This suggests a need for further research to better understand the characteristics of this school and why this might be the case. We will return to this idea later in the discussion section.

Reason 4. AP is compelling to students/ AP adds value to a CS track/pathway

The fact that the new introductory course was an AP course was also mentioned by teachers as a reason for adoption. Of the two respondents who mentioned this, one reported this positively while the other reported it negatively. Viewed positively, one teacher responded: "*Our school has a three course sequence. Last year, we changed the second course from a generic elective called "Programming and Computer Concepts" to AP Computer Science Principles. This was a positive change for enrollment. A lot of high-level students weren't willing to take an unweighted elective in this slot. Now the CS program has two back-to-back AP courses, making it hold sufficiently more value for students. During the prior class, students were doing AP level work, but not getting any credit for it.*" At the same time, another teacher saw the opposite outcome, writing "*added sections of Computer Science Principles AP and Java; CSP-AP sections are needed due to more enrollment caused by a push by to take an easy AP course. This is not a good thing; it causes a decrease in enrollment in legitimate course.*" Similarly to reason 3, the mixed response from teachers speaks to the complexity and challenges related to introducing a new course with broad goals. Specifically, the suggestion that AP CSP might not be a "legitimate course" reflects larger issues related to perceptions of what "real CS" is and the centrality of programming within the discipline.

Reason 5. CSP allows for more flexibility in a CS track

The final reason that emerged from our analysis was given by a single teacher who cited the increased flexibility that came with the AP CSP course as the reason for adoption. *"Last year we changes AP CS A from a two credit (two period) class to a one credit (one period class.) Reason for this change was the double period restricted the number of students enrolling and with AP CS Principles, do not need two class periods.*" This speaks to the quality of the materials associated with the new course and how much care was taken to ensure it could fit within existing educational infrastructure.

5. DISCUSSION

5.1 Shifting Landscape of High School CS

We highlight how the CS landscape in a decentralized state looks profoundly different after the introduction of AP CSP. In the two years since the official introduction of AP CSP, Maryland has had a 3% drop in the number of schools offering any AP CS courses but a significant increase (from 10% to 43%) in high schools that offered AP CSP. Meanwhile, the number of high schools offering AP CS A has dropped from 50% to 38%. It is likely that dropping AP CS A from school CS offerings is responsible for the statewide drop in CS courses offered. In contrast to the overall state-wide decrease in **schools** offering CS, introduction of AP CSP has increased AP CS **classes** by at least 27%. AP CSP has been quickly adopted and is now the most commonly taught CS class in the state (53% of all CS classes taught are AP CSP).

Examining the school-level LEA data we can determine that the introduction of AP CSP has convinced only 3% of Maryland schools to adopt an AP CS course who had not previously offered AP CS to their students. While any increase is a positive outcome, this suggests the impact of AP CSP was less in the form of introducing CS to schools, and instead, was in one of two ways: changing existing CS courses towards something designed to be more broadly appealing and expanding offerings, thus providing more opportunities for learners to take CS. Some schools have added AP CSP to enhance a preexisting CS curriculum, while others have dropped teaching AP CSP in the 2017-18 school year, so that these schools no longer offer any CS course. Unfortunately, because the College Board and MLDSC data are given at the LEA level, there are still some gaps to be uncovered to fully explain trends.

5.2 Varying Needs of Schools

The diversity of reasons given by teachers for why their respective schools chose to introduce the new AP CSP course is an interesting finding. In some instances, the reasons matched the motivations of the designers of the new course, namely, the desire to have a new course that presents a broader picture of what the field of CS includes and frame the discipline in a way that attracts a broader range of students. Teachers also gave justifications that spoke more to institutional requirements, including the desire to have a fourth course to fill out a full four-year CS or the general desire for a course to bridge the existing introductory course and the more challenging AP CS A course. What is interesting about this second line of motivation is that it is orthogonal to the first motivation (and the motivation of the designers). If a school was looking for a fourth CS course to add, it could have just as easily been a course on physical computing or advanced data analysis as one designed to broaden participation.

These differing motivations highlight features and tensions of the decision to both create the AP CSP course and to use the AP mechanism in the first place. Features result in hundreds of schools across the country introducing a new course focused on broadening participation to learners. Tensions can be seen in the data presented above. First, that there are many instances of AP CSP replacing an existing CS course, which does not expand access. While this may be a positive change, it is easy to imagine instances where the net effect is less than desirable, a fact reflected in some of the comments given by teachers. Secondly, that AP CSP is being used to solve numerous different problems. As a result, there may be places where AP CSP is not the ideal solution but the best or easiest available. This is an artifact of the variety of challenges faced by schools seeking to introduce more CS into the curriculum. The fact that a single AP course is being used to fill very different needs across schools in very different situations speaks to the larger need for more research in the world K-12 CS education, from developing curricula to training teachers and educating decision makers. Additional case-specific solutions need to be developed to meet the specific needs of different states, LEAs, and schools.

5.3 Limitations and Future Work

Part of the value of this work is that it affords a very early snapshot into how AP CSP is being adopted at a state level. Working in almost real time, however, limits our ability to attain a complete picture, as we don't yet have access to data regarding student enrollment or the number of sections of AP CSP that are being offered. Longitudinal data will be needed to understand if what we are reporting is a blip or a lasting trend.

6. CONCLUSION

The goal of this work is to understand how a new, national CS course designed to broaden participation in computing affected the high school CS course landscape. To answer this question, we focused on a single state prior to and immediately after the introduction of the AP CSP exam. There are two main findings from our work.

First, the introduction of AP CSP increased the number of CS courses offered by Maryland public high schools. This change took place mainly in schools that were already offering CS courses, so the AP CSP course appears to have had relatively little impact in terms of bringing CS into schools where historically it had not been taught. In this respect, at a school-level, AP CSP did not broaden participation in CS in schools where CS was not historically offered. That being said, the data also show that the new course is achieving its goals. The number of schools that offered only CS A across the state dropped significantly as they either swapped CSP for CS A or added CSP alongside CS A. Likewise, the data reveal examples of expanding pathways and increased enrollment tied to the AP CSP course, highlighting the successes of the program.

Second, AP CSP was incorporated into schools to fill several different needs. Based on the experiences of teachers from across the state, our analysis revealed several different motivations, including the need for an intermediate course between base introductory courses and the existing AP CS A course and the need of an additional course to fulfill a four-year high school CS pathway.

The analysis and findings presented in this work illustrate the complex landscape and dynamic nature of the constantly-shifting state of CS education in American high schools. Further, this paper highlights the different experiences of individual teachers and schools with respect to trying to meet the growing call for CS for all. While more work remains to be done to fully understand the new emerging landscape of CS in high schools across the country, this analysis begins to tell the story of how and why the new AP CSP is changing the landscape of high school CS.

7. REFERENCES

[1] Adrion, R., Fall, R., Ericson, B. and Guzdial, M. 2016. Broadening access to computing education state by state. *Communications of the ACM.* 59, 2 (Jan. 2016), 32–34. DOI:https://doi.org/10.1145/2856455.

[2] Arpaci-Dusseau, A. et al. 2013. Computer Science Principles: Analysis of a Proposed Advanced Placement Course. *Proceeding of the 44th ACM Technical Symposium on Computer Science Education* (New York, NY, USA, 2013), 251–256.

[3] Bort, H., Guha, S. and Brylow, D. 2018. The Impact of Exploring Computer Science in Wisconsin: Where Disadvantage is an Advantage. *Proceedings of the 23rd Annual ACM Conference on Innovation and Technology in Computer Science Education* (New York, NY, USA, 2018), 57–62.

[4] Camp, T., Adrion, W.R., Bizot, B., Davidson, S., Hall, M., Hambrusch, S., Walker, E. and Zweben, S. 2017. Generation CS: the growth of computer science. *ACM Inroads.* 8, 2 (May 2017), 44–50. DOI:https://doi.org/10.1145/3084362.

[5] Cuny, J. 2015. Transforming K-12 Computing Education: An Update and a Call to Action. *ACM Inroads.* 6, 3 (Aug. 2015), 54–57. DOI:https://doi.org/10.1145/2809795.

[6] desJardins, M. and Martin, S. 2013. CE21–Maryland: the state of computer science education in Maryland high schools. *Proceeding of the 44th ACM technical symposium on Computer science education* (2013), 711–716.

[7] Ericson, B., Adrion, W.R., Fall, R. and Guzdial, M. 2016. State-Based Progress Towards Computer Science for All. *ACM Inroads.* 7, 4 (Nov. 2016), 57–60. DOI:https://doi.org/10.1145/2994607.

[8] Fancsali, C., Tigani, L., Toro Isaza, P. and Cole, R. 2018. A Landscape Study of Computer Science Education in NYC: Early Findings and Implications for Policy and Practice. (2018), 44–49.

[9] Garvin, M., Neary, M., Carrigan, K. and desJardins, M. 2018. Maryland Computing Education Growth From 2011-2016. *Paper presented at RESPECT 2018* (Baltimore, MD, 2018).

[10] Goode, J. and Margolis, J. 2011. Exploring Computer Science: A Case Study of School Reform. *ACM Transactions on Computing Education.* 11, 2 (Jul. 2011), 1–16. DOI:https://doi.org/10.1145/1993069.1993076.

[11] Google 2015. *Searching for Computer Science: Access and Barriers in U.S. K-12 Education.*

[12] Google Inc. and Gallup Inc. 2016. *Trends in the State of Computer Science in U.S. K-12 Schools.*

[13] McGee, S., Wilkerson, B., Yanek, D., Rasmussen, A.M., Brylow, D., McGee-Tekula, R., Duck, J., McGee, C., Dettori, L., Greenberg, R.I., Snow, E., Rutstein, D. and Reed, D. 2018. Equal Outcomes 4 All: A Study of Student Learning in ECS. *Proceedings of the 49th ACM Technical Symposium on Computer Science Education - SIGCSE '18* (Baltimore, Maryland, USA, 2018), 50–55.

[14] Partovi, H. 2015. A comprehensive effort to expand access and diversity in computer science. *ACM Inroads.* 6, 3 (Aug. 2015), 67–72. DOI:https://doi.org/10.1145/2807704.

[15] Reed, D., Wilkerson, B., Yanek, D., Dettori, L. and Solin, J. 2015. How exploring computer science (ECS) came to Chicago. *ACM Inroads.* 6, 3 (2015), 75–77.

[16] Ryoo, J.J., Margolis, J., Lee, C.H., Sandoval, C.D. and Goode, J. 2013. Democratizing computer science knowledge: transforming the face of computer science through public high school education. *Learning, Media and Technology.* 38, 2 (Jun. 2013), 161–181. DOI:https://doi.org/10.1080/17439884.2013.756514.

[17] Strauss, A. and Corbin, J. 1994. Grounded Theory Methodology: An Overview. *Strategies of Qualitative Inquiry.* Sage Publications, Inc. 158–183.

[18] Wang, J., Hong, H., Ravitz, J. and Hejazi Moghadam, S. 2016. Landscape of K-12 Computer Science Education in the U.S.: Perceptions, Access, and Barriers. *Proceedings of the 47th ACM Technical Symposium on Computing Science Education - SIGCSE '16* (Memphis, Tennessee, USA, 2016), 645–650.

[19] Wilson, C., Sudol, L.A., Stephenson, C. and Stehlik, M. 2010. *Running on Empty: The Failure to Teach K–12 Computer Science in the Digital Age.* The Association for Computing Machinery and the Computer Science Teachers Association.

An Examination of the Correlation of Exploring Computer Science Course Performance and the Development of Programming Expertise

Steven McGee
The Learning Partnership
Chicago, Illinois
mcgee@lponline.net

Ronald I. Greenberg
Loyola University Chicago
Chicago, Illinois
rig@cs.luc.edu

Randi McGee-Tekula
The Learning Partnership
Chicago, Illinois
rmcgee@lponline.net

Jennifer Duck
The Learning Partnership
Chicago, Illinois
jenn@lponline.net

Andrew M. Rasmussen
Chicago Public Schools
Chicago, Illinois
arasmussen@cps.edu

Lucia Dettori
Chicago Public Schools
Chicago, Illinois
ldettori@cps.edu

Dale F. Reed
University of Illinois at Chicago
Chicago, Illinois
reed@uic.edu

ABSTRACT

This study investigated patterns in the development of computational thinking and programming expertise in the context of the Exploring Computer Science (ECS) program, a high school introductory CS course and professional development program designed to foster deep engagement through equitable inquiry around CS concepts. Prior research on programming expertise has identified three general areas of development – program comprehension, program planning, and program generation. The pedagogical practices in ECS are consistent with problem solving approaches that support the development of programming expertise. The study took place in a large urban district during the 2016–17 school year with 28 ECS teachers and 1,931 students. A validated external assessment was used to measure the development of programming expertise. The results indicate that there were medium-sized, statistically significant increases from pretest to posttest, and there were no statistically significant differences by gender or race/ethnicity. After controlling for prior academic achievement, performance in the ECS course correlated with performance on the posttest. With respect to specific programming concepts, the results also provide evidence on the progression of the development of programming expertise. Students seem to develop comprehension and planning expertise prior to expertise in program generation. In addition, students seem to develop expertise with concrete tasks prior to abstract tasks.

SIGCSE '19, February 27–March 2, 2019, Minneapolis, MN, USA

ACM ISBN 978-1-4503-5890-3/19/02...$15.00
https://doi.org/10.1145/3287324.3287415

CCS CONCEPTS

• **Social and professional topics → Computational thinking**; **Student assessment**; *Model curricula*; *K-12 education*.

KEYWORDS

high school computer science; Exploring Computer Science; computer programming skills

ACM Reference Format:
Steven McGee, Ronald I. Greenberg, Randi McGee-Tekula, Jennifer Duck, Andrew M. Rasmussen, Lucia Dettori, and Dale F. Reed. 2019. An Examination of the Correlation of Exploring Computer Science Course Performance and the Development of Programming Expertise. In *SIGCSE '19: 50th ACM Technical Symposium on Computer Science Education, February 27–March 2, 2019, Minneapolis, MN, USA.* ACM, New York, NY, USA, 7 pages. https://doi.org/10.1145/3287324.3287415

1 INTRODUCTION

"*Our economy is rapidly shifting, and both educators and business leaders are increasingly recognizing that computer science (CS) is a 'new basic' skill necessary for economic opportunity and social mobility.*" – White House Blog [24]

With President Obama's announcement of the Computer Science For All Initiative in 2016, there has been a surge in the number of districts that are planning for or newly implementing computer science (CS) offerings at their schools. Since the dawn of the modern, standards-based era [19], this is the first time that a new subject area is gaining prominence as a core subject. As seen in the White House blog entry, much of the rhetoric around the Computer Science for All initiative has focused on broadening participation by increasing the number of women and minorities who pursue computer science as a career. Broadening participation is an important focus given the dismal levels of participation of women and minorities in computer science. However, without attending to the structural barriers to participation [14], programs that propagate traditional approaches to CS education are unlikely to contribute to the goal of broadening participation.

In a review of computing research, Sheard and colleagues [23] identified a variety of strategies with empirical support on their effectiveness at improving computing outcomes. In particular, they highlight the explicit teaching of planning strategies, pair programming, and collaborative learning. In addition, Robins and colleagues [22] summarize empirical support that a problem solving approach is an effective means to develop programming expertise. On the other hand, Robins and colleagues have also documented that despite this evidence, some CS educators believe that such problem-solving, collaborative approaches to CS can 'dumb down' the curriculum.

Pears and colleagues [20] make a plea for more large-scale, systematic research that examines the relationship between teaching techniques and student outcomes. In order to support generalizations across initiatives, it is important for researchers to be explicit about the pedagogical techniques being used and to use a common framework for characterizing student outcomes. In this study, we examine two research questions related to the correlation between a particular problem-solving approach to teaching high school computer science and the development of programming expertise. (a) To what extent does student performance in the Exploring Computer Science course correlate with performance on the end of course exam? (b) Which aspects of programming expertise are the most difficult for students to develop? In the next section, we discuss a prominent high school computer science curriculum that explicitly incorporates the aforementioned empirically supported pedagogies.

1.1 Exploring Computer Science

The Exploring Computer Science (ECS) curriculum and professional development program was developed at the University of California, Los Angeles and the University of Oregon, with the goal of contributing to broadened participation of women and minorities and increased equity in the field of computer science [14]. Specifically, the ECS curriculum seeks to accomplish this goal of broadening participation by introducing the field of computer science and computational practices in a way that makes the field relevant, engaging, and stimulating for a diverse population of students. The ECS curriculum is composed of activities that are designed to engage students in computer science inquiry around meaningful problems; the ECS professional development program is designed to prepare teachers to implement these inquiry-based activities while also guiding teachers in building a classroom culture that's culturally relevant and inclusive of all students.

When computer science is not taught for deep engagement, but rather as an abstract academic subject, it privileges access to mostly Caucasian, male students [14]. To play an integral role in such classrooms, students must master abstract programming for programming's sake. In contrast, the ECS curriculum is designed to engender deep engagement with important computer science concepts using important features of communities in which youths participate outside the classroom. General technology use outside of school by youths of all races and genders tends to revolve around making social connections and working on practical problems [12]. As suggested by the research reviews cited above, reorienting computer science instruction to focus on problem-solving experiences that are meaningful to students has the potential to increase access to computer science content. In addition, collaborative learning and paired programming techniques create opportunities for students to learn from each other.

At the core of ECS are a set of high-leverage teaching practices [9] that support the three interwoven teaching strands of ECS: equity, inquiry, and CS concepts. The following high-leverage teaching practices enable students to equitably participate in student-led inquiry around important CS concepts: (a) provide a meaningful context for learning; (b) scaffold the development of CS concepts; (c) facilitate peer inquiry and collaboration; and (d) encourage multiple forms of expression [7, pp. 7–8]. Inclusiveness is supported by focusing on ideas that are meaningful to students, and activities in the curriculum provide space for teachers to incorporate students' background and culture. In addition, many activities focus on real-life issues in the community; for example, students can make games that communicate messages about healthy eating or about the plight of undocumented students [15]. Resting on equity are inquiry-based activities in which students are "expected and encouraged to help define the initial conditions of problems, utilize their prior knowledge, work collaboratively, make claims using their own words, and develop multiple representations of particular solutions" [15]. By engaging students in equitable inquiry through the first two strands, students gain access to the domain content of computer science, the third strand.

1.2 Computer Science Content in ECS

For this study, we will use the context of ECS to investigate whether the ECS problem-solving approach correlates with the development of programming expertise. We will also contribute to the literature by engaging in a large-scale, systematic study of ECS implementation. We focused on the development of programming expertise in the context of students in the Chicago Public Schools (CPS) who are participating in an ECS course. CPS is the first school district in the United States to enact computer science as a high school graduation requirement. ECS is a primary course through which students fulfill the requirement. This research has been conducted in the context of the Chicago Alliance For Equity in Computer Science (CAFÉCS), which is an ongoing researcher-practitioner partnership between CPS, The Learning Partnership, DePaul University, Loyola University, and the University of Illinois at Chicago [3, 4]. (Some important prior research results produced by the alliance report on the impact of the ECS course on students' attitudes towards computer science [2], students' choices about future CS coursework [16], and students' development of computational thinking practices [17].)

As recommended by the research review of Robins and colleagues [22], the ECS course first introduces students to general problem solving that is abstracted from any specific language. In the subsequent unit on programming, the ECS sequence generally follows the 'chain of cognitive accomplishments,' involving three general phases as described by Linn and Dalbey [13]. (a) Students first develop comprehension of specific language features by studying their usage within specific case examples. For example, to investigate the concept of conditionals, the teacher engages students in a game of asking them to stand up if something is true, such as if a student is a girl AND wearing a blue shirt. Students are able to develop an appreciation of the feature of a language before engaging in the syntax of a language. (b) Next, the students focus on planning solutions through problem solving scenarios. For example, students apply their knowledge of conditionals to develop a Rock, Paper, Scissors game. They use pseudocode to plan out the possible winning scenarios based on combinations of rock, paper, and scissors. (c) Lastly, the programming unit culminates in students generating code to develop a programming project of their own choosing. The students define the problem, plan out a solution, and then use the features of the programming language to implement their solution.

The development of expertise in comprehending programs, planning, and generation of programs has been studied in the literature [22]. The bulk of this research focused on comprehension of programs — examining the extent to which students demonstrate understanding of an existing program. Research on planning highlights the need for students to organize their thinking prior to translating program specifications into program code. Less research has been done on program generation in which students create part of or a whole program to meet a set of criteria.

These "cognitive aspects of children and novices learning computational concepts were studied extensively in the 1980s" [10, p. 42] but have received less attention since then [10]. Research on planning has shown that students generally spend very little time planning, which suggests a need to focus explicitly on supporting students' planning efforts. Students are able to reason about surface features of a problem, but have difficulty envisioning the unknowns of given problems. In the area of program generation, research has shown that students have particular difficulty with conditionals and loops [18, 21]. In general, educators need to be realistic about what can be accomplished within an introductory CS course.

2 MEASUREMENT OF PROGRAMMING EXPERTISE

To measure the development of programming expertise, we used assessments that were aligned to the computational thinking concepts in ECS [6]. The assessments were developed and field tested by SRI International over two years using Evidence-Centered Design (ECD), an assessment methodology that is especially advantageous when the knowledge and skills to be measured involve complex, multistep performances. The ECD process involved (1) working with various stakeholders to identify the important computer science skills to measure, (2) mapping those skills to a model of evidence that can support inferences about those skills, and (3) developing tasks that elicit that evidence. The assessments were field tested with 941 students over two years [6]. Separate pretest and posttest forms were created. The pretest contains six tasks that measure students' initial understanding of CS concepts and computational thinking. Across the six tasks there are a total of 19 subtasks that are scored independently. The posttest contains five tasks, two of which were on the pretest and three of which were different. The two common tasks were used to equate the two forms and allow for measurement of growth from pretest to posttest. SRI developed scoring rubrics with student work examples for each of the tasks. Across all of the pretest and posttest tasks, there are a total of 30 question prompts that are each scored individually. The assessments and scoring rubrics can be accessed from the SRI assessment website [11]

A subset of the tasks were used for this analysis to examine the development of student expertise in comprehension, planning, and generation. In keeping with the recommendation of being realistic about the expectations for students, the assessment tasks targeted narrow aspects of each ability that were aligned with the expectations of the ECS curriculum.

Within program comprehension, there were two tasks that were assessed. First students were provided with a written algorithm. They were given an input value and asked to determine what the program output would be. Next students were given a scenario in which three drivers with cars needed to pick up 12 passengers for a concert and no more than five people could be in one car. Given an approach to efficiently picking up the passengers, students need to determine whether the algorithm will meet the criteria.

Under planning, students used the same driver and passenger scenario. They were asked to determine which inputs were provided in the scenario and which important inputs were not provided in the scenario. In a separate task, students were asked to provide requirements for a program that would help a teacher track student information.

For program generation, students were provided with an algorithm that is abstracted from any given language. They are then asked to decide which step in the algorithm would use a Scratch conditional block and which step would use a Repeat-Until Loop. Based on the chain of cognitive accomplishments cited above, we hypothesized that comprehension would be the least complex, followed by planning and then generation. As discussed below, this hypothesis about levels of complexity of the tasks was tested using the Rasch scaling method to estimate the relative level of difficulty of each set of tasks.

3 METHODS

This study was undertaken by CAFÉCS in the context of the implementation of ECS in CPS. There were 90 teachers who taught an ECS course during the 2016–17 school year to 6,425 students. The school district invited all of the teachers to administer the pretests at the beginning of the school year and the posttests at the end of the school year. There were 28 teachers with 1,931 students who administered both the pretests and posttests to their students. These teachers and their students were included in the study. The remaining ECS teachers were dropped from the study since they provided only partial data or no data.

Table 1 shows the demographic characteristics of the students who were included in the study, and, for comparison, the demographic characteristics of the remaining ECS students as well as the total district high school population. Statistical comparisons of each demographic characteristic were conducted between the ECS research participants and ECS non-participants. Asterisks indicate those demographic characteristics in which there was a statistically significant difference between the research participants and non-participants.

Table 1: Demographic characteristics of ECS research participants in comparison to non-research ECS students and all district high school students. An asterisk in the research sample column indicates that value is statistically significantly different from the ECS sample.

Characteristics	District	Other ECS	Research Sample
Number of students	**109,053**	**4494**	**1931**
Female	–	45%	42%
Caucasian	8%	12%	15%*
African-American	40%	29%	20%*
Hispanic	46%	46%	58%*
Asian	4%	8%	5%
Low Income	83%	86%	82%*
Special Ed	16%	13%	14%
ESL	8%	9%	9%
Freshman	25%	66%	71%*
Attendance	88%	92%	91%
GPA	–	2.7	2.7

In general, there were fewer females than males who completed the ECS course, but there was no statistical difference between research participants and non-participants. The largest racial demographic group in ECS were Hispanic students followed by African-American students. In the research sample, there was a larger percentage of Hispanic and Caucasian students and a lower percentage of African-American students than the non-research participants. The research population had a lower percentage of low-income students. The proportion of special education, and English language learners was similar as was the rates of attendance and the overall GPA. Given the large sample size, there were sufficient numbers of students in each demographic category to be able to investigate differences in outcomes based on gender and race/ethnicity.

3.1 ECS Professional Development

Curriculum materials and activities represent one component of the ECS program. Implementation of ECS was supported by a robust professional development program. Given the significant shift in the nature of computer science teaching required for successful implementation of ECS, teachers need extended professional development to successfully adapt to the ECS model of teaching [8]. The ECS PD program is intentionally designed to prepare teachers to implement the inquiry-based activities while also guiding them to build a classroom culture that is inclusive of all students [8]. Professional development begins with a weeklong summer workshop prior to implementing ECS. There are five key components of the ECS professional development model, the first being that teachers engage in the process of collaborative inquiry in small groups in the same way that students will engage in inquiry. The second component is that, throughout the first week, teachers participate in inquiry specifically through a teacher-learner-observer model. Each small group is assigned a lesson in which the group co-plans and teaches the lesson to the rest of the participants, who experience the lesson as learners. After the lesson, all the participants engage in reflective discussion about the experience from the point of view of the three ECS teaching strands (equity, inquiry, and CS content). These first two components of ECS professional development are consistent with what Desimone and Garet [1] call active learning in professional development. Their review of professional development found that active learning was an important component of professional development as it significantly influenced changes in teacher practices.

The third component of ECS professional development is explicit discussion and reflection on equitable practices. During the workshop, the teachers read sections of Stuck in the Shallow End [14], which provides rich case study descriptions of the roots of inequity in computer science. The fourth and fifth components of ECS PD are meant to sustain teacher development over long time spans, which is another key dimension of effective PD [1]. The fourth component is ongoing professional development during the school year and a second weeklong workshop the summer after their first year of implementation. The fifth component of ECS PD is the development of a professional learning community. It begins in the summer workshop through the formation of small groups that engage in collaborative inquiry. It is also built up through the trust that teachers develop as they engage in tough, open discussions about equity as well as through open, honest feedback on lesson design and implementation during the workshops.

3.2 Assessments

During the 2016–17 school year, teachers administered the SRI-developed ECS pretest at the beginning of the year and the posttest at the end of the year. SRI has developed rubrics for each of the assessment tasks. These rubrics are designed for classroom teachers to grade their students' assessments. SRI reports that it takes teachers about 5 minutes per student to score the assessments. In order to aggregate assessment result across teachers, we used independent scorers to grade the assessments.

We hired The Graide Network to score the pretests and posttests. The Graide Network recruited and trained 26 undergraduate preservice teachers to score the performances tasks. The scorers were provided training on each of the rubrics prior to scoring. As part of the training, each scorer scored a common set of 80 pretest responses from each question prompt in order to equate the severity of the scorers. For the posttest, we had overlapping subsets of scorers rate the same students. We used the Facets software version 3.71.4 to conduct Many-Facet Rasch Measurement analysis (MFRM) [5] to scale the student responses at each administration. Facets develops a model based on how well the student performed across the range of question prompts with set difficulties taking into account the severity of the scorer relative to the other scorers. Within MFRM, the goal is not for scorers to arrive at agreement on the scores, but instead to model the variation in how the scorers interpreted the rubrics. As long as the raters are internally consistent in how they apply the rubric, Facets can adjust the students' scores based on the severity or leniency of the scores relative to other scorers. We used the pretest tasks as the benchmark for scaling item difficulty. For scaling of the posttest scores, the item difficulties of the two common tasks were fixed based on the pretest scales. The overall model fit of the students, tasks, and scorers at each administration was high. For ease of interpretation, the logit scale produced by Facets was converted to a scale ranging from 0 to 25.

4 RESULTS

To set the context for investigating the development of specific aspects of programming expertise, we first examine the overall pretest to posttest performance as well as examine the extent to which students' performance in the course predicts posttest performance.

In the first model we test the growth of computational thinking from pretest to posttest. The average pretest score was 11.7 out of 25 and the average posttest score was 13.8 for a growth of more than two points. We used a paired t-test to determine that this growth was statistically significant (t(1930)=24.5, $p < 0.001$) with a medium effect size of 0.6 standard deviations, adjusted for the correlation between the pretest and posttest.

In the second model, we investigated the extent to which students' course performance correlates with the development of computational thinking after controlling for student characteristics. Since students were nested within teachers, we conducted hierarchical linear modeling (HLM) on the posttest performance using WHLM software version 7.24q. There are two levels to the HLM model (see Figure 1 for the HLM equation). Given that students of a particular teacher have a shared experience, the HLM analyses account for this shared variance of students within a class by developing a linear model of each student characteristic for the population of students of a given teacher. HLM then aggregates the intercepts and slopes across all of the teachers to model the relationships of each variable to the posttest performance.

At the first level are the student characteristics, which include each student's pretest score, grade level, gender (female), race (African American or Hispanic versus other races), participation in special education, participation in free or reduced lunch program (FRL), which serves as an indicator of low-income status, participation in the English language learning program (ELL), annual attendance rate, cumulative GPA in the year in which the student completed ECS, and grade the student received in the ECS course. The pretest score, attendance, cumulative GPA, and ECS course grade are group mean centered. The level 1 random effect is represented by r_{ij}. At the second level are the teachers. There are no teacher characteristics included in the model. The pretest score coefficient and ECS course grade coefficient are random effects, represented as u_{1j} and u_{11j}, respectively. These random effects allow the slopes of the two coefficients to vary across teachers at level 2. All of the other factors are fixed effects. After controlling for student characteristics, the HLM analyses provide evidence on the extent to which performance in the ECS course correlated with performance on the posttest.

We used students' course grades as an indicator of course performance. In addition, we examined whether there were differences in posttest performance by students of different gender and racial/ethnic backgrounds. Table 2 shows the results of the analysis. After controlling for pretest performance, there were no statistically significant differences in posttest performance by gender, race/ethnicity or level of family income. There were statistically significant negative differences in posttest performance for ELL and special education students. After also controlling for students' overall academic performance as measured by their GPA as well as their school attendance, how well students performed in the course had a statistically significant correlation with posttest performance.

5 DISCUSSION

Given that students significantly increased their overall performance from pretest to posttest and their posttest performance was correlated with performance in the ECS course after controlling for demographic and other behavioral characteristics, we can now examine the results of students' performance on the specific set of programming tasks on the posttest assessment. The process of Rasch scaling provides an estimate of each student's cognitive ability related to the computer science concepts within ECS as measured by the assessments. In addition, the process of Rasch scaling provides an estimate of the difficulty of each task for the population of assessment takers. In the Rasch context, a student is considered competent at a task if the student's ability is greater than or equal to the difficulty of the task. Table 3 shows the percentage of students at pretest and posttest whose estimated Rasch ability level is greater than or equal to the level of difficulty of the tasks in each category of programming competency.

Across all categories, there were more students who achieved competency at posttest than at pretest. Generally the tasks related to comprehension and planning were easier than the tasks related to program generation as indicated by the fact that there is a higher percentage of students whose ability level is greater than or equal to the difficulty level of those tasks. These results are consistent with the 'chain of cognitive accomplishments,' in which tasks related to language features and planning are easier than tasks related to program generation. In addition, tasks that were concrete in nature were generally easier with most students demonstrating competency by posttest. These tasks include determining the output from a written algorithm, identifying the available inputs from a problem scenario, and deciding the general requirements for a teacher's program to track student information. Tasks that were more abstract in nature were generally more difficult, with less than half of the students demonstrating competency on those tasks. These tasks include testing an algorithm against the specifications, identifying inputs that are not given in the problem scenario, and use of loops and conditionals.

6 CONCLUSIONS

School districts across the United States are responding to the call to increase access to computer science for all high school students. It is important for school districts to be mindful of the research on effective practices for the development of computer science expertise as well as research on setting reasonable expectations for student development of expertise.

In this research, we examined the impact of ECS on the development of programming expertise in the context of a large-scale implementation. ECS is a prominent high school introductory compute science course that is closely aligned to effective pedagogical practices that have theoretical and empirical support. A primary goal of the ECS curriculum and professional development program is to contribute to broadened participation of women and minorities and increased equity in the field of computer science. The

$$POSTTEST_{ij} = \gamma_{00} + \gamma_{10} * PRETEST_{ij} + \gamma_{20} * FEMALE_{ij} + \gamma_{30} * GRADE\_LEVEL_{ij} + \gamma_{40} * HISPANIC_{ij} + \gamma_{50} * AFRICAN - AMERICAN_{ij} + \gamma_{60} * IS\_SPECIAL\_ED_{ij} + \gamma_{70} * IS\_FRL_{ij} + \gamma_{80} * IS\_ELL_{ij} + \gamma_{90} * ATTENDANCE_{ij} + \gamma_{100} * GPA_{ij} + \gamma_{110} * ECS\_GRADE_{ij} + u_{0j} + u_{1j} * PRETEST_{ij} + u_{11j} * ECS\_GRADE_{ij} + r_{ij}$$

Figure 1: HLM model equation.

Table 2: HLM Model results for the student posttest scores by student characteristics. The factors in bold are statistically significant.

Characteristic	Coefficient	Standard Error	*t*-ratio	*p*-value
Average	**14.74**	**1.0**	$t(27) = 14.69$	$p < 0.001$
Student Characteristics				
Pretest	**0.15**	**0.03**	$t(27) = 4.97$	$p < 0.001$
Grade Level	−0.08	0.09	$t(221) = -0.83$	$p = 0.407$
Female	−0.17	0.13	$t(252) = -1.34$	$p = 0.181$
Hispanic	0.26	0.18	$t(183) = 1.44$	$p = 0.151$
African-American	−0.25	0.23	$t(287) = -1.08$	$p = 0.283$
Free or Reduced Lunch	−0.04	0.09	$t(177) = -0.51$	$p = 0.611$
ESL	**−0.66**	**0.24**	$t(106) = -2.78$	$p = 0.007$
Special Education	**−1.05**	**0.18**	$t(628) = -5.68$	$p < 0.001$
Rate of Attendance	**−2.59**	**0.89**	$t(39) = -2.95$	$p = 0.005$
Cummulative GPA	**0.72**	**0.15**	$t(61) = 4.70$	$p < 0.001$
ECS Course Grade	**0.26**	**0.13**	$t(27) = 2.04$	$p = 0.051$

Table 3: Percentage of students demonstrating competency on each dimension of programming expertise at pretest and posttest.

Problem type	**Pretest**	**Posttest**
Comprehension		
Determine Output	62%	87%
Will Output Meet Requirement?	14%	34%
Planning		
Available Inputs	46%	78%
Generate Requirements	38%	69%
Missing Inputs	20%	45%
Generation		
Conditional	22%	48%
Loop	7%	21%

curriculum is composed of activities that are designed to engage students in computer science inquiry around meaningful problems in the context of a classroom culture that's culturally relevant and inclusive of all students.

We conducted a large-scale, systematic study, as recommended in the literature [20], to examine whether a curriculum that uses a problem solving approach can support the development of programming expertise. Overall, students achieved medium-sized, statistically significant learning gains from pretest to posttest and those learning gains were spread equitably across gender and race/ethnicity. These learning gains were correlated with students' academic performance in the course after controlling for students' prior academic performance. These results provide evidence that a problem solving approach can support the development of programming expertise.

These results also provide evidence on the progression of the development of programming expertise. Students seem to develop comprehension and planning expertise prior to expertise in program generation. In addition, students seem to develop expertise with concrete tasks prior to abstract tasks. These results provide evidence for the current sequencing of activities in ECS that are consistent with the 'chain of cognitive accomplishments' approach.

ACKNOWLEDGMENTS

This research was supported by the National Science Foundation under grant numbers CNS-1842085, CNS-1738572, CNS-1738776, CNS-1738691, CNS-1738515, DRL-1640215, CNS-1542971, and CNS-1543217. Any opinions, findings, and conclusions or recommendations expressed in this material are those of the authors and do not necessarily reflect the views of the National Science Foundation.

REFERENCES

[1] Laura M. Desimone and Michael S. Garet. 2015. Best Practices in Teachers' Professional Development. *Psychology, Society, and Education* 7, 3 (2015), 252–263.

[2] Lucia Dettori, Ronald I. Greenberg, Steven McGee, and Dale Reed. 2016. The Impact of The Exploring Computer Science Instructional Model in Chicago Public Schools. *Computing in Science & Engineering (Special Issue: Best of RESPECT 2015)* 18, 2 (March/April 2016), 10–17. https://doi.org/10.1109/MCSE.2016.39.

[3] Lucia Dettori, Ronald I. Greenberg, Steven McGee, Dale Reed, Brenda Wilkerson, and Don Yanek. 2018. CS as a Graduation Requirement: Catalyst for Systemic Change. In *SIGCSE '18*. Association for Computing Machinery, 406–407. https://doi.org/10.1145/3159450.3159646.

[4] Lucia Dettori, Don Yanek, Helen Hu, and Dennis Brylow. 2018. The role of researcher-practitioner partnerships in CS4All: Lessons from the field. In *SIGCSE '18*. Association for Computing Machinery, 674–5. https://doi.org/10.1145/3159450.3159626.

[5] Thomas Eckes. 2011. *Introduction to Many-Facet Rasch Measurement*. Peter Lang.

[6] Exploring Computer Science. 2018. Where is ECS? http://www.exploringcs.org/for-teachers-districts/ecs-now. Accessed April 4, 2018.

[7] Joanna Goode and Gail Chapman. 2016. Exploring Computer Science (Version 7.0). http://www.exploringcs.org/curriculum.

[8] Joanna Goode, Jane Margolis, and Gail Chapman. 2014. Curriculum is Not Enough: The Educational Theory and Research Foundation of the Exploring Computer Science Professional Development Model. In *SIGCSE '14*. Association for Computing Machinery, 493–498.

[9] Pam Grossman, Karen Hammerness, and Morva McDonald. 2009. Redefining teaching, re-imagining teacher education. *Teachers and Teaching: Theory and Practice* 15, 2 (2009), 273–289.

[10] Shuchi Grover and Roy D. Pea. 2013. Computational Thinking in K–12 A Review of the State of the Field. *Educational Researcher* 42, 1 (2013), 38–43.

[11] SRI International and Principled Assessment of Computational Thinking (PACT). 2018. PACT | Resources. https://pact.sri.com/ecs-assessments.html. Last accessed 12/1/2018.

[12] Mizuko Ito, Heather Horst, Matteo Bittanti, danah boyd, Becky Herr-Stephenson, Patricia G. Lange, C. J. Pascoe, and Laura Robinson. 2008. Living and Learning with New Media: Summary of Findings from the Digital Youth Project. John D. and Catherine T. MacArthur Foundation Reports on Digital Media and Learning. http://www.macfound.org/media/article_pdfs/DML_ETHNOG_WHITEPAPER.PDF.

[13] Marcia C. Linn and John Dalbey. 1989. Cognitive Consequences of Programming Instruction. In *Studying the novice programmer*, James C. Spohrer and Elliot I. Soloway (Eds.). Lawrence Earlbaum Associates, Chapter 4, 57–81.

[14] Jane Margolis, Rachel Estrella, Joanna Goode, Jennifer Jellison Holme, and Kimberly Nao. 2010. *Stuck in the Shallow End: Education, Race, and Computing*. MIT Press.

[15] Jane Margolis, Jean J. Ryoo, Cueponcaxochitl D. M. Sandoval, Clifford Lee, Joanna Goode, and Gail Chapman. 2012. Beyond Access: Broadening Participation in High School Computer Science. *ACM Inroads* 3, 4 (Dec. 2012), 72–78. https://doi.org/10.1145/2381083.2381102.

[16] Steven McGee, Randi McGee-Tekula, Jennifer Duck, Ronald I. Greenberg, Lucia Dettori, Dale F. Reed, Brenda Wilkerson, Don Yanek, Andrew M. Rasmussen, and Gail Chapman. 2017. Does a Taste of Computing Increase Computer Science Enrollment? *Computing in Science & Engineering (Special Issue: Best of RESPECT 2016)* 19, 3 (April 2017), 8–18. https://doi.org/10.1109/MCSE.2017.50.

[17] Steven McGee, Randi McGee-Tekula, Jennifer Duck, Catherine McGee, Lucia Dettori, Ronald I. Greenberg, Eric Snow, Daisy Rutstein, Dale Reed, Brenda Wilkerson, Don Yanek, Andrew M. Rasmussen, and Dennis Brylow. 2018. Equal Outcomes 4 All: A Study of Student Learning in ECS. In *SIGCSE '18*. Association for Computing Machinery, 50–55. https://doi.org/10.1145/3159450.3159529.

[18] Orni Meerbaum-Salant, Michal Armoni, and Mordechai (Moti) Ben-Ari. 2013. Learning computer science concepts with Scratch. *Computer Science Education* 23, 3 (2013), 239–264. https://doi.org/10.1080/08993408.2013.832022.

[19] National Commission on Excellence in Education. 1983. A nation at risk: The imperative for educational reform. US Department of Education. http://www2.ed.gov/pubs/NatAtRisk.

[20] Arnold Pears, Stephen Seidman, Lauri Malmi, Linda Mannila, Elizabeth Adams, Jens Bennedsen, Marie Devlin, and James Paterson. 2007. A Survey of Literature on the Teaching of Introductory Programming. *ACM SIGCSE Bulletin* 39, 4 (Dec. 2007), 204–223. http://doi.acm.org/10.1145/1345375.1345441.

[21] Yizhou Qian and James Lehman. 2017. Students' Misconceptions and Other Difficulties in Introductory Programming: A Literature Review. *ACM Trans. Computing Education* 18, 1 (Oct. 2017), 1:1–1:24. http://doi.acm.org/10.1145/3077618.

[22] Anthony Robins, Janet Rountree, and Nathan Rountree. 2003. Learning and Teaching Programming: A Review and Discussion. *Computer Science Education* 13, 2 (2003), 137–172. https://doi.org/10.1076/csed.13.2.137.14200.

[23] Judy Sheard, S. Simon, Margaret Hamilton, and Jan Lönnberg. 2009. Analysis of Research into the Teaching and Learning of Programming. In *Proceedings of the Fifth International Workshop on Computing Education Research Workshop (ICER '09)*. 93–104. http://doi.acm.org/10.1145/1584322.1584334.

[24] Megan Smith. 2008. Computer Science For All. White House Blog. https://obamawhitehouse.archives.gov/blog/2016/01/30/computer-science-all.

The History of the SIGCSE Submission and Review Software

From Paper to the Cloud

Henry M. Walker
Computer Science
Grinnell College
Grinnell, IA USA
walker@cs.grinnell.edu

John F. Dooley
Computer Science
Knox College
Galesburg, IL USA
jfdooley@knox.edu

ABSTRACT

The submission and review process for the SIGCSE Symposium has evolved dramatically over the last half-century, reflecting changing expectations among SIGCSE members and advancing capabilities of technology. For almost 30 years, postal mail provided the vehicle for both paper submissions and reviews, and logistical constraints prevented the involvement of reviewers outside North America. Initial electronic submission and review options experimented with new technology and opened reviewing to SIGCSE members internationally. With growing experience, the home-grown submission and review system included new capabilities and could be expanded to additional conferences. Recently, cloud-based software has evolved to provide strong support for professional conferences.

Over the years, the scale of the submission and reviewing process also has increased dramatically. In 1968, 18 papers were accepted from "over 40" submissions, whereas 161 papers were accepted from 459 submissions in 2018. This scale of activity impacts the overall process, and the software systems have required substantial alterations. Throughout, the focus of the submission and review system has remained the same: a fair, peer-reviewed system with a large number of volunteer reviewers, a quick turnaround of all reviews, and ease of use for all the stakeholders - contributors, attendees, reviewers, meta-reviewers, conference leaders, and system administrators.

This article explores the evolution of the SIGCSE submission and review system, focusing on the last twenty years. Each phase of development highlights interactions among stakeholder interests, technological capabilities, and logistical requirements for handling the scope of papers submitted.

SIGCSE '19, February 27-March 2, 2019, Minneapolis, MN, USA.

ACM ISBN 978-1-4503-5890-3/19/02...$15.00.
DOI: https://doi.org/10.1145/3287324.3287427

CCS CONCEPTS

• **Information systems: Database administration**

• **Information systems: Information systems applications**

• **Human-centered computing: Human computer interaction (HCI)**

KEYWORDS

Web-based applications, client-server systems, conference management, database applications.

ACM Reference Format

Henry W. Walker & John F. Dooley. 2019. The History of the SIGCSE Submission and Review Software. *In Proceedings of the 50th ACM Technical Symposium on Computer Science Education (SIGCSE '19),* Feb. 27-March 2, 2019, Minneapolis, MN, USA. ACM, New York, NY, USA, 7 pages. https://doi.org/10.1145/3287324.3287427.

1 Introduction

This article explores the evolution of the SIGCSE submission and review system, focusing on the last twenty years when it moved from paper only to doing all the work in the cloud. Altogether, system development progressed through at least four stages, each described in some detail in its own section.

- Section 2 outlines conferences prior to 2000, for which papers and reviews were submitted as hard copy and sent through postal mail. By 1999 limited email also was utilized.
- Section 3 describes the first Web-based submission and review system. SIGCSE 2000 through SIGCSE 2003 represent a childhood phase of development: Web technologies were relatively young, system development utilized new approaches, backup plans provided alternatives should software malfunction, and each year built upon experiences from the previous year.
- Section 4 reviews the submission/review system between 2004 and 2009—a period that showed careful expansion of capabilities, a maturing of the software into adulthood, and support of multiple conferences, including ITiCSE.
- Section 5 examines software for SIGCSE 2010 to SIGCSE 2015. During this period, the software had matured, while technological advances and personal expectations created an environment far more complex than were present earlier.

- Section 6 reflects upon software after 2015, with the emergence of Web-based systems from third-party organizations and commercial vendors and leading to the retirement of the SIGCSE-oriented system in 2016-2017.
- Finally, Section 7 places in context the SIGCSE-oriented submission and review system between SIGCSE 2000 and SIGCSE 2016. Although the paper focuses on the development of software for SIGCSE symposia, this development shares many characteristics of many other software systems.

Overall, this paper serves as a type of historical case study for software development and evolution. Software generally begins with a vision of addressing specific problems and opportunities, and system evolution reflects changing perspectives of stakeholders, including multiple user-groups, administrators, developers, and hardware maintainers. As this paper illustrates, the SIGCSE submission and review system highlights the interactions of all of these stakeholders within the context of technological advances and evolving stakeholder expectations.

2 Pre-2000: Paper Submissions

Before SIGCSE 2000, the submission and review of papers followed a traditional system. As with many conferences at the time, primary stakeholders included submitters, reviewers, conference leaders (e.g., symposium and program chairs), and the Proceedings Chair. For much of this time, these people participated in a (largely) manual system:

- *Program Chair*: Identified reviewers, often including sending email to the full SIGCSE.members listserv, once the list existed.
- *Submitters*: Created four blinded, paper copies of each paper and submitted them to the Program Chair via postal mail.
- *Program Chair*: Organized three paper copies into sets for each reviewer; typically papers were randomized, so reviewers for one paper would be different from those for another paper. The fourth copy was retained for later reference. Sets of papers were sent via postal mail; due to potential mailing delays, only SIGCSE members in North America could serve as reviewers.
- *Reviewers* sent their feedback to the Program Chair, often in paper form via postal mail.
- *Conference leadership*: Determined paper acceptances and rejections, based on the reviews. All primary authors were notified by postal mail.
- *Submitters of accepted papers*: Revised papers, based on reviewer feedback, and sent revised work to the Proceedings Chair via postal mail.
- *Proceedings chair*: Compiled accepted papers

Although much of this manual process continued throughout this period, by SIGCSE 1999, Program Chair Robert Noonan believed that computing conferences should utilize technology; after all, computing faculty studied, taught, and utilized technology, and he was bothered that the symposium was not using this technology. As a result, he sought to utilize technology for some communications and record keeping [6].

- The Call for Participation identified only paper submissions, but Noonan developed an email-submission option for some electronic submissions (e.g., with html or WordPerfect format). Potential authors (e.g., former reviewers) with known email addresses received email announcements of this possibility.
- Submitters completed an online form with author/title information, stored in an Access database.
- The Program Chair utilized email to inform reviewers of their assignments, encourage reviewers who were late in completing reviews, and inform authors whether or not submissions had been accepted or rejected.
- Email with reviewer assignments included a review template, reviewers sent their reviews via email, and reviews were stored in a Microsoft Access database. Challenges arose when reviewers did not follow the template, preventing the extraction of data with scripts and requiring manual data entry.

Even with these technological advances, several challenges remained:

- Email correspondence utilized a Linux environment, while the Access database involved Windows. Thus, Noonan created numerous scripts to extract material from email, move data between systems, and handle record keeping.
- Most submissions continued to be transmitted via postal mail.
- Some authors were slow in sending materials to the Proceedings Chair. Although the Program Chair had anonymous versions, Proceedings Chairs regularly noted challenges with the transition to a publishable form.

Separate from these logistical matters, from its earliest days the reviewing model for the SIGCSE Symposium differed from many other ACM conferences. In other conferences, the conference committee was charged with reviewing all submissions. For the SIGCSE Technical Symposium the reviewing pool was widened to include any SIGCSE member who volunteered to review—at least members within North America. This allowed a large pool of reviewers, which in turn allowed for each submission to receive 3 or more reviews, and many authors indicated they wanted more!

3 2000-2003: Childhood

Preparation for SIGCSE 2000 began with a vision: Symposium Co-chairs, Boots Cassel and Nell Dale, asked Program Chair Henry Walker to explore the possibility of moving the entire paper submission and review process to a Web-based system. Email would be used for communications, and submission of papers and reviews would utilize Web-based forms. This section outlines the work for SIGCSE 2000 through SIGCSE 2003 and highlights a process of iterative prototyping and development—much in the tradition of the modern agile methods of today [2].

After much discussion, a February 6, 1999, email from Walker to the Symposium Co-chairs proposed the following process:

-- Allow electronic submissions in either paper or html format.
-- Specify that if, after a good faith effort, an electronic

submission remains unreadable (for any reason), then the author will be expected to supply paper copy promptly

-- Make versions of the electronic submissions available on-line to designated referees. (Each referee was restricted to reading only those papers they were assigned.)

-- Papers submitted in hard-copy form would continue to be distributed for review via postal mail.

-- Utilize an updated on-line reviewing process for referee papers [9].

With this high-level process determined, continued discussion identified needed software capabilities, compiled in the following April 22, 1999 document for the software development team.

Software Needs for SIGCSE 2000

- System to accept papers electronically
    - receive cover form, regular copy, author-anonymous copy
    - web-based cover form required; article may come in paper or web form
    - store copies of papers in separate files
    - add author/subject/title information to database
- System to support electronic reviewing
    - allow additions and corrections of reviewer database through web form
    - send messages to reviewers about reviewing assignments
    - make author-anonymous papers accessible on-line to reviewers
    - present reviewing form on line
    - receive reviewer comments and ratings, and place data into the database
    - identify which reviewers have and have not responded
- System to support paper ratings and notification
    - sort papers by ratings and categories
    - present ratings and comments
    - allow designation of which papers are accepted and rejected
    - allow reporting of ratings and comments to authors [10].

For SIGCSE 2000, eight additional comments highlight concerns, approaches, and the state of technology in 1999-2000.

- Since a Web-based system would require authors to submit materials in an electronic form, and since reviewers would have to read those materials online, a fundamental issue involved the format required. Ultimately, SIGCSE 2000 required all electronic submissions to be in html format: some authors could write directly in html, and word processors at the time (e.g., Word, WordPerfect) could save files in html format. In addition, authors could submit images in gif or jpeg format. (The software limited a submission to 14 files, since this simplified system development and seemed sufficient for all submissions for the previous several years.)
- A central part of the SIGCSE 2000 system built upon a Microsoft Access™ database created by Robert Noonan for SIGCSE 1999. The inherited database recorded paper information in one table and all individuals (both authors and reviewers) in another table. In order to maintain backwards compatibility and to speed development, the database design of SIGCSE 1999 was not changed for SIGCSE 2000.
- The new Web-based software utilized a client-server architecture, with two different servers: a Linux server provided the front-end, static, shtml pages, and a Windows server ran ASP scripts that interacted with a Microsoft Access™ database to generate dynamic html pages. This arrangement allowed the front end to function even when the database was down, and the front end could notify users of problems in the dynamic pages.
- To minimize the possible load on the Web server near submission and review deadlines, the original system performed error checking only on the client side using JavaScript. Server-side processing then assumed submitted data were valid, and form-input was formatted directly into SQL queries. Although this seemed reasonable at the time, it was later determined that 30%-40% of SIGCSE members routinely disabled JavaScript as a potential security issue. As a result, when data were submitted without error checking, some SQL queries became invalid. Although a message to that effect was reported, some authors apparently did not notice the error report, and perhaps as many as a dozen submissions may have been lost.
- For overall tracking, authors of both hard-copy and electronic submissions needed to complete a Web form with author/title information, registering the submission, and generating a unique paper ID. Although submitters could review their paper's records, initial limitations in the scripts did not allow submitters to change the author/title data. Changes in author names, institutions, or titles had to be emailed to the Program Chair who then updated the database manually. This led to about 100 manual changes for records of accepted papers.
- All electronic submitters were allowed to upload both full and anonymous versions of their papers, and these uploaded files could be changed (prior to the submission deadline).
- With the availability of submissions online, reviewers outside North America were included in the review of electronic submissions. As in the past, hard copy submissions could be sent only to reviewers in North America.
- Each submitter and reviewer chose a password upon registration. In those early days of Web interactions, transmission and recording of passwords using encryption was not considered a priority, and both the transmission and storage of passwords was accomplished in the clear.

To implement this system in summer 1999, Program Chair Walker worked with two students, Waichao Ma and Morene Mboya, and two consultants, Wayne Twichell and Theresa Walker. Conference deadlines drove development. Remarkably (at least in retrospect), all development milestones were met (sometimes by only 24 hours), and the system worked as required (with only a few minor troubles that were quickly resolved).

As might be expected, the symposium leadership learned much from the new system. For SIGCSE 2001, several substantial changes addressed the most pressing matters:

- Difficulties were noted with some html files, as the files viewed sometimes differed substantially from the appearance a submitter intended. This prompted several changes in the requirements for submitted work, as described in the SIGCSE 2001 Call for Participation:

  What to Send

  Electronic Cover Sheet

  Full version (with full author information)(using formatted postscript, pdf, or hardcopy)

  Anonymous version (using non-formatted html or formatted hardcopy; for html, ok to submit html file as created by word processor from formatted version)

  In the case of electronic submission, a formatted version of the anonymous version may also be submitted in postscript or pdf (optional) [12].
- All error checking for submitted form data was done both client-side and server-side.
- Authors could update their author/title information using an online form—authors no longer had to contact the Program Chair for changes.

Software for SIGCSE 2002 reflected increased learning regarding both Web-based processing and the software system, again involving a major software update. In addition to adjustments in the software, the major changes involved submission options:

- Hardcopy was no longer allowed for papers. (A moderate number of submissions for SIGCSE 2000 came in paper form, but the number dropped substantially for SIGCSE 2001. With the opportunities for international reviewing, there seemed little reason to continue the hardcopy option in 2002.)
- html format was eliminated for submissions, and all submissions had to utilize pdf format. (At that time, tools for the creation of pdf files had become sufficiently common to ensure all submitters could utilize this option. Further, the variability of html documents among browsers was quite high, and reviewers often had difficulty interpreting html documents.)
- Papers could be sent to many reviewers, not just the three dictated by hard-copy limitations. For years, authors had wanted their papers rated by many reviewers; numerous reviews opened the possibility of disregarding a particularly low rating.

SIGCSE 2003 represented another substantial iteration for the submission and review system. Previously, the system focused upon papers; separate Chairs handled the relatively few submissions in other categories—often via email. For SIGCSE 2003, the system was expanded to include panels and special sessions as well as papers. The Panels and Special Sessions Chairs could review their own submission types, and the overall Program Chair could view all submissions. This revised system provided a reasonably uniform environment for all submissions.

As a side note, the automation of the review process enabled a research study that explored a wide range of factors influencing paper ratings. To investigate such factors, for SIGCSE 2000, 10 submissions were each sent to 100 reviewers, providing sufficient data for a reasonable statistical analysis. The study concluded, "few systemic referee factors affect paper ratings. Specifically, the following factors are NOT statistically significant in contributing to overall paper ratings: referee gender, referee's country (U.S. versus non-U.S.), familiarity of referee with subject, or paper format (electronic submission versus hardcopy). However, ratings from referees in groups were lower (by about 0.5) than ratings from those who were not in groups, and this difference is statistically significant." The full analysis is available in [15].

With new understandings and experiences, system development followed an iterative process throughout. Since the system supported an annual conference, each iteration largely spanned a one-year cycle—much longer than is now utilized in various agile methodologies. Each iteration also generally followed an agile philosophy: start with a vision, outline a possible framework, implement the system to meet the currently understood needs, meet with stakeholders to evaluate the current iteration, outline an updated framework, and repeat [3, p. 18]. After these iterations,
the system had fostered considerable insight, and stakeholders had given extensive feedback. The system evolved dramatically through these four iterations, but challenges remained; e.g. sections of code had to be re-written every year to accommodate simple changes, such as the name, location, and logo of the Symposium. The time had arrived to rethink the application—both successes and challenges, in anticipation of an updated, more mature system.

4 2004-2009: Growth into Adulthood

In the summer of 2004 the authors began a complete re-design and re-writing of the submission and review system with the goals of abstracting out many pieces of data in order to make the system more table-driven, simplifying the code, adding additional administrative features, and expanding documentation [11]. We also began the process of adding code to automatically generate the Symposium program. These tasks expanded the list of stakeholders to include the entire conference committee and eventually, Symposium attendees as well.

In addition, at this time we began to receive requests from other ACM and CCSC conferences to use the client-server system for their submissions and reviewing. These requests further expanded our pool of stakeholders and reinforced our desire to make the system easy to change and use.

During the summer 2004, we spent a couple of days together at Grinnell College refining requirements and designing the new system and its interfaces. We then separated to our respective campuses and each wrote the sections of code we'd assigned each other, maintaining a single code base on the Grinnell system, communicating almost daily via email, and talking on the telephone each week.

The improved system was ready for use late in July 2004 and was rolled out, with the usual number of initial bugs, in time for submissions for SIGCSE 2005. Although the initial re-write did not meet all the goals set above, the basic infrastructure of the system was finished. All the original 2004 goals were completed over the next several summers.

Except for 2004 when we worked for most of May, June and July to perform the database abstractions and change the conference interfaces, in subsequent years, we normally worked for at least one month each summer to improve the system and add new functionality as requested by each year's conference committee. Specifically, during this period, we

- Changed the conference interface so that it was largely localized into variables and style sheets. The variables were localized into a single file that would be loaded first to set up the conference parameters.
- Expanded the system to make it easier to accommodate multiple conferences. Each conference would have its own set of variables and its own database. Switching from one conference to another became mostly a matter of filling in the conference-specific variables in a couple of ASP files and creating the new database by copying an existing one and inserting the meta-information.
- Revised each of the stakeholder user interfaces to accommodate the different functions required by each set of stakeholders.
- Expanded the administrative capabilities to allow more administrative functions without requiring code or manual database changes. Direct database edits can be error prone, so we wrote scripts to handle administrative tasks. We also created a permissions table to identify which people on the program committee were allowed to access which data.
- Added the ability to generate the Symposium program, and a feature to allow attendees to generate (but not save) their own personalized program.
- Wrote a set of design documents and a set of user documentation for conference leaders (e.g., [13]).
- Internationalized the system to facilitate submissions from outside North America.
- Added several security features, including more secure administration passwords and session timeouts.
- Increased the types of submissions allowed to add Birds of a Feather sessions, posters, workshops, and video.

The variables and database table entries allowed the system to be generic and easy to configure for each conference. At its peak the system supported about eight (8) conferences. The system fit easily into the overall conference Web presence developed by the conference committee and program chairs—a single link from the main conference page sent the user to the initial submission page, a second link sent potential reviewers to a reviewer registration page, a third yielded assignments for reviewers, a fourth lead to a page for most administrative functions, and a fifth link provided a program to conference attendees.

For the most part, each stakeholder corresponded to a front-end page and an associated directory of scripts. For example, the administrative functions identified by a *dbAdmin.asp* script handled a wide range of tasks for conference leaders. Within each directory, each script largely corresponded to a single dynamic page. Supporting this work, a central directory provided files supporting tasks that were common to several tasks and scripts.

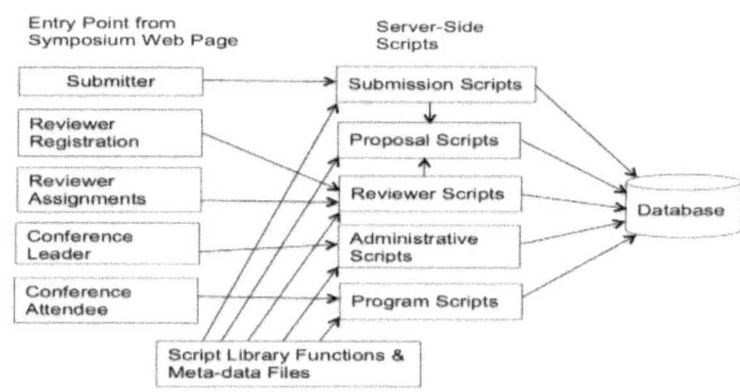

Figure 1. Submission System Architecture

Each of the boxes in Figure 1 represent several shtml and ASP scripts spread across two different servers. Entry from the shtml pages called the ASP scripts based on user input.

5 2009-2015: Maturity in an Increasingly Complex World

Starting around 2010 the conference committees began to request functions that would allow for tightening the reviewing process. This new design was to add more levels of review. Over the next several years a small group of Associate Program Chairs was added to the system. This evolved into a more general set of "meta-reviewers" whose primary function was to use the reviews to make tentative decisions about which papers to accept or reject.

By 2010 the level of effort to make changes to the system had increased and it was becoming clear that another system re-design and re-write was needed to move to more modern web and database tools. With unlimited time, we would have liked to rewrite the system using PHP and an open source RDBMS like MySQL, or using a web development environment like Django which uses an open source RDBMS for its back-end. That would have increased portability, eliminated problems with Microsoft Access, and supported redesign the system. It would also have allowed us to move to a single, stable Linux server.

At the same time, conference management systems were emerging to handle many needed tasks, and it was possible that some of these new systems would take over the needs for the current local SIGCSE system. In 2010 we made the first effort to find a third-party system to replace the current system. When we first looked at the EasyChair (https://easychair.org/) system, it used a different reviewing model than SIGCSE used, it wasn't deemed mature and stable enough to accommodate our increasing number of submissions at that time, and its documentation was quite limited.

In 2012 we examined the OpenConf (https://www.openconf.com/) system and convinced the ITiCSE conference committee to use it as an experimental submission system for the 2012 ITiCSE conference. ITiCSE was a much smaller conference than the SIGCSE Symposium and would give us the opportunity to ease into a change in the submission and reviewing system. The OpenConf reviewing model was close to SIGCSE's, the company would make changes for us for a small charge, and they would host the entire system for us. We ended up using the OpenConf system for the 2012 through 2014 ITiCSE conferences and decided that it was a satisfactory system.

6 2016-2017: Retirement

By 2014 it was becoming clear that we would either have to rewrite the current SIGCSE client-server submission and review system, or move the Symposium permanently to a third-party system. Microsoft was in the process of ending support for the versions of ASP and Microsoft Access that we were using, and the amount of maintenance on two different servers (one Linux, one Windows) was becoming more than volunteers could manage.

The experiment with the OpenConf system at the ITiCSE conference had worked successfully for three years, so the decision was made (with much trepidation from the SIGCSE conference committee) to switch the SIGCSE Symposium submission and review system to OpenConf beginning with the 2014 Symposium.

This switch worked well for two years. In 2016 the current authors decided it was time to retire from their more than decade long stint as database administrators (more like seventeen years for Henry Walker) and two new database admins were brought on board. At the same time the Symposium conference committee decided to switch to a now-improved EasyChair. By 2016 EasyChair was a much more mature system and provided nearly all of the features that the new database administrators and the conference committee required. At this time the committee also decided to make use of the review discussion feature offered in EasyChair in order to further improve the quality of reviews. These review discussions occur after all reviewers have submitted their reviews. They are monitored by the meta-reviewers.

In 2018 the conference committee began requiring abstracts in addition to paper submissions, something that EasyChair can accommodate. The ITiCSE conference has also moved from OpenConf to EasyChair.

The original client-server system continued to support two additional conferences, CCSC Central Plains and CCSC Southwestern in 2014, but the system is now officially retired.

7 Reflections

Some software-development themes illustrated by the evolution of this system over about 17 years:

1. Software projects may begin with a (reasonably) simple vision. [2]. For this system, SIGCSE 1999 experimented with limited communications via email. The vision for SIGCSE 2000 entailed a full Web-based system for communications, submissions, and reviewing, utilizing a back-end database.
2. In modern software development, initial development typically involves identifying stakeholders and fleshing out the vision with use cases for those stakeholders. Work then is organized into stages, perhaps based on an overall timeline, and development proceeds incrementally through multiple stages to yield an initial package [7]. For this system, stakeholders provided a solid focus throughout, and development stages were tied directly to the conference timeline—the system had to support submission/review capabilities as users needed them.
3. In agile programming, a team completes several iterations of the system, each with feedback from stakeholders as well as developers [8]. For this system, each annual conference served as another development iteration. In early years, each year's system represented substantial upgrades. Later changes provided polish and refinements to a maturing system.
4. For many working packages, an initial vision grows steadily, as stakeholders gain experience and desire new capabilities [2]. For the submission/review system, the originally modest system grew to well over 50,000 lines of code over 15 years—dramatically more extensive than originally anticipated.
5. In his reflections on software development, Frederick Brooks, developer of the IBM 360 system, highlighted the need to maintain "Conceptual Integrity" [1, p. 42]. This principle was a mainstay of the submission/review system, adhering to the initial vision and the software's high-level design. New features often could be added and existing elements modified—provided the underlying principles of the system remained.
6. In adhering to system integrity, long-term maintenance requires finding and unifying common elements. Refactoring allows elements throughout a program to utilize common code, yielding simple, general, coherent, and maintainable software [4, p. 184]. For the SIGCSE software, refactoring became a way of life throughout its lifetime.
7. After developing an initial system, Frederick Brooks advises "Plan to Throw One Away" [1, p. 115]. Similarly, in discussing SmallTalk, Dan Ingalls emphasized the great advantages when one can rewrite the entire system, based on learnings from the original system [5]. For this submission/review system, the full redesign of the database and reworking the software for SIGCSE 2004 provided a fresh start, based on several years of feedback from stakeholders and new understandings of database systems and Web-based scripting by the developers.
8. [14] identifies additional reflections and lessons learned from the first decade of experience.

ACKNOWLEDGMENTS

Many, many thanks to all involved helping to shape and improve this system throughout its creation and evolution. Particular thanks are extended to the following.

- Nell Dale and Boots Cassel, SIGCSE 2000 Co-chairs, provided an initial vision and steady support.
- The key development team for the SIGCSE 2000 system included:
  - Dorene Mboya and Weichao Ma, student developers supported by Grinnell College's Fund for Excellence,
  - Wayne Twitchell, technical guidance and support, Grinnell College Computer Services,
  - Theresa P. Walker, Web/database/scripting consultant, and
  - William Francis and Mark Miller, Computer Services Director and Assistant for hardware and software support.
- SIGCSE Symposia leaders, authors, reviewers, and SIGCSE members provided a rich stream of suggestions and feedback.
- Leaders, authors, and reviewers from many CCSC conferences, particularly within the Central Plains region.
- Grinnell College system administrators, John Stone and Wayne Twitchell, of the Linux and Windows servers, respectively, provided extensive support for the submission and review system for over eleven years,
- Grinnell College Computer Services (later Information Technology Services) provided extensive hardware and networking support.
- Robert Noonan, SIGCSE 1999 Program Chair, provided important assistance as the SIGCSE 2000 system emerged. Additional thanks for his feedback regarding this paper.

In addition, author John would like to acknowledge the support of the Dean's office at Knox College which provided travel and conference support every year. Finally, both John Dooley and Henry Walker would like to thank each other for all the fun and collegiality we've had over the years.

REFERENCES

[1] Frederick P. Brooks, *The Mythical Man-Month: Essays on Software Engineering, Silver Anniversary Edition.* Boston, MA: Addison-Wesley, 1995.

[2] Alistair Cockburn. *Agile Software Development.* Boston, MA: Addison-Wesley, 2002.

[3] John F. Dooley, *Software Development, Design and Coding.* 2nd Edition. New York, NY: Apress, 2017.

[4] Andrew Hunt and D. Thomas, *The Pragmatic Programmer: From Journeyman to Master,* Boston: Addison-Wesley, 2000.

[5] Dan Ingalls, *Object-oriented Programming,* Video from University Video Communications, recorded July 1989, now available via https://www.youtube.com/watch?reload=9&v=Ao9W93OxQ7U (accessed August 28, 2018).

[6] Robert. Noonan, Private Communication, 24 August 2018.

[7] M. Poppendieck and T. Poppendieck, *Lean Software Development: An Agile Toolkit,* Upper Saddle River, NJ: Addison-Wesley Professional, 2003.

[8] C. Sims and H. L. Johnson, *The Elements of Scrum,* San Mateo, CA: Dymaxicon, 2011.

[9] Henry M. Walker, Private email to SIGCSE 2000 Symposium Co-chairs regarding submission/review process, February 6, 1999.

[10] Henry M. Walker, "Software Needs for SIGCSE 2000",. private software development document, April 22, 1999.

[11] Henry M. Walker and John F. Dooley, Submission and Reviewing Documentation History at http://www.cs.grinnell.edu/~sigcse/documentation-history.shtml, referenced on 18 August 2018.

[12] Henry M. Walker, SIGCSE 2001 Call for Participation, www.cs.grinnell.edu/~sigcse/2001/call.html (accessed 22 August 2018).

[13] Henry M. Walker and John F. Dooley, Submission and Reviewing Current Documentation at http://www.cs.grinnell.edu/~sigcse/sigcse2010/documentation.shtm l, retrieved on 18 August 2018.

[14] Henry M. Walker and John F. Dooley, "The SIGCSE Submission and Review Software: 10 (hexadecimal) Lessons", Journal of the Consortium for Computing Sciences in Colleges, Volume 25, Number 5 (May 2010), pp. 196-201.

[15] Henry M. Walker, Weichao Ma, and Dorene Mboya, "Variability of Referees' Ratings of Conference Papers," ITiCSE 2002 Proceedings, pp. 178-182.

"I Impressed Myself With How Confident I Felt": Reflections on a Computer Science Assessment for K-8 Teachers

Hannah E. Chipman
Rhodes College
Memphis, Tennessee
chihe-20@rhodes.edu

Fernando J. Rodríguez
University of Florida
Gainesville, Florida
fjrodriguez@ufl.edu

Kristy Elizabeth Boyer
University of Florida
Gainesville, Florida
keboyer@ufl.edu

ABSTRACT

The computer science education community has made great strides in promoting diversity and inclusion in computing fields and bringing K-12 CS learning opportunities to broader groups of learners. However, one area that has not been investigated fully is how assessments can influence a learner's confidence and attitudes towards CS. Stereotype threat and test modality have been shown to affect the performance of CS test takers. This experience report examines how novice CS learners respond to a CS assessment by investigating an increasingly important group of novice CS learners: K-8 classroom teachers. We conducted focus groups with elementary and middle school teachers as part of a week-long CS professional development workshop. The focus groups were held after teachers completed pre- and post-assessments. The assessment instrument featured multiple-choice and short-answer questions with block-based programming snippets. Many teachers reported a positive disposition towards learning CS after completing the pre-assessment, which they attributed to having a growth mindset. Themes related to their confidence involved the difficulty and format of the assessment, with comments about difficulty reducing after the post-assessment. When asked about their thoughts on the assessment from the perspective of their students, they provided suggestions with particular attention to its format. These findings provide insight for CS assessment design and implementation, as well as support further research on the impact of assessments on CS learners.

CCS CONCEPTS

• **Social and professional topics → K-12 education**;

KEYWORDS

Professional development; K-8 teachers; assessment

ACM Reference Format:
Hannah E. Chipman, Fernando J. Rodríguez, and Kristy Elizabeth Boyer. 2019. "I Impressed Myself With How Confident I Felt": Reflections on a Computer Science Assessment for K-8 Teachers. In *Proceedings of the 50th ACM Technical Symposium on Computer Science Education (SIGCSE '19), February 27-March 2, 2019, Minneapolis, MN, USA.* ACM, New York, NY, USA, Article 4, 7 pages. https://doi.org/10.1145/3287324.3287478

SIGCSE '19, February 27-March 2, 2019, Minneapolis, MN, USA

ACM ISBN 978-1-4503-5890-3/19/02...$15.00
https://doi.org/10.1145/3287324.3287478

1 INTRODUCTION

The need to recruit and retain diverse students in computer science is as high as ever. Research on computer science outreach and the role of recruitment interventions has focused on promoting a diverse and inclusive workforce [1, 10, 13], which in turn leads to broader perspectives and new innovations. However, there are still low numbers of women and students from underrepresented groups enrolling in computer science programs [5, 6, 9, 20, 21] due to a wide variety of issues. However, the effects that *knowledge assessments* can have on students' attitudes towards the field have not been fully explored. Studies have shown that test modality and stereotype threat can affect underrepresented groups' performance on computer science examinations [17, 24]. These factors can make computer science tests a deterrent for these underrepresented groups who already self-assess their science, technology, engineering, and math abilities as lower than that of non-minority males [16].

In order to better understand the relationship between CS assessments and attitudes towards CS, we conducted a study with an increasingly important population of novice CS learners: classroom teachers in K-8. Many teachers in the US are being asked to learn computer science and then integrate it into their classroom activities, but most teachers have no formal computer science background. To prepare them, the CS education community relies primarily on professional development workshops and other activities. Research has found that professional development workshops are effective in increasing teachers' and students' confidence in their coding abilities [14].

We conducted this study in the context of a one-week computer science professional development workshop for K-8 teachers. We designed CS assessments to evaluate how well the teachers learned the CS concepts presented to them. Teachers completed the assessments at the start and end of the week-long workshop and participated in focus groups in which we asked them about their experience taking the assessment and their attitudes toward CS. Their focus group responses were analyzed qualitatively through the use of thematic analysis, in which themes were assigned to their responses. We found that teachers expressed high confidence in their ability to learn CS after both the pre- and post-assessments. When they did report low confidence, they attributed it to the assessment's difficulty and format. The teachers also provided insight into how the assessments could be improved for student test takers, with specific recommendations about the assessments' presentation and content. We conclude with a set of practical implications for assessment design and implementation in the classroom. These findings support further research on the impact of assessments on CS learners.

2 RELATED WORK

One of the overarching motivations behind our research is broadening participation in computer science, as there is a significantly low number of women and people of color in computer science and related fields. In 2017, only 18.1% of computer science degrees were awarded to women, while around 9.75% of degrees were awarded to either Black or Hispanic people [11]. There are many barriers to computer science for historically underrepresented groups, including lack of exposure, low self-efficacy, stereotypes about computer scientists, and the societal belief that males are better at science, technology, engineering, and math [2, 16]. We hope to contribute to the literature on this topic by studying the perceptions of a diverse group of teachers and their attitudes toward a CS assessment.

A potential barrier for minorities in computer science that has not been fully explored is CS assessments. How assessment items are presented can significantly impact the performance of women and people of color. In a study of the summative assessment for the AP Computer Science Principles course, code questions were presented to students in either text or block form [24]. The researchers found that students performed better on questions that presented code in a block-based language over questions that showed code in a text-based language. This result was significant for students identifying with underrepresented groups in the field of computer science. A possible explanation discussed in the paper is that some students may be intimidated by text-based languages, which would link the modality to social and cultural influences.

Another factor that can influence how well a person does on a test is stereotype threat, which is when a person's performance is influenced by a known stereotype [19]. In a study of undergraduates in a computer science course, students who were asked for demographic information before a test scored lower on the subsequent computer science exam [17]. By informing and evaluating the design of computer science assessments that reduce bias and stereotype threat, we can ultimately reduce their negative effect on students' attitudes and confidence in computer science.

The assessments designed for teachers in this study were based on literature in block-based assessments. Most prior work has focused on assessing the knowledge of children participating in outreach programs. For example, the Computational Thinking Test (CTt) is a multiple-choice exam in which the questions and answers are presented in block form, focusing on loops and code sequencing [22]. The CTt was tested for convergent validity against assessments that used Bebras Tasks and Dr. Scratch and was found to be partially convergent with both. The K-2 assessment questions, which used code blocks that show directions like north, east, south, and west with the goal of reaching an end point, were based on CTt questions and were meant to demonstrate knowledge of program sequencing. Another study used a block-based test featuring multiple-choice, true/false, and open-ended questions covering topics such as loops, variables, and conditionals to assess what concepts students are learning with block-based curricula [12]. This assessment led us to use short-answer questions in both the K-2 and 3rd-8th assessments, such as questions that ask "What will this program say?" and request a short open answer. The teachers that participated in our workshop learned to program using block-based programming languages, with the goal of using these languages to teach their own students. Therefore, our assessment presented code in a block-based format, drawing from the prior work on block-based assessments.

3 TEACHER CS WORKSHOP STUDY

We conducted the present study in the context of a week-long computer science professional development workshop for K-8 teachers with little to no prior experience in computer science and programming. The workshop's goal was to provide teachers with knowledge and hands-on practice in CS concepts and how to incorporate them into their teaching. It consisted of five 7-hour sessions conducted during the span of a week and included introductions to block-based programming languages and opportunities for the teachers to design activities and lesson plans for their K-8 classrooms.

3.1 Participants

A total of 40 K-8 teachers participated in this professional development, recruited from flyers distributed at several schools in our local county in the Southeastern United States. One teacher did not complete any of the surveys or assessments administered during the workshop, so that teacher's data is excluded from this study. We consider the remaining teachers in two cohorts: K-2 and 3rd-8th grade teachers. As discussed below, these teachers experienced different content and were given different versions of the pre- and post-test. There were 18 teachers in the K-2 cohort and 21 in the 3rd-8th cohort. Table 1 describes the demographic information of these cohorts. Teachers had an average of 10.8 years of teaching experience, with the 3rd-8th teachers specializing in particular subjects: math and science (11), language arts (3), social studies (1), and multiple subjects (6).

3.2 Assessment Design

The goal when designing the assessment was to measure what the teachers would be learning during the professional development workshop, so we carefully aligned the assessment with the workshop's curricular plan. We designed one assessment for each grade cohort based on the programming language each cohort would be using. The two assessments were designed to be similar in question type and difficulty[1]. The workshop activities were designed around block-based languages that the teachers could then directly use in their courses to teach their own students. The workshop content for the K-2 cohort used resources from Code.org's Course A [7], which featured block languages with minimal text and focused on activities that involved moving objects within 2-dimensional environments. The assessment questions drew from examples in the Code.org Course A curriculum and featured the same block images from these materials in the questions and answer choices. The 3rd-8th cohort used Snap*!* in their workshop coding activities [15], and activities were inspired by the Beauty and Joy of Computing curriculum [23]. Assessment questions for these teachers featured Snap*!* code images in their question and answer choices. To assess learning, the same assessment was administered as a pre-assessment and post-assessment.

[1]Both assessment instruments can be found at the following link: https://cise.ufl.edu/research/learndialogue/teacher-workshop/assessments/

Table 1: Teacher demographic information by cohort

Demographic Information	K-2	3rd-8th	Total
Female	17	19	36
Male	1	2	3
Black/African American	3	7	10
Hispanic/Latino	2	2	4
White/Caucasian	13	12	25
Total	18	21	39

In order to better fit into the workshop's schedule, the assessment items consisted of mostly multiple-choice questions with five options, as recommended by prior research on assessment design [4]. Approximately half of the questions were short-answer questions, which were included to get a more accurate assessment of their knowledge, reducing the effects of guessing the right answer on the multiple-choice questions. The K-2 assessment had 14 questions (7 short-answer questions), and the 3rd-8th assessment had 17 questions (7 short-answer questions). Both assessments covered topics on code sequencing, conditionals, loops, and variables. The K-2 assessment focused more on programming tasks related to directional movement in a 2-dimensional space, while the 3rd-8th assessment featured questions on conditions for displaying text or numeric output and conceptual questions (see Figure 1).

We aimed to word questions in a gender-neutral way and avoided questions that could be interpreted as referring to a particular gender, as recommended by prior work on stereotype threat in assessments [17]. We also attempted to avoid questions that required knowledge of more than simple math procedures and science, so as not to elicit negative stereotypes related to science, technology, engineering, and math abilities. Instead, questions were created with the teachers and their students in mind, focusing on what they would find useful, such as the grade calculator question in Figure 1.

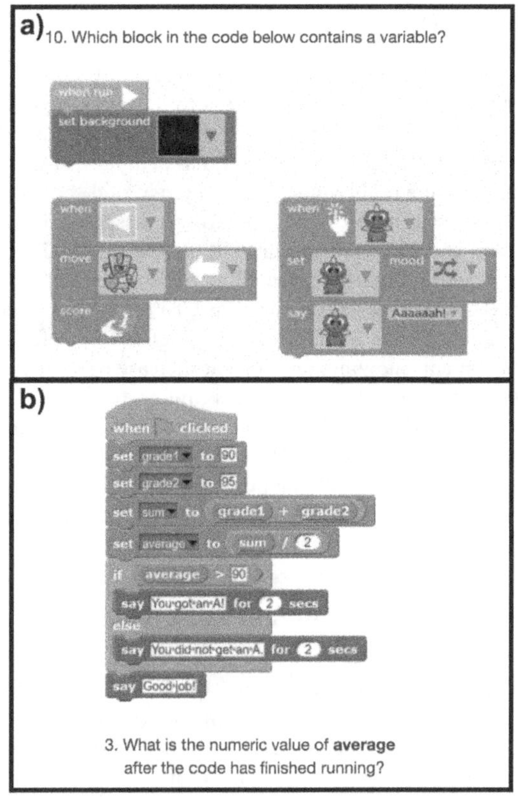

Figure 1: Example assessment items from a) the K-2 assessment and b) the 3rd-8th assessment

3.3 Procedure

The assessments were administered once at the beginning and once more at the end of the workshop. In order to understand the assessment's impact on teachers' understanding of CS concepts, as well as their thoughts on computing and related materials, we conducted focus groups with the teachers after each assessment. The teachers were introduced to their interviewers and split into eight focus groups of three to five participants each, with each group only consisting of teachers from the same grade cohort. The following were the questions asked during the focus groups following the pre-assessment:

- *You just completed a pre-assessment, which we did not expect you to know the answers to. How did you feel about that assessment, in terms of difficulty, content, or format?*
- *How confident do you feel in your ability to succeed in this workshop?*
- *What final thoughts and suggestions do you have regarding this assessment?*

The following were the questions asked during the focus groups following the post-assessment:

- *What are your thoughts regarding the assessment's representation of the topics covered in the workshop?*
- *After taking the assessment the second time, how are you feeling about your computer science abilities?*
- *Now that you are familiar with CS, what recommendations do you have about the assessment?*
- *Research has shown that some assessments have implicit bias. How do you think we could reduce stereotype threat and bias with this assessment?*
- *What final thoughts do you have regarding this assessment?*

3.4 Thematic Analysis

The focus groups were video or audio recorded with permission from the participants, and the recordings were transcribed for further analysis. We used the transcripts to identify emerging themes in the teachers' responses for both focus groups following the pre- and post-assessments. Themes were derived from the most commonly used words in teachers' responses. Each response was assigned a single broad theme based on its content, which was either a new theme or a pre-existing theme that had been assigned to a previous response. After assigning themes to each response, we reviewed the responses once more to assign a subtheme to each response based on the details provided. One focus group was excluded from this analysis because the post-assessment recordings for that focus group were inadvertently not collected.

4 RESULTS

4.1 Assessment Scores

Of the 40 participants, 34 completed both the pre-assessment and post-assessment for their respective grade cohort (14 from the K-2 cohort, 20 from the 3rd-8th cohort). Each item in the assessments was assigned one point value, resulting in a total score of 14 for the K-2 assessment and 17 for the 3rd-8th assessment. The K-2 assessment scores were not normally distributed while the 3rd-8th assessment scores were, according to Shapiro-Wilk tests. The average K-2 pre-assessment score was 60.4% (SD = 19%), and this score increased to an average of 79.1% (SD = 10.6%) for the K-2 post-assessment, showing a significant increase in score from pre- to post-assessment (Wilcoxon signed rank test: $p = 0.0047$; effect size: Cohen's $d = 1.21$). For the 3rd-8th cohort, the average pre-assessment score was 39.4% (SD = 20.1%), increasing to an average of 71.8% (SD = 12.5%) in the post-assessment, also showing a significant increase in score from pre- to post-assessment (t-test: $p < 0.0001$; effect size: Cohen's $d = 1.93$).

4.2 Focus Group Themes Following Pre-Assessment

Table 2 shows a summary of the main themes and subthemes identified from the focus groups following the pre-assessment. The most common theme was **confidence**, mentioned 34 times. Responses in this theme related to questions about how confident the teachers were feeling about their ability to succeed in the professional development workshop. We identified four subthemes for the responses classified under this confidence theme: *confident in ability to succeed* (10 times), *not confident in ability to succeed* (7 times), *neutral confidence in ability to succeed* (3 times), and *positive disposition to learning* (17 times). This last subtheme is distinct in that it refers to responses in which a teacher expressed low confidence in the CS subject matter but a willingness to learn and improve her knowledge, as exemplified by the following quote:

> *"I think you can only go up. At least for me I'm starting with absolutely no knowledge, and so I know that by the end of the week I'm going to have this, all this knowledge. So right now, I'm just sitting here waiting to absorb it and get hands-on practice with it. So right now, I do not have confidence in my ability, but I have confidence in that I'm going to learn this week and be able to do it by the end."* (3rd-8th cohort, 53% on pre-assessment)

The next theme, mentioned 26 times, was that of **question difficulty**. Responses in this theme mentioned the level of effort involved in answering the assessment questions, as well as strategies for completing the assessment. Most teachers mentioned *guessing and using logic* (17 times) as their main strategy, *"I felt like I could guess on some of them through logic, but I wasn't very confident in the answers"* (K-2 cohort, 62% on pre-assessment). Other teachers simply mentioned the *challenging difficulty* (6 times) of the questions, with a few specifically referencing the use of *CS-specific terminology* (3 times) as a source of frustration.

The final theme we identified from the focus group responses related to the assessment's **format** and presentation, and it was mentioned 20 times. Some teachers praised the use of *block-based program images* (9 times) as part of the questions, which helped them more easily visualize the questions. A few teachers indicated a preference towards *fitting all questions into a single window* (5 times) to avoid unnecessary scrolling. Others commented on the *look and feel* (3 times) of the assessment, specifically referencing how selected responses were perceived as being incorrect because they would be highlighted in red, *"We both agree the background color when you click the choice should not be in 'wrong' red"* (K-2 cohort, 46% on pre-assessment). Finally, there were a few mentions about the *variety of question types* (2 times), specifically mentioning the benefits of having different question types.

4.3 Focus Group Themes Following Post-Assessment

Table 3 shows the main themes and subthemes identified from the focus groups following the post-assessment, which was held at the end of the workshop. Once again, the main theme of **confidence** emerged from the teachers' responses to the focus group questions, mentioned 43 times. However, the subthemes were slightly different than in the pre-assessment. The subthemes of *confident in ability to succeed* (17 times) and *not confident in ability to succeed* (3 times) returned, but we also found mentions of *understanding CS concepts* (23 times). The following quote illustrates this subtheme:

> *"Like, I understood the language. The first time I was like, 'what is this?', but this time I'm like 'oh OK,' like I know exactly what they're asking and what the code is saying."* (3rd-8th cohort, 82% on post-assessment)

Teachers also commented on the **format** of the assessments, mentioning it 21 times. Most of their responses involved the survey tool that was being used, referencing the *look and feel* (9 times) and the *variety of question types* (9 times), similar to the responses found in the pre-assessment. Additionally, teachers made comments about the *number of questions* (3 times), mostly relating to insufficient time to cover all of the questions, as described here:

> *"I think there could have been less questions. Even at the beginning, 17 is kind of intimidating. I think it could've been like 10 questions. I think we would've been more comfortable with that. I think we were kind of anxious about 17 and it taking 25 minutes."* (3rd-8th cohort, 65% on post-assessment)

During the focus groups following the post-assessment, we asked teachers for their thoughts on **avoiding bias** (16 times) and for additional suggestions. Some teachers felt that the assessment had *no biased language* (8 times), with mentions on how it does not use gendered pronouns or cultural references. Regarding suggestions, teachers mentioned how the assessment required *English reading and math skills* (5 times) to be completed properly, how *seating arrangements* (2 times) can influence a test taker's confidence if they are sitting next to a highly skilled student, and how students with *limited access to computers* (1 time) could find it more difficult to practice concepts at home.

The last emerging theme from the focus groups following the post-assessment was the **content** of the assessment, mentioned 15 times. In particular, teachers mentioned how the assessment properly covered the topics presented during the workshop, *"I feel like we actually learned what we were assessed on"* (K-2 cohort).

Table 2: Focus group themes following pre-assessment

Theme	Subtheme	Example
Confidence	Positive disposition to learning	*"I have confidence in that I'm going to learn this week and be able to do it by the end."*
	Confident	*"Still confident. I just feel like we'll be able to pick it up."*
	Not confident	*"It made me a little more cautious."*
	Neutral confidence	*"I don't know whether or not I would not want to stop once I got working on a program..."*
Difficulty	Guessing and using logic	*"Yeah, I was guessing and trying to figure out what it all meant."*
	Challenging difficulty	*"It was very difficult, I don't know. When I start reading through it I understand what I don't know and what I need help in."*
	CS-specific terminology	*"Also, some of the language that they use, you have to know that to get through it."*
Format	Block-based program images	*"I agree with the pictures, that definitely helped. Without that, I'd be like 'I don't know.'"*
	Fitting questions to window	*"Sometimes it was so long that you couldn't see the box... so you had to scroll."*
	Look and feel	*"I don't think it should be red because it's like 'oh that's wrong.'"*
	Variety of question types	*"I thought the format was good 'cause it had like multiple choice and typing answers."*

Table 3: Focus group themes following post-assessment

Theme	Subtheme	Example
Confidence	Understanding concepts	*"I understand. The first time it was kind of like a second language."*
	Confident	*"Yes, I was more confident in my answer choices and I wasn't just randomly guessing."*
	Not confident	*"... it would take a lot more for me to really be able to master it."*
Format	Look and feel	*"The red background wasn't a surprise this time."*
	Variety of question types	*"I thought the assessment was good in that it wasn't all multiple choice."*
	Assessment length	*"I think we were kind of anxious about 17 and it taking 25 minutes."*
Avoiding Bias	No biased language	*"It maintained the language of computer science, it didn't say he/she."*
	Reading and math skills	*"I mean obviously you have to have a pretty good grasp of English."*
	Seating arrangements	*"Me sitting next to a male technology savvy, even though I knew him really well, was really intimidating."*
	Limited computer access	*"A lot of students don't have computers so it's gonna be kind of hard for them to do things at home."*
Content	Coverage of topics	*"I think it was really good, like it covered everything we learned in our group."*

5 DISCUSSION

The most common theme across both focus groups following the pre-and post-assessments was confidence. While some teachers expressed low confidence after the pre-assessment, many expressed a positive disposition towards learning more about computer science, regardless of how they felt they performed on the assessment. To that effect, one teacher said, *"I feel like I can learn. I feel like we all have a growth mindset."* (K-2 cohort, 62% on pre-assessment). People with a growth mindset are more likely to view obstacles as learning opportunities rather than as a reflection of their intellectual ability [18]. In a study of undergraduates in an introductory computer science course, researchers found that fostering students' growth mindset led to better performance on assessments compared to students who were not introduced to the concept of a growth mindset [8]. Having this growth mindset may have been the reason for the teachers' self-reported confidence after both the pre-assessment and the post-assessment. The significant improvement in post-assessment score, as well as the reduction of low confidence responses from the focus groups following the post-assessment, echoes prior research on the benefits of having a growth mindset. The increased confidence of the teachers after the post-assessment is exemplified in the following quote:

> *"I was just, I impressed myself with how confident I felt going in taking it and how I could definitively quickly 'yes' this, 'yes' that instead of hemming and hawing about it."* (K-2 cohort, 77% on post-assessment)

When asked to elaborate on the reasons for their lack of confidence in their performance on the pre-assessment, teachers referenced the difficulty of the assessment questions. Some teachers resorted to guessing, *"I felt like I could guess on some of them, through logic"* (K-2 cohort, 62% on pre-assessment), and others mentioned the use of CS-specific terminology as a source of frustration, *"I think there was a lot of terminology that was questionable"* (K-2 cohort, 46% on pre-assessment). They also commented on the format of the assessment and how its presentation could be potentially frustrating to test takers. In particular, teachers expressed a preference towards keeping all relevant question information in a single screen of the assessment, *"... if they have to flip back and forth between the reading passage and the question, they're too conscious about having to find where they were again"* (K-2, 50% on pre-assessment).

Subthemes relating to the assessment's difficulty were not prominent in the focus groups following the post-assessment. Instead, teachers focused more on the format of the assessment and how to improve the test-taking experience overall. This change in theme can be attributed to the professional development workshop's goals of introducing the teachers to CS concepts and encouraging them to reflect on how to integrate CS into their own classrooms. The teachers' newfound familiarity with the CS concepts reduced the difficulty of the assessment, turning their attention instead to the assessment's presentation.

Some positive teacher opinions on the pre-assessment included the use of block-based program images in the question text and the variety of question types. The use of block-based program code in assessment questions has been shown to help improve scores over questions that use traditional code, with the effect being larger on female students and students from underrepresented minorities in CS [24]. One teacher commented on how the block-based program images helped her deduce the answers to the questions, *"...without pictures I wouldn't have been able to figure it out"* (K-2 cohort, 77% on pre-assessment).

In the focus groups following the post-assessment, teachers were asked to identify potential sources of bias within the assessment to get their perspective on ways the assessment could be unintentionally affecting the confidence or performance of test takers. One teacher discussed how her sitting next to a male teacher who was very knowledgeable in the subject intimidated her and decreased her self-esteem, citing stereotypes related to her gender and ability to succeed in STEM. The following quote presents this concern:

> *"Like in our group, there were four of us from the same school, and me sitting next to a male technology savvy, even though I knew him really well, was really intimidating for the whole week."* (3rd-8th cohort, 59% on post-assessment)

In response, another teacher suggested splitting the teachers into cohorts based on skill level. This suggestion is similar to results from prior research on pair programming, which found that students perform better on computer science exams when they work with partners of similar skill level [3].

5.1 Practical Implications

The results presented here highlight some practical considerations for assessing computer science learning:

- When making a digital assessment, make sure each question fits onto one screen so the learners do not need to scroll.
- Tell learners that a pre-test will have vocabulary they are not familiar with, and that is okay. Ask them to do their best.
- Ensure the number of questions is appropriate for the allotted time, taking into account the unfamiliar vocabulary and tendency of many learners to spend time reasoning through items they do not already know how to answer. Good estimates can be obtained by timing volunteers completing your assessment and adjusting the question number accordingly.
- For learners who may not already hold a strong growth mindset, explain the idea of a growth mindset before and/or after assessments and reinforce it throughout your course.
- Test the functionality of online software for administering surveys if this software is to be used for assessments. Its default color choices for user selections (sometimes red) may appear to suggest an incorrect answer.
- Avoid using gendered language in test items.
- Avoid using unnecessarily complex mathematical or scientific content in test items.
- Carefully consider seating arrangements to mitigate the risk that a student who works more slowly or has less prior experience will feel intimidated by a student who works more quickly or has more prior experience. Set classroom norms around what to do when some students finish early.

5.2 Limitations

Our findings have several limitations. We did not formally validate our assessments, but rather they were defined based on our prior experiences in computer science education research and topics covered in the workshop. Additionally, teachers were asked their thoughts on the assessments from their perspectives as K-8 teachers. These opinions may not directly correspond with those of K-8 students, since the teachers may already have stronger preconceived notions about computer science and assessments in general.

6 CONCLUSION

Despite the great strides the community has made in outreach and recruitment, research on how assessments can affect underrepresented groups in computer science is limited. With this study, we explored how our learners, K-8 teachers with very little prior computing experience, responded to an assessment designed as part of a professional development workshop. The assessment featured multiple-choice and short-answer questions, accompanied by block-based program images. The teachers shared their reflections on the assessment, as well as recommendations for improving its design, in focus groups conducted after both the pre- and post-assessment. We identified emerging themes and subthemes, and teachers' responses were classified based on these themes. We found that teachers expressed high levels of confidence after taking both the pre- and post-assessments, which some attributed to their growth mindset. Recommendations for the assessment included accommodations for test takers with low reading comprehension and math skills, limiting the number of questions shown at once, and paying closer attention to the look and feel of the assessment tool.

There are several directions to consider for future work. It is important to conduct similar studies in a classroom where the assessment score factors into the course grade. One teacher remarked they were not being graded during the workshop, so the pressure to perform well on the assessment was much lower, which could have influenced the confidence of the test takers. It is also important for long-term lines of research to continue to investigate assessments in the context of young learners who are still deciding on their career paths. Findings from this research can be used to inform further research on how to improve the test-taking experience for computer science learners.

ACKNOWLEDGMENTS

We would like to thank the LearnDialogue Group for their helpful input. This material is based upon work supported by the National Science Foundation under grants DRL-1640141 and DRL-1721160. Any opinions, findings, and conclusions or recommendations expressed in this material are those of the authors and do not necessarily reflect the views of the National Science Foundation.

REFERENCES

[1] Lecia J. Barker, Charlie McDowell, and Kimberly Kalahar. 2009. Exploring Factors that Influence Computer Science Introductory Course Students to Persist in the Major. In *ACM SIGCSE Bulletin*, Vol. 41. ACM, 153–157.

[2] Skyler J. Bock, Lindsay J. Taylor, Zachary E. Phillips, and Wenying Sun. 2013. Women and Minorities in Computer Science Majors: Results on Barriers from Interviews and a Survey. *Issues in Information Systems* 14, 1 (2013), 143–152.

[3] Grant Braught, John MacCormick, and Tim Wahls. 2010. The Benefits of Pairing by Ability. In *Proceedings of the 41st ACM Technical Symposium on Computer Science Education*. ACM, 249–253.

[4] Philip Sheridan Buffum, Eleni V Lobene, Megan Hardy Frankosky, Kristy Elizabeth Boyer, Eric N. Wiebe, and James C. Lester. 2015. A Practical Guide to Developing and Validating Computer Science Knowledge Assessments with Application to Middle School. In *Proceedings of the 46th ACM Technical Symposium on Computer Science Education*. ACM, 622–627.

[5] Sapna Cheryan, Victoria C. Plaut, Caitlin Handron, and Lauren Hudson. 2013. The Stereotypical Computer Scientist: Gendered Media Representations as a Barrier to Inclusion for Women. *Sex Roles* 69, 1-2 (2013), 58–71.

[6] Sapna Cheryan, Sianna A. Ziegler, Amanda Montoya, and Lily Jiang. 2017. Why are some STEM fields more gender balanced than others? *Psychological Bulletin* 143, 1 (2017), 1–35.

[7] Code.org. 2018. Course A. https://studio.code.org/s/coursea-2018.

[8] Quintin Cutts, Emily Cutts, Stephen Draper, Patrick O'Donnell, and Peter Saffrey. 2010. Manipulating Mindset to Positively Influence Introductory Programming Performance. In *Proceedings of the 41st ACM Technical Symposium on Computer Science Education*. ACM, 431–435.

[9] Wendy DuBow, Joanna Weidler-Lewis, and Alexis Kaminsky. 2016. Multiple Factors Converge to Influence Women's Persistence in Computing: A Qualitative Analysis of Persisters and Nonpersisters. In *2016 Research on Equity and Sustained Participation in Engineering, Computing, and Technology (RESPECT)*. 1–7.

[10] Katrina Falkner, Claudia Szabo, Dee Michell, Anna Szorenyi, and Shantel Thyer. 2015. Gender Gap in Academia: Perceptions of Female Computer Science Academics. In *Proceedings of the 2015 ACM Conference on Innovation and Technology in Computer Science Education*. ACM, 111–116.

[11] National Center for Science and Engineering Statistics (US) (NCSES). 2017. Women, minorities, and persons with disabilities in science and engineering. (2017).

[12] Shuchi Grover and Satabdi Basu. 2017. Measuring Student Learning in Introductory Block-Based Programming: Examining Misconceptions of Loops, Variables, and Boolean Logic. In *Proceedings of the 2017 ACM SIGCSE Technical Symposium on Computer Science Education*. ACM, 267–272.

[13] Margaret Hamilton, Andrew Luxton-Reilly, Naomi Augar, Vanea Chiprianov, Eveling Castro Gutierrez, Elizabeth Vidal Duarte, Helen H. Hu, Shoba Ittyipe, Janice L. Pearce, Michael Oudshoorn, and Emma Wong. 2016. Gender Equity in Computing: International Faculty Perceptions and Current Practices. In *Proceedings of the 2016 ITiCSE Working Group Reports*. ACM, 81–102.

[14] Karla Hamlen, Nigamanth Sridhar, Lisa Bievenue, Debbie K. Jackson, and Anil Lalwani. 2018. Effects of Teacher Training in a Computer Science Principles Curriculum on Teacher and Student Skills, Confidence, and Beliefs. In *Proceedings of the 49th ACM Technical Symposium on Computer Science Education*. ACM, 741–746.

[15] Brian Harvey and Jens Mönig. 2010. Bringing "No Ceiling" to Scratch: Can One Language Serve Kids and Computer Scientists?. In *Constructionism*. 1–10.

[16] Catherine Hill, Christianne Corbett, and Andresse St. Rose. 2010. *Why so Few? Women in Science, Technology, Engineering, and Mathematics*. American Association of University Women.

[17] Amruth N. Kumar. 2012. A Study of Stereotype Threat in Computer Science. In *Proceedings of the 17th ACM Annual Conference on Innovation and Technology in Computer Science Education*. ACM, 273–278.

[18] Laurie Murphy and Lynda Thomas. 2008. Dangers of a Fixed Mindset: Implications of Self-Theories Research for Computer Science Education. In *ACM SIGCSE Bulletin*, Vol. 40. ACM, 271–275.

[19] Hannah-Hanh D. Nguyen and Ann Marie Ryan. 2008. Does Stereotype Threat Affect Test Performance of Minorities and Women? A Meta-Analysis of Experimental Evidence. *Journal of Applied Psychology* 93, 6 (2008), 1314.

[20] Bureau of Labor Statistics. 2018. Employment Projections: Employment by detailed occupation, 2016 and projected 2026.

[21] Bureau of Labor Statistics. 2018. Labor Force Statistics from the Current Population Survey: Employed persons by detailed occupation, sex, race, and Hispanic or Latino ethnicity.

[22] Marcos Román-González, Jesús Moreno-León, and Gregorio Robles. 2017. Complementary Tools for Computational Thinking Assessment. In *Proceedings of International Conference on Computational Thinking Education (CTE 2017), S. C Kong, J Sheldon, and K. Y Li (Eds.). The Education University of Hong Kong*. 154–159.

[23] Lawrence Snyder, Tiffany Barnes, Dan Garcia, Jody Paul, and Beth Simon. 2012. The First Five Computer Science Principles Pilots: Summary and Comparisons. *Inroads* 3, 2 (2012), 54–57.

[24] David Weintrop, Heller Killen, and Baker Franke. 2018. Blocks or Text? How Programming Language Modality Makes a Difference in Assessing Underrepresented Populations. In *Proceedings of the 13th International Conference of the Learning Sciences (ICLS 2018)*. 328–335.

Reflective Diary for Professional Development of Novice Teachers

Martin Ukrop
Masaryk University
Czech Republic
mukrop@mail.muni.cz

Valdemar Švábenský
Masaryk University
Czech Republic
svabensky@ics.muni.cz

Jan Nehyba
Masaryk University
Czech Republic
nehyba@ped.muni.cz

ABSTRACT

Many starting teachers of computer science have great professional skill but often lack pedagogical training. Since providing expert mentorship directly during their lessons would be quite costly, institutions usually offer separate teacher training sessions for novice instructors. However, the reflection on teaching performed with a significant delay after the taught lesson limits the possible impact on teachers. To bridge this gap, we introduced a weekly semi-structured reflective practice to supplement the teacher training sessions at our faculty. We created a paper diary that guides the starting teachers through the process of reflection. Over the course of the semester, the diary poses questions of increasing complexity while also functioning as a reference to the topics covered in teacher training. Piloting the diary on a group of 25 novice teaching assistants resulted in overwhelmingly positive responses and provided the teacher training sessions with valuable input for discussion. The diary also turned out to be applicable in a broader context: it was appreciated and used by several experienced university teachers from multiple faculties and even some high-school teachers. The diary is freely available online, including source and print versions.

KEYWORDS

reflective practice, learning journal, teacher training, teaching assistants, teaching skills

ACM Reference Format:

Martin Ukrop, Valdemar Švábenský, and Jan Nehyba. 2019. Reflective Diary for Professional Development of Novice Teachers. In *Proceedings of the 50th ACM Technical Symposium on Computer Science Education (SIGCSE '19), February 27–March 2, 2019, Minneapolis, MN, USA.* ACM, New York, NY, USA, 7 pages. https://doi.org/10.1145/3287324.3287448

1 INTRODUCTION

Many computer science (CS) faculties employ teaching assistants (TAs) from the ranks of students. This is done for multiple reasons: to integrate prospective Ph.D. and graduate students into academia, to offload the core employees or to cope with the increasing student enrollment [17, 46].

Multiple CS institutions report overwhelmingly positive experience with student TAs [11, 36, 37]. They are proactive, enthusiastic and often able to explain complicated concepts to their fellow students well. Since they still remember the student struggles and can adjust the explanations accordingly, they de facto provide a form of peer tutoring [4], which is often beneficial [44]. Moreover, the TAs themselves strongly benefit from the experience they acquire through teaching. Regardless of whether teaching is their long-term career goal or not, they improve their understanding of CS and soft skills.

The TAs usually have excellent academic performance. However, being knowledgeable in CS does not automatically equal the ability to teach it, and the TAs often have little or no prior pedagogical training[1]. Although the lecturer oversees the development of their technical skills, there is usually nobody helping them improve their pedagogical skills (see fig. 1). Instead, they are often expected to acquire teaching skills "on the fly", which decreases the positive impact they can have as teachers and often also lowers their self-esteem. Therefore, the need for TA training is universal, and there were efforts to address it in the context of CS [14, 32].

In 2016, we established a teacher training course for student TAs at our faculty called the "Teaching Lab". We aim to enhance the quality of teaching CS by improving the skills of new TAs. We also cultivate an active community of CS teachers who share their experiences and best practices. While many interventions can improve teaching, we chose to focus on TAs since they form an important (and often overlooked) portion of the university teaching process.[2]

Apart from several improvements, the Teaching Lab also introduced two major challenges. Firstly, as literature reviews suggest, there is little evidence regarding the impact of training on teaching [19]. Secondly, the effective improvement of university teachers is based on individual feedback, discussion, and mentoring [18], but there are not enough skilled teachers willing to provide such expert feedback.

We decided to alleviate both these issues by guiding the teachers to self-reflection and subsequent analysis of their experience in the community. By doing so, we aim to enhance their teaching skills, since "effective reflective practice is [...] a beginning point in the development of professional knowledge" [28, p. 38].

To support this self-reflection, we created a reflective diary: a semi-structured tool guiding the novice teachers to awareness of their acts (and effects thereof), possible improvements and their strengths/weaknesses. The reflection performed at (or shortly after) the lesson is then revisited and discussed at the regular meeting with other teachers and mentors. The diary also includes a reference to key concepts discussed during the teacher training sessions. Both these aspects allow the diary to bridge the gap between the teacher training sessions and the actual teaching practice of novice TAs.

[1]The TAs in other STEM fields are also poorly prepared for their teaching duties [9].
[2]For the rest of the paper, we will use the term *mentor* as a teacher of the teacher training session, *TA/teacher* as an attendee of the teacher training session, and *student* as a learner who is taught by the TAs.

SIGCSE '19, February 27–March 2, 2019, Minneapolis, MN, USA

ACM ISBN 978-1-4503-5890-3/19/02...$15.00
https://doi.org/10.1145/3287324.3287448

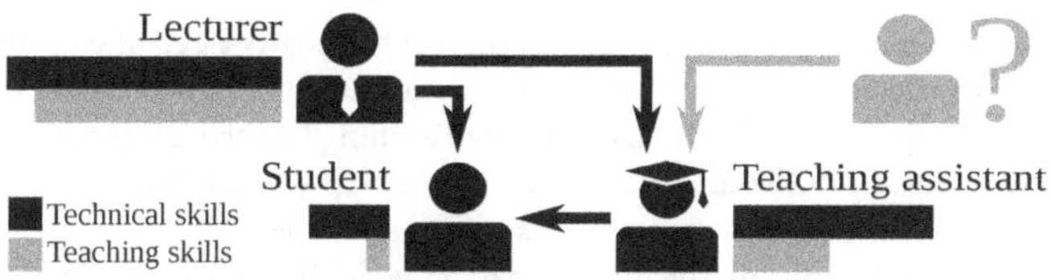

Figure 1: The lecturer oversees the technical development of TAs. But who is helping TAs improve their teaching skills?

This paper reports our experience with using the diary and the lessons we have learned. There are two substantial novelties in our approach. Firstly, to the best of our knowledge, the use of reflective diaries to improve the teaching skills of university TAs has not been published so far. Secondly, the diaries used to support reflection are usually much less structured and lack the methodical section. The diary is publicly available online under a Creative commons license [29], and we encourage all fellow teachers from other institutions to use it or adapt it.

2 RELATED WORK

This section deals with reflective practice and its broader context in CS. In particular, it focuses on multiple versions of reflective diaries and their efficiency.

2.1 Reflective Practice in Teaching

One of the first formalizations of reflective practice can be traced to Dewey's concept of reflective thinking [10]. In the second half of the 20th century, reflective practice was systematically developed in the works of Schön [39], Kolb [24], Boud [6] and Brookfield [7]. Although there is no single accepted definition of reflective practice [21, 33], a common one states it is "a process of learning from experience towards gaining new insights of self and/or practice for future act" [16, p. 15]. Intuitively, reflective practice is systematic thinking about one's own experience focused on future improvement.

Reflective practice is a core concept for educators and one of the major trends and promising innovations in higher education [43]. Reflective practice as a strategy for professional development is applied in many contexts, such as pre-service teaching, nursing education, medical education, psychotherapy training, management education or engineering education (cf. [2]). Furthermore, the concept of reflective practice is connected with many other educational approaches, such as self-regulated learning [47], experiential learning [20] or work-based learning [41]. In these approaches, many methods for supporting professional development are used, including reflective diaries, lesson reports, surveys and questionnaires, audio and video recordings or observation and action research [15].

Reflective writing has been successfully used also in the area of CS education: reflective activities help improve software design using UML [8] and blogging is utilized as a tool for self-directed learning [30] or as a form of feedback for course evaluation [42]. Furthermore, reflective writing is used for the continuous education of primary and secondary school CS teachers [35]. However, reflective diaries as described above mostly focus on supporting the learning of CS *students*. Our approach, on the other hand, innovatively concentrates on novice university *teachers*. Although merely 'thinking about how you teach' may seem obvious, proper reflective practice is hard to carry out and even harder to teach [16]. Therefore, we provide a tool – the reflective diary – to help with performing the reflection.

2.2 The Variety of Reflective Diaries

The reflective diary (a.k.a. learning/teaching journal) is one of the most prominent tools for reflective practice. It is a "container for writing that provides students with a framework to structure their thoughts and reflections" [47, p. 6]. This learner-centered activity provides opportunities for self-education and improves performance.

Although the literature contains general recommendations for reflective diaries (regarding their content, structure or activities performed with it) [31], usually only ad-hoc supplementary materials are available [1, 38, 40] (and often not the complete diaries).

There are many different types of reflective diaries. We can divide them according to three basic criteria [31]: the internal structure, the number of co-authors and the medium they use.

2.2.1 Internal Structure. Different elements can provide the structure within the diary. Examples include a set of standard or contextualized questions, a timeline for a critical incident, comments written or drawn by the learner or a box for an external supervisor (for more examples, see [45]). A well-structured reflective diary can function as a formative assessment of the performer (thus helping the teacher improve their teaching skills). For novice teachers, a more structured reflective diary seems to work better than a less structured one [3].

2.2.2 Number of Authors. A single-author diary serves as a tool for personal development using only self-exploration. A dialogical diary, on the other hand, allows cooperation between the primary author and their supervisor. The access of the supervisor may be limited in some way – e.g., only to observe or to comment on existing sections. A particular kind of dialogical diary is a fully collaborative journal by multiple authors.

2.2.3 Medium Type. A reflective diary can be either paper-based or digital. Although a printed version can be seen as a bit more personal, the digital version is more versatile. Examples include blogs used as personal diaries or to retain a record of events, audio recordings (monologues or dialogues), videos or wiki-based systems for collaborative reflective practice.

2.3 The Evaluation of Reflective Diaries

Research shows that a reflective diary is a useful tool for improving both student and teacher performance. On the one hand, literature reviews document the effectiveness of diaries for university *students*, enabling them to advance in their field of study – examples include pre-service teachers [27], nursing teachers [13] and higher education in general [12]. On the other hand, a reflective diary was used for supporting the career of starting university *teachers* [5]. In an open-ended questionnaire of 64 participants, 80% found journal writing beneficial. According to their opinions, it helped to reflect on their teaching (80%), improved their teaching (81%), and helped link theory and practice (67%) [5]. Our paper is of more qualitative nature, focusing more on the experience from using the reflective journal.

3 THE REFLECTIVE DIARY

This section presents the reflective diary as a tool for integrating teacher training sessions with teaching practice. Firstly, we explain the context leading to the creation of the diary and the principles we employed. Secondly, we outline individual sections of the diary and discuss their aim. Lastly, we give details on a pilot use of the diary that provided us with the lessons learned described in section 4.

3.1 The Wider Context

The diary was created to improve teacher training sessions at the Faculty of Informatics, Masaryk University, Czech Republic. It is a CS faculty with approximately 1,400 students and about 460 people participating in teaching. Out of these, roughly 100 is the regular faculty staff, 80 are members of other faculties and institutions at the university, 110 are external contractors, 55 are Ph.D. students, 50 are graduate (Master's) students, and the remaining 65 are undergraduate (Bachelor's) students. Every semester, about 40 new people start teaching (mostly bright graduates or beginning Ph.D. students who start as TAs). At the same time, a similar number of people stop teaching (mostly graduate students leaving the faculty), keeping the total number somewhat steady.

The TAs participate in a wide variety of courses. Content-wise, the courses span a full CS curriculum, including programming, software engineering, algorithms, formal languages, and discrete mathematics. The form of the courses also varies considerably: from courses featuring explanation in front of the board to those involving individual computer work. As a result, the roles of the TAs vary across the courses: they can lecture, tutor, mentor, grade assignments or consult projects.

As can be seen, students at our faculty form an essential part of teaching. Thus, there is a crucial need to develop their skills. In the past, however, the faculty did not offer any pedagogical training to the student TAs. This situation changed in 2016 when we introduced the Teaching Lab (a teacher training course) and started building the community of skilled teachers open to discussing the issues they face in teaching. The course is intended for approximately 20 attendees who are actively tutoring seminars. It is not mandatory, but 3 credits are awarded for successful accomplishment. In the weekly sessions, we introduce TAs to a variety of relevant topics, including but not limited to: group interactions, asking clear questions, using common teaching tools, creating innovative activities, lesson planning and defining learning outcomes.

We highlight that Teaching Lab is a bottom-up initiative of the TAs from inside the faculty. As a result, the teacher training is not generic but takes into account the specifics of teaching CS. Moreover, it encourages discussion on how to improve particular courses at our institution. So far, the course opened three times.[3] In the latest run, we introduced the reflective diary.

3.2 Creating the Reflective Diary

Our motivation for creating the reflective diary was twofold. Firstly, we wanted the TAs to become reflective practitioners in teaching. Since literature suggests that teachers do not often reflect on their teaching [23], we are focusing (in accord with Hussein [22]) on the means of supporting reflection. The diary can function as the first step to learn from own progress without the costly need of expert mentors. Secondly, we wanted to encourage using the content (such as concepts and tools) discussed in the Teaching Lab classes. If novice teachers apply the discussed concepts and tools themselves, they gain personal experience on what works and when.

When developing the diary, we had two additional design goals: to keep it modular (and thus widely applicable) and easily approachable even by unskilled teachers. The high modularity is necessary because of the heterogeneity of courses taught by our novice teachers. Furthermore, it may allow the adoption of the diary outside of the Teaching Lab community. The reason for easy approachability is that the primary target audience is undergraduate and graduate students teaching their first semester, often with no prior formal teacher training.

Keeping the motivations and design goals in mind, a handful of active and experienced students and teachers (mainly the authors of the paper) drafted the structure of the diary. In comparison with the diaries listed in section 2.2, ours is more structured and enriched with the methodical materials. The process continued by gathering and incorporating suggestions from other members of the Teaching Lab community. It took about three months to develop the first release version from the conception of the idea to print. We preferred paper as a medium as it is easier to develop and work with compared to electronic applications.

3.3 Structure of the Diary

A basic overview of the reflective diary is shown in fig. 2. It has 48 pages in A6 format to comfortably fit into one's pocket. After opening the diary, the introduction explains the importance of reflection. It is followed by the structured space for individual weeks guiding the TA's regular reflection. The diary concludes with a teacher evaluation rubric reminding you what you want to improve and a short reference handbook for concepts and tools discussed in the Teaching Lab sessions. The diary is typeset in LaTeX and version-controlled, allowing for easy modification. It exists in English and Czech versions. Both the sources and the compiled documents ready for print are available on GitHub [29].

3.3.1 Diary Introduction. The diary starts with brief reasoning about the usefulness of reflective practice in teaching and several instructions for use (most notably to use it regularly). To aid the correct use, the main goals of the diary are then transparently summarized: 1) it reminds one to reflect on one's teaching, 2) it provides a convenient place to collect notes for the future, 3) it helps to see different aspects of teaching and 4) it enables to track progress.

3.3.2 Weekly Reflection Pages. The core of the diary is formed by 14 double-page spreads providing enough reflection space for all semester weeks. Each consists of a part to be filled in before the lesson, another part for after the lesson and a full page for notes. The 'before' part encourages the teacher to plan the timeline of the lesson, set learning outcomes or prepare other interaction (e.g., *What precedents do I want to set?, What questions do I plan to ask the group?*). The 'after' part serves for recording subjective satisfaction (*What is my lesson satisfaction?*), highlighting the most prominent successes and opportunities for improvement (*What worked well? What could have been better?*) as well as other useful attributes (e.g.,

[3]In spring 2016, fall 2016 and fall 2017. We are preparing a fourth run for fall 2018.

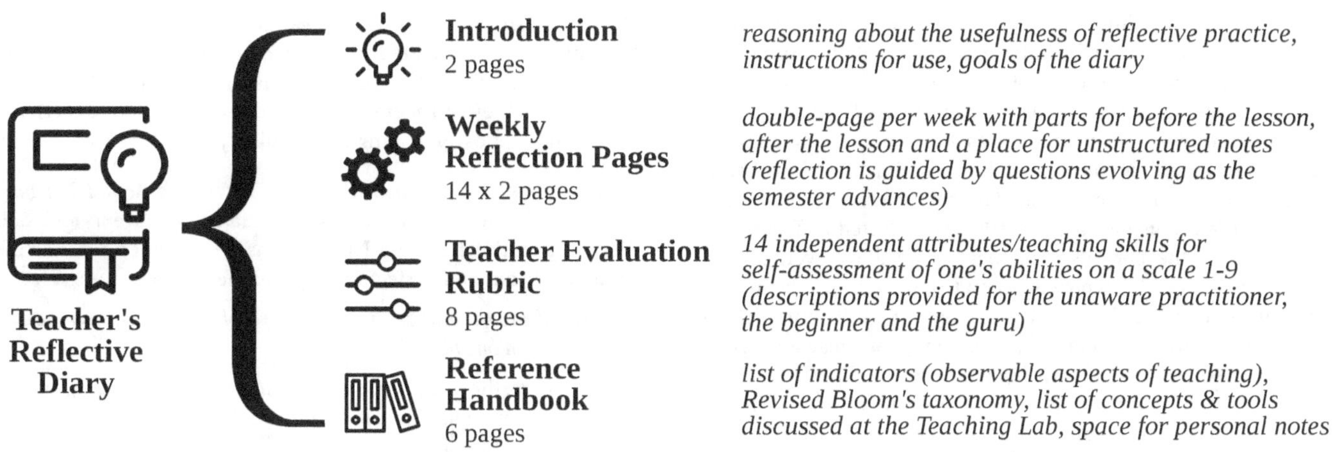

Figure 2: An overview of the Teacher's reflective diary and content of the individual sections. The diary is freely available on GitHub [29] under a Creative Commons license.

Which questions did work in the class? Which did not?). The extra space for comments always has multiple questions pre-printed in gray to guide the teacher if they cannot think of anything to note down (e.g., *How many group questions did I ask? How many questions did the students ask me? Was that too few, enough or too many?*).

The structure and questions on the weekly reflection pages evolve throughout the semester to gradually deepen the reflection. In the beginning, the questions are accompanied by short explanations (e.g., *What is the structure of the lesson? Outline 2–6 blocks on the timeline below.*). Even more importantly, the questions change according to what is relevant in the particular part of the semester: At the beginning, they revolve around precedents, norms, (un)wanted interactions, asking the right questions or identifying teaching problems. In the end of the semester (as more advanced concepts are discussed at the Teaching Lab sessions), they concern higher-level thinking such as what does the course final exam test, whether the course has adequately prepared the students for the exam, how to collect feedback on teaching or what progress did the teacher achieve during the semester.

3.3.3 Teacher Evaluation Rubric. The next part is a scoring rubric for self-assessment of teaching skills, which reminds the teachers of what they want to improve. It consists of 14 independent attributes/teaching skills (not exhaustive but quite representative). For each attribute, one can self-assess their skills on a scale from 1 to 9 with three prominent points described in detail (the unaware, the beginner and the guru). We selected the skills based on what we focus on in the Teaching Lab, which also overlaps with best teaching practices in the literature [26, 34].

Let us illustrate it on an example of a single attribute – *Flexibility/adjustments on the spot.* The label of the teacher unaware of this aspect of teaching reads: *Unaware: I do not consciously respond to situations arising at the lesson.* The beginner practitioner is described as: *Beginner: I am aware of moments where it may be interesting or useful to deviate from the intended lesson plan. Nevertheless, I'm usually unable to react appropriately on the spot.* and the guru level is described as: *Guru: I'm able to adjust my lessons on the fly according to the situation and students' needs. I know enough tools and can use them effectively.*

The usage of the scoring rubric is twofold. Primarily, it allows identifying one's weak spots and tracking improvement. At the beginning of the semester, the owner of the diary assesses themselves in all areas in the rubric and chooses 1–3 skills to concentrate on in the upcoming semester. They can also think of specific indicators if they want to be extra thorough. At the end of the semester, they complete the whole rubric again to see their (self-perceived) progress. Another option is to treat the rubric as a manifesto – the guru descriptions represent our view of the skills great teachers have. Naming and listing these skills enables the teachers to reflect on them with their colleagues.

3.3.4 Reference Handbook. The last part of the diary is a small handbook, which summarizes the concepts and tools discussed during the teacher training sessions. There is a page on indicators (directly observable aspects of teaching) that the teacher can track to help them reflect, evaluate and improve their lessons. Next, the Revised Bloom's taxonomy [25] is summarized along with suggested action verbs to help the teacher think about learning outcomes. Then the diary includes a list of teaching tools introduced at the Teaching Lab sessions. This list eases the adoption of the tools by novice teachers as it works as a short and comprehensive reminder. The tools span across multiple aspects, from the ones that help structure the lesson better, through ones that help assign tasks clearly and efficiently, to ways to create new tasks/exercises or to think about the broader context of the course. The section ends with several empty pages for the owner's personal remarks.

3.4 The Pilot Use of the Diary

In the latest run of the Teaching Lab in fall 2017, we deliberately focused on reflective practice. Before the start of the semester, we handed out reflective diaries to 25 attendees of the course as a compulsory part of the training. Each week, they journaled about their teaching experiences, reflected on them, and shared their findings during the Teaching Lab sessions with their peers and the mentors. Furthermore, we complemented the self-reflection with compulsory peer evaluation, where they observed a peer's teaching practice and provided feedback. Additionally, we offered the diary to several interested senior teachers, who volunteered to try it out. At the end of the semester, we collected feedback from all the participants in an audio-recorded focus group discussion and over e-mail.

Our case study has some limitations. First, there is a strong self-selection bias regarding the users of the diary. Since Teaching Lab is an optional course, its attendees (and thus the users of the diary) are interested in learning how to teach better. The selected staff members intrigued to use the diary also tend to invest an above-average time and effort to perfect their courses. Second, the results may be further biased since we gathered feedback only from a single institution (and only from starting CS teachers and a few language teachers). Nevertheless, the diary was primarily meant to help novice CS teachers, so inapplicability in other fields is not that troublesome. Third, an interviewer bias might be present as the diary authors were present in the focus group discussion and also evaluated the e-mail feedback. To mitigate this, three people analyzed the inputs independently.

4 LESSONS LEARNED

This section presents the lessons learned based on the experience of about 30 teachers from our faculty who used the diary (25 student TAs attending the Teaching Lab and about five members of the regular staff). We share the gathered feedback (including anonymized direct quotations) complemented by our own experience. Furthermore, we discuss the implications and, based on them, suggest future improvements in the next section.

4.1 Successes

We present three significant successes: Using the diary supported the teachers in reflecting on their practice and connected the teacher training sessions to teaching practice more tightly. Moreover, the diary had a broader impact extending outside of our faculty.

4.1.1 Supporting the Reflective Practice. Owning a diary worked as a reminder for the teachers to reflect on their experiences after each lesson. We hypothesize that the diary not only supported but often initiated the process of reflection.

> *"To a great extent, the diary worked as a 'kick' to sit down and think about my lesson."*

> *"Without the Teaching Lab and the diary, I would not think this thoroughly about how I teach."*

Perhaps surprisingly, for some, the diary also worked as a motivator to teach better.

> *"[The diary] had a motivational effect: It made me plan something remarkable so that I would be able to write it into the section listing what went well."*

Next, the diary allowed teachers to gather ideas before, during, and after a lesson. It helped them to keep track of the notes and suggestions for future improvements.

> *"I could tidy up all the ideas of what went well and what didn't in a single place. If the yellow diary didn't shine brightly on my desk, I would probably not do it at all. And since it's in the diary, I know where to find it [...]"*

> *"[I will use it] even more the following year when I'll be checking before every lesson to see what didn't work and what I did wrong."*

Moreover, using the diary raised awareness about reflecting on one's teaching, which cultivated the environment at the faculty. By journaling, the TAs formulated ideas for discussion among themselves. In hindsight, they considered using the diary to be a good experience and did not oppose to having it compulsory.

4.1.2 Connecting Teacher Training Sessions and Actual Teaching. The diary also acts as a handbook: it summarizes concepts and tools discussed in the Teaching Lab sessions. This helped the starting teachers try out and perfect new approaches in their classes.

> *"[Thanks to the diary] I have a list of tools and activities to use together in one place."*

What is more, the diary seems to have increased the teachers' preparation effort, which, arguably, improved their teaching.

> *"[Thanks to the diary] I had put more effort into lesson preparation during the semester. I really filled it in up to about 11th week of the semester."*

> *"[...] before the lesson I noted down 'this must be mentioned to students' so as not to forget."*

4.1.3 Having a Broader Impact. As it was initially not intended, we consider reaching people outside the Teaching Lab community as a major success. The diary attracted the attention of several other student TAs and a few employees of other institutions within our university. Some of them actively used the diary and provided feedback corresponding to the findings above. Furthermore, when we mentioned the diary at relevant events (such as ACM ITiCSE), multiple individuals intended to adapt and use it and promised to share their experience. Teacher training centers at three major Czech universities consider adopting the diary as well. Outside the university realm, a few secondary school teachers were excited and used the diary.

4.2 Challenges

The adopters of the diary encountered three major challenges: irregular use, clashes with other tools and a poor fit for the class format.

4.2.1 Dropout and Irregular Use. As could be expected, not everyone used the diary regularly for the whole semester. Especially people not enrolled in the Teaching Lab (i.e., those not required to use it) dropped out after several weeks.

> *"I wanted to use it, I printed it, but my enthusiasm lasted only for the first few weeks (about four)."*

Others did not use it soon enough after their lesson. This is a problem, since those who did not reflect on a lesson immediately or shortly after usually forgot the details or did not reflect at all.

> *"I have a bad experience with filling the diary in too late [after the lesson] [...] I appeal to everyone to reserve 5–10 minutes right after the lesson [to fill in the diary]."*

What is more, the part 'before the lesson' should be completed before a lesson.

> *"[I would advise] to fill the 'before' part really before the lesson. In 75% of the cases, I filled it in only after the lesson – but in the remaining 25% it really helped me to think more about the upcoming lesson."*

4.2.2 Clashes with Other Tools. Some teachers (both those enrolled in the Teaching Lab and senior ones) already used other means of lesson planning and evaluation (paper or electronic). Therefore, updating the diary sometimes clashed with other tools. For example, some courses require TAs to write weekly reports from the seminars to the leading lecturer. In these cases, people were often unsure of what to write in the diary and what to write in the report.

> *"[...] when we write it [in the report] to the professor, one does not want to rewrite everything into the diary."*

Other courses feature errata documents for the course materials (such as slides or exercises). When a teacher discovers an error and notes it down in the diary (which is conveniently accessible when reflecting), they have to rewrite it elsewhere later on.

4.2.3 Poor Fit for Class Format. The reflective diary was created mainly with weekly lessons in mind. Therefore, the structure did not fit some TAs teaching other types of classes.

> *"I taught two seminar groups – each one bi-weekly and thus the seminars repeated. Apart from that, I taught no theory [...] if I taught [weekly] 'Mathematical Foundations of Computer Science', I would use the diary more often or more effectively."*

As mentioned in section 3.1, the teaching approaches and formats used in different courses vary significantly. The above observation shows that the diary is not yet modular enough to accommodate this.

4.3 Observations

Finally, we share participants' comments that can be classified as neither positive nor negative. These include comments on the medium, format and amount of internal structure. Overall, the diary sections are structured loosely enough to be easily adaptable to one's needs. However, this might have resulted in different ways of use and thus different (and sometimes contradicting) wishes.

4.3.1 Medium and Format. Some TAs suggested that an electronic version (e.g., a mobile app), would be more practical. Others opposed this view and liked the printed version. Of these, some would appreciate a bigger format (e.g., A5-sized) to accommodate more detailed lesson plans while others liked the small and handy A6 size.

4.3.2 Amount of Internal Structure. Finally, some users (especially the beginners) wanted even more questions in the section for free notes to guide their reflection. These generally also wanted more content in the handbook section (e.g., extended and more detailed accounts of tools and concepts discussed at the Teaching Lab). Others (usually the more advanced teachers) sometimes disregarded the guiding questions or had already asked them implicitly and thus used the handbook section minimally.

5 DISCUSSION AND FUTURE WORK

We devise directions for future work from the lessons learned described in the previous section. Considering the successes (section 4.1), we plan to keep the reflective diary a compulsory part of the Teaching Lab, since the usage of the diary turned out to be beneficial according to both the mentors and the teachers. Moreover, we will strengthen guided reflection and experience sharing during the sessions to enhance the connection between teacher training and practice. Finally, as we have seen interest from other groups (language teachers, other institutions), it may be worth initiating proper cooperation with them.

Regarding the challenges (section 4.2), it seems that the dropout is mostly the result of teachers having too much other work and therefore finding the diary expendable. It may be caused by some TAs not perceiving the diary as something that immediately improves their teaching. In the next semester, we will, therefore, emphasize that the benefits of using the diary may become apparent only in the long-term perspective, urging the users to attempt using for a longer time. Furthermore, we will advise them to reserve a short time slot right after the lesson for reflection as doing it later turned out to have limited impact. As for the tool clash (having/using other tools for feedback and reflection), we will ask the teachers what tools they already use and openly discuss how to achieve synergy by incorporating the reflective diary along with them. We will also proactively address how to adjust the individual parts of the diary for teachers with non-standard lessons (e.g., those having only consultations).

As for the observations (section 4.3), we are currently not planning to design an electronic version. Although it could be useful if we wanted to analyze the content of the diaries in more detail, this is not our primary aim, and the development would be quite time-consuming. However, creating two formats (A6 and A5) is feasible and could be helpful for some. Another alternative is a diary with addable/removable pages. Such an adjustable design could optionally accommodate lesson plans or a more detailed version for novices while allowing the advanced teachers to remove the content they would not use anymore.

6 CONCLUSION

We created the Teacher's reflective diary for novice university instructors – a simple yet powerful tool for professional development of CS teachers. Through guided self-reflective journaling combined with a reference handbook, the TAs practically applied concepts from the teacher training and increased self-awareness of their teaching. Since the TAs used the diary in a wide range of CS courses, we gathered rich insight on what worked well and what could be improved. Moreover, the inputs from the TAs' diaries contributed to an open discussion and sharing of experiences in Teaching Lab sessions, cultivating the teaching environment at our institution.

The diary is unique in providing a structured guide for reflection. Based on the thorough literature review, we argue that the diary is the first tool of its kind focused on TAs in CS. Therefore, we encourage fellow CS teachers to use the diary at their institutions and recommend it to TAs. Both the LaTeX sources and the compiled documents ready for printing are available on GitHub [29] for free under a Creative Commons license. While our initial goal was to create the diary for CS university teachers, with very little modification it turned out to work well also outside the context of CS and outside universities.

ACKNOWLEDGMENTS

We thank Ondráš Přibyla for his contributions to the diary and the paper, Martin Macák and the Teaching Lab community for inputs regarding the diary, Bill Siever, Lydia Kraus and Petr Švenda for a thorough internal review and the Faculty of Informatics, Masaryk University for long-term support of the Teaching Lab initiative. Martin Ukrop was also supported by Red Hat Czech.

REFERENCES

[1] Alan Chapman. 2006. Reflective diary/journal process and notes. https://www.businessballs.com/freepdfmaterials/reflective_diary_journal_templates.pdf

[2] Barbara Bassot. 2012. *The reflective diary: enhancing professional development.* Matador, Leicestershire, UK.

[3] Barbara Bassot. 2015. *The reflective practice guide: An interdisciplinary approach to critical reflection.* Routledge, London. https://doi.org/10.4324/9781315768298

[4] Colin Beasley. 1997. Students as teachers: The benefits of peer tutoring. In *Proceedings of the 6th Annual Teaching Learning Forum.* Murdoch University, Perth, 21–30.

[5] Maureen Bell and Max Gillett. 1996. Developing reflective practice in the education of university teachers. In *Proceedings of the 1996 Annual Conference of the Higher Education and Research Development Society of Australaia.* HERDSA, Higher Education and Research Development Society of Australaia, Australia, 46–52.

[6] David Boud, Rosemary Keogh, and David Walker. 1985. *Reflection: Turning experience into learning.* Kogan Page, London.

[7] Stephen D. Brookfield. 1995. *Becoming a critically reflective teacher.* Jossey-Bass, San Francisco.

[8] John W. Coffey. 2017. A Study of the Use of a Reflective Activity to Improve Students' Software Design Capabilities. In *Proceedings of the 2017 ACM SIGCSE Technical Symposium on Computer Science Education.* Association for Computing Machinery, Association for Computing Machinery, Brisbane, Queensland, Australia, 129–134. https://doi.org/10.1145/3017680.3017770

[9] Sue Ellen DeChenne, Natalie Koziol, Mark Needham, and Larry Enochs. 2015. Modeling sources of teaching self-efficacy for science, technology, engineering, and mathematics graduate teaching assistants. *CBE—Life Sciences Education* 14, 3 (2015), ar32. https://doi.org/10.1187/cbe.14-09-0153

[10] John Dewey. 1933. How we think: A restatement of the relation of reflective thinking to the educational process. *Lexington, MA: Heath* 35, 64 (1933), 690–698.

[11] Paul E. Dickson. 2011. Using Undergraduate Teaching Assistants in a Small College Environment. In *Proceedings of the 42nd ACM Technical Symposium on Computer Science Education (SIGCSE '11).* ACM, New York, NY, USA, 75–80. https://doi.org/10.1145/1953163.1953187

[12] Janet E. Dyment and Timothy S. O'Connell. 2011. Assessing the quality of reflection in student journals: A review of the research. *Teaching in Higher Education* 16, 1 (2011), 81–97. https://doi.org/10.1080/13562517.2010.507308

[13] Sheila Epp. 2008. The value of reflective journaling in undergraduate nursing education: A literature review. *International journal of nursing studies* 45, 9 (2008), 1379–1388. https://doi.org/10.1016/j.ijnurstu.2008.01.006

[14] Francisco J. Estrada and Anya Tafliovich. 2017. Bridging the Gap Between Desired and Actual Qualifications of Teaching Assistants: An Experience Report. In *Proceedings of the 2017 ACM Conference on Innovation and Technology in Computer Science Education (ITiCSE '17).* ACM, New York, NY, USA, 134–139. https://doi.org/10.1145/3059009.3059023

[15] Hamidreza Fatemipour. 2013. The Efficiency of the Tools Used for Reflective Teaching in ESL Contexts. *Procedia - Social and Behavioral Sciences* 93 (oct 2013), 1398–1403. https://doi.org/10.1016/j.sbspro.2013.10.051

[16] Linda Finlay. 2008. Reflecting on reflective practice. *PBPL paper* 52 (2008), 1–27.

[17] Jeffrey Forbes, David J. Malan, Heather Pon-Barry, Stuart Reges, and Mehran Sahami. 2017. Scaling Introductory Courses Using Undergraduate Teaching Assistants. In *Proceedings of the 2017 ACM SIGCSE Technical Symposium on Computer Science Education (SIGCSE '17).* ACM, New York, NY, USA, 657–658. https://doi.org/10.1145/3017680.3017694

[18] Graham Gibbs and Martin Coffey. 2004. The Impact of Training of University Teachers on their Teaching Skills, their Approach to Teaching and the Approach to Learning of their Students. *Active Learning in Higher Education* 5, 1 (mar 2004), 87–100. https://doi.org/10.1177/1469787404040463

[19] Annette Gilbert and Graham Gibbs. 1999. A Proposal for an International Collaborative Research Programme to Identify the Impact of Initial Training on University Teachers. In *Research and Development in Higher Education.* HERDSA, Hammondville, 131–143.

[20] Marina Harvey, Debra Coulson, and Anne McMaugh. 2016. Towards a theory of the Ecology of Reflection: Reflective practice for experiential learning in higher education. *Journal of University Teaching & Learning Practice* 13, 2 (2016), 2.

[21] Neville Hatton and David Smith. 1995. Reflection in teacher education: Towards definition and implementation. *Teaching and Teacher Education* 11, 1 (1995), 33–49. https://doi.org/10.1016/0742-051x(94)00012-u

[22] Jeylan Wolyie Hussein. 2006. Which One Is Better: Saying Student Teachers Don't Reflect or Systematically Unlocking Their Reflective Potentials: A Positive Experience from a Poor Teacher Education Faculty in Ethiopia. *Australian Journal of Teacher Education* 31, 2 (2006), 1.

[23] Heng Jiang and Mary F. Hill (Eds.). 2018. *Teacher Learning with Classroom Assessment.* Springer, Singapore. https://doi.org/10.1007/978-981-10-9053-0

[24] David Kolb. 1984. *Experiential learning as the science of learning and development.* Prentice Hall, Englewood Cliffs, NJ.

[25] David R. Krathwohl. 2002. A revision of Bloom's taxonomy: An overview. *Theory into practice* 41, 4 (2002), 212–218. https://doi.org/10.1207/s15430421tip4104_2

[26] Dan Leyzberg, Jérémie Lumbroso, and Christopher Moretti. 2017. Nailing the TA Interview: Using a Rubric to Hire Teaching Assistants. In *Proceedings of the 2017 ACM Conference on Innovation and Technology in Computer Science Education (ITiCSE '17).* ACM, New York, NY, USA, 128–133. https://doi.org/10.1145/3059009.3059057

[27] James T. Lindroth. 2015. Reflective journals: A review of the literature. *Update: Applications of Research in Music Education* 34, 1 (2015), 66–72. https://doi.org/10.1177/8755123314548046

[28] John Loughran. 2002. Effective reflective practice: In search of meaning in learning about teaching. *Journal of teacher education* 53, 1 (2002), 33–43. https://doi.org/10.1177/0022487102053001004

[29] Martin Ukrop, Ondřej Přibyla, Valdemar Švábenský, and Martin Macák. 2017. Teacher's Reflective Diary. https://github.com/teaching-lab/reflective-diary

[30] Roger McDermott, Garry Brindley, and Gordon Eccleston. 2010. Developing tools to encourage reflection in first year students blogs. In *Proceedings of the fifteenth annual conference on Innovation and technology in computer science education.* ACM, Association for Computing Machinery, Bilkent, Ankara, Turkey, 147–151. https://doi.org/10.1145/1822090.1822132

[31] Jennifer A. Moon. 2006. *Learning journals: A handbook for reflective practice and professional development.* Routledge, London. https://doi.org/10.4324/9780429448836-8

[32] Elizabeth Patitsas. 2013. A Case Study of the Development of CS Teaching Assistants and Their Experiences with Team Teaching. In *Proceedings of the 13th Koli Calling International Conference on Computing Education Research (Koli Calling '13).* ACM, New York, NY, USA, 115–124. https://doi.org/10.1145/2526968.2526981

[33] Joan Y. Pedro. 2005. Reflection in teacher education: exploring pre-service teachers' meanings of reflective practice. *Reflective practice* 6, 1 (2005), 49–66. https://doi.org/10.1080/1462394042000326860

[34] Geoffrey Petty. 2009. *Teaching Today: A Practical Guide.* Nelson Thornes, Cheltenham, UK.

[35] Tracie E. Reding and Brian Dorn. 2017. Understanding the "Teacher Experience" in Primary and Secondary CS Professional Development. In *Proceedings of the 2017 ACM Conference on International Computing Education Research - ICER '17.* Association for Computing Machinery, Tacoma, WA, 155–163. https://doi.org/10.1145/3105726.3106185

[36] Stuart Reges. 2003. Using Undergraduates as Teaching Assistants at a State University. In *Proceedings of the 34th SIGCSE Technical Symposium on Computer Science Education (SIGCSE '03).* ACM, New York, NY, USA, 103–107. https://doi.org/10.1145/611892.611943

[37] Eric Roberts, John Lilly, and Bryan Rollins. 1995. Using Undergraduates as Teaching Assistants in Introductory Programming Courses: An Update on the Stanford Experience. In *Proceedings of the Twenty-sixth SIGCSE Technical Symposium on Computer Science Education (SIGCSE '95).* ACM, New York, NY, USA, 48–52. https://doi.org/10.1145/199688.199716

[38] Royal College of Nursing. 2015. Reflective Diary. http://rcneolnutritionhydration.org.uk/wp-content/uploads/sites/6/2015/11/reflective-diary-V3.pdf

[39] Donald Schön. 1983. *The reflective practitioner: How practitioners think in action.* Temple Smith, London.

[40] Scottish Social Services Council. 2011. Reflective Diary. http://workforcesolutions.sssc.uk.com/PracticeSim/scenario_02/Diary/Reflective%20Diary.pdf

[41] Sabina Siebert and Anita Walsh. 2013. Reflection in work-based learning: Self-regulation or self-liberation? *Teaching in Higher Education* 18, 2 (2013), 167–178. https://doi.org/10.1080/13562517.2012.696539

[42] Jeffrey A. Stone. 2012. Using reflective blogs for pedagogical feedback in CS1. In *Proceedings of the 43rd ACM technical symposium on Computer Science Education.* ACM, Association for Computing Machinery, Raleigh, NC, USA, 259–264. https://doi.org/10.1145/2157136.2157216

[43] Lara Tembrioti and Niki Tsangaridou. 2013. Reflective practice in dance: a review of the literature. *Research in Dance Education* 15, 1 (jul 2013), 4–22. https://doi.org/10.1080/14647893.2013.809521

[44] Keith J. Topping. 1996. The effectiveness of peer tutoring in further and higher education: A typology and review of the literature. *Higher Education* 32, 3 (oct 1996), 321–345. https://doi.org/10.1007/bf00138870

[45] Letitia Trif and Teodora Popescu. 2013. The reflective diary, an effective professional training instrument for future teachers. *Procedia-Social and Behavioral Sciences* 93 (2013), 1070–1074. https://doi.org/10.1016/j.sbspro.2013.09.332

[46] Arto Vihavainen, Thomas Vikberg, Matti Luukkainen, and Jaakko Kurhila. 2013. Massive Increase in Eager TAs: Experiences from Extreme Apprenticeship-based CS1. In *Proceedings of the 18th ACM Conference on Innovation and Technology in Computer Science Education (ITiCSE '13).* ACM, New York, NY, USA, 123–128. https://doi.org/10.1145/2462476.2462508

[47] Patric Wallin and Tom Adawi. 2018. The reflective diary as a method for the formative assessment of self-regulated learning. *European Journal of Engineering Education* 43, 4 (2018), 507–521. https://doi.org/10.1080/03043797.2017.1290585

Helping K–12 Teachers Get Unstuck with Scratch: The Design of an Online Professional Learning Experience

Paulina Haduong
Harvard Graduate School of Education
Cambridge, MA
haduong@g.harvard.edu

Karen Brennan
Harvard Graduate School of Education
Cambridge, MA
karen_brennan@gse.harvard.edu

ABSTRACT

K–12 introductory programming experiences are often highly scaffolded, and it can be challenging for teachers and learners to transition from these scaffolded experiences to experiences of learner-directed creative work, where learners are solving problems and fluently expressing ideas through code. Learners can often "get stuck" in this creative process due to a number of different factors: (1) *imagination*, (2) *concepts*, (3) *bugs*, (4) *doubt*, and (5) *pedagogy*. Teachers can support learners in overcoming these factors, but K–12 computing teachers often have minimal preparation and lack computer science backgrounds. However, effective professional development can support teachers in developing the computing skills and pedagogical frameworks for facilitating powerful learning experiences for young people.

In this paper, we describe the design and implementation of *Getting Unstuck*, a 21-day, email-based learning experience for K–12 teachers interested in developing greater familiarity and fluency with Scratch. More than 1,900 people subscribed to the mailing list, with 400 people completing at least one day and 73 people completing all 21 days of activities. Participants received a daily email that invited them to: (1) create a Scratch project in response to a creative prompt that focused on a particular programming concept or Scratch feature, (2) share their work in the online community, and (3) reflect on their learning. We discuss our design decisions and how participants responded to them. We hope that this rich description of the course design will offer insights and inspiration for other CS educators who are designing similar K–12 professional development experiences.

CCS CONCEPTS

• **Social and professional topics → Computational thinking; Informal education; K-12 education;** • **Applied computing → Collaborative learning; Distance learning;**

KEYWORDS

debugging, K–12 professional development, distance/online education, Scratch, teachers

SIGCSE '19, February 27-March 2, 2019, Minneapolis, MN, USA

ACM ISBN 978-1-4503-5890-3/19/02...$15.00
https://doi.org/10.1145/3287324.3287479

ACM Reference Format:
Paulina Haduong and Karen Brennan. 2019. Helping K–12 Teachers Get Unstuck with Scratch: The Design of an Online Professional Learning Experience. In *Proceedings of the 50th ACM Technical Symposium on Computer Science Education (SIGCSE '19), February 27-March 2, 2019, Minneapolis, MN, USA.* ACM, New York, NY, USA, 7 pages. https://doi.org/10.1145/3287324.3287479

1 INTRODUCTION

This is a truly exciting time for K–12 computing education. Never before have there been so many tools and curricula to support introductory experiences for novice programmers. But how do we go beyond these introductory experiences, which are often highly scaffolded? How do we help K–12 teachers and students develop greater fluency and familiarity with programming, eventually leading to greater independence and creative capacity for solving problems and expressing ideas through code?

In this paper, we describe the design and implementation of *Getting Unstuck*, a 21-day, email-based learning experience for K–12 teachers interested in developing greater familiarity and fluency with Scratch. This professional development experience featured daily messages that invited teachers to: (1) create a Scratch project in response to a creative prompt that focused on a particular programming concept or Scratch feature, (2) share their work in the Scratch online community, and (3) reflect on their learning. First, we discuss what motivated the design of *Getting Unstuck*, outlining five factors that often limit deeper participation. We then describe our design principles and participant responses in three sections: *Create*, *Share*, and *Reflect*. Finally, we suggest future directions for supporting K–12 teachers in facilitating learning experiences for novices.

2 BACKGROUND AND MOTIVATION

Introductory programming experiences are often highly scaffolded (e.g., step-by-step video tutorials that rely on direct instruction, whole-group activities that involve making an identical project, puzzle-based experiences that have a single correct answer). Identifying what to do next—how to follow these introductory, scaffolded learning experiences—is often challenging for K–12 teachers; transitioning from these scaffolded experiences to learner-directed creative work can be complicated and require a lot of time and experience for both the teacher and learner. Over the past decade, largely through our work developing ScratchEd, an ecosystem of support for K–12 educators working with Scratch, we have been fascinated by how teachers and learners deal with this leap into independent creative work and the various ways they, as one young learner described, "get stuck."

2.1 What can make creative work challenging

We have identified five factors that contribute to teachers and learners "getting stuck" in creative work. These factors are neither mutually exclusive nor jointly exhaustive; they are recurring themes from conversations with teachers and students about what can make creative work more challenging. These factors have informed our approach to designing learning experiences, and they are: (1) *imagination*, (2) *concepts*, (3) *bugs*, (4) *doubt*, and (5) *pedagogy*.

2.1.1 Imagination. Programming is a new medium for personal expression and problem solving for most teachers and students. So, even with a scaffolded introductory experience, it can be challenging to grasp what is possible to create with code, and an invitation to "create whatever you want" can feel more inhibiting than liberating. However, offering constraints can be a powerful way to unleash the creative imagination and can be a useful way of helping people engage in creative work [22].

2.1.2 Concepts. After a student has identified something that they are excited to make, the next challenge for teachers and students can be a lack of familiarity with the programming language concepts or features necessary to make their dream project. Introductory experiences, of course, cannot acquaint a learner with the entire expressive capacity of a programming language, which leads to a gap between code that is familiar and code that is needed to achieve certain desired creative outcomes. Creating opportunities for learners to encounter new concepts and features, particularly concepts and features that are necessary to achieve their creative aspirations, is essential for evolving fluency.

2.1.3 Bugs. The frustration of not knowing why a program does not behave as anticipated, or not knowing how to fix a buggy program, has been a common refrain from both teachers and students [17]. Especially for younger learners, who have evolving metacognitive skills, the type of bugs that one encounters in creative work can be discouraging. As teachers, being explicit about debugging strategies, as well as encouraging metacognitive development, can support learners through these types of challenges.

2.1.4 Doubt. K–12 teachers often lack computer science backgrounds and receive minimal or no preparation for facilitating computer science curriculum, although there are many ongoing initiatives seeking to provide computer science professional development [15, 18]. With insufficient preparation, teachers can feel unsure about how to personalize existing curriculum to their specific context and classroom, which can lead to using less open-ended and more step-by-step curriculum that may not resonate with, or excite, their population of learners [3]. Students and teachers may also feel held back by assumptions that they are not creative "enough" or "aren't good enough at computing." By creating conditions where learners can see others' projects and get to know others in the computing community, teachers can help learners see a broader range of what programmers look like, as well as what creative work is possible.

2.1.5 Pedagogy. Teachers often describe the pedagogical challenges of supporting more open-ended creative work in the computing classroom, an approach that is unfamiliar to them, both in terms of their professional preparation and their own experiences as learners. This type of learning experience is often also unfamiliar and uncomfortable to their students. Creating opportunities for teachers to experience creative work themselves is an important aspect of making creative work possible in the classroom; congruence between teachers' experiences and learners' experiences is key to classroom pedagogical change [16].

2.2 How to support teachers in supporting creative work

One way to support teachers is through the facilitation of professional development opportunities. Professional development can help teachers gain the skills they need, in addition to developing communities of practice, which can act as valuable supports for teachers. But these opportunities are often ineffective [11], either because they are not tailored to teachers' contexts or because the ideas are hard to implement in practice [5, 13]. Currently, the majority of computer science professional development programs are short (less than a week long), occur only once, and require in-person participation [18]. Although in-person learning experiences can more easily facilitate hands-on and active learning, they can also be cost-prohibitive and limited to resource-dense areas, therefore reaching a smaller audience. And because Scratch has an extremely active international audience, offering online professional development enabled us to connect with educators worldwide.

As Dede et al. [7] write, "the need for professional development that can fit with teachers' busy schedules, that draws on powerful resources often not available locally" has given rise to many online teacher professional development programs (p.9). As learning experience designers interested in supporting teachers and students with developing greater fluency with programming, we wondered: "How can we design an online teacher professional development experience to support teachers in developing their creative confidence, technical capacity, and professional community connections?"

3 DESIGN OF GETTING UNSTUCK

With teacher creative confidence, technical capacity, and professional community connections in mind, we designed a program called *Getting Unstuck*, a free, email-based professional learning experience for teachers. From July 5-25, 2018, we sent out daily emails to participants, predominantly K–12 educators, asking them to create a Scratch project in response to a programming challenge (e.g., "Create a project that shows different backgrounds depending on how loud the room is"), share their creation in a Scratch studio (e.g., "Share your project to the Day 4 studio and look at/comment on others' projects"), and reflect on their creative process (e.g., "What would you do with it next, if you had more time?"). If learners got stuck, we encouraged them to reach out for help, through their Scratch project comments, in the "Teaching with Scratch" Facebook community, or on Twitter. The *Getting Unstuck* email course was free, and although the majority of participants signed up on July 5, there were others who began later and nonetheless completed many, if not all activities. In the remainder of this section, we describe the design of each of these experience elements (i.e., *Create*, *Share*, and *Reflect*) and how participants engaged with them.

3.1 Create

3.1.1 Short, daily prompts. Block-based programming environments, like Scratch, readily display all of the blocks that might be used to create a project, whereas text-based languages, with a "blank slate" approach, often require a novice to memorize a certain amount of vocabulary in order to create a program. However, just because all of the different blocks are visible does not imply that those blocks will either be used or understood. Because of the focus on sprites, backdrops, and other media assets, novices often gravitate towards the *Motion*, *Looks*, and *Sound* block categories in Scratch, with an occasional nod towards the *Control* category when needed.

The core of our design approach in *Getting Unstuck* involved inviting participants to engage in creating a project every day for 21 days, focusing on aspects of the Scratch programming environment that are not necessarily intuitive or obvious to a novice. In designing each daily challenge, we considered which blocks and computational concepts were challenging and/or underutilized in novice projects we have seen through our previous work. We designed prompts for blocks related to traditionally difficult concepts, such as loops and variables [21], as well as blocks related to Scratch-specific concepts, such as the *Pen* category or video/sound sensing blocks.

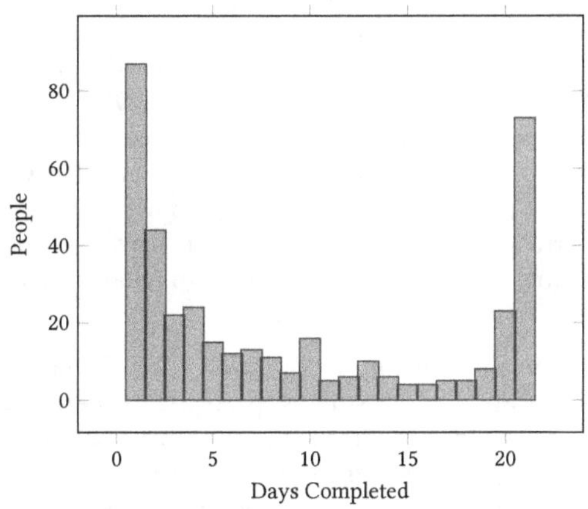

Figure 1: How many challenges did people complete?

Building on the role and value of constraints in supporting learners' creativity, we designed the prompts to be open-ended (i.e., invited a range of responses, not a single solution) and short (i.e., could be completed in less than an hour). Because there was a new prompt available daily, we hoped that even if participants became stuck on a particular concept that was challenging for them, they would not feel discouraged for too long, because there was something entirely different to try the following day. This was intentional in our design; although some learning initiatives have a specific sequence in mind, so that learners cannot progress to the next concept without mastering the first, we argue that part of the work of introducing novices to the breadth of creative programming possibilities involves preventing them from getting too bogged down in unproductive and frustrating failure. The complete collection of daily prompts is available at bit.ly/GettingUnstuckChallenges.

3.1.2 How people participated. More than 1,900 people signed up for the *Getting Unstuck* mailing list. Of those subscribed, 400 people completed one or more of the 21 days, and 73 people completed all 21 days synchronously. As Evans and Baker [9] noted, persistence and participation in online learning experiences can look very different from traditional, face-to-face courses, largely because it can be very easy to enroll but more challenging to consistently participate. Given this, many online learning experiences have large discrepancies between the number of registrants and the number of participants who complete the entire experience. Segmenting the participation of these 400 people into quartiles, the first quartile completed one day, the second quartile completed 2 to 5 days, the third quartile completed 6 to 19 days, and the fourth quartile completed 20 or 21 days. Figure 1 illustrates this distribution of participation. Many participants, through social media postings as well as notes on their Scratch projects, reported spending 20 minutes to several hours on each daily project.

Participants had varying degrees of prior familiarity and fluency with Scratch. Of the 1,900 people who subscribed, 6% were brand new to Scratch, 14% had heard of Scratch but had not used it themselves, 33% had helped someone else make a project, 24% had made a few projects, and 23% felt well-acquainted with Scratch. This variability in prior experience was evident in how people engaged with the daily prompt. As in a classroom, learners bring different understandings and experiences to the learning context, and should be able to make connections to the learning in their own ways. As just one example of how people took the same prompt and responded in very different ways, consider Day 6 of *Getting Unstuck*, which invited participants to create a project that uses the random block. The complete collection of Day 6 projects is available at scratch.mit.edu/studios/5142691, but we will highlight four examples. One participant used the random block to create a Magic 8 Ball, another participant created a random-joke generator for teachers, another participant implemented the Monty Hall problem, and another participant used the random block to generate abstract art. Figure 2 includes code excerpts from each of these four projects, illustrating the different ways people used the random block in their project implementation.

In addition, we were pleasantly surprised by how much people created. As the designers of *Getting Unstuck*, we were also participating in the act of daily project creation, so we had a visceral appreciation for the intensity of the experience. We had considered different deployment methods (e.g., more days or fewer days, weekly vs. daily), but had converged on 21 days based on the literature around habits and development of expertise [14]. In retrospect, we wished that we had built in some time off during the experience (e.g., weekends off), for participants and for us to get caught up, and would certainly consider adopting that as a strategy in future designs, where the entire experience of 21 challenges could take place during the entire month of July. Because most of our participants were U.S. K–12 educators, and the majority of U.S. K–12 schools are on the 9-month September-May academic calendar, July can be an ideal month for an intensive professional development experience.

3.1.3 Participant persistence. Given the intensity of this daily practice over three weeks, we wondered what motivated people to persist, particularly the 100 people who completed 20 or 21 days. We

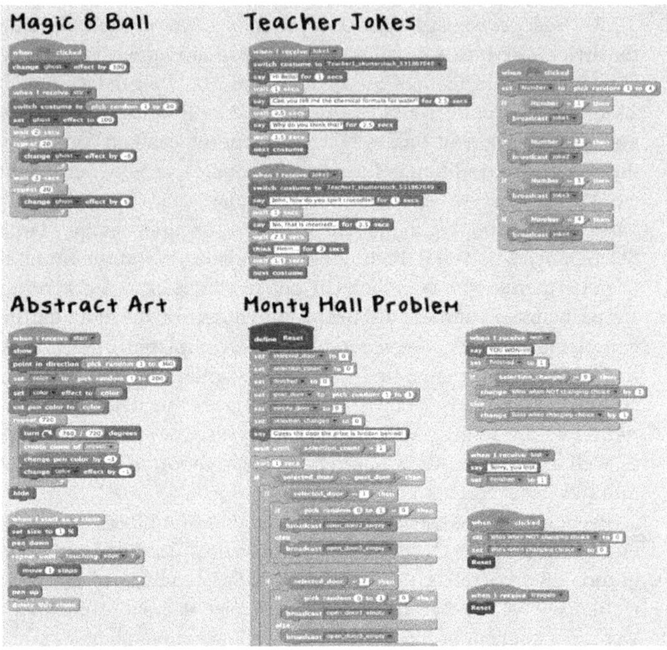

Figure 2: Four projects that involve the random block. Clockwise, from top left: Magic 8 ball, random joke generator, Monty Hall, and abstract art.

incorporated a trivial form of extrinsic motivation into *Getting Unstuck*; anyone who completed all 21 days of the experience would be eligible to receive a set of three stickers. We included this as a recognition of sustained effort, a very small token of our appreciation to people for participating, rather than a serious form of extrinsic motivation. We were amused to see the sticker pack jokingly being identified as the reason for completing all of the activities. More earnestly, though—in project comments, on social media, and via end-of-experience survey data—participants regularly mentioned the intrinsic motivation that supported their sustained participation. One participant shared that, "This course was addictive! The everyday challenge was super motivating!", while another shared that the pleasure of creating encourage her to expand her efforts: "When it started, I thought I would just spend a little bit of time each morning doing a little project, but I actually started planning part of my day around it because I had so much fun!" Numerous people, independent of prior experience level, talked about the motivation that accompanies learning new things. As a participant with prior proficiency noted, "I consider myself to be a 'Scratch Expert,' but Getting Unstuck showed me things from a new angle and I learned a lot."

3.2 Share

3.2.1 Daily challenge studios. After creating a response to the daily prompt, participants were asked to share their project in a studio dedicated to that particular prompt. Many participants commented that it was helpful to see how many different ways there were to approach the work. On Day 2, for example, participants received the following prompt: *Display a flower each time that the user clicks on the background. There are at least three different ways of programming this in Scratch—what will your approach be?*

Figure 3: Day 2: Making flowers appear.

Participants shared projects with aesthetic variations: some participants used pre-made sprites from the library, some designed flowers using the Scratch Paint Editor, and some found images of their favorite flowers online. Participants shared projects with implementation variations: using hidden objects to detect clicks, using built-in background-sensing blocks to detect clicks, and using polling with mouse clicks to detect clicks. Participants looked at each other's work and, in some instances, revised their project, based on ideas they encountered in others' work. Some participants posted their projects with bugs, and others commented with suggestions or even remixed the original projects to offer new solutions. As one participant wrote, "Collaboration is key to getting unstuck. Viewing other projects and talking through issues with others was very helpful."

3.2.2 Building community more broadly. In addition to sharing work within the Scratch studios, participants were encouraged to share and ask for support via the #CreativeComputing Twitter hashtag and in the *Teaching with Scratch* Facebook group. As designers, we hoped to not only introduce teachers to the various opportunities for social interaction within the Scratch community, we also aspired to strengthen teachers' networks and communities of practice.

While the majority of the social interaction happened within the Scratch studios, on the projects themselves, we also saw teachers sharing their projects and asking for help (for a specific day's challenge, as well as concepts more broadly) through Twitter and Facebook. From July 1 to July 25, membership in the *Teaching with Scratch* Facebook group went up 58% (to 1,900 total members), and there were 212 posts and 773 comments, primarily about *Getting Unstuck*, which represents 473% and 244% increases, respectively. Although there were fewer requests for help on Twitter, we did see many participants proudly sharing their creations via Twitter and participating in conversations with other non-Scratch educators. While Twitter was used less often than Facebook by the teaching team, it served as a key promotional tool before and during the learning experience, and Twitter chats have often been relied on by educators as a source of professional development [6].

The *Getting Unstuck* online community was not only a place to find help, but also a way to cultivate an appreciative audience, which served as an additional motivating factor. One participant shared, "I found a new appreciation for the Scratch community. I had never engaged in it myself before, so I enjoyed commenting on other projects and receiving comments on mine!" As adults on the Scratch platform, which is primarily designed for young people, it can be challenging to find fellow learners with the same motivation and goals. Another participant wrote, "I believed I was part of a small community within Scratch with the members of Unstuck. This was something new for me. With the vastness of Scratch, I did not have that sense of connection with others until now."

3.2.3 Barriers to Sharing. When learners create projects with others, these connections can support learners debugging their current work and spark ideas for future projects. This social nature of learning has been well-documented as essential for supporting both young people and teachers [4, 10, 12]. Within in-person learning environments, the learning community is often conceptualized as the classroom environment. But Scratch is both a blocks-based programming environment and a large online community, where kids are making friends, making projects together, and learning from one another.

Although K–12 classroom educators may be aware of the value of sharing work with peers, both within the classroom and more broadly, there are many barriers that may prevent educators from supporting Scratch community interaction in the classroom, and as a result, there are many educators primarily using the Scratch 2 Offline Editor. Some of the barriers are technical in nature; for example, poor internet connectivity can be challenging when all of the students in a classroom are trying to use Scratch simultaneously. Many public schools also block or filter social media sites on campus [1], due to concerns about student attention and data privacy, and we have also heard from teachers that these network management systems occasionally mistakenly block the Scratch website.

Teachers might also be concerned about being new to the online community, as well as trying to maintain their in-person classroom as an independent learning ecosystem. Because Scratch projects must be public before they can be shared to any studio, this means that it is possible for other Scratch users to interact with a student's project, and teachers may not be prepared to act as a moderator if or when other students comment on a project. There may also be concerns about whether "likes" are merely an extrinsic motivator or are actually useful in supporting a learner's development. Within *Getting Unstuck*, we modeled meaningful engagement with others' work—"liking" projects and adding comments about specific things we appreciated or asking questions about how something in the project was made. One participant remarked at the end, "I don't use 'likes' in class because I find it can be a distraction, but if I encourage a comment along with it, it may prove to be more useful."

There may also be educational concerns about how much or where the learning is happening when students are not clearly focused on their own work. Because the Scratch homepage features different projects that the community currently loves and is remixing, it can be easy for young learners to be distracted by playing engrossing games, and those projects can also scare novices away because of their technical complexity. But if learners are able to spend time looking at different projects for inspiration, there are exciting opportunities for learning. On Day 2, one participant tweeted that she "spent less time programming, but a lot of time admiring all the cool projects in today's studio." This participant made a project that responded to the prompt, learning from and being inspired by what others had made. Because the studio had a specific focus through the daily prompt, it was easier for learners to draw connections from others' projects to their own work.

3.3 Reflect

We asked participants to publicly post daily reflections along with their projects, answering questions such as, "What was challenging about this project? What was exciting? Which debugging strategies did you use?" Over the 21 days, we saw how reflection supported individual learning, how the public nature of reflection supported the learning of others, and how reflection on process enabled participants to develop greater understandings of students' experiences of the programming process.

3.3.1 No learning without reflection. The experience of creating and sharing can support learning, but the act of reflecting deepens a learner's understanding of what they have learned, why they learned it, and how that learning took place [8]. This is particularly true when the learning is challenging or unsuccessful. In those instances, "reflection can often give us insights into what may have gone wrong with our learning, and how on a future occasion we might avoid now-known pitfalls" [19].

Although we were interested in supporting participants in developing greater computational fluency through the act of creating projects, we also wanted to encourage participants to practice writing reflectively on their project artifacts and processes. We invited participants to write their reflections in the *Notes/Credits* text box on the project page. While some only wrote a few words about a block or two that was challenging, others wrote not only about what blocks and bugs they struggled with, but also some of the emotional challenges that are a natural part of the process. For example, one participant wrote about how looking at some complete projects felt initially inhibiting, but after choosing a creative direction and trying out new blocks, realized that the prompt was not as difficult as originally perceived.

> *"This was fun. After looking at the first couple projects submitted I was paralyzed! They were so good! Then I realized I could counter that with something sooo baaad-ddd! I have used operator blocks more and more during the last two weeks. However, I really have not used the list blocks before. I saw them in someone else's project, realized how it could be used, and tested them out. Much easier than I anticipated. That, added to the realization earlier that I could randomized broadcasts, didn't make this too hard in the end."*

However, not all participants contributed written reflections on their product or process. As illustrated by Figure 4, of the projects submitted for the initial prompt, often only two-thirds of the projects had text in the *Notes/Credits* sections of their projects (i.e., the blue bars), while one-third left that area blank and didn't respond to the reflection prompts (i.e., the red bars). As participants dropped off and there were fewer projects submitted overall, the

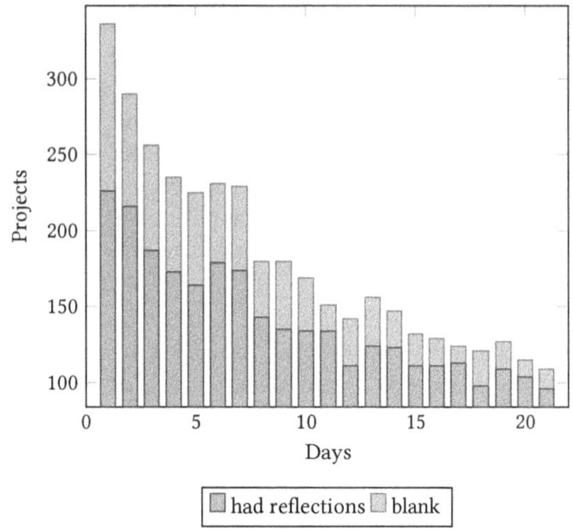

Figure 4: Who wrote notes/credits for their projects?

number of projects without reflections decreased, likely because participants noticed that posting reflections was a norm.

3.3.2 Public reflection normalizes the struggle. Although reflection is primarily an individual act, reflection-in-public by one learner can support other learners in better understanding their own learning. These public reflections, collectively, can also support learners in normalizing some of the challenges and struggles that are natural and necessary components of learning to program [20].

> *"The most difficult part for me with this remix was figuring out how to prevent players from scoring points after the timer went off. After getting seriously stuck and getting help from a friend, we came up with a variable based on the game's state as either "on" or "off." Such a simple, powerful idea."*

Learning to program can be difficult and isolating [2, 21], and debugging is a natural part of the process. For every *GettingUnstuck* prompt, though, there were a number of different bugs that learners might have encountered, and it was unlikely that any individual learner would practice debugging all of those errors in a single project. Being able to see a range of reflections, then, helped learners understand the wider range of possibilities, in terms of what could be created, what bugs might be encountered, and what debugging strategies might be employed. For example, one participant wrote about a specific issue they were struggling with, but they also wrote about how they got unstuck by asking for help from a friend, and how their specific solution worked.

3.3.3 Reflection as empathy building. Towards the end of *Getting Unstuck*, participant reflections began to turn towards classroom practice, both in terms of how they might use *Getting Unstuck* prompts in the classroom, as well as how their experiences as learners with Scratch were congruent with their students' experiences. One participant wrote, "As I approached these daily exercises in a 'student mode,' I truly experienced the excitements, the frustrations, the struggles that my students face in the classroom. Specifically, the pressure of time constraint that I have experienced really hit home with me. I work with students in the after-school setting and they only get to spend one hour with me each week." Another said, "I now know far more about using Scratch. Also, when things worked, I got an enormous sense of satisfaction. The other side of this is that I gained real insight into how the children must feel when they really don't get it."

4 CONCLUSION

Through creating, sharing, and reflecting, *Getting Unstuck* participants challenged themselves to try unfamiliar computational concepts and Scratch features, learned with and from one another, and deepened their understanding of their own and their students' experiences with programming. Some educators talked more openly about the anxieties and fears that arose as they worked through their projects, while others wrote about not realizing what kinds of projects were possible with a deceptively simple prompt. There are many ways to struggle with the creative programming process beyond encountering bugs within the code, and we are excited to see how an experience like *Getting Unstuck* can help educators grapple with some of the additional barriers to supporting creative computing, whether they ask students to try more open-ended prompts or develop more in-class sharing and reflecting strategies. As participants practiced getting unstuck, they developed more awareness of the different kinds of factors that can pose challenges to learners' ability to successfully produce creative work.

However, it is important to recognize that even if these factors—of imagination, concepts, bugs, doubts, and pedagogy—are overcome, there may still be contextual and logistical challenges which may pose difficulties in achieving equitable computer science participation. For instance, educators in school districts that lack sufficient computers and bandwidth may not be able to support learners exploring the online Scratch community. Others may work in schools preoccupied with high-stakes testing, or schools with required programming curriculum, so it may be more challenging to implement these kinds of learning experiences. These were not challenges that we experienced as facilitators of this online learning experience, but they may very well be ones that arise for many educators.

In addition to challenges educators may face in their classrooms, we also want to highlight that there are limitations in who is able to participate in this particular kind of online teacher professional development. Although *Getting Unstuck* activities were not intended to be time-intensive, some participants were able to spend much longer on their projects than others. Although July is generally an optimal month for many teachers on the 9-month academic calendar, there are also K–12 teachers who work at 12-month schools, or teachers who hold additional summer jobs, and these educators may not be able to devote the necessary time and resources to a free, but also unpaid, learning experience.

As we continue to work to broaden participation in K–12 computing education, we look to deepen our understandings of what kinds of supports can enable teachers and learners to get unstuck. In particular, we are excited to consider new iterations of online teacher professional development to help teachers develop their own confidence and facilitate more opportunities for creative computing in the classroom.

REFERENCES

[1] June Ahn, Lauren K. Bivona, and Jeffrey DiScala. 2011. Social media access in K-12 schools: Intractable policy controversies in an evolving world. *Proceedings of the American Society for Information Science and Technology* 48, 1 (2011), 1–10. https://doi.org/doi:10.1002/meet.2011.14504801044

[2] Sarah B Berenson, Kelli M Slaten, Laurie Williams, and Chih-Wei Ho. 2004. Voices of women in a software engineering course: reflections on collaboration. *Journal on Educational Resources in Computing (JERIC)* 4, 1 (2004), 3.

[3] Karen Brennan. 2015. Beyond right or wrong: Challenges of including creative design activities in the classroom. *Journal of Technology and Teacher Education* 23, 3 (2015), 279–299.

[4] David Buckingham and R Willett. 2006. *Digital Generations: Children, Young People, and the New Media.* Routledge, London.

[5] Linda Darling-Hammond, Maria E Hyler, and Madelyn Gardner. 2017. Effective teacher professional development. *Palo Alto, CA: Learning Policy Institute* (2017).

[6] Kerry Davis. 2015. Teachers' perceptions of Twitter for professional development. *Disability and Rehabilitation* 37, 17 (2015), 1551–1558. https://doi.org/10.3109/09638288.2015.1052576

[7] Chris Dede, Diane Jass Ketelhut, Pamela Whitehouse, Lisa Breit, and Erin M. McCloskey. 2008. A Research Agenda for Online Teacher Professional Development. *Journal of Teacher Education* 60, 1 (2008), 8–19. https://doi.org/10.1177/0022487108327554

[8] John Dewey. 1933. How we think: A restatement of the relation of reflective thinking to the educational process. *Lexington, MA: Heath* 35, 64 (1933), 690–698.

[9] Brent J. Evans and Rachel B. Baker. 2016. MOOCs and Persistence: Definitions and Predictors. *New Directions for Institutional Research* 2015, 167 (2016), 69–85. https://doi.org/10.1002/ir.20155

[10] Barry J Fishman and Elizabeth A Davis. 2006. *Teacher learning research and the learning sciences.* Cambridge University Press, Cambridge, 535–550.

[11] Heather C. Hill, Mary Beisiegel, and Robin Jacob. 2013. Professional Development Research: Consensus, Crossroads, and Challenges. *Educational Researcher* 42, 9 (2013), 476–487. https://doi.org/10.3102/0013189X13512674

[12] Mizuko Ito. 2009. *Engineering play: A cultural history of children's software.* MIT Press.

[13] Andy Jacob and Kate McGovern. 2015. The Mirage: Confronting the Hard Truth about Our Quest for Teacher Development. *TNTP* (2015).

[14] Phillippa Lally and Benjamin Gardner. 2013. Promoting habit formation. *Health Psychology Review* 7, sup1 (2013), S137–S158. https://doi.org/10.1080/17437199.2011.603640

[15] Dan Leyzberg and Christopher Moretti. 2017. Teaching CS to CS Teachers: Addressing the Need for Advanced Content in K-12 Professional Development. *Proceedings of the 2017 ACM SIGCSE Technical Symposium on Computer Science Education* (2017), 369–374. https://doi.org/10.1145/3017680.3017798

[16] Ann Lieberman. 1995. Practices that support teacher development: Transforming conceptions of professional learning. *Innovating and evaluating science education* (1995), 67–78.

[17] Renée McCauley, Sue Fitzgerald, Gary Lewandowski, Laurie Murphy, Beth Simon, Lynda Thomas, and Carol Zander. 2008. Debugging: a review of the literature from an educational perspective. *Computer Science Education* 18, 2 (2008), 67–92. https://doi.org/10.1080/08993400802114581

[18] Muhsin Menekse. 2015. Computer science teacher professional development in the United States: a review of studies published between 2004 and 2014. *Computer Science Education* 25, 4 (2015), 325–350. https://doi.org/10.1080/08993408.2015.1111645

[19] Phil Race. 2002. Evidencing reflection: putting the âĂIJwâĂİ into reflection. *Retrieved May* 30 (2002), 2013.

[20] Joseph A. Raelin. 2001. Public Reflection as the Basis of Learning. *Management Learning* 32, 1 (2001), 11–30. https://doi.org/10.1177/1350507601321002

[21] Anthony Robins, Janet Rountree, and Nathan Rountree. 2003. Learning and Teaching Programming: A Review and Discussion. *Computer Science Education* 13, 2 (2003), 137–172. https://doi.org/10.1076/csed.13.2.137.14200

[22] Patricia D Stokes. 2005. *Creativity from constraints: The psychology of breakthrough.* Springer Publishing Company.

Perfect Match: Facilitating Study Partner Matching

Tam Nguyen Thanh
Monash University
Melbourne, Australia
thanh.nguyen@monash.edu

Michael Morgan
Monash University
Melbourne, Australia
michael.morgan@monash.edu

Matthew Butler
Monash University
Melbourne, Australia
matthew.butler@monash.edu

Kim Marriott
Monash University
Melbourne, Australia
kim.marriott@monash.edu

ABSTRACT

With the massive growth of online learning, there has been a decrease in students' face-to-face interactions, leading to rising feelings of isolation. This in turn contributes to several issues such as motivation loss, increased course attrition rates and poor learning experiences. Strong Online Learning Communities (OLCs) have been suggested as a means to help improve the situation, however the formation of OLCs is strongly influenced by learners' individual characteristics and their preferences regarding how and with whom they would want to form study groups. Taking students as its focus, this research attempts to develop a learning partner recommender system (LPRS) to facilitate finding compatible study peers in order to promote informal learning communities among students. From a synthesis of related literature and using data from a study of the student' preferences, a collection of learners' individual characteristics has been identified as a set of matching criteria in our LPRS model. A proof of concept based on the conceptual model has been developed and evaluated with a small group of target users. Results of the investigation showed positive feedback from participants and good prospects of the recommender system.

CCS CONCEPTS

• **Social and professional topics → Computing education**;

KEYWORDS

Online Learning Communities, Learning Partners, Recommender Systems

ACM Reference Format:

Tam Nguyen Thanh, Michael Morgan, Matthew Butler, and Kim Marriott. 2019. Perfect Match: Facilitating Study Partner Matching. In *Proceedings of the 50th ACM Technical Symposium on Computer Science Education (SIGCSE '19), February 27-March 2, 2019, Minneapolis, MN, USA.* ACM, New York, NY, USA, 7 pages. https://doi.org/10.1145/3287324.3287344

SIGCSE '19, February 27-March 2, 2019, Minneapolis, MN, USA

ACM ISBN 978-1-4503-5890-3/19/02...$15.00
https://doi.org/10.1145/3287324.3287344

1 INTRODUCTION

An innate feature of online learning is the reduced availability of face-to-face interactions and communication through which a sense of learning community is created, which in turn is often responsible for students feeling isolated. It is unsurprising that students feel isolated in fully online courses. However, in the higher education context with an increased reliance on blended learning a feeling of disconnectedness is not uncommon [38, 46]. The issues emerging from disconnected students are many, including a loss of motivation, poor academic performance, and higher drop out rates. In such a context, supporting Online Learning Communities (OLCs) has become a more significant issue [6].

Students' individual characteristics are asserted to have significant impact on the formation of OLCs [4]. Therefore, finding peers compatible with these characteristics is a key factor for having a safe and supportive OLC emerge. In online learning environments, Learning Analytics (LA) data and processes have the potential for facilitating the collection and analysis of data about students' characteristics and preferences regarding those with whom they would want to do their study.

With an ambition of promoting informal online learning communities among learners through stimulation of positive interactions, the research describes the design and implementation of a recommender system (Learning Partner Recommender System - LPRS) which provides students with suggestions on learning partners based on their individual characteristics, what they look for in peers, and preferences in learning partners. A conceptual model of the system was developed with criteria used for generation of recommendations. These criteria were collated from previous literature on Collaboration Learning (CL), Learning Communities (LCs), and Group Formation (GF). This was combined with data on students' perspectives on appropriate matching criteria. A proof of concept of the system was then developed and preliminary user acceptance testing has been conducted. Results of the initial testing have shown that the LPRS is considered to have the potential to facilitate students to overcome some existing obstacles in order to find suitable learning partners and improve their learning experiences.

2 BACKGROUND AND CONTEXT

This section provides an overview of the importance of online learning communities, factors influencing group formation and the use of Learning Analytics to support Recommender Systems.

2.1 Online learning communities

Feelings of isolation are common in fully online courses and MOOCs [5, 24]. In higher education (HE) there is an increasing adoption of blended learning (referring to the integration of online learning activities into the traditional classroom) and therefore on-campus attendance has been declining. This trend is closely related to a major challenge, students' feeling that they are disconnected from their peers [38, 46]. In this context, OLCs have been asserted to play a significant role in improving issues highly associated with students' feelings of isolation, such as low course retention rates, loss of motivation and poor learning experiences.

Although different approaches to encourage OLCs in HE have been studied, the majority of studies have focused on issues such as syllabus design, the instructor's role and behaviour, and strategies to encourage students' interaction [6, 45]. However, the interactions encouraged tend to be centred around subject content in formal learning contexts with an emphasis mainly on cognitive processes [25, 51]. Little attention has been placed on affective social-emotional interactions among students and their role in facilitating OLCs.

2.2 Group formation

Group formation has been a critical task in facilitating collaborative learning (CL) in HE since negative effects might emerge if there is lack of careful consideration in the process of grouping students into teams working together [9]. Being derived from best pedagogical practices, grouping criteria are typically highly associated with learning aspects of students such as their understanding level on a given topic [26] or the collaborative goals set by the teachers such as forming groups of students with heterogeneity in marks or learning styles [34].

Many of students' individual characteristics and preferences have been used as grouping criteria in previous research including personality [22, 28], learning styles [31], topic-specific knowledge level [52], demographic traits [34], communication skills [33], and topic preferences [48]. However, each study investigated an individual characteristic or a small set of factors; and most of the time considered learning performance (grades) as the ultimate goal of encouraging collaborative activities. Also, previous work has mainly focused on supporting teachers assigning students into short-term groups primarily based on topic- or project-specific requirements rather than for the formation of more generic task-free and longer lasting informal study groups.

Nevertheless, research in this area has strongly suggested that students' characteristics and preferences play an important part in grouping them into a team. These factors are even more vital when it comes to attempts to promote informal learning communities. The present project aims to create an accessible platform where learners can find peers with compatible characteristics which fit their preferences in order for a comfortable and trusting atmosphere to be created, which is the key for a learning community to emerge.

2.3 Recommender systems for study partners

In education contexts, recommender systems play an important role in the effort to improve learning experiences, with a focus on generating recommendations for learning materials or courses content to access. Recently, there has been an increased interest in research to develop systems to support students to find study partners, emphasising the reciprocal nature of recommendation requirements [37]. Different factors have been used to generate recommendations such as knowledge level, availability, preferences [23], demographics, interests [40], or on an ad-hoc basis in cases where students need help with specific problems [11, 12]. These studies have brought valuable contributions to research in the field and showed the potential for improving learners' experience through suggesting suitable peers. However, factors used in those studies for recommendation generation are based on researchers' rationale or academics' requirements. The students' attitudes and perspectives have not been explored. Evaluation approaches used to assess these systems have often employed synthetic data, focusing mainly on technical aspects such as scalability, coverage, precision and recall [23, 40]. Again, students' experience and satisfaction have not been investigated.

Moreover, in the context of remarkable growth of online learning, Learning Analytics (LA) has the potential to collect data about students' characteristics and preferences in an objective manner. Thus, LA can serve as one of the primary data sources for such a recommender system. However, in the context of this paper, establishment of the system has the highest priority in order for the matching process to be investigated. Therefore, integration of LA data from external sources will be deferred to further research.

3 METHODOLOGY

Considering the identified research problem, that forming a meaningful informal learning community in higher education contexts can be challenging, this paper presents a learning partner recommender system where students are provided with suggestions on peers who might learn well with them based on compatible characteristics and preferences.The research questions are:

> RQ1: What are the characteristics of students which can be used as matching criteria?
> RQ2: How to design and implement the proposed LPRS?

In order to tackle these research questions, two phases of the study have been established employing a mixed method. Phase 1 focuses on identifying a set of students' characteristics which can be used as matching criteria in the system. In this stage, studies in relevant areas have been reviewed to compile a collection of students' characteristics conducive to OLCs which can be used as study partner matching criteria. Then data collection was carried out with IT students to explore their perspectives on the collated characteristics and potential of the proposed LPRS. Next, Phase 2 of the research aimed at implementing the proposed learning partner recommender system. A working proof of concept of the recommender system has been designed, implemented and investigated with a focus group.

4 ANALYSIS AND RESULTS

By reviewing literature on areas including Collaborative Learning (CL), Online Learning Communities (OLCs) and Group Formation (GF), a collection of students' individual characteristics which are considered as influential factors in their participation in collaborative activities, and in the formation of a learning community in online environments, was collated.

The identified characteristics were classified into two categories: (1) Academic factors: motivation, self-efficacy, skills, learning styles, learning patterns, academic interests and education level; and (2) Socio-psychological factors: personality, willingness to communicate (WTC), self-perception of being connected, hobbies, demographics, and preferred communication channels. Table 4 gives a summary of the important students' characteristics from literature conductive to collaborative learning, knowledge sharing, and the development of OLCs.

Characteristics	Research Base	Data Source
Education Level	[4]	LA
Learning Styles	[1, 31]	Felder-Silverman questionnaire
Learning Patterns	[15, 50]	LA
Academic Interests	[10, 26, 52]	LA & Self-report data
Motivation	[18, 43]	MSLQ Quiz (Motivation subscale)
Self-efficacy	[10, 18]	MSLQ Quiz (Self-efficacy subscale)
Skills & Experiences	[10, 15, 31, 32, 48]	LA & Self-report data
Willingness to Communicate (WTC)	[8]	WTC Questionnaire
Personality Traits	[18, 48, 49]	Personality Questionnaire
Self-perception of being connected / separated	[4, 44]	Self-report data
Demographics	[4, 21, 34]	LA (profile data) or Self-report data
Preferred Communication Media	[4, 47]	Self-report data
Hobbies	[27]	Self-report data
Students' Preferences	[17, 48, 49]	Self-report data & Interaction data

*** Blue = academic factors. Pink = socio-psychological factors.**

Table 1: Students' characteristics conductive to OLCs

4.1 Phase 1: Confirming Preferences

Since the proposed LPRS is student focused, aiming to match peers with compatible characteristics and preferences, it is essential to explore; (1) students' perspectives on factors they consider important when looking for study mates, and (2) their attitudes towards the proposed recommender system. An online survey and semi-structured interviews with undergraduate IT students of Monash University were carried out to obtain these insights.

The online survey instrument was designed based on the types of LCs [42] and Sense of Community [30] factors. The focus was on students' experience on three forms of Learning Communities, including: Knowledge-based, Practice-based and Task-based LCs [42]. Also examined were the perceived benefits of being a part of an LC, difficulties when working/learning with others, and factors which they find important in peers when working in a group. Follow-up interviews were conducted to obtain deeper insight into factors covered in the survey. From April to June 2017 when the online survey was available, 35 students responded (24 males and 11 females). Out of the 35 survey respondents, ten students (7 males and 3 females) agreed to take part in the follow-up interview session.

Findings from the Phase 1 data collection (both online survey and interviews) are presented below. First of all, among the three forms of LCs, informal learning communities (Practice-based) received more negative remarks compared to the other forms. Students tended to feel less comfortable and valued this form of LC least. An insight regarding this trend relates to how the three forms of LCs take place in the current learning environment. For Task-based learning activities, group members usually have a clear idea of what they have to do, which tasks to accomplish and a suitable manner to collaborate together. Therefore, while conflicts regarding how to work together towards a common goal might occur, students would tend to make efforts in resolving collaboration issues emerging so that the collective work would not be jeopardised and harmfully affect learning outcomes (such as grades). In terms of Knowledge-based LCs, participants share common interests in a particular area. Also, they do not have the pressure of completing a task/project towards a deadline. Consequently, Knowledge-based LC members are likely to feel less tense and more relaxed working with each other. This is in contrast to Practice-based LCs. Here, students have to figure out how to collaboratively work and learn together mostly by themselves outside of classroom and beyond the initial instruction period. This is where students might best develop their self-regulated and collaborative learning, but also where difficulties would emerge in respect of how to effectively collaborate with others, how to juggle lectures, tutorials, self-study and outside classroom learning activities, and how to benefit from participating in this form of LCs. This is an area where the present research has the potential to make significant impact.

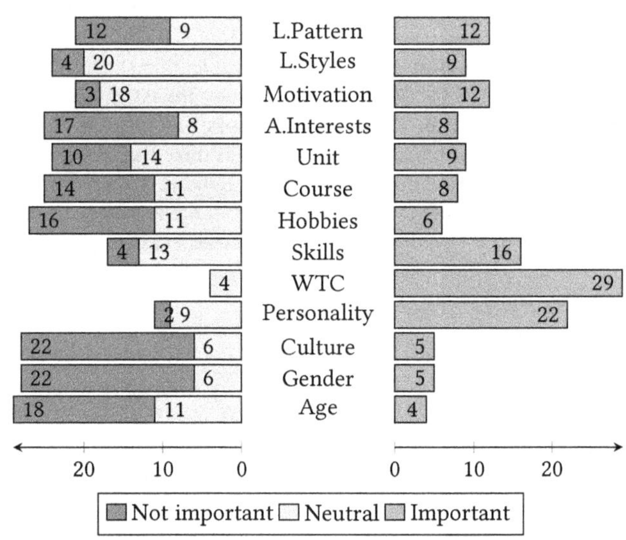

Figure 1: Students' perceived importance of different characteristics (N=33)

Second finding was about valued factors in peers. 33 out of 35 students who participated in the online survey responded to a question

SIGCSE '19, February 27-March 2, 2019, Minneapolis, MN, USA

asking them to specify which characteristics they consider important when looking for study partners. Survey data revealed that characteristics in other peers which were appreciated by most students included willingness to communicate, personality, academic skills/experience, motivation and learning patterns (see Figure 1). Other factors which received varying lower levels of significance by the participants were learning styles, interests, hobbies, demographics and education levels. Similar perception was found in interview results except for learning patterns where students mentioned that one's learning patterns might result from one's degree of self-motivation and personality. Also, it should be noted that self-efficacy was not examined in the initial survey. This factor only emerged during the interviews and was later searched for in previous literature and integrated into the list of important characteristics (Table 4). Importantly, responses showed that there existed a need among learners for finding peers who possess favourable features and to make connections with those peers.

Finally, as for the proposed LPRS, 96% of survey respondents contended that compatible characteristics among learners could help improve (or had possibilities in improving) their learning experience. Also, the majority of interviewees' opinions suggested that students believed such a system could facilitate matching learners with compatible characteristics and fitted individual preferences (such as similar interests and complementary skills).

4.2 LPRS Conceptual Model

Based on the synthesis of literature and results retrieved from the Phase 1 data collection on IT students' perspectives, a model of a partnership recommender system for students is shown in Figure 2. Results from Phase 1 suggested that different characteristics are perceived with varying level of significance by students. That suggested an idea for assigning weights to characteristics in determining the compatibility level of two arbitrary learners.

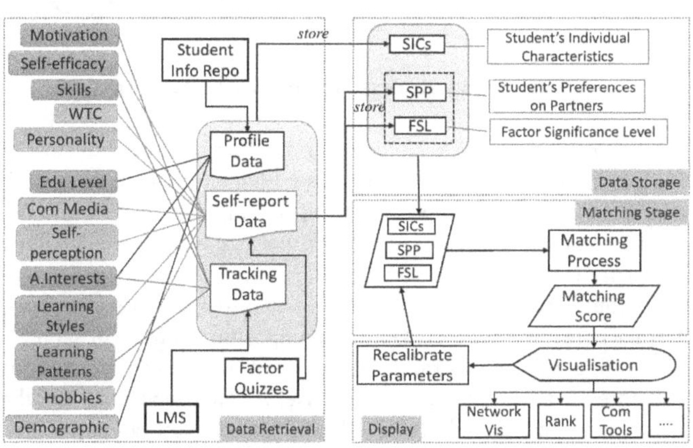

Figure 2: LPRS Conceptual Model

The proposed LPRS model consists of four stages - Data Retrieval, Data Storage, Matching, and Display. In the model, 13 factors (Figure 2 left) are used as matching criteria, the five listed on the top being the ones that either received high perceived significance according to the survey results or emerged from the interviews. The other factors at the bottom (including learning patterns and seven other factors) are those with varying levels of importance as perceived by students who participated in both the survey and interviews. Values of these factors are suggested to be retrieved from three main sources including: profile data, tracking data and self-report data. Profile data involves students' basic information such as demographics, education level, degree, major, year and academic interests. Tracking data, derived from a Learning Management System (LMS), keeps track of students' activity within the online learning environment. Self-reported data refers to data provided by students themselves through explicit indication or completion of characteristic forms. After that, the retrieved data is stored, being categorised into (1) student's profile, data about their own characteristics, and (2) student's preferences, which consist of preferences on learning partners and significance levels of different factors. Next, data is fed into a matching process to generate compatibility scores. An interactive visualisation is suggested to be used to present recommended peers so that students can have a better insight into the displayed results.

4.3 Phase 2: LPRS Design and Development

Although there are 13 factors suggested to be used as matching criteria in LPRS, as a proof of concept six out of the 13 are used as key matching factors. The five factors which are perceived as important to students include: Willingness to communicate, Personality, Self-efficacy, Motivation, Skills; and the sixth factor - Learning styles - has been employed intensively in group formation area. Factors, such as Demographics, Education level and Academic interests, are used as recommendation filtering conditions. Value of the motivation factor is currently collected in self-rating form, but will potentially be retrieved from an external source (LMS).

4.3.1 Design blocks. The system proof of concept is comprised of four main blocks - Profile, Preference, Recommendation, and Utilisation, as demonstrated in Figure 3. Profile is made up of results from characteristic forms. Preference keeps track of what students look for in preferred learning partners. Recommendation takes care of the presentation of recommended peers generated from the matching process; while Utilisation aims to facilitate initial contact among students as well as future evaluation of the system.

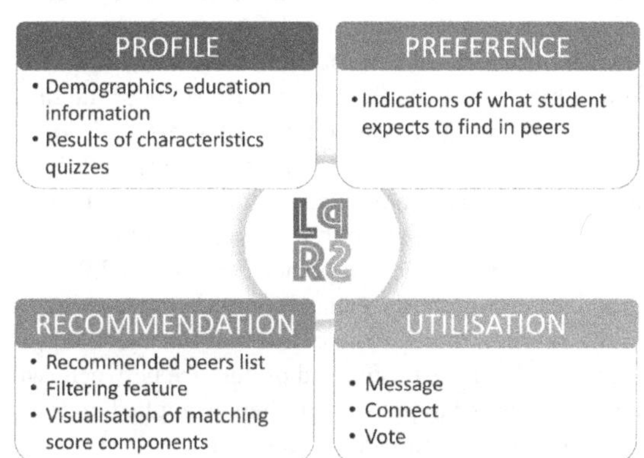

Figure 3: LPRS Design Blocks

4.3.2 Student Profile and choice of characteristic questionnaires. Four characteristics (WTC, Personality, Self-efficacy, Learning styles) are retrieved via questionnaires. The questionnaires employed are those which have been designed and reported on in literature (see Table 2). Although some studies were conducted to automatically identify students' characteristics such as Personality traits [2, 16], or Learning styles [3, 7, 19] based on students' online activities in LMSs, those studies had to resort to corresponding questionnaires to evaluate the automatic approaches' performance and accuracy. Thus, although there is an awareness that users would have to be involved more in data retrieval phase of the system, for the purpose of quality data, self-report questionnaires are the key data sources.

Characteristic	Questionnaire	#Qs
WTC	WTC Scale [29]	12
Personality	BFI-10 [41]	10
Self-efficacy	Self-efficacy subscale from the (MSLQ) for College students [35]	8
Learning Styles	Felder-Silverman questionnaire (Active/Reflective & Global/Sequential) [13, 14]	22

Table 2: Characteristic Questionnaires

4.3.3 Matching approach. The matching approach identified is known as a two-way or reciprocal recommendation [36, 37]. This is distinguishable from common recommender systems where the recommended items are objects and suggested to human users with their individual taste/preference. Suggesting learning partners would not work if a recommendation only satisfies one party. It is essential to take into account characteristics and preferences of both the recommended peer, as well as the one who receives the recommendation.

In reciprocal recommendation, there are two main methods: Content-based and Collaborative Filtering (CF) [36, 37]. The former refers to an approach where a target user is suggested to make connections with people who possess similar attribute values as the ones the target user has connected to. The latter can be either Item-based or User-based. Item-based assumes that if many of A's connections are also connected to B, then A might also like to connect to B too. User-based assumes that similar users might wish to connect with the same people. A Content-based approach is applicable when there is a substantial amount of user interaction data, which is not the case at an early stage of the LPRS [39]. CF is conducted mainly based on similar users' opinions which tend to be more social network oriented. This research focuses on students' more intrinsic characteristics, their preferences and how they impact their participation in learning communities.

Thus, the recommendation approach employed in LPRS has been established: profile-preference matching and content-based. At the start of the process, matching is performed through calculation of the degree to which the profile and preference between two users match. Content-based approach can then be applied once a certain amount of user interactions have occurred.

This part presents the matching algorithm used in the system - Profile-preference matching. Data of a user (referred to as user A) in the system is comprised of A's characteristics (which consists of values of the six factors) and A's preferences (which includes (i) A's preferred value of factors in peers, and (ii) A's perceived significance level of characteristics when looking for learning partners). For each pair of two users referred to as users A and B, firstly one-way matching scores $score_{(B \to A)}$ are generated. This indicates how user B's characteristics fit user A's preferences. Then the reverse one-way matching score $score_{(A \to B)}$ is calculated, which indicates how user A's characteristics fit user B's preferences. It is to be noted that the calculation of one-way matching scores takes into account the weight (significance level) of factors which were assigned by the users. The calculation of $score_{(B \to A)}$ can be formulated as:

$$\sum_{i=1}^{N} fit(V_{C_i(B)}, V_{C_i Pref(A)}) * W_{C_i(A)}$$

N is the number of characteristics used as matching criteria ($N = 6$ in this research). $V_{C(B)}$ is user B's values of a specific characteristic C. $V_{C_{Pref}(A)}$ is value of the characteristic C which user A would want to find in learning peers. $W_{C(A)}$ is the weight user A has assigned to the factor C. Then the harmonic mean [37] of the two scores is generated to obtain the compatibility score between the two users. Figure 4 demonstrates a way in which recommendations on peers can be represented. Information includes the peers' user name, compatibility score, education and demographics, their skills, as well as interests. Here, users can filter the recommendations based on these kinds of information.

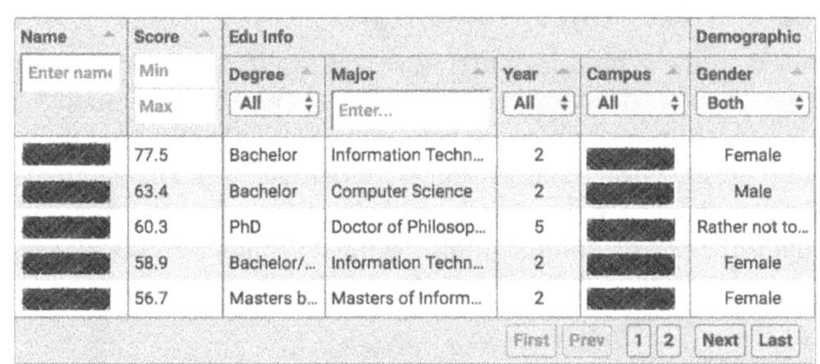

Figure 4: Recommendations with peers' info

4.3.4 Presentation of Recommendations. Inspired by the work of [20] about a visualisation technique which employs bar charts to create an interactive representation of multi-attribute rankings, an inline horizontal stacked bar chart was used to visualise how compatible a target user is with other users in the system.

Recommendation results are presented to a target student in a form of compatibility scores with decomposition of the score components. Figure 5 demonstrates the visualisation of recommendations presented to a target student (called user A). Here, column 1 lists the name of recommended peers, followed by the *Score* column which indicates the compatibility score of user A with a corresponding peer. This compatibility score is made up of components represented in column 3 and 4. Column 3 (*They fit you*) illustrates the extent to which the peers' characteristics fit user A's preferences; while column 4 (*You fit them*) represents the degree to which user A's characteristics suits the peers' preferences. Characteristics are colour-coded and the length of each portion represents the weight which user A has assigned to that characteristics when the user entered their preferences. The order of coloured bars is based on how user A ranked/weighed the importance of the characteristics. As for the shades of a colour, the darker shade of a colour represents how much one's characteristic fits the other's preference regarding that particular matching criterion, While the lighter shade illustrates the unmatched portion.

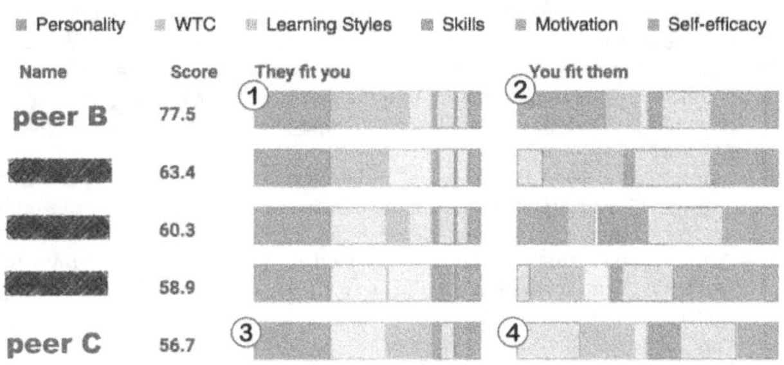

Figure 5: Recommendations with compatibility score decomposed

To illustrate, in Figure 5, user A (the student who receives the recommendations) ranked the characteristics as Personality, WTC, Learning styles, Skills, Motivation and Self-efficacy in descending order of importance. Therefore, stacked bars in both column 3 and 4 are arranged consistently in this order. Regarding individual matching factors (characteristic), user A considers personality as the most important characteristics while looking for learning partners and similar personality is preferred.

Considering the recommended peer in the first row (peer B), the peer has the highest compatibility score of 77.5 (out of 100). At ①, user A's preference regarding Personality is satisfied by peer B's Personality. Similarly, as can be seen at ②, peer B perceives personality as the most important and prefers study partners with similar personality traits. User A and peer B fit quite well in terms of other factor as well. In contrast, peer C - who has the lowest compatibility score in user A's top 5 recommendations - ranks Skills as the most important factor, followed by Personality, WTC, Motivation, Self-efficacy and learning styles. Although peer C's value of Personality fits user A's preference concerning this factor ③, peer C prefers those with different personality traits ④. Similarly, user A's requirement on WTC is not met by peer C. Also peer C's Skills preference is not fully satisfied by user A's experiences. These mismatches all affect the final compatibility score of the two users.

4.4 LPRS User Acceptance Testing

In order to investigate usability of the proposed LPRS and gather its target user's opinions about the system, a second round of data collection involving a focus group (FG) was conducted. Activities in the session involved system interactions (account creation, data inputs, system outputs), group discussion, 8-item usability questionnaire, and seeking user comments. An invitation to the FG was advertised in three units of Faculty of IT, Monash University. Eight students agreed to take part in the FG activities. By the time of the FG commencement (31st May 2018), key system blocks had been preliminarily developed including user profile, preferences, generation and presentation of recommendations.

In FG discussions participants confirmed that there exist difficulties when it comes to looking for peers to learn with due to mismatches of characteristics among peers. Specific characteristics mentioned included work attitude, personality, commitment, learning styles, skill-level, and motivation. One participant stated:

> There's no existing platform which allows students who are strangers to study together [...] Normally you can meet people at lectures and tutorials, but not people from other streams or timetables.

As for system usability, positive feedback was given by the participants. All the students were positive about the potential of the system to facilitate students finding informal learning partners with compatible features. The majority of the participants (7 out of 8) found LPRS simple to use. They managed to become familiar with the system with little effort or detailed instructions. Interestingly, participants also mentioned that the 'characteristics' questionnaires seemed to generate similar results to the ones which they had previously taken, particularly those for personality and learning styles. Also, the students reported that the visualisation of recommendations were interesting and tended to meet their expectations. They reported that the inline bar chart (see Figure 5) could help users make sense of the compatibility scores which indicate the degree to which they and their peers fit.

Importantly, useful suggestions emerged from the FG activities and discussion which have contributed to further refinements being applied to the development of the LPRS. The main points suggested were: (1) using additional matching criteria (such as location, degree, major, interests), (2) changes to make the visualisation of the recommendation easier to understand, (3) features to generate better user experience, such as an improved process for completing the characteristic forms, and (4) supporting users' decision making, such as providing more relevant information about connected peers. These minor changes will be implemented before further usability testing and deployment of the system at large scale.

5 CONCLUSION AND FURTHER RESEARCH

This paper describes the model of LPRS and the process in which its proof of concept was developed employing a collection of students' characteristics as matching criteria. The identification of the characteristic set (to address RQ1) involved (1) literature view on relevant areas, and (2) investigation of students' perspectives on LCs and preferences for a partner recommender system. A working system was implemented (to address RQ2) with different components including system data retrieval, matching approach and implementation, recommendation presentation implementation, and integration of utilisation tools. An initial user acceptance test has been conducted. Results have shown interest from students as the target user of the system, and good prospects of the LPRS to facilitating finding peers with compatible characteristics to form informal learning communities.

The next steps in refining the LPRS include: system modifications based on student feedback from the FG, additional user testing prior to wide scale deployment, combination of both qualitative and measurable quantitative approaches in evaluation, and integration of data retrieved from LMS systems to incorporate LA on their online activity.

REFERENCES

[1] Enrique Alfonseca, Rosa M Carro, Estefanía Martín, Alvaro Ortigosa, and Pedro Paredes. 2006. The impact of learning styles on student grouping for collaborative learning: a case study. *User Modeling and User-Adapted Interaction* 16, 3 (2006), 377–401.

[2] Yair Amichai-Hamburger and Gideon Vinitzky. 2010. Social network use and personality. *Computers in Human Behavior* 26, 6 (2010), 1289–1295.

[3] Jason Bernard, Ting-Wen Chang, Elvira Popescu, and Sabine Graf. 2017. Learning style Identifier: Improving the precision of learning style identification through computational intelligence algorithms. *Expert Systems with Applications* 75 (2017), 94–108.

[4] Chris Brook and Ron Oliver. 2003. Online learning communities: Investigating a design framework. *Australasian Journal of Educational Technology* 19, 2 (2003).

[5] Monica Bulger, Jonathan Bright, and Cristóbal Cobo. 2015. The real component of virtual learning: motivations for face-to-face MOOC meetings in developing and industrialised countries. *Information, Communication & Society* 18, 10 (2015), 1200–1216.

[6] Daniel W Calhoun and Lucy Santos Green. 2015. Utilizing online learning communities in student affairs. *New Directions for Student Services* 2015, 149 (2015), 55–66.

[7] Yi-Chun Chang, Wen-Yan Kao, Chih-Ping Chu, and Chiung-Hui Chiu. 2009. A learning style classification mechanism for e-learning. *Computers & Education* 53, 2 (2009), 273–285.

[8] Hichang Cho, Geri Gay, Barry Davidson, and Anthony Ingraffea. 2007. Social networks, communication styles, and learning performance in a CSCL community. *Computers & Education* 49, 2 (2007), 309–329.

[9] Wilmax Marreiro Cruz and Seiji Isotani. 2014. Group formation algorithms in collaborative learning contexts: A systematic mapping of the literature. In *CYTED-RITOS International Workshop on Groupware*. Springer, 199–214.

[10] Maria-Iuliana Dascalu, Constanta-Nicoleta Bodea, Miltiadis Lytras, Patricia Ordoñez De Pablos, and Alexandru Burlacu. 2014. Improving e-learning communities through optimal composition of multidisciplinary learning groups. *Computers in Human Behavior* 30 (2014), 362–371.

[11] Moushir M El-Bishouty, Hiroaki Ogata, Samia Rahman, and Yoneo Yano. 2010. Social knowledge awareness map for computer supported ubiquitous learning environment. *Educational Technology & Society* 13, 4 (2010), 27–37.

[12] Moushir M El-Bishouty, Hiroaki Ogata, and Yoneo Yano. 2007. PERKAM: Personalized knowledge awareness map for computer supported ubiquitous learning. *Journal of Educational Technology & Society* 10, 3 (2007).

[13] Richard M Felder, Linda K Silverman, et al. 1988. Learning and teaching styles in engineering education. *Engineering Education* 78, 7 (1988), 674–681.

[14] Richard M Felder and Barbara A Soloman. 1999. Index of learning styles (ILS). *On-line at http://www2. ncsu. edu/unity/lockers/users/f/felder/public/ILSpage. html* (1999).

[15] Martha A Gabriel. 2004. Learning together: Exploring group interactions online. *Journal of Distance Education* 19, 1 (2004), 54.

[16] Fatemeh Ghorbani and Gholam Ali Montazer. 2015. E-learners' personality identifying using their network behaviors. *Computers in Human Behavior* 51 (2015), 42–52.

[17] Peter Goodyear and Symeon Retalis. 2010. Technology-enhanced Learning. *Rotterdam: Sense Publishers* (2010).

[18] Sabine Graf, Rahel Bekele, et al. 2006. Forming heterogeneous groups for intelligent collaborative learning systems with ant colony optimization. In *Intelligent Tutoring Systems*, Vol. 4053. Springer, 217–226.

[19] Sabine Graf and Tzu-Chien Liu. 2009. Supporting Teachers in Identifying Students' Learning Styles in Learning Management Systems: An Automatic Student Modelling Approach. *Journal of Educational Technology & Society* 12, 4 (2009).

[20] Samuel Gratzl, Alexander Lex, Nils Gehlenborg, Hanspeter Pfister, and Marc Streit. 2013. Lineup: Visual analysis of multi-attribute rankings. *IEEE transactions on visualization and computer graphics* 19, 12 (2013), 2277–2286.

[21] Kaj Holmberg. 2014. *Formation of Student Groups with the Help of Optimization.* Linköping University Electronic Press.

[22] Tanja Jadin, Timo Gnambs, and Bernad Batinic. 2013. Personality traits and knowledge sharing in online communities. *Computers in Human Behavior* 29, 1 (2013), 210–216.

[23] Hassan Khosravi. 2017. Recommendation in Personalised Peer-Learning Environments. *arXiv preprint arXiv:1712.03077* (2017).

[24] Whitney Kilgore and Patrick R Lowenthal. 2015. The Human Element MOOC. *Student-teacher Interaction in Online Learning Environments* (2015), 373–391.

[25] Karel Kreijns, Paul A Kirschner, and Wim Jochems. 2003. Identifying the pitfalls for social interaction in computer-supported collaborative learning environments: a review of the research. *Computers in human behavior* 19, 3 (2003), 335–353.

[26] Yen-Ting Lin, Yueh-Min Huang, and Shu-Chen Cheng. 2010. An automatic group composition system for composing collaborative learning groups using enhanced particle swarm optimization. *Computers & Education* 55, 4 (2010), 1483–1493.

[27] Youmei Liu. 2010. Social media tools as a learning resource. *Journal of Educational Technology Development and Exchange (JETDE)* 3, 1 (2010), 8.

[28] Kurt Matzler, Birgit Renzl, Julia Müller, Stephan Herting, and Todd A Mooradian. 2008. Personality traits and knowledge sharing. *Journal of economic psychology* 29, 3 (2008), 301–313.

[29] James C McCroskey. 1992. Reliability and validity of the willingness to communicate scale. *Communication Quarterly* 40, 1 (1992), 16–25.

[30] David W McMillan and David M Chavis. 1986. Sense of community: A definition and theory. *Journal of Community Psychology* 14, 1 (1986), 6–23.

[31] Zohra Mehennaoui, Yacine Lafifi, Hassina Seridi, and Asma Boudria. 2014. A new approach for grouping learners in CSCL systems. In *Proceedings of International Conference on Multimedia Computing and Systems (ICMCS), 2014.* IEEE, 628–632.

[32] Andrés Moreno, Erkki Sutinen, and Mike Joy. 2014. Defining and evaluating conflictive animations for programming education: The case of Jeliot ConAn. In *Proceedings of the 45th ACM Technical Symposium on Computer Science Education.* ACM, 629–634.

[33] Julián Moreno, Demetrio A Ovalle, and Rosa M Vicari. 2012. A genetic algorithm approach for group formation in collaborative learning considering multiple student characteristics. *Computers & Education* 58, 1 (2012), 560–569.

[34] Asma Ounnas, Hugh C Davis, and David E Millard. 2009. A framework for semantic group formation in education. *Journal of Educational Technology & Society* 12, 4 (2009).

[35] Paul R Pintrich et al. 1991. A manual for the use of the Motivated Strategies for Learning Questionnaire (MSLQ). (1991).

[36] Luiz Pizzato, Tomasz Rej, Joshua Akehurst, Irena Koprinska, Kalina Yacef, and Judy Kay. 2013. Recommending people to people: the nature of reciprocal recommenders with a case study in online dating. *User Modeling and User-Adapted Interaction* 23, 5 (2013), 447–488.

[37] Luiz Pizzato, Tomek Rej, Thomas Chung, Irena Koprinska, and Judy Kay. 2010. RECON: a reciprocal recommender for online dating. In *Proceedings of the fourth ACM conference on Recommender systems.* ACM, 207–214.

[38] Joanna Poon. 2013. Blended learning: An institutional approach for enhancing students' learning experiences. *Journal of Online Learning and Teaching* 9, 2 (2013), 271.

[39] Boyd A Potts, Hassan Khosravi, Carl Reidsema, Aneesha Bakharia, Mark Belonogoff, and Melanie Fleming. 2018. Reciprocal peer recommendation for learning purposes. In *Proceedings of the 8th International Conference on Learning Analytics and Knowledge.* ACM, 226–235.

[40] Sankalp Prabhakar, Gerasimos Spanakis, and Osmar Zaiane. 2017. Reciprocal Recommender System for Learners in Massive Open Online Courses (MOOCs). In *International Conference on Web-Based Learning.* Springer, 157–167.

[41] Beatrice Rammstedt and Oliver P John. 2007. Measuring personality in one minute or less: A 10-item short version of the Big Five Inventory in English and German. *Journal of research in Personality* 41, 1 (2007), 203–212.

[42] Margaret Riel and Linda Polin. 2004. Learning communities: Common ground and critical differences in designing technical support. *Designing for Virtual Communities in the Service of Learning* (2004), 16–52.

[43] Bart Rienties, Dirk Tempelaar, Piet Van den Bossche, Wim Gijselaers, and Mien Segers. 2009. The role of academic motivation in Computer-Supported Collaborative Learning. *Computers in Human Behavior* 25, 6 (2009), 1195–1206.

[44] Alfred P Rovai. 2002. Development of an instrument to measure classroom community. *The Internet and Higher Education* 5, 3 (2002), 197–211.

[45] Peter Shea. 2006. A study of students' sense of learning community in online environments. *Journal of Asynchronous Learning Networks* 10, 1 (2006), 35–44.

[46] Siobhan Smyth, Catherine Houghton, Adeline Cooney, and Dympna Casey. 2012. Students' experiences of blended learning across a range of postgraduate programmes. *Nurse Education Today* 32, 4 (2012), 464–468.

[47] Hyo-Jeong So and Thomas A Brush. 2008. Student perceptions of collaborative learning, social presence and satisfaction in a blended learning environment: Relationships and critical factors. *Computers & Education* 51, 1 (2008), 318–336.

[48] Howard Spoelstra, Peter Van Rosmalen, Evert Van de Vrie, Matija Obreza, and Peter Sloep. 2013. A Team formation and project-based learning support service for social learning networks. *Journal of Universal Computer Science* 19, 10 (2013), 1474–1495.

[49] Ivan Srba and Maria Bielikova. 2015. Dynamic group formation as an approach to collaborative learning support. *IEEE Transactions on Learning Technologies* 8, 2 (2015), 173–186.

[50] Emma J Stodel, Terrie Lynn Thompson, and Colla J MacDonald. 2006. Learners' perspectives on what is missing from online learning: Interpretations through the community of inquiry framework. *The International Review of Research in Open and Distributed Learning* 7, 3 (2006).

[51] Eunmo Sung and Richard E Mayer. 2012. Five facets of social presence in online distance education. *Computers in Human Behavior* 28, 5 (2012), 1738–1747.

[52] Virginia Yannibelli, Marcelo Armentano, Franco Berdun, and Analía Amandi. 2016. A Steady-State Evolutionary Algorithm for Building Collaborative Learning Teams in Educational Environments Considering the Understanding Levels and Interest Levels of the Students. *J. UCS* 22, 10 (2016), 1298–1318.

A Structured Mentorship Model for Computer Science University Students in Kenya

Chao Mbogo
Kenya Methodist University
Nairobi, Kenya
chaombogho@gmail.com

ABSTRACT

The Kenyan university education system has been criticized for graduating students who are underprepared to meet the skills demand of the modern workplace, and who cannot formulate effective solutions to our most pressing socio-economic problems. To address the skills gap for Computer Science (CS) students, a structured 6-month mentorship program was designed to offer skills in personal and professional development, innovation, scholarship application, and community engagement. This paper presents the results of a mixed-method study comprising of 95 CS students from 12 Kenyan universities who have participated in the mentorship program since September 2016. The study examines if structured mentorship leads to successful upskilling for CS students. The findings indicate that at least 81% of the students in the mentorship program improve in skills such as innovation and professional preparedness. Results from this study demonstrate how CS education can be complemented with a structured mentorship model towards global competitiveness.

ACM Reference format:

C. Mbogo. 2018. A Structured Mentorship Model for Computer Science University Students in Kenya. In *Proceedings of the 50th ACM Technical Symposium on Computer Science Education (SIGCSE'19), Feb. 27-Mar. 2, 2019, Minneapolis, MN, USA.* ACM, New York, NY, USA, 7 pages. DOI: https://doi.org/10.1145/3287324.3287447

1 INTRODUCTION

The Kenyan university education system has been criticized for graduating students who are underprepared to meet the skills demand of the modern workplace, and who struggle to formulate effective solutions to our most pressing socio-economic problems. Many authors [1-4] have linked the reduced quality of university education to factors such as a dramatic increase in the number of institutions of higher learning in Kenya over the last ten years, inadequate teaching facilities and qualified staff, overwhelming workload among faculty, declining funds to universities, and lack of mentorship. Also, a study by the Inter-University Council for East Africa [5] indicates that employees are lacking crucial skills, such as problem-solving, teamwork, and communication skills, in the university graduates that they hire. Equally, employers have expressed dissatisfaction with the quality of ICT professionals graduating from educational institutions in Kenya [6,7]. Perhaps due to this skills-gap among university graduates Kenya is seeing an increase in non-university institutions that exclusively teach computing and problem-solving skills, such as Moringa School [8] and Andela [9]. Yet, with Information and Communication Technologies (ICT) being one of the key drivers of any knowledge economy, the need to effectively train and upskill CS university students cannot be overstated. In fact, Kenya's Vision 2030 report [10] cites ICT workforce as one of the key foundations to acquiring the status of a knowledge economy by the year 2030.

While many factors, such as improved policies, qualified staff, and adequate resources, contribute to high-quality university education, we argue that structured mentorship that complements classroom learning could contribute towards preparing CS students for the job market and improve personal development. Also, as indicated in a 'Closing the Skills Gap' project by the World Economic Forum [11], if education systems are to keep up with the changing demands in skills there needs to be continual reskilling and upskilling among students. To address this need, a 6-month mentorship program was initiated for Computer Science university students in Kenya. The structured model of the program incorporates student-driven pillars and measurable goals with the aim to bridge the skills gap. Mentorship is provided in out-of-the-classroom sessions through industry linkages and peer mentorship.

This paper discusses the structured mentorship model and the impact, experiences, and lessons drawn from 95 students in 12 universities in Kenya who have participated in the program since September 2016. The contributions of this paper are: (i) to provide data-based evidence on the potential impact of a structured mentorship model; (ii) to share lessons and experiences from the mentorship program; (iii) to contribute to insights on mentoring CS students in a developing country's context; and (iv) to demonstrate how learning of CS students can be complemented with a structured mentorship program.

The following sections review related work, followed by a description of the structured mentorship program, the methods used and findings.

2 RELATED WORK

Mentoring occurs when a mentor serves as a trusted role model, counselor, or teacher for a mentee [12]. The benefits of mentorship have been realized in youth employability [13],

SIGCSE '19, February 27-March 2, 2019, Minneapolis, MN, USA

ACM ISBN 978-1-4503-5890-3/19/02…$15.00
https://doi.org/10.1145/3287324.3287447

choice of careers [14], interest in CS subjects [15], students' performance [16], and even the mentor's skills growth [17]. Indeed, the impact of mentorship has been evident among initiatives by non-profit organizations in Kenya such as Akili Dada [18] and AkiraChix [19] that focus on training, mentoring, and empowering girls from disadvantaged backgrounds in ICT and leadership skills. Other examples include university-initiated mentorship programs such as the Greenhorn Mentorship Program [20] based at the University of Nairobi, Kenya, that focuses on students taking Business-related courses. These examples show that mentorship has been recognized as key in the development and learning among students, beyond the classroom.

Outside Kenya, there have been successful mentorship programs for university students that focused on more than just academic development. For example, a mentorship program at the University of Cape Town in South Africa, by the Educational Development Unit (EDU), uses a holistic approach, rather than focusing on academic skills, to strengthen life skills, industry exposure, and giving back to the community [21]. The EDU approach is reported to generate results that out-perform most undergraduate courses, with increased graduation rates and professional achievements among its participants. The study in this paper seeks to emulate such mentorship examples in implementing out-of-the classroom skills that could potentially improve personal and professional skills.

In spite of the benefits that mentorship provides to students, mentorship efforts are yet to take root in many Kenyan universities, especially for students taking technical subjects such as Computer Science. Additionally, most existing mentorship programs in Kenya focus on only girls [18,19,22], high school students [24], and out-of-school youth [23]. Few sustainable mentorship programs are focused on university students. Further, a comprehensive study on the role of mentorship in enhancing youth employability in Kenya [13] showed that university graduates need exposure to various other interventions to scale-up their competitiveness in the local and global market. The program described in this paper aims to fill this gap.

While some mentorship programs take an informal and non-structured format, studies [25] have shown that students express a need for a formalized mentorship program in order to increase accountability. Also, mentorship programs that are organized such that participants are held accountable for the mentorship activities [12] have shown an impact in increasing the students' skills and confidence to succeed in the computing field. In the context of this study, organized mentorship, with specific goals and measurable expectations, is defined as a *structured mentorship*. Thus, this paper discusses the effect of a free structured mentorship program, which complements classroom learning, for Computer Science university students in Kenya.

3 THE STRUCTURED MENTORSHIP MODEL

The mentorship project started in September 2016 as a response to various mentorship requests from students. Over the two years, the growth of the program has influenced the development of a structure that is discussed under program pillars, cohort-based model, mentor involvement, format of mentorship sessions, mentorship curriculum development, and evaluation criteria. The author is the Program Lead and Founder of the mentorship program.

3.1 Program Pillars

The first cohort of 40 students completed an online survey, an exercise whose aim was to understand the skills' gaps that they wished addressed. Four common themes emerged from the students' responses:

3.1.1 Innovation and ICT Skills. 60% of the students indicated that they wished to learn how to use their ICT skills to solve societal issues and challenges, as well as learn relevant ICT skills not taught in the classroom.

3.1.2 Personal and Professional Development. 80% of the students indicated that they wished to develop their professional and soft skills such as writing, interview preparation, and presentation skills.

3.1.3 Scholarship application and awareness. 85% of the students indicated that they were not aware of scholarship opportunities in the field of Computer Science, nor did they possess the skills to write scholarship essays and applications.

3.1.4 Community Engagement. 80% of the students indicated that they had not participated in any tech and community events outside the university. Additionally, students expressed the desire to have an avenue that could link them to the local community where they could give back to volunteer-driven initiatives.

The above skills were analyzed alongside the objectives of successful mentorship programs [21] as well as those cited in the study by the Inter-University Council for East Africa [5], as needed by higher education graduates to succeed in the workplace. Thus, these skills were deemed as appropriate to form the pillars of the program.

3.2 Cohort-based Model

The program maintains the same group of students over a period of 6-months, as opposed to walk-ins, which could mean mentorship to different students at any given time. This choice was deemed appropriate to promote more effective evaluation of the impact of the program. Before joining the program, students apply through an online application form that includes two essays that describe the motivation of the student's application to the program. Such an application model is practiced by established mentorship programs like Techwomen [26]. The selection of students to the program is by the Program Lead, peer mentors, and industry stakeholders. The first cohort of the mentorship program took place from September 2016 to March 2017, excluding the December Holidays. The second cohort of the mentorship program took place in May 2017 to December 2017, and the third cohort of the mentorship program started in March 2018 and ended in September 2018, including a one-month break when most of the students had their university examinations.

3.3 Mentor Involvement

Mentors to the students are drawn from three pools of individuals: Program Lead, Industry Professionals, and Peer Mentors.

3.3.1 Program Lead

The Founder and Program Lead of the mentorship program conducts sessions on all the five pillars as well as one-on-one follow up sessions with each mentee over the period of the program.

3.3.2 Industry Professionals

Industry professionals from various computing and professional disciplines volunteer to facilitate sessions that address the various pillars. Additionally, ICT and Community-based organizations have partnered with the program to offer professional mentorship, as well as provide opportunities for the students to get involved in community projects as volunteers.

3.3.3 Peer Mentors

Peer mentors are students who have gone through a full cycle of the program and who give back by mentoring new students who join the program. Therefore, the peer mentorship model commenced in the second cohort of the program. This model has been successful in other projects, such as the near-peer mentorship model for middle school mentees [27]. At the start of the cohort, the peer mentors are trained in mentorship principles. The peer mentorship model involves the pairing of a maximum of three mentees per peer mentor, scheduled meetings that involve group and individual tasks, and a review after each peer session.

3.4 Curriculum Development

After the end of the second cohort, and after collecting sufficient student feedback to encourage proceeding with the project, a curriculum was designed and developed by the Program Lead with input from peer mentors and industry stakeholders. This curriculum was tested for the first time with the third cohort of mentees and was reviewed at the end of that phase of the mentorship program. The curriculum contains two main parts: training, and implementation. The training occurs in the first four months when the students take part in workshop sessions that address the pillars of the program. The implementation occurs in the last two months when the students take part in stakeholder-driven competitions to practice what they have learned. For all the competitions, professionals from the industry and who practice in relevant sectors volunteer to judge the competitions.

3.4.1 Innovation Training and Competitions

Training on Innovation involves impacting skills that enable the students to identify socioeconomic issues in the Kenyan society and use the ICT skills they learn in the classroom to provide solutions, through design thinking and prototyping. Further, the students are taught how to write pitch proposals and to pitch their solutions. Thereafter, the competition phase simulates a real-life innovation process of a solution, applying for a seed-grant and pitching an idea. The students are grouped into teams of up to six students and throughout the mentorship program, they work together to design an innovative solution to a socio-economic problem in Kenya. In the final two months, each team writes a seed-grant proposal and prepares and presents a pitch to a panel of industry professionals.

An example of an innovation that was designed and developed by the students is *Eternal Vote,* a project that was inspired by the 2017 Kenyan elections, which were marred with claims of rigged elections that led to repeated voting. The innovation considered the use of blockchain technology to improve accountability in voting.

3.4.2 Public Speaking Training and Competitions

Training on Public Speaking involves impacting skills in speech writing, presentation skills, and speech delivery, in order to improve students' self-confidence as well as confidence in presentations and speaking in front of a crowd. The objective of the competition phase is to simulate a real-life speech or presentation opportunity. The students compete individually in various rounds by giving speeches on various topics using various speech formats such as humorous, topical, and impromptu speeches.

3.4.3 Professional Development Training and Competitions

Training on Professional Development involves impacting skills such as CV writing, interview preparation, and professional communication. The objective of the competition phase is to simulate a real-life environment of applying for a technical role, such as that of a Software Engineer, as well as to practice professional communication and writing. The students compete individually in various rounds of mock-interviews that simulate real-life interviews. After each stage, the students receive feedback on their performance from the professional mentors who take part in the review process.

3.4.4 Scholarship Application Training and Competitions

Training on Scholarships involves creating awareness of scholarship opportunities as well as training student how to write award-winning scholarship applications and essays. The objective of the competition phase is to simulate a real-life competition of applying for highly competitive scholarships and grants, as well as to practice professional communication and writing.

3.5 Format of Mentorship Sessions

The mentorship sessions consist of non-technical workshops in a seminar room and technical workshops in a computer laboratory. Additionally, the mentees complete various tasks remotely, such as an assignment to practice their CV and scholarship writing skills. The students are also hosted in various ICT companies and tech events over the period of the program. Examples of companies that have participated in the program are Google and IBM.

The mentorship meetings are held once a week on Wednesday evenings and on two Saturdays a month. These times were deemed appropriate to enable students to attend their university classes during the week-day, as well as accommodate students who are on internship or have full-time employment. The program's timetable includes breaks from the sessions when the students have their university exams. All mentorship sessions are held within Nairobi, the capital city of Kenya.

3.6 Program Funding

The mentorship program has been funded using donations from friends and family, as well as event-specific grants from Google and Systers Pass-it-on Award.

3.7 Evaluation Criteria of the Program

The program is evaluated using various criteria to determine the impact that the mentorship is having on the students. The criteria used are discussed in section 4.3.

4 METHOD

The purpose of this study was to explore the impact of the structured mentorship program for CS university students in Kenya. The research questions that guided this study are: (i) Does structured mentorship lead to successful upskilling of Computer Science University students? (ii) Does structured mentorship lead to local and international exposure of CS students to the ICT industry? (iii) How do CS students perceive their experience in a structured mentorship program? A mixed-method approach was used to answer the research questions. Surveys were used to collect data before the start, during and at the end of the mentorship program.

4.1 Participants

Table 1 shows the number of mentees and peer mentors who completed the program, as well as the number of universities represented by the students. All students pursue degrees in Computing and related subjects. The number of universities represented by the students has increased since cohort one, showing that the program's popularity is rising as well as the need for mentorship by students. All the students who completed the program are from universities located within Nairobi. Table 2 shows that there has been an increase in the number of industry mentors and partners from the first cohort to the third. The program consists of both male and female students with an objective to maintain a 50-50 representation of male and female students in order to embody Dr. Anita Borg's vision of maintaining a 50-50 representation by the year 2020 [28] in computing workforce, which aims at achieving a 50% representation of women in Computer Science.

4.2 Data Collection

During the first cohort, only an end of program survey was issued. The students in the second and third cohort completed a pre-program survey, a mid-program survey, and a final impact survey. Interviews were used to validate the results of the survey and to gain further insights into how and if structured mentorship leads to increased local and international exposure of CS students, as well as how students perceive their experiences in the program.

4.3 Criteria for Measurement

4.3.1 *Previous experience in mentorship*

When applying to the program the students indicate what prior experience they have had with mentorship while at the university.

4.3.2 *Retention rate*

This criterion measures how many students start the program and how many finish the program.

Table 1: Number of mentees, peer mentors, and universities in Cohort one to three

Cohort	Number of universities	Mentees who completed the program	Peer Mentor
1	5	33	0
2	7	27	14
3	9	35	12
Total unique counts	**12**	**95**	**26**

Table 2: Number of individual industry contributors and companies

Cohort	Number of individual industry mentors	Number of company partners
1	3	1
2	23	5
3	28	6
Total Unique counts	**42**	**5**

4.3.3 *Student's participation in the program*

This criterion is measured by the attendance rate of the students during the program using a point-based system. When a student attends a mentorship workshop or submits an assigned task, their attendance is awarded 7 points, while if they send an apology they are awarded 1 point. If a student attends an ICT event outside the ones planned within the program, they submit a mini-report of the lessons learned to our closed Google Plus community and earn 5 bonus points. The minimum attendance rate required to be considered as having successfully completed the program is 70%. This is deemed sufficient to have covered the basic mentorship skills while allowing the students room to focus on their university studies.

4.3.4 *Skills improvement*

This criterion is measured using a pre and post survey, where the students indicate their level of skills in the five pillars of the program at the start of the program, during the program, and at the end of the program.

4.3.5 *Students' achievements*

This criterion is measured by tracking the achievements of students across the five pillars in terms of innovative solutions designed, internship and employment opportunities earned, improvement in public speaking, number of community involvement initiatives, or number of scholarships won.

4.3.6 *Students' satisfaction*

This criterion is measured by asking individual students of their perceived satisfaction with the mentorship program in terms of whether it is meeting their mentorship objectives.

5 RESULTS

Table 3 shows a summary of the results discussed in this section.

5.1 Previous experience with Mentorship

Majority of the students had not received any form of mentorship while at university, prior to joining the program. These results confirm the claims that most Kenyan universities do not offer consistent mentorship outside the classroom. Further, the fact that students from various universities apply to join the program could be an indication that there is a high demand for interventions that support university students to learn new skills that are not taught in the classroom.

5.2 Retention Rate

83%, 77%, and 88% of the students who started the program in the first, second, and third cohorts, respectively, completed the program successfully. The students who do not complete the program usually drop out within the first two months, and the main reason given for dropping out is new school and work commitments that demand more of their time.

5.3 Students' Participation Rate

The participation rate is measured by calculating the total number of points earned by a student and then dividing by the gross total that would be earned from participating in all the workshops and completing all the tasks. The overall average attendance rate by all the mentees at the end of the second cohort was 84%, and 95% at the third cohort. The point-based system had not been designed during the first cohort and hence was not used to measure attendance rates. The high attendance rates in the second and third cohorts indicate that students are finding value in the program. Further, the increase in attendance rate from the second to the third cohort indicates that the program is improving in meeting the objectives of the mentees.

5.4 Students' Achievements

Table 3 shows the number of students who won various scholarships or were accepted into internships in cohort one to three. There has been an increase in the number of students who won scholarships, across the three cohorts, after receiving mentorship training on writing award-winning scholarship applications. All the scholarships that the students won are in the CS field. For example, in cohort three, 22 of the students were awarded the Google Africa Udacity scholarship that sponsors students to take certified online courses in Web and Android Development. At the same time, two of the female students won full scholarships to attend the Grace Hopper Celebration of Women in Computing in the US for the first time.

5.5 Skills Improvement

Across all the skills students in the second and third cohorts demonstrated more improvement than those in the first cohort, showing that the program has improved in meeting the students' objectives. Further, at least three-quarters of the students who signed up for the mentorship program perceived to have significantly improved in most of the skills offered in the program. Table 4 and Table 5 show a comparison that was made between the number of students who indicated to be skilled to 'a great extent' at select skills, at the start and at the end of cohort two and cohort three. The findings in Table 4 and Table 5 show that at least 81% of the students who join the mentorship program improve in most of the skills by the time they complete the program.

5.6 Student Satisfaction

Table 3 shows the percentage of students who indicated that the program is either meeting their mentorship expectations or if it is exceeding their expectations, in cohort two and three. At the end of cohort two, 80% of the students indicated that the program has met their mentorship expectations, and 20% indicated that the program has exceeded their mentorship expectations. At the end of cohort three 41% of the students indicated that the mentorship program so far has met their expectations and 59% indicated that the mentorship program so far has exceeded their expectations. Additionally, in all cohorts, 100% of the students indicated that they would recommend a friend to apply to the mentorship program.

Further, some of the sample feedback from students are cited verbatim as below:

"I have become more confident in my skills, and have learnt to conduct myself in a highly professional manner as I exit college."

"I was really scared before the pitching sessions but after pitching several times my confidence was really boosted."

"I gained the opportunity to learn skills not taught in school."

"I was able to overcome my impostor syndrome"

"I have improved in my innovation skills."

"I am inspired to grow as an ICT developer and to do more in my career."

6 DISCUSSION, LESSONS, AND LIMITATIONS

The results show that a structured mentorship program, where students have measurable goals in terms of attendance and objectives, provides an organized and guided platform where students can learn new skills for their personal and professional development, especially for skills that are not typically offered in the university curricula. The findings also indicate that CS students benefit from guidance and support to identify and prepare for local and international opportunities, which are usually highly competitive.

6.1 Lessons Learned

Since September 2016 the program has restructured to respond to students needs as well as to the growing interest from potential participants and contributors. Thus, it is imperative to embrace flexibility throughout the program so as to adapt to what works and improve or change what does not work. While some mentorship programs work with students from just one institution, incorporating students from various institutions

Table 3: Summary of results from cohort one, two and three

Cohort	Number of students who started the program	% of students who had *no* previous mentorship experience	Number of students who completed the program	Average overall participation rate	Students who won scholarships and internships	expectations met vs those whose expectations were exceeded
1	40	85%	33	-	1	-
2	35	60%	27	84%	4	80%: 20%
3	40	80%	35	95%	26	41%: 59%

Table 4: Comparison of % of students who are skilled to a 'great extent' at the start and end of cohort two

Skill	Start of program	End of program
Innovation	13%	81%
Communication	22%	82%
CV-writing	19%	84%
Scholarship application	8%	54%
Community involvement	35%	85%

Table 5: Comparison of % of students who are skilled to a 'great extent' at the start and end of cohort three

Skill	Start of program	End of program
Innovation	13%	87%
Communication	25%	81%
CV-writing	10%	88%
Scholarship application	5%	83%
Community involvement	10%	82%

creates an environment for vast idea-sharing, thus leading to a more conducive environment for teamwork and collaboration.

A key lesson that emerged right from the beginning is that student-driven goals for a mentorship program offers significant potential to meet students' objectives. Further, a stakeholder-driven mentorship curriculum is likely to have more impact than one without stakeholder input. In addition, such a mentorship program gives industry contributors a platform to give back to academia through fostering industry-academia linkages and offering mentorship.

6.2 Limitations

While the mentorship program described in this study has demonstrated a positive growth and early impact on the 95 students who have taken part in it so far, several limitations have been observed that need improvement.

The 6-month duration could be short considering that the program serves students who have to juggle a full-time university workload with an additional mentorship workload.

The impact of the program was not sufficiently tracked right from the first cohort, thus important lessons could have been missed. However, as the program grows the required criteria that would demonstrate improvement of skills and impact would be measured for each cohort.

The program still lacks a follow-up model that would determine if the mentees are using the skills they learn after the program has ended. In future, such a model would be designed in order to gain a broader understanding of the impact of a structured mentorship program.

7 CONCLUSION

The Kenyan university education system has been criticised for producing CS graduates who are not ready for the job market. However, the findings in this study suggest that for institutions in developing countries that face limited human and technical resources in their higher education systems, a consistent, measurable and structured mentorship program that combines industry expertise, peer mentorship, and relevant skills for out-of-the-classroom learning, could potentially contribute towards filling any skills gap. Such a mentorship program can offer training on how students can apply their ICT skills to innovative projects. Further, in order to adequately communicate their ICT expertise and efficiently disseminate their information, tech students are expected to develop their professional skills. In addition, tech students should be able to tap into the numerous opportunities which would expose them to the vibrant tech community. However, structured mentorship programs should be adaptable to the needs of the mentees and of the environment.

REFERENCES

[1] Wycliffe Wanzala. 2013. Quest for quality and relevant higher education, training and learning in Kenya: an overview. *Education Journal* 2, 2 (March 2013), 36–49. DOI: 10.11648/j.edu.20130202.13

[2] Ishmael Munene. 2016. Kenya's universities are in the grip of a quality crisis. (February 2016). Retrieved from https://qz.com/618436/kenyas-universities-are-in-the-grip-of-a-quality-crisis/

[3] Josephat M. Mukhanji. 2017. Stakeholders' Perception on Instructional Effectiveness in Maseno University, Kenya. *The International Journal of Social Sciences and Humanities Invention* 4, 43. (March 2017). DOI: 10.18535/ijsshi/v4i3.05

[4] Kumwenda Save, Niang E. Hadji, Orondo Pauline, William Pote, Oyinlola Lateefah, Bongo Gedeon, and Chiwona Bernadette. 2017. Challenges facing young African scientists in their research careers: A qualitative exploratory study. *Malawi Medical Journal* 29, 1, (March 2017), 1–4.

[5] IUCEA. 2014. Status of Higher Education Qualifications Systems and their Contributions to Human Resources Development in East Africa. (June 2014). Retrieved from https://iucea.org/index.php?option=com_phocadownload&view=category&download=127:iucea-study-report-on-status-of-higher-education-status-in-eac-2014&id=14:qa-policy-documents&Itemid=613

[6] Audrey Cheng. 2016. Bringing World-Class Tertiary Education to Sub Saharan Africa. (December 2016). Retrieved from https://challenges.openideo.com/challenge/youth-empowerment-challenge/beneficiary-feedback/bringing-world-class-tertiary-education-matched-to-emerging-markets/comments

[7] IDC. 2011. *Kenya* ICT Market Survey 2011. (November 2011) Retrieved from https://www.scribd.com/presentation/73453205/Julisha-Kenya-ICT-Market-Survey-2011

[8] Moringa School. 2018. Retrieved from http://www.moringaschool.com/

[9] Andela. 2018. Retrieved from https://andela.com/

[10] Government of Kenya. 2013. Kenya Vision 2030: Towards a Globally Competitive and Prosperous Kenya. Retrieved from https://www.researchictafrica.net/countries/kenya/Kenya_Vision_2030_-_2007.pdf

[11] World Economic Forum. 2016. The Future of Jobs: Employment, Skills and Workforce Strategy for the Fourth Industrial Revolution. Retrieved from http://www3.weforum.org/docs/WEF_System_Initiative_Future_Education_Gender_Work_Closing_Skills_Gap_pagers....pdf

[12] Kristy E. Boyer, Thomas, E. Nathan, Audrey S. Rorrer, and Mladen Vouk. 2010. Increasing Technical Excellence, Leadership and Commitment of Computing Students through Identity-Based Mentoring. *SIGCSE' 10.* (March 2010). DOI:10.1145/1734263.1734320

[13] Esther W. Muchiri. 2013. *The Role of Mentorship in Enhancing Youth Employability in Kenya.* Master's thesis. United States International University (USIU), Nairobi, Kenya.

[14] Kipkoech Rotich, and Koech Julius. 2014. Factors Influencing the Choice of College Among Undergraduate Students in Public Universities in Kenya: A Case Study of the University of Eldoret. *Australian Journal of Commerce Study* 4, (January 2014), 1-11. ISSN: 2308-1365

[15] Daryl D'souza, Margaret Hamilton, James Harland, Peter, Muir, P, Charles Thevathayan, Cecily Walker. Transforming Learning of Programming: A Mentoring Project. *Tenth Australasian Computing Education Conference (ACE2008).* (January 2008).

[16] Betty, Karanja, and John Gikungu. 2014. Effect of Mentorship Programmes on the Performance of Students in Secondary Schools in Mbooni East District, Makueni County - Kenya. *Mediterranean Journal of Social Sciences 5,* 5, (April 2014), 345–349.

[17] Jody Clarke-Midura, Vicki Allan, and Kevin Close. 2016. Investigating the Role of Being a Mentor as a Way of Increasing Interest in CS. In *Proceedings of the 47th ACM Technical Symposium on Computing Science Education - SIGCSE '16,* (March 2016), 297–302.

[18] Akili Dada. 2018. Retrieved from http://www.akilidada.org/

[19] AkiraChix. 2018. Retrieved from http://akirachix.com/

[20] Greenhorn Mentorship. 2018. Retrieved from http://www.greenhornmentorship.com/interface/index.php

[21] British Council. 2015. Universities, Employability and Inclusive Development: Reposition Higher Education in Ghana, Kenya, Nigeria and South Africa. Retrieved from https://ereadiness.kenet.or.ke/sites/default/files/ctools/Graduate employability final report.pdf

[22] Joyce Kinyanjui. Mentoring for Kenya's Marginalized Girls: Benefits, Challenges, and Policies. 2016. *The 2016 ECHIDNA Global Scholars Policy Brief.* (December 2016).

[23] Undugu Mentorship 2016. Retrieved from http://www.undugumentorship.org/

[24] e-mentoring Africa. 2017. Retrieved from http://ementoringafrica.or.ke/transition-programs/

[25] Andrew S. Ssemata, Sophia Gladding, Chandy C. John and Sarah Kiguli. Developing mentorship in a resource-limited context: a qualitative research study of the experiences and perceptions of the Makerere university student and faculty mentorship programme. *BMC Medical Education 17,* 1. 123. (July 2017).

[26] Techwomen. 2018. Retrieved from https://www.techwomen.org/program/overview

[27] Jody Clarke-Midura, Fredrick Poole, Katarina Pantic, Megan Hamilton, Chongning Sun, and Vicki Allan. 2018. How Near Peer Mentoring Affects Middle School Mentees. *SIGCSE'18,* 664-669. (February 2018). DOI: 10.1145/3159450.3159525

[28] Anita Borg's 2020. 2018. Retrieved from https://medium.com/@meena24dhanani/pbc-2018-50-50-by-2020-why-do-i-care-429f0ac8dfca

A Flexible Curriculum for Promoting Inclusion through Peer Mentorship

Heather Pon-Barry
Mount Holyoke College
South Hadley, MA
ponbarry@mtholyoke.edu

Audrey St. John
Mount Holyoke College
South Hadley, MA
astjohn@mtholyoke.edu

Becky Wai-Ling Packard
Mount Holyoke College
South Hadley, MA
bpackard@mtholyoke.edu

Barbara Rotundo
Mount Holyoke College
South Hadley, MA
barbara.rotundo@mtholyoke.edu

ABSTRACT

The MaGE Training curriculum prepares computer science students for the task of inclusive peer mentoring and teaching. The curriculum raises awareness of the role of social identity in learning, emphasizes active learning within computer science, and provides preparation for technical code review. This article presents an overview of the MaGE Training curriculum where it has been used to train six cohorts of near-peer mentors and its impact on more than 500 students at a liberal arts college. While rapid growth in course enrollments has presented many challenges, results suggest that the MaGE curriculum has helped to address some of these challenges by maintaining high quality feedback to, and close interaction with, introductory students. Effectiveness is evidenced through increases in mentor self-efficacy, positive impact on student belongingness and continued enrollment, and reports of buffering the instructor workload. The flexibility of the curriculum is supported through a set of modules that can be engaged with via in-person discussions or viewed remotely. This enables easier adoption of the curriculum for use at other institutions.

KEYWORDS

Peer mentor preparation; Inclusion; Effective learning; Modular curriculum

ACM Reference Format:

Heather Pon-Barry, Audrey St. John, Becky Wai-Ling Packard, and Barbara Rotundo. 2019. A Flexible Curriculum for Promoting Inclusion, through Peer Mentorship. In *Proceedings of the 50th ACM Technical Symposium on Computer Science Education (SIGCSE '19), February 27-March 2, 2019, Minneapolis, MN, USA.* ACM, New York, NY, USA, 7 pages. https://doi.org/10.1145/3287324.3287434

1 INTRODUCTION

Computer science (CS) programs are striving to become more inclusive and engaging of all students; the MaGE (Megas and Gigas Educate) Training curriculum focuses on inclusion as a key tool for creating a welcoming environment that fosters a community of learning, especially for students who may not initially see themselves as computer scientists or see themselves reflected in the existing computer science community. The course provides research-based instruction on effective learning (motivation, strategic learning, self-efficacy, and growth mindset), enabling peer mentors to strengthen their education toolkits by self-assessing their strengths, engaging in group discussions, practicing effective feedback strategies, and adjusting and stretching their personal perspectives on the computer science community as well as their technical peer code review skills.

The MaGE Training curriculum was developed in 2015. In three years, 72 undergraduate peer mentors in computer science at Mount Holyoke College have participated in the training, serving as mentors to 532 near-peer novice CS learners. This article describes the curriculum and its impact at Mount Holyoke College. The curriculum, structured as a flexible set of online modules, can be customized for in-person or remote participation over varying time spans; complete lesson plans are intended to be as self-contained as possible, offering clear instructions to the novice and expert alike. Curricular materials, including four formats from a half-day workshop to a half-semester course, are available online[1]. We discuss suggestions for others who wish to adopt the curriculum for use at their institution.

1.1 Motivation

Many new faculty members, although experts in their own fields of study, enter college classrooms without a research-based understanding of how novices learn. While faculty often draw upon their own learning experiences as a resource, this alone can be insufficient as students vary in their strengths, stumbling blocks, and strategies. Decades of research have demonstrated the value of faculty learning communities, where faculty deepen research-based teaching strategies, including active learning and and inclusive pedagogical strategies [7, 11].

Peer mentors come to the task with their own knowledge base; although less extensive than faculty, their experience is more recent. While some peer mentors may use their own intuition to reach a wide variety of students, just as many, if not more, appreciate the

SIGCSE '19, February 27-March 2, 2019, Minneapolis, MN, USA

ACM ISBN 978-1-4503-5890-3/19/02.
https://doi.org/10.1145/3287324.3287434

[1] https://sites.google.com/mtholyoke.edu/student-training-resources

opportunity to learn about best practices from the literature (such as [15]), from more experienced others (whether more seasoned peer mentors, lab directors, or faculty), and in colleagueship or consultation with other peer mentors [18]. Thus, providing training for mentors is beneficial [10]. Specifically, investing in peer mentors as a cohort can professionalize the program, leading peer mentors become ambassadors for the department, with better outcomes for both mentors and newer students [1, 4].

Beyond improving the general teaching effectiveness, which is important, we also grappled with increased enrollments in our introductory course; we wanted to maintain high quality feedback, as the first CS course is so important to a student continuing on [3]. Furthermore, our college student population is racially and socioeconomically diverse–and almost exclusively women–while the computer science field historically has not been. Peer mentoring as well as peer-led team learning in introductory CS courses have been shown to increase enrollment, performance, and retention of students from underrepresented groups [8, 14]. We wanted to take an intentionally inclusive approach to our preparation of peer mentors in order to deliberately invite student participation.

With this motivation in mind, the MaGE Training curriculum is designed to enable peer mentors to hone their technical skills, improve their knowledge of learning processes, and develop their understanding of the fundamentals of effective peer mentoring and inclusive pedagogy, all of which will improve their teaching effectiveness with increasingly diverse student populations.

1.2 Context

With growing student interest (echoing national trends), our Computer Science department faced the challenge of meeting capacity demands with limited resources. As a women's liberal arts college, we aimed to scale our CS offerings while maintaining quality feedback when teaching a diverse community that includes groups traditionally underrepresented in CS. The MaGE program was designed to address these challenges because we were particularly cognizant of the importance of the quality of the introductory computer science course experience in students' decisions to persist [3, 16].

2 MAGE TRAINING CURRICULUM

The MaGE Training curriculum prepares students for the task of peer mentoring and teaching others inclusively. This training course raises awareness of the role of social identity in learning, emphasizes active learning within computer science, and provides preparation for technical peer code review. The curriculum was developed by computer science faculty in collaboration with a colleague in psychology and education who has research expertise in motivation, identity, and mentoring diverse student populations [15].

The core curriculum is grouped into the following modules:

- Learning processes (including self-regulated learning, active learning, peer instruction)
- Motivational factors that promote learning (including self-efficacy, growth mindset)
- Effective feedback and emotional intelligence
- Inclusiveness and climate

The module dependencies are shown in Figure 1.

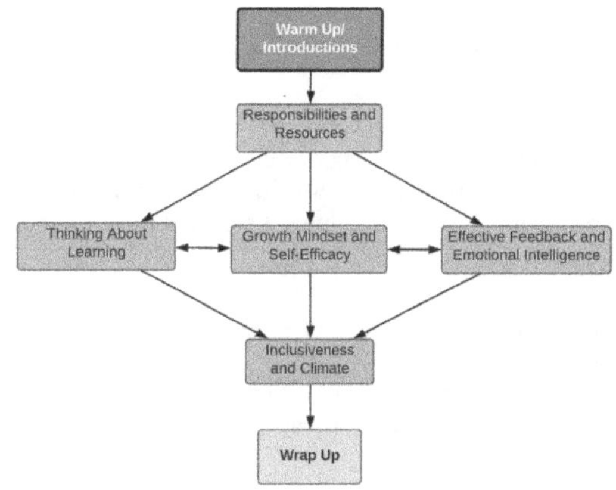

Figure 1: Core modules in the MaGE Training curriculum.

Each module is comprised of a set of curricular materials intended for instructors who are new to engaging with these topics. These materials include:

- A topic overview that introduces concepts, terminology, and tips for instructors
- Relevant readings including primary research articles
- Lesson plans for in-class activities, discussion question prompts, case scenarios for reflection and discussion, and handouts
- A flowchart showing the recommended order of the subtopics within the module, for example, Figure 2 shows the flowchart for the growth mindset and self-efficacy module

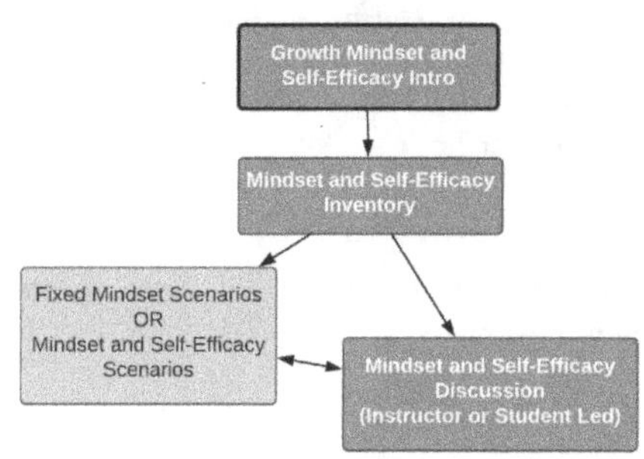

Figure 2: Recommended order for leading the growth mindset and self-efficacy modules. Darker modules are the highest priority if time is limited.

We anticipate that institutional constraints will impact the way others might engage with the curriculum and have been deliberate to maintain flexibility in this modular approach. Whenever possible, we provide multiple options within a module for engaging with the material. For example, a topic introduction could be a short video or a set of scholarly papers. Section 5 discusses this in more depth.

We also include suggested strategies for facilitating discussions and helping peer mentors engage with and reflect upon the topics, for instructors who are more comfortable with traditional lecture-based classroom environments than discussion. The material is intended to be as self-contained and "off-the-shelf" as possible to allow for minimal overhead when adopting the curriculum.

2.1 Sample Training Schedule

An example schedule for a single full-day (approximately 8-hour) training session is outlined below. This schedule includes a subset of activities from all of the modules. Lesson plans are included for each activity.

```
Introductions [10 min]
Guidelines and Expectations [10 min]
Technology Pact [10 min]
Ice-breaker: Tell Me Something [15 min]
Initial Reflection About Learning [10 min]
Talking About Learning [30 min]
Break
Mindset and Self-Efficacy Intro [10 min]
Mindset and Self-Efficacy Inventory [10 min]
Mindset and Self-Efficacy Scenarios [30 min]
General Discussion on Mindset and Self-Efficacy [20 min]
Lunch
Criticism and Tone [15 min]
Discussing Effective Feedback [15 min]
Coach vs Mirror [10 min]
Trying Out the Coach and Mirror Roles [10 min]
Thinking About Roles [15 min]
Naming Emotions Worksheet [5 min]
What is Emotional Intelligence [10 min]
Why does Emotional Intelligence Matter [30 min]
Emotional Intelligence Scenarios [30 min]
Break
Pet Peeves and Pop Ups [20 min]
Climate and Learning Outcomes [20 min]
Universal Design for Learning [20 min]
Intersectionality and Lived Experience [30 min]
Bringing It All Back [15 min]
Framing [20 min]
Exit Feedback [10 min]
```

2.2 Sample Lesson Plan

An abridged lesson plan for the *Climate and Learning Outcomes* activity is shown below.

Topic: Inclusiveness and Climate
Approximate Time: 20 – 30 min
Ideal Group Size: 2 – everyone
Summary: Facilitate discussion about the ways our learning environment influences how effectively we learn
Objectives:

- Start students reflecting about their own experiences with classroom climates
- Encourage students to reflect on the experiences of others

Potential prompts:

- Can you think of a time when you felt as though you didn't belong in a class? Why do you think you felt that way? Were there things that the instructor or other students did to make you feel that way (or make the feeling stronger)? What impact do you think that had on your ability to learn effectively in that class?
- Can you think of a time when you felt very at home in a class? What contributed to your comfort level? What did you have in common with the instructor or the other students?
- Have you noticed any patterns for when you're likely to feel comfortable in a class and when you're likely to feel out of place? Is it related to the subject? The way the class is being taught? Your own level of knowledge going in? Feeling like the only person of a certain identity in the room?
- Based on the conversations we've had so far, can you think of things that you can do (or avoid doing) to help other students feel comfortable?

3 ESTABLISHING MAGE

We created the MaGE Training curriculum as a *precursor* to establishing the MaGE peer mentorship program. While the initial curriculum was specifically tailored to our program mentors' responsibilities, we have revised the materials to enable its use by a broader audience. We envision that the curriculum will be useful both for establishing new mentorship programs, as well as augmenting established mentoring programs or teaching assistant training.

At our institution, trained peer mentors work with a small (6-9 person) group of CS1 or CS2 students for a whole semester. At regular intervals[2], the peer mentors perform written code reviews on completed student assignments and give feedback in one-on-one 10-minute meetings. Some mentors additionally lead active learning lessons or assist with student questions in lab sections. The cohort of peer mentors meets weekly for a MaGE Practicum course with the program coordinator and a faculty member to discuss topics related to the MaGE Training course and further develop as mentors.

The MaGE program was initially supported by external funding. The goal was to address rising enrollments while maintaining close interactions and feedback in the introductory courses without requiring additional staffing for multiple sections of the course. The MaGE program leverages a peer mentorship solution. Providing peer mentors with a rigorous foundation in both pedagogical approaches and technical skills can create an inclusive and supportive climate that empowers a diverse population of students to learn effectively, with positive outcomes for the peer mentors' developing leadership and longer-term trajectories [13]. To develop the MaGE program, we looked to existing programs with similar goals in the literature, at other institutions, and on our campus. Past research supports the use of a seminar-style course to organize and deliver the peer mentor training [19]. On our own campus, we were inspired by the success of a half-semester, seminar-style course to train peer mentors for another program and worked closely with the director of that program to understand the structure, benefits and potential stumbling blocks to bear in mind when creating our own. The factors we considered varied from student motivation and selection to approval requirements for credit-bearing courses to logistical questions of scheduling. We also drew upon literature of previous efforts to support peer-led workshops (e.g., [12]) as our peer mentors were expected to lead active learning workshops, in addition to engaging in peer code review.

[2]For the 2015-2018 period reported on in this paper, the feedback and meetings occurred weekly.

Table 1: Teaching self-efficacy changes among peer mentors 2016–2017.

Item: "I am confident in my ability to..."	Pre-survey mean	Post-survey mean	significance
Create a positive climate for learning	3.81	4.19	t(47)=4.31, p<.01, d=.63
Promote a positive attitude towards learning in my students	4.04	4.34	t(47)=2.25, p<.06, d=.32
Provide support to students who are having difficulty learning	4.15	4.47	t(47)=2.90, p<.05, d=.42
Provide effective written feedback to students	3.85	4.36	t(47)=3.51, p<.01, d=.51
Provide effective feedback one-on-one	3.74	4.28	t(47)=4.70, p<.01, d=.69
Lead an active learning session	3.13	3.71	t(47)=6.19, p<.01, d=.90

Developing the initial curriculum was a collaborative process, drawing on the experience and perspectives of the computer science faculty and the expertise in effective learning and mentorship strategies from the faculty colleague in psychology and education. To kickstart the program, we first ran the training course as a "bootcamp" with a small group of students over a 10-day period immediately preceding the semester. Their feedback helped us refine the materials for the credit-bearing half-semester course, which has been offered for a three-year period. The course has counted towards the instructor's teaching load, which reduced the total courses that the department could offer. We are still iterating to find the right balance and anticipate that increasingly modular, "off-the-shelf" materials will greatly reduce the time required to lead the course in the future.

4 OUTCOMES

4.1 On Mentors

Our findings demonstrate the efficacy of the training curriculum on student mentors. In-line with previous findings of improved teaching efficacy for mentors and teaching assistants [5, 9], we found that during Year 1, peer mentors grew in their teaching self-efficacy throughout the training and practicum, and the intro CS students consistently rated the mentors' knowledge, approachability, and flexibility/creativity as strong or very strong [17]. Intro CS students also credited the one-on-one sessions with peer mentors with improving their self-efficacy and understanding of material [16].

In this paper, in Table 1, we share the peer mentor analyses from Year 2. Based on repeated measures t-tests to analyze changes within individual mentors pre-to-post training, peer mentors grew significantly in their teaching confidence, with moderate (0.32-0.51) to larger (0.63-0.90) effect sizes.

Interviews with over 20 peer mentors provided additional insights about the value of the curriculum used in the training. Peer mentors emphasized that the curriculum provided 1) practice with the role; 2) a research foundation that provided useful explanations and helpful language, with an emphasis on growth mindset, self-efficacy, and feedback; and 3) a learning community to support their development as peer mentors. MaGE mentors shared that when they interviewed for internships or post-graduation employment, whether for technical or non-technical positions, they were able to speak in specific concrete terms about what they learned, such as teaching and working in diverse teams, providing and receiving feedback, and improving their technical ability to debug code. Therefore, the curriculum was not only useful for their role as peer mentors, but also transferred to new contexts of employment.

One powerful strategy leveraged in the training was to videotape the mentors as they provided mock one-on-one feedback to each other. Mentors viewed their own videos privately, and watched, in small groups, short video snippets of their peers' interactions. One mentor explained the value: "We saw each other's videos– seeing how other people introduced themselves helped. How they gave criticism– how they would make it better, and make it more effective." Another voiced the importance of being able to practice a mock active learning module (ALM), sharing "the most valuable experience in the preparation course was doing the mock ALM– public speaking is a concern of mine...having experience and doing it in a safe environment in front of your peers is so helpful."

4.2 On Introductory Learners

The MaGE program was introduced initially in CS1 in the 2015-16 academic year, then in CS2 in the 2016-17 academic year. In these same years, course enrollments and the total number of computer science majors rose rapidly at our institution as well as nationally [2]. Table 2 shows the enrollment growth in CS1 and CS2 from 2014 through 2018.

Table 2: Increases in enrollment in CS1 and CS2 from 2014–2018. The bolded values indicate the years with MaGE mentors integrated into the courses.

Academic Year	CS1 enrollment	CS2 enrollment
2014–15	90	56
2015–16	**122**	83
2016–17	**123**	**77**
2017–18	**138**	**72**
2018–19	**165**	**113**

In this context of enrollment growth, the course-by-course student retention from CS1–CS2 and CS2–CS3 show increased retention rates upon the introduction of MaGE. Table 3 shows these retention estimates (data is based on course enrollment numbers rather than tracking of individual students; 2018–19 retention data is for half the year).

We observe that during the years after implementing this new curriculum, the retention from CS1–CS2 improved, was maintained, and recently has risen. For the CS2–CS3 transition, which reflects

Table 3: Retention proportion of first to second course (CS1–CS2) and second to third course (CS2–CS3). The bolded values indicate the years with MaGE mentors integrated into the courses.

Academic Year	CS1–CS2	CS2–CS3
2014–15	0.46	0.73
2015–16	**0.60**	0.78
2016–17	**0.62**	**0.88**
2017–18	**0.60**	**0.68**
2018–19*	**0.76**	**0.88**

the conversion to a computer science major, we observe a peak, a dip, and then a return. This dip is likely due to limitations on instructor staffing and the number of course sections offered. Open-ended survey responses suggest that retention was supported by the encouragement and personalized feedback from mentors. In one student's words, "[My mentor] helped me a lot in terms of emotional support. She motivated me whenever I thought CS was so challenging that I could not continue." In another's: "Any questions I had about the course material or computer science in general my mentor was able to answer. Moreover, my mentor boosted my confidence and made me feel like I was good enough at computer science to continue on in the program." We saw the peer mentors as normalizing the challenges faced by students in computer science, so introductory students were less likely to internalize the struggles as something inherently problematic with them as individual learners of computer science.

Survey data collected at the end of each semester from the novice students who were mentored in the MaGE program further supports the impact of mentors on student confidence. The percentage of students completing the end-of-semester surveys ranged from 63% to 89%. Table 4 shows mean student responses to the following statements: *"My mentor's written feedback contributed to my confidence with the material"*, *"The weekly meetings with my mentor contributed to my confidence with the material"*. A 6-point scale was used, with 1 indicating 'strongly disagree' and 6 indicating 'strongly agree'. The data shows consistently high levels of agreement for both CS1 and CS2 students over the two-year assessment period from 2016-2018, suggesting their validation of the quality of the mentoring and by extension the impact of the MaGE training curriculum.

Table 4: Introductory students' ratings of mentor contributions to improved confidence.

Course	Acad. Year	Written feedback	In-person meetings
CS1	2016–17	4.99	4.98
CS1	2017–18	5.34	5.42
CS2	2016–17	5.59	5.51
CS2	2017–18	5.12	5.23

Another goal of the MaGE curriculum is to foster a community where novice students feel a sense of belonging. Students were surveyed at the start and end-of-semester using a survey of belonging [6]. Students indicated their level of agreement, on the same 6-point scale, with the following statements: *"I feel that I belong to the computer science community"*, and *"I feel a connection with the computer science community"*. Table 5 shows the mean responses, indicating increased sense of belonging in all but one of the groups reported. It is possible that belonging increased over time due to other factors beyond the peer mentoring. However, we underscore the student open-ended comments pointing to the contribution of the peer mentors as at least a contributing factor. One student explained: "I not only learned CS from my mentor, I also learned more about Mount Holyoke as a school and formed a community with my mentor and fellow students."

Table 5: Introductory students' increased belonging and connection ratings 2016–2018.

Course	Acad. Year	belong pre	belong post	connect pre	connect post
CS1	2016–17	3.92	4.23	3.76	3.95
CS1	2017–18	3.21	3.96	3.19	3.77
CS2	2016–17	4.36	4.33	4.28	4.29
CS2	2017–18	4.22	4.35	4.20	4.31

4.3 On Instructors

We found that the instructors of CS1 and CS2 were able to reduce their workload, even for larger class sizes, due to (1) less time providing technical feedback, given initial mentor code reviews, (2) embedded mentors in labs eliminating the need for faculty instructors to be present alongside lab instructors, and (3) fewer students requesting support via office hours, appointments and emails. In addition, engaging in the MaGE Training curriculum alongside students provides instructors with an opportunity to acquire a framework for more effectively interacting with a diverse group of students. As one instructor noted, "Preparing to teach the MaGE training course had a profound impact on me, my relationships with my colleagues and students, and my teaching style. I've always viewed myself as personable, empathetic and understanding of difference. This course helped me to see that there is no endpoint for emotional intelligence and that my empathy was biased in favor of situations I had personally experienced. I realized that, while understandable, addressing my biases would help me grow as an educator and fundamentally shape my students' experiences."

4.4 At the Institution

Modules from the MaGE curriculum are being piloted on campus more broadly, as the core topics focus on effective, inclusive teaching and learning strategies. Some modules have been already been incorporated into an introductory mathematics class and into the training for mentors who assist peers in oral and written communication skills. A new course for preparing peer mentors embedded in the campus makerspace has been closely structured around the MaGE curriculum. A group of STEM faculty plan to adapt the half-day workshop materials for training their TAs and mentors. We are currently collecting reports of how other campuses (larger research universities as well as small colleges) are modifying the modules to suit the needs of their own peer mentor or TA preparation, in and beyond computer science.

5 PRACTICAL SUGGESTIONS FOR ADAPTING THE FLEXIBLE MAGE CURRICULUM MODULES

The curriculum is designed to be as modular as possible, providing flexibility for those wishing to adopt it. Materials are intended to be as instructional and self-contained as possible, so that a lack of familiarity with the associated topics is not a barrier to adoption. Indeed, we have observed that instructors engaging alongside their mentors as fellow learners can result in more robust and meaningful interactions. Factors that should be taken into consideration when choosing curricular modules include logistical constraints, mentor responsibilities and prioritization of training goals. While we designed the course originally around 7 weekly 3-hour sessions, we provide additional curricular formats for single-day, half-day or 5 hourly sessions on our website[3].

Logistical constraints and facilitating discussion. The *number of mentors* has an impact on the delivery of discussion-based modules; we have found groups of about 12-15 allow for a level of trust and familiarity to be established that leads to deeper conversations. When working with a large group of mentors, we suggest breaking into smaller groups and, if possible, having a facilitator for each; facilitators could be instructors or previously trained mentors, suggesting that this model can be scaled. The curricular materials include tips for how to facilitate inclusive discussions, as well as suggestions for different formats. While we have only delivered the curriculum to groups of students in the context of one *discipline*, most of the topics are more universal, so training mentors across a variety of disciplines may be possible. We suggest being mindful, however, of discipline-specific factors that may impact the discussions; for example, gender identity may play a different role when considering mentorship of computer science students versus biology students. There may be particular technical nuances as well, such as a focus on debugging errors that are difficult among novice learners as compared to those at a more advanced level.

Schedule constraints pose limitations on in-session activities, pre-session requirements and post-session reflections. Whenever possible, we provide choices on how to engage with a module; for example, in-session short videos may be chosen to introduce a topic instead of more scholarly pre-session articles if training does not allow for multiple meetings or assigned work.

Mentor responsibilities. The MaGE mentors held an array of responsibilities, from providing on-the-fly assistance in lab to written and oral feedback on completed work (1-on-1 meetings founded in a code review) to leading active learning group activities. When adapting the curriculum, choose topics that align with the responsibilities of the mentors being trained; e.g., if mentors are only performing code review (and not directly interacting with students), the module on emotional intelligence may be less important than the module on effective feedback. We suggest targeting activities to the specific responsibilities that mentors will undertake.

[3]https://sites.google.com/mtholyoke.edu/student-training-resources

For example, we used mock 1-on-1 meetings to prompt reflection on the mentorship role our students would undertake; for a program where mentors only interact with larger groups of students, a different activity (e.g., modeling a short interactive lecture) would be more appropriate. Whatever the activity, we found that videotaping it followed by independent (private) reflection and small group discussion of clips was often the training experience mentors found most impactful.

Training goals. When choosing and structuring training sessions for peer mentors, it helps to list and prioritize the goals for the program and convey them to the mentors. Are mentors reducing workload on faculty and staff (e.g., via code review)? Is the program aiming to create a more inclusive climate to increase representation of underrepresented groups? Do intended outcomes include cohort-building or construction of a supportive community? The curriculum is designed to have flexibility for embedding skill-based activities throughout, training students in specific responsibilities as well as providing material for reflection and discussion about the more abstract pedagogical topics. For example, if mentors will be performing code review, we suggest pairing mock code review with a discussion around providing effective feedback in inclusive ways.

Structure and flow. The suggested formats are a starting point for structuring the topics and finding a flow that is most effective. An initial discussion about mentorship, particularly regarding program goals, followed by the modules on thinking about learning (e.g., topics of self-regulated learning, self-efficacy and mindset) can organically prompt reflection around the importance of inclusive approaches to mentorship. We noticed that placing these discussions and reflection opportunities before explicitly addressing the role of identity helped establish a group dynamic where participants were more open to digging into the deeper and often more difficult discussions. As many campuses have the goal to improve racial, gender, and socioeconomic diversity, among other identity dimensions, having the capacity to talk among peer mentors and TAs, as well as department instructors more generally, is critically important to reach these goals.

6 CONCLUSION

Asking how one's department, college, or university curriculum serves to invite a wide variety of learners to participate in the broader learning community, and sustain challenge, may be facilitated by engaging TAs and peer mentors in the process. These seasoned and more advanced students often act as ambassadors to our majors and programs of study. Equipping them to be effective technical and inclusive teachers is an important step in the right direction. This paper offers an overview of the MaGE Training curriculum and evidence of the efficacy of the program for the peer mentors, introductory learners, and instructors. The flexibility of the modules facilitates customization for different campuses and uses within and beyond computer science. The online availability also increases access. Importantly, the curriculum addresses effective learning and inclusivity goals which are important on the national level. Adapting the curriculum and sharing the outcomes of similar initiatives can only help computer science to reach collective expansion and diversity goals.

ACKNOWLEDGEMENTS

This work was funded by a Google CS Capacity Award. We are grateful for the support of Mount Holyoke College, the computer science department, and all the students who have participated in MaGE and shared their feedback with us.

REFERENCES

[1] Thalia Anagnos, Alicia Lyman-Holt, Claudia Marin-Artieda, and Ellen Momsen. 2014. Impact of engineering ambassador programs on student development. *Journal of STEM Education: Innovations and Research* 15, 3 (2014), 14–20.

[2] Computing Research Association. 2017. Generation CS: Computer Science Undergraduate Enrollments Surge Since 2006. http://cra.org/data/Generation-CS/ Accessed November 28, 2018.

[3] Sylvia Beyer. 2014. Why are women underrepresented in computer science? Gender differences in stereotypes, self-efficacy, values, and interests and predictors of future CS course-taking and grades. *Computer Science Education* 24 (2014), 153–192.

[4] Bethany Bowling, Maureen Doyle, Jennifer Taylor, and Alison Antes. 2015. Professionalizing the role of peer leaders in STEM. *Journal of STEM Education* 16 (2015), 30–39.

[5] Sue Ellen DeChenne, Larry G. Enochs, and Mark Needham. 2012. Science, technology, engineering, and mathematics graduate teaching assistants teaching self-efficacy. *Journal of Scholarship in Teaching Learning* 12 (2012), 102–123.

[6] Catherine Good, Aneeta Rattan, and Carol S. Dweck. 2012. Why do women opt out? Sense of belonging and women's representation in mathematics. *Journal of Personality and Social Psychology* 102, 4 (2012), 700–717.

[7] Charles Henderson, Andrea Beach, and Noah Finkelstein. 2011. Facilitating change in undergraduate STEM instructional practices: An analytic review of the literature. *Journal of Research in Science Teaching* 48, 8 (2011), 952–984.

[8] Susan Horwitz, Susan H. Rodger, Maureen Biggers, David Binkley, C. Kolin Frantz, Dawn Gundermann, Susanne Hambrusch, Steven Huss-Lederman, Ethan Munson, Barbara Ryder, and Monica Sweat. 2009. Using peer-led team learning to increase participation and success of under-represented groups in introductory computer science. In *Proceedings of the 40th ACM Technical Symposium on Computer Science Education (SIGCSE '09)*. ACM, New York, NY, USA, 163–167. https://doi.org/10.1145/1508865.1508925

[9] Sarah Hug, Heather Thiry, and Phyllis Tedford. 2011. Learning to love computer science: Peer leaders gain teaching skill, communicative ability and content knowledge in the CS classroom. In *Proceedings of the 42nd ACM Technical Symposium on Computer Science Education (SIGCSE '11)*. ACM, New York, NY, USA, 201–206. https://doi.org/10.1145/1953163.1953225

[10] Christina Algiere Kasprisin, Peg Boyle Single, Richard M. Single, and Carol B. Muller. 2003. Building a better bridge: Testing e-training to improve e-mentoring programs for diversity in higher education. *Mentoring & Tutoring* 11, 1 (2003), 67–78.

[11] Clifton Kussmaul. 2012. Process oriented guided inquiry learning (POGIL) for computer science. In *Proceedings of the 43rd ACM Technical Symposium on Computer Science Education (SIGCSE '12)*. ACM, New York, NY, USA, 373–378. https://doi.org/10.1145/2157136.2157246

[12] Janet Liou-Mark, A. E. Dreyfuss, and Lori Younge. 2010. Peer assisted learning workshops in precalculus: An approach to increasing student success. *Mathematics and Computer Education* 44 (2010), 249–260.

[13] Marina Micari, Army Knife Gould, and Louie Lainez. 2010. Becoming a leader along the way: Embedding training into a large-scale peer learning program in the STEM disciplines. *Journal of College Student Development* 51, 2 (2010), 218–230.

[14] Tia Newhall, Lisa Meeden, Andrew Danner, Ameet Soni, Frances Ruiz, and Richard Wicentowski. 2014. A support program for introductory CS courses that improves student performance and retains students from underrepresented groups. In *Proceedings of the 45th ACM Technical Symposium on Computer Science Education (SIGCSE '14)*. ACM, New York, NY, USA, 433–438. https://doi.org/10.1145/2538862.2538923

[15] Becky Wai-Ling Packard. 2016. *Successful STEM mentoring for underrepresented students: A research-based guide for faculty and administrators.* Stylus Publishing, Sterling, VA.

[16] Heather Pon-Barry, Audrey St. John, Becky Wai-Ling Packard, and Chris Stephenson. 2017. Addressing the CS capacity challenge by improving undergraduate peer mentoring. *ACM Inroads* 8, 3 (2017), 43–47. https://doi.org/10.1145/3123732

[17] Heather Pon-Barry, Becky Wai-Ling Packard, and Audrey St. John. 2017. Expanding capacity and promoting inclusion in introductory computer science: A focus on near-peer mentor preparation and code review. *Computer Science Education* 27, 1 (2017), 54–77. https://doi.org/10.1080/08993408.2017.1333270

[18] Bernhard Streitwieser and Gregory Light. 2010. When undergraduates teach undergraduates: Conceptions of and approaches to teaching in a peer led team learning intervention in the STEM disciplines: Results of a two year study. *International Journal of Teaching and Learning in Higher Education* 22 (2010), 346–356.

[19] Lydia T. Tien, Vicki Roth, and J.A. Kampmeier. 2004. A course to prepare peer leaders to implement a student-assisted learning method. *Journal of Chemical Education* 81 (2004), 1313–1321.

Student Engagement is Key to Broadening Participation in CS

Beryl Hoffman
Elms College
Chicopee, MA
hoffmanb@elms.edu

Ralph Morelli
Trinity College
Hartford, CT
ralph.morelli@trincoll.edu

Jennifer Rosato
College of St. Scholastica
Duluth, MN
jrosato@css.edu

ABSTRACT

The Mobile CS Principles (Mobile CSP) course is one of the NSF-supported, College Board-endorsed curricula for the new Computer Science Principles AP course. Since 2013, the Mobile CSP project has trained more than 700 teachers, and the course has been offered to more than 20,000 students throughout the United States. The organizing philosophy behind the Mobile CSP course is that student engagement in the classroom is the key to getting students, especially those traditionally underrepresented in CS, interested in pursuing further study and careers in CS. The main strategies used to engage Mobile CSP students are: (1) a focus on mobile computing throughout the course, taking advantage of current student interest in smartphones; (2) an emphasis on getting students building mobile apps from day one, by utilizing the highly accessible App Inventor programming language; and (3) an emphasis on building creative, 'socially useful' apps to get students thinking about ways that computing can help their communities. In this paper we present and summarize two years of data of various types (i.e., student surveys, teacher surveys, objective assessments, and anecdotal reports from students and teachers) to support the hypothesis that engagement of the sort practiced in the Mobile CSP course not only helps broaden participation in CS among hard-to-reach demographics, but also provides them with a solid grounding in computer science principles and practices.

CCS CONCEPTS

• **Social and professional topics** → **Computing education**; • **Software and its engineering** → *Visual languages*;

KEYWORDS

Mobile CSP, AP CSP, App Inventor, Broadening Participation, Student Engagement

ACM Reference Format:
Beryl Hoffman, Ralph Morelli, and Jennifer Rosato. 2019. Student Engagement is Key to Broadening Participation in CS. In *Proceedings of the 50th ACM Technical Symposium on Computer Science Education (SIGCSE '19), February 27-March 2, 2019, Minneapolis, MN, USA.* ACM, New York, NY, USA, 7 pages. https://doi.org/10.1145/3287324.3287438

ACM ISBN 978-1-4503-5890-3/19/02...$15.00
https://doi.org/10.1145/3287324.3287438

1 INTRODUCTION

Student engagement, defined as "the student's active participation in academic...activities, and commitment to educational goals and learning" [4], is essential to learning. Engagement can be measured along four dimensions: behavioral, affective (or emotional), academic, and cognitive [1]. In this study we are focused on cognitive engagement which has been defined as "thoughtfulness and willingness to exert the effort necessary to comprehend complex ideas and master difficult skills" [11]. Cognitive engagement can be readily observed by teachers and self-reported by students. Students often feel cognitively engaged in activities they perceive to be relevant to their lives and that have the potential to impact their communities.

While it is possible to have strong student engagement in a lecture-based classroom, in the current K-12 environment it is typically associated with active learning approaches which require the student to participate in the learning process. Active learning classrooms employ a core of pedagogical approaches, including collaborative, cooperative, inquiry-based, and problem-based learning strategies. NCWIT's Engagement Practices include a number of strategies for computer science educators to use both within and outside the classroom [8].

In computer science (CS) education, active learning can be traced back to the work of Seymour Papert. In the late 1960s, Papert and his colleagues [22] created Logo, the first programming language that was designed with student engagement and student learning in mind. It was Papert's revolutionary view that students should be learning to program computers rather than being controlled by them. This emphasis on creative student-initiated projects is a basic tenet of the Papert's contructionist approach to education, which views learning as an active process of building mental models and physical artifacts [17].

In this paper we describe research results derived from the past two years of study of the attitudes and achievements of students and teachers participating in the Mobile CS Principles (Mobile CSP) course, a CS Principles course deliberately designed to foster student creativity and engagement in the spirit of Papert.

1.1 AP CSP

The Advanced Placement (AP) CSP curriculum is roughly equivalent to an introductory college CS0 course for non-majors. It offers a broad overview of CS, focusing on seven big ideas: abstraction, algorithms, programming, data, the Internet, creativity, and the social impact of computing [2]. It emphasizes cooperation, collaboration and project-based creativity. It was specifically designed with the goal of broadening participation in computer science both in terms of the number of students taking high school CS courses as well as the increased inclusion of underrepresented groups, such as women and minorities [5].

The AP CSP exam was officially launched in May 2017 with 50,000 examinees, breaking the record for the largest roll out of a new AP course; in the second year of 2018, more than 75,000 took the exam [10]. A unique part of the AP CSP exam is that students submit two performance tasks that are included in their score as well as taking a multiple-choice exam: the Explore task, a research project on a computing innovation, and the Create task, a programming project in any programming language. A key feature of the AP CSP framework is that it does not prescribe a programming language (in contrast to the AP CS A course, which is based on Java). Curriculum providers and teachers are free to use any programming language. For the purposes of the written exam, pseudocode and generic block code are used to express programming and algorithm questions and solutions. In the two years of the exam, a wide range of languages have been used by students to complete the performance task, including both blocks-based languages (App Inventor, Alice, Scratch) and text-based languages (JavaScript, Python).

The 2017 and 2018 AP CSP course broadened participation among female and underrepresented minority students compared to the AP CS A course. However, there is still much work to be done to increase these percentages which still leave out many female and minority students as can be seen in Figure 1. Mobile CSP students who took the AP exam had similar demographics to the total AP CSP students among all CSP curricula. Interestingly, Mobile CSP does have a higher percentage of minorities in its course registration which includes students who are not taking it as an AP course (20% Latinx, 11% African-American, for 20,000+ students).

Figure 1: Demographics of 2017 and 2018 AP CSP (n=115,967) and Mobile CSP Students (n=7,569)

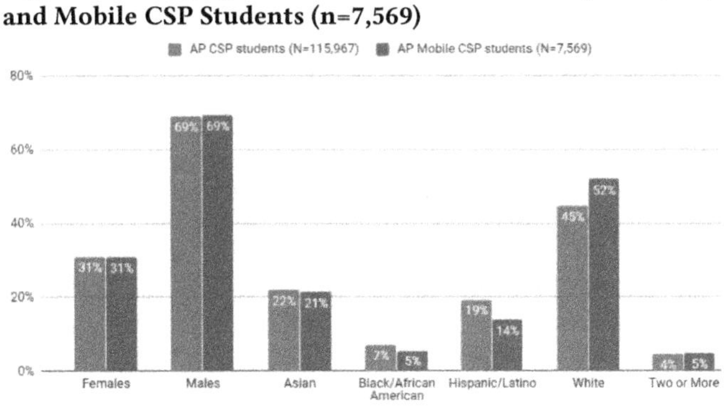

1.2 Mobile CSP

The Mobile CSP course [6, 14, 20] is one of the NSF-supported, College Board-endorsed curricula for the new Computer Science Principles AP framework. Mobile CSP began as a college CS0 course in 2011 and then joined the College Board's Phase 2 pilot program. With support of a 2013 NSF grant, the course became the vehicle for training local teachers in summer professional development (PD) courses. With support of a second NSF grant in 2014, the project was expanded nationally with both local and online PD modalities. Since then, the Mobile CSP course has been used to train more than 700 teachers and it has been offered to more than 20,000 students throughout the United States.

The Mobile CSP course uses creative mobile app-building projects as a fundamental element of the learning experience, giving students the opportunity to create solutions to problems they care about. The curriculum consists of a set of 80-100 45 minute lessons with a mixture of coding and CS theory taught in a hands-on interactive fashion.[1] About half of the course's lessons focus on programming and algorithms (i.e., app building). Programming lessons use a combination of three approaches: video and text tutorials to introduce new concepts, small projects where students use pair programming to solve open-ended problems, and creative projects where students are encouraged to express their own ideas. The other half of the lessons covers non-programming CS Principles (CSP) topics, such as data, the Internet, and computing impact. Table 1 provides an overview of the types of lessons in the course. Multiple modes of learning are provided such as video tutorials, text tutorials, guided-inquiry group activities based on POGIL (Process Oriented Guided Inquiry Learning) [18], and interactive simulations. While both programming and non-programming lessons take an active-learning approach, our data (see Table 4) show that app-building lessons clearly provide the motivational "hook" that gets students engaged in learning challenging concepts.

Table 1: Types of Mobile CSP Lessons

Lesson Type	Number of 45 min lessons
App coding	26
CSP topics	24
CSP POGIL topics (group work)	10
Impacts of CS	11
AP Create Tasks (app coding)	24
AP Explore Tasks (impacts)	16

With its emphasis on mobile app building the Mobile CSP curriculum provides a robust model for engaging a diverse population of students to improve their skills and attitudes towards computer science. The course's organizing philosophy is that student engagement in the classroom is the key to getting students, especially those who are traditionally underrepresented in CS, interested in pursuing further study and possible careers in CS. The main strategies used to engage students are a focus on mobile computing and its social impact throughout the course, taking advantage of current interest in smartphones; an emphasis on getting students building mobile apps from Day 1; and an emphasis on building creative, "socially useful" apps that solve real-world problems. Learning to program by learning to program mobile apps is an example of contextualized learning, similar to media computation which has been shown to be effective in motivating underrepresented students to learn CS within a context they are interested in [9].

To focus on mobile computing, the Mobile CSP curriculum uses App Inventor as the programming language. Created originally by Hal Abelson of MIT during a sabbatical at Google, App Inventor was deliberately designed in the Papertian tradition [16, 25, 26].

[1] The curriculum is freely available at course.mobilecsp.org.

Like other blocks-based languages, such as Scratch and Alice, App Inventor's use of blocks makes programming accessible to complete novices. Block languages have been shown to improve learning for all students, and especially for those traditionally underrepresented in CS. In a comparative study of over 5,000 students answering block-based and text-based questions, researchers [24] found that all students performed better when questions were presented in the block-based form, with female and underrepresented minority students showing the largest improvements.

The significance of App Inventor's accessibility and computational power cannot be overstated. With App Inventor, students are able to create mobile apps from Day 1 of the course – i.e., apps that work the same way as apps that they are familiar with on their mobile devices. The language provides access to all of the device's hardware and communication features.[2] For example, one of the lessons in the course focuses on using the mobile device with its camera or voice recognition or text-to-speech generation. Unlike most other blocks languages, App Inventor's programming abstractions are rooted to actual mobile devices. The degree of abstraction in App Inventor components makes working on real world problems more feasible, providing functions such as sprite animation, text to speech generation, speech recognition, text translation, databases, maps, etc.

For the AP CSP's Create Performance Task, students design their own mobile apps and are encouraged to make them "socially useful". Some of the apps that students have designed are quite ambitious, and several of these have been used outside the classroom in student-initiated extra-curricular projects, demonstrating a high level of engagement. For example, one group of four Hartford high school girls worked with the local police department to create the Emergency Messenger App, a crowd-sourcing app to report crimes and suspicious activity in their neighborhood, and won first prize in the first annual Congressional App Challenge (previously named the Congressional STEM Competition) [19]. Many teachers report that they organize show-and-tell activities in their schools where students can display their apps to parents and school officials. For example, each spring a Mobile Apps Expo is held at Trinity College where students from area high schools demo their apps. Several of the apps that began as performance tasks have gone on to win regional or national contests [23].

An emphasis on building "socially-useful" apps is essential to getting students thinking about ways that computing technology can help their communities in classrooms, families, and neighborhoods. Students learn better when their classroom experience is connected to their lives [3]. The nature of the projects will depend on the interests and abilities of the students themselves. We observe that even simple apps, such as quiz apps that help students study a particular subject or apps that do something beneficial for one's school, can engage students in creative, constructionist learning.

Taken together these strategies not only help broaden participation in CS among hard-to-reach demographics, but also provide students with a solid grounding in computer science principles and practices.

[2]App Inventor was originally designed for Android devices. But a beta release of the language now supports iOS (Apple iPhones). The Mobile CSP course has been adapted to use both Android and iOS platforms.

2 RESULTS

2.1 Methods

The Mobile CSP project provided professional development (PD) for 275 high school teachers in the summers of 2016 and 2017 for those teaching the course in the following academic years (2016-17 and 2017-18). The PD of approximately 100 hours included an introduction to the course, its lessons, and the pedagogical strategies used to teach the course. It was offered in hybrid or online formats; hybrid included two weeks of in-person instruction with two weeks of online instruction. The summer PD was led by master teachers, largely high school teachers who had previously taught the course and received training on offering PD. During the academic year, the master teachers also led monthly web conferences to discuss progress in the course and provide support to first-time teachers. The larger Mobile CSP community of teachers interacted through a discussion forum and had access to monthly webinars from the project team. The teachers trained in the PDs participated in the research project to gather student data in their classes. They administered pre and post surveys and a midterm and final exam to approximately 6,000 students in 2016-2018.

The following data was collected from teachers and students in the research study:

- Teacher pre-PD, post-PD, and post-course surveys,
- Student pre-course and post-course surveys,
- Student midterm and final exam scores
- Student Create and Explore performance task scores (graded by their teachers using the AP rubrics

Data was collected on student engagement through a survey administered to teachers after the course was completed. Students were given a pre-and post-course survey on their attitudes and interest in CS. Data on student performance was similar to the AP exam itself with scores for final exams and the create and explore performance tasks. A common final exam was used with autograding while teachers used the AP rubrics for each performance task to report a score to researchers.

The demographics of students in the Mobile CSP research study in the past two years is detailed in Table 2. As can be seen, the percentage of females at 29% is very close to the 31% rate participating in AP CSP. The underrepresented minorities (African-American, Hispanic/Latino, American Indian/Alaska Native, Native Hawaiian/Pacific Islanders) make up 32% of the students in the research study. We are not reporting the results for minorities for which there were too small numbers (American Indian/Alaska Native, Native Hawaiian/Pacific Islanders).

Table 2: Student Demographics in 2016-2018 Research (n=6492 in pre-surveys)

Demographics	Number	Percentage
Male	4609	71%
Female	1883	29%
Black	858	13%
Latino	1260	19%
Total URM	2118	32%

2.2 Engagement

As described above, the project's data measures student cognitive engagement through a number a different instruments from both teachers and the students themselves. In post-course surveys, teachers report very high levels of engagement among students; nearly 80% of teachers reported that three-quarters or more of their students found the course "engaging" (Figure 2). Although the survey did not explicitly define "engaging" in terms of cognitive engagement, we believe it is the most relevant interpretation of the term given the context.

Figure 2: Teacher post-survey 2016-2018: What proportion of your class found the course engaging (n=226)

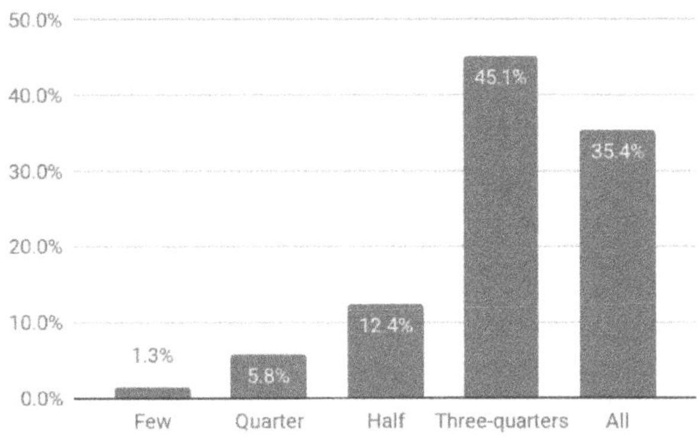

The Mobile CSP PD for teachers emphasizes pedagogy that engages students and broadens participation. In teacher post-surveys in 2016-2018, 72% of the teachers agreed or strongly agreed that the Mobile CSP program helped them to better understand how to implement strategies to support underrepresented populations in CS as seen in Figure 3.

Figure 3: Teacher post-survey 2016-2018: The Mobile CSP program helped me better understand how to implement strategies to support underrepresented populations in CS (n=230)

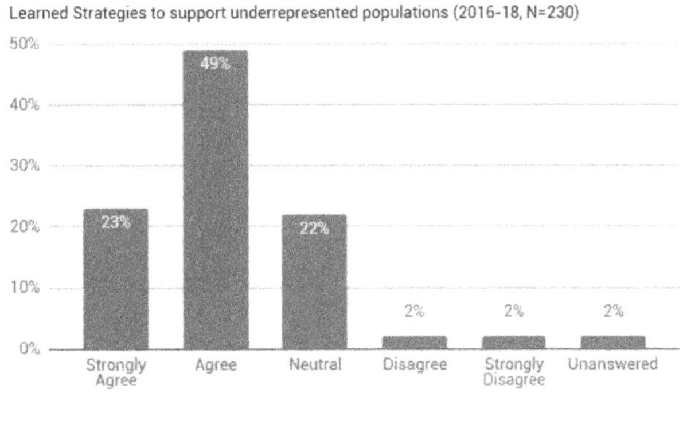

Teachers in the Mobile CSP PD are taught pedagogical strategies to improve student engagement and learning for all students, especially reaching those underrepresented and perhaps new to computer science. Strategies taught include growth mindset, pair programming, welcoming physical environment, project based learning, etc. Teachers are encouraged to use pair programming in class which has been shown to improve student learning, success and persistence [12, 13]. Physical environments that are not gender-biased are welcoming to all students [15]. Encouraging growth mindset in students leads to persistence [7].

In the 2016-2018 post-course surveys, teachers were asked how well they were able to implement the following pedagogies that they learned during the PD in teaching the course as seen in Table 3. Teachers were able to successfully use these strategies in their classes. With pair programming, some teachers report problems such as finding pairs that worked well together, and making sure both students did equal amounts of work.

Table 3: Teacher post-survey 2016-2018: How well were you able to implement the following strategies (n=230)

Worked	very well	well	some	no
Growth Mindset	20%	47%	23%	0%
Pair Programming	27%	27%	37%	4%
Welcoming Environment	47%	40%	8%	1%
Project based learning	47%	36%	4%	1%

Teachers in general report that App Inventor lessons are more popular and engaging with their students than the theory CS principles lessons, even with those involving group work, as seen in Table 4. This supports the view that students are engaged by lessons involving active learning that are contextually relevant and applicable to their lives and interests.

Table 4: Teacher post-survey 2017: How well did lessons work (n=147)

	Very Well	Well	Both
App Inventor Lessons (22)	42%	41%	84%
Other Lessons (30)	22%	49%	71%

2.3 Student Learning

Student engagement can also be demonstrated through student success in learning. In the first year of the AP CSP exam in 2017, 3,611 Mobile CSP students took the AP CSP exam with a pass rate of 78%, 4 points above the national average of 74% for passing the AP exam with a score of 3 or higher. In 2018, 4,031 Mobile CSP students took the AP CSP exam with a 76% pass rate, 7 points higher than the national average of 69%. Mobile CSP students met or exceeded the national average in every content area and performance task. In addition, Mobile CSP students out-performed the national average in every demographic group as seen in the Figure 4 for 2017 and in most groups as seen in Figure 5 for 2018. We were pleased to see that female and male students were very close in their success using the Mobile CSP curriculum. This data supports the view that using a curriculum like Mobile CSP which engages students with a variety of methods, including an accessible block language with highly abstract, useful blocks to create apps for problems that matter to them, may show better gains for underrepresented groups. However, there is still much room for improvement in both recruiting underrepresented groups (see Figure 1) and in ensuring their success (see Figure 4 and Figure 5).

Figure 4: Success of 2017 AP CSP and Mobile CSP Students who passed the AP CSP exam with 3 or higher

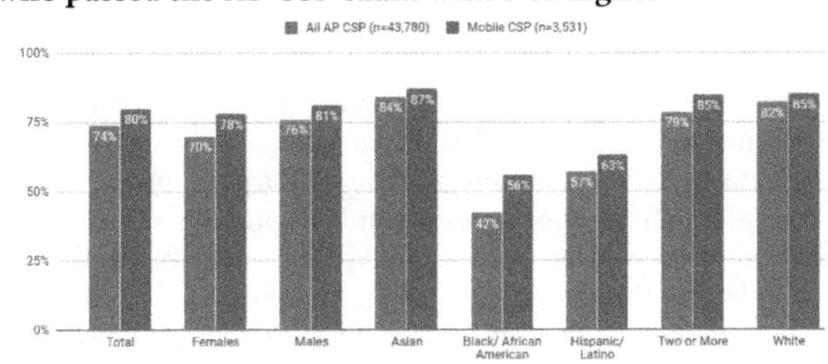

Figure 5: Success of 2018 AP CSP and Mobile CSP Students who passed the AP CSP exam with 3 or higher

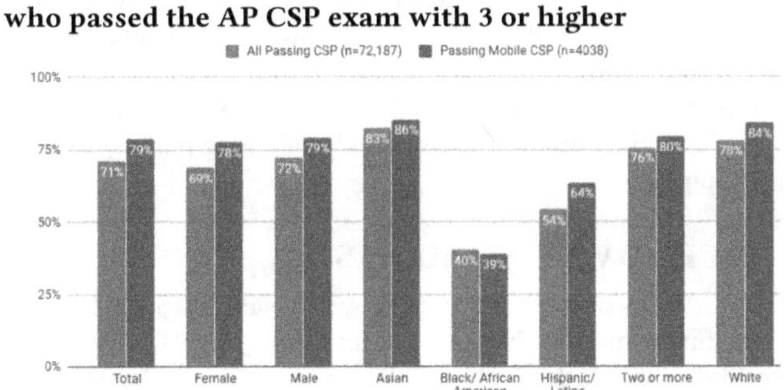

Table 5: Mobile CSP Student Average Grades in Class (2017 and 2018).

	All	Female	Black	Latino
Final Exam ave.	80%	83%	72%	74%
Create 2	84%	87%	74%	79%
Explore 2	70%	67%	56%	62%
Final Grade (2017)	82%	84%	75%	75%

Mobile CSP PD teachers participating in the research study are asked to give a standard Mobile CSP final exam and submit data about their students' success in their classes. Table 5 from 2016-2018 shows that female and underrepresented minority students did better in their Mobile CSP final exam, Create project, and their final grade in the class than on the AP exam. This makes sense due to the high stakes one day test for the AP exam which makes up the bulk of their AP score. Many students enjoyed and did well on the creative programming projects that are reflected in their course grade and performance task grades.

2.4 Student Attitudes

Although our student surveys have no questions that directly measure student engagement, there are several questions that indirectly speak to student engagement. In post-course surveys students were asked various attitudinal questions about their experiences in the course (Table 6). Large majorities of students (76%) reported that the course improved their understanding of computer science. Importantly, these results were consistent or higher across the targeted underrepresented groups, with 79% of female, 77% of Black/African-American, and 79% of Hispanic/Latino students reporting improved understanding. Similarly, more than two-thirds of students (66%) reported that the course improved their attitude toward computer science, which was consistent or higher across female and underrepresented minorities (68-72%). Students also reported an increased interest in CS (59%) and, importantly, that they discovered a new talent for programming (58%) with higher percentages for underrepresented minorities for whom this may have been a first experience in programming.

Table 6: Percent "quite true" or "completely true" on improvement in attitudes about CS after taking Mobile CSP 2017 (n=2218)

	All	Female	Black	Latino
The course improved my understanding of CS	76%	79%	77%	79%
The course improved my attitude towards CS	66%	68%	72%	72%
I learned that I have more programming talent than I was aware of	58%	61%	66%	65%
I have become more interested in CS	59%	56%	56%	66%

2.5 Student Future CS Plans

Strong student engagement is also suggested indirectly by student responses on questions focusing on their future plans. Table 8 presents a summary of gender vs. minority status with respect to future plans while Table 7 presents the full results for three different statements of increasing commitment to a future in CS: "I plan to take more CS in college", "I am considering a Computer Science major in college", and "I am considering a career in Computer Science and technology". In the 2017 and 2018 student post-surveys, nearly two-thirds (64%) of students expressed interest in either majoring in CS in college or pursuing a career in CS as seen in Table 8 which aggregates several questions. Even higher percentages (83%) answered Yes or Maybe to a statement "I plan to take more CS in college" as seen in Table 7. Female students did not feel as strongly committed to this plan as seen by more Maybe answers than Yes answers. Especially encouraging is the fact that there were no differences in the future CS plans of underrepresented minority students (African-American, Latino) compared with all the students. These results are strong evidence that the course is providing a positive view of computer science and helping to reinforce students' desire to continue their study of CS.

On the other hand, while 72% of the male students had future CS plans only 48% of female students reported such plans, suggesting that there is still work to be done in broadening CS participation. However, the fact that 48% of female students reported that they plan to major or work in CS is still a strong result considering that currently the computing workforce is only 26% female and less than 20% of CS/CIS majors are female [21].

Table 7: Student post-course survey 2017 and 2018: future CS plans (n=3024)

Plans for		All	Female	Black	Latino
More CS in college	No	17%	24%	23%	19%
	Maybe	37%	44%	40%	35%
	Yes	46%	32%	37%	45%
	YesOrMaybe	83%	76%	77%	80%
CS major	No	33%	49%	41%	36%
	Maybe	32%	29%	31%	29%
	Yes	35%	22%	28%	35%
	YesOrMaybe	67%	51%	59%	64%
CS career	No	31%	48%	42%	32%
	Maybe	33%	31%	27%	31%
	Yes	36%	22%	42%	37%
	YesOrMaybe	69%	52%	69%	68%

Table 8: Combining students considering or planning CS in college and/or career by URM and gender

Future CS Plans	In Total Students	In URM Students
Total	64%	62%
Female	48%	45%
Male	72%	72%

3 DISCUSSION

Our data suggest that the Mobile CSP course leads to a high level of engagement and learning in the classroom (and outside the classroom in some cases). Nearly 80% of teachers report that more than three-quarters of their students found the course engaging. Students from all demographic groups report increased interest in CS and improved attitudes towards CS. We believe the essential elements of student engagement in this course are: (1) a focus on mobile computing, which is important in students day-to-day lives; (2) the use of a programming environment (App Inventor) that makes it possible for students to create real world apps from the very beginning of the course; and (3) a requirement that students focus on apps that have some personal, community or social benefit.

Although one can't draw a direct causal connection between classroom engagement and success on the AP CSP exam, it certainly seems plausible to expect better performance from students that are more engaged in the way described here. While there is still an unacceptable lag in AP exam scores among females and underrepresented minorities, our data suggest perhaps that engagement can help diminish some of that gap. To help bridge these gaps a variety of extracurricular steps could be taken. More consideration could be given to the types of projects and apps that are developed to ensure they appeal broadly across genders and cultural groups. More attention can be paid to recruiting underrepresented students to bring them into closer alignment with school demographics. Efforts to promote positive role models and address implicit biases can help create a more welcoming classroom environment for all students.

As noted above, in our post-course surveys, students report strong interest in further CS study in college or as a career. The fact that the CSP course emphasizes creativity and project-based learning are strong incentives towards improving students attitudes towards CS. Even further, the type of hands-on engagement emphasized in the Mobile CSP course (and presumably other CSP courses) provides even stronger incentives. Our worry, however, is that students who experience computer science through the CSP or Mobile CSP lens will be disappointed and discouraged to find that not all introductory CS courses emphasize this type of engagement.

Hopefully some of the positive strategies and pedagogical lessons learned from the CSP experience can flow into the courses that follow CSP, such as in AP CS A or the CS1 and CS2 courses in college. That would ensure that students will find a similarly engaging environment, one that leverages their interests and active learning strategies and continues the trend of broadening participation in the CS pipeline.

4 ACKNOWLEDGEMENTS

This work was partially supported by the National Science Foundation under grants CNS-1240841 and CNS-1440947. We would also like to thank the Mobile CSP team for their dedication and contribution to this project.

REFERENCES

[1] James Appleton, Sandra Christenson, and Michael Furlong. 2008. Student engagement with school: Critical conceptual and methodological issues of the construct. 45 (05 2008), 369 – 386.

[2] College Board. 2017. AP Computer Science Principles: Course and Exam Description. Retrieved August 31, 2018 from https://secure-media.collegeboard.org/digitalServices/pdf/ap/ap-computer-science-principles-course-and-exam-description.pdf

[3] Lisa M Bouillion and Louis M Gomez. 2001. Connecting school and community with science learning: Real world problems and school–community partnerships as contextual scaffolds. *Journal of Research in Science Teaching: The Official Journal of the National Association for Research in Science Teaching* 38, 8 (2001), 878–898.

[4] Sandra L Christenson, Amy L Reschly, and Cathy Wylie. 2012. *Handbook of research on student engagement.* Springer Science & Business Media. 816–7 pages.

[5] Jan Cuny. 2015. Transforming K-12 Computing Education: AP&Reg; Computer Science Principles. *ACM Inroads* 6, 4 (Nov. 2015), 58–59. https://doi.org/10.1145/2832916

[6] Mobile CSP Curriculum. 2018. Course site: http://course.mobilecsp.org , Teacher site: http://teach.mobilecsp.org. Retrieved November 1, 2018 from https://mobile-csp.org/

[7] Carol S. Dweck. 2006. *Mindset: The New Psychology of Success.* Ballantine Books.

[8] NCWIT Engage CS Edu. 2018. Retrieved August 31, 2018 from https://www.engage-csedu.org/engagement/make-it-matter

[9] Mark Guzdial. 2015. Learner-centered design of computing education: Research on computing for everyone. *Synthesis Lectures on Human-Centered Informatics* 8, 6 (2015), 1–165.

[10] Sasha Jones. 2018. Participation in AP Computer Science Principles Grows Again. Retrieved August 31, 2018 from http://blogs.edweek.org/edweek/curriculum/2018/06/by_guest_blogger_sasha_jones.html

[11] Duhita Mahatmya, Brenda J Lohman, Jennifer L Matjasko, and Amy Feldman Farb. 2012. Engagement across developmental periods. In *Handbook of research on student engagement*. Springer, 45–63.

[12] Charlie McDowell, Linda Werner, Heather Bullock, and Julian Fernald. 2002. The effects of pair-programming on performance in an introductory programming course. *ACM SIGCSE Bulletin* 34, 1 (2002), 38–42.

[13] Charlie McDowell, Linda Werner, Heather E Bullock, and Julian Fernald. 2006. Pair programming improves student retention, confidence, and program quality. *Commun. ACM* 49, 8 (2006), 90–95.

[14] Ralph Morelli, Chinma Uche, Pauline Lake, and Lawrence Baldwin. 2015. Analyzing year one of a CS Principles PD project. In *Proceedings of the 46th ACM technical symposium on Computer science education*. ACM, 368–373.

[15] NCWIT. [n. d.]. How Does the Physical Environment Affect WomenâĂŹs Entry and Persistence in Computing? Retrieved August 31, 2018 from https://www.ncwit.org/resources/how-does-physical-environment-affect-women%E2%80%99s-entry-and-persistence-computing

[16] MIT News Office. 2010. The MIT roots of GoogleâĂŹs new software. Retrieved August 31, 2018 from http://news.mit.edu/2010/android-abelson-0819

[17] Seymour Papert and Idit Harel. 1991. Situating constructionism. *Constructionism* 36, 2 (1991), 1–11.

[18] CS Pogil. 2019. Retrieved August 31, 2018 from http://cspogil.org

[19] Press Release. 2014. Retrieved August 31, 2018 from https://esty.house.gov/media-center/press-releases/rep-elizabeth-esty-announces-congressional-design-your-own-app-contest

[20] Jennifer Rosato, Chery Lucarelli, Cassandra Beckworth, and Ralph Morelli. 2017. A Comparison of Online and Hybrid Professional Development for CS Principles Teachers. In *Proceedings of the 2017 ACM Conference on Innovation and Technology in Computer Science Education*. ACM, 140–145.

[21] NCWIT By the Numbers. 2017. Retrieved August 15, 2018 from https://www.ncwit.org/sites/default/files/resources/btn_04042018_web.pdf

[22] Paulo Blikstein (Stanford University). [n. d.]. Seymour Papert's Legacy: Thinking About Learning, and Learning About Thinking. Retrieved August 31, 2018 from https://tltl.stanford.edu/content/seymour-papert-s-legacy-thinking-about-learning-and-learning-about-thinking

[23] WCVB. 2016. 5 for Good: Local high School students win Congressional App Challenge. Retrieved August 31, 2018 from https://www.wcvb.com/article/5-for-good-local-high-school-students-win-congressional-app-challenge/8096710

[24] David Weintrop, Heather Killen, and Baker Franke. 2018. Blocks or Text? How programming language modality makes a difference in assessing underrepresented populations. In *Proceedings of the International Conference on the Learning Sciences 2018, At London, UK*.

[25] David Wolber. 2011. App inventor and real-world motivation. In *Proceedings of the 42nd ACM technical symposium on Computer science education*. ACM, 601–606.

[26] David Wolber, Hal Abelson, Ellen Spertus, and Liz Looney. 2011. *App Inventor.* " O'Reilly Media, Inc.".

Evaluating the Impact of Combination of Engagement Strategies in SEP-CyLE on Improve Student Learning of Programming Concepts

Mourya Reddy Narasareddygari [a], Gursimran S. Walia [a], Debra M. Duke [b], Vijayalakshmi Ramasamy [c], James D. Kiper [c], Debra Lee Davis [d], Andrew A. Allen [d], Hakam W. Alomari [c]
[a] North Dakota State University, [b] Virginia Commonwealth University, [c] Miami University, [d] Florida International University

ABSTRACT

Programming is a skill, which could be acquired through repeated practice, feedback. In lectures, many students are neither practicing nor obtaining feedback on anything. Practice and feedback would energize the student's motivation, direct their focus on gaining the knowledge. But, from instructor's perspective offering manually quality evaluation for even a smaller class implies that feedback cannot be as instant as one-to-one tutoring. Also, becomes hard as the class size grows. This could be achieved with the help of some supporting tools apart from the lectures, that help in attracting students and motivates them to spend significant time on tasks. SEP-CyLE (Software Engineering and Programming Cyber Learning Environment) is a cyber learning environment that contains digital learning content of software programming and testing concepts. SEP-CyLE incorporates collaborative learning, social networking and gamification strategies that provides students motivation, practice and instant feedback. This paper aims to assess the impact of different combinations of these learning engagement strategies (LESs) of SEP-CyLE on student learning and understanding of programming concepts. We conducted a multi-institution study wherein different combination of LESs were utilized using SEP-CyLE in CS1 classrooms. We analyzed the impact of LESs on students' acquisition of programming concepts, their engagement and usage of SEP-CyLE. The pre and post test results indicated that the assorted LEs have shown a positive impact on student learning across all the institutions. The correlation results demonstrated that there is meaningful relationship between the LEs and the student performance in the course

CCS CONCEPTS

• CS1/2 • Learning Environment • Software Engineering

KEYWORDS: SEP-CyLE, CS1, Gamification, Learning Objects, Collaborative Learning, Social Interaction

SIGCSE '19, February 27-March 2, 2019, Minneapolis, MN, USA

ACM ISBN 978-1-4503-5890-3/19/02...$15.00
https://doi.org/10.1145/3287324.3287413

ACM Reference format:

Mourya Reddy Narasareddygari, Gursimran S. Walia, Debra M. Duke, Vijayalakshmi Ramasamy, James D. Kiper, Debra Lee Davis, Andrew A. Allen, Hakam W. Alomari. 2019. Evaluating the Impact of Combination of Engagement Strategies in SEP-CyLE on Improve Student Learning of Programming Concepts. In *Proceedings of 50th ACM Technical Symposium on Computer Science Education (SIGCSE '19), February 27-March 2, 2019, Minneapolis, MN, USA.* ACM, New York, NY, USA, 7 pages. https://doi.org/10.1145/3287324.3287413

1 Introduction

Like all educators, as instructors of computer science, we continually search for ways to facilitate student learning. To be effective in this task, we need to be aware of the habits and characteristics of our current set of Millennial college students [1]. In her book Reality is Broken [2], Jane McGonigal explores the influence of games on society in general and on millennials in particular. The subtitle of her book "Why Games Make Us Better " explains the increasing significance of gaming. The general question that we address in this work is what learning engagement strategies will be most effective with millennial computer science students.

This paper describes a group of experiments conducted at several universities to explore several specific learning engagement strategies: social interaction, collaborative learning, and gamification. Of course, there are many other ways to engage students [11]. However, we believe that these are some that fit the characteristics of current students. The set of universities who participated in these studies vary in geographic location, in the balance between teaching and research, and in the nature of the students (ages and demographic characteristics). The one commonality is that all of the experiments use a particular cyber-learning support system: *SEP-CyLE - Software Engineering and Programming – A Cyber Learning Environment* [3]. This web-based system supports instructors in providing appropriate CS content to students and supports CS students in using that content through text and video. The features of SEP-CyLE that are particularly relevant to this paper are the learning strategies that are supported: social interaction, collaborative learning, and gamification.

The paper is organized as follows. Section 2 provides background information about learning engagement strategies; section 3 gives more information about the cyber-learning tool SEP-CyLE. In section 4, we describe the study design. This is followed by results and analyses in section 5 and a discussion of the results in section 6.

2 Background

Strategies to improve student engagement continues to be at the forefront of research on education as engaged students take an active role in their learning. Fredricks et al [7] suggest that engagement can be defined as behavioral - where participation and social interactions are seen as indicators for academic success; emotional - where reactions to the ecosystem of their education influences willingness to do work and therefore succeed academically; and cognitive - where the willingness to exert effort to understand and master difficult ideas correlates to academic success. For this work we focus on three learning engagement strategies (LESs) that crosscut the behavioral, cognitive and emotional. We present an overview of the three LESs.

- *Gamification*: Educators continue to leverage strategies from the entertainment domain [4] with gamification increasingly being recognized as an effective method of improving student motivation and engagement [5]. Gamification leverages the competitive nature of students and the feeling of community through the use of familiar gaming elements such as ranking of users, badges and points as rewards for completing tasks or challenges [9,10].
- *Social Interaction*: Social interaction has many aspects, including the idea of exchanges [8,11] - interactions that provide something of value to others that can be rewarded. For students, that reward could be directly grade-related or visible appreciation by the community for some contribution [12].
- *Collaborative Learning*: Collaborative learning is a learning engagement strategy that enables a group of students to contribute and work together on the completion of tasks toward an academic goal, leading to shared understanding and long-term retention [11]. Teams may be self-selected or are assigned by the instructor and tasks assigned that require all team members to contribute / participate to be considered completed. Team completed tasks are rewarded, potentially motivating team members to contribute so they do not let the team down.

The application of these LESs in a virtual online environment is described in Section 3.

3 SEP-CyLE – Software Engineering and Programming Cyber Learning Environment

SEP-CyLE[1] is a configurable cyberlearning platform for Software Engineering and Programming that currently implements these three learning engagement strategies: gamification, social interaction and collaborative learning. The contents of SEP-CyLE are packaged as digital learning objects (LOs), which includes multimedia instructions and tutorials as well as auto graded quizzes. We present an overview of the way that SEP-CyLE implements these learning engagement strategies.

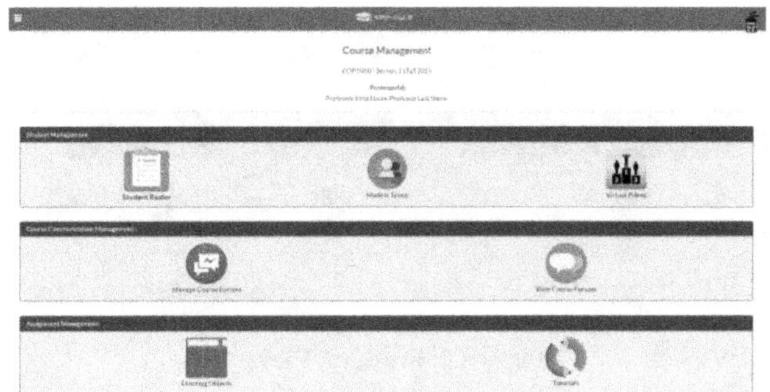

Figure 1: Instructor View

Gamification: Specifically, SEP-CyLE includes the gaming elements of 1) reward: points for completing tasks, and 2) leaderboard: displaying student point rank as a comparative incentive. The rewards element is enabled through the awarding of points for successful completion of a task (quizzes, forum posts, commenting, etc). The leaderboard aggregates the points for all students in the course and displays a ranking of the students. This element may encourage the competitive students to participate in more activities in the system to improve their ranking.

Social Interaction: In SEP-CyLE social interaction is defined as some social exchange between the students that is rewarded. The intent of this learning engagement strategy is to develop a community of learners. Teams are assigned by the instructors; team members use SEP-CyLE's facilities to upload their own profile picture and provide personal details on their profile that they want to share. Students are also encouraged to provide comments in the discussion forum and pose questions to other teams or other students in the class and to the larger SEP-CyLE community.

Collaborative Learning: In SEP-CyLE, groups are created by the instructor. Each task is assigned virtual points and each student's successful completion of a task is rewarded with the task points. Additional points are awarded based on the aggregate performance of each member of the team in completing each of the tasks. The primary performance metrics are 1) tasks completed by all members of the team and 2) speed of completing task by the group.

The instructor view of SEP-CyLE provides the course management options as seen in Figure 1. Students enrollment is accomplished in *Student Roster* via a roster file upload or, if preferred, entering individual student's information. For collaborative work or engagement strategies, each student can be assigned to a group using *Student Teams*. The prebuilt LOs tutorials are assigned to the course through *Learning Objects* and *Tutorials* respectively. The instructor can enable any combination of the available LESs through *Course Settings* and assign points to task through *Virtual Points*.

[1] "SEP-CyLE – Software Engineering and Programming Cyber Learning Environment" https://stem-cyle.cis.fiu.edu/. Accessed 31 Aug. 2018.

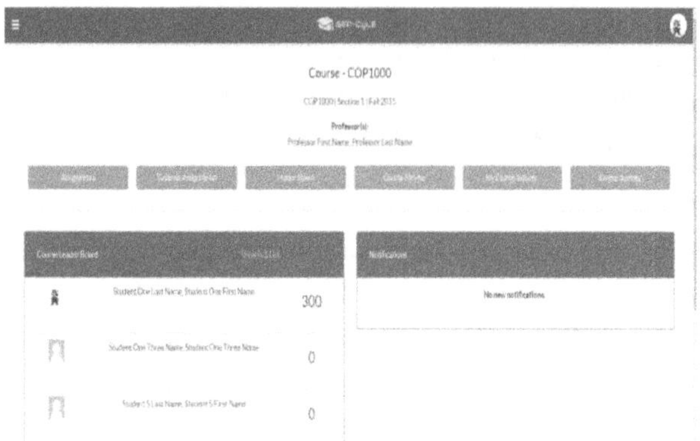

Figure 2: Student View

Figure 2 shows the student view of SEP-CyLE. Once the student is logged in to her course, she can proceed to her LO assignments, or her tutorial assignments. The *Course Forum* provides an avenue to interact with her team or the class by asking or answering questions. *My Activity* provides a list of her completed tasks and interactions, while *Course Activity* provides course-wide information. The *Leaderboard* displays the current ranking of the students based on their points accumulation.

Several Studies have been conducted in the past few years. Some of these studies have investigated the impact of single LESs in one institution, or impact of two of the LESs in another institution.

4 Study Design

This study was designed to investigate the impact of student learning and understanding of programming concepts of various combinations of learning engagement strategies (LESs), i.e., Social Interaction (SI), Collaborative Learning (CL), and Gamification (G) in SEP-CyLE at two major universities, which could be seen in Table 1.

The study was conducted across two institutions where various combinations of LESs were utilized using SEP-CyLE in CS1 courses. Each institution had a different experimental condition (i.e., utilized SEP-CyLE with different LESs enabled). The studies utilized a pre- and post-test design to measure the impact of using SEP-CyLE with various combinations of LESs on-student learning outcomes.

At every institution, a pretest was conducted at the start of the semester prior to the introduction of SEP-CyLE. Students then advanced through the course wherein they worked individually and completed their assigned programming labs but were periodically assigned SEP-CyLE LOs to supplement classroom and laboratory instruction. toward the end of the semester, students were tested again with post-test instrument which utilized the same set of questions as used in the pretest. More details of the study are provided in the following sections

4.1 Study Goals and Hypothesis

The main objective of the study is to analyze the impact of different combination of learning engagement strategies of SEP-CyLE on student learning. More formally, the high-level research goal was to:

Investigate the impact of different combinations of learning engagement strategies (i.e., CL, G, SI) used in SEP-CyLE on student's understanding and learning of programming concepts in an introductory programming course at multiple institutions.

The design of SEP-CyLE and the motivation to include CL, G and SI as major learning engagement strategies (LESs) were based on the results from literature findings (details provided in Section 2). We hypothesized that inclusion of 3 LESs (CL+G+SI) would be more beneficial to support CS1 pedagogy when compared to using 2 LESs (CL+G or CL+SI or G + SI) which in turn would be more beneficial than using 1 LES (CL or G or SI). More formally, The higher the number of LESs utilized in SEP-CyLE, the larger the improvement in student performance and their understanding of programming concepts in CS1 courses.

4.2 Independent and Dependent Variables

The following independent variables were manipulated:

- *Virtual Points (VP):* These are the reward points that are earned by the students for the activities they perform within the SEP-CyLE.

Table 1: Participation Subjects and Interventions

# of LESs	Groups	Site	Year/Semester	# of subjects
3	G+SI+C	North Dakota State University	Fall' 2017 and Spring 18	14
	G+SI+C	Virginia Commonwealth University	Fall 2017	36
2	G+SI	North Dakota State University	Fall 2017	16
	G+CL	Virginia Commonwealth University	Fall 2017	26
	SI + CL	North Dakota State University	Fall 2017	19
1	G	Virginia Commonwealth University	Spring 2018	29
	SI	Virginia Commonwealth University	Spring 2018	32
	CL	NA	NA	NA

0	None - SEP-CyLE with no LESs enabled	Virginia Commonwealth University	Fall 2017	29

Table 2: Comparison of Pre and Post-test Scores Across Different Intervention Groups

Average Score	3 LESs	G+SI	CL+SI	CL+G	SI	G	None
# of subjects	50	16	19	26	32	29	29
Pre-test Scores	8.6	7.81	8.16	8.88	7.03	8.21	8.52
Post-test	11.56	13	11.57895	10.73077	10.1875	11.13793	10.21
Improvement	+2.96	+5.19	+3.42	+1.85	+3.16	+2.93	+1.69
Significance (p-value)	<0.001	<0.001	<0.001	0.012	<0.001	<0.001	0.036

- *Number of LOs assigned:* the number of digital learning objects that were assigned by instructors at each site and for each intervention.
- *Number of **LO**s **A**ttempted (LOA):* the number of learning objects that each student attempted from the assigned list of learning objects.
- *Number of **LO**s **C**ompleted (LOC):* the number of learning objects that a student passed with at least 80% of the questions correctly answered.

Researchers measured the effect of above independent variables on the following dependent variables *Pre/Post-test Score:* measured based on the responses to the 21 questions contained in the pre/posttest instrument. Each question was worth one point; students were graded on range of 0 (none of the questions correctly answered) to 21 (all questions were correctly answered).

- *Higher-level Programming Concepts:* We also measured students' understanding of 8 high-level programming concepts (i.e., memory management, conditional statements, basic operators, methods, arrays, loops, OOP, software testing). We mapped each of the 21 questions in the pre/post-test to one of these 8 categories in order to evaluate students' understanding of these 8 conceptual categories.
- *Course Grade (CG):* measured as the course grade (in terms of percentage out of 100) achieved by a student.
- *Assignment Grade (AG):* measured as the average of the assignment scores (in terms of percentage out of 100) for each of the subjects during the semester.
- *Exam Grade (EG):* measured as the average of exam grades scored by the students in a semester.

4.3 Participating Subjects

A total of 209 students participated in this study. These subjects are divided in groups (or sections of CS1) at three different institutions. Each group (or section) utilized SEP-CyLE with different combination of LESs (3 or 2 or 1 or none). A brief summary of the intervention groups and subjects are provided in Table 1.

4.4 Study Procedure

- *Step 1 -- Pretest:* At the beginning of the semester, a pretest was conducted to establish a baseline regarding the student's understanding of software programming concepts. The test consisted of 21 questions that assessed knowledge of students on various programming concepts like arrays, pointers, software testing, memory management, etc.,
- *Step 2 -- Introducing SEP-CyLE to students:* The students were shown how to use SEP-CyLE including how to peruse video tutorials and learning content, how can they track their progress, how to change their profile pictures, interact with their peers in the cyberlearning environment, and how to post to the discussion forums. Each section of university site was trained separately depending upon the LESs that have been enabled to them.

Step 3 -- post-test: Toward the end of the semester, the students were re-tested on the knowledge of their proficiency on software programming and testing concepts. The post-test contained the same set of questions as of the pretest. This was done across all the sites to understand the impact of different combinations of LEs on improvement in their conceptual knowledge. We additionally assessed the students course grade, assignment grades, and exam grades to comprehend the effect SEP-CyLE had on their course performance.

5 Results and Analysis

The principal data source are students' responses to the pre- and post-test data. We calculated students' pre and post-test scores in different intervention groups (groups that used 3 LESs versus 2 LESs versus 1 LES versus none) to evaluate the impact of different LESs on students' acquisition of programming concept.

To provide an overview of the results, Table 2 presents the averages of the pre- and post-test scores for all subjects in each group. Table 2 also shows the improvement in post-test scores to support comparing different treatment groups. Additionally, an independent samples t-test was conducted to evaluate the statistical significance of the improvement in post versus pre-test scores. A threshold of p-value < 0.05 was used to judge the statistical significance.

Based on the results presented in Table 2, the following major observations were made:

Overall, SEP-CyLE was able to improve students' knowledge upon completing CS1 (post-test) as compared to their knowledge when entering CS1 (pre-test). Though significantly better than the pre-test scores, the post-test scores show that students are not learning everything that they are expected to learn in CS1. This result is discussed later in Section 6.

In terms of LESs used, "*G + SI*" had the largest impact on students' knowledge gain (+5.19). Additionally, students exposed to SEP-CyLE with SI and G enabled were able to demonstrate largest post-test scores (correctly answered 13 of 21 questions on average) when compared to other groups.

CL did not seem to add substantially to knowledge gains for students in this study. This is evident throughout the study groups. SI or G, when used independently had similar or higher gains compared to when CL was added to SI or G. Additionally, adding CL to "G+SI" did not have a positive impact on students' knowledge gains. Reflecting back on how CL is implemented in SEP-CyLE, we plan to improve the design by involving more collaborative activities to increase student engagement and their knowledge gains (also discussed in Section 6).

We additionally gathered SEP-CyLE information for every student in terms of the number of LOs assigned to them, the number of LOs attempted by them, the number of LO's passed by them, and their performance in the course in terms of their grades, assignment scores and exam scores. Note that, while SEP-CyLE is a cyber learning environment (used outside of classroom), participating institutions had developed LOs (available for everyone) specifically to help improve some common knowledge deficient areas (e.g., OOPs concepts, Methods, Loops, Conditional Statements). Based on students' feedback from earlier SEP-CyLE studies [6], LOs help students self-assess their knowledge areas and also contribute to their motivation to improve their skill-set. Therefore, the goal of this analysis was to understand if the availability of LOs can supplement in-class instruction and improve students' performance (especially their assignment scores) in classroom.

Based on the results presented in Table 3; the following major observations were made:

- Students enrolled in "*G+SI*", "*G*", and "*SI*" groups (the columns in gray in Table 3) attempted and subsequently completed (passed with at least 80% of questions correctly answered) the largest number of LOs. This may have been because of the following reasons:
- Firstly, for each LO completed by students, students are awarded certain virtual points (VPs). VP is a gamification element and students only receive VPs when "G-gamification" is enabled. Similarly, there are VPs associated with SI (social interaction) activities. Only groups that have SI enabled will receive VPs for those activities (e.g., profile pic, posting/replying to discussion thread).
- Second, students with the most VPs also show up in the "leaderboard", so students are motivated (perhaps extrinsically) to be more engaged on SEP-CyLE and get more visibility with their peers.
- Looking at the high course scores (percentage out of 100), this result were based on the inclusion of subjects that completed pretest and post-test and used SEP-CyLE. It could be that, more motivated students tend to go beyond normal teaching resources and are likely to perform better. We plan to investigate whether SEP-CyLE can be made more inclusive in the course so that everyone can benefit from it.

An examination of the average scores from these schools in Table 3 may seem higher than is typical for CS1 courses. Note that the average of assignment scores ranges from 61.8% to 81.3%; for exam scores from 74.8 to 88.0%; for class grade from 79.1% to 87.2%. This may be explained by the fact that these data were collected only for students who completed the pretest and post-test and who used SEP-CyLE. Thus, these are likely more motivated students, that is, self-selection. It may be the case that general CS1 student performance could be improved if use of SEP-CyLE or a similar cyber-learning tool was a required part of the course rather than voluntary.

Next, we performed multiple regression analysis to evaluate the impact of SEP-CyLE usage metrics (i.e., VP - *average virtual points earned*; LOA - *average # of LOs attempted*; and LOC - *average # of LOs completed*) on student's course performance (i.e., AS - *average assignment Score*; ES - *average exam score*; CG - *average course grade*) for different LESs combinations. The goal of this analysis was to understand if certain usage areas of SEP-CyLE can be encouraged to students in future implementations of SEP-CyLE. Based on the correlation analysis, major results (only the significant results) are discussed as follows:

- For CL+G treatment group, VPs were *positively* correlated to assignment scores. The results showed a significant but weak correlation (r2=0.2 and p= 0.03) between VPs and AS.
- For G treatment group; VPs, LOA and LOC were all positively and significantly correlated to CG and AS.
  - VPs - weak correlations with CG (r2=0.16 and p= 0.04); and with AS (r2=0.26 and p= 0.04)
  - LOA - weak correlation with CG (r2=0.17 and p= 0.02); moderate correlation with AS (r2=0.40 and p= <0.001)
  - LOC - weak correlations with CG (r2=0.28 and p= 0.003) and with ES (r2=0.17 and p= 0.02); moderate correlation (r2=0.40 and p= 0.001) with AS
- For SI treatment group; VPs, LOA and LOC were all positively correlated to CG
  - VPs - weak correlation (r2=0.14 and p= 0.03) with CG;
  - LOA - weak correlation (r2=0.11 and p= 0.06) with CG;
  - LOC - weak correlation (r2=0.17 and p= 0.02) with CG;

Based on these results, only the number of LOs attempted (LOA) seemed to have a significant and moderate size effect on assignment scores (AS) of students in treatment group that used

Gamification. As mentioned earlier, only the "G" group rewards students for completing LOs (in term of VPs) and so students may have been extrinsically motivated to earn VPs.

6 Discussion of Results

This section summarizes the results presented in Section 5 and then discuss results in light of hypothesis formulated in Section 4 and the impact of the results on SEP-CyLE design and its future implementations. Finally, we provide concluding remarks and briefly mention studies to evaluate future implementations of SEP-CyLE.

Summary of Results: A brief summary of results presented in Section 5 is as follows:

- SEP-CyLE in any manner can help students improve their conceptual knowledge of computer programming;
- Gamification (G) and Social-Interaction (SI) learning engagement strategies are more useful (when used individually or in combination) than Collaborative Learning (CL);
- Ability to earn VPs (element of Gamification) and to be more visible to peers (via Leaderboard) is a good motivator for students to be more engaged on SEP-CyLE when used in CS1 classrooms;
- LOs helped students improve their assignment scores and course grades.
- The number of LOs attempted had a moderate and significant impact on the assignment scores of subjects in "Gamification - G" group.

In terms of **testing of hypothesis** listed in Section4, we conclude the following:

- Using SEP-CyLE with some LESs enabled is better for student knowledge gains versus SEP-CyLE with no LESs enabled.
- We reject the hypothesis that 3 LESs is better than 2 LESs
- Using G+SI is better than all other groups.

SEP-CyLE Design and Implementation Changes: Based on the results from this study and feedback from students and instructors, we discuss the possibility of incorporating the following changes

- *Collaborative Learning* (CL)- Currently, CL is being used in SEP-CyLE in a virtual sense where students can be made a part of team but they never collaborate on tasks. We plan to address this by having team members work on a shared space to solve a more complicated problem for additional bonus VPs after successfully passing individual LOs.
- *Levels of LOs*- It was noted that some of the same LOs were too hard or too easy for students which impacts student perception of SEP-CyLE. We are working on having different levels of LOs (e.g., beginner, expert) to mitigate this issue and improve future implementations of SEP-CyLE.
- *Tracking time spent*: We plan to collect time spent by students on different areas of SEP-CyLE to better understand their usage patterns and improve SEP-CyLE usage;
- *Number of LOs*: This study used 11 LOs that were developed, and subsequently vetted by the involved researchers. Since then, we have developed additional LOs and are working on LOs specifically focused on areas where CS1 students are still deficient at the end of the course.

ACKNOWLEDGMENTS

This work is supported in part by the National Science Foundation under grants DUE-1225742, DUE-1525414, DUE-1525112, DUE-1525208 and DUE-1661610. Any opinions, findings, and conclusions or recommendations expressed in this material are those of the author(s) and do not necessarily reflect the views of the National Science Foundation.

REFERENCES

[1] H. Neil., and W.Strauss. Millennials Go to College: [*strategies for a New Generation On Campus : Recruiting and Admissions, Campus Life, and the Classroom*]. 2nd ed. Great Falls, Va.: LifeCourse Associates, 2007.

[2] J. McGonigal, *Reality is Broken, Why Games Make Us Better and How They Can Change the World*, Penguin Books, 2011.

[3] R. Chang-lau and P. J. Clarke. Software engineering and programming cyberlearning environment (SEP-CyLE), 2018. https://stem-cyle.cis.fiu.edu/instances (retrieved Jan. 2018).

[4] M. Dickey, Engaging By Design: How Engagement Strategies in Popular Computer and Video Games Can Inform Instructional Design, *Educational Technology Research and Development*. Vol 53, Issue 2 June 2005

[5] M R Narasareddygari, G. S. Walia, and A. Radermacher. Gamification in Computer Science Education: a Systematic Literature Review. *The 125th ASEE Annual Conference & Exposition. – Computers in Education Division, June 2018*

[6] M. R. Narasareddygari, G.S. Walia, O. Borchert, and A. Radermacher. "Evaluating Learning Engagement Strategies in a Cyber Learning Environment during Introductory Computer Programming Courses-- An Empirical investigation" *125th Annual ASEE Conference, June 24 - 27, 2018, Salt Lake City, Utah*

[7] A.J. Fredricks,P.C. Blumenfeld, & A.H. Paris, (2004). School Engagement: Potential of the Concept, State of the Evidence. *Review of Educational Research*, 74(1), 59-109.

[8] M. H. Jacobsen, & S. Kristiansen, (2015). *Goffman's sociology of everyday life interaction. In Social Thinkers: The social thought of Erving Goffman* (pp. 67-84). Thousand Oaks, CA: SAGE Publications, Inc. doi: 10.4135/9781483381725.n5

[9] J. Hamari, J. Koivisto, and H. Sarsa, "Does Gamification Work?–A Literature Review of Empirical Studies on Gamification" in *System Sciences (HICSS), 2014 47th Hawaii International Conference* on, 2014, pp. 3025–3034.

[10] I, M.B., A.Di-Serio, C. D. Kloos.: "Gamification for engaging computer science students in learning activities: a case study". *IEEE Trans. Technol.* 7(3), 291 301(2014).

[11] K.Karel & K. Paul & J. Wim. (2003). Identifying the Pitfalls for Social Interaction in Computer-Supported Collaborative Learning Environments: A Review of the Research. *Computers in Human Behavior.* 19. 335-353. 10.1016/S0747-5632(02)00057-2.

[12] D.R. Garrison, T. Anderson, W. Archer Critical thinking and computer conferencing: a model and tool to access cognitive presence. *American Journal of Distance Education*, 15 (1) (2001), pp. 7-23.

[11] OECD, PISA 2009 Results: Learning to Learn–Student Engagement, Strategies and Practices, vol. 3. Paris, France: OECD Publishing,2010.

[12] G. D. Kuh, "Assessing what really matters to student learning inside the national survey of student engagement," *Change: Mag. Higher Learn.*, vol. 33, no. 3, pp. 10–17, 2010.

[13] V Ramasamy, H. Alomari, J. Kiper and G. Potvin, "A Minimally Disruptive Approach of Integrating Testing into Computer Programming Courses," 2018 IEEE/ACM International Workshop on Software Engineering Education for Millennials (SEEM), Gothenburg, Sweden, 2018, pp. 1-7. https://www.computer.org/csdl/proceedings/seem/2018/5750/00/575001a001-abs.html

Non-Programming Activities for Engagement with Foundational Concepts in Introductory Programming

Shuchi Grover
Looking Glass Ventures
Palo Alto, CA, USA
shuchi.grover@gmail.com

Patrik Lundh
SRI International
Menlo Park, CA, USA
patrik.lundh@sri.com

Nicholas Jackiw
SRI International
Menlo Park, CA, USA
nicholas.jackiw@sri.com

ABSTRACT

Programming—in a text-based or visual language—is a complex activity that novices find difficult to learn. In this paper, we present an experience report on how novel activities designed for early conceptual exploration can support middle school students' engagement with and learning of foundational programming concepts beginning programmers often struggle with, specifically, variables, expressions (Boolean, arithmetic, relational), loops, and abstraction. We drew on mathematics education research on dynamic representations to design and develop a set of four non-programming, (open access) web-based, interactive activities and micro-worlds and two unplugged activities as part of a suite of activities that can be embedded in a typical introductory programming curriculum to introduce learners to the target concepts before they encounter them in programming. This report describes the activities as well as our experience with their use as part of an introductory computer science course in three diverse, urban, middle school classrooms in the US.

ACM Reference format:
Shuchi Grover, Patrik Lundh and Nicholas Jackiw. 2019. Non-Programming Activities for Engagement with Foundational Concepts in Introductory Programming. In *SIGCSE '19: 50th ACM Technical Symposium on Computer Science Education, Feb. 27–Mar.2, 2019, Minneapolis, MN, USA.* ACM, NY, NY, USA, 7 pages. https://doi.org/10.1145/3287324.3287468

1 Introduction

Learning to program is a central feature of most K-12 computer science (CS) curricula. As K-12 CS education grows, stakeholders are working on varied approaches to support the development of programming skills among diverse, young learners.

Novice CS learners are typically introduced to programming in a block-based language such as Scratch, Blockly, Alice, App Inventor, and Snap!. These languages shift the programming focus from syntax to semantics since the blocks all but eliminate syntax errors. However, syntax is not the only aspect of programming that novices find challenging. Learners also struggle with learning the semantics and pragmatics of programming, be it in a text-based [e.g 3, 15, 19] or a visual language [e.g. 5, 8, 10]. Research suggests that weak mental models and conceptual understandings prevent deeper learning of foundational CS concepts [3, 16]. Recent research on middle school programming in Scratch also found that some concepts—such as variables, expressions with variables, Boolean logic, loops (with variables), and abstraction—are more difficult than others for learners [9].

To address the need to support students' early CS conceptual skill development, we designed a curriculum, 'VELA', built around programming and six non-programming activities for middle school students to learn key CS concepts: including variables, expressions, loops, abstraction and conditionals. The VELA non-programming activities are designed to help students explore and use these concepts in interesting ways in non-programming contexts (digital or unplugged) ***before they encounter them in programming contexts*** in environments like Scratch.

The VELA activities (along with teacher materials) and a curricular sequence involving Scratch were implemented as a 4-week intervention (as part of their middle school CS course) in three diverse middle school classrooms in a large urban school district in the United States. This experience report presents our findings from this implementation as well as lessons learned. We believe this report will be valuable in informing the use of these activities and materials (available at http://csforall.sri.com) in their curriculum regardless of programming language being used.

2 Related Work & Research Framework

Novices struggle with naïve notions about variable assignment (assuming variables can have multiple values at the same time) [21]; with distinguishing between what goes inside a loop and what precedes or follows a loop [3] and with designing mathematical and logical expressions and naming variables [6] Problems pertaining to the understanding of conditionals are also often attributed to a lack of understanding of Boolean operators [4]. Recent research with Scratch also reports that students struggle with constructing terminating conditions for loops involving variables and Boolean expressions [8]. Some students working in Scratch were found to believe a variable must be a letter that stands for an "unknown number" (as in math class), and students often assume multiple actions in a loop are repeated not as a block but rather individually one after the other [10].

Activities in introductory programming classrooms are often centered on open-ended projects and tinkering involving minimal guidance. Lack of conscious pedagogic attention to student engagement with conceptual ideas often exacerbates the problems

SIGCSE '19, February 27-March 2, 2019, Minneapolis, MN, USA

ACM 978-1-4503-5890-3/19/02...$15.00
https://doi.org/10.1145/3287324.3287468

novices face in understanding programming [16,17]. Our activity designs draw specifically on innovations in interactive dynamic representations in mathematics such as those in Geometer's Sketchpad [12] or Cabri Géometre [14]. Research has shown the important role such dynamic representations play in supporting diverse students' development of conceptual understanding in topics of algebra and geometry [2, 20].

3. Design of Non-Programming Activities for Conceptual Learning

In this section, we describe the design and classroom use of four interactive digital activities and two unplugged activities that support early exploration and understanding of foundational CS concepts. This process entailed conceptualization, design, and development of digital (and two companion non-digital activities for introductory CS middle school curricula that can serve as precursorial "conceptual sandboxes" to explore these key concepts before employing them in programming. The names of the activities and computing concepts targeted are in Table 1.

Table 1. Non-Programming Conceptual Activities Suite

Name	Type	Introductory Concept(s)
Story Variables	Unplugged	Variables (variation, naming, types)
Cats & Ladders	Digital	Variables, Numeric Expressions
Graphical Looping	Digital	Repeating pattern, Looping
Dice Game	Unplugged	If-Then, Boolean outcomes
Three Switches	Digital	Boolean Logic, Boolean Expressions
Alarm Clock	Digital	Numeric and Boolean Expressions, Data Types, String Data, Modeling

3.1 Activity Design Guidelines

The activity design process was guided by a precise set of learning goals (LGs) that our activities (and companion curriculum) targeted. These LGs, informed by emergent standards and frameworks and recent research in the context of middle school programming [1, 8, 13], are listed below.

Students will learn/understand–

1. How programs are executed sequentially
2. Simple loops (fixed/predetermined number of repetitions)
3. How to create different pathways in algorithms using conditional statements
4. Algorithmic flow of control- how instructions are executed in sequence sometimes with loops/conditionals
5. That in control structures (like loops and conditionals), a collection of an arbitrary number of statements can be declared to act as a single statement by grouping them
6. What Initialization (in general and of variables, specifically) is and why it is needed
7. That variables can only hold one value at a time
8. How types define the set of values a variable can have, and the set of operators that can be used
9. How variables are created, assigned values, and updated
10. How variable values change within loops
11. How to use expressions to make new variables from old ones
12. Boolean variables, operators & expressions
13. How to control loops and conditionals using Boolean conditions (that may involve variables and expressions)
14. Boolean as a data type
15. How variables are an abstraction or representation of data in the program and the real world
16. Computational solutions are abstractions; and that these abstractions can be represented in different ways
17. Identifying and specifying patterns in real-world phenomena and abstracting them into structural components of program.

Guided by the LGs, the main focus of designed activities was to introduce *Variables* as named quantities that can change value; *Expressions* as defining new changing values by applying value-appropriate operations to existing variables; *Looping* as countable repetitions of some identifiable "repeating unit"; *Abstraction* as the process of giving a name to a specific collection of details to reference its purpose without quoting or enumerating its detail; and *Conditionals* as enabling alternate pathways that are determined based on evaluation of expressions involving arithmetic, relational, and Boolean operators.

The initial activity concepts were designed with inputs from classroom teachers from a large, diverse urban school district in Northern California in a participatory design model. Over a 12-month period, the activities were iteratively designed and refined with inputs from a multi-disciplinary, multi-stakeholder team that included researchers, teachers, and students. The research team included computer scientists, CS education researchers, learning scientists, and math education researchers.

The current version of the web-based digital activities is available at (URL suppressed). We describe the activities and lesson sequence in brief in the remainder of this section.

3.2 VELA Non-Programming Activities

All our activities are designed to be completed in pairs along with a worksheet and intermittent whole class discussions.

3.1.1 Story Variables (Unplugged) In Story Variables, students work collaboratively in pairs to investigate a series of short "stories" all containing everyday examples of quantities that vary (Figure 1). For example, "Excuse me—last week I bought one of these pens here for $1.50. Are you really telling me they now cost $3?" Or "I watched the basketball game last night. At halftime we were tied, but in the end, they beat us 94-90." Through discussions, students come up with a definition of 'variable' as a named quantity whose value can change, practice identifying and naming variables meaningfully, and analyze a variable's changing values to determine its specific types and expected ranges. Students identify their own real-world scenarios that involve "variables". As a final activity, they watch a video clip of the Pacman game and list the different variables they observe, and their ranges.

3.1.2 Cats & Ladders (Digital) The Cats and Ladders digital "game" (Figure 2) formalizes this idea of variables as named quantities whose values can change. In the context of an interactive game that involves rescuing cats from various floors of buildings, they encounter ideas of variation (of the ladder height), data types (numerical ladder height or alphabetic building label), arithmetic expressions on varying inputs (stacking two ladders—an orange and blue one, whose heights are added to get "total ladder height", and the relevance of descriptive and meaningful names for variables in an operational context (e.g. BlueLadderHeight). The activity is divided into multiple stages, each of which is "unlocked" as the students proceed through the activity. Students also discuss the range of possible values of the variables involved. They explore abstraction through creating arithmetic expressions that synthesize new variables (e.g. TotalLadderHeight) from existing ones using operators.

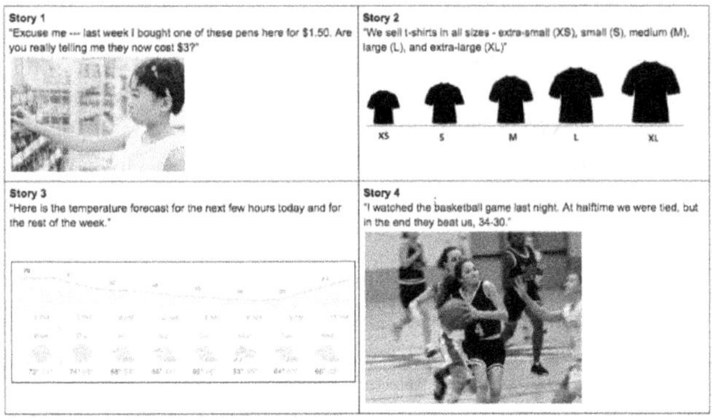

Figure 1. Real-world variables/scenarios in "Story Variables"

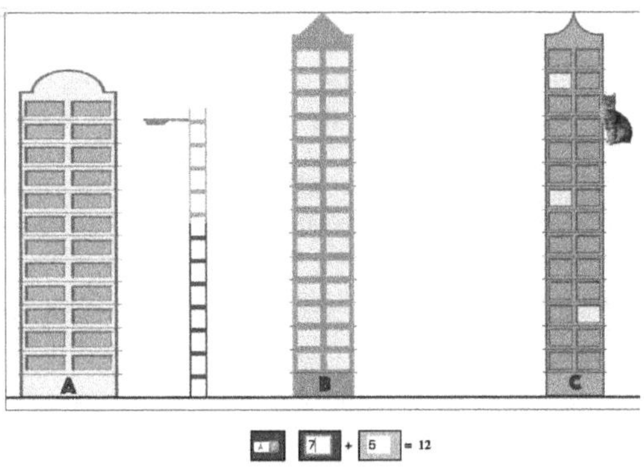

Figure 2. Screenshot of Cats & Ladders Digital Activity

3.1.3 Graphical Looping (Digital) Here, students are introduced to sequential and iterative control flow through comic-strip panels that provide an accessible, graphical interface in which linear sequence directly shapes coherence and meaning. Students first arrange a collection of panels into "a sensible story," representing one back-and-forth lap of a swimmer in a pool (Figure 3a). They then evolve their narrative into a story with a pattern, whereby repeating the "inner story" of swimming one lap (the "repeating unit"), generates different stories in which any number of laps can be completed (Figure 3b). The dynamic visualization of the total laps with the variable number of the laps, is in essence a visual "unfurling" of a loop where the number of repeats is based on the value of a variable. Students answer questions such as: What happens when the inner story is repeated 10 times, how many pool lengths will the swimmer swim? How might the total length swum increase with each lap?

3.1.4 Dice Conditionals (Unplugged) Our introduction to conditionals involves learning how to evaluate expressions that result in a TRUE or FALSE. Through a series of fun, unplugged activities, student learn to evaluate whether or not to take a course of action. In the warmup to the game, students play "Simon Says," where all students begin by standing, and sit if a statement the teacher says is true (e.g. I am wearing sneakers) and then progress to taking action based on evaluating an IF statement (e.g. "If I am wearing sneakers, raise my right hand") and finally based on an IF-ELSE statement (e.g. "If I am wearing any red, then stand on one leg, ELSE raise your right hand"). The activity then moves to a game played in pairs with online or physical dice, where player 1 or 2 gets a point based on evaluating an expression involving arithmetic and relational operators (e.g. IF **Dice1 + Dice2 < 12,** THEN player 1 gets a point).

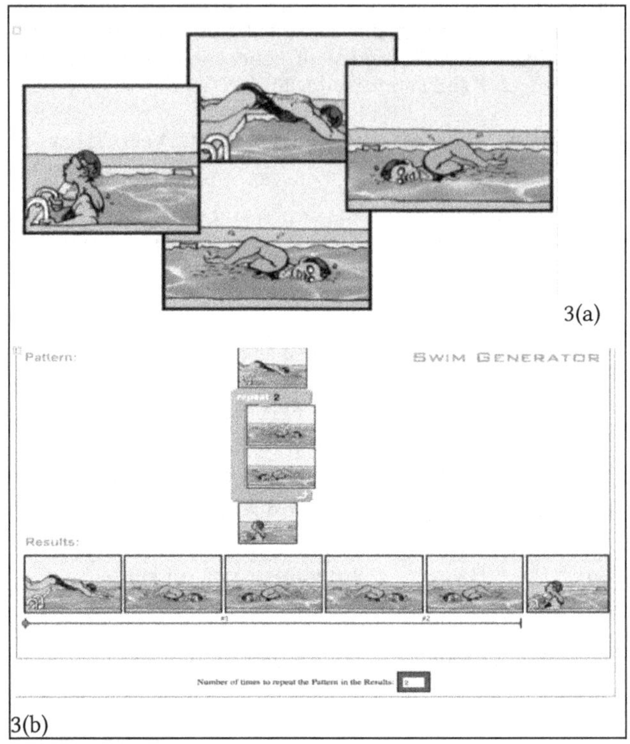

Figure 3. Screenshot of the Graphical Looping Activity

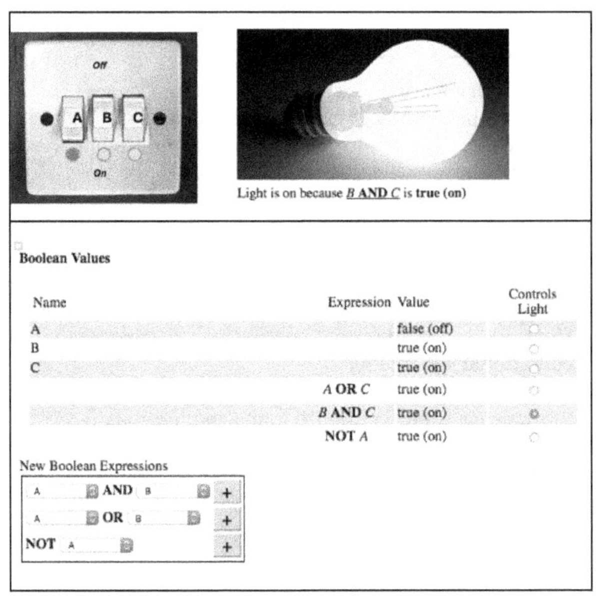

Figure 4. Screenshot of the 3 Switches Interactive Activity

3.1.5 Three Switches (Digital) Though introductory exploratory "challenges" in an interactive expression-authoring microworld, students explore how Boolean operators (AND, OR, NOT) work, and what the resulting expressions evaluate to using an example of three switches that toggle between two states —ON and OFF/

TRUE and FALSE (Figure 4). They then extend the ideas to create and evaluate Boolean expressions that use these operators either in simple expressions or compound expressions that combine one or more operators. The activity ends with an exploration of connections between variables and Boolean expressions in real-world scenarios through discussions, in which students articulate the outcome variable, the controlling variables, the Boolean operators used, and the Boolean expression (e.g. A car gives a warning beep if – Driver's seat-belt is not locked; Passenger's seat-belt is not locked; Car is being driven).

3.1.6 Alarm Clock (Digital) The final VELA non-programming activity uses the same underlying microworld and expression builder as Three Switches, but the context in this case is an Alarm Clock (Figure 5) that should ring at certain times e.g. to wake one up for school (or when *isAlarmTime* is true) based on expressions created using variables (Boolean, numerical, and string) and expressions (relational, arithmetic, and Boolean). By assigning names to these new expressions, and by incorporating those new names (rather than the full symbolic expressions defining them) into new expressions that reference those intermediate results, students develop a hierarchy of abstractions to manage the growing symbolic and conceptual complexity of a family of equations expressed only in terms of foundational variables. The activity can be expanded to be woken only on *weekdays* where an expression like (*isAlarmTime AND isWeekday*) encodes a complex amount of decision-making involving times, and day-calendars.

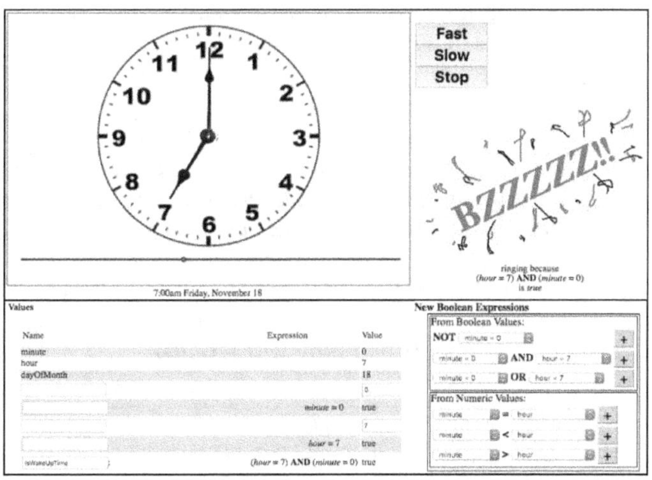

Figure 5. Screenshot of the Alarm Clock Interactive Activity

3.3 Teacher Materials and Curricular Sequence for VELA & Programming Activities

Each of the non-programming activities described included teacher lesson plans, student worksheets that guided the activity trajectory (to be completed by students in pairs), and formative assessments (or "review sheets", to be completed individually). In addition to these designed activities and materials, we designed lesson plans to introduce students to basic Scratch constructs and programming concepts. The Scratch lesson plans attempted to also make connections to relevant ideas in VELA activities in an effort to mediate transfer. For example, the Scratch activities related to loops with variables made explicit connections to *Graphical Looping*. Learners were introduced to the idea of using a "Repeat" block to swim three laps, change the (swimmer's) Energy value, and also "watch" this value decrease (using the 'Say' block) with each lap (or iteration of the loop). They then progressed to the idea of a generalized solution where the number of laps was based on an input from the user to be used as a variable in the Repeat block (Figure 6).

All the lesson plans and materials were refined with feedback from 3 middle school classroom teachers who were planning to implement them in their classrooms. We also worked with the teachers to embed the entire VELA intervention (of non-programming and programming lessons) into a 20-day period within a 9-week introductory programming middle school course that they were teaching. <URL> shows the entire curricular sequence for those 4 weeks.

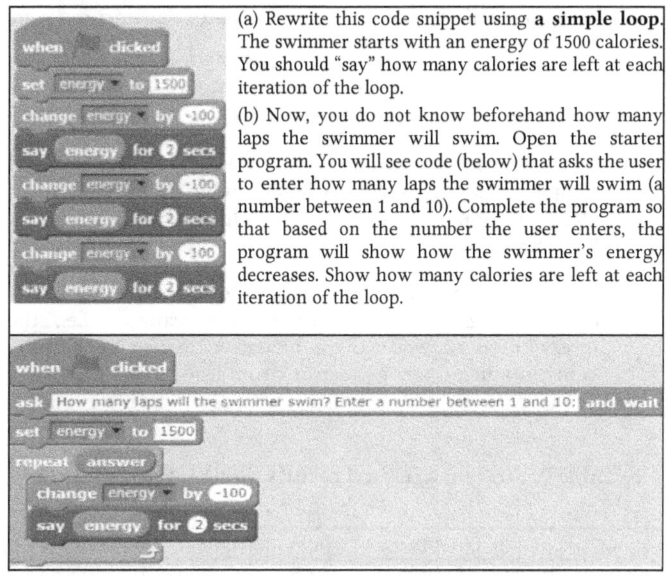

Figure 6. Scratch activities using loops and variables that bridge to Graphical Looping

4. Classroom Study, Data Gathered & Findings

VELA activities and the Scratch curriculum were used in 3 middle school classrooms (N=72; Gr. 6: 17 male, 10 female; Gr. 7: 15 male, 16 female; Gr. 8: 11 male, 3 female) in 3 different schools in a large, diverse, urban school district in the U.S., as part of an introductory CS course. Grades 6 and 8 schools serve high-poverty and underserved populations, whereas grade 7 was in a high-achieving school. The three teachers participated in 20 hours of professional development before implementing the curriculum.

We gathered data on (a) ***Pre-post assessment scores*** from an assessment [7] that we designed through iterative rounds of piloting in classrooms and the use of a robust assessment design framework. It included multiple-choice and open response question types using snippets of Scratch code, or real-world (narrative) scenarios; (b) ***Post-survey*** on students' reactions to the activities; (c) ***Classroom observations*** when the non-programming activities were used; (d) ***Teacher and Student interviews***; (e) ***Final (open-ended) projects*** in Scratch done (individually or in pairs) that we analyzed using an elaborate rubric [11]. The rubric supports analysis for correctness as well as program sophistication. We compared these to final Scratch projects from ~60 students randomly selected from middle school classrooms across the district who were not part of this study (who used a version of [22] as their introductory CS course); and

(f) ***Prior academic preparation*** (math & English scores) ***and ethnicity*** provided by the district (anonymized).

4.1 Findings

This section presents salient findings from statistical analyses of posttest scores and learning gain (pre-to-post change).

- All three classrooms showed statistically significant gains on the pre-post assessment (Table 2).
- Grades 7 & 8 had statistically higher pre- and post-scores than Grade 6, and there was no statistical difference between Grades 7 & 8 pre- or post-score.
- No differences by gender in pre-/post-score or learning gain
- Prior math score significantly predicted pre-score; English did not. However, when controlling for pre-score, neither math nor English were significant predictors of post-score.
- Ethnicity-wise distribution of students was uneven and sample sizes very small for some groups. That said, there were no significant differences by ethnicity in post-score or learning gain.
- Learning gain was not statistically different by gender, grade, ethnicity, or prior math or English score – i.e., the intervention showed no significant difference in learning gains in students by gender or prior academic preparation, and all grades showed statistically similar learning gains.

Table 2. Student pre-post results on VELA assessment

	pre	post	p	Cohen's *d*
Grade6 (n=26)	39.2	52.5	0.00	0.65
Grade7 (n=31)	65.5	80.0	0.00	1.02
Grade8 (n=14)	56.3	68.5	0.00	0.67

Table 3. Average scores on final open-ended projects for VELA (N=54) and non-VELA students (N=60)

	VELA	Non-VELA	p
Total Score	96.0	71.8	0.01
General Factors	31.4	29.2	0.22
Mechanics of Design	17.5	16.4	0.67
User Experience	4.6	3.4	0.93
Basic Coding Constructs	31.83	18.17	0.00
Advanced Constructs	10.72	4.6	0.01
Variables	1.3	0.9	0.10
Boolean Operators	2.8	0.9	0.01
Relational Operators	4.3	2.7	0.06
Repeat-Until Loops	1.7	1.1	0.21

A comparison of scored free-choice final projects of our sample students and those of a comparison sample from the same district showed significantly better performance by VELA students (for all three grade levels) especially on coding constructs and the use of operators. Use of 'Variables', and 'Repeat-untils' also showed higher (though not statistically significant) use on average in VELA projects than non-VELA projects (Table 3).

Table 4. Student and teacher reactions to the activities

Teacher and Student Reactions to Cats & Ladders
Teacher: *"maybe it is having that tool that reaches the student on so many levels being that it is animated, there is sort of an emotional interest, all of that, so that story sticks out better. And so it may not really have huge payoff in that it shows you how to build an expression, but as the teacher emphasizes over and over again now that expressions are made from variables and operators and how that comes up later, it refers back to cats and ladders it is like oh yeah, cats and ladders, the two ladders, the two ladders. So the power becomes more on how the teacher refers back to the tool in later discussion in referencing the story plots."*
7th Grade Student: *"I thought it was interesting because this happens in real life, and I like cats, and I like the idea of saving them..I thought it was more challenging and interesting because you would have to not only type in the blue ladder height and orange ladder height, but also which building it was in. It made it more connected to realize because in the city that I live in, there's a lot of buildings."*
8th grade student:*"It's... to show us about height. And like the variables change. Because like you could change the numbers...It shows us variables. Like how high the ladder could go, like how we could change it."*
6th Grade Student: *"Cats & Ladders was fun and cool"* **(a few other students had similar reactions)**
7th Grade Student: *"I liked cats and ladders because it was like a real game."*
Student Reactions to Graphical Looping
8th Grade Student: *"It's sort of like a puzzle...It teaches you the purpose of what loops do...It reminded like if we go to a grocery store and we could come back and get more food from there and then come back...Like each day like ... it can be from like school, you go back home. And from the home you go back to school"*
7th Grade Student: *"Graphical Looping was too easy and boring"* **(a few other students had similar reactions)**
Teacher and Student Reactions to Alarm Clock
6th Grade Student: *"I did not really understand it"*
8th Grade Student: *"I liked alarm clock the most because it was most challenging"*
8th Grade Student:*"It was most interesting"*
6th Grade Student: *"It took too long"*
Teacher: *""And then the Boolean 3 switches and the alarm clock, I think are too big for the kids, as an activity to handle on their own. And so they become very teacher directed, and along that way you lose a lot of kids.."*
Teacher: *"The interface is confusing, in particular with regard to drawing attention to which features are more important than others... Some kids might get it and understand what to ignore and what to work with, but it's not clear at first. And so even some of the naming schemes for what the boxes are, what the tables are, this table is how you're going to use this, and this table is how you're going to use that.*

Students' post-survey feedback and teacher interviews (Table 4) reflects that, overall, students found *Cats & Ladders* to be most engaging and fun, *Graphical Looping* activity was found to be lacking in challenge by some, though students readily made real-world connections, and the micro-world expression-building interface for *Three Switches and Alarm Clock* was confusing for some students. Additionally, one teacher noted that on the topic of abstraction, the bridging between the Scratch activities and the VELA activities should be stronger. One teacher said that while students were highly engaged with the activities and they learned, they would benefit from more time to return to the ideas, solidify them, calibrate misunderstandings, and *build deeper understanding over time.*

Our classroom observations revealed that teachers' challenges keeping students on topic, the number of students in class, and classroom cultures that did not always support student-driven whole class discussion. The paired activities also lacked explicit strategies for supporting collaboration.

At the same time, one of the teachers felt strongly that participating in the PD and teaching the activities deepened her own conceptual understanding, especially of abstraction. She recommended that the activities (especially those relating to Boolean expressions and abstraction) be used in the district teacher PD— *"I felt like it really educated me quite a bit, deeply and powerfully. And so it was a huge learning process for me, not quite on the level of how to be a teacher in the classroom, but the content itself. So it developed my content knowledge really well. And I'm excited to now kind of apply it in the classroom, and try to marry our current curriculum to some of these ideas and flesh it out more."*

5. Lessons Learned

Reflecting on our findings, some particular insights may inform future use of these activities.

1. All three classrooms showed significant gains on the pre-post assessment (see Figure 1). Examining the VELA classroom as a curricular activity system, we see that students engaged well with many of the VELA activities, demonstrating promise of our approach, our digital and unplugged activities, and relevant examples and contexts.
2. One of the most promising findings that points to the value of using this curriculum widely is that learning gains were not linked to specific grades or student characteristics (gender, prior math/English scores). It demonstrates the promise of this approach and curriculum to reach all students regardless of prior academic preparation.
3. The finding that students' use of more Boolean operators and Repeat-untils in their free-choice final projects suggests that our strategy to deliberately introduce these key concepts impacted transfer to programming. This is significant since these topics are often ignored in programming curricula despite being listed in CS frameworks and standards [1, 13]
4. Our activities need to be refined to incorporate better ways to engage younger learners (in grade 6), as their performance in the pre-posttest left much room for improvement. We also need to determine if the assessment itself is better suited to grades 7 and 8 students by studying it more widely with larger samples. Also, the wording of one question in the test was found to be ambiguous and is being improved upon. The assessment and related analyses can be found in [7].
5. Classroom culture needs attention when using a curriculum like this. Even in the high achieving school (grade 7), there were issues with regard to time for exploration, pacing, differentiation, leveraging whole class discussions productively, trouble shooting opportunities, and iterations of key learning moments. Evidence related to the relationships between instruction, classroom environment, and the activities raised questions about how to deepen students' engagement with, and learning of, our target programming concepts. We found that students needed time to explore the concepts in different ways through the activities, opportunities to collaborate with peers in order to problem solve together, have their own thinking articulated and challenged, and to return to prior learning experiences to iterate on their growing conceptual insights. Unfortunately, when teachers make instructional choices to address these needs, they have to concurrently contend with the limits of the system, such as class size, varied levels of student understanding, time, student habits and mindsets, as well as their own beliefs and practices.
6. One teacher felt that given the number of students and time constraints, she could only do superficial differentiation. This was reinforced by our classroom observations.
7. Our unique conceptual activities can also be used for CS teacher PD (as one of the teachers noted) to introduce novice CS teachers to—and deepen their understanding of—foundational concepts, and especially Boolean expressions and abstraction.
8. Perhaps our most gratifying takeaway from this project is that at the urging of our participant teachers, the district has incorporated most of our non-programming activities into their regular introductory middle school CS course, as a result of which our unique conceptual activities are reaching over 10,000 students in the large urban school district.

6. Conclusion

In this experience report we described our unique innovation—a suite of non-programming activities for introducing learners to variables, expressions, loops, conditionals, Boolean logic, and abstraction—that targets these concepts that novice learners often find challenging. We shared results from the use of these digital and unplugged interactive activities in grade 6,7, and 8 classrooms in a large urban district in the U.S., representing ethnic and socio-economic diversity. Our findings reflect the promise of our approach while our lessons learned provide useful pointers for others who may be interested in using these activities as part of their introductory CS course (using any programming language).

ACKNOWLEDGMENTS

We thank NSF (#1543062) for grant funding. Thanks to Matthias Hauswirth, Jeremy Roschelle, Satabdi Basu and SRI colleagues, Bryan Twarek, Xander Piper, and middle school teachers and their students for participating and partnering in this research.

REFERENCES

[1] Computer Science Teachers Association. 2017. *CSTA K-12 Computer Science Standards*, Revised 2017. Retrieved from http://www.csteachers.org/standards.

[2] Drijvers, P., Kieran, C., Mariotti, M. A., et al. (2010). Integrating technology into mathematics education: Theoretical perspectives. In C. Hoyles , & J. P. Lagrange (Ed.), *Mathematics education and technology-rethinking the terrain* (pp. 89-132). New York, NY: Springer.

[3] du Boulay, B. (1986). Some difficulties of learning to program. Journal of Ed Computing Research, 2(1), 57-73.

[4] Ebrahimi, A. (1994). Novice programmer errors: Language constructs and plan composition. International Journal of Human-Computer Studies, 41(4), 457-480.

[5] Franklin, D., Skifstad, G., Rolock, R., Mehrotra, I., Ding, V., Hansen, A., ... & Harlow, D. (2017, March). Using upper-elementary student performance to understand conceptual sequencing in a blocks-based curriculum. In Proceedings of the 2017 ACM SIGCSE Technical Symposium on Computer Science Education (pp. 231-236). ACM.

[6] Gobil, A. R. M., Shukor, Z., & Mohtar, I. A. (2009). Novice difficulties in selection structure. In International Conference on Electrical Engineering and Informatics, 2, 351–356. New Jersey, USA: IEEE.

[7] Grover, S. 2019. An Assessment for Introductory Programming Concepts in Middle School Computer Science. In *Proceedings of the 2019 Annual Meeting of the National Council on Measurement in Education (NCME), Toronto, CA*

[8] Grover, S., Pea, R., Cooper, S. (2015). Designing for Deeper Learning in a Blended Computer Science Course for Middle School Students. Computer Science Education, 25(2), 199-237.

[9] Grover, S., Pea, R. & Cooper, S. (2016). Factors Influencing Computer Science Learning in Middle School. In Proceedings of the 47th ACM Technical Symposium on CS Ed. (SIGCSE '16). ACM.

[10] Grover, S. & Basu, S. (2017). Measuring Student Learning in Introductory Block-Based Programming: Examining Misconceptions of Loops, Variables, and Boolean Logic. In Proceedings of the 48th ACM Technical Symposium on Computer Science Education (SIGCSE '17). Seattle, WA: ACM.

[11] Grover, S., Basu, S., & Schank, P. 2018. What We Can Learn About Student Learning From Open-Ended Programming Projects in Middle School Computer Science. In *Proceedings of the 49th ACM Technical Symposium on Computer Science Education* (pp. 999-1004). ACM.

[12] Jackiw, N. 1991, 2009. *The Geometer's Sketchpad* (computer software V1, V5). Emeryville, CA: Key Curriculum Press.

[13] K-12 CS Framework Committee. 2016. K-12 Computer Science Framework. Retrieved from http://www.k12cs.org.

[14] Laborde, J. M, & Strässer, R. 1990. Cabri-géomètre: A microworld of geometry for guided discovery learning. *Zentralblatt für didaktik der athematic*, 90(5), 171-177.

[15] Lahtinen, E., Ala-Mutka, K., & Järvinen, H. M. (2005). A study of the difficulties of novice programmers. ACM SIGCSE Bulletin, 37(3), 14-18.

[16] Mayer, R. E. (2004). Should there be a three-strikes rule against pure discovery learning?. American Psychologist, 59(1), 14.

[17] Pea, R., & Kurland, D. (1984). On the cognitive effects of learning computer programming. New Ideas In Psychology, 2, 137–168.

[18] Pears et al. (2007). A Survey of Literature on the Teaching of Introductory Programming. In Proceedings of the 38th Technical Symposium on CS Education. ACM.

[19] Robins, A., Rountree, J. and Rountree, N., 2003. Learning and teaching programming: A review and discussion. *Computer scien education*, *13*(2), pp.137-172.

[20] Roschelle, J. et al. (2010). Integration of technology, curriculum, and professional development for advancing middle school mathematics: Three large-scale studies. American Educational Research Journal, 47(4), 833-878.

[21] Samurcay, R. (1989). The concept of variable in programming: Its meaning and use in problem-solving by novice programmers. In E. Soloway and J. C. Spohrer, editors, Studying the Novice Programmer, 161–178.

[22] Schofield, E., Erlinger, M., & Dodds, Z. (2014). MyCS: CS for middle-years students and their teachers. In Proceedings of the 45th ACM technical symposium on Computer science education (pp. 337-342). ACM.

A Teacher Workshop for Introducing Computational Thinking in Rural and Vulnerable Environments

Jocelyn Simmonds
Department of Computer Science
University of Chile
Santiago, Chile
jsimmond@dcc.uchile.cl

Francisco J. Gutierrez
Department of Computer Science
University of Chile
Santiago, Chile
frgutier@dcc.uchile.cl

Cecilia Casanova
Department of Computer Science
University of Chile
Santiago, Chile
ccasanov@dcc.uchile.cl

Cecilia Sotomayor
Graduate School, FCFM
University of Chile
Santiago, Chile
cecilia.sotomayor@u.uchile.cl

Nancy Hitschfeld
Department of Computer Science
University of Chile
Santiago, Chile
nancy@dcc.uchile.cl

ABSTRACT

In Latin America, computational thinking workshops are mostly developed in urban areas, charging participation fees. And although teachers are increasingly being expected to include technology in their classrooms, computational thinking and programming are not mandatory topics in teacher training programs. This hinders the development of digital skills among Latino students, and we expect that the digital gap between urban and rural populations will expand over time, especially in socio-economically vulnerable populations. Believing that teachers can be agents of change, we designed a 12 hour workshop to train the K-8 teaching staff in a rural and vulnerable school. The goal of this experience was to help these teachers develop basic computational thinking skills and devise new ways to incorporate what they learned in their classrooms. In this paper, we report our experience facilitating this workshop, and analyze the teacher perceptions before and after the intervention. Teacher attitudes changed drastically during the execution of the workshop, and they were able to come up with creative ways of incorporating computational thinking activities into their subjects. The reported experience can be used as input to develop public policies with respect to how computational thinking should be introduced in rural and vulnerable environments.

CCS CONCEPTS

• **Social and professional topics → Computational thinking**;

KEYWORDS

Teacher development, computational thinking, rural environments, socio-economic vulnerability, Latin America

SIGCSE '19, February 27-March 2, 2019, Minneapolis, MN, USA

ACM ISBN 978-1-4503-5890-3/19/02...$15.00
https://doi.org/10.1145/3287324.3287456

ACM Reference Format:
Jocelyn Simmonds, Francisco J. Gutierrez, Cecilia Casanova, Cecilia Sotomayor, and Nancy Hitschfeld. 2019. A Teacher Workshop for Introducing Computational Thinking in Rural and Vulnerable Environments. In *Proceedings of the 50th ACM Technical Symposium on Computer Science Education (SIGCSE '19), February 27-March 2, 2019, Minneapolis, MN, USA.* ACM, New York, NY, USA, 7 pages. https://doi.org/10.1145/3287324.3287456

1 INTRODUCTION

Computational Thinking (CT) research and practice is having an impact on education worldwide, both inside and outside the classroom, from primary school to adult learning. More and more countries are recognizing the importance of including CT in the classroom, sometimes as early as in primary school. Initiatives such as CSForALL and Code.org have motivated students and K-12 teachers to learn how to code. However, it is apparent that a large majority of the teachers in these communities do not feel adequately prepared to teach CT [9]. Another important issue raised by some teachers, is how to merge the "closed" teaching paths provided by the Code.org material with the need of providing more "open" venues, where both teachers and students can express their creativity [8].

This is an open issue in the research community [24], where part of the community advocates for puzzle-based activities, while another part takes a project-based approach to teaching CT and computer science (CS). Programs like Computer Science for High School (CS4HS, New Zealand)[1] try to address these issues, holding teacher training workshops that focus on how CT and CS can be integrated into the classroom. Experiences like these effectively increase participants' understanding of CT and CS [4, 5], and there is evidence of integration of these topics in the curriculum.

Introducing CT in the classroom can help break the cycle of poverty in vulnerable populations [22], since the use of technology has a positive impact on learning between different age groups and in most areas of the curriculum. In Latin America, coding bootcamps like *Laboratoria*[2] have successfully trained vulnerable young women, helping them develop careers in front-end development. Unfortunately, these types of programs rarely make it to the rural

[1] https://www.cs4hs.aut.ac.nz/
[2] https://www.laboratoria.la/en/impact (currently run in Peru, Mexico, and Chile)

areas of Chile, meaning that the digital divide between urban and rural areas only continues to grow.

To address these issues, we have designed a teacher workshop for introducing CT in vulnerable populations living in rural areas in Chile. The goal is to give teachers an additional tool to support student learning and improve engagement, where the CT skills that students develop can help them overcome situations of social disadvantage. In this setting, there are two important barriers to overcome. First, it is critical to manage expectations: teachers need to shed the idea that new technology will automatically lead to greater student achievements. It is important to plan how the use of technology is expected to improve learning, and how this experience can be replicated in the future. The second major barrier is that teachers need support and time to learn to use the new technology efficiently. In other words, it is not enough to just to teach them how to use technology; our workshop must also include support for understanding how it can be used for learning. Teachers need to guide students in discovering how to use technology, they do not need to become expert programmers.

In this experience report, we describe a 12-hour workshop, carried out over three consecutive afternoons, which we designed for teachers in rural and vulnerable environments. We ran the workshop at a rural K-8 school, where more than 75% of the students are classified as socio-economically vulnerable. We used Scratch[3] since it can be used to create audiovisual projects, and is geared toward non-programmers. None of the workshop participants had any previous programming experience. The entire teaching staff of the school attended the workshop, including preschool and differentiated educators, as well as the school principal, the pedagogical assessor, and the guidance counsellor, which gave us a total of 17 participants. This workshop is an adaption of a 5-day workshop for 10-12 year old learners that we run at the University of Chile (in Santiago, the capital city of Chile) [13].

We also present the evidence we collected during the workshop, where we tried to answer the following research questions:

- RQ1: Was our workshop able to change teacher attitudes about using CT to develop pedagogical projects?
- RQ2: How do teachers envision using CT in rural and vulnerable classrooms?

With respect to RQ1, we did observe a change in teacher attitudes. During the first day, the participants were wary of the workshop, unsure of what to expect. The only exception was the school principal, who had contacted us in order to carry out the workshop. The teachers did not believe that they were capable of learning how to program in such a short time span. However, by the second day, the participants were already designing and implementing pedagogical projects in Scratch. Participants worked in groups of 2 - 3, some focusing on one subject, while others combined subjects, which allows us to answer RQ2. By the end of the workshop, the participants felt that they would be able to design new pedagogical projects using CT and Scratch, but they would still need our support when introducing these activities in the classroom.

We believe that the answers to these two research questions will help researchers and practitioners interested in designing and/or adapting interventions for developing CT skills in K-8 learners in Latin America, as well as public policy makers. Concretely, this paper makes the following contributions:

- The structure of a teacher workshop for introducing CT in rural and vulnerable populations, using project-based learning and Scratch.
- A set of lessons learned about introducing CT without overwhelming teachers. These lessons can be used to update teacher training programs, as well as define public policy about how CT should be introduced in classrooms in Chile.

[3]https://scratch.mit.edu/

2 RELATED WORK

Several Western countries have already integrated CT and coding in their formal educational systems [1]. Albeit at a slower pace, in Latin America the idea of developing CT skills in primary and secondary education has been increasingly gaining attention [13].

Recent literature reports various successful approaches for introducing school teachers to programming and consequently equipping them with conceptual tools for delivering CT and CS instructional programs for their students. For instance, unplugged activities [3, 11], hands-on robot programming [15], and professional development programs [12, 21] have all been effective in achieving this goal. Likewise, block-based programming environments (such as Scratch) are perceived as more effective than traditional text-based languages (such as Java and Python) for introducing pre-service and in-service teachers to coding [6].

Certainly, teacher self-efficacy in CT and basic coding skills is critical for effectively conducting this kind of training programs and providing K-12 learners the confidence needed for developing 21st-century skills [18]. This underlying expectation on teacher performance is usually reflected on their attitudes and overall performance in training sessions for acquiring such a set of skills. For example, while conducting informal workshops for training primary school teachers with no prior experience in programming, Bell et al. [3] identified that teachers are frequently anxious about teaching CS and doubt their ability to deliver these topics independently. Likewise, Reding and Dorn [23] emphasize that, although teachers experience insecurity and are concerned about losing control due to not being proficient in programming, they also want to be well prepared for the practical implementation of their envisioned pedagogical plans. On a more positive note, Curzon et al. [11] identified that empowering teachers through positive actions in CT development workshops has a positive effect, allowing them to build confidence and develop a better understanding of the involved concepts to transfer in their lessons.

Following that line of reasoning, contextualizing the development of CT skills integrated with the topical lessons that are planned in the general curriculum (e.g., using CT concepts in parallel to teaching more "traditional" subjects, such as arts, social science, and mathematics) increases the chance of effective adoption. In that respect, according to Bean et al. [2], pre-service teachers that are exposed to acquiring CT and programming skills, end up praising the effects of applying CT-related activities in their lessons plans despite an initial negative attitude toward the topic. Likewise, Corradini et al. [9], stress that external factors (such as a formal preparation of elementary school teachers) directly impact on the level of preparation for teaching CT topics, which could lead to positive (or negative) viewpoints and attitudes on the integration of CT and programming in the classroom [25]. In more concrete terms, after participating in CT training workshops, teachers spend a considerable amount of time considering how the newly acquired skills can be adapted to their lessons plans, which are not always related to CS. Therefore, pedagogical connections between the current topics covered in the regular curriculum can be facilitated using CT topics and activities, hence providing a solid foundation for practical application [23].

Most of the current evidence on the effects and experiences of teachers acquiring CT skills and transferring them into their lessons plans come from Western countries in large, urban areas. Naturally, given the differences between urban and rural schools, the acquired skills and current teaching programs are not necessarily transferable between both scenarios. Furthermore, there is large level of diversity within the enrolled students in public and state education, which reinforces the need to better understand the complexity and contextual nuances of deploying instructional programs as a way to truly achieve "Computer Science For All".

For instance, in the US, some notable exceptions reported in the literature come from New Mexico and Wyoming. On the one hand, Lee et al. [16] report their experience on running the NM-CSforAll project, an outreach program in New Mexico targeting rural and under-represented groups in the state. This intervention aims to train STEM teachers on becoming future CS teachers. Although the project results were fairly positive, the authors identified administrative challenges, particularly in managing course schedules, unbalanced support from external actors (such as other schools or districts), and a lack of access to computers and high-speed internet connection in the participating schools. On the other hand, Croff [10] ran a series of outreach activities targeted to raise awareness and the involvement of the educational community in CT activities in rural Wyoming. In this project, the authors established a link between the local community college and primary and secondary schools as a way to teach basic concepts of CT, in-classroom CT skills and patterns, and practical ways to transfer this knowledge to students (e.g., through video games and simulations). By providing highly contextual and real-life examples, teachers can motivate their students to engage in their learning experience, hence raising awareness in STEM job opportunities. As a follow up to this project, Leonard et al. [17] analyzed the instructional approaches followed in educating rural communities in Wyoming. By enhancing self-efficacy, teachers could structure new pedagogical plans to create unique learning opportunities based in STEM, and particularly, in developing CT skills.

A final challenge that emerges when envisioning to scale this kind of workshops is to engage school leadership in the process. In that respect, Heinz and Mannila [14] reported their experience on designing and running an effective workshop for developing CT in Linköping, Sweden. Among the factors, according to the authors, that may jeopardize scalability of this kind of intervention, are: a lack of time for conducting the activities, a lack of school leadership—particularly not counting with the explicit support of the school principal—, and a lack of focus when envisioning how to introduce CT and coding in future endeavors.

In summary, the experience reports and research projects described above, all contribute to develop new course curricula and understand the implications of introducing CS and CT to pre-service and in-service teachers. However, there is also a significant gap in how these interventions can be mapped to more diverse populations, such as under-represented groups in urban areas and students in rural communities. In that respect, to the best of our knowledge, the main differences of our intervention to the ones already reported in the literature are: (1) we focus our intervention in a rural and socio-economically vulnerable population in Chile; (2) we explicitly involve the whole teaching staff, ranging from the whole variety of subjects covered in the formal national education curriculum (e.g., Spanish, English, mathematics, science, social science, physical education and sports); (3) we also worked hand-in-hand with the school principal and other administrative staff in our workshop, who actively followed the proposed activities; and (4) following a project-based learning approach and hands-on activities, we enhanced the school sense of community by making them embrace CT as an effective tool for supporting learning and creativity.

3 TEACHER WORKSHOP

We designed a 12-hour workshop for teachers at a rural and vulnerable K-8 school. Our main goal was to present CT as a tool for creating pedagogical projects in the classroom. The workshop was held at the school where all the participants work, during the afternoons since this was during the school term (14:00 - 18:00). As mentioned in Section 1, more than 75% of the students are classified as vulnerable, and the school is below average in standardized language and mathematics tests. The school also has preschool and differentiated students, and students do not pay tuition to attend.

We had 17 participants: 14 teachers, the principal, the pedagogical assessor, and the guidance counsellor (12 female and 5 male). As this was the full teaching staff, the 14 teachers included: preschool and differentiated educators, as well as Spanish, English, science, social science, physical education, and mathematics teachers. Age-wise, the participants were evenly distributed: three aged 23-29, four aged 30-39, three aged 40-49, three aged 50-59, and one participant is over 60 years old. Two participants did not indicate their age. None of the participants had programmed before.

At the beginning of the workshop, each participant received the workbook that we use to teach Scratch to 10-12 year old children in an informal setting [13]. Note that, since 2012, we run the children's workshop twice a year at the University of Chile. We also created additional material for this workshop: 1) an introductory slide deck on algorithms and CT, and 2) an introduction to project-based learning (PBL, based on [19]). During the first day, each participant worked on their own, and then worked in groups of 2-3 on the second and third days. The workshop had three facilitators, all of which have experience running the children's workshop.

We now describe the topics and activities included on each day. Accompanying workbooks, slide decks, and programs (in Spanish) are available for download at: http://bit.ly/scratch-profesores-dcc.

Day 1: We started by explaining what an algorithm is, what CT is, etc. We also talked about PBL: how to define, plan, and execute pedagogical projects, and strategies that can help make this a more fruitful experience for both the students and the teacher. During the second half of this session, the participants had their first hands-on experience with programming, with each one working on their own computer. The Scratch environment was presented as a way for students to code in a more intuitive fashion, incorporating audiovisual elements. Since nobody had programming experience, we used the Scratch workbooks and programs for the childrens' workshop. These activities have been designed so as to steadily introduce the concepts of CT and problem solving. We only completed parts of the workbook during this session: creating and interacting with actors and events, using control structures, and defining and using variables. We asked the participants to read the rest of the workbook at home, using Scratch if possible. This was intentional, since we wanted the participants to explore the environment on their own, and not rely on us to guide them every step of the way. Finally, towards the end of the session, we asked the participants to start brainstorming project ideas, taking into account what they learned about CT, PBL, and Scratch.

Day 2: We started this session by showing the participants some pedagogical projects that we have developed: an animation that lets children experiment with water phase changes (solid to liquid to gas), another showing the water cycle, and finally a program that lets children experiment with projectile motion by throwing cannonballs with varying speed and launch angle. We then asked participants to think about the projects that they had roughed out the day before, and now specify the actors and interactions that they would need in order to program these projects. This was done in groups of 2-3, where some mixed topics (e.g., the English teacher and a physical education teacher formed a group), while others were more homogeneous (e.g., all the differentiated educators worked together). During this session, we answered questions about Scratch, developed and showed code samples, or helped think of ways to implement some of the functionality that the participants wanted to include in their project. The idea was to let the participants explore the Scratch environment, and to let them figure out what they needed, as opposed to following us blindly in guided exercises.

Day 3: During the first half of this session, the participants continued working on their projects, in the same groups as the day before. The final activity for this workshop was a presentation session, where the participants showed their work to the rest of the group. We asked each group to first explain their project: topic, expected learning outcomes, target students, etc. They then demonstrated their project, explaining what they had implemented and how. They then received feedback from both the group and us.

4 EVALUATION

In order to formally evaluate the experience described in the previous section, we followed a systematic qualitative data analysis approach. The goal of such evaluation was to better understand and derive lessons learned on how the studied sample of teachers in a rural and highly socio-economically vulnerable school accept the proposed activities for developing CT-related topics and conceive project-based learning activities to introduce CT in the classroom as a complement to formal educational plans.

4.1 Data Sources

Given our research questions, the following data sources were considered relevant for analyzing and reporting our experience: (1) basic demographic information, (2) workshop exit survey, (3) handwritten notes taken by the workshop facilitators, and (4) the projects created by the workshop participants. We now discuss each data source, indicating what data was collected and how.

Demographic information about the participants. The first two authors of this paper and a volunteer teaching assistant, who acted as facilitators in charge of the workshop, collected data like the age and gender of the participants, as well as the main subject taught at the school. This data is kept anonymized and participants are identified using a randomized numeric id.

Exit surveys applied to workshop participants. We adapted the instrument proposed by Choi [7], relating different dimensions of working with Scratch: (1) perceptions on the technological aspects, (2) reflections on the technological aspects, (3) perceptions on the pedagogical aspects, and (4) reflections on the pedagogical aspect. Participants were identified using the previously assigned numeric id. In order to analyze this dataset, the responses to all items were transcribed and tabulated by three co-authors of this paper. Data analysis was structured in a systematic way around a grounded theory approach, consisting on iterative open, axial, and selective coding, and then theory framing using affinity diagrams and triangulation with the collected socio-demographic data.

Handwritten notes and participant observation. The workshop facilitators took detailed handwritten notes on the involvement, attitudes, and common errors expressed by the participants. The observation was led by one of the facilitators at a time. In order to mitigate the effects of potential observer bias, the observations and related notes were taken individually and independently by the facilitators. Collected data were analyzed using group affinity and thematic analysis, jointly by the two first authors of this paper.

Projects created by the workshop participants. The enrolled participants in the workshop were expected to design and prototype a small-scale project-based learning activity to be applied in their classes, using Scratch and emphasizing CT concepts. Participants were encouraged to work with a colleague teaching different subjects, as a way to foster collaboration and interdisciplinary exchanges. Participants were free to pick the particular topic for motivating the activity, and could either start from scratch or choose to extend one or more of the sample projects provided during the workshop. These projects were downloaded for analysis at the end of the workshop and were identified using the numeric id assigned to each workshop participant.

4.2 Description of Teacher Projects

Workshop participants were organized in seven groups that worked together. All participants managed to complete a partially functional prototype by the end of the third session. Two projects were small stories without user interaction, while the rest were simple games (all available upon request). Figure 1 shows 4 of these projects, we now describe the main characteristics of each project.

Group 1: *Vowels and consonants.* The student has to interact by clicking elements according to the displayed question. Vowels, consonants, and numbers are moving on the screen until they are clicked. This activity was designed by differentiated educators.

Group 2: *Verbs and nouns.* The student has to choose between a noun and a verb to complete a sentence, respecting their grammatical agreement, both in English and Spanish. In order to promote

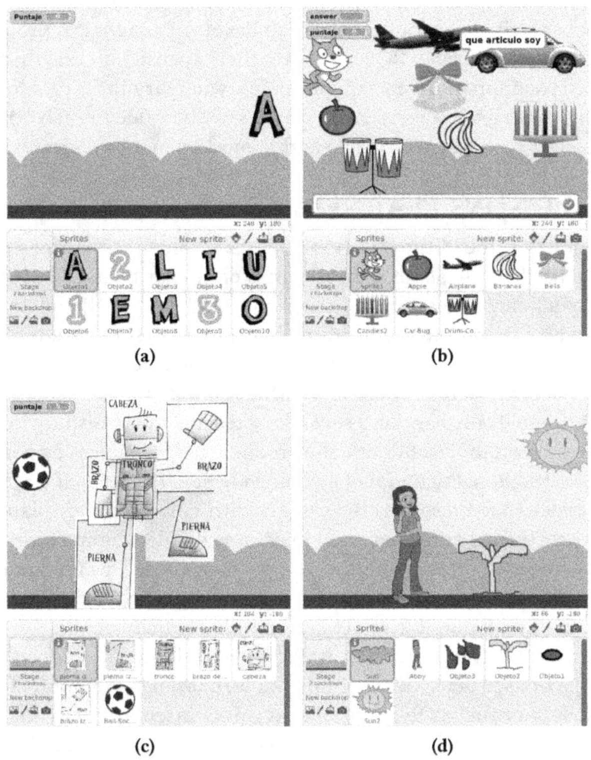

Figure 1: a) Group 1, b) Group 5, c) Group 6, d) Group 7.

student engagement, the game simulates a soccer match, a sport that is quite popular among boys in the country. This project was developed jointly by the Spanish and English teachers, alongside a physical education teacher.

Group 3: *Discovery of America.* An animated story without interaction is built to show people and ships involved in the discovery of America. This project was collaboratively produced by social science teachers from grades 3 and 4.

Group 4: *Multiplication.* The student is immerse in a fantasy story, where he has to play with a wizard for learning basic times tables. This project was collaboratively produced by one of the math teachers and the school's pedagogical assessor.

Group 5: *Articles.* This project, collaboratively designed by the language teacher for grades 5 through 8 and a preschool teacher, is a game for promoting the understanding of gender/noun differences in Spanish. In this game, several objects are shown and the student has to click one and write the correct article.

Group 6: *Body parts: left/right.* The parts of the body are shown in the background. At each time, a question is shown to evaluate if the student identify correctly the right/left parts of a body. This project was designed by the physical education and sport teachers in collaboration with a math teacher.

Group 7: *Plant growth.* This project is a story used to show the main nature actors involved in the plant growth process. While there is no interaction with end-users, this project was conceived by preschool teachers to motivate and stimulate their students.

Table 1: Project Dr. Scratch scores, by dimension

Dimension	G1	G2	G3	G4	G5	G6	G7
flow control	2	3	1	2	2	2	2
data representation	2	2	1	1	2	3	1
abstraction	1	1	1	0	1	1	1
user interactivity	2	2	1	2	2	2	1
synchronization	2	3	1	0	2	1	1
parallelism	1	3	1	0	1	0	1
logic	0	3	0	2	2	3	0

Both teachers provided voice acting for this animation, since the computers were not equipped with sound cards.

4.3 Evaluating Teacher Projects

In order to evaluate the acquisition of basic CT skills, we evaluated the produced projects with Dr. Scratch[4]. This is an automatic assessment tool, specifically tailored to measure CT skills in Scratch projects showing a high degree of correlation between human and automatic evaluations [20]. This instrument measures specific CT dimensions, based on the structure of Scratch applications: (1) logical thinking, (2) data representation, (3) user interactivity, (4) flow control, (5) abstraction and problem decomposition, (6) parallelism, and (7) synchronization. Each dimension has 4 mastery levels: None, denoting little or no mastery; Beginner, denoting a basic mastery; Developing, denoting that there is some mastery, and Competent, denoting competency. Being competent assigns the highest score (3), whereas None does not assign any points (0).

5 FINDINGS

Table 1 shows the results of evaluating the teacher projects using Dr. Scratch. According to the values returned by Dr. Scratch, we observe that most of the teachers show basic or developing programming skills. For example, most of the projects scored as *Developing* for the flow control and user interactivity dimensions, which was expected since these concepts were included in the Scratch session we held on the first day. The scores for abstraction are similar, achieving only a *Basic* level. This was also expected, since the workshop only lasted 12 hours, of which approximately 8 were spent working in Scratch. The scores for the other dimensions are much more varied, ranging from *None* to *Competent*. Group 4 obtained the most *None* scores, which may seem surprising, since one of the math teachers was in this group. This teacher was also very vocal about wanting a more guided workshop. As such, he was reluctant to experiment with the Scratch environment, and was not open to suggestions about his project, especially not from the much younger teaching assistant. In general, most of the participating teachers were able to design and build a small prototype for a teaching activity in a short time, after they were convinced that they could do it.

Looking at the exit surveys, we found that most of the participants positively evaluated their experience in the workshop. We also found that most of the participants think that it is important that their students learn CT and programming skills, with some even pointing out that it is a necessary part of the current technological and social context. Only the principal and pedagogical

[4]http://www.drscratch.org

assessor thought this before the workshop. They also indicated that they believe that what they learned in the workshop can be incorporated into their classrooms, where they would be responsible for designing new projects. There is still a challenge of how to carry out this transfer of knowledge at the school level, and also to the school community. For example, one could establish training programs for the school community, where most parents currently earn minimum wage in the agricultural sector.

Despite the positive evaluation of this experience, the participants do exhibit certain stereotypes about the technological effects of using Scratch. Concretely, most of them describe themselves as insecure and fearful of this new scenario. They also pointed out that this experience is a positive one for the school, since they now see how their students can use technology for more than just social networking. In other words, they started associating programming with non-technical content and with learning outcomes.

Note that there are no significant differences in the evaluation of the program based on the age of the participants. Also, all participants indicate that the workshop should be longer. Finally, there are no differences between the teachers, the subjects they teach and the way in which they propose to replicate in the classroom the knowledge that they acquired in the workshop. When asked about what they would do to include technology in their classrooms, they all indicated general actions.

We did observe entrance barriers that can impede the inclusion of programming and CT skills in this type of environment. During the first days, the participants presented strong concerns with respect to the following aspects: (1) not seeing a direct way to transfer the acquired knowledge in their classroom; (2) thinking that they have to build an interactive tool for their students, where they can play and learn. They did not see that these children can learn science, language, or math, among others, by programming; and (3) believing that they need to become strong programmers before ever thinking of using Scratch in the classroom.

These barriers are a threat to the introduction of CT in the classroom, because they generate biases in the vision that teachers have of students' abilities and their real capabilities, which may lead to a weak adoption of CT and Scratch in the classroom. Teachers, like everybody, have implicit biases, in this case about their students' socio-economic status, which may lead them to assume that their students are not capable of creating or understanding the abstractions required to program something more complex.

One advantage of the rural setting is that the entire teaching staff of the school participated in the workshop, since the facilitators had committed to travelling several hours each day to carry out the workshop. The principal is also a respected figure within her community, and her participation in the workshop also helped communicate how important she thought CT was for their students. In Santiago, it is usually easier for us to hold teacher workshops at the university, so schools usually only end up sending 1-2 representatives each, who must then individually communicate the value of what they learn to their colleagues. What we did not see was anything specific to the vulnerable context, apart from the fact that 3 of the 14 teachers were differential educators. However, we need to analyze this in a future study, since we only interacted with the teachers, who have a better socio-economic status than the students and their parents.

We can now answer RQ1: the described workshop did change teacher attitudes about using CT to develop pedagogical projects. We can also answer RQ2: some teachers focused on creating interactive animations to explain topics, whereas others developed more game-like projects. Participants saw the value in each others' projects, especially the teachers that worked in mixed groups.

6 LESSONS LEARNED

Although some of the reported findings resonate with prior literature, particularly about initial feelings of insecurity and anxiety on the very early stages of the intervention [3, 9, 11, 23], our experience also shows particular traits that can inform the design of CT workshops to be deployed in scenarios similar to the one studied. We can summarize our lessons learned as follows:

Lesson 1: Primary and secondary teachers may display initial concerns on the usefulness of introducing CT practices as part of the instructional material of a planned lesson. However, if teachers consider that these practices align with current topics planned in their formal curricula, they may consider developing working prototypes to extend with their students in class. This implies that pedagogical support needs to be aligned with teacher expectations and deal with possible reluctance in a timely manner.

Lesson 2: Teachers can learn how to develop small snippets and project-based activities in a short time, but long-term motivation and support needs to be offered, as initial insecurity may rapidly lead to frustration. Provide "follow-up" sessions as required.

Lesson 3: Teachers are eager to collaborate with each other, even when coming from different subjects and grade levels. For instance, developing PBL activities, using CT as common ground, may lead to surprisingly rich course material. In particular, this has the potential to enhance the school sense of community, by making clear that CT is an effective way to support learning and creativity.

Lesson 4: Principals and other members of the administrative staff are key for building and sustaining continuous CT programs, particularly in schools where there is little to no support coming from formal education services. The buy-in from a well-respected school administrator who also participates in the workshop, can help ameliorate teachers' initial concerns and fears about CT.

Lesson 5: It is important to address the barriers to entry by designing a national strategy for introducing CT in the classroom. This training program should promote self-efficacy of both teachers and students, be entertaining, and respond to the interests and needs of the students. This national strategy should also define a support structure for schools, for example, pairing up schools with local universities or institutions that can help with training and replication. Moreover, teachers should be considered as another type of student in this national strategy, since most do not have any programming experience but are increasingly being asked to participate in CT experiences. Finally, this national strategy should also update teacher training programs so as to teach CT to all teachers, not just those traditionally associated to CT, like maths.

7 CONCLUSION AND FUTURE WORK

In Latin America, coding bootcamps and informal workshops have been successful in introducing basic CT skills, but rarely make it to rural areas. In order to bridge this gap, we ran a teacher workshop in rural and socio-economically vulnerable school, as a way to give teachers an additional tool to support student learning and improve engagement. Our results show that we did observe a change in teacher attitudes: participants were initially wary of the workshop, but later gained confidence and felt that they would be able to design new pedagogical projects using CT and Scratch, although they would still need our support during the first few times when introducing these activities in the classroom. Our experience report contributes to CS Education by providing empirical evidence of changing teacher attitudes towards CT as a result of the workshop, as well as a set of lessons learned about introducing CT without overwhelming teachers. These lessons can be used to update teacher training programs, as well as define public policy about how CT and CS should be introduced in classrooms.

Although valuable, our results are not exempt from limitations. First, we acknowledge that our results are highly dependent on the particular location where we conducted our intervention, observations, and analysis. In addition, this experience report only provides evidence in favor of a single scenario, that possibly needs to be replicated in other similar cases as a way to formally assess validity. Finally, our results, in this research stage, are not generalizable to broader populations given the reduced sample size that does not allow for statistical inference. For example, can we shorten the workshop and still be effective at changing teacher perceptions? This is important, since it is not always feasible to gather the entire teaching staff of a school for a 12-hour workshop.

We are now designing a longitudinal study, aiming to carefully monitor how the workshop participants—teacher staff and other participants—relate to their students, in order to assess how effective the followed approach would be for promoting effective CT interventions in this context. This is in collaboration with the Chilean Ministry of Education, that is rolling out a nationwide CT teacher training program: *Plan Nacional de Lenguajes Digitales* (http://sitios.mineduc.cl/lenguajesdigitales/).

REFERENCES

[1] Anja Balanskat and Katja Engelhardt. 2015. Computing our future: computer programing and coding – priorities, school curricula and initiatives across Europe. (2015). Retrieved August 28, 2018 from http://www.eun.org/resources/detail?publicationID=661

[2] Nathan Bean, Joshua Weese, Russell Feldhausen, and R. Scott Bell. 2015. Starting From scratch: developing a pre-service teacher training program in computational thinking. In *Proceedings of the IEEE Frontiers in Education Conference (FIE'15)*. IEEE, New York, NY, USA. https://doi.org/10.1109/FIE.2015.7344237

[3] Tim Bell, Caitlin Duncan, and James Atlas. 2016. Teacher feedback on delivering computational thinking in primary school. In *Proceedings of the Workshop in Primary and Secondary Computing Education (WiPSCE'16)*. ACM, New York, NY, USA, 100–101. https://doi.org/10.1145/2978249.2978266

[4] Lenore Blum and Thomas J. Cortina. 2007. CS4HS: an outreach program for high school CS teachers. In *Proceedings of the ACM Technical Symposium on Computer Science Education (SIGCSE'07)*. ACM, New York, NY, USA, 19–23. https://doi.org/10.1145/1227310.1227320

[5] Heather Bort and Dennis Brylow. 2013. CCS4Impact: measuring computational thinking concepts present in CS4HS participant lesson plans. In *Proceedings of the ACM Technical Symposium on Computer Science Education (SIGCSE'13)*. ACM, New York, NY, USA, 427–432. https://doi.org/10.1145/2445196.2445323

[6] Ibrahim Cetin. 2016. Preservice teachers' introduction to computing: exploring utilization of Scratch. *Journal of Educational Computing Research* 54, 7 (2016), 997–1021. https://doi.org/10.1177/0735633116642774

[7] Hyungshin Choi. 2013. Pre-service teachers' conceptions and reflections of computer programming using Scratch: technological and pedagogical perspectives. *International Journal for Educational Media and Technology* 7, 1 (2013), 15–25.

[8] Isabella Corradini, Michael Lodi, and Enrico Nardelli. 2017. Computational thinking in Italian schools: quantitative data and teachers' sentiment analysis after two years of "Programma il Futuro" project. In *Proceedings of the Innovation and Technology in Computer Science Education Conference (ITiCSE'17)*. ACM, New York, NY, USA, 224–229. https://doi.org/10.1145/3059009.3059040

[9] Isabella Corradini, Michael Lodi, and Enrico Nardelli. 2017. Conceptions and misconceptions about computational thinking among Italian primary school teachers. In *Proceedings of the International Computing Education Research Conference (ICER'17)*. ACM, New York, NY, USA, 136–144. https://doi.org/10.1145/3105726.3106194

[10] Carla Hester Croff. 2017. Teaching computational thinking patterns in rural communities. In *Emerging Research, Practice, and Policy on Computational Thinking*, Peter J. Rich and Charles B. Hodges (Eds.). Springer International Publishing, Cham, 175–188. https://doi.org/10.1007/978-3-319-52691-1_11

[11] Paul Curzon, Peter W. McOwan, Nicola Plant, and Laura R. Meagher. 2014. Introducing teachers to computational thinking using unplugged storytelling. In *Proceedings of the Workshop in Primary and Secondary Computing Education (WiPSCE'14)*. ACM, New York, NY, USA, 89–92. https://doi.org/10.1145/2670757.2670767

[12] Barbara J. Ericson, Mark Guzdial, and Tom McKlin. 2014. Preparing secondary computer science teachers through an iterative development process. In *Proceedings of the Workshop in Primary and Secondary Computing Education (WiPSCE'14)*. ACM, New York, NY, USA, 116–119. https://doi.org/10.1145/2670757.2670781

[13] Francisco J. Gutierrez, Jocelyn Simmonds, Cecilia Casanova, Cecilia Sotomayor, and Nancy Hitschfeld. 2018. Coding or hacking?: exploring inaccurate views on computing and computer scientists among K-6 learners in Chile. In *Proceedings of the ACM Technical Symposium on Computer Science Education (SIGCSE'18)*. ACM, New York, NY, USA, 993–998. https://doi.org/10.1145/3159450.3159598

[14] Fredrik Heintz and Linda Mannila. 2018. Computational thinking for all – an experience report on scaling up teaching computational thinking to all students in a major city in Sweden. In *Proceedings of the ACM Technical Symposium on Computer Science Education (SIGCSE'18)*. ACM, New York, NY, USA, 137–142. https://doi.org/10.1145/3159450.3159586

[15] Jennifer S. Kay, Janet G. Moss, Shelly Engelman, and Tom McKlin. 2014. Sneaking in through the back door: introducing K-12 teachers to robot programming. In *Proceedings of the ACM Technical Symposium on Computer Science Education (SIGCSE'14)*. ACM, New York, NY, USA, 499–504. https://doi.org/10.1145/2538862.2538972

[16] Irene A. Lee, Maureen Psaila Dombrowski, and Ed Angel. 2017. Preparing STEM teachers to offer New Mexico Computer Science for All. In *Proceedings of the ACM Technical Symposium on Computer Science Education (SIGCSE'17)*. ACM, New York, NY, USA, 363–368. https://doi.org/10.1145/3017680.3017719

[17] Jacqueline Leonard, Monica Mitchell, Joy Barnes-Johnson, Adrienne Unertl, Jill Outka-Hill, Roland Robinson, and Carla Hester Croff. 2017. Preparing teachers to engage rural students in computational thinking through robotics, game design, and culturally responsive teaching. *Journal of Teacher Education* 69, 4 (2017), 386–407. https://doi.org/10.1177/0022487117732317

[18] Linda Mannila, Lars-Åke Nordén, and Arnold Pears. 2017. Digital competence, teacher self-efficacy and training needs. In *Proceedings of the International Computing Education Research Conference (ICER'18)*. ACM, New York, NY, USA, 78–85. https://doi.org/10.1145/3230977.3230993

[19] Thom Markham, John Larmer, and Jason Ravitz. 2003. *Project-Based Learning Handbook: A Guide to Standards Focused Project-Based Learning for Middle and High School Teachers.* Buck Institute for Education, Novato, CA, USA.

[20] Jesús Moreno-León, Marcos Román-González, Casper Harteveld, and Gregorio Robles. 2017. On the automatic assessment of computational thinking skills: a comparison with human experts. In *Extended Abstracts of the ACM SIGCHI Conference on Human Factors in Computing Systems (CHI'17)*. ACM, New York, NY, USA, 2788–2795. https://doi.org/10.1145/3027063.3053216

[21] Tom Neutens and Francis Wyffels. 2018. Bringing computer science education to secondary school: a teacher first approach. In *Proceedings of the ACM Technical Symposium on Computer Science Education (SIGCSE'18)*. ACM, New York, NY, USA, 840–845. https://doi.org/10.1145/3159450.3159568

[22] Organisation for Economic Co-operation and Development. 2017. *Enhancing Social Inclusion in Latin America: Key Issues and the Role of Social Protection Systems.* Technical Report.

[23] Tracie Evans Reding and Brian Dorn. 2017. Understanding the "teacher experience" in primary and secondary CS professional development. In *Proceedings of the International Computing Education Research Conference (ICER'17)*. ACM, New York, NY, USA, 155–163. https://doi.org/10.1145/3105726.3106185

[24] Mitchel Resnick and David Siegel. 2015. A different approach to coding: how kids are making and remaking themselves from Scratch. (2015). Retrieved August 28, 2018 from https://brightthemag.com/a-different-approach-to-coding-d679b06d83a

[25] Aman Yadav, Chris Mayfield, Ninger Zhou, Susanne Hambrusch, and John T. Korb. 2014. Computational thinking in elementary and secondary teacher education. *ACM Transactions on Computing Education* 14, 1 (2014), article 5. http://dx.doi.org/10.1145/2576872

An Analysis through an Equity Lens of the Implementation of Computer Science in K-8 Classrooms in a Large, Urban School District

Jean Salac, Max White, Ashley Wang, Diana Franklin
University of Chicago
Chicago, Illinois
{salac,mnwhite,awang21,dmfranklin}@uchicago.edu

ABSTRACT

Major metropolitan school districts around the United States are implementing computer science in elementary school classrooms as part of the CS for All (CS4All) initiative. Little is known, however, about the success of such a large-scale rollout, especially in terms of equity. In this study we analyze the performance of 4th grade classrooms completing three modules of an introductory computational thinking curriculum, looking at not only overall results but also the variance in performance between high-, mid-, and low-performing schools (as identified by their school report cards). We find that all classrooms are benefiting from the computational thinking (CT) curriculum, making great strides in providing equitable access to CT education. However, statistically-significant differences in performance are present, especially between the high- and low-performing schools, showing that there is still room for improvement in developing strategies and curricula for struggling learners.

CCS CONCEPTS

• **Social and professional topics → Computer science education**; *Computational thinking*; *K-12 education*;

KEYWORDS

K-8 education, diversity, Scratch

ACM Reference Format:
Jean Salac, Max White, Ashley Wang, Diana Franklin. 2019. An Analysis through an Equity Lens of the Implementation of Computer Science in K-8 Classrooms in a Large, Urban School District. In *Proceedings of the 50th ACM Technical Symposium on Computer Science Education (SIGCSE '19), February 27-March 2, 2019, Minneapolis, MN, USA.* ACM, New York, NY, USA, 7 pages. https://doi.org/10.1145/3287324.3287353

1 INTRODUCTION

The CS4All movement in the United States has gained momentum in the past decade. Its genesis might be the landmark research and interventions in the Los Angeles Unified School District chronicled in Stuck in the Shallow End [14] coupled with the National Science Foundation CS10K program's goal of training ten thousand teachers to teach computer science in high schools across the country [1].

Several public school districts, including Chicago, New York City, and San Francisco, have added computer science (CS) graduation requirements, with accompanying teacher professional development (PD). This provides fertile ground to understand the impacts of CS efforts on student learning.

This study analyzes the equity of CS learning outcomes across three different-performing schools in the district. School performance has been shown to be a proxy for the race, income, and parental involvement of their students [13, 15] and related to resources and teacher turnover rates [2]. Such disparities are realities in school districts nationwide, and thus need to be addressed to advance equity in K-12 CS education.

This study focuses on a large urban school district's nascent CS4All effort, which will provide CS instruction to all pre-K-12th grade students. This study focuses on 4th grade, using an adaptation of the Creative Computing Curriculum [5] that teaches sequence, events, and iteration.

Our study was guided by the following research questions:

- What is the level of understanding and sources of confusion overall in learning the core concepts of events and iteration?
- To what extent does school performance influence results?

This paper presents key findings from assessments given at the conclusion of each module. In the next section, we present relevant literature on large CS4All initiatives and student learning. In Section 3, we describe our methods and experimental design. We present our results in Section 4, along with a discussion of the implications of the results. Section 5 describes limitations of this study. Finally, we provide concluding remarks in Section 6.

2 RELATED WORK

We present two bodies of work that overlap with this study's goals. First, we present studies that have added to the collective understanding of large-scale efforts to improve computer science education. Second, we present studies that focus on student learning of basic computing concepts.

Margolis et al. began research on interventions to improve K-12 equity in LAUSD [14]. They focused on structural barriers, curriculum shortcomings and professional development shortcomings. This heavily influenced CS10K, a movement to develop high school curricula and train ten thousand teachers. A national landscape study was performed for CS10K to understand the professional development opportunities for teachers in the United States [8],

SIGCSE '19, February 27-March 2, 2019, Minneapolis, MN, USA

ACM ISBN 978-1-4503-5890-3/19/02...$15.00
https://doi.org/10.1145/3287324.3287353

identifying gaps in offerings at the time. Wang et al. surveyed households and schools, finding that while there was a high demand for CS education from both parents and students, over 75% of principals reported their school did not offer computer science with programming/coding [17].

Major school districts have published early results of CS4All efforts. A study in New York City found that schools with CS courses and activities served fewer Black and Latino students and more White and Asian students, compared with schools without CS courses [6]. Research in Broward County in Florida found an association between completing more Code.org computer science lessons and higher literacy scores [3].

A growing body of work has researched challenges and successes students have had using visual block-based languages (VBBLs) [12] as they learn initialization [9], variables and loops [11], what concepts are appropriate for what age groups [7, 10, 16], and the patterns that emerge from starting with Scratch that might impact later instruction [18].

This work reinforces prior CS research in novice learning in two ways. First, it provides insight into equity at a district level with respect to student learning. Second, it is a larger-scale study researching student learning in the concepts of sequence, events, and repetition.

3 METHODS

This study consisted of nine 4th grade classrooms (204 9-10 year old students): three classrooms from three schools (identified as high-, mid-, and low-performing by the school district) in a large urban school district. In their classification, they use characteristics of both students (e.g. percentage of minority students, English language learners, students with special needs, students in poverty, etc) and teachers (e.g. years of experiences, turnover rates, etc).

All teachers in the study underwent the same professional development and taught the same curriculum. In each school, the same teacher taught all three classrooms. Each school has balanced gender splits. Ethnic breakdowns are shown in Table 1, matching prior research that underrepresented minorities are over-represented in mid- and low-performing schools [13, 15], allowing equity in terms of overall school performance to function as a proxy for equity in terms of minority status.

School	Ethnicity (%)				
	Asian	Black	His/Lat	Pac Is	White
High	49	0	13	2	21
Mid	2	14	54	5	18
Low	5	8	26	31	0

Table 1: Demographics of study schools.

Students completed three modules in an introductory CT curriculum in Scratch, which was a modification of the Creative Computing Curriculum [5]. Upon completion of Unit 2 (events) and Unit 3 (loops), students took a pen-and-paper assessment designed for this curriculum by a team of researchers, practitioners, and a reading comprehension specialist, with several rounds of review by each of the five team members. Each assessment consisted of a mix of multiple-choice, fill-in-the-blank and open response questions, and was designed to take students about 20 to 30 minutes to complete. Multiple-choice answer options were scrambled randomly on each exam. The assessments were graded by undergraduate researchers. The open response question was qualitatively coded by two undergraduate researchers to ensure inter-rater reliability.

Our study follows the completely randomized hierarchical *CRH-pq(A)* design. The linear model is as follows:

$$Y_{ijk} = \mu + \alpha_j + \beta_{k(j)} + \epsilon_{i(jk)} \quad (1)$$

where:

- Y_{ijk} is the question score for the ith student in classroom k within school j,
- μ is the grand mean of the question score,
- α_j is the effect of school j,
- $\beta_{k(j)}$ is the effect of classroom k within school j,
- and $\epsilon_{i(jk)}$ is the error effect associated with Y_{ijk}.

The independent variable in this study is the type of school, with classrooms nested within them. Both the type of school and individual classrooms are fixed factors. The classrooms in our study are of different sizes, so we randomly sampled classrooms of 18 students (the smallest classroom size in our study) and ran the linear model based on the sampled classrooms. This process was repeated 1000 times, and the average of the linear model outputs over all iterations was calculated; the mean of the outputs was used.

Because there are three schools, analysis was performed in two steps to find statistical significance. First, an ANOVA F-test was used to find whether there are any statistically-significant differences between schools. Then, a Fisher-Hayter Post Hoc test was performed pairwise on the three pair choices to determine which pairs' result differences were statistically significant. Both tests provide p values – $p < 0.05$ is statistically significant. The ANOVA F-test also provides an F value for a significance test, which is compared to values in the F distribution. Effect sizes (ω^2) were also calculated, where ω^2 values of 0.010, 0.059, and 0.138 are small, medium, and large associations, respectively [4]. With the large sample size, the power of all tests was at least 80%.

4 RESULTS

Analysis seeks to answer two questions, one about overall learning and confusion with events (Q1-2) and loops (Q3-7,EC) and one about the correlation between school performance and student learning. Question-level results are presented, both overall and per-school, along with discussion of what those results reveal about understanding within the concept. We then discuss overall implications of the study in the discussion.

4.1 Q1: Events Starting One Script

Question 1 asked students to circle which script(s) out of the four shown would run if they clicked on the sprite. Two scripts started with 'when sprite clicked', one with 'when green flag clicked', and one with 'when space key pressed'. Students received two points for every correct script circled and lost one for any incorrect script circled, for 0-4 points.

The overall average score on Q1 was 2.49 (Figure 1). 61.4% of students circled only correct scripts, but only 43.4% of students

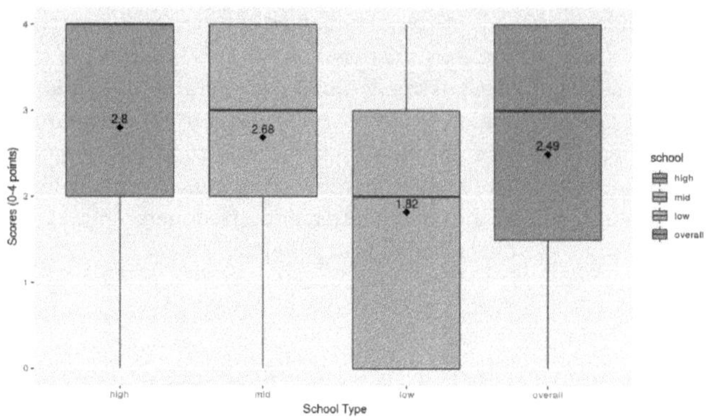

Figure 1: Q1 Events Scores(0-4 points)

circled all correct scripts (and no incorrect ones). Across all three schools, there is a statistically-significant difference (F(2,144)=7.43, $p < 0.001$, ω^2=0.282). Between pairs of schools, there are significant differences between the low-performing school and both the high- and mid-performing schools with a Fisher-Hayter Post Hoc ($p < 0.05$).

To better understand how students answered, student responses are categorized as: (1) NO correct - students who circled none of the correct answers, (2) BOTH correct & incorrect - students who circled some some correct and some incorrect answers, (3) ONLY correct - students who circled correct but not incorrect answers, and (4) ALL correct & NO incorrect - students who circled all the correct answers and none of the incorrect ones. As shown in Table 2, students in the high-performing school circled correct options (ONLY C) most frequently and provided the most complete answers, followed by the mid- and low-performing schools. Conversely, students in the low-performing school circled incorrect options (NO C, Both C/I) most frequently and were most likely to miss correct options, followed by the mid- and high-performing school.

Sch	Category			
	NO C	Both C/I	ONLY C	ALL C/NO I
H	19.3%	7.9%	72.7%	59.1%
M	24.5%	15.9%	59.5%	41.1%
L	33.3%	16.7%	50%	26.7%
All	24.8	13.8%	61.4%	43.4%

Table 2: Q1 Qualitative Results

4.2 Q2: Events Starting Multiple Scripts

Question 2 consists of two actions (playing drum and changing costume) in three scripts across two sprites (Pico & Giga), all started by `when green flag clicked`. Pico's single script performs the actions sequentially, whereas Giga's two scripts run in parallel (Figure 2). To assess students' understanding of multiple events in multiple scripts versus sequential events in one script, students were asked to circle the true statements from the following:

a) Pico plays the drum 7 times THEN changes costumes 4 times.
b) Giga plays the drum 7 times THEN changes costumes 4 times.

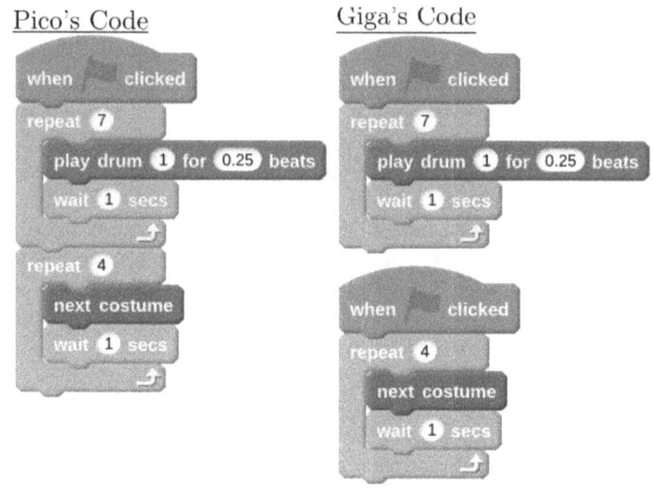

Figure 2: Q2 Sequential (left) and Parallel (right) Scripts

c) Pico plays the drum AND changes costumes at the same time.
d) Giga plays the drum AND changes costumes at the same time.
e) Pico and Giga both play the drum 7 times THEN change costumes 4 times.

The correct answers were a and d. Students earned 2 points for each correct answer circled and lost 1 point for each incorrect answer circled, for 0-4 points. Most students struggled with Q2, with an overall average score of 1.11 points. When broken down by school, the average scores were 1.31, 1.4 and 0.53 points for high-, mid-, and low-performing schools, respectively. Across all three schools, there is a statistically-significant difference (F(2,144)=7.82, $p < 0.001$, ω^2=0.289). Between pairs of schools, there are significant differences between the low-performing school and both the high- and mid-performing schools with a Fisher-Hayter Post Hoc ($p < 0.05$).

64.37%, 70.13%, and 46.55 % of students in high-, mid-, and low-performing schools, respectively, correctly identified Pico's sequential behavior. Only 41.38%, 36.91%, and 35.79% of students in high-, mid-, and low-performing schools, respectively, however, circled Giga's parallel behavior.

Some very common errors include: 44.82% circled Giga having sequential behavior; 22.07% circled Pico having parallel behavior; and 53.85% circled option 5 (both sprites have sequential behavior). The higher frequency of answers with sequential behavior suggest that students may not understand parallelism as deeply as sequential execution in Scratch.

However, students may also have had difficulty comprehending the answer choices – 25.75% of students selected incompatible answers (such as circling both a and c or b and d). Determining whether the difference in performance was due to different levels of CS understanding or different reading abilities is further study.

4.3 Q3: Repeat Iteration Count

Students were shown a repeat block and asked how many times the loop would repeat.

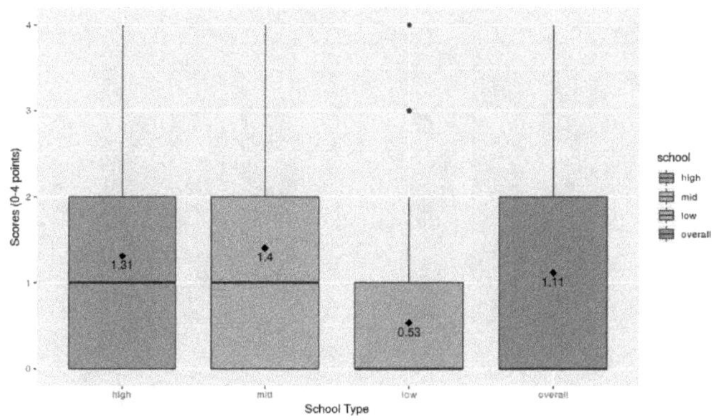

Figure 3: Q2 Parallel Scripts Scores (0-4 points)

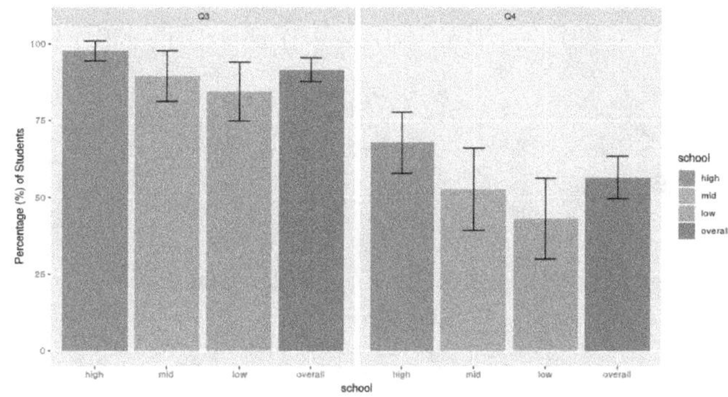

Figure 4: Q3 Iteration Count vs Q4 Loop Unrolling Results

Almost all of the students from each school were able to answer correctly, with 98.85%, 88.31%, and 84.48% of the students in the high-, mid-, and low-performing schools, respectively getting the answer correct (Figure 4). Comparing the differences in the number of students who answered correctly, we found a statistically-significant difference ($F(2,144)=5.05$, $p < 0.01$, $\omega^2=0.192$) among the schools. A Fisher-Hayter Post Hoc pairwise analysis shows a significant difference between the high- and low-performing schools ($p < 0.05$).

Students performed very well on Q3. However, there is still a performance gap between the high- and low-performing schools.

4.4 Q4: Unrolling a Loop

Students were shown a repeat 4 loop consisting of two blocks.They were given choices of those two blocks repeated 1, 2, 3, and 4 times. Students were then asked to choose the unrolled code that did the same thing as the loop.

Students struggled on Q4, with only 56.44% overall answering it correctly. Within individual schools, 70.11%, 53.05%, and 44.83% of the students in the high-, mid-, and low-performing schools, respectively, answered correctly (Figure 4). There is a statistically-significant difference among schools for Q2 ($F(2,144)=5.25$, $p < 0.01$, $\omega^2=0.214$), with only a significant difference between high- and low-performing schools from a Fisher-Hayter Post Hoc ($p < 0.05$).

When we put Q3 and Q4 performance in perspective, we see that while students are able to identify how many times a repeat loop is run, many students do not truly understand what that means. This implies a limited understanding of loop functionality, especially in the low-performing school.

4.5 Q5: Repeated Blocks vs Repeat Loops

Students were asked to circle the scripts that would make a sprite perform some actions exactly three times. Students were provided one set of blocks (a) alone and (b) inside a repeat 3 loop, and three sets of sequential blocks (c) alone and (d) within a repeat block (Figure 5). Q5 was designed based on a common misconception observed by teachers - not understanding the relationship between repeated code within a loop and repeated loop iterations. Choices were provided in random order on different assessments.

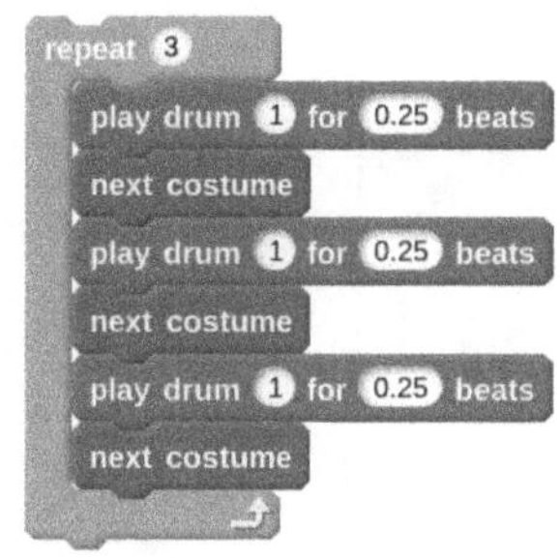

Figure 5: Q5 Answer Option (d) and inspiration for question.

Q5 had two correct answers (b and c described above); students received two points for each correct answer circled and lost one point for each incorrect answer circled, for 0-4 points. Overall, the median score was 2 and mean score was 2.07. Comparing performance over all three schools, we found a significant difference ($F(2,144)=7.00$, $p < 0.01$, $\omega^2=0.272$). A Fisher-Hayter Post Hoc revealed a significant difference between the high-performing school and the other two schools ($p < 0.05$).

Of the incorrect options, the option with only one pair of blocks was the least common, with 3.45%, 5.15%, and 1.72% of students choosing that option in the high-, mid-, and low-performing schools, respectively. In contrast, 25.29%, 28.57%, and 44.83% of students in high-, mid-, and low-performing schools selected the option with three pairs of blocks within a 'Repeat 3' block, supporting the observation made by the teachers.

4.6 Q6: Loops Within Sequence

Question 6 consisted of a repeat loop sandwiched between two blocks and asked them three sub-questions: which blocks run (a) *in*, (b) *before*, and (c) *after* the loop. On each sub-question, students earned 2 points for each correct answer circled and lost 1 point for each incorrect answer circle, for 0-4 points (a) or 0-2 points (b, c).

We found a significant difference in scores across schools for all three parts (a: $F(2,144)=7.00$, $p < 0.01$, $\omega^2=0.289$; b: $F(2,144)=7.78$, $p < 0.001$, $\omega^2=0.292$; c: $F(2,144)=9.40$, $p < 0.001$, $\omega^2=0.329$). A Fisher-Hayter Post Hoc shows a significant difference between the high-performing school and the other two schools ($p < 0.05$).

Students from the high-performing school outperformed the rest of the students on all parts of Q6. Part (a) tests their understanding of

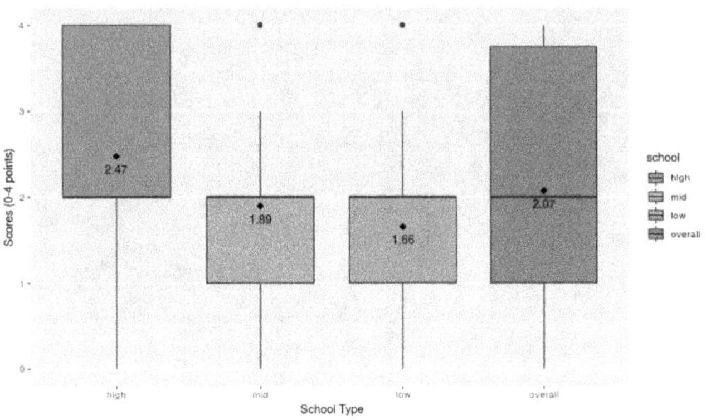

Figure 6: Q5: Repeated Blocks vs Loops Scores (0-4 points)

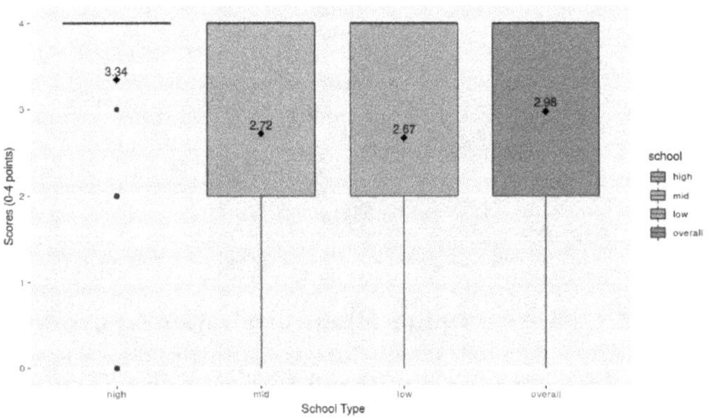

Figure 7: Q4(a) Code in Loop Scores (0-4 points)

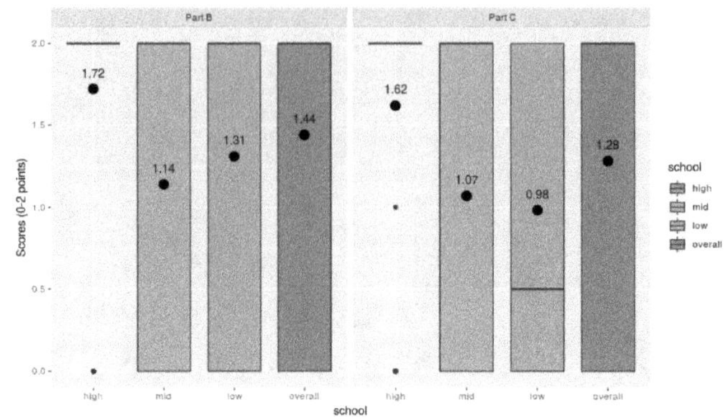

Figure 8: Q4 Code before (b) and code after (c) Loop Scores (0-2 points)

loops, while parts (b) and (c) test their understanding of sequence, a topic that was covered earlier in the curriculum. This result suggests the students from the high-performing school were better able to retain CT concepts.

However, two similar-looking blocks used in Q6 may have unintentionally confused students in part c. We found that the `play drum` block, which looks similar to the correct `play sound` block, was a frequent incorrect answer, selected by 9.2%, 11.04% and 27.59% of students in the high-, mid-, and low-performing school, respectively. Future work will explore whether reading comprehension skills may have influenced their performance on Q6.

4.7 Q7: Explain In Your Own Words

Students were shown a loop and asked to explain what the loop would do in their own words. Answers were given between 0-10 points depending on accuracy and completeness.

Students performed fairly well, with an average score of 8.36. When broken down by school, the average scores were 9.33, 8.04 and 7.21 points for high-, mid-, and low-performing schools, respectively. Across all three schools, there is a statistically-significant difference (F(2,144)=24.63, $p < 10^{-11}$, ω^2=0.524). There are statistically-significant differences between all pairs of schools from a Fisher-Hayter Post Hoc ($p < 0.05$).

Qualitative coding of student responses reveals some patterns. In the high-performing school, all students described the loop itself and at least one of the blocks in the loop. In the mid-performing school, 5.19% described neither the loop nor any blocks within it, and 1.30% did not describe any blocks in the loop. In the low-performing school, these figures jump to 10.1% for the former feature and 6.74% for the latter feature.

While both features were less frequent in high- and mid-performing schools, other answer features were more prevalent in their responses. 14.04% and 16.3% of students in the high- and mid-performing schools, respectively, left out block parameters in their responses, compared with 10.11% of students in the low-performing school. 14.04% and 20% of students in the high- and mid-performing schools, respectively, neglected to describe at least one block in their responses, compared with 6.74% of students in the low-performing school. 17.5% and 9.09% of students in the high- and mid-performing schools, respectively copied the text from the Scratch blocks verbatim, compared with 3.37% of students in the low-performing school.

These patterns in answer features suggest that, in the low-performing school, struggling students answered minimally. In contrast, struggling students in the high- and mid-performing schools attempted to write correct answers, but would either leave parts out or copy them directly from the Scratch code. Determining whether these patterns are due to different levels of CS understanding, or different reading and writing abilities will require further study.

4.8 EC: Nested Loop Iteration Count

The last problem, an Extra Challenge question, presented a nested loop, which was not explicitly taught in the curriculum. It consisted of a repeat 2 outer loop and a `repeat 10` inner loop, and we asked students how many times the blocks in the inner loop would run.

Overall, only 25.25% of students gave the correct answer of 20. When broken down by school, we found that 38.76%, 24.08%, and 8.62% of students answered correctly in the high-, mid-, and low-performing schools, respectively. Comparing across schools, there is a statistically-significant difference in performance (F(2,144)=7.85,$p < 0.001$, ω^2=0.285). Between pairs of schools, students in both the

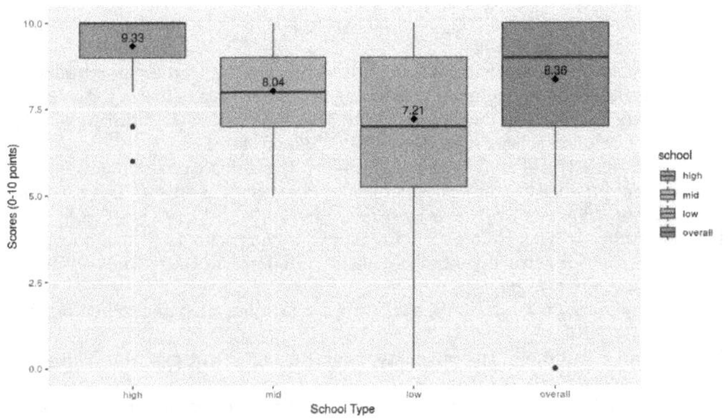

Figure 9: Q7 Explain In Your Own Words Scores(0-10 points)

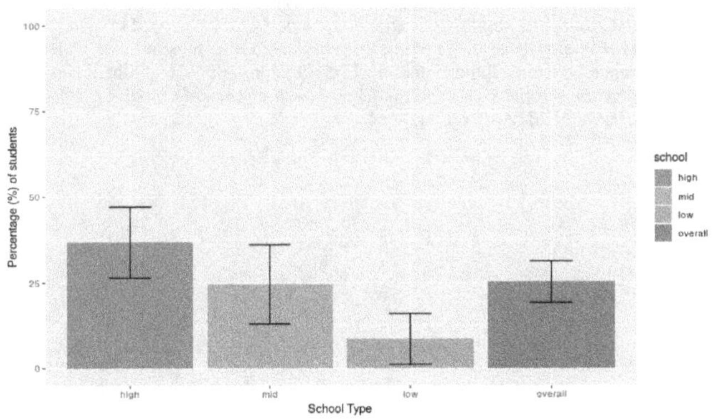

Figure 10: EC Nested Loop Results

high- and mid-performing schools significantly outperformed students from the low-performing school from a Fisher-Hayter Post Hoc ($p < 0.05$).

Our results suggest that students in the high- and mid-performing schools were more likely to apply what they learned about repetition to nested loops, compared to students in the low-performing school. Nonetheless, two responses displayed an understanding of basic loops, if not nested loops. A plurality (40.13%) of students wrote 10, the number in the innermost loop, and 7.36% of students wrote 2, the number in the outermost loops.

4.9 Discussion

We now revisit our two original research questions:

- What is the level of understanding and sources of confusion overall in learning the core concepts of events and iteration?
- To what extent does school performance influence results?

Students in high-performing schools, in general, show a good understanding of events and loops. Most students know the number of iterations a repeat loop performs (Q3), can see the relationship between the loop and equivalent sequential code (Q4, Q5), understand the order of blocks in a loop compared to blocks before and after the loop (Q6), and can articulately describe what a loop does with fidelity (Q7). Only two concepts, parallelism (Q2) and nested loops (EC) were beyond their grasp.

Q	Mean			Significant Differences		
	High	Mid	Low	H*M	H*L	M*L
Q1 (4)	2.80	2.69	1.84		*	*
Q2 (4)	1.31	1.4	0.53		*	*
Q3 (1)	0.99	0.88	0.84		*	
Q4 (1)	0.70	0.53	0.45		*	
Q5 (4)	2.47	1.89	1.56	*	*	
Q6a (4)	3.34	2.72	2.67	*	*	
Q6b (2)	1.72	1.14	1.31	*	*	
Q6c (2)	1.62	1.07	0.98	*	*	
Q7 (10)	9.33	8.04	7.21	*	*	*
EC (1)	0.39	0.24	0.09		*	*

Table 3: Summary of student performance and statistically-significant differences between schools.

However, our results show that students at mid- and low-performance schools exhibit a much shallower understanding of loops. While they can specify how many times a repeat loop will iterate (86%), fewer than half can identify the unrolled equivalent of a repeat loop and identify both constructs that repeat actions (repeat loop and sequential code). Overall, there was a statistically-significant difference between students in the high- and low-performing school on all questions, and the mid- and low-performing schools on Q5, Q6, and Q7.

In terms of ethnic equity, the high-performing school contains high percentages of students already well-represented in the computing field (Asian and White), whereas the majority of Black, Hispanic/Latino, and Pacific Islander students were at mid- and low-performing schools.

5 LIMITATIONS

There are several limitations to this study. First, due to the lack of validated assessments for this age group, this assessment was created specifically for this curriculum, and is therefore not validated. However, our design team included practitioners, CS Ed researchers, and a specialist in students with disabilities. Also, the classrooms, students, and teachers were not randomly sampled throughout the individual school district, nor school districts in the US or world. The same teacher taught all three classrooms within each school; therefore differences could be attributed to teaching methods. Finally, the demographics of study schools may not hold for other examples of high-, mid-, and low-performing schools. More research on a large sample set is necessary to understand district- and nation-wide implications of such results.

6 CONCLUSION

This study shows the successes and challenges of providing elementary school computational thinking instruction with the goal of providing equitable outcomes. This curriculum supports some students in learning sequence, events, and loops well. However, special care should be taken to improve the depth of understanding in mid- and low-performing schools, especially for loops.

REFERENCES

[1] Owen Astrachan et al. "The CS10K project: mobilizing the community to transform high school computing". In: *Proceedings of the 42nd ACM technical symposium on Computer science education.* ACM. 2011, pp. 85–86.

[2] Jack Buckley, Mark Schneider, and Yi Shang. "Fix it and they might stay: School facility quality and teacher retention in Washington, DC". In: *Teachers College Record* 107.5 (2005), pp. 1107–1123.

[3] Jeanne Century, Kaitlyn Ferris, and Huifang Zuo. *Finding Time for Computer Science in the Elementary Day.* URL: http://outlier.uchicago.edu/TimeforCS/findings/.

[4] Jacob Cohen. *Statistical power analysis for the behavioural sciences.* 1988.

[5] Creative Computing. *An introductory computing curriculum using Scratch.*

[6] Cheri Fancsali et al. "A Landscape Study of Computer Science Education in NYC: Early Findings and Implications for Policy and Practice". In: *Proceedings of the 49th ACM Technical Symposium on Computer Science Education.* ACM. 2018, pp. 44–49.

[7] Louise P Flannery et al. "Designing ScratchJr: support for early childhood learning through computer programming". In: *Proceedings of the 12th International Conference on Interaction Design and Children.* ACM. 2013, pp. 1–10.

[8] Baker Franke et al. "Expanding access to K-12 computer science education: research on the landscape of computer science professional development". In: *Proceeding of the 44th ACM technical symposium on Computer science education.* ACM. 2013, pp. 541–542.

[9] Diana Franklin et al. "Initialization in scratch: Seeking knowledge transfer". In: *Proceedings of the 47th ACM Technical Symposium on Computing Science Education.* ACM. 2016, pp. 217–222.

[10] Diana Franklin et al. "Using upper-elementary student performance to understand conceptual sequencing in a blocks-based curriculum". In: *Proceedings of the 2017 ACM SIGCSE Technical Symposium on Computer Science Education.* ACM. 2017, pp. 231–236.

[11] Shuchi Grover and Satabdi Basu. "Measuring student learning in introductory block-based programming: Examining misconceptions of loops, variables, and boolean logic". In: *Proceedings of the 2017 ACM SIGCSE Technical Symposium on Computer Science Education.* ACM. 2017, pp. 267–272.

[12] Charlotte Hill et al. "Floors and Flexibility: Designing a programming environment for 4th-6th grade classrooms". In: *Proceedings of the 46th ACM Technical Symposium on Computer Science Education.* ACM. 2015, pp. 546–551.

[13] Jennifer Jellison Holme. "Buying homes, buying schools: School choice and the social construction of school quality". In: *Harvard Educational Review* 72.2 (2002), pp. 177–206.

[14] Jane Margolis. *Stuck in the shallow end: Education, race, and computing.* MIT Press, 2010.

[15] Sean F Reardon. "The widening income achievement gap". In: *Educational Leadership* 70.8 (2013), pp. 10–16.

[16] Linda Seiter and Brendan Foreman. "Modeling the learning progressions of computational thinking of primary grade students". In: *Proceedings of the ninth annual international ACM conference on International computing education research.* ACM. 2013, pp. 59–66.

[17] Jennifer Wang et al. "Landscape of K-12 computer science education in the US: Perceptions, access, and barriers". In: *Proceedings of the 47th ACM Technical Symposium on Computing Science Education.* ACM. 2016, pp. 645–650.

[18] David Weintrop et al. "Starting from Scratch: Outcomes of Early Computer Science Learning Experiences and Implications for What Comes Next". In: *Proceedings of the 2018 ACM Conference on International Computing Education Research.* ACM. 2018, pp. 142–150.

Increasing Capacity for Computer Science Education in Rural Areas through a Large-Scale Collective Impact Model

Jayce R. Warner
University of Texas at Austin
jaycewarner@utexas.edu

Carol L. Fletcher
University of Texas at Austin
carol.fletcher@utexas.edu

Ryan Torbey
University of Texas at Austin
ryan.torbey@utexas.edu

Lisa S. Garbrecht
University of Texas at Austin
lgarbrecht@utexas.edu

ABSTRACT

Students living in rural areas are less likely to attend schools that offer computer science (CS) courses largely because educational institutions in these remote areas lack the resources to staff teaching positions for these courses. This study investigated the impact of WeTeach_CS, a program designed to train teachers to become certified to teach high school CS in Texas. The WeTeach_CS collective impact model may be well suited to influence rural areas at scale because it utilizes an existing network of organizations across the state to bring high-quality professional development opportunities to teachers in remote areas. Results from a comparative interrupted time series analysis showed a significant, positive change in the rate in which the number of certified CS teachers in rural areas increased during the period of time after WeTeach_CS began compared to the period before the program was implemented, whereas the number of teachers certified in technology applications showed no such change. Furthermore, the growth rate in the number of certified CS teachers was much higher for rural schools than urban, suggesting that collective impact models like WeTeach_CS may be especially beneficial for rural communities.

KEYWORDS

rural education, teacher professional development, educator certification, high school teachers, equitable access to computer science education, broadening participation in computing

ACM Reference Format:

Jayce R. Warner, Carol L. Fletcher, Ryan Torbey, and Lisa S. Garbrecht. 2019. Increasing Capacity for Computer Science Education in Rural Areas through a Large-Scale Collective Impact Model. In *Proceedings of the 50th ACM Technical Symposium on Computer Science Education (SIGCSE '19), February 27-March 2, 2019, Minneapolis, MN, USA.* ACM, New York, NY, USA, 7 pages. https://doi.org/10.1145/3287324.3287418

SIGCSE '19, February 27-March 2, 2019, Minneapolis, MN, USA

ACM ISBN 978-1-4503-5890-3/19/02...$15.00
https://doi.org/10.1145/3287324.3287418

1 INTRODUCTION

Schools in rural areas are behind their more urbanized counterparts in terms of access to CS education [12]. Rural schools constituted only 10% all U.S. public schools that offered an AP computer science course in 2017 [2], even though the latest estimates show that 28% of all public schools in the U.S. are designated as rural and 42% as rural or small-town [7]. At the core of this issue is that the lack of qualified CS teachers overall is exacerbated in rural areas, where schools have a relatively harder time funding new teaching positions and recruiting highly qualified teachers to fill those positions. Schools simply cannot offer courses for which they have no qualified teacher, implying that one crucial antecedent to increasing access to CS education for underserved students is increasing the CS teacher workforce in those areas.

Efforts to increase the number of qualified CS teachers are invariably met with challenges of scalability and sustainability. Collective impact models [13], which unite interdisciplinary partners towards a common goal, may be better suited to overcome these challenges than stand-alone interventions. A collective impact model has the potential to effect change in rural schools because it connects local education agencies with resources and expertise to which they may not otherwise have access. The WeTeach_CS program has worked extensively with rural schools and teachers over the past three years to build capacity for K-12 CS Education. Approximately 40% of the 640 schools served by WeTeach_CS in 2016-17 are in rural or small-town districts. WeTeach_CS, which serves teachers across multiple districts, is particularly helpful in creating an economy of scale for CS teacher professional development that is not possible to obtain for individual small, rural districts. WeTeach_CS supports sustainability of program effects by using a network of professional development partners to support local teachers before and after becoming certified to teach CS. This research project examines the effectiveness of the WeTeach_CS collective impact model for increasing the number of certified CS teachers in rural schools.

2 BACKGROUND

2.1 Equitable Access to CS Education in K-12

A growing consensus is emerging around the need for computer science (CS) education for all K-12 students. CSforAll as a national movement was catalyzed by President Obama's announcement in January of 2016 of a new initiative focused on making sure every student had the computer science and computational thinking experiences they needed to become "active citizens in our technology-driven world" [19]. Economic competitiveness in the United States rests in large part on the ability to develop and leverage technology to fuel progress and innovation. The CS field is booming, with jobs like Software Developer positioned to have hundreds of thousands of openings between now and 2026 [16]. The value for students who study CS is immense. Computer science majors earn an average of $1.67 million throughout their lifetimes, 40% greater than the average of all college graduates [18]. Even for those students who will not eventually pursue a post-secondary career specific to CS or information technology, learning to reason and solve problems computationally may be of value. Computational thinking has been marked as a transferable problem-solving skill, and computational literacy is seen as a modern way of learning and representing knowledge [1].

Equitable access to CS education is important since the opportunity to study CS opens doors to above-average earning potential and the ability to create, rather than simply consume, in the digital world. Schools, however, are struggling to adequately meet the challenge of providing equitable access to CS education opportunities for all students. Despite the fact that the majority of teachers and parents believe that CS should be a required part of K-12 education, only 40% of schools are estimated to offer at least one CS course [11]. Access to CS courses is even lower for students in rural areas, students of color, and students from low-income families [10]. One of the most significant barriers to the ability of schools to offer CS courses is the lack of certified teachers [6]. Many schools, especially those in poorer districts, simply lack the resources to train new CS teachers. For this reason, scalable interventions to incentivize and train teachers across a diverse range of schools and districts are needed to achieve the goals of increasing the number of certified CS teachers and providing all students opportunities to study CS. Little is known, however, about the effectiveness of such large-scale programs in relatively new subject areas like computer science and in rural areas.

2.2 Interventions to Increase the Teacher Workforce in High-Need Areas

District and state programs have utilized professional development and financial incentives as a means to influence teacher choices related to where they work and what they teach. For example, in New York City public schools, where teachers must have the relevant coursework to be qualified to teach a particular subject, the New York City Department of Education offers current teachers tuition reimbursement to gain additional certification in hard-to-staff subject areas [17]. Research on the effectiveness of similar programs has produced mixed results [4]. An analysis of Florida's Critical Teacher Shortage Program showed that tuition reimbursement programs and one-time bonuses had positive effects on the retention of teachers in math and special education [5]. Other research, however, calls into question the effectiveness of financial incentives that do not also provide teachers with professional support. Massachusetts and North Carolina implemented teacher bonus programs to incentivize teachers to teach hard-to-staff subjects at high-poverty schools. Over half of the Massachusetts teachers in the study ended up leaving before the four year program was complete [15], and the North Carolina program was mired by misunderstanding and low perceived value among teachers [3]. Another study showed that although a financial incentive increased the likelihood of having teachers to teach in low-performing schools, teachers who received the incentive were just as likely to leave the school as teachers who did not receive the incentive [20]. A common theme of the findings from these studies is that financial incentives alone may not be enough if not coupled with proper training and support. In addition, the majority of the studies in this field focus on the impact of incentives on the retention of teachers, whereas few studies take up the initial question of whether and how these incentives impact recruitment or the achievement of new certifications to teach additional, high-need subjects.

We have highlighted research regarding large, statewide programs because of their ability to effect change across a broad range of economically- and resource-diverse districts. Incentive and professional development programs designed for implementation by individual school districts can have the unfortunate result of perpetuating educational inequities since only those districts with adequate resources can successfully implement such programs. For example, one study found that larger school districts were more likely to implement incentive programs than smaller school districts [14]. Thus, to meet the needs of smaller, rural school districts, we need large-scale, collective impact programs that bring together educational institutions with similar goals, pool resources across geographic boundaries, and create a sustainable network of these institutions and resources to support efforts beyond the program's initial stages.

2.3 Collective Impact Models

Collective impact models have grown in prominence as viable solutions to complex social sector challenges. Projects applying a collective impact approach address a wide range of challenges including addressing worldwide malnutrition, reducing teenage binge drinking, combating childhood obesity, and tackling environmental cleanup efforts [8]. Other collective impact projects are addressing educational challenges. The Strive Partnership in Cinncinatti is a prime example of the potential of collective impact models to make significant and sustainable changes to student educational outcome measures, with 81% of its 34 measures of student achievement showing postive improvement over four years [8].

Collective impact models incorporate five key components: a backbone organization that supports the entire system, a common agenda regarding the problem to be solved, shared measurement systems to track progress toward goals, mutually reinforcing activities, and continuous communication across all stakeholders [13]. By leveraging the expertise of multiple players across the system, collective impact models can address a variety of variables that influence the problem of practice simultaneously. In the education sector, this includes building teacher content knowledge, developing administrator leadership, addressing school funding and teacher incentives, and identifying and modifying when possible state or local policies that impede progress.

2.4 The WeTeach_CS Program

The University of Texas at Austin (UT Austin) STEM Center's WeTeach_CS program trains K-12 educators to improve access to high quality CS experiences for a broad and diverse range of students. The objectives of the WeTeach_CS program are to increase the number of CS certified high school teachers, increase the number of high schools offering CS courses, increase the number and diversity of students enrolled in CS courses, and expand access to computational thinking, coding and programming experiences for all students in K-8.

The WeTeach_CS program is a collective impact model currently serving the entire state of Texas. The program offers a $1,000 stipend to Texas teachers who successfully achieved certification in computer science. To help teachers learn the content, WeTeach_CS provides a 7-week online certification preparation course along with a 2-day in-person training that was offered at various locations around the state. In order to reach and serve teachers across all geographic and economic areas of the state, WeTeach_CS utilizes an existing network of 30 region-level organizations (e.g., education service centers, universities) within the state to publicize and implement the program.

The WeTeach_CS program reflects the five key characteristics of collective impact models mentioned above. The UT Austin STEM Center serves as the WeTeach_CS **backbone organization**, coordinating all state level professional development, CS Collaborative funding and support, data collection, and convening of leaders and teacher participants. Teachers, schools, universities, non-profits, industry partners, and professional development providers who participate in the WeTeach_CS program all share the **common agenda** of broadening participation in K-12 computing. The common goal is grounded in four key building blocks of broadening participation in K-12: 1) Capacity, 2) Access, 3) Participation, and 4) Equity. While the final goal is equitable participation of all students in CS-related experiences in K-12, the three prior components are necessary antecedents to reaching equity at scale. In this study we focus on the first of those components, capacity, operationalized here as the availability of qualified teachers certified to teach computer science. Partner organizations within WeTeach_CS all use the same **shared measurement systems**. For example, to become certified to teach computer science in Texas, all teachers must pass the same state certification exam specific to computer science. Additionally, public schools and districts across the state are all required to use one common data reporting system for all teacher and student data. **Mutually reinforcing activities** of the WeTeach_CS network include professional development related to teacher certification as well as other training that builds teacher content knowledge, equitable practices, and instructional skills. UT Austin also hosts an annual 3-day WeTeach_CS Summit, attended by over 400 educators in 2018, to provide professional development and build community across the statewide network. Finally, the WeTeach_CS community is connected through an ecosystem of support and **continuous communication**. The WeTeach_CS blog is a weekly online newsletter subscribed to by over 1,300 stakeholders focused on keeping teachers aware of various professional development opportunities, funding and policy updates related to CS education, instructional resources, and student opportunities. Over 2,400 people follow the WeTeach_CS Facebook and Twitter feeds. Each WeTeach_CS Collaborative teacher also receives regular communication from their own CS Collaborative Project Director related to their regional professional development program and meets regularly with the teachers in their CS Collaborative (20-40 teacher per cohort). WeTeach_CS Project Directors are supported by UT Austin staff through virtual and in-person meetings as well as CS workshops and training opportunities.

Many of the teachers and schools served by the collaborative organizations within this collective impact model were located in school districts that lacked the resources typical of larger districts in more affluent areas. The purpose of this study was to investigate whether and to what extent the WeTeach_CS program increased the number of certified CS teachers in rural areas of Texas.

3 METHOD

Comparative interrupted times series (CITS) analysis was used to investigate the impact of the WeTeach_CS program on the number of certified computer science teachers in rural schools. CITS is a quasi-experimental method that tests whether the introduction of an intervention produces a change in the target outcome over time for the treatment group to a greater degree than a comparison group. We refer to the periods of time before and after the introduction of the program as the pre-intervention and intervention phases, respectively. Two types of causal effects can be estimated with CITS: level change and slope change. In the current analysis, the presence of a level change would mean a change in the number of certified teachers immediately following the introduction of the WeTeach_CS program that could not be explained by the overall trend. A statistically significant slope change would indicate that the intervention phase trend differs from the pre-intervention phase trend. Similar level and slope changes for the comparison group would suggest that the observed changes for the treatment group were due to some other factor not accounted for in the model.

We hypothesized that the WeTeach_CS program would positively impact the number of certified CS teachers in rural schools but that this effect would happen gradually over time. Accordingly, we expected results to reveal a statistically significant, positive change in slope but no significant level change. We further expected null results for changes in the level and slope of the number of certified teachers in the comparison group.

In contrast to standard interrupted time series (ITS) analyses, CITS seeks to rule out the possibility of unknown confounders by including a comparison group that is similar to the treatment group such that it would be influenced by the same unknown confounding factors as the treatment group but remain unaffected by the treatment. We included teachers who obtained certification in technology applications to serve as the comparison group for a couple reasons. First, technology applications is the certification most similar to the computer science licensure in terms of the content knowledge covered on the certification exam and the curricular content of the courses that a teacher holding that certification would be qualified to teach. Second, technology applications and computer science had relatively similar slopes for the pre-intervention phase. For both computer science and technology applications, the number of certified teachers steadily increased over the four years prior to the start of WeTeach_CS, whereas other certification fields (e.g., mathematics) showed less stable increases or no increases during that time period.

3.1 Data Sources

Education data were collected through the Texas Educational Research Center, a data clearinghouse that contains a broad range of data on every public school and public school teacher and student in the state. This clearinghouse includes data maintained by the State Board of Educator Certification (SBEC), which oversees and administers educator certifications for the state. To obtain a certification for a particular subject area in Texas, teachers are required to hold a bachelor's degree, complete an approved certification program, and pass the appropriate certification exam for that subject. Teachers who already hold certification in one area can become certified in another area by passing the appropriate content exam and applying for certification. The SBEC maintains records of all exam administrations and all certifications issued. Access to these data allowed us to determine precise counts of the number of active CS certifications each month across several years. By merging these data with data on teacher assignment, we were able to determine for all certified teachers the name and location of the school in which they were teaching at the time they became certified and each time point thereafter. We included data spanning six years, from the beginning of the 2011-12 school year through the end of 2016-17.

To determine whether teachers taught in rural or urban/suburban school districts, we used the district type designations developed and assigned by the Texas Education Agency (TEA). These include eight categories, which we list here in order from the largest, most urban type of school districts to the smallest, most remote type of districts: major urban, major suburban, other central city, other central city suburban, independent town, non-metropolitan fast-growing, non-metropolitan stable, and rural. (A ninth category, charter school districts, was excluded from the analysis because the criteria for inclusion in this category was entirely unrelated to geographic location. Computer science teachers in this category comprised approximately two percent of the total population of certified CS teachers employed in the state at the start of the intervention.) Because the TEA designation of "rural" includes only the smallest, most remote school districts, we further grouped these eight categories into two super categories: urban-suburban and rural. To determine whether each of the eight TEA district types should be classified as urban-suburban or rural, we considered several factors, including average district size (in terms of student enrollment), average number of campuses per district, and remoteness. Clear distinctions were evident between the first three categories and the latter five in terms of district size and number of campuses per district, as shown in Table 1. Visual inspection of the districts within each category confirmed the remoteness of the latter five district types. Thus, these five district types were designated as rural in the current study.

Table 1: District Type Designations

Designation in Current Study	TEA District Type	Avg. No. of Campuses Per District	Avg. Student Enrollment
Urban-Suburban	Major Urban	124	89,059
	Major Suburban	26	22,066
	Other Central City	29	21,142
Rural	O.C.C. Suburban	7	4,603
	Independent Town	6	3,744
	Non-Met Growing	3	1,057
	Non-Met Stable	4	1,687
	Rural	2	388

4 RESULTS

Huitema's [9] guidelines for two-stage model selection were followed to conduct model fit tests to identify the appropriate parameters to include in the model and determine correct model specifications. Results from these tests suggested that a four-parameter model that accounted for autocorrelated errors would be the best fit to analyze the data. The resulting model assumed this form:

$$Y_t = \beta_0 + \beta_1 T_t + \beta_2 L_t + \beta_3 S_t + \phi_1 e_{t-1} + u_t \quad (1)$$

where Y_t is the number of certified teachers at time t; β_0 is the intercept; β_1 is the pre-intervention slope; β_2 is the level-change at the time of the intervention; β_3 is the change in slope from pre-intervention phase to intervention phase; T_t is the value of the time variable at time t; L_t represents the level-change and is a dummy-code variable that denotes the phase at time t; S_t represents the slope-change variable and is defined as $[T_t - (n_1 + 1)]L$; n_1 is the number of observations in the first phase; ϕ_1 is the first-order autoregressive coefficient; e_{t-1} is the residual at time $t-1$; and u_t is the residual at time t.

Inspection of scatter plots of the data revealed evidence of seasonal trends recurring annually. Specifically, the number of certified teachers decreased slightly each year between the months of August and September. These decreases are likely the result of some teachers allowing their certifications to lapse before renewing them again, since certifications are often set to expire at the end of the school year. To account for this seasonality, we added 11 dummy-coded variables to the model to indicate the month of the year for each time point. Due to space constraints, we omitted these variables from the results tables.

Table 2: Time Series Regression Results: Rural CS Teachers

	B	SE	t	p
Pre-intervention slope	0.33	0.15	2.14	.037
Level change	3.09	3.79	0.82	.418
Slope change	6.46	0.44	14.59	.000
Constant	56.47	4.91	11.48	.000

ρ=.83

Results showed that, as expected, the level change was not statistically significant ($t(57)=0.82$, $p=.418$), indicating that there was no immediate change in the number of certified CS teachers that could not be explained by the overall trend (see Table 2). However, the slope change was statistically significant ($t(57)=14.59$, $p<.001$), signaling that the intervention slope differed from the pre-intervention slope. The coefficient for this estimate (B=6.46) suggests that an average of approximately 6 more teachers were certified each month in the intervention phase than in the pre-intervention phase. By adding the slope-change coefficient to the coefficient for the pre-intervention slope (B=0.33), we can calculate the actual slope for the intervention phase. In doing so, we note that an average of about 7 new teachers were certified each month during the time after WeTeach_CS began compared to an average of less than 1 new teacher per month during the time before WeTeach_CS was implemented. Figure 1 illustrates these trends.

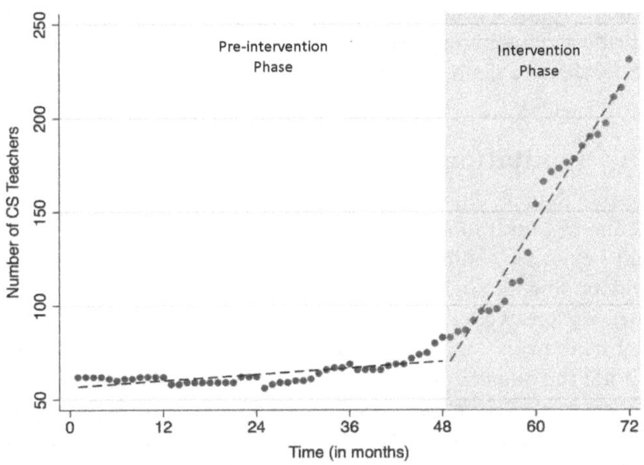

Figure 1: The number of certified CS teachers in rural areas before and after the start of the WeTeach_CS program

To check whether these trends were similar or dissimilar to the trends for urban-suburban school districts, we conducted the same analysis for CS teachers in those areas. The statistical significance of this analysis was similar to that of rural schools in that there was no level change but there was a significant change in slope from the pre-intervention to the intervention phase ($t(57)=9.11$, $p<.001$), indicating that there was a significant increase in the rate at which teachers in urban-suburban districts became certified after the start of WeTeach_CS compared to the period of time before the program. However, the rate at which teachers became certified in rural areas was substantially larger than urban-suburban areas. Whereas the number of certified CS teachers in urban-suburban areas increased by 88% during the intervention phase, it increased by 169% in rural areas during the same period (see Figure 2).

To ensure this difference between rural and urban-suburban areas was unique to the intervention phase and not simply a continuation of differences that existed prior to the intervention, we calculated the percent change for comparable periods of time before and after the start of the WeTeach_CS program. Because the intervention phase comprised a two-year period and the pre-intervention phase comprised a period of four years in the analysis, we calculated the pre-intervention percent change using just the two years prior to the start of WeTeach_CS and found that the number of CS teachers increased by 31% in urban-suburban areas and 34% in rural areas during this time period. Thus, whereas the rate in which teachers became certified in urban-suburban areas was twice as large during the two years of the intervention phase than the last two years of pre-intervention phase (63% vs 31%, respectively), it was over five times greater in rural areas (178% vs 34%).

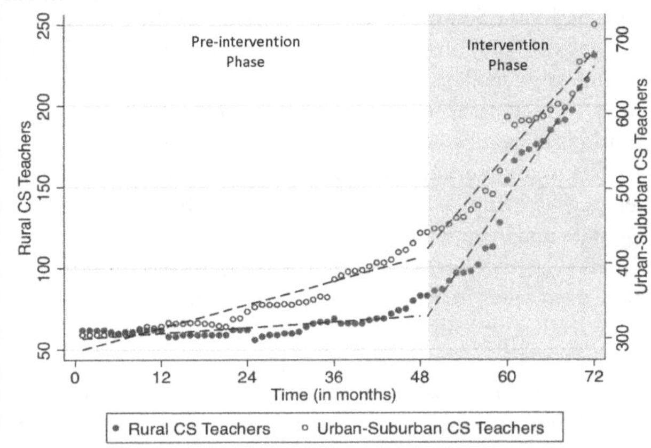

Figure 2: The number of certified CS teachers in rural and urban-suburban areas before and after the start of the WeTeach_CS program

To aid in ruling out the presence of unknown confounding factors, an interrupted time series analysis was run on the comparison group, rural teachers obtaining certification in Technology Applications. In conducting this analysis, we followed the same procedures used to conduct the analysis for rural CS teachers. We followed Huitema's [9] two-stage model selection guidelines to determine appropriate model specification, tested and accounted for autocorrelation, and included month dummy variables to control for seasonality. Results showed no statistically significance change in level or slope (see Table 3). Thus, we conclude that there were no changes in the number of certified Technology Applications teachers immediately after the start of the intervention phase that could not be accounted for by the overall trend, nor was there any difference between the trends in the intervention and pre-intervention phases.

Table 3: Time Series Regression Results: Rural Technology Applications Teachers

	B	SE	t	p
Pre-intervention slope	4.33	0.63	6.83	.000
Level change	-2.24	11.55	-0.19	.847
Slope change	1.27	1.73	0.73	.467
Constant	1060.44	20.70	51.24	.000

5 DISCUSSION

The results of this study demonstrate that large-scale collective impact interventions can be effective in increasing the number of certified CS teachers. Moreover, given the statistically significant change in slope between the pre-intervention and intervention phases, this study shows that program effects can be sustained over time. Perhaps most importantly, the WeTeach_CS program seemed to have had an even greater impact in rural schools, where the number of certified CS teachers increased by 178% compared to 63% in urban-suburban areas. As advocates make the case for expanding K-12 CS education for all students in the United States, initiatives that demonstrate success in rural locations will be of great importance. There has been a focus on closing the digital divide, in which rural schools have lagged behind urban-suburban institutions in gaining access to technical advances. Unless effective strategies in broadening participation in CS in rural districts are developed and implemented, there is a risk that this divide will perpetuate and even widen.

Whereas previous research on increasing the teacher workforce in high-need areas focused on interventions enacted on relatively smaller scales (typically at the district level), this study provides evidence for the effectiveness of a large-scale intervention as it was implemented across an entire state. WeTeach_CS appears to be implementing a promising strategy yielding positive results across a state which has large socioeconomic and geographic diversity. We believe the distinguishing factors that have contributed to the success of the WeTeach_CS program lay in its utilization of the collective impact model as well as its combination of financial incentives with ample available training. The results of this study provide strong evidence for the value of collective impact models for effecting change in rural areas and across large geographic regions generally.

The unique impact on rural areas may have been due to three challenges that rural school districts face to a greater degree than urban and suburban districts. First, while many school districts, regardless of geography, lack computer science expertise, school districts in urban and suburban areas can often tap into nearby institutions of higher education and industry partners to access resources. Second, administrators and teachers in rural communities often have overlapping responsibilities due to the small school size and simply lack the bandwidth to launch and support new initiatives in which they lack personal expertise. Finally, it if often the case that rural school districts simply lack the ability to afford expensive initiatives, such as implementing new courses and training teachers in new content areas.

We theorize that WeTeach_CS has been more successful in rural communities because it addresses these specific challenges. Collective impact models like WeTeach_CS, which function at a large scale and create collaborative networks of like-minded organizations, can be especially beneficial for educational institutions in remote areas. With the collective impact model, small rural schools can leverage the expertise of the network to compensate for limited CS expertise within their organizations. While these schools are geographically isolated, through collective impact they become connected to institutions of higher education, industry partners, and other teachers and schools all focused on addressing the same challenges. Because rural schools have relatively few teachers, it is difficult for individual school districts to achieve an economy of scale to support the creation and growth a CS program. However, in a collective impact model the investment can be distributed across an entire statewide network, thus achieving the economy of scale that would be too inefficient for rural districts to do on their own. The CS certification preparation training provided by the WeTeach_CS program purposefully leverages the strengths of the collaborative network, allowing the local organizations to utilize their existing relationships with teachers to propagate the online course and promote in-person training sessions. This allowed the initiative to scale more quickly into all areas of the state while keeping the financial cost to schools and districts at manageable levels.

Another distinguishing feature of the WeTeach_CS program is its focus on training and incentivizing inservice teachers as opposed to preservice teachers. This approach may have provided additional benefits to rural districts since training existing teachers who are already serving in rural schools means reducing the need to recruit CS teachers to remote areas.

5.1 Limitations

Despite the fact that we used a comparative design to strengthen claims of causal inference, it is important to consider the possibility of other confounding factors. The existence of unknown confounding factors would be more plausible if other programs or interventions were implemented at the same time as WeTeach_CS that were likely to influence the number of certified CS teachers but not the number of certified Technology Applications teachers. However, we believe the presence of such factors to be highly unlikely given the fact that the WeTeach_CS program was the only statewide CS program in effect at the time.

One limitation of this study is the fact that rules and regulations concerning teacher certification vary from state to state in the United States and country to country worldwide. Texas teacher certification rules enable currently certified teachers to take a subject-matter certification exam and then add that subject to their teaching certificate. This can be done without any additional coursework, allowing for a relatively flexible teacher workforce in terms of adding additional academic subjects to teaching credentials. Where certification requirements differ in other states, interventions like the one examined in this study may need to be altered to be effective.

5.2 Conclusion

A major strength of this study lies in the fact that it was done at scale, as the intervention canvassed the entire state of Texas and the analysis took into account the whole of certification data in the state. This has important implications for efforts to improve equitable access to CS education. The lack of qualified teachers is one of the foremost barriers to students' access to CS courses in their schools. This study is an important step forward in understanding how to improve equitable access to CS education for all students because it examines and demonstrates the effectiveness of a large-scale collective impact model to build capacity in rural communities.

REFERENCES

[1] Paulo Blikstein. 2018. *Pre-college computer science education: A survey of the field.* Report. https://goo.gl/gmS1Vm.

[2] College Board. 2018. *AP computer science expansion.* Report. https://reports.collegeboard.org/ap-program-results/ap-computer-science-expansion

[3] Charles T. Clotfelter, Elizabeth J. Glennie, Helen F. Ladd, and Jacob L. Vigdor. 2008. Teacher bonuses and teacher retention in low-performing schools. *Public Finance Review* 36, 1 (2008), 63–87.

[4] Jane L. David. 2008. Teacher recruitment incentives. *Educational Leadership* 65, 7 (2008), 84–86.

[5] Li Feng and Tim R. Sass. 2018. The impact of incentives to recruit and retain teachers in âĂIJhard-to-staffâĂİ subjects. *Journal of Policy Analysis and Management* 37, 1 (2018), 112âĂŞ135.

[6] Carol L. Fletcher. 2014. *Building the Texas computer science pipeline: Strategic recommendations for success.* Report. The University of Texas at Austin. https://www.thetrc.org/web/assets/files/pdfs/Building-the-Texas-CS-Pipeline_Fletcher.pdf

[7] National Center for Education Statistics. 2014. *Rural education in America.* Data Table. https://nces.ed.gov/surveys/ruraled/tables/a.1.a.-2.asp

[8] Fay Hanleybrown, John Kania, and Mark Kramer. 2012. Channeling Change: Making Collective Impact Work. *Stanford Social Innovation Review* (2012). https://ssir.org/articles/entry/channeling_change_making_collective_impact_work

[9] Bradley E. Huitema. 2011. *The analysis of covariance and alternatives: Statistical methods for experiments, quasi-experiments, and single-case studies (2nd edition).* John Wiley & Sons, New Jersey.

[10] Google Inc. and Gallup Inc. 2015. *Searching for computer science: Access and barriers in U.S. K-12 Education.* Report. https://services.google.com/fh/files/misc/searching-for-computer-science_report.pdf

[11] Google Inc. and Gallup Inc. 2016. *Trends in the state of computer science in U.S. K-12 schools.* Report. http://goo.gl/j291E0

[12] Google Inc. and Gallup Inc. 2017. *Computer science learning: Closing the Gap: Rural and Small Town School Districts.* Report. http://goo.gl/hYxqCr

[13] John Kania and Mark Kramer. 2011. Collective impact. *Stanford Social Innovation Review* 9, 1 (2011), 36–41. https://ssir.org/articles/entry/collective_impact

[14] Guodong Liang and Motoko Akiba. 2015. Characteristics of teacher incentive pay programs: a statewide district survey. *Journal of Educational Administration* 53, 6 (2015), 702–717. https://doi.org/10.1108/jea-09-2013-0106

[15] Edward Liu, Susan Moore Johnson, and Heather G. Peske. 2004. New teachers and the Massachusetts signing bonus: The limits of inducements. *Educational Evaluation and Policy Analysis* 26, 3 (2004), 217–236.

[16] Bureau of Labor Statistics. 2018. *Occupational Outlook Handbook.* Report. U.S. Department of Labor,. https://www.bls.gov/ooh/computer-and-information-technology/software-developers.htm

[17] Alfred S. Posamentier and Joyce R. Coppin. 2005. How the nation's largest city is managing one of its severest math teacher shortages. *The Mathematics Teacher* 98, 9 (2005), 582–584. http://www.jstor.org/stable/27971820

[18] The Hamilton Project. 2014. Career earnings by college major. http://www.hamiltonproject.org/charts/career_earnings_by_college_major/

[19] Megan Smith. 2016. Computer science for all. https://obamawhitehouse.archives.gov/blog/2016/01/30/computer-science-all

[20] Jennifer L. Steele, Richard J. Murnane, and John B. Willett. 2010. Do financial incentives help low-performing schools attract and keep academically talented teachers? Evidence from California. *Journal of Policy Analysis and Management* 29, 3 (2010), 451–478. https://doi.org/10.1002/pam.20505

The Role of Translanguaging in Computational Literacies

Documenting Middle School Bilinguals' Practices in Computer Science Integrated Units

Sara Vogel
The Graduate Center, City University of New York
New York, NY

Christopher Hoadley
New York University
Brooklyn, NY

Laura Ascenzi-Moreno
Brooklyn College, City University of New York
Brooklyn, NY

Kate Menken
Queens College, City University of New York
Queens, NY

ABSTRACT

Bilingual education has described a process called translanguaging by which students use linguistic resources across and beyond multiple named languages to learn. Here, we examine how bilingual learners translanguage while learning computer science. These middle schoolers participated in a curricular intervention which infused computational thinking into their Spanish-English bilingual language arts class. Through a descriptive qualitative methodology, we document classroom moments supporting four claims: 1) students' translanguaging blurs linguistic, disciplinary, and modal boundaries, 2) computational literacies are intertwined with students' other literacies , 3) students' attitudes about language and the contexts around them play a role in their translanguaging, and 4) students translanguage to engage in specific CT practices.

CCS CONCEPTS

• **Social and professional topics → Computational thinking; K-12 education; Cultural characteristics;**

KEYWORDS

Computer Science for All, Middle School, Bilinguals, Translanguaging, Computational Literacies, English Language Learners

ACM Reference Format:

Sara Vogel, Christopher Hoadley, Laura Ascenzi-Moreno, and Kate Menken. 2019. The Role of Translanguaging in Computational Literacies : Documenting Middle School Bilinguals' Practices in Computer Science Integrated Units. In *Proceedings of the 50th ACM Technical Symposium on Computer Science Education (SIGCSE '19), February 27-March 2, 2019, Minneapolis, MN, USA.* ACM, New York, NY, USA, 7 pages. https://doi.org/10.1145/3287324.3287368

1 INTRODUCTION AND THEORETICAL FRAMEWORK

Humans use language as a primary way to communicate and to learn. This is as true in computer science as it is in other school subjects. Translanguaging, a recent theory from the fields of applied linguistics and bilingual education, posits that people fluidly call into action their full meaning-making repertoires, including their linguistic resources (e.g. knowledge of Spanish and/or English vocabulary), semiotic resources (e.g. drawing, intonation) and social practices (e.g. conventions for greeting, joking, etc.) [13]. Translanguaging argues that the way people – especially bilingual and multilingual people – assemble language features often defies categorization into traditional named languages (like "Spanish" or "French") [29]: in a single interaction, people may use words from multiple languages, gestures, and even emoji and other resources from the environment and technology to make meaning.

Translanguaging is a relevant theory to apply in K-12 CS learning environments. In such classrooms, students are not just expected to write compilable code, they are expected to collaborate to produce meaningful projects for particular users, to deepen their understanding of concepts in a particular subject area, and to think critically about the impacts of technology [2]. In these activities, language takes on a central role. Students communicate to a range of audiences using dynamic configurations of spoken and written human and programming languages, through modalities such as comments in code, paper prototypes, UML diagrams, and a host of other resources: in other words, they translanguage. In introducing translanguaging to the CS education field, we do not equate programming languages with named languages like French or Chinese (as some states have controversially done by enabling students to fulfill foreign language graduation credits with CS courses [4]), but rather recognize the ways computer science is taught and learned with and through language.

As CS for All initiatives are implemented in more schools serving multilingual students, it's imperative to consider the role that students' language resources might play in learning. There is, however, an absence of research documenting translanguaging in CS education. How do students, especially emergent bilinguals (students with diverse linguistic backgrounds who may be learning English in school), draw upon their diverse language repertoires? How might teachers support students to translanguage in ways that promote engagement with CS concepts and practices? How can classroom communities work across language differences so all can learn? Past studies demonstrated how "talk, specifically, when used consciously and productively in an introductory CS curriculum for young learners can shape the process of development of CT [computational thinking]" [16]. We build on this by considering how students make meaning in CS ed using language beyond "talk,"

SIGCSE '19, February 27-March 2, 2019, Minneapolis, MN, USA

ACM ISBN 978-1-4503-5890-3/19/02...$15.00
https://doi.org/10.1145/3287324.3287368

and how their language use is shaped by their diverse profiles and experiences. Translanguaging has been mentioned in CS education studies of Indian tertiary schooling contexts, mostly to describe how teachers used both English and Hindi [30] or Tamil [32] to teach programming to students who have been schooled through a vernacular language. Those studies, however, do not provide researchers and practitioners with an understanding of the characteristics of students'–especially young bilingual students'–language practices while they engage in CS, and the relationship of students' translanguaging to computational thinking concepts or practices.

In this paper, we report preliminary findings from a study we conducted using a descriptive qualitative research methodology at a bilingual Spanish-English middle school program where teachers infused computational thinking into other subjects. Specifically, we document a series of classroom moments which help support four main claims: 1) students' translanguaging practices in CS learning contexts blur linguistic, disciplinary, and modal boundaries; 2) computational literacies are intertwined with the many other literacies students bring with them; 3) students' language attitudes and activity contexts around them play a role in their translanguaging; 4) students translanguage in order to engage in specific CT practices (like remixing and abstraction). Finally, we discuss how evidence of translanguaging among bilingual learners has implications not only for how bilingual students might learn computer science but for understanding monolingual learners' use of language during CS activities, and how teachers might support students to translanguage purposefully while they learn CS.

2 RESEARCH CONTEXT

2.1 Bilingual Students and CS Education

The context for this study is a research practice partnership (RPP) called Participating in Literacies and Computer Science (PiLaCS), which grapples with a core problem of practice facing schools and districts implementing CS for All policies: how to meaningfully include emergent bilingual students. The linguistic diversity of the country's school-aged student population is the highest it has ever been [19]. The close to 10 percent of the US public school students that are classified as "English Language Learners" [5] often face many challenges as they navigate the school system: nearly 60 percent of ELLs in every state live in families whose income falls below 185 percent of the federal poverty line [15], they often attend schools of variable quality [8] where administrators and teachers have limited knowledge about language learning and bilingualism [26], they are unfairly evaluated by assessment policies that measure them against monolingual English standards [24], and often experience subtractive models of education that do not build on their language or cultural backgrounds [25]. For these and other factors, emergent bilinguals graduated at below-average rates (66 percent to 84 percent nationally in the 2015-16 school year) [3]. There is no data available on the rates of these students' participation in CS education.

2.2 The New York City Context

The home base of our RPP is New York City, where this problem of practice is a particularly important one. Here, the Department of Education has committed to teaching CS perspectives, practices, and concepts in at least one meaningful, 10-25 hour instructional unit per grade band (K-2, 3-5, 6-8, 9-12) to all 1.1 million students in NYC. While there are tools such as the NYC DOE Computer Science Education Blueprint [27] to guide this implementation, there are few resources for teachers of emergent bilinguals. In NYC, 41% percent of students speak languages other than English at home [28], and 12.5% were categorized as English Language Learners in the 2015-16 school year [9]. Simply translating curricula and software into multiple languages is insufficient to deal with our city's variability in learners' linguistic backgrounds which includes 155 languages other than English [9]. Students use a variety of language practices, and vary in terms of country of birth, educational history, race, and language, among other factors [10]. Because of this diversity within the population and because this diversity is not static, schools implementing NYC's CS4All policy must come to understand their students' languaging practices, and devise responsive and flexible approaches to CS curriculum design and implementation.

To address these challenges, the PiLaCS RPP brought together New York City-based university researchers with teachers at three public schools in the Washington Heights neighborhood of Manhattan. Multilingualism is woven into the fabric of that community. Forty-eight percent of area residents are foreign-born, with two-thirds of them from the Dominican Republic. The neighborhood is within the NYC DOE's District 6, which had the highest share of students classified as ELLs in the City (nearly 29 percent) [1]. This study focuses in on one of the schools that participated in the RPP in the 2017-18 school year: a public 6th-8th grade middle school where 51% of the student population was categorized with the ELL designation that year. At this school, parents and caregivers of Spanish-speaking emergent bilingual students can opt their children into a bilingual program, where the school policy is to alternate the language of instruction between Spanish and English by day. This paper will focus on data from two sixth and seventh grade dual-language arts classes where teachers and students tend to use language flexibly despite the official language allocation policy. (Other schools in the project integrated CS into other subjects such as Science.)

2.3 Our Curriculum Design Lenses and Process

Teachers and researchers in the RPP co-designed CS-integrated units of study, taking into consideration students' language backgrounds, language objectives they were expected to meet in English and Spanish, content objectives in Language Arts, and computational thinking (CT) objectives. Our team designed projects for students to complete within the Scratch programming environment and community, because it is available in more than 40 languages, and can be used in many disciplines and kinds of projects. As we selected the CT objectives to focus on in the units, we drew on Brennan et al.'s [6] definition of CT in Scratch, which includes concepts (e.g. loops and conditionals), practices (e.g. debugging and remixing), and perspectives (e.g. participating in computing to express, connect, question).

Two other key concepts framing the collaborative design process were translanguaging pedagogy and literate programming [20]. Translanguaging pedagogy–the idea that teachers should leverage students' dynamic language resources to support their learning –

has been applied in many teaching and learning fields to advance equity in education, especially for emergent bilinguals [11]. Traditional bilingual pedagogies focus on the extent to which students' practices conform to standard named languages, locating "problems" in students that schools could "fix" [33]. Translanguaging pedagogy instead embraces speakers who have been traditionally marginalized for their language practices in education and policy. This pedagogy encourages teachers to understand and build on students' repertoires [12], much in the way that culturally relevant and responsive models ask teachers to build on students' cultural practices [21, 22]. Culturally relevant [14] and responsive [31] computing approaches have been readily taken up in the CS education community as part of efforts to broaden participation in the field. In this study, we applied translanguaging pedagogy to the design of CS learning environments to promote equity in this discipline for emergent bilinguals. Our other guiding principle, literate programming, is a concept many associate with Donald Knuth's programming environments, which supported turning English into pseudocode, and finally into computer code plus embedded comments. His broader philosophy helps us view programming not as the mere construction of code for a computer to execute, but as texts humans will read, write, and discuss, just as people interact around other texts.

With these lenses in mind, we developed curriculum that provided multiple opportunities for students to draw upon their language resources and to communicate about, with, and through code. First, teachers described their knowledge of students and their languages practices. Then, they surfaced the specific subject-area content objectives that they were expected to cover in their typical units of study. Together, we discussed how language and content objectives might be enhanced through integration with CS and students' interests and practices. This process led to unique CS-integrated unit plans which were relevant to students' experiences and language resources. At the school in this study, we were inspired by another initiative at the school that had brought authors of young adult novels to classrooms to read and dialogue with students. Sixth and 7th grade language arts students produced three Scratch projects: a remix of a simple "telenovela" dialogue, a remix of a project where users could practice conducting a bilingual "interview" of a character or an author of a story they read, and a "talk show" style project featuring a bilingual dialogue between book characters or authors. Teachers planned individual lessons in the unit to ensure that there were ample opportunities for students to make sense of code through writing, drawing, and speaking about it bilingually, for example, though annotations of code printed on paper, and the commenting feature within Scratch.

3 RESEARCH QUESTIONS AND METHODS

The research question guiding our analysis was: how, when, and why do students translanguage (draw on a range of linguistic, social, and semiotic resources) as they learn computational thinking? Given that not much is known about the performance of emergent bilinguals in CS education, our study seeks to explore the terrain: we are not interested in evaluating a particular intervention against a set of criteria, but rather, aim to better describe students' language use. For this, our study follows a naturalistic, qualitative descriptive paradigm [23]. We draw from a methodology in applied linguistics called "moment analysis" [34], which seeks to analyze the creativity and criticality of multilinguals' language-in-use at important "translanguaging moments" as well as research participants' sense-making and metacommentary about those practices.

To conduct moment analysis, the researcher collects both recordings of naturally occurring interactions and metalanguaging data – the commentary of language users about their language practices and decisions. In this study, researchers conducted 50 hours of classroom observation during periods when teachers were conducting the CS-integrated units. During observations, researchers recorded field notes and audio of whole class discussions, and of small groups of particular focal students at work on unit activities. We took photographs of students' screens, and collected student work samples. We also conducted focus groups with students, which combined questions from artifact-based interviews [7] – meant to elicit communication about particular computational thinking practices like remixing, debugging, and experimenting – with questions meant to elicit students' meta-commentary about their language choices.

The findings we present below were generated through a series of analysis procedures. We flagged moments in our field notes and student work samples that showcased the creativity of students' translanguaging, and/or their engagement with computational thinking. We brought some of these examples to the broader RPP team to reflect upon. Two collaborative descriptive inquiry sessions (CDI) [17] were conducted with our team's teachers and researchers, centered around these artifacts. CDI protocols set out a focus question, ask those present to first describe using non-evaluative language what they noticed, and then to use those noticings to prompt inferential answers to the focus question, plus recommendations and action. During CDI sessions, researchers and teachers from these schools and others described student work examples and commentary from focus groups, sharing what we thought they demonstrated about students' learning.

4 FINDINGS

Our analysis substantiated four "existence proof" claims about student translanguaging. We saw that 1) students' translanguaging practices in CS learning contexts blur linguistic, disciplinary, and modal boundaries, 2) computational literacies are intertwined with the many other literacies students bring with them, 3) students' language attitudes and activity contexts around them play a role in their translanguaging, and 4) students translanguage in order to engage in specific CT practices (like remixing and abstraction). In the section below, we describe sample critical moments that illustrate each of these claims. Due to space limitations we can not include all of the relevant critical moments supporting these claims, however, we detected no contradictory examples in our much larger dataset of field notes and analytic memos.

4.1 Moment 1: "Predicting" Code

In one activity, seventh graders were given "Scratch cards"–a resource produced by the Scratch Education community to serve as starter "recipes" for projects. These particular cards were written in English. Students were asked to predict on a sticky note what they thought the code on the card would make happen on the screen.

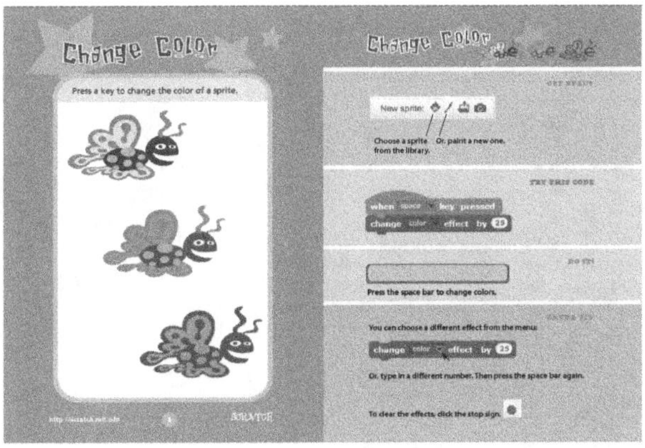

Figure 1: The Scratch card that Julio used to make his sticky-note prediction.

One student Julio, who had arrived in New York from the Dominican Republic the previous school year, wrote: "El personaje cabia el color conforme a la vanderita por ejemplo: rojo azul y verde. Son mi predision." Translation: "The character changes color along with the little flag, for example, red blue and green, is my prediction."

This example supports claims one and two. First, it demonstrates how students' translanguaging blurs linguistic boundaries between named languages. Julio told us he was more comfortable using Spanish over English. At the same time, he drew on the English he knew and English/Spanish cognates such as color/color to help him interpret the English text and Scratch codes on the card. He then recast his understanding of the English card on his sticky note in a way that made sense to him (using Spanish). In this example, Julio also translanguaged "beyond" named languages. His response employs the word "vanderita" a term that he and peers spontaneously generated to refer to the green flag button in Scratch ("vanderita" is a diminutive form of the Spanish word bandera, meaning flag, spelled phonetically by Julio). Even if his response is written using language forms that might not appear in formal dictionaries, he is using his repertoire to help him make meaning of the code. Julio may also be interpreting the graphic features of the Scratch card, such as the images of the butterfly changing color. Supporting claim two is the idea that his response features words that are frequently employed in the language arts discipline, such as "el personaje" (the character) and "predision" (prediction, spelled by Julio in Spanish with invented spelling). By drawing on all of his linguistic and semiotic resources – including English/Spanish cognates, images, and discipline-specific words – Julio expresses his budding understanding of concepts such as how computer programs include events that trigger various behaviors.

4.2 Moment 2: "I don't like Spanish"

In one activity, students were asked to remix a simple project where two sprites dialogue in Spanish with each other in a kind of "telenovela." As Jack, a sixth grade student who said he grew up in the US but identified as Dominican, was working on his remix, he expressed that he wanted to change the conversation to English, stating: "I don't like Spanish, it's too hard." Many of the peers he called on for support with his project, however, typically used Spanish in their interactions with him. One student spoke in mostly Spanish as she showed him how to use Google Translate to change the text strings of his project from one language to another.

As the unit progressed, Jack wanted to share his work on Scratch with his peers, and it became necessary for him to translanguage. At times he used English words he knew his bilingual peers would understand, at other times, he practiced oral and written Spanish, supplementing words with gestures (pointing at particular parts of the screen), and also engaging with them digitally through "likes" on Scratch projects (selecting the heart or star icons on project pages). In one instance Jack observed another student remixing his own project in the Spanish language interface of Scratch, then modified his own code using the English language interface to match hers. (Scratch's interface allows changing not only the user interface elements between English and many other languages, it also changes the keywords displayed on the code blocks.)

Jack's teacher, knowing he was reluctant to practice Spanish, consciously paired him with a student who more often used Spanish, and would benefit from Jack's preference for English. In this way, both students had authentic contexts for practicing new language, and in the end, Jack's remix featured a great deal of Spanish text, which helped him ensure his work would be accessible to his classmates. After presenting his project to the class, he stated: "When I was working with [female student], she was helping me with some of the words, because they were had misspellings in Spanish. And I was helping her with the ones that she had misspellings in English... I liked peer editing because I need help sometimes with my grammar."

This example supports our third claim that students' language attitudes and the activity contexts around them play a role in their translanguaging. Jack's initial attitude made him resistant to use Spanish in his Scratch projects and interactions with peers around Scratch. As he discovered, given his peers' language preferences and his desire to share his Scratch project and process with them, he would benefit from occasionally using language he found "too hard." The teacher's strategic pairing of Jack with a student more comfortable using Spanish pushed both students to practice new forms of language, expanding their repertoires.

4.3 Moment 3: Interviewing a *bachatero*

In one activity, students were shown an interactive Scratch project in which the user simulates interviewing the author of a novel through multiple choice Q&A. The teachers at this school recommended that students remix the project by choosing a different author or book character to interview—but students had other ideas. Students selected figures from sports such as Stephen Curry, or pop culture, like Nicki Minaj and the reggaeton artists, Bad Bunny and Osuna. One 7th grade student, Diani, decided she wanted users of her project to interview her favorite bachata singer, Romeo Santos. This required her to draw on what she knew about this artist to ask him informed questions, and to import photos from the internet. This detail provides evidence for our second claim, that students think about computational practices such as remixing in integrated ways with their own interests and literacy practices they are familiar with – in this case, her knowledge of pop culture. As Diani planned

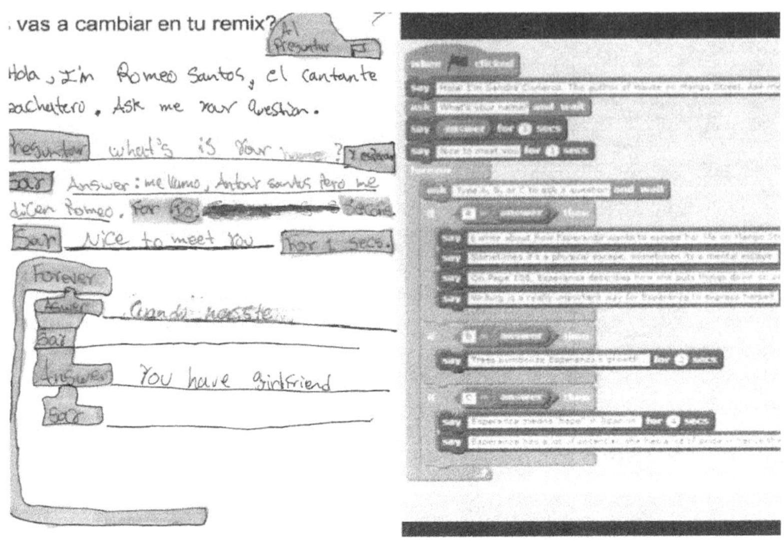

Figure 2: The remix plan that Diani drew on paper before coding in Scratch.

her remix of the "Meet the Author" project, her teacher gave her an opportunity to look at the code for the project – represented with English code blocks on the right side of a handout – and to plan out her modifications on the left side of the handout before using the digital Scratch interface. To complete this task, Diani engaged in translanguaging across linguistic and modal boundaries, supporting our first claim. She translanguaged across named language boundaries because the subject of her interview was himself, a well-known bilingual person. For this, her character Santos "says" to users: "Hola, I'm Romeo Santos, el cantante bachatero [the bachata singer]. Ask me your question," and the questions she would enable users to ask the singer included: "What's is your name?" "Cuando naciste" [When were you born?] and "You have girlfriend."

The representation of her remix plan also employed modes beyond written language. She drew representations of Scratch code blocks using English keywords (the "say... for one sec" and "forever" blocks in the figure). While the handout was printed in black and white, Diani colored certain code blocks in orange corresponding to the color of many common Scratch blocks. She also drew invented blocks which featured Spanish and English keywords, such as the first orange block pictured at the top of her drawing which has the keywords "Al preguntar [flag]," which would literally translate to "When you ask the flag." This representation combines the "Al presionar [flag]" block and the "preguntar" blocks in the Spanish interface of Scratch ("When [flag] clicked" and "ask" blocks in the English interface.) The way she translanguages across modal and linguistic boundaries in this example is reminiscent of the way beginning writers sound out words and use invented spelling to help them write a story. This aspect of the classroom moment demonstrates the range of linguistic and modal resources students draw upon, supporting claim 1.

Further down the page, she combined the commands "answer - say - answer" in a representation of a block next to English and Spanish text of questions she wanted Santos to answer. While there is no such code block, it captures a simple algorithm for a back-and-forth conversation between people in an interview. In this instance, Diani translanguages as she employs the computational thinking practice "abstraction," or creating steps to represent the real-world phenomena she is interested in. Diani translanguages as she plans her remix and engages in abstraction. This moment supports our fourth claim that students translanguage in order to engage in specific CT practices.

4.4 Moment 4: Bilingual conversation with Shakira

In a second project, students were asked to use Scratch to portray a dialogue between an interviewer and a character of a book. Julio and his partner, Yadira, decided their interviewee would be Esperanza, the main character of the novel House on Mango Street. They took their time deciding who the interviewer would be. First, they discussed choosing Nicki Minaj, the pop singer, but decided against it since she only speaks English. They then considered a Spanish-speaking pop singer, but decided that her particular accent in Spanish would be too difficult for them to emulate when recording. It was important to the students that they be able to provide the voices for these characters. Shakira, they determined, would be the perfect person to interview Esperanza, because she can bridge two languages, and would help amplify the audience of their Scratch project. When asked why it was important that the interviewer speak both languages, Julio responded, "porque también la gente que hable inglés también al verlo puede entender un poco de lo que se está hablando y la gente que hable español también no se desincluye" [because people who also speak English can understand a little bit of what's being talked about, and the people who speak Spanish also won't be excluded.] The dialog between Julio and Yadira as they discuss their chosen characters, and Julio's comments describing why he values the bilingualism in his project, supports claim three that students' language attitudes and the activity context play a role in translanguaging. We also

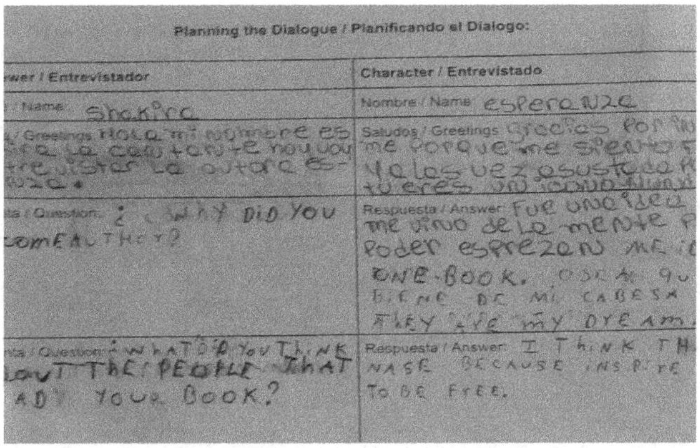

Figure 3: Julio and Yadira's script for their Scratch dialogue, featuring Shakira.

see students' translanguaging help them use computing to express and connect with local audiences – key computational thinking perspectives [6], supporting claim 4.

Julio and Yadira wrote a script for their characters using both English and Spanish. Given they wanted to ask at least one question using all English, they chose to practice writing out the standard English sentence structure for questions. As they recorded (and re-recorded) their dialogue as audio in the "sound" section of the Scratch software, the students translanguaged between modes – their written text, and their oral interpretation of it. Students drew on disciplinary literacies that are encouraged in their language arts class (making inferences about characters' emotions based on text-based evidence) as they imagined how the character's tone of voice would change if she were to meet the famous Shakira. As they sequenced the code blocks to animate their sprites, their speech was peppered with Scratch keywords in both Spanish and English. Throughout the planning process and as they built their project, this pair of students translanguaged across and beyond named languages, modalities, and code (supporting claim 1).

5 DISCUSSION

Guided by the theory of translanguaging, this study aimed to document the diverse language practices of bilingual students, and to validate them as meaning-making resources in computer science education. Through moment analysis, we generated four claims that we illustrated with examples, namely: 1) that students' translanguaging practices in CS learning contexts blur linguistic, disciplinary, and modal boundaries, 2) computational literacies are intertwined with the many other literacies students bring with them, 3) students' language attitudes and activity contexts around them play a role in their translanguaging, and 4) students translanguage in order to engage in specific CT practices (like remixing and abstraction).

Similar to the literate programming philosophy, we see evidence that students can and do use their full linguistic repertoire as they leverage into new competencies and discourses. They express computational ideas through code and many other associated representations such as sprites, audiofiles, text and so on. These ideas are not divorced from other literacies the students bring to bear, whether it is their literacy in the norms and forms of a telenovela, or their understandings of how to craft a message for a particular audience. Nor are their computing practices divorced from their values about languages and bilingualism. Students' computing in this project was driven by their desire to connect with their bilingual peers who had varying experiences with English and Spanish, which meant their choices about sprites and scripts were tied up with their perceptions of their own and others' language use. Moreover, as students came to value their own fluency in Scratch, it was deeply influenced by how that skill intersected with their cultural, linguistic, and disciplinary literacies.

Our original research question asked about the use of translanguaging while students learn computational thinking. In the classroom profiled in this study, doing computer science meant becoming a part of the classroom community though use of multiple named languages, code, and shared references to pop culture and books. These moments shifted our view away from translanguaging as a process that co-occurs with or mediates learning computational thinking, and encouraged us to begin considering computational literacies as the real goal, through the lens of translanguaging. By "computational literacies" we mean ways of creating and communicating about, with, and through computational artifacts (like code, datasets, and models) for particular purposes, and in and for communities. In this way, computation is participating in a community of discourse, i.e., being able to co-construct meaning with a larger community of interlocutors [18]. Viewing CS as participating in computational literacies prompts educators to ask the question: "What conversation is this code a part of?"

Translanguaging has implications not only for how emergent bilingual students use home language and English as they participate in computational literacies, but also how all students, including monolingual students, leverage across and beyond human and computational languages and representations. It also means that educators should not treat computer science education as pursuing fixed learning progressions of computational concepts with 'remediation' or 'differentiation' for emergent bilinguals. Rather, educators must think more about how to join the varied literacies students bring to the classroom with potential computational literacies they could participate in through translanguaging. This is as true for teachers of monolingual learners as it is for emergent bilinguals, since each student brings their distinct repertoires and values to the domain of computation. Translanguaging provides an important lens to help us describe and support this process. Understanding students' translanguaging can help teachers design CS projects and lessons that support all learners more equitably.

ACKNOWLEDGMENTS

The authors would like to thank the students and teachers that participated in this research. This material is based on work supported by the US National Science Foundation under Grant Nos. CNS-1738645 and DRL-1837446. Any opinions, findings, and conclusions or recommendations expressed in this material are those of the author(s) and do not necessarily reflect the views of the National Science Foundation.

REFERENCES

[1] 2015. *An Economic Snapshot of Washington Heights and Inwood.* Technical Report 2-2016. Office of the State Comptroller, New York City. https://www.osc.state.ny.us/osdc/rpt2-2016.pdf

[2] 2016. A Framework for K-12 Computer Science Education. https://k12cs.org/

[3] 2017. *Common Core of Data: America's Public Schools.* Technical Report. National Center for Education Statistics. https://nces.ed.gov/ccd/tables/ACGR_RE_and_characteristics_2015-16.asp

[4] 2017. Supporting the Study of World Languages and Computer Science. https://www.actfl.org/news/position-statements/supporting-the-study-world-languages-and-computer-science

[5] 2018. *The Condition of Education: English Language Learners in Public Schools.* Technical Report. National Center for Education Statistics. https://nces.ed.gov/programs/coe/indicator_cgf.asp

[6] Karen Brennan, Michelle Chung, Wendy Martin, Francisco Cervantes, Bill Tally, and Mitchel Resnick. [n. d.]. *Computational Thinking With Scratch.* Online. Harvard Graduate School of Education and the Education Development Center Inc. http://scratched.gse.harvard.edu/ct/index.html

[7] Karen Brennan and Mitchel Resnick. 2012. Using artifact-based interviews to study the development of computational thinking in interactive media design. Vancouver, BC, Canada. http://scratched.gse.harvard.edu/ct/files/AERA2012.pdf

[8] Virginia P. Collier and Wayne P. Thomas. 2017. Validating the Power of Bilingual Schooling: Thirty-Two Years of Large-Scale, Longitudinal Research. *Annual Review of Applied Linguistics* 37 (Sept. 2017), 203–217. https://doi.org/10.1017/S0267190517000034

[9] Division of English Language Learners and Student Support. 2018. *English Language Learner Demographics Report for the 2016-17 School Year.* Technical Report. New York City Department of Education, New York, NY. http://schools.nyc.gov/NR/rdonlyres/3A4AEC4C-14BD-49C4-B2E6-8EDF5D873BE4/223369/201617DemographicReportFINALSpring20191.pdf

[10] Ofelia García. 2009. *Bilingual Education in the 21st Century: A Global Perspective* (1 edition ed.). Wiley-Blackwell, Malden, MA ; Oxford.

[11] Ofelia García, Susana Ibarra Johnson, and Kate Seltzer. 2017. *The Translanguaging Classroom: Leveraging Student Bilingualism for Learning.* Caslon Publishing, Philadelphia.

[12] Ofelia García and Tatyana Kleyn (Eds.). 2016. *Translanguaging with Multilingual Students: Learning from Classroom Moments.* Routledge, New York.

[13] Ofelia García and Li Wei. 2014. *Translanguaging: Language, bilingualism and education.* Palgrave Macmillan Pivot, London, United Kingdom. http://www.palgrave.com%2Fpage%2Fdetail%2Ftranslanguaging-ofelia-garcia%2F%3Fisb%3D9781137385758

[14] Joanna Goode and Jane Margolis. 2011. Exploring Computer Science: A Case Study of School Reform. *TOCE* 11, 2 (2011), 12. https://doi.org/10.1145/1993069.1993076

[15] Grantmakers for Education. 2013. *Educating English Language Learners: Grantmaking Strategies for Closing America's Other Achievement Gap.* Technical Report. https://edfunders.org/sites/default/files/Educating%20English%20Language%20Learners_April%202013.pdf

[16] Shuchi Grover and Roy Pea. 2013. Using a Discourse-intensive Pedagogy and Android's App Inventor for Introducing Computational Concepts to Middle School Students. In *Proceeding of the 44th ACM Technical Symposium on Computer Science Education (SIGCSE '13).* ACM, New York, NY, USA, 723–728. https://doi.org/10.1145/2445196.2445404

[17] Margaret Himley and Patricia F. Carini. 2000. *From Another Angle: Children's Strengths and School Standards : the Prospect Center's Descriptive Review of the Child.* Teachers College Press. Google-Books-ID: ERNnJChzRywC.

[18] Chris Hoadley and S Favaro. [n. d.]. Digital literacy in higher education. In *The SAGE Encyclopedia of Educational Technology* (1 edition ed.), J. Michael Spector (Ed.). SAGE Publications, Inc, 221–223.

[19] Megan Hopkins. 2016. Beliefs in context: Understanding language policy implementation at a systems level. *Educational Policy* 30, 4 (2016), 573–605. http://journals.sagepub.com/doi/abs/10.1177/0895904814550073

[20] D. E. Knuth. 1984. Literate Programming. *Comput. J.* 27, 2 (Jan. 1984), 97–111. https://doi.org/10.1093/comjnl/27.2.97

[21] Gloria Ladson-Billings. 1995. But that's just good teaching! The case for culturally relevant pedagogy. *Theory into practice* 34, 3 (1995), 159–165. http://www.tandfonline.com.ezproxy.gc.cuny.edu/doi/pdf/10.1080/00405849509543675

[22] Gloria Ladson-Billings. 2007. Pushing Past the Achievement Gap: An Essay on the Language of Deficit. *Journal of Negro Education* 76, 3 (2007), 316–323.

[23] Lincoln, Yvonna S. and Guba, Egon G. 1985. *Naturalistic Inquiry* (1st edition ed.). SAGE Publications, Beverly Hills, Calif.

[24] Kate Menken. 2010. NCLB and English Language Learners: Challenges and Consequences. *Theory Into Practice* 49, 2 (April 2010), 121–128. http://dx.doi.org/10.1080/00405841003626619

[25] Kate Menken, Tatyana Kleyn, Laura Ascenzi-Moreno, Nabin Chae, Nelson Flores, and Alexander Funk. 2009. *Meeting the Needs of Long-Term English Language Learners in High School, Phase II.* Technical Report. Report submitted to New York City Department of Education.

[26] Kate Menken and Cristian Solorza. 2015. Principals as linchpins in bilingual education: The need for prepared school leaders. *International Journal of Bilingual Education and Bilingualism* 18, 6 (2015), 676–697. https://katemenken.files.wordpress.com/2011/10/menken-solorza-2015-principals-as-linchpins-published.pdf

[27] New York City Department of Education. [n. d.]. *CS4All "Blueprint".* Technical Report. New York City.

[28] Office of English Language Learners. 2013. *2013 Demographic Report.* Technical Report. New York City Department of Education, New York, NY. http://schools.nyc.gov/NR/rdonlyres/FD5EB945-5C27-44F8-BE4B-E4C65D7176F8/0/2013DemographicReport_june2013_revised.pdf

[29] Ricardo Otheguy, Ofelia García, and Wallis Reid. 2015. Clarifying translanguaging and deconstructing named languages: A perspective from linguistics. *Applied Linguistics Review* 6, 3 (2015), 281–307. https://doi.org/10.1515/applirev-2015-0014

[30] Yogendra Pal and Sridhar Iyer. 2015. Classroom Versus Screencast for Native Language Learners: Effect of Medium of Instruction on Knowledge of Programming. In *Proceedings of the 2015 ACM Conference on Innovation and Technology in Computer Science Education (ITiCSE '15).* ACM, New York, NY, USA, 290–295. https://doi.org/10.1145/2729094.2742618

[31] Kimberly A. Scott, Kimberly M. Sheridan, and Kevin Clark. 2015. Culturally responsive computing: a theory revisited. *Learning, Media and Technology* 40, 4 (2015), 412–436. http://www.tandfonline.com.ezproxy.gc.cuny.edu/doi/abs/10.1080/17439884.2014.924966

[32] Adalbert Gerald Soosai Raj, Kasama Ketsuriyonk, Jignesh M. Patel, and Richard Halverson. 2018. Does Native Language Play a Role in Learning a Programming Language?. In *Proceedings of the 49th ACM Technical Symposium on Computer Science Education (SIGCSE '18).* ACM, New York, NY, USA, 417–422. https://doi.org/10.1145/3159450.3159531

[33] Richard R. Valencia. 2010. *Dismantling contemporary deficit thinking: Educational thought and practice.* Routledge, New York & London. https://books-google-com.ezproxy.gc.cuny.edu/books?hl=en&lr=&id=80tZBwAAQBAJ&oi=fnd&pg=PP1&ots=RIXnFaVYlx&sig=XxQZsK_KNg66wj3bxzoQ6aL9Qp8

[34] Li Wei. 2011. Moment Analysis and translanguaging space: Discursive construction of identities by multilingual Chinese youth in Britain. *Journal of Pragmatics* 43, 5 (April 2011), 1222–1235. https://doi.org/10.1016/j.pragma.2010.07.035

A Cultural Computing Curriculum

James Davis
Rensselaer Polytechnic Institute
Troy, New York
DavisJ20@rpi.edu

Michael Lachney
Michigan State University
East Lansing, Michigan
LachneyM@msu.edu

Zoe Zatz
Rensselaer Polytechnic Institute
Troy, New York
zatzz@rpi.edu

William Babbitt
Rensselaer Polytechnic Institute
Troy, New York
babbw2@rpi.edu

Ron Eglash
University of Michigan
Ann Arbor, Michigan
eglash@umich.edu

ABSTRACT

Broadening the participation of underrepresented students in computer science fields requires careful design and implementation of culturally responsive curricula and technologies. Culturally Situated Design Tools (CSDTs) address this by engaging students in historic, cultural, and meaningful design projects based on community practices. To date, CSDT research has only been conducted in short interventions outside of CS classrooms. This paper reports on the first semester-long introductory CS course based on CSDTs, which was piloted with 51 high school students during the 2017-2018 school year. The goal of this study was to examine if a culturally responsive computing curriculum could teach computer science principles and improve student engagement. Pre-post tests, field notes, weekly teacher meetings, formative assessments, and teacher and student interviews were analyzed to assess successes and failures during implementation. The results indicate students learned the conceptual material in 6 months rather than in the 9 months previously required by the teacher. Students were also able to apply these concepts afterward when programming in Python, implying knowledge transfer. However, student opinions about culture and computing didnâĂŹt improve, and student engagement was below initial expectations. Thus we explore some of the many challenges: keeping a fully integrated cultural curriculum while satisfying CS standards, maintaining student engagement, and building student agency and self-regulation. We end with a brief description for how we intend to address some of these challenges in the second iteration of this program, scheduled for fall 2018. After which a study is planned to compare this curriculum to others.

CCS CONCEPTS

• **Applied computing → Education**; *Interactive learning environments*; *Collaborative learning*;

KEYWORDS

Pilot, Mixed-method, Culture, Curriculum, High School, Introductory, Computer Science, Design, Culturally Situated Design Tools

ACM Reference Format:
James Davis, Michael Lachney, Zoe Zatz, William Babbitt, and Ron Eglash. 2019. A Cultural Computing Curriculum. In *Proceedings of the 50th ACM Technical Symposium on Computer Science Education (SIGCSE '19), February 27-March 2, 2019, Minneapolis, MN, USA.* ACM, New York, NY, USA, 5 pages. https://doi.org/10.1145/3287324.3287439

1 INTRODUCTION

In July of 2017, a high school computer science (CS) teacher lamented that when students in his introductory CS course used Interactive Python they were neither learning nor engaged, and worse yet did not experience the personal and creative satisfaction that programming offers. This teacher works in an urban high school in Upstate New York which included over 50% students underrepresented in CS. Counter to findings by Margolis et. al. [15] that reveal students of color are often faced with shallow CS offerings, this teacher provided students with a rigorous CS curriculum that would lay a foundation to take more advanced CS courses in high school and college. Yet, while the LOGO turtle had been reported by Seymour Papert [16] and colleagues as a motivating factor for young people's engagement with programming decades earlier, its implementation in Interactive Python proved, like the course in general, to be of little interest to his students. Indeed, in this school CS had become yet another course with content decontextualized from students' lives and passions.

To address these challenges, a team of social scientists, technologists, and this teacher collaborated to develop an equally rigorous curriculum called Cultural Computing. It used a suite of culturally responsive educational technologies called Culturally Situated Design Tools (CSDTs) to contextualize CS within African American and Native American cultural practices. The idea behind CSDTs is that computational thinking is already present in many cultural practices; and thus students can benefit by using tools that allow them to "translate" between indigenous or vernacular knowledge in cultural context, and equivalent concepts in the classroom. With CSDTs, students are asked to examine the history and personal significance of cultural practices like cornrow braiding, quilting, and science fiction, then to computationally duplicate existing designs before creating artifacts of their own. This contextualization is a critical component of culturally responsive education, in which

SIGCSE '19, February 27-March 2, 2019, Minneapolis, MN, USA

ACM ISBN 978-1-4503-5890-3/19/02.
https://doi.org/10.1145/3287324.3287439

community, national, and political identities are connected in support of learning [13]. Unlike prior research with CSDTs in small scale workshops of a week or two, this paper reports on a semester long curriculum intended to be implemented in a CS course over several months.

2 BACKGROUND

CS undergraduate degree attainment is notoriously low in terms of gender (17.1% women) and ethnic (1.1% black) diversity [19]. This cannot be entirely accounted for by access. Black students have access to 23% fewer classes than white students, and 17% fewer computers [20], but there is a 1400% underrepresentation in CS degree attainment [19, 20]. Thus there may be other social, economic, and/or psychological barriers for why students do not enter CS in high school and college. To make matters worse, students in CS classes face many of the same challenges as in other classes: uninteresting lecture styles, regimented curricula, and poor scaffolding for future courses. There have been many broad criticisms of CS education in the U.S. as a result.

Some claim that classes are too didactic and do not support the development of formal thinking [16], which may hurt all students, but especially those resistant to authority. Others suggest that student disengagement may be from stereotype threat [6], where students in CS courses may feel, explicit or implicit, as though they cannot succeed because of false, though widespread, societal stereotypes about their race or gender [18]. There are additional claims that students simply do not engage because CS is not an obviously visible and representative part of their culture or community [4], or that teachers can have a genuine interest in their students but there is a cultural gap that can result in miscommunication and frustration [8].

Constructionism is one learning theory that has sought to use coding and design to overcome these issues via low-control exploration in an open and inviting environment [16]. For example, Scratch, a constructionist visual programming environment, aims to address the didactic nature of education by giving students more freedom to design their own programs. Another learning theory tackling these issues is culturally responsive teaching, which grounds teachers' classroom content in the unique cultural competencies of their students [10, 13]. Thus reducing or eliminating false impressions of cultural or racial limitations and supporting better communication with students of different backgrounds. Culturally responsive teaching treats community expertise and cultural competencies as important academic assets and culturally rich sources for student engagement. One offshoot of culturally responsive teaching is culturally responsive computing, which highlights the computational qualities of such community assets and expertise [12, 17].

CSDTs is a suite of culturally responsive computing applications that leverages constructionist design and implementation strategies. Like Scratch, CSDTs have students work within a visual programming environment to design and reverse engineer media but, unlike Scratch, grounds that media in computationally rich cultural artifacts (e.g. Native American quilts and African American braiding techniques). As part of this process, students conduct research on cultural and community practices in small groups to frame the historical, social, and/or political significance of the design they are working with. In the past, CSDTs have been shown to improve student engagement and knowledge acquisition in short term implementations [1, 7]. There has been no research on semester or year long curricula using CSDTs, and the research supporting their design and development has taken place outside of CS courses. As a result, major challenges remain for creating CSDTs and associated curriculum for CS classrooms.

3 CURRICULUM DEVELOPMENT

Based on Interactive Python, which this curriculum was designed to replace, students needed to explore critical CS concepts including: Parameters, Loops, Variables, Conditionals, and Functions while practicing program writing, reading, and debugging. This method of introducing various concepts is less constructionist than desired, but needed to maintain instructor support. To ground material and engage students up front, this material was put first. Then concepts were introduced in the order above because they were considered easiest to hardest. Students were then introduced to programming with tutorials which had previously been shown to be effective<cite pending paper>. Each new unit was introduced by the instructor, who provided a guided practice session, in which they demonstrated the relevant CS concepts while students simultaneously performed the same actions on their own computers. This too came from the instructors personal experience. Then students were provided with cultural artifacts to be created. These artifacts were based on prior work and experiences with various cultural groups. It was hypothesized that some of the scripts would be too challenging for students to create on their own, and so they were provided with parts that were already completed. Students were then asked to create their own designs using their new knowledge.

4 METHODS

A CSDT based curriculum called Cultural Computing was administered in four high school classes, attended by a total 51 students. To assess the curriculum a pre-post test was created. Of the 51 students, we were able to match 33 pre and post tests. Based on the pre-post test demographics, the class identified as, 48% white, 24% black or African American, 6% Hispanic, 3% Asian, and 18% multiracial. Furthermore 24 identified as male, 9 identified as female.

The pre-post assessment consisted of seven main parts, each designed by the research team in collaboration with two external evaluators. Section one of the assessment contained demographic information (e.g. gender and ethnicity). Section two contained four items designed to gather students' perception related to computing. The third section measured students' perceptions related to culture and section four contained students' perceptions as they related to the relationships between computing and culture. The above mentioned close-ended items used a series of six-point "Likert-type" [5] scale: 1=Strongly Disagree, 2=Disagree, 3=Slightly Disagree, 4=Slightly Agree, 5=Agree, 6=Strongly Agree. The fifth section of the assessment used eight vocabulary items with a word bank. The sixth section contained two items asking students to write pseudo code and a multiple choice code question. Seventh and finally, there was a section with three questions on geometric transformations.

While this was a CS course, we sought to measure students' understanding of transformational geometry because each of the CS-DTs that students used to create cultural designs drew on cultural traditions in which the geometric transformations (i.e. rotation, translation, reflection, and dilation) are embedded. Thus the seventh section on this topic helped examine knowledge, transfer, and possible fringe mathematical benefits. This test, and the results, were reviewed and scored by external evaluators.

Additionally, researchers attended most sessions to take field notes and scheduled weekly meetings with the teacher to discuss students' progress and provide constructive criticism that was noted for future iterations of the curriculum. Field notes and teacher meetings focused on class activities and student engagement, with particular attention paid to students' difficulties interacting with the software and online platform. Formative assessments in which students were provided with an end goal, starting costumes, and a list of steps / outcomes and points for each new topic before being asked to complete the design without peer or instructor support. Ethnographic interviews were conducted with three students, which focused on their feelings and future plans as they related to CS and culture. Finally, interviews with the teacher both at the end of the curriculum and after moving to Interactive Python were conducted to assess his perspective on successes and failures of the Cultural Computing curriculum in preparing students to move to a text-based programming environment.

An initial pre-test was administered before students set up accounts and profiles on the CSDT online learning community (csdt .rpi.edu). On this site they learned about the political, social, and historical relevance of the cultural designs they were to spend the semester working with (African American cornrow braiding; Native American, African American, Appalachian quilting traditions; and feminist, indigenous, black and speculative science fiction). After their exploration of these topics they shared what they learned with the rest of the class in the form of Google presentations. They then took an introductory programming tutorial. This was followed by a sequence of units on "parameters," "loops," "variables," "conditionals," and "functions." As part of each unit, a guided practice session given by the teacher, in which he demonstrated the relevant CS concepts while students simultaneously performed the same actions on their own computers. After the guided practice, students were given a programming challenge in which they were to study and manipulate code to finish an incomplete design from one of the cultural areas. After the conditionals unit, but before functions, students were then asked to work in pairs to create their own designs and then physically fabricate them. After the completion of the Cultural Computing curriculum students took a post test before proceeding to an Interactive Python curriculum.

5 RESULTS

No significant differences were found when examining the mean differences within subscores for student perceptions on computing, culture or their relationship on the pre-post assessment (see Table 1). This is consistent with observational data. When students were informally surveyed at the end of the semester, less than one-third of them intended to continue with CS. It is also consistent with our interviews in which two of three students were not able to recognize the relationship between CS and history, politics, community, or culture originally intended to be integrated. One student didn't remember covering the material at all.

Table 1: Within groups attitude differences [11]

Subscore (n=33)	Pre	Post
Perceptions Related to Computing	16.09	16.03
Perceptions Related to Culture	12.91	12.79
Perceptions related to Computing and Culture	12.79	11.09

When looking at individual items in each of these three constructs some notable changes standout beyond interest in pursuing CS (see Table 2). This includes students confidence in explaining CS concepts to middle school students. In addition, while results show a negative change in students' interest in learning about their own culture, students' were more interested in cultural and artistic practices from other cultures. Consistent with these two positive changes, there was a slight positive change in students' confidence that they can use cultural art and designs to teach computer programming to people in their community. Students were also less likely to say CS supported cultural understanding, or cultural practices supported understanding CS. This further confirms the aforementioned observational and interview data. This may have been due to the fact that the teacher front loaded all of the political, historical, and social aspects of the CSDTs and exclusively focused on the CS aspects of the tools for the remainder of the course.

A paired-samples t test was calculated to compare the mean pretest score to the mean post test score for vocabulary: Conditionals, Recursion, Loops, Functions, Variable, Heritage Algorithm, Script and List. The mean on the pretest was 2.67 (sd=1.493) and the mean on the posttest was 4.03 (sd=1.649). A significant increase from pretest to posttest was found ($t(32)=-3.697$, $p<.05$ (see Table 3). These results are well couched in fact that the units of the Cultural Computing curriculum were largely designed around many of these terms (e.g. students spent a whole unit on loops, another on conditionals, and so on). What is more, the teacher taught and reinforced these CS concepts in the course through both lectures and guided practices.

Finally, a paired samples t test was calculated to compared the mean pretest score to the mean post test score for open ended questions around math and programming . The mean on the pretest was 3.70 (sd=2.568), and the mean on the post test was 7.55 (sd=3.193). A significant increase from pretest to post test was found ($t(32)=7.608$, $p<.001$ (Table 4).

This too was consistent with our formative assessments and observations. Some students during the first unit, parameters, challenges required instructor intervention to move images on the screen. In the final unit nearly all students were able to make their own designs that included the concepts from every unit. While the first three formative assessment showed several students completely copying from old projects, and many struggling, the final formative assessment showed most students were able to nearly complete a challenging design independently.

Table 2: Treatment Group Responses to Survey Items [11]

Statement	Pre % agree	Post % agree	Change
I look forward to learning more about how computer programs work.	64	58	-6
I feel confident explaining what computer programming is to someone in middle school.	24	42	+18
I am interested in learning about computer programming in college or in my future work.	52	49	-3
I am interested in learning computer programming on my own time, outside of school.	27	33	+6
I am interested in learning about different cultures and their artistic practices.	39	46	+16
I am interested in learning more about my own cultural heritage.	49	35	-14
Including knowledge of different cultures in school improves learning	46	48	+2
I think that knowing about cultural designs and art will make someone a better computer programmer	42	30	-12
I think that understanding computer programming will better help me understand cultural designs and art such as quilting, braiding and science fiction.	49	30	-19
I can use cultural design and art to teach computer programming to people in my community.	18	30	+12

Table 3: Mean Scores from Pre and Post on Vocabulary Questions [11]

Treatment Group	N	Mean	SD	Change pre to post
Pre	33	2.67	1.493	
Post	33	4.03	1.649	+1.46

Table 4: Paired samples statistics on open-ended math and computing questions [11]

Treatment Group	N	Mean	SD	Change pre to post
Pre	33	3.70	2.568	
Post	33	7.55	3.193	+3.60

However, the rate of this learning was extremely varied. The variables unit, intended for only 2 weeks, lasted 6, with the instructor repeating material and challenges constantly until satisfied students understood it. However, of conditionals and if-else loops the teacher said "I think they [students] immediately grasped it." The teacher frequently stressed that the curricula performed much better than Interactive Python, with students learning all the same material in 6 rather than 9 months. Furthermore, when students moved to text based programming, the teacher stated that they were able to transfer the relevant concepts.

6 DISCUSSION

It is important to note that this study had major limitations. Neither the attitude constructs nor the individual items of the survey were tested for validity or reliability. However, the survey, observations, and interviews indicate together may suggest that student attitude toward CS, culture, and their relationship did not improve. And perhaps equally importantly, students didn't seem to enjoy the class. The questions on the ability of students to program were similarly not validated, but again, agree with formative assessments, observation, and teacher perception that students did learn the material. This failure to engage students is particularly troubling as it's a core goal of both constructionism and culturally responsive teaching. This may be related to separate failures to both maintain a cultural connection and student agency.

Considering the emphasis on culturally responsive computing, the most dramatic issue for this implementation of the Cultural Computing curriculum was the inability to maintain the connections between culture and CS. After initially reading about the historical, political, and economic background sections associated with the CSDTs, the teacher did not address any of these social l dimensions of the cultural designs again. Moreover, the cultural context was constantly switched for different directed lessons, preventing any deeper exploration of the social aspects of the cultural designs by students. Consequently, while some students continued to see the embedded cultural connection, by the time students were working on physical renderings, some had also completely forgotten there was any cultural relevance.

The teacher did not explain why they were reluctant to revisit the social dimensions of the cultural material. Perhaps the fact that it was a CS course and this was what the teacher is trained in, not social studies or history, reflects a lack of cultural competencies and an uncomfortableness in talking about cultural traditions with students in their courses. Like many other technical disciplines, CS often reproduces a social/technical dichotomy. Commonly understood, this dichotomy privileges what is seen as "technical"–the application of math or science–over what is deemed "social" or person-centered activities [9]. The field of science and technology studies has critiqued this dichotomy, arguing what is technical is also social and cultural and, conversely, what is social and cultural is also technical [3]. This multi-directional understanding is exactly what the CSDTs seek to make clear. To overcome this dichotomy, one strategy is to help teachers make strong connections between CS and culture by including and collaborating with those cultural expertise (e.g. an expert in African American braiding techniques) during a programming lesson [2, 12, 14]. While this requires extra effort on the part of the teacher, it has the added benefit of fostering classroom environments that are representative of and inviting for community experts, including people some students may be familiar with and even know personally.

The curriculum failed to instill student agency or allow self-regulation. Students were never allowed to pick their cultural context, as originally planned. Projects were limited or stripped down to make more time for guided lessons. Students were not allowed to set their own goals, overcome their own challenges, or asked to plan out work. Instead guided instruction, in which students performed tasks with the teacher, was so specific that even minor errors in entered values needed instructor intervention. Students were dropped into pre-existing programs, and many of them took longer to struggle to understand how a program worked than to complete a project (making their own script). This lack of control, choice, and relevancy may have influenced students' inattention or disinterest in the classroom.

Despite this, the success of students to learn material is some consolation. Furthermore, this has been extremely effective in collecting data for future improvements. Areas that have changed this coming year include improvements from small technical details, tasks, curricular details, and methodological details. The small technical details include defaulting to saving to the cloud and log in methods; tasks include giving a gradient in challenge difficulty, embedding cultural descriptions in the code, and starting from nothing rather than existing code; curricular details include eliminating lectures, including self-regulatory assignments, and asking students to reach out to their community; and methodological details include collecting more student interviews, structuring observations, and using validated tests where possible.

7 CONCLUSION

Cultural computing successfully improved student learning and performance over the school year. This is a strong indicator that CSDTs can be successfully used to form a year long curricula. However, the end goal of making this introductory high school programming course extremely engaging and facilitating rapid mastery of critical concepts like loops, variables, conditionals, and functions will require further iteration. As such the curriculum will be redesigned and deployed. It is hoped that a controlled study can be arranged.

ACKNOWLEDGMENTS

This work was supported by the National Science Foundation through NSF grant #1640014. Any opinions, findings, and conclusions or recommendations expressed in this material are those of the author(s) and do not necessarily reflect the views of the National Science Foundation.

REFERENCES

[1] William Babbitt, Michael Lachney, Enoch Bulley, and Ron Eglash. 2015. Adinkra Mathematics: A study of Ethnocomputing in Ghana. *Multidisciplinary Journal of Educational Research* 5, 2 (June 2015), 110–135. https://doi.org/10.17583/remie.2015.1399

[2] Audrey Bennett, Ron Eglash, Michael Lachney, and William Babbitt. 2016. Design Agency: Diversifying Computer Science at the Intersections of Creativity and Culture. *Revolutionizing Education through Web-Based Instruction* (2016), 35–56. https://doi.org/10.4018/978-1-4666-9932-8.ch003

[3] Wiebe E. Bijker, Thomas Parke Hughes, and Trevor J. Pinch. 1989. *The Social Construction of Technological Systems: New Directions in the Sociology and History of Technology.* MIT Press. Google-Books-ID: SUCtOwns7TEC.

[4] Sapna Cheryan, Allison Master, and Andrew N. Meltzoff. 2015. Cultural stereotypes as gatekeepers: increasing girls' interest in computer science and engineering by diversifying stereotypes. *Frontiers in Psychology* 6 (2015). https://doi.org/10.3389/fpsyg.2015.00049

[5] Dennis L Clason and Thomas J Dormody. 1994. Analyzing data measured by individual Likert-type items. *Journal of agricultural education* 35 (1994), 4.

[6] Ron Eglash, Juan E. Gilbert, and Ellen Foster. 2013. Toward Culturally Responsive Computing Education. *Commun. ACM* 56, 7 (July 2013), 33–36. https://doi.org/10.1145/2483852.2483864

[7] Ron Eglash, Mukkai Krishnamoorthy, Jason Sanchez, and Andrew Woodbridge. 2011. Fractal Simulations of African Design in Pre-College Computing Education. *Trans. Comput. Educ.* 11, 3 (Oct. 2011), 17:1–17:14. https://doi.org/10.1145/2037276.2037281

[8] Christopher Emdin. 2017. *For White Folks Who Teach in the Hood... and the Rest of Y'all Too: Reality Pedagogy and Urban Education* (reprint edition ed.). Beacon Press.

[9] Wendy Faulkner. 2000. Dualisms, Hierarchies and Gender in Engineering. *Social Studies of Science* 30, 5 (Oct. 2000), 759–792. https://doi.org/10.1177/030631200030005005

[10] Geneva Gay and James A. Banks. 2010. *Culturally Responsive Teaching: Theory, Research, and Practice* (2 edition ed.). Teachers College Press, New York.

[11] Z Score Inc. 2018. Evaluation Memo: RPI STEM+C Partnership, Summer 2018. (2018).

[12] Michael Lachney. 2017. Culturally responsive computing as brokerage: toward asset building with education-based social movements. *Learning, Media and Technology* 42, 4 (Oct. 2017), 420–439. https://doi.org/10.1080/17439884.2016.1211679

[13] Gloria Ladson-Billings. 2013. *The Dreamkeepers: Successful Teachers of African American Children.* John Wiley & Sons. Google-Books-ID: _GQMZsAX0igC.

[14] Dan Lyles, Michael Lachney, Ellen Foster, and Zoe Zatz. 2016. Generative Contexts: Generating value between community and educational settings. *Teknokultura* 13, 2 (2016), 613–637. https://dialnet.unirioja.es/servlet/articulo?codigo=5764112

[15] Jane Margolis, Rachel Estrella, Joanna Goode, Jennifer Jellison Holme, and Kim Nao. 2010. *Stuck in the Shallow End: Education, Race, and Computing.* The MIT Press, Cambridge, MA.

[16] Seymour Papert. 1980. *Mindstorms: Children, Computers, and Powerful Ideas.* Basic Books, Inc., New York, NY, USA.

[17] Kimberly A. Scott and Patricia Garcia. 2016. Techno-Social Change Agents: Fostering Activist Dispositions Among Girls of Color. *Meridians* 15, 1 (2016), 65–85. https://doi.org/10.2979/meridians.15.1.05

[18] Claude M. Steele. 2011. *Whistling Vivaldi: How Stereotypes Affect Us and What We Can Do* (reprint edition ed.). W. W. Norton & Company, New York.

[19] Stuart Zweben and Betsy Bizot. 2017. *Generation CS Continues to Produce Record Undergrad Enrollment; Graduate Degree Production Rises at both Master's and Doctoral Levels.* Technical Report. Computing Research Association. 3–51 pages. https://cra.org/crn/wp-content/uploads/sites/7/2017/05/2016-Taulbee-Survey.pdf

[20] US Census. 2017. *Race and Ethnicity.* Technical Report. U.S. Department of Commerce. https://www.census.gov/mso/www/training/pdf/race-ethnicity-onepager.pdf

Stitching the Loop with Electronic Textiles

Promoting Equity in High School Students' Competencies and Perceptions of Computer Science

Yasmin B. Kafai[†] kafai@upenn.edu
Deborah A. Fields* deborah.fields@usu.edu
Debora A. Lui[†] deblui@upenn.edu
Justice T. Walker[†] justicew@gse.upenn.edu
Mia S. Shaw[†] mshaw12@gse.upenn.edu
Gayithri Jayathirtha[†] gayithri@gse.upenn.edu
Tomoko M. Nakajima° tnak@493@g.ucla.edu
Joanna Goode‡ goodej@uoregon.edu
Michael T. Giang^ mtgiang@cpp.edu

[†]Graduate School of Education, University of Pennsylvania, Philadelphia, PA, U.S.A.
*Instructional Technologies and Learning Sciences, Utah State University, Logan, UT U.S.A.
°Urban Schooling, University of California, Los Angeles, Los Angeles, CA U.S.A.
‡Education Studies, University of Oregon, Eugene, OR, U.S.A.
^Psychology and Sociology, Cal Poly Pomona, Pomona, CA U.S.A.

ABSTRACT

Many efforts of curricula design have concentrated on expanding participation in K-12 CS education by introducing innovative approaches but few have focused on addressing longstanding equity issues through their choices of culturally relevant materials and activities. In this paper, we describe our efforts in using electronic textiles which include Arduino-based microcontrollers that are sewn with conductive thread on fabrics to connect actuators and sensors and create interactive wearables. We report on the implementation of an electronic textiles curricular unit in the *Exploring Computer Science* introductory computing course in 13 high schools involving 272 high school students largely from underrepresented groups in a major metropolitan school district. We examined two issues relevant to broadening equitable participation in CS: (1) students' changed perceptions of computing, and (2) students' depth of learning of computing, circuitry and crafting in the final project. Pre/post surveys on students' perceptions of computing showed positive, significant gains in students' self-confidence in solving CS problems, fascination with computing and ability to be creative with computing. Teacher evaluations of students' final projects revealed robust learning in the areas of basic programming and computational circuitry as well as strong learning across more challenging computational concepts, with room for growth. We discuss factors that impacted student outcomes and outline steps for further analysis.

SIGCSE '19, February 27-March 2, 2019, Minneapolis, MN, USA

ACM ISBN 978-1-4503-5890-3/19/02...$15.00
https://doi.org/10.1145/3287324.3287426

CCS CONCEPTS

• Social and professional topics → Computer science education; Computational thinking • K-12 Education

KEYWORDS

high school computer science, electronic textiles, equity, computer science education, curriculum, Exploring Computer Science, computer science attitudes

ACM Reference format:

Yasmin B. Kafai, Deborah A. Fields, Debora A. Lui, Justice T. Walker, Mia S. Shaw, Gayithri Jayathirtha, Tomoko M. Nakajima, Joanna Goode, and Michael T. Giang. 2019. Stitching the Loop: Results from an Electronic Textiles Curriculum on High School Students' Competencies and Perspectives of Computer Science. In *Proceedings of 50th ACM Technical Symposium on Computer Science Education (SIGCSE '19), February 27-Mar. 2, 2019, Minneapolis, MN, USA.* ACM, New York, NY, USA, 7 pages. https://doi.org/10.1145/3287324.3287426

1 Introduction

Current national initiatives to expand computer science to all through K-12 education face many formidable challenges in addressing the lack of access to computers, courses, and teachers [23] as well as missing teacher preparation and certification [7]. Efforts have also concentrated on developing curricula for K-12 education that contextualize introductory CS concepts and practices by using application design or integrating CS into other disciplinary content (e.g., science [35], mathematics [32]); however, few efforts have focused on promoting culturally-relevant contexts and activities [14] that address the needs of underrepresented groups.

Most well-known efforts in culturally-relevant computing design and tools (e.g., [8]) leverage connections between existing cultural practices and concepts of computing. More recent developments have focused on bringing in materials and practices that promote the design of new computing artifacts. One example includes electronic textiles (hereafter: e-textiles) that connect sewable microcontrollers with conductive thread to actuators such as LEDs as well as sound, light or touch sensors to make interactive craft projects [3]. Such projects are far more popular with female designers than traditional Arduino projects whose designers tend to be predominantly male and focus on robot and drone designs [4]. Research on e-textiles in K-12 education has shown their potential to introduce basic circuitry [29] and computing to high school students [19]. However, studies in which students design multiple and more advanced e-textile projects and in which classroom teachers (rather than researchers) lead the intervention are still rare and the focus of this paper.

In this paper, we describe the implementation of our e-textile high school curriculum unit and how this influenced student perceptions and learning competencies. Our unit is situated within the larger context of *Exploring Computer Science* [12], an introductory year-long computer science curriculum. Three equity issues—broadening access, diversifying representation (by privileging non-dominant CS learners, techniques, and artifacts), and deepening participation—formed the impetus for developing the e-textiles curriculum [9]. We report on the content of the curriculum unit and its implementation in 15 classrooms (in 13 schools) with 272 high school students from largely underserved communities in a major metropolitan school district to address the following research questions: (1) To what degree was there equity in changing perceptions of CS across students? and (2) To what degree did all students demonstrate depth of competence in computing, circuitry and crafting, in finishing the final, and most challenging project of the unit? To evaluate these questions, we used pre/post surveys on students' perceptions of CS and teacher evaluations of students' final projects. In the discussion, we address opportunities and challenges of implementing equitable CS activities.

2 Background

The focus on curriculum reform in CS education began in the early 2000s with NSF's support in the development, piloting, and scaling of year-long introductory and advanced computer science courses, resulting in *Exploring Computer Science* and *AP Computer Science Principles* [6]. These courses were explicitly designed with the belief that a more engaging and culturally responsive curriculum would attract and retain students from historically underrepresented groups. In addition to these well-established foundational courses, there has been a rhizomatic spread of curricular efforts that have showcased innovative and novel approaches to teaching high school students about particular topics or approaches to computing. These include (1) courses with a foundational breadth approach to teaching computer science (e.g., *CS Discoveries* by code.org), (2) courses which focus on particular application design such as games [30], and (3) courses which are situated within disciplinary STEM contexts such as *Bootstrap* for algebra [32] or *StarLogo* for complex systems in science [35].

There have been far fewer efforts in course development which situate key computational concepts and practices in culturally-relevant contexts [8]. For instance, *Exploring Computer Science* (hereafter: ECS) was specifically developed to challenge the persisting underrepresentation of women and people of Color in computing, as well as the systemic and political barriers that continue to exist in computer science education [14]. In ECS, students learn through inquiry and project-based activities, and develop a repertoire of computational practices [12] which connect computing with students' everyday experiences [33]. Over the last 10 years, ECS has prepared over 3000 teachers through a comprehensive two-year professional development program. Each year, approximately 50,000 diverse high school students enroll in ECS courses across the nation.

We chose to situate our e-textile unit within ECS because the design of its curriculum activities and teaching already addresses aspects considered critical for equity-minded and inquiry-oriented programming instruction [27] such as (1) *time* because students are introduced to a variety of CS concepts and practices within the context of a year-long curriculum, (2) *diversity* because students engage with a range of different CS contexts such as data science, robotics, programming and HCI, and (3) *reflection* because students review and describe their learning throughout the curriculum. Previous evaluations have consistently demonstrated that ECS is successful in significantly increasing students' perceptions of CS [13, 24].

In this larger scale implementation across many classrooms, we wanted to examine whether these initial successes of broadening students' perspectives and deepening their learning about CS would extend to the new e-textile unit. We wondered if the introduction of personalized handcrafts in conjunction with electronics in academic CS classes within schools that serve marginalized populations, would help broaden students' interest and perspectives about CS. Handcrafts practices are more inclusive of gendered [28] and indigenous [25] influences, can help students strengthen connections to history and cultures, and can be linked to content knowledge in school. Although such work has been long considered vocational, non-academic, and low-tech [31] in contrast to most CS activities that require programming, engineering skills, and high-tech tools, their inclusion diversifies materials and practices to promote interest and broaden application. Furthermore, designing open-ended projects with e-textiles is unlike the more constrained design of robotics or games in other ECS units and allows students to personalize their designs.

In terms of deepening student learning about CS, we entered new territory. Most previous e-textile activities in K-12 education focused on students' learning simple circuits or relatively basic lighting sequences rather than engaging more extensively with computing [15]. In designing our curriculum, we included a series of increasingly difficult e-textile projects that introduced challenging concepts in coding, circuitry, and crafting [9]. Furthermore, prior e-textiles activities in after-school, museum, and even classroom settings were almost all facilitated by researchers (e.g., [2, 18, 21]), whereas existing CS classroom teachers led our program implementation with their own students. We know from pilot implementations of the e-textile unit within two ECS classrooms that teachers used equitable practices such as modeling mistakes, legitimizing student expertise, and promoting connected learning in their public-school classrooms with up to 35 students [9, 10, 11]. In this study we expanded our pilot implementation to 15 classrooms and examined to what degree the e-textiles unit was able to reach all students in breadth of interest and depth of learning.

3 Methods

3.1 Curriculum Content

ECS and e-textile experts co-developed the curricular unit to be taught as one of the final units of the ECS course, replacing either the *Data* or *Robotics* units. The resulting e-textile activities follows the ECS model, containing big ideas and recommended lesson plans, with much room for teachers to interpret and bring in their own approaches. In the design of the four e-textiles projects, we prioritized helping students learn challenging concepts in computing, electronics, and crafting while also supporting personal expression and design (for design principles of the unit, see [17]; for descriptions of all projects, see [9, 10]). The fourth and final project incorporates a handmade human sensor created from two aluminum foil conductive patches that when squeezed generate a range of data (see Figure 1, Project #4). Students must determine the range of data useful for their project (how hard they want people to squeeze) and break that into a set of at least four conditions that trigger different lighting patterns (e.g., no squeezing, light squeezing, hard squeezing, etc.).

Figure 1: Samples of the four types of e-textile projects.

While introducing new circuitry and crafting skills, the e-textiles unit builds on students' prior programming skills developed through the ECS Scratch unit. Drawing upon student understanding of computational concepts such as sequences, loops, conditionals, and variables, it requires students to apply these in a new context: a text-based programming language (Arduino). In addition, students learn new programming skills such as nested conditionals, data input from sensors, and functions. Learning these challenging skills in the context of making handcrafted, personalized objects helped support our goal of diversifying the computational artifacts used in CS classes.

3.2 Participants

In Spring 2017, the ECS-school district liaison in a large metropolitan area in California sent an invitation to the ECS-teacher listserv for educators to participate in the third and final year of the e-textiles pilot study. Teachers and school sites were chosen by the liaison for their diverse teaching styles, to maximize the variety of feedback on the curriculum. The liaison included himself as a pilot teacher. Lastly, when two teachers announced their need to take maternity leave mid-pilot, the replacement teachers were identified through snowball sampling. The final number of educators was 15 with teaching experience ranging from 3 and 37 years; most but not all also had taught ECS for several years. All teachers engaged in four days of e-textile professional development over a period of four months, where they became familiar with the curriculum by creating the projects from the unit and reflecting on the pedagogy used during professional development.

In Spring 2018, 15 teachers implemented the e-textile unit in their ECS classes; classes ranged from 20-42 students. The unit lasted between 8 and 13 weeks, depending on the classroom. There was a wide variety in approaches and modifications among implementing teachers. Over 430 students participated but only 359 provided consent to collect their data for research purposes. Of these 272 completed both pre- and post-surveys. For participating schools, percentages of students from ethnically underrepresented groups (i.e., non-white) ranged between 72% and 99%; English as a second language between 2% and 41%; and those with reduced lunch between 47% and 97%.

3.3 Data Collection

To investigate student perceptions and learning, we focused on two sources of data: (1) students' perceptions of CS and their own competence using a pre-post survey, and (2) teachers' evaluations of student competence (via a grading rubric assessment of students' final e-textile project #4, with human sensors).

3.3.1 Student Pre-Post Surveys. Students were given a CS in E-Textiles Survey before (pre-survey) and immediately after (post-survey) participating with the ECS electronic textiles unit. At the demographic level, students answered questions about gender, ethnic identification, prior experience with CS courses, language spoken at home, and family college attainment. In terms of their perceptions about CS, five categories were assessed using a 4-point Likert scale (ranged from strongly disagree (1) to strongly agree (4): (1) *self-confidence* in solving CS-based problems (5 items; e.g., "I think I am very good at explaining my solutions to technical problems"), (2) *fascination* with CS (4 items; e.g., "Designing new things makes me feel excited"), (3) *value* of CS in future endeavors (2 items; e.g., "knowing computer science is important for contributing to my community"), (4) the ability to *express personally* through CS activities (3 items; e.g., I can be creative in computer science"), and (5) the ability to carry out *electronic textile-based activities* (post-survey only, 9 items; e.g., "identify a problem in someone else's circuit diagram for an e-textile project"). The self-confidence, fascination, and value of CS items were based on an instrument previously published by the Activation Lab [1, 26] which measures the affective and cognitive aspects of student interests toward science topics or tasks. The survey items were adjusted from reflecting on science to computer science while items focused on personal expression with CS were newly created.

3.3.2 Grading Rubric. As part of the curriculum, teachers were provided a grading rubric to evaluate students' performance on the final project of the unit using human sensors. This rubric was organized as follows:

• *Coding* (30 points) for having the general structure of code including variable declaration, input/output setup and the appropriate conditionals (15 points), four complete lighting pattern functions (5 points), appropriately commented code (5 points), and functional sensors (5 points).

• *Circuity* (20 points) for the completion and clarity of the circuit design (15 points), and functionality of the LED circuits themselves (5 points).

• *Design & Craft* (50 points) for fulfilling the basic requirements of having four independently controllable lights and two sensor patches (10 points), aesthetics and finishing (15 points), sewing (15 points), and design notebook completion (10 points).

Following the unit, teachers were asked to evaluate their students' projects based on this rubric and submit these to the researchers.

3.4 Data Analysis

Student Demographics. In all analyses, we used the following demographic information provided by students. Gender was defined across three categories including: male, female and decline to indicate. Race/ethnic identification was defined across seven categories including: Hispanic/Latinx, African-American/Black, Asian-American, White/Caucasian, Other, Biracial and decline to indicate. Primary home language was a measure of the extent to which students spoke a language other than English at home (responding "never, once in a while, most of the time, and all of the time."). Family college attendance was defined as whether or not a student had an immediate or extended family member who had attended college.

3.4.1 Student Pre-Post Surveys. We evaluated the entire sample of students who completed both a pre- and post-survey for all constructs except for those related to e-textile activities. We first validated each of the five survey constructs empirically by calculating Cronbach alpha reliability scores using survey items in each construct. Scores with $\alpha > 0.800$ reflect good consistency among items in a given construct. Scores with $\alpha > 0.700$ reflect fair consistency. The self-confidence construct had a pre and post Cronbach alpha score of $\alpha=0.747$ and $\alpha=0.848$, respectively; fascination pre and post scores were $\alpha=0.767$ and $\alpha=0.800$; CS value pre and post scores were $\alpha=0.721$ and $\alpha=0.770$; personal expression pre and post scores were $\alpha=0.893$ and $\alpha=0.860$; e-textiles skills (post-survey only) score was $\alpha=0.890$. Thus, all constructs passed the threshold for survey validation.

To provide insights into overall differences in student perspectives before and after participating in the e-textiles curricular unit, paired sample t-tests were conducted for (1) confidence, (2) fascination, (3) value and (4) expression. Analyses of variance (ANOVAs) were conducted to assess differences that may exist across the self-reported social and economic demographic categories (gender, race/ethnicity, home language, and family college attendance). These ANOVAs were conducted with the post-survey composite in order to ascertain differences in student perspectives after having participated in the e-textiles curricular unit.

3.4.2 Grading Rubric. As a measure of learning, we compiled rubric scores from teachers and calculated descriptive statistics mean, range, and median) across individual students' total scores, composite theme scores (Coding, Circuitry, Design & Crafting), and subtopic scores, (e.g., sensor functionality, circuit diagram) to compare student accomplishments in these different areas. Because students were scored using four fixed levels across each subtopic, we also performed a count and percentage of student scores (e.g., for a range of 10, a score of 0, 3, 6, or 10) and compared these across the other subtopics as another point of comparison.

For this grading rubric analysis, only 8 of 15 classrooms are included for a total of N=174 students. The other classes were not included because either they did not finish all four projects and therefore did not submit human sensor rubric scores (N=5), or they did complete the human sensor projects but provided incomplete rubric scores for the project, specifically, the total score out of 100 rather than the individual theme and subtopic scores (e.g., Circuitry, Sensor Functionality) (N=2).

4 Findings

4.1 Student Perceptions of CS

Across student perceptions of CS, we found significant increases in three of the four constructs after participating in the e-textile curriculum (see Table 1). The self-confidence outcome suggests that overall, students perceived themselves as more confident in solving CS-related technical problems or challenges after participating in the e-textiles activity. The fascination outcome suggests that students reported being more interested in learning about computer science after having participated in the e-textiles activity. The CS expression outcome suggests that students felt that they could engage with activities that are of personal interest in computer science. However, there was no change ($p>0.05$) in student responses about their perceived CS value of computer science for future endeavors.

Variable	Pre-Survey Mean (SD)	Post-Survey Mean (SD)	Demographic Differences
Confidence	15.04 (2.2)	15.54 (2.397)*	None
Fascination	12.58 (2.334)	12.89 (2.307)*	None
Expression	9.6 (2.00)	10.03(1.808)*	None
Value	6.33 (1.314)	6.27 (1.364)*	Gender**

Note *p<0.05, **p<0.001

Table 1: Differences between pre- and post-surveys (N=272).

Demographic comparisons did not yield any significant differences in how students responded to post-survey questions related to confidence in CS, fascination with CS, and overall e-textiles skills and capabilities (ANOVA), suggesting that the e-textiles unit was relevant to students' interest, confidence, and sense of creativity with CS regardless of gender, ethnicity, language and family education. Furthermore, while there were no overall pre- and post-survey differences on constructs related to student CS value, an ANOVA revealed that male students reported valuing computer science for future academic and professional studies more than female students after working with e-textiles. These findings suggest that in some categories traditional inequities can persist and require further work.

Regarding e-textile abilities, mean scores show that students felt "very confident" or "confident" in all areas, with some minor differences. Overall students showed high confidence (mean scores between 3.10-3.59) in areas of crafting, circuitry, and basic coding sequences. Students were slightly less confident (mean scores between 2.97-3.00) in areas of diagnosing coding problems with sensors (which require Boolean logic and conditionals) and troubleshooting another person's code. There were no differences regarding the four demographic areas in an ANOVA. As we will show, these self-assessed areas of confidence matched well with the areas of teacher-rated competence in the final project.

4.2 Student CS Competence

One of the goals for the e-textiles unit was that students create personally relevant e-textile artifacts through open-ended projects with creative constraints to support depth of learning [17]. This goal was met in all 15 classrooms. Preliminary examination of student artifacts illustrated diversity of project designs despite having the same requirements and materials provided in the curriculum. Whereas some students 'hacked' existing fabric artifacts such as their own t-shirts, hats, and stuffed animals by adding LEDs and sensors, still others created original soft projects (both flat and 3-D) such as banners or pillows using felt and glue (see Figure 1). Students drew from diverse sources for inspiration including popular culture (e.g., *Spiderman*, *Finding Nemo*, *M&M* candies), personal interests and affiliations (e.g., an outer space scene, a school logo t-shirt), and/or their own names (i.e., nicknames, initials). The findings that students could be creative in the unit was reflected in their survey answers, particularly in the category of personal expression.

4.2.1 Teacher Evaluation of Coding and Circuitry. Turning to teachers' evaluations of the final human sensor project from eight classrooms, students' total scores ranged from 16 to 100 (out of a possible 100 points), with a mean of 79.4, and a median of 83. Overall students performed well on the final projects. We further considered the spread of scores in different areas of the rubric. Students scored the highest in the overall themes of Design & Crafting (average of 87.5% out of 50 pts), and Circuitry (average of 87% out of 20 pts), and lowest in *Coding* (average of 61% out of 30 pts). We investigate these areas more deeply below.

The overall *Circuitry* score was calculated from two underlying subtopics: a workable circuitry blueprint and actual working LED circuits (see section 3.3.2). Overall, students scored relatively well on both. Regarding clear and workable circuitry blueprints, 93.1% of students received the top two scores, with 76.4% of students receiving the highest possible score. Regarding functional LED circuits that turned on, 87.4% of students scored in the top two scores with 70.7% of students receiving the highest score. Scoring in the top two categories demonstrates strong performance in these areas with either perfect work (highest score) or close to perfect work (second highest score). From this vantage point, nearly all students generally gained a strong understanding of circuit fundamentals in the class, including knowledge of polarity, short circuits, and spatial design of programmable circuits.

The overall *Coding* score was calculated from four underlying categories (see section 3.3.2): having four lighting patterns, clearly structured program code, commented code, and functional sensors. Compared to other categories, students generally received the highest scores for having four distinct lighting patterns as custom functions for controlling the LEDs (82.8% for the top two scores, including 68.4% for the highest score). This trend makes sense considering that sequencing commands to create distinct light patterns was something students also did in project #3, the collaborative mural project. However, students generally scored lower on both code structure—having the appropriate variable declarations, input/output setup, and conditional statements (65.5% for the top two scores, including 51.1% with the highest score)—and functional sensors—having sensor code that read four distinct levels of pressure from working handmade sensors (61.5% with the top two scores, 50% with the highest score). Considering that students were newly introduced to these concepts during the final human sensor project, the lower score averages in these subtopics are not surprising. Further, students worked in pairs during the collaborative mural project but independently in the final project, meaning no one could lean on a more capable partner for coding.

In the area of commented code, only 28.2% of students scored in the two upper levels (19% with the highest score), while 69.5% of students did not comment code at all (0 points). While commenting is considered a fundamental skill in collaborative and large-scale software development, students perhaps felt less interested in doing so for the human sensor project since they were working alone. Similarly, they may also have prioritized completion over comments: focusing more on completing the actual code rather than leaving comments for others to decipher.

Looking across teachers' rubrics we noted that students in the classrooms where teachers had 1-2 years prior experience leading the e-textiles unit had consistently higher scores in all rubric subtopics except aesthetics and finishing, having functional LED circuits, and coding four lighting patterns (which were already high scoring areas overall). This suggests that as with other curricular implementations [24], teachers with more experience (even one year) can teach the e-textiles unit in a more successful way that leads to greater depth of student learning. It also fits with our knowledge of the classroom implementations, where the experienced e-textiles teachers finished the unit with time to spare whereas most inexperienced e-textiles teachers struggled to complete the unit at all (i.e., the five teachers who did not start the final human sensor project and the remaining teachers who were pressed for time at the end). We reflect more on this in the discussion.

5 Discussion

In this paper, we presented our efforts to implement, on a larger scale, an e-textile unit within the ECS curriculum designed to increase interest in CS and understanding of key circuit and computing concepts in high school students from predominantly underrepresented groups. Overall, our findings indicate that there was success in broadening interest in CS as reported by students themselves and to a lesser degree, in deepening the learning of computing, circuitry and crafting as evaluated by the teachers. In the following sections, we discuss these aspects in more detail in addition to considering the role of teachers.

5.1 Broadening Student Perceptions of CS

Our first finding is in line with outcomes from prior large-scale ECS implementations in which the course has been consistently successful in significantly increasing students' positive perceptions of CS [14, 24]. While our e-textile unit followed the general format of ECS, it also introduced new elements such as textile materials, open-ended project designs, and a much greater emphasis on personalization of CS artifacts that provided the context for learning about computing. We know from prior research that using different materials and practices changes who participates in CS activities [4], but it was unclear whether this would extend to high school students unfamiliar with CS. Overall, our analysis revealed no gender or other demographic differences: all participants, including male high school students, indicated a broadened CS interest after working with e-textiles except in the area of future aspirations. Though many prior studies have utilized e-textiles to reach specifically to women or to underrepresented ethnic groups, our study suggests that e-textiles can be an effective means to broaden interest in CS for all students. Furthermore, we examined students' perceptions of creativity with CS, an area prominently featured in AP Computer Science Principles [5], but rarely quantitatively assessed. We know from prior research with e-textiles [2, 18, 17, 34] that this is an important dimension in how students connect to CS. We hope this new survey construct allows for further comparisons of creativity and personal expression in other CS education contexts.

5.2 Deepening Student Learning of CS

In this study, we also tackled relatively new ground for equity-oriented curricular initiatives such as ECS by assessing student learning of computing and engineering concepts from their final projects rather than a test. We observed that student performance was strong for those computing and engineering concepts that they had encountered in previous projects, while there was room for growth for those CS concepts that they encountered for the first time in the final project. These findings are not surprising given the complexities of learning to make e-textiles that require students to develop an understanding of not only functional circuits but also programmable circuits [21] in the context of challenging three-dimensional crafts [20]. The rubrics allowed us to base assessment on students' actual work in an authentic manner. However, the focus on the final project limits our understanding into the processes and problem-solving students engaged in during the unit. To this end, in the future we plan to examine students' reflective portfolios which have shown promise for evaluating computational practices such as iteration, debugging, and testing [16, 22]. Such portfolios may also illuminate more about students' sense of creativity with CS.

5.3 Designing Inclusive Curriculum Activities

We began our investigation of implementing an e-textile unit within the ECS curriculum to understand whether new materials and practices can contribute to the overall equity agenda of broadening student perceptions of and participation in CS. While broadening perceptions is critical, we also need to make sure that students can develop a better understanding of key CS concepts and practices within the context of designing personally-relevant artifacts. Our findings suggest that providing opportunities for personal and collaborative designs are promising steps into the right direction.

Yet we recognize more needs to be done to understand teacher implementation and how to support productive classroom practices that robustly strengthen equity [11]. Thus far we already have hints that prior experience in teaching e-textiles may result in stronger student learning. Looking more closely at teacher practices may yield more specific suggestions on how to support more students in going deeper with their projects. It is clear that curriculum design alone "is not enough" [14], but that professional development and pedagogy play an equally powerful role in enacting and realizing equity in classrooms. Supporting teachers across multiple years is a continuing challenge, especially in a discipline and field at large that has a long history of being exclusive of the very groups it seeks to embrace now.

Our large-scale implementation of the e-textiles unit offers one way to challenge preconceived notions of what CS can be by juxtaposing and connecting the high technologies of computing and engineering with the "low" perceived technologies of crafting and sewing. This study shows evidence that open-ended e-textiles projects can be done by teachers in regular public-school classrooms with positive effects for students. Such introductions begin to unlock the doors to the clubhouses of computing [23].

ACKNOWLEDGMENTS

This work was supported by the National Science Foundation grant to Yasmin Kafai, Jane Margolis, and Joanna Goode (#1509245/1512760/1510725). Any opinions, findings, and conclusions or recommendations expressed in this paper are those of the authors and do not necessarily reflect the views of either NSF, the University of Pennsylvania, Utah State University, University of California, Los Angeles, University of Oregon or Cal Poly Pomona.

REFERENCES

[1] Activation Lab. 2018. Retrieved on August 20, 2018 from http://activationlab.org/

[2] Beth Buchholz, Kate Shively, Kylie Peppler, and Karen Wohlwend. 2014. Hands on, hands off: Gendered access in crafting and electronics practices. *Mind, Culture, and Activity, 21*, 4, (July 2014) 278-297.

[3] Leah Buechley, Mike Eisenberg, Jaime Catchen, and Ali Crockett. 2008. The LilyPad Arduino: using computational textiles to investigate engagement, aesthetics, and diversity in computer science education. In Proceedings of the SIGCHI Conference on Human Factors in Computing Systems (CHI '08). ACM, New York, NY, USA, 423-432. DOI: https://doi.org/10.1145/1357054.1357123

[4] Leah Buechley and Benjamin Mako Hill. 2010. LilyPad in the wild: how hardware's long tail is supporting new engineering and design communities. In Proceedings of the 8th ACM Conference on Designing Interactive Systems (DIS '10). ACM, New York, NY, USA, 199-207. DOI=10.1145/1858171.1858206 http://doi.acm.org/10.1145/1858171.1858206

[5] College Board. 2017. Advanced Placement Computer Science Principles. Retrieved on April 20, 2018 from https://apcentral.collegeboard.org/courses/ap-computer-science-principles.

[6] Jan Cuny. 2015. Transforming K-12 computing education: an update and a call to action. ACM Inroads 6, 3 (August 2015), 54-57. DOI: https://doi.org/10.1145/2809795

[7] Leigh Ann Delyser, Joanna Goode, Mark Guzdial, Yasmin Kafai, Aman Yadav. 2018. Priming the computer science teacher pump: Integrating computer science education into schools of education. CSforAll, New York, NY.

[8] Ron Eglash, Juan E. Gilbert, and Ellen Foster. 2013. Toward culturally responsive computing education. Commun. ACM 56, 7 (July 2013), 33-36. DOI: https://doi.org/10.1145/2483852.2483864

[9] Deborah A. Fields, Yasmin Kafai, Tomoko Nakajima, Joanna Goode, and Jane Margolis. 2018. Putting Making into High School Computer Science Classrooms: Promoting Equity in Teaching and Learning with Electronic Textiles in Exploring Computer Science. *Equity & Excellence in Education,* 51, 1 (May 2018): 21-35.

[10] Deborah A. Fields, Debora Lui, and Yasmin B. Kafai. 2017. Teaching computational thinking with electronic textiles: High school teachers' contextualizing strategies in Exploring Computer Science. In Proceedings of the International Conference on Computational Thinking Education (CTE '17), The Education University of Hong Kong, Hong Kong, China, pp. 67-72.

[11] Deborah A. Fields, Debora Lui, and Yasmin B. Kafai, Y. B. (in press). Teaching practices that support iterative design in the electronic textiles Exploring Computer Science unit. In S. C. Hong and H. Abelson (Eds.) *Computational Thinking, Education.* Springer.

[12] Joanna Goode, Gail Chapman, and Jane Margolis. 2012. Beyond curriculum: the exploring computer science program. ACM Inroads 3, 2 (June 2012), 47-53. DOI: https://doi.org/10.1145/2189835.2189851

[13] Joanna Goode and Jane Margolis. 2011. Exploring Computer Science: A Case Study of School Reform. Trans. Comput. Educ. 11, 2, Article 12 (July 2011), 16 pages. DOI=http://dx.doi.org/10.1145/1993069.1993076

[14] Joanna Goode, Jane Margolis, and Gail Chapman. 2014. Curriculum is not enough: the educational theory and research foundation of the exploring computer science professional development model. In Proceedings of the 45th ACM technical symposium on Computer Science Education (SIGCSE '14). ACM, New York, NY, USA, 493-498. DOI: https://doi.org/10.1145/2538862.2538948

[15] Gayithri Jayathirtha and Yasmin B. Kafai. (in press). Electronic Textiles in Computer Science Education: A Synthesis of Efforts to Broaden Participation, Increase Interest, and Deepen Learning. In *Proceedings of ACM SIGCSE conference (SIGCSE '19).* ACM, Minneapolis, MN USA.

[16] Gayithri Jayathirtha, Deborah A. Fields, and Yasmin B. Kafai. 2018. Computational concepts, practices, and collaboration in high school students' debugging electronic textile projects. *Conference Proceedings of International Conference on Computational Thinking Education 2018,* Hong Kong: The Education University of Hong Kong.

[17] Yasmin B. Kafai, and Deborah A. Fields. 2018. Some Reflections on Designing Constructionist Activities for Classrooms. In Proceedings of the Constructionism Conference 2018. Vilnius, Lithuania.

[18] Yasmin B. Kafai, Deborah A. Fields, and Kristin A. Searle. 2014. Electronic textiles as disruptive designs in schools: Supporting and challenging maker activities for learning. *Harvard Educational Review,* 84(4), 532-556.

[19] Yasmin B. Kafai, Eunkyoung Lee, Kristin Searle, Deborah Fields, Eliot Kaplan, and Debora Lui. 2014. A Crafts-Oriented Approach to Computing in High School: Introducing Computational Concepts, Practices, and Perspectives with Electronic Textiles. Trans. Comput. Educ. 14, 1, Article 1 (March 2014), 20 pages. DOI=http://dx.doi.org/10.1145/2576874

[20] Victor R. Lee and Deborah A. Fields. 2017. Changes in undergraduate student competencies in the areas of circuitry, crafting, and computation after a course using e-textiles. *International Journal of Information and Learning Technology,* 34, 5 (2017), 372-384.

[21] Breanne. K. Litts, Yasmin B. Kafai, Debora A. Lui, Justice T. Walker, and Sari A. Widman. 2017. Stitching Codeable Circuits: High School Students' Learning About Circuitry and Coding with Electronic Textiles. *Journal of Science Education and Technology, 26,* 5 (May 2017), 494-507.

[22] Debora Lui, Justice T. Walker, Sherry Hanna, Yasmin B. Kafai, Deborah A. Fields, & Gayithri Jayathirtha, (in press). Communicating computational concepts and practices within high school students' portfolios of making electronic textiles. *Interactive Learning Environments.*

[23] Jane Margolis, Rachel Estrella, Joanna Goode, Jennifer J. Holme, & Kimberly Nao. 2017. *Stuck in the Shallow End: Education, Race and Computing, updated ed.* MIT Press, Cambridge, MA.

[24] Steven McGee, Randi McGee-Tekula, Jennifer Duck, Catherine McGee, Lucia Dettori, Ronald I. Greenberg, Eric Snow, Daisy Rutstein, Dale Reed, Brenda Wilkerson, Don Yanek, Andrew M. Rasmussen, and Dennis Brylow. 2018. Equal Outcomes 4 All: A Study of Student Learning in ECS. In Proceedings of the 49th ACM Technical Symposium on Computer Science Education (SIGCSE '18). ACM, New York, NY, USA, 50-55. DOI: https://doi.org/10.1145/3159450.3159529

[25] Douglas L. Medin, and Megan Bang. 2014. *Who's asking?: Native science, western science, and science education.* MIT Press, Cambridge, MA.

[26] Moore, D. W., Bathgate, M. E., Chung, J., & Cannady, M. A. (2011). Technical report: Measuring activation and engagement; Activation Lab, Enables Success Study. Retrieved July 21, 2018 from http://activationlab.org/wp-content/resources/aera2013/aera_research/AERA_2013_0_1_ALES2011_TechReport.pdf

[27] David. B. Palumbo. 1990. Programming language/problem-solving research: A review of relevant issues. *Review of Educational Research, 60,* 1 (March 1990), 65-89.

[28] Rozsika Parker. 1984. The subversive stitch: Embroidery and the making of the feminine. Palgrave Macmillan, New York, NY.

[29] Kylie Peppler and Diane Glosson. 2013. Stitching circuits: Learning about circuitry through e-textile materials. *Journal of Science Education and Technology* 22, 5 (2013), 751-763.

[30] Alexander Repenning, David Webb, and Andri Ioannidou. 2010. Scalable game design and the development of a checklist for getting computational thinking into public schools. In Proceedings of the 41st ACM technical symposium on Computer science education (SIGCSE '10). ACM, New York, NY, USA, 265-269. DOI: https://doi.org/10.1145/1734263.1734357

[31] Mike Rose. 2014. *Why school? Reclaiming education for all of us.* The New Press, New York, NY.

[32] Emmanuel Schanzer, Kathi Fisler, Shriram Krishnamurthi, and Matthias Felleisen. 2015. Transferring Skills at Solving Word Problems from Computing to Algebra Through Bootstrap. In Proceedings of the 46th ACM Technical Symposium on Computer Science Education (SIGCSE '15). ACM, New York, NY, USA, 616-621. DOI: https://doi.org/10.1145/2676723.2677238

[33] Kimberly A. Scott, Kimberly M. Sheridan, and Kevin Clark. 2014. Culturally responsive computing: a theory revisited. *Learning, Media and Technology* 40, 4 (June 2014), 412-436.

[34] Mia S. Shaw, Deborah A. Fields, and Yasmin B. Kafai, Y. B. (under review). Crafting identities: Portfolios as meta-artifacts for narrating selves in portfolios in an e-textiles class.

[35] Susan A. Yoon, Emma Anderson, Jessica Koehler-Yom, Chad Evans, Miyoung Park, Josh Sheldon, Ilana Schoenfeld, Daniel Wendel, Hal Scheintaub, and Eric Klopfer. Teaching about complex systems is no simple matter: building effective professional development for computer-supported complex systems instruction. *Instructional Science* 45, 1 (Feb. 2017), 99-121.

How Faculty Negotiate "Inclusive Educational Practice" in Computer Science

Heather Thiry
Golden Evaluation
Golden, CO; USA
Heather.thiry@colorado.edu

Sarah Hug
Colorado Evaluation & Research Consulting
Westminster, CO; USA
hug@colorado.edu

ABSTRACT

This paper builds from over a decade of engagement with an equity-focused initiative, the Computing Alliance for Hispanic Serving Institutions, an effort to both transform and supplement the educational experiences of computing students attending HSIs. This grassroots effort engages faculty, primarily department chairs in computer science and computer engineering programs at Hispanic-serving Institutions, in developing and implementing research-based educational practices to support the recruitment, retention, and advancement of Hispanics in computing fields. While we have addressed how CAHSI activities influence student experiences in becoming computer scientists in other work [1,2,3] we turn to the faculty to understand how faculty at Hispanic Serving Institutions act on their roles as educators at institutions with traditions of inclusive missions in a technical field. The research questions that direct the paper are:

How do faculty perceive their role in educating underrepresented students in STEM?

How do institutional contexts and current events in computing education constrain and support faculty action towards equitable practice in computing?

KEYWORDS

Faculty perspectives, equity, teaching and learning, qualitative research

ACM Reference format:

Heather Thiry and Sarah Hug. 2019. How Faculty Negotiate "Inclusive Educational Practice" in Computer Science. In Proceedings of the 50th ACM Technical Symposium on Computer Science Education *(SIGCSE'19) Feb. 27-March 2, 2019, Minneapolis, MN, USA. ACM, NY, NY, USA, 7 pages.* https://doi.org/10.1145/3287324.3287388

SIGCSE '19, February 27-March 2, 2019, Minneapolis, MN, USA

ACM ISBN 978-1-4503-5890-3/19/02...$15.00
https://doi.org/10.1145/3287324.3287388

Introduction

"Institutions should leverage the increasing interest in computer science and related fields, among both non-majors and intended majors, to engage, recruit, and retain more women and underrepresented minorities into the field and help address the diversity problem proactively."

The National Academy of Sciences proposed institutions could mobilize under the current U.S. phenomenon of booming enrollments in computer science to diversify the student population, and ultimately, the workforce of technical professionals [4]. In this era of booming enrollments, it is particularly important to consider policy and practice that supports equity and promotes CS for all learners, as financial, space, and human resource constraints make rigorous standards for admission seem necessary for managing growth [4].Yet narrowing the pool of prospective students based on traditional metrics of academic merit may limit the diversity of computer science students, as African American, Hispanic/LatinX, Native American and Pacific Islanders are less likely to have familial experience with college, and more likely to attend K-12 schools negatively impacted by poverty and teacher turnover.

Broadening participation in computer science has become a movement to provide opportunity to those who are underrepresented in the field, defined in the United States context as individuals belonging to one or more demographic groups currently participating in computing less than would be expected compared to their prevalence in the population. Broadening participation activities may take an additive approach, where the goal is to *complement* or *supplement* experiences of students with (historically) less access to high quality learning opportunities, or they may take a *transformative* approach, which shifts the common experience of students towards more inclusive practice, at once transforming the field and the experiences of students [5].

Computing departments may have intentions to diversify, yet the ways in which booming enrollments influence departmental culture—larger class sizes, greater pools of students to advise, less space for student interaction, competition for courses—may be at odds with these goals. The compounding issue of shrinking state funding for state institutions (like the HSIs under study) exacerbates the problem [6] Yet faculty, particularly faculty from HSIs, must consider how to support inclusive educational practices under these circumstances to promote their students' success. In this study, we address how faculty consider their roles in promoting inclusive educational practice, and consider how institutional, and temporal contexts influence their work towards equitable education for underrepresented students.

Context of the Study

This paper builds from over a decade of engagement with an equity-focused initiative, the Computing Alliance for Hispanic Serving Institutions, an effort to both transform and supplement the educational experiences of computing students attending HSIs. This grassroots effort engages faculty, primarily department chairs in computer science and computer engineering programs at Hispanic-serving Institutions, in developing and implementing research-based educational practices to support the recruitment, retention, and advancement of Hispanics in computing fields.

While we have addressed how CAHSI activities influence student experiences in becoming computer scientists in other work [1,2,3] we turn to the faculty to understand how faculty at Hispanic Serving Institutions act out their roles as educators at institutions with traditions of inclusive missions in a field that historically recruits from "high performing" student populations [7,8] We view the cultural tensions between these two concepts, inclusive practices of HSIs versus selective, sometimes exclusive cultures of computer science [9] as vibrant for understanding how inclusion is negotiated in computer science higher education departments at HSIs. The research questions that direct the paper are:

1. How do faculty perceive their role in educating underrepresented students in STEM?
2. How do institutional contexts and current events in computing education constrain and support faculty action towards equitable practice in computing?

Theoretical Foundations

The authors utilize a socio-cultural approach to the study of teaching and learning computer science [10,11]. We build on the notion of "identity development" [12,13] in the field, and the role more capable others have in shaping knowledge acquisition, development of repertoires of practice, and the "ways of thinking" supportive of success in the field [14, 15]. We acknowledge that some attempts to diversify computing may perpetuate deficit, rather than promote asset-based thinking about students' capabilities—we tried to focus on inclusive pedagogical practices in this paper that showed faculty acknowledgements of student needs, rather than assumptions of difference that can lead to victim blaming or continued oppression of underrepresented students [16].

Methods

This paper is part of a mixed-method research project that benefits from 10 years of affiliation with the Computing Alliance for Hispanic Serving Institutions (CAHSI). Data for this work were generated in site visits to two of the member institutions, both considered "Hispanic Serving Institutions" because of the proportion of their students who identify as Hispanic/LatinX. Site visits included the following data collection strategies:

1. Course observations using the Teaching Dimensions Observation Protocol (TDOP) (approx., 10 per institution)
2. Peer led team learning session observations at each site (n=4 site A; n=2 site B)
3. Faculty interviews (n= 7, site A); faculty and staff interviews (n=7, site B)
4. Student focus groups, (n= 5 site A; and n=6 site B)
5. Interviews with student leaders (e.g., President of ACM chapter, etc.) at site A (n=5)

Interviews were audio recorded and transcribed verbatim. Seventeen faculty and staff interviews were the primary source of data for this paper, while observations, focus groups with students, and interviews with student leaders were used as secondary sources for triangulation of data [17].

Data analysis began with both authors reviewing each interview, then meeting to collectively develop a code book, using passages from the interviews as exemplars for each code developed. The team co-coded four interviews and separately coded the remaining interviews.

Codes were developed both deductively and inductively, with theory informing the development of codes while emergent themes were simultaneously considered for analysis. Theory regarding equity, diversity, inclusive pedagogy, mentoring, and identity development in computing informed code trees. The lead codes under which related themes were subsumed were:

6. Departmental growth and change
7. Climate and belonging
8. Student success
9. Student preparedness
10. Institutional and computing pathways
11. Pedagogy/teaching and learning

We report on our themes privileging faculty member voices, though triangulated evidence supports the "self-report" nature of this qualitative study. In other words, student focus groups, observations, and document analyses are used as secondary sources to ensure the self-report is accurate, when appropriate. For example, focus groups with students indicate they go to faculty members with personal and professional concerns, which supports the quotes below regarding mentoring and support.

Results Question 1: Faculty views on their role in education for underrepresented students

Faculty held varying views on their role in supporting underrepresented students within computing departments. A small number of faculty adopted a deficit-based approach that underrepresented students are somehow "lacking" and/or might not be capable of successfully completing computing degrees. However, even this perspective was often more nuanced, and the overwhelming majority of faculty viewed their role as providing the support that students need to be successful in their degree programs. This support took three forms: 1) helping students to navigate complex institutional and computing pathways, 2) providing mentoring and support for students, and 3) understanding the complexity of students' lives.

Navigating institutional and computing pathways

Because many students in CAHSI departments were the first in their families to attend college and came from underserved communities with limited or no access to computer science in their K-12 education, most faculty viewed their role as helping students to navigate unfamiliar computing and higher education pathways. Many faculty felt that it was important to provide students with clear pathways so they would not become "lost" in the computing department.

> "We have a diverse population of students. Sometimes they come from underrepresented communities and underserved communities as well. So they do not have too much exposure. So when they come in, they sometimes, kind of, are lost. So, to make them successful, we have to mostly communicate with them, talk with them, and provide them a clear path of things and to tell them what lies ahead and motivate them. That's the only thing I believe that works."

Students often had little previous exposure to computer science or computing careers, so faculty also felt it was their responsibility to prepare students for the workforce and life after the university. Many faculty took it upon themselves to advise and guide students towards graduate school or professional positions. For instance, one professor invited a career counselor to come to one of his courses on two separate occasions to discuss resume development, cover letters, and interviewing techniques for computer science positions. Students were required to create a resume and conduct a mock interview as part of the assignment. Faculty also personally advised students who did not have the social capital to easily traverse graduate school trajectories, serving as institutional brokers to share knowledge and provide resources to help students navigate graduate school pathways. For example, one faculty member commented in her interview that she had just advised a student about graduate school and encouraged him to apply.

> "It happened like a half hour ago, there was a student here, I was pushing him to apply for graduate school. He was very smart, very motivated, but because sometimes they haven't gone through the process, he didn't know he needed to apply early. Actually, he's going to graduate next spring. He should apply now. He didn't know it. But always, I advise them to look for job early, I advise them to think about it."

Similarly, some faculty rejected traditional notions of success that rely on quantitative metrics, such as completion rates, and, instead, considered student success to be students who have achieved their own personal goals and positively contribute to society, as mentioned in the following comment from a computer science chair. In this definition, success is personalized and individualized and defined by the student and not defined by an external metric or committee.

> "So if the student reaches his or her goal and is able to contribute to society, I think that would be student success. Not just graduating. Because if you graduate and don't get a job ... if you get a job, I'm not sure that's success because he or she may not like it. So it has to be something that is his or her goal and be able to do that job to contribute to society. I think that would be considered student success. I'm hoping the students get to that. It's difficult to define student success. Everyone has their own definition, it's not easy.

Another aspect of helping students to navigate computing pathways, was helping students to explore their fit with computing and to find their place within the complex array of computing possibilities. Some departments had instigated different degree pathways with varying amounts of math requirements with the goal of preparing students for different types of careers within computing (e.g., a computer science degree for software developers and a computer technology degree for homeland security professionals and domain expert technicians, among other career possibilities). Other departments created different tracks that students could explore and specialize in with a graduate degree, such as a master's program in Data Analytics. With these distinct possibilities, faculty and career counselors could advise students on the path that best fits their interests and goals.

> "When students are faltering ... Even when they're Computer Science, they know they want to do something with computers, but they just don't know what. Okay, is it Information Science, or is it Computer Science? I've developed a little chart so they can see the differences. "You've got to have those strong math skills, how are your math skills? Do you enjoy math?" Those kinds of things that hopefully can help them, once they start thinking about it." (career counselor)

Providing mentoring and support

Faculty also saw it as their responsibility to provide mentoring and support to their students as many of them came from underserved communities. One faculty who had worked at three different institutions commented that he had much more interaction with students in his current department and felt a greater need to provide support for them than he had at his other institutions which served less diverse populations.

> "Actually this is my third school, very different. My first school was a state university but it's Midwest and lots of white students and also very diverse, many migrants. My second school was a private institution and majority are white graduate kids from very affluent families. The third one is my current school. Most of our students are underserved students. And they're probably most of them are first-generation college students. For example, for my current school, I really try to be motivational. I just let them feel I'm one of them. I really want to help them. I have more interaction with my current students compared to my first two schools."

Beyond the need for basic mentoring and support, faculty also discussed the importance of providing opportunities for students to engage in professional practice to form a community with other computer scientists and to develop a professional identity. Many faculty engaged in research with undergraduate students and encouraged them to take advantage of opportunities to engage with the larger computing community, such as attending and presenting at professional conferences. This type of professional mentoring and support encouraged some students to pursue graduate school.

> "Most of the interactions here are academic oriented. For example, I really encourage students to have some research opportunities. I really encourage some of them to work with me and to submit their research results to an international conference or national conference. Give them lots of encouragement on how to present at an international conference or national conference. I am constantly reminding them, 'Hey, you know

I have some money I can support you.' Like CAHSI right? CAHSI has generous support. I encourage some students to go. For example, one of my students he just went to the Washington DC to present his research in an emerging researcher national conference. He was an undergraduate student last year and then because of our interaction and because of his own motivation he is now our graduate student."

In this way, faculty not only provided emotional and social support to students, but also academic and professional mentoring and support.

Understanding the complexity of students' lives

Because most students were from underserved communities, many faculty felt that it was important to understand their students and the complexity of their lives. Many students had transferred from community colleges or other institutions, were non-traditional aged, first-generation college students, low-income, and some of them supported families. Faculty tried to understand students' complex and busy lives, often viewing this complexity as an asset, and not a deficit.

"These are the best students I ever had because they really are motivated because they already spend so much effort just to come to the school. Working part time, and then trying to pay the bills, then they have to make an extra effort to come to school, so they are already motivated. So it's much easier and you get to teach people who are already motivated. So much easier in that aspect and I really enjoy it."

Many faculty also made an effort to be accessible and available to students outside of class sessions and office hours. Faculty realized that students had many stresses beyond their academic work and that they might need a supportive person in their department to discuss these issues.

"A lot of them talk about a lot of issues and some of them might be stressed out, some may have issues at home. We've talked a little bit here and there. I have an open-door policy, so they can come ... I have office hours for advising, but they can always walk in if I'm available, I'll tell them to come in. So they come in for advice."

Understanding the complexity of students' lives also prompted faculty to adopt an equity-based perspective in their courses and in their interactions with students. For instance, a professor at one institution contrasted the approach towards students in his department with that of other departments. Faculty in his department sought to understand students' perspectives and to support their persistence and success, in contrast to the lack of care and support found in many departments.

"So to understand from a students' perspective, sometimes they come in and they say that they were not able to do a homework on time. I mean, as an instructor you can just say 'okay, I follow the syllabus, I give them a zero and I'm done with it.' But then, we have to go a little deeper and understand why the student was not able to do it. Because there might be other issues that are beyond the control of the student. Of course, we cannot accommodate everything but as a human being and trying to help the students, this is a different type of campus."

Question 2: Institutional contexts that constrain or support faculty toward equitable practice

While faculty cultivated equitable student learning and support, institutions also cultivated environments that facilitated faculty engagement in these practices. Institutional contexts supported equitable environments and practices in ways that were deliberate and intentional and in unintentional ways that were byproducts of the nature and character of the Hispanic-Serving Institutions. Although, most of the ways that institutions supported faculty were deliberate, suggesting that even diverse institutions need to intentionally cultivate environments that are equitable for diverse learners. The ways that institutions supported equity were through: 1) providing resources for faculty to support students, 2) promoting curricular changes that advance equity, and 3) providing inclusive leadership. Contextual factors such as the small size of the departments at the research sites was an unintentional source of support for faculty, but also an emerging constraint with the growth of computer science enrollments in recent years.

Providing resources

Institutions and departments provided resources to enable faculty to support underrepresented students. Some of these resources were formal programs to support first-generation college or other underserved students. These programs often placed faculty in a formal mentoring role to students and created a peer mentoring network as well. A comprehensive support program on one of the campuses also distributed a regular "newsletter" that contained information about scholarships, internships, and other opportunities. This newsletter was also distributed to faculty so they could provide better advising and make their students aware of these opportunities. Institutions offered other supports to reinforce student learning, such as peer-led team learning and tutoring, to reinforce faculty classroom instruction.

Because the campuses of many Hispanic-Serving Institutions are commuter campuses, there is often not a place for students to go in between classes. Faculty on one campus noticed that students were spending time in their cars between classes and so they remedied the situation by providing a common area in the department for students to eat, study, and socialize during their down time. A faculty member described the situation:

"You can see a lot of students sitting in their car in the parking lots. Then I talk to a few other faculty at the same time. The students don't know where to go outside of class. So they come in, arrive, Los Angeles traffic is pretty bad. When they come here, they just sit outside. It's a lack of getting together in a common room, or the union, or any lab... So, there's a lack of sense of community as well. That pertains to it being a commuter campus, not too many people stay around. So if you can help in that aspect, like we have a cyber security lab upstairs in the library. We open it up to other students as well. We ask them if you can come in, have some lunch, sit there, talk with other students, get help with homework, be part of the community, so if we can do that, then students become a lot more successful."

A professor from a different campus affirmed that the commuter campus aspect of HSIs interfered with students' ability to form communities and places a constraint on students' time. As students spend more time commuting to-and-from campus, they also have less time to interact with their peers and faculty.

"Well for our students, it's a little bit more difficult because we are not a traditional university and we don't have dorms. Our students, a lot of them come from economically disadvantaged families. So for one thing, they have a commute back and forth and that takes up a lot of time.

Some students told me that it may take four hours, every day, to come here and then to go home. And also, because there's no dorms, there's a lesser chance for them to interact with their peers. So we try to improve that, we've used student lounges, and that gave the students a place to meet, to socialize. But compared to a traditional university, that's a weakness."

Promoting curricular changes

Because many students lacked prior exposure to computing in their K-12 education, departments initiated curricular changes to support students. Faculty changed curricula, taught introductory, preparatory courses, and advised students of the appropriate coursework they would require based on their background experience. The preparatory CS-0 course emphasized an introduction to algorithmic thinking and computer science. One of the goals of the course was to introduce students to problem-solving techniques that they would utilize throughout the computer science degree, as mentioned by a faculty member.

"It's a good question that I can ... The 115 course, it really is to try introduce them the concept of problem solving, how to solve problems with some software kind of built in, but really trying to get the problem solving a little bit more ingrained in how they approach things."

In addition to providing a pre-computer science preparatory experience, students still struggle with the math requirements of the computer science degree. Many students were returning learners or had not had adequate math preparation in their earlier education. Faculty must communicate frequently, including across departments, to ensure a continuous, curricular pathway that works for students with limited computing or math backgrounds. A department chair stated:

"One of things is students lack of preparation and that's what we have this CS0, but still the math is one of things that is causing a little issue for the students. We do have these remedial courses, but as I mentioned.... And I talk to the math department, , what did you cover?.... We have faculty, CS0, CS1, CS2, CS3 talk to each other. CS1, I tell them what are the problems that we have CS1? Let's add them to CS0. We make sure [math curriculum] is reflected in the previous courses, because if we don't do it all the way [through], it will cause a problem."

One of the ways that departments and institutions ensured student success was to focus attention on student advising and mentoring, especially for math pathways in computer science, as described by an assistant dean. Math pathways were vitally important to students who may have lacked access to rigorous math opportunities in their previous education.

"So the university has a faculty mentoring program where each college kind of allots different faculty to mentor incoming students and so that's one way that computer science majors are able to sort of identify, in the beginning, their interests and be paired up with a faculty member in computer science hopefully that is able to sort of guide them on that beginning track. We also have mandatory advising for all of our first-year students, central advising by a college advisor that kind of makes sure they're on the right track. The hardest part and the part where student support plays a big role is the math for our students. Most of our students come in at college algebra level, sometimes even developmental, which makes it hard because the first CS course in the major requires them to be at a certain level and so they've got to be credit or enrolled in Precalc track or finished with track and the Precalc portion and so a lot of students aren't able to get the flavor in the first class until second, sometimes third semester."

To support students in the major, institutions and departments also focused on adopting high-impact practices to improve student engagement and learning outcomes. In some cases, this involved individual faculty adopting high-impact practices in their particular courses, such as implementing research modules or other in-depth, open-ended learning experiences. For instance, in one of the departments, the capstone course focused on student research projects and weekly student presentations. In this way, students gained experience with extended projects and gained comfort with presentation skills that more closely modeled a professional workplace than traditional instructional methods.

Providing inclusive leadership

Another way that faculty were supported in their work in educating underrepresented students was through inclusive departmental leadership that focused on student and faculty development. Inclusive leadership was equity-focused and student-centered, yet also focused on supporting faculty in their work with students. A faculty member noted that his chair motivated and inspired all of the faculty in the department to be student-centered. Departmental leadership also helped to set the tone and climate for the department, creating a positive space for both students and faculty.

"We have a great chair who really motivates all of us to work hard. He's the one really to fight for us. Sometimes I feel like he's the one we really feel we like this department. So he has lots of money so the students can travel to conferences. I guess that's something I feel very fortunate for. I am really happy to work under his leadership. Our faculty is we are all busy with our own teaching but we are very supportive to each other."

Inclusive leaders also supported their departments in their interactions with the broader institutions. For instance, inclusive leaders advocated for resources, such as more tenure lines or funding, for the departments to support their students and faculty.

"They have the department chair meeting at our institution. They call it every month. Our chair is very vocal in that meeting, always fighting for our department .... He's very active and good at fighting for our department. He's really trying to hire more faculty."

Other faculty commented that the departmental leadership provided a safe space where they could grow and develop professionally. For example, one faculty member commented that he had made some mistakes early in his tenure in the department, but he was allowed to learn and develop from those early missteps.

"It's a small department and I like it a lot. After my PhD program I directly came here and I made some mistakes. I received a lot of help from the department; from the chair, peers, you know. This is a small department; really nice. Everybody is really nice. Also you can see this, we have a very diverse faculty body here and everybody is very nice. We have a new faculty coming and it's a woman."

Therefore, departmental leadership was essential in setting a supportive climate for faculty where they could have positive peer relationships and positive student-faculty interactions. In this setting, faculty growth and development was prioritized along with student success.

Student enrollment and department size

Department size at the Hispanic-Serving Institutions served as both a support and a constraint on professor's ability to serve underrepresented students. Small departments offered small class sizes which fostered more student-faculty interaction and better student advising. Faculty were more able to advise students on professional pathways in addition to academic topics. Small departments also facilitated a positive departmental climate through generally friendly interactions among faculty and students.

"I think [the department] is very friendly and relaxed. We don't have very big classes, so we focus on small classes. So my biggest class is less than 40 students. So I can quickly get familiar with every student. So they also feel free, they're not nervous when they see me. Yeah, they feel free to ask me questions, and we also communicate on other things, in addition to the course topics. Maybe some students, they are looking for job. I will provide some suggestions. And some student preparing for their interviews. I will also give some information about this."

Another faculty member commented that a small department facilitated more student opportunities for undergraduate research.

"I think we are really good at interacting with students. We have small class-sizes, and our faculty are really engaged with the students. For undergrad research, you probably don't see any other university that has this high-intensity of undergrad research. I know every faculty is involved, is working with some number of undergrad students, doing some research topic. And the result is phenomenal. We have a lot of undergrad student publications and they got published, they go to conferences, it's all peer-reviewed conferences, it's not just some random conference. So they got to present and to publish their work at proceedings and in scientific journals. I think it's really phenomenal, compared to some other universities."

However, a small department and under-resourced institutions provided many constraints in a time of booming computer science enrollments. Departments lack faculty to teach the increasing number of course sections. Departments also lacked space, funding, and other resources to accommodate the enrollment shifts.

A chair discussed the lack of space and resources to adapt to rising enrollment, but also to meet faculty research interests and needs.

"Space is almost impossible to get. They are doing some reconstruction on lots of areas. When the new building gets built, we hope to gain some space so we can expand. We need some additional computer rooms and we need some additional labs. We've got people working in AI and robotics, and all we have, really is one little room where we've got the computers. They all have to figure out how to work through that space. An additional lab or two for the faculty, especially the robotics part, because they have so many students."

Besides creating squeezed spaces and resources, rising enrollments created a burden for faculty in small departments. Faculty had to take on unreasonable advising loads that hindered their ability to provide the type of student-centered, highly personalized advising that many faculty in CAHSI departments have provided in the past. A department chair described how his advising load is currently 300 students on top of all of the other responsibilities that come with the chair position.

"I usually have advising time that I do, every student has to come here for advising. Once a semester at least to advise for their courses. I used to get all of the students a couple of years ago. It became too much, so I get maybe 300 hundred that come to me and then others go among other faculty. They all come to me, so I advise them one by one. We have this folder to see what we're going to advise, so we know exactly who advises what, when and what to track. We've shared this folder with all of the faculty. Especially when the schedule comes out for next semester, that's when they come more than before because they want to see what courses they have to take next semester."

Departments also had to employ more adjunct and part-time faculty to meet the growing demand for course sections. However, part-time faculty do not lessen the advising burden on the tenure-track faculty. Part-time faculty also do not engage in the service or shared governance commitments of tenure-track faculty.

"So the thing is we take help from a lot of part timers. So we have I think more than ten part timers. So they can teach a few courses. But they do not do any advising or any other work that faulty has to do. Then in terms of finances, this is a state university so the state gives the funding and then it comes down to the college and the college decides which department gets what. Everyone understands it but due to financial constraints we are being held back. We are trying to make the best of whatever we have." We're expanding of course. We have too much course load to actually balance. So that effects our advising and meeting all the students outside of classroom."

The faculty member continued to explain that the department also has new degree pathways and programs that are just beginning and will need to be staffed as well. The growth of degree programs and student enrollment has placed constraints on faculty and their ability to adequately serve students.

"And then we have new programs coming in as well. So right now we have four programs and are supposed to start a Masters of science in cyber security next fall. So we will have five programs with six faculty members –that cannot be promising."

Other Constraints

The institutional contexts of HSIs themselves also provided constraints on the ability of faculty to adopt a student-centered, equity-based approach. In a time when computer science enrollments are booming and placing pressure on CS departments, the overall institutional enrollment of some HSIs is declining. For instance, the chair of one of the departments discussed this paradox.

"Well, I think the biggest problem we have is that the university seems to be strapped for funds all the time. They're not giving sufficient funds to our departments so that we can support travel and those kinds of things the way we should. In fact, this year, earlier, we were told there could be a five percent reduction. Then there was some additional money that is generated from course fees. We've always received a pretty good amount there that helps us fund our labs and our senior projects and things like that. The dean has had to shift a lot of that money to something else that didn't get funded. I guess this year I'm really being very careful in terms of what I can approve and what I can't."

Discussion

Results indicate that faculty at Hispanic Serving Institutions have developed strategies for supporting their diverse students in the computing field, and that institutional and temporal contexts can support and inhibit inclusive educational practices. Faculty-student relationships are necessary for developing nurturing computer science learning environments [17] and thus faculty perspectives are important for considering how to recruit, retain and advance a more diverse student body in computing. While our data were collected at HSIs and may be most applicable to faculty in these settings, we submit that lessons learned in this effort may be applicable to other types of institutions, and could inform larger, more systemic efforts to broaden participation in computing.

REFERENCES

[1] Gates, A. Q., Hug, S., Thiry, H., Aló, R., Beheshti, M., Fernandez, J., ... & Adjouadi, M. (2011). The computing alliance of Hispanic-serving institutions: Supporting Hispanics at critical transition points. ACM Transactions on Computing Education (TOCE), 11(3), 16.

[2] Thiry, H., & Hug, S. (2014). "We should all help each other": Latina undergraduates' practices and identities in the figured world of computing. Boulder, CO: International Society of the Learning Sciences.

[3] Hug, S., Thiry, H., & Tedford, P. (2011, March). Learning to love computer science: Peer leaders gain teaching skill, communicative ability and content knowledge in the CS classroom. In Proceedings of the 42nd ACM technical symposium on Computer science education (pp. 201-206). ACM.

[4] National Academies of Sciences Engineering and Medicine. Assessing and Responding to the Growth of Computer Science Undergraduate Enrollments. The National Academies Press, Washington, DC, 2018.

[5] Bang M, Warren B, Rosebery A, S, Medin D, Desettling Expectations in Science Education. Human Development 2012;55:302-318

[6] Mitchell, M., Palacios, V., & Leachman, M. States are Still Funding Higher Education below Pre-Recession Levels (Washington, DC: Center on Budget and Policy Priorities, 2014).

[7] Bullock, E. (2017). Only STEM can save us? Examining race, place, and STEM education as property. Educational Studies, 53(6), 628-641

[8] Ladson-Billings, G., & Tate IV, W. F. (2016). Toward a critical race theory of education. In Critical race theory in education(pp. 21-41). Routledge.

[9] Goode, J., Estrella, R., & Margolis, J. (2006). Lost in translation: Gender and high school computer science. The MIT Press.

[10] Vygotsky, L. (1978). Interaction between learning and development. Readings on the development of children, 23(3), 34-41.

[11] Gutiérrez, K. D., & Rogoff, B. (2003). Cultural ways of learning: Individual traits or repertoires of practice. Educational researcher, 32(5), 19-25.

[12] Holland, D., Fox, G., & Daro, V. (2008). Social movements and collective identity: A decentered, dialogic view. Anthropological Quarterly, 95-126.

[13] Carlone, H. B., & Johnson, A. (2007). Understanding the science experiences of successful women of color: Science identity as an analytic lens. Journal of research in science teaching, 44(8), 1187-1218.

[14] Rogoff, B. (1990). Apprenticeship in thinking: Cognitive development in social context. Oxford University Press.

[15] Collins, A., Brown, J. S., & Newman, S. E. (1989). Cognitive apprenticeship: Teaching the crafts of reading, writing, and mathematics. Knowing, learning, and instruction: Essays in honor of Robert Glaser, 18, 32-42.

[16] Valencia, R. R. (2010). Dismantling contemporary deficit thinking: Educational thought and practice. Routledge.

[17] Patton, M. Q. (1999). Enhancing the quality and credibility of qualitative analysis. Health services research, 34(5 Pt 2), 1189.

Infusing Cooperative Learning into AP Computer Science Principles Courses to Promote Engagement and Diversity

Jeff Gray
University of Alabama
Tuscaloosa, AL
gray@cs.ua.edu

Kathy Haynie
Haynie Research & Evaluation
Skillman, NJ
kchaynie@alumni.stanford.edu

Fran Trees
Rutgers University
New Brunswick, NJ
fpt9@cs.rutgers.edu

Owen Astrachan
Duke University
Durham, NC
ola@cs.duke.edu

Chinma Uche
Academy of Aerospace & Engineering
Windsor, CT
chinmauche@gmail.com

Siobhan Cooney
Cooney Collaborative
Narbeth, PA
siobhan@cooneycollaborative.com

Richard Kick
Newbury Park High School
Newbury Park, CA
kickrg@gmail.com

ABSTRACT

The Advanced Placement Computer Science Principles (AP CSP) course was the culmination of an eight-year NSF/College Board pilot project that exceeded all expectations in terms of enrollment in its first two official years. Four NSF-sponsored projects and six other projects have endorsed AP CSP curricula and professional development (PD), a first for an AP course. In this paper, we report on an NSF-sponsored multi-year effort to infuse cooperative learning (CL) structures into AP CSP classrooms to improve class participation and student learning. As we report, CL structures have been beneficial for both new and experienced teachers and across the curricula of the endorsed providers. Since AP CSP was designed to engage all learners, the CL structures used in our PD workshops and the CL resources designed by participating teachers in our project have the potential to positively impact all AP CSP classrooms.

Research was conducted on the extent to which use of CL structures impacted student efficacy and student achievement. Three cohorts of AP CSP teachers participated in PD that focused on AP CSP pedagogical content knowledge using CL structures. A cumulative 143 teachers attended one-week PD workshops spanning July 2015, 2016, and 2017. We studied the effect of CL structures on student learning using AP scores as an outcomes measure. Use of CL structures was a statistically significant and positive predictor of student AP scores for participating classes in cohorts 2 and 3. Additionally, the use of pair programming was a significant and positive predictor of AP scores.

ACM Reference format:

J. Gray, K. Haynie, F. Trees, O. Astrachan, C. Uche, S. Cooney, R. Kick. 2019. Infusing Cooperative Learning into AP Computer Science Principles Courses to Promote Engagement and Diversity. In *Proceedings of 50th ACM Technical Symposium on Computer Science Education (SIGCSE '19), February 27-March 2, 2019, Minneapolis, MN, USA.* ACM, New York, NY, USA, 7 pages. http://dx.doi.org/10.1145/3287324.3287421

ACM ISBN 978-1-4503-5890-3/19/02...$15.00. http://dx.doi.org/10.1145/3287324.3287421

1 Introduction

Broadening the accessibility of computing to include a diverse population of students has been a fundamental design goal of the AP CSP curriculum framework (CF). The "Big Ideas" of AP CSP provide more breadth of topic coverage than the current AP CSA exam in a manner that is appealing to students with varied interests and abilities. The recognition and celebration of the social impacts of computing, within a context that encourages students to explore their own creativity through the creation of computational artifacts, opens more opportunities for teachers to engage students.

However, *curriculum alone does not necessarily engender engagement.* The most interesting and innovative curriculum can be taught in a disengaged manner, leading to lost opportunities for broadening interest in computing across a diverse student population. The objectives of the project described in this paper are to demonstrate the benefits of infusing an AP CSP course with a pedagogical approach that has been demonstrated to engage diverse learners who are in the same classroom. The learning science literature on Cooperative Learning (CL) [1] has been shown to increase class participation and student learning using pedagogical structures and strategies that offer an environment where every student is encouraged to participate equally toward their own academic achievement, while simultaneously working toward a positive common goal with teammates from different backgrounds and mixed abilities. This paper introduces our investigation into infusing CL into AP CSP and provides the results of observed best practices of CL that can be applied across the AP CSP curriculum framework.

1.1 Cooperative Learning for Computer Science

The phrase "group learning" has been used to describe educational activities in which students work in clusters or groups of two or more. However, such group work [2] is not cooperative learning, and the two are often misunderstood [3, 4]. Group work (or group discussion) is an unstructured activity in which the teacher asks a question or announces a topic to a class that has been physically organized in groups of 3-4 students. The students are then instructed to discuss the topic or solve the problem in their groups. In group learning, there are no specific guidelines on who speaks first and how long each student speaks. Characteristics of this type of discussion include unequal participation with the chance that one student dominates the discussion and others do not participate at all. This may foster a competitive, rather than cooperative, learning environment [5]. In contrast to group work, CL has built-in structures that naturally drive the equal participation of all students. Cooperative learning focuses on four key concepts (called "PIES" by Kagan [4]):

1. *Positive Interdependence*: Positive interdependence is realized when group members perceive that group success is based on every group member succeeding. Each member's efforts benefit the entire group [6], gains for one imply benefits for the others, and cooperation replaces competition. CL activities are structured so that no one person can work alone, but all group members must work together to succeed. This interdependence fuels cooperation.
2. *Individual Accountability*: In addition to group accountability, individual accountability exists when an individual in the group is able to perform and succeed without assistance. The assessment of the individual is made public to the group. It is the responsibility of the group to provide assistance, support, and encouragement to individual members who need it [6].
3. *Equal Participation*: CL structures ensure that each group member participates in the learning activity, and no one can just be a passive listener. Student participation contributes to achieving expected outcomes [7].
4. *Simultaneous Interaction*: With CL structures, the amount of active engagement increases. Participation of many class members occurs simultaneously. In groups of four, 25% of the students in the class are speaking and the others are actively listening at any one time.

Although CL structures are content-independent, this paper describes our three-year project that has incorporated CS content (particularly AP CSP content) to provide activities that are engaging and that address AP CSP learning objectives. Our project invited teacher participants who have adopted all of the various endorsed AP CSP curricula – our project was not focused on any specific AP CSP curriculum provider. The pedagogical approach that drives our CL activities involves the equal participation of 100% of the students in the class. No student has the opportunity to "tune-out." We have dozens of CL structures that we have applied to AP CSP. Below are just a few example CL structures and example activities we have used:

1. *Round Robin* is a CL structure that provides each student with an opportunity to speak exclusively for an equal amount of time, alternating between students at specified time intervals. As an example of applying CL to AP CSP, we introduce Round Robin with an activity that asks students to share their thoughts on effects of computing in other fields, or the beneficial (or harmful) effects of social media. Active involvement (speaking) occurs with 25% - 50% of the students in class at any one time.
2. To access higher-order thinking skills, a teacher may use *The Debate Team Carousel* [8]. In this activity, the students are in teams of four. Each student is given a worksheet with a yes-no question on the top of the worksheet that will require them to analyze a problem prompted by the teacher. Think-time is provided. The remainder of the worksheet is divided into four quadrants. The upper-left quadrant provides the prompt, "Write your opinion and one reason why you think that way." Students are given a specified amount of time to write their answer in the designated quadrant. Students pass their worksheet to the person on their right. A specified amount of time is given to respond to the prompt in the upper-right quadrant, "Read your partner's response and add another reason that you would **support** what your partner wrote." Again, the papers are passed to the right for the third prompt in the lower-left quadrant to be answered in a specified amount of time: "Write a reason that might be used to argue **against** what is written in the boxes above." And finally, passing the papers one more time, the prompt in the last quadrant is, "Read what is written in all three boxes. Add YOUR opinion and YOUR reason here."
3. To work on teambuilding skills, a teacher may announce a topic, set a time limit, give all students a short quiet (think) time to formulate ideas or answers to a question such as, "How does the Internet impact your privacy?" The teacher will then initiate CL by setting a timer. During a prescribed time (~1 min) students, in turn, will say an answer, write it on a slip of paper, and place the paper in the center of their group table with no papers overlapping. This structured activity (called *Jot Thoughts* by Kagan [4]) involves active listening, encouragement, praise, and a chance to build on the ideas of classmates.
4. Pair programming is an example of CL that has been used in CS classes for decades and encouraged for use in AP CSP. In pair programming, two students work together at one computer. One student is the driver and types the code; the other is the navigator and reviews and suggests as the program is being developed. The roles change after a specified time. This requires 100% active involvement.

This paper is organized as follows. Section 2 overviews the specific project details concerning teacher recruitment and professional development (PD) during our multi-year project. Section 3 provides details of our research methods, followed by a summary of our project evaluation results in Section 4. We offer our project observations and lessons learned in Section 5 and concluding remarks in Section 6.

2 Project Background

Students with less computing experience are likely to have greater anxiety when using a computer. Such anxiety is related to lower achievement in computation-based activities and leads to lower competence/self-efficacy. Female students and underrepresented minority (URM) students have historically had fewer computational experiences (e.g., [9, 10]), and therefore greater anxiety and lower self-efficacy regarding computational topics. Experiential anxiety is also related to experience and familiarity with computational thinking. Busch [11] found that students with lower computational self-efficacy (i.e., URM students), when given the choice, selected cooperative learning techniques. In addition, cooperative groups were found to score significantly better on achievement tests, self-concept, and sense of control-mastery (i.e., self-efficacy) than groups receiving direct instruction [12]. A study by Ericson and Guzdial [13] performed an aggregated analysis of gender and ethnicity. It is critically important to consider if CL structures within AP CSP offer benefits to diverse groups of students, leading to outcomes such as greater self-efficacy, higher achievement, and broadened participation in CS. Given these research findings, we expect:

Hypothesis 1: The impact of using CL structures will be cumulative; use of CL structures will increase students' computing self-efficacy, particularly for URM and female students.

Hypothesis 2: More opportunities to learn collaboratively will support stronger learning outcomes (as measured by AP scores).

Hypothesis 3: Students' achievement in AP CSP classes that used CL structures will exceed those of the national AP sample, particularly for females and URM students.

The implementation of teacher PD, teachers' use of CL structures, and student outcomes were externally evaluated using a goals-based approach. Research was conducted on the extent to which use of CL structures impacted student efficacy and achievement.

2.1 Teacher Professional Development

Three cohorts of AP CSP teachers were offered PD in using CL structures as classroom pedagogy, with activities to support student learning while focusing on strategies that promote positive interdependence, individual accountability, equal participation, and simultaneous interaction. From our grant support, we offered week-long summer PD (with travel support, stipend, and academic year followup) to three separate cohorts spanning July 2015 (at the CSTA conference in Dallas, Texas), 2016, and 2017 (both at CSPdWeek in Golden, Colorado), with a total of 143 teachers participating. Figure 1 shows the location of teachers selected across the US from the three cohort groups.

Teachers' quality ratings for the workshop on a scale of 1 to 5 averaged 4.4 in year 1, 4.5 in year 2 and 4.7 in year 3, indicating that in all three years teachers found the workshop to be of high quality. Moreover, teachers made significant pre- to post-PD gains in understanding CL structures, confidence, and perceived preparedness to teach the AP CSP course in all three years.

Figure 1. Location of Project Teacher Participants Cohort1 (Blue), Cohort2 (Red), Cohort3 (Yellow)

The PD training evolved in effectiveness from years 1 to 3, and workshop content increasingly integrated CL structures within the course content of AP CSP; those teachers in Cohort 1 (July 2015) were offering CSP in their schools a year before the official AP CSP exam was available. In open-ended survey responses to items asking about the best aspects of the PD, teachers often discussed 1) the energy, experience and knowledge of the instructors; 2) having CL modeled for them, thereby giving them opportunities to practice and participate in CL themselves; and 3) networking with other CS teachers and learning alongside them.

3 Research Methods Overview

To address the research questions, we utilized data collected via teacher reports of CL practices used during course implementations, student-reported pre/post-course computing self-efficacy surveys, teacher-reported student enrollment data and demographics, and teacher-reported student AP scores provided by the College Board. Measures included:

- A teacher pre-PD background information survey
- Teacher surveys of the frequency and average length of time each CL structure was used in class
- A 15-item measure (5-point Likert scale) of student computing self-efficacy adapted from [14]
- Classroom-level aggregate student enrollment and grade results, including gender and race/ethnicity
- Individual student AP scores (scale of 1-5)
- National AP data available publically

3.1 Study Sites and Data Collection

Our research study aimed to include classrooms led by 30 cohort 2 and 3 teachers who completed the PD the preceding summer. The AP CSP exam was first given in the 2016-17 school year; therefore, cohort 1 teachers and their students are not included in the present study. With each cohort, in the spring prior to the PD, we contacted the teachers and asked them to participate in our research and to facilitate their students' participation by distributing and collecting consent/assent forms, administering the pre- and post-course student surveys, and submitting student enrollment data, course grades, and AP CSP exam scores. Teachers who agreed to participate and facilitate the participation of their students were then asked to solicit and document school-level or district-level permission for the research. We included in the study those teachers for whom student participation in the research was approved by an administrator. Ultimately, our study sample was comprised of 14 Cohort 2 and 13 Cohort 3 teachers from 27 high schools across 14 states. The study's 27 schools include 22 public schools, 3 charter or magnet schools, a technology center, and a homeschool network. The analysis sample is 613 students, the majority of whom are male (58%) and/or non-URM (61%). All students assented to the research and if less than 18 years old, had a parent/guardian give permission.

All 27 teachers in this study completed a pre-PD survey of background information in June-July 2016 (Cohort 2) or June-July 2017 (Cohort 3), a mid-course classroom implementation survey in January 2017 (Cohort 2) or January 2018 (Cohort 3) and a final implementation survey the following May. Students completed a pre-course survey in September 2016 (Cohort 2) or September 2017 (Cohort 3) and a post-course survey the following May. Of the 253 Cohort 2 students, 154 (61%) completed the post-course survey; 223 (62%) of the 361 Cohort 3 students completed the post-course survey. AP scores were reported by teachers for 230 (91%) Cohort 2 students and for 240 (67%) Cohort 3 students. National AP data from each May exam administration were drawn from publically available AP data the following November.

3.2 Analytical Procedures

We explored our first hypothesis related to whether students' gains in computing self-efficacy were associated with the use of CL structures. The first step was to calculate opportunity to learn collaboratively (OTLC) scores for each participating classroom for three time periods based on teacher survey data: (1) the first half of the course, named OTLC1, (2) the second half of the course, named OTLC2, and (3) the entire course, named OTLCTot. Scores for use of pair programming for the same three time periods were also calculated. Total pre- and post-course computing self-efficacy scores were determined based on student survey data. Finally, student gender and URM status were variables drawn from student surveys.

We measured the extent to which a student had opportunities to engage with CL structures (of which pair programming was one) by summing across CL structures the product of how often a structure was used (0=not at all, 1=once or twice during this time period, 2=once a month, 3=a few times a month, 4=once a week, 5= every day or a few times a week) with the average length of time per use (0=not at all, 1=1-5 minutes, 2=6-10 minutes, 3=11-15 minutes, 4=more than 30 minutes). We use the term "opportunity to learn cooperatively" so as to make no assumptions about the extent to which a student engages in a particular cooperative learning activity, but to indicate the degree to which the opportunities to engage were available. Therefore:

$$\text{OTLC} = \Sigma\ (\text{frequency of use}) \times (\text{avg length of use})$$

To control for the number of CLs queried in a given time period (e.g., surveys did not ask about the *exact same set* of CLs each time), we divided each sum by the number of CLs surveyed.

We calculated total self-efficacy as the sum of the 15 computing self-efficacy items given on the pre- and post-course student surveys. Student URM status was coded as '1' where a student indicated race as African American or American Indian/Native American, or ethnicity as Hispanic/Latino. If race/ethnicity was indicated but did not include these categories, URM status was coded as '0'.

To test the first hypothesis, two linear regression models were constructed with class-level OTLCs (and pair programming only) as the independent variables: model 1 with gain in computer self-efficacy as the dependent variable and model 2 with post-course self-efficacy as the dependent variable.

We explored our second hypothesis related to whether students' CS learning (as measured by AP scores) was associated with OTLC. A mediating variable was each teacher's number of years teaching high school computer science. Our belief was that teachers newer to teaching high school CS could benefit more from CL structures since their pedagogical skills were earlier on the developmental curve. The dependent variable was student AP score; independent variables (at the class level) included OTLC1, OTLC2, and OTLCTot. The mediating variable, number of years teaching high school (HS) CS, was used to divide the sample into different analysis groups.

To test this hypothesis, three linear regression models were run with class-level OTLCs as independent variables. The models conditioned AP scores on independent variable combinations for three different samples: (1) students of all teachers, (2) students of teachers with 0-2 years of experience teaching HS CS, and (3) students of teachers with 3+ years of experience teaching HS CS.

Our third hypothesis explored the impact of CL structures in comparison with national AP CSP exam results, disaggregated by gender and by race/ethnicity. We aggregated the separate race/ethnicity distributions into a URM and a non-URM distribution (see above definitions). To test whether each CL distribution was significantly different than the corresponding national distribution, chi-square tests were run for: total group, female students, male students, URM students, and non-URM students. For distributions that were significantly different, group passing rates (a score of 3 or more on the AP exam) were compared and percentage differences were calculated.

4 Results from our Project Evaluation

4.1 Computing Self-Efficacy and OTLC

The 15-item computing self-efficacy measure exhibited excellent post-course reliabilities for both cohorts (Cohort 2 alpha=.92; Cohort 3 alpha=.83). Computing self-efficacy scores were initially higher for non-URM students (Cohort 2 $p<.05$; Cohort 3, $p<.02$) compared with URM students, and for males (Cohort 2, $p<.05$; Cohort 3, $p=.001$) compared with females. Pre-post gains in self-efficacy were not significant for either cohort. In fact, Cohort 2 students' average pre/post-course self-efficacy scores were identical (3.1 on a 5-point scale). The gain in self-efficacy score was non-significant for Cohort 3 students; however, gains for

Cohort 3 non-URM students (n=116) were significantly higher than those of URM students (n=31; p<.01, with a small effect size of .07). Gains in computing self-efficacy did not differ by gender. Linear regressions of self-efficacy gains and post-course self-efficacy scores were conditioned on OTLC scores. For both cohorts, OTLC was not a significant predictor of gains in computing self-efficacy scores or post-course self-efficacy scores.

4.2 Student Learning and OTLC

For the combined student sample (cohorts 2 and 3), passing rates were higher than expected, based on total sample, for non-URM students ($X^2_{1,}$ p<.05), lower than expected for URM students ($X^2_{1,}$ p<.01), and lower than expected for female students ($X^2_{1,}$ p<.05). However, there were no group-level passing rate differences for Cohort 2 alone, and no differences in passing rates by gender for Cohort 3 alone. AP scores were significantly and positively associated with students' initial self-efficacy scores (p<.01) and with gains in computing self-efficacy (p=.000).

We studied the effect of CLs on student learning (measured by AP scores) for the same combined cohort sample with promising results. Use of CLs positively predicted AP scores. OTLC1 was a significant and positive predictor of AP scores (n=467, p=.000, R^2=.04); OTLC2 also positively predicted AP scores (n=400, p=.03, R^2=.01), as well as OTLCTot (n=400, p=.02, R^2=.01).

Student AP scores are positively predicted by teachers' years of teaching HS CS (n=23 teachers, n=469 students, p=.000, R^2=.10). Interestingly, when the teaching sample was restricted to teachers with less than three-years experience teaching high school CS (n=11 teachers), use of CLs was a stronger positive predictor: OTLC1 (n=234, p=.000, R^2=.13), OTLC2 (n=188, p=.000, R^2=.09) and OTLCTot (n=188, p=.000, R^2=.09).

We also considered the impact on AP scores when using just the pair programming CL structure. The use of pair programming in the first half of the course significantly (and positively) predicted AP scores (n=467, p=.000, R^2=.05), particularly for students of teachers with less than three years of experience teaching high school CS (n=234, p=.000, R^2=.09). The relatively stronger effect of OTLC (and particularly pair programming early in the course) in the hands of newer teachers is particularly promising, given the immediate need for successful pedagogical approaches in the early years of teaching CS.

4.3 Comparison with National Sample

AP scores of students in CL classes were compared with the AP National (AP-N) samples for 2017 and 2018. The combined analytic sample for Cooperative Learning (n=469) is 34.5% female (n=162), 57.4% male (n=269), 36.0% URM (n=169), and 55.9% non-URM (n=262). The AP-N sample (n=114,644) is 31.0% female (n=35,492), 69.0% male (n=79,152), 31.0% URM (n=35,561), and 66.5% non-URM (n=76,222).

Cohorts 2 and 3 AP score results were compared with the combined AP National samples from 2017 and 2018. Figure 2 shows the percentages of students who received each AP score for the CL and AP-N samples by and across student groups. The passing rate (score of 3 or above) for all students in the CL sample, 76.8%, was significantly higher than the AP-N sample, 72.3% ($X^2_{1,}$ p<.05). The passing rate for URM students in the CL sample, 66.3%, was significantly higher than the AP-N sample, 55.0% ($X^2_{1,}$ p<.01) – a difference of over 11 percentage points! The passing rate for CL male students, 79.9%, was significantly higher than male students in the AP-N sample, 73.7% ($X^2_{1,}$ p<.05) - a difference of over 6 percentage points. Finally, the passing rates for female students and for non-URM students were not different for the two samples (female CL= 69.1% vs. 69.2% for AP-N; non-URM CL=82.4% vs. 80.6% for AP-N).

Figure 2. AP Scores for Cohorts 2+3 Cooperative Learning and 2017+2018 AP National Samples

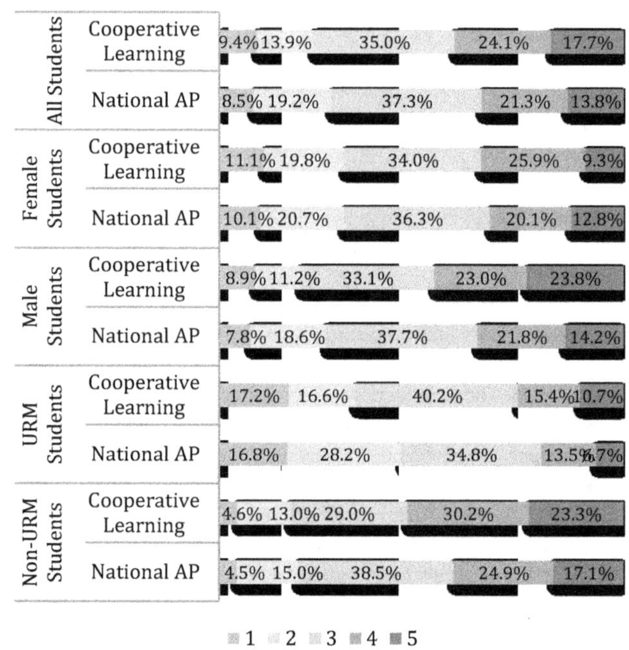

5 Discussion and Lessons Learned

Drawing on previous research, we set out to prepare three cohorts of AP CSP teachers to infuse CL techniques into their courses and then examine the results of our efforts. Specifically, we hypothesized that opportunity to learn collaboratively would have a positive and cumulative impact on students' computing self-efficacy, particularly for URM and female students. Additionally, we anticipated that opportunities to learn collaboratively would positively impact students' AP scores, and that our sample of students learning with CL would have higher AP CSP exam scores than those of the national sample, particularly for females and URM students.

As anticipated, baseline assessments of students' computing self-efficacy indicated lower self-efficacy for URM than non-URM students, and for female than male students. Unexpectedly, gains from pre-post gains were non-significant in both cohorts 2 and 3, and opportunities to learn collaboratively predicted neither pre-post gains in self-efficacy nor post-course self-efficacy. In Cohort 3, non-URM students gained more than URM students between pre- and post-measures of self-efficacy. The lack of apparent association between OTLC and computing self-efficacy was surprising and may be an area of future research in CS courses.

When examining AP CSP exam scores, we found that students' scores, like scores on our measure of computing self-efficacy, were lower for URM than non-URM students, and for female than male students. Furthermore, these two measures were correlated: computing self-efficacy, and gains in self-efficacy from pre- to post-course, positively predicted student AP exam scores. As expected, students with more opportunities to learn collaboratively, both overall and using pair programming in particular, tended to have higher AP CSP scores. The positive impact of CL appeared most substantial for teachers with fewer than three years of CS teaching experience, a promising and important finding given that newer teachers do not yet have the same pedagogical experience and expertise than veteran teachers.

When we compared students in our research Cohorts 2 and 3 to the national cohort of AP CSP exam takers in 2017 and 2018, we see that the CL study students had passing rates (i.e., scoring 3 or higher) above or equal to the national sample in ***all*** groups of interest (female, male, URM, non-URM, and total). This is a promising finding, made more so when looking at particular passing rates for these groups: while 55% of URMs in the national sample passed, 66% did in our study, and while 74% of the male students in the national sample passed, 80% did in our study. Furthermore, all students in our combined cohort (n=469) outperformed the extremely large national AP sample (n=144,644) by 5 percentage points. Broadly, these findings may suggest that CL can particularly be advantageous to URM students and helpful to male students, while having a potentially positive impact on female students (the CL sample had a larger % of female students, when compared with the AP-N sample; this larger female sample did as well as the national sample).

5.1 Limitations and Threats to Validity

We note some limitations of the present study. In this research, we engaged in numerous and varied data collection activities with the participating teachers, and to a lesser extent, their students, in order to understand the effects of the PD on teachers; whether, how, and to what extent the teachers implemented CL in their AP CSP classrooms; and whether and to what extent the CL activities had an impact on student self-efficacy and AP exam scores. In this study, however, we know little about the students in the national sample and their AP CSP teachers - whose outcomes constitute the counterfactual in this research. For example, we are unaware of the extent to which the nation's AP CSP teachers are trained in CL techniques, and the extent to which they may also use CL in their CSP classrooms - an important point when we are examining their average exam scores compared to the CL study sample. We also must consider that in addition to CL, the summer workshops included content on the AP CSP exam more generally. In this study, we did not examine in a national sample the extent to which AP CSP teachers are formally trained on and understand, for example, the AP CSP curriculum framework and how the exam is structured and scored - all of which may impact their students' exam scores. Finally, we acknowledge that the teachers who self-selected into our PD opportunity are likely different to some extent from their peers across the country, and that these differences may drive some or even all of the findings comparing the CL study sample to the national sample - in essence, a threat to internal validity. These limitations could be addressed in future research with an experimental or quasi-experimental design in which both study groups (research and comparison/control) are fully engaged with data collection activities.

6 Conclusion

Cooperative learning has been studied deeply in many areas, including STEM subjects, but little is known about its application in the context of CS courses. This paper described our investigation into the best practices that lead to the creation and evaluation of PD that infuses the ideas of CL structures within the AP CSP context. Although student opportunities to learn collaboratively (OTLC) was generally not a significant predictor of gains in computing self-efficacy scores or final (post-course) self-efficacy scores, student learning in CL classrooms (as measured by AP CSP scores) demonstrated positive results when compared to national scores. This is particularly notable for female students and URM students. The use of pair programming in the early part of the course significantly and positively predicted AP scores, particularly for students of teachers with less than three years of experience teaching high school. This is encouraging, given the immediate need for successful pedagogical approaches in the early years of teaching CS.

One of the goals of this project is to create a publicly available collection of resources (e.g., workbook and accompanying videos) that document the best practices of applying cooperative learning structures within the AP CSP context. To that end, a subset of 22 teachers from Cohorts 2 and 3 met for two days in July 2018 to share AP CSP lessons that integrate CL structures designed by the teachers for use in their own AP CSP classes. Each of the participating teachers had the responsibility of documenting lessons using a predetermined template that specifies the AP CSP learning objectives targeted in the lesson, as well as the CL structures used. The lessons are documented such that they could be reproduced in any AP CSP class. In addition, video clips of current AP CSP teachers demonstrating selected CL structures in their AP CSP classes are available (http://bit.ly/apcsp-cl).

As future work, we plan to investigate the impact of CL structures in other curricula, such as AP CSA. Additionally, CL has been investigated in the context of college courses [15], but we are not aware of how CL can be extended or modified for use in college CS courses in large lecture groups (particularly when the seating arrangement is fixed and does not support the arrangement of students into groups). Other interesting areas for further investigation include online tools for supporting distance learning of CS courses that are taught with CL structures, where the participants may be in different geographical locations.

ACKNOWLEDGMENTS

We thank Lien Diaz for her support in encouraging us to consider the application of cooperative learning to CS Principles. We also thank the CSTA and our colleagues at CSPdWeek in Golden, Colorado for helping to host our summer workshops. This project was funded in part by NSF STEM-C award #1441045.

REFERENCES

[1] Gillies, R. M. (2016). Cooperative Learning: Review of Research and Practice. *Australian Journal of Teacher Education*, 41(3).

[2] Dillenbourg, P. *Collaborative Learning: Cognitive and Computational Approaches*. Elsevier Science / Pergamon, 1999.

[3] Slavin, R E. Cooperative Learning: Student Teams. What Research Says to the Teacher. Second Edition. NEA publishing, West Haven Connecticut 1987.

[4] Kagan, S. Kagan, M., Kagan *Cooperative Learning*. Kagan Publishing. 2015.

[5] Garvin-Doxas, K., Barker, L. Communication in computer science classrooms: understanding defensive climates as a means of creating supportive behaviors. J. Educ. Resour. Comput. 4, 1, Article 2 (March 2004).

[6] Johnson, D., Johnson, R., Holubec, E. The New Circles of Learning: Cooperation in the Classroom and School. ACSD. Alexandria, VA. 1994.

[7] Frey, N. Fisher, D., Everlove, S. *Productive Group Work: How to Engage Students, Build TeamWork, and Promote Understanding*. ACSD. Alexandria, VA. 2009.

[8] Himmele, W., Himmele, P., How to Know What Students Know: Total participation techniques get all students engaged with content, giving teachers feedback about what they know. Educational Leadership. ASCD. 2012.

[9] Margolis J, Estrella, R., Goode, J., Holme, J., Nao, K. Stuck in the shallow end: education race and computing. MIT press, Cambridge, MA, 2008.

[10] Margolis, J. & Fisher, A. (2003). Unlocking the clubhouse: Women in computing. Cambridge, MA: MIT Press.

[11] Busch, T. (1996). Gender, group composition, cooperation, and self-efficacy in computer studies. In Journal of Educational Computing Research. Vol. 15, No.2. 125-135.

[12] McInerney, V., McInerney, D., & Marsh, H. (1997). Effects of metacognitive strategy training within a cooperative group learning context on computer achievement and anxiety: An aptitude–treatment interaction study. Journal of Educational Psychology, Vol 89(4), Dec 1997, 686-695.

[13] Ericson, B., Guzdial M., Measuring Demographics and Performance in Computer Science Education at a Nationwide Scale Using AP CS Data, In *Proceedings of the 45th ACM technical symposium on Computer science education (SIGCSE '14)*. 2014.

[14] Compeau, D.R & Higgins, C.A. Computer Self-Efficacy: Development of a Measure and Initial Test. *MIS Quarterly*, Vol. 19 (2): 189-211, 1995.

[15] Premo, J., Cavagnetto, A., Davis, W., Promoting Collaborative Classrooms: The Impacts of Interdependent Cooperative Learning on Undergraduate Interactions and Achievement. May 2018. CBE life sciences education 17(2).

Computer Science Educators Stack Exchange: Perceptions of Equity and Gender Diversity in Computer Science

Sukanya Kannan Moudgalya
Michigan State University
College of Education
moudgal1@msu.edu

Kathryn M. Rich
Michigan State University
College of Education
richkat3@msu.edu

Aman Yadav
Michigan State University
College of Education
ayadav@msu.edu

Matthew J. Koehler
Michigan State University
College of Education
mkoehler@msu.edu

ABSTRACT

The representation of women in computer science (CS) is low in the United States and has been declining over the past few decades. Prior research has demonstrated that educators play an important role in increasing gender diversity. Not much, however, is known about their views regarding gender diversity in CS. Educators are often isolated as the only ones teaching CS in their schools, with limited opportunity to converse with each other about the underrepresentation of women in CS and other issues facing the field. Thus, to better understand educators' questions and concerns about gender diversity, we conducted a qualitative exploratory study within an online discussion forum, Stack Exchange for CS educators. The conversations gave us insights into gender diversity issues that the forum members were interested in, such as enrollment, retention, and roles of teachers. We also analyzed the lenses through which the forum members spoke about gender representation. Results from this study suggest that researchers need to continue to examine educator perceptions so that we can design appropriate online teacher communities, teacher education courses, and professional development workshops to address equity and gender diversity issues in CS.

CCS CONCEPTS

• **Social and professional topics → Computer science education;**

KEYWORDS

Computer Science Education; Gender Diversity; Equity; Educator Perceptions; Discussion Forums

ACM Reference Format:
Sukanya Kannan Moudgalya, Kathryn M. Rich, Aman Yadav, and Matthew J. Koehler. 2019. Computer Science Educators Stack Exchange: Perceptions of Equity and Gender Diversity in Computer Science. In *SIGCSE '19: 50th ACM Technical Symposium on Computer Science Education, February 27–March 2, 2019, Minneapolis, MN, USA.* ACM, New York, NY, USA, 7 pages. https://doi.org/10.1145/3287324.3287365

ACM ISBN 978-1-4503-5890-3/19/2...$15.00
https://doi.org/10.1145/3287324.3287365

1 INTRODUCTION

Computer science (CS) is fast becoming an essential discipline in the 21st century with knowledge and tools of computing being required in almost every field. In particular, the Bureau of Labor Statistics has projected that between 2016 and 2026, there will be a faster than average employment growth (13.7%) in the field of computer and mathematical occupations in the United States [6].

To address such demands, Computer Science Education (CSEd) is now at a junction where many organizations across the K-12 and postsecondary education, government, industry, and professional and not-for-profit institutions are coming together to expand access to computer science [5]. For instance, the CS10K initiative, founded by the National Science Foundation (NSF), started the push to train CS teachers for high schools [5].

Although organizations are taking such positive steps to expand access to CS, there remain some glaring issues. For instance, not everyone has an equal opportunity to access CS education and resources, especially women [21]. Educators play an important role in addressing this inequity. Therefore, their views on gender diversity and equity issues are important to explore and understand [20].

The purpose of this paper is to explore the views of the participants in an online discussion forum, catered specifically towards CS education, on the topic of gender diversity. This forum will afford a non-intrusive mechanism to understand the views of educators on the topic.

2 BACKGROUND

A recent Google-Gallup report [23] brought to light that female students are less likely than male students to know of opportunities to learn CS. Compared to males, they are also less likely to observe 'people like them' involved in CS, less likely to be told they will be good in CS by both teachers and parents, and more likely to rate themselves lower on skills relating to CS [23]. Female students may also face certain stereotype threats that decrease their interest in CS [10]. Indeed in the United States (US), of the all people who earn Bachelor's degree in CS, the percentage of women has steadily decreased over the last three decades, down from 37% in 1984 to only 18% in 2016 [30]. With many women and minorities missing out on opportunities in CS, equitable access has become a crucial issue. Equity and diversity are important for CS as a field, as they allow for multiple perspectives to be heard and more innovative ideas to develop [28, 31].

Fortunately, emerging research has uncovered strategies to help increase gender diversity in CS. Another report from Google [22] demonstrated that social encouragement from family and educators, positive self-perception, academic exposure, and career perception are important for increasing female participation in CS.

Since many of the solutions to broaden participation in CS involve educators, it is important to better understand their role in increasing gender diversity in CS. Educators have even been touted as potential 'change agents' [27] to increase diversity in CS. Researchers have suggested that educators can increase gender diversity in their CS classrooms by increasing their pedagogical content knowledge, cultural diversity content knowledge, interests in teaching, and interactions with students. Researchers also suggest that educators develop relations with local communities, colleges, and industries and join teacher communities [12, 19, 27]. The last suggestion appears to be especially important, as many CS teachers are 'singletons', or the only ones teaching CS in their high schools with little chance to share and discuss problems, such as underrepresentation of women, while teaching the subject [43]. Margolis et al. suggested the importance having a community of CS teachers, citing an example where an educator shared with her peers a successful recruitment technique that increased diversity in her classroom [27]. Moreover, high school CS teacher networks were proved important for promoting a sense of community, increasing teacher reflection and creating a change in teaching practices [32]. Recently, many online CS educator communities have formed, where teachers can discuss with their peers the issues they face while teaching CS [4]. For instance, Alice Community forum [3], CSTA online K-12 repository [16], CS10K community [15], Computing at Schools (CAS) [8], and ISTE [24] have discussion forums online.

One of the largest online discussion networks, Stack Exchange (SE) [39], also has a discussion forum for CS educators. Stack Exchange is a Question and Answer (Q&A) platform that comprises many different websites. These websites are categorised into six major domains: *Technology, Culture/Recreation, Life/Arts, Science, Professional,* and *Business.* The website *Computer Science Educators Stack Exchange* (CSEd SE) [13] is a part of the Stack Exchange network that specifically caters to those interested in the field of Computer Science Education and it is listed under the *'professional'* domain. The formal introduction to the forum hails it as *'Q&A for those involved in the field of teaching Computer Science.'* People interested in this field can pose questions on the forum. These questions can later be answered by other fellow users on the forum. Each question can be tagged with descriptive categories such as 'classroom management', 'curriculum design', 'lesson plan', and so on, to describe the context of the questions asked. Users have many opportunities to interact on the forum, by asking questions, responding to questions, commenting on questions and responses, and up-voting or down-voting questions and responses. Thus, this forum acts as a platform for CS educators and those interested in this field to build their professional and learning networks.

To better understand the questions, views, and concerns that CS educators have regarding gender diversity in CS, we studied discussions on the SE platform. This exploratory research will help us begin to understand what questions or concerns CS educators may have, especially as little research has been done in this area so far.

The following research questions guided the study:

(1) What kind of topics do community members of CSEd Stack Exchange discuss when talking about issues of gender diversity in CS?
(2) What are some lenses through which community members of CSEd Stack Exchange discuss gender roles with regards to CS?

3 METHODS

We used data mining and qualitative coding to better understand the educator perceptions of gender, equity, and diversity expressed in the forum. We also address ethics and privacy concerns of using internet data in this section.

3.1 Data mining

To find evidence of perceptions of equity and gender diversity within CSEd SE, we used the stackr package [40] and the R software to mine the website for all the descriptive tags that were associated with the research questions. We found 207 tags in total as of August 2018. We then hand coded the data to find tags that seemed relevant to gender diversity. After this process, we chose the tags 'equity'[1] and 'diversity gap'[2]. Then, we mined all the questions tagged with 'equity' and 'diversity gap' and the associated answers, also with the stackr package. The stackr package returned only the metadata such as the question id, answer id, number of votes, user id, view count, and url for the post. With the help of web crawling and the metadata (question id and answer id), we extracted the text related to the questions and answers from the website. We then merged the textual data with the relevant metadata and wrote them into csv files using R. These spreadsheets were then used for qualitative coding.

3.2 Data Analysis

We used a process of content analysis to code the data. Kirppendorff [11, 26] describes content analysis as a 'research technique for making replicable and valid inferences from texts (or other meaningful matter) to the contexts of their use'. It has origins from analysis of mass media and is applicable to 'substantive problems at the intersection of culture, social structure, and social interaction' [11, 42]. It has been used to study 'knowledge generation' in discussion forums [36]. Thus, this approach was suitable to code the data. We followed the procedure for content analysis as described in Cohen et al [11].

[1]From CSEd SE: 'Questions on promoting fairness, especially the inclusion of groups underrepresented in computer science.'

[2]From CSEd SE: 'Diversity Gap refers to the fact that in some countries with a diverse population, such as the US, certain groups, especially minorities, but also women, are not represented equally in CS education, nor in the workplace. Use this tag for questions relating to how educators can overcome this gap.'

We chose sentence as the unit of analysis. To determine the codes from the data (more specific, level two) and then construct categories (more general, level one), the first author engaged in open coding by assigning themes for the ideas reflected in the written data. After multiple rounds of generating themes and collapsing them into related codes, the author decided on finalizing eleven codes. Later, the author grouped these codes into five larger categories, then again went through the data and decided where a sentence or a group of sentences that formed an idea would fall under the codes. The author also wrote a codebook with relevant themes, codes, categories, descriptions of what they represent, and rules to be used while coding the data, such as the codes not being mutually exclusive. Finally, to calculate the inter-rater reliability (IRR), the second author read the codebook and using it, coded about one third of the data in a new spreadsheet using the same strategy as the first author. [3]

The mean percent agreement across all the codes and categories was 92%. The IRR using Cohen's Kappa was 0.79, with sd = 0.15, which is a substantial agreement [21].

Finally, the metadata for the users, which included the user id and a url for the users' profile, was used to determine the profession of the users and the countries they were from.

3.3 Privacy & Ethics of Internet Research

The information available in the website are publicly observable data and are not human research data, as the data are posts on the CSEd SE website that are open to all without any password or login. The authors received clearance from their institutional IRB for this purpose. Although all data used in this paper are publicly available, in order to maintain confidentiality and respect the privacy of the users on the website, we have not written complete quotes and other identifiers from the participants in a way that they can lead to the participant by an internet keyword search. We have only used short phrases and a few quotes. We request readers to keep this in mind as they read the results section.

4 RESULTS

Here, we describe some data regarding the CSEd SE website to better contextualize the research questions. As of August 2018, there were 571 questions that had been asked on the platform, with an average of five answers per question and 100% of the questions answered. In addition, there were approximately 5500 registered users of the website and a visit rate of around 150 people per day.

The equity tag had five questions and the diversity gap tag had one question, with an average of eight answers per question. The equity and diversity tags had very few questions compared to the curriculum design tag (79 questions), with the highest number. In terms of view count, the tags ranked quite high, however, with two of the six questions in top fifteen and approximately 32,500 views between the two questions. Of the four different users who asked the six questions, three were educators (including both K-12 and college teachers) and the fourth was anonymous. Of the 50 total answers, 46 were answered by unique users. Of these 46 users, 9 had specified themselves as educators (including both K-12 and college teachers), 5 as working professionals, 3 as students, and 29 chose to be anonymous. The users were from several different countries, including the US, UK, Ireland, and India. The questions asked, however, seemed to be directed towards the issues relating to the US, such as asking about the fall of women's representation in CS in the US and about CS1/CS2 courses. The participants who asked these questions were also from the US.

4.1 RQ1: What kind of topics do community members of CSEd Stack Exchange discuss when talking about issues of gender diversity in CS?

As mentioned earlier, there were six total questions in the gender diversity topic area. Of these, two specifically were related to finding out more about the percentage of women enrolled in CS and how they have dropped over the years. Three were about how to increase, encourage, and maintain gender diversity and representation in CS programs. The last question was about sharing appropriate role models and examples of women in CS that could be included in CS1 and CS2 courses. In the forum gender was mostly discussed in binary terms (male and female), hence our categories reflect the same. The topic areas that were discussed within these two tags were broadly about

(1) Gender roles in CS
(2) CS enrollment and retention
(3) The role of teachers, schools, and workplaces (referred to collectively as features of context)
(4) CS course and program enhancements
(5) The nature of CS and CS education over the years

We discuss the material on gender roles in CS in section 4.2 in detail. Here, we concentrate on the four other topics.

4.1.1 Enrollment and Retention. The discussions (N=13, with N representing number of answers with this theme here and throughout) that centered around ***enrollment*** had to do with suggestions on how to increase gender diversity in enrollment in CS programs. The suggestions included eliminating *'gatekeepers'*, having at least one CS class with no prerequisites, having active encouragement and face to face recruitment events that have an over-representation female students as recruiters, reaching out to students at a young age, having faculty and administrative buy-in for policies such as *'all students register'* for CS courses, and having parents on board.

There was also discussion of reasons why women entered CS in the past. A few people stressed that when CS was a newly emerging field, many pioneers were women. They attributed this to computers being associated with typing or data entry and how such jobs were considered feminine. The difficulties discussed with regards to dropping female enrollment since that initial female presence in CS had to do with social dynamics in the field of CS. A couple of people spoke about how the early personal computers and computer games were catered more towards boys, and how the social image and advertisements have only boosted this image that computers are for boys. One person referred to peer reviewed studies that spoke about lower exposure of females to CS and their perception of lower self-efficacy compared to males.

[3]The authors who coded the data consider themselves to be women in computing. Hence, the coding scheme could potentially reflect biases that are associated with being a woman in CS.

There were a few discussions centered around how to increase ***retention*** (N=8). One person wrote how it was important to support continued motivation early on, with perhaps non-traditional grading, so that low grades do not decrease the desire for students to persist. Another user discussed how changing classroom environments to avoid stereotypically male paraphernalia (e.g., *Star Trek* posters) was important, quoting a research study to support the point. Yet another user conveyed that having high performance requirements was important and that holding students to high standards this would enable students to dispute any biases they face. Finally, while discussing barriers to retention, a person expressed that since CS has had more males than females, the classes have always been more catered towards men, which make women feel like *'fish out of water.'* Another user mentioned how the CS programs have now taken on the culture and lifestyle of engineering programs and thus have fewer females enrolling and persisting in them.

4.1.2 Role of Context. Teachers, classrooms, schools, and workplaces played a significant role in the CSEd SE discussions when users spoke about the issues regarding enrollment and retention of women in CS. So, in this section, we explore the users' perceptions of the roles of context in gender diversity and equity.

There were several questions that **teachers and educators** asked regarding what role they could play to increase gender diversity in classrooms and CS programs. In response, the CSEd Stack community mentioned several strategies (N=20), such as actively encouraging women to be involved in CS courses, removing obstacles students may face, representing a range of diversity in CS courses to disclaim a monolithic gender view around CS, and refraining from just giving token diversity examples. Participants in the forum also discussed other strategies that teachers could use such as making a note of classroom and group dynamics, observing who dominates in discussions then acting appropriately, changing the classroom's physical environment to favour women and girls, and so on. A few other suggestions centered around finding out more from the students themselves about how they feel about biases and gender issues. These included talking to students, administering surveys, encouraging students to define what unacceptable behavior means for them, asking them how they would respond to gray-area discrimination, treating them as individuals, and letting them know that they are not alone.

The CSEd Stack users also had a few conversations (N=10) in terms of what roles ***schools and universities*** could play. One user mentioned the rules in their school, in which even freshmen could register for CS courses and students did not need math or advanced placement/accelerated courses. Another user emphasized how in their university there were diverse professors and guest speakers, including women of color, in all the CS programs. Yet another user gave the example of Carnegie Mellon University where the students had lifelong access to their email ids and mailing lists, adding to it the example of their own university where students could maintain email distribution lists and thus form strong bonds across different graduation years and geographical locations. They emphasized that faculty should be involved in this apart from the alumni office. Finally, a user spoke about having connections outside the university, such as colloquium series with high schools, panel discussions with companies in their industrial-advisory board, and so on.

The third component that users spoke about was the preparedness of students for the ***workplace*** environment (N=9). One educator, in particular, was concerned about supporting students' transitions from a liberal university environment to a perhaps more biased workplace environment. Users offered potential solutions, such as career counselling with a focus on students examining company reputation and environment, preparing their resumes and professional networks, keeping alumni connections, offering ways to respond to discrimination such as taking assistance from the management or human resources, actively seeking good working environments, and so on. A person also mentioned that people may need glasses or *'geeky'* t-shirts and short-sleeved shirts to conform.

4.1.3 CS course and program enhancements. A lot of the queries, conversations, and suggestions centered around how teachers and other educators could make CS courses and program plans more impactful. The ***affective and non-technical*** ways (N=7) that people discussed to improve a CS program experience were to have support groups for women, role models and mentors from the community, alumni and guest speaker interactions and to have the students themselves reach out and act as mentors, help students address their imposter syndrome, and so on.

Some of the more ***technical enhancements*** (N=6) to CS programs that users talked about were to encourage attending conferences and tech summits, such as Grace Hopper Celebration of Women in Computing, have more hands-on opportunities for coding, including 3D printing, asking students it they feel prepared on a technical basis, and so on. There was also a discussion on using contributions of women in computing for CS1 and CS2 courses, especially to explain the Liskov Substitution Principle (Barbara Liskov), Universal Systems Language (Margaret Hamilton), and COBOL (Grace Hopper).

4.1.4 State of CS and CS education. Lastly, people mentioned how ***the state of CS as a field has been changing over the years*** (N=11), which had influenced much of what is discussed in the previous sections. For instance, one user mentioned that as the views around what computer science is changes, it may affect those who want to be involved. Another user gave an example of how CS used to be more about chip design but is now considered to be mostly programming. One person stated that historically, computing was a female-dominated field and later when people realized the importance of programming, men started joining the field in huge numbers. Additionally, people discussed how the perception of "AI Winter" around 1984 may have affected women entering the field. Also, someone expressed how they felt the baby boomer generation might have been more concerned with gender roles than the silent generation and hence *'unintentionally imbuing'* youngsters with certain gender roles, which made young men have a higher tendency to like CS. According to them, this could explain why there were far more women in computing during earlier years than presently.

Finally, a user emphasized that in schools, CS is still considered an advanced elective, and how the school staff may not realize that such policies might reduce diversity in CS. They mentioned this needed to change as there was value in providing exposure to CS even if it was not for college preparation.

Thus, the topics discussed on the forum have ranged quite widely from trying to better understand enrollment and retention of women to specific strategies educators can follow to increase gender diversity. Now, we will look more specifically into the user perceptions of gender roles in CS.

4.2 RQ2: What are some lenses through which community members of CSEd Stack Exchange discuss gender roles with regards to CS?

Broadly, the members of the community talked about gender through three lenses. These were gender stereotypes, gender comparison, and gender positivity.

First, they spoke about various ***gender stereotypes*** (N=18) that exist and/or impede diversity in CS. A couple of people mentioned that teachers could have unconscious or conscious biases. One feared that it might be difficult to demonstrate to students that biases still exist today, especially if students are shown historically significant movies such as the Hidden Figures, which they thought may end up indicating that biases were a thing of the past. Yet another was concerned that it may take a long while to address these issues, as discriminations take a long time to die. In particular, a person expressed that popular culture potrayed only men as *'computer geeks'*.

There were also people who made generic statements with little differentiation between the members of the group the user was talking about, which we considered 'stereotypes' as well. One person mentioned that according to them, the reasons there are fewer women in CS was that women inherently like some majors more than others. Another mentioned that the reason women have ended up quitting CS was because they did not like it and this was the *'whole explanation'* for fewer women in CS.

Second, there were users who ***compared gender roles*** (or gender comparison) (N=14), that is, the roles they felt men and women played in CS. To explain why there were more women involved in the field during the early days of computing, a person mentioned that men did not get involved as CS was associated with typing. According to them, in those days people thought that typing was for secretaries, something women did while they *'waited'* to get married. On the other hand, to explain why there were fewer women in CS currently, a person said that men liked fields which were *'least social'* like CS and Engineering whereas women liked fields which were *'highly social'* and focused on helping others, like health professions, education, social work, etc. Another person seemed to resonate with this view and conveyed that men tend to find programming more interesting than women do. On the other hand, a user mentioned boys simply end up coding more than girls for some reason, and did not think it was because boys like coding more than girls. A user also wondered if there were incentives directed towards women which might have made them choose fields other than CS. Finally, someone mentioned that *'smart students'* might be viewed negatively by fellow students and this happened more for women as compared to men. Another person also added that in social situations students tended to give lower priority to *'being smart'*.

Third, people also discussed the importance of equity, diversity, and of women's crucial role in computing, and thus were considered ***gender positive*** (N=26). While discussing the important contributions of women that would be relevant to discuss in CS1 and CS2 courses, many (N=18) used phrases such as *'pioneer'*, *'major developer'*, *'renowned scientist'*, *'expert'*, and so on for computer scientists like Ada Lovelace, Lynn Conaway, Grace Hopper, Dorothy Vaughan, Nancy Lynch, and many more. For instance, a person said that Klari von Neumann did a lot of the coding that made her husband *'look so good'* and another stated that women were an important and irreplaceable aspect of the early computing days.

There were fewer instances of gender positivity while discussing present day classroom scenarios or strategies. One person mentioned that since elementary teachers were predominantly women they are able to serve as role models for young girls, but this trend does not keep up in later years due to fewer female teachers. Another mentioned that it was important to see gender empowering examples at home too in addition to classrooms.

Table 1 gives the percentage of answers using each gender lenses for the three types of questions discussed in section 4.1. Please note that stereotypes also refers to the kind of biases users think women may have to deal/dealt with in addition to any biased statement they had made themselves.

5 DISCUSSION AND CONCLUSION

One of the main contributions of the paper is that the CSEd SE forum affords a non-intrusive technique to understand and analyze the thoughts educators might have about gender diversity and equity in CS. As we described in section 4.1, some conversations seemed crucial to the educators, such as the discussion about transitioning from a liberal university environment to a workplace environment, wanting examples of women scientists for CS1 and CS2, and wishing to know how to make classes equitable and diverse students feel welcomed. In fact, an educator in the discussions lamented that although diversity issues were receiving a lot of national attention he had not seen good solutions. He also added that he hoped to get new and useful insights from the discussions on the forum. One more person mentioned they would be interested to hear other educators' experiences with addressing gender diversity concerns and if they could make a *'perceptible difference'*. Such thoughts, combined with the number of visitors to the forum per day, the large number of views for the equity tagged questions, and that most teachers are singletons, are testament to the fact that having such conversations are important for educators.

The topics that users discussed regarding gender roles ranged from highly insightful, gender positive conversations to some that had more rigid views or stereotypes, such as attributing liking or disliking CS to gender and assuming certain external appearances were crucial to survival in CS as a field. Further, intersectional identities were not spoken about often, such as particular biases women of color or women with disabilities might face. These are crucial to take into account and merit further investigation. Thus, this paper sets a base for future research, as explained in section 5.1.

Table 1: Percent of Answers Using Each Gender Lens

Type of Question	Gender Positive	Gender Stereotypes	Gender Comparison
Examples of women in CS	100%	0%	6%
Understanding reduction of women in CS	12%	53%	53%
Increasing/maintaining gender diversity in CS	33%	40%	27%

Also as mentioned previously in the introduction section, educators may be less likely to be telling women they will fare well in CS, but in fact need to be encouraging them to participate more so as to ensure more representation of women. Analyses, such as the one shown in Table 1, can give us insights about the areas that might need more attention from the educators in terms of ensuring more gender positive views, better understanding of the nuances of gender stereotypes in the society, and so on. Given all of this, the results from this study sets a base for exploring ways in which we can support educators to broaden participation in CS. We focus here on two concrete areas of practice: building online teacher networks and teacher development, which have been elaborated in sections 5.2 and 5.3.

5.1 Implications for Future Research

There were many claims made in CSEd SE which were either stereotypical in nature or points of view which have been invalidated by research. Despite this, such comments were often received rather well. For instance, the answer which put forth that men find programming more interesting than women was voted the second highest out of fifteen for a particular question. A thorough look into how these discussion points have been supported or refuted by prior research and how they have been received by the community in CSEd SE is required. We need to investigate the possible roles of both community moderation and official moderation.

Apart from this, there was a small discussion about how information on representation of intersectional minorities in CS was difficult to access, and thus, address. Though an important topic, the question generated very few answers compared to some other questions about representation of women in general. More investigation is required to fully understand the implications of this fact. We plan to conduct analyses in future studies which target both these crucial topics.

5.2 Implications for Building Online Teacher Networks

Many researchers have brought to light the isolation problems singleton teachers face in CS [27, 43]. There also have been positive reports for CS educators of having a community and peer-interactions, both online and in-person [9, 14, 32, 35] such as the recent example of Lighthouse CC, a diversity-focused online professional development course with a discussion component [9]. While in-person interactions are crucial, they might experience challenges due to geographical separation between teachers [29] and their busy schedules. So researchers and practitioners also need to start examining the components and requirements that online teacher networks might require. For instance, some questions that we can answer in the future could be: Is having a diverse range of people in a forum from different countries including teachers, professors, students, working professionals, etc., a positive element? Would it be okay to have anonymous members in a forum? How should sharing potentially harmful stereotypes in such forums be dealt with? Would it better to have membership registration to post questions and answers in such forums? Or should registration not be mandatory? It is important that we are able to direct teachers to appropriate forums and places where they can discuss important issues in CS, since reflective practices are important for addressing diversity issues [1] and discussion forums have been suggested as a place to do so [37].

5.3 Implications for Teacher Development

Educators may be dealing with both explicit and implicit biases regarding women. In the past such biases have shown to be reduced using diversity training courses [7, 25], although such courses can also be tricky to execute and critically evaluate [33]. Specifically, researchers have suggested educators have training and intergroup contact, interaction with diverse groups of students during field experiences, exposure to counter-stereotypical exemplars, such as of women in positions of power, collect data to bring to notice patterns of unconscious but disparate treatment of individuals, and so on [17, 34, 38, 41]. In addition, educators may also require specific strategies and tips that they can follow in their classrooms. We think that this insight into existing educator perceptions of equity and diversity in CS will help us develop better diversity courses and professional development workshops, think about appropriate 'counter-stereotypical exemplars' or other gender positive examples to provide, and so on. We hope to continue examining educator perceptions and interactions so that we as a community can cater to their needs appropriately and take a step towards making CS more equitable and diverse.

6 LIMITATIONS

This was an exploratory study conducted in an online environment. Due to this, we could not ask follow up questions to the users of the forum or do member checking. To account for these shortcomings, we followed the suggestions mentioned in the literature for conducting qualitative research in online environments [18]. Thus, we had peer debriefing or multiple investigators to code the data, used thick descriptions of the methods followed (see section 3), and clarified researcher bias (see section 3.2, footnote 3).

REFERENCES

[1] Betty Achinstein and Steven Z Athanases. 2005. Focusing new teachers on diversity and equity: Toward a knowledge base for mentors. *Teaching and Teacher Education* 21, 7 (2005), 843–862.

[2] Motoko Akiba. 2011. Identifying program characteristics for preparing pre-service teachers for diversity. *Teachers College Record* 113, 3 (2011), 658–697.

[3] Alice Community Forums -. Retrieved August 31, 2018 from http://www.alice.org/community/

[4] Neil Christopher Charles Brown and Michael Kölling. 2013. A tale of three sites: Resource and knowledge sharing amongst computer science educators. In *Proceedings of the ninth annual international ACM conference on International computing education research.* ACM, 27–34.

[5] Quincy Brown and Amy Briggs. 2015. The cs10k initiative: progress in k-12 through exploring computer science part 1. *ACM Inroads* 6, 3 (2015), 52–53.

[6] Bureau of Labor Statistics 2017. EMPLOYMENT PROJECTIONS - 2016-26. Retrieved August 31, 2018 from https://www.bls.gov/news.release/pdf/ecopro.pdf

[7] Molly Carnes, Patricia G Devine, Carol Isaac, Linda Baier Manwell, Cecelia E Ford, Angela Byars-Winston, Eve Fine, and Jennifer Sheridan. 2012. Promoting institutional change through bias literacy. *Journal of Diversity in Higher Education* 5, 2 (2012), 63.

[8] CAS Online -. Retrieved August 31, 2018 from http://community.computingatschool.org.uk/

[9] Yunjeong Chang, Leslie Cintron, James P Cohoon, and Luther Tychonievich. 2018. Diversity-focused Online Professional Development for Community College Computing Faculty: Participant Motivations and Perceptions. In *Proceedings of the 49th ACM Technical Symposium on Computer Science Education.* ACM, 783–788.

[10] Sapna Cheryan, Victoria C Plaut, Paul G Davies, and Claude M Steele. 2009. Ambient belonging: How stereotypical cues impact gender participation in computer science. *Journal of personality and social psychology* 97, 6 (2009), 1045.

[11] Louis Cohen, Lawrence Manion, and Keith Morrison. 2002. *Research methods in education.* Routledge.

[12] J McGrath Cohoon. 2002. Recruiting and retaining women in undergraduate computing majors. *ACM SIGCSE Bulletin* 34, 2 (2002), 48–52.

[13] Computer Science Educators Stack Exchange -. Retrieved August 31, 2018 from https://cseducators.stackexchange.com/

[14] Stephen Cooper, Susan H Rodger, Madeleine Schep, RoxAnn H Stalvey, and Wanda Dann. 2015. Growing a k-12 community of practice. In *Proceedings of the 46th ACM Technical Symposium on Computer Science Education.* ACM, 290–295.

[15] CS10K Community -. Retrieved August 31, 2018 from http://cs10kcommunity.org/

[16] CSTA Source Online K-12 Repository -. Retrieved August 31, 2018 from http://drupdev.csc.villanova.edu/csta7/

[17] Nilanjana Dasgupta and Shaki Asgari. 2004. Seeing is believing: Exposure to counterstereotypic women leaders and its effect on the malleability of automatic gender stereotyping. *Journal of Experimental Social Psychology* 40, 5 (2004), 642–658.

[18] Hannah R Gerber, Sandra Schamroth Abrams, Jen Scott Curwood, and Alecia Marie Magnifico. 2016. *Conducting qualitative research of learning in online spaces.* SAGE Publications.

[19] Joanna Goode. 2008. Increasing Diversity in K-12 computer science: Strategies from the field. In *ACM SIGCSE Bulletin*, Vol. 40. ACM, 362–366.

[20] Sarah Gretter, Aman Yadav, Phil Sands, and Susanne Hambrusch. in press. Equitable Learning Environments in K-12 Computing: Teachers' Views on Barriers to Diversity. *ACM Transactions on Computing Education (TOCE)* (in press).

[21] Kevin A Hallgren. 2012. Computing inter-rater reliability for observational data: an overview and tutorial. *Tutorials in quantitative methods for psychology* 8, 1 (2012), 23.

[22] Google Inc. 2014. *Women who choose Computer Science: What Really Matter.* Technical Report.

[23] Google Inc. and Gallup Inc. 2016. *Diversity Gaps in Computer Science: Exploring the Underrepresentation of Girls, Blacks and Hispanics.* Technical Report.

[24] ISTE Connect, Computer Science Network -. Retrieved August 31, 2018 from https://connect.iste.org/community/learningnetworks

[25] Sarah M Jackson, Amy L Hillard, and Tamera R Schneider. 2014. Using implicit bias training to improve attitudes toward women in STEM. *Social Psychology of Education* 17, 3 (2014), 419–438.

[26] Krippendorff Klaus. 2004. Content analysis: An introduction to its methodology.

[27] Jane Margolis. 2010. *Stuck in the shallow end: Education, race, and computing.* MIT Press.

[28] Jane Margolis and Allan Fisher. 2003. *Unlocking the clubhouse: Women in computing.* MIT press.

[29] Jane Margolis, Jean Ryoo, and Joanna Goode. 2017. Seeing Myself through Someone Else's Eyes: The Value of In-Classroom Coaching for Computer Science Teaching and Learning. *ACM Transactions on Computing Education (TOCE)* 17, 2 (2017), 6.

[30] National Center for Educational Statistics 2016. Degrees in computer and information sciences conferred by postsecondary institutions, by level of degree and sex of student: 1970-71 through 2014-15. Retrieved August 31, 2018 from https://nces.ed.gov/programs/digest/d16/tables/dt16_325.35.asp

[31] National Science Foundation [n. d.]. Why Diversity in Computer Science Is Important. Retrieved August 31, 2018 from https://www.nsf.gov/news/mmg/mmg_disp.jsp?med_id=73862

[32] Lijun Ni, Mark Guzdial, Allison Elliott Tew, Briana Morrison, and Ria Galanos. 2011. Building a community to support HS CS teachers: the disciplinary commons for computing educators. In *Proceedings of the 42nd ACM technical symposium on Computer science education.* ACM, 553–558.

[33] Elizabeth Levy Paluck and Donald P Green. 2009. Prejudice reduction: What works? A review and assessment of research and practice. *Annual review of psychology* 60 (2009), 339–367.

[34] Thomas F Pettigrew and Linda R Tropp. 2006. A meta-analytic test of intergroup contact theory. *Journal of personality and social psychology* 90, 5 (2006), 751.

[35] Jean Ryoo, Joanna Goode, and Jane Margolis. 2015. It takes a village: supporting inquiry-and equity-oriented computer science pedagogy through a professional learning community. *Computer Science Education* 25, 4 (2015), 351–370.

[36] Sarah Schrire. 2006. Knowledge building in asynchronous discussion groups: Going beyond quantitative analysis. *Computers & Education* 46, 1 (2006), 49–70.

[37] Melanie Shoffner. 2009. The place of the personal: Exploring the affective domain through reflection in teacher preparation. *Teaching and Teacher Education* 25, 6 (2009), 783–789.

[38] Cheryl Staats. 2016. Understanding Implicit Bias: What Educators Should Know. *American Educator* 39, 4 (2016), 29.

[39] Stack Exchange -. Retrieved August 31, 2018 from https://stackexchange.com/

[40] stackr: an R package for connecting to the Stack Exchange API -. Retrieved August 31, 2018 from https://github.com/dgrtwo/stackr

[41] Sylvia Valentíin. 2006. Addressing diversity in teacher education programs. *Education* 127, 2 (2006).

[42] Robert Philip Weber. 1990. *Basic content analysis.* Vol. 49. Sage.

[43] Aman Yadav, Sarah Gretter, and Susanne Hambrusch. 2015. Challenges of a computer science classroom: Initial perspectives from teachers. In *Proceedings of the Workshop in Primary and Secondary Computing Education.* ACM, 136–137.

Defining Tinkering Behavior in Open-ended Block-based Programming Assignments

Yihuan Dong, Samiha Marwan, Veronica Cateté, Thomas Price, Tiffany Barnes
North Carolina State University
Raleigh, North Carolina
{ydong2,samarwan,vmcatete,twprice,tmbarnes}@ncsu.edu

ABSTRACT

Tinkering has been shown to have a positive influence on students in open-ended making activities. Open-ended programming assignments in block-based programming resemble making activities in that both of them encourage students to tinker with tools to create their own solutions to achieve a goal. However, previous studies of tinkering in programming discussed tinkering as a broad, ambiguous term, and investigated only self-reported data. To our knowledge, no research has studied student tinkering behaviors while solving problems in block-based programming environments. In this position paper, we propose a definition for tinkering in block-based programming environments as a kind of behavior that students exhibit when testing, exploring, and struggling during problem-solving. We introduce three general categories of tinkering behaviors (test-based, prototype-based, and construction-based tinkering) derived from student data, and use case studies to demonstrate how students exhibited these behaviors in problem-solving. We created the definitions using a mixed-methods research design combining a literature review with data-driven insights from submissions of two open-ended programming assignments in iSnap, a block-based programming environment. We discuss the implication of each type of tinkering behavior for learning. Our study and results are the first in this domain to define tinkering based on student behaviors in a block-based programming environment.

CCS CONCEPTS

• **Social and professional topics → Computing education**; • **Applied computing → Interactive learning environments**;

KEYWORDS

Tinkering; programming; novice; block-based

ACM Reference Format:
Yihuan Dong, Samiha Marwan, Veronica Catetė, Thomas Price, Tiffany Barnes. 2019. Defining Tinkering Behavior in Open-ended Block-based Programming Assignments. In *Proceedings of the 50th ACM Technical Symposium on Computer Science Education (SIGCSE '19), February 27-March 2, 2019, Minneapolis, MN, USA.* ACM, New York, NY, USA, 7 pages. https://doi.org/10.1145/3287324.3287437

SIGCSE '19, February 27-March 2, 2019, Minneapolis, MN, USA

ACM ISBN 978-1-4503-5890-3/19/02...$15.00
https://doi.org/10.1145/3287324.3287437

1 INTRODUCTION

Block-based programming environments are specifically designed to help novices tinker and explore to learn programming. By using blocks over text-based languages, these environments reduce the learner's cognitive demands by limiting possible syntactic and grammatical mistakes and focusing only on developing algorithmic thinking [2, 8]. Additionally, block-based programming environments has been shown to increase learning and programming efficiency [16, 24]. Together with other known benefits [23], these attributes make block-based programming ideal in introductory programming courses [24], especially those targeted for novices.

When teaching with block-based programming, open-ended creative assignments are often used as a way to motivate students to learn. Block-based programming environments such as Scratch and Snap! are designed to encourage learners to explore the blocks and discover different ways of solving problems through tinkering [18]. Tinkering has been proven to have a positive effect on the makers in terms of their ability to express new realizations and offer explanations for strategies and tools [21]. Tinkering embraces creativity and gives learners the opportunity to explore and learn with hands-on experience. Open-ended programming assignments in block-based programming environments resemble making activities in that both of them encourage students to tinker with tools, virtually or physically, and create a solution to a problem. Thus, it is intuitive to assume that tinkering will help learners progress while problem-solving. However, to our knowledge, no previous research has defined what tinkering is in block-based programming, or studied the tinkering behaviors the learners exhibit in open-ended programming assignments, which may provide insights for the design and use of tinkering-focused interventions for learning.

We seek to better understand tinkering behaviors, and to eventually build automated systems to detect and support productive tinkering. In this work, we focus on the following two questions:

(1) What is tinkering behavior in open-ended block-based programming assignments?
(2) What are the different types of tinkering behaviors among novices during problem-solving?

In this position paper, we first discuss related work on tinkering and introduce Snap!, a block-based programming environment. Afterwards, we describe the methodology we used to analyze exploratory tinkering behaviors in two assignments from a non-majors introduction to computers course. Then, we propose three types of tinkering that we observed in the student block programming trace data, illustrating these types with case studies. Finally, we discuss the purpose of identifying tinkering and its potential to benefit programming education. This work takes the first step in defining tinkering in block-based programming environments, especially for open-ended programming activities.

2 BACKGROUND

2.1 Tinkering

In recent decades, researchers have investigated methods and techniques that increase learning motivation and capability of exploration. In return, these techniques will increase the capability of learning and performing tasks effectively [7, 22]. As a result, the term tinkering emerges from makerspace activities. Some researchers considered tinkering as a "mindset" that involves a playful approach to solving problems through "direct experience, experimentation, and discovery" [10], which the mindset can cut across intentional building and disciplinary construction activities [21]. Other researchers considered tinkering as a type of making activities, instead of mindset [14, 19]. However, none of the previous tinkering research provide actionable definition to identify tinkering behaviors in the making activities.

A number of studies have assessed the efficacy of tinkering behavior in improving the motivation in learning and exploring in different fields, like making, engineering, robotics and computer programming [3, 9, 21]. In addition to these studies, some previous tinkering research focused on analyzing tinkering as a way to explore gender differences in approaches to problem solving [1, 6]. The Coursera course "Tinkering Fundamentals, A Constructionist Approach to STEM Learning" argues for the use of tinkering by educators and learners to develop their learning [13]. In [1], authors introduced tinkering as a behavior similar to debugging, as a trial-and-error process.

The first broad definition of tinkering in computer science was introduced by Krieger et al [6]. Authors categorized tinkering behavior used by undergraduate students in computer science into four categories, named: Exploratory behaviors, Deviation from instructions, Lack of reliance on formal methods of learning and instruction, and Use of trial and error techniques. Authors used these categories to investigate the differences in tinkering between genders. Although the authors provide tinkering categorizations, their data is collected from surveys and questionnaires about previous programming assignments and not on actual student work during problem solving.

To our knowledge, there are no prior studies that provide a precise definition or categorization of tinkering based on student problem-solving data in block based programming environments.

2.2 Block-based Programming Environments

In this section, we first provide an overview of the Snap! block-based programming environment and then give a brief discussion of the related literature illustrating how it has been specifically designed to promote tinkering. Scratch is a block-based environment designed to inspire children aged around 10-12 years old to explore programming by constructing creations of their own [18]. Snap! was inspired by Scratch, but was built specifically to support more advanced computer science and programming constructs, including custom blocks and recursion, for the "Beauty and Joy of Computing" version of the Computer Science Principles Advanced Placement course [5]. Figure 1 shows the interface of Snap!. The left palette holds the blocks, organized in 8 categories, that can be used to write a program. The user can drag and drop the blocks into the scripting area and snap the blocks together to make scripts. The user is able to create variables and custom blocks. The custom block resembles functions or methods in other programming languages and can be edited in the block editor. The stage is where the user can see the script outputs. The user can run a script either by clicking on the green flag to run the scripts attached to the "when green-flag clicked" block, or by clicking on an individual script. Below the stage is a Sprite palette that stores the sprites, which resembles the idea of an object in object-oriented programming languages. Each sprite can have its own behavior dictated by its variables and scripts and the user can switch between the sprites by clicking on the sprite icon.

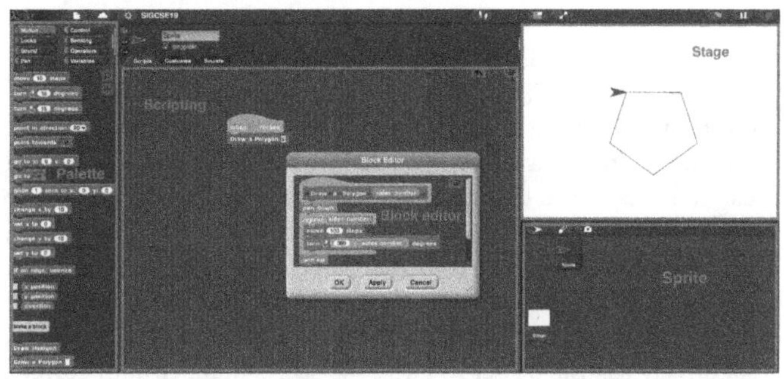

Figure 1: SNAP!, a Block-based Programming Environment.

Block-based programming environments are specifically designed to support a constructionist theory of learning [8]. They are considered easier to use than text-based alternatives [16, 24], helping prevent most syntactic errors [2]. The drag-and-drop interaction style mitigates the low proficiency of typing skills among young learners, and provides a visual way to learn the available commands. The natural language labels on the blocks make them easier to understand [8].

Moreover, block-based programming environments are designed to support construction, creativity, and learning through tinkering [20]. Blocks serve as virtual manipulatives like the mechanical and/or electronic objects in typical making activities. Blocks can be snapped together to make script snippets where both the blocks and the scripts can be tested by a single click. This sandbox-style, rapid feedback is meant to facilitate and encourage tinkering and construction. As such, block-based programming environments encourage users to tinker by creating and testing small features, then combining the features to reach a user-identified goal.

Although block-based programming environments are designed to support tinkering, there is no guarantee that the users are tinkering in a meaningful, productive way [20]. Studying the ways that students tinker may provide insights for designing curricula, interventions, and tools that improve student learning.

3 METHOD

In order to identify and categorize tinkering behavior, we looked at submissions of two programming assignments used in a non-majors "Introduction to Computers" course with 68 students. One section of

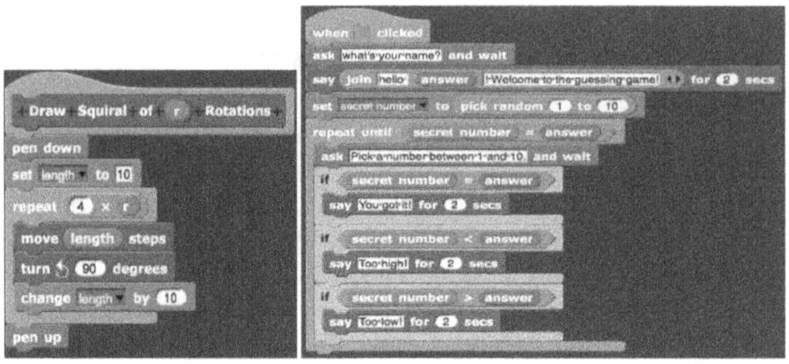

(a) Squiral Solution **(b) Guessing Game Solution**

Figure 2: Sample solutions for the Squiral assignment and the Guessing Game Assignment

the course uses labs from the BJC curriculum [5], including *Squiral* and *Guessing game*. Figure 2 shows the sample solutions for both the Squiral and Guessing game assignments. In the Squiral assignment, students make a custom block to draw a square-like spiral. The custom block needs to take a parameter that controls the number of full rotations for the Squiral. In the Guessing Game assignment, students create an interactive game where the player tries to guess a secret number. The game should start by asking and greeting the player by name, set a (random) secret number between 1 and 10, repetitively ask the player to guess the secret number until correct, tell the player if the player's guess was too high or too low, and then congratulate the player if the guess was correct.

The students programmed the assignments in iSnap, a variant of the Snap! programming environment that has the ability to provide students with next-step-hints upon student request [17]. iSnap captures a student's interactions inside the environment as a *trace* and is able to recreate the process of the student making the solution from the trace. Our analysis included student traces who requested next-step-hints during the assignments because the student needed to tinker to understand the hints and make progress. However, we filtered out 11 Squiral traces and 3 Guessing Game traces which completed the assignment by blindly requesting and following the next-step hints. The remaining dataset includes 46 Squiral traces and 62 Guessing Game traces.

Two experts, the first and second authors, took a mixed-methods research approach to define the observed tinkering behaviors. Both experts are proficient in programming in Snap! and one of them has extensive experience researching and analyzing student interactions in Snap!. The process of defining tinkering behaviors was conducted in 3 phases: initial definition, consensus, and verification, described as follows:

Phase 1 - Initial definition: The two experts started off by reviewing the literature on tinkering behaviors in makerspaces, programming, and similar activities, to get a general idea of how tinkering behavior is defined in previous research. Next, the two experts manually looked through the step-by-step interactions of all the traces on both assignments independently. Each expert created an initial definition of tinkering behaviors they observed in the interaction traces and categorized those behaviors. Then, the two experts discussed the tinkering behavior categorization they found in the dataset and merged their findings into one definition and categorization that they both agreed on.

Phase 2 - Consensus: The two experts then analyzed a shared set of 10 Squiral traces and 10 Guessing game traces. A random selection algorithm was used to select the 20 traces so that distribution of the samples across grade bins of 0-24, 25-50, 51-75, and 76-100 matched that of the total set of traces for each assignment. The experts took notes on the occurrences of each type of tinkering behavior on each of the 20 traces. Then, the experts discussed their notes to see if they agreed on all the occurences and types of tinkering, and resolved disagreements through discussion and updates to the definition and categorizations. This ensured that the experts had the same understanding of the definition and categories.

Phase 3 - Verification: Finally, the experts divided the remaining 88 traces, tagged the traces individually with the existing definitions, and made sure no tinkering behavior in the dataset was omitted from the definition and categorization. We note that different tinkering behaviors can occur at different times and for different reasons while students work on an assignment.

We present our results on defining tinkering behaviors by giving the definition of each type of tinkering behavior and illustrating the behavior through representative case studies. Purposive sampling is "based on the assumption that one wants to discover, understand, or gain insight; therefore one needs to select a sample from which one can learn the most" [12]. Therefore, the following case studies were selected using purposive sampling to demonstrate typical or interesting behaviors that can provide insights into each type of tinkering behavior.

4 TINKERING BEHAVIOR IN BLOCK-BASED PROGRAMMING ASSIGNMENTS

Our work focuses on defining tinkering behaviors in open-ended assignments using block-based programming environments. Open-ended programming assignments often provide students a set of goals to achieve, but do not restrict the students to have a single correct solution. These assignments, as opposed to step-by-step, prescriptive programming activities, give students more opportunities to freely explore the programming environment and embrace creative solutions to the given problem. As such, we expect students to display more tinkering behaviors in the process of completing open-ended programming assignments.

In this work, we define tinkering as a kind of behavior that students exhibit when *testing, exploring, and struggling* with their code to *achieve a goal* in a programming assignment. We consider a main theme of tinkering is a sense of *uncertainty* or *hesitation* within the student behavior, which can often be observed when a student moves a block back-and-forth or inserts and removes a block indecisively. We do not consider a student to be tinkering if the student knows exactly what to do and completes a feature or the whole assignment quickly and with minimal hesitation or revision. On the other hand, our definition's inclusion of working towards a goal requires tinkering to be purposeful. In this paper, the intention of the tinkering actions, whether tinkering with the "correct" blocks

Table 1: Number of traces that exhibited each type of tinkering behavior in Phase 2.

	Test-based		prototype-based		Const.-based	No tinker
	debugging	running	side-project	expanding		
Squiral (n=10)	6	8	4	3	6	2
Guessing Game (n=10)	4	3	4	8	9	1
Total	10	11	8	11	15	3

used in the final solution or not, should be to achieve a goal or a subgoal in the assignment. Since programming assignments are usually designed with learning objectives in mind, we consider completely irrelevant, playful behaviors as more of an off-task behavior than a tinkering behavior, even though they can be considered as tinkering behaviors in some contexts [20]. Similarly, we excluded painting sprite costumes from our tinkering definition, because this type of tinkering is not related to learning programming.

We identified three general categories of tinkering behaviors in the two programming assignments: test-based tinkering, prototype-based tinkering, and construction-based tinkering. Test-based tinkering can be further categorized into debugging and running, and Prototype-based tinkering can be further categorized into side-project and expanding. Table 1 shows the number of tinkering behaviors observed in the 20 traces analyzed in the consensus phase. The considerable number of examples suggests that all of these behaviors are prevalent in student programming traces, with only 3 of the 20 samples exhibiting no tinkering. We describe the detailed definition for each type of tinkering behavior in the following sections. We note that our categorization is not meant to be exhaustive. Instead of attempting to fit a tinkering behavior into a single category, we focused more on depicting the main characteristics present in each tinkering behavior we observed. Therefore some tinkering behaviors may fit into two or more categories, and each trace may contain many examples of tinkering.

4.1 Test-based Tinkering

Test-based tinkering is a type of behavior that involves executing the part of the code the student is editing. Students who exhibit test-based tinkering tend to test their scripts frequently within a few edits or in a short amount of time. Test-based tinkering can be further categorized into two sub-categories: debugging and running.

Debugging

Debugging refers to students who adopt trial-and-error behaviors when fixing a bug, defined as an unexpected or undesirable script output. Debugging is a well-known process where programmers make small changes to the code to locate and correct an error. In the context of block-based programming, students with this debugging behavior generally start with a script not working as intended, usually for an unknown reason. The student would make minor changes in the script followed by immediate testing in an attempt to fix the anomaly. Here, "minor changesâĂİ refers to changes that do not impact the overall structure of the code, for example, tweaking the parameters of blocks, reordering, and adding or removing blocks. This behavior can help students explore the functionality of the blocks and identify the reason for the differences between the desired and actual output. It is worth noting that novices tend to debug unconsciously without using a systematic approach as opposed to professionals.

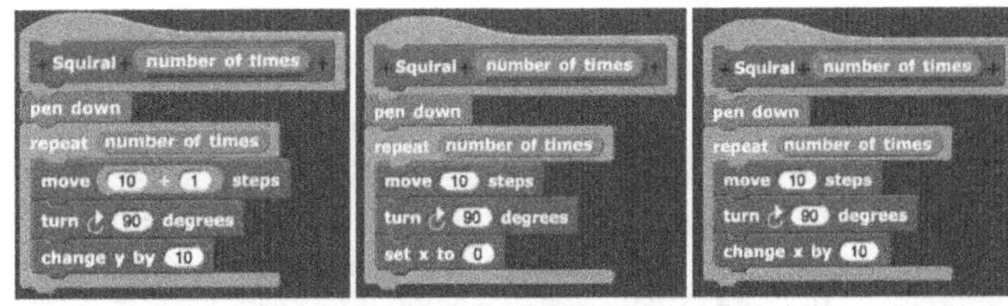

Figure 3: Debugging case study 1

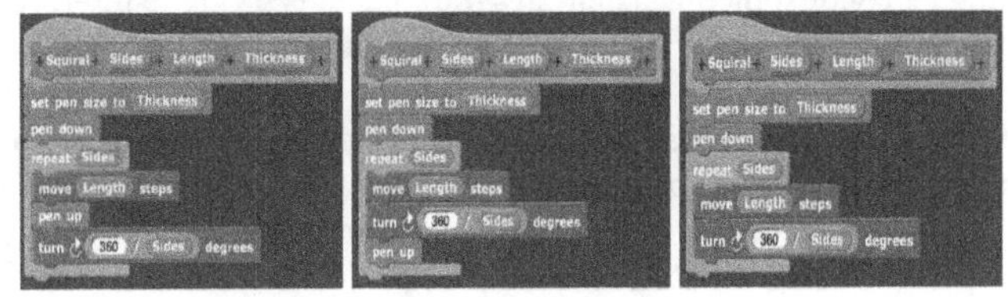

Figure 4: Debugging case study 2

In one case, a student, whom we will call Alex, got stuck trying to code correct blocks in the loop to draw a Squiral. Alex started to tinker with no purpose by using irrelevant blocks and testing the updated code afterwards. As shown in Figure 3, Alex first used the "change y" block, which is used to change the y-coordinate value and this is completely irrelevant to the activity. Afterwards, she tried using the "set x" block, which is used to set the x-coordinate, afterwards she used the "change x" block and tested again and still did not get a desired output. It is relatively clear that the student's goal was to increase side length after each turn. Although this behavior did not help the student approach the solution, it might have helped rule out those blocks from the solution and explore those blocks' functionalities.

On the other hand, while solving the Squiral exercise, a student whom we call Tay, got stuck determining where to place the "PenUp" block, as shown in Figure 4. Tay started debugging and tinkering by placing the "PenUp" block in the middle of a loop, and then tested the code. Tay found that the sprite, instead of drawing a square, only draws a line. Next, Tay tried to place the "PenUp" block at the end of the loop then tested the script again. The output was, again, only drawing a line. At this point, Tay seemed to realize that the "PenUp" block does not belong inside the loop and finally removed the "PenUp" block from the script. This behavior clearly illustrates a trial and error manner that is useful in exploring the arrangement of the blocks.

Running

Running describes a case when the student runs the code several times consecutively after some edits. The main difference between Running and Debugging is that Running involves multiple runs without making any code edits in between, while Debugging requires the student to make progress by regularly running the code with meaningful edits between the runs. Running behavior can be either helpful or harmful in different cases. On the one hand, Running behavior sometimes indicates the student is trying to interpret how the script works by looking at the output of each run. This usually happens when the code can execute without runtime errors but the output is undesirable. On the other hand, running behavior could be an indicator of frustration. For example, one student ran a script over 15 times, even though the script couldn't run properly because of using a variable named "Length" with a capital L instead of "length". The student was frustrated by not being able to figure out why the code did not work as expected. In this case, running behavior is considered an anti-pattern.

4.2 Prototype-based Tinkering

Prototype-based tinkering behavior is a way to complete a feature by first creating and testing a prototype of the feature. The prototype could be a part of a feature, with clear similarities to other parts, for example three consecutive if blocks to model three different conditions in a feature. The prototype could also be a feature assembled and tested aside from the main script, and later integrated or replicated in the main script. This behavior is similar to the bottom-up programming habits described in Meerbaum-Salant's research on novice programmer habits in text-based environments [11]. While Meerbaum-Salant considered the bottom-up programming habit to be a general problem-solving behavior, the prototype-based tinkering that we propose here is smaller in scope, e.g. completing a feature or even a part of a feature, and can appear alternately with other tinkering behaviors in student interactions. We categorized prototyping-based tinkering behaviors into two subcategories: side-project, and expanding.

Side Project

Side-project describes a behaviour where students build up code blocks (no matter the size) outside of an identifiable part of the main solution script. For example, a student tinkers with a set of blocks to assemble a small feature of the assignment. After testing its correctness or sometimes reasoning with logic, the student integrates the side-project into the main script. Another example is a student who builds up several small functionalities, each one on its own and then integrates them. Figure 5 presents an example where a student created a condition, tested it, and then added it to the main script. It is interesting that this student adopted this testing behavior multiple times throughout their work.

Expanding

Expanding describes a behaviour where the student shows a strong intention of prototyping and testing a part of a feature and then expands or just replicates it to develop the whole feature. The part of the feature usually is a representative chunk that appears multiple

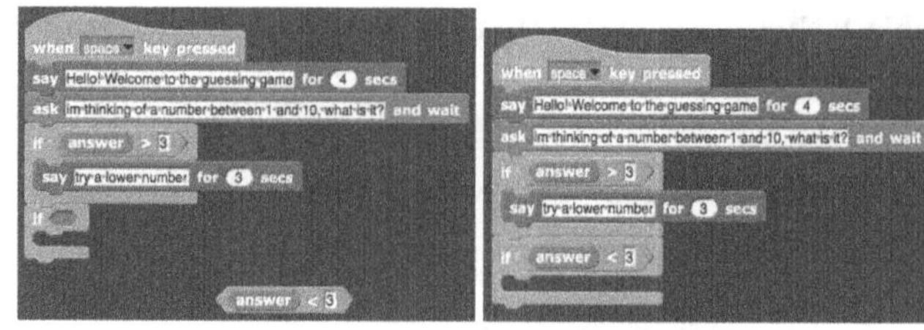

Figure 5: Side Project case study

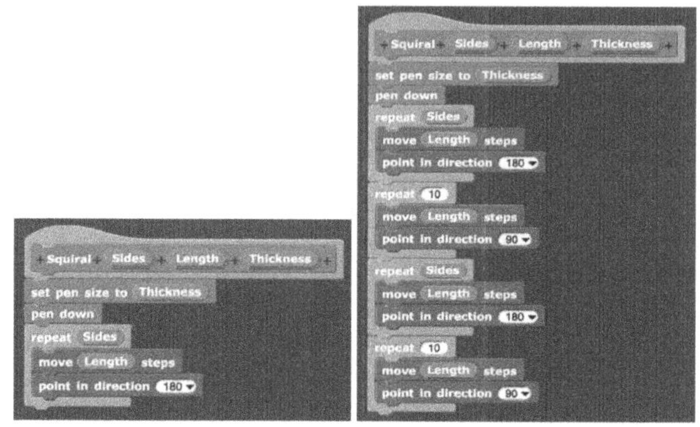

Figure 6: A Case Study on Unproductive Expanding

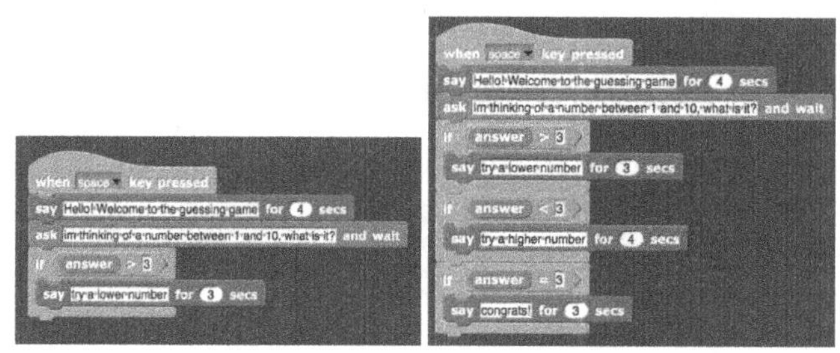

Figure 7: A Case Study on Productive Expanding

times in the feature with similar functionality. Expanding can be done both productively and unproductively, as illustrated by two cases below. Our first case study of Em represents an unproductive example of Expanding while solving the Squiral exercise, as shown in, Figure 6.. Em started a sequence of three blocks, then ran it, duplicated it and ran it again, and so on. Although this behavior reflects tinkering, we argue that it is not productive, since the use of blocks in this way misguides Em away from the correct use of the repeat pattern.

On the other hand, Figure 7 shows a case study of a student, Max, who adopts a productive Expanding behavior on the Guessing game. Max created an if-condition and made three copies of it to cover all the cases needed for the solution. Although the figure does not show the final solution, these three if conditions are needed to guarantee a correct final solution.

4.3 Construction-based Tinkering

Construction-based Tinkering is a behavior where students spend a good amount of time making major changes in the code, like

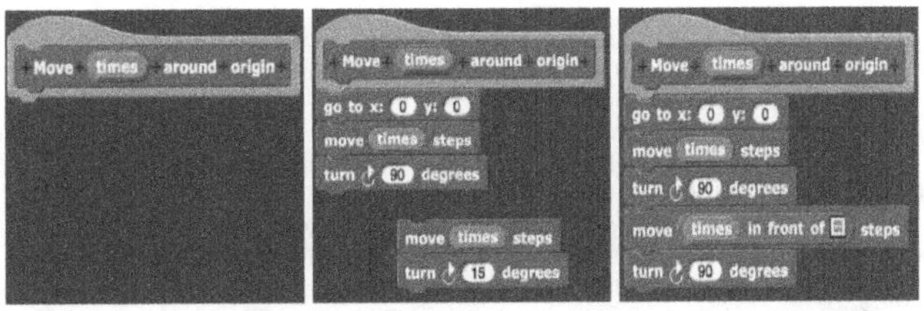

Figure 8: A Case Study on Construction based Tinkering

adding, deleting, or rearranging blocks, before any testing. Figure 8 shows an example of a student with Construction-based tinkering behavior, where the student constantly manipulated the blocks and inputs without testing. Construction-based tinkering behavior indicates that the student is likely pursuing an idea on how to solve the exercise, but still demonstrates some hesitation or uncertainty. We differentiate Construction-based tinkering from non-tinkering construction behavior based on the amount of hesitation or uncertainty exhibited. Construction-based tinkering involves pauses, or uncertainty in student actions, including major edits, or repeatedly adding and deleting large numbers of blocks. When students quickly construct large chunks of a solution with minimal hesitation, this indicates that the student has a prescribed idea on how to reach the solution without the need for exploration. Hence, we do not classify this expert-like construction behavior as tinkering.

Construction-based tinkering differs from debugging based on larger script changes with infrequent testing. Test-based tinkering is characterized by student tests after small edits, while construction-based tinkerers test complete features all at once.

5 DISCUSSION

The purpose of identifying and categorizing tinkering behavior is not to say which tinkering behaviors are good or bad. In fact, any of the tinkering behaviors identified, depending on the student mindset, can turn out to be productive or detrimental. For example, with the test-based running behavior, a student could run a piece of script multiple times, attempting to understand how the script works by analyzing the output after each run. This is often encouraged and considered as a positive behavior. In other cases, students could be running the script numerous times, not trying to understand how the script works, but only as a sign of frustration.

Our purpose in studying tinkering behavior is to learn about students' behavior when approaching a problem, and to identify moments of productive struggle. Struggling with some perplexity, confusion, or doubt has been considered a necessary component of learning by both mathematicians and cognitive scientists. Struggle becomes productive when it leads to a process of restructuring a disequilibrium towards new understanding [15]. By identifying student tinkering behavior, we hope to find ways to encourage and support productive struggle that helps students gain understanding, and prevent unproductive struggle that may lead to fatigue, boredom, or frustration.

Studying students' tinkering behavior opens up new opportunities to support student learning. One goal for identifying tinkering behavior is to automatically identify and categorize student's behavior in real time or for a static summary. One example where this can be used is to improve hint algorithms. Much research has been done to provide hints to help students complete programming assignments. While most hint generation algorithms focus on how to bring the students closer to a correct solution, few consider how to select meaningful hints that meet a student's most important current need. Irrelevant hints may lead to student distrust and as a result students may decide not to use hint features even when struggling [17]. Identifying student tinkering behavior may not only help to pinpoint the location where the student is struggling, but it may also help to track student's subgoals. Consequently, this process will help filter out hints not related to a student's struggle before presenting them to the student. In addition, automated tinkering detection can be used in building a dashboard [4] for instructors so that they can see students' tinkering behaviors in the programming environment and provide interventions accordingly.

This research may help us discover tinkering behaviors that need for a different kind of help. For example, if a student is showing running behavior indicating frustration, it maybe appropriate to suggest a hint or in-person help from the instructors. However, if a student is exhibiting construction-based tinkering behavior for a while, it may be better to suggest the student to test the code first instead of suggesting a next-step hint.

Moreover, studying tinkering behavior could guide the design of curricula for block-based programming environments. Since tinkering has been shown to have a positive effect in "making" activities, it is reasonable to hypothesize that tinkering behavior, when used meaningfully, can have a positive effect on learning to program. If proven, block-based programming tutorials can be improved to show students how they can productively tinker to discover the functionality of the blocks on their own.

One limitation of this work is that it only analyzed 108 code traces from two programming assignments in a college-level, non-major course. Thus, the tinkering behaviors identified are by no means exhaustive. Additional tinkering behaviors may exist among different age groups (e.g. K-12 students) and in different types of programming assignments (e.g. making adventure games).

6 CONCLUSIONS AND FUTURE WORK

In this position paper, we proposed a goal-oriented definition for tinkering in order to study exploratory behaviors in block-based programming. We took a data-driven, mixed-methods approach to investigate tinkering in 108 sample novice programs. Based on our analysis of two assignments in a non-majors intro to computers course, we identified three categories of tinkering behaviors: test-based, prototype-based, and construction-based tinkering. Our study shows that tinkering behavior can be productive and unproductive depending on how the student tinker in different cases. Our findings do suggest ways to differentiate between productive and unproductive tinkering. We were able to classify tinkering behaviors using programming traces, suggesting that it may be feasible to realize our goal to build an automated system to detect, support, and promote productive tinkering.

ACKNOWLEDGMENTS

This material is based upon work supported by the National Science Foundation under grant number 1623470.

REFERENCES

[1] Laura Beckwith, Cory Kissinger, Margaret Burnett, Susan Wiedenbeck, Joseph Lawrance, Alan Blackwell, and Curtis Cook. 2006. Tinkering and gender in end-user programmers' debugging. In *Proceedings of the SIGCHI conference on Human Factors in computing systems*. ACM, 231–240.

[2] Andrew Begel. 1996. LogoBlocks: A graphical programming language for interacting with the world. *Electrical Engineering and Computer Science Department, MIT, Boston, MA* (1996), 62–64.

[3] Marina Umaschi Bers, Louise Flannery, Elizabeth R Kazakoff, and Amanda Sullivan. 2014. Computational thinking and tinkering: Exploration of an early childhood robotics curriculum. *Computers & Education* 72 (2014), 145–157.

[4] Nicholas Diana, Michael Eagle, John Stamper, Shuchi Grover, Marie Bienkowski, and Satabdi Basu. 2017. An instructor dashboard for real-time analytics in interactive programming assignments. In *Proceedings of the Seventh International Learning Analytics & Knowledge Conference*. ACM, 272–279.

[5] Dan Garcia, Brian Harvey, and Tiffany Barnes. 2015. The beauty and joy of computing. *ACM Inroads* 6, 4 (2015), 71–79.

[6] Samantha Krieger, Meghan Allen, and Catherine Rawn. 2015. Are females disinclined to tinker in computer science?. In *Proceedings of the 46th ACM Technical Symposium on Computer Science Education*. ACM, 102–107.

[7] Mark Lepper. 1987. Intrinsic motivation and instructional effectiveness in computer-based education. *Aptitude, learning, and instruction: III. Conative and affective process analyses* (1987), 255–296.

[8] John Maloney, Mitchel Resnick, Natalie Rusk, Brian Silverman, and Evelyn Eastmond. 2010. The scratch programming language and environment. *ACM Transactions on Computing Education (TOCE)* 10, 4 (2010), 16.

[9] Richard Martin and Andrew Klein. 2017. Improved student independence through competitive tinkering. In *Frontiers in Education Conference (FIE)*. IEEE, 1–8.

[10] Sylvia Libow Martinez and Gary Stager. 2013. *Invent to learn: Making, tinkering, and engineering in the classroom*. Constructing modern knowledge press Torrance, CA.

[11] Orni Meerbaum-Salant, Michal Armoni, and Mordechai Ben-Ari. 2011. Habits of programming in scratch. In *Proceedings of the 16th annual joint conference on Innovation and technology in computer science education*. ACM, 168–172.

[12] Sharan B Merriam. 1988. *Case study research in education: A qualitative approach*. Jossey-Bass.

[13] Mike Petrich, Karen Wilkinson, and Luigi Anzivino. 2014. Tinkering Fundamentals: A Constructionist Approach to STEM Learning. Coursera. (August 2014). www.coursera.org/course/tinkering

[14] Mike Petrich, Karen Wilkinson, and Bronwyn Bevan. 2013. It looks like fun, but are they learning. *Design, make, play: Growing the next generation of STEM innovators* (2013), 50–70.

[15] Jean Piaget. 2005. *The psychology of intelligence*. Routledge.

[16] Thomas W Price and Tiffany Barnes. 2015. Comparing textual and block interfaces in a novice programming environment. In *Proceedings of the eleventh annual International Conference on International Computing Education Research*. ACM, 91–99.

[17] Thomas W Price, Yihuan Dong, and Dragan Lipovac. 2017. iSnap: towards intelligent tutoring in novice programming environments. In *Proceedings of the 2017 ACM SIGCSE Technical Symposium on Computer Science Education*. ACM, 483–488.

[18] Mitchel Resnick, John Maloney, Andrés Monroy-Hernández, Natalie Rusk, Evelyn Eastmond, Karen Brennan, Amon Millner, Eric Rosenbaum, Jay Silver, Brian Silverman, et al. 2009. Scratch: programming for all. *Commun. ACM* 52, 11 (2009), 60–67.

[19] Mitchel Resnick and Eric Rosenbaum. 2013. Designing for tinkerability. *Design, make, play: Growing the next generation of STEM innovators* (2013), 163–181.

[20] Ian Utting, Stephen Cooper, Michael Kölling, John Maloney, and Mitchel Resnick. 2010. Alice, greenfoot, and scratch–a discussion. *ACM Transactions on Computing Education (TOCE)* 10, 4 (2010), 17.

[21] Shirin Vossoughi and Bronwyn Bevan. 2014. Making and tinkering: A review of the literature. *National Research Council Committee on Out of School Time STEM* (2014), 1–55.

[22] Jane Webster and Joseph J Martocchio. 1993. Turning work into play: Implications for microcomputer software training. *Journal of Management* 19, 1 (1993), 127–146.

[23] David Weintrop and Uri Wilensky. 2015. To block or not to block, that is the question: students' perceptions of blocks-based programming. In *Proceedings of the 14th International Conference on Interaction Design and Children*. ACM, 199–208.

[24] David Weintrop and Uri Wilensky. 2017. Comparing block-based and text-based programming in high school computer science classrooms. *ACM Transactions on Computing Education (TOCE)* 18, 1 (2017), 3.

Using Rubrics Integrating Design and Coding to Assess Middle School Students' Open-ended Block-based Programming Projects

Satabdi Basu
Center for Education Research and Innovation, SRI International
Menlo Park California U.S.A.
satabdi.basu@sri.com

ABSTRACT

Free-choice, open-ended projects are commonly used to assess student learning in introductory block-based programming (BBP) environments. They are generally assessed in school based on criteria such as the social impact conveyed, whether the projects work without errors, and whether they are creative and engaging. Additionally, researchers have assessed such projects based on the frequency of use of various coding constructs like variables, conditionals, and iterations. This paper presents a novel multi-dimensional rubric for analyzing open-ended BBP projects that integrates assessment of front-end project design and back-end sophistication of use of coding constructs. Further, the novelty of the rubric lies in the fact that instead of relying solely on frequencies, it uses scaled scores based on sophistication of rubric components. Using this rubric, 160 Scratch and App Inventor projects were scored and analyzed. The paper establishes external validity of the rubric and examines what we can learn about student learning from this analysis. Our findings will help K-12 CS educators and curriculum developers recognize what aspects of CS middle school students need most support on, and how to leverage programming environments to provide this support.

KEYWORDS

Block based programming; K-12 CS assessment; CSForAll

ACM Reference format:

Satabdi Basu. 2019. Using rubrics integrating design and coding to assess middle school students' open-ended block-based programming projects. In *Proceedings of 50th ACM Technical Symposium on Computer Science Education (SIGCSE '19), February 27-March 2, 2019, Minneapolis, MN, USA.* ACM, NY, NY, USA, 7 pages. https://doi.org/10.1145/3287324.3287412

1 Introduction

The recent impetus for making CSForAll a reality has seen a surge of efforts to introduce K-12 students to Computer Science (CS) and Computational Thinking (CT) concepts from an early age, preferably during elementary school or at least during middle school. Block-based programming (BBP) environments such as Scratch, Snap!, Alice, and App Inventor (AI) have become an integral part of these introductory K-12 CS experiences [3]. The ease of use of these environments help motivate young learners and support their confidence as they learn to express themselves through creative and personally meaningful programming projects [14]. However, there still remains a need to carefully design instruction around the affordances of these environments, as well as to measure students' learning in these environments. Assessment is one of the most salient drivers of education at scale [5], and the need for a variety of thoughtful K-12 CS assessments cannot be overemphasized for scaling up CS in K-12.

ACM ISBN 978-1-4503-5890-3/19/02...$15.00 https://doi.org/10.1145/3287324.3287412

Students' open-ended, free choice final projects are often used to assess student learning in BBP environments. While computational artifacts created for free-choice CS assignments represent authentic evidence of students' developing proficiency, they can represent imperfect and incomplete measures of student learning when used as the only form of assessment [7]. Because the complexity of a project is dependent on a student's design choices, it may not showcase all the skills the student has attained. Additionally, it is difficult for someone who only has access to a student's final product to gauge whether a given student has received substantial help or remixed existing code to accomplish their project. Also hidden from view are the processes and practices that form an important aspect of computer science learning [1, 6]. Similarly, it is not possible to see the student's design process, how they framed the problem, prototyped, incorporated feedback, etc. The above caveats notwithstanding, final projects do afford important evidence of student learning, especially considering the lack of other standardized CS assessments for younger students.

This paper presents a novel approach for analyzing middle school students' free-choice BBP projects, accounting for project interface design and user interactivity along with programming correctness and complexity. The novelty of the approach is two-fold: (i) it uses rubrics integrating assessment of front-end design and back-end coding; and (ii) moves away from solely focusing on frequency of use of constructs to assessment primarily based on sophistication of use of constructs. Two rubrics for analyzing Scratch and AI projects were developed using this approach and represent significant improvements over existing rubrics in the field [4, 7, 8, 10, 13]. The paper discusses these rubrics and their application to analyze 160 middle school Scratch and AI projects. We find that the rubrics are successfully able to distinguish between different levels of student proficiencies and are able to identify aspects of programming where students would benefit from greater instructional support. Additionally, the paper also establishes external validity for the rubric by correlating project scores with students' CS GPA.

We believe that these rubrics can prove to be invaluable tools for K-12 CS educators. While the rubrics might be too elaborate to use for assigning grades to a large number of student projects in class, they will provide educators and researchers a thorough and detailed lens for judging student learning, gaps in student understanding, and effectiveness of curricula. In addition, our findings from application of the rubrics to student projects in one large school district in the U.S. can provide valuable insights to K-12 CS teachers, and curriculum and assessment developers who are designing and implementing curriculum for middle school CS.

2 Related work

Frequency of use of constructs has been commonly used in the past to analyze students' programming projects though it is not the most accurate measure of student learning [2]. For example, Scratch programs analyzed based on frequency of use of CT concepts revealed that the frequencies were higher for simple CT concepts and progressively lower for more complex concepts like variables, conditionals and Boolean logic [9]. Similarly, millions of AI projects have been analyzed for program complexity using frequency-based measures of CT constructs and presence/absence of specific blocks [15].

Among efforts that have deviated from the frequency-based approach, most are deficient in the coverage of criteria examined through the rubrics. For example, a Scratch rubric for a creative CS principles lab [4] uses a scale of 1-4 for each criterion, but examines only 4 criteria, namely accuracy, efficiency, reasoning and readability. Another rubric for mobile CT analyzes AI projects using 14 criteria, some general criteria like loops and variables, and some mobile criteria like screen interface and public web services, each on a scale of 1-4 [13]. However, this rubric also does not account for some important design criteria like code readability, user interactivity, use of media, use of interface layouts, and use of special effects. In fact, very few rubrics integrate aspects of design and coding simultaneously [e.g., 7, 8, 10]. But, these rubrics again rely on frequency counts for several design and coding elements. Total project scores are based on weighted sum of frequencies of use of different CS constructs and design mechanics like 'Frequency of use of forever loops', and 'Frequency of use of keyboard inputs' [7].

3. Methodology

This paper attempts to answer the following research questions: (1) How can open-ended BBP projects be assessed without solely relying on frequency counts, and accounting for elements of both design and code?; (2) How can we establish validity and reliability evidence for the developed rubrics?; (3) What can free-choice projects tell us about students' proficiencies and difficulties with introductory CS concepts?; and (4) How do these programming artifacts differ based on student, teacher and school level variables?

3.1 Rubric development

The rubrics described in this paper were adapted from previous rubrics designed to integrate elements of design and coding [7], but instead of relying solely on frequency counts, scores each rubric criterion on a scale of 0-3, with 3 representing the highest level of proficiency. The rubrics evaluate student projects in depth along various criteria across three dimensions: overall proficiency, user experience (design elements) and coding & CS constructs. Table 1 presents the 19-criteria rubric for Scratch projects. Most criteria were scored along a 3-point scale, with 0 representing lack of use or lack of proficiency, and 3 representing 'exceeding grade level proficiency'.

The rubric for examining AI projects is similar to that for Scratch and consists of 20 rubric criteria across the same three rubric dimensions. Some criteria are specific to AI such as the screen layout, the dynamic nature of the interface, the use of sensors, and the use of connectivity and storage. On the other hand, some rubric criteria like message passing and program termination are Scratch specific and not shared by the AI rubric. Even for criteria shared across rubrics, the interpretation of scores along the scale tend to vary slightly. For example, code readability for Scratch projects is based on how well commented the code is, and the extent of user instructions provided, but it also accounts for meaningful naming of design components for AI projects.

While these rubrics were developed keeping in mind expected proficiency at the middle school level, they can be scaled to other grade levels with slight modifications. For example, several of the criteria for emerging proficiency in middle school can be considered to be criteria for proficiency for younger students.

3.2 Data measures

Students' end-of-semester Scratch and AI projects were collected from all middle school classes in a large urban school district in Western US. Classes were excluded if they followed a modified curriculum, used different programming languages or ran significantly longer than normal. The district was in its 3rd year of middle school CS implementation, and offered a first level CS course using Scratch, and a second level course using AI. The Scratch course comprised mostly 6th grade students and some 7th grade students, while the AI course comprised mostly 7th grade students and some 8th grade students. Both courses typically ran for 9 or 12 weeks. All students received similar instructions to combine what they had learnt as part of the course in their final free-choice projects. In all, an initial set of 153 Scratch projects and 87 AI projects were collected from which the evaluation sample of 80 Scratch and 80 AI projects were selected. For each project collected, data was also collected on a range of variables at the student, teacher and school level that might be associated with project performance and learning outcomes.

In order to select 160 projects from the 240 collected projects, a random sampling was performed, while also trying to match the ethnicity and gender distribution with that of the district enrolment at the middle school level. For the 80 Scratch projects selected, the distribution generally reflected the diverse student population of the district—48% female, 52% male; 7% African Americans, 38% Asian Americans, 27% Latinos, 12% Whites, 24% ELL and 12% students with special needs. However, for AI projects, since we had to select a sample of 80 projects from the set of only 87 collected projects, we were limited in how closely we could match our sample with the district population.

Table 1: Multi-dimensional rubrics for analyzing free-choice Scratch programming projects

OVERALL PROFICIENCY				
	Lacking basic proficiency 0 point	**Emerging proficiency 1 point**	**Proficient 2 points**	**Exceeding grade level proficiency 3 points**
Program Correctness	Programs contains several errors	Program contains a few errors	Program runs without errors, but the functionality and/or output is inappropriate (semantic errors)	Program runs correctly without errors and the output is appropriate
Code Readability	There are no comments or user instruction for running the code	The source code is somewhat readable; it is partly commented or has some partial user instruction	The source code is either fully commented or has complete user instruction	The source code is fully commented and has complete user instruction
Novelty	Not meeting minimal requirements	Not very novel	Some novelty	Very novel
Engagement	Not meeting minimal requirements	Not very engaging	Somewhat engaging	Very engaging
Complexity	Not meeting minimal requirements	Not very complex	Somewhat complex	Very complex
USER EXPERIENCE				
	Lacking basic proficiency 0 point	**Emerging proficiency 1 point**	**Proficient 2 points**	**Exceeding grade level proficiency 3 points**
User Inputs	No user inputs (no Ask blocks)	Program asks for user input (Use of Ask block) but the program does not respond to the user input	At least 1 user input (using the Ask block) that the program responds to	More than 1 user input (using the Ask block) that the program responds to
Keyboard Interactivity	No event handler used	One or more instances of only 1 type of event handler	Use of 2-3 types of event handlers	Use of 4 or more types of event handlers
Motion of Sprites	No motion of sprites	Motion of sprites on their own or user-controlled navigation; No collision detection	Motion of sprites on their own or user-controlled navigation, but with collision detection	Motion of sprites on their own and user-controlled navigation, along with collision detection
Use of Media	No use of user-created media or music	Use of music, but no user-created media	At least 1 type of use of user-created media	More than 1 type of use of user-created media, and use of music
Use of Special Effects	No special effects (No ongoing/frequent changes in size, costume, color, scene, or show/hide of sprite, etc.)	Minimal special effects (few ongoing/frequent changes in size, costume, color, scene, or show/hide of sprite, etc.)	Moderate special effects (some ongoing/frequent changes in size, costume, color, scene, etc.)	Complex special effects (many ongoing/frequent changes in size, costume, color, scene, or show/hide of sprite, etc.)
CODING & CS CONSTRUCTS				
	Lack of use 0 point	**Simplistic use 1 point**	**Proficient use 2 points**	**Exceeding grade level proficiency 3 points**
Use of Variables	No use of user-created variables	Variables were created and used, but not named meaningfully or not initialized explicitly	1-2 variables were created with meaningful names, initialized correctly, and used appropriately	More than 2 variables were created with meaningful names, initialized correctly, and used appropriately
Use of Loops	No use of loops	Use of forever loops or simple loops that repeat a constant number of times	Use of 1-2 complex loops. Complex loops include repeat-until loops and loops involving variables to indicate the number of repetitions.	More than 2 uses of complex loops. Complex loops include repeat-until loops, and loops involving variables to indicate the number of repetitions.
Use of Conditionals	No use of conditionals	Use of simple IF-THEN or IF-THEN-ELSE not involving any variables in the condition	Use of 1-2 nested conditionals, or use of 1-2 conditionals involving variables and expressions in the condition	More than 2 nested conditionals, or more than 2 conditionals involving variables and expressions in the condition
Use of Operators & Expressions	No use of operators	Use of only arithmetic and/or relational operators (No Boolean operators), and no evidence of nested operators in an expression	Use of 1-3 operators, with at least one Boolean operator, or one instance of nested operators in an expression	More than 3 operators, with at least one Boolean operator or one instance of nested operators in an expression
Message – Passing	No use of "Broadcast" or use of "Broadcast" with no "When I receive"	Use of "Broadcast" with 1 "When I receive" per "Broadcast"	1-2 instances with multiple "When I receive" per "Broadcast" message	More than 2 instances with multiple "When I receive" per "Broadcast" message
Use of Procedures	No procedures defined or used	Procedures defined and called once	1 procedure defined and used more than once	More than 1 procedure defined and used more than once
Use of Complex Data Structures	Lists were not defined or used	Lists were defined but not used	At least one list defined and used	More than 1 list defined and used
Program Initialization	Incorrect initialization or did not attempt to initialize when required	Partially correct initialization or initialization not applicable	Initialization required and correctly done	
Program termination	Program does not terminate	Program terminates		

Our selected sample of projects comprised 80 Scratch projects completed by 93 students, and 80 AI projects completed by 121 students. Only 19% Scratch projects were completed collaboratively, while the majority of AI projects (54%) were completed by students working in pairs. As expected, the majority of the Scratch projects (77.5%) were from 6th grade students; only 22.5% were completed by 7th grade students. For AI projects, 81% projects were from 7th grade students, while 19% projects were by 8th grade students. The

Scratch sample was gender balanced, with projects from 53% female students and 47% male students. The AI sample however had over twice as many male students (30%) as female (70%). Students worked on their projects for varied amounts of time ranging from 3-5 days to 11-15 days. For the AI projects, all students were allowed at least 9-10 days for working on their projects. Most students had a high degree of creative license to create projects as they wished.

3.3 Rubric-based coding and analyses

The responsibility for applying the rubrics and scoring 160 projects was divided between a team of 3 researchers and 8 district CS teachers. The researchers scored an initial subset of projects, while CS teachers helped score the remaining projects.

For Scratch projects, the author trained two other researchers using 3 projects of varying complexity. To establish inter-researcher reliability, 9 Scratch projects were double scored, with each researcher responsible for scoring 6 projects. After comparing and discussing scores (Cohen's kappa=0.92), the researchers resolved all discrepancies, and refined the rubric language to ensure a more consistent understanding. Next, the researchers individually graded a total of 11 Scratch projects. A similar process ensued for AI projects, with the researchers scoring a total of 23 Scratch projects and 23 AI projects.

Next, two half day workshops were conducted, one for Scratch and one for AI, where 8 CS teachers were trained on the rubrics by the researchers using 3 projects that had already been scored. Each teacher scored 2 projects already scored by the researchers to establish reliability between teachers and researchers. The teachers and researchers reviewed the scores together to resolve discrepancies (Cohen's kappa=0.9), and the teachers then scored additional projects independently. This process provided additional opportunity to further refine aspects of the rubric based on teacher feedback. The inter-rater reliability of 0.9 or above that was established between the researchers, and between teachers and researchers, speaks for the **reliability of the rubric**.

In addition to scoring each project according to the rubric, the projects were also categorized as follows: games, stories, and utility applications. Once all projects had been scored, score distributions were examined, and relationships between scores and metadata were analyzed. Since we had nine different self-reported ethnicities from students, they were grouped into four categories as follows: (i) Asian: includes students who identified as Asian and Filipino; (ii) White, (iii) Under-represented: includes students who identified as African American, LatinX, American Indian and Pacific Islander, and (iv) Two or more/ Declined to state.

4. Results

4.1 Analysis of Scratch and AI projects

Student projects were found to vary widely in terms of complexity and the type of artifact created. Most Scratch projects (55%) were games, while the majority of AI projects (57%) were utility applications, such as apps about pollution, recycling, and cyberbullying. Few Scratch projects were stories, but none of the AI projects represented stories. This result is not surprising, given that AI projects are designed to be mobile apps, and mobile apps are generally built more for games and utility functions than for storytelling. For both Scratch and AI, the types of projects that students created were similar across male and female students, though females chose to create a slightly higher number of utility apps and male students made a slightly higher number of games.

Students' Scratch projects ranged from very simple ones with one or few sprites and a few lines of code to extremely complex ones with numerous sprites, complex synchronization between sprites, and outstanding special effects. Students' AI projects also displayed a wide range. The rubrics were able to successfully distinguish between projects of varying complexity. The total project score (sum of scores on the 3 rubric dimensions) for Scratch projects ranged from 1 to 39 (maximum possible score = 54) with a median of 18, a mean of 18.56 and a standard deviation of 8.34. The total project scores for AI projects ranged from 1 to 41 (maximum possible score = 59) with a median of 15.5, a mean of 17.33 and a standard deviation of 10.55.

The projects were classified into four proficiency levels: Lacking proficiency, Emerging proficiency, Proficient, and Exceeding grade level proficiency, based on their total scores, and an understanding of what students should know and be able to do at the middle school level, informed by emerging national standards and frameworks [12]. Figure 1 depicts the distribution of Scratch and AI projects by proficiency levels. Projects lacking proficiency scored poorly on all three dimensions of the rubrics. They were very simple and/or buggy, were poorly designed, and used very few programming constructs. Projects with emerging proficiency showed evidence of either some simplistic use of programming constructs or some attention to user experience and were generally low in novelty and engagement. Proficient projects had few to no bugs and were novel and engaging. Some demonstrated use of many basic and limited sophisticated programming constructs and focused on a few aspects of user experience. Other proficient projects displayed only a simplistic use of programming constructs but emphasized a sophisticated user experience. Projects exceeding grade level proficiency scored high on all 3 rubric dimensions. They had no bugs, were well designed with scope for user interactivity, and involved considerable sophisticated use of programming constructs.

The projects were also examined for proficiency on the individual rubric dimensions. For Scratch projects, 40% were proficient on the 'overall dimension', but fewer projects demonstrated proficiency on the user experience (19%) and CS constructs (12%) dimensions. However, about half the AI projects (49%) were proficient or exceeded grade level proficiency on the user experience dimension of the rubric, unlike a mere 19% in case of Scratch projects. This result can be attributed to affordances of the AI programming environment that is, by design, intended to focus more on visual layout and user interaction, as well as the AI curriculum used in the district that focuses on user-centered design. For the CS score dimension, a majority of AI projects seem to be lacking proficiency. But, it is important to note that a lack of use of CS constructs does not necessarily equate to lack of CS proficiency. In fact, we often see reasonably complex and very creative AI projects that are visually engaging but have very simple CS code; the complexity primarily arising from the user interface and media used.

The attention to both design and coding in the rubric helps characterize these projects as proficient.

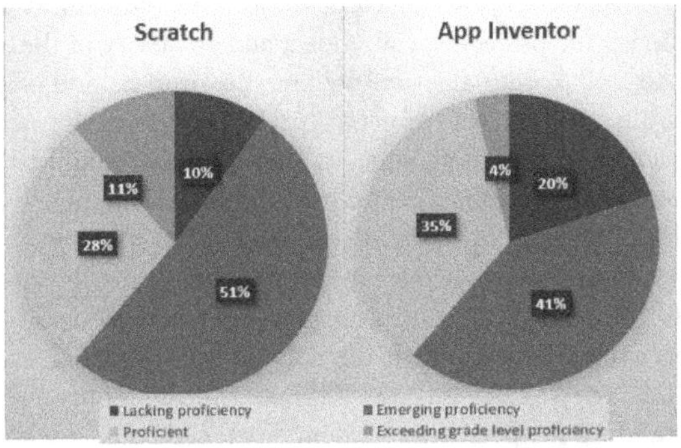

Figure 1. Scratch and AI projects by proficiency levels

Overall, most students were well versed in programming simple concepts like collision detection, keyboard interactivity, and broadcasting and receiving messages. Projects revealed students' comfort with creating sprites with a multitude of changing costumes in Scratch, and mobile apps with nuanced layouts in AI. Most projects were without syntax errors, and several contained neither syntax nor semantic errors. As students progressed from Scratch in Year 1 of middle school to AI in Year 2, they attempted more complex projects. Perhaps, this difference in complexity is reflected in overall lower program correctness for AI projects compared to Scratch projects. A number of very simple Scratch projects were found where the lack of complexity minimized the probability of syntax or semantic errors.

In both these environments, students showed skill in simplistic use of most CS constructs like loops, conditionals, operators, and variables, but did not often demonstrate sophisticated use, such as use of repeat-until loops, nested conditionals, loops and conditionals involving variables and expressions, and Boolean operators. Students showed some degree of proficiency with the creation, initialization, and use of variables, with 38 Scratch projects and 25 AI projects achieving proficiency. Students may have been less inclined to use variables in AI because they were able to find ways to update values, such as a timer or a score, on the user interface by updating labels without using variables. Very few students demonstrated proficiency with functional abstraction or use of procedures in both Scratch and AI projects. Also, very few projects demonstrated proficiency with producing readable code that was well commented and documented with user instructions. Still, code readability is notably higher for AI projects compared to Scratch students. Students also improved on program initialization from Scratch to AI.

4.2 Effects of student and teacher level variables

We examined the effects of different student-level, school-level, and course-level variables on students' total project scores to examine whether there was any difference in performance based on these variables. The primary findings are summarized.

Students with higher CS course grades generally have higher project scores. Students' project grades received in class were not available for comparison, but the CS course grades include performance on multiple assignments and assessments beyond the final project. Students with CS grades of A also had highest project scores and students with CS grades of F had lowest project scores. Putting the grades A-F on a scale of 5 through 1, we find a statistically significant positive correlation between CS grades and Scratch project scores ($r=0.58$, $p<0.001$), and a nearly significant correlation between CS grades and AI project scores ($r=0.17$, $p=.058$). Figure 2 shows the distribution of Scratch project scores for students with different CS course grades – A through F. This result provides criterion related validity for the rubric [11].

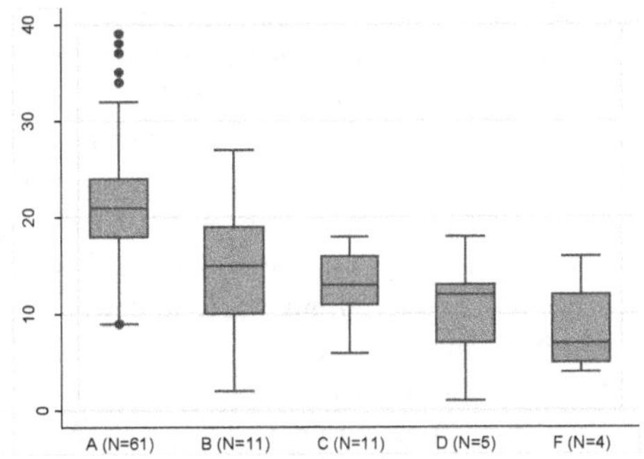

Figure 2. Scratch scores for students with different CS grades

Students with higher middle school GPA generally have higher project scores. We found significant positive correlations between GPA and Scratch project scores ($r=0.55$, $p<0.001$), as well as between GPA and AI project scores ($r=0.41$, $p<0.001$).

Students with higher English Language Arts (ELA) and Math scores generally have higher project scores. We found significant positive correlations between ELA scores and Scratch scores ($r=0.56$, $p<0.001$), ELA scores and AI scores ($r=0.60$, $p<0.001$), Math scores and Scratch scores ($r=0.59$, $p<0.001$), and Math scores and AI scores ($r=0.61$, $p<0.001$).

Schools with lower percentage of students receiving free lunch have projects with higher scores. We found significant negative correlations between the school-level variable 'Percentage of students receiving free lunch' and Scratch project scores ($r=-0.35$, $p<0.001$), as well as between the variable and AI project scores ($r=-0.65$, $p<0.001$).

No significant difference in total project score by English Language status, but students with special needs have significantly lower project scores, especially for AI.

No difference in project scores by gender, but significant differences in project scores by ethnicity. Asian and White students have significantly higher total Scratch and AI project scores ($p<0.05$) than students from under-represented ethnicities. Further examination reveals that under-represented students have significantly lower GPA, ELA and Math scores compared to other students, and come from schools with higher eligibility of free lunch, all of which are factors correlated with lower project scores. However, the disparity between their CS project scores and that of other students is greater than this general disparity.

No effect of collaboration or type of partnership formation on Scratch project score, but collaborative AI projects have significantly higher total project scores compared to AI projects done individually, and students perform significantly better when paired by their teachers based on similar interests. Students who chose their own partners had significantly lower project scores than student for whom teachers chose partners (p<0.001), and students performed significantly better when their teachers paired them by similar interests versus similar ability levels (p<0.05).

No overall difference in total project score by amount of time assigned for working on project, but students who were allowed higher flexibility had higher project scores, especially for AI.

5. Discussion

This paper presents a novel approach for analyzing students' free-choice BBP projects by developing a multi-dimensional rubric that integrates elements of students' design and coding, and assigns scores based on sophistication of use of constructs instead of solely relying on frequency of use of constructs. The rubric criteria were informed by past work [7, 13] and national frameworks like the K-12 CS framework, and went through an additional expert review, helping establish construct-validity for the rubric [11]. Also, the rubrics were used by CS teachers from a large urban school district during a workshop for scoring 160 middle school Scratch and AI projects, helping establish face-validity [11]. During the workshop, inter-rater reliability of 90% or higher was also reached between CS teachers and researchers applying the rubrics. In addition, criterion-related validity [11] was established by correlating project scores with an external criterion – students' CS GPA. The rubric also successfully distinguished between projects at varying levels of proficiency. Finally, formative validity [11] was reached by applying the rubric to identify aspects of programming that middle school students were proficient at, and aspects on which they struggled, providing pointers for refining middle school CS instruction.

Applying the rubric to score 160 middle school Scratch and AI projects from a large urban school district in the U.S., we find that students demonstrated a wide range of CS skills and were able to create a wide variety of projects spanning diverse contexts when given free choice. Students mostly create programs without syntax errors, and several programs contain neither syntax nor semantic errors. They are proficient with message passing and use of event handlers in Scratch and demonstrate improved proficiency in program initialization and generating readable code in AI as compared to Scratch. In both environments, students demonstrate comfort with simplistic use of most CS constructs like loops, conditionals, operators, and variables, but do not demonstrate sophisticated use of these constructs. Students also lack proficiency with modularization of code and use of procedures.

We found that gender or ELL differences do not appear to be a predictor of project scores. However, there are differences in performance based on ethnicity, special education status, and free lunch eligibility. Students from under-represented ethnicities underperformed, students with special needs had lower project scores for AI, and projects generally had lower scores in schools with high percentages of free lunch eligibility.

5.1 Implications for pedagogy

The rubric itself has potential to be pedagogically useful for K-12 educators and researchers by drawing attention to the various criteria of interest in a project, and what varying levels of sophistication look like for different criteria. Criteria currently used by teachers to grade student projects include ability to plan and propose the project, social impact and creativity of the project, ability to collaborate respectfully on the project, and ability to successfully present the project. Programming requirements are either absent or limited such as the project should start, be complete, have comments and directions, and contain at least one variable or at least one loop. Discussions with middle school CS teachers indicated that they generally lack time to use such detailed rubrics to assign project grades. But, these rubrics need not necessarily be used with the sole aim of awarding grades to students. They can enable educators to identify gaps in understanding for particular students or the class as a whole, and critically reflect on and adjust their teaching strategies.

Further, the analysis of student work using the rubrics can provide valuable insights to CS educators by providing concrete examples of learners' struggles as they work to develop programming skills in the context of BBP environments. While results from one cohort of middle school students in one district in one state of the U.S. cannot be generalized across all middle school students, these results are similar to those from past research in the field [7, 16], and can serve as examples. They can be used by CS teachers to improve upon their pedagogy and by instruction designers to carefully design instruction around the affordances of the different environments. K-12 CS instruction needs to emphasize important CS constructs like use of variables, procedures, Boolean operators, and loops and conditionals involving operators and expressions. It should also highlight the importance of producing comprehensible, generalizable code that is well commented and contains explicit user instructions.

Our analysis also provides the basis for allowing teachers to choose student pairs based on similar interests. It appears that student pairs performed better when teachers chose partners instead of allowing students to choose their own partners, and especially when teachers chose partners with similar interests instead of partners with similar abilities. Another important implication of this work is the recognition that differentiated instruction and extra support is vital for students from underrepresented ethnicities and students with special needs. This entails further research into the specific challenges these students face, and ways to compensate for lower academic preparation to support success in CS learning. Teachers will need support targeted towards improving their capacity to meet these goals.

Finally, though our analysis has yielded some very useful information about middle school students' CS learning, we need to remember that open-ended project-based assessments come with their limitations. When this analysis is coupled with other forms of assessment, it can offer a more complete picture of students' CS proficiencies [7]. Further, all open-ended projects may not be truly freely-choice. When evaluating BBP projects created to satisfy specific constraints or model specific scenarios, a very different set of rubric criteria are required. Without sufficient attention to thoughtful measurement of learning, CS can have little hope of scaling in formal K-12 settings.

ACKNOWLEDGMENTS

We thank all the CS teachers who helped us collect and score projects, and the researchers who helped score the projects.

REFERENCES

[1] Basu, S., Biswas, G., & Kinnebrew, J. S. (2017). Learner modeling for adaptive scaffolding in a computational thinking-based science learning environment. User Modeling and User-Adapted Interaction, 27(1), 5-53.

[2] Basu, S., Kinnebrew, J. S., & Biswas, G. (2014, June). Assessing student performance in a computational-thinking based science learning environment. In International conference on intelligent tutoring systems (pp. 476-481). Springer, Cham.

[3] Bau, D., Gray, J., Kelleher, C., Sheldon, J., & Turbak, F. 2017. Learnable programming: blocks and beyond. *Communications of the ACM*, 60(6), 72-80.

[4] Cateté, V., Snider, E., & Barnes, T. (2016, July). Developing a rubric for a creative CS Principles lab. In *Proceedings of the 2016 ACM Conference on Innovation and Technology in Computer Science Education* (pp. 290-295). ACM.

[5] Cuban, L. (1993). How teachers taught: Constancy and change in American classrooms, 1890-1990. Teachers College Press.

[6] Grover, S., Basu, S., Bienkowski, M., Eagle, M., Diana, N., & Stamper, J. (2017). A Framework for Using Hypothesis-Driven Approaches to Support Data-Driven Learning Analytics in Measuring Computational Thinking in Block-Based Programming Environments. *ACM Transactions on Computing Education (TOCE)*, *17*(3), 14.

[7] Grover, S., Basu, S., & Schank, P. (2018, February). What We Can Learn About Student Learning from Open-Ended Programming Projects in Middle School Computer Science. In *Proceedings of the 49th ACM Technical Symposium on Computer Science Education* (pp. 999-1004). ACM.

[8] Grover, S., Pea, R., & Cooper, S. (2015). Designing for deeper learning in a blended computer science course for middle school students. *Computer Science Education*, *25*(2), 199-237.

[9] Maloney, J., Peppler, K., Kafai, Y.B., Resnick, M., & Rusk, N. 2008. Programming by choice: Urban youth learning programming with Scratch. *Proceedings of SIGCSE '08*. New York, NY: ACM Press.

[10] Martin, C.K., Walter, S., & Barron, B. 2009. Looking at learning through student designed computer games: A rubric approach with novice programming projects. Stanford U.

[11] Moskal, B.M., & Leydens, J.A. (2000). Scoring rubric development: Validity and reliability. Practical Assessment, Research & Evaluation, 7(10). [Available online: http://pareonline.net/getvn.asp?v=7&n=10].

[12] Parker, M. C., & DeLyser, L. A. (2017). Concepts and Practices: Designing and Developing A Modern K-12 CS Framework. In *Proceedings of the 2017 ACM SIGCSE Technical Symposium on Computer Science Education* (pp. 453-458). New York, NY, USSA: ACM.

[13] Sherman, M., & Martin, F. (2015). The assessment of mobile computational thinking. *Journal of Computing Sciences in Colleges*, *30*(6), 53-59.

[14] Weintrop, D., & Wilensky, U. (2015, June). To block or not to block, that is the question: students' perceptions of blocks-based programming. In *Proceedings of the 14th International Conference on Interaction Design and Children* (pp. 199-208). ACM.

[15] Xie, B., & Abelson, H. (2016, September). Skill progression in MIT app inventor. In *Visual Languages and Human-Centric Computing (VL/HCC), 2016 IEEE Symposium on* (pp. 213-217). IEEE.

[16] Grover, S., & Basu, S. (2017, March). Measuring student learning in introductory block-based programming: Examining misconceptions of loops, variables, and boolean logic. In *Proceedings of the 2017 ACM SIGCSE Technical Symposium on Computer Science Education* (pp. 267-272). ACM.

Block-based Comprehension: Exploring and Explaining Student Outcomes from a Read-only Block-based Exam

David Weintrop
University of Maryland
College Park, MD, USA
weintrop@umd.edu

Heather Killen
University of Maryland
College Park, MD, USA
hkillen@umd.edu

Talal Munzar
University of Maryland College Park, MD, USA
tmunzar@terpmail.umd.edu

Baker Franke
Code.org
Seattle, WA, USA
baker@code.org

ABSTRACT

The success of block-based programming environments like Scratch and Alice has resulted in a growing presence of the block-based modality in classrooms. For example, in the United States, a new, nationally-administered computer science exam is evaluating students' understanding of programming concepts using both block-based and text-based presentations of short programs written in a custom pseudocode. The presence of the block-based modality on a written exam in an unimplemented pseudocode is a far cry from the informal, creative, and live coding contexts where block-based programming initially gained popularity. Further, the design of the block-based pseudocode used on the exam includes few of the features cited in the research as contributing to positive learner experiences. In this paper, we seek to understand the implications of the inclusion of an unimplemented block-based pseudocode on a written exam. To do so, we analyze responses from over 5,000 students to a 20 item assessment that included both block-based and text-based questions written in the same pseudocode as the national exam. Our analysis shows students performing better on questions presented in the block-based form compared to text-based questions. Further analysis shows that this difference is consistent across conceptual categories. This paper contributes to our understanding of the affordances of block-based programming and if and how the modality can help learners succeed in early computer science learning experiences.

ACM Reference format:

D. Weintrop, H. Killen, T. Munzar, and B. Franke. 2019. Block-based Comprehension: Exploring and Explaining Student Outcomes from a Read-only Block-based Exam In Proceedings of the 50th ACM Technical Symposium on Computer Science Education (SIGCSE '19). *February 27-March 2, 2019, Minneapolis, MN, USA,* ACM, NY, NY, USA, 7 pages. https://doi.org/10.1145/3287324.3287348

KEYWORDS

Introductory Programming Environments; High School Computer Science Education; Block-based Programming; Assessment

1 INTRODUCTION

The last five years have seen a steady flow of block-based programming tools into K-12 classrooms. While some block-based programming environments have a long history in formal educational contexts (e.g. Alice), other block-based tools were specifically designed for informal learning spaces (e.g. Scratch). As part of the transition of block-based programming into K-12 classrooms, the modality is starting to be used in ways quite distinct from how it was initially designed. Nowhere is this clearer than when it comes to assessment.

ACM 978-1-4503-5890-3/19/02...$15.00
https://doi.org/10.1145/3287324.3287348

Many introductory computer science courses assess student knowledge through written exams that ask students questions about specific syntactic features of a programming language and evaluate student comprehension of programs. While not ideal, such questions lend themselves well to the multiple-choice question format and thus can be graded quickly and objectively. As a result, written, multiple choice assessments are common in introductory computing contexts.

The rise of block-based programming environments in classrooms presents an interesting challenge for educators. What happens when we use learning environments designed for informal spaces that prioritize creativity and expression and situate them in formal contexts where they are subject to conventional educational institutional constraints, such as summative written examinations? Often the result is for educators to create pen-and-paper written exams or other static presentations of material based on the block-based programming environments students used in their classrooms. In moving from the programming environment itself to the written assessment context, many of the affordances of these environments are lost as the graphical representation is recreated in static, often black-and-white printed exam booklets. This raises interesting research questions on the affordances of block-based tools and if and how they support learning beyond the programming environment itself. It is these questions we are pursuing with this research. Specifically, we seek to answer the following questions:

> *Does the block-based programming modality support novice programmers' program comprehension on static, read-only assessments? And, if so, how?*

To answer these questions, we designed a 20-item assessment asking questions using both block-based and text-based forms of a custom pseudocode (Fig. 1). The exam was then included as an optional activity in materials distributed nationally, resulting in over 5,000 students completing the assessment.

```
x ← 10
IF (x > 7)
{
    DISPLAY ("inside the if.")
}
ELSE
{
    DISPLAY ("Inside the else.")
}
DISPLAY ("All done.")
```

(a)

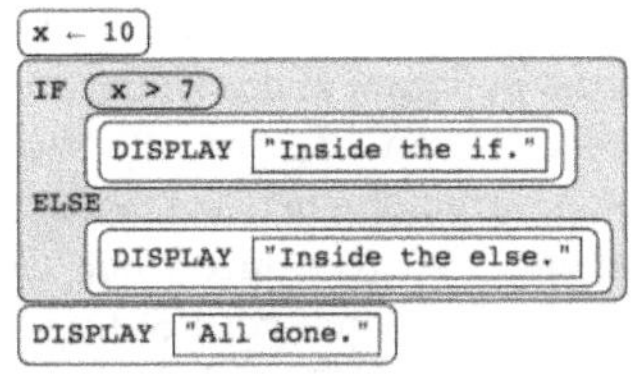

(b)

Figure 1. A sample text-based (left) and block-based (right) program written in the AP CSP pseudocode.

The paper begins with a review of relevant literature. We then describe the block-based pseudocode that was used in the assessment and present a comparison of the pseudocode to widely-used block-based languages to understand how they are similar and where they diverge. Next, we present information on the assessment we created and the methods and participants of the study. The findings section follows and the paper concludes with potential explanations for the findings and a discussion of the implications of this work.

2. PRIOR WORK

2.1 The Role of Representation in Learning

The first and most foundational literature that this paper builds on is prior work studying the role of representation in learning. This work has come under a few labels. Kaput and colleagues use the term *representational system* in their investigation of the cognitive impacts of different symbol systems used in mathematics and how they affect cognitive aspects of engaging with mathematics [21]. Moving beyond the individual, they expand this idea through the concept of *representational infrastructure* as a way to talk about how a representational system supports the cultural and social dimensions of thinking and communicating about ideas [20]. Much of this work is specifically in relation to technology and the new representations and interaction patterns the medium affords. In his conceptualization of *Computational Literacy*, diSessa builds on this idea with the notion of material intelligence, saying "we don't always have ideas and then express them in the medium. We have ideas *with* the medium" [7, emphasis in the original].

While often assumed to be static, Wilensky and Papert show how representational infrastructures can and should change over time [46]. As part of their *Restructuration Theory*, they present examples of such representational shifts, or restructurations, and provide criteria to evaluate the different capacities that representational systems play. Our exploration of the impact of presenting programs using block-based representations builds directly on this work as it is trying to make sense of representational affordances and understand if and how the way ideas are represented shapes learners ability to interpret the ideas presented. In doing so, this work shares a goal with Sherin's investigation into the role of representations in learning physics [33] and Gilmore and Green in looking at declarative versus procedural notation [13].

2.2 Block-based Programming

The second body this study builds off of and contributes to is work on block-based programming. Block-based programming (Fig. 2) is a graphical programming modality that presents programming commands as visual blocks that can be assembled via a drag-and-drop interaction [3]. The environment provides a direct manipulation interface for authoring programs [34]. While not a recent innovation (e.g. [4]), the block-based approach to programming has become widespread in introductory contexts due to the success of tools such as Scratch [30], Alice [6], and the Blockly library [12].

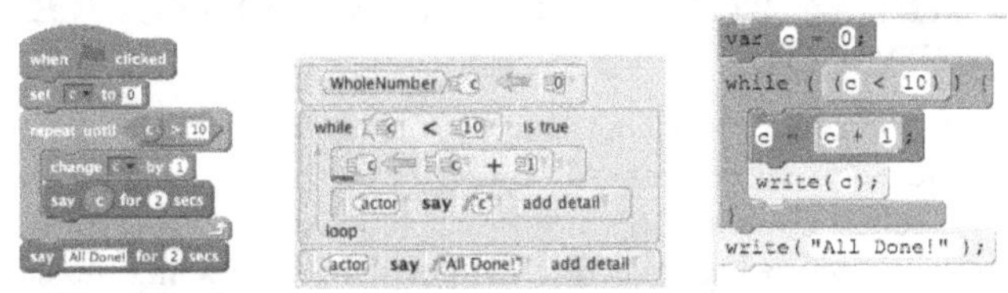

(a) (b) (c)

Figure 2. Three examples of block-based programming environments: (a) Scratch (b) Alice and (c) Code.org's AppLab.

A growing body of research is revealing how, where, and in what ways block-based programming is effective for introducing novices to the practice of programming and the field of computer science more broadly. This includes research documenting novice programmers' learning gains [10, 17, 29, 42], as well as attitudinal and perceptual shifts in interest in the field of computer science [22, 25, 26]. Research has also investigated how block-based environments can serve as a context around which participatory cultures can form, further bolstering learners identities as computational doers [9, 19, 32]. Section 4 of this paper presents a more detailed account of the specific affordances of block-based programming as these design features are central to this paper.

2.3 Evaluating Programming Knowledge

In their review of assessments of introductory programming, Gross and Powers [14] found that "some of the least studied questions are those that focus on how the environments impact a student's learning process and understanding from a formative perspective." In the decade since that statement was written, a growing body of research has started to answer some of these open questions [16]. This work includes creating and validating traditional summative assessments that use multiple choice questions to assess knowledge (e.g. [26]), performance-based assessments where students are asked to complete a specific task (e.g. [45]), and portfolio or artifact-based assessments that used student-produced work as a way to measure students level of understanding (e.g. [5]).

The work presented in this paper most closely builds off research into program comprehension of statically presented programs used in summative assessments. This includes assessments such as the Foundations for Advancing Computational Thinking assessment [17] which has been used to investigate learner misconceptions in block-based programs [15]. A second line of work this study builds off is research comparing block-based and text-based comprehension using the Commutative Assessment [44]. Studies using the Commutative Assessment have shown how students perform better on questions presented in block-based forms, even when students' preceding programming instruction was in a text-based programming environment [42]. The work presented in this paper contributes to this literature by focusing on a relatively feature-light block-based programming language: the AP Computers Science Principles Pseudocode.

3. THE AP COMPUTER SCIENCE PRINCIPLES PSEUDOCODE

In the 2016-2017 school year, the College Board introduced a new Advanced Placement (AP) course to be taught in the United States called Computer Science Principles (CSP) [2]. The course focuses on seven big ideas of computer science, meaning, unlike many other introductory computing courses, AP CSP does not prioritize programming over other computer science content. One feature of the course is that it is programming language agnostic, meaning teachers are free to choose the programming language and environments they will use in instruction. This presents a challenge for the nationally-administered summative assessment of the course as the programming questions need to reflect the programming plurality welcomed in the design of the curriculum.

In response to this challenge, the AP CSP development committee invented a pseudocode that had both text-based and visual block-based representations (Fig. 1). The summative AP CSP exam includes questions asked in BOTH block-based and text-based modalities, meaning all students answer questions asked in both forms. The goal of this decision is to ensure that students are not rewarded or penalized for using one type of programming tool or another during the school year.

The AP pseudocode developed for the AP CSP exam consists of 23 keywords including looping constructs (e.g. REPEAT), conditional operators (e.g. IF), and I/O (e.g. DISPLAY). The block-based and text-based representations of the commands are isomorphic, meaning that anything that can be represented in one form can also be represented in the other. The place the two representations differ with respect to the symbols used is in relation to scope, where the text form uses ()s, []s, and {}s while the block-based form conveys this information through the boundaries of the blocks. In the opinion of the authors, the block-based form of the pseudocode can be described as the text-based form with ovals and rectangles drawn around the commands. The full documentation for this pseudocode can be found on pages 14-20 of the AP Computer Science Principles Assessment Overview and Performance Task Directions for Students [1].

4. AFFORDANCES OF BLOCK-BASED PROGRAMMING

In this section, we review specific features of block-based tools that the literature has documented as supporting novices and discuss if and how it is present or absent in the AP CSP pseudocode. Following the strategy of Robins et al. in their review of the literature and learning and teaching programming [31], we break the affordances into two main categories: supports for program comprehension and supports for program generation, although we recognize some design features may support both roles. The following list of features is compiled from a number of resources delineating the characteristics and affordances of block-based environments [3, 8, 11, 24, 27, 37, 43]. After discussing the design feature, we briefly discuss if and how the feature is present in the AP CSP pseudocode that is the focus of this study.

4.1 Supports for Program Comprehension

4.1.1 Visual Rendering of Blocks. The defining feature of block-based programming environments is that each command is rendered as a block. These blocks present visual cues denoting information about the command. This information includes a specific shape showing how and where the block can be used (e.g. commands having notches at the top and bottom, Boolean variables presented as hexagons, and "hat" blocks having rounded tops to make clear that nothing can precede it). Similarly, blocks that accept arguments can render their argument slots using the same shape, making it clear the types of inputs the block will accept. Blocks are also often color-coordinated, so families of blocks related to a concept share a color (e.g. all control blocks in Scratch are yellow). Block-based environments also use shape to denote scope through "c-shaped" blocks that wrap commands and render the nested inside the structure as can be seen in Fig. 2a and Fig. 2c.

While the AP CSP block-based pseudocode includes some of these features, such as encircling commands with lines to give the appearance of blocks and nesting blocks inside each other, most of the visual features cited in the literature are absent. For example, the AP CSP blocks do not include notches to denote how blocks fit together and do not use color to convey the block category.

4.1.2 Natural Language Block Labels. Another oft-cited affordance of block-based environments is their ability to use natural language expressions within the command themselves. Since the block rendering itself defines the scope of each command and how it is to be parsed by the compiler, the language designer is free of the syntactic and keyword constraints of text-based languages. As a result, it is possible to create block-based commands that read like sentences (e.g. the `change x by 1` block shown in Fig. 2a) as well as domain-specific block languages with commands tailored to the specific domain (e.g. Frog Pond [18] or CoBlox [39]).

Given the constraint that the AP CSP pseudocode needed to support both block-based and text-based forms, the pseudocode was not able to take advantage of this feature of the block-based modality. This can be seen in the character-by-character similarities between the programs shown in Fig. 1a and Fig. 1b.

4.1.3 Browsability. The third feature of block-based tools we highlight is not a characteristic of the language itself, but rather, a feature of the larger block-based apparatus that makes block-based programming possible. Block-based programming environments present users with the set of available blocks in a logically ordered and easily browsed set of "drawers" since blocks need to be present somewhere on the screen in order for the user to drag them into their program. One benefit of this feature is that it makes blocks "browsable", meaning learners need not have commands memorized, but instead can easily discover blocks, which can then be used to bootstrap programming ideas.

A version of this feature is available to students for the AP CSP pseudocode. During the exam, students have access to a reference sheet describing the pseudocode and the keywords that comprise the language, meaning they can "browse" the blocks. However, the static, black-and-white reference sheet is a simplified version of the interface of most block-based environments.

4.2 Supports for Program Generation

In this section, we document additional features of block-based programming that the literature has identified as contributing to making it an effective way to introduce novices to programming. Due to the fact that the AP CSP pseudocode was only designed for comprehension on a written test, the language itself has never been implemented. Thus, none of the benefits listed in this section are present in the AP CSP Pseudocode.

4.2.1 Drag-and-Drop Composition. Unlike text-based languages where statements are typed in one character at a time, authoring programs in block-based tools allows learners to assemble commands using a drag-and-drop interaction. The information provided by the visual rendering of the command gives the user information about how and where a block can be used. If two blocks cannot be joined to form a valid statement, then the block-based editor prevents the commands from snapping together, thus preventing most types of syntax errors. This drag-and-drop construction also lends a feeling of "tinkerability" and playfulness, as changes can be made quickly and easily, especially for novice computer users who may find typing commands cumbersome.

4.2.2 Dynamic Rendering. Given the graphical nature of the block-based representation, the visual presentation of commands allows for a number of additional dynamic rendering features that can support the user. For example, the shapes of blocks can change to fit changing characteristics of the program (e.g. c-shaped blocks can grow to wrap a larger number of sub-commands). Additionally, block-based tools can provide hover-over tooltips, include images or short animations, or allow the user to modify the shape of the block on the fly (e.g. Blockly's mutator feature). While such features are possible in text-based editors (e.g. Citrus [23]), they are not as widely used or as central to the modality as the dynamic rendering features of block-based tools.

5. METHODS AND PARTICIPANTS

To answer our stated research questions we gathered data on students answering questions in both the block-based and text-based forms of the AP CSP Pseudocode. To do so, we created a 20 question multiple choice assessment in the same form as the multiple choice question portion of the AP CSP written exam. We then included the assessment as an optional "Practice AP Programming exam questions" module at the end of the programming module of Code.org's CSP curriculum (http://code.org/csp). Code.org's CSP curriculum is a full-year, rigorous, entry-level course that introduces high school students to the foundations of modern computing and prepares them for the AP CSP Exam. Programming in the course is done in App Lab (Fig. 2c, http://code.org/applab), which is a JavaScript-based, dual-modality environment where students can construct programs in both block-based and text-based modalities.

5.1 The AP CSP Pseudocode Assessment

The assessment used in this study is comprised of 20 multiple choice questions, 10 in the block-based form and 10 in the text-based form of the AP CSP pseudocode. The questions were drawn from a previously used and validated assessment used in similar research studies [41]. Each question on the assessment begins with a short code snippet and is followed by the question: "What will the output of the program be?" There are also a series of questions that present short programs that use the prompt "What does this program do?" These comprehension questions are intended to evaluate a student's ability to identify the purpose of a program as opposed to just mentally running the program and reporting the output. The assessment covers five programming topics: variables, loops, conditionals, functions, and program comprehension. For each of the five topics, the assessment asked two questions in the block-based pseudocode form and two in the text-based pseudocode. This counter-balance design ensures that every student answered two questions for each concept in both forms of the pseudocode. A sample question is shown in Fig. 1.

5.2 Data collection and participants

The assessment was administered through Code.org's content management system that tracks individual students as well as classroom progress through the curriculum. At the beginning of the course, students create a profile which includes optionally self-reporting their gender, age, and race. The responses collected by Code.org were de-identified and then shared with researchers. All necessary institutional approval was acquired for conducting this research.

The dataset for this study consists of 5,427 students and over 105,000 individual question responses. The sample includes 1,218 (22.4%) female students, 3,198 (58.9%) male students, and 1,011 students (18.6%) who chose to not provide gender information. Of the 5,427 students, 1,040 (19.2%) learners self-identified as being from an underrepresented minority in computing (URM), while 2,199 (40.5%) of students were classified as not URM and 2,188 (40.3%) of student did not self-report their race. For this work, students that self-identified as Black, Hispanic, LatinX, Native American, or Pacific Islander were categorized as being from a URM. Finally, a majority of participants were between the ages of 15 and 18, which corresponds to the four years of American high-school (9.6% 15 years old; 22.5% 16 years old; 30.7% 17 years old; 27.2 % 18 years old).

6. FINDINGS

6.1 Performance by Modality

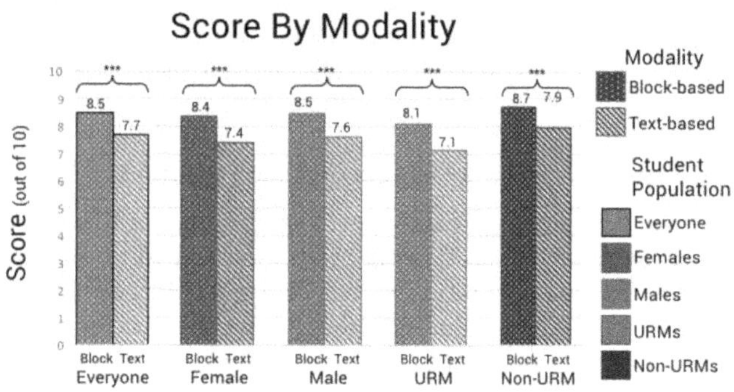

Figure 3. Average scores on the assessment by modality.

6.1.1 Overall Performance. To answer our first research question on the impact of modality, we first look at overall student performance on the 20-question assessment. The leftmost column of Fig. 3 shows student performance on the block-based questions compared to the text-based questions. Overall, students scored an average of 8.5 out of 10 on block-based questions (*SD* 1.9) and 7.7 out of 10 on text-based questions (*SD* 2.2), a difference that is statistically significant $t(4761) = 38.14$, $p < .001$, $d = .40$. This means, overall, students performed better on the block-based questions than the text-based questions.

6.1.2 Performance by Gender. Looking at gender, we find that both male and female students perform significantly better on block-based questions: Female $t(1081) = 20.25$, $p < .001$, $d = 0.62$ and Male $t(2852) = 29.344$, $p < .001$, $d = 0.55$ (columns 2 and 3 in Fig. 3 respectively). In the case of female students, this resulted in a .92 point improvement on average while males had a .85 point increase, as can be seen by the larger effect size for female students.

6.1.3 Performance by Race. When conducting the same analysis and dividing the participant population by race, we see a similar pattern. Both URM and non-URM students performed significantly better on block-based questions versus text-based questions: URM students $t(878) = 18.20$, $p < .001$, $d = 0.61$ and non-URM students $t(2000) = 23.74$, $p < .001$, $d = 0.53$ (the two right-most pairs of columns in Fig. 3). For participants that self-identified as a URM, there was, on average a full point difference between mean block-based score and mean text-based score. Non-URM students saw on average score improvement of .76 points between block-based and text-based questions. A longer, more detailed analysis of the impact of modality on learners from historically underrepresented populations can be found in [41].

6.1.4 Performance by Concept. Along with analyzing results by characteristics of the learner, we can also look at student performance by modality across the concept being assessed. Fig. 4 reports the percentage of students that got each question correct grouped by modality and concept.

Across all five content areas, students scored better on questions asked in the block-based modality over the text-based modality. Given students only answered 2 questions for each modality-concept pairing, we present only averages in Fig. 4. A redesign of the assessment is underway that will give us greater power to further investigate the interaction of modality and concept in code comprehension questions.

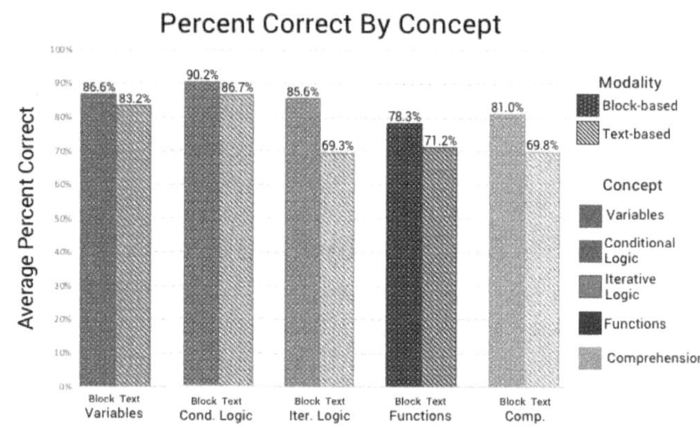

Figure 4. Average number of students who answered a question correctly grouped by concept and modality

Taken together, this collection of results is slightly surprising as the block-based format used in this assessment lacks many of the features the literature has identified as making block-based tools easier to comprehend. This suggests that the features that are present, namely the block-shapes created by outlining each command, play a central role in facilitating the comprehension of programs by novice programmers.

7. DISCUSSION

7.1 Potential Explanations for these Findings

The main finding from this study is that students do better on questions presented in a block-based form compared to isomorphic text-based presentations. This on its own is not that surprising as previous studies have found similar results (e.g. [44]). What is surprising is that we see these same patterns using the AP CSP pseudocode block-based presentation which includes relatively few of the features that learners and researchers cite as being responsible for the ease-of-comprehension. Further, the AP CSP pseudocode is not a real language, meaning learners have never written a program using it. In this section, we explore a number of potential explanations for the findings presented.

7.1.1 The Simple Visual Cues are Sufficient. The first potential explanation is that the basic visual cues that are present in the AP CSP pseudocode are enough to cause the differences found in the data. By visual cues, we are referring to both the rectangular and oval lines encircling commands that give them their block-based appearance and the nesting of commands. It is also possible that the opposite is true, that the absence of potentially confusing or difficult-to-parse language features that are present in the text-based questions, such as `{ }`s and `( )`s are the cause of student difficulty in the text-based form. This explanation is supported by prior research on the difficulty novices have with syntactic features of programming languages, including the use of less familiar symbols like the brackets and braces [36].

7.1.2 The Block-based Pseudocode is Closer to Prior Programming Experiences. While the AP CSP Pseudocode used on the assessment was created specifically for the written test, students did have prior programming experience that could have shaped these results. For example, if students had spent the two months leading up to the exam programming in a block-based environment such as Scratch it is possible that would make them more likely to do better on the block-based questions. Similarly, if students came into the test on the heels of a unit learning JavaScript, the text-based questions may appear more familiar and thus easier. While the AP CSP exam was designed to prevent this, it is still possible.

The assessment used in this study was embedded in a curricular unit based on Code.org's AppLab environment (Fig. 2b). While AppLab includes both a block-based and text-based interface, research shows that novices generally prefer the block-based modality [28, 40, 43], which also matches the anecdotal evidence received from teachers of the course. Given these facts, the prior experience explanation is certainly plausible. However, prior research has not found a strong coupling of the modality used for learning programming and ability to answer questions on a static exam. In two separate studies, Weintrop and Wilensky found students who worked in block-based environments performed better on text-based programming questions than peers who had learned using text-based programming tools [42, 44].

7.1.3 Block-based Programs are Friendlier. A third potential explanation focuses not on a feature of the language itself or on learners' prior experiences, but on learners perception of the language and how they relate to it. This explanation draws from the literature on stereotype threat, which finds that students underperform when there is a risk of their performance confirming an existing stereotype [35]. This explanation posits that when learners see the block-based pseudocode, the form is closer to the fun and playful programming they relate to, as opposed the serious and professional programming languages they make them feel unwelcome. While there is more work that needs to be done to confirm (or refute) this account, it does provide a plausible explanation for the differences observed in the analysis of gender and race presented in sections 6.1.2 and 6.1.3.

7.1.4 Classroom or Curricular Factors. Given that this study took place in classrooms across the United States there are many other possible environmental factors that may contribute to these findings. For example, it is possible that teacher effects played a role in this pattern. If a teacher was new to computer science, he or she may have felt more comfortable with, and therefore chosen to work in the block-based modality, resulting in block-based examples during classroom instruction. Likewise, the curriculum used in the classroom may have prioritized the block-based modality over the text-based form.

While we think there is merit to all these explanations and suspect the truth includes a bit of all of them. More work remains to be done to further tease apart these potential explanations.

7.2 Broadening Participation in Computing

A second important discussion point from this work is how these findings speak to the goal of broadening participation in computing. One of the objectives of the AP CSP course was to introduce learners from populations historically underrepresented in computing to the field of computer science. By framing the course around seven-big ideas, as opposed to just programming, the hope was to present a broader (and more accurate) picture of what computer science is. From this perspective, the finding that students who self-identify as members of historically underrepresented groups, like female, Black and Hispanic learners, performed better on the block-based form is important. Having early successes in computing experiences, especially for AP classes, which are designed to be more challenging than traditional high school coursework, has the potential to positively impact their attitudes towards the field and reshape how they perceive themselves with respect to whether or not they are (or can be) a computer scientist.

8. IMPLICATIONS AND CONCLUSION

As this work was based on a newly introduced exam taken by thousands of learners across the United States, there are a number of implications for the findings. First, the finding that learners perform better on questions presented in the block-based modality has direct implications for educators and their choice of learning environment and curricula. Second, the findings have implications for designers of introductory programming tools and their decisions about whether to include block-based features and if so, how. This research suggests that even the most basic block-based features are enough to improve learning outcomes. A final potential implication for this work is related to assessing emerging computing knowledge. The results from this research suggest that the block-based pseudocode created for the exam was successful in providing supports for novices. This means efforts to include features of block-based tools into assessment contexts is a potentially productive decision.

The growing interest in computing education across the K-12 spectrum has produced a variety of initiatives intended to bring computer science to all. As part of this larger effort, educators, curriculum designers, and assessment creators have drawn inspiration from the successes and popularity of block-based tools as a way to introduce learners to computer science in formal contexts. This paper provides further evidence that the block-based modality does help learners on static written assessments. Further, it is particularly helpful for learners from historically underrepresented groups. This finding validates some of the decisions made by the designers of the AP CSP written exam. With this finding, we continue to advance our understanding of the role block-based programming might play in helping learners at the beginning of their journey into the world of computer science.

9. REFERENCES

[1] AP Computer Science Principles Assessment Overview and Performance Task Directions for Students: *https://apcentral.collegeboard.org/pdf/ap-csp-student-task-directions.pdf* Accessed: 2018-04-06.

[2] Arpaci-Dusseau, A. et al. 2013. Computer Science Principles: Analysis of a Proposed Advanced Placement Course. *Proceeding of the 44th ACM Technical Symposium on Computer Science Education* (New York, NY, USA, 2013), 251–256.

[3] Bau, D., Gray, J., Kelleher, C., Sheldon, J. and Turbak, F. 2017. Learnable programming: blocks and beyond. *Communications of the ACM.* 60, 6 (May 2017), 72–80. DOI:https://doi.org/10.1145/3015455.

[4] Begel, A. 1996. *LogoBlocks: A graphical programming language for interacting with the world.* Electrical Engineering and Computer Science Department. MIT.

[5] Brennan, K. and Resnick, M. 2012. New frameworks for studying and assessing the development of computational thinking. (Vancouver, Canada, 2012).

[6] Cooper, S., Dann, W. and Pausch, R. 2000. Alice: a 3-D tool for introductory programming concepts. *Journal of Computing Sciences in Colleges.* 15, 5 (2000), 107–116.

[7] diSessa, A.A. 2000. *Changing minds: Computers, learning, and literacy.* MIT Press.

[8] Dwyer, H., Hill, C., Hansen, A., Iveland, A., Franklin, D. and Harlow, D. 2015. Fourth Grade Students Reading Block-Based Programs: Predictions, Visual Cues, and Affordances. *Proceedings of the eleventh annual International Conference on International Computing Education Research* (2015), 111–119.

[9] Fields, D., Giang, M. and Kafai, Y. 2014. Programming in the wild: trends in youth computational participation in the online Scratch community. *Proceedings of the 9th Workshop in Primary and Secondary Computing Education* (2014), 2–11.

[10] Franklin, D., Skifstad, G., Rolock, R., Mehrotra, I., Ding, V., Hansen, A., Weintrop, D. and Harlow, D. 2017. Using Upper-Elementary Student Performance to Understand Conceptual Sequencing in a Blocks-based Curriculum. *Proceedings of the 2017 ACM SIGCSE Technical Symposium on Computer Science Education* (New York, NY, USA, 2017), 231–236.

[11] Fraser, N. 2013. *Blockly.* Google.

[12] Fraser, N. 2015. Ten things we've learned from Blockly. *2015 IEEE Blocks and Beyond Workshop (Blocks and Beyond)* (Oct. 2015), 49–50.

[13] Gilmore, D.J. and Green, T.R.G. 1984. Comprehension and recall of miniature programs. *International Journal of Man-Machine Studies.* 21, 1 (Jul. 1984), 31–48. DOI:https://doi.org/10.1016/S0020-7373(84)80037-1.

[14] Gross, P. and Powers, K. 2005. Evaluating Assessments of Novice Programming Environments. *Proceedings of the First International Workshop on Computing Education Research* (New York, NY, USA, 2005), 99–110.

[15] Grover, S. and Basu, S. 2017. Measuring Student Learning in Introductory Block-Based Programming: Examining Misconceptions of Loops, Variables, and Boolean Logic. *Proceedings of the 2017 ACM SIGCSE Technical Symposium on Computer Science Education* (New York, NY, 2017), 267–272.

[16] Grover, S., Cooper, S. and Pea, R. 2014. Assessing computational learning in K-12. (2014), 57–62.

[17] Grover, S., Pea, R. and Cooper, S. 2015. Designing for deeper learning in a blended computer science course for middle school students. *Computer Science Education.* 25, 2 (Apr. 2015), 199–237. DOI:https://doi.org/10.1080/08993408.2015.1033142.

[18] Horn, M.S., Brady, C., Hjorth, A., Wagh, A. and Wilensky, U. 2014. Frog pond: a codefirst learning environment on evolution and natural selection. *Proceedings of the 2014 conference on Interaction design and children* (2014), 357–360.

[19] Kafai, Y.B. and Burke, Q. 2014. *Connected Code: Why Children Need to Learn Programming.* MIT Press.

[20] Kaput, J., Noss, R. and Hoyles, C. 2002. Developing new notations for a learnable mathematics in the computational era. *Handbook of international research in mathematics education.* (2002), 51–75.

[21] Kaput, J.J. 1987. Towards a Theory of Symbol. *Problems of Representation in the Teaching and Learning of Mathematics.* C. Janvier, ed. Lawrence Erlbaum Associates. 159.

[22] Kelleher, C., Pausch, R. and Kiesler, S. 2007. Storytelling alice motivates middle school girls to learn computer programming. *Proceedings of the SIGCHI conference on Human factors in computing systems* (2007), 1455–1464.

[23] Ko, A.J. and Myers, B.A. 2005. Citrus: a language and toolkit for simplifying the creation of structured editors for code and data. *Proceedings of the 18th annual ACM symposium on User interface software and technology* (2005), 3–12.

[24] Kölling, M., Brown, N.C.C. and Altadmri, A. 2015. Frame-Based Editing: Easing the Transition from Blocks to Text-Based Programming. *Proceedings of the Workshop in Primary and Secondary Computing Education* (New York, NY, USA, 2015), 29–38.

[25] Lewis, C.M. 2010. How programming environment shapes perception, learning and goals: Logo vs. Scratch. *Proceedings of the 41st ACM Technical Symposium on Computer Science Education* (New York, NY, 2010), 346–350.

[26] Maloney, J.H., Peppler, K., Kafai, Y., Resnick, M. and Rusk, N. 2008. Programming by choice: Urban youth learning programming with Scratch. *ACM SIGCSE Bulletin.* 40, 1 (2008), 367–371.

[27] Maloney, J.H., Resnick, M., Rusk, N., Silverman, B. and Eastmond, E. 2010. The Scratch programming language and environment. *ACM Transactions on Computing Education (TOCE).* 10, 4 (2010), 16.

[28] Matsuzawa, Y., Ohata, T., Sugiura, M. and Sakai, S. 2015. Language Migration in non-CS Introductory Programming through Mutual Language Translation Environment. *Proceedings of the 46th ACM Technical Symposium on Computer Science Education* (2015), 185–190.

[29] Price, T.W. and Barnes, T. 2015. Comparing Textual and Block Interfaces in a Novice Programming Environment. (2015), 91–99.

[30] Resnick, M., Silverman, B., Kafai, Y., Maloney, J., Monroy-Hernández, A., Rusk, N., Eastmond, E., Brennan, K., Millner, A., Rosenbaum, E. and Silver, J. 2009. Scratch: Programming for all. *Communications of the ACM.* 52, 11 (Nov. 2009), 60.

[31] Robins, A., Rountree, J. and Rountree, N. 2003. Learning and teaching programming: A review and discussion. *Computer Science Education.* 13, 2 (2003), 137–172.

[32] Roque, R., Kafai, Y. and Fields, D. 2012. From tools to communities: Designs to support online creative collaboration in Scratch. *Proceedings of the 11th International Conference on Interaction Design and Children* (2012), 220–223.

[33] Sherin, B.L. 2001. A comparison of programming languages and algebraic notation as expressive languages for physics. *International Journal of Computers for Mathematical Learning.* 6, 1 (2001), 1–61.

[34] Shneiderman, B. 1983. Direct manipulation: a step beyond programming languages. *Computer.* 16, 8 (1983), 57–69.

[35] Steele, C.M. and Aronson, J. 1995. Stereotype threat and the intellectual test performance of African Americans. *Journal of personality and social psychology.* 69, 5 (1995), 797.

[36] Stefik, A. and Siebert, S. 2013. An Empirical Investigation into Programming Language Syntax. *ACM Transactions on Computing Education.* 13, 4 (Nov. 2013), 1–40. DOI:https://doi.org/10.1145/2534973.

[37] Tempel, M. 2013. Blocks Programming. *CSTA Voice.* 9, 1 (2013).

[38] Tew, A.E. and Guzdial, M. 2011. The FCS1: a language independent assessment of CS1 knowledge. *Proceedings of the 42nd ACM technical symposium on Computer science education* (2011), 111–116.

[39] Weintrop, D., Afzal, A., Salac, J., Francis, P., Li, B., Shepherd, D.C. and Franklin, D. 2018. Evaluating CoBlox: A Comparative Study of Robotics Programming Environments for Adult Novices. *Proceedings of the 2018 CHI Conference on Human Factors in Computing Systems* (Montreal QC, Canada, 2018), 366:1–12.

[40] Weintrop, D. and Holbert, N. 2017. From Blocks to Text and Back: Programming Patterns in a Dual-Modality Environment. *Proceedings of the 2017 ACM SIGCSE Technical Symposium on Computer Science Education* (New York, NY, USA, 2017), 633–638.

[41] Weintrop, D., Killen, H. and Franke, B. 2018. Blocks or Text? How programming language modality makes a difference in assessing underrepresented populations. *Proceedings of the International Conference on the Learning Sciences 2018* (London, UK, 2018), 328–335.

[42] Weintrop, D. and Wilensky, U. 2017. Comparing Block-Based and Text-Based Programming in High School Computer Science Classrooms. *ACM Transactions on Computing Education (TOCE).* 18, 1 (Oct. 2017), 3. DOI:https://doi.org/10.1145/3089799.

[43] Weintrop, D. and Wilensky, U. 2015. To Block or Not to Block, That is the Question: Students' Perceptions of Blocks-based Programming. *Proceedings of the 14th International Conference on Interaction Design and Children* (New York, NY, USA, 2015), 199–208.

[44] Weintrop, D. and Wilensky, U. 2015. Using Commutative Assessments to Compare Conceptual Understanding in Blocks-based and Text-based Programs. *Proceedings of the Eleventh Annual International Conference on International Computing Education Research* (New York, NY, USA, 2015), 101–110.

[45] Werner, L., Denner, J., Campe, S. and Kawamoto, D.C. 2012. The fairy performance assessment: measuring computational thinking in middle school. *Proceedings of the 43rd ACM technical symposium on Computer Science Education* (2012), 215–220.

[46] Wilensky, U. and Papert, S. 2010. Restructurations: Reformulating knowledge disciplines through new representational forms. *Proceedings of the Constructionism 2010 conference* (Paris, France, 2010).

Women and Girls of Color in Computing

Exploring Current Trends, Emerging Opportunities, and Strategies for Meaningful Impact

Frieda McAlear[1*], Allison Scott[1], Kimberly Scott[2], Jamika Burge[3], Sonia Koshy[1]

[1] Kapor Center, 2148 Broadway, Oakland, CA {friedam; allison; sonia@kaporcenter.org}
[2] CGEST, Arizona State University, Tempe, AZ {Kascott3@asu.edu}
[3] Thurgood Marshall College Fund (TMCF), Washington, DC {Jamika.burge@gmail.com}
*Moderator

ABSTRACT

Women of color comprise a critical segment of the United States population, yet they remain underrepresented in computing education and the workforce and often overlooked in data collection and reporting, research, and interventions to increase diversity in computing. This panel of researchers will provide an overview of the current challenges facing women of color, and highlight initiatives to develop, test, and scale strategies to improve the outcomes of women of color in computing. This panel aims to increase audience understanding of the challenges and opportunities, while inspiring the audience to take action and apply emerging insights and strategies to their local contexts, in order to improve outcomes for women of color. The intention is that this panel is not merely intended to highlight programs, but more importantly, to begin to strategically, scientifically, and collaboratively improve the outcomes for women and girls of color across the computing pipeline. The intended audience for this panel include K-12 computing educators, computing faculty, education nonprofit leaders, researchers and the philanthropic community.

Categories and Subject Descriptors

• Computing Industry • Computing Education
• Race/Ethnicity • Gender

Keywords

Women of Color; Intersectionality; Computing Research; Computing Education; Workforce

1. SUMMARY

Women of color comprise nearly 40% of the female-identified population in the United States (and will comprise the majority by 2060) [1], yet they remain underrepresented in Advanced Placement Computer Science participation, computing degree completion, the computing workforce, and among technology entrepreneurs and venture capitalists [2]. Transformation across all levels of the computing ecosystem is needed in order to address barriers and increase participation, persistence, and success of underrepresented women of color in computing. Given that there is a need for foundational grounding and level-setting on the challenges and experience of women of color in computing, this panel aims to first provide the audience with a comprehensive understanding of the barriers facing women and girls of color in computing, including current landscape and data trends. The panelists will then provide an overview of three innovative interventions which offer insights into emerging strategies for increasing participation and persistence in K-12 computing education and across the broader computing ecosystem for women and girls of color. Each of the programs being highlighted has research-driven, innovative interventions and is coupled with a rigorous research and evaluation strategy to ensure empirical measurement of impact is prioritized. Each panelist will also highlight efforts to expand research and data collection, and share promising evidence-based strategies with the broader community to improve outcomes for girls of color across the computing ecosystem. This panel aims to increase audience understanding of the challenges and opportunities, while inspiring the audience to take action and apply emerging insights and strategies to their local contexts, in order to improve outcomes for women of color. The intention is that this panel is not merely intended to highlight programs, but more importantly, to begin to strategically, scientifically, and collaboratively improve the outcomes for women and girls of color across the computing pipeline.

SIGCSE'19, February 27-March 2, 2019, Minneapolis, MN, USA.

ACM ISBN 978-1-4503-5890-3/19/02.
DOI: http://dx.doi.org/10.1145/3287324.3287341

2. PANEL STRUCTURE

The moderator will open by setting the context for the discussion, highlighting current data and trends on the participation and persistence of women of color across the computing ecosystem, and then introducing each panelist. Each panelist will be given 15 minutes to describe their initiative or intervention, its potential for improving outcomes for women of color, and how their work can inform and build capacity among the broader computer science education community. The moderator will then facilitate a discussion with the audience around three key themes: piloting promising evidence-based interventions and strategies into existing programs; testing the efficacy of interventions to further inform program and scaling effective strategies to move the move the needle on women and girls of color in computing, particularly in post-secondary education.

3. DR. ALLISON SCOTT

As Chief Research Officer of the Kapor Center, Dr. Scott leads a research team that aims to increase diversity in the tech ecosystem by conducting and disseminating landscape studies, research on interventions, strategies, resources, and practices within education and the technology workplace. Dr. Scott's research examined the influence of perceived barriers and stereotypes in the sciences, the double-bind facing women of color, and the effectiveness of research-based interventions in improving STEM outcomes for underrepresented groups. In collaboration with the Center for Gender Equity in Science and Technology (CGEST) at Arizona State University, Dr. Scott launched the Women of Color in Computing Researcher/Practitioner Collaborative in 2018 to build a foundational body of literature on barriers and interventions for girls and women of color across the computing ecosystem. This initiative aims to develop, test, and scale interventions to increase the number of women of color entering and persisting in computing. Dr. Scott will describe the initiative's inaugural landscape and experimental research projects, highlight early findings, and discuss emerging strategies for practitioners to implement.

4. DR. KIMBERLY A. SCOTT

As the Founding Executive Director at the Center for Gender Equity in Science and Technology (CGEST) at Arizona State University, Dr. Scott has been a prolific writer and educator on experiences and interventions for girls of color, and developed the CompuGIRLS program to empower girls of color across 5 states to develop technological skills and become techno-social change agents [3]. Under Dr. Scott's leadership, CGEST also operates the annual Women of Color in STEM Entrepreneurship Conference. In collaboration with the Kapor Center, Dr. Scott launched the Women of Color in Computing Researcher/Practitioner Collaborative to increase the number of girls and women of color in computing. Dr. Scott will describe the research projects conducted by the inaugural cohort of Women of Color in Computing Fellows, discuss the role of intersectionality as a heuristic to examine the double-bind in computing, and discuss the Collaborative's researcher-practitioner partnership strategies in improving outcomes for girls and women of color in computing.

5. DR. JAMIKA D. BURGE

Dr. Burge leads Communities of Practice for One Design at Capital One, is an affiliate researcher at the Thurgood Marshall College Fund, and co-PI for Girls ROCK! Tech, a partnership with Black Girls ROCK! She is an authority in research investigating the intersectionality of black women and girls in computing and serves as a co-founder of blackcomputeHER.org. Through her research projects, she has developed a leadership curriculum that combines computational thinking with cultural and gender empowerment for middle and high school girls, and supported computational and workforce development and ecosystems for black women and girls. She will describe lessons learned from the BRIGHT-CS research project, which uses a cohort model and peer-peer/near-peer mentoring to emphasize (1) empowerment and leadership development for black girls, (2) computer science and computational thinking experiences, and (3) partnerships with schools, universities, and non-profit and community organizations. She will describe the effectiveness of learning ecosystems and her research will inform best practices for broadening participation for girls of color and other marginalized groups.

6. DR. SONIA KOSHY

As the Director of Measurement, Evaluation, and Learning, Dr. Koshy conducts rigorous longitudinal impact evaluation assessments of the Kapor Center's Summer Math and Science Honors Academy (SMASH). The SMASH program provides underrepresented high school students of color (50% of whom are girls) with rigorous STEM and CS education each summer for 3 years (15 weeks total). In response to previous research conducted by Dr. Koshy and colleagues [4, 5], several interventions within the SMASH program have been developed and implemented to improve outcomes for the girls of color in the program. Dr. Koshy will describe the intervention, provide highlights of the findings, and recommendations for adapting interventions to multiple different contexts. In addition, Dr. Koshy will speak to the importance of measuring experiences and outcomes to inform program development and continuous improvement cycles to ensure programs targeting girls of color are producing intended outcomes.

7. DEFINITIONS:

A broad definition is used to define "women of color" which includes individuals who identify as female and as a member of a racial/ethnic group other than white (specifically, Black/African-American, Latinx/Hispanic, Asian, Native American/Alaskan Native, Native Hawaiian/Pacific Islander). Underrepresented women of color are distinguished as women from racial/ ethnic groups who are traditionally underrepresented in computing education, degree completion, the tech workforce, and entrepreneurship/VC, in comparison to their representation in the U.S. population and representation among potential pools of candidates (e.g., the total labor force, CS degree-earners).

8. REFERENCES

[1] U.S. Bureau of the Census. 2014. National Population Projections Tables. Table 10: Projections of the Population by Sex, Hispanic Origin, and Race for the United States (2015-2060):https://www.census.gov/data/tables/2014/demo/popproj/2014-summary-tables.html

[2] McAlear, F., Scott, A., Scott, K., and Weiss, S. 2018. Data Brief: Women of Color in Computing: http://wocincomputing.org.

[3] Scott, K. A., & White, M. 2013. COMPUGIRLS' Standpoint: Culturally responsive computing and its effect on girls of color. *Urban Education, 48*(5), 657–681.

[4] Scott, A., Martin, A., & McAlear, F. 2017. Enhancing participation in computer science among girls of color: An examination of an AP preparatory computer science intervention. In A. Rankin & J. Thomas (Eds.), *Moving Students of Color from Consumers to Producers of Technology.* Hershey, PA: IGI Global Publishing.

[5] Scott, A., McAlear, F., Martin, A., Koshy, S. 2017. Broadening participation in computing: Examining experiences of girls of color. DOI: https://doi.org/10.1145/3059009.3059054

Demystifying Language about Students' Varied Identities

Jason T. Black
School of Business and Industry
Florida A&M Univ.
Jason.Black@famu.edu

Kamau Bobb
Constellations Center for Equity & Computing
Georgia Tech
kamau.bobb@cc.gatech.edu

April Browne
Computer Science Dept.
Butte College
Oroville, CA, USA
browneap@butte.edu

Phillip T. Conrad
Computer Science Dept.
UC Santa Barbara
Santa Barbara, CA
conrad@acm.org

Colleen M. Lewis
Computer Science Dept.
Harvey Mudd College
Claremont, CA, USA
lewis@cs.hmc.edu

Cherly A. Swanier
Math and CS Dept.
Claflin University
Orangeburg, SC, USA
cswanier@claflin.edu

Sheila Tejada
Computer Science Dept.
University of Southern California
Los Angeles, CA, USA
stejada@usc.edu

ABSTRACT

The goal of the session is to help attendees who are committed to diversity and inclusion learn to talk about different dimensions of identity (e.g., race, class, gender, sex, sexuality, etc.). The landscape of terms is always changing and we want SIGCSE attendees to feel more comfortable using current language to talk about issues related to diversity and inclusion. This special session will include six lightning talks, individual reflection, small-group discussion, and a Q&A with presenters. This is a reprise of a special session held at the NCWIT Summit in 2018; it was well received and we hope to offer it to the larger SIGCSE audience.

1 SUMMARY AND GOALS

We seek to provide resources and definitions for discussing students' identities. After each lightning talk, attendees will have the opportunity to practice applying these ideas through individual reflection and small-group discussion. On the NCWIT Summit survey, the session was described as amazing, actionable, inspiring, interactive, and valuable. 88.7% of survey respondents (N=141) agreed or strongly agreed that they feel more comfortable discussing complex topics such as race, ethnicity, and sexual orientation in their classroom after the session.

2 STRUCTURE AND TOPICS

We will begin by repeating the following structure three times:

- Two lightning talks (~7 min with transitions)
- Individual reflection on discussion prompts (~3 min)
- Discussion in small groups (~7 min).

The remaining time will be used for Q&A with the presenters.

SIGCSE '19, February 27-March 2, 2019, Minneapolis, MN, USA

ACM ISBN 978-1-4503-5890-3/19/02.
https://doi.org/10.1145/3287324.3287513

The session will be facilitated by Dr. Cheryl Swanier. Dr. Swanier is the Department Chair of Mathematics and CS and an Associate Professor of CS at Claflin University where she is named the Henry N. and Alice Carson Tisdale Endowed Professor.

2.1 Family Friendly—April Browne

Students with caregiving responsibilities are a hidden diversity with their own set of challenges. There are many ways that institutions, as well as faculty, can be more family friendly. Attendees will discuss:

- What additional problems or supports for student caregivers have you seen or heard about?
- What course policies do you have that could have a differentially negative impact on student caregivers?
- What kinds of supports does your school or community have for student parents? How might they be improved?

April Browne is a Computer Science instructor at Butte College in northern California. She has been teaching introductory level programming classes at Butte for the past three years She has had the opportunity to interact with student parents while her children have participated in the on-campus childcare. This has led to her interest in advocating for student caregivers.

2.2 Ability and Ableism—Colleen Lewis

We might think about classroom accommodations as valid when they apply to physical health, but not mental health. While no accommodation is going to be perfect, mental health is physical and it is probably wise to trust experts to help make our classroom accessible. There are ways we can change our language and behavior to avoid ableism, i.e., bias or discrimination in favor of able bodied people. Attendees will discuss:

- How do you (or could you) make accommodations just part of your regular teaching practice?
- Can you think of tasks in tech careers that are similar to tests? Are these tasks required in all roles?

- How might you respond to your colleagues who are resistant to providing accommodations?

Colleen Lewis is the McGregor-Girand Associate Professor of CS. Her research seeks to identify effective teaching practices for creating equitable learning spaces for all students. Lewis curates CSTeachingTips.org, a NSF-sponsored project for disseminating effective CS teaching practices.

2.3 Gender and Sexuality—Phill Conrad

Are gender, sex and sexuality issues in the CS classroom? We address this with real-world stories. We discuss the benefits of sharing one's pronouns (she/her/hers vs. he/him/his vs. they/them/their) and inviting students to share theirs. We identify four aspects of personal identify: sex, gender identity, gender expression and sexual orientation, and invite attendees to discuss:

- "Someone left their umbrella; I hope they get it." Is this sentence grammatically correct? What is your level of comfort with the singular they?
- We may ask students: "What are your preferred gender pronouns" or may simply ask "what are your pronouns". Discuss: pros/cons, why it might matter.
- Which aspects of personal identity (sex, gender identity, gender expression and sexual orientation) are you the most (or least) comfortable discussing, and why?
- Cameron uses the pronouns "they/them/their." Try using Cameron's name and their pronouns in a sentence.

Phill Conrad is a Senior Lecturer at the University of California, Santa Barbara; he has been on the UCSB CS faculty since 2008. Before that, he was CS faculty at Temple University, and the University of Delaware, where he earned his Ph.D. in CS.

2.4 Privilege, Racism, and Implicit Bias—from the Eyes of Black Men—Jason Black

This presentation discusses the racism and bias that black men face daily, both in society and more specifically in academia, and how these biases create stereotypes that prove a deterrent to their educational and personal progress. Also presented is a frank discussion of racism and privilege and how many of us can hold racist or prejudicial views toward black men as a consequence of being a member of a "privileged" group. An additional focus is on strategies for counteracting bias. Attendees will discuss:

- Would you consider yourself part of a privileged group? How has that shaped your view of Black Men?
- Do you hold any of the stereotypes or biases presented? If so, how do you plan to address this? If not, how do you think you have been able to avoid these?
- What is the most significant take-away from today that will shape your future interactions with Black Men?
- Do you belong to a group that has been traditionally hostile in its views toward Black Men? If so, how do you plan to address that group on this issue?

Dr. Black, Associate Professor in Business Information Systems, holds a MS degree in CS from Georgia Tech, and a PhD in CS from Florida State University. Dr. Black has a research background in mobile computing, collaborative learning and educational technology. Dr. Black founded and directed the NSF-funded African-American Women in CS Scholarship program, and was a founding partner in the NSF-funded STARS Alliance for Diversity in Computing. Dr. Black also is working in Big Data, Social Computing, Social Media, and Entrepreneurship.

2.5 Race Labels—Kamau Bobb

This presentation explains the introduction and evolution of racial categorization and race as a social construct. Racial categorization obscures multiple dimensions of heterogeneity within racial groups. The talk will explain why the terms "minority" and "non-White" have been critiqued and how they can be replaced by "minoritized" and "person of color." Attendees will discuss:

- In your role at your institution, when/why does it matter to refer to anyone or any group by racial identity?
- Have you ever wanted to know someone's race? If so, why? Was it necessary for you to know?
- Have you noticed a tendency to avoid race labels and instead refer to individuals or groups as "diverse" or "ethnic" or "minority"? Why might this be problematic?

Dr. Bobb's work focuses on the relationship between equity for students and communities of color in the STEM enterprise, society, and large educational systems. Dr. Bobb holds a PhD in Science and Technology Policy from Georgia Tech and M.S. and B.S. degrees in Mechanical Engineering from UC Berkeley.

2.6 Model Minority—Sheila Tejada

While the term "Model Minority" might seem like a complement, it is a myth that can place additional pressure on people of Asian descent and serve to silence students from asking for help they may need. It can reinforce racial hierarchies that denigrate other marginalized groups, and hide the variations in experiences among people of Asian descent. Attendees will discuss:

- Stereotypes can treat a group of people as homogeneous. In what ways can this be harmful?
- As educators, how we can become more aware of bias?
- What resources can we give our students to educate them about stereotypes and bias?
- About 20% of CS undergrads are Asian. At your school, what challenges and stereotypes may they face?

Dr. Tejada is currently a professor in the CS Department at the University of Southern California, in Los Angeles (LA), where she teaches courses and performs research applying artificial intelligence, machine learning and robotics in education. As the academic community leader for Anita Borg Institute.LA, she is passionate about empowering a diverse tech community in LA.

Nifty Assignments

Nick Parlante
Julie Zelenski
Stanford University
nick.parlante@cs.stanford.edu
zelenski@cs.stanford.edu

Jeffrey L. Popyack
William M. Mongan
Drexel University
popyack@drexel.edu
wmm24@drexel.edu

Benjamin Dicken
University of Arizona
bddicken@cs.arizona.edu

Kendall Bingham
University of Missouri Kansas City
binghamkl@umkc.edu

Allison Obourn
University of Arizona
aeobourn@cs.arizona.edu

Ben Stephenson
University of Calgary
ben.stephenson@ucalgary.ca

Diane Horton
David Liu
University of Toronto
dianeh@cs.toronto.edu
david@cs.toronto.edu

ABSTRACT

The Nifty Assignments special session is all about promoting and sharing the ideas and ready-to-use materials of successful assignments.

Each presenter will introduce their assignment, give a quick demo, and describe its niche in the curriculum and its strengths and weaknesses. The presentations (and the descriptions below) merely introduce the assignment. A key part of Nifty Assignments is the mundane but vital role of distributing the materials – handouts, data files, starter code, rubrics – that make each assignment ready to adopt. Each assignment presented has complete materials freely available on the Nifty Assignments home page **nifty.stanford.edu**.

If you have an assignment that works well and would be of interest to the CSE community, please consider applying to present at Nifty Assignments.

CCS CONCEPTS

• Applied computing~Digital libraries and archives

KEYWORDS

Education; assignments; homeworks; examples; repository; library; nifty; pedagogy

SIGCSE '19, February 27-March 2, 2019, Minneapolis, MN, USA

ACM ISBN 978-1-4503-5890-3/19/02.
https://doi.org/10.1145/3287324.3293871

Post-It Pandemonium (CS0/CS1) – Jeffrey L. Popyack and William M. Mongan

In this unplugged activity, students collectively reconstruct an image using Post-Its for pixels. Students are given the GIF data divided into subsections, an indexed table of Post-It colors, and instructions for run-length encoding. The image is assembled on a large, numbered grid.

The resulting image is not known to the students beforehand, but is revealed incrementally as they place subsections on the grid. The subsections are dispersed and assembled in random order, which adds intrigue as the image gradually takes form.

We use this as a lecture or lab exercise in a CS Principles course to illustrate abstraction, algorithms, data compression, efficiency, and creative expression through digital images. We have also used it in a variety of venues for informal education, e.g., open houses, middle-school camps, and STEM community events. Audiences have proven enthusiastic, understand the instructions, and enjoy the resulting photo opportunity.

Exercise preparation requires the instructor to design a suitably sized GIF image with color palette restricted to the available Post-Its. Using other media, e.g., construction paper or colored pencils, permits a more extensive palette. We have created software to generate the instruction sheets from a given GIF image.

Motion Parallax (CS0/CS1) – Ben Dicken

Motion parallax is a visual phenomenon that allows people to perceive depth when moving. Whether they know it or not, most people experience the phenomenon of motion parallax on a regular basis. If you are staring out the window of a moving vehicle, a nearby road sign will move quickly across your field of vision while a distant mountain range will move much more slowly.

Students are assigned the task of creating a scene that emulates the effect of motion parallax. The program draws a simple landscape on a canvas and the emulated perspective in the scene changes in response to the motion of the mouse.

This assignment covers a number of CS0/CS1 topics such as mathematics, loops, functions, randomness, and graphical coordinate systems. This assignment also lends itself nicely to theme modifications and adjustments in difficulty.

Phonetic Pronunciation of Hawaiian Words (CS1) — Kendall Bingham

In preparation for the tropical vacation we aspire to enjoy someday, this program shows how to pronounce a Hawaiian word such as humuhumunukunukuapua'a. The Hawaiian language uses only 5 vowels and 7 consonants and has straightforward rules for how the pronunciation varies based on letter combination and position.

This fun exercise gives students practice with simple string manipulation. The program iterates over the input word, looking ahead and behind as needed, and builds a new string with the correct pronunciation. This task is approachable by a novice student who has learned basic control structures (while, if, for) and the string data type. It is also possible to adapt the assignment to test more advanced skills, such as file input and output and dictionaries.

Computing Gerrymandering (CS1) — Allison Obourn

Gerrymandering is creating voting districts to give one party an unfair advantage. Students write a program to analyze voting data from a prior election and report whether a state exhibits evidence of having been gerrymandered according to a mathematical definition.

The core of this assignment is a straightforward calculation; the difficulty can be adjusted by changing how the results are visualized. This assignment has been given in a CS1 course taught in Python and a CS1.5 level web programming course.

The data used is interesting and real-world but yet still manageable to visualize and debug. Gerrymandering is topical and relevant for modern citizenship. The non-computer science learning that they do to complete this assignment provides student with deeper insight into the political process.

Code Crusher (CS1) — Ben Stephenson

Candy Crush is a popular puzzle game where players swap adjacent pieces on a rectangular board to form horizontal or vertical lines of matching pieces.

This assignment asks students to create a limited variation of Candy Crush, with computer-science themed game pieces, that we named Code Crusher. We provide the graphics and user interface code and students are responsible for implementing the game logic. The required tasks give the students ample opportunity to work with 2D lists and nested loops.

We have used this as the third of four assignments in an objects-late CS1 course for non-majors. Two weeks was sufficient time for most of our students to complete it successfully. The assignment difficulty can be adjusted by providing more or less starter code and by adding or removing gameplay elements.

Recursive Blocky Game (CS2) — Diane Horton and David Liu

"Blocky" is a colorful, visual game that has simple rules but is challenging to play. The game board is a recursive structure of blocks within blocks, and players apply operations such as rotations and swaps in an attempt to reach a particular goal state. These operations can be applied at any level within the nested structure.

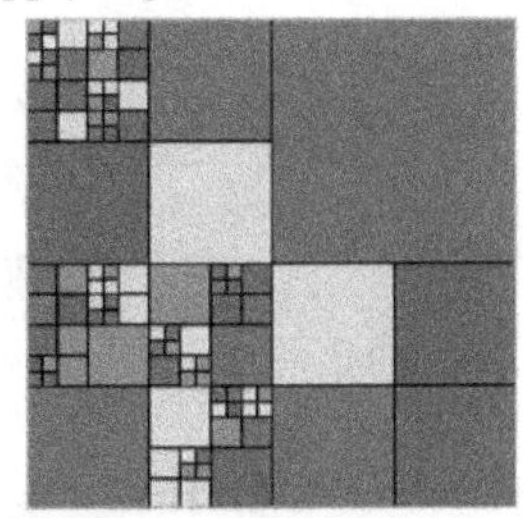

This assignment provides lots of practice with recursion, ranging from straightforward structural recursion to some interesting and quite challenging algorithms, such as one to find the size of the largest connected region of a given color. Students also experience a problem for which a dual representation (as a quad-tree and as a two-dimensional structure) is motivated. Students use inheritance and polymorphism for modeling different types of game goal and for the types of player (solo, human, computer).

One of our favorite things about this assignment is that the code includes many non-trivial and critically important invariants and preconditions. Because these are lifelines when students write the code, the value of carefully documenting code properties like invariants and preconditions becomes clear.

Panel: Making K-12 CS Education Accessibility a Norm, not an Exception

Maya Israel
University of Florida
Gainsville, FL
misrael@coe.ufl.edu

Shireen Hafeez
Deaf Kids Code
Lafayette, IN
contact@deafkidscode.org

Emmanuel Schanzer
Bootstrap
Alexandria, VA
schanzer@bootstrapworld.org

Rebecca Dovi
CodeVA
Richmond, VA
rebeccadovi@codevirginia.org

Emma Koslow
Programming Pals
Warren, NJ
emma@programmingpals.org

Todd Lash
University of Illinois
Champaign, IL
toddlash@illinois.edu

CCS CONCEPTS

• **Social and professional topics → Computing education**;

KEYWORDS

CSforALL; accessibility; inclusion; equity; students with disabilities; curriculum development; professional development; K12 CS Education

ACM Reference format:
Maya Israel, Shireen Hafeez, Emmanuel Schanzer, Rebecca Dovi, Emma Koslow, and Todd Lash. 2019. Panel: Making K-12 CS Education Accessibility a Norm, not an Exception. In *Proceedings of Proceedings of the 50th ACM Technical Symposium on Computer Science Education, Minneapolis, MN, USA, February 27-March 2, 2019 (SIGCSE '19),* 2 pages.
https://doi.org/10.1145/3287324.3287340

1 SUMMARY

Computer science (CS) education is rapidly expanding in the United States[4]. That said, the CS education field is still grappling with coming to consensus about definitions of K-12 CS and how to reach all students. While the CS education community has made great efforts to expand opportunity for under served groups, students with disabilities have regularly been left out of the conversation. According to the National Center for Education Statistics, approximately 13% of all students enrolled in public schools in the US receive special education services and 95% of these students are taught either part or full time in the regular classroom[3] . One aim of CSforALL is to increase equity in CS education and opportunities[5]. Recent studies have examined the challenges faced by students with disabilities in K12 CS education[1][2]. Including students with disabilities in CS classes not only increases their access to academic and career opportunities in CS, but it also gives them the opportunity to develop new ways of thinking and participating in the world that they would otherwise be potentially without. This panel addresses the inclusion of students with disabilities as part of the national all movement and seeks to augment the discussion initiated by the CSforALL Consortium and AccessCSforALL with the introduction of the Accessibility Pledge at the annual CSforALL Summit. This panel brings together four different experts, with a wide range of experience in regards to computer science education and students with disabilities, in an effort to expand both the national conversation and increase efforts related to including students with disabilities equitably in CS education.

In this panel we present a group of CS education community members who represent multiple approaches to accessibility and serving students with disabilities, as well as diverse implementations; peer-to-peer mentoring, initiatives focused on a single subpopulation of students with disabilities, curriculum and platform providers, and district and state-wide solutions. The panelists, and the organizations they represent have a diversity of experiences to share, including current high school students and parents of students with disabilities.

ACM ISBN 978-1-4503-5890-3/19/02.
https://doi.org/10.1145/3287324.3287340

2 PANELISTS

Together the panelists represent multiple types of expertise in the advancement of CS Education for student with disabilities. Each panelist is described here, both for their role in the CS education community as well as the way in which their experience and expertise may drive the discussion of inclusion of students with disabilities in the broader CSforALL movement.

2.1 Shireen Hafeez, Deaf Kids Code

Shireen Hafeez is a mother of a deaf/hard of hearing son and founder the nonprofit DEAF KIDS CODE. The grassroots organizations quickly became a national outreach organization. Has worked with over 1000 Deaf or Hard of Hearing students in over 15 states in over 30 different locations. The organization promotes design thinking, computer science, and technology skills through small group, hands-on, project based interactive experiences. Hafeez believes that the digital age is the great equalizer and computer science skills will allow greater participation in our world for the next generation. Computer science is to her a matter of human rights, self-determination, and workforce development.

2.2 Emmanuel Schanzer, Bootstrap

Emmanuel Schanzer spent several years as a program manager and developer before becoming a public high school teacher and middle school academic coach in Boston. He is the founder and co-director of Bootstrap, which integrates computing into mainstream classes that are required for all students. With accessibility being a requirement for these classes, Bootstrap has worked with AccessCSforAll as a development partner for several years, and has re-engineered their student-facing software to be fully accessible. In the process, Emmanuel has spoken publicly about BootstrapâĂŹs work in this area, and made all of the engineering open-source in order to benefit the community. He has presented BootstrapâĂŹs work on accessibility at several state and national events, worked directly with differently-abled students and developers, and feels passionately about accessibility.

2.3 Rebecca Dovi, CodeVA

Rebecca Dovi is the Director of Education for CodeVA, a Virginia non-profit focused on making computer science available to all Virginia students. CodeVA is participating in an NSF funded grant centered on the integration of computer science in K-5 inclusive classrooms to support students with high incidence disabilities. As someone with dyslexia, parenting a dyslexic child, this is an area of particular interest for her in the work to make computer science available to all students. One of the most damaging misconceptions is that students that experience the world in different ways are experiencing the world through a deficit. The field of computer science has tremendous potential, and responsibility, to disrupt this belief and expand opportunities for these students. Rebecca has twenty years experience as a high school computer science teacher, and was a Google Fellow Trailblazer and a recipient of the Aspirations in Computing award from the National Council of Women in Information Technology.

2.4 Emma Koslow, Programming Pals

Emma Koslow is a high school senior and a disability advocate for computer science. She started coding with HTML and Scratch at six years, has currently learned almost 20 programming languages, and is the founder of Programming Pals, an online coding tutoring service for students with disabilities. For her work with Programming Pals, she has been recognized by NCWIT, Stanford She++, National Coding Week, and Girls Who Code. Emma also suffers from Misophonia, a rare neurological condition that causes severe sensitivity to sound and Motor and Vocal tic disorder.

2.5 Moderator: Maya Israel, University of Florida

Maya Israel, Ph.D. is an associate professor of educational technology at the University of Florida where she leads the Creative Technology Research Lab (CTRL) in research related to K-12 computational thinking. Her primary areas of specialization include supporting students' meaningful access to science, technology, engineering, and mathematics (STEM) learning with an emphasis on computational thinking and computer programming. She studies how to use instructional approaches such as Universal Design for Learning, metacognitive learning strategies, and technologies to help students become more successful learners.

3 PANEL GOALS

In this panel we present a group of CS education community members who represent very different roles and organizations, each of which bring a different expertise to the conversation around CS education and the inclusion of students with disabilities. The goals of this panel are to prompt discussion among the panelists, as well as with the audience, to elicit lessons learned and generalizable best practices for the inclusion of students with disabilities in K12 instructional settings, on the creation of accessible tool and curriculum and professional development. The panel will also provide guidance to funders of CS educational initiatives as to how they may best serve all students, including those with disabilities.

During the panel session, each panelist will give a brief overview of their organization and how they view their role in the movement, and more specifically the CSforALL Accessibility Pledge led by CSforALL and AccessCSforALL. The goal of the panel is to bring to light real-world examples of successful CS education accessibility initiatives and inspire SIGCSE community members to consider accessibility among the core underrepresented groups, and proactively address the multiple dimensions of accessibility and needs of students with disabilities in the design of curricula, programs and initiatives. We will also share the emerging outcomes of the CSforALL Accessibility Pledge, and action steps required to make CSforALL truly inclusive. Panelists will be provided the moderator's questions in advance in order to prepare short answers and the moderator will emphasize discussion and interaction between panelists and the audience. The moderator will then devote the remaining time to questions from the audience, again focusing on interaction between panelists and the audience.

REFERENCES

[1] M. Israel, J. N. Pearson, T. Tapia, Q. M. Wherfel, and G. Reese. Supporting all learners in school-wide computational thinking: A cross-case qualitative analysis. *Computers & Education*, 82:263–279, 2015.
[2] R. E. Ladner and A. Stefik. Accesscsforall: making computer science accessible to k-12 students in the united states. *ACM SIGACCESS Accessibility and Computing*, (118):3–8, 2017.
[3] J. McFarland, B. Hussar, C. de Brey, T. Snyder, X. Wang, S. Wilkinson-Flicker, S. Gebrekristos, J. Zhang, A. Rathbun, A. Barmer, et al. The condition of education 2017. nces 2017-144. *National Center for Education Statistics*, 2017.
[4] M. Smith. Computer science for all. Website, January 2016.
[5] S. Wille, J. Century, and M. Pike. Exploratory research to expand opportunities in computer science for students with learning differences. *Computing in Science & Engineering*, 19(3):40–50, 2017.

Wednesday Workshops

Embracing our Future: CS Courses and Curriculum for Non-CS-majors

Paul Ruvolo, *Olin College*
Darakhshan Mir, *Bucknell University*
Zachary Dodds, *Harvey Mudd College*
Contact: dodds@cs.hmc.edu

CS majors are certainly not disappearing, but the interest and demand for computing from non-CS majors is a far larger part of our future, as members of CS departments, than those on the disciplinary-major path. As computing evolves from valuable specialty to a professional literacy, CS departments face several challenges. How do we support both the traditional CS-major path and provide computing curriculum to a far broader audience? How do we partner with sibling departments in order to foster their sense of ownership and identity with computing's mindsets and toolsets? And, perhaps especially poignant in 2018, how do we invest energy into the CS-for-All future during a time that demand in our major pathway is at historic highs?

This workshop distills the experiences of three faculty members who have tried to answer these questions within the context of their departments. The presenters will share the results of those experiments, will offer hands-on exploration of a representative subset of the curricular materials, and will scaffold a strategic discussion of CS's future and identity in the era of "CS for All."

Keywords: Computing for Non-CS majors, CS for All

DOI: https://doi.org/10.1145/3287324.3287553

Exploring Parallel Computing with OpenMP on the Raspberry Pi

Suzanne J. Matthews, *West Point*
Joel C. Adams, *Calvin College*
Richard A. Brown, *St. Olaf College*
Elizabeth Shoop, *Macalester College*
Contact: suzanne.matthews@westpoint.edu

The ACM/IEEE CS 2013 report recommends fifteen hours of parallel & distributed computing (PDC) education for every undergraduate. This workshop illustrates the use of the Raspberry Pi as an inexpensive, multicore platform for teaching shared-memory parallel programming. The inexpensive and tactile nature of the Raspberry Pi enables each student to experience her own parallel multiprocessor through sight and touch. In this hands-on workshop, we will teach attendees how they can leverage the Raspberry Pi and the OpenMP library to teach shared-memory parallel concepts in their own classrooms. All CS educators who are interested in learning about the Raspberry Pi, shared memory parallelism, and OpenMP are encouraged to attend. In Part I of the workshop, each participant will connect to and learn about the Raspberry Pi's multicore capabilities. In Part II, each participant will engage in self-paced, hands-on exploration of basic parallel computing concepts using the OpenMP "patternlets" from *CSinParallel.org*. In Part III, participants will investigate more complex applications, such as numeric integration and drug design and study how these applications can be parallelized using OpenMP. We will conclude the workshop with a series of lightning talks discussing how the Raspberry Pi has been used to teach parallel computing concepts at different institutions. We will also present a summary of student perceptions of the Raspberry Pi. All materials from this workshop will be freely available from *CSinParallel.org*. Space is limited to 20 participants. **A laptop is required**.

Keywords: Raspberry PI; OpenMP; multicore; parallel computing

DOI: https://doi.org/10.1145/3287324.3287535

Transform Your Computer Science Course with Specifications Grading

James W. McGuffee, *Christian Brothers University*
David L. Largent, *Ball State University*
Christian Roberson, *Florida Southern College*
Contact: jmcguff1@cbu.edu

As proposed by Linda B. Nilson in *Specifications Grading: Restoring Rigor, Motivating Students, and Saving Faculty Time*, specifications grading is an assessment construct that relies on pass/fail grading of assignments and assessments, the structuring of course content into modules linked to learning outcomes, and the bundling of assignments and assessments within those modules. One of the intentions of this type of course grading construct is to more closely align assessment with student attainment of intended learning outcomes. While there has been very visible work in incorporating specifications grading in some academic areas (e.g. in mathematics), examples of the use of specifications grading in computer science courses are less common. The goal of this workshop is to introduce the concepts of specifications grading, explain how to apply these concepts to a wide range of computing courses, and have the participants apply these concepts to one of their current or upcoming computer science courses. Each participant should leave the workshop with at least one revised course syllabus or assignment that incorporates specifications grading.

Keywords: Specifications Grading; Assessment; Syllabus

DOI: https://doi.org/10.1145/3287324.3287528

Narratives and Evaluation: How to Write Competitive NSF CS Education Proposals

Stephanie E. August, *National Science Foundation*
S. Megan Che, Eileen T. Kraemer, *Clemson University*
Mark Pauley, *National Science Foundation*
Murali Sitaraman, *Clemson University*
Contact: saugust@nsf.gov

You develop a plan for testing the prototype for a new learning strategy in your class or across institutions. How can you ensure

ACM ISBN 978-1-4503-5890-3/19/02.

that your plan is clearly understood by reviewers and the managing NSF program officer? What goes through the reviewer's mind once a proposal is submitted? What prompts one proposal to be recommended for funding but another declined? Close examination of the panel review process can inform proposal writing and ensure that reviewers will understand an idea, identify its merit, and value a PI's vision of how the work will broaden participation in STEM education. This workshop steps through the NSF proposal review process from submission of proposal to award or decline, touching on NSF intellectual merit and broader impact criteria, mapping the project pipeline to appropriate evaluation. Participants gain insight into writing a good review and improving one's own proposal writing. ***For further information and travel support see:***
https://people.cs.clemson.edu/~etkraem/UPCSEd/.
Laptops recommended.

Keywords: CS Education; Ed research proposals; Illustrative projects

DOI: https://doi.org/10.1145/3287324.3287531

Bringing Real-World Data and Visualizations of Student-Implemented Data Structures into Sophomore CS Courses Using BRIDGES

Kalpathi Subramanian,
University of North Carolina at Charlotte
Jamie Payton, *Temple University*
Erik Saule, *University of North Carolina at Charlotte*
Contact: krs@uncc.edu

This workshop introduces participants to the concepts and use of BRIDGES, a software infrastructure for programming assignments in data structures and algorithms courses. BRIDGES provides two key capabilities,
(1) easy to use interface to real world datasets spanning social networks, entertainment (movies on IMDB, song lyrics), scientific data (real-time USGIS Earthquake Data), civic issues (crime data), and literature (books); and (2) a visualization of the acquired data can be used in assignments by students to populate their implemented data structures, including the capability to bring out attributes of the dataset. The visualizations are displayed on the BRIDGES website and are easily shared (with family, friends, peers, etc) via a weblink. Workshop attendees will engage in hands-on experience with BRIDGES and multiple datasets and will have the opportunity to discuss how BRIDGES can be used in their own courses, as well as partner with the BRIDGES team.

Keywords: real-world dataset, visualization, data structures

DOI: https://doi.org/10.1145/3287324.3287536

Guiding Students to Discover CS Concepts and Develop Process Skills Using POGIL

Chris Mayfield, *James Madison University*
Debra Duke, *Virginia Commonwealth University*
Margarethe Posch, *Salt Lake Community College*
Contact: mayfiecs@jmu.edu

This workshop introduces Process-Oriented Guided Inquiry Learning (POGIL) to anyone who teaches CS or related subjects. In a POGIL classroom, teams of 3-4 learners work on activities with a particular structure based on learning cycles. Through scripted inquiry and investigation, learners discover concepts and construct their own knowledge. Using assigned team roles and other scaffolding, learners develop process skills and individual responsibility. The teacher is not a lecturer, but an active facilitator who helps all students to be engaged and achieve the learning objectives. POGIL is an evidence-based approach that has been shown to improve student performance significantly. Workshop participants will work through POGIL activities as students and complete meta-activities designed to introduce core POGIL concepts, practices, and benefits. We will share POGIL materials for a variety of CS courses. For more information, see pogil.org and cspogil.org, where you will find activities for CS1, CS2, and other courses. Laptops optional.

Keywords: Active Learning; Cooperative Learning; Inquiry Learning; Teams

DOI: https://doi.org/10.1145/3287324.3287539

Security Labs for Software Defined Networks in CloudLab

Younghee Park, *San Jose State University*
Hongxin Hu, *Clemson University*
Xiaohong Yuan, *North Carolina A&T University*
Contact: younghee.park@sjsu.edu

Software-Defined Networking (SDN) has been changing inflexible networks in software-based programmable networks for more flexibility, scalability, and visibility into networking. At the same time, it brings many new security challenges, but there are very few educational materials for students in learning about SDN security. In this workshop, we present our newly designed SDN security education materials, which can be used to meet the ever-increasing demand for high-quality cybersecurity professionals with expertise in SDN security. For effective hands-on learning, the security labs are designed in CloudLab, a free open cloud platform supported by NSF. Participants receive handouts describing security problems, lab instructions, techniques to use CloudLab, and worksheets for Q&A, which can be directly used for their networking classes at their home institutions. The workshop proceeds in three sessions in which we: present the way to use CloudLab and to understand SDN; practice in simulating three networking attacks in SDN on CloudLab; and discussion and critique in small groups for new SDN security labs.

Keywords: Software-Defined Networking (SDN); Security; CloudLab

DOI: https://doi.org/10.1145/3287324.3287538

Programming Smart Contracts in Ethereum Blockchain using Solidity

Debasis Bhattacharya, Mario Canul, Saxon Knight, *University of Hawaii Maui College*
Mohammad Q. Azhar, *BMCC, The City University of New York*
Rajiv Malkan, *Lone Star College*
Contact: debasisb@hawaii.edu

This workshop introduces participants to programming smart contracts using Ethereum Blockchains and the Solidity programming language. Cryptocurrencies such as Bitcoins use Blockchains and Smart Contracts to enforce transactions. Given the popularity of Bitcoins and related technologies in the press, this module provides a module for CS educators to introduce the underlying technology into their classrooms. Participants receive handouts describing sample programming techniques and worksheets for creating basic smart contracts. The workshop proceeds in three sessions in which we: present the underlying technology of Ethereum; practice the creation of smart contracts using the Solidity programming language; and discuss the implementation of this module in our classrooms in small groups. Further information, sample code and workshop handouts are at: http://maui.hawaii.edu/cybersecurity. ***Note: A laptop is needed for this workshop and handouts will be given out.***

Keywords: blockchain; smart contracts; Solidity; Ethereum; bitcoins; programming

DOI: https://doi.org/10.1145/3287324.3287542

Assessing Writing in CS: A Hands-on Workshop

Phillip Barry, *University of Minnesota*
Mia Minnes, *University of California, San Diego*
Stephanie R. Taylor, *Colby College*
Contact: barry@umn.edu

Although many educators acknowledge the importance of written communication in computer science education, there are a number of challenges to using writing assignments in classes. These include assessing writing effectively and efficiently, especially in larger classes. The workshop will consist of a combination of short presentations, hands-on exercises, and discussion of a number of items related to writing assessment: the role of writing in computer science classes and how different types of assessment apply to different types of writing; how clarifying the goals of writing assignments often leads to better assessment; different techniques, such as rubrics, for grading writing; and strategies --- such as peer review and breaking a substantial writing assignment into a sequence of subassignments --- for scaling writing and its assessment to larger classes.

Keywords: Writing; Professional development; Communication; Curriculum design; Assessment; Rubric design

DOI: https://doi.org/10.1145/3287324.3287544

Computing Infrastructure and Curriculum Design for Introductory Data Science

Mine Çetinkaya-Rundel, *Duke University + RStudio*
Contact: cetinkaya.mine@gmail.com

The goal of this workshop is to equip educators with concrete information on content and infrastructure for designing and painlessly running a modern data science course. This is a three-part workshop. Part 1 will outline a curriculum for an introductory data science course and discuss pedagogical decisions that go into the choice of topics and concepts as well as the choice of programming language (R) and syntax (primarily tidyverse), and the emphasis on literate programming for reproducibility (with R Markdown). Part 2 will discuss infrastructure choices around teaching data science with R: RStudio as an integrated development environment, cloud-based access with RStudio Cloud and Server, version control with Git, and collaboration with GitHub. Part 3 will focus on classroom management on GitHub (with ghclass). Workshop attendees will work through several exercises from the course and get first-hand experience with using the tool-chains and techniques described above. While the workshop content will focus on usage of R, many of the pedagogical takeaways will be language agnostic. All workshop content, including teacher facing documentation and student facing course materials, will also be available to participants via datasciencebox.org. Please bring a laptop with you.

Keywords: data science; pedagogy; reproducibility; R; version control

DOI: https://doi.org/10.1145/3287324.3287556

ACM ISBN 978-1-4503-5890-3/19/02.

Friday Workshops

Adopting, Integrating, and Evaluating Computational Creativity Exercises to Improve Student Learning

Leen-Kiat Soh, Markeya S. Peteranetz,
University of Nebraska-Lincoln
Contact: lksoh@cse.unl.edu

Abstract: In this workshop, participants will learn how to integrate in their classes computational thinking and creative thinking activities that have been shown via rigorous research to significantly improve student learning and performance. Specifically, participants will be familiarized with the suite of Computational Creativity Exercises (non-programming-based, group-based, active learning exercises), take part in completing two of the exercises, learn how to integrate and adapt them into their courses, and be exposed to the educational research studies behind the development, design, and administration of these exercises. Participants will also learn how to conduct evidence-based, educational research studies. Workshop sessions will include presentations, panel-based Q&A, breakout group discussions, and hands-on activities. More information can be found at cse.unl.edu/agents/ic2think/CCEWorkshop

Keywords: Computational thinking; Creativity; Computational creativity

DOI: https://doi.org/10.1145/3287324.3287529

Using Raspberry Pi as a Platform for Teaching Cybersecurity Concepts

Andreea Cotoranu, Li-Chiou Chen, *Pace University*
Contact: acotoranu@pace.edu

This workshop aims to assist high school and college educators with implementing cybersecurity into their existing curriculum. This workshop will introduce Raspberry Pi as a teaching platform for topics such as network traffic analysis, cryptography and web security. We will discuss the Raspberry Pi hardware and software requirements, and will demonstrate network traffic analysis using Wireshark. Participants will receive a fully configured Raspberry Pi kit to use during the workshop and then take home at the end. Manuals on Raspberry Pi configuration will be shared for both Windows and Mac platforms, along with sample lesson plans on network analysis and its security implications. The workshop will send all participants home with flexible tools and new expertise in implementing cybersecurity curricula. Bring a laptop with an Ethernet port or adapter, and ensure that you have full administrator privileges to configure settings and install software on your device. Seats are limited.

Keywords: Raspberry Pi; IoT Security; network security; cryptography; computer science principles

DOI: https://doi.org/10.1145/3287324.3287534

ACM ISBN 978-1-4503-5890-3/19/02.

Using Subgoal Labeling in Teaching CS1

Briana Morrison, *University of Nebraska Omaha*
Lauren Margulieux, *Georgia State University*
Adrienne Decker, *University at Buffalo*
Contact: bbmorrison@unomaha.edu

Subgoal labeling is an instructional design framework for breaking down problems into pieces that are small enough for novices to grasp, and often difficult for instructors (i.e., experts) to articulate. Subgoal labels have been shown to improve student performance during problem solving in disciplines both in and out of computing. Improved student performance occurs because subgoal labels improve student transfer and retention of knowledge. With support from NSF (DUE-1712025, #1712231), subgoal labels have been identified and integrated into a CS1 course (variables, expressions, conditionals, loops, arrays, classes). This workshop will introduce participants to the materials and demonstrate how the subgoal labels and worked examples are integrated throughout the course. Materials include over 100 worked examples and practice problem pairs that increase in complexity and difficulty within each topic. The materials are designed to be integrated into CS1 courses as homework or classroom examples and activities. Assessment of topics using subgoal labels will also be discussed. Participants will also engage in an activity where they create an example for their own course using subgoal labels.

Keywords: subgoal labels; CS1; introductory programming; worked examples; cognitive load theory

DOI: https://doi.org/10.1145/3287324.3287540

Micro:bit Magic: Engaging K-12, CS1/2, and non-majors with IoT & Embedded

Bill Siever, *Washington University in St. Louis*
Michael P. Rogers, *Northwest Missouri State University*
Contact: bsiever@gmail.com

Are you interested in a fun way to introduce a variety of students to significant contemporary CS topics, like wireless networking, robotics, and the Internet of Things (IoT)? Do you want to do so using a platform that is cheap, has a low-barrier to entry, but where learning can translate to the real world and where advanced students can pursue advanced topics? If so, you need a micro:bit!

The micro:bit is a platform developed by the British Broadcasting Corporation (BBC) to encourage children to pursue computing and electronics. Although designed for children, its capabilities are sufficient for a variety of postsecondary applications. It includes a 32-bit processor, lights, buttons, an accelerometer, digital I/O, and wireless communication, making it ideal for wearables and robotics. It also leverages some of the latest trends in introductory computing, like support for block-based languages (àla Scratch), while also being sophisticated enough for complex topics in Operating Systems and Networking.

This workshop will introduce the micro:bit and focus on engaging, lightweight coverage of complex topics, including robotics, mesh networks, and IoT. Participants will work through classroom-ready exercises suitable for K-12 workshops, student recruiting events, CS0/1/2, or as bootstrap topics in IoT courses. The workshop will include some subjects not commonly covered in existing micro:bit material, like integration with mobile apps and IoT applications. Participants will be provided with hardware but will need a laptop with internet access and a mobile device (any OSes, but some features work better with iOS).

Keywords: micro:bit; STEM Outreach; CS Outreach

DOI: https://doi.org/10.1145/3287324.3287527

Integrating Agent-based Modeling in STEM Classes: From Blocks to Text and Back?

Connor Bain, Gabriella Anton, *Northwestern University*
Contact: connorbain@u.northwestern.edu

Agent-based modeling (ABM) is a form of computational modeling whereby a phenomenon is modeled in terms of agents and their interactions. By looking at scientific phenomenon using ABMs, students can learn to understand the micro interactions that are responsible for so many of the seemingly complex systems in the world around them. In addition, by integrating CT skills into science classrooms, we can simultaneously broaden participation in computing, provide a more authentic scientific experience for learners, and encourage deeper scientific content learning.

In this hands-on workshop, we introduce participants to two parallel agent-based modeling environments: NetTango (Olson & Horn, 2011), a blocks-based language, and NetLogo (Wilensky, 1999), a text-based language. The workshop will focus on contextualizing agent-based modeling activities within high school STEM classrooms, allowing participants to explore how computer science can be integrated into existing high school STEM curricula. Over the course of the workshop, participants will gain first-hand experience with ABM and how to design ABM activities in classrooms using NetTango and NetLogo. In addition, the workshop will feature open discussions in which participants will discuss the learning trajectories and affordances of the different programming modalities, brainstorm models that could be built for student exploration, and design activities that incorporate both scientific and computer science content for existing curricula.

Keywords: computing education; computational thinking; blocks-based programming; science education; agent-based modeling; teacher education

DOI: https://doi.org/10.1145/3287324.3287546

ACM ISBN 978-1-4503-5890-3/19/02.

SciGirls Code: Creative Robotics for Tween Girls in Out of School Time

Joan Freese, *Twin Cities PBS*
Heather Benedict, *Heather Benedict Consulting*
Sarah Carter, *Twin Cities PBS*
Katie Hessen, *Twin Cities PBS*
Rita Karl, *Twin Cities PBS*
Karen Peterson, *National Girls Collaborative Project*
Cassandra Scharber, *University of Minnesota*
Contact: jfreese@tpt.org

This workshop introduces participants to SciGirls Code, a unique, connected learning model for engaging middle school girls in computer science (CS) in out of school time. The pilot project, which ran nationally at 16 sites across the United States in 2017-18, included: three curriculum strands (mobile apps, robotics, and e-textiles); role model training for female technology professionals; professional development for informal STEM educators; and a research study that investigates the ways in which learning experiences impact the development of girls' computational thinking as well as their interest and attitudes toward computer science. Workshop participants will learn best strategies for engaging girls in CS and see how those strategies play out in a creative robotics activity using Hummingbird robots. (See https://sites.google.com/tpt.org/scigirlscode/robotics/12-hummingbird-art-bot.)

Keywords: gender equity; broadening participation; computational thinking; connected learning; robotics; e-textiles, app development; curriculum; middle school; professional development; role models

DOI: https://doi.org/10.1145/3287324.3287552

Competency-Based Education: The Future of Learning

Amardeep Kahlon, Ann Kennedy,
Linda Smarzik, *Austin Community College*
Contact: akahlon@austincc.edu

Competency-based education (CBE) has been the focus of much attention lately –from institutions, employers, and policy makers alike. Institutions - from ivy leagues to community colleges to K-12 - are incorporating some form of CBE. In computer science, CBE is an excellent modality to measure mastery and thus prepare students for the next phase whether it is further education or a job. This workshop introduces participants to CBE with an emphasis on CBE course design and competency development. This workshop will be useful for faculty and course designers at all levels – from K-12 through graduate school.

Keywords: Competency-based; cs education; mastery-based education; course design

DOI: https://doi.org/10.1145/3287324.3287555

Playing with and Creating Practice Spaces for Equitable Teaching

Joshua Littenberg-Tobias, Amanda Aparicio,
Justin Reich, *MIT*
Contact: jltobias@mit.edu

In computer science classrooms, the assumptions teachers have about students can significantly shape their interactions. Deeper understandings of the decisions impacting equity offers teacher educators and researchers new leverage in cultivating equitable teaching. Our work uses interactive online practice spaces to focus on specific teaching decisions that may be affected by teachers' assumptions about students. Teacher practice spaces are learning experiences, inspired by games and simulations, that allow teachers to rehearse and reflect on important decisions in teaching. Practice spaces are a potentially powerful approach for encoding equitable teaching strategies because they have the potential to reveal the different assumptions and interpretations which drive different teaching decisions We developed these practice spaces and embedded them within CS teacher preparation programs where they have been used by over 6,000 teachers. In this workshop, we'll use online practice spaces as a novel way to approach discussions about equity in computer science classrooms. We'll have participants try out different variations on these practice spaces, brainstorm ideas for improving existing practice space, and invite reflection about challenges they've observed in training CS teachers in equitable teaching. Participants will leave with links to practice spaces and related curriculum materials they can use in their own work.

Keywords: Equity; Simulations; Teacher Preparation; Culturally Responsive Teaching

DOI: https://doi.org/10.1145/3287324.3287530

Code Crafting Curriculum, A Textile Craft Approach To Computer Science, Remember the 250 Word Count Limit

Ursula Wolz, *Bennington College*
Seoyeon (Stella) Lee, *Grinnell College*
James Mulligan, *Bennington College*
Paulina Valdivieso, *Bennington College*
Contact: ursulawolz@bennington.edu

This reprise of a highly successful SIGCSE 2018 workshop provides a novel perspective on : skills that are often labeled 'women's work' are the foundational principles of computer science developed from textile crafts. The 'Code Crafters' curriculum, which expands Andrea Mayer's Snap-based TurtleStitch embroidery programming project, is being successfully taught in 3 ways: as a full semester undergraduate course, as a weeklong summer workshop for middle and high school students, and as a half day event. The SIGCSE workshop will introduce participants to potential adaptations of this curriculum, report on its use as both a CS 0, and CS 1 course, and give participants hands-on experience in designing and rendering a machine embroidery pattern in TurtleStitch and Processing Stitch (Java). Key concepts from the full semester curriculum will be demonstrated: (1) crocheting as a vehicle for learning about primitive operations instruction codes for process control, and reading and writing patterns (algorithms); (2) programing machine embroidery provides exposure to agile design; (3) contrasting embroidery with quilting provides experience in abstraction and reuse; (4) weaving and tapestry provide concrete illustrations of manipulating two dimensional data structures; (5) studying embroidery machine file formats demonstrates how language translation takes place; (6) sharing a limited resource (a $500 programmable, single thread machine) provides concrete experience in scheduling, and product testing; (7) collaborative crochet and quilted projects provide experience in team dynamics. Participants in this workshop will be invited to join an online community of mutual support.

Keywords: Code crafting, machine embroidery, turtle graphics, computational thinking.

DOI: https://doi.org/10.1145/3287324.3287532

Make and Take an Ethics Module: Ethics Across the CS Curriculum

Darakhshan Mir, *Bucknell University*
Iris Howley, *Williams College*
Janet Davis, *Whitman College*
Evan Peck, *Bucknell University*
Deborah Tatar, *Virginia Tech*
Contact: d.mir@bucknell.edu

This Workshop is intended to be a generative space for participants to create a module on ethics in a Computer Science course of their choice. Participants will choose an existing course in the typical CS curriculum; and coalesce around common themes to create a module that integrates critical reflection on ethical choices and societal impact of computing with the practice of computing. The workshop will offer a space to collaboratively work on designing an ethics module for a CS course chosen by the participants. The ethics module would integrate teaching specific concepts and practices in computing alongside a critical reflection of these practices. Ideally, these modules would be flexible enough to fit into curricula at various institutions.

Keywords: Ethics in CS curricula; Integrate ethics in the practice of CS

DOI: http://doi.org/10.1145/3287324.3287543

ACM ISBN 978-1-4503-5890-3/19/02.

Saturday Workshops

Using and Customizing Open-Source Runestone Ebooks for Computer Science Classes

Barbara Ericson, Jaclyn Cohen, *University of Michigan*
Brad Miller, *Runestone Interactive, LLC*
Contact: barbarer@umich.edu

Runestone Interactive is an open-source ebook platform designed to create and publish interactive computer science textbooks. (See http://runestoneinteractive.org). Runestone ebooks support programming in the browser, code visualizations, and a wide variety of practice activities, from multiple choice and fill-in-the-blank questions to Parsons Problems (drag-and-drop mixed-up code). Free textbooks have been created for CS1, CS2, and Advanced Placement (AP) CS. The presenters have several years of experience creating and using Runestone ebooks. Several studies have demonstrated good usability and positive learning and attitude impacts on students using these ebooks. Runestone ebooks can be customizable to meet the needs of individual courses and teachers. Over 20,000 people a day use Runestone ebooks.

The goal of this workshop is to introduce computer science teachers (both secondary and post-secondary) to Runestone ebooks. This hands-on session will start by leading participants through use of the ebooks as if they were students. Participants will try each of the interactive features. They will also create a custom course from an existing ebook, use the instructor dashboard to review student activity, modify the course, and grade students. Participants will create their own assignments using existing active learning components. They will also be shown how to create new material for assignments, such as multiple-choice questions for a quiz. ***Laptop Required.***

Keywords: ebooks; electronic books; Parsons problems; Parson's problems; active learning

DOI: https://doi.org/10.1145/3287324.3287545

To Dissemination... And Beyond! Building Better Propagation Plans for Computer Science Education Innovations

Christopher Lynnly Hovey,
University of Colorado Boulder
Cynthia Taylor, *Oberlin College*
Heather Bort, *Marquette University*
David P. Bunde, *Knox College*
Zack Butler, *Rochester Institute of Technology*
Contact: hoveyc@colorado.edu

In computer science, educational innovation is constant, but many great ideas never achieve the type of widespread adoption necessary to make lasting and effective change to the way we teach and learn. Research across STEM education has shown that propagation planning is often an overlooked or undervalued part of educational innovation. Whether promoting our own projects or an outside innovation, barriers to success are more difficult to overcome when encountered without sufficient preparation. Plans for adoption and scaling of innovations are not one-size-fits-all, but there are lessons we can learn from both successful and unsuccessful previous projects. We will present a summary of these lessons based on our recent ITiCSE working group research experience on the topic. This writing workshop will focus on building propagation plans informed by best practices, within the context of individual project definitions of success. We will work in small groups to identify potential barriers to the success of our projects, learn about best practices for overcoming those barriers, and put in place a measurable and actionable plan for adoption and propagation. Participants will work toward a better plan for propagation while garnering advice from their peers, learning and generating new ideas about and methods for dissemination and adoption, and building a community of resources for future collaboration, champions for change, and peer feedback. Bringing a laptop is recommended.

Keywords: increasing use; faculty adoption; educational innovations; propagation

DOI: https://doi.org/10.1145/3287324.3287550

Architecting Serverless Microservices on the Cloud with AWS

Ariel Ortiz, *Tecnologico de Monterrey, Campus Estado de México*
Contact: ariel.ortiz@itesm.mx

A microservice architecture decomposes the entire functionally of an application into a set of services that can be deployed and scaled independently. Each service does only one job and does it well. Thus, it's simpler to develop, test and maintain. Additionally, it has its own database and provides access to datasets and services through a well-defined application programming interface (API). Highly successful Internet companies, such as Amazon, Netflix, and Twitter, use microservice architectures to build their software. This workshop is aimed at CS instructors that wish to teach students how to design and build microservice-based applications using cloud services and products provided by the Amazon Web Services (AWS) free tier. We'll start creating a cloud development environment with the AWS Cloud9 IDE. Afterwards, we'll code in Python several RESTful web services using AWS Lambda functions, which are serverless cloud computing services that are executed in response to events. The advantage of going serverless is that you build and run applications and services without thinking about servers. Your application still runs on servers, but all the server management is done by AWS. Finally, we'll demonstrate how to persist our information in a NoSQL database using the Amazon DynamoDB service. More information available at: *http://microservices.arielortiz.info/* **Laptop required.**

Keywords: Microservices; Serverless Computing; Cloud Computing; RESTful API

DOI: https://doi.org/10.1145/3287324.3287533

ACM ISBN 978-1-4503-5890-3/19/02.

NSF Interactive Discussion: Computer Science Undergraduate Education in 2026 and Beyond

Stephanie E. August, Alexandra Medina-Borja,
Mark Pauley, Michael M. Rook,
National Science Foundation
Contact: saugust@nsf.gov

By 2026, today's fifth graders will be entering college and our first-year college students will be the assistant professors. The workforce will see (r)evolutionary changes in the workplace at the human-technology frontier. Participants will be asked to think strategically about how we will reach the future we want to live. Content delivery mechanisms and active learning/project-based experiences for undergraduate students have developed and matured at a dramatic pace in recent years. How can we leverage what we already know, working to improve and broaden undergraduate STEM education and computing education in particular? How do we prepare students to solve the wicked societal problems of the future? Will students require problem-solving skills that transcend disciplines? Is interdisciplinarity teachable at the undergraduate computer science level? Which skills/knowledge will employers and graduate schools require in 10/20 years? The National Science Foundation Division of Undergraduate Education is preparing to have a nationwide dialogue with STEM communities and industry partners on this topic. Participants in this highly interactive session will collectively construct a shared vision for the future of computing sciences education, and outline a research agenda for the future.

Keywords: computer science education; STEM education; future of education; workforce; National Science Foundation; wicked societal problems; human-technology frontier

DOI: https://doi.org/10.1145/3287324.3287537

CyberPaths: Cyber Security Labs for Liberal Arts Institutions Using the NSF Global Environment for Network Innovations (GENI)

Xenia Mountrouidou, *College of Charleston*
Vic Thomas, *Architecture Technology Corporation*
Contact: mountrouidoux@cofc.edu,
vicraj.thomas@gmail.com

The primary purpose of this workshop is to help undergraduate liberal arts colleges integrate cyber security seamlessly into the curriculum with little to no additional investment. We believe Liberal Arts Colleges can provide to the cyber security workforce well-rounded individuals equipped to tackle new and complex problems. However, liberal arts colleges rarely have the resources needed to provide the hands-on labs critical to attracting students to cyber security classes and for preparing students for the workforce. Our NSF funded project "CyberPaths" addresses this by devising several active learning labs on topics such as ransomware, authentication, Distributed Denial of Service (DDoS), and remote network attacks. These labs are implemented on the cloud infrastructure GENI, an NSF funded free academic cloud infrastructure for realistic networking experimentation. We have developed a variety of labs that are suitable for non-CS majors as well as CS upper level courses. In addition, we propose interdisciplinary cyber security modules and multiple paths that can lead to the cyber security professions, starting from the general education courses, moving to an intro to cyber security course, and upper level CS courses. Our goal is to offer solutions to liberal arts institutions with cyber security active learning and introducing cyber security early in the curriculum with low overhead. *This workshop will be highly interactive using a combination of hands-on labs and discussions. If you wish to do the hands-on exercises please bring a laptop with a browser and ssh client installed.*

Keywords: Cybersecurity; Liberal Arts; General Education; GENI; Active Learning Labs

DOI: https://doi.org/10.1145/3287324.3287541

Modernizing Early CS Courses with Parallel and Distributed Computing

Sushil Prasad, *Georgia State University*
Sheikh Ghafoor, *Tennessee Technical University*
Charles Weems *University of Massachusetts Amherst*
Alan Sussman *University of Maryland*
Contact: sprasad@gsu.edu

Parallel and distributed computing (PDC) is now a pervasive aspect of deployed systems, and thus it is essential that students include parallelism and distribution in the computational thinking that they apply to problem solving, from the very beginning. Our students all have multicore laptops. Most of their favorite applications use vast numbers of distributed processors. Why are we still teaching them to solve problems using only sequential thinking? Come to this workshop to see how easy it is to open their eyes to exploiting concurrency in problem solving, starting in their earliest courses. You'll hear about and experience some unplugged activities, learn how to help students recognize examples of concurrency in the world around them, see how event driven user interfaces can easily exemplify issues related to multithreading, and how freely available libraries can be used to naturally exploit parallelism in working with large data structures. We will also highlight the two summer training programs that we are organizing, for which we have funding to support attendance by instructors. **Having a laptop that can run Java and C++ will allow you to follow along with some code examples, but isn't necessary.**

Keywords: Parallel and distributed computing; introductory computer science; data structures; unplugged activities

DOI: https://doi.org/10.1145/3287324.3287548

An Afternoon with an AP Computer Science A Exam Reader

Ria Galanos, *Thomas Jefferson High School for Science and Technology*
Timothy Gallagher, *Winter Springs High School*
Briana Morrison, *University of Nebraska Omaha*
Contact: authoremail@mandatoryhere.com

Advanced Placement (AP) Computer Science A (CS A) is an introductory high school Java course equivalent to a CS1 course at the undergraduate level. Over 66,000 high school students sat for the AP CS A end-of-course examination in May 2018. The exam contains four free-response questions (FRQs) where students are to implement methods or a full class according to specifications. Each June, these exams are graded at the AP CS A Reading. This workshop provides a behind-the-scenes look at the Reading, during which the FRQs are read (scored) by more than 325 college faculty and high school AP teachers. You will learn how the FRQs are scored, the roles of the various Reading participants, and the steps to ensure consistent grading. You will engage in an AP Reading–style training by applying a rubric based on a past free-response question and then participate in a mock reading using the rubric. After attending this workshop, you will be able to understand the role and responsibilities of the Chief Reader, Question Leader, and Table Leader at the AP Reading; develop strategies for creating rubrics for code questions; consistently apply rubrics for free-response questions and similar assignments; and apply strategies to prepare students for the free-response portion of the AP Exam or to similar style questions in an introductory college-level course.

Keywords: computer science education; CS1; K-12 education; student assessment
DOI: https://doi.org/10.1145/3287324.3287549

Interactive Programming Environments for Teachers and Students

David J. Malan, Doug Lloyd, Kareem Zidane, *Harvard University*
Contact: malan@harvard.edu

We present in this hands-on workshop a suite of interactive programming environments for teachers and students, each of them cloud-based and free. The first is CS50 Sandbox, a web app at sandbox.cs50.io that enables teachers and students to create temporary programming environments quickly and share copies of those sandboxes with others. With this app can a teacher start programs in class that students can then finish, distribute starter code for problems, and post interactive solutions. The second tool is CS50 Lab, a web app at lab.cs50.io that enables teachers to create step-by-step programming lessons, providing incremental feedback at each step, and enables students to progress from an empty file (or starter code) to working code, with hints and feedback along the way. Via this app can teachers author their own Codecademy-style lessons using just a GitHub repository of their own. And third in the suite is CS50 IDE, a web app at ide.cs50.io built atop Cloud9 that provides students with their own cloud-based Linux environment. Each of these environments offers a built-in file browser and code editor and, most importantly, an interactive terminal window with shell access to their very own container. And each enables students to write programs in any language. Throughout this workshop will we discuss lessons learned from having deployed these tools in CS50 at Harvard to hundreds of students on campus and thousands of students online. And we'll discuss challenges encountered and best practices adopted.

Keywords: IDE; programming; sandbox

DOI: https://doi.org/10.1145/3287324.3287554

Big Data Analytics with Spark

Mark C. Lewis, *Trinity University*
Contact: mlewis@trinity.edu

Born from a Berkeley graduate project, the Apache Spark library has grown to be the most broadly used big data analytics platform. While Spark integrates with the older Hadoop ecosystem, it provides much more intuitive, faster, and powerful abstractions for manipulating distributed data than MapReduce.

In this workshop, we will cover the basics of the Spark library with the goal of getting participants up to speed so that they can use the library or teach it in courses that involve big data or distributed processing. Participants will work with examples that range from calculating basic summary statistics to using the Spark Machine Learning library for performing sophisticated machine learning analyses on large datasets.

Tasks during the session will be performed on smaller samples using the Spark local standalone implementation on participant's laptops. We will also discuss how Spark can be run on a local or cloud-based cluster and point participants toward resources for setting up those environments for their students.

Participants are encouraged to bring their own laptops. Code samples and configuration files will be provided in a GitHub repository.

Keywords: big data; data science; distributed computing; Spark

DOI: https://doi.org/10.1145/3287324.3287551

Booting Into AI: Startup Instructions for Teaching Artificial Intelligence

Brian K. Hare, *University of Missouri-Kansas City*
David Heise, *Lincoln University*
Contact: hareb@umkc.edu

This tutorial will provide a foundation for faculty members either teaching a course in artificial intelligence for the first time or renewing a course that has been dormant. The growing ubiquity of AI and machine learning dictates that departments offer a course in this area, regardless of whether any such expertise exists locally. Furthermore, there are many possible approaches, from a general overview to a tight focus on a particular application area, either as a single elective or a specialization area within an undergraduate degree. An increasingly wide range of resources is available, but intelligent selection from the plethora of information can be a challenge particularly in smaller programs where no local expertise is available.

ACM ISBN 978-1-4503-5890-3/19/02.

The tutorial is in two parts. Part 1 focuses on background knowledge, discussing major divisions within the broad field of AI, research trends and application areas, and commonly used tools.Part 2 addresses classroom implementation, assessment, textbook options, and online resources including code libraries, free-to-use data sets, development environments, and visualization tools. Participants will have the opportunity to brainstorm and discuss options for course focus. Sample syllabi using differing course approaches, sample exams and assignments, and a non-exhaustive list of useful resources will be provided.

Keywords: curriculum; course design; artificial intelligence; machine learning
DOI: https://doi.org/10.1145/3287324.3287547

ACM ISBN 978-1-4503-5890-3/19/02.

Birds of Feather: Flock 1

Towards a More Inclusive Tech Culture: Promoting Professionalism in CS Classrooms and Labs

Ursula Wolz, *Bennington College*
Stephanie R. Taylor, *Colby College*
Contact: ursulawolz@bennington.edu, srtaylor@colby.edu

Professional behavior in the workplace needs to promote broad participation and inclusion. The competitive nature of the traditional classroom can thwart pedagogical goals to model, support and give practice to collaborative professionalism in the Tech industry and graduate level computing-based disciplines. Diverse populations, ingrained cultural expectations, and a significant range of opportunities for developing computing expertise prior to undergraduate opportunities can all exacerbate this problem. The goal of this BoF is to bring together educators who want to promote inclusive professionalism in the classroom and their community. We hope to use this collaborative setting to identify major issues and to set an agenda for further collaboration among the participants. The long-term goal is to create vehicles for best practice such as stories, curricular activities, and standards that can effect change in the CS community.

Keywords: professionalism; community; competitiveness

DOI: https://dx.doi.org/10.1145/3287324.3293742

AI for K-12: Making Room for AI in K-12 CS Curricula

Christina Gardner-McCune, *University of Florida*
David Touretzky, *Carnegie Mellon University*
Fred Martin, *University of Massachusetts Lowell*
Deborah Seehorn, *CSTA Curriculum Committee*
Contact: gmccune@ufl.edu

As CS expands into more K-12 classrooms and children become familiar with computational thinking, advances in AI pose new challenges for CS educators. Children now enjoy conversing with AI-powered agents such as Alexa and Siri, while their parents worry about the imminent arrival of autonomous robots and self-driving cars. As AI technologies become more prominent in our lives, we need to consider what every child should know about AI. This BOF provides a timely opportunity to introduce CS educators and researchers to several AI for K-12 efforts, including available curricula, tools, and resources. Attendees will discuss how AI can best be incorporated into the K-12 CS curriculum, the tools/resources that will be needed to support students and teachers learning about AI, and how AI education might impact their own work. This BOF is complementary to the SIGCSE 2019 Special Session: AI for K-12 Guidelines Initiative that introduces the current draft of our "Big Ideas in AI." Further information about the initiative and resources is available at http://ai4k12.org.

Keywords: AI education; Artificial Intelligence; K-12 CS Education; standards; curriculum; AI4K12

DOI: https://doi.org/10.1145/3287324.3293729

Toward an Anti-Racist Theory of Computational Curricula

Matt Jadud, *Bates College*
Jamika Burge, *Capital One*
Jeffrey Forbes, *Duke University*
Celine Latulipe, *UNC Charlotte*
Yolanda Rankin, *Florida State University*
Kristin Searle, *Utah State University*
Ben Shapiro, *University of Colorado Boulder*
Contact: matthew.c@jadud.com

Ibram X. Kendi, in his book "Stamped from the Beginning," lays out the argument that structures (political, economic) drive inequitable systems, and it is our enculturation in those systems that lead to ignorance and bigotry. Our goal, in this BOF, is to discuss the dominant social, political, and curricular structures of the discipline of computing, and how we might strengthen or challenge those structures to increase access, equity, and justice within computing. To do so, we must confront the manifold ways in which the existing structures and practices of computing are exclusionary, from curricula to epistemology and the expressions of identity that typically represent what it means to be (and be recognized as) a computer scientist.

Keywords: access; equity; justice; anti-racism; epistemology; identity

DOI: https://doi.org/10.1145/3287324.3293738

What to Make of Makerspaces

Michael P. Rogers, *Northwest Missouri State University*
Bill Siever, *Washington University at St. Louis*
Contact: mprogers@mac.com

Makerspaces are areas set aside in schools, libraries, and other locations, where inventors and Do-It-Yourselfers gather to create and collaborate. Activities run the gamut from high(er) tech, such as electronic kit making and Arduino programming, 3D design and printing, to more traditional crafts such as sewing and woodworking.

As makerspaces become more prevalent, the question arises where, if anywhere, do they fit into the post secondary environment, and specifically, in the computer science realm? Should computer science departments host them? What, exactly, can we do with them? They would be appear to be a good outlet for our students, allowing them to exercise their creative side, but can they do more? Can we use them to draw in non-majors, or to encourage collaboration between students in different fields? Can they be used to supplement various

ACM ISBN 978-1-4503-5890-3/19/02

courses? If so, which, and how might they be used? We are interested in talking to others who have makerspace experience at the post-secondary level so that we can share ideas.

Keywords: makerspace; outreach; collaboration; creativity; curriculum

DOI: https://doi.org/10.1145/3287324.3297796

Can Game Elements Make Computer Science Courses More Attractive?

Darina Dicheva, Christo Dichev, Keith Irwin, Elva J Jones, *Winston-Salem State University*
Lillian (Boots) Cassel, *Villanova University*
Peter J Clarke, *Florida International University*
Contact: dichevad@wssu.edu

Having to compete harder than ever for students' attention against cool social media sites, mobile apps, video games, messaging, etc., instructors are struggling to find new ways to motivate and engage learners. Gamification offers a promising framework for educational interventions that can increase students' motivation and engagement. This BOF will bring together instructors who have already explored the use of various game driven strategies and elements to increase the motivation of their students and also those who are looking for promising interventions to do that. The facilitators conducted a similar BOF at SIGCSE 2018, which was well attended, well received and sparked an interesting and lively discussion. This BOF will continue the conversation on what might be useful ways of incorporating game elements in Computer Science courses, what tools might be needed to support such efforts, how can the student experience of gamified learning be personalized, etc. Two NSF sponsored projects related to the use of gamification in STEM courses will seed the discussion. We hope to collectively contribute to the ongoing important discussion on successful strategies for applying of gamification in Computer Science education.

Keywords: Gamified learning; gamification; student engagement

DOI: https://doi.org/10.1145/3287324.3293726

Discussion of Integrating Hands-on Cybersecurity Exercises into the Curriculum in 2019

Richard Weiss, *Evergreen State College*
Jens Mache, *Lewis & Clark College*
Blair Taylor, Siddharth Kaza, *Towson University*
Ankur Chattopadhyay,
University of Wisconsin at Green Bay
Contact: weissr@evergreen.edu

The critical shortage of cyber security professionals remains an unsolved problem. We need to greatly expand the community in order to meet the increasing demand. The number of security-focused competitions and exercises has increased in recent years. As faculty we need to choose those that we can best integrate into our courses. As a community, we can think about how to create a more unified environment to contribute to each other's projects. We would like to bring together new and experienced faculty to build community and engage in this work. We have set up a dedicated Facebook to allow us to work together outside of SIGCSE events. During the BoF, we will encourage participants to sign up for the closed group, and we will ask the questions, "What do you want from this learning community? What exercises have you heard about or tried?"

One benefit of having a learning community is that it will be easier to provide support for new members to learn about resources and get help. These resources include exercises, webinars, and slides. We will share experiences, practices and ongoing efforts (NSA's National Cybersecurity Curriculum Program), including our own (e.g. Security Injections, Security Knitting Kit, EDURange and UWGB GenCyber). The BoF also benefits experienced members, helping them to disseminate their work and reach other faculty with similar interests. We will discuss what works and what problems students and instructors have encountered. We will discuss ways to integrate security-related exercises into existing courses.

Keywords: security; laboratory exercises; hacker curriculum; secure coding; cybersecurity

DOI: https://doi.org/10.1145/3287324.3293746

Teaching Track Faculty in CS

Chris Gregg, *Stanford University*
Shawn Lupoli, *Texas A&M University*
Laney Strange, *Northeastern University*
Contact: cgregg@stanford.edu

Many computer science departments have chosen to hire faculty to teach in teaching-track positions that parallel the standard tenure-track position, providing the possibility of promotion, longer- term contracts, and higher pay for excellence in teaching and service. This birds-of-a-feather is designed to gather educators, both experienced and new to teaching track positions, who are currently in such a position to share their experiences as members of the faculty of their departments and schools, and to provide opportunities for schools considering such positions to gather information. In particular, we will discuss how to support for new teaching track faculty, as many CS departments are expanding and adding teaching track positions.

Keywords: Teaching Track Faculty; Teaching; Non-tenure

DOI: https://doi.org/10.1145/3287324.3293722

Computing Competencies and the CC2020 Project

Alison Clear, *Eastern Institute of Technology, NZ*
John Impagliazzo, *Hofstra University, USA*
Ming Zhang, *Peking University, China*
Contact: AClear@eit.ac.nz

This birds-of-a-feather session discusses the global project Computing Curricula 2020 (CC2020), a joint project launched by

ACM ISBN 978-1-4503-5890-3/19/02

professional computing societies worldwide. CC2020 is a priority of the ACM Education Council; its sponsors include ACM, IEEE Computer Society, and eight professional organizations from around the world. The project team consists of a task force of 38 members representing 16 countries and six continents. A steering committee of 13 members functions as an executive board to manage the project. CC2020 examines the current state of curricular guidelines for academic programs granting bachelor's degrees in computing and it provides a vision for the future of computing. Audience discussion encompasses new ways computing programs can prepare graduates both academically and professionally. Since computing competencies is an underlying theme of the project, this birds-of-a-feather session discusses competencies, their definition, and their inclusion into future curricular reports. Discussion surrounds competencies in computing, their effect, and the possible ways to visualize their meaning. This birds-of-a-feather session also allows the audience to provide comment on the elements of the project, to engage them to serve as potential project reviewers, and to provide a forum for lively interaction on a global and encompassing computing project.

Keywords: Computing curricula; CC2020; global perspectives

DOI: https://doi.org/10.1145/3287324.3293724

A Town Meeting: SIGCSE Committee on Expanding the Women-in-Computing Community

Paula Gabbert, *Furman University*
Wendy Powley, *Queen's University*
Gloria Childress Townsend, *DePauw University*
Contact: gct@depauw.edu

In January 2004, we organized the second SIGCSE Committee ("Expanding the Women-in-Computing Community"). The SIGCSE Board approved the charter, because the underrepresentation of women in computing is an international problem and an embarrassment for our profession. A BOF provides SIGCSE program advertising that will create a large audience for dissemination of information concerning successful gender issues projects and can provide time for discussion and brainstorming. We select projects to highlight through listserv communication and through our connections with ACM-W, NCWIT, ABI, CDC, CRA-W, etc. The forum provides an important annual meeting for a large group of people, who work to increase the representation of women in computing in their separate organization and who do not customarily have an opportunity to share ideas face-to-face.

Keywords: Gender Issues

DOI: https://doi.org/10.1145/3287324.3293725

ACM ISBN 978-1-4503-5890-3/19/02

The Problem of Packaging Curricular Materials

Austin Cory Bart, *University of Delaware*
Michael Hilton, *Carnegie-Mellon University*
Bob Edmison, *Virginia Tech*
Phill Conrad, *UC Santa Barbara*
Contact: acbart@udel.edu

Packaging materials is a generalized term to capture a broad array of tasks (creating, revising, sharing, finding, crediting, etc.) for materials such as assignments, teacher notes, and evaluation data. Substantial effort has gone into creating materials over the years, but the community still struggles to find ways to effectively manage these. This BoF provides an opportunity to identify needs, concerns, prior efforts, and future plans. A primary goal is the formation of a Working Group tasked to develop a standard for curricular material creation and sharing, joining with broader efforts of standardization (e.g., CSSPLICE) and existing initiatives for creating repositories, tools, and materials.

Keywords: Curriculum Materials; Instructional Design; Packaging; Assignments; Standardization

DOI: https://doi.org/10.1145/3287324.3293732

Modernizing the Mathematics Taught in Computer Science

Barbara Anthony, *Southwestern University*
Mia Minnes, *University of California, San Diego*
David Liben-Nowell, *Carleton College*
Peter-Michael Osera, *Grinnell College*
Contact: osera@cs.grinnell.edu

The undergraduate computer science curriculum is ever-changing but has seen particular turmoil recently. Topics such as machine learning, data science, and concurrency and parallelism have grown in importance over the last few years. As the content of our curriculum changes, so too does the mathematical foundations on which it rests. Do our current theoretical courses adequately support these foundations or must we consider new pedagogy that is more relevant to our students' needs? In this BoF, we will discuss *what* a modern mathematics curriculum for computer scientists should cover and *how* we should go about accomplishing this in our classrooms.

Keywords: Computer science education; discrete mathematics

DOI: https://doi.org/10.1145/3287324.3293748

Teaching Human-Centered Design in CSE Programs

Tamara Peyton, *Harrisburg University*
Aarathi Prasad, *Skidmore College*
Sa Liu, *Harrisburg University*
Joslenne Pena, *Pennysvania State University*
Contact: tpeyton@harrisburgu.edu

Many CSE programs have begun to mandate a human-centered design (HCD) course as part of degree requirements. Rather than abstracting out messy humans to a single generic 'user', HCD requires solution designers to use their innate creativity and empathy to work alongside a varied group of people who will be most impacted by a new system. However, many CSE students tend to keep a narrowed focus on system-only behavior and the human inter-relation skills necessary to do HCD well may not come naturally to CSE students. Within HCD projects, this becomes a problem given that project teams consist not just of designers, developers and project managers, but also increasingly of core users, in a co-design or participatory design process. Figuring out ways to get students to define a problem completely, account for human needs in solution ideas, and work alongside actual users can be a struggle for many in the CSE education field. This BOF is intended to share ideas for how to appropriately teach the mindset and methods skillset of HCD to typical CSE students. This session is directed at the sharing and collaborating around teaching resources, techniques, in-class activities and assignments for HCD education. *Handouts.*

Keywords: Human-centered design; teaching; techniques; resources; undergraduate education; design

DOI: https://doi.org/10.1145/3287324.3293731

Incorporating Computing for Social Good in Computing Education

Gregory W. Hislop, *Drexel University*
Darci Burdge, *Nassau Community College*
Michael Goldweber, *Xavier University*
Samuel Rebelsky, *Grinnell College*
Stewart Weiss, *Hunter College of CUNY*
Contact: hislop@drexel.edu

Computing often makes headlines for negative social impacts such as data breaches, algorithmic bias, and cyber warfare. The many ways that computing can create social good are similarly powerful but seem to get much less attention. This BoF will explore ways to incorporate the positive potential of computing for social good in undergraduate courses. The organizers are especially interested in active learning approaches where students can experience first-hand the positive social impact of computing. The discussion will allow faculty who have included computing for social good in their courses to exchange ideas and share their experiences. Faculty who are interested in this area but have not yet tried it in their courses are encouraged to join the discussion.

Keywords: computing for social good; active learning; service learning

DOI: https://doi.org/10.1145/3287324.3293740

ACM ISBN 978-1-4503-5890-3/19/02

How Can We Make Office Hours Better?

Kristin Stephens-Martinez, *Duke University*
Brian Railing, *Carnegie Mellon University*
Contact: ksm@cs.duke.edu

Most student personal interactions with the course staff come through office hours. Particularly in large courses, the office hours are predominantly run by teaching assistants (TAs). TAs are best advantaged by support and training from more senior instructional staff, especially faculty. This BOF will provide a forum for discussing mentoring techniques and other individualized support of the TAs (particularly in computer science courses) to improve student learning and experience, as well as longer-term gains to the discipline. Second, we will be discussing what technological support exists, such as queue software or internal wikis, to improve student learning and experience in office hours. Finally, we will discuss ideas for more significant changes in office hour structures that could lead to future collaborations or research experiments.

Keywords: Office Hours; teaching assistant training; course tools;

DOI: https://doi.org/10.1145/3287324.3293741

Supporting Students Living With Mental Illness

Christian Murphy, *University of Pennsylvania*
Linda DuHadway, *Weber State University*
Matthew Hanson, *University of Minnesota*
Contact: cdmurphy@seas.upenn.edu

Long hours, pressure to meet deadlines, and fear of failure are just some of the stressors that affect CS students and professionals alike, leading to burnout, anxiety and depression. These issues are particularly amplified in students who are already living with diagnosed mental illnesses such as bipolar mood disorder, schizophrenia, or autism spectrum disorder. A quarter of the world's population lives with some form of mental illness, and recent research suggests that 50% of those working in the tech community have been diagnosed with a mental illness, a statistic that may actually underestimate the problem because of stigmas in certain cultures and communities around seeking mental health services. These numbers suggest a significant need for awareness and support in the CS education community. This BOF will provide attendees an opportunity to discuss the mental illnesses that affect CS students and how to create a culture of understanding and support within their communities.

Keywords: mental health; mental illness; wellness; well-being

DOI: http://doi.org/10.1145/3287324.3293730

Birds of Feather: Flock 2

Academic Cybersecurity Disciplinary Foundations and Accreditation

Allen Parrish, *Mississippi State University*
Rajendra K. Raj, *Rochester Institute of Technology*
Lawrence Jones, *ABET*
Contact: allen.parrish@msstate.edu

This session is designed to attract participants with an interest in post-secondary academic cybersecurity programs. Despite the extraordinary interest in cybersecurity due to the job market, relatively little consensus exists on how to design academic programs. Divergence on issues such as degree title, program objectives and outcomes, program scope, whether only one distinct discipline of cybersecurity exists or several, whether a separate academic unit is needed to offer such degrees, and what role other (non-computing) disciplines should play in cybersecurity programs. Prior efforts in defining cybersecurity at the collegiate level include the US Department of Homeland Security and the US National Security Agency's Centers for Academic Excellence (CAE) programs, NIST's National Initiative for Cybersecurity Education (NICE), the Cyber Education Project, the Joint Task Force's CSEC 2017 draft curricular guidelines, and ABET accreditation criteria for cybersecurity programs. The audience is expected to consist of college faculty and administrators who are either in the process of starting cybersecurity programs or are seeking guidance for developing security content for other computing programs that must now teach security. This session will allow participants to share ideas regarding how to develop and teach cybersecurity in four-year, post-secondary academic programs.

Keywords: Cybersecurity education; computing education; degree program development; program accreditation.

DOI: https://doi.org/10.1145/3287324.3293728

Sponsoring Girls Who Code Clubs

Pamela Cutter, *Kalamazoo College*
Contact: Pam.Cutter@kzoo.edu

Girls Who Code (GWC) Clubs are springing up all around the country, with almost 90,000 girls involved from all 50 states. Have you ever wondered what it takes to get a club started? How do clubs make use of the curriculum that GWC provides? Do clubs ever take their girls on field trips to local places that would show them the possibilities of what they can do in computing? Maybe you're already involved with a club and would like to know what other clubs are doing, or you're doing some cool things with your club that you'd like to share. Or maybe you've been thinking about getting a club started and would like some ideas. This BOF will provide a platform for the discussion of starting and running a GWC club, as well as for sharing ideas of the interesting things clubs have been doing.

Keywords: Girls Who Code; outreach; K-12;

DOI: https://doi.org/10.1145/3287324.3293736

Developing a Contemporary and Innovative Operating Systems Course

Saverio Perugini, *University of Dayton*
David J. Wright, *University of Dayton*
Contact: saverio@udayton.edu

This birds-of-a-feather provides a discussion forum to foster innovation in teaching operating systems (os) at the undergraduate level. This birds-of-a-feather seeks to generate discussion and ideas around pedagogy for os and, in particular, how we might develop a contemporary and innovative model, in both content and delivery, for an os course—that plays a central role in a cs curriculum—and addresses significant issues of misalignment between existing os courses and employee professional skills and knowledge requirements. We would like to exchange ideas regarding a re-conceptualized course model of os curriculum and related pedagogy, especially in the areas of mobile OSs and Internet of Things; concurrent programming and synchronization; and cloud computing and big data processing.

Keywords: Course re-design; operating systems pedagogy.

DOI: https://doi.org/10.1145/3287324.3293734

Co-Curricular Activities in Computer Science Departments

Kathleen Freeman Hennessy, University of Oregon
Jennifer Parham-Mocello, Oregon State University
Henry Walker, Grinnell College
Contact: kfh@uoregon.edu

Academic co-curricular activities (e.g., programming contests, hackathons, student ACM clubs, tutoring, internships, undergrad research) are popular with students, may promote academic engagement, and can give a leg up to students applying for jobs and grad schools. Yet information about co-curricular activities in departments and schools can be hard to come by. This BOF will provide participants with a forum for comparing notes: What co-curricular opportunities exist in your department? Does your department or school explicitly support or promote undergraduate co-curricular activities? If so, how (e.g., staff positions, faculty release time, student leadership – volunteer or for pay or credit)? What have you learned from your experiences with co-curricular activities? Are co-curricular activities a good investment of department resources?

Keywords: co-curricular; student activities; student organizations; student experience

DOI: https://doi.org/10.1145/3287324.3293735

Access to Computing Education for Students with Disabilities

Richard E. Ladner, *University of Washington*
Andreas Stefik, *University of Nevada, Las Vegas*
Andrew J. Ko, *University of Washington*
Brianna Blaser, *University of Washington*
Contact: accesscomp@uw.edu

Approximately 10% of computer science and engineering majors have a disability. Students with disabilities are more likely to drop out of the major than those without disabilities. At the K-12 level, many tools used to teach computing have limited accessibility to students with disabilities. This BOF will bring together individuals who are interested in increasing the representation of students with disabilities in computing and improving their success. Participants will share strategies to help each other do a better job of including these students in our classes and research projects. Resources, including those produced by AccessComputing and AccessCSforAll, will be shared.

Keywords: accessibility; disability; universal design; broadening participation

DOI: https://doi.org/10.1145/3287324.3293723

Building Bridges for Data Science Education

Mine Çetinkaya-Rundel, *Duke University + RStudio*
Andrea Danyluk, *Williams College*
Jeff Forbes, *Duke University*
Michael Posner, *Villanova Universirty*
Contact: cetinkaya.mine@gmail.com

Data science encompasses elements of statistics, computer science, and mathematics as well as domain-specific knowledge, suggesting that with interdisciplinary conversations and collaborations we can make data science curricula more comprehensive and successful. Development of such programs provide an exciting collaboration opportunity for faculty in statistical and computer and mathematical sciences as well as a wide array of other disciplines. This BOF provides an opportunity for faculty involved/interested in the development of undergraduate data science curricula to come together and discuss forming collaborations across disciplines and what the disciplines can learn from each other. The discussion will be led by faculty from computer science and statistics departments who have been involved with both disciplinary and interdisciplinary data science education initiatives. One of the goals of this BOF is to jumpstart conversations across disciplines, which we hope the audience will continue at their home and/or nearby institutions.

Keywords: Data Science; Statistics; Interdisciplinary; Curriculum; Undergraduate

DOI: https://dx.doi.org/10.1145/3287324.3293745

ACM ISBN 978-1-4503-5890-3/19/02

Birds of a Feather Who'd Like to Share Software Together: Teaching Tools that Improve Efficiency and Outcomes

David J. Malan, Doug Lloyd, Erin Carvalho,
Harvard University
Contact: malan@harvard.edu

Odds are we've all used (or tried!) quite a few tools to facilitate efficiency inside and outside of the classroom and empower students to learn more effectively. Some of those tools are perhaps homegrown and unique to one's own institution, but freely available educational technologies abound as well, some in the cloud, some for Macs and PCs, some open-source. And quite a few commercial tools offer free or discounted educational plans as well. In this BoF, we'll begin with a whirlwind tour of the tools we ourselves use, identifying the problems they solve and how well, then quickly open the floor to everyone to share their favorites as well. Along the way, we'll jot down every tool mentioned and share the results. Attendees should exit this session with a better understanding of the educational-technology landscape, familiarized with innovations they can bring back to their own classes.

Keywords: edtech; tools; software; teaching; learning; innovation; efficiency

DOI: https://doi.org/10.1145/3287324.3297795

Bringing Reflection into Computer Science Education

Paul E. Dickson, *Ithaca College*
John Barr, *Ithaca College*
Contact: pdickson@ithaca.edu

Computer Science is a rapidly changing field where code bases and development strategies can change in months even if core concepts stay largely the same. In order to prepare our students for this environment we need to enable them to learn on their own and this concept appears in the literature as self-directed or self-regulated learning (SRL). The literature on SRL suggests that reflection is one of the most effective ways of promoting SRL. Reflective diaries, blogs, journals and questionnaires have all been used successfully in fields from the humanities to medicine to engineering to encourage students to engage in SRL. We believe that reflection has not caught on in CS as heavily as in some other fields because our students dismiss these common methods of reflection as mere busy work. The benefit of reflection, however, is not the writing itself but the process of thinking about and analyzing the actions and experiences of learning in order to master them. With this BOF we will describe reflection and its use in CS and start a discussion of reflective exercises relevant to computer science. As an example, students can reflect on how they learn new material by creating YouTube tutorials for others and adding to community knowledge. The intended result of this BOF is to begin the development of a repository of reflective activities that can be used in computer science classes.

Keywords: Reflection, Problem Based-Learning; Project Based-Learning; Self-Regulated Learning; Open-Ended Group Projects

DOI: https://doi.org/10.1145/3287324.3293733

Undergraduate TA and Mentor Programs in Computer Science

Diba Mirza, *UC Santa Barbara*
Phillip Conrad, *UC Santa Barbara*
Colleen Lewis, *Harvey Mudd College*
Cynthia Lee, *Stanford University*
Contact: diba@ucsb.edu

Undergraduates have been an important part of the teaching staff at many universities for decades, but this is not a universal practice. This BOF provides a forum to discuss undergraduate TA/mentor programs at various stages in their evolution. Attendees will have an opportunity to discuss the benefits, best practices, and research questions related to the use of undergraduates as teaching assistants and/or mentors. The audience is expected to consist of faculty that have already implemented such programs, and those who might be considering doing so, and want to share information about successes and challenges.

Keywords: Undergraduate Teaching Assistants; Undergraduate Tutors; Undergraduate Mentors

DOI: https://doi.org/10.1145/3287324.3293744

Auto-graded Programming Labs: Dos and Don'ts for Less-Stressed Higher-Performing Students, Reduced Grading Time, and Happier Teachers

Frank Vahid, *Univ. of California, Riverside*
Roman Lysecky, *Univ. of Arizona*
Contact: vahid@cs.ucr.edu

Program auto-graders used to be tough applications to install and use by instructors, meaning many instructors avoided them, and for those that used them, most assignments were created by specialists with scripting and other expertise. As such, creating new auto-graded programming assignments was a rare event done by just a few people. But modern cloud-based program auto-graders enable nearly any instructor or TA to create new auto-graded assignments in just tens of minutes, fully created and carried out via the web. This capability has led to an explosion in the number of instructors and TAs creating auto-graded programming assignments, benefiting students via immediate feedback and the option to resubmit, and saving teachers huge amounts of grading time. BUT, this new frontier is very different from hand-graded assignments, with plenty of pitfalls for teachers to avoid, and emerging best practices. This BOF allows teachers to share do's and don'ts, so each can improve their use of auto-graded labs, and teachers new to auto-graded labs can benefit from others' experiences. Special focus is on early CS classes (CS0, CS1, CS2) but topics may apply to many CS classes.

Keywords: Program auto-grading; grading; automation; feedback; CS1; labs; programming assignments

DOI: https://doi.org/10.1145/3287324.3293727

ACM ISBN 978-1-4503-5890-3/19/02

POGIL in Computer Science for Beginners and Experts

Debra Duke, *Virginia Commonwealth University*
Margarethe Posch, *Salt Lake Community College*
Contact: s2dmduke@vcu.edu

Process-Oriented Guided Inquiry Learning (POGIL) is a form of student-centered, engaged learning. It is a research-based instructional strategy with a proven history across STEM disciplines. In a POGIL classroom, teams of students work on activities that are specifically designed to guide them to construct their own understanding of key concepts. At the same time, students develop process skills such as communication, teamwork, problem solving, and critical thinking. POGIL incorporates practices shown to be particularly helpful for students from underrepresented populations. In a POGIL classroom, teachers are facilitators, not lecturers. Multiple studies have shown that students in POGIL classes do better on common exams and in subsequent courses. For more information, see http://cspogil.org and http://pogil.org. This BOF will (1) enable people unfamiliar with POGIL to experience it first-hand, and (2) bring together experienced POGIL practitioners to share experiences, insights, ideas, and concerns. As in a POGIL classroom, we will discuss topics in small teams and report out to the larger group.

Keywords: Active Learning; POGIL; Learning Cycle

DOI: https://doi.org/10.1145/3287324.3293737

Broadening Participation in Computing: A Call to Action for Universities and Community Colleges

Amardeep Kahlon, *Austin Community College*
Deborah Boisvert, *University of Massachusetts Boston*
Cheryl Calhoun, *Santa Fe College*
Louise Ann Lyon, Jill Denner, *ETR*
Wendy DuBow, *NCWIT*
Melanie Williamson, *Bluegrass Community and Technical College*
Contact: akahlon@austincc.edu

Over half of community college (CC) students are non-white, and more than half of all Hispanic and Black undergraduates start at community college. Given that community colleges (CCs) enroll minorities and women in larger numbers than universities, it is imperative for both universities and CCs to engage in collaborative efforts to broaden the participation of diverse peoples in the computing field. Such efforts could include, but not be limited to, the creation of a national broadening participation in computing (BPC) alliance, structured transfer pathways from the CC to the university, inclusion of a CS Principles course for college, and changing the commonly held perceptions of CCs. Brainstorming, and then building, these strategic partnerships requires that experts from various backgrounds come together to share knowledge and experiences that contribute to a better understanding of the role such collaborative efforts could play with universities and CCs in BPC efforts in CS and information technology (IT).

Keywords: Community College; Transfer Pathways; Broadening Participation; CS Principles

DOI: https://doi.org/10.1145/3287324.3293747

Enriching Courses on Computers and Society and Computer Ethics

Ronald M. Baecker, University of Toronto
Elliot B. Koffman, Temple University
Contact: ron@taglab.ca

We shall discuss ways of enriching courses on Computers and Society and Computer Ethics to better engage and stimulate students, including those from Computer Science as well as other disciplines. This topic is significant because society is experiencing increasing stress due to data breaches, privacy invasions, fake news, election hacking, corporate concentration with increased power by a few dominant high-tech firms; and recent advances in AI. Based upon participant interest, we shall discuss and share experiences dealing with issues such as: 1) prerequisites, 2) kinds of assignments and projects; 3) teaching materials including media; 4) the mix of individual and group assignments; 5) how to handle the increasing numbers of desirable topics; 6) how much of the course to focus on AI; 7) methods of teaching ethics; 8) level at which to teach the course, including use in secondary schools; 9) differences between CS courses and general education courses; 10) integration with other CS courses; 11) follow-on options for students wanting to learn more. BOF attendees will be able to hear multiple viewpoints and connect with other people in similar situations, so they can share resources and techniques for teaching such courses. The audience is expected to consist of professors and lecturers who teach, are planning to, or are considering teaching such courses.

Keywords: Computers, society, ethics, social implications, course

DOI: https://doi.org/10.1145/3287324.3293721

Exploring Programming Instruction in Multidisciplinary Contexts

Leo C. Ureel II, Michelle Jarvie-Eggart,
Melanie Kueber Watkins, Russell Louks, Briana Bettin,
Michigan Technological University
Contact: ureel@mtu.edu

Programming is becoming skill required by a wide range of students, not just CS majors. Furthermore, not only are non-CS majors learning to program, but many non-CS faculty find themselves teaching programming courses. Introducing these faculty and students to the craft of programming is accompanied by a number of unique challenges. How can non-CS faculty position themselves as programming experts, given they are not CS people? How can we convince non-CS students that coding is a necessary skill? Often our non-computing majors are reluctant, stating "Programming isn't what I signed up for!" Many non-CS students are not receptive to learning new programming languages due to a lack of intrinsic motivation coupled with technological anxiety. These factors often result in low-self efficacy, which must be overcome in order to explore, play, and learn. This Birds of a Feather discussion brings together instructors from diverse disciplines to discuss the teaching of programming to a range of students, the barriers that exist for non-computing students, and the interventions that attempt to mitigate these issues.

Keywords: Teaching Programming; Non-CS Faculty; Non-Majors; Multidisciplinary; CS0

DOI: https://doi.org/10.1145/3287324.3293739

How Can We Engage in Inclusive, Culturally Responsive Computer Science?

Eileen T. Kraemer, *Clemson University*
Murali Sitaraman, *Clemson University*
S. Megan Che, *Clemson University*
Contact: etkraem@clemson.edu

In this BoF we discuss the tenets of culturally responsive computer science and how teachers, professors and providers of professional development can include culturally responsive perspectives in their classes. In contrast to other academic fields, which typically include rigid curricular tracks ostensibly based on academic performance, talent, or ability that pose structural barriers to access to rigorous academic instruction for underrepresented students, the field of computer science education is explicitly focused on broadening participation, as evidenced by the SIGCSE community's consistent emphasis on equitable representation. Culturally responsive computing (CRC) is founded on culturally responsive teaching (CRT) and on CRT's three tenets: asset building (in contrast to deficit approaches), reflection, and connectedness. CRC frames these tenets for the specifics of computing education. CRC's tenet that all students are capable of digital innovation should drive teachers' interactions and relationships with students. CRC also requires that teachers be continually reflective about their privilege and constraints and how those are connected with our worldviews. This topic is significant because teachers must be connected to their students in non-traditional ways that prize diversity as an asset to innovation. The participants are expected to include professors, lecturers, high school teachers and industry experts who are interested in employing culturally responsive computing approaches in their own teaching and professional development activities. A major goal of the BoF is to establish connections among the participants to promote the sharing of resources and best practices.

Keywords: computer science; culturally responsive; broadening participation

DOI: https://doi.org/10.1145/3287324.3293743

ACM ISBN 978-1-4503-5890-3/19/02

Poster Session 1

Coding Pedagogy for the Liberal Arts: An Online Publication

Jeremy Sarachan, Sean O'Leary, *St. John Fisher College*
Contact: jsarachan@sjfc.edu

Professors across various disciplines in the liberal arts increasingly find themselves incorporating programming into their classes. Examples include media professors teaching web design and video game development, art professors teaching Processing, and statistics and political science professors teaching R. In order to help meet the professional development needs of this group, an online publication published in late fall 2018 covers both the general trends related to coding across the liberal arts disciplines, as well as specific pedagogical strategies and assignments related primarily to media production. Specifically, the chapters are: 1) an overview of the use of coding within media departments nationwide; 2) a literature review and analysis of coding pedagogical discourse as it relates to the liberal arts; 3) a discussion of why journalism and media students need to know coding; and six case studies: 4) mobile app creation; 5) p5.js; 6) HTML/CSS 7) interactive documentaries; 8) data visualizations; 9) video games. This book takes an innovative trajectory by never being entirely complete. Authors may submit additional chapters for consideration at anytime with the goal of creating a large repository of coding pedagogy strategies for professors teaching programming outside of traditional Computer Science (and hopefully, Computer Science professors may find this source useful as well). This poster showcases some of the content of the online publication and invites new authors to consider submitting—after discussion with the editor who will be available at the poster session.

Keywords: coding pedagogy; media production; non-majors; publishing opportunity; HTML/CSS; R; video games

DOI: https://doi.org/10.1145/3287324.3297797

Online or In Person? Student Motivations in the Choice of a CS1 Experience

Melinda McDaniel, *Georgia Institute of Technology*
David Joyner, *Georgia Institute of Technology*
Contact: mcdaniel@cc.gatech.edu

As online offerings have matured and expanded, new efforts have recently been devoted to opening fully-accredited online versions of traditional on-campus classes. Such classes may be offered to on-campus students for greater flexibility during busy semesters, or to allow them to continue to make progress toward their degrees during internships or semesters away from campus. This trend intersects with a growing CS for All movement that sees more and more non-computer science majors enrolling in CS classes. As online offerings expand, it is important for us to understand who enrolls in online sections and the reasons for their choices, both to make sure that learning outcomes are similar across different delivery mechanisms, and to take advantage of opportunities to tailor course content to specific audiences. In this analysis, we look at two versions, one online and one traditional, of a CS1 class offered at a major public research university. We investigate demographic, motivational, and experiential components to identify which types of students are most likely to select each version and what implications this decision has for student success and course design.

Keywords: CS1; online education; CS for All

DOI: https://doi.org/10.1145/3287324.3293783

ViCyber: An Intelligent Curriculum Design Tool for Cybersecurity Education

Shamim Khan, Shuangbao Wang, Rania Hodhod, *Columbus State University*
Contact: hodhod_rania@columbusstate.edu

Unauthorized access to confidential information with malicious intent has become a growing challenge to individuals, businesses and governments. Recent media reports of attempted foreign interference in the domestic politics highlights the threat to data security from both within as well as outside the country. Adequate protection of information systems urgently requires a cybersecurity-educated workforce trained using a curriculum that covers the essential skills required for different cybersecurity work roles. The demand for effective cybersecurity education has led to efforts at the national level like the National Initiative for Cybersecurity Education (NICE) framework to guide cybersecurity curriculum design. However, the many-to-may relationships among components of the NICE framework makes it difficult for anyone but experienced cybersecurity experts to design courses or training programs. The much needed rapid expansion of cybersecurity education depends on the ability of educators to understand and reflect in their curriculum frameworks like NICE. This poster presentation describes the design and use of viCyber, an intelligent cybersecurity course design tool, currently under development with support from the National Security Agency. The goal of this tool is to guide inexperienced instructors through the curriculum design process and provide an evaluation of their design with suggestions for possible improvements. viCyber is available as a web-based tool for trial and evaluation by the cybersecurity education community. It is hoped that the dissemination of information through this presentation will help make educators aware of this publicly available web-based tool and elicit valuable feedback from cybersecurity educators.

Keywords: cybersecurity education; NICE framework; curriculum design; intelligent system

DOI: https://doi.org/10.1145/3287324.3293788

ACM ISBN 978-1-4503-5890-3/19/02

Establishing Computational Thinking as Just Another Tool in the Problem Solving Tool Box

Hillary Fleenor, *Columbus State University*
Contact: fleenor_hillary@columbusstate.edu

Even though the computer science education community has not definitively established exactly what "Computational Thinking" entails, most will agree that it is using a computing machine to solve problems. Like all tools for solving problems, this knowledge should be made available to everyone. Jeannette Wing sounded this call in 2006, writing that "computational methods and models give us the courage to solve problems and design systems that no one of us would be capable of tackling alone." These skills are not just for computer scientists, but for anyone and everyone who plans to solve problems. We already teach other forms of problem solving to all our students including: Mathematical Thinking, Critical Thinking, and Scientific Reasoning. Computational Thinking, as well as engineering and design's Design Thinking, should be equally exposed to all students. It is also important to illuminate that these tools are not used in isolation to solve problems. Perhaps the key to the acceptance of Computational Thinking (as well as Design Thinking) as essential educational tools is to highlight their overlap and interdependence with other problem solving skills. The next generation will need practice with every tool at their disposal to be prepared to solve tomorrow's problems. I propose embedding Computational Thinking in a problem solving framework that leverages teachers' (and students') existing knowledge of problem solving in mathematics, science, and language arts in order to encourage teachers in non CS disciplines to teach Computational Thinking in their classrooms.

Keywords: computational thinking; problem solving; computer science education

DOI: https://doi.org/10.1145/3287324.3293792

Questioning the Board in Computer Science Education Board Games

Caroline Hardin, Alexander Brooks, Joshua Gabai, Anthony Pellicone, and Isaac Sung,
University of Wisconsin-Madison
Contact: caroline.hardin@wisc.edu

In the space between the well documented shortage of access to computer science educational (CSed) opportunities, especially those that broaden participation, and the increasing consensus that computer science knowledgeis a fundamental modern literacy lie an eclectic collection of non-traditional and informal CSed projects. An increasingly popular form of interest-based CSed product are board games, which are often justified as inter-ventions due to their 'unplugged' nature and their supposedly natural appeal to diverse audiences of children. Through an exploration of the popular and academic discourses around the CSed board game genre, we found over 30 games which specifically aim to teach core CS content, often with a wide variety of rationales for utilizing a board game format. This poster will display the results of our preliminary work investigating how designers position cardboard as the exciting new alternative for teaching computer science education. Our examination of game makers' documentation and related research suggests that further work is required to determine how well the board game medium serves the various justifications presented by the game makers in our sample.

Keywords: Computer Science Education; Board Games; Design

DOI: https://doi.org/10.1145/3287324.3293793

Creating a Tech-in-Residence Corps of Industry Adjuncts: An Academic/Government/Industry Partnership

Susan P. Imberman, *City University of New York*
Robert J. Domanski, *NYC Tech Talent Pipeline*
Contact: susan.imberman@csi.cuny.edu

Responding to NYC Mayor Bill de Blasio's call to double the number of students graduating with Bachelor degrees in computer science, in 2017, the Tech-in-Residence Corps program – a first-of-its-kind multistakeholder partnership between academia, government, and private industry, was established to specifically address two challenges at the City University of New York; the capacity problem (not enough faculty to accommodate the growing student body) and creating curriculum that incorporates in-demand "applied knowledge" areas to increase students' job competitiveness. Moving industry practitioners into the classroom posed problems that both mirrored and went beyond those posed by the typical adjunct hire. First, accommodations had to be instituted to consider the industry adjunct's work schedule. Second, industry professionals professed a fear of not being able to develop materials and teach effectively. To address these concerns, we set up an administrative structure that paired industry adjuncts with campuses that fit their pedagogical strengths and goals, as well as their logistical needs. Industry adjuncts were assigned campus faulty mentors so that there was a point person with which to communicate other than the chairperson. Both industry adjuncts and faculty attended a two-day workshop focused on pedagogical best practices as well as campus logistics. This poster outlines the Tech-in-Residence Corps model and presents our initial results. Early data indicates that this program has proven quite effective for driving curriculum innovation and raising student awareness of industry trends and hiring practices, however, the jury is still out as to whether it helps address the institutional capacity problem.

Keywords: Adjuncts; training; curriculum; capacity; enrollment; applied knowledge;

DOI: https://doi.org/10.1145/3287324.3293801

Encouraging Reflection in Support of Learning Data Structures

Cheryl Resch, *University of Florida*
Christina Gardner-McCune, *University of Florida*
Contact: cheryl.resch@ufl.edu

Our research looks at using reflection in teaching Data Structures and Algorithms (DSA) to promote meaningful learning. This poster examines the differences in reflections produced by two different programming assignments in DSA at the University of Florida. In the first assignment, students were asked to implement a line editor using a linked list and in the reflection prompt students were asked to reflect on the use of the assigned data structure and what they would do differently if they could do the assignment again. In this assignment, the dominant reflection was a simple recounting of material taught in class. In 15% of the reflections, students identified an implementation improvement that could be used. In 25% of the reflections, students identified non-technical issues such as time management when reflecting on what they would do differently if they had to do the assignment again. In the second assignment, students were asked to code Google's page-rank algorithm and were allowed to choose a graph implementation. They were asked to reflect on their implementation and what they would do differently if they could do the assignment again. In this assignment, the dominant reflection, ?%, was about the appropriateness of the chosen graph implementation compared to other implementations. In their reflection on what they would do differently, only 12% of the reflections mentioned non-technical issues. This data suggests that giving students an opportunity to decide the implementation approach and providing more specific reflection prompts produces more technical reflections.

Keywords: reflection; data structures and algorithms; problem solving

DOI: https://doi.org/10.1145/3287324.3293802

The Development and Validation of Survey Items on Upper Elementary Students' Perspectives and Attitudes on CS

Jessica Vandenberg, *North Carolina State University*
Jennifer Tsan, *North Carolina State University*
Zarifa Zakaria, *North Carolina State University*
Kristy Elizabeth Boyer, *University of Florida*
Collin Lynch, *North Carolina State University*
Eric Wiebe, *North Carolina State University*
Contact: jvanden2@ncsu.edu

Demand for K-6 computer science (CS) curricula is growing considerably. Many of the existing curricula have been developed by domain experts who are comfortable with specific and technical terminology, which they expect students to master. However, children are not always comfortable with these terms nor do they understand general concepts like 'coding' in the way that the curriculum designers intend. This is a problem because many researchers use self-report and attitudinal survey instruments with the implicit belief that the students' understanding of the terms and concepts resemble their own. This mismatch may invalidate results. For this project, we report on our modification of a validated survey to measure upper elementary students' attitudes about and perspectives on CS by attempting to understand the appropriate language to use when querying children about these topics. We use an iterative, design-based research approach that is informed by educational and psychological cognitive interview processes. We interviewed two groups (N=64) of upper elementary students on their understanding of computer science concepts and attitudes toward coding. Our findings indicate that 4th and 5th grade students could not explain the terms *computer programs* nor *computer science* as we had expected and that they struggled to understand how coding may connect with or support their learning in other domains. These results will help to guide the development of appropriate survey instruments and course materials for K-6 students, which both match their use of broad domain concepts and therefore inform their understanding and improve their outcomes.

Keywords: Elementary school; computer science attitudes; survey development

DOI: https://doi.org/10.1145/3287324.3293829

Fostering State-level Change in CS Education: The Expanding Computing Education Pathways Alliance

Jeffrey Xavier, Alan Peterfreund, Rebecca Zarch, *SageFox Consulting Group*
W. Richards Adrion, Renee Fall, *UMass Amherst*
Mark Guzdial, Barbara Ericson, *University of Michigan*
Sarah Dunton, *UMass Amherst*
Tom Mcklin, *The Findings Group*
Contact: jxavier@sagefoxgroup.com

Efforts to improve and promote CS education characterized by greater participation of underrepresented groups have taken off sharply in the six years since the Expanding Computing Education Pathways (ECEP) NSF alliance was first funded. Though many of these initiatives are occurring at the student and teacher level, ECEP and other national-level organizations have demonstrated the importance of focusing on change at the state level, as this can have important, long-term implications on policy and infrastructure. This poster describes ECEP's emergent design as a backbone organization helping state-level teams achieve educational change around CS. It also highlights key lessons learned through the alliance about how to foster CS education change at the state level. Four key lessons stand out. 1) The importance of understanding that engaging states requires appreciating the commonality of a framework around key areas to change (such as state standards, teacher certification and graduation requirements) but also respecting the uniqueness of state circumstances in these change areas. 2) The shared value created through a collective impact model to build a community that can support rich discussion and sharing of ideas. 3) The utility of an empirically derived a 4-stage model of state change used by ECEP that emphasized defining leaders, understanding the CS education landscape and finding allies to support efforts. and 4) The role of state team structures that can facilitate change when they are guided by identifying and engaging key stakeholders within a state and giving them a voice in driving the strategies and plans.

Keywords: CS education; state-level change; National Science Foundation; Broadening Participation in Computing

DOI: https://doi.org/10.1145/3287324.3293812

Teaching and Assessing Debugging, Testing, and Coding Style with Recursive Pedagogy using Spinoza

Fatima Abu Deeb,
King Saud bin Abulaziz University for Health Sciences
Timothy Hickey, *Brandeis University*
Contact: tjhickey@brandeis.edu, deebf@ksau-hs.edu.sa

There has been a rapid proliferation of auto-graders for introductory programming courses to cope with rapidly expanding Computer Science enrollments. In this poster we report on our research in developing and deploying a problem solving learning environment, Spinoza 3.0, which goes beyond auto-grading and provides active learning exercises to teach debugging, testing, and good coding style in addition to providing immediate feedback on program correctness. The key idea is to collect all of the attempts by all students to a particular problem generated by a particular class and to form them into equivalence classes where two attempts are equivalent if they produce exactly the same values on all of the unit tests. This allows the system to find the most common errors made by that class. The system then generates a variety of different kinds of problems by selecting either one of the most common errors or one of the correct solutions and asking the students to critique it. After a student makes a critique they are shown (a subset of) the critiques of their fellow students and are asked to pick the best one before proceeding to the next problem. Since the system generates new problems precisely tailored to this particular class, by turning selected attempts into new problems, we call this approach Recursive Pedagogy. This poster reports on preliminary results we have obtained using Recursive Pedagogy in an Introduction to Python Programming course with 19 college students.

Keywords: auto-grading; problem solving learning environment; CS1; Recursive Pedagogy

DOI: https://doi.org/10.1145/3287324.3293814

Towards Learning Analytics in Cybersecurity Capture the Flag Games

Valdemar Švábenský, Jan Vykopal, Pavel Čeleda,
Masaryk University
Contact: svabensky@ics.muni.cz

Capture the Flag games are software applications designed to exercise cybersecurity concepts, practice using security tools, and understand cyber attacks and defense. We develop and employ these games at our university for training purposes, unlike in the traditional competitive setting. During the gameplay, it is possible to collect data about players' in-game actions, such as typed commands or solution attempts, including the timing of these actions. Although such data was previously employed in computer security research, to the best of our knowledge, there were few attempts to use this data primarily to improve education. In particular, we see an open and challenging research problem in creating an artificial intelligence assistant that would facilitate the learning of each player. Our goal is to propose, apply, and experimentally evaluate data analysis and machine learning techniques to derive information about the players' interactions from the in-game data. We want to use this information to automatically provide each player with a personalized formative assessment. Such assessment will help the players identify their mastered concepts and areas for improvement, along with suggestions and actionable steps to take. Furthermore, we want to identify high- or low-performing players during the game, and subsequently, offer them game tasks more suitable to their skill level. These interventions would supplement or even replace feedback from instructors, which would significantly increase the learning impact of the games, enable more students to learn cybersecurity skills at an individual pace, and lower the costs.

Keywords: Cybersecurity games; Capture the flag; Learning analytics

DOI: https://doi.org/10.1145/3287324.3293816

Boxes, Bumps & Breakfast: Object Lessons for Teaching Undergraduates the Importance of Human-centered Research & Analysis

Tamara Peyton, Harrisburg University of Science and Technology
Contact: tpeyton@harrisburgu.edu

The interdisciplinary fields of Computer Science & Engineering and Human Computer Interaction are increasingly faced with developing human-centered solutions faster, with fewer project members. As a result, while learning the process of humancentered research and design within human-computer interaction classes, CSE students often appear to feel pressured to just go ahead and start building as quickly as possible. This is not the right approach, as students will then ignore the crucial problem identification phase of any project. In order to foster the right research and analysis mindset in students, it is often necessary to get them to think outside the box, break down the bumps in the project path, and analyze the action of everyday activities. This poster presents three different object lessons I have used in the undergraduate and graduate classroom that wake students up to the need to research issues, analyze evidence and think critically about connections between people, information and technology - all before they code or make.

Keywords: Human-centered design; teaching; techniques; resources; undergraduate education; design

DOI: https://doi.org/10.1145/3287324.3293817

Situated Learning in Systems-Level Coursework

Jeremiah Blanchard, *University of Florida*
Contact: jblanch@cise.ufl.edu

Computer science coursework at the undergraduate level at most institutions includes low-level systems coursework. Such coursework is often largely theoretical. When students complete assignments which involve writing software, they often do so in the context of operating systems not identified and/or connected with their everyday experiences (e.g., Minix or XINU). Approaches also tend to focus on kernel-level operations – leaving out the connections to higher levels of the OS (e.g. graphical user

ACM ISBN 978-1-4503-5890-3/19/02

interfaces). To connect systems concepts and assignments to students' personal experiences and provide a mechanism to discuss high-level layers of interactive operating systems, we assembled a Linux/Android operating system variant specifically geared to be accessible to students taking introductory systems courses, dubbed "Reptilian". Reptilian, available as an Open Virtual Appliance (OVA) image, provides both an Ubuntu-derived user-space and the standard Android GUI user-space. The appliance provides a typical Linux kernel development environment for assignments while facilitating demonstration of connections between layers in a modern operating system. To investigate the impact of the use of Reptilian, we compared questions on student evaluations between two semesters – one using Minix as the target system for student assignments and another using Reptilian. The curricula topics were identical, and both courses were taught by the same instructor. Students the cohorts completed comparable projects focused on the process table and filesystem, while the Reptilian cohort also completed a GUI layering assignment. We found that students rated content relevance, learning, and engagement of critical thinking more highly in the Reptilian cohort compared to the Minix cohort.

Keywords: Operating Systems; Situated Learning; Android

DOI: https://doi.org/10.1145/3287324.3293818

Messy Learning: When Problem-based Learning Just Isn't Enough

Paul E. Dickson, John Barr, *Ithaca College*
Contact: pdickson@ithaca.edu

In computer science (CS) classes it is common to give students a large ill-defined problem and let them struggle with it. The mess of the problem forces students to identify knowledge needed to solve the problem and to learn problem-solving skills. This is the concept behind problem-based learning (PBL), a learner-centered pedagogy that has become a popular research topic in computer science. PBL in CS has 3 defining characteristics: 1) presenting students with large authentic projects, 2) enabling students to independently learn necessary concepts, and 3) enabling them to learn while working in groups. An examination of the CS PBL/project-based learning (PrBL) literature reveals that step 2, self-directed or self-regulated learning (SRL), is lacking in almost every description of PBL. However, extensive CS research literature explores effective methods of SRL, and these methods revolve around the concept of reflection. We therefore propose a new structure for PBL/PrBL that we term messy learning that explicitly incorporates large, ill-defined, authentic projects and reflective activities. We also describe our experience with using messy learning in a game development course and present some examples of how to apply messy learning.

Keywords: Messy Learning; Reflection, Problem Based Learning; Project Based-Learning; Self-Regulated Learning; Open-Ended Group Projects

DOI: https://doi.org/10.1145/3287324.3293819

Evaluating the Effect of Follow-up Questions in an Online Exercise

Yifei Dong, Michelle Craig, Jennifer Campbell,
University of Toronto
Contact: mcraig@cs.toronto.edu

Studies in other disciplines demonstrate that writing summaries of videos or readings is an effective strategy for increasing student understanding. We explore a related strategy in computer science where we ask students to write explanations of program behaviour. Our experiments are conducted through an online application used by students to prepare for class by watching videos and solving follow-up exercises. With students randomly assigned to treatment groups, we evaluate the effect of different kinds of video follow-up questions by analyzing pre- and post-performance on subsequent select-all-that-apply multiple-choice questions. In experiment one, we found no difference in post-performance between students who wrote explanations and those who were not asked to do so. When the same prompt for explanations was accompanied by a motivational sentence, the quality of the student answers increased, but post-performance was unchanged. In a second experiment, students received either no experimental questions, questions requiring a written explanation or short-answer questions with a single correct response. Again, we found no difference in post-performance across the different treatments. This non-significant result might be explained by the post-performance question difficulty — the question might not be hard enough to reveal differences in understanding. The question timing might also be a factor, since students complete all the questions soon after watching the video and there may not be enough time for students to need the extra retention benefit gained by doing the experimental questions.

Keywords: summarizing; motivation

DOI: http://dx.doi.org/10.1145/3287324.3293827

What Can the Reid List of First Programming Languages Teach Us About Teaching CS1?

Robert M. Siegfried, *Adelphi University*
Diane Liporace, *Montclair State University*
Katherine G. Herbert-Berger, *Montclair State University*
Contact: siegfrie@adelphi.edu

The CS1 course is arguably the most important course offered in a Computer Science major; if students struggle in the course, they are likely to drop out of the major, and if certain key topics are covered, they may struggle in other courses later in their undergraduate program. For this reason, it is not surprising that the programming language used in a CS1 course as well as the teaching methodology is frequently a contentious subject. Richard Reid of Michigan State University kept a list of programming languages used in CS1 courses from the early 1990s until his retirement in 1999, and Reid's former student, Frances Van Scoy, continued compiling the List until 2006. Siegfried et al. updated the List in 2011 and 2015. The historical data shows the different languages (and in some cases, approaches) used by the schools reported on the Reid List. Additionally, in compiling the last two lists, there were trends spotted, with some feedback from faculty at the Reid List schools, stating the reasons for changes that they made as well as why they currently use and previously used the various languages.

Keywords: Introductory programming; objects early approach; programming languages

DOI: https://doi.org/10.1145/3287324.3293830

Game Engines Construction to Motivate Computing Concepts: Build from Scratch or Leverage Existing Systems

Christopher A. Egert, *Rochester Institute of Technology*
Contact: caeics@rit.edu

Game engine design and development is a highly desirable area of exploration for students involved in the computing sciences. Equally, faculty find the use of game engines to be highly compelling in upper division computing courses as they consolidate application of systems topics and usually require a team-based approach in their architectural design and implementation. As an application domain, game engines exhibit a high degree of complexity and present students with challenges related to many areas of the curricula, including graphics programming, computer architecture, operating systems, compiler theory, artificial intelligence, and much more. However, at a practical level, the use of game engines as a motivator for computing concepts and large-scale software development is beginning to change. Educators are starting to question the utility of games engines in the computing classroom given the availability of high quality, easily accessible commercial engines. In this poster, the author examines how this changing landscape influences computing educators that wish to utilize game engines as a motivator in the computing classroom. The poster provides insight into the challenges related to the software construction of game engines and the reality of new approaches and techniques that are on the horizon. The poster provides examples of means and methods to provide balance, incorporating lessons learned from new industry approaches in relation to (and not exclusion) the foundational practices of the computing sciences.

Keywords: Game engine; Large application architecture; Problem solving

DOI: https://doi.org/10.1145/3287324.3293831

An Analysis of Upper Elementary and Middle Grade Teachers' Perceptions, Concerns and Goals for Integrating CS into Classrooms

Mehmet Celepkolu, Erin O'Halloran, Jamieka Wilkinson, Kristy Elizabeth Boyer, *University of Florida*
Contact: mckolu@ufl.edu

As efforts to integrate computer science into K-8 teaching in the US are dramatically rising, professional development workshops for teachers are becoming widespread. An open challenge for the CS education research community is to understand teachers' needs and develop empirically grounded best practices for professional development. This poster displays our findings from a five-day professional development workshop in which 22 third through eighth grade teachers from various subjects learned about fundamental CS concepts, practiced coding, and created lesson plans for integrating what they learned into their classroom. We present quantitative and qualitative outcomes, with emphasis on teachers' perception of CS and how to integrate CS into their classrooms. The quantitative results, based on pre- and post-tests, reveal that the teachers gained significant technical knowledge and improved their attitudes toward CS. The qualitative results, based on the focus groups conducted before and after the workshop, indicated that teachers' limited exposure to CS can lead to misconceptions and some negative attitudes. Moreover, limitations such as time constraints and lack of understanding of CS are barriers to integrating CS into classrooms. On the other hand, the workshop provided teachers a clearer sense of the potential of CS to enhance their classroom plans. Teachers noted that they felt able to use CS to help students learn critical thinking, prepare them for their futures, and address their individual needs. These results can inform future workshops that address the needs of teachers and students.

Keywords: CS Education, Professional Development, Teacher Training

DOI: https://doi.org/10.1145/3287324.3293821

Integrating Computational Thinking in Informal and Formal Science and Math Activities for Preschool Learners

Shuchi Grover, *Looking Glass Ventures*
Ximena Dominguez, *Digital Promise Global*
Danae Kamdar, *Digital Promise Global*
Phil Vahey, *SRI International*
Savitha Moorthy, *Digital Promise Global*
Ken Rafanan, *SRI International*
Sara Gracely, *SRI International*
Contact: shuchi.grover@gmail.com

How do we integrate requisite thinking skills into children's earliest informal and formal learning experiences in order to prepare the next generation of problem solvers? This project examines how Computational Thinking (CT) skills align to the abilities and interests of young children and can be integrated with other STEM learning activities in order to promote school readiness. The goals of the project are to (1) build a knowledge base on how CT can be promoted in early childhood through integration with mathematics and science, (2) develop learning blueprints to guide the development of integrated classroom and family resources, and (3) develop and evaluate prototype activities to identify design principles useful to future development efforts integrating CT and STEM in early childhood. In this work, a multidisciplinary research team with expertise in CT, early science and mathematics, technology and media, and home and school learning partners with preschool educators and parents to co-design and pilot test prototype activities. Emerging prototypes presented integrate fundamental science and mathematics concepts and practices with CT skills such as problem decomposition, logical and algorithmic thinking, abstraction and debugging. They include hands-on activities with manipulatives familiar to young children and developmentally appropriate technology with unique affordances for complementing and reinforcing the learning that

ACM ISBN 978-1-4503-5890-3/19/02

occurs during hands-on experiences. With a goal of addressing CS For All, the co-design, development and pilot testing of prototype activities aim to take into account the needs and strengths of preschool programs and families from low-income and culturally diverse communities.

Keywords: Computational Thinking; Science; Mathematics; preschool; informal learning; formal learning

DOI: https://doi.org/10.1145/3287324.3293837

Undergraduate Computer Science Student Perceptions of their Own Field

Katelyn Manzo, *University of Maine*
Stacy A. Doore, Sarah Harmon, *Bowdoin College*
Contact: sdoore@bowdoin.edu

It is not just K-12 students that have misconceptions about computer science. Undergraduate students entering into a post-secondary computer science major also have significant misconceptions about what a computer scientist actually does on a day-to-day basis, even at the end of their four-year undergraduate computer science program. While the Draw-A-Scientist Test (DAST) investigates student perceptions of scientists in general (Chambers, 1983) and the Draw-An- Engineer Test (DAET) examines student perceptions of engineers (Knight and Cunningham, 2004), there have been few adaptations investigating student perceptions of computer scientists (Martin, 2004). Based on previous research, our study assessed undergraduate computer science student perceptions of computer scientists at both a mid-size research university and a small liberal arts college. Students (n=120) were asked to describe computer scientists in both a visual format and a written format using an adaptation of the DAST. The authors share comparative results for computer science students (pre-test, post-test) perceptions when 1) exposed to an intentional but not explicit curriculum with diverse representation of computer scientist images and a broad range of computer science research areas, and 2) exposed to a regular curriculum without intentional messages about the diversity of computer scientists and the diversity of research areas within the discipline. The poster describes additional scoring measures introduced beyond those in previous instruments which help to better categorize and interpret perceptions of computer science students about their own discipline.

Keywords: undergraduate students; perceptions of computer science; broadening participation

DOI: https://doi.org/10.1145/3287324.3293838

Overcoming Doubt: Workshop Aimed at Giving Students Strategies to Build Their Authentic Self-Esteem Within Their Computing Major

Rachelle Kristof Hippler, *Baldwin Wallace University*
Contact: rhippler@bw.edu

Much research has been conducted demonstrating that women often have different experiences in computer science than their male classmates. Self-esteem research provides one way we can understand the effects of these experiences as self-esteem has long been associated with well-being and academic success. Some experiences may be positive and enhance self-esteem, where others may be negative and decrease self-esteem leaving students to doubt whether they belong in their computing major. This poster presents a workshop for students that is grounded in research on building what is called "authentic" self-esteem. Authentic self-esteem can be understood as a balance between competence (skills) and worthiness (feelings of connectedness and acceptance). Recent research by the poster presenter based on these two factors of self-esteem revealed that female computing student's feelings of worthiness and competence are unbalanced: (1) their feelings of worthiness are lower than their feelings of competence within their computing major; and, (2) the gap is largest among seniors. This gap between competence and worthiness manifests as doubt just at the time that students should be excited about graduation and interviewing for jobs. The workshop presented in this poster was developed with psychologist Christopher Mruk and is based on his Competence and Worthiness Training (CWT) program. The workshop is aimed at providing students with tools to build their authentic self-esteem through helping to close the gap between their feelings of competence and worthiness.

Keywords: women in computing; authentic self-esteem; competence; worthiness

DOI: https://doi.org/10.1145/3287324.3293839

Debriefing Lab Content Using Active Learning

Michael J. McCarthy, *Carnegie Mellon University*
Joseph Mertz, *Carnegie Mellon University*
Martin L. Barrett, *Carnegie Mellon University*
Michael Melville, *Carnegie Mellon University*
Contact: martinba@cmu.edu

Labs in a large lecture course provide highly scaffolded programming exercises. Despite positive student feedback, some students were not achieving the learning goals. This project attempted to increase student's conceptual understanding using short active learning exercises. The first iteration of this project used two versions of active learning: present several multiple-choice questions about the lab material, then either provide a full debrief of all answers or a partial debrief of only the correct answer. The control group was the previous semester's course when no debriefing was done. Two research questions were evaluated. First, does debriefing enhance learning in a computer science course? We found that students performed significantly better on debriefed items compared to students that were not debriefed. These results were unaffected by individual student GPA as a predictor. Second, does level of depth of debriefing affect learning? We found no significant difference between full debrief and partial debrief groups. These results were replicated in a second trial that compared full, partial, and no debriefing.

In the second iteration of the project, each of three sections were given a full debrief, partial debrief, or no debrief (only the correct answer was given with no explanation). The full debrief group and the partial debrief group used the Think-Pair-Share method: pairs of students discussed the questions and various answers; one pair was chosen at random to answer each question. The research question is, does the level of depth of the debriefing intervention among the three treatments affect learning?

Keywords: Active learning; Think-pair-share; Lab debrief

DOI: https://doi.org/10.1145/3287324.3293843

Graduate Curriculum Initiative — COSMIC: Change Opportunity - Start Masters in Computing

Gary Krenz, Thomas Kaczmarek, *Marquette University*
Contact: gary.krenz@marquette.edu

The new graduate curriculum initiative, COSMIC: Change Opportunity - Start Masters in Computing, is aimed at an adult population that is typically under-served by computing programs at institutions of higher education. The COSMIC initiative provides an accelerated pathway to a professional Master of Science (MS) degree for individuals who do not have an undergraduate degree in computing, but who wish to cross over into the computing field. The COSMIC initiative is based on a highly focused summer bridge course combined with a customized curriculum pathway that allows people without computer science degrees to merge quickly and efficiently into a professional MS in Computing degree program. In this poster, we discuss our bridge course, additional bridge curriculum and its connection to our MS in Computing program; and present preliminary data from initial COSMIC cohorts. The COSMIC initiative's goal is to provide the computing profession with a documented model for training students that seek to cross over from non-computer science undergraduate degrees to work in the computing field.

Keywords: Masters; Curriculum Initiative; Non-traditional Students; Bridge Course

DOI: http://dx.doi.org/10.1145/3287324.3293846

An Investigation of Learning Outcomes Between Two Teaching Modalities to Improve Student Learning in Online Courses

Audrey Rorrer, *UNC Charlotte*
Julio César Bahamón, *UNC Charlotte*
Contact: jbahamon@uncc.edu

We describe a study of learning outcomes in an undergraduate C Programming course taught in two modalities: in-person and online. Because this course has been taught by the same instructor, using the same scaffolding activities, materials and approaches, we were uniquely positioned to conduct a quasi-experimental study of learning outcomes between courses and within students. Our goal was to glean knowledge and implications about assessment practices for undergraduate courses that are taught in two modalities. The objectives of our research are to discern what differential impacts are found between in-person and online delivery modalities. We aimed to discover learning outcome patterns among the students who participate in these modalities. Findings from this study provide valuable information for undergraduate Computer Science programs by identifying any differential learning outcomes that students experience between in-person and online course instruction. The research questions addressed were: 1) What impact does modality have on student learning outcomes? 2) What patterns are discernable across student groups 3) What relationship is there between final course grades and assignment module learning outcomes? We were surprised that no significant differences were obtained between course modality. While this is an encouraging finding, we believe that further data collection and analysis are needed, before making general conclusions. We are planning future studies to account for additional variables, such as instructor, multiple modalities, and online course design approaches.

Keywords: Course modality; Online Education; Programming; Retention; Sex; Gender; Race

DOI: https://doi.org/10.1145/3287324.3293848

University-Industry Collaboration in Curriculum Design: A Case Study of Curriculum Design for Early Undergraduate Computer Science Coursework with an Eye on Equity

Lauren E. Provost, *Simmons University*
Christopher Harrington, *Dell*
Contact: Lauren.Provost@Simmons.edu

This poster session will discuss several dimensions of bias in curricular design that must be considered in the development of curriculum materials in undergraduate computer science education if we are to broaden interest, engagement and ultimately participation. Multiple dimensions of bias were used to identify gender, race and other biases in curricula that led to the authors' redesign of coursework materials and activities in two undergraduate courses: Computer Networks and Cybersecurity. Our goal was to assess current curricula and ultimately redesign curricula to include topics and authentic activities connected to industry while also broadening learner interest, engagement and accessibility. The design of materials intentionally shifted to social problems, data-driven problem solving and other new curricula foci areas that have been shown to broaden interest and engagement. In addition, materials are aligned with national standards and competencies in cybersecurity while maintaining course rigor. The expanded study includes the use of multiple measures to assess the effectiveness of curriculum design in relation to interest and other factors that influence the engagement of learners in their first two years of computer science coursework. The Computer Science Cultural Attitude and Identity Survey (CSAIS) was revised and used to measure constructs that influence the attitudes and identity of undergraduate students in computer science including interest as well as other factors such as self-efficacy and identity.

Keywords: curriculum; equity; diversity; identity; self-efficacy; undergraduate

DOI: https://doi.org/10.1145/3287324.3293850

A Peer Based Tutoring and Mentoring Model for First Year Computer Science Courses Based on Strategies Used by Songbirds for Learning

Ashwin Satyanarayana, *Computer Systems Technology, New York City College of Technology, Brooklyn, NY*
Lior Baron, *Computer Science, Graduate Center, City University of New York, New York, NY*
Contact: asatyanarayana@citytech.cuny.edu

Effective tutoring is not limited to humans alone. A significant amount of research in songbird learning has shown that birds' songs are not coded in the DNA like other behavioral features but learned over time through one-on-one tutoring involving experimentation, error detection and adaptation. Like students, juvenile songbirds use active listening to learn a tutor's song that is repeated multiple times. The songbird first divides the complex song into short syllables and later uses trial and error to match the syllables sequence to the tutor's song. Birds learn more effectively when listening to an adult bird from the same species. We draw a parallel to bird learning in humans by implementing one-on-one peer-based tutoring of first-year students by senior students, who share the same culture. This poster presents a successful ongoing mentoring and tutoring model used at the Computer Systems Technology department of New York City College of Technology (CUNY) for over five years. This peer-based model utilizes strategies shared by both first-year students and young birds involving social interaction, active learning and problem decomposition. Furthermore, the tutors hired were trained to use the same strategies observed in songbirds tutoring. This project has shown an increase in first-year student retention rate of 83% for students who participated in this program as compared to 61% retention for students who did not. The tutoring program impact demonstrated that the students' academic performance increased significantly (mixed model anova $F(1, 247) = 29.11$, $p < 0.001$).

Keywords: Peer tutoring; First-year students; Bird learning; Active Learning; Social interaction

DOI: https://doi.org/10.1145/3287324.3293853

Changing Teaching Assistant's Behavior Based on Learning Support Strategies for Programming Exercise

Yuuki Yokoyama, Hironori Egi,
The University of Electro-Communications
Contact: y1730120@edu.cc.uec.ac.jp,

In this research, we devised learning support strategies to change how teaching assistants (TAs) for basic university courses in information technology (IT) behave toward students during programming classes. Based on learning support strategies, we developed and evaluated a TA support system that presents student learning situations on mobile devices. In basic IT courses, a TA support system is often used to help and guide individual students. To help TAs using such support, a previous study visualizes the learning situation and offers advice. However, support in addition to presenting learning situations to the TA should include guidelines for interaction with the students. In order to provide adequate support to students, we propose learning support strategies for TAs. In practical computer science exercises, TAs mainly advise and answer questions from students. However, it is not clear how TAs could best support students. Therefore, we propose the following learning support three types of strategies: "Hope", "Priority", "Motivation". Futhermore, we researched what learning support from the TA was desired by the students and developed a TA support system that presents learning support strategies. According to each learning support strategy, the classroom's map governs seat colors for each student who is the recipient of advice. The TA prioritizes helping the students presented by the learning support strategy as mapped by the seat charts. The system we developed was practiced in class, and as a result we found that even students who wanted to work on sophisticated content did not consider the teacher and TA unnecessary.

Keywords: Classroom Management; Teaching Assistant; Learning Support Strategies; Programming Exercise

DOI: https://doi.org/10.1145/3287324.3293857

Using Bloom's Taxonomy to Write Effective Programming Questions for Autograding Tools

Lina Battestilli, Sarah Korkes,
North Carolina State University
Olivia Smith, *University of Minnesota*
Tiffany Barnes, *North Carolina State University*
Contact: lbattestilli@ncsu.edu

Automated grading has become crucial in supporting large introductory Computer Science courses by assisting instructors in reducing grading time and course costs. However, novice programmers are often frustrated by auto-grading tools as they often provide minimal feedback or the questions are too complex. We propose using Bloom's Taxonomy to gradually increase the complexity of the programming question in an auto-grading tool. The easiest questions are based on Knowledge and Comprehension. Next are questions that require Application and Analysis. The most complex questions require Design and Creativity. We have developed programming questions that fit these categories. For example, when debugging the students have to understand and Analyze code. However, in order to write a program with more complex logic the students have to be Creative. The main goal is to lead novice programmers to learn more effectively and efficiently. In this poster, we present examples of the developed auto-graded programming problems based on Bloom's Taxonomy and explain a pilot study done in a CS-1 non-majors course.

Keywords: automated grader; teaching tools; learning programming; Bloom's Taxonomy; CS1

DOI: http://doi.org/10.1145/3287324.3293858

Utilizing Participatory Design to Develop a Culturally Relevant Computer Science Curriculum

Merijke Coenraad, *University of Maryland, College Park*
Jen Palmer, Diana Franklin, *University of Chicago*
David Weintrop, *University of Maryland, College Park*
Contact: mcoenraa@umd.edu

The underrepresentation of women and minorities in the field of computer science is well documented. Due to this lack of representation, efforts to broaden participation in computing abound. One manner with which to do this is through the development of culturally relevant curricula. Education literature encourages the use of culturally relevant techniques and topics to teach school content through the knowledge of diverse groups as well as teach about culturally diverse populations. In addition, partnering with the students who will learn with the curriculum is encouraged in order to co-develop ideas and learn more about students' interests and experiences. This poster describes the outcomes from a series of participatory design sessions with a diverse group of stakeholders (students, teachers, parents, and administrators) to design an intermediate computing curriculum for 5th – 7th grade students. Specifically, we examine the topics developed by the participants that are being utilized as themes for curricular units. Preliminary analysis shows that participants of all ages brainstormed and utilized themes related to both cultural heritage and contemporary culture, but more focus was placed on youth culture and pop culture topics. The poster will describe the design methods used during the participatory design sessions as well as the themes developed and an overall analysis of the categories from which the themes are drawn.

Keywords: participatory design; computer science education; culturally relevant; middle grades

DOI: https://doi.org/10.1145/3287324.3293803

Exploring the Mental Models of Undergraduate Programmers in the Context of Linked Lists

Harrison Chotzen, *Claremont McKenna College*
Alasdair J. Johnson, Parth M. Desai, *Pitzer College*

This paper describes misconceptions students encounter as they design algorithms to implement linked list operations. The research was conducted in a qualitative manner [1], and aims to inform pedagogical practice in the data structures space. The design of our study involved conducting interviews with five undergraduate students, who were given a packet consisting of four questions involving arrays, linked lists, or binary search trees.

Though participants showed a confident understanding of the way that linked lists work as static diagrams, when asked to reason about the reassignment of pointers during the design of insert and remove operations, the students seemed to struggle. The details of the representation of pointers as members of the linked list class appeared unclear to our participants, and we posit this gap of understanding was a primary source confusion.

We posit increased attention to the object oriented implantation of linked lists in data structures education may result in improved learning outcomes.

Keywords: Linked Lists; Pointers; Data Structures; Misconceptions; Students; Pedagogy

DOI: https://doi.org/10.1145/3287324.3293862

ACM ISBN 978-1-4503-5890-3/19/02

Poster Session 2

Enhancing Essential Data Skills for College-wide Students

Qiong Cheng, *University of North Carolina at Charlotte*
Contact: qcheng1@uncc.edu

In the Big Data era, essential data skills are critical for everybody in full participation of the workforce and modern society to better understand decisions from diverse levels of society. However not all graduates exit college with these needed skills.

In this poster, the author(s) report on the integrating of data literacy into a college-wide computer and information literacy course with collaborative practices of project-based learning, which aims at increasing students' awareness of data science and boosting essential data skills of college-wide students.

In the poster, we will demonstrate our module design on training essential data skills through examples, case students, and team-based projects within a college-wide computer and information literacy course. We will also present our comparative analysis on one data-enhanced course session with other two course regular sessions as control. In the data-enhanced session, students formed a team, choose a topic in the engaging context, specified questions that they want to ask and answered through data, analyzed data from different perspectives, evaluated results, and present in the course poster session. Two measures are used in assessing the effectiveness of exploratory and collaborative learning in data literacy: student performance in a poster session and student perceptions on Likert scales. Thus far the evaluation results and statistical analysis showed the innovative practice significantly intrigued students' interest in data science and boosted students' fundamental data skills, for both computer science or non-computer science majors.

Keywords: Add your own keywords here & enter the same; on the submission page; separated; with semi-colons

DOI: https://doi.org/10.1145/3287324.3293782

Data Protection with SMSD Labware

Hossain Shahriar, *Kennesaw State University*
Kai Qian, *Kennesaw State University*
Md Arabin Islam Talukder, *Kennesaw State University*
Reza Parizi, *Kennesaw State University*
Contact: hshahria@kennesaw.edu

The majority of malicious mobile attacks take advantage of vulnerabilities in mobile applications, such as sensitive data leakage via inadvertent or side channel, unsecured sensitive data storage, data transmission, and many others. Most of these mobile vulnerabilities can be detected in the mobile software testing phase. However, most development teams often have virtually no time to address them due to critical project deadlines. To combat this, the more defect removal filters there are in the software development life cycle, the fewer defects that can lead to vulnerabilities will remain in the software product when it is released. As part of Secure Mobile Software Development (SMSD) project, we are currently developing capacity to address the lack of pedagogical materials and real world learning environment in secure mobile software development through effective, engaging, and investigative approaches. In this session, we provide details of a new implemented module named *data protection.* We also share our initial experience and feedback on the developed module.

Keywords: Mobile Software; Data sanitization; input validation; SQL injection;

DOI: http://dx.doi.org/10.1145/3287324.3293785.

Applying Project-Based Learning for an Online Object-Oriented Systems Course

Kalpathi Subramanian, Kiran Budhrani,
Univ. of North Carolina at Charlotte
Contact: krs@uncc.edu

Traditionally, students are introduced to programming oriented courses by covering a series of topics and having a programming project due at the end of each topic. Assigned projects are often not connected to each other, but are rather used to expose students to a variety programming constructs and concepts. Students take the most direct approach such as trial and error to complete these projects. While this scenario utilizes projects, it approaches the use of projects as a means to assess learning rather than a means for learning. In this poster, we present results from a project-based online course in object-oriented analysis and design. We present a model for structuring project modules that provide opportunities for students to prepare, design, implement and reflect on each project module. By providing multiple points for feedback and reflection, as well as assigning projects with visual components, the course aims to promote engagement of undergraduate students, while at the same time maintaining rigor. Preliminary results from this course are encouraging, and could potentially become a model for project based learning.

Keywords: project based learning; object oriented systems; reflection;

DOI: https://doi.org/10.1145/3287324.3293786

Use Bots to Improve GitHub Pull-Request Feedback

Zhewei Hu, Edward Gehringer,
North Carolina State University
Contact: zhu6@ncsu.edu

Rising enrollments make it difficult for instructors and teaching assistants to give adequate feedback on each student's work. In our software engineering course, we have 50–120 students each semester. Our course projects require students to submit GitHub

ACM ISBN 978-1-4503-5890-3/19/02

pull requests as deliverables for their open-source software (OSS) projects. We have set up a static code analyzer and a continuous integration service on GitHub to help students check code style and functionality. However, these tools cannot enforce system-specific customized guidelines and do not explicitly display detailed information. In this study, we discuss how we bypass the limitations of existing tools by implementing three Internet bots. The *Expertiza Bot* can help detect violations of more than 35 system-specific guidelines. The *Travis CI Bot* can explicitly display instant test execution results on the GitHub pull-request page. The *Code Climate Bot* can insert pull-request comments to remind students to fix issues detected by the static code analyzer. These bots are either open source or free for OSS projects, and can be easily integrated with GitHub repositories. Our survey results show that more than 70% of students think the advice given by the bots is useful. We tallied the amount of feedback given by the bots and the teaching staff for each GitHub pull request. Results show that bots can provide significantly more feedback (six times more on average) than teaching staff. Bots can also offer more timely feedback than teaching staff and help student contributions avoid more than 33% system-specific guideline violations.

Keywords: Internet bots; open-source software; software engineering; open-source curriculum; Expertiza

DOI: http://dx.doi.org/10.1145/3287324.3293787

Student Debuggging Practices and Their Relationships with Project Outcomes

Ayaan M. Kazerouni, Rifat Sabbir Mansur,
Stephen H. Edwards, Clifford A. Shaffer, *Virginia Tech*
Contact: ayaan@vt.edu

Debugging is an important part of the software development process, studied by both the CS education and software engineering communities. Most prior work has focused either on novice or professional programmers. Intermediate-to-advanced students (such as those enrolled in post-CS2 Data Structures courses) who are working on large and complex projects have largely been ignored. We present results from an empirical observational study that examined junior-level undergraduate students' debugging practices on relatively large (4-week lifecycle) projects, using IDE clickstream data collected by a custom Eclipse plugin. Specifically, we hypothesize that there are differing debugging behaviors exhibited, and that differing behaviors lead to differing project outcomes. For example, how often do students use the symbolic debugger available in modern IDEs, versus how often do they use diagnostic print statements, or both? What triggers a debugging session? What follows a debugging session? Does it matter *when* in the project lifecycle that debugging takes place? We have a number of interesting preliminary results. When using the debugger, there was a negative relationship between step-over and step-into actions versus final course grades, indicating that when students "spin their wheels" while debugging, they tend to perform more poorly. Students also tend to perform better on the project when debugging takes place earlier in the overall project life-cycle. We developed an algorithm to identify diagnostic print statements in the students' projects. We found that over 90% used at least one diagnostic print statement, and about 75% used the symbolic debugger, at least once in any given project.

Keywords: debugging; incremental development; intermediate students

DOI: https://doi.org/10.1145/3287324.3293794

Using Interactive Visualization and Programmed Instruction to Teach Formal Languages

Mostafa Mohammed, Clifford A. Shaffer, *Virginia Tech*
Susan H. Rodger, *Duke University*
Contact: profmdn@vt.edu

The material taught in a Formal languages course is mathematical in nature and requires students to practice proofs and algorithms to understand the content. Traditional Formal Languages textbooks are heavy on prose rather than visuals, and homework consists of solving many paper exercises. Some instructors make use of Finite State Machine simulators like JFLAP. JFLAP allows students to build different models and apply algorithms on these models, which improves student interaction with the material. However, students still need to read a significant amount of text without direct and immediate feedback on their understanding. Inspired by the Programmed Instruction (PI) teaching method, we have begun developing a new Formal Languages eTextbook capable of conveying these concepts more intuitively (through visualizations) and more interactively (through the use of PI methods). Under PI methods, students read a little, ideally a sentence or a paragraph, and then answer a question related to that information. Based on the question response, students can go further and complete other frames of information or retry to solve the same question. To evaluate the pedagogical effectiveness of our new eTextbook, we will conduct time and performance evaluations across two offerings of a Formal Languages course. We will compare the time spent by students using materials with text and exercises only, with text and visualizations, and with the PI frames to determine levels of students engagement. Students grades will be compared to assess learning gains.

Keywords: Formal Languages; Programmed Instruction; visualization; pedagogical evaluation; automated assessment; Turing Machine; Finite Automata.

DOI: https://doi.org/10.1145/3287324.3293795

Benefits of Physical Interaction with Array Elements and Code Consolidation on Student Comprehension of Sorting Algorithms

Anisha Kaul, Julia Pinedo, *Scripps College*
Anya Wallace, *Harvey Mudd College*
Contact: jpinedo1459@scrippscollege.edu

This study was a qualitative analysis of introductory-level computer science students' comprehension of sorting algorithms. We asked six students to read and summarize the code of a sorting algorithm. Next, we asked them to trace through the code, first using a provided array with pencil and paper, then again using sticky-notes to represent the array. Focused analysis of one interview found that a student who struggled to comprehend the algorithm during the pencil-and-paper trace quickly gained

ACM ISBN 978-1-4503-5890-3/19/02

understanding when physically tracing the sticky-note array. We hypothesize that physical interaction with a sticky-note representation of an array facilitated student comprehension of sorting algorithms by consolidating multiple lines of code (LOC) into a single repeatable action. This research is relevant to computer science educators who may teach sorting algorithms to introductory-level students.

Keywords: Sorting Algorithm; Introductory; Consolidation; Bubble Sort; Insertion Sort; Graphics/Visualization; Undergraduate Instruction

DOI: http://doi.org/10.1145/3287324.3293797

An Investigation of Conflicts Between Upper-Elementary Pair Programmers

Jennifer Tsan, Jessica Vandenberg, Xiaoting Fu, *North Carolina State University*
Jamieka Wilkinson, *University of Florida*
Danielle Boulden, *North Carolina State University*
Kristy Elizabeth Boyer, *University of Florida*
Collin Lynch, Eric Wiebe, *North Carolina State University*
Contact: jtsan@ncsu.edu

Extensive prior research suggests that pair programming holds many benefits for novices. Pair programming has been well studied at the undergraduate level, and recently, the CS education research community has started to realize that younger learners may also benefit from pair programming. However, an important factor in pair programming success for young learners is the ability to resolve conflicts during the process. Little is known about what types of conflicts occur while elementary students pair program or how those conflicts are, or are not, resolved. To investigate this phenomenon, we analyzed the videos of six pairs of students completing a programming activity. We found that conflicts evolve in four general stages, which may not all be present in each conflict: initiation, escalation, de-escalation, and conclusion. Some conflicts are resolved when the students come to an agreement, others end passively. The analysis revealed that the pairs' conflicts began around disagreements about code, who should have control of the keyboard and mouse, and other interpersonal events. This research indicates that conflicts are a significant concern for young students, and supporting young learners in developing improved collaboration skills is a key direction for CS education research.

Keywords: Elementary school; pair programming; collaboration; conflict.

DOI: http://dx.doi.org/10.1145/3287324.3293799

ACM ISBN 978-1-4503-5890-3/19/02

Job Placement Experience of Alumni from a 3-year CS Program

Miguel Lara, *California State University, Monterey Bay*
Kathryn Cunningham, *University of Michigan*
Bude Su, *California State University, Monterey Bay*
Contact: milara@csumb.edu

Computing educators entice students with information about stable, readily available, and lucrative careers in computing. Do our promises turn into reality for all students? We report on an in-depth alumni survey of 50 college graduates from a 3-year cohort-based program (CSin3), one year post-graduation. The majority of graduates from the two first cohorts surveyed are Hispanic, first-generation college students from a rural area in California. More than a third of the respondents (36%) are female. Notwithstanding the fast pace of the program (three years instead of the traditional four), the vast majority of graduates (88%) were full-time employed at the time of the survey and were hired less than 3 months after graduation, on average.

The most common challenges that alumni reported facing professionally are: Work-life balance (36%) Cost of living (36%) Lack of diversity (25%), and Stress in current position (25%) (they could select multiple choices). While no correlation was found between GPA and job satisfaction level or annual salary, significant low grades in upper division programming courses were a common factor among unemployed alumni. We also examined differences, based on gender, in annual salary and job satisfaction level; intention to remain in the technology sector; their level of satisfaction about how well the CSin3 program prepared them professionally; correlation between job satisfaction level and choice of CS as a career; and factors and alumni's perceptions of what contributed to their success in the job market, such as their participation in an internship program and the academic enrichment activities.

Keywords: alumni; employment; workplace satisfaction; cohort-based learning; accelerated degree program; first-generation college students; underrepresented minority students.

DOI: https://doi.org/10.1145/3287324.3293805

Creating Co-curricular Programs to Improve CS Student Identity and Sense of Belonging

Cynthia Y. Lester, *Georgia State University*
Pamela Leggett-Robinson, *PLR Consulting*
Contact: clester6@gsu.edu

In 2016, Georgia Perimeter College consolidated with Georgia State University. The new Georgia State University with a student population of over 51,000 has become a national model in serving students from diverse backgrounds. Perimeter College is the 2-year arm of the university and provides instruction to approximately 18,000 students. As of fall 2018, there were over 1200 students who had declared computer science as a pathway and 40 percent were from groups historically underrepresented in STEM. The purpose of this poster to describe co-curricular programs that began in 2012, with the establishment of the Perimeter College STEM Office whose mission was to increase access and success. The poster will present programs that were developed and continue to be utilized to broaden participation, improve retention, and increase CS student identity and a sense of belonging especially among students who are first generation, at-risk, and from minority populations. Although created for students especially at the 2-year college level, programs are scalable to senior institutions. Data and findings will be presented to also include how the STEM Office helped grow programming at Perimeter College by 175 percent and how partnerships have helped to provide sustainability.

Keywords: CS student identity; co-curricular programming; broadening participation; retention; community college; STEM

DOI: https://doi.org/10.1145/3287324.3293808

Engaging Alumni Mentors in Software Engineering Project Courses

C.F. Larry Heimann, Sara Moussawi, Jeria Quesenberry, Raja Sooriamurthi, *Carnegie Mellon University*
Contact: lheimann@andrew.cmu.edu

Getting alumni effectively engaged as mentors with students is a topic that is of great interest to universities but often hard to do in practice. We have found that with proper structure and support, software project courses provide a good avenue to make these connections between alumni and student and that alumni input can improve the quality of outcomes in these project courses. In this poster the authors describe the alumni mentoring process and how it has evolved over the past three years. In addition, we have begun to collect data from both student teams and alumni to answer three questions: (1) what information are alumni sharing with student teams? (2) is a student team's perception of what was said matching up well with the mentor's perception?, (3) are student teams able to convert alumni feedback into actionable project items?, and (4) at what phase in a software engineering project are alumni mentors most effective? The poster will demonstrate the details of our mentoring process and display our preliminary findings in a colorful fashion convenient to allow others to assess for themselves the potential value of using alumni mentors in software project courses.

Keywords: mentoring; alumni engagement; project courses; software engineering; academic-industry partnerships

DOI: https://doi.org/10.1145/3287324.3293811

Improving Programming Skills Through Classroom Presentation of Assignments

Abhimanyu Ghosh, Daniel Sinkovits,
Keith Wojciechowski, *University of Wisconsin-Stout* Contact: ghosha@uwstout.edu

Students in non-CS STEM majors often have specific difficulties with programming content in their coursework. Instructor feedback is usually limited to the results obtained and major algorithmic errors, due to the nature of coding assignments. The authors' aim is to investigate whether presenting code and receiving feedback from their peers in class makes an appreciable difference in non-CS STEM-major students' learning of programming. The poster will present data collected over two semesters from five sections of three programming-heavy chemistry, engineering and math courses taught at the University of Wisconsin-Stout. Student groups were asked to present their homework attempts to the class, their peers were asked to fill out surveys containing Yes/No questions and comments on the attempts, and this feedback was passed on to the presenting students, who were then given time to improve their work before submitting their final versions. Comparison of student performance statistics in exams, between semesters during which the study was implemented and prior semesters, is used as a tool to assess student learning. Results of the study from two semesters have shown that group composition and the type of questions asked in the survey are the two major factors at play. The poster will also discuss the enhanced design of the study during the third and final semester in spring 2019 that will take these results into account.

Keywords: peer review; programming for non-CS majors; collaborative learning; programming instruction

DOI: http://doi.org/10.1145/3287324.3293820

Mobile App Development: Android or iOS? An Experience Report from Teaching Both Platforms

Gina Sprint, *Gonzaga University*
Contact: sprint@gonzaga.edu

Despite student interest in mobile app development (MAD) and a rise in demand for mobile app developers, many computer science departments have not yet incorporated a MAD course into their curriculum. For such departments, barriers such as resource and curriculum limitations stand in the way of offering a MAD course. To elaborate, it can be difficult to find an instructor with the expertise to teach a MAD course. If such expertise is not available, it can be time consuming for an educator to train him/herself to gain the necessary knowledge to the teach the course. Furthermore, the instructor must decide which MAD platform to utilize, Android, iOS, hybrid, or web? Since MAD is a relatively new field, there are few resources in the literature that can help with MAD course preparation and design. In this poster, I present my experiences navigating these MAD course barriers at a primarily undergraduate institution. Recently, I have designed and taught a 300-level Android/Java course (Fall 2017) and a 300-level iOS/Swift course (Fall 2018). My experience report includes a summary of MAD course preparation, design, and implementation for both courses. To help guide choosing a platform, I include a detailed comparison of Android and iOS for supporting undergraduate CS learning outcomes. The comparison is based on resources required, maintenance considerations, software design principles covered (OOP and design patterns), and student work and feedback. The experiences reported in this poster offer guidance and insights for educators considering teaching a MAD course at their own university.

Keywords: Mobile App Development; iOS; Android; Computer Science Education; Teaching Experience Report

DOI: https://doi.org/10.1145/3287324.3293822

Building Trust in Computer Science Research-Practice Partnerships: A Theme Study

Todd Lash, *UIUC*
Stephanie Wortel-London, Leigh Ann Delyser, Lauren Wright, *CSforALL*
Contact: toddlash@illinois.edu

Creating equitable, sustainable, and productive partnerships between computer science (CS) education researchers and practitioners is essential if we are to further improve CS educational outcomes, practice, and equity. Research-practice partnerships (RPPs) provide one promising approach for expanding how practice may inform research and research may inform practice. This early work, centered around a framework proposed by Henrick et al., and utilizing interview data from 11 participants, explores the ways in which six diverse RPP teams went about developing trusting and collaborative relationships as they worked together to solve local problems of practice. Barriers and challenges to collaboration and trust building, as well as mechanisms by which teams overcame those challenges, are discussed. The study revealed discrete team behaviors, norms, and structures that may contribute to building more collaborative, trusting, and sustainable RPP relationships. Limitations are presented and implications for current and future RPP teams, as well as possible future research directions, are addressed.

Keywords: Research-practice Partnerships; K-12 education; Collaboration

DOI: https://doi.org/10.1145/3287324.3293815

Understand the Emerging Demands of Computing Education for Non-CS Major Students

Meng Han, Zhigang Li, Jing Selena He, Xin Shirley Tian, Kennesaw State University

In this poster, the investigators report their experience in teaching five computer science courses that were developed specifically for non-CS major students. These courses were taught in a four-year period in a public research institution in the South-eastern region of the United States. The whole study demonstrates an emerging demand for computing education from non-CS major students. The investigators collected data from both the students and the instructors in the hope to seek empirical answers to the questions of why there are such emerging demands for computing education, where are the demands coming from, and what non-CS major students are looking for in computer science classes. The answers to these questions can help shed the light on what educators should provide to the students in these courses. Based on the analysis of the data gathered, the investigators proposed a list of four recommendations to help guide fellow educators in the development of non-CS major computer science courses: (a) focus on high-level programming and modeling with low syntactic overhead; (b) broaden the breath of application demonstration to help non-CS major students to apply the knowledge to their specific domain; (c) introduction of computational tools; (d) hands on projects that match students' background and interests.

Keywords: Education; Computer Science; Course Development; Non-major; Instruction

DOI: https://doi.org/10.1145/3287324.3293826

Infusing CS Graduate Transition Curriculum with Professional, Technical and Data Science Competencies

Katherine G. Herbert-Berger, Nina Goodey,
Stephen Ruczszyk, Scott Kight, *Montclair State University*
Thomas J. Marlowe, *Seton Hall University*
Contact: herbertk@montclair.edu

The United States does not produce sufficient numbers of well-qualified professionals in STEM, and in computing/ technology in particular. The number of students pursuing undergraduate degrees in computer science or related field continues to grow but is still not pacing industry growth. Employers repeatedly suggest that good professional and technical competencies, including "soft skills", are a major factor in both obtaining and succeeding in STEM careers. Moreover, both the Council on Graduate Studies and the National Science Board in the NSF 2018 STEM Trends report support the need of such skills for success in STEM. These competencies comprise (1) communication, oral and written, and in technical, business and general settings; (2) working in and leading teams, in varying roles; (3) managing business and professional relationships; (4) planning, problem solving, and critical thinking; (5) mathematical capabilities including numeracy; and (6) an understanding of ethical, social, managerial, and economic perspectives; plus, responding to recent developments in science and science careers, (7) an interdisciplinary perspective and overview understanding of data science. In this poster we present a proposal for a post baccalaureate certificate curriculum, which we suggest also assists students transitioning from other fields, and can be applied more widely across STEM.

Keywords: Graduate education; professional and technical competencies; soft skills; post-baccalaureate certificate

DOI: https://doi.org/10.1145/3287324.3293828

Towards Encapsulated Cyber Security Labs: A Container Based Approach

Selvarajah Mohanarajah, *UNC - Pembroke*
Gregory Ross, *SPAWAR, Charleston*
Shan Suthaharan, *UNC- Greensboro*
Contact: smohanarajah@acm.org

Platform-independent encapsulated and self-contained labs can enhance the delivery of cybersecurity teaching modules in resource-limited academic institutions. Cybersecurity teaching modules usually incorporate hands-on labs using tools such as NETLAB+, NS-3, SEED, GENI, etc. There are two major problems in using such labs; students need to learn the underlying tool before doing labs, and setting-up a lab may require significant IT support and resources. In addition, development and delivery of security labs is barricaded by two other technical realities: built-in security controls in computer systems and networks (e.g. NX-bits, ASL-Randomization, Canaries, Firewalls, etc.), and heterogeneity in students-owned operating environments. In our proposed work, we have studied the concept of container-based educational solutions by leveraging the unique features of Docker containers (i.e., light-weight packaging of code and all of its system dependencies) to build platform-independent encapsulated cybersecurity labs. The benefits of our approach includes, cost-effective teaching environment, scalability over heterogeneous operating platforms, independence from hardware, software, and network controls, and hassle-free learning experience for students. As a proof of concept, we have developed an interoperable encapsulated lab for giving hands-on experience to students in one aspect of cybersecurity, buffer overflow. The lab was created using Docker and uploaded to a central repository. Students can pull this lab from anywhere, and can execute it on any platform that runs Docker daemon. We will use the knowledge and experience gained in this study to build our future research in the areas of building Learning Objects for cybersecurity education.

Keywords: Cyber Security Education; Docker; Learning Objects; Buffer Overflow; Cyber Security Labs; Security and Privacy

DOI: https://doi.org/10.1145/3287324.3293832.

The Institute of Coding: A University-Industry Collaboration to Address the UK Digital Skills Crisis

James H. Davenport, Rachid Hourizi, *University of Bath*
Contact: J.H.Davenport@bath.ac.uk

The UK is not the only country with a serious digital skills crisis, but it is one with a formal Government inquiry (The Shadbolt Report) and response. It also has very detailed tracking of people into, through and out of higher education into employment. The Institute of Coding (https://instituteofcoding.org/) is a new £40m+ initiative by the UK Government to transform the digital skills profile of England. It responds to the apparently contradictory data that the country has a digital skills shortage across a variety of sectors, yet has unemployed computing graduates every year.

The Institute is a large-scale national intervention funded by Government, industry and universities to address some of the perceived issues with formal education versus industry skills and training, for example: technical skills versus soft skills, industry-readiness versus "deep education", and managing expectations for the diverse digital, data and computational skills demands of employers across a wide range of economic sectors. Its work ranges from the development of specialist, in-demand digital skills to the provision of work experience, employability skills and ensuring work-readiness of computing graduates, and the provision of digital skills for those from a non-digital background. It is also addressing under-representation and under-achievement by a variety of groups, notably women (only 16% of university students) but also ethnic minorities and other groups.

Keywords: Digital skills; employability; industry-academia collaboration; gender

DOI: https://doi.org/10.1145/3287324.3293834

ACM ISBN 978-1-4503-5890-3/19/02

Computer Science Problem Solving Course: Practical and Technical Thinking Skills for CS Majors

Margaret Ellis, *Virginia Polytechnic Institute and State University*
Contact: maellis1@vt.edu

Solving problems in various current subfields of computer science improves student motivation and helps level the playing field for students who are less-likely to be exposed to such topics and tools outside of their coursework. The importance of student mindset is well studied in education, confident students who find course material useful and interesting are likely to be motivated and perform well. For several decades computer science educators have recognized the need for computer science students to enhance and practice their problem-solving skills. More recently, computer science educators have become attentive to barriers to student success, particularly barriers that impact students from groups that are underrepresented in the field. Students with more computing experience outside of their college coursework, such as high school coursework or extracurricular computing activities, have an advantage and the students who lack such experience are likely to be intimidated in addition to less skilled. This updated version of a Computer Science Problem Solving course still addresses the long-recognized need for undergraduates to improve metacognitive and problem-solving skills, but also improves student motivation and engagement by using current computer science tools and demystifying potentially intimidating topics such as version control, security, command line tools, web development and machine learning. In this poster the author reports on the philosophy and design of a newly updated Computer Science Problem Solving course for computer science majors and presents preliminary data regarding student mindset, metacognition and computing experience outside of coursework. Sample schedule and activites are available: http://people.cs.vt.edu/~maellis1/teaching_resources/

Keywords: problem solving; diversity; extra-curricular

DOI: https://doi.org/10.1145/3287324.3293844

Design of a Gateway for Open Source Software Development in a Traditional CS Curriculum

Stewart N. Weiss, *Hunter College of the City University of New York*
Contact: stewart.weiss@acm.org

Many computer science students are eager to learn about how to contribute to Free and Open Source Software (FOSS) projects, but like most computer science departments, ours has no courses to help them achieve that goal. Creating such courses requires buy-in by deans, department chairs, and other faculty, who, because of lack of knowledge, can have little interest in supporting such efforts. Our poster shows how we solved this problem and created a means for students to simultaneously learn how to be contributors to FOSS projects and earn credit toward their major. It shows how we sought and found interested students and engaged them through repeated, informal meetings, which we used to gain the support of the chair and dean, and how we simulated a prototype course by having the students sign up for independent study credit. The group then met at regular intervals, communicated and shared work using discussion forums, source code repositories, and IRC chat. All course content is based on open source materials, including free textbooks, an abundance of on-line tutorials and reference materials, lecture notes and assignments that we wrote, with open source licenses, and other materials borrowed from *http://foss2serve.org*. The success of this simulated course led to the creation of a pilot course for the Spring 2019 semester, endorsed by the college.

The poster presents several assignments, discusses preliminary findings, and provides links to materials that we created for this course. It also shows how we encouraged students to work on humanitarian FOSS (HFOSS) projects.

Keywords: free and open-source software; curriculum development; FOSS; HFOSS

DOI: https://doi.org/10.1145/3287324.3293847

Inclusive Experiences Using HFOSS in a Senior Computer Science Elective

Becka Morgan, *Western Oregon University*
Contact: morganb@wou.edu

Humanitarian Free/Open Source Software (HFOSS) participation has been shown to promote real world experience and a create a portfolio of work for students that prove to be valuable assets for entering the work force. Creating a senior level software engineering elective that provides the scaffolding for students to participate in an HFOSS project allows professors to ease the often daunting steep learning curve that exists in contributing to these projects. Educators in computer science have recognized that building community within student cohorts provides many benefits for all students as well as being important for creating inclusive environments for underrepresented minorities. Based on the Communities of Practice model, developed by Lave and Wenger, mentorship also plays an important role in bridging entrance into professional communities. Using a classroom model that incorporates both levels of community by putting students into self-selected groups and using mentors from an HFOSS project provides the mechanisms for the aforementioned scaffolding. This poster will show the student perceived benefits of this course for their overall understanding of their place within the community of CS practitioners, their ability to participate with a diverse group of developers, and how this experience influences how they see their skills in relation to a project of this size. Included will also be lessons learned by teaching this course and resources for teachers to build the knowledge for teaching a course in HFOSS development.

Handouts will be available outlining the work that has been done and include the resources.

Keywords: HFOSS; Humanitarian Computing; Free and Open Source Software; Computing Education

DOI: https://doi.org/10.1145/3287324.3293849

ACM ISBN 978-1-4503-5890-3/19/02

A Neural Network Model for a Tutoring Companion Supporting Students in a Programming with Java Course

Melissa Day, Javier Gonzalez-Sanchez, *Arizona State University*
Contact: melissa.day@asu.edu

With large class sizes and instructors who may not be equipped to assist struggling students, many students abandon the field, deeming it to be too difficult and not for them. Consistent, constructive, supportive feedback through a Tutoring Companion can scaffold the learning process for students. This poster describes a reasoning model, using neural networks techniques, for a tutoring companion embedded into the Eclipse IDE. The companion provides support for students in a first-year university Java programming course. The companion collects data from students' events and programming assignments, analyzes it for relevant trends, and estimates each student's situation. The input data for the neural network comes from areas with which beginning computer science students often struggle, such as the presence of important keywords and the amount of time spent in a state with errors. Then, it determines the feedback to be provided for students to overcome a detected challenging situation, providing both hints on how to fix the problem with the code, as well as encouragement to help keep students motivated and learning. The effectiveness of the approach is examined among first-year computer science students through the completion of recursion and control flow programming assignments. The students complete surveys regarding their learning experience to assist in evaluating the companion's pedagogical effectiveness, which is discussed with an emphasis on the value of feedback provided.

Keywords: Computer science education; Tutoring companion; Neural networks; Programming tutoring; Teaching programming; Eclipse IDE

DOI: https://doi.org/10.1145/3287324.3293851

Assessing Middle School Students' Computational Thinking Through Programming Trajectory Analysis

Bita Akram, Wookhee Min, Eric Wiebe, Bradford Mott, *North Carolina State University*
Kristy Elizabeth Boyer, *University of Florida*
James Lester, *North Carolina State University*
Contact: bakram@ncsu.edu

With national K-12 education initiatives such as "CSForAll," block-based programming environments have emerged as widely used tools for teaching novice programming. A key challenge presented by block-based programming environments is assessing students' computational thinking (CT) and programming competencies. Developing assessment methods that can evaluate students' use of CT practices such as testing and refining, and developing and using appropriate algorithms, can help teachers evaluate students learning and provide appropriate scaffolding. In this work, we utilize an evidence-centered assessment design approach to devise a three-dimensional assessment to evaluate students' CT competencies based on evidence extracted from their programming trajectories in a block-based programming environment. In this assessment, the first dimension assesses students' knowledge of essential CT concepts, the second dimension assesses students' dynamic testing and refining strategies, and the third dimension assesses their overall problem-solving efficiency. We apply the assessment framework to data collected from students' interactions with a game-based learning environment designed to develop middle-grade students' CT competencies and programming skills. The results demonstrate that students' knowledge of basic CT constructs, such as appropriate use and combination of control structure, serves as the foundation for designing and implementing effective algorithms. Further, we assessed students testing and refining strategies over the three dimensions of novelty, positivity, and scale. The results demonstrate that students with higher algorithmic capabilities tend to make more novel, positive, and small-scale changes. The results reveal distinctive patterns in students' approaches to computational thinking problem solving and make a step toward identifying and assessing productive computational thinking practices.

Keywords: Computational Thinking Assessment; Evidence-Centered Design; Block-Based Programming; Programming Trajectories; Game-based Learning

DOI: https://doi.org/10.1145/3287324.3293798

Evaluating Student Engagement towards Integrating Parallel and Distributed Computing (PDC) Topics in Undergraduate Level Computer Science Curriculum

Mary Smith, *Hawaii Pacific University*
Srishti Srivastava, *University of Southern Indiana*
Contact: srishti.srivastava.phd@gmail.com

This research is a cross university study of evaluating whether there are differences between demographic factors (gender, age, class standing) and student engagement via unplugged activities introducing parallel and distributed computing (PDC) topics in CS1, CS2, and CS3 level courses in an undergraduate computer science (CS) curriculum. The collaboration stemmed from attending a NSF Center for Parallel and Distributed Computing Curriculum Development and Educational Resources (CDER) PDC Curriculum Early Adopter Grant and Summer Training Program. Initiatives by the National Science Foundation in conjunction with the Institute for Electronic and Electrical Engineers' Technical Committee of Parallel Processing (NSF/IEEE-TCPP) encourage and promote the introduction of PDC concepts in the early CS undergraduate courses. The researchers used the [Wiggins, 2017: Assessing Student Perspective of Engagement in Class (ASPECT)] survey to collect data from ~105 undergraduate CS students after each unplugged activity. Demographic data (gender, age, class standing) was added to the survey to determine if there are differences in these and student engagement. For the study, the researchers designed two unplugged activities to demonstrate the fundamental concepts of PDC. The first activity help students learn the key benefits of parallel computing, and the limitations imposed by Amdahl's and Gustafson's law. The second activity exhibits the concepts of scheduling and load balancing. Our findings indicate there are no significant differences between gender, age, class standing and student engagement. The researchers plan to continue their research on unplugged activities and student engagement. Additional activities will be developed to introduce other PDC topics.

Keywords: parallel computing; active learning; student engagement; unplugged activity

DOI: https://doi.org/10.1145/3287324.3293854

Dynamic Recitation: A Student-Focused, Goal-Oriented Recitation Management Platform

Joseph A. Boyle, Georgiana Haldeman, Andrew Tjang, Monica Babeş-Vroman, Ana Paula Centeno, Thu D. Nguyen, *Rutgers University*
Contact: joseph.a.boyle@rutgers.edu

Computer science universities and colleges around the nation are experiencing large growth in enrollments. To maintain in-person interaction with students, large courses typically include multiple recitations, each led by a Teaching Assistant (TA). Students in each group struggle with various course content, and these weaknesses are best evaluated by the TAs working closely with the students. TAs, however, have only a superficial understanding of education theory, and instructors must closely monitor and evaluate the content of recitations. Existing instruction management systems can be used to organize course-wide content, but, to our knowledge, none of them operate at the granularity of recitations. This poster presents Dynamic Recitation, an open-source platform through which TAs and instructors can create and share practice problems and lesson plans tagged with the learning objectives that they cover. The poster illustrates the interface offered to the TAs for creating problems, designing lesson plans for individual sections, and submitting feedback about student progress. It shows examples of lesson plans created in the system, as well as reports that can be used to identify elements that promote desired learning objectives and refine recitations.

Keywords: programming course recitation; learning management system; recitation feedback; in-class programming exercises; customized lesson plans

DOI: https://doi.org/10.1145/3287324.3293859

Sentiment Analysis across the Courses of a MOOC Specialization

Kenny Wong, *University of Alberta*
Contact: kenw@cs.ualberta.ca

A Massive Open Online Course (MOOC) is an effective way for a university to deliver course content that reaches a global audience. Such developments are not without substantial costs and risks [1]. On the Coursera platform, there are MOOC specializations, which package a sequence of related courses. Retaining learners is of particular interest to instructors as they progress through the courses of a long specialization. Learners that encounter delays, unfairness, or plagiarism in peer evaluations of assignments could become dissatisfied enough to withdraw, for example. We describe using trends in sentiment analysis of discussion forum postings across the courses. The idea is to detect, interpret, and address points of lower sentiment in a MOOC specialization, to avoid losing learners. We outline our findings with a MOOC specialization on software product management, which consists of six courses, involving a nominal 24 weeks of content [2,3]. Interestingly, higher sentiment in a course's content did not necessarily preserve enrollment numbers for the subsequent course.

Keywords: Massive Open Online Course; MOOC retention; Coursera specialization; sentiment analysis; natural language processing; discussion forum; software product management

DOI: https://doi.org/10.1145/3287324.3293864

Using an Art Museum Field Trip to Spark Classroom Discussions About Mobile App Design

Aarathi Prasad, *Skidmore College*
Contact: aprasad@skidmore.edu

Classes on mobile computing are popular in schools all over the country, however, the author is not aware of any that include sessions on mobile app design. How do you help students understand what constitutes a good design? Faculty have used wireframes and affinity diagrams to teach design in the classroom, included user experience and design in final course projects, and incorporated problem-based learning, opportunities for service and video-making to develop further HCI skills. One option the author has tried in the past to teach mobile app design is to ask students to choose a few mobile apps that they consider the best and a few that they consider the worst in terms of aesthetics and usability and then lead a discussion on the different factors that make the app aesthetically pleasing and usable. A new approach the author attempted this year was to hold the class meeting at the art museum instead. Looking at the different art pieces, the class engaged in a discussion of the factors that allowed the artists to capture the attention of the audience and convey their message. This activity also introduces a cross-disciplinary approach into a computer science class.

Keywords: mobile app; hci; art museum; app design

DOI: https://doi.org/10.1145/3287324.3293865

Lichen: Customizable, Open Source Plagiarism Detection in Submitty

Matthew Peveler, *Rensselaer Polytechnic Institute*
Tushar Gurjar, *IIT Kanpur*
Evan Maicus, Andrew Aikens, Alexander Christoforides,
Barbara Cutler, *Rensselaer Polytechnic Institute*
Contact: pevelm@rpi.edu

Prior education research, including Computer Science, has established that students will attempt to cheat and violate academic integrity, with one of the more common forms being code plagiarism. The majority of existing tools for software plagiarism are closed source, requiring instructors to use them in a prescribed configuration and sending student code to a third-party server for analysis. At the core of this analysis is the need to perform a language-specific tokenization of the input program and then to use "digital fingerprinting" on the code to identify significant markers. This has required developers to write their own parser for each supported language, which is time-consuming to create and keep up-to-date, and thus a barrier to creation of these tools. Instead we bootstrap new languages into our plagiarism system by leveraging the "Language Server Protocol", an initiative to create open-source parsers and tokenizers for many languages (principally to be used within a range of popular IDEs). In this poster, we present our work on Lichen, the open source plagiarism detection tool that is integrated into the Submitty course management platform we use at Rensselaer Polytechnic Institute. This tool is a pipeline of modules for the specific tasks of tokenizing, fingerprinting, and then comparing the fingerprints for any number of files. Through this, a similarity score is generated for pairs of files, and these are used to help instructors determine to what extent code plagiarism has occurred.

Keywords: Lichen; Plagiarism; Code Plagiarism

DOI: https://doi.org/10.1145/3287324.3287507

Facilitating Discussion-Based Grading and Private Channels via an Integrated Forum

Andrew Aikens, *Rensselaer Polytechnic Institute*
Gagan Kumar, *Indian Institute of Technology Patna*
Shail Patel, Evan Maicus, Matthew Peveler,
Barbara Cutler, *Rensselaer Polytechnic Institute*
Contact: aikena@rpi.edu

Submitty is an open-source course management platform for assignment submission with automated testing and grading, immediate feedback with an option for resubmission, and manual grading from course instructors and TAs. We have added an integrated discussion forum to the Submitty environment, which enables the students to communicate with their peers and have a public dialogue with the teaching staff outside of the classroom. Compared to a collection of closed-source external applications, our single-system login for distribution of course materials, assignment submission, and discussion forum participation is more convenient and accessible for students and simplifies administrative tasks. Students use the forum to ask questions about course logistics, homework help, exam review problems, and Submitty-related questions. The forum supports image and code segment posts, which facilitates targeted debugging help and sharing of additional reference material. An instructor-moderated forum is especially helpful in larger classes where students can feel it is otherwise difficult to get their questions answered. Every thread is tagged with course-specific categories and we provide full-text search of the forum. The forum becomes a curated collection of relevant frequently asked questions, which reduces the number of duplicate questions that must be answered by the staff. The forum includes customizable system and email notifications for important events such as: instructor announcement, assignment posted, team invitation, forum question answered, grades released, etc. Our current work focuses on private channels to facilitate team assignments (which can be monitored for participation by staff) and a grading interface for discussion-based assignments within the forum.

Keywords: Educational Software; Discussion Forum; Grading; Teaching

DOI: https://doi.org/10.1145/3287324.3293869

Poster Session 3

Introducing Theoretical Computer Concepts in Secondary Education

Rafael del Vado Vírseda,
Universidad Complutense de Madrid
Contact: rdelvado@sip.ucm.es

The purpose of this poster is to provide practical arguments to stimulate debate and discussion on whether or not to introduce concepts of theoretical computer science in the pre-university education system, conveniently adapted within students' capability. Theoretical computer science is a hard subject to teach at the university level. Many students who enter the computer sciences courses have very little mathematical or theoretical background. For this reason, it is important that students acquire an appreciation of these concepts before they leave the secondary education. In anticipation that these contents would not be included or addressed in the context of a subject of Computer Science, a work in progress educational experience is presented during the 2018-2019 academic year for enhancing the algorithmic curriculum of pre-university computing and mathematical courses. We describe a collection of selected problems, puzzles and riddles from high school mathematics and introductory logic, to be added to the current secondary curriculum. We want to show attendees the use of our educational activities, offering practical aspects that could not be shown through the reading of a paper, so that they can learn to use them in their own classes. The preliminary experimental results show that the students who have undergone this educational experience have obtained a higher motivation that those who have followed the course in its traditional form. We believe that introducing these theoretical computer concepts can help students to perform better in some areas of computer science and be increasingly prepared and motivated for their university studies.

Keywords: Computability theory; Algorithmic complexity; Computing curricula; Curriculum issues; Undergraduate studies

DOI: https://doi.org/10.1145/3287324.3293784

Girls in Engineering Draw a Computer Scientist

Sabrina Tsui, *University of California, Santa Cruz*
Contact: sctsui@ucsc.edu

There is a large gender disparity in computing: women are underrepresented. By exposing girls to computing activities in a summer day camp, and using near-peers as teachers, we found differences in perceptions the girls held about computer scientists between those on the first day of camp with those on the last day of camp. We describe the day camp program, the participants, and the activity used to investigate the girls' perceptions of computer scientists. The 'Draw a Computer Scientist' activity was used to determine how the stereotypes of a computer scientist and the day camp have influenced the girls. The only instruction given to the participants was to draw what they thought a computer scientist looked like. Key drawing characteristics were identified and quantified in a blind coding process, then compared across pre-camp and post-camp drawings. The results suggest that exposing girls to other female engineers and engaging them in age-appropriate engineering activities broadened their perspectives on what a computer scientist looks like.

Keywords: Gender; Stereotypes; Outreach; Middle School; K-12

DOI: https://doi.org/10.1145/3287324.3293789

What does it take to Teach K12 Computer Science? Exploring Teachers' Attitudes Towards Teaching CS K12 in Georgia

Alfredo Perez, *Columbus State University*
Hillary Fleenor, *Columbus State University*
Contact: perez_alfredo@columbusstate.edu

Currently, the state of Georgia requires a CS teacher endorsement (or the passing of the CS GACE exam) to teach middle/high school computer science in public schools. However, issues such as the cost of a CS endorsement and a lack of incentives to take the endorsement may undermine the long-term efforts to establish high-quality K12 CS education in the state. This may negatively affect the broadening of CS participation efforts in the state (47% of the population in GA belongs to a minority group). In this poster, we will present preliminary results of a survey conducted with more than 200 K-12 teachers across the state of Georgia in which we explore the attitudes towards teaching K12 computer science in the state. Our goal with the collection of the data is to understand better what it would take to become a long-term CS teacher in the state.

Keywords: computer science education; computer science teacher training; computer science teacher preparation

DOI: https://doi.org/10.1145/3287324.3293790

Implementing CS0 with Computer Science Principles Curriculum

D. Cenk Erdil, *Sacred Heart University*
Darcy Ronan, *Sacred Heart University*
Contact: erdild@sacredheart.edu

As a prerequisite to ACM-IEEE CS1/CS2 curricula, common objectives of a CS0 course are: (i) to introduce CS to students who are interested, but do not have any prior CS skills, (ii) support student success while adapting to college life, and (iii) improve recruitment and retention of CS majors using the 'common first year' theme of many STEM programs. A previous CSO survey course at our institution focused on abstract logic, without any hands-on component, resulting in a CS0 "gate" course- a dull first encounter with computer science for most and an 'extremely fun and interesting' course for the few with pre-existing abstract

ACM ISBN 978-1-4503-5890-3/19/02

thinking and reasoning skills. The missed opportunity to engage more students with CS, and thereby contribute to program viability and growth, spurred curriculum renewal. Given the existence of multiple high-quality offerings of CS curricula geared toward P-12 students, including at the AP-level, and also relying on our existing institutional partnership with a national non-profit organization dedicated to expanding access to CS in schools and addressing patterns of underrepresentation, we have implemented a new course based on a Computer Science Principles curriculum. This poster provides details of implementation as well as student experience and feedback with the first cohort of this brand-new course.

Keywords: Active learning model; flipped classroom; computer science principles; college teaching; CS0 curricula

DOI: https://doi.org/10.1145/3287324.3293791

Linear Data Structures: A Comparison of Novice and Expert Teacher Pedagogical Content Knowledge

Aleata Hubbard, *WestEd*
Contact: ahubbar@wested.org

Pedagogical content knowledge (PCK), which includes knowledge of student understanding and knowledge of instructional strategies to support learning, is a component of teaching expertise that develops over time and with experience. In this poster, I present exploratory work to identify and categorize PCK amongst secondary teachers new to computing. Four teachers participating in a multi-year case study completed a questionnaire where they (a) listed student difficulties with linear data structures and (b) described how they address the topic in their teaching. Using a content analysis approach, I analyzed the quantity and type of responses provided. Since little research exists describing computing PCK, I also compared responses against public data sources gathered from experienced teachers who completed similar tasks. Results show that participants provided more ideas about student difficulties than teaching strategies and they focused equally on difficulties with programming notation and with programming pragmatics and plans. In contrast, the experienced educator list included a wider range of difficulty types. Ideas about teaching strategies focused mostly on presenting information, while the experienced educator list focused mostly on providing problem solving tasks. Unlike participants, the experienced educator list referenced real-life examples as an instructional strategy. Lastly, the responses provided by participants were not simply a subset of the experienced educator list and included unique ideas. On the poster I suggest possible contextual and experiential differences between new and experienced computing teachers that might lead to these differences.

Keywords: Pedagogical content knowledge; computer science teachers; high school teachers

DOI: https://doi.org/10.1145/3287324.3293796

ACM ISBN 978-1-4503-5890-3/19/02

SciGirls Code: Computational Participation for Middle School Girls

Cassandra Scharber, Yu-Hui Chang, Sarah Barksdale, Lana Peterson, Angelina Constantine, Ramya Sivaraj, Jennifer Englund, *University of Minnesota*
Contact: scharber@umn.edu

SciGirls Code is a project which used the principles of connected learning with 16 STEM outreach partners to provide 160+ middle school girls with computational thinking (CT) and coding skills within informal education spaces. Programs completed 3 curricular strands (Mobile Apps, Robotics, E-Textiles) between September 2017-May 2018. SciGirls Code integrates a computational participation framework with connected learning. The research study investigates the ways in which computational learning experiences impact girls' development of CT; interest and attitudes toward computer science; and their understanding of how participation in technology creation impacts themselves and the world around them. This study utilizes an interpretive multi-site case study design. There are multiple data sources with different data collected at focal and participating sites. The seven (7) focal cases represent an array of settings (rural, suburban, urban) as well as a variety of programming contexts (museums, community centers, after school). The remaining nine (9) sites comprise the participating cases. Notably, interviews (in-person) from focal sites and shorts (videos) from participating sites were collected at three moments in the programming (beginning, middle, end) to document changes in understandings and skills. Content analysis was conducted, and further triangulated in teams, to develop themes for each case and cross-case comparison. Thus far, the study has found that a connected learning approach boosted the development of middle school girls' CT skills, positively impacted attitudes towards computing pathways/careers, and increased understandings of computational participation.

Keywords: Case studies; Computational thinking; Computational participation; Connected learning; Gender

DOI: https://doi.org/10.1145/3287324.3293800

Every Little Bit Counts: Experiences and Lessons Learned Building a Community Outreach Program from the Ground Up

Brian Krupp, Paul Peters, Tyler Hardy, Sydney Leither, Baldwin Wallace University, Zach Egler, *Baldwin Wallace University*
Contact: bkrupp@bw.edu

Large scale efforts, such as CS4All and Hour of Code, have made significant progress in attracting more students to computing as well as attracting underrepresented groups. However, even with these large efforts, there is still work to be done to help increase diversity and ensure computing jobs are not left unfilled. The authors will present their experiences in creating a Community Outreach program known as CS+ at Baldwin Wallace University. They will share the model that was created for CS+ to ensure continuity and scalability in the program. Even with a small team, CS+ has made significant progress towards their mission in providing opportunities for students to learn computing that have limited access to similar programs. The poster will include organizational details of the group including recruitment of students, positions they hold, and the vision and mission of the program. The poster will also share experiences in partnering with teachers at local school districts, attracting students to the program, and partnering with the education department as well as community organizations. The poster will include sample content that is used in camps and clubs as well as a site where all of the content can be accessed. While our efforts alone may not have the same impact as large organizations, by inspiring other institutions to start similar programs, we can reach underrepresented groups and those that lack confidence in computing to help bridge the gap in diversity and meet the demand of computing jobs that are available.

Keywords: Computer Science Education; Community Outreach

DOI: https://doi.org/10.1145/3287324.3293804

Machine Learning: An Introductory Unit of Study for Secondary Education

Ramsey Young, *University of Nebraska Omaha*
Jonathan Ringenberg, *University of Nebraska Omaha*
Contact: rdyoung@mpsomaha.org

Machine learning and neural networks have become key techniques for solving some of society's most difficult problems. Many students are intimidated by, or ignorant of the mechanics of AI. Teaching machine learning to early computing students is possible; in doing so students will gain further confidence and interest in the field of Computer Science.

Through an NSF funded grant to the University of Nebraska Omaha, a unit of study was created to teach machine learning to high school students. Focuses for the unit include; neural networks, genetic algorithms, sigmoid and perceptron networks, social impacts, ethics, history, and supervised and unsupervised learning techniques. The unit employs hands on learning approaches and media elements. Also included is a lab where students train an autonomous car.

Students were administered pre and post Likert surveys for this unit using the Computing Attitude Survey V4.1 with additional topic specific questions. The study size was sixteen students from two sections of AP Computer Science Principles. Based on survey results, student perceived machine learning comprehension showed a positive delta value growth of 27.84% and negative results showed a delta value shrink of 20.45%. For questions related to computer science interest and confidence, students showed a positive delta value growth of 14.58% and a negative delta value shrink of 11.8%. We believe these results demonstrate that teaching machine learning topics to high school students is effective and has a positive impact on student desire and confidence to pursue further study in the field.

Keywords: machine learning; neural networks; CS0; AP Computer Science Principles; genetic algorithms; AI; secondary education

DOI: https://doi.org/10.1145/3287324.3293806

ACM ISBN 978-1-4503-5890-3/19/02

Comparing the Effects of Using a Tangible Object or a Simulation in Learning Elementary CS Concepts: A Case Study with Block-Based Programming

Grégoire Fessard, Ilaria Renna, Patrick Wang,
Institut Supérieur d'Électronique de Paris
Contact: gregoire.fessard@gmail.com

Learning elementary Computer Science (CS) concepts can often be difficult for young students. The literature presents two main practices to introduce programming: using digital environments (e.g., integrated development environments, command-line tools) or exploiting manipulations on programmable tangible objects such as robots. This second practice has recently gained traction thanks to the positive results concerning the use of programmable objects in introductory programming courses. However, and to the best of our knowledge, there is no study comparing learning gains between 'digital' and 'physical' computing.

Our study focuses on highlighting possible differences between these two practices to learn CS at an introductory level. We compare the learning progress of two groups of students (total=36, male=27, female=9, aged 14-17) with little or no previous knowledge of programming; both groups are presented with the same pre-test, programming exercises, and post-test. All participants exploit a block-based programming environment to do the exercises and program either a tangible BBC micro:bit card or its digital simulation. The proposed programming exercises concern basic CS concepts: variables, conditional structures, and iterative structures. By running their programs on the tangible or digital card, students are able to visualize the results of their exercises thanks to the grid of LEDs that is present on the BBC micro:bit.

Our objective is to determine if the learning of a specific CS concept is better achieved through the programming of a tangible object or an exact equivalent digital simulation of it.

A statistical analysis will be presented to evaluate the results of this experiment.

Keywords: Computer Science Education; Physical Computing; Digital Computing; Block-Based Programming

DOI: https://doi.org/10.1145/3287324.3293809

Collaborative Coding and Composing of *JazzHands*: Integrating the Learning of Advanced Computational Concepts with Electronic Textiles to Make Music Wearables

Gayithri Jayathirtha, Yasmin B. Kafai, Debora A. Lui,
Mia S. Shaw, *University of Pennsylvania*
Ji Yong Cho, *Cornell University*
Contact: gayithri@gse.upenn.edu

The links between music and computation date back at least three decades. This trend has led to the development of learning environments for novices to make music and learn computational concepts. However, research connecting music and computation is mostly situated within the context of on-screen programming, with little research involving hybrid, tangible environments.

Electronic textiles (e-textiles) is one such hybrid context where learners craft interactive physical artifacts by sewing microcontrollers, sensors, and actuators onto toys, clothes, or other fabric accessories. Prior studies show that Arduino-based e-textiles afford opportunities for students to learn basic concepts such as variables and control flow but not more advanced concepts such as arrays and *for* loops. In our study, we expand learning with e-textiles as learners compose and code music to address the following research question: What are the affordances of designing musical wearables to deepen computational conceptual learning? We present a case study of a group of four 15-17-year-old youth and an adult co-making a musical wearable—*JazzHands*—a glove augmented with actuators such as LEDs and speaker, and motion, touch, and light sensors. We analyzed videos of the group's collaborative design sessions, student daily journals, multiple versions of the code, and post-workshop, artifact-based interviews with the youth. Our analysis revealed that making musical wearables not only allowed the youth to express themselves and relate to computing as a creative endeavor but also afforded unique opportunities to work with constructs such as arrays indices, sensor data integration, and logical expressions to control *for* loops.

Keywords: musical wearables; electronic textiles; for loops; arrays; creative computing

DOI: https://doi.org/10.1145/3287324.3293810

Collaboration: Developing and Piloting a Cybersecurity Curriculum for Middle School

Hillary Fleenor, *Columbus State University*
Yesem Peker, *Columbus State University*
Ebone Cutts, *Muscogee County School District*
Contact: fleenor_hillary@columbusstate.edu

Investing in raising a generation with more security-aware minds is essential in preventing many of the security incidents that threaten us and our nation. In addition there is a high need for well-trained cybersecurity professionals to protect our networks, computer systems, and infrastructure. Early exposure is key to developing awareness, piquing student interest, and laying a foundation for more complex skill development. Students of today are parents, professionals, and leaders of tomorrow. The impact of their actions is significant for the future. In this work, TSYS School of Computer Science at Columbus State University and Rothschild Leadership Academy, a Title I middle school in the Muscogee County School District of Georgia collaborated to develop, deliver, and assess a middle school cybersecurity curriculum for U.S. grade 8 students. The project had three student achievement goals:

1. Provide a good foundation for students in cybersecurity knowledge and skills,

2. Enhance students' ability to secure their environment, and

3. Increase students' interest in cybersecurity education

The project included development of the standards, objectives, lessons, and assessment instruments for implementation within a year-long business and computer science course and training of the teacher in cybersecurity. The course was piloted with sixty grade 8 students in two classes during the 2017-2018 school year. Results show significant growth in mastery of key cybersecurity concepts via a pre- and post- test and artifacts from the course indicate an increase in student interest in cybersecurity.

Keywords: computer science education; cybersecurity education; middle school;

DOI: https://doi.org/10.1145/3287324.3293824

Building Computer Science K-12 PLCs in Rural Communities

Allison Sauppé, *University of Wisconsin–La Crosse*
Samantha S. Foley, *University of Wisconsin–La Crosse*
Thomas Gendreau, *University of Wisconsin–La Crosse* Joshua T. Hertel, *University of Wisconsin–La Crosse*
Mao Zheng, *University of Wisconsin–La Crosse*
Contact: asauppe@uwlax.edu

Computer science is in increasing demand at the K-12 level. However, due to a lack of qualified educators, numerous programs (e.g., Google's CS4HS, NSF's CSForAll) have been created to train teachers and increase student access to computer science. Although these programs have seen some success, schools in areas with lower population density continue to struggle to offer computer science opportunities. These schools face unique challenges due to their low population density, including increasing teaching demands in core subjects, smaller teaching staff, and a smaller pipeline of students, making it difficult to justify offering a course in computer science. This poster draws on our experience of collaborating with K-12 teachers in rural schools in western Wisconsin to help mitigate these unique challenges. We have obtained two Google CS4HS grants to hold educational computer science workshops with teachers from across the region. These workshops allowed us to work closely with teachers and help them become more comfortable with incorporating computer science into their classrooms, while also helping us to form relationships with both teachers and administrators in a number of districts. Building on these relationships, we are taking the next step of working more closely with individual school districts to form professional learning communities. Our goal in this work is to connect K-12 teachers within each district and help facilitate a robust pipeline of students interested in computer science and justify offering AP CS courses at the high school level.

Keywords: K-12 computer science education; rural computer science education

DOI: https://doi.org/10.1145/3287324.3293825

Computational Thinking in the Making: Lessons for Second Graders in a STEM Computer Science Immersion School

Lindsey Scheppegrell, *Charlotte Teachers Institute*
Elyse Hiatt, *Charlotte Teachers Institute*
Johanna Okerlund, *University of NC at Charlotte*
David Wilson, *University of NC at Charlotte*
Contact: davils@uncc.edu

Recently, there has been significant interest in integrating Maker-related experiences into formal education. A challenge is reconciling open-ended making and non-deterministic learning goals with standards that drive traditional education. In the context of our CS-focused STEM magnet school, we designed two 2nd grade lessons that not only align with grade-level standards and our school's computer science-oriented pedagogy, but also incorporate 3D printing and the philosophy of Makerspaces. The integrated Maker experience serves to scaffold computational thinking practices such as abstraction, modeling, and decomposition, which are essential for long-term success in STEM learning. To bring these aspects together, we created a rubric based on existing evaluation tools. Using this rubric, we evaluated the two lessons with a small sample of participants. Our pilot study shows promise of mastery in standard-related content, evidence of a making mindset, engagement in the activity, innovation in design, and solidarity in working with peers. Aligning state standards with open-ended Maker activities has potential for fostering student growth and engagement in the classroom. An additional component of our research was reflecting on our experience as teachers with no Makerspace experience who were newly submerged in the digital fabrication world. We present the two 3D printing-based lessons, one addressing extreme weather standards, the other incorporating understanding of urban, suburban, and rural communities. We also present the rubric we designed, the literature that guided this work, and reflections and recommendations from our experience of learning digital fabrication for the first time and integrating it into curriculum.

Keywords: Makerspace; Computational Thinking; Maker Movement; Evaluation Tools; STEM Learning; Digital Fabrication; Digital Education

DOI: https://doi.org/10.1145/3287324.3293833

CodeNC: Integrating Computational Thinking into K-12 Instructional Activities using Animated Videos

N. Rich Nguyen, *University of Virginia*
Iuliia Poliakova, Sahithi Meduri, Joshua Hutcheson, Ryan Ke, *University of North Carolina Charlotte*
Contact: nn4pj@virginia.edu

Increasing the representation of minorities in computer science (CS) has become a national priority. One of the many reasons minority students nationwide choose not to study CS is that they often lack mentors and role models to encourage them early in their learning. However, a big issue facing this initiative is that many K-12 teachers finds themselves lack of (1) relevant materials, (2) systematic training, and (3) a supportive community. The democratization of media, such as photos and videos, has provided a great variety of options to educate a broad audience on myriad topics. In this poster, we will describe the challenges and successes of using animated videos including its beauty, soundness, and utility as critical elements in establishing a strong CT comprehension while engaging K-12 teachers in a non-threatening way via http://codenc.org. Using a process of iterative design, we have integrated CT concepts in six non-CS disciplines in the K-12 curriculum. The teachers who have collaborated with us respond positively that this design approach provides them with a greater comprehension of the CT concepts while giving them exciting instructional activities. Therefore, this poster may be of interest to any CS educator who wishes to improve the engagement of K-12 teachers while sustaining a CT training program at their institution.

Keywords: computational thinking; K-12; instructional activities; animated videos

DOI: https://doi.org/10.1145/3287324.3293835

An Interactive Teaching Tool for Introducing Novices to Machine Translation

Huda Khayrallah, Rebecca Knowles, Kevin Duh, Matt Post, *Johns Hopkins University*
Contact: huda@jhu.edu

The first step in the research process is developing an understanding of the problem at hand. Novices may be interested in learning about machine translation (MT), but often lack experience and intuition about the task of translation (either by human or machine) and its challenges. The goal of this work is to allow students to interactively discover why MT is an open problem, and encourage them to ask questions, propose solutions, and test intuitions. We present a hands-on activity in which students build and evaluate their own MT systems using curated parallel texts. By having students hand-engineer MT system rules in a simple user interface, which they can then run on real data, they gain intuition about why early MT research took this approach, where it fails, and what features of language make MT a challenging problem even today. Developing translation rules typically strikes novices as an obvious approach that should succeed, but the idea quickly struggles in the face of natural language complexity. This interactive, intuition-building exercise can be augmented by a discussion of state-of-the-art MT techniques and challenges, focusing on areas or aspects of linguistic complexity that the students found difficult. We envision this lesson plan being used in the framework of a larger AI or natural language processing course (where only a small amount of time can be dedicated to MT) or as a standalone activity. We describe and release the tool that supports this lesson, as well as accompanying data.

Keywords: Machine translation; Active learning

DOI: https://doi.org/10.1145/3287324.3293840

ACM ISBN 978-1-4503-5890-3/19/02

Teacher Beliefs in Student Capabilities as a Mediating Factor in a Novel Understanding of Enactment of CT Curriculum

Paige Prescott, *University of New Mexico*,
Irene A. Lee, *Massachusetts Institute of Technology*
Kersti Tyson, *University of New Mexico*
Contact: pprescott@unm.edu

The integration of computer science (CS) and computational thinking (CT) in STEM classes has been promoted as one strategy to engage all students in CS education. This approach aims to reduce inequities in access to computing education by placing CS within compulsory science classes. The Project GUTS CS in Science curriculum supports the integration of CT-rich computer modeling and simulation activities and has been promoted to serve the dual goals of exposing students to CS in a powerful context while simultaneously promoting students' understanding of modern scientific practices. This case study follows two middle school science teachers as they implement the curriculum that integrates CS within science classrooms through the use, modification, and creation of computer models of scientific phenomena. Their implementation stories represent the range of enactments from "use-only" in which computer models are used to demonstrate the behavior of a system, to "modify/create" in which teachers support students in the using, decoding and modifying computer models that are used as experimental test beds. These cases illuminate teacher characteristics and pedagogical decisions that impact enactment of the curriculum. Evidence is provided that teacher's belief in student capabilities is a factor correlated with enactment, and that has the potential to impact students' opportunities to learn. This finding suggests that addressing CS/CT skill building, content knowledge, and pedagogy within teacher professional development (PD) programs may be necessary but not sufficient to lead to enactment of CT-rich curricula and may inform others seeking to integrate CS in K-12 education.

Keywords: teacher beliefs; pedagogy; CS in Science; CT in Science; CS integration; inquiry in CS

DOI: https://doi.org/10.1145/3287324.3293841

Exploring the Definition of Computational Thinking in Research and the Classroom

Tony Lowe, Sean Brophy, Monica Cardella,
Purdue University
Contact: lowe46@purdue.edu

Our research group has studied how Kindergarteners through second graders can be introduced to the ideas of Computational Thinking (CT) through engineer design, unplugged, and programming activities. We often found it difficult to explain the boundaries and clear definitions for CT in research, to students and their teachers. Literature provides a variety of definitions from various perspectives, but these definitions often seem like capturing smoke. We see evidence CT, indicating fire, but how hot or lasting it burns cannot be measured by smoke alone. CT is typically defined by siloed concepts and skills. Some silos describe concrete ideas, which tend to be tied to programming principles. Many describe essential ideas, but over generalized becoming hard to teach and measure and distinguish from other types of problem solving. Is there a middle ground where we can clearly observe the presence and growing maturing of CT yet not limit the ways it can manifest, particularly without requiring coding? We hope this poster inspires conversation on 1.) the intersection of CT and programming skills, 2.) the priority and order for learning those skills, and 3.) how we can promote CT in disciplines who interact with and help define computational solutions yet are never expected to learn to program. We hope to share our perspective as well as garner feedback and possibly collaboration on better refining curriculum within Computer Science as well as promoting CT in other disciplines.

Keywords: Computational Thinking

DOI: https://doi.org/10.1145/3287324.3293842

Curated Pathways to Innovation: Personalized CS Education to Promote Diversity

Natalie Linnell, *Santa Clara University*
Phil Gonsalves , *YWCA Silicon Valley*
Mayank Kakodkar, *Purdue University*
Vanessa Martinez, *YWCA Silicon Valley*
Tim Urdan, *Santa Clara University*
Bruno Ribiero, *Purdue University*
Janice Zdankus, *Hewlett Packard Enterprise*
Contact: nlinnell@scu.edu

The lack of diversity in computing is a well-known issue. This poster is a work-in-progress report on Curated Pathways to Innovation (CPI), a web-based tool which gathers existing online resources for computer science (CS) engagement and learning to allow students to learn more about CS careers and content, with a particular focus on improving participation of K-12 girls and under-represented minorities in CS. This project is a collaboration of people from academia in CS and social science, K-12 education, non-profit, and industry. We are about halfway through a 3-year pilot deployment of CPI with all students in a low-income, primarily Latino/a middle school with nearly 500 students, and smaller deployments have been undertaken and are planned for 2018-19. In addition to online content, we have created in-person experiences, including reverse science fairs, summer camps, and a hackathon, which are tracked in the CPI tool. To measure impact, we conduct regular surveys with the students measuring their interest in CS, self-efficacy, and other metrics. Our evaluation of the system based on survey data has helped inform the development of the system and curriculum, but remains preliminary.

This poster also discusses the tool itself. It uses gamification in the form of badges to measure student progress. From the beginning, the vision was to use machine learning to customize recommendations based on students' demographics, background, and past performance. This integration is coming to fruition at the same time we are including more interesting visuals in the UI, such as an avatar and animations.

Keywords: Diversity; Tools; Machine Learning

DOI: https://doi.org/10.1145/3287324.3293845

Using Music to Foster Engagement in Introductory Computing Courses

Fatemeh Jamshidi, Daniela Marghitu *Auburn University*
Contact: fzj0007@tigermail.auburn.edu

The importance of imaginative assignments and innovative curriculum design in computer science (CS) education has been researched for some time now. In this poster, the authors discuss an interdisciplinary K12 informal education course called "Computational Thinking in Music". The goal is to engage students in computer science by prioritizing personal expression, creativity, and aesthetics. The research includes a creative curriculum based on modeling theory of evidence-based pedagogical research, and an empirical one: by the time of the SIGCSE Symposium, the authors expect to have comparative results for control courses, where active learning curriculum was not used at all, as well as for the course with active learning curriculum. The "Computational Thinking in Music" course intends to broaden the number of individuals, particularly from underrepresented groups, who show interest and persist in the field of computer science through the use of student's intrinsic interests. Specifically, this study built an authentic STEAM learning environment through the use of EarSketch (https://earsketch.gatech.edu) and Scratch (https://scratch.mit.edu/) two creative computing programs.

The poster will display our findings in a creative fashion convenient for drawing informative conclusions. Two measures are used in assessing the effectiveness of creative curriculum: student scores on typical assessment instruments and student perceptions on Likert scales. Thus far the data are remarkably consistent over the various settings and indicates that participants of this camp benefitted more from an authentic learning environment allowing for music, creativity, and imagination than from a more traditional computing camp without the addition of musical concepts.

Keywords: k-12 CS education; creativity; music; STEAM; performamatics; Scratch; EarSketch

DOI: https://doi.org/10.1145/3287324.3293855

Sorting Out Algorithms: What Makes One Better than Another?

Connor Bain, *Northwestern University*
Uri Northwestern, *Northwestern University*
Contact: connorbain@u.northwestern.edu

For many years, beginning computer science students have been asked the seemingly simple question: *what makes one algorithm better than another*? Usually, this concept of "best-ness" is introduced with the many algorithms that are used to sort data. Thus, students are overwhelmed by the intricacies of sorting while simultaneously trying to understand one of the greatest questions in computer science. In this work we take inspiration from *embodied cognition* and describe a new, *constructionist* curriculum for approaching algorithmic efficiency. In order to help students construct understandings of both sorting algorithms and algorithmic efficiency, we present a curriculum that focuses around *participatory simulations* (PartSims) where students "play as" datapoints and experience sorting algorithms from an entirely different perspective. Instead of first experiencing the usual top-down approach to sorting where datapoints are manipulated by an "observer," each student follows a simple set of rules which, collectively, end in an emergent sorting algorithm. In this way, instead of talking in the abstract about the different pros and cons of sorting algorithms, students have different physical experiences across the different algorithms. With this embodied, grounded experience, students then construct for themselves metrics for comparing the different algorithms by evaluating the differences in their physical experiences. This two-week curriculum is targeted towards beginning computer science students (high-school or collegiate level) and utilizes the Parallax hackable *Electronic Conference Badge* and NetLogo to track the students experience in the PartSims throughout the curriculum.

Keywords: computing education; sorting; algorithms; participatory simulations

DOI: https://doi.org/10.1145/3287324.3293856

Four Scope-Related Misconceptions Held by Computer Science Students

Wynne Becker, Kayley James, *Scripps College*
Maya Minier, *Harvey Mudd College*
Contact: WBecker0192@scrippscollege.edu

Scope is a fundamental topic of computer science and its pervasive nature affects how programmers interpret code on every level. Thus, a strong understanding of scope is necessary for reading and writing code as well as tracing memory usage. This paper qualitatively analyzes students' misconceptions about scope, specifically involving parameters, variable declarations, and loop variables. Our study consisted of five one-on-one interviews where participants were given a set of scope-related problems in Java and Python to solve. We noticed that, despite demonstrating a general understanding of scope, some students became confused about the particular subtypes of scope mentioned previously. Our paper identifies four misconceptions about scope involving parameters, variable declarations, and loop variables: that variable declaration and use are indistinguishable, that where the variable is declared (eg. inside/outside of a method) is not relevant, that passing in a value as a parameter changes the parameter's value globally within the code, and that a loop variable defined to iterate through a for loop is accessible outside of the loop it is declared within. Many of these misconceptions indicate that some participants have an abstract notion about scope that is not equivalent to the programming languages' rules about scope. The information we gathered in this study could potentially help computer science (CS) teachers present scope in a way that prevents the four misconceptions and thus encourage a stronger understanding of scope as a whole.

Keywords: scope; variable; loop; paramete ; Java; Python; misconception

DOI: https://doi.org/10.1145/3287324.3293860

ACM ISBN 978-1-4503-5890-3/19/02

Snap! A Look at 5 Years, 250,000 Users and 2 Million Projects

Michael Ball, *UC Berkeley*
Jens Mönig, *SAP*
Bernat Romagosa, *Independent*
Brian Harvey *UC Berkeley*
Contact: contact@snap.berkeley.edu

Snap! is blocks-based programming language that inherits a design and vocabulary from Scratch, but has been extended with support for user-defined functions, and robust built-in libraries. The Snap! Cloud software has been running for over 5 years and recently passed 250,000 users and 2 million projects of which nearly 600,000 are shared publicly. We have been to do an exploratory analysis the database of public projects to better understand how students are programming an using Snap!. This analysis is being conducted using a cleaned up XML-based representation of Snap! projects, which allows querying for data using SQL to extract information from project files. So far, we've seen that projects in Snap! computationally more complex than those found in Scratch, and make use of Snap!'s advanced features. Combined with growing use, we hope to give context to the ways which Snap! (and other) blocks-based languages are being used in classrooms. While there has been a discussion of code smells in Scratch, we haven't seen any discussions using Snap! and hope to show its additional functionality helps write clean code. Finally, we are interested in presenting a clear story of growing use for Snap! that is a compelling case to teachers (and subsequently their students) that blocks-based languages can be quite popular.

Keywords: Snap!; visual programming language; blocks-based programming; cloud software; program analysis

DOI: https://doi.org/10.1145/3287324.3293863

ECS4Alabama: A State-Wide Effort to Provide Access to Authentic Computer Science Education in Predominantly Rural and High Minority Schools

Mohammed A. Qazi, *Tuskegee University*
Jeff Gray, *University of Alabama*
Melody Russell, *Auburn University*
David M. Shannon, *Auburn University*
Contact: mqazi@tuskegee.edu

This poster provides a description of an NSF-sponsored project entitled "ECS4Alabama" that addresses one of the nation's areas of highest priority in K-12 education: To offer all children opportunities for preparation in authentic Computer Science, with a specific focus on students from rural high-minority schools. ECS4Alabama addresses this need locally in Alabama by preparing teachers to offer a stand-alone, College preparatory Computer Science course - Exploring Computer Science (ECS) – in the participating high schools. Over the last two years, 52 in-service teachers have received training on ECS who in turn are teaching the course to nearly 1,500 students. Approximately 80% of the enrollment is minority and 48% of the students are young women. In many communities, ECS4Alabama is bringing access to challenging Computer Science curricula in school districts that often lack preparatory experiences that are typically only available to students in more affluent districts. Teachers Leaders are emerging and are spearheading Professional Development Communities to assist their peers with ECS implementation. In addition to sharing ECS4Alabama's implementation successes and challenges, the poster will also describe the project's rigorous evaluative and Social Science research components. Initial findings reveal that ECS professional development opportunities enhance teachers' self-efficacy and confidence in teaching CS through a problem-based, engaging curriculum that teachers view as relatable and relevant to students' daily lives. Students report that teachers make great efforts to facilitate their involvement in cognitively demanding work to solve real problems, encourage autonomy and stimulate student interest in CS.

ACM ISBN 978-1-4503-5890-3/19/02

Keywords: Exploring Computer Science; K-12; Under-represented minorities, Girls, Equity, Diversity, Mixed Methods Study

DOI: https://doi.org/10.1145/3287324.3293866

Don't Forget About Us: Understanding Rural and Small Town Principals' Values Toward Computer Science

Christopher Shively, *SUNY Buffalo State College*
Sarbani Banerjee, *SUNY Buffalo State College*
Neal Mazur, *SUNY Buffalo State College*
Joseph Zawicki, *SUNY Buffalo State College*
Contact: shivelct@buffalostate.edu

Buffalo State College has hosted a number of summer institutes and conferences over the years to increase the availability of computer science (CS) courses taught in western and central New York high schools. These institutes and conferences have contributed to strong CS programs in suburban and private schools, but not in urban and rural/small town schools. In the summer of 2018, Buffalo State invited high school principals from across the area to a summit to discuss the future of CS. Forty-six principals participated in the summit and of those school leaders, 30% of them were from rural/small towns. In this poster, the research team will present the results of a mixed-methods school leadership study based on the value rural/small town principals place on CS. Results from a survey, conducted at the summit, and semi-structured interviews will be presented. A sociocultural approach was used to analyze the data, since the principals' values and mediated actions toward CS were influenced by the socially situated environment of the schools they lead.

Handouts will be provided for all research results and a link to an online forum hosted by Buffalo State will be given so that the conversation can continue beyond the conference.

DOI: https://doi.org/10.1145/3287324.3293868

Integrated Stem+C Learning for K-2 Aged Children: Ct Skills as a Precursor to K-2 Computer Science Education

Tikyna M. Dandridge, Hoda Ehsan, Elizabeth Gajdzik
Tony Lowe, Carson Ohland, Ibrahim H. Yeter,
Sean Brophy, Monica E. Cardella, *Purdue University*
Contact: tdandrid@purdue.edu

As computer science education is incorporated into the United States educational system, it is imperative that children, educators, and caregivers understand the requisite competencies called "computational thinking" (CT). CT has advanced since first described by Wing in 2006 as an algorithmic problem-solving approach. For three years, the INSPIRE Research Institute for Pre-College Engineering (INSPIRE) has studied integrated science, technology, engineering, mathematics, and computational thinking (STEM+C) learning for K-2 aged children, in both formal and informal settings. At the project's origin, the team focused on characterizing and operationalizing the CT competencies. Our studies then followed how children, instructors, and families engaged in the CT competencies within school and out-of-school contexts. As the project evolved, our team created curricula to be used in K-2 classrooms, activities for out-of-school settings, a summer training for educators, a CT exhibit at a small Midwestern science center, and facilitated a field trip for elementary students. Our poster presents findings from all stages of our NSF-funded STEM+C project. For classroom settings, we report discoveries from integrated STEM+C curricula development and children's CT capabilities and engagement within the classroom and during homeschooling. For informal settings, we report children's abilities to engage in CT when engaging with a specially designed CT exhibit and an open-ended problem-solving task. We also discuss our data management for our project. Finally, we report the lessons and implications of CT for K-2 as a viable skill for computer science education. ***For additional information and findings, handouts will be given during poster presentation.***

Keywords: computational thinking; integrated STEM+C

DOI: https://doi.org/10.1145/3287324.3293870

Using an Intelligent Tutoring System to Teach Red Black Trees

Chun Wai Liew, *Lafayette College*
Huy Nguyen, *Carnegie Mellon University*
Contact: liewc@lafayette.edu

There are many tutoring systems that are being used to teach basic concepts in grade schools and high schools. There are few that address the issues involved in teaching complex skills and concepts such as are taught in CS2. We designed, developed and implemented an intelligent tutoring system (ITS) to help teach the concepts underlying red black trees. Red black trees are a balanced tree structure that are created and maintained with fairly complex insertion and deletion algorithms. The ITS helped the students improve their understanding of red black trees and also changed the instructors view of the causes of the students' difficulties. This paper describes effects on student learning, the lessons we learned from using the ITS and how it affected the way in which teach red black trees in our class. We have used the ITS for four years in our data structures class and it has benefited us in many ways.

Keywords: balanced trees;red black trees; CS2; tutoring systems

DOI: https://doi.org/10.1145/3287324.3293823

Code For Her: Exploring Female and Gender-Diverse Computing Workshops for Faculty, Staff, and Students

Joslenne Pena, Carmen Cole, Mary Beth Rosson,
The Pennsylvania State University
Contact: jop5190@psu.edu

Inspired by initiatives like Girls Who Code, the authors developed a similar learning opportunity in a higher education environment. Code for Her, a nine-week coding workshop series, was piloted to determine if interest existed in the academic community. With an overwhelming response (over 100 applicants), the authors saw a need in the community for an informal learning space targeting women and gender-diverse individuals. Currently, two distinct workshop sections, one for students and one for faculty and staff, are being conducted in a single academic semester, each focusing on learning three web development languages. The goal of this study is to investigate the impacts of the workshop series on its participants using a mixed methods approach. The authors will examine measures of self-efficacy, computing behavior, knowledge, and learning to determine, at an exploratory level, how the workshops have an effect on their learning, motivation, attitudes, and computational thinking. Preliminary results from a baseline survey indicate that keeping a flexible curriculum and learning environment is imperative to the ever-changing needs of participants week to week. Further, results indicate a slightly positive attitude towards achieving programming tasks, future predictors of their behavior after the workshop, and self-efficacy. The authors plan to conduct a post survey, collect participant projects as artifacts for analysis, and arrange follow-up focus groups to determine if participant attitudes, motivation, and retention of the content have changed over a period of time. The authors hope to improve future workshop offerings and expand our research efforts.

Keywords: coding workshop; gender and diversity; programming

DOI: https://doi.org/10.1145/3287324.3293852

Rubric to Evaluate Programming Learning of Elementary School Students

Daisuke Saito, Hironori Washizaki, Yoshiaki Fukazawa,
Waseda University
Mariko Tamura, Yuki Sakuragi, *D2C inc*
Contact: d.saito@fuji.waseda.jp

As more children are exposed to computer science and programming, numerous indicators have been proposed to evaluate programming learning. Because these indicators are not divided by step in a learning goal, learner's growth cannot be evaluated in detail. Our research focuses on resolving this issue in the field of programming. Herein we propose a rubric to measure

ACM ISBN 978-1-4503-5890-3/19/02

the progress of programming learning for elementary school students. This rubric, which is comprised of indices, aims to evaluate learning achievement of logical skills such as logical thinking and problem solving using a unified learning goal. Furthermore, this rubric consists of 30 evaluation items in 8 categories. Then we investigate whether this rubric can be adapted to existing workshops of programming learning. The workshops occurred in 2016 and 2017. in addition, A total of 101 students between 6 and 12 years old participated in the workshops. The rubric successfully evaluates programming learning workshops as it provides a unified evaluation that covers common learning objectives in existing indicators. Our rubric is available at https://g7programming.jp/plr/.

Keywords: Rubric; Programming Learning; Learning Evaluation

DOI: https://doi.org/10.1145/3287324.3293807

Giving Students Canned Code using Typing Exercises

Adam M. Gaweda, Collin F. Lynch,
North Carolina State University
Contact: agaweda@ncsu.edu

This poster presents two studies using typing exercises to provide worked examples of CS concepts that students retype through our online platform called TYPOS. In a usability and interaction study, 11 students completed typing, fill-in-the-blank, and self-explanation style exercises. Students with "Poor"-labeled self-explanations experienced more typing errors and took more time to complete exercises. In a semester-long study, 99 students in a CS2 course voluntarily completed 538 submissions of 66 weekly typing exercises. The students were classified into four groups: users that joined but never used the platform, users that barely used the platform, regular viewers of exercises, and regular completers of exercises. We found that the regular completers all earned a minimum final letter grade of a B in the course. But we also found that they were not simply high performing students that did additional work, as 40% of the completers scored a C or lower on the course's first midterm exam. Overall, students who used the system performed similarly or better than students who did not. Thus we conclude that typing exercises (and other novel exercises) can serve as a viable tool for teaching Computer Science and boosting low-performing students' abilities.

Keywords: typing exercises; worked examples

DOI: https://doi.org/10.1145/3287324.3293836

Using an Art Show in CS1 to Spark Interest in Computer Science

David L. Largent, *Ball State University*
Contact: dllargent@bsu.edu

Media computation provides a context within which computation can more easily be learned, allowing students to be creative while learning fundamental programming building blocks (like sequencing, iteration, selection, and two-dimensional arrays). Focusing on images, students can alter a picture's appearance by selectively changing its pixels. By combining different images, students can create collages. Creativity and success in CS1 have been studied. The effect media computation and an art show might have on student satisfaction and persistence, and promotion of the department is less understood. We articulate our experiences from five years of implementing media computation in CS1, with a strong focus on an accompanying public art show held to showcase the best student work produced each semester.

We implemented the art show with a goal of raising visibility of our department within the university, and to highlight the ability to be creative in a CS degree program, with the hope of attracting students. It also allows our students to showcase their work to their peers and others, while motivating them to be creative and engaged.

We briefly describe how we implement media computation within CS1 and describe in full detail how we conduct the public art show. Specifics about the student image collage project that is entered into the art show, the selection process, judging, show production, and promotion are provided. We describe how things have evolved over the ten shows spread over five years to provide perspective for others considering implementation of a similar experience for their students.

Keywords: Art show; Collage; Creativity; CS1; Department promotion; Media computation; Software project; Student engagement; Student motivation

DOI: https://doi.org/10.1145/3287324.3293861

ACM ISBN 978-1-4503-5890-3/19/02

Lightning Talks Session 1

Building a Community of Undergraduate Women: Ambassadors for Computing Outreach

Kathryn Atchison, Jandelyn Plane,
University of Maryland, College Park
Contact: katea@cs.umd.edu

This lightning talk describes the Maryland Center for Women in Computing (MCWIC) ambassador program that was designed to empower current undergraduate women to lead K-12 outreach efforts for MCWIC and build a community of within the undergraduate students interested in diversity, inclusion and education. For the last 7 years, the MCWIC ambassadors led summer camps, after school programs in schools, weekend workshops, and programs that support current undergraduate population. The program has grown to the point that we now employ over 15 undergraduate students each semester to support these activities. Come to this talk to learn more about how this program was created, how it is sustained, and how the ambassadors benefit from being a part of the program while also serving the greater community.

Keywords: community; outreach; women; undergraduate; K-12; growth; education; new programs

DOI: https://doi.org/10.1145/3287324.3293771

Introduction to Ipsative Assessment

Jared O'Leary, *BootUp PD*
Contact: jared@BootUpPD.org

This lightning talk introduces ipsative assessment, which is an assessment undertaken by a student for the purpose of learning through reflection of prior work. This process differs from self-assessment where students evaluate their own efforts or results without making connections to prior creations or demonstrations of understandings. I begin this session by briefly reviewing applications of formative and summative assessment techniques and then introduce ipsative assessment as another possibility for assessing student work. After this brief introduction, I elaborate by providing examples of how I used ipsative assessment within the K-8 coding classes I designed and facilitated, and conclude the lightning talk by sharing assessment resources I created for elementary CS education professional development.

Keywords: Assessment; Ipsative Assessment; Reflection; Self-assessment

DOI: http://dx.doi.org/10.1145/3287324.3293776

ACM ISBN 978-1-4503-5890-3/19/02

Sports Analytics as a Context for Computational Thinking in K-12 Education

Steven Paul Floyd, *Western University*
Contact: stevenpfloyd@gmail.com
Luigi Sorbara, *Boston Celtics, Fanshawe College*
Contact: luigi@celtics.com

As educational jurisdictions around the world begin to integrate computational thinking (CT) into their K-12 mandatory curriculum, there is a need to ensure that classroom activities are engaging, relate to student interests, and effectively promote the development of CT skills. The analysis of sports performance data fulfills this criteria for some students and teachers and presents an exciting context in which students from all K-12 grades can access complex CT concepts. This lightning talk investigates sports analytic tasks within the context of the CT in mathematics and science taxonomy introduced by Weintrop et al. (2015). Specific classroom activities are presented including analyzing the distribution of soccer goals, baseball salaries, the location of successful basketball shots, and the placement of volleyball serves. Examples of data analytics projects will be shared and the four main components of the taxonomy (data practices, modelling and simulation practices, computational problem-solving practices and systems thinking practices) will be identified within each project.

Keywords: K-12 education; computer science; computational thinking; sports; analytics; sports analytics; data analytics; modelling; mathematics;

DOI: https://doi.org/10.1145/3287324.3293773

Programming Politics: Using p5.js to Create Interactive Art Connected to Current Events

Jeremy H. Sarachan, *St. John Fisher College*
Contact: jsarachan@sjfc.edu

This lightning talk describes a proposal for a class that includes a mix of programming and politics. Students would use the p5.js library to learn basic programming, making this class appropriate to undergraduate non-majors. With a focus on interfacing with an audience, students learn variables and arrays, loops, if...then statements, text animation, and functions, as well as p5.js specific libraries for video and the Kinect. For a major/final project, students are asked to consider a social issue (e.g., poverty, global warming, gun reform) and create an interactive art exhibit using a PC, Kinect, keyboard, and/or mouse, and their choice of photography/graphics/video. All viewpoints are accepted. The integration of social science (e.g., Political Science, Sociology), humanities (e.g., American Studies, Gender Studies), and programming would offer a wide spectrum of students with an immediate and tangible product, while also broadening their concept of what can be accomplished and communicated through code. Additionally, students would study other example of interactive installations as a means to see what is possible and come to terms with what forms may constitute art. Most significantly, this alternative version of project-based learning would motivate students to apply and continue to learn what is necessary to implement their artistic vision and communicate their views. Furthermore, each student's unique project would minimize the risk of cheating and require students to synthesize not only specific programming tasks, but also an understanding of audience and concepts of usability relevant to the brief time a user may interact with the installation.

Keywords: p5.js; Javascript; CS1; Kinect; installation art; politics; social issues

DOI: https://doi.org/10.1145/3287324.3293762

Online Mob Programming: Effective Collaborative Project-Based Learning

Michael Hilton, Sreecharan Sankaranarayanan,
Carnegie Mellon University
Contact: mhilton@cs.cmu.edu; sreechas@cs.cmu.edu

This lightning talk presents an ongoing effort investigating the use of a collaborative programming paradigm originating in industry called Mob Programming, for effective collaborative learning in the classroom. In industry, Mob Programming involves the participation of a group of developers solving one problem at the same time and place. Developers take turns cycling through a structured process for collaboration having been assigned pre-defined roles responsible for brainstorming ideas, deciding on a path forward and implementing the consensus decision respectively. Pedagogically, there are several compelling reasons to motivate the adoption of Mob Programming in learning settings . First, the collaboration is well-structured meaning that the interaction between even a large group of students will not descend into chaos. Second, students are assigned to roles, which allows for the differentiation of responsibilities and development of skills in different aspects of solving the problem. Third, the rotation of assigned roles allows students to learn and exhibit multiple competencies as well as appreciate bringing different perspectives to bear on solving the problem. In order to investigate whether this promise is borne out in practice, the paradigm is currently being investigated in the context of a Cloud Computing course offered online to undergraduate and graduate students at a large American university and its satellite campuses. Since this effort is still underway, faculty who implement or are interested in implementing collaborative learning for this classrooms are invited to attend and provide feedback or consider joining the effort to investigate this paradigm for use in learning settings.

Keywords: Mob Programming; Online Mob Programming; Collaborative Learning; Project-Based Learning; Computer-Supported Collaborative Learning

DOI: http://doi.org/10.1145/3287324.3293774

Thinking about Computational Thinking: Lessons from Education Research

Shuchi Grover, *Looking Glass Ventures, LLC*
Contact: shuchi.grover@gmail.com

Computational thinking (CT) is a means to help learners engage in authentic disciplinary and problem-solving practices of computer science (CS). For CS classrooms, CT is considered "thinking like a computer scientist". CT is believed to be an important learning goal of introductory CS in addition to CS concepts and programming. Despite the growing attention on CT in K-12 CS education, there is lingering confusion on the what and how of CT, and CT's relationship to coding and CS. Education research on disciplinary thinking skills in science and mathematics education can provide guidance for teaching and learning of CT. For example, (a) The shift in emphasis on disciplinary thinking helps focus on deeper conceptual understanding rather than rote learning of knowledge and facts. Hence thinking like a scientist, or mathematician, historian or computer scientist, draws attention to authentic practices of those disciplines. (b) Thinking skills are best taught in context. Therefore, CT should be taught in CS classrooms or integrated into learning of other subjects rather than taught as a separate skill or subject. (c) Even if there is no transfer beyond the context in which they are taught, a focus on thinking skills helps in deeper conceptual learning; (d) Like critical or creative thinking, CT should be integrated into other subjects to enrich learning. Research on meaningful technology integration across subjects provides useful frameworks to inform CT integration efforts. This talk aims to productively move the discourse on CT toward concrete ideas for K-12 educators, researchers, and curricular designers.

Keywords: computational thinking; K-12 computer science; disciplinary thinking skills; problem solving

DOI: https://doi.org/10.1145/3287324.3293763

Assessing the Impact of Sustainability-Themed Programming Assignments

Jeffrey A. Stone, *Pennsylvania State University*

This lightning talk describes initial research to assess the impact of a set of multidisciplinary programming projects in introductory CS and IS courses. Students in these courses are given a series of programming projects designed around various components of sustainability (e.g. air pollution, wind power). These projects are intended to provide students with a lightweight, non-intrusive introduction to sustainability concepts while still assessing their ability to perform introductory programming tasks. This approach is intended to show students the applicability of programming towards sustainability concepts, but it is also intended help build students' knowledge and spark interest in applying sustainability concepts in their own communities and daily routine. Recently, we have undertaken an effort to more accurately assess the impact of these projects on students' knowledge, understanding, appreciation, and practice of sustainability concepts. Small post-project reflective writing exercises have been used to assess the influence that the sustainability-based projects have had on students' knowledge and behavior. This work has included initial development of custom reflective writing exercises and an accompanying grading rubric, as well as pre- and post-course surveys, but more work is needed to develop and/or refine these instruments and the overall approach. This assessment effort began in Spring 2018 and is currently in pilot. We are seeking additional interested faculty collaborators and feedback on the approach. Especially welcome are faculty who may have an interest in adopting and/or helping to develop assessment materials or sustainability-themed projects.

Keywords: CS1; sustainability; programming; active learning.

DOI: https://doi.org/10.1145/3287324.3293764

ACM ISBN 978-1-4503-5890-3/19/02

More than a Bootcamp, Less than a Degree: A One-Year Program to Retrain Industry Employees as Developers

Gail Carmichael, *Shopify*
Contact: authoremail@mandatoryhere.com

We are designing a year-long program for internal Shopify employees who want to retrain as software developers. Our aim is to provide a better base in core computer science concepts than boot camps, but be less comprehensive than a degree. The design leverages the best of our Dev Degree work-integrated learning program that combines developer skills training and team placements at Shopify with a fully accredited computer science degree. Participants will spend six months on education full time, and six months in a team at Shopify with some continuing education an hour or two a week. By the end of the program, participants will have the opportunity to join a team as a back-end web developer. Our lightning talk will share key aspects of the program design and solicit feedback offline.

Keywords: professional training; bootcamp; industry education

DOI: https://doi.org/10.1145/3287324.3293766

Experiences using Discord as Platform for Online Tutoring and Building a CS Community

Kenrick Mock, *University of Alaska Anchorage*
Contact: kjmock@alaska.edu

This lightning talk describes our experience using Discord as a platform for online tutoring at the University of Alaska Anchorage (UAA) for the past two and a half semesters. Discord is a free online chat system that is accessible via a web browser, computer program, or mobile app. It competes with apps including Skype, Slack, and TeamSpeak. We initially pitched Discord to our students as a way to deliver online tutoring. However, once a critical mass of students joined the system they began to use it for socializing, finding study partners, and other community-building activities. Utilization has been much higher than other online communication tools we have implemented in the past. With approximately 250 majors there are currently 261 users subscribed to our server with users actively posting messages every day. Students have reported positive experiences with the platform. To further facilitate tutoring in the future we are developing a bot and web tools into the platform to make it easier to share and run snippets of code.

Keywords: Online Tutoring; Student Engagement

DOI: https://doi.org/10.1145/3287324.3293769

A Research-Oriented EPIC Course – Applying Mobile Technologies to Biomedical Research Questions

Chen-Hsiang Yu, *Wentworth Institute of Technology*
Contact: yuj6@wit.edu

At Wentworth Institute of Technology, we have advocated Externally-collaborative, Project-based, Interdisciplinary Curricula (EPIC) learning for years. EPIC learning provides opportunities for the students from different majors to work together on interdisciplinary projects, which have been proved interesting, useful and influential to the students' future career, either academia or industry. In 2016, we reported the success of applying mobile application development to biomedical education for creating a mobile health system for the students. To extend this success, we spent one year designing and teaching a new research-oriented interdisciplinary EPIC course for guiding undergraduate students to conduct research projects in biomedical field. In this talk, I will summarize our learning from this process, including (1) Why is it more difficult to teach a research-oriented EPIC course than a regular course for undergraduate students from different majors? (2) How to conquer some difficulties found in this process? (3) How to design suitable lectures and laboratory assignments to facilitate research collaboration? (4) How to motivate the undergraduate students to work on research projects? Although three out of six student teams' research work were accepted at a research conference, we believe there is a space to improve this process for this kind of research-oriented EPIC course in the future.

Keywords: A research-oriented course; EPIC learning; mobile technologies

DOI: http://dx.doi.org/10.1145/3287324.3293777

Every Marathon Starts with the First Mile: Early Successes in Broadening Participation in K-12 CS

Carol L. Fletcher, *University of Texas at Austin*
Contact: carol.fletcher@utexas.edu

Broadening participation in K-12 CS education at a statewide level is a challenge that requires substantial structural changes that need to be addressed across the K-12 system. At the same time, it is vital to find early successes in order to build both political and financial support for broadening participation in computing (BPC) efforts. Leadership teams from Expanding Computing Education Pathways (ECEP) Alliance states are responding to these two apparently conflicting drivers as they develop goals and metrics that measure outcomes that are both realistic in the short term and that will lead to long-term success. This lightening talk will discuss a framework for goal development used by Texas that addresses four interdependent components of the K-12 CS education system: capacity, access, participation, and equity. Focusing on measurable outcomes for each of these components can both lead to early "wins" that are meaningful and easily communicated to stakeholders and that lay the foundation for substantive changes in CS engagement and success for students from traditionally underrepresented groups including women, students of color, and students of low socio-economic status.

Keywords: Equity; policy; K-12 computing; broadening participation; teacher; professional development

DOI: https://doi.org/10.1145/3287324.3293760

ACM ISBN 978-1-4503-5890-3/19/02

Lightning Talks Session 2

Micro-Volunteering and Virtual-Volunteering as Pedagogical Tools in Computer Science Instruction

Valerie Summet, *Rollins College*
Contact: vsummet@rollins.edu

Many universities and students look for opportunities to volunteer and contribute to their communities in a variety of ways. However, a host of factors including time, expense, and duration effect instructor adoption, student commitment and student perception of volunteer tasks. In CS curriculums, volunteer work most often takes the form of projects for local charities through a specific course (e.g., a senior capstone or software engineering course) or work in local elementary schools teaching younger students to program. The purpose of this talk is to stimulate a conversation about low-cost, low-commitment ways to incorporate service learning via micro-volunteering and virtual-volunteering into CS classes as pedagogically relevant assignments. Micro-volunteering refers to volunteer actions which take little time (usually less than 30 minutes) and have no expectation of continued involvement. Virtual-volunteering is defined as volunteering which a person can complete via the Internet from any location. While there exist many opportunities for semester-long, service learning-based projects in upper level courses, there is a lack of practical project ideas and assignments which could be incorporated into courses of all levels on a smaller scale. The goal of this project is to develop concrete assignments and short projects which incorporate micro- and virtual-volunteer opportunities in a variety of core Computer Science courses including introductory and non-major courses.

Keywords: service education; volunteering

DOI: https://doi.org/10.1145/3287324.3293775

5 Lessons on Supporting CSforAll in K12 School Districts

Rafi Santo, *CSforAll*
Contact: rafi.santo@nyu.edu

This lightning talk shares emerging lessons on helping K12 school districts plan around CSforAll. The CSed community rightly spends a lot time thinking about what CS to teach and how to teach it. And as efforts to bring CSed to K12 schools grow, we're starting to think more about how to support teachers through effective professional development. But we don't really know a lot about how the institutional contexts in which CSforAll efforts will succeed, or, potentially, fail - K12 districts - can approach CSed holistically. If we want to reach all kids, then districts are going to be a key leverage point to ensure that CSed efforts are equitable, rigorous and sustainable. We also know that they're incredibly complex systems that are difficult to change.

ACM ISBN 978-1-4503-5890-3/19/02

In this talk we share lessons emerging from a research-practice partnership with sixteen K12 school districts. Based on studying how these districts have engaged in strategic planning and decision making, we share five emerging lessons for supporting K12 districts on their journey to make CSforAll to their schools. We focus on (1) the importance answering the question of "why CS for all students?", (2) developing a local definition of what 'counts' as CS learning goals, (3) mapping existing activities and expertise related to CS, (4) integrating CSed efforts not just with existing curricula but also broader, existing institutional infrastructures, and (5) establishing coherence across learning goals, professional development, curricula and a guiding vision for CS education in a district.

Keywords: K12 school districts; education policy implementation; CS for All

DOI: https://doi.org/10.1145/3287324.3293767

Promoting Mastery Learning in an Introductory Programming Course

Paul Salvador Inventado,
California State University Fullerton
Contact: pinventado@fullerton.edu

Programming is a complex skill requiring computational thinking, knowledge of the programming language, and the ability to distinguish, combine, and manipulate appropriate components to solve a problem. Practice is an effective strategy for teaching programming because it fosters skill mastery especially when students get sufficient experience and feedback. However, properly implementing programming practice is difficult because instructors need to assign appropriate problems for each student, evaluate solutions, and provide feedback. We conducted a pilot study on an introductory C++ programming class that applied mastery learning to optimize practice, used a repository of programming problems to reduce instructor effort, and leveraged unit tests to provide feedback and facilitate grading. The class had a lecture component to introduce programming concepts and a lab component for practice. We used mastery learning to control the number of practice-problems students solved on a topic before moving to a more advanced one. We assumed mastery when students answered three programming problems correctly in a row without help. If they sought help, they had to successfully solve a new set of three problems in a row. We also assumed mastery if they solved ten problems because it should have given them sufficient practice. We observed that experienced students asked fewer questions and quickly progressed across topics, while other students got much-needed help from instructors. The repository saved time for preparing problems and the unit tests helped answer students' low-level questions. Unit tests already checked students' solutions against expected results, so it significantly reduced checking time.

Keywords: mastery learning; introductory programming; unit testing; programming problem repository

DOI: https://doi.org/10.1145/3287324.3293780

Teaching RSA: What Happens When One of Your Primes Isn't?

Barry Fagin, *US Air Force Academy*
Contact: barry.fagin@usafa.edu

Once you introduce RSA and probabilistic primality testing to your cryptography class, one of your brighter students will ask "What happens if the test is wrong?" It turns out the answer can vary from "You'll find out immediately" to "It makes no difference" to "It depends". We explain the mathematics that determine where the answer lies, and illustrate with examples suitable for use in the undergraduate classroom. We conclude by showing how to construct a key pair that produces correct RSA results from composite numbers p and q, and thus whose composite nature is not detectable through RSA encryption and decryption alone.

Suppose you are teaching RSA, and your students have just learned about probabilistic primality detection. Someone in the front row is likely to ask: "What happens if a composite number passes the test?" You might say "That's a great question. When you encrypt and then decrypt, you won't get the message back." You might then head to the board to show an example. It turns out, however, that if you pick the wrong numbers, you'll be in for a surprise.

Keywords: cryptography; cryptography education; RSA; number theory; discrete mathematics

DOI: https://doi.org/10.1145/3287324.3293761

Recognizing and Questioning the CT Education Paradigm

Vance Kite, Soonhye Park, Eric Wiebe
North Carolina State University
Contact: vkite@ncsu.edu

In 1962, Thomas Kuhn changed our understanding of scientific progress through his explanation of scientific paradigms and attribution of scientific advances to paradigm shifts. According to Kuhn, a discipline's paradigm drives research, provides explanations, and directs the accumulation of discipline-specific knowledge. In 2006 and 2008 Jeanette Wing authored articles that reignited interest in computational thinking (CT) education and CT education research. Wing's articles, arguably, set in place the conceptual foundations of the paradigm currently guiding CT education and paved the way for a fruitful decade of CT education research. We are concerned, however, that the present direction of CT education and research will not support CT as an integral part of K-12 education. In its current form, CT instruction focuses almost exclusively on teaching students to program and isolates CT from disciplinary content; perpetuating the persistent misconception that programming = CT. This approach to CT education may deprive students of the opportunity to adequately develop foundational CT skills (e.g. systems thinking, abstraction and generalization, data collection and utilization, solution evaluation) and may prevent teachers from persistently and meaningfully integrating CT into their curriculum. Through this talk, we identify features of the current CT paradigm, question their alignment with Wing's ideal of "computational thinking for everyone," and propose specific recommendations for expanding the current CT paradigm.

Keywords: computational thinking; computational thinking paradigm

DOI: https://doi.org/10.1145.32873224.3293765

Consistency when Teaching Multiple Sections: Live Lecture Recordings Reviewed and Discussed with Students

Olivera Grujic, *University of Southern California*
Contact: grujic@usc.edu

Recent popularity of computer science courses has caused class enrollments to skyrocket to mega level of several hundred students. Due to space and other constraints, multiple sections of each class are often taught by the same instructor. Students attending different section are taking the same exam, which requires the instructor to keep teaching repeating lectures consistently. This can be difficult and is further complicated by the varying number of students and questions posed during different sections. The lightning talk explores one faculty's solution to lecture consistency issue by making use of technology in the classroom: review and discussion of lecture recordings with students in attendance. All lectures were recorded during the first session. During the subsequent session, those recordings were played back to students in attendance on the large projector screen. This practice offered the opportunity to the instructor to further clarify concepts taught in class and receive continuous feedback how to improve her teaching in addition to delivering consistent lectures. More importantly, it offered students an opportunity to hear the questions asked by the students in attendance of the recorded session, before asking their own or offering additional discussion points. Class participation increased significantly as a result of this practice.

Keywords: Consistency Teaching Lectures; Technology in Classroom; Student Attendance and Participation

DOI: https://doi.org/10.1145/3287324.3293768

Improving Access to Internships with an On-Campus Software Development Center

Zachary J. Oster, *University of Wisconsin-Whitewater*
Contact: osterz@uww.edu

Internships are widely recognized as a high-impact educational practice that effectively prepares students for successful careers in the computing industry. Unfortunately, not all students have equal access to computing internships. Students are often expected to find internships independently, but their classes generally do not teach them the skills needed to search for computing internships or to succeed in a technical interview. Furthermore, at a university in a rural area with little or no public transportation, students may not be able to accept an internship offer unless they have a car and enough time to travel to and from a work site in a nearby city. These problems are especially severe for students of opportunity (e.g., students with low socioeconomic status, first-generation students): the exact students for whom an internship can have the greatest impact. To address this problem, our university is starting a software development center to provide campus-based internships in which student teams develop software products for clients. Students hired by the center will benefit from dedicated

SIGCSE '19, February 27-March 2, 2019, Minneapolis, MN, USA.

ACM ISBN 978-1-4503-5890-3/19/02

workspace on or near our campus, ongoing training in common software development practices (e.g., version control, project management, requirements engineering) that are not covered consistently in a classroom setting, and on-site mentoring from experienced software professionals. We believe that this co-curricular experience will improve participants' ability to begin and persist in a career in software development after graduation. We will discuss our experience with several pilot projects and our vision and goals for the center.

Keywords: Internships; Industry partnerships; Software engineering

DOI: https://doi.org/10.1145/3287324.3293779

Increase K-12 Cyber Competency to Prevent Cyberbullying

Rachel Stange, *Sherando High School & Lord Fairfax Community College*
Contact: rms25145@email.vccs.edu

The efforts of a Generation Z student to improve K-12 cyber competency through curriculum design and educator professional development, is having a positive impact in Virginia. School Systems in Virginia and across the nation tend to focus on cyber bullying as the primary issue. The issue that is not addressed is what cyber mechanisms allow cyber bullying to occur. This is often due to administrators and educators themselves not understanding what cyber competencies are needed to protect oneself in today's technological world. Studies show that social engineering, hacking and defending, cyber awareness, and personal connections have more impact on Generation Z and Generation Alpha students. My efforts started out to help my peers and have spiraled into a crusade to improve cyber competency of K-12 students and educators. One school system has created a Digital Citizenship Committee to support the concept of cyber competency beyond just teaching cybersecurity courses to a select few. This is a pay forward approach as the student leading the charge was impacted by two other students who were bullied through cyber stalking and classroom discussion boards. This effort is being aided by national organizations such as Safe Surfin' Foundation, National Center for Women & IT (NCWIT), and National CyberWatch Center. My presentation will show attendees how to expand this movement into their community to help slow down some of the cyber challenges facing Generation Z and beyond.

Keywords: Cyber Security, Cyber Awareness, Cyber Bullying, K-12 Educator PD, Curriculum Issues, Ethics, K-12 Curriculum, K-12 Instruction, Learning Environment, Privacy/Security, Problem Solving, Generation Z and beyond

DOI: https://doi.org/10.1145/3287324.3293770

Historical High School Computer Science Curriculum and Current K-12 Initiatives

Steven Paul Floyd, *Western University*
Contact: stevenpfloyd@gmail.com

It's an exciting time in computer science education on the K-12 landscape. Educational jurisdictions around the world are incorporating computer science concepts, as well as related computational thinking components, into their mandatory, K-12 curriculum. As we develop and implement curriculum initiatives with an eye on the future and the 21st century learner and citizen, what wisdom can we gleam from the past?

In Ontario, Canada computer science education dates back to 1966 with the release of the Ministry of Education's Data Processing course that included a number of computer science and computer programming concepts and ideas. The document also frames computer education within the context of an emerging field and highlights the importance of students developing appropriate computer skills in to thrive in the labour market and society. While we often consider computer science curriculum initiatives in K-12 education nascent, are important historical policy and initiatives being overlooked? This lightning talk encourages curriculum policy makers, educators and researchers to situate their current computer science curriculum initiatives within a historical context and to search for best practice in previous policies from their own educational jurisdictions.

Keywords: K-12 education; curriculum; computer science; computing; computational thinking; historical analysis; educational policy; computer programming; 21st century learning

DOI: https://doi.org/10.1145/3287324.3293772

Improving Retention through Team-Based Learning Finch Labs and Peer-Educators in Intro to Programming

Sotirios Kentros, Manish Wadhwa, Lakshmidevi Sreeramareddy, Komalpreet Kaur, *Salem State University*
Contact: skentros@salemstate.edu

We have introduced Peer-Educators through the Supplemental Instruction program and four Team-Based Learning laboratory assignments in our Introduction to Programming course. These four laboratory assignments are using Finch Robots to facilitate student comprehension of basic object-oriented programming concepts. In contrast to other lab assignments, Finch labs are team-based activities that revolve around programming Finch, a programmable robot to do activities like moving, sensing the environment, playing music, etc. Introducing the Finch labs has multiple benefits for the students. It helps better anchor the basic concepts of object-oriented programming, since interacting with the Finch robot is done by instantiating a Finch object and performing method calls on the object. This helps students understand many of the object oriented topics of the course, like object instantiation, method calls, passing arguments to a method and changing the state of an object. Furthermore, the labs facilitate peer learning in a natural way, since students group to work on a physical object. The goal of our intervention is to increase retention in our introduction to programming offerings. We are currently on the third year of our project and after having concluded in the interventions we want to adopt we are evaluating them through post-activity surveys, end of the semester surveys and comparison of retention data.

Keywords: Introduction to Programming; Peer Learning; Active Learning; Supplemental Instruction; Finch Robots; Object-oriented Programming; Retention

DOI: https://doi.org/10.1145/3287324.3293781

ACM ISBN 978-1-4503-5890-3/19/02

Demonstrations

Applying Bioinformatics to Assignment Evaluation: A New Approach for Pattern Recognition in Open-Ended CS Assignments

Seth Haberman, Kereb Perry-Shamir, *Sense Education*
Contact: keren@sense.education

At universities around the world, class sizes in Computer Science and other STEM courses are rapidly growing, as these skills become increasingly sought after in the marketplace, promising lucrative careers to graduates. Staffing-up to support the influx of students in this field presents challenges of its own. Hiring and training TAs to allow for quality and personal interactions with students, even as the class sizes grow, is expensive and difficult to maintain. Existing tools provide some automation by focusing mainly on output correctness but often overlook the student's approach to solving a problem. A solution is required in order to provide high-quality personalized feedback to very large numbers of student submissions for open-ended assignments, and in the timeframe that will keep today's instant-feedback-seeking students moving forward and not discouraged. The Sense platform utilizes algorithms from bioinformatics and genomics to identify patterns in student submissions and quickly surface insights about how students solved a problem. This enables the educator to provide rapid, equitable, in-depth feedback to each and every student, regardless of class size, and to use insights gained from this process to optimize their teaching methods and choice of assignments. In our presentation, we will show how our system identifies patterns in student submissions and uses those to generate clusters of students who have approached the problem in a similar way. We will use this time to facilitate a discussion about the specific insights that can be gleaned from the results for the students and for the educator.

Keywords: feedback; assessment; personalized education; optimizing content

DOI: https://doi.org/10.1145/3287324.3293752

Integrating Computational Modeling in K-12 STEM Classrooms

Gautam Biswas, Nicole Hutchins, Ákos Lédeczi,
Vanderbilt University
Shuchi Grover, *Looking Glass Ventures*
Satabdi Basu, *SRI International*
Contact: gautam.biswas@vanderbilt.edu

C2STEM is a web-based learning environment founded on a novel paradigm that combines block-structured, visual programming with the concept of domain specific modeling languages (DSMLs) to promote the synergistic learning of discipline-specific and computational thinking (CT) concepts and practices. Our design-based, collaborative learning environment aims to provide students in K-12 classrooms with immersive experiences in CT through computational modeling in realistic scenarios (e.g., building models of scientific phenomena). The goal is to increase student engagement and include inclusive opportunities for developing key computational skills needed for the 21st century workforce. Research implementations that include a semester-long high school physics classroom study have demonstrated the effectiveness of our approach in supporting synergistic learning of STEM and CS/CT concepts and practices, especially when compared to a traditional classroom approach. This technology demonstration will showcase our CS+X (X = physics, marine biology, or earth science) learning environment and associated curricula. Participants can engage in our design process and learn how to develop curricular modules that cover STEM and CS/CT concepts and practices. Our work is supported by an NSF STEM+C grant and involves a multi-institutional team comprising Vanderbilt University, SRI International, Looking Glass Ventures, Stanford University, Salem State University, and ETR. More information, including example computational modeling tasks, can be found at C2STEM.org.

Keywords: computational thinking; CS+X; modeling; K12

DOI: https://doi.org/10.1145/3287324.3293757

Building Simple Games With BRIDGES

David Burlinson, Erik Saule, Kalpathi Subramanian,
The Universityof North Carolina at Charlotte
Contact: krs@uncc.edu

Many newcomers to programming and computational thinking have been brought up on interactive, gamified learning environments. Introductory computer science courses at the university level need to dig deeper into these topics, but must do so with similarly engaging technologies and projects. To address this need, we have built a framework for a grid-based game API with event-based blocking and continuous non-blocking interfaces. The framework abstracts away much of the complexity of inputs and rendering and exposes a simple game grid similar to a 2D array indexed by rows and columns. As such, our project helps reinforce basic computing concepts (arrays, loops, OOP, recursion) with a customizable and engaging game interface. We have discussed the valuable influence of visual representations of student's data structures using BRIDGES in previous publications, and believe our game API can provide significance and intrigue for students in introductory courses and beyond. Our Bridges Games App website (http://bridges-games.herokuapp.com/) presents descriptions and instructions.

Keywords: 2d games; visualization; game grid

DOI: https://doi.org/10.1145/3287324.3293758

ACM ISBN 978-1-4503-5890-3/19/02

Engaging in Logical Code Reasoning with an Activity-Based Online Tool

Joseph E. Hollingsworth, *Rose-Hulman Insitute of Technology*
Eileen T. Kraemer, Murali Sitaraman, *Clemson University*
Contact: hollings@rose-hulman.edu

Using freely available online automated reasoning tools, we will demonstrate a sequence of engaging reasoning activities that are suitable to introduce beginning programmers and software engineering students to reason logically and symbolically about code. The automated tools have an underlying verification engine that makes it possible for the tool to offer activities and directed logical feedback not possible with typical development environments. The tools have been used in undergraduate classrooms for multiple years by well over a thousand students. The imperative language used by the tool is integrated with the underlying verification engine, and because it closely resembles many commercial languages, it presents little barrier to student usage. A comprehensive activity-based "Reason with Components" tool takes 5-10 minutes of instructor introduction and allows student exploration of contracts, objects, loops, recursion, and reusable concepts. Multiple versions of "Begin to Reason" tools are designed to help students learn the basics of code tracing in intro CS courses "on their own". Students and instructors can create new activities and can fine-tune the existing activities to their specific needs. Attendees can pair, share, and engage in the activities on their own laptops during the demo.

Keywords: active learning; code tracing; contracts; online tool; symbolic reasoning

DOI: https://doi.org/10.1145/3287324.3293754

Hands-on Cybersecurity Exercises that are Easy to Access

Richard Weiss, *Evergreen State College*
Jens Mache, *Lewis and Clark College*
Contact: weissr@evergreen.edu

The critical shortage of cyber security professionals has driven faculty interest in adding this to the curriculum, and it was added to the ACM/ IEEE Model Curriculum of 2013. This is a subject that demands hands-on exercises. There has been a modest increase in the number of such exercises, but the limit is usability. Most faculty do not have the time to create their own exercises, modify and install VMs, and set up assessment mechanisms. EDURange is a framework for accessing, developing and assessing interactive cybersecurity exercises. It has a range of exercises from introductory to advanced. We will demo an introductory exercise about using the command line and an advanced exercise about network scanning. We want to reach and engage as many faculty as possible, so that they can develop their own exercises. EDURange uses VMs in the cloud. Students only need an ssh-client. We have built tools to give faculty detailed information on how students are doing. This allows instructors to more easily see when students are stuck or heading in the wrong direction. The exercises we have created have manuals that instructors can use. Information about EDURange can be found at https://edurange.org.

Keywords: cybersecurity, hands-on exercise

DOI: https://doi.org/10.1145/3287324.3293759

Gamifying Computer Science Courses with OneUp

Keith Irwin, Austin Hodge, Darina Dicheva,
Winston-Salem State University
Contact: dichevad@wssu.edu

The low performance and drop-outs in Computer Science classes are frequently attributed to lack of engagement and motivation. Meanwhile, gamification – the application of game design principles and game mechanics to a non-game context – increasingly attracts the interest of educators due to its potential to foster motivation and behavioral changes in learning contexts. This Demo will introduce OneUp Learning, a platform aimed at facilitating the gamification of academic courses. OneUp enables instructors to define course activities and create exercise problems for practicing and self-assessment, as well as exams or quizzes for testing particular skills. The platform enables gamifying these practice activities. It is highly configurable and supports tailoring gamification features to meet the vision of the instructor. The gamification related configuration includes the choice of the game elements to be used along with specification of gaming rules for them. The system currently supports the following game elements: points (challenge points, skill points, and activity points), progress bar, virtual currency, badges, leaderboard, skill board, learning dashboard, and avatars. In the demo, we will show interested instructors how they can use OneUp in their classes. In particular, we will show them how to create problems and challenges, how to configure the gamification features they like to use, how to define their own badges, how to define rules for earning and spending virtual currency (in the course shop), and how to monitor the engagement and progress of their students. This work is supported by the NSF under Grants HBCU-UP TIP-1623236 and DUE-1821189.

Keywords: Gamified learning; course gamification; student engagement

DOI: https://doi.org/10.1145/3287324.3293751

Code Defenders: A Mutation Testing Game

Gordon Fraser, *University of Passau*
Contact: gordon.fraser@uni-passau.de

Software testing is an essential skill for software developers, but it is challenging to get students engaged in this activity. The Code Defenders game aims to address this problem by letting students compete over code under test by either introducing faults ("attacking") or by writing tests ("defending") to reveal these faults. We have empirically established that the game is engaging and players write better tests than outside the game scenario, and we have successfully integrated Code Defenders as a semester-long activity of an undergraduate and graduate level university course on software testing. This demonstration provides an introduction to Code Defenders from a student point of view (How to play the game?) as well as from a teacher point of view (How to set up

SIGCSE '19, February 27-March 2, 2019, Minneapolis, MN, USA.

ACM ISBN 978-1-4503-5890-3/19/02

games for my students, and how to integrate the game into my course?) A laptop is recommended to join in and try out the game.

Keywords: Software testing education; mutation analysis; testing game; software engineering education; unit testing

DOI: https://doi.org/10.1145/3287324.3293753

An Interactive, Graphical Simulator for Teaching Operating Systems

Joshua W. Buck, *University of Dayton*
Saverio Perugini, *University of Dayton*
Contact: saverio@udayton.edu

We demonstrate a graphical simulation tool for visually and interactively exploring the processing of a variety of events handled by an operating system when running a program. Our graphical simulator is available for use on the web by both instructors and students for purposes of pedagogy. Instructors can use it for live demonstrations of course concepts in class, while students can use it outside of class to explore the concepts. The graphical simulation tool is implemented using the React library for the fancy ui elements of the Node.js framework and is available as a web application at https://cpudemo.azurewebsites.net. The goals of this demonstration are to showcase the demonstrative capabilities of the tool for instruction, share student experiences in developing the engine underlying the simulation, and to inspire its use by other educators. An article describing this software simulation and demonstrating its pedagogical capabilities is available at https://arxiv.org/abs/1812.05160.

Keywords: Node.js; operating systems pedagogy; process scheduling; React library; semaphore processing.

DOI: https://doi.org/10.1145/3287324.3293756

NetsBlox and Wireless Robots Make Cybersecurity Fun

Ákos Lédeczi, *Vanderbilt University*
Hamid Zare, *Vanderbilt University*
Gordon Stein, *Vanderbilt University*
Contact: akos.ledeczi@vanderbilt.edu

NetsBlox (https://netsblox.org) is a web-based collaborative learning environment extending Snap! with a few carefully selected abstractions that enable students to create distributed applications. These include online multi-player games and client-server applications that access online STEAM data such as maps, weather, earthquakes, movie information, etc. The distributed computing abstractions supported by NetsBlox also make it possible to write robot control programs. These programs issue wireless commands to the robots which in turn reply with acknowledgements and sensor readings. The programs run in the browser making debugging much easier and eliminating the need to download anything to the robots. Furthermore, the environment makes it possible for other users to eavesdrop on the wireless messages and hijack the robots of others. This provides an excellent motivation for cybersecurity and makes it easy to teach it in a hands-on manner. We have created a cybersecurity curriculum for a week-long summer camp for high school students. Lessons include Denial of Service attacks, their detection and mitigation, cryptography, secure key exchange, replay attacks, etc. Each day student teams solve challenge problems that their robots have to carry out while under cyber-attack by the other participants. This technology demonstration is a companion to the paper "Teaching Cybersecurity with Networked Robots." It will provide the audience with a more practical view of this novel approach to hands-on cybersecurity education.

Keywords: visual programming; robotics; cybersecurity; K12

DOI: https://doi.org/10.1145/3287324.3293749

Blocks4All: Making Blocks-Based Programming Languages Accessible for Children with Visual Impairments

Lauren R. Milne, *Macalester College*
Richard E. Ladner, *University of Washington*
Contact: lmilne@macalester.edu

Block-based programming environments such as Scratch are designed to make programming easier to learn for both children and adults. Unfortunately, these environments rely so heavily on visual features that they are inaccessible to people who are blind and use screen readers. To address this problem, we created Blocks4All, a block-based environment for the Apple iPad, which uses the touchscreen and VoiceOver, the built-in screen reader for iOS, to help make the environment accessible. Blocks4All differs from existing block-based environments in three main ways: (1) it uses select, select, drop instead of drag and drop to move blocks, (2) the blocks are placed on the bottom of the screen and are a fixed size so that they can easily be found by touch even without sight, and (3) it uses both audio and spatial cues to convey information about statements nested inside repeat loops and conditionals. In our presentation, we will show the features we developed and demonstrate how to write code that uses both conditional statements and repeat loops. We anticipate the demo will be useful both for instructors with students with visual impairments and developers of block-based environments. Handouts will be provided that describe Blocks4All and information about how to download a beta version.

Keywords: block-based programming languages; accessibility; students with disabilities; introductory programming environments; visual impairments

DOI: https://doi.org/10.1145/3287324.3293755

CodeBuddy (Collaborative Software Development Environment): In- & Out-Class Practice for Remote Pair-Programming with Monitoring Coding Students' Progress

Teerapong Leelanupab, Tiwipab Meephruek,
King Mongkut's Institute of Technology Ladkrabang
Contact: teerapong@it.kmitl.ac.th

Pair-programming is an Agile technique in Extreme Programming (XP) where traditionally two programmers need to be collocated

ACM ISBN 978-1-4503-5890-3/19/02

and work together at one workstation. Previous research has shown that pair-programming is very beneficial in software engineering education. However, learning and practicing pair-programming are mostly limited in a class where students can only learn to collaboratively program with another student in controlled or laboratory settings. Although nowadays there exist some collaborative tools, such as CodePilot, Google Colaboratory and Git, they are not specifically pair-programming-oriented. This impedes a pairing's ability to discuss effective strategies in problem solving, to form productive or mutually learning pairs, and to predict pair compatibility. To encourage students in out-class practice of pair-programming, we present a demonstration of a novel web-based software development environment, called CodeBuddy, for remote pair-programming. CodeBuddy provides instructors and students with several features for managing laboratory classes and practicing pair-programming. Examples of CodeBuddy's features include: coding screen mirroring between a pair, output terminal to show compiled results, face-to-face like communication channels (i.e., video calling and instant text messaging), automatic and manual role switching, code quality analysis for monitoring coding students' progress and recommending a pair with targeted pairing goals, implicit code reviews using face detection for tracking a reviewer's engagement, line-by-line code commenting, etc. The demonstration consists of a walkthrough of two use-case scenarios: an instructor assigns a problem-solving task and two students remotely work together in a pair using CodeBuddy on two different workstations to solve it.

Keywords: Pair Programming; Remote Collaboration and Learning; Agile Software Development; Software Engineering

DOI: https://doi.org/10.1145/3287324.3293750

ACM ISBN 978-1-4503-5890-3/19/02

ACM SRC: ACM Student Research Competition

Subgoals, Problem Solving Phases, and Sources of Knowledge

Kevin Lin, David DeLiema,
University of California, Berkeley
Contact: kevinlin1@berkeley.edu

Educational researchers have increasingly drawn attention to how students develop computational thinking (CT) skills, including in science, math, and literacy contexts. A key component of CT is the process of abstraction, a particularly challenging concept for novice programmers, but one vital to problem solving. We propose a framework based on situated cognition that can be used to document how instructors and students communicate about abstractions during the problem solving process. We develop this framework in a multimodal interaction analysis of a 32-minute long excerpt of a middle school student working in the PixelBots JavaScript programming environment at a two-week summer programming workshop taught by undergraduate CS majors. Through a microgenetic analysis of the process of teaching and learning about abstraction in this excerpt, we document the extemporaneous prioritization of subgoals and the back-and-forth coordination of problem solving phases. In our case study, we identify that (a) problem solving phases are nested with several instances of context-switching within a single phase; (b) the introduction of new ideas and information creates bridges or opportunities to move between different problem solving phases; (c) planning to solve a problem is a non-linear process; and (d) pedagogical moves such as modeling and prompting highlight situated resources and advance problem solving. Future research should address how to help students structure subgoals and reflect on connections between problem solving phases, and how to help instructors reflect on their routes to supporting students in the problem solving process.

Keywords: Computational Thinking; Education; Situated Cognition; Debugging; Abstraction; Problem Solving

DOI: https://doi.org/10.1145/3287324.3293712

Young Aspirants Developer Contest

Vinitha Subburaj, *West Texas A&M University*
Jacob McInite, *West Texas A&M University*
Jordan Fite, *West Texas A&M University*
Petterson Pham, *West Texas A&M University*
Contact: pnpham1@buffs.wtamu.edu

Online contests often have a wide skill range between each participant, making it feel overwhelming for high school students to compete in. On sites like HackerRank or TopCoder, students could be competing against professionals with years of work. The project narrows down the skill gap to a young audience so that they can compete against one another without having to compete with these professionals. In addition, this project provides the participants with the necessary environment and tools to run their programs without the hassle of having to installing necessary tools and its required files to run these programs. During the contest, participants can access a scoreboard, giving them a view of their progress against other participants. The purpose of the scoreboard is to show each participant their progress, as well as motivating them to achieve higher scores. The contest tool then grades based on time before correctness to provide fairness towards most students as the goal to solve problems early rather than optimize their program. With this, the focus is to improve their problem solving skills, pique curiosity, or serve as an impetus, to become a computer science engineering student.

Keywords: Education; Programming; Computers and Society; Student Involvement; Online Programming Contest;

DOI: https://doi.org/10.1145/3287324.3293713

Problem Decomposition in Introductory Computer Science and Spatial Reasoning

Ka Ki Fung, *Claremont McKenna College*
Thitaree Tanprasert, *Harvey Mudd College*
Contact: kfung20@cmc.edu

Previous research has documented correlations between spatial reasoning ability and success in STEM fields [7-9]. While connection between spatial reasoning and other STEM fields like physics and calculus may seem obvious, there are no theories to explain this correlation of CS (computer science) performance and spatial reasoning. [5,7,8]. We aim to better understand this correlation, specifically between CS performance in an introductory course and spatial reasoning by observing the common characteristics between students' strategies in solving CS and spatial reasoning problems. We conducted interviews with eight students who have prior experience in CS but have taken only two introductory CS courses. In the interview, we asked the participants to solve a total of four problems; two CS problems and two spatial reasoning problems. [1,6]. The CS problems were code-reading problems in Python, which focus on basic programming concepts, including nested loops and functions. We analyzed the participants' problem-solving strategies and recorded their explanation for each problem. We observed for both types of problem, participants appeared to first observe the problem for its fundamental structures then decomposes the problem into smaller sub-problems. We conjecture that problem decomposition may be a required skill to solve both CS and spatial reasoning problems, and thus, could be a possible factor that contributes to the correlation between the two fields. Further study into utilization of problem decomposition in CS and spatial reasoning may provide more insights into the correlation between success in CS and spatial reasoning ability.

Keywords: problem decomposition; computer programming; introductory CS, problem solving; spatial reasoning

DOI: https://doi.org/10.1145/3287324.3293710

SIGCSE '19, February 27-March 2, 2019, Minneapolis, MN, USA.

ACM ISBN 978-1-4503-5890-3/19/02

Accessible American Sign Language Recognition with the Leap Motion Controller

Sarah Almeda, *The College of New Jersey*
Contact: almedas1@tcnj.edu

Communities that use visual languages like American Sign Language (ASL) to communicate are underrepresented in the domain of translation and language learning tools. Translating between a visual, gestural language like ASL and a spoken, written language like English presents multiple unique challenges. The visual elements of hand shape, location, orientation, and motion used in ASL can be challenging to detect, interpret, and represent.
We present an algorithm to recognize the 24 static signs in the ASL fingerspelling alphabet using the Leap Motion Controller. This algorithm can be used in ASL teaching applications, as well as to translate finger-spelled words. Existing Sign Language Recognition systems use cameras to extract low resolution images of hands where positions of individual fingers are difficult to detect. Our program utilizes the Leap Motion device, a motion sensor that provides skeletal hand tracking functionality. Based on joint coordinate and orientation information provided by the device, we extract a number of features including finger configuration (extended, bent, or curled), distance between fingers, and palm orientation. We then use a decision tree to classify signs as individual letters. This method does not require large amounts of training data like other machine learning based approaches. Preliminary results indicate that our method is successful in recognizing most of the static signs in the ASL fingerspelling alphabet.

Keywords: American Sign Language; Fingerspelling; Accessibility; Human computer interaction (HCI); Sign Language Recognition

DOI: https://doi.org/10.1145/3287324.3293718

Visualizing Classic Synchronization Problems

Elizabeth Koning, Joel C. Adams, Calvin College
Christiaan D. Hazlett, University of Illinois, Urbana-Champaign
Contact: erk24@students.calvin.edu

Classic synchronization problems are often used to introduce students to the subtleties of concurrency and synchronization mechanisms, such as semaphores, monitors, locks, and condition variables. The Dining Philosophers, Producers-Consumers, and Readers-Writers are all classic problems in which a correct solution requires the actions of multiple processes or threads to be synchronized. In this work, we present visualizations for these three problems and demonstrate their use in helping students build accurate mental models of concurrency abstractions. We also present the results of an experiment that indicate students find using these visualizations to be significantly more engaging than reading a textbook, with no significant difference in learning.

Keywords: Dining Philosophers; Graphics; Parallel; Producers Consumers; Readers Writers; Synchronization; Threads; Visualization

DOI: https://doi.org/10.1145/3287324.3293708

Understanding the Usage and Familiarity of Home Network Terminology Using Open Card Sorting Analysis

Jackie Chan, Kirby Mitchell, *Carleton College*
Contact: chanj3@carleton.edu

Research around computer networks has been rapidly expanding as the Internet becomes more prevalent in day-to-day life. Despite this rapid expansion in academic interest, computer networks, especially home networks, remain a challenge for inexperienced users to configure and maintain. To remedy this, new data needs to be collected to understand this new audience as computer networks move from academic/institutional to residential settings. This study examines the terminology that homeowners prefer when discussing bandwidth and connectivity issues on their home networks. We generated a list of common terms from web forums and user interviews and had participants classify these terms using an open card sort to determine their effectiveness. Our initial results indicate that participants were more likely to misclassify bandwidth-related and technical terms. This study demonstrates the importance of designing home networks to better meet the needs and diverse expertise levels of users.

Keywords: computer networks; home networks; usability; human-computer interaction; user studies; card sorting; vocabulary

DOI: http://dx.doi.org/10.1145/3287324.3293716

A Qualitative Analysis of Students' Understanding of Conditional Control Structures

Shannon Collier, Mara Downing, *Harvey Mudd College*
Contact: scollier@g.hmc.edu

Conditional logic and control structures are typically considered an important part of introductory computer science education, yet novices often struggle to correctly write and navigate such program logic. Previous research has largely attended to student difficulties with parsing Boolean expressions, but has not had much focus on the control structures themselves. To investigate how students work through complicated logic, we conducted a qualitative analysis of four one-on-one interviews with undergraduate students in which we gave students a piece of code with a complicated conditional control structure and asked them to write test cases for all paths. We found that several students struggled to determine the output the function would provide for a given input, and we hypothesize this occurred because they incorrectly treated an if statement as an else-if statement. One student simply wrote an incorrect output, which we believe occurred because they made this particular mistake, while another student got partway through the problem before verbally seeming to correct themself and re-identify a statement as an else-if. Based on our results, we hypothesize that novices

ACM ISBN 978-1-4503-5890-3/19/02

may sometimes misidentify a sequential if statement as an else-if, which may lead them to incorrectly interpret a conditional control structure.

Keywords: Conditionals; Conditional Control Structures; Education; Expert Blind Spot; Students

DOI: https://doi.org/10.1145/3287324.3293704

The Adventures of ScriptKitty: Teaching Middle School Students Cyber Awareness with Comics on the Raspberry Pi

Ovidiu-Gabriel Baciu-Ureche, Carlie Sleeman, Karlee Scott, William Moody, Suzanne J. Matthews, *United States Military Academy*
Contact: suzanne.matthews@westpoint.edu

Cyber security and on-line safety practices are not commonly taught in schools. However, there is an increasing need for education in these topics as children are joining the Internet community at a much earlier age than previous generations. It is crucial that young people understand the risks they may face on-line and how to mitigate them, ideally as soon as they begin using the Internet unsupervised. *The Adventures of ScriptKitty* (AOSK) introduces students to basic cyber security concepts using the Raspberry Pi, a single board computer that retails for $35.00. We created AOSK to help facilitate a culture of good cyber security practices and raise interest in STEM. The material is presented in the form of comics paired with instructional sections, including sections of more detailed technical information for readers who wish to learn more about key concepts. We piloted a portion of AOSK to a group of local middle school students. Our time with the students was limited, so we administered a short quiz, then discussed the Raspberry Pi. Next, students completed the packet sniffing exercise from Chapter 2, with the authors available to answer questions and help troubleshoot. Students were asked to re-take the quiz afterward. Our preliminary results show that students achieved a greater understanding of the material, with improved scores of 14%. A custom Pi image preloaded with Kali Linux and all needed software is included with the material. All the materials are published and available for free through GitBook at: https://suzannejmatthews.gitbooks.io/aosk/content

Keywords: Raspberry Pi; Kali Linux; Wireshark; Cyber security; Education; Comics; ScriptKitty

DOI: https://doi.org/10.1145/3287324.3293702

A Qualitative Study of Wisconsin Computer Science in K-12

Darren Jefferson, Tina Boyle Whyte, *Marquette University*
Contact: darren.jefferson@marquette.edu

The number of students enrolling into CS (Computer Science) is currently recovering from a period of declining numbers. Although the number of students enrolling in CS isn't declining anymore, there is still a lot of ground to be covered as far as student enrollment in CS goes. This is because the number of computer science jobs, on the other hand, is and has been steadily rising. The disconnect between students enrolling in CS and the increase of Jobs for CS leaves a deficiency for in the CS work field for qualified workers. We wish to look for ways to increase K-12 student interest in CS related fields in an attempt to increase the number of students pursuing CS. This first starts with the teachers teaching the class. To address these issues, we investigated the implementation of teachers who had been through Computer Science professional developments in the K12 school environment. Using the data, gathered from a qualitative study approach, we present results found from interviews conducted on K12 teachers from all across Wisconsin to demonstrate the impact of professional development on teacher's ability to teach.

Keywords: Computer Science; Education; Professional Development; Student Enrollment

DOI: http://doi.org/10.1145./3287324.3293719

Improving Student Self-efficacy in CS 1 Using Examples of Erroneous Code

Adam Koehler, *University of California, Riverside*
Contact: akoeh001@cs.ucr.edu

Research has shown that self-efficacy, a student's confidence in his or her ability, contributes to student success. Here, we examine if teaching students to recognize common programming errors increases student self-efficacy in an introductory programming course. We provided students with exercises containing examples of typical novice programming errors and methods for fixing them. At the beginning of the course we assess self-efficacy and administer a test to measure programming competence. We repeat these measurements at the end of the course. To assess self-efficacy, students rate their confidence in completing various programming tasks on a scale of 0 to 100. The test has fourteen questions; thirteen are short answer and one is multiple choice. Short answer questions require the student to write at most a few lines of C++ code, with most requiring only a single line. We analyze student self-efficacy in relation to our pre- and post-test, student course grade, assignment grade, and final exam grade. Our analysis shows improvements between the experimental term compared to the control terms across eleven measures of self-efficacy, but only three of these improvements are significant ($p < 0.05$).

Keywords: computer science education; CS 1; self-efficacy; erroneous examples

DOI: https://doi.org/10.1145/3287324.3293720

A Corpus-assisted Discourse Analysis of Chiptune-related Practices Discussed within Chipmusic.org

Jared O'Leary, *Arizona State University*
Contact: jared.oleary@asu.edu

This study examined 245,098 discussion forum posts within a website dedicated to chiptunes, which are electronic music compositions or performances either emulating the sounds of or created through early computer and video game sound chips. Corpus-assisted discourse analysis tools and techniques assisted with revealing patterns of discourse across 10,892,645 words

ACM ISBN 978-1-4503-5890-3/19/02

written between December 30th, 2009 and November 13th, 2017 within chipmusic.org.

Findings indicate seven interconnected themes of chiptune-related practices that demonstrate potential transdisciplinary connections between computer science education and music education: (a) music composition practices, (b) music performance practices, (c) maker practices, (d) coding practices, (e) entrepreneurial practices, (f), visual art practices, and (g) community practices.

Members of chipmusic.org engaged in computer science practices such as designing, manufacturing, and modifying electronic hardware for performing and recording chiptunes, as well as coding practices such as creating or modifying software for chiptune-related purposes. Such practices were guided by an interest in making music through old computer and video game hardware, and demonstrate several potential connections between computer science education and music education. For example, members engaged in computer science practices such as hardware and software modification to enable the ability to compose and perform music through the Nintendo Game Boy.

Findings from this study not only demonstrate potential connections between computer science education and music education, they also raise questions about spaces and curricula with blurred disciplinary boundaries. For example, where might chiptune-related practices that blur concepts and practices from a multitude of disciplines and standards occur within a formalized education environment?

Keywords: Chiptunes; Music-centered Making; Transdisciplinary; Interdiscipline; Curriculum; Computer Science Education; Music Education

DOI: http://dx.doi.org/10.1145/3287324.3293706

Analyzing User Interactions with Cybersecurity Games

Valdemar Švábenský, *Masaryk University*
Contact: svabensky@ics.muni.cz

Capture the Flag games are software applications designed to exercise cybersecurity concepts, practice using security tools, and understand cyber-attacks and defense. We develop and employ these games at our university for training purposes, unlike in the traditional competitive setting. During the gameplay, it is possible to collect data about players' in-game actions, such as typed commands or solution attempts, including the timing of these actions. Although such data was previously employed in computer security research, to the best of our knowledge, there were few attempts to use this data primarily to improve education. In particular, we see an open and challenging research problem in creating an artificial intelligence assistant that would facilitate the learning of each player. Our goal is to propose, apply, and experimentally evaluate data analysis and machine learning techniques to derive information about the players' interactions from the in-game data. We want to use this information to automatically provide each player with a personalized formative assessment. Such assessment will help the players identify their mastered concepts and areas for improvement, along with suggestions and actionable steps to take. Furthermore, we want to identify high- or low-performing players during the game, and subsequently, offer them game tasks more suitable to their skill level. These interventions would supplement or even replace feedback from instructors, which would significantly increase the learning impact of the games, enable more students to learn cybersecurity skills at an individual pace, and lower the costs.

Keywords: Cybersecurity games; Capture the flag; Learning analytics

DOI: https://doi.org/10.1145/3287324.3293717

Applying Alignment to Improve the Effectiveness of CS Education

Noha Elsherbiny, Virginia Tech
Contact: noha@vt.edu

Course alignment refers to the degree to which curriculum, assessments and instruction methods are in agreement with each other. Course alignment can be used by instructors to evaluate the effectiveness of their instructional content and assessments and whether they are meeting their learning objectives. Applying alignment models is time consuming and laborious, making them difficult for a course instructor to use. Current alignment models require a panel of experts to review documents and make judgments about the degree of alignment of the course objectives and assessments. With that in mind, we devised a practical strategy to be used by a course instructor, as part of course design, to assess the alignment between the course content, learning objectives and assessment methods. We developed a process for evaluating the degree of alignment of a course based on attributes from Webb's alignment model and we developed data structures based on Porter's matrix to facilitate the assessment of the alignment. The devised strategy will be applied to various CS courses by instructors and the results of the process will be used to refine the alignment strategy. An alignment process that can be applied timely and simple to follow may encourage instructors to apply it to their course, becoming a common practice for any instructor when modifying their course.

KEYWORDS: Alignment Models, Course Evaluation, Course Design

DOI: https://doi.org/10.1145/3287324.3293705

Reinforcement Learning: Improve Feedback Mechanism with Indicator based Reward, VirtualTA towards Growth Mindset

Zhiyi Li, *Virginia Tech*
Contact: zli04@vt.edu

Automatic grading systems such as Web-CAT are widely used when students learn programming, especially in CS1/CS2 courses in colleges and universities. Current feedback mechanism in these systems benefits students with performance-based information. They have negative effects to often frustrate students especially novice programmers to belief of fixed mindset – their programming abilities are native and limited. Students with fixed mindset can seriously influence female and minority enrollment

ACM ISBN 978-1-4503-5890-3/19/02

and retention rate in CS major. It is important to move students to growth mindset instead – belief their programming skills can be improved by practice and hard work. Recently effort were made to improve feedback mechanism in automatic grading systems. One effort was the design and implementation of a group of indicators to reflect students' progress and effort, based on their programming submissions. Another effort was the design of virutalTA Maria to deliver positive comments to encourage and reinforce students. We demonstrate the design of boosters (rewards) component and positive encourage and reinforcement comments feedback by virtualTA, based on indicators information. We simulated boosters (rewards) and comments component with a historical programming dataset to validate boosters (rewards) strategy. Simulated results found only 32 percent students did not get any Booster (rewards). 68 percent students won four types of booster range from Tier 1 to Tier 4. This result is what we are as expected. We also designed positive encouraging and reinforcement comments feedback from VirtualTA in adaptive style, based on indicator information. We plan to apply these two designed components to classroom for evaluation.

Keywords: Feedback; Growth Mindset; Reward; Booster; VirtualTA

DOI: https://doi.org/10.1145/3287324.3293703

Engaging African American Elementary School Children in Code Understanding

Olivia Nche, *Clemson University*
Contact: oncheey@g.clemson.edu

This paper summarizes the results of a research project to broaden access to computing. The project is aimed at improving the attitudes and computational thinking skills for African American elementary school children in the 3rd to 5th grades and to understand their difficulties in reasoning about code. This was done within the context of a five-week summer camp. There were 40 children of whom about half were females. Along with instruction, we used a custom video game to teach code tracing. We used video game data and pre and posttests to assess students' performance. Qualitative and quantitative results from our mixed method design show cognitive and affective improvements as well as improvements in computational thinking skills. The data we collected also highlighted potential common mistakes that elementary school children might make as they attempt to reason about code. It shows the potential in games to motivate code understanding practice and improve learning.

Keywords: Broadening participation; code tracing; computational thinking; video game; integrative approach; problem solving.

DOI: https://doi.org/10.1145/3287324.3293715

ACM ISBN 978-1-4503-5890-3/19/02

Empirical Assessment of Software Documentation Strategies: A Randomized Controlled Trial

Scott Kolodziej, *Texas A&M University*
Contact: scottk@tamu.edu

Source code documentation is an important part of teaching students how to be effective programmers. But what evidence do we have to support what good documentation looks like? This study utilizes a randomized controlled trial to experimentally compare several different types of documentation, including traditional comments, self-documenting naming, and an automatic documentation generator. The results of this experiment show that the relationship between documentation and source code understanding is more complex than simply "more is better," and poorly documented code may even lead to a more correct understanding of the source code.

Keywords: Software documentation; empirical study; randomized controlled trial; automatic documentation generation; self-documenting code

DOI: https://doi.org/10.1145/3287324.3293714

Online Mob Programming: Effective Collaborative Project-Based Learning

Sreecharan Sankaranarayanan, *Carnegie Mellon University*
Contact: sreechas@cs.cmu.edu

This work presents a new paradigm for collaborative project-based computer science education called Online Mob Programming (OMP). OMP is adapted from the industrial practice of Mob Programming, where groups of developers work on the same problem, at the same time, in the same place. OMP was designed and implemented as a technique where a group of 4-6 students collaborate online through a structured process for solving programming tasks. In OMP, students rotate through clearly defined roles to collectively contribute towards a solution to a programming challenge. These roles require students to brainstorm potential solutions, decide on a path forward, and implement the correct course of action respectively. OMP was investigated in the context of a 6-week free online course on Cloud Computing. During the course, students participated in four intelligent conversational agent-coordinated OMP sessions. By instrumenting the online development environment, all student code revisions and chat logs were collected in addition to qualitative data from questionnaires. Analyses show evidence of success in terms of students following the structure of OMP and further investigations into differences in mob behavior based on the size, and problem outcome provide pedagogically valuable insights and a path toward building OMP into the computer science education curriculum.

Keywords: Mob Programming; Online Mob Programming; Collaborative Learning; Project-Based Learning; Computer-Supported Collaborative Learning

DOI: https://doi.org/10.1145/3287324.3293709

Deconstructing Successful and Unsuccessful Computer Science Undergraduate Interns

Amanpreet Kapoor, *University of Florida*
Contact: kapooramanpreet@ufl.edu

Internships play a crucial role in helping CS undergraduate students to commit to CS degrees and computing careers. Internships also promote students' personal and professional growth. Studies have also shown that pursuing an internship is positively correlated with an improved chance of getting a full-time job offer and a higher starting salary. However, previous research has shown that only 52.1% of undergraduate students pursue an internship before they graduate. In this poster, we present findings from a cross-sectional study focused on understanding the characteristics of CS undergraduate students who have interned at one or more companies and those who have not interned. We surveyed 97 and interviewed 14 CS undergraduates. We found that 41.2% of 97 students participated in one or more internships. The key characteristics that distinguish students who successfully interned and those who did not were: 1) 95% students who interned had career goals - either to join industry or pursue graduate school after they graduate. In contrast, 21% of the students who did not intern were unsure or confused about their career goals; 2) students who interned were more likely to have participated in an undergraduate research experience or a student organization; 3) students who interned intentionally prepared for interviews, while those who did not intern were not actively preparing, not confident enough to apply, or were unsuccessful in the interview process because of lack of preparation. This poster provides insight into CS students' competitiveness for securing internships and for developing programs to support professional development.

Keywords: Internship; Professional development; Curricula improvement; Computing careers; Industry; Retention

DOI: https://doi.org/10.1145/3287324.3293711

Using Touch and Sound to Program Scratch

Zirui Wang, *Birmingham-Southern College*
Contact: zwang@bsc.edu

Computer Science in K-12 is continuing to become more prevalent. Because learning syntax and debugging can be burdensome, many teachers in K-12 use block languages to teach their students. Block languages, such as Scratch, allow students to focus on simple programming concepts and logic, and therefore, make computer programming easier and more approachable to students. However, block languages are not accessible to students with visual impairments because of block-environments' high dependence on visual aspects. CodeBox64 is a possible solution, offering a tactile approach to input. It is a peripheral device containing six buttons. Four of them allow users to control the mouse, and the other two allow users to select different menus and drag and join the blocks in the block editor. As users navigate through the block programming language, CodeBox64 generates auditory cues to indicate the name of the block when the mouse lands on it. In order to test the usability and efficiency of CodeBox64, an experiment was designed and conducted. It required the use of CodeBox64 to access Scratch and complete three small programs ten times without looking at the screen. The purpose of the evaluation was primarily to test that the device was working as intended with three test cases, and the results showed CodeBox64 functioned properly with all cases.

Keywords: Accessibility; auditory cues; block languages; computer science education; tactile input modality; visual impairments

DOI: http://doi.org/10.1145/3287324.3293707

ACM ISBN 978-1-4503-5890-3/19/02

Author Index

NOTES

www.ingramcontent.com/pod-product-compliance
Lightning Source LLC
LaVergne TN
LVHW080109011026
849160LV00013B/1057